November 13–17, 2016
Malta

I0060975

Association for Computing Machinery

Advancing Computing as a Science & Profession

MSWiM'16

Proceedings of the 19th ACM International Conference on

Modeling, Analysis and Simulation of Wireless and Mobile Systems

Sponsored by:
ACM SIGSIM

Association for Computing Machinery

The Association for Computing Machinery
2 Penn Plaza, Suite 701
New York, New York 10121-0701

Advancing Computing as a Science & Profession

Notice to Past Authors of ACM-Published Articles

ISBN: 978-1-4503-4502-6

Additional copies may be ordered prepaid from:

ACM Order Department
PO Box 30777
New York, NY 10087-0777, USA

Phone: 1-800-342-6626 (USA and Canada)
+1-212-626-0500 (Global)
Fax: +1-212-944-1318
E-mail: acmhelp@acm.org
Hours of Operation: 8:30 am – 4:30 pm ET

Printed in the USA.

Welcome Message from General Chair

Welcome to the 19th ACM International Conference on Modelling, Analysis and Simulation of Wireless and Mobile Systems (MSWiM), held this year in astonishing Malta. Located in the central area of the Mediterranean between South of Sicily and North Africa, Malta is culturally very rich due to being in a strategic naval position, which has been successively ruled by several civilizations and empires along its long history. The warm climate and its pleasant beaches washed by the Mediterranean perfectly complement its 7000 years of history with architectural and historical monuments, including UNESCO World Heritage sites: Hypogeum of Hal-Saflieni, Valleta, and the seven Megalithic Temples, consisting of some of the oldest free-standing structures in the world.

MSWiM has established itself over the years as a leading venue where some of the best research in the area of performance evaluation of wireless and mobile systems is presented, and this is no exception. Putting together a high-quality conference like MSWiM is an enormous undertaking that requires a great team effort. We thank Geyong Min and Antonio F. Loureiro for putting together the technical program, from the Call for Papers to the final program selection and its schedule. We also acknowledge the volunteer efforts of TPC members and external reviewers whose expertise and hard work culminated in selecting excellent papers. This year, MSWiM presents strong poster and demonstration sessions, managed by Robson E. De Grande, the Poster Sessions Chair, and Laura-Marie Feeney, the Demo Session Chair. Finally, the technical program includes two distinguished keynotes addresses by the following two outstanding experts, Prof. Jean-Pierre Hubaux from EPFL, Switzerland, and Prof. Kin K. Leung from Imperial College, UK.

To recognize excellence in research work in the field of Wireless Communications and Mobile Networking from academia and industry, the *ACM MSWiM Reginald G. Fessenden Award* has been established two years ago, and it is granted to a distinguished researcher for the remarkable contributions that he has achieved in the area. In 2015, the award was presented to Professor Mario Gerla from UCLA in recognition of *"his pioneering contributions for his outstanding work in the development of Routing, Transport Protocols, and Applications in Mobile Wireless Networks"*. The winner for this year will be announced at the ACM MSWiM 2016 banquet dinner.

Four symposia and two tutorials will be held this year along with the main conference program, covering several specializations within mobile and wireless systems. The four symposia are: *MobiWAC, PE-WASUN, DIVANET* and *Q2SWinet*. Over the years, these symposia have become successful and quite competitive in their own right.

We also wish to express our gratitude to those who have managed the many practical details of the event. These individuals include Mirela Notare and Salil Kanhere as the Publicity Co-Chairs; and Thomas Begin and Jalel Ben-Othman for organizing the tutorials in the Conference. We also express our appreciation to the MSWiM Steering Committee for their guidance and support, which helped us to bring together an exceptional conference program this year. Last but not least, we wish to thank our main sponsor, ACM SIGSIM.

We are very pleased to welcome you to MSWiM 2016 and fascinating Malta. We are certain that you will find this year's event full of stimulating ideas and discussions.

Albert Zomaya, General Chair
University of Sydney, Australia

Technical Program Chairs' Welcome

The technical program of the 19th ACM International Conference on Modeling, Analysis and Simulation of Wireless and Mobile Systems (MSWiM), held in Malta in 2016 continues to build upon the high standards set by previous editions of the conference.

In 2016, the call for papers attracted 138 registered papers in all areas of mobile and wireless systems. The submitted papers came from 36 countries. Members of the Technical Program Committee are affiliated to universities and industry in 17 countries spread over five continents, reflecting the truly international profile of MSWiM. The five most commonly listed topics for submissions to MSWiM'15 were:

- Performance evaluation and modeling
- Wireless network algorithms and protocols
- Wireless mesh networks, mobile ad hoc networks, Vehicular networks
- Algorithms and protocols for energy efficiency and power control
- Analytical models

The submissions included a large number of papers of very high quality making the selection process difficult and competitive. In the end, we selected 36 regular papers, which correspond to an acceptance rate of approximately 27%. An additional 10 short papers were recommended for the program owing to their quality and contribution.

Among the regular papers, the following four papers were shortlisted as candidates for the best paper award:

- *"Coverage Properties of One-Dimensional Infrastructure-Based Wireless Networks,"* Naveen Kolar Purushothama (Indian Institute of Technology Madras, India) and Anurag Kumar (Indian Institute of Science, India);
- *"Effective Selection of Targeted Advertisements for Vehicular Users,"* Gil Einziger (Politecnico di Torino, Italy), Carla-Fabiana Chiasserini (Politecnico di Torino, Italy), and Francesco Malandrino (Politecnico di Torino, Italy);
- *"Preference and Mobility-Aware Task Assignment in Participatory Sensing,"* Rim Ben Messaoud (Universite Paris Est Marne La Vallee, France), Yacine Ghamri-Doudane (University of La Rochelle, France), and Dmitri Botvich (TSSG, Waterford Institute of Technology, Ireland);
- *"Theoretical Interference Analysis of Inter-vehicular Communication at Intersection with Power Control,"* Tatsuaki Kimura (NTT Corporation, Japan) and Hiroshi Saito (NTT Corporation, Japan).

The winner among these three papers will be announced at the conference banquet, and will be reported in the proceedings of MSWiM 2016. At this point, we take the opportunity to congratulate the winners of the best paper award for MSWiM 2015:

- *"Data Dependency based Parallel Simulation of Wireless Networks,"* Mirko Stoffers, Torsten Sehy, James Gross, and Klaus Wehrle.

TPC Co-Chairs

Antonio A. F. Loureiro
Federal University of Minas Gerais, Brazil

Geyong Min
University of Exeter, UK

Table of Contents

Session: Wireless Networks — Performance Modeling

Session: Wireless Access

Session: Wireless Cloud and IoT

Session: Cellular Networks and Mobility Management

Session: Wireless Sensor Networks

Session: Wireless Communication

Session: D2D and Wearable Devices

Session: Sensing and Tracking

Session: Wireless Networks

19th ACM MSWiM 2016 Conference Organization

General Co-Chair: Albert Zomaya *(University of Sydney, Australia)*

Program Co-Chairs: Geyong Min *(University of Exeter, UK)*
Antonio F. Loureiro *(Federal University of Minas Gerais, Brazil)*

Workshop Co-Chairs: Periklis Chatzimisios *(Alexander TEI of Thessaloniki, Greece)*
SungBum Hong *(Jackson State University, USA)*

Poster Chair: Robson E. De Grande *(DIVA Strategic Research Network, Canada)*

Demo/Tools Chair: Laura Marie Feeney *(Swedish Institute of Computer Science, Sweden)*

Tutorials Co-Chairs: Thomas Begin *(University Claude Bernard Lyon, France)*
Jalel Ben-Othman *(University Paris 13, France)*

Publicity Co-Chairs: Salil Kanhere *(University of New South Wales, Australia)*
Mirela. A. M. Notare *(Sao Jose Municipal University, Brazil)*

PhD Forum Chair: Bjorn Landfeldt *(Lund University, Sweden)*

Registration Chair: Ibrahim Hajjeh *(Fransec, France)*

Steering Committee: Azzedine Boukerche *(University of Ottawa, Canada)*
Sajal K. Das *(University of Texas at Arlington, USA)*
Albert Zomaya *(University of Sydney, Australia)*
Lorenzo Donatiello *(Università di Bologna, Bologna, Italy)*
Jason Yi-Bing Lin *(National Chiao-Tung University, Taiwan)*
William C.Y.Lee *(AirTouch Inc., USA)*
Simon Taylor *(Brunel University, UK)*
Robson E. De Grande *(University of Ottawa, Canada)*

Program Committee: Antonio A.F. Loureiro *(Federal University of Minas Gerais, Brazil)*
Adam Wolisz *(Technische Universität Berlin, Germany)*
Andrea Passarella *(IIT-CNR, Italy)*
Andreas Willig *(University of Canterbury, New Zealand)*
Angel Cuevas *(Universidad Carlos III de Madri, Spain)*
Azzedine Boukerche *(University of Ottawa, Canada)*
Bjorn Landfeldt *(Lund University)*
Brahim Bensaou *(The Hong Kong University of Science and Technology, Hong Kong)*
Carla-Fabiana Chiasserini *(Politecnico di Torino, Italy)*
Cheng Li *(Memorial University of Newfoundland, Canada)*
David Eckhoff *(University of Erlangen, Germany)*
Dirk Staehle *(Docomo Euro-Labs, Germany)*
Ehab Elmallah *(University of Alberta, Canada)*

Privacy Challenges in Mobile and Pervasive Networks

Jean-Pierre Hubaux
Department of Computer Science
Ecole Polytechnique Federale de Lausanne
Lausanne, Switzerland
jean-pierre.hubaux@epfl.ch

ABSTRACT

This last decade has witnessed a wide adoption of connected mobile devices able to capture the context of their owners from embedded sensors (GPS, Wi-Fi, Bluetooth, accelerometers). The advent of mobile and pervasive computing has enabled rich social and contextual applications, but the use of such technologies raises severe privacy issues and challenges. The privacy threats come from diverse adversaries, ranging from curious service providers and other users of the same service to eavesdroppers and curious applications running on the device. The information that can be collected from mobile device owners includes their locations, their social relationships, and their current activity. All of this, once analyzed and combined together through inference, can be very telling about the users' private lives.

In this talk, we will describe privacy threats in mobile and pervasive networks. We will also show how to quantify the privacy of the users of such networks and explain how information on co-location can be taken into account. We will describe the role that privacy enhancing technologies (PETs) can play and describe some of them. We will also explain how to prevent apps from sifting too many personal data under Android. We will conclude by mentioning the privacy and security challenges raised by the "quantified self" and digital medicine.

Bio

Jean-Pierre Hubaux is a full professor at EPFL. Through his research, he contributes to laying the foundations and developing the tools to protect privacy in tomorrow's hyper-connected world. He is focusing notably on network privacy and security, with an emphasis on mobile/wireless networks and on data protection, with an emphasis on health-related data and especially genomic data. He has also studied privacy and security mechanisms (especially for mobile networks) in the presence of selfish players. Previously, he pioneered the areas of wireless network security and secure vehicular communications. Since 2007, he has been one of the seven commissioners of the Swiss FCC. He was recently appointed to the "Information Security Task Force", set up by the Swiss federal government. He is a Fellow of both IEEE (2008) and ACM (2010).

CCS Concepts

•Security and privacy → Privacy-preserving protocols; Authorization; •Human-centered computing → *Ubiquitous computing; Mobile computing;*

Keywords

Privacy and Security; Mobile Networks; Pervasive Networks

MSWiM '16 November 13-17, 2016, Malta, Malta

© 2016 Copyright held by the owner/author(s).

ACM ISBN 978-1-4503-4502-6/16/11.

DOI: http://dx.doi.org/10.1145/2988287.2998439

Use of Optimization Models for Resource Allocation in Wireless Ad-Hoc and Sensor Networks

Kin K. Leung
Department of Electrical and Electronic Engineering
Imperial College, London
kin.leung@imperial.ac.uk

ABSTRACT

Optimization models and techniques are often used to achieve efficient allocation of limited network resources to competing demands in communication networks. In this talk, the speaker will give a brief overview of distributed optimization theory, including convex optimization problems for which iterative solution techniques exist and converge. The well-known Transport Control Protocol (TCP) is shown to be equivalent a distributed solution that achieves the optimal allocation of bandwidth in communication networks. As for wireless ad-hoc and sensor networks, each link capacity depends on the transmission power of other links due to co-channel interference. In addition, the quality of multimedia services supported by these networks cannot be represented by a concave function of the amount of allocated bandwidth. These factors unfortunately make the resource allocation problem for the wireless networks become a non-convex optimization problem. New distributed solution techniques will be presented to solve these problems and numerical examples will also be provided.

This talk will also consider the in-network data processing in wireless sensor networks where data are aggregated (fused) along the way they are transferred toward the end user. It will be shown that finding the optimal solution for the distributed processing problem is NP-hard, but for specific parameter settings, the problem can lead to a distributed framework for achieving the optimal tradeoff between communications and computation costs. Future work on integrating data or signal processing techniques with the distributed solution framework will be discussed.

CCS Concepts

•Computing methodologies → Modeling methodologies; •Networks → In-network processing;

MSWiM '16, November 13-17, 2016, Malta

© 2016 Copyright held by the owner/author(s).

ACM ISBN 978-1-4503-4502-6/16/11.

DOI: http://dx.doi.org/10.1145/2988287.2998440

Keywords

Optimization; resource allocation; wireless ad-hoc and sensor networks; in-network data processing

Bio

Kin K. Leung received his B.S. degree from the Chinese University of Hong Kong in 1980, and his M.S. and Ph.D. degrees from University of California, Los Angeles, in 1982 and 1985, respectively. He joined AT&T Bell Labs in New Jersey in 1986 and worked at its successor companies, AT&T Labs and Bell Labs of Lucent Technologies, until 2004. Since then, he has been the Tanaka Chair Professor in the Electrical and Electronic Engineering (EEE), and Computing Departments at Imperial College in London. He serves as the Head of Communications and Signal Processing Group in the EEE Department at Imperial. His research focuses on networking, protocols, optimization and modeling issues of wireless broadband, sensor and ad-hoc networks. He also works on multi-antenna systems and cross-layer optimization of these networks.

He received the Distinguished Member of Technical Staff Award from AT&T Bell Labs in 1994, and was a co-recipient of the 1997 Lanchester Prize Honorable Mention Award. He was elected as an IEEE Fellow in 2001. He received the Royal Society Wolfson Research Merits Award from 2004 to 2009 and became a member of Academia Europaea in 2012. Along with his co-authors, he also received a number of best paper awards at major conferences, including the IEEE PIMRC 2012 and ICDCS 2013. He serves as a member (2009-11) and the chairman (2012-15) of the IEEE Fellow Evaluation Committee for Communications Society. He was a guest editor for the IEEE JSAC, IEEE Wireless Communications and the MONET journal, and as an editor for the JSAC: Wireless Series, IEEE Transactions on Wireless Communications and IEEE Transactions on Communications. Currently, he is an editor for the ACM Computing Survey and International Journal on Sensor Networks.

Theoretical Interference Analysis of Inter-vehicular Communication at Intersection with Power Control

Tatsuaki Kimura
NTT Network Technology Laboratories
NTT Corporation
Musashino-shi, Tokyo, Japan
kimura.tatsuaki@lab.ntt.co.jp

Hiroshi Saito
NTT Network Technology Laboratories
NTT Corporation
Musashino-shi, Tokyo, Japan
saito.hiroshi@lab.ntt.co.jp

ABSTRACT

Interference problems caused by congestion of vehicles at intersections or on highways may significantly affect vehicle-to-vehicle (V2V) communications, especially for active-safety assistance systems due to the importance of emergency information. In this paper, we propose a theoretical interference model of V2V communications at an intersection that uses transmission power control method. To evaluate and address the interference problem at an intersection, we derived an analytical expression of the outage probability of a *typical* vehicle at an intersection and provide guidelines for an optimal power control method, which cannot be obtained through simulations. We model the location of vehicles in *queueing* segments and *running* segments separately and analyze their interference based on a stochastic geometry approach. In our model, a simple power control method is used: the transmission power of each vehicle is determined by the status of the vehicle, i.e., stopping or running. By changing the transmission power of vehicles in queueing segments, we can mitigate the interference received at vehicles running closer to an intersection. By using the theoretical results, we obtain an optimal power control method, which can balance the trade-off between the outage probabilities of vehicles in queueing segments and running segments. We validated our analytical results and the effect of the power control on V2V communications through numerical experiments.

CCS Concepts

•**General and reference** → **Performance;** •**Networks** → **Network performance modeling; Network performance analysis;** •**Mathematics of computing** → *Stochastic processes;*

Keywords

ITS; V2V communication; VANET; power control; stochastic geometry; Poisson point process; outage probability; intersection

1. INTRODUCTION

Intelligent transportation systems (ITSs) have been attracting much attention because they have various applications for not only ve-

MSWiM '16, November 13-17, 2016, Malta, Malta

ⓒ 2016 ACM. ISBN 978-1-4503-4502-6/16/11. . . $15.00

DOI: http://dx.doi.org/10.1145/2988287.2989156

hicles but also for passengers and pedestrians. The applications include traffic and congestion control, safety assistance, and auto-driving, all of which will drastically change and provide tremendous benefits to our lives [13, 15]. The key technologies for ITSs, called vehicle-to-infrastructure (V2I) or vehicle-to-vehicle (V2V) communications, involve the networking of vehicles and other communication devices e.g., road side units (RSUs). The wireless communications protocols commonly used in V2I and V2V communications are dedicated short range communications (DSRC). For example, IEEE 802.11p is used in the U.S. and provides media access control (MAC) and physical layer design in DSRC [15]. In addition, other protocols, such as device-to-device communication mode in LTE, may be used in future ITSs.

Contrary to current mobile ad-hoc networks (MANETs), V2V communications in urban environments include new research issues. Interferences caused by congestion at intersections or on highways may significantly affect V2V communications [2, 16, 23]. To reduce the interference caused by a large number of vehicles using the same channels, several adaptive control schemes of transmission power or broadcasting rate have recently been proposed in the area of active-safety assistance systems [8, 9, 23]. For example, method proposed by Moreno *et al.* [23] adaptively controls the transmission power of vehicles so that their max-min fairness is satisfied.

In spite of their impact, theoretical analysis for the interference problems of V2V communications in urban environments have not been sufficiently studied. Most of their performance evaluations are simulation-based [6, 11, 23], or specific protocol behaviors (e.g. IEEE 802.11p) are considered [5, 19, 22], and few studies have been focused on interference caused by congestion of vehicles such as at intersections. However, theoretical analysis is important for optimizing power- or rate-control without a heuristic because time-consuming simulations are needed. Not only for optimization, theoretical understanding may be useful for sensitivity analysis of system parameters, which will help in designing future ITSs.

In this paper, we propose a theoretical interference model for V2V communications at an intersection that uses a simple transmission power control method. By deriving the mathematical expression of performance metrics, we reveal the effect of power control on the interference problem and obtain a guideline for optimizing the power control method, which cannot be obtained through simulations. To model the locations of vehicles at an intersection, we consider *queueing* (i.e., stopping) and *running* segments separately. Vehicles in running segments are assumed to be distributed according to a Poisson point process (PPP). By taking the stochastic geometry approach, we derive a theoretical expression of the outage probability of a *typical* vehicle in queueing or running segments. The outage probability is defined as the probability that the signal-to-interference ratio (SIR) of a vehicle exceeds a certain threshold. To address the interference problem at intersections, we consider the power control method in our model: each vehicle in queueing segments is assigned less transmission power than that in running segments, i.e., the transmission power is determined based on the status of vehicles, stopping or running. By changing the transmission power of vehicles in queueing segments, vehicles in running segments can reduce the interference from those in queueing segments, which can mitigate the interference problem at intersections. By computing the mathematical expression of the outage probability, we reveal not only the interference problem at an intersection but also the effect of the power control in a theoretical manner. Furthermore, we obtain a guideline for optimization of the power control method, which balances the trade-off relationship between the outage probability of vehicles in the queueing and running segments. We validated our model through numerical experiments and confirmed that the power control method can be optimized through theoretical analysis.

Stochastic geometry has recently been applied to theoretical modeling of wireless vehicular communications [5, 10, 16, 19, 22]. In short, stochastic geometry is a tool for a spatial modeling of random objects (see e.g., [21]). By applying a spatial point process to the locations of communication devices, we can obtain theoretical expressions of performance metrics, e.g., SIR or outage probability, which give mathematical insights to the design or optimization of wireless systems. In previous studies [19, 22], the behaviors of the carrier sense multiple access (CSMA) protocol used in DSRC (especially in IEEE802.11p) were analyzed; however, the impacts of urban structures, such as intersections, were not considered. Some studies took such structures into account: e.g., highways [10] and streets in cities [4, 12, 16, 17]. Steinmetz *et al.* considered a simple intersection model [20]; however, the results contained errors and they did not consider congestion or power control.

The remainder of this paper is organized as follows. In Section 2, we explain the proposed model considered in this paper. We provide the theoretical expression of the outage probability in vehicular communication in Section 3. Based on these results, we discuss our transmission power control method and its optimization in Section 4. In Section 5, we discuss several numerical experiments and conclude the paper in Section 6.

2. SYSTEM MODEL

In this section, we explain the proposed model. Figure 1 shows a conceptual image of our model. First, there is an intersection crossing two streets, one of which is along the x-axis and the other is along the y-axis. Each street is classified into segments, a segment occupied by vehicles queueing (i.e., stopping) at the intersection and the other segment. We call the former a queueing segment S_Q and the latter a running segment S_R. Running segments are subclassified into *approaching* segments and *leaving* segments. They are the S_Rs used for vehicles approaching and leaving from an intersection, respectively. We assume that vehicles authorized to transmit in S_Rs are distributed according to a homogeneous PPP in the approaching and leaving segments of each street, respectively. Let $\lambda_{x,+}$, $\lambda_{x,-}$, $\lambda_{y,+}$, and $\lambda_{y,-}$ [1/km] denote the intensity of vehicles in an arriving segment of each part. The subscript $(\cdot, +)$ (resp. $(\cdot, -)$) represents the positive (resp. negative) direction on each axis. From these notations, we call each part a $(z, *)$ part ($z \in \{x, y\}, * \in \{+, -\}$). Similarly, let $\nu_{x,+}$, $\nu_{x,-}$, $\nu_{y,+}$, and $\nu_{y,-}$ be the intensity of vehicles in a leaving segment of each part, respectively. We define $n_{x,+}$, $n_{x,-}$, $n_{y,+}$, and $n_{y,-}$ as random variables representing the numbers of vehicles stopping at an intersection in each part. We assume that the positions of vehicles in

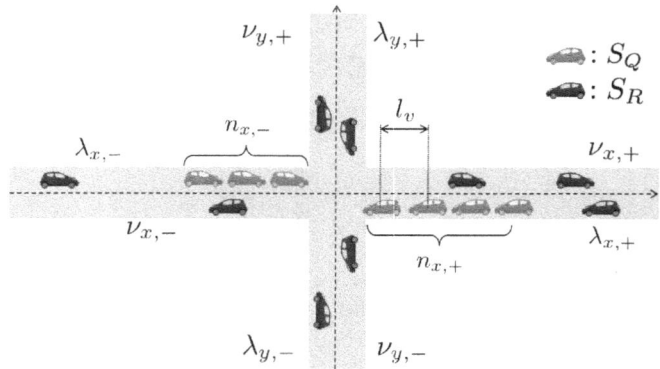

Figure 1: System model. Vehicles are in queueing segments (S_Qs) or in running segments (S_Rs). Vehicles in approaching (resp. leaving) of S_Rs are distributed according to homogeneous PPP with intensity $\lambda_{z,*}$ (resp. $\nu_{z,*}$) ($z \in \{x, y\}, * \in \{+, -\}$). $n_{z,*}$ represents number of vehicles stopping at intersection.

S_Qs are at equal intervals l_v (including vehicle's length) and the widths of the streets are equal to zero.

Vehicles transmit and receive radio signals between them (i.e., V2V communications). We assume that vehicles in an S_Q independently transmit radio signals with probability ρ. In addition, we assume the following power control method in our model. The transmission power assigned for vehicles in an S_R is constant $1/\mu$, and that for vehicles in an S_Q is θ/μ ($\theta > 0$), respectively. The parameter θ corresponds to the power control ratio and $\theta = 1$ implies that power control is off. By changing the value of θ, we can mitigate the interference problem at the intersection (details are discussed in Section 4). Antenna gain is assumed to be equal to 1 in the remainder of this paper. We also assume that all transmission channels have an effect of the same fading whose random variable is denoted as h_i for vehicle i. The path loss model is assumed as $r^{-\alpha}$ for distance $r \in \mathbb{R}_+$, where $\alpha > 2$ is a path loss component. Thus, for instance, the received power from vehicle i at distance r in an S_R can be expressed as $h_i r^{-\alpha}/\mu$. Table 1 summarizes the notations used in this paper.

Table 1: List of notations

S_R	set of vehicles running on street
S_Q	set of vehicles stopping/queueing at intersection
ρ	probability that vehicles in S_Q are sending signals
l_v	interval of vehicles in S_Qs (including vehicle's length)
$\lambda_{z,*}$	intensity of vehicles in arriving segment in $(z, *)$ part ($z \in \{x, y\}, * \in \{+, -\}$)
$\nu_{z,*}$	intensity of vehicles in leaving segment in each part
$n_{z,*}$	number or vehicles stopping at intersection in each part
$1/\mu$	transmission power of vehicles in S_R
θ	ratio of transmission power of vehicles in S_Q to S_R
h_i	fading variable

Note that CSMA is designed as the MAC layer protocol in IEEE 802.11p [15]. Since vehicles that are close to each other do not transmit simultaneously in CSMA, hard-core point processes have been used for modeling such CSMA-based protocols [7, 18, 22]; however, they are not mathematically tractable because they are obtained by *dependent* thinning of a PPP. In addition, Nguyen et al. [19] claimed that CSMA behaves like an ALOHA-type transmission pattern in dense networks. Therefore, to focus on the effect of power control on interference and maintain the mathematical tractability, we assume that transmitting vehicles use the Aloha MAC protocol and follow a PPP in this paper.

3. ANALYSIS

In this section, we derive the theoretical expression of the outage probability of a vehicle in an S_Q and S_R. To do this, we first consider the total interference received at the *tagged* vehicle in an S_R and S_Q and derive their Laplace transforms. By combining these results, we derive the outage probability of the tagged vehicle in the V2V communication scenario in which vehicles communicate with the nearest ones.

3.1 Interference from vehicles in S_Qs

We first consider the interference from vehicles in S_Qs. To do this, we consider the tagged vehicle on the x-axis as a typical vehicle. Let d_i denote the distance from the i-th vehicle in an S_Q to the tagged vehicle. If the i-th vehicle transmits a radio signal, the received power at the tagged vehicle is equal to $\theta h_i d_i^{-\alpha}/\mu$. Then, the total interference I_Q is given by $\sum_{i \in S_Q} \theta h_i \delta_i d_i^{-\alpha}/\mu$ where $\delta_i = 1$ if the i-th vehicle transmits, and $\delta_i = 0$ otherwise. Therefore, if we denote the set of the distances from the vehicles in S_Qs to the tagged vehicle as $\mathcal{D}$, then the Laplace transform of I_Q can be obtained as

$$
\begin{aligned}
\mathcal{L}_{I_Q}(s \mid \mathcal{D}) &\equiv \mathbb{E}[e^{-sI_Q}] = \prod_{d_i \in \mathcal{D}} \mathbb{E}[e^{-s\theta h_i \delta_i d_i^{-\alpha}/\mu}] \\
&= \prod_{d_i \in \mathcal{D}} \mathbb{E}_{h_i}[\rho e^{-s\theta h_i d_i^{-\alpha}/\mu} + (1-\rho)] \\
&= \prod_{d_i \in \mathcal{D}} \left(\rho \mathcal{L}_h(s\theta d_i^{-\alpha}/\mu) + (1-\rho) \right),
\end{aligned} \quad (1)
$$

where $\mathcal{L}_h(s)$ represents the Laplace transform of h.

3.2 Interference from vehicles in S_Rs

We next consider the interference from the vehicles in S_Rs. Suppose that the tagged vehicle is at distance $t_v > 0$ from the intersection in the $(x,+)$ part. Let Φ_R^X and Φ_R^Y denote PPPs corresponding to an S_R in the $(x,\cdot)$ and $(y,\cdot)$ parts, respectively. Then, the total interference from Φ_R^X can be represented as $I_R^X = \sum_{x_i \in \Phi_R^X} h_i |x_i - t_v|^{-\alpha}/\mu$. Note that the distance from the tagged vehicle to a vehicle at distance y from the intersection on the y-axis is equal to $\sqrt{y^2 + t_v^2}$. Thus, if I_R^Y denotes the total interference from Φ_R^Y, we have $I_R^Y = \sum_{y_i \in \Phi_R^Y} h_i (y_i^2 + t_v^2)^{-\alpha/2}/\mu$. If the intensity of a PPP is λ, then the Laplace transform of the interference received from the vehicles in an S_R in segments $(a, \infty]$ in $(x,\cdot)$ and $(y,\cdot)$ parts are given by (see, e.g. Proposition 1.5 and Corollary 2.9 in [3]),

$$
\begin{aligned}
\mathcal{L}_{I_R, a}^X(s \mid t_v, \lambda) &\triangleq \mathbb{E}\left[\exp\left(-s \sum_{x_i \in \Phi_R^X \cap (a,\infty]} \frac{h_i}{\mu |x_i - t_v|^\alpha} \right) \right] \\
&= \exp\left(-\lambda \int_a^\infty 1 - \mathcal{L}_h\left(\frac{s}{\mu |x - t_v|^\alpha} \right) dx \right),
\end{aligned} \quad (2)
$$

$$
\begin{aligned}
\mathcal{L}_{I_R, a}^Y(s \mid t_v, \lambda) &\triangleq \mathbb{E}\left[\exp\left(-s \sum_{y_i \in \Phi_R^Y \cap (a,\infty]} \frac{h_i}{\mu (y_i^2 + t_v^2)^{\frac{\alpha}{2}}} \right) \right] \\
&= \exp\left(-\lambda \int_a^\infty 1 - \mathcal{L}_h\left(\frac{s}{\mu (y^2 + t_v^2)^{\frac{\alpha}{2}}} \right) dy \right).
\end{aligned} \quad (3)
$$

3.3 Interference from all the vehicles

From the above results, we can obtain the total interference from all the vehicles when the tagged vehicle is in an S_R and S_Q.

3.3.1 Tagged vehicle in S_R

We first consider the case in which the tagged vehicle is in an S_R. To this end, we assume that the tagged vehicle is at t_v on the x-axis in the $(x,+)$ part. Since the positions of the vehicles in S_Qs are at equal intervals, we have

$$
\begin{aligned}
\{d_i; i \in S_Q\} = &\{t_v - il_v; -n_{x,-} \le i \le n_{x,+}, \ i \ne 0\} \\
&\bigcup \{\sqrt{t_v^2 + (il_v)^2}; -n_{y,-} \le i \le n_{y,+}, \ i \ne 0)\}.
\end{aligned}
$$

Therefore, the Laplace transform of the total interference from vehicles in S_Qs becomes a function of t_v:

$$
\begin{aligned}
&\mathcal{L}_{I_Q}(s \mid \{t_v - il_v; -n_{x,-} \le i \le n_{x,+}, \ i \ne 0\}) \\
&\times \mathcal{L}_{I_Q}(s \mid \{\sqrt{t_v^2 + (il_v)^2}; -n_{y,-} \le i \le n_{y,+}, \ i \ne 0)\}).
\end{aligned}
$$

According to Slivnyak's theorem, the Palm measure regarding the vehicle's location in S_Rs given that the tagged vehicle is in an S_R is identical to the probabilistic measure of the vehicle's location in S_Rs (see e.g. [21]). Thus, the total interference from vehicles in an S_R is given as follows:

$$
\begin{aligned}
&\mathcal{L}_{I_R}(s \mid t_v, n_{x,+}, n_{x,-}, n_{y,+}, n_{y,-}) \\
&= \mathcal{L}_{I_R, l_v n_{x,-}}^X(s \mid -t_v, \lambda_{x,-}) \mathcal{L}_{I_R, 0}^X(s \mid -t_v, \nu_{x,-}) \\
&\quad \times \mathcal{L}_{I_R, l_v n_{x,+}}^X(s \mid t_v, \lambda_{x,+}) \mathcal{L}_{I_R, 0}^X(s \mid t_v, \nu_{x,+}) \\
&\quad \times \mathcal{L}_{I_R, l_v n_{y,-}}^Y(s \mid -t_v, \lambda_{y,-}) \mathcal{L}_{I_R, 0}^Y(s \mid -t_v, \nu_{y,-}) \\
&\quad \times \mathcal{L}_{I_R, l_v n_{y,+}}^Y(s \mid t_v, \lambda_{y,+}) \mathcal{L}_{I_R, 0}^Y(s \mid t_v, \nu_{y,+}),
\end{aligned} \quad (4)
$$

where $\mathcal{L}_{I_R,a}^X(\cdot \mid \cdot)$ and $\mathcal{L}_{I_R,a}^Y(\cdot \mid \cdot)$ are given in (2) and (3). As a result, the Laplace transform of the total interference received at the tagged vehicle in S_Rs is given by

$$
\begin{aligned}
&\mathcal{L}_I^{[R]}(s \mid t_v, n_{x,+}, n_{x,-}, n_{y,+}, n_{y,-}) \\
&= \mathcal{L}_{I_Q}(s \mid \{t_v - il_v; -n_{x,-} \le i \le n_{x,+}, \ i \ne 0\}) \\
&\quad \times \mathcal{L}_{I_Q}(s \mid \{\sqrt{t_v^2 + (il_v)^2}; -n_{y,-} \le i \le n_{y,+}, \ i \ne 0)\}) \\
&\quad \times \mathcal{L}_{I_R}(s \mid t_v, n_{x,+}, n_{x,-}, n_{y,+}, n_{y,-}).
\end{aligned} \quad (5)
$$

3.3.2 Tagged vehicle in S_Q

We next consider the case in which the tagged vehicle is in an S_Q. We assume that the tagged vehicle is the I_v-th vehicle in the $(x,+)$ part. Note that $n_{x,+}$ includes the tagged vehicle and that $I_v \equiv t_v/l_v$ is an integer. We then have

$$
\begin{aligned}
\{d_i; i \in S_Q\} = &\{|I_v - i|l_v \mid -n_{x,-} \le i \le n_{x,+}; i \ne 0, I_v\} \\
&\bigcup \{l_v \sqrt{I_v^2 + i^2} \mid -n_{y,-} \le i \le n_{y,+}; i \ne 0\}.
\end{aligned}
$$

Therefore, the Laplace transform of the total interference from vehicles in S_Qs is equal to

$$
\begin{aligned}
&\mathcal{L}_{I_Q}(s \mid \{|I_v - i|l_v \mid -n_{x,-} \le i \le n_{x,+}; i \ne 0, I_v\}) \\
&\times \mathcal{L}_{I_Q}(s \mid \{l_v \sqrt{I_v^2 + i^2} \mid -n_{y,-} \le i \le n_{y,+}; i \ne 0\}).
\end{aligned}
$$

On the other hand, the total interference from vehicles in S_Rs is equal to (4) when $t_v = I_v l_v$. As a result, the Laplace transform of the total interference at the tagged vehicle in an S_Q is given by

$$
\begin{aligned}
&\mathcal{L}_I^{[Q]}(s \mid I_v, n_{x,+}, n_{x,-}, n_{y,+}, n_{y,-}) \\
&= \mathcal{L}_{I_Q}(s \mid \{|I_v - i|l_v \mid -n_{x,-} \le i \le n_{x,+}; i \ne 0, I_v\}) \\
&\quad \times \mathcal{L}_{I_Q}(s \mid \{l_v \sqrt{I_v^2 + i^2} \mid -n_{y,-} \le i \le n_{y,+}; i \ne 0\}) \\
&\quad \times \mathcal{L}_{I_R}(s \mid I_v l_v, n_{x,+}, n_{x,-}, n_{y,+}, n_{y,-}).
\end{aligned} \quad (6)
$$

3.4 Queue length distribution

We next consider the probability distribution of queue length. We assume that vehicles run at a constant speed ϕ [km/sec.]. We also assume that all vehicles stopping in S_Qs leave the intersection and S_Qs become empty when a traffic signal changes to green. In other words, vehicles join in S_Qs only when traffic signals are red. Let τ denote the elapsed time after a traffic signal changes to red. Since vehicles in the $(x,+)$ part arrives to the intersection according to a Poisson process with the rate $\lambda_{x,+}\phi$, the variable $n_{x,+}$ becomes a Poisson variable with mean $\lambda_{x,+}\phi\tau$. We then have, for $k = 0, 1, \ldots,$

$$q_+(k \mid \tau) \triangleq \mathsf{P}(n_{x,+} = k \mid \tau) = e^{-\lambda_{x,+}\phi\tau}\frac{(\lambda_{x,+}\phi\tau)^k}{k!}. \quad (7)$$

Similarly, queue length distributions for the other parts, such as $q_-(k \mid \tau) \triangleq \mathsf{P}(n_{x,-} = k \mid \tau)$, can be obtained.

3.5 Outage probability

We next derive the mathematical expression of the outage probability of downlink transmission to the tagged vehicle. Vehicles are assumed to communicate with the nearest vehicles in both S_Rs and S_Qs. The outage probability is defined as the probability that the SIR of the tagged vehicle is smaller than a certain threshold T. Without loss of generality, the tagged vehicle is assumed to be in the S_R or S_Q in the $(x,+)$ part. To focus on the effect of the congestion at the intersections, we only consider the case in which $n_{x,+}, n_{x,-} \geq 1$. In addition, we consider the case in which the traffic signals on the y-axis are green, i.e., $n_{y,+} = n_{y,-} = 0$. Note that we can apply a similar argument to other cases, such as those in which traffic signals on the y-axis are red, or the tagged vehicle is in the $(y, \cdot)$ parts.

In addition, all channels are assumed to have only Rayleigh fading with unit mean. Thus, the Laplace transform of h is equal to $\mathcal{L}_h(s) = \frac{1}{1+s}$. We also assume that the nearest vehicle in an S_Q to the tagged vehicle is chosen regardless of whether or not the vehicle are sending signals, i.e., the I_v-th $(1 < I_v < n_{x,+})$ vehicle in an S_Q selects $(I_v - 1)$-th or $(I_v + 1)$-th vehicle from the intersection as the nearest vehicle if there is no vehicle in the leaving segment between them; and the tagged vehicle in an S_R selects the vehicle at the end of the queue if there is no running vehicle between them. Furthermore, to simplify the notation, we omit the parameter $n_{y,*}$ $(* \in \{+, -\})$ appearing in several functions (e.g. $\mathcal{L}_{I_R}(\cdot \mid \cdot)$, $\mathcal{L}_I^{[R]}(\cdot \mid \cdot)$, and $\mathcal{L}_I^{[Q]}(\cdot \mid \cdot)$) as

$$\mathcal{L}_{I_R}^{[R]}(s \mid t_v, n_{x,+}, n_{x,-}, n_{y,+}, n_{y,-}) \equiv \mathcal{L}_{I_R}^{[R]}(s \mid t_v, n_{x,+}, n_{x,-}).$$

Theorem 1 (Outage probability of tagged vehicle in S_R) *Suppose that the tagged vehicle is in an S_R at distance t_v from the intersection. Then, the outage probability of the tagged vehicle is given by*

$$p_o^{[R]}(T \mid t_v) = 1 - \frac{1}{Q_{t_v}} \sum_{k=1}^{\lfloor t_v/l_v \rfloor} \sum_{m=1}^{\infty} q_+(k \mid \tau)q_-(m \mid \tau).$$
$$\times p_o^{[R]}(T \mid t_v, k, m), \quad (8)$$

where Q_{t_v} denotes the probability that the queue length in the $(x,+)$ part is less than t_v such that

$$Q_{t_v} = \sum_{k=1}^{\lfloor t_v/l_v \rfloor} q_+(k \mid \tau), \quad (9)$$

where $p_o^{[R]}(T \mid t_v, k, m)$ is the outage probability of the tagged vehicle in an S_R given that $n_{x,+} = k$ and $n_{x,-} = m$ such that

$$
\begin{aligned}
p_o^{[R]}(T \mid t_v, k, m) &= e^{-2(\lambda_{x,+}+\nu_{x,+})(t_v - kl_v)} \\
&\times \mathcal{L}_{I,t_v-kl_v}^{[R]}(\mu T(t_v - kl_v)^\alpha/\theta \mid t_v, k, m) + 2(\lambda_{x,+}+\nu_{x,+}) \\
&\times \int_0^{t_v-kl_v} e^{-2(\lambda_{x,+}+\nu_{x,+})r}\mathcal{L}_{I,r}^{[R]}(\mu Tr^\alpha \mid t_v, k, m)\mathrm{d}r, \quad (10)
\end{aligned}
$$

and, for $0 \leq r \leq t_v - kl_v$,

$$
\begin{aligned}
\mathcal{L}_{I,r}^{[R]}(s \mid t_v, n_{x,+}, n_{x,-}) &= \mathcal{L}_I^{[R]}(s \mid t_v, n_{x,+}, n_{x,-}) \\
&\times \exp\left((\lambda_{x,+}+\nu_{x,+})\int_{-r}^{r}\frac{s}{\mu|x|^\alpha + s}\mathrm{d}x\right), \quad (11)
\end{aligned}
$$

which is equal to the Laplace transform of the interference received at the tagged vehicle in the S_R under the condition that there is no vehicle within r of the tagged vehicle.

PROOF. The proof of this theorem is given in Appendix. □

Theorem 2 (Outage probability of tagged vehicle in S_Q) *Suppose that the tagged vehicle is the I_v-th vehicle from the intersection in an S_Q and $1 < I_v < n_{x,+}$, i.e., the tagged vehicle is not the head or the end of the queue. The outage probability of the tagged vehicle is equal to*

$$
\begin{aligned}
p_o^{[Q]}(T \mid I_v) &= 1 - \frac{1}{\overline{Q}_{I_v}} \sum_{k=I_v+1}^{\infty} \sum_{m=0}^{\infty} q_+(k \mid \tau)q_-(m \mid \tau) \\
&\times p_o^{[Q]}(T \mid I_v, k, m), \quad (12)
\end{aligned}
$$

where $\overline{Q}_{I_v}$ denotes the probability that the queue length in the $(x,+)$ part is larger than I_v such that

$$\overline{Q}_{I_v} = \sum_{k=I_v+1}^{\infty} q_+(k \mid \tau) = 1 - \sum_{k=0}^{I_v} q_+(k \mid \tau),$$

and where $p_o^{[Q]}(T \mid I_v, k, m)$ is the outage probability of the tagged vehicle in an S_Q given that $n_{x,+} = k$ and $n_{x,-} = m$ such that

$$
\begin{aligned}
p_o^{[Q]}(T \mid I_v, k, m) &= e^{-2\nu_{x,+}l_v}\mathcal{L}_{I,l_v}^{[Q]}(\mu Tl_v^\alpha/\theta \mid I_v, k, m) \\
&+ \int_0^{l_v} 2\nu_{x,+}e^{-2\nu_{x,+}r}\mathcal{L}_{I,r}^{[Q]}(\mu Tr^\alpha \mid I_v, k, m),
\end{aligned}
$$

and for $0 \leq r \leq l_v$,

$$
\begin{aligned}
&\mathcal{L}_{I,r}^{[Q]}(s \mid I_v, n_{x,+}, n_{x,-}) \\
&= \mathcal{L}_I^{[Q]}(s \mid I_v, n_{x,+}, n_{x,-})\exp\left(\nu_{x,+}\int_{-r}^{r}\frac{s}{\mu|x|^\alpha + s}\mathrm{d}x\right).
\end{aligned}
$$

PROOF. This theorem can be proved in a similar way to Theorem 1. Thus, we omit the proof. □

Note that we assume $1 < I_v < n_{x,+}$ in Theorem 2, however, we can similarly consider the case in which $I_v = 1$ or $I_v = n_{x,+}$. For example, if $I_v = n_{x,+}$, we need to consider the case that y_0 is an approaching vehicle in the $(x,+)$ part. Due to space limitation, we omit these cases.

4. TRANSMISSION POWER CONTROL

In this section, we discuss the transmission power control method in our model. Based on the results in the previous section, we give theoretical explanation to the trade-off relationship between the outage probability of the tagged vehicle in an S_R and S_Q. By mathematically representing the trade-off as a cost function and deriving its explicit expression as a function of θ, we optimize θ so that the trade-off can be well-balanced.

We assume that each vehicle obtains its stopping/running status by using a speedometer and controls its transmission power based on its current status. Vehicles determine power control parameter θ by receiving the information from RSUs or piggy-backing on packets used in V2V communications. In this paper, we consider the stationary or static situations such that all vehicles in the intersection are controlled using the same power control scheme. The adaptive control or transient situation are out of the scope of this paper. For simplicity, we assume the following conditions hereafter: $\lambda_{z,*} \equiv \lambda$ and $\nu_{z,*} \equiv \nu$, for all $z \in \{x, y\}$ and $* \in \{+, -\}$.

4.1 Trade-off and cost function

It is natural to consider that there exists a trade-off between the outage probability of the tagged vehicle in an S_Q or S_R depending on the value of θ. If θ is small, the tagged vehicle in an S_R has less interference from vehicles in S_Qs; however, the tagged vehicle in an S_Q has less transmission power, which may lead to the degradation in the SIR of the tagged vehicle in the S_Q. Thus, it is important to balance the outage probabilities of the tagged vehicles in an S_Q and S_R. To illustrate the trade-off relationship, we set the following metric as a cost function:

$$U(\theta, \gamma, T, t_v^*, I_v^*) = \gamma p_o^{[R]}(T \mid t_v^*) + (1 - \gamma)p_o^{[Q]}(T \mid I_v^*), \quad (13)$$

where t_v^* and I_v^* denote *reference points* of vehicles in an S_R and S_Q, respectively and $\gamma \in [0, 1]$ denotes a balancing parameter. The reference points are chosen as typical points in an S_R and S_Q and are determined by system designers or administrators. From the definition, the cost function can be considered as the average outage probability of a typical vehicle in S_Rs and S_Qs. In what follows, we derive an explicit expression of the cost function as a function of θ and study its characteristics.

It follows from (1) and $\mathcal{L}_h(s) = \frac{1}{1+s}$ that, for any set $\mathcal{D}$ and $r \in \mathbb{R}_+$,

$$\mathcal{L}_{I_Q}(\mu T r^\alpha \mid \mathcal{D}) = \prod_{d_i \in \mathcal{D}} \left[\frac{\rho}{1 + \theta T (r/d_i)^\alpha} + 1 - \rho \right]. \quad (14)$$

Furthermore, (2) leads to

$$\mathcal{L}_{I_R,a}^X(\mu T r^\alpha / \theta \mid t_v, \lambda)$$
$$= \exp\left(-\lambda \int_a^\infty \frac{T r^\alpha}{\theta|x - t_v|^\alpha + T r^\alpha} \mathrm{d}x \right), \quad (15)$$

which implies that $\mathcal{L}_{I_R,a}^X(\mu T r^\alpha / \theta \mid t_v, \lambda)$ is a function of θ. Similar to (15), we obtain

$$\mathcal{L}_{I_R,a}^Y(\mu T r^\alpha / \theta \mid t_v, \lambda)$$
$$= \exp\left(-\lambda \int_a^\infty \frac{T r^\alpha}{\theta(y^2 + t_v^2)^{\alpha/2} + T r^\alpha} \mathrm{d}y \right). \quad (16)$$

Thus, combining (14)–(16) with (4), (5), and (10) yields

$$p_o^{[R]}(T|t_v^*) = 1 - \frac{1}{Q t_v^*} \sum_{k=1}^{\lfloor t_v^*/l_v \rfloor} \sum_{m=1}^\infty q_+(k \mid \tau) q_-(m \mid \tau)$$
$$\times [C_0(k, m) D(\theta \mid t_v^* - k l_v, t_v^*, k, m)$$
$$+ \int_0^{t_v^* - k l_v} C_1(r, k, m) K(\theta \mid r, t_v^*, k, m) \mathrm{d}r \Bigg], \quad (17)$$

where

$$D(\theta \mid r, t_v, k, m) = \exp\left(-(\lambda + \nu) \int_{-\infty}^\infty \frac{T r^\alpha}{\theta(y^2 + t_v^2)^{\frac{\alpha}{2}} + T r^\alpha} \mathrm{d}y \right.$$
$$-(\lambda + \nu) \int_{(-\infty, \infty) \setminus [-r, r]} \frac{T r^\alpha}{\theta|x|^\alpha + T r^\alpha} \mathrm{d}x$$
$$\left. + \lambda \int_{-m l_v}^{k l_v} \frac{T r^\alpha}{\theta|x - t_v|^\alpha + T r^\alpha} \mathrm{d}x \right), \quad (18)$$

$$K(\theta \mid r, t_v, k, m) = \prod_{\substack{-m \le i \le k \\ i \ne 0}} \left[\frac{\rho}{1 + \theta T r^\alpha |t_v - i l_v|^{-\alpha}} + 1 - \rho \right], \quad (19)$$

and $C_0(k, m) = e^{-2(\lambda + \nu)(t_v^* - k l_v)} K(1 \mid t_v^* - k l_v, t_v^*, k, m)$ and $C_1(r, k, m) = 2(\lambda + \nu)e^{-2(\lambda + \nu)r} D(1 \mid r, t_v^*, k, m)$ are independent factors of θ. On the other hand, applying (14)–(16) to (4)–(6) and (12) leads to

$$p_o^{[Q]}(T \mid I_v^*) \equiv 1 - \frac{1}{\overline{Q}_{I_v^*}} \sum_{k=I_v^*+1}^\infty \sum_{m=1}^\infty q_+(k \mid \tau) q_-(m \mid \tau)$$
$$\times [C_2(k, m) D(\theta \mid l_v, I_v^* l_v, k, m)$$
$$- \int_0^{l_v} C_3(r, k, m) K(\theta \mid l_v, I_v^* l_v, k, m) \mathrm{d}r \Bigg], \quad (20)$$

where $C_2(k, m) = e^{-2\nu l_v} K(1 \mid l_v, I_v^* l_v, k, m)$ and $C_3(r, k, m) = 2\nu e^{-2\nu r} D(1 \mid r, I_v^* l_v, k, m)$, which are independent factors of θ. As a result, (13), (17) and (20) give an explicit expression of U as a function of θ.

4.2 Optimization of power control

To balance the trade-off between the outage probability of the tagged vehicle in an S_Q and S_R, it is sufficient to consider and find an optimal θ such that

$$\tilde{\theta} = \arg\min_{\theta > 0} U(\theta, \gamma, T, t_v^*, I_v^*).$$

The above optimization problem can be solved using numerical methods (e.g., Newton's method). Although $U(\cdot)$ cannot be expressed in an explicit way, $U(\cdot)$ and θ have the following simple relationship, which can be easily confirmed from (18) and (19).

Lemma 1 *For any $t_v, r \ge 0$, $k, m \in \mathbb{N}$, and $\theta \ge 0$, the following are true:*

(a) $D(\theta \mid r, t_v, k, m)$ *is an increasing function of θ; and*

(b) $K(\theta \mid r, t_v, k, m)$ *is a decreasing function of θ.*

Lemma 1 and (17) indicate that $p_o^{[R]}(T \mid t_v^*)$ can be represented as the sum of a decreasing function (the second term in (17)) and a increasing function (the last term in (17)). Similar to this, (20) shows that $p_o^{[R]}(T \mid t_v^*)$ is also the sum of a decreasing function (the second term in (20)) and a increasing function (the last term in (20)). As a result, the definition of $U(\cdot)$ and Lemma 1 indicate that the optimization problem of θ is equal to that of the trade-off between the sum of the increasing functions and the sum of the decreasing functions. Due to this simple characteristic of θ and the cost function, it is easy to understand the impact of θ on the outage probability and to obtain the optimal $\tilde{\theta}$ using a numerical optimization method, which are confirmed in Section 5.

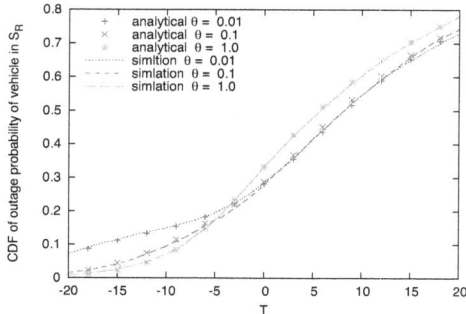

Figure 2: CDF of $p_o^{[R]}(T \mid t_v^*)$ with different θ when $t_v^* = 100$ m, $\rho = 0.75$.

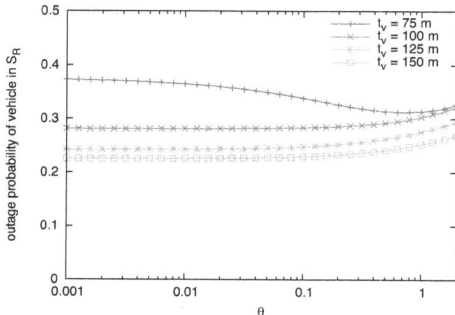

Figure 3: Comparison of $p_o^{[R]}(T \mid t_v^*)$ with different θ and t_v^* when $T = 0$ dB and $\rho = 0.75$.

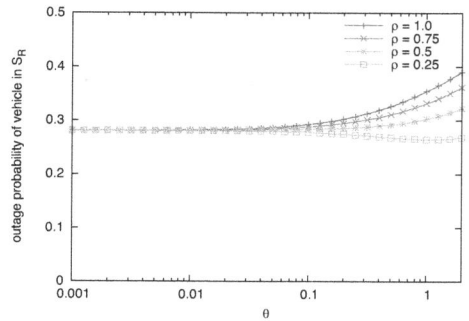

Figure 4: Comparison of $p_o^{[R]}(T \mid t_v^*)$ with different θ and ρ when $T = 0$ dB and $t_v^* = 100$ m.

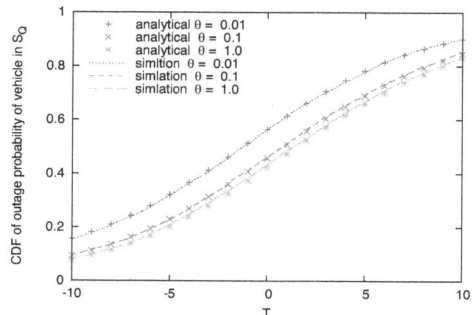

Figure 5: CDF of $p_o^Q(T \mid I_v)$ with different θ when $I_v^* = 5$ and $\rho = 0.75$.

5. EXPERIMENTS

In this section, we discuss the results from several numerical experiments. First, our analytical results were validated through simulation experiments. We then evaluated the effect of our power control on the interference problem at an intersection. In addition, we evaluated the impact of the various parameters on the power control method and its optimization.

Before reporting the results, we explain the experimental setting. Considering practical and typical situations, we choose $l_v = 6$ m, and $\lambda = 10 \sim 30$ [1/km]. Furthermore, we fixed $\gamma = 1/2$, $\nu = 5$ [1/km], $\phi = 60/3600$ [km/sec.], $\tau = 30$ [sec.], and $\alpha = 4$ in all experiments. In each round of simulation, we first generate vehicles in S_Qs based on the queue length distribution (see Section 3.4); and then generate those in S_Rs according to PPPs on roads with length of 10 km. We conducted 10,000 times simulation rounds for each experiment.

5.1 Effect of power control on interference

We first discuss the effect of the power control on the outage probability of the tagged vehicle in an S_R and S_Q. Figure 2 shows the cumulative distribution function (CDF) of the outage probability of the tagged vehicle in an S_R, i.e, $p_o^{[R]}(T \mid t_v^*)$, with different T. We set $\lambda = 10$, $t_v^* = 100$ m, and $\rho = 0.75$. Note that $\theta = 1$ means that power control is off and if θ is smaller, then power control is stronger, i.e., the power of vehicles in S_Qs is smaller. As we can see from the figure that if θ decreases, the outage probability becomes lower in the region where T is larger than -5 dB. This fact shows that the power control can reduce the outage probability of the vehicle in an S_R. The figure also indicates that roughly 10% of the outage probability can be reduced when $T = 0$ dB.

Figures 3 and 4 show the results of $p_o^{[R]}(T \mid t_v^*)$ when varying

the values of θ with different t_v^* and ρ, respectively. We set $T = 0$ dB. Similar to Figure 2, if θ decreases, the outage probability becomes lower when $t_v^* \geq 100$ m and $\rho \geq 0.5$. In addition, the results of Figure 3 show that if t_v^* decreases, the outage probability of the tagged vehicle in an S_R increases. This fact indicates that the vehicle closer to the intersection has high interference. Furthermore, if the vehicle drives away from the intersection, then the improvement in the outage probability becomes small. This is because the interference from vehicles in S_Qs becomes smaller when t_v^* is larger. On the other hand, Figure 4 shows that if ρ is small, the outage probability of the tagged vehicle in an S_R becomes low because it has lower interference. Due to the same reason, the improvement in the outage probability also decreases if ρ is small. Note that $p_o^{[R]}(T \mid t_v^*)$ can be represented as the sum of a increasing function and decreasing function of θ (see (17) and Lemma 1). Figures 2–4 show that $p_o^{[R]}(T \mid t_v^*)$ behaves like a increasing function of θ when $\rho \geq 0.5$ or $t_v^* \geq 100$ m. These results indicate that the impact from the decreasing function (i.e., the second term in (17)) was relatively small in these experimental setting. On the other hand, if $t_v^* = 75$ m, the decreasing function was dominant. Since the decreasing function, i.e., the second term in (17), corresponds to the probability that the tagged vehicle in S_R receives from the vehicle at the end of the queue, this fact shows that if t_v^* is small, the vehicle at the end of the queue is selected as a sender, i.e., the nearest vehicle, with high probability.

We next show the CDF of $p_o^{[Q]}(T \mid I_v^*)$ with different θ in Figure 5. The other parameters are $I_v^* = 5$, $\lambda = 10$, and $\rho = 0.75$. We can see from the figure that if the value of θ decreases, the outage probability becomes higher in all cases. Figure 6 shows the results of $p_o^{[Q]}(T \mid I_v^*)$ when varying θ with different ρ. We can see from the figure that if ρ decreases, $p_o^{[Q]}(T \mid I_v^*)$ increases. This

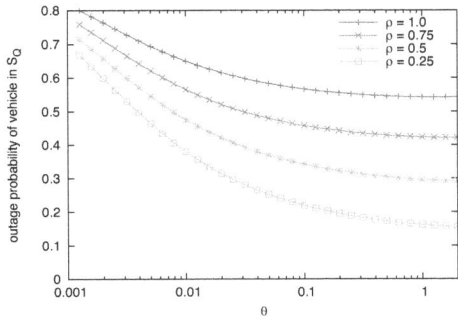

Figure 6: Comparison of $p_o^{[Q]}(T \mid I_v^*)$ with different θ and ρ when $I_v^* = 5$, and $T = 0$ dB.

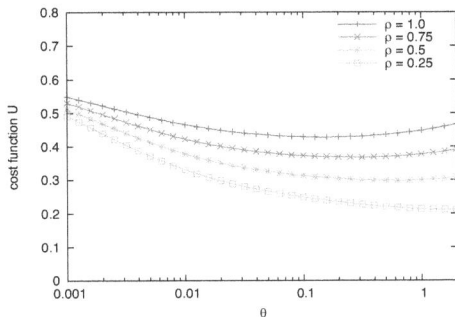

Figure 7: Comparison of $U(\theta, \gamma, T, t_v^*, I_v^*)$ with different θ and ρ when $t_v^* = 100$ m, $I_v^* = 5$, $T = 0$ dB, and $\gamma = 1/2$.

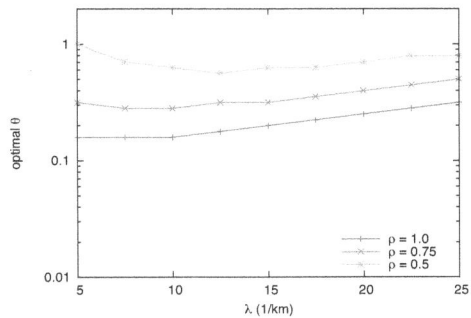

Figure 8: Comparison of $\tilde{\theta}$ with different λ and ρ. $t_v^* = 100$ m, $I_v^* = 5$, and $T = 0$ dB.

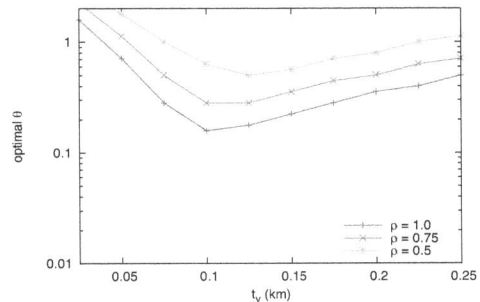

Figure 9: Comparison of $\tilde{\theta}$ with different t_v^* and ρ. $I_v^* = 5$, $T = 0$ dB, and $\gamma = 1/2$.

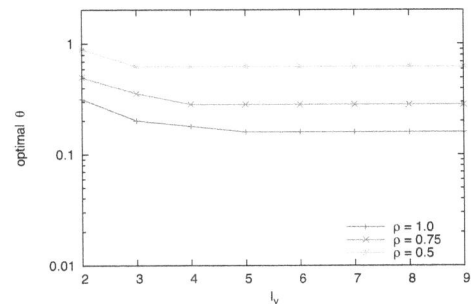

Figure 10: Comparison of $\tilde{\theta}$ with different I_v^* and ρ. $t_v^* = 100$ m, $T = 0$ dB, and $\gamma = 1/2$.

is because the total interference received from the vehicles in S_Qs decreases. In addition, Figures 5 and 6 show that $p_o^{[Q]}(T \mid I_v^*)$ behaves as an increasing function of θ. These results show that the impact from the increasing function (i.e., the second term in (20)) was dominant in this experimental setting (see Lemma 1). As a result, Figures 4 and 6 show that there exists a trade-off between the outage probability of the tagged vehicle in an S_R and S_Q.

We show the results of the cost function when varying θ in Figure 7. Note that the cost function is equal to the weighted sum of $p_o^{[R]}(T \mid t_v^*)$ and $p_o^{[Q]}(T \mid I_v^*)$ (see (13)). Thus, Figure 7 can be obtained by combining the results of Figures 4 and 6. We can see from Figure 7 that the cost function does not have very complicated form, which implies that the optimal θ can be easily found using a numerical method.

5.2 Impacts of traffic intensity

We next evaluated the impacts of the traffic intensity on the optimal θ. Figure 8 shows the results of numerically obtained optimal θ when varying λ. By definition, large λ implies that the number of vehicles in S_Rs is large and the queue length is long. We can see from the figure that if λ increases, the optimal θ increases slightly. This fact can be considered as follows: if λ increases, then the total interference received from the vehicles in S_Rs becomes large because the traffic intensity at S_Rs becomes high. On the other hand, the total interference from S_Qs also increases because the queue length tends to be long. As a result, $\tilde{\theta}$ increased slightly because of these offset.

5.3 Impacts of reference points

Finally, we considered the impact of the reference point locations. Figure 9 shows the results of $\tilde{\theta}$ when varying the reference point t_v^*. As shown in the graph, when t_v^* is small, the optimal θ tends to be high, while if t_v^* is larger than $100 \sim 120$ m, $\tilde{\theta}$ increases. The reason for this can be considered as follows: if the reference point in an S_R is closer to the end of the queue, then the nearest vehicle is likely to be that at the end of the queue. As a result, the vehicle at the reference point does not benefit much from the power control. In other words, if t_v^* is small, then the second term in (17) becomes dominant, which corresponds to the outage probability of the tagged vehicle in an S_R communicating with the vehicle at the end of the queue. On the other hand, Figure 10 shows the results for $\tilde{\theta}$ with different values of I_v^*. We can see that $\tilde{\theta}$ takes similar values when $I_v^* \geq 4$ and if I_v^* turns away from 4, $\tilde{\theta}$ increases. This is because the vehicle close to the intersection tends to have higher interference from S_Rs in the $(y, \cdot)$ parts. Thus, $\tilde{\theta}$ is large because the effect of the power control method is small.

6. CONCLUSIONS

We proposed a mathematical interference model with a simple power control method for intersections. Using a stochastic geometry approach, we derived the theoretical values of the outage probability of a typical vehicle in an S_Q an S_R. By mathematically expressing the trade-off relationship between the outage probability of the tagged vehicle in an S_Qs and S_R as a cost function, we obtain a guideline for an optimal power control method, which cannot be obtained through simulations. Although we assumed a simple power control method in our model, we believe that such a theoretical analysis of power control can help in efficient system design and control in future ITSs.

In this paper, we only considered uni-cast communication as a typical type of V2V communications, i.e., a tagged vehicle communicates with only the nearest vehicle. However, in active-safety management systems, vehicles broadcast their information periodically. Thus, taking into account such broadcast communications is for future work. The analysis of broadcast-rate control is also important because it can reduce the interference on the time axis. More realistic modeling of the location patterns of vehicles and the MAC layer design are also for future work.

7. REFERENCES

[1] J. G. Andrews, F. Baccelli, and R. K. Ganti. A tractable approach to coverage and rate in cellular networks. *IEEE Trans. on Commun.*, 59(11):3122–3134, 2011.

[2] S. Azimi, G. Bhatia, R. R. Rajkumar, and P. Mudalige. Reliable intersection protocols using vehicular networks. In *ICCPS*, 2013.

[3] F. Baccelli and B. Blaszczyszyn. *Stochastic Geometry and Wireless Networks, Volume I -Theory.* Hanover: Now Publishers, 2009.

[4] F. Baccelli and X. Zhang. A correlated shadowing model for urban wireless networks. In *INFOCOM*, 2015.

[5] B. Blaszczyszyn, P. Muhlethaler, and Y. Toor. Stochastic analysis of Aloha in vehicular ad-hoc networks. *Ann. Telecommun.*, 68(1):95–106, 2012.

[6] S. Eichler. Performance evaluation of the IEEE 802.11p WAVE communication standard. In *VTC*, 2007.

[7] H. ElSawy and E. Hossain. A modified hard core point process for analysis of random CSMA wireless networks in general fading environments. *IEEE Trans. Commun.*, 61(4):1520–1534, 2013.

[8] Y. P. Fallah, C. Huang, R. Sengupta, and H. Krishnan. Congestion control based on channel occupancy in vehicular broadcast networks. In *VTC*, 2010.

[9] Y. P. Fallah, N. Nasiriani, and H. Krishnan. Stable and fair power control in vehicle safety networks. *IEEE Trans. on Veh. Technol.*, 65(3):1662–1675, 2016.

[10] M. J. Farooq, H. ElSawy, and M.-S. Alouini. Modeling inter-vehicle communication in multi-lane highways: a stochastic geometry approach. In *VTC*, 2015.

[11] A. T. Gian and A. Busson. Modeling CSMA/CA in VANET. In *ASMTA*, 2012.

[12] C. Gloaguen, F. Voss, and V. Schmidt. Parametric distributions of connection lengths for the efficient analysis of fixed access networks. *Ann. Telecommun.*, 66:103–117, 2011.

[13] H. Hartenstein and K. Laberteaux. *VANET Vehicular Applications and Inter-Networking Technologies.* New York: Wiley, 2009.

[14] M. Haenggi, J. G. Andrews, F. Baccelli, O. Dousse, and M. Franceschetti. Stochastic geometry and random graphs for the analysis and design of wireless networks. *IEEE J. Sel. A. Commun.*, 27(7):1029–1046, 2009.

[15] G. Karagiannis, O. Altintas, E. Ekici, G. Heijenk, B. Jarupan, K. Lin, and T. Wei. Vehicular networking: a survey and tutorial on requirements, architectures, challenges, standards and solutions. *IEEE Commun. Surveys Tuts.*, 13(4):584–616, 2011.

[16] T. Kimura, H. Saito, H. Honda, and R. Kawahara. Modeling urban ITS communication via stochastic geometry approach. *to appear in VTC*, 2016.

[17] F. Morlot. A population model based on a Poisson line tessellation. In *WiOpt*, 2012.

[18] T. V. Nguyen, F. Baccelli, and D. Kofman. A stochastic geometry analysis of dense IEEE 802.11 networks. In *INFOCOM*, 2007.

[19] T. V. Nguyen, F. Baccelli, K. Zhu, S. Subramanian, and W. Wu. A performance analysis of CSMA based broadcast protocol in VANETs. In *INFOCOM*, 2013.

[20] E. Steinmetz, M. Wildemeersch, and H. Wymeersch. WiP abstract: reception probability model for vehicular ad-Hoc networks in the vicinity of intersections. In *ICCPS*, 2014.

[21] D. Stoyan, W. S. Kendall, and J. Mecke. *Stochastic Geometry and its Applications.* Chichester: John Wiley & Sons, 1995.

[22] Z. Tong, H. Lu, M. Haenggi, and C. Poellabauer. A stochastic geometry approach to the modeling of DSRC for vehicular safety communication. *IEEE Trans. on Intell. Transp. Syst.*, 17(5):1448-1458, 2016.

[23] M. T.-Moreno, J. Mittag, P. Santi, and H. Hartenstein. Vehicle-to-vehicle communication: fair transmit power control for safety-critical information. *IEEE Trans. on Veh. Technol.*, 58(7):3684–3703, 2009.

APPENDIX

PROOF OF THEOREM 1. By conditioning on the queue length in the $(x, +)$ and $(x, -)$ parts, the outage probability of the tagged vehicle in an S_R can be expressed as

$$p_o^{[R]}(T \mid t_v) = 1 - \frac{1}{Q_{t_v}} \sum_{k=1}^{\lfloor t_v/l_v \rfloor} \sum_{m=1}^{\infty} q_+(k \mid \tau) q_-(m \mid \tau) \times \mathsf{P}(\mathsf{SIR}^{[R]} > T \mid t_v, k, m), \quad (21)$$

where $\mathsf{SIR}^{[R]}$ represents the SIR of the tagged vehicle in the S_R and $\mathsf{P}(\mathsf{SIR}^{[R]} > T \mid t_v, k, m)$ is equal to $p_o^{[R]}(T \mid t_v, k, m)$. Let y_0 denote the nearest vehicle (a desired transmitter) of the tagged vehicle. By conditioning on whether y_0 is in an S_Q or S_R, we have

$$p_o^{[R]}(T \mid t_v, k, m) = \mathsf{P}(\mathsf{SIR}^{[R]} > T, y_0 \in S_Q \mid t_v, k, m) + \mathsf{P}(\mathsf{SIR}^{[R]} > T, y_0 \in S_R \mid t_v, k, m). \quad (22)$$

We first consider the case where $y_0 \in S_Q$. In this case, y_0 is the vehicle at the end of the queue; thus, the distance from the tagged vehicle to y_0 is $t_v - kl_v$. By definition, the probability that there is no vehicle between the tagged vehicle with y_0 is equal to $e^{-2(\lambda_{x,+} + \nu_{x,+})(t_v - kl_v)}$. Since the desired channel (between y_0 and the tagged vehicle) has Rayleigh fading, the complementary cumulative distribution function of the SIR of the tagged vehicle can be computed as follows (see e.g. Theorem 1 in [1]):

$$\mathsf{P}(\mathsf{SIR}^{[R]} > T, y_0 \in S_Q \mid t_v, k, m)$$
$$= \mathsf{P}(\text{no vehicle within distance } t_v - kl_v)$$
$$\times \mathsf{P}\left(\frac{\theta h(t_v - kl_v)^{-\alpha}}{\mu I^{[R]}} > T \mid t_v, y_0 \in S_Q, n_{x,+} = k, n_{x,-} = m\right)$$
$$= e^{-2(\lambda_{x,+} + \nu_{x,+})(t_v - kl_v)} \mathcal{L}_{I, t_v - kl_v}^{[R]}(\mu T(t_v - kl_v)^{\alpha}/\theta \mid t_v, k, m), \quad (23)$$

where $I^{[R]}$ denotes the total interference received at the tagged vehicle in an S_R and the second equality holds because h is exponential. Similarly, conditioning on the distance to y_0 yields

$$\mathsf{P}(\mathsf{SIR}^{[R]} > T, y_0 \in S_R \mid t_v, k, m)$$
$$= \int_0^{t_v - kl_v} \mathsf{P}(\text{distance to } y_0 \text{ is } r) \mathcal{L}_{I, r}^{[R]}(\mu T r^{\alpha} \mid t_v, k, m) dr$$
$$= \int_0^{t_v - kl_v} 2(\lambda_{x,+} + \nu_{x,+}) e^{-2(\lambda_{x,+} + \nu_{x,+})r} \mathcal{L}_{I, r}^{[R]}(\mu T r^{\alpha} \mid t_v, k, m) dr. \quad (24)$$

Finally, combining (22), (23) and (24) with (21), we have (8)–(11). □

Effective Selection of Targeted Advertisements for Vehicular Users

Gil Einziger
Politecnico di Torino, Italy

Carla Fabiana Chiasserini
Politecnico di Torino, Italy

Francesco Malandrino
Politecnico di Torino, Italy

ABSTRACT

This paper focuses on targeted advertising for vehicular users, where users receive advertisements (ads) from roadside units and the vehicle onboard system displays only ads that are relevant to the user. A broker broadcasts ads and is paid by advertisers based on the number of vehicles that displayed each ad. The problem we study is the following: given that the broker can broadcast a limited number of ads, what is the strategy for ad selection that maximizes the broker's revenue? We first identify the conflict existing between users' interests and broker's revenue as a critical feature of this scenario, which may dramatically reduce the broker's revenue. Then, given the problem complexity, we propose Volfied, an algorithm that solves this conflict, allows for near-optimal broker's revenue and has very limited computational complexity. Our results show that Volfied increases the broker's revenue by up to 70% with respect to state-of-the-art alternatives.

Keywords

Performance evaluation; algorithms; services for mobile users

1. INTRODUCTION

As mobile devices outnumber TV sets and desktop PCs [1], advertisers have recently rushed to this media. Mobile advertising is therefore growing globally at a rapid rate, involving an increasing variety of mobile devices [2]. This paper focuses on targeted advertising for vehicular users, although our problem formulation and solution can be easily extended to the case of pedestrian users. Vehicular users are indeed expected to represent a large portion of the mobile users population in a few years, and several types of business (shops, restaurants, touristic attractions) are interested in advertising their products and services through, e.g., onboard devices as an alternative to static advertisement billboards.

In particular, targeted advertising (such as Google AdWords and Ink TAD) aims at displaying advertisements (ads) only to interested users, by analyzing their online profiles or behaviors [3]. This approach has been shown to be very beneficial for both advertisers and users [4]. On one hand, the probability of an ad being effective increases significantly with the user interest in the product or service. On the other, users are not bothered with irrelevant information. This is particularly important in a mobile scenario, where users cannot be exposed to too many ads at the same time, due to their reduced screen size and attention span.

In accordance with Internet advertising systems [5, 6], our work addresses a scenario where advertisers sign a contract with a broker (e.g., an advertising platform) to display an ad to interested users. The user exposure to the ad is referred to as an *impression* [7]. Each ad may have a different value depending on the advertised product/service, and the broker is paid by advertisers based on both the ad value and the number of ad impressions. In our vehicular environment, the broker delivers ads by broadcasting them through roadside units (e.g., base stations or APs), and the number of broadcast ads is constrained by bandwidth limitations. Vehicular users passing by a roadside unit (RSU) will receive the transmitted ads; however, as mentioned, the onboard system will display only ads that are relevant to the user. The actual number of impressions can then be reported to the broker by vehicles, periodically (e.g., once a day) and in a secure manner.

Under this framework, our goal is to solve the problem of real-time ads selection that the broker should perform in order to maximize its revenue while meeting the constraint on the number of ads that can be broadcast. The broker's revenue is defined as the number of ad impressions, each weighted by the value of the displayed ad. To find the best ad selection strategy, the broker exploits information on radio coverage and users' interests. The former can be obtained through RSUs, the latter can be obtained from the user profile upon service subscription.

The main contributions of our work are as follows.

(i) We present a system model that jointly captures ads features and users' interests. We show that when ads are broadcast by the RSUs and the users can choose which ads to display, there exists a conflict between the broker and users' interests. This implies that increasing the number of broadcast ads may actually reduce the broker's revenue. We then formulate the following optimization problem: which is the best set of ads that the broker should select to maximize its revenue? Due to its complexity, we design a greedy algorithm, named after the computer game Volfied. Our algorithm solves the above conflict and provides an efficient solution.

(ii) In order to further speed up the ad selection procedure, we propose a technique to reduce the number of ads to process. By applying Volfied to such simplified system representation, we ensure a swifter on-line ad selection, with negligible performance loss.

(iii) Finally, we evaluate Volfied in a realistic vehicular environment and show that its performance is nearly optimal in a small-scale scenario. In a large-scale scenario, Volfied is compared to other heuristics, such as Top-k and Random, and it is shown to

MSWiM '16, November 13-17, 2016, Malta, Malta
© 2016 ACM. ISBN 978-1-4503-4502-6/16/11...$15.00
DOI: http://dx.doi.org/10.1145/2988287.2989136

Table 1: Notation

Symbol	Description
$\mathcal{A} = \{a\}$	Set of advertisements
$\mathcal{V} = \{v\}$	Set of vehicular users
$\mathcal{U} = \{u\}$	Set of RSUs
$\mathcal{A}_\epsilon^{(M)}$	M-sparse approximation of set $\mathcal{A}$
$D(\cdot, \cdot)$	Distance between users' interests and/or ads
K	No. of ads each RSU can broadcast in one time step
M	No. of ads each vehicle can display in one time step
$r(a, u)$	Value of ad a under the coverage of RSU u
$R(a, u)$	Estimated total revenue for ad $a \in \mathcal{A}$ at RSU u

increase the broker's revenue by up to 70% and the generated impressions by up to 50%.

Our model and problem formulation share some common elements with previous work, as discussed in Sec. 2. However, to the best of our knowledge, our work is the first to present a unified model capturing the main aspects of mobile advertising, to identify the conflict issue between users' interests and broker's revenue, and to propose a highly efficient algorithm for ad selection that meets the system constraints.

2. RELATED WORK

Advertisement scheduling is an important problem that can be studied from multiple perspectives, as it provides different challenges for advertisers, brokers and users. Existing works typically employ machine learning [8] or game theory approaches [9], and either focus on ad pricing or attempt to maximize social welfare. For example, [10, 11] suggest methods for advertisers to configure their ads features and generation speed to maximize ads visibility. Similarly, [12] suggests ad scheduling techniques to maximize revenue over a shared medium. This approach requires advertisers to make complex decisions, which are not practical in a vehicular environment. Other approaches aim at maximizing social welfare [13] in ad auctions, or address social influence in on-line advertising [6]. Another research direction is to treat selection of on-line ads as an optimization problem [7, 14], which however cannot scale to large systems due to solution complexity. The work in [15] addresses a scenario and problem similar to ours, albeit with a simpler display policy at the vehicle level. The strategy in [15] is radically different from ours: decisions are made by solving an ILP optimization problem, which would be too computationally intensive in our scenario. Finally, several works have addressed privacy in targeted advertising (see, e.g., [5]) – a relevant issue that, however, is out of the scope of this work.

3. SYSTEM MODEL AND PROBLEM FORMULATION

We consider that advertisers rely on an ad platform, called *broker*, to deliver targeted ads to vehicular users. Each user has a profile from which the user's interests can be deduced. The delivery of ads takes place through an infrastructure-based vehicular network, composed of vehicles and RSUs. Through such a network, the broker can disseminate ads to vehicular users.

For simplicity, we consider that time is divided into discrete steps. Vehicles receive ads broadcast by the RSUs under whose coverage they pass, and display the ones that are relevant (i.e., of interest) to the user. At each step, vehicles can display a limited number of ads, M, and ads are not cached. Also, a vehicle displays an ad at most once[1];The number of ads that can be broadcast by RSUs is constrained by bandwidth and cost limitations. We denote the maximum number of ads that each RSU can broadcast in one time step by K.

It is the broker's job to select the sets of ads to be broadcast at each time step by each RSU. In order to make this decision, the broker can use the following information:
(i) users' interests and preferences;
(ii) the vehicles that are currently under coverage by RSUs;
(iii) the ads that have been broadcast by RSUs in the past;
(iv) the RSUs visited by vehicles in the past.

Information about users' interests can be provided by the users themselves upon subscription to the service, or obtained through nowadays-common profiling techniques. Information about the presence of vehicles under RSUs coverage can be obtained from the RSUs themselves, by exploiting the beacons vehicles periodically transmit [16]; in our performance evaluation, we also study how errors in acquiring such information affect the performance.

Model entities. The main entities we need to model are: (i) *vehicles* (also referred as users), $v \in \mathcal{V}$, and (ii) *ads* $a \in \mathcal{A}$. Each ad a has an associated *value*, $r(a, u)$. Having RSU-specific ad values allows us to model both *local* ads, which are worthless at RSUs out of their target location, and *global* ones, whose value is constant at all RSUs. Every time ad a is displayed to a vehicle, the onboard platform notifies the broker, which gets a *revenue* equal to the ad value. Thus the broker's total revenue is given by the number of impressions, each weighted by the value of the displayed ad.

The content of ads and the interest of vehicles are both described in terms of *features* $\vec{f} \in \mathbb{F}$. Therefore, both ads and vehicles can be mapped onto points in an n-dimensional *feature space*, $\mathbb{F} \subseteq \mathbb{R}^n$, where n is the number of features.

Distance and relevance. We can define the *distance* between two points $\vec{f_1}, \vec{f_2} \in \mathbb{F}$ (either ads or vehicular users) as:

$$D(\vec{f_1}, \vec{f_2}) = \left\| \vec{f_1} - \vec{f_2} \right\|_0. \tag{1}$$

If both $\vec{f_1}$ and $\vec{f_2}$ are vehicles, the distance defined in (1) expresses how similar their interests are. If both are ads, (1) conveys how similar the ads themselves, and their potential audience, are. Finally, if $\vec{f_1}$ is an ad $a \in \mathcal{A}$ and $\vec{f_2}$ is a vehicle $v \in \mathcal{V}$, the distance $D(a, v)$ represents how *relevant* ad a is to vehicle v.

We also define a *relevance threshold* $D_{\max}$: only ads closer than $D_{\max}$ are relevant to a user.

The above notation, along with the one used in the following, is summarized in Tab. 1.

3.1 Problem definition

It is the broker's task to define and enact what we formally call a *selection strategy*: given the set $\mathcal{A}$ of ads, the number of ads that can be broadcast (K) and displayed (M), and the vehicles under RSU coverage, the broker has to select those ads that maximize its revenue. Intuitively, the broker should select ads that will be displayed by many vehicles and have a high value r. The former implies that the selected ads should be relevant *and* new to as many vehicles as possible, but, quite surprisingly, these two conditions are not sufficient to ensure that a broadcast ad is actually displayed by the vehicle. Indeed, the broker decides which ads to broadcast, but vehicles decide which of these ads to display. The aims of these two actors are different and potentially *conflicting*: the broker would aim at selecting ads with high value r, while vehicles display ads based on their relevance to the user. Thus, *whenever the broker*

---

[1] Ads that generate a revenue when displayed multiple times can be represented by separate elements of $\mathcal{A}$.

can broadcast more ads than vehicles can display (i.e., $K > M$), a conflict between the broker and the users' interests may arise. We remark that indeed $K > M$ in all practical cases, and that, as highlighted in the example below, conflicts do not only waste radio resources, but they can also severely reduce the broker's revenue.

Example. Consider a toy case with one RSU ($\mathcal{U} = \{u\}$), one vehicle ($\mathcal{V} = \{v\}$) and two ads ($\mathcal{A} = \{a_1, a_2\}$). Assume: $r(a_1) = 10$, $r(a_2) = 1$, $D(a_1, v) = 0.1$ and $D(a_2, v) = 0.05$. Also, let us focus on one time step and assume $M = 1$, i.e., the vehicle can display only one ad, and $D_{\max} = 0.15$. First, consider $K = 1$, i.e., the RSU can transmit only one ad, and that the RSU sends a_1. Then the vehicle will display a_1 and the broker will earn $r(a_1, u) = 10$. Now, assume $K = 2$ and that the RSU sends a_1 and a_2: one would expect that by sending more ads, the broker would earn *at least* the same revenue. However, owing to the fact that $M = 1$, vehicle v will disregard a_1 and only display a_2, being the most relevant to itself. Thus, the broker's revenue will be $r(a_2, u) = 1$.

In light of this, we introduce the following definition.

DEFINITION 3.1 (CONFLICT-FREE SET). *A set of selected ads, $\mathcal{S} \subseteq \mathcal{A}$, is conflict free if, for each vehicle $v \in \mathcal{V}$, the set includes at most M ads that are relevant to v.*

3.2 Problem formulation

We now formulate the ad selection problem as an optimization problem. We denote the current time step by t_c, and the set of past and current steps by $\mathcal{T}$. Then the set of binary flags $\chi(u, v, t) \in \{0, 1\}$ express whether RSU u covers vehicle v at time $t \in \mathcal{T}$.

Our formulation involves two binary decision variables: $\beta(a, u, t_c)$ and $\delta(a, v, t_c)$. The former concerns the broker, and it indicates whether an ad a is broadcast by RSU u at the current time step or not. The latter concerns individual vehicles, and it indicates whether ad a is displayed by vehicle v at time t_c. Note that, although the vehicles and the broker make different decisions for different, and indeed conflicting, purposes, we are able to reproduce both decisions in the *same* optimization problem, as laid out next.

Constraints. A vehicle v can display only the relevant ads that it receives from the current RSU, i.e., for any $a \in \mathcal{A}$ and $v \in \mathcal{V}$

$$\delta(a, v, t_c) \leq \chi(u, v, t_c)\beta(a, u, t_c)\mathbf{1}_{[D(a,v) \leq D_{\max}]}, \quad (2)$$

where u is the RSU, and $\mathbf{1}_{[D(a,v) \leq D_{\max}]}$ takes 1 if $D(a, v) \leq D_{\max}$ and 0 otherwise. Next, vehicles can display at most M ads:

$$\sum_{a \in \mathcal{A}} \delta(a, v, t_c) \leq M, \quad \forall v \in \mathcal{V}. \quad (3)$$

Each ad can be shown at most once by every vehicle:

$$\sum_{t \in \mathcal{T}} \delta(a, v, t) \leq 1, \quad \forall a \in \mathcal{A}, v \in \mathcal{V}. \quad (4)$$

Note that the δ values that refer to previous time steps are input parameters to the problem.

Last, we must make sure that a vehicle v selects the ads to display based on their relevance to itself. In other words, vehicle v will not display an ad a if it receives from the RSU M (or more) ads whose relevance to v is higher than a's:

$$\delta(a, v, t_c) \leq \max \left\{ 0, M - \sum_{\substack{a' \in \mathcal{A}: \\ D(a',v) > D(a,v)}} \left[\chi(u, v, t_c)\beta(a', u, t_c) \right. \right.$$
$$\left. \left. \left(1 - \sum_{t \in \mathcal{T} \setminus \{t_c\}} \delta(a', v, t) \right) \right] \right\} \quad \forall a \in \mathcal{A}, v \in \mathcal{V}. (5)$$

As far as the broker is concerned, the sole constraint is on the maximum number of ads that each RSU can broadcast at a given time step:

$$\sum_{a \in \mathcal{A}} \beta(a, u, t_c) \leq K \quad \forall u \in \mathcal{U}. \quad (6)$$

Objective. Given the above constraints, the broker's objective is to maximize its revenue:

$$\max \sum_{a \in \mathcal{A}} \sum_{v \in \mathcal{V}} \sum_{u \in \mathcal{U}} \delta(a, v, t_c)\chi(u, v, t_c)r(a, u). \quad (7)$$

Discussion. The above formulation has the interesting property of accounting for the way *both* vehicles and broker make decisions. Constraint (5) describes how vehicles will select ads based on the ads' relevance to themselves, while objective (7) represents the broker's aim to maximize its own revenue. Thus, conflicts are accounted for: by solving the optimization problem, the broker will maximize its revenue *subject to* the behavior of the vehicles. On the negative side, the problem complexity prevents its solution in large-scale scenarios. Specifically, the ad selection is a $0-1$ knapsack problem with constant weights, whose item values are the outcome of another $0-1$ knapsack problem (the selection of the ads to display). Thus, the optimization problem is NP-hard. In light of this, we present below a heuristic approach.

4. ON-LINE DECISION MAKING

Our problem exhibits two main challenges. The first has to do with the *conflict* between the broker's revenue and the user interests, which may significantly impair the broker's revenue. The second is *complexity*, since the set of ads $\mathcal{A}$ is potentially very large, as are the sets of ads relevant to individual vehicles. We address these two challenges separately. First, we propose a way to make *conflict-free* decisions leveraging on the estimated revenue that ads can generate. Then we introduce a *sparse-set* approximation that bounds the complexity of estimating ad revenues. For ease of presentation, we describe our decision-making scheme with reference to one RSU and one time step only, and we drop the RSU and time indices when discussing this scenario. Sec. 4.3 explains how to extend the proposed schemes to the multi-step and multi-RSU cases.

4.1 Conflict-free decisions: Volfied

In order to select a set of ads that maximizes its revenue, the broker has to first estimate the revenue it will get from broadcasting a generic ad a. Let $R(a)$ denote such estimated revenue. $R(a)$ is computed by adding $r(a)$ thereto every time a vehicle v, to which a is relevant, enters the RSU coverage area, and subtracting the same amount when v leaves the coverage area.

Armed with the estimated revenues $R(a)$, the broker applies an ad selection strategy. The most straightforward strategy would be *Top-k*, which selects the K ads with highest estimated revenue $R(a)$. However, Top-k has the major disadvantage of ignoring the fact that vehicles can display at most M ads each, thus it may create conflicts that harm the broker's revenue and waste radio resources on ads that will not be displayed (see Sec. 3.1). To avoid this, we devise a *conflict-free* alternative, called Volfied and presented in Alg. 1.

The objective of Alg. 1 is to identify the set $\mathcal{S} \subseteq \mathcal{A}$ of ads to broadcast, initialized in line 1. Volfied starts by sorting set $\mathcal{A}$ by estimated revenue, in line 2. Then, for each ad a, it checks how many ads are already in $\mathcal{S}$ closer to a than $2D_{\max}$ (line 4). If less than M, a is added to the set of ads to serve, in line 5. The algorithm ends when either all ads have been evaluated, or K ads have been selected (line 6).

13

Algorithm 1 Conflict-free ad selection: Volfied

Require: $\mathcal{A}, K, M, D_{\max}, R(a)$
1: $\mathcal{S} \leftarrow \emptyset$
2: **sort** $a \in \mathcal{A}$ **by** $R(a)$ in decreasing order
3: **for all** $a \in \mathcal{A}$ **do**
4:     **if** $|\{b \in \mathcal{S}: D(a,b) \leq 2D_{\max}\}| < M$ **then**
5:         $\mathcal{S} \leftarrow \mathcal{S} \cup \{a\}$
6:     **if** $|\mathcal{S}| \geq K$ **then**
7:         break
    return $\mathcal{S}$

Below, we formally prove that Volfied always generates a conflict-free set of ads, i.e., no vehicle gets more than M relevant ads.

Theorem 1. *The set of ads $\mathcal{S}$ selected by Volfied is conflict free.*

PROOF. Consider a set with one ad only; this is clearly conflict free. Then, by construction (line 4), Volfied selects an additional ad only if, for any ad $a \in \mathcal{S}$, there are less than M ads within distance $2D_{\max}$. This implies that, for any vehicle v, $\mathcal{S}$ includes at most M ads relevant to v, i.e., $\mathcal{S}$ remains conflict free. Indeed, due to triangle inequality, for any two ads a and b s.t. $D(a,b) > 2D_{\max}$, we have: $D(a,v) + D(v,b) \geq D(a,b) > 2D_{\max}$, for any vehicle v. That is, given an ad a, which is relevant to v, only ads within distance $2D_{\max}$ from a may be relevant to v too. $\square$

Furthermore, for sake of completeness, we remark that, in the special case $M = K$, Volfied outputs the same ad set as Top-k, and such set maximizes the broker's revenue. In other words, both Volfied and Top-k are optimal when $K = M$. This is because, by selecting the first K top-revenue ads, the condition in line 4 in Alg. 1 is always met (as $K = M$), thus Volfied and Top-k select the same ads. By Theorem 1, the set is conflict free; also it maximizes the broker's revenue since, by construction, it includes the K ads with top estimated revenue $R(a)$. Next, we show that Volfied has linear complexity in the size of the ads set.

Theorem 2. *The worst case runtime complexity of Volfied is $O(|\mathcal{A}| \cdot K)$.*

PROOF. From Algorithm 1, one can see that the loop in line 3 iterates over all the ads $a \in \mathcal{A}$, thus in the worst case all ads in $\mathcal{A}$ are processed. In line 4, we compare each ad against all previously selected ads, which are at most $K - 1$. The operations in the remaining lines have complexity $O(1)$ and thus the overall complexity of Algorithm 1 is $O(|\mathcal{A}| \cdot K)$. $\square$

Finally, we remark that Volfied relies on the estimated revenues, i.e., the $R(a)$ values. Such estimates need to be refreshed every time a vehicle enters or exits the coverage area of an RSU. Every update has a linear cost in the number of ads, as shown below.

Property 1. *The worst case complexity of updating the revenue estimation is $|\mathcal{A}|$.*

PROOF. Consider a vehicle v and that all ads are relevant to v. When v enters or leaves the coverage of an RSU, the revenue estimation of all ads has to be updated, thus the complexity is $|\mathcal{A}|$. $\square$

Clearly, when the number of ads and vehicles involved is large, the update procedure becomes cumbersome. To overcome this issue, below we propose an effective approach which greatly reduces the number of ads to consider.

4.2 Sparse-set approximation

An intuitive solution to speed up the ad selection procedure consists in limiting the size of the set of ads $\mathcal{A}$. However, blindly removing ads would wantonly impair the system performance: the problem is not that there are too many ads, but there are too many ads *similar to each other*, hence with the same target audience. We therefore replace the set $\mathcal{A}$ with its *sparse approximation*, as defined below. For the sake of clarity, we start by considering $M = 1$, i.e., each vehicle can display at most one ad per time step.

DEFINITION 4.1 (SPARSE SET). *$\mathcal{X} \subseteq \mathbb{F}$ is a sparse set if, for any two points $\vec{f}_1, \vec{f}_2 \in \mathcal{X}$, $D(\vec{f}_1, \vec{f}_2) > 2\epsilon$.*

It is important to note that, due to local ads that are relevant only to RSUs within their target location, different RSUs may select different ads to be part of their sparse approximation.

The following result states that, given a sparse set of ads $\mathcal{X} \subseteq \mathbb{F}$, the distance between a point in $\mathcal{X}$ and any other point either in $\mathcal{X}$ or in $\mathcal{V}$ ($\mathcal{V} \subseteq \mathbb{F}$), is at least ϵ. It follows that, given $D_{\max}$, a vehicle cannot find in $\mathcal{X}$ more than $\lceil (D_{\max}/\epsilon)^n \rceil$ ads that are relevant to itself.

Theorem 3. *Given a sparse set $\mathcal{X} \subseteq \mathcal{A}$, for every point $\vec{f} \in \mathcal{X} \cup \mathcal{V}$, a closed ball of radius ϵ around $\vec{f}$ contains at most a single ad $a \in \mathcal{X}$.*

PROOF. In the case where $\vec{f} \in \mathcal{X}$ is an ad, the theorem holds given the definition of sparse set. Next, consider that $\vec{f}$ is a vehicle. we prevent the selection of any additional ad within a ball of $2 \cdot \varepsilon$ from a. Assume that there are two ads a_1 and a_2 in $\mathcal{X}$ s.t. $D(a_1, \vec{f}) \leq \epsilon$ and $D(a_2, \vec{f}) \leq \epsilon$. Then, by triangular inequality, $D(a_1, a_2) \leq D(a_1, \vec{f}) + D(a_2, \vec{f}) \leq 2\epsilon$, which contradicts the definition of sparse set. Thus the thesis is proven. $\square$

Let us now introduce the sparse approximation of an ad set.

DEFINITION 4.2 (SPARSE APPROXIMATION). *The sparse approximation of a set of ads $\mathcal{A}$ is a set $\mathcal{A}_\epsilon^{(1)} \subseteq \mathcal{A}$ such that: (i) $\mathcal{A}_\epsilon^{(1)}$ is a sparse set, and (ii) for each ad $a \in \mathcal{A} \setminus \mathcal{A}_\epsilon^{(1)}$, there exists $a' \in \mathcal{A}_\epsilon^{(1)}$ with $r(a') \geq r(a)$ and $D(a, a') \leq 2\epsilon$.*

Intuitively, $\mathcal{A}_\epsilon^{(1)}$ is a sparse set obtained by removing redundant, low-value ads from $\mathcal{A}$. Alg. 2 provides a technique to build the sparse approximation of $\mathcal{A}$.

Algorithm 2 Building a sparse approximation of the ad set (function `EpsilonSet`)

Require: $\mathcal{A}, \epsilon$
1: $\mathcal{A}_\epsilon^{(1)} \leftarrow \emptyset$
2: **sort** $a \in \mathcal{A}$ **by** $r(a)$ in decreasing order
3: **for all** $a \in \mathcal{A}$ **do**
4:     $\mathcal{A}_\epsilon^{(1)} \leftarrow \mathcal{A}_\epsilon^{(1)} \cup \{a\}$
5:     $\mathcal{A} \leftarrow \mathcal{A} \setminus \{b \in \mathcal{A}: D(a,b) \leq 2\epsilon\}$
    return $\mathcal{A}_\epsilon^{(1)}$

The algorithm first sorts the ads in the original set by their value (line 2). Then, at each iteration, it adds the top (i.e., highest-value) ad to the sparse set (line 4) and removes all other ads in $\mathcal{A}$ at distance less than or equal to 2ϵ from said ad (line 5). An example of how Alg. 2 works is presented in Fig. 1. It is straightforward to see that, by construction, the resulting set $\mathcal{A}_\epsilon^{(1)}$ is the sparse approximation of $\mathcal{A}$, as by Definition 4.2.

Next, we consider $M > 1$ (i.e., vehicles can display more than one ad per time step). In this case, the broker should select multiple

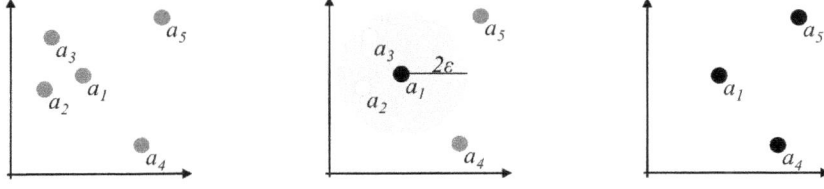

Figure 1: How Alg. 2 works: given the initial set $\mathcal{A}$ with $r(a_1) > r(a_2) > \ldots > r(a_5)$ (left), it first includes a_1 in the sparse set $\mathcal{A}_\epsilon^{(1)}$. Then, a_2 and a_3 are excluded as stated in line 5 (center). Finally, a_4 and a_5 are added to $\mathcal{A}_\epsilon^{(1)}$ (right).

ads targeting the same audience. We therefore introduce the notion of M-sparse set and M-sparse approximation, $\mathcal{A}_\epsilon^{(M)}$.

DEFINITION 4.3 (M-SPARSE SET). $\mathcal{X}^{(M)} \subseteq \mathbb{F}$ is an M-sparse set if, for any point $\vec{f} \in \mathcal{X}^{(M)}$, there are at most M points within distance 2ϵ from $\vec{f}$ (including $\vec{f}$ itself).

DEFINITION 4.4 (M-SPARSE APPROXIMATION). The M-sparse approximation of a set of ads $\mathcal{A}$ is a set $\mathcal{A}_\epsilon^{(M)} \subseteq \mathcal{A}$ such that (i) $\mathcal{A}_\epsilon^{(M)}$ is M-sparse, and (ii) for each subset $\mathcal{B} \subseteq \mathcal{A}$ with $|\mathcal{B}| \leq M$, there exists a subset $\mathcal{B}_\epsilon^{(M)} \subseteq \mathcal{A}_\epsilon^{(M)}$ with $|\mathcal{B}_\epsilon^{(M)}| = |\mathcal{B}|$ and bijection function, $g : \mathcal{B} \to \mathcal{B}_\epsilon^{(M)}$, s.t. $\forall b \in \mathcal{B}$: $r(g(b)) \geq r(b)$ and $D(b, g(b)) \leq 2\epsilon$.

Algorithm 3 Building the M-sparse approximation of the ad set

---
Require: $\mathcal{A}, \epsilon, M$
1: $\mathcal{A}_\epsilon^{(0)} \leftarrow \emptyset$
2: **for** $j = 1$ **to** M **do**
3: $\quad \mathcal{A}_\epsilon^{(j)} \leftarrow \mathcal{A}_\epsilon^{(j-1)} \cup \texttt{EpsilonSet}(\mathcal{A} \setminus \mathcal{A}_\epsilon^{(j-1)}, \epsilon)$
$\quad$ **return** $\mathcal{A}_\epsilon^{(M)}$

It is easy to see that, by construction, Alg. 3 builds the M-sparse approximation of the ad set $\mathcal{A}$. Indeed, it repeatedly calls the $\texttt{EpsilonSet}$ function defined in Alg. 2. As shown by the following theorem, the sparse set resulting from Alg. 3 includes groups of up to M similar ads that are relevant to the same vehicle.

Theorem 4. Given an M-sparse set $\mathcal{A}_\epsilon^{(M)}$ output by Alg. 3, for every vehicle $v \in \mathcal{V}$, a closed ball of radius ϵ around v contains at most M ads.

PROOF. The set $\mathcal{A}_\epsilon^{(M)}$ is generated recursively by forming M sparse sets (as it can be seen in Algorithm 3). Each sparse set satisfies Theorem 3 and, thus, contributes with at most a single ad s.t. $D(a, v) \leq \epsilon$. It follows that the maximum number of ads within a closed ball of radius ϵ, centered in v, is equal to M. $\square$

Replacing the original set of ads $\mathcal{A}$ with its sparse approximation $\mathcal{A}_\epsilon^{(M)}$ makes it possible for the broker to streamline the ad selection procedure. In particular, the estimate of the revenue, $R(a)$, can be updated with limited complexity.

Theorem 5. When performed on $\mathcal{A}_\epsilon^{(M)}$, the complexity of the revenue estimation update is: $\min \left\{ \lceil \left(\frac{M \cdot D_{\max}}{\epsilon} \right)^n \rceil, |\mathcal{A}_\epsilon^{(M)}| \right\}$.

PROOF. It follows from Theorem 4 that for each vehicle v a closed ball of radius ϵ around v contains at most M ads. Therefore, we are left to consider how many such balls fit into a closed ball of radius $D_{\max}$. The maximum number of balls of radius ϵ that fit in such a volume is: $\lceil \left(\frac{M \cdot D_{\max}}{\epsilon} \right)^n \rceil$. Thus the maximum number of ads within distance $D_{\max}$ from the vehicle is the minimum between such a value and the total number of ads in $\mathcal{A}_\epsilon^{(M)}$. $\square$

Clearly, larger values of ϵ allow a greater reduction of the number of ads, hence a faster ad selection. However, as ϵ grows, $a \in \mathcal{A}$ and its corresponding ad, $a' \in \mathcal{A}_\epsilon^{(M)}$, become less similar. It follows that a' may become not relevant to a certain vehicle (i.e., $D(a', v) > D_{\max}$) while a was (i.e., $D(a, v) \leq D_{\max}$). This means that the opportunities of a selection strategy to pick M relevant ads for a vehicle may diminish when the strategy is applied to $\mathcal{A}_\epsilon^{(M)}$ instead of $\mathcal{A}$. However, in Sec. 5 we show that such a performance loss is negligible even for large values of ϵ, e.g., $\epsilon = D_{\max}/4$.

Finally, we remark that the sparse approximation of the ad set needs to be computed only *once*, while the selection algorithm runs every time a new set of ads to be broadcast has to be identified.

4.3 Multi-RSU, multi-step

The ad selection algorithm can be easily extended to networks comprising multiple RSUs and operating for multiple time steps, such as the one considered in our performance evaluation in Sec. 5.

Specifically, when considering multiple time steps, there is no profit in serving vehicles with the same ad multiple times. Thus, the way the estimated revenues R are computed is enhanced as follows: $R(a, u)$ is increased by $r(a, u)$ only if a has not been broadcast to the vehicle before.

Similarly, we can account for the presence of multiple RSUs, i.e., for the fact that vehicles may have received an ad from some RSU they visited in the past. If a vehicle under the coverage of an RSU, $u \in \mathcal{U}$, has been served ad $a \in \mathcal{A}$ in the past by another RSU, $u' \in \mathcal{U}$, the corresponding $r(a, u)$ value is discounted from the revenue estimation $R(a, u)$. This requires the broker (not the advertisers) to know which RSUs the vehicles visited, a piece of information that can be easily gathered from the beacons cars are required to periodically send and that will be available in next-generation network systems [16]. It does *not* require to know which ads were displayed by cars.

5. PERFORMANCE EVALUATION

We evaluate Volfied using a vehicular trace [17] depicting car mobility in Cologne, Germany. The trace refers to a urban area of 28×32 km^2, and models over 110,000 vehicles, during the course of 8 hours. As shown in Fig. 2, 1,000 RSUs were deployed (black dots in the figure) along the busiest roads and at the center of intersections so that vehicles are under radio coverage for approximately 60% of the time they appear in the trace. The RSU radio range is set to 150 m.

Each vehicle is assigned a five-dimensional feature vector. Feature values are sampled from the normal distribution with a mean of 0.5 and standard deviation of 0.15. Similarly, each ad is assigned a five-dimensional feature vector and a value r, both sampled uniformly in the range $(0, 1)$. 90% of the ads are global, the others are local. Recall that local ads can be displayed only within the coverage area of a specific RSU, which is selected at random.

15

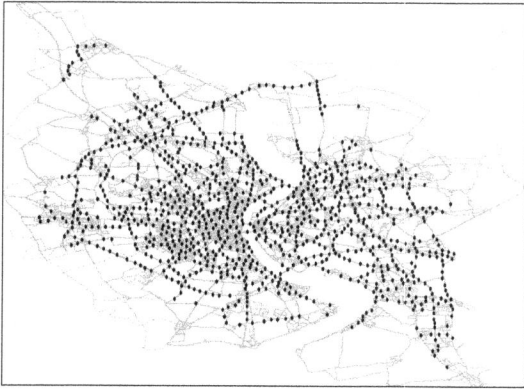

Figure 2: Road layout (grey lines); deployed RSUs are represented by black dots.

We evaluate Volfied, Top-k and a Random strategy by simulating the system over 480 time steps, with each step lasting one minute. At each time step, RSUs broadcast the ads selected by the broker. The tested algorithms only differ from each other in the ad selection strategy, i.e., all of them can access the same information on ads, vehicles and ads values. Specifically, Top-k selects the K ads with highest estimated revenue R, Random selects K random ads among those that have a positive revenue R, and Volfied makes conflict free selection as described in Sec. 4.1. We first perform our evaluation with respect to a *default configuration*, whose settings are: $K = 5$, $M = 1$, $|\mathcal{A}| = 10,000$, $D_{max} = 0.15$, and $\epsilon = 0.025$, and under the assumption that the presence of vehicles under an RSU can be detected without error. Note that the default configuration implies that the tested algorithms use as input the sparse set $\mathcal{A}_{0.025}^{(1)}$. The performance metrics we plot are:
(i) Total revenue, which reflects the amount of money paid to the broker by advertisers and is computed as the sum of the revenue generated by all broadcast ads (recall that the revenue is equal to the ad value r multiplied by the number of ad impressions);
(ii) Total number of impressions, i.e., the total number of ads that have been displayed by vehicles. This metric reflects the point of view of advertisers who would like to maximize ad visibility;
(iii) The average impression distance, which represents how relevant, on average, a displayed ad is to the user. This last metric clearly accounts for the user's point of view. The lower the distance, the more relevant the displayed ads are to the users. The average distance never exceeds D_{max}.

We remark that other performance metrics such as bandwidth consumption are the same for all tested algorithms and are therefore omitted. Higher performance in any of the metrics we present could also be perceived as more efficient bandwidth utilization.

Table 2: Comparison against the optimum for a single time step

Metric	Top-k	Random	Volfied	Optimum
Revenue	1444.3	810.1	1712.0	1770.3
Impressions	1647	1573	1910	1889
Distance	0.107	0.115	0.125	0.119

Comparison against the optimal solution. We compare the performance of Volfied, as well as that of Top-k and Random, against the optimum derived through (7). To this end, we restrict ourselves to a single-step scenario so that the computation of the optimal so-

lution is viable. The results in Tab. 2 show that Volfied provides near-optimal performance: its revenue is just 3.4% lower than the optimum, while it generates 1% more impressions and similar distance. Note that, since the optimum maximizes the revenue, there may be cases where it selects ads with very high value r but that are displayed by slightly fewer users, while Volfied always generates a conflict-free set thus resulting in a higher number of impressions. The performance gap between the optimum and the other two schemes is much larger: the revenue gain is 25% and 55% when compared to Top-k and Random, respectively.

Performance over time. Fig. 3 shows the time evolution of our performance metrics for the default configuration. As can be observed, Volfied generates 70% higher revenue and 50% more impressions than Top-k. This implies that Volfied satisfies the interests of both broker and advertisers. Because Volfied aims at maximizing the broker's revenue, it may select ads that are slightly (by about 0.01) less relevant to users with respect to Top-k and Random, as shown by the right plot in Fig. 3.

Effect of the ad set size. Fig. 4 shows the impact of the ad set size, $|\mathcal{A}|$, on the system performance. Intuitively, the larger $|\mathcal{A}|$, the easier it is to find relevant ads to each vehicle. Indeed, revenue (and also impressions, omitted for brevity) improves for larger values of $|\mathcal{A}|$. Interestingly, for 1,000 ads the difference between the algorithms is small and Volfied generates 30% more revenue than its alternatives. However, as $|\mathcal{A}|$ increases, the performance gap also grows, and when $|\mathcal{A}| = 20,000$, Volfied increases revenue by 70% with respect to the other schemes. Indeed, the more ads in the system, the more critical their selection becomes and the more severe the revenue loss that occurs due to the conflict discussed in Sec. 3.1. Hence the advantage provided by Volfied becomes more evident.

How many ads to serve? The value of K corresponds to the bandwidth that is consumed by ad broadcasting. The left plot in Fig. 5 shows that, for small values of K, the broker's revenue increases with K. However, it is interesting to notice that the revenue saturates as eventually the vehicles' ability to display ads and the number of possible advertisements become a performance bottleneck. Thus, there is a preferred value of K (which depends on the system settings) that the broker should use.

Furthermore, it is surprising to notice that the performance of Top-k and Random is not monotone with K: increasing K beyond a certain point actually hurts the system performance. The reason is twofold. First, the larger K, the more likely the conflicts. Second, ads that were broadcast before are not considered as profitable anymore (although they can still generate revenue if not all vehicles displayed them); thus, once the top K ads have been broadcast, it becomes increasingly harder to identify the best ads to transmit. Interestingly, Top-k reaches its peak value of revenue for a lower K than Random, due to the fact that the ads selected by Top-k create conflicts more often than those that are randomly chosen. This is confirmed by the right plot in Fig. 5, which shows that the conflicts generated by Top-k reduce the distance between ad and user, hence providing slightly smaller average distance than Random.

Effect of M. We now fix $K = 5$ and study the performance as M varies. Recall that a small value of M accounts for the reduced screen size aboard a vehicle and for the limited driver's attention span, and that typically $M < K$. As shown in Fig. 6, Top-k and Random are very sensitive to M. For $M < K$, they provide much lower revenue and number of impressions; only when M approaches K, i.e., when conflicts seldom occur, Top-k gives good performance. Volfied, instead, is much more robust, as its performance varies very little with M. It generates just 10% lower revenue and 15% fewer impressions when $M = 1$ than when $M = K$.

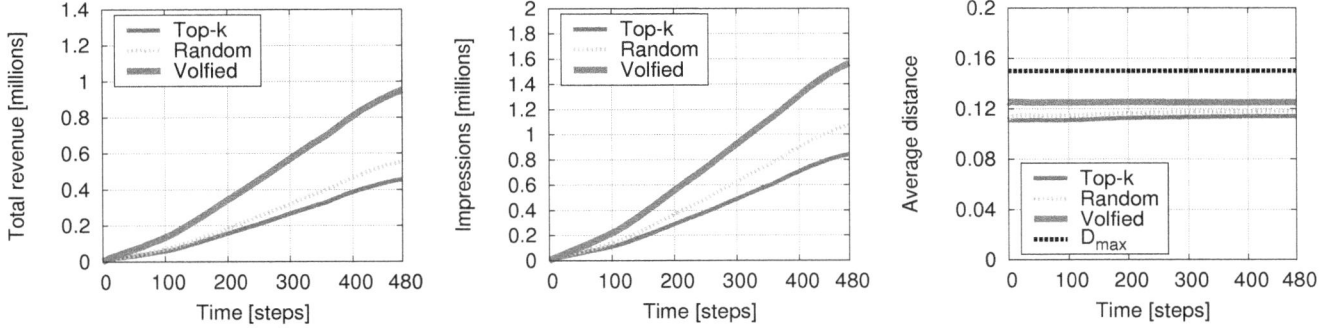

Figure 3: Time evolution of the cumulative revenue, cumulative number of impressions and average distance for Volfied, Top-k and Random (default configuration).

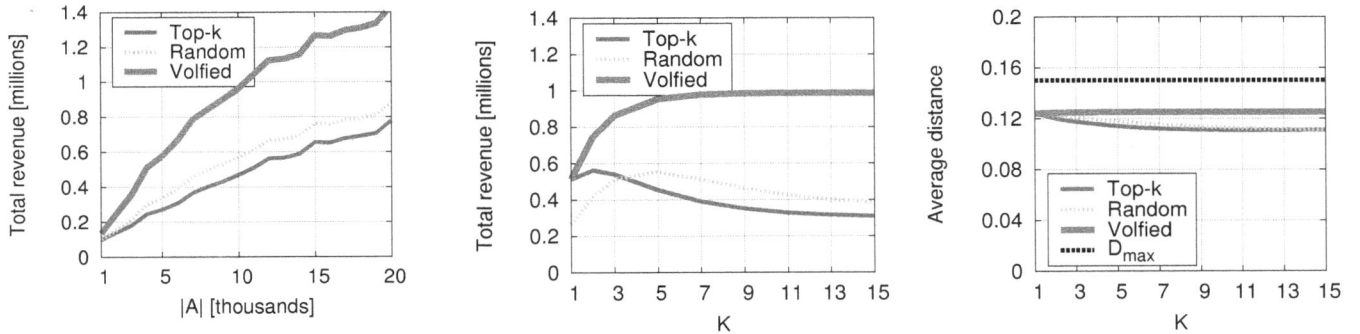

Figure 4: Effect of the ad set size on broker's revenue, when $K = 5$ and $M = 1$.

Figure 5: Effect of number of broadcast ads (K) per time step, with fixed $M = 1$.

We remark that the latter is the special case where Volfied and Top-k yield the same revenue, which coincides with the optimum (see also Sec. 4.1). Thus, the fact that Volfied gives a similar revenue for $M = 1$ and for $M = K$, confirms that its performance is near-optimal for any $M < K$.

Effect of ϵ. The left plot in Fig. 7 depicts the broker's revenue as ϵ varies, when $D_{\max} = 0.15$. As can be observed, for values of $\epsilon \leq D_{\max}/4$, the revenue loss due to the sparse approximation is negligible. Also, for such values of ϵ we limit the number of ads that have to be processed per vehicle arrival/departure. As shown in Theorem 5, the number of processed ads is bounded by: $\lceil \left(\frac{D_{\max}}{\epsilon} \right)^n \rceil$ regardless of the size of the ad set $\mathcal{A}$, which, for $\epsilon = D_{\max}/4$, amounts to $4^5 = 1024$.

Vehicle detection accuracy. While deriving the previous results, we assumed that an RSU could reliably detect all vehicles under its coverage thanks to their beacon messages. The right plot in Fig. 7 shows the impact of different levels of accuracy, i.e., probability of successfully detecting a vehicle under an RSU. Remarkably, Volfied with 0.3 accuracy provides higher revenue than the best alternative with accuracy equal to 1. It follows that Volfied is very effective even with incomplete knowledge of the scenario, since it can still successfully avoid conflicts.

$D_{\max}$ **and average distance.** $D_{\max}$ is another important parameter as it determines which ads are relevant to a user. Intuitively, the larger $D_{\max}$, the easier it is to select relevant ads that will be displayed by a vehicle, but also the larger the average ad-user distance. Fig. 8 confirms these trends for all selection strategies. However, we can see that, when $D_{\max}$ is very small, all strategies yield similar revenue and average distance as the set of ads with positive

revenue, hence that can be selected, is very small. Likely each vehicle has at most one ad within distance $D_{\max}$ in $\mathcal{A}_{\epsilon}^{(1)}$. For larger values of $D_{\max}$, instead, Volfied provides higher revenue than the other schemes, as conflicts become increasingly likely and cause revenue loss (left plot in Fig. 8). For Volfied, the price to pay is a slight increase in the average ad-user distance (right plot in Fig. 8).

6. CONCLUSIONS

We addressed targeted advertising in vehicular networks and envisioned a system where advertisers pay a broker based on the value and the number of impressions of each ad. We considered the broker's perspective and formulated the problem of selecting the ads to broadcast that maximize the broker's revenue, subject to a maximum number of ads that can be transmitted. While doing this, we identified a conflict between user and broker's interests, which severely hurts the broker's revenue if not properly addressed. Then, in light of the problem complexity, we introduced Volfied, an efficient greedy algorithm that always selects a conflict-free set of ads while maximizing the broker's revenue. The complexity of Volfied has been proved to be linear with the number of ads. In addition, we proposed a sparse approximation of the ad set, which further speeds up ad selection. We evaluated Volfied and our sparse approximation technique in a realistic vehicular environment, against the optimum in a single-time step scenario and against the Top-k and Random strategies in a multi-time step scenario. Our results show that Volfied provides near-optimal performance. Also, it improves the broker's revenue by up to 70%, and the number of displayed ads by up to 50%, with respect to Top-k.

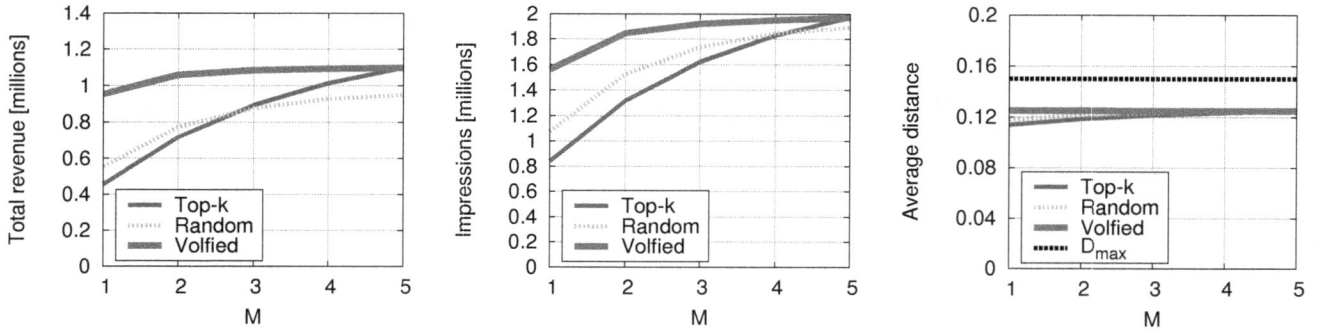

Figure 6: Effect of the number of displayable ads (M) on performance metrics for fixed $K = 5$.

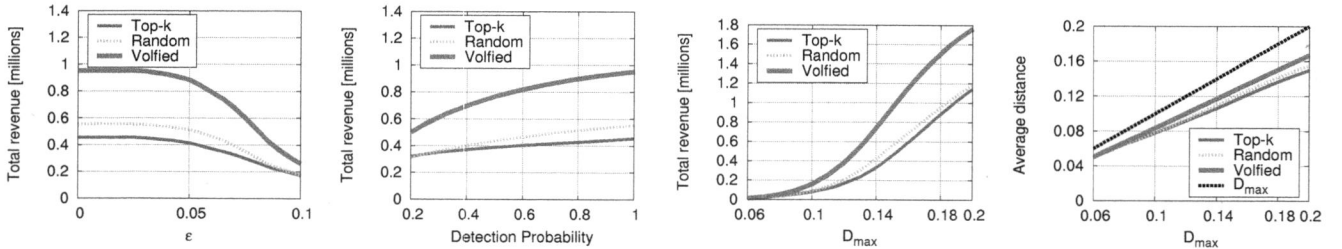

Figure 7: Effect of ϵ (left) and of accuracy in vehicle detection (right) on the broker's revenue.

Figure 8: Effect of $D_{\max}$ on performance metrics.

7. ACKNOWLEDGMENT

This paper was made possible by NPRP grant ♯ $5-782-2-322$ from the Qatar National Research Fund (a member of Qatar Foundation). The statements made herein are solely the responsibility of the authors.

8. REFERENCES

[1] G. Sterling, "It's official: Google says more searches now on mobile than on desktop," *SearchEngineLand*, 2015.

[2] R. van der Meulen and J. Rivera, "Gartner says mobile advertising spending will reach 18 billion dollars in 2014," 2014, Gartner Press Release.

[3] A. Rao, F. Schaub, and N. M. Sadeh, "What do they know about me? Contents and concerns of online behavioral profiles," *CoRR*, vol. abs/1506.01675, 2015.

[4] H. Beales, "The value of behavioral targeting," *Network Advertising Initiative*, Jan. 2010.

[5] W. Wang, L. Yang, Y. Chen, and Q. Zhang, "A privacy-aware framework for targeted advertising," *Computer Networks*, vol. 79, pp. 17–29, Mar. 2015.

[6] Z. Abbassi, A. Bhaskara, and V. Misra, "Optimizing display advertising in online social networks," in *ACM WWW*, 2015.

[7] J. Feldman, N. Korula, V. Mirrokni, S. Muthukrishnan, and M. Pál, "Online ad assignment with free disposal," in *Internet and Network Economics*, ser. Lecture Notes in Computer Science, S. Leonardi, Ed.   Springer Berlin Heidelberg, 2009, vol. 5929, pp. 374–385.

[8] R. Friedman and A. Libov, "An advertising mechanism for p2p networks," in *IEEE P2P*, 2013.

[9] G. Aust, *Vertical Cooperative Advertising and Pricing Decisions in a Manufacturer-Retailer Supply Chain: A Game-Theoretic Approach*.   Cham: Springer International Publishing, 2015, pp. 65–99.

[10] A. Reiffers-Masson, E. Altman, and Y. Hayel, "A time and space routing game model applied to visibility competition on online social networks," in *NETGCOOP*, 2014.

[11] A. Reiffers-Masson, Y. Hayel, and E. Altman, "Game theory approach for modeling competition over visibility on social networks," in *COMSNETS*, 2014.

[12] E. Altman and N. Shimkin, "Strategic posting times over a shared publication medium," in *NETGCOOP*, 2014.

[13] F. P. Kelly, P. Key, and N. S. Walton, "Incentivized optimal advert assignment via utility decomposition," *ACM Conference on Economics and Computation*, 2014.

[14] E. Vee, S. Vassilvitskii, and J. Shanmugasundaram, "Optimal online assignment with forecasts," in *ACM Conference on Electronic Commerce*, 2010.

[15] C. Borgiattino, C.-F. Chiasserini, F. Malandrino, and M. Sereno, "Advertisement delivery and display in vehicular networks," in *IEEE VTC-Fall*, 2015.

[16] E. T. P. for Communications Networks and Services, http://networld2020.eu/wp-content/uploads/2015/01/Joint-Whitepaper-V12-clean-after-consultation.pdf.

[17] D. Naboulsi and M. Fiore, "On the instantaneous topology of a large-scale urban vehicular network: The Cologne case," in *ACM MobiHoc*, 2013.

A Fully-distributed Traffic Management System to Improve the Overall Traffic Efficiency

Allan M. de Souza and Leandro A. Villas

University of Campinas, Campinas, SP, Brazil
allanms@lrc.ic.unicamp.br, leandro@ic.unicamp.br

ABSTRACT

In recent years, the number of vehicles has increased faster than the available infrastructure. Consequently, traffic congestion has become a daily problem affecting several aspects of modern society, including regional economic development. In this way, Traffic Management System (TMS) have been proposed to improve the traffic efficient and minimize traffic congestion problems. These systems rely on gather traffic-related data in a central entity to identify congestion and suggest alternative routes. However such approach adds load in communication channel depending on the traffic density. In this way, this paper introduces FASTER, a fully-distributed TMS to improve the overall vehicle traffic efficiency that does not overloads the communication channel, providing a suitable distributed solution. Simulation results indicate that our FASTER outperforms the assessed solutions in different scenarios and in different key requirements of TMS.

Keywords

Traffic Management System; VANETs; Traffic efficiency

1. INTRODUCTION

Mobility is one of the most challenging concern in large cities around the world. This takes place due to the fast population growth [9]. On the other hand, the transport infrastructure has not grown at the same pace as the number of vehicles. As a consequence of this, traffic congestion has become a daily problem, creating several negative issues for the society, including traffic congestiton, high number of traffic accidents, effects in the economic development, monetary losses and impacts in the environment [12].

To cope with such problem, modern societies rely on Traffic Management Systems (TMS), which are composed of a set of applications and management tools to improve the efficiency and the safety of the transportation system. TMS integrate information, communication and sensory technologies to collect traffc-related data from heterogeneous sources such as vehicles, traffic ligths, in-road and road side sensors and so on [9, 6]. Upon collecting and aggregating such data, they are exploited to identify traffic hazards

MSWiM '16, November 13-17, 2016, Malta, Malta

© 2016 ACM. ISBN 978-1-4503-4502-6/16/11...$15.00

DOI: http://dx.doi.org/10.1145/2988287.2989167

which may degrade the traffic efficiency, to them deliver services to overcome these hazards.

One building block to develop an efficient TMS is the Vehicular Ad hoc Network (VANET). It considers vehicles as mobile nodes with embedded sensors, processing units, and wireless communication interfaces [12, 19, 18]. Thanks to these features, vehicles can cooperate among themselves and create an ad hoc network to provide and receive data to other entities. In addition, though an infrastructure is not a requirement, it can be used such as Road Side Units (RSU) to improve the its capacity and provide another features. In general, VANETs acts as the sensing, communication and actuation platforms for TMS [9].

Several TMS to improve the traffic efficiency have been proposed [10, 1, 15, 6, 5, 16, 8, 7]. However, these solutions perform the exchange of traffic information in an inefficient way, which may overload the communication network. In general, they also assume that the entire city is covered by RSU in order to detect, control and reduce traffic congestion. However most cities are not fully covered by RSU. Moreover, as far as we are aware, there is no attempt to solve the vehicular congestion problem in a fully-distributed way as does our proposed.

In order to overcome such problem, we introduce the FASTER, a fully-distributed VANET-based system designed to improve the vehicle traffic efficiency. FASTER relies to four main phases: *(i)* Information gathering; *(ii)* Information aggregation; *(iii)* Information dissemination; and *(iv)* Congestion detection and avoidance. It addresses network challenges during the data dissemination process, which includes the *broadcast storm problem* [19] and *resynchronization problem* introduced by the IEEE 802.11p protocol [18]. The broadcast storm takes place whenever multiple vehicles attempt to transmit simultaneously, causing network overload, packet collisions and additional delay at the medium access control (MAC) layer. On the other hand, the resynchronization occurs due to multichannel operation of the IEEE 802.11p standard.

Aiming to provide a better understanding of the behaviour of FASTER, we present an extensive set of experiments that shows the need of novel solutions to improve vehicle traffic efficiency as well as clearly indicates its superior performance when compared to existing proposal.

This paper is organized as follows. Section 2 provides an overview of the existing TMS approaches and presents the related work. Section 3 introduce our proposed solution. The performance evaluation is described in Section 4 and, finally, Section 5 presents our conclusions and future work.

2. RELATED WORK

This section describes some related solutions to improve traffic efficiency found in the literature. However, is important to stress that no fully-distributed solution aware about the overall traffic condition was found in the literature. There are some fully-distributed solutions which focus on control traffic jam caused by traffic accidents [8, 7]. Other solutions such as [1, 15, 2] focus on detect and control traffic jam cooperatively, but they did not have a full knowledge about the traffic condition. On the other hand, some centralized solutions uses a central entity to collect information periodically to create a this knowledge and to compute alternative routes for vehicles [6, 5]. Other solutions use a central entity to collect a full knowledge of traffic condition, but routes are computed in each vehicle, which may lead to not suitable alternative routes [1, 15] and overload the network [10, 6, 5].

Meneguette et al. [15] introduce the Urban CONgestion Detection System (UCONDES), a TMS based on inter-vehicle communication to detect and reduce urban congestion. UCONDES uses an Artificial Neural Network (ANN) to detect and classify the levels of congestion on roads. To identify and classify the traffic congestion, it uses the average speed and the density of vehicles on the road, which are periodically obtained via beacons sent by them all. After classifying the target road, the information is sent to the other vehicles via beacon messages. Upon receiving a congested road message, a vehicle decides if it keeps the current route or computes an alternative route. However, the mechanism to alert the vehicles about congested roads may overload the network since several vehicles in the same road can produce the same road classification and disseminate the same messages.

Bauza et al. [2] propose CoTEC (Cooperative Traffic congestion detEChtion), a novel cooperative vehicular system based on V2V communications to detect traffic congestion using fuzzy logic. CoTEC uses CAM (Cooperative Awareness Messages) or beacon messages to periodically broadcast the road traffic condition. In addition, CoTEC uses fuzzy logic to detect a potential road traffic congestion locally at each vehicle. The fuzzy logic system was built based on Level-of-Service (LOS) present in Highway Capacity Manual (HCM) [4]. The LOS represents a quality measurement used to describe the operational conditions within a traffic flow. Therefore, when a traffic jam is detected, at first, each vehicle broadcasts its own estimation about the traffic jam and, then, with all estimations, vehicles collaboratively detect and characterize the road traffic congestion.

Similarly to CoTEC, Araujo et al. [1] propose CARTIM (Cooperative vehiculAR Traffic congestion Identification and Minimization) which is a proposal for collaborative identification and minimization of traffic congestion. Like CoTEC, CARTIM uses V2V communications to cooperatively measure the level of traffic congestion. CARTIM collects data from the vehicles (speed and density) periodically sent through beacons by all vehicles and with these information by using a fuzzy logic system it is able to measures the level of congestion. However, despite of CARTIM use a fuzzy logic system as well as CoTEC the rules were built using different metrics presented in HCM, thus CARTIM and CoTEC differ in the fuzzy logic rules and in the mechanism to spread the local traffic measurement through the network. Furthermore, when a traffic congestion is detected, CARTIM proposes a heuristic to change the vehicles route to minimize the traffic congestion detected.

Doolan and Muntean [10] introduce EcoTrec, a novel eco-friendly routing system for vehicular traffic that relies on V2V communication. EcoTrec, assumes that all vehicles are equipped with GPS receiver, tilt sensor and accelerometer, that gather information about position, angle, acceleration of the vehicle and road surface condition. Moreover, with these information, EcoTrec builds a *Vehicle Model* that is the vehicle behavior. Furthermore, every vehicle

sends periodically beacon messages with its ID, position and speed, where this beacon is sent to the other vehicles. Upon receiving these beacon messages, every vehicle aggregates it with existing data and builds a *Traffic Model*. In addition, the messages are sent using *Endemic routing*, in order to make sure that the vehicles will receive it. Moreover, EcoTrec builds a *Road Model* that considers the traffic condition on the road. This *Road Model* are stored in a central server and is fed by the *Traffic Model* of each vehicle. Finally, EcoTrec computes the recommended routes for each vehicle. Its routing algorithm takes into account two main factors: *(i)* the road characteristics and; *(ii)* traffic condition, which are used to set the weights of each road and build a scenario overview. Thereafter, this scenario overview is sent to the vehicles through the VANET, and the vehicles are then routed according to the Dijkstra lowest edge weight algorithm. Each time that a vehicle receives new scenario overview, it re-computes its route.

The proposal mencioned above have some limitations such as: network overload [6, 5, 10] and no knowledge about traffic condition to reroute vehicles [1, 15, 10, 2, 16]. To overcome such limitations, we propose FASTER which is a fully-distributed TMS to improve the overall traffic efficiency that does not overloads the network nor introduces an undesire overhead for the system.

3. PROPOSED SOLUTION

This section describes FASTER, a fully-distributed VANET-based TMS to improve vehicle traffic efficiency. FASTER relies only on V2V communication to gather traffic information, detect congested roads and compute alternative routes and yet producing low overhead.

The main challenge is how to provide to all vehicles the full knowledge about the traffic condition of the entire scenario with low overhead. To this aim, in FASTER all vehicles share information with their neighbors, by doing that, each vehicle can increase its knowledge about the traffic condition. Furthermore, every vehicle shares its local knowledge with all vehicles. However, to overcome VANETs challenges, such as broadcast storm and the resynchronization. It segments the scenario in districts and proposes an aggregation mechanism to reduce the number of transmissions and a data dissemination protocol to incur in low overhead, short delays and large coverage. Finally, upon getting full knowledge of traffic condition each vehicle can detect congested roads and compute alternative routes to avoid them.

Consider a VANET environment where the road network can be modeled by a directed and weighted graph $G = (V, E)$, where the set $V = \{v_1, v_2, \ldots, v_i\}$ corresponds to the set of intersections (vertices), the set $E = \{e_{01}, e_{12} \ldots, e_{ij}\}$ corresponds to the set of roads (edges) which connects the intersections $E \subseteq V \times V$. Each edge e_{ij} is defined by a pair of subsequent vertices $(v_i, v_j) \in V$. Moreover, $W = \{w_1, w_2, \ldots, w_i\}$ is a set of weights representing the traffic condition, in which $w : E \rightarrow \mathbb{R}_+^*$. Let $N = \{n_1, n_2, \ldots, n_i\}$ be a set of vehicles (nodes) and $\langle e_{ij}, \ldots, e_{mn} \rangle \mid e_{ij}, \ldots, e_{mn} \in E$ be a route $\forall n \in N$. Furthermore, let C be the communication range of $\forall n \in N$. In FASTER, each vehicle builds an subgraph $G' = (V', E')$, whose $V' \subseteq V$ is the subset of vertices covered by C, and $E' \subseteq E$ is the set of incident and out-going edges of each vertex in V'. Furthermore, each vehicle builds a local knowledge about the traffic condition E''. In this way, to provide a precise knowledge, each vehicle shares its local knowledge with all vehicles in the network. Finally with this precise knowledge built, each vehicle can detect a congested road e_{pq} verifying its weight w_{pq}, and compute an alternative route in case that it will pass through this road $\exists e_{pq} \in \langle e_{ij}, \ldots, e_{mn} \rangle$.

FASTER relies to four main phases: *A)* Information Gathering;

B) Information Aggregation; and *C)* Information Dissemination; and *D)* Congestion Detection and Avoidance which are described below.

3.1 Information Gathering

Each vehicle gathers information from its one hop neighbors to build a local knowledge about the traffic condition. For this, every vehicle provides information to its neighbors through *beacon messages*.

Beacon message: *is an IEEE 802.11p 2-layer periodic message sent by all vehicles in the Control Channel (CCH) every 2 seconds, which contains the current vehicle position $e_{pq} \in \langle e_{ij}, \ldots, e_{mn} \rangle \mid e_{pq}, e_{ij} \ldots, e_{mn} \in E$ and its average speed s_{mean}.*

Upon receiving beacon messages, each vehicle stores these messages received and in a predefined interval t, each vehicle creates a *Local knowledge about the traffic condition E''*, that have all roads e_{ij} within its coverage and their respective average speed $S_{e_{ij}}$. Additionally, these roads are classified as fully covered roads or partially covered roads, this classification is given by the function $\xi(n)$.

$$\xi(n) = \begin{cases} 1 & e_{ij} \in E' \\ 0 & \exists v \in e_{ij} \mid e_{ij} \notin E', v \in V' \end{cases}$$

where, 1 represents the case of fully covered road, in which an edge $e_{ij} \in E'$ is covered by vehicle n, and 0 represents the case of partially covered road, in which just one vertex $\exists v \in V'$ that composing an edge $e_{ij} \notin E'$ is covered by the vehicle n. Figure 1 shows an example of this classification, in which the road e_{ij} is fully covered and the road e_{jk} is partially covered.

Finally with all covered roads, at a predefined time t, each vehicle computes the average speed $S_{e_{ij}} \forall e \in E''$ based on associated speed s_{mean} of each *beacon message* received related to that road. However, in case that a vehicle covers a road e_{ij} and it does not receives any beacon related to that road, it sets the average speed $S_{e_{ij}}$ of that road with the road *max speed*, because it means that the road is free.

3.2 Information Aggregation

FASTER segments the scenario in districts and employs an aggregation mechanism to aggregate the *local knowledge about the traffic condition* of all vehicles in the same district in order to create a knowledge about the traffic condition of the district. To define the number of districts, FASTER uses Equation 1.

$$\kappa = \left\lceil \frac{A}{\pi \cdot C^2} \right\rceil \tag{1}$$

where, A is the scenario area, C is the vehicle communication range and κ is the number of districts.

Upon defining the number of districts, FASTER uses the kmeans clustering algorithm [14] to segment the κ districts. The key idea is to define κ centroids, one for each district, then associate a set of nearest vertices of a centroid to each district. Therefore a set of κ vertices $v_0, \ldots, v_\kappa \mid v_0, \ldots, v_\kappa \in V$ are selected to represent the centroids, then every vertex is bind to nearest centroid, forming a district. Furthermore the κ centroids are re-calculated and a new bind is done. This process is employed until the κ centroids stay the same. The district selecting process aims at minimizing an objective function, in this case a squared error function. The objective function is defined by Equation 2.

$$\underset{V}{\arg\min} \sum_{j=1}^{\kappa} \sum_{v \in V_j} \| v - c_j \|^2 \tag{2}$$

where, $\| v - c_j \|^2$ is the distance measure between vertex v and the district centre c_j, V_j is the set of vertices associated to the district j and κ is the number of districts.

Figure 1 shows an example of district segmentation, and its centroids to a scenario with an area of $1km^2$ and vehicles with communication range of 300 m.

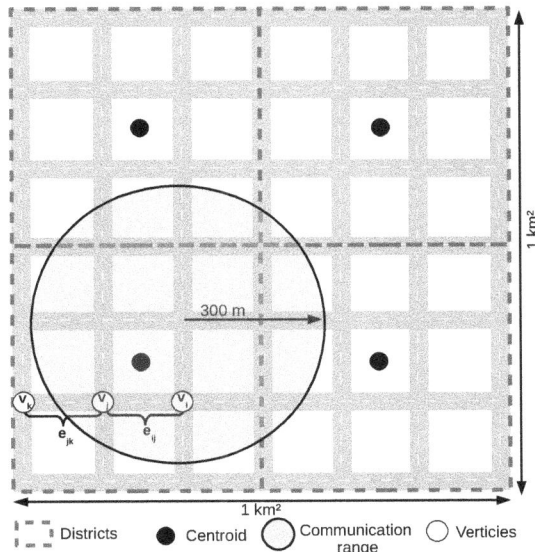

Figure 1: District organization.

After each vehicle creates its local knowledge of traffic condition, a *Local knowledge message* is created to share its local knowledge about the traffic condition with all one hop neighbors in the same district.

Local knowledge message: *is an IEEE 802.11p 2-layer periodic message sent by all vehicles in the Service Channel (SCH) in an interval $t + \gamma$, which contains all covered roads $e_{ij} \in E''$, the average road speed $S_{e_{ij}}$ and the road type $[0, 1]$, where 0 is to partially covered roads and 1 to fully covered roads.*

When a vehicle n_i receives a *Local knowledge messages* from a vehicle n_j it creates a *District knowledge*, which have all roads and their average speed in relation to its district. Algorithm 1 shows the creation of a district knowledge.

In this way, for each entry of each *Local knowledge message* received from the vehicle n_j. First, the vehicle n_i verifies if it already knows the traffic condition of the that road (Line 4). To this, it verifies if it already has the road e_{ij} in its *District knowledge*. If it does not knows the traffic condition of the road e_{ij} received from vehicle n_j, it adds the road to its *District knowledge* (Lines 5-6). On the other hand, if it already knows the traffic condition of the road e_{ij}, it verifies the road type (Line 9) and in case of the road in its *District knowledge* is fully covered, the vehicle keeps its local knowledge about the traffic condition of that road. Otherwise in the case that the road in its *District knowledge* is partially covered and the road in the *Local knowledge message* received is full covered, its updates its knowledge of the road traffic condition (Lines 10-12). However if both roads (the road which the vehicle n_i has in its District knowledge and the road received from the local knowledge of vehicle n_j) have type partially covered, vehicle n_i updates its *District knowledge* using the minimum of the both roads average speed (Line 15).

Despite of each vehicle has knowledge about the traffic condition in its *District knowledge*, this knowledge is far from of the full

---
Algorithm 1: District knowledge creation

Input : E''_{n_i} // Set of all covered roads of vehicle n_i

  1   E''_{n_j} // Local knowledge received from vehicle n_j

Output: District knowledge built by the vehicle n_i, which contains each district road e_{ij} and its average speed $S_{e_{ij}}$

  // set the local knowledge of vehicle n_i to its district knowledge D

2 $D \leftarrow E''_{n_i}$;

3 **foreach** $e_{ij} \in E''_{n_j}$ **do**

    // verifies if the edge e_{ij} already is in its district knowledge

4   **if** $e_{ij} \notin D$ **then**

      // vehicle n_i adds the edge e_{ij}, average speed $S_{e_{ij}}$ and the edge type received from vehicle n_j to its district knowledge

5       $D[e_{ij}].S_{e_{ij}} \leftarrow E''_{n_j}[e_{ij}].S_{e_{ij}}$;

6       $D[e_{ij}].type \leftarrow E''_{n_j}[e_{ij}].type$;

7   **end**

8   **else**

      // verifies if the edge e_{ij} in its district knowledge has type partially covered

9   **if** $D[e_{ij}].type$ *is partially covered* **then**

        // verifies if the edge e_{ij} received from vehicle n_j is full covered

10   **if** *if* $E''_{n_j}[e_{ij}].type$ *is fully covered* **then**

          // updates the edge speed and the type

11         $D[e_{ij}].S_{e_{ij}} \leftarrow E''_{n_j}[e_{ij}].S_{e_{ij}}$;

12         $D[e_{ij}].type \leftarrow 1$;

13   **end**

14   **else**

         // updates the average speed

15         $D[e_{ij}].S_{e_{ij}} \leftarrow \min(D[e_{ij}].S_{e_{ij}}, E''_{n_j}[e_{ij}].S_{e_{ij}})$

16   **end**

17   **end**

18   **end**

19 **end**

---

scenario knowledge desired. Therefore to have such full knowledge, each vehicle needs to know the *District knowledge* of all κ districts. In other words, each vehicle needs to have knowledge about the traffic condition of the others districts. To this, FASTER implements an inter-district data dissemination protocol, which is explained below, to spread each *District knowledge* to other districts.

3.3 Information Dissemination

FASTER employs a multi hop delay-based data dissemination protocol, which is composed by three main modules: *(i)* Transmitter selection; *(ii)* Broadcast suppression; and *(iii)* Packet collision minimization.

Due to aggregation mechanism employed, all vehicles within the same district potentially share the same *District knowledge*. In this way, a single transmission of this knowledge is sufficient to forward it to the others districts. In order to provide such issue, FASTER uses its *Transmitter selection* module, to select the best vehicle to transmit its *District knowledge*. In a predefined interval $t + \lambda \mid \lambda > \gamma$, all vehicles create a *District knowledge message*, which contains its *District knowledge*. A delay is computed to schedule this message based on the euclidean distance between its current position and the district centre. The main idea of *Transmitter selection* is to prioritize the transmission of the vehicle nearest to the center. The vehicle closest to the center will

transmit first then the others; when the other vehicles receive a *District knowledge message* from its district, they cancel their *District knowledge message* scheduled. Moreover the *District knowledge message* needs to be forward to the other districts by employing a multi-hop process starting the *Broadcast suppression* module.

The *Broadcast suppression* module addresses the broadcast storm problem by reducing the number of transmissions, providing different delays and canceling duplicated messages. To this, is used a *preference zone* concept [20], which is an area where the vehicles are best suited to continue performing forwarding. In other words, among all vehicles that received data to be forwarded, the transmission of a single vehicle within the *preference zone* is sufficient to perform the data dissemination efficiently. Therefore, vehicles within a *preference zone* have a lower delay then the vehicles outside this area. Figure 2 shows the *preference zone* organization to a transmitter vehicle, and the respective delays for vehicles within the *preference zone* and as well as outside this zone.

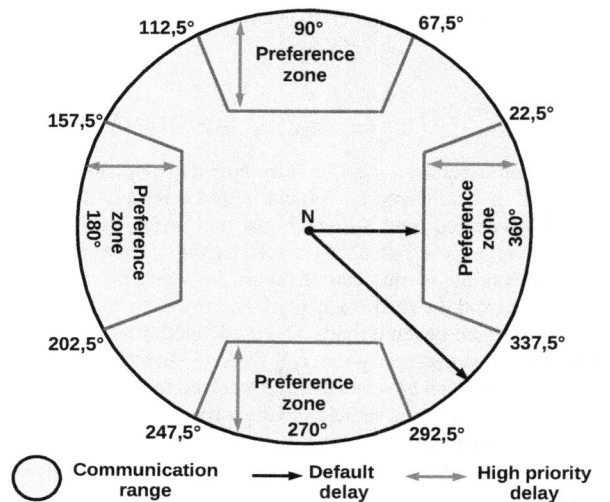

Figure 2: Preference zone organization.

FASTER also employs a desynchronization mechanism to avoid the *synchronization problem* introduced by the IEEE 802.11p standard [11, 18]. The desynchronization mechanism proposed aims to reduce packet collision. For this, it verifies if the delay computed by the *Broadcast suppression* module will occur when the service channel becomes active. In case this delay happens, the *desynchronization mechanism* adds an additional delay to allow transmission in the service channel, where the additional delay at most 50 ms (the time the IEEE 802.11p standard uses to swap from CCH to SCH). If a transmission is scheduled when the control channel is active, the additional delay is added to allow the transmission to occur during the SCH. Figure 3 shows how the desynchronization mechanism works. In this figure, a vehicle receives a *District knowledge message* at time T_1, and the *Broadcast suppression* computes a delay to forward the *District knowledge message* in 60 ms. After 60 ms, at time T_2 the CCH will be active, avoiding the synchronization, then the desynchronize mechanism computes again the delay and changes it to 115 ms.

3.4 Congestion Detection and Avoidance

After a vehicle receive all κ *District knowledge*, at time $t + \rho \mid \rho > \lambda$, it creates a *Scenario knowledge*, which contains all roads and average speed received from all κ districts. Each vehicle builds

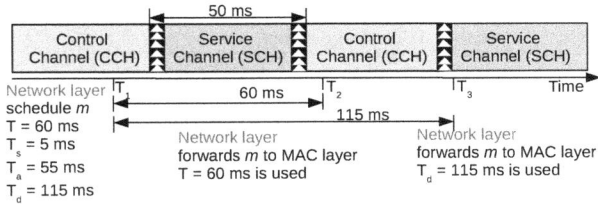

Figure 3: Desynchronized meachism.

Table 1: Relation of weight, LOS and traffic classification

Road weight	LOS	Traffic classification
$(0, 0.15]$	A	Free-flow
$(0.15, 0.33]$	B	Free-flow
$(0.33, 0.50]$	C	Sligth congestion
$(0.50, 0.60]$	D	Sligth congestion
$(0.60, 0.70]$	E	Congested
$(0.70, 1.00]$	F	Congested

a graph $G = (V, E)$ based on *Scenario knowledge* and for each road $e_{ij} \in E$ it computes a weight w_{ij} based on Equation 3. The weight equation was modeled to be inversely proportional to the road average speed value. In this way, faster roads have lower weights then slower roads, as follows:

$$w_{ij} = 1 - \frac{S_{e_{ij}}}{S_{e_{ij}}^{max}} \quad (3)$$

where $S_{e_{ij}}$ and $S_{e_{ij}}^{max}$ denote the max speed, and the average speed in *Scenario knowledge* of road e_{ij}, respectively.

Each vehicle can classify the traffic condition in each road e_{ij} based on the each weight w_{ij} value. The *Congestion detection* module is based on the Level-Of-Service (LOS) of the Highway Capacity Manual (HCM) [4]. The LOS represents a quality measurement used to describe the operational conditions within a traffic flow, which defines six different levels of service, with LOS A representing free-flow conditions and LOS F representing high congested level. Furthermore each level defines the minimum and the maximum speed based on the road maximum speed. Table 1 shows the minimum and maximum road weight to each LOS from HCM.

The *Congestion detection and avoidance* module is divided in two phases: *(i)* Real-time decision making, which each vehicle verifies if it will pass through a congested road and *(ii)* Alternative route computation, which relies to compute an alternative route if the vehicles will pass through a congested road. In this context, relating to *Real-time decision making* phase, to enable a detection of a congested road, each vehicle verifies all weights of the roads that compose its route, and if it has a road with a weight greater than a predefined threshold it knows that the road is congested. The a threshold is defined based on the HCM manual with the value of 0.50 (LOS D). The *Real-time decision making* function $\delta(n)$ is given by.

$$\delta(n) = \begin{cases} 1 & \exists e_{pq} \in \langle e_{ij}, \ldots, e_{mn} \rangle \mid w_{pq} \geq 0.50, e_{pq} \in E \\ 0 & Otherwise \end{cases}$$

The value 1 means that a vehicle has road e_{pq} in its route $\langle e_{ij}, \ldots, e_{mn} \rangle$ which has weight w_{pq} up to the defined threshold and 0 otherwise.

In case that a vehicle will go through a congested road, the *Alternative route computation* phase starts. In this way, the vehicle computes an alternative route using the Probabilistic k-Shortest Path

(PkSP) based on the road weights. PkSP uses the Boltzmann probabilistic algorithm [13] to select the route to the vehicle among the ones in a set of k possible routes.

4. PERFORMANCE ANALYSIS

This section describes the performance evaluation of FASTER. First of all, in Subsection 4.1 the simulation tools is presented as well as the scenario used in our simulations. Subsections 4.2 and 4.3 present the network cost and traffic efficiency results respectively. The results were organized as the following. First we analysed the network cost of our solution by evaluating the aggregation mechanism and the data dissemination protocol. Second, we compared FASTER with some TMS solutions to evaluate the traffic efficiency.

4.1 Methodology

For the simulations, we use the Network Simulator OMNeT++ 4.3[1] and the framework SUMO (Simulator for UrbanMObility) [3], version 0.25.0, to manage the scenario and the mobility of vehicles. We obtained realistic map scenarios from OpenStreetMap tool. For the vehicular network, we used the framework Veins 4.3 [17] that implements the IEEE 802.11p and the signal attenuation model considering obstacles.

We used as scenario a fragment (1 km^2) of Manhattan, USA, with several blocks and two-way streets for vehicles moving in opposite directions. The route of the vehicles is composed by the shortest path between two vertices $v_i, v_j \in V$ which are selected randomly. Furthermore to ensure close to real overtaking, their speeds range from 0 kilometres per hour to the maximum speed allowed on the road. In addition, to provide different traffic conditions, we used densties from 700 to 1500 vehicles/km^2. In this way, as main parameters, we set the bit rate to 18 Mbit/s at the MAC layer and the transmission power to 2.2 mW, resulting in a communication range of approximately 300 m under a two-ray ground propagation model [17]. Table 2 shows a summary of the main simulation parameters used in our assessment.

Table 2: Simulation parameters

Parameters	Values
Transmission power	2.2 mW
Communication range	300 m
Bit rate	18 Mbit/s
Scenario	Manhattan grid
Scenario size	1 km^2
Densities	from 700 to 1500 vehicles/km^2
Number of simulations	33
Confidence interval	95%

4.2 Network Cost evaluation

As there is no other fully-distributed solution with the same purpose of FASTER in literature, we evaluate the network cost comparing with the Baseline, in which all vehicles disseminate their local knowledge using the data dissemination protocol proposed with no aggregation. The assessed metrics for the network cost evaluation were:

- **Coverage**: the percentage of messages generated by the vehicles regarding to the delivered messages;

---

[1]http://omnetpp.org/

Table 3: Coverage		
Vehicles/Km^2	Baseline	FASTER
700	61.13%	93.39%
900	57.49%	95.11%
1100	51.31%	95.26%
1300	51.78%	94.63%
1500	45.27%	95.18%

Table 4: Average delay (s)		
Vehicles/Km^2	Baseline	FASTER
700	114.46	0.44
900	102.88	0.45
1100	137.81	0.47
1300	288.58	0.48
1500	533.20	0.49

Table 5: Transmitted messages		
Vehicles/Km^2	Baseline	FASTER
700	2910	179
900	4834	206
1100	6864	216
1300	10201	246
1500	13833	279

Table 6: Overall traffic knowledge		
Vehicles/Km^2	Baseline	FASTER
700	62.63%	97.58%
900	49.37%	95.63%
1100	40.53%	96.23%
1300	31.13%	95.82%
1500	12.66%	95.6%

- **Delay**: the average time to spread district knowledge messages to all vehicles;

- **Transmitted messages**: total number of district knowledge messages transmitted;

- **Overall traffic knowledge**: accuracy of the knowledge about the traffic condition that each vehicle have about the traffic condition of the entire scenario.

Tables 3, 4, 5 and 6 show results for all assessed networks metrics in function of the vehicle density. Table 3 shows the results for coverage. In particular, FASTER reaches a coverage of approximately 95% when the density of 700 vehicles/km^2, due its efficient aggregation mechanism that aggregates all knowledges of each district in a single one, thus reducing the number of transmitted messages. On the other hand,the Baseline presents a coverage of approximately 60%. Its low coverage presented occurs because it does not implements any mechanism to aggregate messages in order to reduce the number of transmissions, consequently as all vehicles need to transmit their local knowledge the number of transmitted messages increase and overloads the network. However, this overload worsens as the density increases. Therefore, with the density of 1500 vehicles/km^2 the Baseline system presents a coverage of only 45%, because it is not able to deliver all messages transmitted by all vehicles. Meanwhile, FASTER maintains its coverage of 95%. It is effect of the efficient aggregation mechanism employed by FASTER, which reduce the number transmitted messages (see Table 5) and consequently it does not overload the network.

Overloading the network creates several negative impacts for the system, it introduces an undesired overhead that affects its overall performance. In Table 4 is shown the average delay that each system introduces to spread the knowledge messages through the network. As can be expected, the overload caused by the Baseline system introduces a high overhead which presents a delay greater than 100 seconds for all densities. This overhead degrades the overall performance of the system, in which in scenarios with frequent traffic hazards such as hush hours, that a fast response is desired to provide information about the traffic condition for the vehicles, it may take almost 10 minutes to spread the knowledge, and also it may not be a precise one (see Table 6), thus infeasible to provide a suitable solution. Differently, FASTER does not overloads the network, therefore it is able to spread the knowledge through the network in a fast way, specifically it takes less than 1 second. Such results in FASTER is consequence of the adoption of the efficient

aggregation mechanism, which drastically reduces the amount of transmitted messages.

Table 5 shows the total number messages transmitted in each system for all densities. As discussed above, the Baseline system produces a high number of messages because it does not implements an aggregation mechanism, so all vehicles need to transmit their messages at least once. However, this approach transmits several of redundant messages which could be aggregate in a single one to make a better usage of the network. This feature, is implemented in FASTER, and as can be seen it generates approximately 97% less messages when compared to Baseline. Such result shows that FASTER does not waste bandwidth with unnecessary transmissions.

Finally, the impact of the network overload present in Baseline system can be seen in Table 6, which presents the overall knowledge that each vehicle has about the traffic condition of the entire scenario. The Baseline system, starts with an accuracy of 62% with the density of 700 vehicles/km^2. Despite this is not a good accuracy, it get worse as the density increases, because more messages are transmitted, consequently this further overloads the network and increases the overhead. Consequently, Baseline presents an accuracy of 12% with the density of 1500 vehicles/km^2. However, thanks for the efficient mechanisms employed by FASTER, it presents an accuracy between 98% and 95% for all densities. This results shows how efficient is FASTER to spread the information in order to build a precise knowledge about the traffic condition of the entire scenario.

4.3 Traffic Efficiency evaluation

In this section, we evaluate the efficiency of vehicular traffic flow using FASTER and UCONDES [15], compared with the original vehicle mobility traffic (OVMT). The assessed metrics for the vehicular traffic efficiency were: *(i)* Travel time; *(ii)* Congestion time; and *(iii)* Average speed. Regarding FASTER parameters, we used $t = 15$ seconds, $\gamma = 1$ second, $\lambda = 1$ second, and $\rho = 2$ seconds.

Figure 4 shows the results for all vehicular traffic efficiency metrics. In particular, Figure 4(a) shows the travel time results. It is important to note that OVMT represents the original mobility (i.e. it does not alternates any route of all vehicles). Therefore, as can be seen the more the density increases, the travel time increases as well, reaching approximately 15 minutes with density of 1500 vehicles/km^2. However, UCONDES presents the highest travel time increasing up to 30% compared to OVMT. This is consequence of the absence of the knowledge about the traffic condition

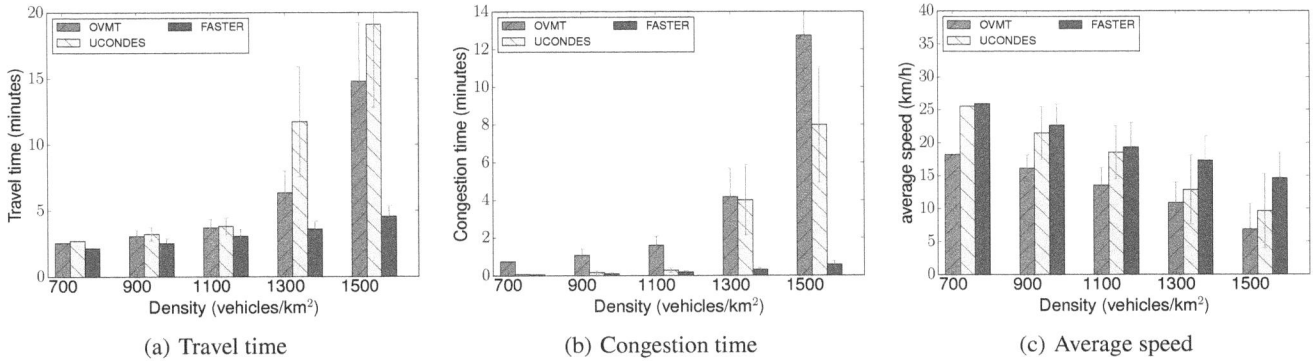

Figure 4: Traffic efficiency evaluation results.

in the entire scenario. Vehicles in UCONDES only know about the roads that are congested within its coverage. Therefore, they compute an alternative route to avoid the congested roads just based on the distance between its current position and its destination. Hence, they may get stuck in another congestion (see Figure 4(b)). On the other hand, as vehicles in FASTER have an overall knowledge about the traffic condition, they can compute improved alternative routes to avoid congested roads avoiding to enter in another congestion. Moreover, it reduces the average travel time in 58% and 68% compared with OVMT and UCONDES respectively.

Regarding congestion time, in Figure 4(b) OVMT presents the higher congestion time. Vehicles spend up to 12 minutes of their entire travel time in the congestion. In other words, vehicles spend up to 80% of their entire route stuck in some congestion. UCONDES reduces this time spent in some congestion to approximately 7 minutes, reducing the congestion time in up to 45% compared to OVMT. However, as it does not compute efficient routes, the vehicles still spend 33% of its route stuck in some congestion. On the other hand, FASTER presents the lower congestion time, which is reduce to approximately 1 minute. it reduces the congestion time in 93% and 87% compared to OVMT and UCONDES. FASTER reaches better results because all vehicles have a precise knowledge about the traffic condition of the entire scenario. In addition, it is possible because it does not overload the network to provide such knowledge using the efficient aggregation and the data dissemination mechanisms, consequently it does not introduces a higher overhead for the system making possible that vehicles detect and avoid traffic hazards in a fast way. Finally, as consequence of the lower travel and congestion time FASTER enables a smooth traffic flow increasing the average speed in up to 90% when compared to OVMT and 50% when compared to UCONDES.

The better traffic efficiency presented in FASTER is consequence of low overhead and the high accuracy of the overall traffic knowledge, thus it can detect congestion first than UCONDES [15]. Such low overhead is because FASTER is fully-distributed, where each vehicle can detect a traffic hazard and compute an alternative to itself. Differently form centralized systems which concentrate the calculation of an alternative route to all vehicles in a single entity, in which can introduce high overhead depending on the traffic density.

5. CONCLUSION

Vehicle congestion has become a daily problem affecting several aspects of modern society. Nowadays it is extremely necessary a distributed TMS to improve the flow of vehicle traffic once the centralized TMS present several issues. In this work we present the FASTER, a fully-distributed VANET-based TMS to improve the overall vehicle traffic efficiency as well as to avoid traffic congestion. FASTER was extensively compared to other known solutions regarding travel time, congestion time, and average speed and several network metrics. The obtained results indicate that our FASTER outperforms the assessed solutions in different scenarios and in different key requirements of TMS. As future work, we intend to analyze FASTER in more realistic scenarios, using real environments mobility traces. In addition, we intend to extend our solution implementing more sophisticated re-reroute algorithms.

6. ACKNOWLEDGMENTS

The authors would like to thank the grant 2015/07538-1, Sao Paulo Research Foundation (FAPESP) for the financial support. This work also has received funding from the European Union's Horizon 2020 for research, technological development, and demonstration under grant agreement no. 688941 (FUTEBOL), as well from the Brazilian Ministry of Science, Technology and Innovation (MCTI) through RNP and CTIC.

7. REFERENCES

[1] G. Araujo, M. Queiroz, F. Duarte-Figueiredo, A. Tostes, and A. Loureiro. Cartim: A proposal toward identification and minimization of vehicular traffic congestion for vanet. In *Computers and Communication (ISCC), 2014 IEEE Symposium on*, pages 1–6, June 2014.

[2] R. Bauza and J. Gozalvez. Traffic congestion detection in large-scale scenarios using vehicle-to-vehicle communications. *Journal of Network and Computer Applications*, 36(5):1295 – 1307, 2013.

[3] M. Behrisch, L. Bieker, J. Erdmann, and D. Krajzewicz. SUMO - Simulation of Urban MObility: An Overview. In *International Conference on Advances in System Simulation (SIMUL '11)*, pages 63–68, 2011.

[4] T. R. Board. *HCM 2010 - Highway capacity manual*. National Research Council, 2010.

[5] A. M. de Souza, R. S. Yokoyama, L. C. Botega, R. I. Meneguette, and L. A. Villas. Scorpion: A solution using cooperative rerouting to prevent congestion and improve traffic condition. In *Computer and Information Technology; Ubiquitous Computing and Communications; Dependable, Autonomic and Secure Computing; Pervasive Intelligence and Computing (CIT/IUCC/DASC/PICOM), 2015 IEEE International Conference on*, pages 497–503, Oct 2015.

[6] A. M. de Souza, R. S. Yokoyama, G. Maia, A. Loureiro, and L. Villas. Real-time path planning to prevent traffic jam through an intelligent transportation system. In *2016 IEEE Symposium on Computers and Communication (ISCC)*, pages 726–731, June 2016.

[7] A. M. de Souza, R. S. Yokoyama, G. Maia, A. A. F. Loureiro, and L. A. Villas. Minimizing traffic jams in urban centers using vehicular ad hoc networks. In *2015 7th International Conference on New Technologies, Mobility and Security (NTMS)*, pages 1–5, July 2015.

[8] A. M. de Souza R. S. Yokoyama Nelson L. S. da Fonseca Rodolfo I. Meneguette and L. A. Villas. Garuda: A new geographical accident aware solution to reduce urban congestion. In *Proceedings of the 15th IEEE International Conference on Computer and Information Techinology*, 2015.

[9] S. Djahel, R. Doolan, G.-M. Muntean, and J. Murphy. A Communications-Oriented Perspective on Traffic Management Systems for Smart Cities: Challenges and Innovative Approaches. *IEEE Communications Surveys Tutorials*, 17(1):125–151, 2015.

[10] R. Doolan and G.-M. Muntean. Vanet-enabled eco-friendly road characteristics-aware routing for vehicular traffic. In *Vehicular Technology Conference (VTC Spring), 2013 IEEE 77th*, pages 1–5, June 2013.

[11] D. Eckhoff, C. Sommer, and F. Dressler. On the necessity of accurate ieee 802.11p models for ivc protocol simulation. In *Vehicular Technology Conference (VTC Spring), 2012 IEEE 75th*, pages 1–5, May 2012.

[12] G. Karagiannis, O. Altintas, E. Ekici, G. Heijenk, B. Jarupan, K. Lin, and T. Weil. Vehicular networking: A survey and tutorial on requirements, architectures, challenges, standards and solutions. *Communications Surveys Tutorials, IEEE*, 13(4):584–616, 2011.

[13] S. Kirkpatrick, C. D. Gelatt, M. P. Vecchi, et al. Optimization by simmulated annealing. *science*, 220(4598):671–680, 1983.

[14] J. B. MacQueen. Some methods for classification and analysis of multivariate observations. In *Proceedings of 5-th Berkeley Symposium on Mathematical Statistics and Probability*, 1967.

[15] R. I. Meneguette, J. Ueyama, G. P. R. Filho, B. Krishnamachari, L. F. Bittencourt, and L. A. Villas. Enhancing intelligence in inter-vehicle communications to detect and reduce congestion in urban centers. In *IEEE Symposium on Computers and Communication (ISCC)*, 2015.

[16] J. Pan, I. S. Popa, and C. Borcea. Divert: A distributed vehicular traffic re-routing system for congestion avoidance. *IEEE Transactions on Mobile Computing*, PP(99):1–1, 2016.

[17] C. Sommer, R. German, and F. Dressler. Bidirectionally coupled network and road traffic simulation for improved ivc analysis. *Mobile Computing, IEEE Transactions on*, 10(1):3–15, Jan 2011.

[18] A. M. Souza, G. Maia, and L. A. Villas. Add: A data dissemination solution for highly dynamic highway environments. In *Network Computing and Applications (NCA), 2014 IEEE 13th International Symposium on*, pages 17–23, Aug 2014.

[19] L. Villas, A. Boukerche, R. Araujo, A. Loureiro, and J. Ueyama. Network partition-aware geographical data dissemination. In *Communications (ICC), 2013 IEEE International Conference on*, pages 1439–1443, 2013.

[20] L. A. Villas, A. Boukerche, G. Maia, R. W. Pazzi, and A. A. Loureiro. Drive: An efficient and robust data dissemination protocol for highway and urban vehicular ad hoc networks. *Computer Networks*, 2014.

Revisiting 802.11 Rate Adaptation
from Energy Consumption's Perspective

Iñaki Ucar*, Carlos Donato†, Pablo Serrano*, Andres Garcia-Saavedra‡,
Arturo Azcorra*†, Albert Banchs*†
inaki.ucar@uc3m.es, {pablo,azcorra,banchs}@it.uc3m.es,
carlos.donato@imdea.org, andres.garcia.saavedra@neclab.eu

*Universidad Carlos III de Madrid	†IMDEA Networks Institute	‡NEC Labs Europe
Avda. Universidad, 30	Avda. Mar Mediterráneo, 22	Kurfürsten-Anlage, 36
28911 Leganés, Spain	28918 Leganés, Spain	69115 Heidelberg, Germany

ABSTRACT

Rate adaptation in 802.11 WLANs has received a lot of attention from the research community, with most of the proposals aiming at maximising throughput based on network conditions. Considering energy consumption, an implicit assumption is that optimality in throughput implies optimality in energy efficiency, but this assumption has been recently put into question. In this paper, we address via analysis and experimentation the relation between throughput performance and energy efficiency in multi-rate 802.11 scenarios. We demonstrate the trade-off between these performance figures, confirming that they may not be simultaneously optimised, and analyse their sensitivity towards the energy consumption parameters of the device. Our results provide the means to design novel rate adaptation schemes that takes energy consumption into account.

Keywords

WLAN; 802.11; Rate Adaptation; Energy Efficiency

1. INTRODUCTION

In recent years, along with the exponential growth in mobile data applications and the corresponding traffic volume demand (see e.g. [1]), we have witnessed an increased attention towards "green operation" of networks, which is required to support a sustainable growth of the communication infrastructures. For the case of wireless communications, there is the added motivation of a limited energy supply (i.e., batteries), which has triggered a relatively large amount of work on energy efficiency [9]. It turns out, though, that energy efficiency and performance do not necessarily come hand in hand, as some recent research has pointed out [2,3], and that a criterion may be required to set a proper balance between them.

This paper is devoted to the problem of rate adaptation

MSWiM '16, November 13 - 17, 2016, Malta, Malta

© 2016 Copyright held by the owner/author(s). Publication rights licensed to ACM.
ISBN 978-1-4503-4502-6/16/11... $15.00

DOI: http://dx.doi.org/10.1145/2988287.2989149

(RA) in 802.11 WLANs from the energy consumption's perspective. RA algorithms are responsible for selecting the most appropriate modulation and coding scheme (MCS) and transmission power (TXP) to use, given an estimation of the link conditions, and have received a vast amount of attention from the research community (see e.g. [4] and references therein). In general, the challenge lies in distinguishing between those loses due to collisions and those due to poor radio conditions, because they should trigger different reactions. In addition, the performance figure to optimise is commonly the throughput or a related one such as, e.g., the time required to deliver a frame.

It is generally assumed that optimality in terms of throughput also implies optimality in terms of energy efficiency. However, some recent work [6,7] has shown that throughput maximisation does not result in energy efficiency maximisation, at least for 802.11n. However, we still lack a proper understanding of the causes behind this "non-duality", as it may be caused by the specific design of the algorithms studied, the extra consumption caused by the complexity of MIMO techniques, or any other reason. In fact, it could be an inherent trade-off given by the power consumption characteristics of 802.11 interfaces, and, if so, RA techniques should not be agnostic to this case.

This work tackles the latter question from a formal standpoint. A question which, to the best of the authors' knowledge, has never been addressed in the literature. For this purpose, and with the aim of isolating the variables of interest, we present a joint goodput and energy consumption model for single 802.11 spatial streams in the absence of interfering traffic. Packet losses occur due to poor channel conditions and RA can tune only two variables: MCS and TXP.

Building on this model, we provide the following contributions: (*i*) we demonstrate through an extensive numerical evaluation that energy consumption and throughput performance are different optimisation objectives in 802.11, and not only an effect of MIMO or certain algorithms' suboptimalities; (*ii*) we analyse the relative impact of each energy consumption component on the resulting performance of RA, which serves to identify the critical factors to consider for the design of RA algorithms, and illustrate that different hardware should employ different configurations; and (*iii*) we experimentally validate our numerical results.

The rest of this paper is organised as follows. In Section 2, we develop the theoretical framework: a joint goodput-energy model built around separate previous models. In Section 3, we provide a detailed analysis of the trade-off between energy efficiency and maximum goodput, including a discussion of the role of the different energy parameters involved. In Section 4, we support our numerical analysis with experimental results. Finally, Section 5 summarises the paper.

2. JOINT GOODPUT-ENERGY MODEL

In this section, we develop a joint goodput-energy model for a single 802.11 spatial stream and the absence of interfering traffic. It is based on previous studies about goodput and energy consumption of wireless devices. As stated in the introduction, the aim of this model is the isolation of the relevant variables (MCS and TXP) to let us delve in the relationship between goodput and energy consumption optimality in the absence of other effects such as collisions or MIMO.

Beyond this primary intent, it is worth noting that these assumptions conform with real-world scenarios in the scope of recent trends in the IEEE 802.11 standard development, namely, the amendments 11ac and 11ad, where device-to-device communications (mainly through beamforming and MU-MIMO) are of paramount importance.

2.1 Goodput Model

We base our study on the work by Qiao *et al.* [8], which develops a robust goodput model that meets the established requirements. This model analyses the IEEE 802.11a Distributed Coordination Function (DCF) over the assumption of an AWGN (Additive White Gaussian Noise) channel without interfering traffic.

Let us briefly introduce the reader to the main concepts, essential to our analysis, of the goodput model by Qiao *et al.*. Given a packet of length l ready to be sent, a frame retry limit $n_{\max}$ and a set of channel conditions $\hat{s} = \{s_1, \ldots, s_{n_{\max}}\}$ and modulations $\hat{m} = \{m_1, \ldots, m_{n_{\max}}\}$ used during the potential transmission attempts, the *expected effective goodput* $\mathcal{G}$ is modelled as the ratio between the expected delivered data payload and the expected transmission time as follows:

$$\mathcal{G}(l, \hat{s}, \hat{m}) = \frac{\mathbb{E}[\text{data}]}{\mathbb{E}[\mathcal{D}_{\text{data}}]} = \frac{\Pr[\text{succ} \mid l, \hat{s}, \hat{m}] \cdot l}{\mathbb{E}[\mathcal{D}_{\text{data}}]} \quad (1)$$

where $\Pr[\text{succ} \mid l, \hat{s}, \hat{m}]$ is the probability of successful transmission conditioned to $l, \hat{s}, \hat{m}$, given by Equation (5) in [8]. The expected transmission time is defined as follows:

$$\mathbb{E}[\mathcal{D}_{\text{data}}] = (1 - \Pr[\text{succ} \mid l, \hat{s}, \hat{m}]) \cdot \mathcal{D}_{\text{fail}|l, \hat{s}, \hat{m}} \quad (2)$$
$$+ \Pr[\text{succ} \mid l, \hat{s}, \hat{m}] \cdot \mathcal{D}_{\text{succ}|l, \hat{s}, \hat{m}}$$

where

$$\mathcal{D}_{\text{succ}|l, \hat{s}, \hat{m}} = \sum_{n=1}^{n_{\max}} \Pr[n \text{ succ} \mid l, \hat{s}, \hat{m}] \cdot \left\{ \sum_{i=2}^{n_{\max}} \left[\overline{T}_{\text{bkoff}}(i) \right. \right.$$
$$+ T_{\text{data}}(l, m_i) + \overline{\mathcal{D}}_{\text{wait}}(i) \right]$$
$$+ \overline{T}_{\text{bkoff}}(1) + T_{\text{data}}(l, m_1) + T_{\text{SIFS}}$$
$$\left. + T_{\text{ACK}}(m'_n) + T_{\text{DIFS}} \right\} \quad (3)$$

is the average duration of a successful transmission and

$$\mathcal{D}_{\text{fail}|l, \hat{s}, \hat{m}} = \sum_{i=1}^{n_{\max}} \left[\overline{T}_{\text{bkoff}}(i) \right. \quad (4)$$
$$\left. + T_{\text{data}}(l, m_i) + \overline{\mathcal{D}}_{\text{wait}}(i+1) \right]$$

is the average time wasted during the $n_{\max}$ attempts when the transmission fails.

$\Pr[n \text{ succ} \mid l, \hat{s}, \hat{m}]$ is the probability of successful transmission at the n-th attempt conditioned to $l, \hat{s}, \hat{m}$, and $\overline{\mathcal{D}}_{\text{wait}}(i)$ is the average waiting time before the i-th attempt. Their expressions are given by Equations (7) and (8) in [8]. The transmission time (T_{data}), ACK time (T_{ACK}) and average backoff time ($\overline{T}_{\text{bkoff}}$) are given by Equations (1), (2) and (3) in [8]. Finally, T_{SIFS} and T_{DIFS} are 802.11a parameters, and they can be found also in Table 2 in [8].

2.2 Energy Consumption Model

The selected energy model is our previous work of [10], which has been further validated via ad-hoc circuitry and specialised hardware [11] and, to the best of our knowledge, stands as the most accurate energy model for 802.11 devices published so far, because it accounts not only the energy consumed by the wireless card, but the consumption of the whole device. While classical models focused on the wireless interface solely, this one demonstrates empirically that the energy consumed by the device itself cannot be neglected as a device-dependent constant contribution. Conversely, devices incur an energy cost derived from the frame processing, which may impact the relationship that we want to evaluate in this paper.

This model can be summarised as follows:

$$\overline{P} = \rho_{\text{id}} + \sum_{i \in \{\text{tx}, \text{rx}\}} \rho_i \tau_i + \sum_{i \in \{\text{g}, \text{r}\}} \gamma_{\text{x}i} \lambda_i \quad (5)$$

where $\rho_{\text{id}}, \rho_{\text{tx}}, \rho_{\text{rx}}$ are the power consumed by the device in idle, transmission and reception states respectively; $\tau_{\text{tx}}, \tau_{\text{rx}}$ are the airtime percentages in transmission and reception; $\gamma_{\text{xg}}, \gamma_{\text{xr}}$ are the so called *cross-factors*, a per-frame energy toll for generation and reception respectively; and $\lambda_{\text{g}}, \lambda_{\text{r}}$ are the frame generation and reception rates.

Therefore, the average power consumed $\overline{P}$ is a function of five device-dependent parameters ($\rho_i, \gamma_{\text{x}i}$) and four traffic-dependent ones (τ_i, λ_i).

2.3 Energy Efficiency Analysis

Putting together both models, we are now in a position to build a joint goodput-energy model for 802.11a DCF. Let us consider the average durations (3) and (4). Based on their expressions, we multiply the idle time ($\overline{\mathcal{D}}_{\text{wait}}, \overline{T}_{\text{bkoff}}, T_{\text{SIFS}}, T_{\text{DIFS}}$) by ρ_{id}, the transmission time (T_{data}) by ρ_{tx}, and the reception time (T_{ACK}) by ρ_{rx}. The resulting expressions are the average energy consumed in a successful transmission $\mathcal{E}_{\text{succ}|l, \hat{s}, \hat{m}}$ and the average energy wasted when a transmission fails $\mathcal{E}_{\mathrm{fail}|l,\hat{s},\hat{m}}$:

$$\mathcal{E}_{\mathrm{succ}|l,\hat{s},\hat{m}} = \sum_{n=1}^{n_{\max}} \Pr[n \text{ succ} \mid l,\hat{s},\hat{m}] \cdot \left\{ \sum_{i=2}^{n_{\max}} \left[\rho_{\mathrm{id}}\overline{T}_{\mathrm{bkoff}}(i) \right.\right.$$
$$+ \rho_{\mathrm{tx}}T_{\mathrm{data}}(l,m_i) + \rho_{\mathrm{id}}\overline{\mathcal{D}}_{\mathrm{wait}}(i) \big]$$
$$+ \rho_{\mathrm{id}}\overline{T}_{\mathrm{bkoff}}(1) + \rho_{\mathrm{tx}}T_{\mathrm{data}}(l,m_1) + \rho_{\mathrm{id}}T_{\mathrm{SIFS}}$$
$$\left. + \rho_{\mathrm{rx}}T_{\mathrm{ACK}}(m'_n) + \rho_{\mathrm{id}}T_{\mathrm{DIFS}} \right\} \qquad (6)$$

$$\mathcal{E}_{\mathrm{fail}|l,\hat{s},\hat{m}} = \sum_{i=1}^{n_{\max}} \left[\rho_{\mathrm{id}}\overline{T}_{\mathrm{bkoff}}(i) \right. \qquad (7)$$
$$\left. + \rho_{\mathrm{tx}}T_{\mathrm{data}}(l,m_i) + \rho_{\mathrm{id}}\overline{\mathcal{D}}_{\mathrm{wait}}(i+1) \right]$$

Then, by analogy with (2), the *expected energy consumed per frame transmitted*, $\mathbb{E}\left[\mathcal{E}_{\mathrm{data}}\right]$, can be written as follows:

$$\mathbb{E}\left[\mathcal{E}_{\mathrm{data}}\right] = \gamma_{\mathrm{xg}} + (1 - \Pr[\mathrm{succ} \mid l,\hat{s},\hat{m}]) \cdot \mathcal{E}_{\mathrm{fail}|l,\hat{s},\hat{m}} \qquad (8)$$
$$+ \Pr[\mathrm{succ} \mid l,\hat{s},\hat{m}] \cdot \mathcal{E}_{\mathrm{succ}|l,\hat{s},\hat{m}}$$

It is noteworthy that the receiving cross-factor does not appear in this expression because ACKs (acknowledgements) are processed in the network card exclusively, and thus its processing toll is negligible.

Finally, we define the *expected effective energy efficiency* μ as the ratio between the expected delivered data payload and the expected energy consumed per frame, which can be expressed in *bits per Joule* (bpJ):

$$\mu(l,\hat{s},\hat{m}) = \frac{\mathbb{E}\left[\mathrm{data}\right]}{\mathbb{E}\left[\mathcal{E}_{\mathrm{data}}\right]} \qquad (9)$$

3. NUMERICAL RESULTS

Building on the joint model presented in the previous section, here we explore the relationship between optimal goodput and energy efficiency in 802.11a. More specifically, our objective is to understand the behaviour of the energy efficiency of a single spatial stream as the MCS and TXP change following our model to meet the optimal goodput.

3.1 Optimal Goodput

We note that the main goal of RA, generally, is to maximise the effective goodput that a station can achieve by varying the parameters of the interface. In terms of the model discussed in the previous section, a rate adaptation algorithm would aspire to fit the following curve:

$$\max \mathcal{G}(l,\hat{s},\hat{m}) \qquad (10)$$

We provide the numerical results for this goodput maximisation problem in Fig. 1, which are in good agreement with those obtained in [8]. For the sake of simplicity but without loss of generality we fix $l = 1500$ octets and $n_{\max} = 7$ retries, and assume that the channel conditions and the transmission strategy are constant across retries ($\hat{s} = \{s_1, \ldots, s_1\}$ and $\hat{m} = \{m_1, \ldots, m_1\}$).

Fig. 1 illustrates which mode (see Table 1) is optimal in terms of goodput, given an SNR level. We next address the question of whether this optimisation is aligned with energy efficiency maximisation.

3.2 Extension of the Energy Parametrisation

The next step is to delve into the energy consumption of wireless devices. [10] provides real measurements for five

Table 1: Modes of the IEEE 802.11a PHY

Mode Index	1	2	3	4	5	6	7	8
MCS (Mbps)	6	9	12	18	24	36	48	54

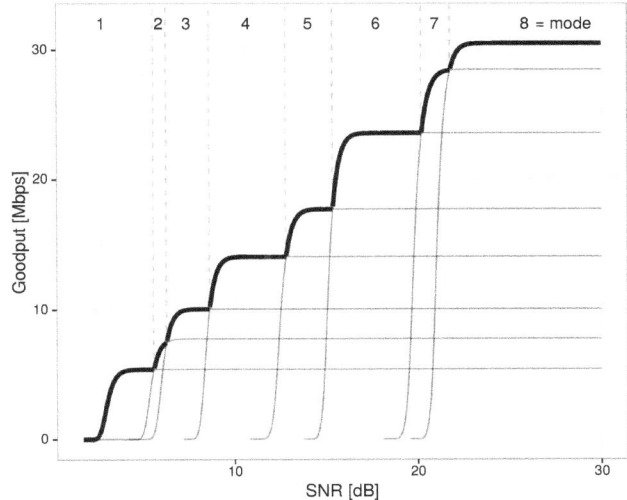

Figure 1: Optimal goodput (bold envelope) as a function of SNR.

devices: three AP-like platforms (Linksys WRT54G, Raspberry Pi and Soekris net4826-48) and two hand-held devices (HTC Legend and Samsung Galaxy Note 10.1). Two of the four parameters needed are constant ($\rho_{\mathrm{id}}, \gamma_{\mathrm{xg}}$), and the other two ($\rho_{\mathrm{tx}}, \rho_{\mathrm{rx}}$) depend on the MCS and the TXP used. However, the characterisation done in [10] is performed for a subset of the MCS and TXP available, so we next detail how we extend the model to account for a larger set of operation parameters.

A detailed analysis of the numerical figures presented in [10] suggests that ρ_{rx} depends linearly on the MCS, and that ρ_{tx} depends linearly on the MCS and the TXP (in mW). Based on these observations, we define the following linear models:

$$\rho_{\mathrm{tx}} = \alpha_0 + \alpha_1 \cdot \mathrm{MCS} + \alpha_2 \cdot \mathrm{TXP} \qquad (11)$$
$$\rho_{\mathrm{rx}} = \beta_0 + \beta_1 \cdot \mathrm{MCS} \qquad (12)$$

The models are fed with the data reported in [10], and the resulting fitting is illustrated in Figs. 2a and 2b, while Table 2 collects the model estimates for each device (with errors between parentheses), as well as the adjusted r-squared. Since these linear models show a very good fit, they support the generation of synthetic data for the different MCS and TXP required.

3.3 Energy Consumption

To compute the energy consumption using the above parametrisation, first we have to define the assumptions for the considered scenario. We assume for simplicity a device-to-device communication, with fixed and reciprocal channel conditions during a sufficient period of time (i.e., low or no mobility). As we have discussed before, our primary goal is to isolate MCS and TXP as variables of interest, but we must not forget that these are also reasonable assumptions in

Table 2: Linear Regressions

Device	ρ_{tx} model estimates (α_i)				ρ_{rx} model estimates (β_i)		
	(Intercept) [W]	MCS [Mbps]	TXP [mW]	adj. r^2	(Intercept) [W]	MCS [Mbps]	adj. r^2
HTC Legend	0.354(14)	0.0052(3)	0.021(3)	0.97	0.013(3)	0.00643(11)	>0.99
Linksys WRT54G	0.540(12)	0.0028(2)	0.075(3)	0.98	0.14(2)	0.0130(7)	0.96
Raspberry Pi	0.478(19)	0.0008(4)	0.044(5)	0.88	-0.0062(14)	0.00146(5)	0.98
Galaxy Note 10.1	0.572(4)	0.0017(1)	0.0105(9)	0.98	0.0409(10)	0.00173(4)	0.99
Soekris net4826-48	0.17(3)	0.0170(6)	0.101(7)	0.99	0.010(8)	0.0237(3)	>0.99

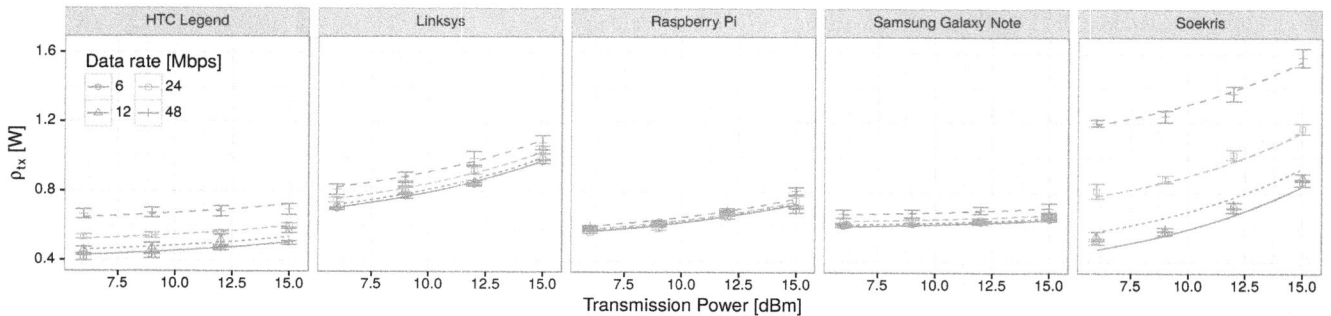

(a) ρ_{tx} fit as a function of MCS and TXP.

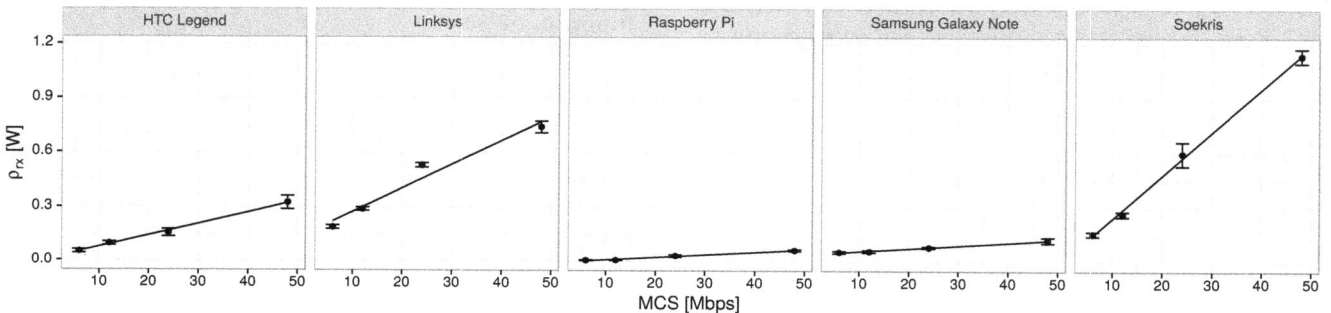

(b) ρ_{rx} fit as a function of MCS.

Figure 2: Linear regressions.

scenarios targeted by recent 802.11 standard developments (11ac, 11ad).

For instance, given channel state information from a receiver, the transmitter may decide to increase the TXP in order to increase the receiver's SNR (and thus the expected goodput), or to decrease it if the channel quality is high enough. Although the actual relationship between TXP and SNR depends on the specific channel model (e.g., distance, obstacles, noise), without loss of generality, we choose a noise floor of $N = -85$ dBm in an office scenario with a link distance of $d = 18$ m in order to explore numerically the whole range of SNR while using reasonable values of TXP. The ITU model for indoor attenuation [5] gives a path loss of $L \approx 85$ dBm. Then, we can use (8) to obtain the expected energy consumed per frame and MCS mode, with TXP being directly related to the SNR level.

The results are reported in Fig. 3. As the figure illustrates, consumption first falls abruptly as the TXP increases for all modes, which is caused when the SNR reaches a sharp threshold level such that the number of retransmis-

sions changes from 6 to 0 (i.e., no frame is discarded). From this threshold on, the consumption increases with TXP because, although the number of retransmissions is 0, the wireless interface consumes more power. We note that the actual value of the TXP when the consumption drops depends on the specifics of the scenario considered, but the qualitative conclusions hold for a variety of scenarios.

3.4 Energy Efficiency vs. Optimal Goodput

We can finally merge previous numerical analyses and confront energy efficiency, given by (9), and optimal goodput, given by (10), for all devices and under the aforementioned assumptions. To this aim, we plot in the same figure the energy efficiency for the configuration that maximises goodput given an SNR value vs. the obtained goodput, with the results being depicted in Fig. 4. We next discuss the main findings from the figure.

First of all, we can see that the energy efficiency grows sub-linearly with the optimal goodput (the optimal goodput for each SNR value) in all cases. We may distinguish three

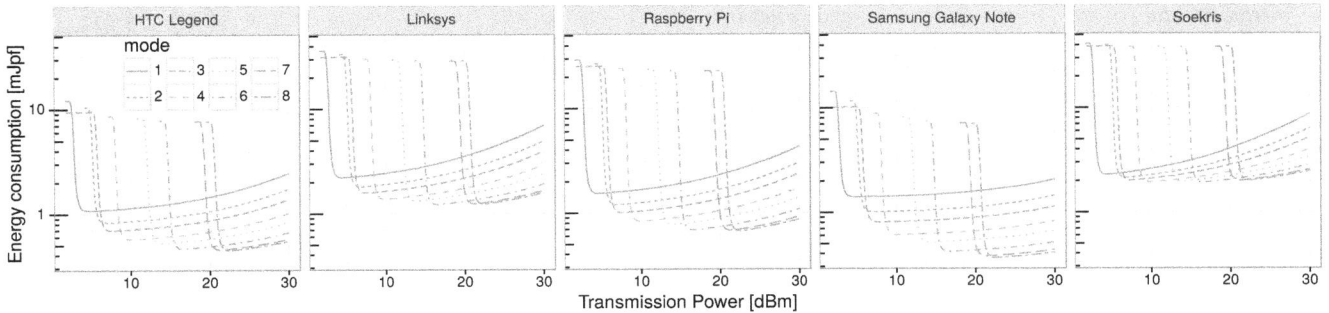

Figure 3: Expected energy consumption per frame in *millijoules per frame* (mJpf) under fixed channel conditions.

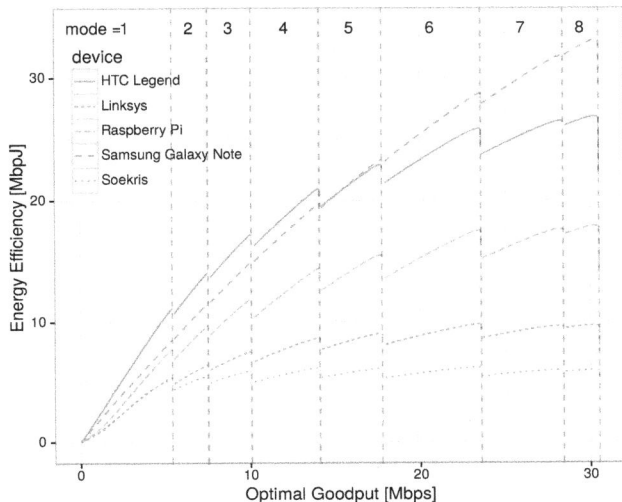

Figure 4: Energy Efficiency vs. Optimal Goodput under fixed channel conditions.

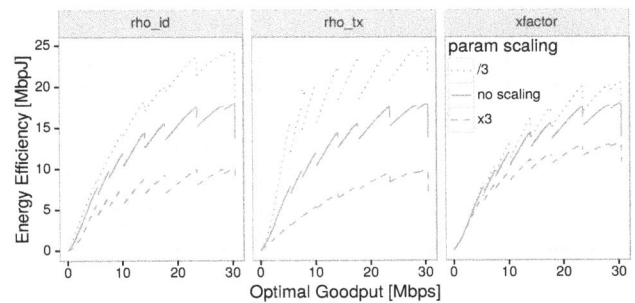

(a) Overall effect.

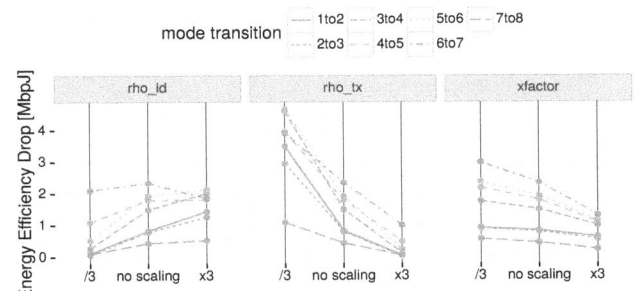

(b) Impact on mode transitions.

Figure 5: Impact of energy parameter scaling on the energy efficiency.

different cases in terms of energy efficiency: high (Samsung Galaxy Note and HTC Legend), medium (Raspberry Pi) and low energy efficiency (Linksys and Soekris). Furthermore, for the case of the Soekris, we note that the "central modes" (namely, 4 and 5) are more efficient in their optimal region than the subsequent ones.

Another finding (more relevant perhaps) is that it becomes evident that increasing the goodput does not always improve the energy efficiency: there are more or less drastic leaps, depending on the device, between mode transitions. From the transmitter point of view, in the described scenario, this can be read as follows: we may increase the TXP to increase the SNR, but if the optimal goodput entails a mode transition, the energy efficiency may be affected.

As a conclusion, we have demonstrated that optimal goodput and energy efficiency do not go hand in hand, even in a single spatial stream, in 802.11. There is a trade-off in some circumstances that current rate adaptation algorithms cannot take into account, as they are oblivious to the energy consumption characteristic of the device.

3.5 Sensitivity to Energy Parameter Scaling

We next explore how the different energy parameters af-

fect the energy efficiency vs. optimal goodput relationship. For this purpose, we selected the Raspberry Pi curve from Fig. 4 (results are analogous with the other devices) and we scale up and down, and one at a time, the four energy parameters ρ_{id}, ρ_{tx}, ρ_{rx}, and γ_{xg}. The scaling up and down is done by multiplying and dividing by 3, respectively, the numerical value of the considered parameter. One of the first results is that the impact of ρ_{rx} is negligible, a result somehow expected as the cost of receiving the ACK is practically zero. From this point on, we do not consider further this parameter.

We show in Fig. 5a the overall effect of this parameter scaling. The solid line represents the base case with no scaling (same curve as in Fig. 4), and in dashed and dotted lines the corresponding parameter was multiplied or divided by a factor of 3, respectively. As expected, larger parameters contribute to lower the overall energy efficiency. However, the impact on the energy efficiency drops between mode transitions is far from being obvious, as in some cases transitions are more subtle while in others they become more abrupt.

To delve into these transitions, we illustrate in Fig. 5b the "drop" in energy efficiency when changing between modes. As it can be seen, the cross-factor is the less sensitive parameter of the three, because its overall effect is limited and, more importantly, it scales all the leaps between mode transitions homogeneously. This means that a higher or lower cross-factor, which resides almost entirely in the device and not in the wireless card, does not alter the energy efficiency vs. optimal goodput relationship (note that this parameter results in a constant term in (8)). Thus, the cross-factor is not relevant from the RA point of view, and energy-aware RA algorithms can be implemented by leveraging energy parameters local to the wireless card.

On the other hand, ρ_{id} and ρ_{tx} have a larger overall effect, plus an inhomogeneous and, in general, opposite impact on mode transitions. While a larger ρ_{id} contributes to larger leaps, for the case of ρ_{tx}, the larger energy efficiency drops occur with smaller values of that parameter. Still, the reason behind this behavior is the same for both cases: the wireless card spends more time in idle (and less time transmitting) when a transition to the next mode occurs, which has a higher data rate.

This effect is also evident if we compare the Samsung Galaxy Note and the HTC Legend curves in Fig. 4. Both devices have ρ_{id} and ρ_{tx} in the same order of magnitude, but the HTC Legend has a larger ρ_{id} and a smaller ρ_{tx}. The combined outcome is a more dramatic sub-linear behaviour and an increased energy efficiency drop between mode transitions.

4. EXPERIMENTAL VALIDATION

This section is devoted to experimentally validate the results from the numerical analysis and, therefore, the resulting conclusions. To this aim, we describe our experimental setup and the validation procedure, first specifying the methodology and then the results achieved.

4.1 Experimental Setup

We deployed the testbed illustrated in Fig. 6, which consists of a station (STA) transmitting evenly-spaced maximum-sized UDP packets to an access point (AP). The AP is an x86-based Alix6f2 board with a Mini PCI Qualcomm Atheros AR9220 wireless network adapter, running Voyage Linux with kernel version 3.16.7 and the ath9k driver. The STA is a desktop PC with a Mini PCI Express Qualcomm Atheros QCA9880 wireless network adapter, running Fedora Linux 23 with kernel version 4.2.5 and the ath10k driver. We also installed at the STA a Mini PCI Qualcomm Atheros AR9220 wireless network adapter to monitor the wireless channel.

The QCA9880 card is connected to the PC through a *x1 PCI Express to Mini PCI Express* adapter from Amfeltec. This adapter connects the PCI bus' data channels to the host and provides an ATX port so that the wireless card can be supplied by an external power source. The power supply is a Keithley 2304A DC Power Supply, and it powers the wireless card through an *ad-hoc* measurement circuit that extracts

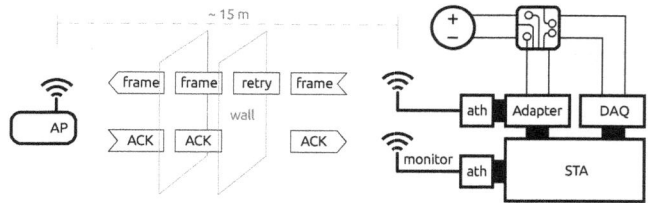

Figure 6: Experimental setup.

the voltage and converts the current with a high-precision sensing resistor and amplifier. These signals are measured using a National Instruments PCI-6289 multifunction data acquisition (DAQ) device, which is also connected to the STA. Thanks to this configuration, the STA can simultaneously measure the instant power consumed by the QCA9880 card[1] and the goodput achieved.

As the figure illustrates, the STA is located in an office space and the AP is placed in a laboratory 15 m away, and transmitted frames have to transverse two thin brick walls. The wireless card uses only one antenna and a practically-empty channel in the 5-GHz band. Throughout the experiments, the STA is constantly backlogged with data to send to the AP, and measures the throughput obtained by counting the number of received acknowledgements (ACKs).

4.2 Methodology and Results

In order to validate our results, our aim is to replicate the qualitative behaviour of Fig. 4, in which there are energy efficiency "drops" as the optimal goodput increases. However, in our experimental setting, channel conditions are far from steady, which introduces a notable variability in the results as it affects both the x-axis (goodput) and the y-axis (energy efficiency). To reduce the impact of this variability, we decided to change the variable in the x-axis from the optimal goodput to the transmission power –a variable that is directly configured in the wireless card. In this way, the qualitative behaviour to replicate is the one illustrated in Fig. 7, where we can still identify the performance "drops" causing the loss in energy efficiency.

Building on this figure, we perform a sweep through all available combinations of MCS (see Table 1) and TXP[2]. Furthermore, we also tested two different configurations of the AP's TXP at different times of the day, to confirm that this qualitative behaviour is still present under different channel conditions. For each configuration, we performed 2-second experiments in which we measure the total bytes successfully sent and the energy consumed by the QCA9880 card with sub-microsecond precision. From this data, the energy efficiency is computed, with the results depicted in Fig. 8 (each figure corresponds to a different TXP value configured at the AP).

In the figure, each line type represents the STA's mode that achieved the highest goodput for each TXP interval, therefore in some cases low modes do not appear because a higher mode achieved a higher goodput. Despite the in-

---

[1]Following the discussion on Section 3.5, the device's cross-factor is not involved in the trade-off, thus we will expect to reproduce it by measuring the wireless interface alone.

[2]The model explores a range between 0 and 30 dBm to get the big picture, but this particular wireless card only allows us to sweep from 0 to 20 dBm.

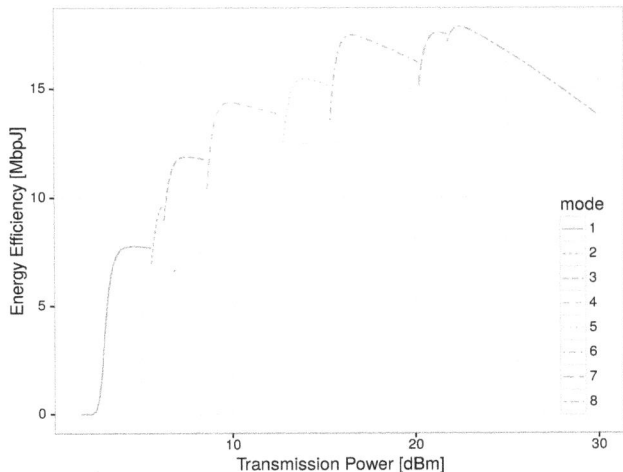

Figure 7: Energy Efficiency vs. Transmission Power under fixed channel conditions for the Raspberry Pi case.

herent experimental difficulties, namely, the low granularity of 1-dBm steps and the random variability of the channel, the experimental results validate the analytical ones, as the qualitative behaviour of both figures follows the one illustrated in Fig. 7. In particular, the performance "drops" of each dominant mode can be clearly observed (especially for the 36, 48 and 54 Mbps MCSs) despite the variability in the results.

5. SUMMARY AND FUTURE WORK

In this paper, we have revisited 802.11 rate adaptation by taking energy consumption into account. While some previous studies pointed out that MIMO rate adaptation is not energy efficient, we have demonstrated through numerical analysis that, even for single spatial streams without interfering traffic, energy consumption and throughput performance are different optimisation objectives. Furthermore, we have validated our results via experimentation.

Our findings show that this trade-off emerges at certain "mode transitions" when maximising the goodput, suggesting that small goodput degradations may lead to energy efficiency gains. Moreover, our analyses have showed that these trade-offs arise as a consequence of the power consumption behaviour of wireless cards and does not depend on the energy consumed in the rest of the device. In this way, energy-aware rate adaptation may be achieved building on information local to the wireless interface. Still, to develop energy-aware rate adaptation algorithms, further research is needed to understand how the findings of this work can be leveraged in suboptimal conditions, and how other effects, such as collisions and MIMO, affect the established trade-off.

6. ACKNOWLEDGEMENTS

This work has been performed in the framework of the H2020-ICT-2014-2 projects 5GNORMA (grant agreement no. 671584) and Flex5Gware (grant agreement no. 671563). The authors would like to acknowledge the contributions of their colleagues. This information reflects the consortium's view, but the consortium is not liable for any use that may be made of any of the information contained therein.

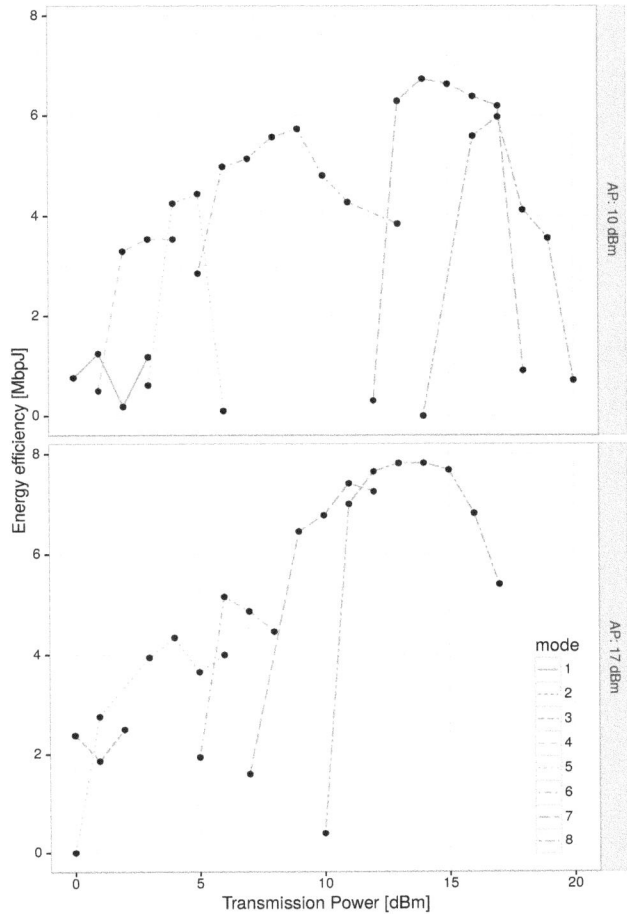

Figure 8: Experimental study of Fig. 7 for two AP configurations.

7. REFERENCES

[1] Cisco. Cisco visual networking index: forecast and methodology, 2014-2019. Technical report, Cisco, 2015.

[2] S. Eryigit, G. Gur, S. Bayhan, and T. Tugcu. Energy efficiency is a subtle concept: fundamental trade-offs for cognitive radio networks. *Communications Magazine, IEEE*, 52(7):30–36, July 2014.

[3] A. Garcia-Saavedra, P. Serrano, A. Banchs, and M. Hollick. Balancing energy efficiency and throughput fairness in IEEE 802.11 WLANs. *Pervasive and Mobile Computing*, 8(5):631 – 645, 2012.

[4] K. Huang, K. Duffy, and D. Malone. H-RCA: 802.11 Collision-Aware Rate Control. *Networking, IEEE/ACM Transactions on*, 21(4):1021–1034, Aug 2013.

[5] ITU-R. Recommendation P.1238, International Telecommunication Union, July, 2015.

[6] M. O. Khan, V. Dave, Y.-C. Chen, O. Jensen, L. Qiu, A. Bhartia, and S. Rallapalli. Model-driven energy-aware rate adaptation. In *Proceedings of the*

Fourteenth ACM International Symposium on Mobile Ad Hoc Networking and Computing, MobiHoc '13, pages 217–226, New York, NY, USA, 2013. ACM.

[7] C.-Y. Li, C. Peng, S. Lu, and X. Wang. Energy-based Rate Adaptation for 802.11n. In *Proceedings of the 18th Annual International Conference on Mobile Computing and Networking*, Mobicom '12, pages 341–352, New York, NY, USA, 2012. ACM.

[8] D. Qiao, S. Choi, and K. Shin. Goodput analysis and link adaptation for IEEE 802.11a wireless LANs. *Mobile Computing, IEEE Transactions on*, 1(4):278–292, Oct 2002.

[9] P. Serrano, A. de la Oliva, P. Patras, V. Mancuso, and A. Banchs. Greening wireless communications: Status and future directions. *Computer Communications*, 35(14):1651 – 1661, 2012. Special issue: Wireless Green Communications and Networking.

[10] P. Serrano, A. Garcia-Saavedra, G. Bianchi, A. Banchs, and A. Azcorra. Per-Frame Energy Consumption in 802.11 Devices and Its Implication on Modeling and Design. *IEEE/ACM Transactions on Networking*, PP(99):1–1, 2014.

[11] I. Ucar and A. Azcorra. Deseeding Energy Consumption of Network Stacks. In *Research and Technologies for Society and Industry Leveraging a better tomorrow (RTSI), 2015 IEEE 1st International Forum on*, pages 7–16, Sept 2015.

Energy Efficiency in Mixed Access Networks*

Christian Vitale
IMDEA Networks Institute
and Universidad Carlos III de Madrid
Madrid, Spain
christian.vitale@imdea.org

Vincenzo Mancuso
IMDEA Networks Institute
Madrid, Spain
vincenzo.mancuso@imdea.org

ABSTRACT

This paper tackles the multifaceted challenges of controlling *mixed access networks* with base stations, access points and D2D relay stations. Mixed access networks are of uncompelling importance since the next generation cellular access networks are envisioned to use different access technologies at once. We propose a unified framework to model throughput, airtime and power consumption of mobile terminals under any workload conditions in SDN-controlled mixed access networks. With our analysis, we formulate an access selection problem to optimize energy efficiency at the terminal side, while providing fair throughput guarantees. We show that the problem is NP-hard and propose an online low-complexity heuristic that largely outperforms legacy access selection policies. Our results indicate that energy efficiency can be traded off for fairness and that D2D relay is key to increase *both* energy efficiency and fairness.

Keywords

Access Selection; Device-to-Device Communications; 5G; SDN

1. INTRODUCTION

Mixed-technology access networks with heterogeneous protocols and resource allocation schemes are sprouting. On the one hand, telco operators already implement WiFi hotspots alongside the traditional cellular infrastructure [16]. On the other hand, the standardization of Device-to-Device (D2D)-assisted cellular networks is now becoming reality [2] and future cellular networks (e.g., 5G) are envisioned to support D2D communications. Currently available multi-homed mobile devices are already supporting D2D communications in addition to cellular and WiFi connectivity. In addition, many other short-range communication technologies, such as millimeter-Wave and Visible-Light Communi-

cations (VLC), are drawing the attention of industries and the research community [15, 17]. In this context, D2D-assisted cellular access networks might allow bundling user traffic in groups and implement dynamic relay, without requiring additional infrastructure deployments. So they allow improving the service towards destinations experiencing poor channel quality. Therefore *D2D can be seen as an alternative network access technology*. In the following, we focus on access networks in which D2D connectivity complements the presence of standard access points (APs) and base stations (eNBs). We refer to such networks as *mixed access networks* with heterogeneous devices acting as Points of Access (PoAs).

Energy efficiency becomes of paramount importance in mixed access networks. Indeed, mobile terminals, which may occasionally act as D2D PoAs, want to seamlessly experience broadband connectivity while preserving their battery lifetime [12]. D2D-assisted cellular access networks have been proven to substantially improve throughput and fairness compared to standard cellular access networks, although they often increase power consumption [3, 4]. Unfortunately, existing network access techniques rarely account for energy efficiency and throughput at the same time. They mostly aim to either improve battery lifetime of devices [14] or seek for throughput [18]. Moreover, energy efficient-aware approaches like [11] neglect the coupling between uplink and downlink resource allocation, or between cellular and 802.11 utilization due to the operation of D2D relays. As of today there is no model or technique available to make informed access selection decisions based on analytical estimate of throughput and power consumption, and hence energy efficiency, in a mixed access network.

We start our work by deriving a *novel comprehensive model which accounts for the intertwined nature of cellular and* 802.11 *resource allocation when D2D comes into play*. In fact, while the bandwidth available at the cellular access affects the load of D2D over 802.11 channels, it is also true that the performance of 802.11 mobile terminals connected to APs and D2D transmissions are entangled and affect the quantity of traffic that can be offloaded, and therefore cellular users. Our model includes an innovative approach to the characterization of 802.11 cliques under any traffic load condition, using a simple yet effective description of 802.11 as a system with a variable number of fully backlogged terminals. With our approach, standard tools like Bianchi's analysis [5] can be reinterpreted and applied. With our model, we compute the *airtime* used by terminals for communicating to any kind of PoAs, even when experiencing heterogeneous channel qualities and under variable load conditions. The airtime characterization is novel and key in our proposal, since it is needed to compute throughput and power consumption of the terminals. Building on our model, we *formulate a new network-controlled access selection problem* that aims to maximize the energy efficiency achieved at terminal side

---

*Work supported by the Spanish Ministry of Economy and Competitiveness under Ramon y Cajal grant (ref: RYC-2014-01335) and HyperAdapt grant (ref: TEC2014-55713-R) and by the European Commission in the framework of the H2020-ICT-2014-2 project Flex5Gware (grant agreement no. 671563). This research was also partially supported by the Madrid Regional Government through the TIGRE5-CM program (S2013/ICE-2919).

MSWiM '16, November 13-17, 2016, Malta, Malta
© 2016 ACM. ISBN 978-1-4503-4502-6/16/11. . . $15.00
DOI: http://dx.doi.org/10.1145/2988287.2989151

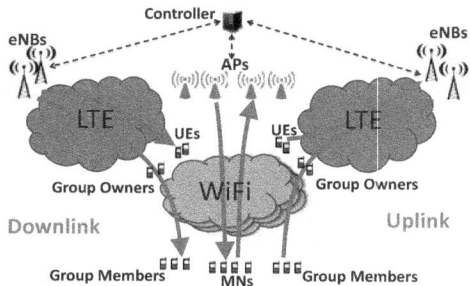

Figure 1: SDN-controlled mixed access network.

when the SDN control paradigm is enforced. As a major point, in the proposed formulation, not only uplink and downlink are simultaneously considered, but also they are jointly optimized in terms of cellular and 802.11 resource allocation. Since the resulting problem is NP-Hard, we design a *novel and efficient heuristic for access selection in SDN-controlled mixed access networks*. We validate our model and the heuristic via packet-level simulations and show that, thanks to D2D-enabled relay, the access selection mechanism we propose achieves up to 75% higher efficiency and much fairer throughput distributions than standard access selection procedures. Notably, our results scale well with the density of terminals.

2. MIXED ACCESS NETWORKS

In a mixed access network, users can attach to a single PoA, i.e., an AP, an eNB or a D2D relay. Users directly connected to an eNB can act as relay for uplink and downlink transmissions of other users, using D2D. We denote by MNs the users attached to an AP, and by UEs the ones attached to an eNB, whereas for relays and users attached to relays we use WiFi-Direct terminology, i.e., Group Owners (GOs) and Group Members (GMs), respectively. Each UE can become GO and form and manage a single WiFi-Direct group to handle the traffic of all the users (GMs) accessing the network through that GO. D2D transmissions use 802.11 frequencies and therefore do not interfere with cellular communications. Resource allocation relies on SDN, with a controller collecting info from PoAs to enforce policies dynamically.

Figure 1 illustrates the above-mentioned network elements. To avoid wasting valuable resources, the SDN controller collects info on channel qualities and traffic demands of mobile terminals, and estimates the throughput each user can achieve under the current PoA association by means of the analytical scheme we present in Section 3. Then the controller enforces rate limiting, to ensure that no resource is misused. The controller also manages access selection decisions, to optimize the energy efficiency at the terminal side, following the scheme we present in Section 4.

3. SYSTEM MODEL

To evaluate access selection policies, we start by proposing a novel model for the estimation of throughput and power consumption at terminal side. We first model cellular and 802.11 throughput and power consumption under given loads. Then we model the impact of the coupling between cellular and 802.11 due to D2D relay.

3.1 Analytical framework

Network. We denote by B the number of eNBs in the access network, whereas $\mathcal{B}$ represents the set of eNBs. The set $K_J = \{k_{1J}, ..., k_{iJ}, ..., k_{n_J J}\}$ is the set of users attached to eNB J. The number of GMs attached to the WiFi-Direct group managed by k_{iJ} is denoted by g_{iJ}. If k_{iJ} is not a GO, $g_{iJ} = 0$. The uplink demand of k_{iJ} is d_{iJ}^u. Such demand includes the uplink traffic of k_{iJ} plus

the uplink traffic of the g_{iJ} GMs attached to it. The downlink demand is instead indicated as d_{iJ}^d, which includes the demand of k_{iJ} and of all its GMs. We define a set $\mathcal{A}_q$ composed by A_q APs/GOs using the same channel and in radio range with each other (i.e., in the same clique q). However, we omit the index q when analyzing a given clique. Accordingly, we denote the set of users attached to a particular AP/GO $W \in \mathcal{A}$ by $K_W = \{k_{1W}, ..., k_{iW}, ..., k_{n_W W}\}$. The 802.11 traffic demands of k_{iW} are indicated as d_{iW}^u and d_{iW}^d in uplink and downlink, respectively. Therefore, the notation used for 802.11 users is similar to the one used for cellular users, although the exact meaning will be clear from the context.

Uplink and downlink coupling. We analyze the uplink and downlink jointly, accounting for the fact that they are coupled. For example, if the downlink throughput achieved by a GO over the cellular link changes, we consider the change in the downlink relay, which will affect the uplink traffic from GMs, and, consequently, the uplink load over the cellular link of the GO.

Cellular transmissions. We assume that power control is operated only in the uplink channel, and that uplink and downlink occur on different frequencies. Furthermore, we assume that all the eNBs use the same cellular bandwidth, i.e., frequency reuse 1 is used. We assume that the cellular transmissions adopt OFDMA to allocate resources to the users. We also assume that eNBs are always active in downlink (e.g., due to intense download activity), whereas the uplink might be not saturated (e.g., due to bottlenecks at GOs).

Cellular scheduling. We assume that eNBs operate independently from each other and that use a Vertical First Scheduling (VFS) [10], i.e., users are scheduled over consecutive subframes with a Weighted Round Robin (WRR) policy and subframes are filled avoiding empty spaces. VFS reduces the airtime by design and achieves high energy saving.

Scheduling of GOs. Since GOs haul the traffic of other users, we assume that their weight in WRR is proportional to the number of GMs connected plus one (the GO itself).

D2D and 802.11 operation. The model follows 802.11 a/b/g specifications with no power control. Furthermore, we assume that APs or GOs serve their users in Round Robin (RR) order.

802.11 cliques. We assume that, due to the use of different channels or due to distance, we have N_W independent (non-interfering) 802.11 sets. Since many orthogonal channels are available, and since GO and GMs have to be in proximity, we further assume that all users and APs in a set form a clique.

Demands and arrival processes. We assume demands and arrival processes are stationary and independent, but not identically distributed for each user and for uplink and downlink. Arrivals are packets with the same average size for all cases.

It is worth noticing that different assumptions on the scheduling, resource allocation, packet size or on the network control operation can be easily accommodated in our model.

3.2 Analysis of cellular operation

The throughput in the cellular network is strictly related to the bit efficiency achieved and the airtime used, i.e., the portion of time during which transmissions are active. Similarly, the power consumption under VFS scheduling is proportional to the airtime of the terminals [10]. Therefore, we develop an analytical method to compute bit efficiency and airtime.

3.2.1 Uplink

Let us first consider uplink transmissions to the eNB. Let π_{iJ} be the transmission power used by UE k_{iJ}, which is the result of the uplink power control mechanism in place and it is set to $\pi_{iJ} = \min\left(\frac{SNR_T \cdot \mathcal{N}}{L(k_{iJ}, J)}, \pi^{\max}\right)$, where SNR_T is the target SNR that each user tries to achieve in uplink transmissions [1], $\mathcal{N}$ is the noise power, $L(k_{iJ}, J)$ is the path loss in the transmissions from k_{iJ} to eNB J, while $\pi^{\max}$ is the maximum power transmission allowed.

We now show how to calculate the average uplink bit efficiency b_{iJ}^u achieved by each uplink transmitter, that is, the average number of bits that each UE can transmit per Hertz and per second. The average level of interference sensed by each eNB is the power received from users attached to other eNBs. Thus, using the Shannon formula (normalized to the bandwidth used) and considering that distinct eNBs operate independently, the bit efficiency is:

$$b_{iJ}^u = \log_2\left(1 + \frac{\pi_{iJ} L(k_{iJ}, J)}{\mathcal{N} + \sum_{M \in \mathcal{B}\backslash\{J\}} \sum_{x=1}^{n_M} a_{xM}^u \pi_{xM} L(k_{xM}, J)}\right), \quad (1)$$

where a_{xM}^u is the uplink airtime of an interfering user in a different cell, and the second term in the argument of the log function is the signal-to-noise-plus-interference ratio (SINR).

With VFS, the airtime used in uplink is the portion of symbols needed to serve the throughput T_{iJ}^u, out of a total of N_S symbols transmitted per second over the entire uplink bandwidth. Since the number of symbols per second required is $T_{iJ}^u/(T_S B_S b_{iJ}^u)$, where T_S and B_S are time and bandwidth used to transmit an OFDM symbol, the airtime is:

$$a_{iJ}^u = \frac{T_{iJ}^u}{T_S B_S b_{iJ}^u N_S}. \quad (2)$$

The above formulas show that there is a complex relation between airtime, bit efficiency and throughput. Indeed, bit efficiency and airtime achieved by a particular user depend on bit efficiency and airtime of interfering users, which in turn depend on bit efficiency and airtime of the user under analysis.

Denoting by r_{iJ}^u the unsatisfied demand (in terms of symbols/s), the airtime is also expressed as:

$$a_{iJ}^u = \frac{1}{N_S}\left(\frac{d_{iJ}^u}{T_S B_S b_{iJ}^u} - r_{iJ}^u\right), \quad (3)$$

in which r_{iJ}^u can be computed iteratively.

We propose Algorithm 1 to solve the problem without approximations, for a given set of users, demands, and channel qualities. The algorithm, which is a recursive fixed point algorithm, estimates iteratively the uplink airtime of each user in the scenario and its achieved average bit efficiency. The algorithm starts by assigning users airtime proportionally to the relay group size $g_{iJ} + 1$. Then, Algorithm 1 estimates the bit efficiency, fixing the resource allocation, and the new resulting resource allocation, given the bit efficiency just computed. In the algorithm, the available N_S symbols/s are distributed to users according to the weights of the WRR scheduler. Unused resources are then assigned to the users whose demands are higher than their fair share.

Upon convergence, or after a maximum number of iterations, Algorithm 1 returns the airtime allocation that corresponds to the served demand (computed as in line 20 of the algorithm's pseudocode). The throughput can be then computed by inverting (2), and the uplink power consumption P_{iJ}^u is computed based on uplink airtime and transmission power [10]:

$$P_{iJ}^u = a_{iJ}^u\left(P_0 + \alpha \pi_{iJ}^{(dBm)}\right) + (1 - a_{iJ}^u) P_{idle}, \quad (4)$$

where P_0 is the power consumed by the terminals when the transmission power is $1\,mW$, α is a proportionality factor (in W/dBm), $\pi_{iJ}^{(dBm)} = 10\log_{10}\frac{\pi_{iJ}}{1mW}$, and P_{idle} is the power consumption of the terminals when no transmission is in place.

Algorithm 1 Uplink cellular bit efficiency and airtime computation

---

Input: $g_{iJ}, \pi_{iJ}, d_{iJ}^u \forall k_{iJ} \in K_J, \forall J \in \mathcal{B}$,
  $L(k_{iJ}, J) \ \forall k_{iJ} \in K_J, \forall J \in \mathcal{B}$,
  $L(k_{iM}, J) \ \forall k_{iM} \in K_M, \forall M \neq J \in \mathcal{B}, \forall J \in \mathcal{B}$,
  $cnt^{\max}, N_S, b^{\max}, T_S, B_S, \mathcal{N}$

Initialization:
Compute WRR weights w_{iJ}, initialize airtimes a_{iJ}^u, a_{iJ}^o and counter cnt:
$$w_{iJ} = \frac{g_{iJ} + 1}{\sum\limits_{x=1}^{n_J}(g_{xJ} + 1)}, \forall k_{iJ} \in K_J, \forall J \in \mathcal{B}$$

$a_{iJ}^u = w_{iJ}, \ \forall k_{iJ} \in K_J, \forall J \in \mathcal{B}$
$a_{iJ}^o = 0, \ \forall k_{iJ} \in K_J, \forall J \in \mathcal{B}$ [for previous round's values]
$cnt = 1$

Procedure
 Iterative procedure (at most $cnt^{\max}$ loops).
1: **while** $cnt \leq cnt^{\max} \ \&\& \ (\exists J \in \mathcal{B} \text{ and } k_{iJ} \in K_J : a_{iJ}^u \neq a_{iJ}^o)$ **do**
 First, update bit efficiency:
2: **for** $\forall k_{iJ} \in K_J, \forall J \in \mathcal{B}$ **do**
3:   Compute b_{iJ}^u using (1)
4:   $b_{iJ}^u = \min(b_{iJ}^u, b^{\max})$; [bit efficiency has an upper limit]
5: **end for**
 Second, update resource allocation (symbols assigned proportionally to w_{iJ}; unused resources redistributed iteratively):
6: **for** $J \in \mathcal{B}$ **do**
7:   $N_R = N_S$; [available uplink symbols/s]
8:   $r_{iJ}^u = \frac{d_{iJ}^u}{T_S B_S b_{iJ}^u}, \forall k_{iJ} \in K_J$; [unsatisfied demand of k_{iJ}]
  Iterative resource allocation:
9:   **while** $N_R > 0 \ \&\& \ \exists i : r_{iJ}^u > 0$ **do**
10:    $N_a = 0$; [symbols/s allocated by eNB J]
11:    **for** $i : r_{iJ}^u > 0$ **do**
12:     $r_a = \min\left(r_{iJ}^u, \frac{w_{iJ} N_R}{\sum\limits_{x:r_{xJ}^u > 0} w_{xJ}}\right)$; [symbols/s for k_{iJ}]
13:     $N_a = N_a + r_a$
14:     $r_{iJ}^u = r_{iJ}^u - r_a$
15:    **end for**
16:    $N_R = N_R - N_a$
17:   **end while**
  Update airtime values:
18:   **for** $k_{iJ} \in K_J$ **do**
19:    $a_{iJ}^o = a_{iJ}^u$
20:    Compute a_{iJ}^u with (3)
21:   **end for**
22: **end for**
23: $cnt = cnt + 1$
24: **end while**
Output: $b_{iJ}^u, a_{iJ}^u, \forall k_{iJ} \in K_J, \forall J \in \mathcal{B}$

3.2.2 Downlink

The downlink transmission power of an eNB is constant over time and equal to π_J. The bit efficiency depends on inter-cell interference generated by the transmissions of other eNBs, which are always active. As a result, the average bit efficiency achieved b_{iJ}^d by eNB J in the transmissions to user k_{iJ}, can be computed as:

$$b_{iJ}^d = \log_2\left(1 + \frac{\pi_J L(J, k_{iJ})}{\mathcal{N} + \sum_{M \in \mathcal{B}\backslash\{J\}} \pi_M L(M, k_{iJ})}\right), \quad (5)$$

where $L(M, k_{iJ})$ represents the path loss among eNB M and user k_{iJ}. Note that, differently from the uplink case, the bit efficiency in downlink is not affected by the user airtime, and so it can be computed without iterations.

Downlink resource allocation follows the same VFS scheduling policy used in uplink, so that an expression equivalent to (2) holds by replacing the superscript u with d. So, to compute the downlink user airtime and throughput, we only need to compute the amount of unsatisfied demand r_{iJ}^d, using the WRR policy for resource allocation. For such computation we use an algorithm similar to Algorithm 1, and omitted for sake of brevity, in which the "while-do" statement is not necessary. In fact, a single iteration (equivalent to lines 6-22 of Algorithm 1) suffices to return the downlink airtime of each user, from which we compute the downlink throughput:

$$T_{iJ}^d = T_S B_S b_{iJ}^d a_{iJ}^d N_S. \tag{6}$$

Finally, the power consumption due to downlink activity is:

$$P_{iJ}^d = a_{iJ}^d P_R + (1 - a_{iJ}^d)P_I, \tag{7}$$

where P_R is the power consumed by the terminal while receiving and P_I is consumed when the terminal is idle.

3.3 Analysis of 802.11 operation

In order to compute the throughput and the power consumption achieved in 802.11, we analyze a generic clique. We first show how to compute the bit efficiency of 802.11 transmitters. Second, with the bit efficiencies we propose a new model to compute the throughput based on system *states*. We then compute the duration of the states, which is key to estimate the power consumption.

Bit efficiency. The bit efficiency b_{iW}^d achieved by each PoA W is univocally determined by the particular destination k_{iW}:

$$b_{iW}^d = \log_2 \left(1 + \frac{\pi_W L(W, k_{iW})}{\mathcal{N}}\right), \tag{8}$$

where π_W is the fixed transmission power of W and $L(W, k_{iW})$ is the path loss from W to k_{iW}. Eq. (8) does not include interference because successful 802.11 transmissions in a clique occur when only one device transmits.

However, the average bit efficiency of W depends on the distribution of transmissions from W to the terminals attached to W. Indeed, differently from what assumed in state-of-the-art proposals, the average bit efficiency is neither an input of the problem nor a constant, since it changes with the traffic distribution across terminals served by W, and the traffic distribution changes with the number of devices in the clique and with their demand. For this reason we present here a novel approximation method to compute throughput and power consumption.

The basic idea behind our model is that, in each 802.11 channel, operations can be split in intervals of time during which the set of active (backlogged) devices remains unchanged. In each of such intervals, active APs, GOs, MNs and GMs can be regarded as a saturated system for which the analysis of Bianchi for a clique [5] can be used. Thereby, each interval corresponds to a *system state* for which we can compute bit efficiencies, throughputs and airtimes.

Let us consider the PoAs $W \in \mathcal{A}$. In a generic state s, terminals with packets to transmit to W are denoted as set $Q_W^u(s)$, whereas $Q_W^d(s)$ is the set of terminals with packets to receive from W. Now, while the average bit efficiency b_{iW}^d of terminal $k_{iW} \in Q_W^u(s)$ is computed with an expression similar to (8), the bit efficiency of PoA W is the average of its bit efficiencies experienced when transmitting to its attached terminals in round robin in state s (packets have the same average length, otherwise per-user average packet sizes shall be used as weights in the following expression):

$$b_W(s) = \left|Q_W^d(s)\right| \bigg/ \sum_{i:k_{iW} \in Q_W^d(s)} \frac{1}{b_{iW}^d}. \tag{9}$$

Throughput and state duration. Due to the packet-fairness of the 802.11 MAC protocol, all transmitters achieve the same throughput (in packets per second). Having assumed a common average packet lengths for all transmitters, all throughputs in a clique are statistically identical. Such common value is the throughput $R(s)$ computed in state s with Bianchi's formula [5], in which the average transmission time is computed with the bit efficiencies derived as described above. Note that $R(s)$ accounts for the presence of *all* active PoAs and for their attached terminals active in state s, so it expresses the coupling between different PoAs using the same channel in the same area. Moreover, the throughput of a PoA is fairly shared between its MNs or GMs. Therefore uplink throughputs $T_{iW}^u(s)$ and downlink throughputs $T_{iW}^d(s)$ of the MNs (or GMs) of W, in state s, are as follows:

$$T_{iW}^u(s) = R(s); \qquad T_{iW}^d(s) = \frac{R(s)}{|Q_W^d(s)|}. \tag{10}$$

We now need to compute the time spent in each state. To this aim, we note that the order in which states are visited is not important, because the arrival processes are independent. So we consider a unit interval and the demand corresponding to that interval, and reorder the states occurring in such interval. We start with the state with more active devices, namely s_1: the system remains in such state until the uplink or downlink demand of one device is completely served. This is simply given by:

$$t_1 = \min_{i:k_{iJ} \in \bigcup_{W \in \mathcal{A}} (Q_W^u(s_1) \cup Q_W^d(s_1)),\ x \in \{d,u\}} \left(\frac{d_{iW}^x}{T_{iW}^x(s_1)}\right). \tag{11}$$

After t_1, the system switches to state s_2 in which one less 802.11 downlink/uplink flow is active, which changes the average system throughput. Thus, the computation of t_2 and of the durations of the successive states can be done sequentially, until all demands are served or $\sum_i t_i = 1$.

Having used a unit interval in the computation, the values t_i represent the fractions of time spent in each state. The resulting average throughputs on 802.11 are therefore as follows:

$$T_{iW}^u = \sum_i t_i R(s_i); \qquad T_{iW}^d = \sum_i \frac{t_i R(s_i)}{|Q_W^d(s_i)|}. \tag{12}$$

Note that the approach proposed is an approximation, since it assumes that after a flow activates or deactivates, the system reaches instantaneously its steady state, in which Bianchi's formula holds. However, we will show via simulation that this approximation introduces negligible error.

Airtime and power consumption. In order to compute the power consumption of APs and MNs (or GOs and GMs in 802.11), we exploit the results of [9]. Throughput and airtime determine the power consumption of PoAs (P_W) and terminals (P_{iW}):

$$P_W = P_{idle} + \gamma_{tx} a_W^{tx} + \gamma_{rx} a_W^{rx} + \sum_{k_{iW} \in K_W} \left(\beta_{tx} \frac{T_{iW}^d}{E[S_p]} + \beta_{rx} \frac{T_{iW}^u}{E[S_p]}\right); \tag{13}$$

$$P_{iW} = P_{idle} + \gamma_{tx} a_{iW}^{tx} + \gamma_{rx} a_{iW}^{rx} + \beta_{tx} \frac{T_{iW}^u}{E[S_p]} + \beta_{rx} \frac{T_{iW}^d}{E[S_p]}; \tag{14}$$

where P_{idle} is power consumed by an 802.11 device when idle, γ_{tx} and γ_{rx} are the powers consumed by a device per airtime unit in transmission/reception, β_{tx} and β_{rx} are the powers consumed per packet transmitted/received per second, and $E[S_p]$ is the average packet length. In the formulas, we have denoted by a_{iW}^{tx} and a_{iW}^{rx} the transmission/reception airtime of k_{iW}, whereas a_W^{tx} and a_W^{rx} denote airtimes at PoA W.

We now show how to compute the airtime as an average over states s. We denote by τ_s and p_s respectively the probability that a system slot (which has variable length, as defined in [5]) contains a transmission and the conditional probability that a transmission is successful in state s, given that the transmission occurs. Using the same approach of [5], we can compute τ_s and p_s from the number $D(s)$ of transmitting devices (PoAs and terminals) in state s:

$$D(s) = \left| \bigcup_{W \in \mathcal{A}} Q_W^u(s) \right| + \left| \left\{ W \in \mathcal{A} : \exists k_{iW} \in Q_W^d(s) \right\} \right|; \quad (15)$$

$$p_s = 1 - (1 - \tau_s)^{D(s)-1}; \quad (16)$$

$$\tau_s = \frac{2(1 - 2p_s)}{(1 - 2p_s)(C + 1) + p_s C[1 - (2p_s)^m]}; \quad (17)$$

where C is the the minimum congestion window size of 802.11 and m is the maximum number of transmission attempts for a packet. The absolute probability to have a success for any of the transmitters is then $P_s = \tau_s(1 - \tau_s)^{D(s)-1}$, so that the probability of collision in a slot for a given transmitter is $\tau_s - P_s$. Thus, solving (16) and (17) for τ_s, leads to the airtime computation for state s:

$$a_W^{tx}(s) = \frac{\left(P_s / |Q_W^d| \right) \sum_{k_{iW} \in Q_W^d} \delta_{iW}^d + (\tau_s - P_s)\delta_c}{\bar{\delta}_s}; \quad (18)$$

$$a_W^{rx}(s) = P_s \frac{\sum_{k_{iW} \in Q_W^u} \delta_{iW}^u}{\bar{\delta}_s}; \quad (19)$$

$$a_{iW}^{tx}(s) = \frac{P_s \delta_{iW}^u + (\tau_s - P_s)\delta_c}{\bar{\delta}_s}; \quad (20)$$

$$a_{iW}^{rx}(s) = \frac{P_s}{|Q_W^d|} \frac{\delta_{iW}^d}{\bar{\delta}_s}; \quad (21)$$

where δ_c is the duration of a slot containing a collision (either an RTS frame or a packet), whereas δ_{iW}^u and δ_{iW}^d are successful transmission durations (including 802.11 overheads) from k_{iW} to PoA W and vice versa, respectively. Considering that unused slots have fixed duration δ_e, the average slot duration $\bar{\delta}_s$ in state s is:

$$\bar{\delta}_s = P_s \sum_{W \in \mathcal{A}} \left(\sum_{k_{iW} \in Q_W^u} \delta_{iW}^u + \frac{1}{|Q_W^d|} \sum_{k_{iW} \in Q_W^d} \delta_{iW}^d \right)$$
$$+ (1 - \tau_s)^{D(s)} \delta_e + \left(1 - D(s)P_s - (1 - \tau_s)^{D(s)} \right) \delta_c. \quad (22)$$

Finally, the average airtime values are computed by averaging each of (18)–(21) according to the state durations t_i. Note that, differently from existing studies, the above equations take into consideration the presence of several PoAs in a clique, and the fact that PoAs serve terminals with different channel qualities.

3.4 Network-controlled coupling

So far we have considered traffic demands of GOs as an input of the model. However the real demand of GOs depends on what they receive to relay. Moreover, it is possible that the traffic to relay cannot be handled in full. It is therefore possible that cellular resources are wasted for traffic that can not be relayed by the GOs.

However, an SDN network controller may avoid such problem by acting as coordinator among the cellular network and the 802.11 groups. The controller needs to estimate the quantity of traffic that GOs can actually relay given the limitation of cellular and 802.11 resources and enforce a rate limiting on the activity of GOs and GMs. Such control beneficially impacts the resource allocation of UEs that do not act as relays, since more resources are freed for UEs. In addition, since GOs' activity on the 802.11 channels is reduced with respect to the uncontrolled case, also APs and their MNs indirectly benefit from the presence of a controller. The controller operates iteratively, as described in what follows.

Step 0: Cellular downlink resources are allocated with the procedure presented in Section 3.2.2, the demand of GOs being computed as the local GO traffic plus the demands of GMs:

$$d_{iJ}^d = d_W^d + \sum_{k_{iW}} d_{iW}^d, \quad \forall \text{UE } k_{iJ} \text{ acting as PoA } W. \quad (23)$$

In the notation adopted in the above expression, we have used the fact that a GO acts as UE for the eNB and as AP for GMs. The controller computes the cellular downlink throughput T_{iJ}^d of any GO k_{iJ} (alias PoA W). Only part of such throughput belongs to k_{iJ}, namely $T_W^d \leq T_{iJ}^d$, while the rest is for relay.

Step 1: Using RR and T_{iJ}^d, compute downlink throughputs of GO k_{iJ} and its GMs, for all GOs.

Step 2: Compute uplink 802.11 throughput T_{iW}^u of all GMs using the procedure described in Section 3.3, but replacing d_{iW}^d with the GM downlink throughputs found in **Step 1**.

Step 3: Use the procedure of Section 3.2.1 to compute cellular uplink, using GMs' 802.11 throughputs computed in **Step 2** as GO relay uplink demands.

Step 4: The resulting cellular uplink throughput of each GO is split across its GMs as in downlink (with RR). Such throughput values are set by the controller as rate limits of the GMs.

Step 5: Recompute the operational point of 802.11 with the limits fixed for relay traffic in **Step 1** and **Step 4**. Any GM obtains exactly the rate fixed with rate limiting, while a GO can receive no more than what imposed in **Step 1**.

Step 6: Recompute cellular downlink allocation with the procedure of Section 3.2.2, using as GO downlink relay demands the relay throughputs (in 802.11) computed in **Step 5**.

Step 7: If any of the downlink GO throughputs computed at **Step 6** differ from what used in **Step 1** of this iteration, unused resources are redistributed to UEs and GOs for which the allocation did not change from **Step 1** to **Step 6**, and whose demand is not satisfied. The redistribution uses WRR with weights $g_{iJ} + 1$. Then a new iteration starts from **Step 1**.

Uplink cellular resources and 802.11 resources are univocally determined for each downlink cellular allocation, so the algorithm converges as soon as downlink cellular resource allocation converges. The convergence of iterations is guaranteed because downlink resources are limited and, at each iteration, the amount of downlink cellular resources assigned to UEs increases.

With the above, we have computed not only throughputs, but also the rate limits to impose. So we can also compute airtimes and power consumptions as described in Sections 3.2 and 3.3.

4. ACCESS SELECTION

In this section we present a new access selection mechanism that improves the energy efficiency of wireless terminals in mixed access networks. Exploiting the fact that carefully selecting the attachment of the terminals to proper PoAs leads to different throughputs and power consumptions, our access selection mechanism aims to maximize the total terminal energy efficiency figure:

$$E = \sum_{y \in \mathcal{M}} (T_y^u + T_y^d)/P_y, \quad (24)$$

where $\mathcal{M}$ is the set of UEs (some of which acting as GOs), MNs, and GMs present in the system, T_y^u and T_y^d are the throughputs achieved by terminal y in uplink and downlink, respectively, whereas P_y is the power consumed by y.

In our access selection mechanism, UEs become GOs *if needed*, i.e., if there is a benefit in terms of total energy efficiency (24). However, purely pursuing the total energy efficiency might lead to low and unfairly distributed throughputs. For instance, an AP might be more energy efficient than an eNB but guarantee less throughput when the number of MNs becomes large and collisions drastically degrade the throughput in 802.11. Furthermore, when acting as a GO, a UE may use a non-negligible part of its energy to relay the traffic of the attached GMs. This *cannot be more energy efficient* for the GO, i.e., the individual energy efficiency of a GO is negatively impaired by the relay traffic, and being a GO is not beneficial for the UE acting as GO. However, the presence of GOs improves connectivity, and a GO might turn to be a GM at some point in time, so there is a clear incentive for keeping GOs in the loop.

To account for the above considerations, in the following, we formulate an access selection problem that aims to maximize the total energy efficiency under throughput and energy constraints defined on a per-terminal basis.

4.1 Problem Formulation

We use the total energy efficiency as utility function, and we add per-terminal constraints to guarantee that (i) the achieved terminal throughput is at least α_T times the highest throughput potentially achieved under any other access choice, $\alpha_T \in (0, 1]$, and (ii) the energy efficiency achieved by a GO is at least the α_E times the energy efficiency achieved by acting as a simple UE, $\alpha_E \in (0, 1]$. Denoting by E_y the energy efficiency of terminal y, and by $\mathcal{V}$ the set of feasible terminal access combinations, the resulting formulation of our optimization problem is as follows:

$$
\max_{\substack{V = \{K_J : J \in \mathcal{B}, \forall J; \\ K_W : W \in \bigcup_q \mathcal{A}_q, \forall W\} \in \mathcal{V}}} \quad \sum_{k_{iW} : W \in \bigcup_q \mathcal{A}_q} \frac{T_{iW}^u + T_{iW}^d}{P_{iW}}
$$

$$
+ \sum_{J \in \mathcal{B}} \left(\sum_{k_{iJ} \notin \bigcup_q \mathcal{A}_q} \frac{T_{iJ}^u + T_{iJ}^d}{P_{iJ}^u + P_{iJ}^d} + \sum_{k_{iJ} \in \bigcup_q \mathcal{A}_q} \frac{T_{k_{iJ}}^u + T_{k_{iJ}}^d}{P_{iJ}^u + P_{iJ}^d + P_{k_{iJ}}} \right) ;
$$

s.t.:

$$
\forall y : y = k_{iW} \qquad T_{iW}^u + T_{iW}^u \geq \alpha_T \max_{\mathcal{V}} \left(T_y^u + T_y^d \right) ;
$$

$$
\forall y : y = k_{iJ} \notin \bigcup_q \mathcal{A}_q \quad T_{iJ}^u + T_{iJ}^d \geq \alpha_T \max_{\mathcal{V}} \left(T_y^u + T_y^d \right) ;
$$

$$
\forall y : y = k_{iJ} \in \bigcup_q \mathcal{A}_q \quad T_{k_{iJ}}^u + T_{k_{iJ}}^d \geq \alpha_T \max_{\mathcal{V}} \left(T_y^u + T_y^d \right) ;
$$

$$
\forall y : y = k_{iJ} \in \bigcup_q \mathcal{A}_q \quad E_{k_{iJ}} \geq \alpha_E \max_{\mathcal{V}} E_y .
$$

$$
(25)
$$

Above we have split the contribution to the total energy efficiency in terms of MNs (the first summation) and UEs (second summation). The contribution of UEs is further split between non-GOs (UEs $k_{iJ} \notin \bigcup_q \mathcal{A}_q$) and GOs (UEs $k_{iJ} \in \bigcup_q \mathcal{A}_q$).

Due to the fact that, in a real mixed access network, the access selection mechanism has to take separate decisions every time a new terminal enters the network, we actually tackle the above optimization problem in on-line fashion. The resulting on-line problem can be reduced to an on-line Generalized Assignment Problem (GAP) [6], in which items arrive one after the other and they have to be assigned to bins of fixed capacity. In GAP a decision has to be made at the arrival of each item and cannot be changed later. When assigned to a bin, the item requires a given capacity and provides a given benefit. Depending on the bin, capacity and benefit may change. In our on-line problem each terminal can be seen as an item in GAP, while each of the PoAs is a bin. Depending on the PoA, the capacity required and the energy efficiency (the benefit) achieved by a terminal changes. However, our problem is more constrained than GAP. First, assigning a terminal to a given PoA also changes the capacity required and the energy efficiency (the benefit) achieved by other terminals. Second, we need to assign a PoA to each terminal. Therefore, if the capacity requested by a subset of terminals to a PoA is higher than the actual capacity of the PoA, each terminal has to shrink its capacity request so to fit into the PoA, at the expenses of reduced efficiency. So, our problem is a GAP with extra constraints and with bin-occupancy-dependent benefits. Since GAP is NP-Hard, so is our on-line problem.

4.2 On-line Energy Efficient Access Selection

In order to find a solution to our optimization problem, we propose the *Marginal Benefit Heuristic* (MBH), inspired by the well known heuristic that has been proposed for solving a GAP [6]. Upon the arrival of a terminal, MBH works as follows:

1. MBH computes the energy efficiency of each terminal before the attachment of the new terminal.

2. MBH evaluates the attachment of the new terminal to any feasible PoA. For each possibility, MBH computes the energy efficiency of affected terminals.

3. At this point, all the PoAs not ensuring at least α_T of the maximum throughput that could be received by the new terminal are discarded. Likewise, when the PoA is a GO, the MBH algorithm evaluates the energy efficiency degradation experienced by the GO. To have a reference point, all the GMs attached to the GO under analysis are considered as attached directly to their closer eNBs and the GO energy efficiency is computed. If by serving all its GMs and the new terminal the energy efficiency of the GO drops below α_E times the energy efficiency it would achieve while acting as a simple UE, then this GO is no further considered.

4. The MBH choses a PoA which guarantees the highest marginal benefit w.r.t. the same PoA without the new terminal attached.

MBH differs from the classic heuristic used for GAP mainly because it does not require to evaluate the allocation of a new incoming terminal to each and every possible PoA. In fact, the additional constraints we introduced, i.e., on throughput and energy guarantees for the incoming terminal, identify a subset of possible target PoAs. Another difference is the fact that MBH, differently from GAP heuristics, accepts negative marginal benefits, since MBH needs to allocate the new terminal to one PoA in any case. Moreover, and most importantly, our heuristic has to recompute the resource allocation for each possible assignment.

5. NUMERICAL EVALUATION

In this section we first validate our method to analyze 802.11 performance. The cellular part of the model is quite straightforward so we skip validation results here. Afterwards, we show how our MBH scheme outperforms state of the art approaches and we shed light on the trade-off between maximizing system energy efficiency and achieving fair throughputs.

5.1 802.11 model validation

To validate the throughput and power consumption model we presented in Section 3.3, we used a packet-level simulator written in MatLab. In our simulations, a GO and a number of GMs randomly picked among 2 and 10 were positioned in a squared area of size $50m \times 50m$, following a uniform distribution. The channel quality among the GO and the different GMs (and vice versa) was computed as in (8). The simulator considers that all the GMs and the GO can listen to the transmission of all the others. Transmissions were therefore regulated by the 802.11 MAC protocol, whose main parameters are show in Table 1. Packet arrivals followed Pois-

Table 1: 802.11 parameters

Carrier	$2.5\,GHz$
C (Min congestion window)	16
m Max retry	5
Other MAC param. (SIFS, DIFS,...)	$802.11n$
Max Transmission rate	$144\,Mbps$
$\mathcal{N}$ Noise Level	$3.98 \times 10^{-18} W/Hz$
Bandwidth	$20\,MHz$
Path Loss	Log-Distance, Exponent 3
Transmission Power	$100mW$

Table 2: Cellular transmission and power parameters

Carrier	$2.45\,GHz$
Bandwidth	$20\,MHz$
Subframe Duration	$1\,ms$
Symbols per RB	84
Max Power Uplink	$200\,mW$
Power Downlink	$1\,W$
SNR target Power Control	$20dB$
Max Symbol Efficiency	$5.55\,b/sym$
Noise Level	$3.98 \times 10^{-18}\,W/Hz$
Path Loss Model	Log-Distance, Exponent 3
P_{idle}	$0\,W$
P_0	$2.3815\,W$
α	$0.0649\,W/dbm$
P_R	$0.225\,W$
γ_{tx}	$0.11\,mW$
γ_{rx}	$0.09\,mW$
β_{tx}	$0.55\,W$
β_{rx}	$0.4\,W$

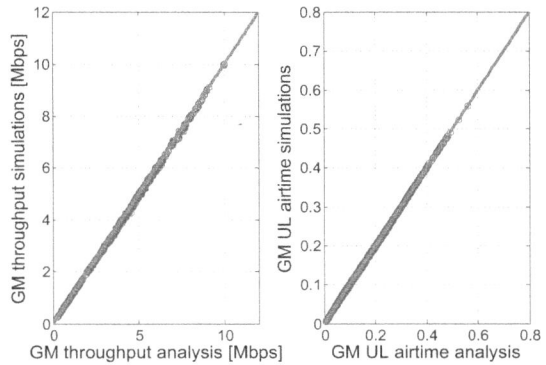

Figure 2: 802.11 model validation.

son processes with intensity fixed during the simulation and picked uniformly at random in the set $\{0.25, 0.5, 1, 2, 3, 5, 7.5, 10\}\,Mbps$.

In Figure 2 we compare simulated and analytically computed throughput and airtime of terminals. Each point corresponds to a simulated throughput (airtime), whereas the red line indicates where the point should be if the model was error-free. As it is easy to see, the approximation introduced with our state-based analysis is practically negligible, and the largest relative error is 7.43% for throughput and 9.31% for airtime. Although not explicitly shown in the figure, the 95% percentiles of the error on throughput and airtime are as low as the 3.04% and 3.17%, respectively.

5.2 Access Selection Performance

In this section we evaluate the performance of our access selection mechanism MBH. In particular, we quantify the gain in terms of energy efficiency achieved by MBH against state of the art solutions when the values of α_T and α_E change. We also consider the effects of access selection decisions on aggregate throughput and its fair distribution among terminals.

In an area of $400m \times 400m$, we first fixed the position of 7 eNBs so to have an inter-site distance equal to 100m. Furthermore, in each experiment, we positioned randomly 10 APs with uniform distribution. The APs select the particular channel they use depending on their location (the same holds for UEs acting as GOs). In this way, terminals scheduled on the same channel are co-located and form a clique. We further introduce 500 users, one after the other, at random positions. At their arrival, we apply MBH under different configurations for α_T and α_E. User demands are like described in Section 5.1, and downlink and uplink demands of a terminal are picked independently. Note that we evaluate the performance of MBH under increasing density of terminals.

802.11 and cellular parameters are set up as shown in Table 1 and Table 2, respectively. The latter also shows the particular power consumption parameters used, extracted from [10], [9], and [8]. Furthermore, we set P_{idle} to zero. In this way we effectively evaluate only the power consumption due to active transceivers.

Figure 3 presents the results achieved in terms of utility (i.e., energy efficiency), aggregate throughput and fairness varying the values assumed by α_T and α_E. Results are compared with a standard *WiFi First policy* [18], in which a new user is attached to the strongest AP, if available, or to the strongest eNB if no AP is available. Results are also compared with a version of MBH which ignores D2D relay opportunities. The number of independent 802.11 channels considered in Figure 3 is 3, but similar results have been achieved with more channels.

The main tendency shown by Figure 3 is that MBH is able to achieve huge energy efficiency gains when compared to WiFi First policy if there is no guarantee on per-user throughput and GO power efficiency. When α_T and α_E are set to zero, indeed, MBH improves energy efficiency at terminal side by about the 75% if compared to the WiFi First policy. However, a careful inspection of the results shows that MBH with α_T and α_E set to zero aggregates the traffic and the energy efficiency to a small number of users present in the scenario. As a result, both the aggregate traffic and the per-user fairness decrease w.r.t. the WiFi First policy. Increasing the value of α_T allows coping with this problem. Indeed, restricting the access selection of the new users to the subset of PoAs ensuring at least α_T times the maximum achievable throughput improves drastically the aggregate throughput and fairness. However, such result is achieved at the expense of GO energy efficiency, and the figure shows that utility drops when throughput grows. For instance, when α_T is 1 (and $\alpha_E = 0$), a new user always attaches to the PoA ensuring the larger achievable throughput, and MBH energy efficiency gain drops to 35%—which is still remarkable—with 15% higher fairness w.r.t. WiFi First.

By increasing α_E, we can ensure that GOs limit their D2D relay activity, i.e., we reduce the average number of GOs in the system. In turn, this reduces the achievable energy efficiency gain. Nevertheless, Figure 3 shows that a trade-off between system energy efficiency, fairness and power consumption wasted due to relay is possible. For instance, when we select $\alpha_T = 0.5$ and $\alpha_E = 0.5$, we achieve gain in energy efficiency close to 50%, while achieving competitive aggregate throughput and fairness w.r.t. WiFi First. We also ensure that at most half of the power consumed by a GO is reserved for relay. We also note that D2D is key to enable energy efficient access networks. In fact, when MBH is not allowed to create relay links, performance figures drop and become very close to (though better than) what achievable with WiFi First. Note also that, interestingly, the utility gain is barely affected by the population density, which tells that MBH scales well.

6. RELATED WORK

Several techniques exists that deal with access selection and energy efficiency. Nguyen-Vuong *et al.* [14] propose to increase the

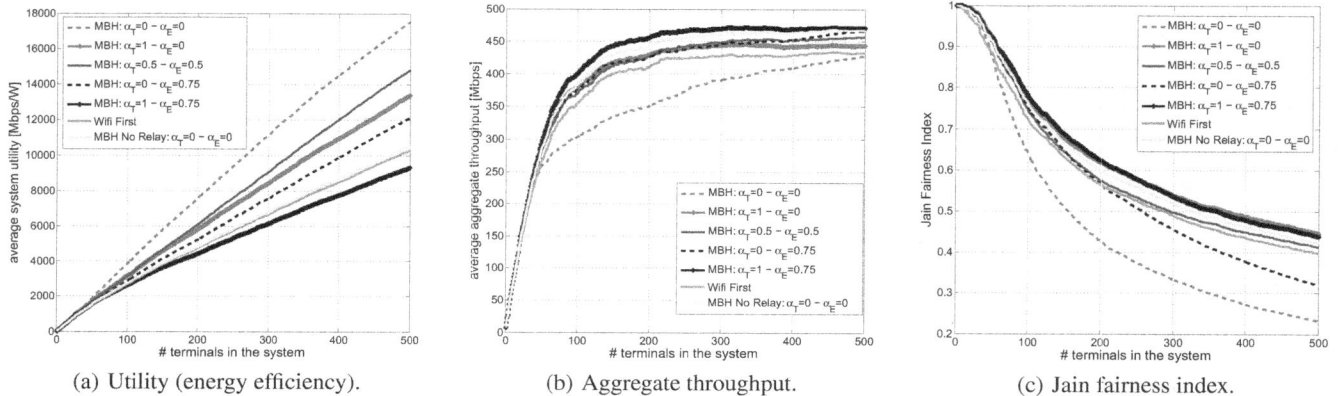

| (a) Utility (energy efficiency). | (b) Aggregate throughput. | (c) Jain fairness index. |

Figure 3: Performance of MBH considering different values of α_T and α_E (with 3 channels for 802.11).

battery lifetime of terminals by connecting them to the least power expensive technology among the ones available. No guarantees on the throughput achieved and no consideration on the different loads of the PoAs is taken into account. Desset *et al.* [7] assume uplink and downlink demands are known at the terminal. The user then chooses the access technology that is able to serve its traffic with the lowest cost. However, in their scheme, access selection effects on neighboring terminals are not considered and terminals are not allowed to access the network if there is no PoA that can satisfy their demand. Lee *et al.* [11] account for D2D relay in down-link, though the energy efficiency of each terminal is considered as independent, and resource allocation as PoA-independent. Access selection is then solved as a knapsack problem. Malandrino *et al.* [13]—even if their work does not explicitly address an access selection mechanism—show how, in an access network with un-derlay D2D support, scheduling the least interfering users at once may reduce terminals power consumption, which is in line with our findings. However, we provide analytical reasons behind this phenomenon, which goes well beyond what hinted in [13].

We remark that, differently from previous proposals, our ap-proach dynamically adapts to load distributions, works at any sys-tem load with both uplink and downlink traffic, accounts for the fact that throughput and power consumption of users connected to the same PoA are tightly coupled, and that resource allocation for distinct PoAs using distinct access technologies can be coupled.

7. CONCLUSIONS

We have proposed a framework to compute throughput, airtime and power consumption in SDN-controlled mixed access networks. A controller is envisioned to avoid waste of cellular and 802.11 re-sources by enforcing rate limiting on the generation of traffic han-dled by means of D2D communications. Our model is unique and accurate, and its novelty consists not only in accounting for the cou-pling between cellular and 802.11 resource allocation/utilization in uplink and downlink with D2D relay, but also in the method used to analyze the 802.11 operation by identifying network states. With the analysis, we have formulated an on-line access selection prob-lem for energy efficiency. Given the NP-hardness of the problem, we have proposed MBH, an on-line heuristic that largely outper-forms existing association policies and provides enhanced levels of fairness by means of D2D-based relay.

8. REFERENCES

[1] 3GPP. Evolved Universal Terrestrial Radio Access (E-UTRA); Physical layer procedures (Release 12). TS 36.213, 3rd Generation Partnership Project (3GPP), 2015.

[2] 3GPP. Proximity-based services (ProSe); stage 2. TS 23.303, 3rd Generation Partnership Project (3GPP), 09 2015.

[3] S. Andreev, A. Pyattaev, K. Johnsson, O. Galinina, and Y. Koucheryavy. Cellular Traffic Offloading onto Network-Assisted Device-to-Device Connections. *IEEE Comm. Magazine*, 2014.

[4] A. Asadi, Q. Wang, and V. Mancuso. A survey on device-to-device communication in cellular networks. *Communications Surveys &Tutorials, IEEE*, 16(4):1801–1819, 2014.

[5] G. Bianchi. Performance analysis of the IEEE 802.11 distributed coordination function. *IEEE JSAC*, 18(3):535–547, 2000.

[6] D. G. Cattrysse and L. N. Van Wassenhove. A survey of algorithms for the generalized assignment problem. *European Journal of Operational Research*, 60(3):260–272, 1992.

[7] C. Desset, N. Ahmed, and A. Dejonghe. Energy savings for wireless terminals through smart vertical handover. In *ICC*. IEEE, 2009.

[8] B. Dusza, C. Ide, L. Cheng, and C. Wietfeld. An accurate measurement-based power consumption model for LTE uplink transmissions. In *IEEE INFOCOM (Poster)*, Turin, Italy, April 2013.

[9] A. Garcia-Saavedra, P. Serrano, A. Banchs, and G. Bianchi. Energy consumption anatomy of 802.11 devices and its implication on modeling and design. In *CoNEXT*, pages 169–180, 2012.

[10] T. Israeli, E. Biton, and O. Gurewitz. Experimental assessment of power-save behavior of commercial IEEE 802.16 network. *IEEE Trans. on Wireless Communications*, 14(3):1169–1182, March 2015.

[11] S. Lee, K. Sriram, K. Kim, Y. H. Kim, and N. Golmie. Vertical handoff decision algorithms for providing optimized performance in heterogeneous wireless networks. *IEEE T. Vehicular Technology*, 58(2):865–881, 2009.

[12] G. Y. Li, Z. Xu, C. Xiong, C. Yang, S. Zhang, Y. Chen, and S. Xu. Energy-efficient wireless communications: tutorial, survey, and open issues. *IEEE Wireless Commun.*, 18(6):28–35, 2011.

[13] F. Malandrino, Z. Limani, C. Casetti, and C. Chiasserini. Interference-aware downlink and uplink resource allocation in HetNets with D2D support. *IEEE Transactions on Wireless Communications*, 14(5):2729–2741, 2015.

[14] Q. Nguyen-Vuong, N. Agoulmine, and Y. Ghamri-Doudane. A user-centric and context-aware solution to interface management and access network selection in heterogeneous wireless environments. *Computer Networks*, 52(18):3358 – 3372, 2008.

[15] Y. Niu, Y. Li, D. Jin, L. Su, and A. V. Vasilakos. A survey of millimeter wave communications (mmWave) for 5G: opportunities and challenges. *Wireless Networks*, 21(8):2657–2676, 2015.

[16] Nokia. Integrated Wi-Fi supports superior mobile broadband. Technical report, Nokia Siemens Networks, 2014.

[17] P. H. Pathak, X. Feng, P. Hu, and P. Mohapatra. Visible light communication, networking, and sensing: A survey, potential and challenges. *Communications Surveys & Tutorials, IEEE*, 17(4):2047–2077, 2015.

[18] W. Song, H. Jiang, and W. Zhuang. Performance analysis of the WLAN-first scheme in cellular/WLAN interworking. *IEEE Transactions on Wireless Communications*, 6(5):1932–1952, 2007.

Energy Aware Network Formation in Peer-to-Peer Wireless Power Transfer

Adelina Madhja
Computer Technology Institute
and Press "Diophantus" (CTI)
& University of Patras, Greece
madia@ceid.upatras.gr

Sotiris Nikoletseas
Computer Technology Institute
and Press "Diophantus" (CTI)
& University of Patras, Greece
nikole@cti.gr

Christoforos Raptopoulos
Computer Technology Institute
and Press "Diophantus" (CTI)
& University of Patras, Greece
raptopox@ceid.upatras.gr

Dimitrios Tsolovos
Computer Technology Institute
and Press "Diophantus" (CTI)
& University of Patras, Greece
tsolobos@ceid.upatras.gr

ABSTRACT

This paper addresses wirelessly networked populations of nodes (agents) that can both transmit and receive wireless power among each other, interacting locally in a peer to peer manner. In this setting, we study the important problem of network formation, in particular how the agents can distributively create a star structure. Extending the state of the art, we introduce energy considerations in network formation: in addition to the star construction, our goal is to achieve a certain target energy distribution among the agents. We assume a generalized, more realistic energy loss factor which may differ for each pairwise power exchange.

We propose four interaction protocols aiming both to construct the star structure and also converge to the target energy distribution. Our protocols assume different amounts of network knowledge, achieving different efficient trade-offs with performance, measured in terms of how close they get to the targeted energy distribution, as well as their energy efficiency and convergence time.

Keywords

network formation, energy aware protocols, wireless energy transfer, generalized population protocols

1. INTRODUCTION

Next generation wirelessly networked populations are expected to consist of very large numbers of distributed portable devices carried by mobile agents that follow unpredictable and uncontrollable mobility patterns. Recently, there has been an increasing interest to combine near-field communication capabilities and *wireless energy transfer* in the same portable device, allowing mobile agents carrying the devices

to wirelessly exchange energy. For example, the same antenna, designed to exploit its far-field properties for communication purposes, can be suitably configured for simultaneously realizing wireless energy transfer via its near-field properties. The near-field behavior of a pair of closely coupled transmitting and receiving dual-band printed monopole antennas (suitable for mobile phone applications) can make it possible to achieve both far-field performance and near-field power transfer efficiency (between 35% to 10%) for mobile phones located few centimeters apart [17]. Further developments on the circuit design can render a device capable of achieving bi-directional, highly efficient wireless energy transfer and be used *both as a transmitter and as a receiver of energy* [6, 20]. In this context, energy harvesting and wireless energy transfer capabilities are integrated, enabling each device to act on demand either as a wireless energy provider or as an energy harvester.

An important goal in the design and efficient implementation of large networked systems is to save energy and keep the network functional for as long as possible [9, 19]. In the above setting, this goal can be achieved by using wireless energy transfer as an energy exchange enabling technology and applying interaction protocols among agents/devices which guarantee that the available energy in the network can be eventually distributed in a desirable way.

In a recent paper [15], the authors present a new model for abstracting *populations of agents* that are capable of *peer-to-peer wireless energy exchange* and study the problem of achieving *approximate energy balance* in the population through pairwise interactions at the minimum total energy loss. It is also pointed out in that paper that, to allow scalability of any algorithmic solutions, devices in such settings have to operate under severe limitations in their computational power, data storage, the quality of communication and most crucially, their available amount of energy. For this reason, the efficient distributed cooperation of the agents towards collectively achieving global computational and communication goals is a challenging task. It is worth noting that a restricting assumption in [15] is that the energy lost in any wireless energy transfer follows a fixed linear law; here, we relax this assumption by *allowing the energy loss factor β to be different* in every agent interaction.

In this paper, embarking from the model of network con-

MSWiM '16, November 13-17, 2016, Malta, Malta
© 2016 ACM. ISBN 978-1-4503-4502-6/16/11...$15.00
DOI: http://dx.doi.org/10.1145/2988287.2989166

structors of [14], we *significantly generalize* the ultimate global task of the population of agents, thus generalizing the computational problem considered in [15]. In particular, agents are required to form (either virtually or physically) a predefined target network structure(i.e., a graph) by using their in-between states and at the same time *converge to an energy distribution* that depends on the target network itself. To present our algorithmic solutions, we consider the construction of *one of the most basic network structures, namely the star* as depicted in Fig. 1. Furthermore, we assume that the target distribution is such that the relative energy level of each node is proportional to its degree. Our motivation for this problem comes from the fact that star formations usually arise in wireless networks when nodes are organized in a cluster, in which case a cluster-head is selected to which all communication is forwarded. In view of this, the energy level of the cluster-head should be proportional to the number of nodes in its cluster.

Our contribution: The main contributions of this paper are the following.

- For the first time, we *introduce energy issues* in network construction protocols. More specifically, the network agents can exchange energy when they interact. In this paper, the selected network structure is *the star* and we propose *a corresponding target energy distribution*.

- We propose *a new model*, which is a generalization of that in [15], where we let the *energy loss factor β to be different in each energy exchange* between any pair of agents. This abstracts the difference on the environmental conditions and the wireless energy transfer technology characteristics.

- We design and evaluate (via simulations) *four interaction protocols* which construct the star structure and try to converge to the targeted energy distribution as well. We study different network knowledge levels and provide *efficient trade-offs* between the cost of obtaining higher amount of knowledge and achieving higher performance gain.

2. RELATED WORK

Wireless Power Transfer is an emerging technology which recently has been studied in various perspectives. Most of them use powerful entities called chargers which are able to carry large amounts of energy and transfer it to the network devices. In [16] the authors conducted experiments using real devices to evaluate their proposed protocols that maximize the energy efficiency and achieve energy balance. In [11, 12, 21] the authors proposed coordination protocols for multiple chargers. The minimum number of the required chargers is investigated in [5]. Both data gathering and energy transfer is studied in [8] and [23].

In [22] the authors study the case of collaborative charging where chargers can charge each other, which in [12] was extended to a hierarchical structure. In [2] the authors investigated the case where the nodes are mobile, as in [16], but the charger is mobile too.

Using bi-directional wireless energy transfer technology [6], it is possible to both transmit and receive energy. The corresponding circuits can be embedded to the mobile agents in the population protocols a fundamental study of which is

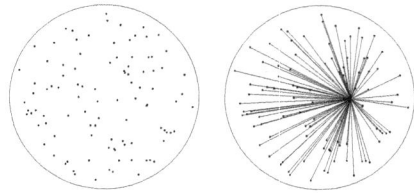

Figure 1: The network before / after the star construction.

provided in [4]. In [13] authors introduced the Arithmetic Population Protocol model where the agents with limited capabilities are able to compute order statistics of their arithmetic input values. More specifically, the agents have a fixed number of registers and the joint transition function allows them to only make comparisons and copy/paste operations on the values stored on their registers. In contrast, our model allows the agents to compare their registered values and to update them, according to the protocols. It is possible to construct a specific network structure as described in [14]. In [15] the authors proposed the model where the agents are able to perform peer-to-peer energy exchanges. We extend their model by letting the energy loss factor be different in each energy exchange.

3. THE MODEL

We consider a population of m mobile agents denoted as $\mathcal{M} = \{u_1, u_2, \ldots, u_m\}$, each one equipped with a *battery cell*, a *wireless energy transmitter* and a *wireless energy receiver*. Additionally, each agent u has a *state* from a set of states $\mathcal{Q}$ and a small *local memory* consisting of a small number of registers. For any time $t \geq 0$ and agent u, we denote by $C_u(t) \stackrel{def}{=} (E_u(t), q_u(t), R_u(t))$ the *configuration* of u at t, where $E_u(t)$ (resp. $q_u(t), R_u(t)$) is the *energy level* (resp. state and memory) of agent u at time t. The *relationship* between any pair of agents $\{u, v\}$ is further characterized by a *connection state* from a set of states $\mathcal{Q}'$ (different from $\mathcal{Q}$). Following [14] and since in this paper we consider energy aware network formation, we set $\mathcal{Q}' = \{0, 1\}$. In particular, for any pair of agents u, v, if their connection state $q_{\{u,v\}}(t)$ at time t is equal to 1, then we say that u is connected to v at t; otherwise (i.e. if $q_{\{u,v\}}(t) = 0$) they are disconnected.

The movement of the agents does not follow any specific pattern, but whenever two agents meet (e.g. whenever their trajectory paths intersect or the agents come sufficiently close), they can interact according to an *interaction protocol* $\mathcal{P}$; all agents run the *same* protocol $\mathcal{P}$. In particular, whenever agents u, v interact, they modify their respective configurations (i.e. they exchange energy, modify their states and local memory) and their connection state according to $\mathcal{P}$. Formally, we assume that time is discrete and that if agents u, v interact at time t, they communicate their configurations and current connection state and they jointly modify them as follows:

$$(C_u(t+1), C_v(t+1), q_{\{u,v\}}(t+1)) = \mathcal{P}(C_u(t), C_v(t), q_{\{u,v\}}(t)). \quad (1)$$

The configurations of all other agents, as well as every other connection state (even those involving agents u or v with other agents) remain unchanged.

Due to the nature of wireless energy technology (e.g. RF-to-DC conversion, materials and wiring used in the system, objects near the devices, etc.), any transfer of energy induces *energy loss*. Therefore, whenever an agent u transfers energy ε to agent v, the amount of energy that the latter actually receives is $(1 - \beta) \cdot \varepsilon$, where β is a constant depending on the environment and the equipment for energy transfer available to the agents. In fact, we will consider the quite general scenario, where β is *not known* by the agents and can be *different* in every interaction (in our experimental evaluation, we assume that in every interaction β is an independent random variable that follows the normal distribution; see section 6). For simplicity, we do not take into account energy loss due to movement or other activities of the agents explicitly, as this is besides the focus of the current paper.

In fact, we assume that most devices can be carried by individuals or other moving entities that have their own agenda, and thus devices interact when the latter happen to come in close proximity. In the most general setting, interactions between agents are planned by a *scheduler* (that satisfies certain fairness conditions ensuring that all possible interactions will eventually occur), which can be used to abstract the movement of the agents. To allow for non-trivial results in our experimental evaluation of our algorithmic solutions, in this paper, we consider a widely accepted special case of fair scheduler, namely the *probabilistic scheduler*, which was introduced in [3]. According to the probabilistic scheduler, in every time step, a single interacting pair of agents is selected independently and uniformly at random among all $\binom{m}{2}$ pairs of agents in the population.

A crucial assumption of this model (which is inspired by the population protocols model [3] and network constructors [14]) is that agents do not share memory or exchange messages unless they interact. Furthermore, agents are computationally weak machines that cannot grasp the full structure and status of the entire population. Nevertheless, through pairwise interactions agents are required to collectively eventually *converge* to a stable state.

4. PROBLEM DEFINITION AND METRICS

In [14], the authors define the *population network* at time t to be the simple, undirected graph G_t with vertex set the set of agents $\mathcal{M}$ and edge set the set of pairs of agents u, v that have $q_{\{u,v\}} = 1$. In particular, they design protocols (which they call *network constructors*) that eventually converge to certain graph structures. We significantly generalize the definition of network constructors to take into account the energy levels of the agents in the population; we call this *energy aware network formation*. To this end, we use two metrics: the *structural distance* and the *energy distance*.

Formally, let H be a *target graph* on m vertices. For two graphs H, G on the same vertex set $\mathcal{M}$, we denote by $H \triangle G$ the hamming distance between those graphs, i.e. $H \triangle G \overset{def}{=} \sum_e |\mathbf{1}_e(H) - \mathbf{1}_e(G)|$, where the summation is over all $\binom{m}{2}$ possible edges and $\mathbf{1}_e(H)$ (resp. $\mathbf{1}_e(G)$) is the indicator variable for the existence of e in H (resp. G). We define the *structural distance* of the population from the target graph H at time t as follows:

$$\delta_t^s(H, G_t) \overset{def}{=} \min_{G \sim G_t} H \triangle G, \qquad (2)$$

where G_t is the population network at time t and the minimum is taken over all graphs G that are isomorphic to G_t.

The energy distance is defined in analogy to the *total variation distance* in probability theory and stochastic processes [1, 7]. Let $\mathcal{E}^*$ be a *target distribution*, defined on $[m] = \{1, 2, \ldots, m\}$ and, for any $t \geq 0$, let $\mathcal{E}(t)$ be the relative energy distribution at time t given by $\mathcal{E}_u(t) = \frac{E_u(t)}{\sum_u E_u}, u \in \mathcal{M}$. Let also $\Sigma(m)$ be the set of permutations of $[m]$. We define the *energy distance* of the population from the target energy distribution $\mathcal{E}^*$ at time t as follows:

$$\delta_t^e(\mathcal{E}^*, \mathcal{E}(t)) \overset{def}{=} \min_{\sigma \in \Sigma(m)} \frac{1}{2} \sum_{i=1}^m |\mathcal{E}_i^* - \mathcal{E}_{\sigma(u_i)}(t)|, \qquad (3)$$

where the minimum is among all permutations of $[m]$, $\mathcal{E}_{\sigma(u_i)}(t)$ is the relative energy level of agent $\sigma(u_i)$ at time t and $\mathcal{E}_i^*$ is the target distribution at point i of its domain.

The general formulation of the problem that we consider in this paper is as follows:

DEFINITION 1 (ENERGY AWARE NETWORK FORMATION). *Consider a population $\mathcal{M}$ of agents. Let H be a target graph on $\mathcal{M}$ and $\mathcal{E}^*$ a target distribution. Let also ϵ be a small positive constant. Assuming the probabilistic scheduler, find a protocol that, when run by the agents in the population, there is $t \geq 0$ such that (a) $\delta_t^s(H, G_t) = 0$, (b) $\delta_t^e(\mathcal{E}^*, \mathcal{E}(t)) \leq \epsilon$ and (c) the total energy loss is minimized, i.e. $E_{total}(0) - E_{total}(t) = \sum_u E_u(0) - \sum_u E_u(t)$ is as small as possible.*

In this paper, in particular, we consider the construction of one of the most basic graph structures, namely the star. Furthermore, we assume that the target distribution is such that *the relative energy level of each node is proportional to its degree*. Our motivation for this problem comes from the fact that star formations usually arise in wireless networks when nodes are organized in a cluster, in which case a cluster-head is selected to which all communication is forwarded. In view of this, the energy level of the cluster-head should be proportional to the number of nodes in its cluster. Therefore, the target energy level of the central node of the star at time t should be $a = \frac{E_{total}(t)}{2}$, while the target energy level of a peripheral node should be $b = \frac{E_{total}(t)}{2(m-1)}$. Setting without loss of generality $\mathcal{E}^* = \{a, b, b, \ldots, b\}$, the minimum of $\frac{1}{2} \sum_{i=1}^m |\mathcal{E}_i^* - \mathcal{E}_{\sigma(u_i)}(t)|$ (which is equal to the energy distance $\delta_t^e(\mathcal{E}^*, \mathcal{E}(t))$) is attained by choosing any permutation σ that assigns the agent with the largest energy level to u_1.

5. THE PROTOCOLS

In this section we present our proposed interaction protocols that form a star network structure and aim to minimize the energy distance metric as defined above. The pseudo-code for all proposed protocols is presented in the full version of this paper [10]. At any time t, the probabilistic scheduler selects two agents u, v to interact and the protocols run in order to change the configuration of each agent. The protocols differ on the way that two agents interact, on the amount of energy that two agents exchange and on the size of the agents' memory. The set of states is defined as $\mathcal{Q} = \{c, p, h_1, \ldots, h_d\}$. If the state of an agent is c (resp. p), the agent is characterized as central (resp. peripheral). The states h_i, $i \in \{1, \ldots, d\}$ are not network structure states but are used to allow the algorithms to improve their decisions. However, these states are not used by all proposed algorithms. More specifically, in the Full

Transfer and the Half Transfer protocols the agent may be either central or peripheral. Initially, in all protocols, the agents are considered to be central.

5.1 Full Transfer Protocol

In this section we present a straightforward protocol that can be seen as a lower bound to the performance of the other proposed protocols discussed in sections below.

In this protocol there are three main interaction cases. The first case is when both agents are central. In this case one of them will randomly be selected to remain central and the other one will become peripheral and it will transmit all its available energy (except a small amount of it, denoted as E_{min}, which is needed in order for the agent to remain operational) to the central agent. In addition, a connection between them will be established. In the second case, both agents are peripherals. If a connection between them exists, the algorithm removes it and no energy is transferred between them. In the final case, one agent is considered to be central, and the other one is peripheral. In this case, if there is no connection between them, the algorithm establishes it and like in the previous case, no energy is transferred between them.

We expect this protocol, to have high energy loss and energy distance from the target distribution, due to its random nature. In addition, we expect it to converge to its final energy distribution in a low number of interactions.

5.2 Half Transfer Protocol

In this section we describe the Half Transfer protocol, which allows the agents to store their own initial energy level in their memory. Notice that this does not constitute global knowledge by the agents.

The decisions made by this protocol differ from the Full Transfer in two ways. When two central agents interact, the agent with highest energy level at that time will remain central, while the other one will become peripheral. The second difference lies in the amount of energy that is transferred when there is an energy exchange. The peripheral agent will keep half of its initial energy and will transmit the rest. This decision is based on the observation that in order to achieve the desired energy distribution, the central agent will have to acquire half of the total energy of the network. Aside from these two differences, the Half Transfer protocol operates exactly like the Full Transfer protocol.

We expect this protocol to improve on the results of the Full transfer protocol on both the energy loss and energy distance due to the non random selection of agents and the amount of energy that is transferred.

5.3 Degree Aware Protocol

The Degree Aware protocol *aims to estimate the total number of agents* that are present in the network. This information is useful since each agent can adapt its energy exchanges in order to reduce the energy distance. Each central agent's estimation is the number of their connected neighbors. The non central agents store the maximum estimation among the agents that they have interacted with. The maximum estimation is exchanged in each interaction, thus ensuring its propagation to every agent.

In order to improve the estimation, each agent goes through d halted states $(h_1, h_2, \ldots, h_d)$; d is a parameter whose choice will be fine-tuned. The transition from a halted state to the next one is performed whenever the agent interacts with a central agent, that has a higher estimation. Each agent, will only transmit energy to agents with a higher estimation than its own, after they have passed through every halted state and have become peripherals. There are four main interaction cases in this protocol.

In the case where both agents are centrals, the agent with the lowest estimation becomes a 1st level halted agent. A connection between them is established, the estimation of the central agent is increased by one and the estimation of the halted agent is updated to this maximum value as well.

In the case where each agent is either peripheral or halted, the agents exchange the maximum estimation and delete their connection if it exists.

In the case where one agent is central and the other one is peripheral, if the central agent has lower estimation than the peripheral, it becomes a 1st level halted agent and updates its estimation. Otherwise, their states remain the same, but if the agents are not connected, they establish a connection and update their estimations to the new maximum one. If the energy level of an agent times the maximum estimation (between these two agents) is larger than the energy level of the other agent, it will transmit to it an amount of energy that is equal to $(1/k) \times (E_u \times E_v)/(E_u + E_v)$ where parameter *k is used to limit the energy exchanged between the agents and thus the energy loss*, when the estimation is not equal to the actual network size.

In the fourth case where one agent is central and the other one is halted, if the halted agent has larger estimation than the central, the latter becomes halted as well. Else, if the central agent has the larger estimation but the level of the halted agents is not d, i.e. its state is not the h_d, it moves to the next level halted state. Otherwise, if the central agent has the highest estimation and the halted agent's state is the last one, then the halted agent becomes peripheral. If the agents are not connected, they establish a connection between them, and increase the estimation of the central agent by one. If the energy level of an agent times the maximum estimation (between these two agents) is larger than the energy level of the other agent, it will transmit to it an amount of energy that is equal to $(1/k) \times (E_u \times E_v)/(E_u + E_v)$. Also, both agents will update their estimation to the maximum one between them.

We expect this protocol to achieve near-zero energy distance, low energy loss, but an increase on the number of interaction until the energy distribution is achieved.

5.4 Fully Adaptive Protocol

The Fully Adaptive protocol aims to improve on the ideas of the Degree Aware protocol which assumes slightly stronger agents with the ability to store more information on their memory. In addition to storing the estimation of the network size, each agent also stores the energy level (at the time of their interaction) of the last central agent (e_c) it has interacted with. This protocol works in the same way as the Degree Aware protocol. The main difference lies in the way the agents exchange energy. There are two different types of energy exchanges.

(a) When a central agent (u) interacts with either a peripheral or a d-level halted agent (v), the energy to be exchanged between them is calculated with this formula $e_{sent} = (1/k) \times (E_u(R_u - 1) - E_v)/(R_u + 1)$. When this value is negative (resp. positive), it means that u has less (resp. more) energy than it is required in order to achieve the desired energy distribution and thus it receives (resp. transmits) that (absolute) amount of energy from (resp. to) v.

(b) When two peripheral agents (u, v) interact, before they exchange energy, they attempt to find the optimal energy level a peripheral agent should have according to the desired energy distribution. This is done by using the stored value for the energy of the last central agent they have interacted with and is defined as $e_p^{u/v} = E_c/(R_{u/v} - 1)$. Both agents calculate this value and they exchange energy if and only if they are on opposite sides of both these calculated values (i.e. $E_u > e_p^u$ & $E_v < e_p^u$ & $E_u > e_p^v$ & $E_v < e_p^v$). If all these conditions are true, then the agent with the highest energy level (e.g. agent u) transmits energy according to the following formula: $e_{sent} = (1/k) \times (E_v - E_u)/2$. As in the previous protocol, k is used to limit the energy exchanged between the agents and thus the energy loss, when the estimation is not equal to the actual network size.

This protocol aims to improve the outcomes of the Degree Aware protocol, especially in the energy loss metric because of the way that the energy is exchanged between agents.

6. EVALUATION

We conducted simulations in order to evaluate the performance of the proposed protocols. The simulation environment is Matlab R2016a. In order to abstract the real network of diverse portable devices, we apply a non-uniform initial energy distribution among the agents. The numbers of agents vary, from 20 to 100. The total initial energy is analogous to the number of agents. More specifically, the total energy is set to $6 \cdot 10^4 \times [1:5]$ for $[20:20:100]$ agents respectively. Our protocols are designed to run constantly, but for the purposes of this paper, we plot their performance until the desired energy distance is achieved. The wireless energy loss factor β is different at each interaction and follows the Normal Distribution. More specifically, $\beta \sim N(0.2, 0.05)$. For statistical smoothness we conducted each simulation 100 times. The statistical analysis of the findings (the median, the lower and upper quartiles, outliers of the samples) demonstrate very high concentration around the mean and so, in the following simulation results we depict only the average values.

In this section we provide our simulation results on various metrics. At first we find the best value of the parameters d and k for various metrics and various number of agents. In order to select the best values for d and k for each protocol, we design *a metric that takes into account both the energy loss and the speed of each protocol trying to optimize their trade-off*. This metric is defined as follows:

$$y = t \times energy\_loss(t) \times energy\_distance(t) \qquad (4)$$

where t is the time when the protocol with the worst performance reaches its best energy distance and the factors $energy\_distance(t)$ and $energy\_loss(t)$ are the energy distance and total energy loss of each protocol at time t respectively. The values of d and k which give the minimum value for y are selected.

These selected values are used to investigate the protocols' performance on the following metrics: (a) structural distance, (b) energy distance, (c) energy loss and (d) speed. The metrics (a) and (b) are already described in section 4. Metric (c) refers to the amount of energy lost due to energy

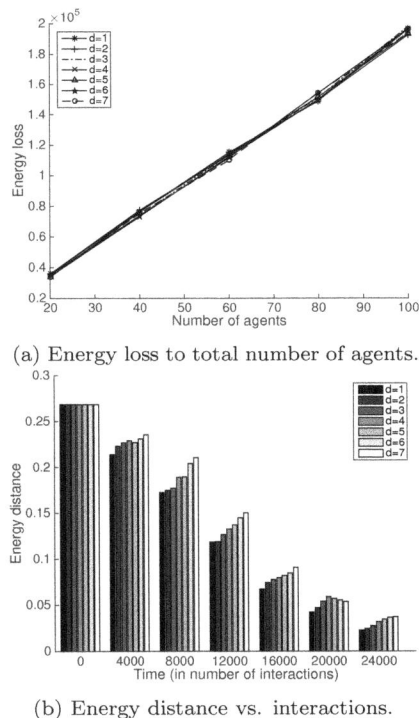

(a) Energy loss to total number of agents.

(b) Energy distance vs. interactions.

Figure 2: Evaluation of the parameter d for the DA protocol.

exchanges and metric (d) represents how fast, i.e. the number of interactions, the protocols achieve the desired energy distance.

6.1 Fine tuning of parameter d

In this section, we conduct simulations in order to evaluate the performance of the Degree Aware and the Fully Adaptive protocols for different values of the parameter d which indicates the number of halted states an agent will have to pass through, before its state becomes peripheral. We select various number of agents $[20:20:100]$ and we set the value of k, which is used to withhold the amount of transmitted energy, to $k = 1$ in order to evaluate the effect of d independently of k.

Degree Aware protocol. Fig. 2 presents the effect of d on the Degree Aware protocol. More specifically, Fig. 2a depicts the impact of d on the total energy loss when the protocol achieved an energy distance equal to 0.2. Interestingly, the energy loss is not affected by the value of d. This means that even a value of $d = 1$ is sufficient for the Degree Aware protocol to reach its optimal energy loss.

In order to further evaluate the effect of d, we also need to take into account its effect on the speed of the protocol (i.e. how many interactions are required to achieve the desired energy distribution). In Fig 2b, as expected, we observe that the lower the value of d the faster the Degree Aware protocol achieves the energy distribution. This is natural since the agent does not have to pass through many halted states in order to begin transmitting its energy to prospective central agents.

Fully Adaptive protocol. Fig. 3 presents the effect of d on the Fully Adaptive protocol. More specifically, Fig. 3a depicts the impact of d on the total energy loss. We observe that for lower values of d the total energy loss is higher. This

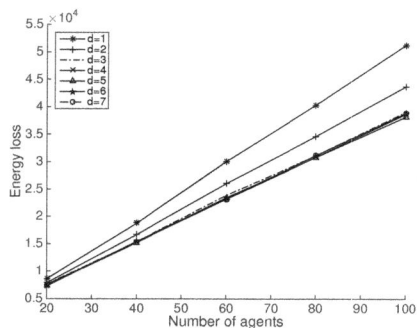

(a) Energy loss to total number of agents.

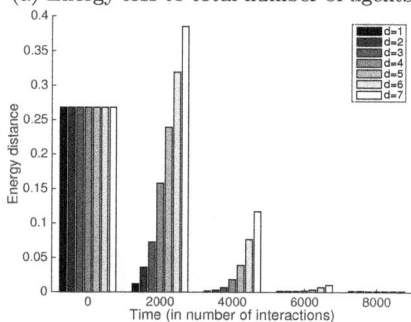

(b) Energy distance vs. interactions.

Figure 3: Evaluation of the parameter d for the FA protocol.

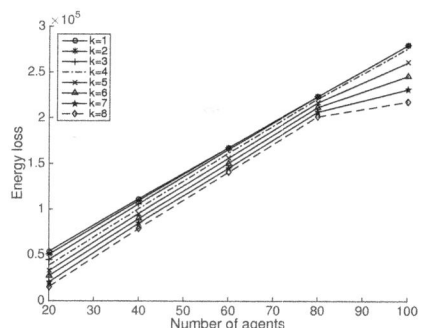

(a) Energy loss to total number of agents.

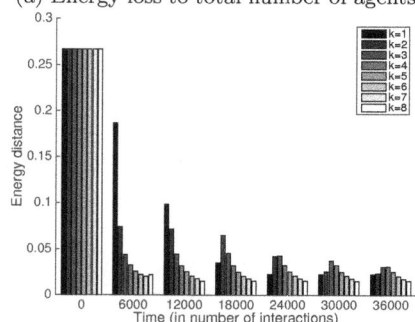

(b) Energy distance vs. interactions.

Figure 4: Evaluation of the parameter k for the DA protocol.

is explained by the fact that an agent, when in a halted state, will not make any energy exchanges. The more halted states the agent has to pass through, the higher the confidence will be about the estimated size of the network, thus making any energy exchanges more precise. We also observe that for larger network size, the total energy loss is higher. This is expected because the number of energy exchanges is much larger. Another observation that can be made by Fig. 3a is that for values of $d \geq 3$ the effect on the energy loss is diminished.

We further investigate the effect of d on the speed of the protocol. As in the Degree Aware protocol, in Fig 3b, we observe that the lower the value of d, the faster the adaptive protocol achieves the targeted energy distribution. In fact, we see that for $d \geq 6$ the adaptive protocol, in the first interactions, increases the energy distance significantly. This can be explained by the fact that the structural distance is being decreased, but the necessary energy exchanges are not being performed. We will refer to the period, in the lifetime of a protocol, during which there are many fluctuations in the energy distance metric as *metastability period*.

After the execution of the protocols, we calculate the value d from the equation 4. The values for both the Degree Aware and the Fully Adaptive protocol are d(Degree Aware) = d(Fully Adaptive) = 1.

6.2 Fine tuning of parameter k

In this section, we conduct simulations in order to evaluate the performance of the Degree Aware and the Fully Adaptive protocols for different values of the parameter k which is used to withhold the amount of transmitted energy. More specifically, if in any given interaction, an agent is supposed to transmit amount of energy e_x, with the addition of k it will transmit $\frac{e_x}{k}$. In order to evaluate the effect of k solely, we set the value of the parameter $d = 1$. As in the previous

section, we conduct simulations with a various number of network sizes, comprised of [20:20:100] agents respectively.

Degree Aware protocol. Fig. 4a presents the effect of k on the energy loss factor. We observe that with higher values of k the Degree Aware protocol, achieves lower energy loss. This is expected, because during the first few energy exchanges we are in the metastability period. The performed energy exchanges during this period are not optimal.

Fig. 4b depicts the effect of k on the speed of the Degree Aware protocol. The results clearly show that k's effect is minuscule and can be dismissed.

Fully Adaptive protocol. In Fig. 5a, similarly to the Degree Aware and Half Transfer protocols, it is observed that higher values of k lead to lower energy loss. It is worth noting that for values of $k \geq 4$, the performance of the protocol is similar with respect to this metric.

In Fig. 5b we can clearly see that for lower values of k the Fully Adaptive protocol reaches energy distance close to the desired energy distribution much faster.

Similarly to the parameter d, by using equation 4 we find the optimal value of k for each protocol. More specifically, we select k(Degree Aware) = 7 and k(Fully Adaptive) = 1.

In the following sections we present the performance of the four protocols described in the previous sections, after the fine tunning of the various parameters. We conducted simulations with different network sizes, i.e., with 20, 60 and 100 agents respectively. We observed that each protocol has similar performance for each network size. Thus we select to present the results for a network with 100 agents.

6.3 Performance on time to converge

In this section we compare the protocols performance on the number of interactions they need to build a global star network structure, as well as to achieve a low energy distance. In Fig. 6a, we can clearly see that during the metasta-

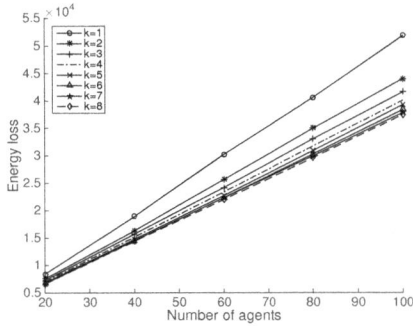

(a) Energy loss to total number of agents.

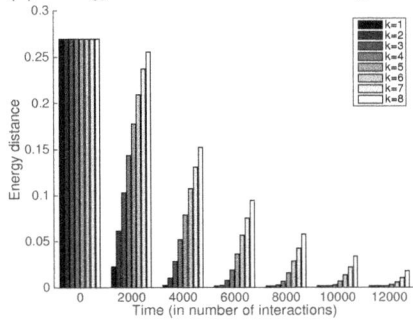

(b) Energy distance vs. interactions.

Figure 5: Evaluation of the parameter k for the FA protocol.

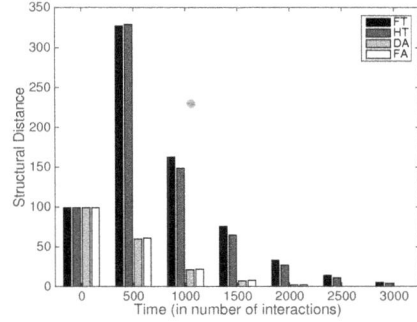

(a) Structural Distance vs. interactions.

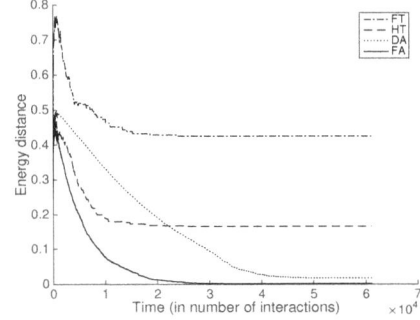

(b) Energy distance vs. interactions.

Figure 6: Speed comparison of the different protocols.

bility period the Full Transfer and Half Transfer protocols increase the structural distance. This is explained by the fact that the agents do not have any knowledge on the network size. Whenever a central agent interacts with a peripheral agent, a connection will be established, resulting in a large number of unnecessary connections between agents. When the metastability period ends, these protocols will eventually build a star network as well. The Degree Aware and Fully Adaptive protocols have similar performance in this metric as they build the structure relatively quickly, compared to the other two protocols. The performance gap between the two types of protocols can be explained by the power of two choices [18] that the halted states provide.

Fig. 6b depicts the performance of the protocols on the number of interactions needed in order to achieve a relatively low energy distance. We clearly observe that the Fully Adaptive protocol, outperforms all other protocols. It reaches almost zero energy distance in relatively few interactions. The Degree Aware protocol also reaches the desired energy distribution but does so with almost double number of interactions than the Fully Adaptive. The Full Transfer and Half Transfer protocols do not achieve a good energy distribution. They achieve their best energy distance with relatively few interactions but that energy distance is far from the desired distribution.

6.4 Overall performance

In this section we perform simulations in order to compare the performance of the protocols w.r.t. the energy spent in order to achieve the target energy distribution and their performance on how close they come to that distribution.

Fig. 7a depicts the total energy lost during the energy exchanges by each protocol with respect to the total initial amount of available energy in the network. As expected

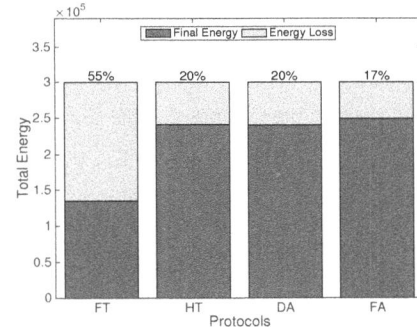

(a) Energy loss to total energy.

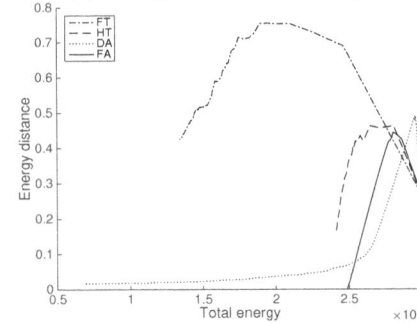

(b) Energy distance to total energy.

Figure 7: Energy comparison of the different protocols.

the Adaptive protocol achieves the lowest energy loss since the energy exchanges made are more precise and focused. In order to make the comparison fair, the amount of lost energy depicted for the Degree Aware protocol is the value when the protocol reaches sufficiently low energy distance (0.05). The

Half Transfer protocol also has a similar performance in this metric. In contrast, the Full Transfer protocol has the worst performance, spending more than half of the initial energy. This is expected due to the completely random nature of the protocol.

In Fig. 7b we observe that during the metastability period, the Degree Aware protocol is actually better than the Fully Adaptive. This can be explained by the value of $k = 7$ that was selected. After this period, the Fully Adaptive clearly outperforms all protocols on both the energy distance metric as well as the energy loss. The Degree Aware protocol approaches the desired energy distribution but in doing so, it spends all the available energy in the network. The Half Transfer protocol manages to reduce the energy distance but it fails in approaching the Degree Aware protocols. As expected, the Full Transfer protocol performs badly in this metric as well.

The lossless case. Finally, we conduct simulations in order to evaluate the performance of the protocols in the lossless case ($\beta = 0$). The only metric that is affected by the loss factor is the energy distance. The Fully Adaptive protocol, as expected, outperforms the other protocols. In [10], the full analysis for the lossless case is provided.

7. CONCLUSION AND FUTURE WORK

In this paper, we presented a more realistic generalization of the model proposed in [15] for wireless power transfer in population of agents, where the energy exchanges between agents are subject to variable energy loss factor β. Under this model, we introduce energy aspects in distributed network formation, particularly for creating a star structure. We designed four protocols that construct a star network structure with a desirable energy distribution motivated by applications (e.g. clustering). These protocols assume different amount of knowledge of the network. We evaluated the performance of these protocols via simulations, and identified their trade-offs, w.r.t. energy efficiency and time.

For future research, we plan to investigate the formation of different network structures (e.g. line, ring, etc.). Moreover, it would be interesting to study an extension of our model, that allows more than two agents to interact at any time.

8. ACKNOWLEDGMENTS

This research was partially supported by the EU/FIRE IoT Lab project - STREP ICT-610477.

9. REFERENCES

[1] D. Aldous and J. A. Fill. Reversible markov chains and random walks on graphs, 2002.

[2] C. M. Angelopoulos, J. Buwaya, O. Evangelatos, and J. D. P. Rolim. Traversal strategies for wireless power transfer in mobile ad-hoc networks. In *MSWiM*, 2015.

[3] D. Angluin, J. Aspnes, and D. Eisenstat. Fast computation by population protocols with a leader. *Distributed Computing*, 2008.

[4] J. Aspnes and E. Ruppert. *An Introduction to Population Protocols*. Springer Berlin Heidelberg, 2009.

[5] H. Dai, X. Wu, G. Chen, L. Xu, and S. Lin. Minimizing the number of mobile chargers for large-scale wireless rechargeable sensor networks. *Computer Communications*, 2014.

[6] M. del Prete, A. Costanzo, A. Georgiadis, A. Collado, D. Masotti, and Z. Popović. Energy-autonomous bi-directional wireless power transmission (wpt) and energy harvesting circuit. In *IEEE MTT-S International Microwave Symposium*, 2015.

[7] D. A. Levin, Y. Peres, and E. L. Wilmer. *Markov chains and mixing times*. 2006.

[8] Z. Li, Y. Peng, W. Zhang, and D. Qiao. J-roc: A joint routing and charging scheme to prolong sensor network lifetime. In *ICNP*, 2011.

[9] J. Luo and Y. He. Geoquorum: Load balancing and energy efficient data access in wireless sensor networks. In *INFOCOM*, 2011.

[10] A. Madhja, S. Nikoletseas, C. Raptopoulos, and D. Tsolovos. Energy aware network formation in peer-to-peer wireless power transfer, full paper. http://students.ceid.upatras.gr/~madia/fullpaper.pdf.

[11] A. Madhja, S. E. Nikoletseas, and T. P. Raptis. Distributed wireless power transfer in sensor networks with multiple mobile chargers. *Computer Networks*, 2015.

[12] A. Madhja, S. E. Nikoletseas, and T. P. Raptis. Hierarchical, collaborative wireless energy transfer in sensor networks with multiple mobile chargers. *Computer Networks*, 2016.

[13] G. Mertzios, S. Nikoletseas, C. Raptopoulos, and P. Spirakis. Stably computing order statistics with arithmetic population protocols. To appear in MFCS 2016.

[14] O. Michail and P. G. Spirakis. Simple and efficient local codes for distributed stable network construction. In *PODC*, 2014.

[15] S. Nikoletseas, T. Raptis, and C. Raptopoulos. Interactive wireless charging for energy balance. In *ICDCS*, 2016.

[16] S. Nikoletseas, T. P. Raptis, A. SThis, and D. Tsolovos. An experimental evaluation of wireless power transfer protocols in mobile ad hoc networks. In *WPTC*, 2015.

[17] M. D. Prete, F. Berra, A. Costanzo, and D. Masotti. Exploitation of a dual-band cell phone antenna for near-field wpt. In *WPTC*, 2015.

[18] A. W. Richa, M. Mitzenmacher, and R. Sitaraman. The power of two random choices: A survey of techniques and results. *Combinatorial Optimization*, 2001.

[19] J. D. P. Rolim. *Energy Balance Mechanisms and Lifetime Optimization of Wireless Networks*. Springer Berlin Heidelberg, 2011.

[20] S. Schafer, M. Coffey, and Z. Popović. X-band wireless power transfer with two-stage high-efficiency gan pa/ rectifier. In *WPTC*, 2015.

[21] C. Wang, J. Li, F. Ye, and Y. Yang. Multi-vehicle coordination for wireless energy replenishment in sensor networks. In *IPDPS*, 2013.

[22] S. Zhang, J. Wu, and S. Lu. Collaborative mobile charging for sensor networks. In *MASS*, 2012.

[23] M. Zhao, J. Li, and Y. Yang. A framework of joint mobile energy replenishment and data gathering in wireless rechargeable sensor networks. *IEEE Transactions on Mobile Computing*, 2014.

Passive Classification of Wi-Fi Enabled Devices

Alessandro E. C. Redondi, Davide Sanvito, Matteo Cesana
Dipartimento di Elettronica, Bioingegneria e Informazione (DEIB)
Politecnico di Milano
Piazza Leonardo da Vinci, 32
Milano, Italy
name.surname@polimi.it

ABSTRACT

We propose a method for classifying Wi-Fi enabled mobile handheld devices (smartphones) and non-handheld devices (laptops) in a completely passive way, that is resorting neither to traffic probes on network edge devices nor to deep packet inspection techniques to read application layer information. Instead, classification is performed starting from *probe requests* Wi-Fi frames, which can be sniffed with inexpensive commercial hardware. We extract distinctive features from probe request frames (how many probe requests are transmitted by each device, how frequently, etc.) and take a machine learning approach, training four different classifiers to recognize the two types of devices. We compare the performance of the different classifiers and identify a solution based on a Random Decision Forest that correctly classify devices 95% of the times. The classification method is then used as a pre-processing stage to analyze network traffic traces from the wireless network of a university building, with interesting considerations on the way different types of devices uses the network (amount of data exchanged, duration of connections, etc.). The proposed methodology finds application in many scenarios related to Wi-Fi network management/optimization and Wi-Fi based services.

Keywords

Device classification; probe requests analysis; traffic analysis

1. INTRODUCTION

Network traffic from wireless devices will exceed traffic from wired devices by 2019, accounting for 66% of the total IP traffic [1]. That is almost double with respect to 2013, when non-PC devices generated 33 percent of the total IP traffic.

For this reason, in the last few years there has been a constantly increasing attention towards the analysis and the profiling of traffic generated by WiFi-enabled devices, with particular focus on the so called Bring Your Own Devices

MSWiM '16, November 13-17, 2016, Malta, Malta
© 2016 ACM. ISBN 978-1-4503-4502-6/16/11...$15.00
DOI: http://dx.doi.org/10.1145/2988287.2989161

(BYOD), that is smartphones, laptops and tablets more and more frequently brought by people on their workplaces or study places. Such a class of devices is substantially different compared to traditional wired PCs for what concerns the users behavior and the traffic pattern they produce. Indeed, BYODs join and leave the network frequently and their shape and size makes it possible to use them almost everywhere. In addition, the vast range of networked applications running on top of such devices (instant messaging, social networking, video streaming, online videogames, etc...) makes them a concern for a series of reasons, including network management and security [7].

At the same time, WiFi-enabled BYOD devices can be separated in two different classes: mobile handheld devices (MHD), composed of smartphones and tablets, and non handheld devices (NHD) or laptops. The two classes differ in a series of physical and technical features (size, weight, battery capacity, type of wireless connectivity, operating system, etc.) and are generally used for different purposes, with direct implication on the network traffic pattern they produce. In this context, the knowledge (or prediction) of what type of traffic (and devices) is actually using the network can be leveraged to optimize the network configuration and/or implement and support several services (e.g., management of wide WiFi networks, smart content caching approaches, etc.) [11, 8, 3, 15, 9, 10, 19, 18].

Clearly, any analysis on the traffic differences between MHD and NHD builds on the capability to classify traffic flows as belonging to MHD or NHD devices. The available work in the field can be broadly grouped in two classes: (i) approaches that exploit only the Medium Access Control (MAC) addresses contained in WiFi frames generated by the devices, (ii) approaches that resort to some type of *active* traffic/packet inspection tool available in the reference network (e.g., direct access to DHCP logs, inspection of the *User-Agent* field of HTTP headers, etc.). Both classes though have drawbacks. Namely, the approaches based on MAC addresses perform device classification just by looking at the vendor information contained in the Organizationally Unique Identifiers (OUIs) of the MAC address; however, since some of the most popular vendors (e.g. Apple, Samsung) produce both handheld and non-handheld devices, many devices are excluded from the classification due to the impossibility to assign them to a specific class only by looking at their vendor.

On the other hand, the approaches based on active traffic/packet inspection do have two major drawbacks: deploying traffic/packet inspection probes in the network might not be always possible, and, even when this is possible, the increase in encrypted traffic makes it hard to extract useful information out of such tools; it's a matter of fact that web giants (Google, Amazon, Facebook, etc.) protect the traffic through their servers with HTTPS: as an example, a recent transparency report from Google [2] stated that 77% of the requests to its servers used encrypted connections, with such percentage destined to increase dramatically in the next few years. Such trend imposes tight limits on the use of those methods based on the inspection of application layer information such as the *User-Agent* header field, which is encrypted in HTTPS and thus hard to analyze.

For these reasons, we propose here a less invasive but still effective way to perform device classification. Our proposal is entirely *passive*, in that it does resort neither to traffic probes on network edge devices nor to deep packet inspection techniques to read out application layer information. Instead, we claim that device classification can be performed by collecting (and parsing) only *probe requests* Wi-Fi management frames. Such frames are transmitted in-the-clear by any Wi-Fi enabled device to requests information from in-range access points, can be captured with almost any low-cost commercially available Wi-Fi interface and carry enough information to perform device classification accurately. Our proposed classification framework first labels each device with a set of *features* extracted from the probe request frames the device itself is generating; the reference set of features captures information on the temporal process of probe requests transmission (how frequently probe requests are transmitted) and the power levels used in the probe request transmission. Then, a supervised learning approach is used to train different classifiers able to predict the type of transmitting device just by looking at its corresponding *features*.

The rest of this paper is structured in the following way: Section 2 and Section 3 describe how we collected the data used to train the classifiers and which are the features extracted from the captured probe request frames. Section 4 describes the supervised classification approaches and reports on their performance evaluation. A selected classification method is then used to perform the analysis of Wi-Fi network traffic in a university campus: results of such an analysis are reported in Section 5. Section 6 summarizes recent works related to MHD / NHD traffic analysis, focusing in particular on the device classification methods used, as well as works related to probe request frames analysis. Finally, Section 7 concludes the paper.

2. DATA COLLECTION

Our dataset consists of network data traces lasting several hours and containing only sniffed probe request frames collected during particular university classes ("tutorials" or "hands-on" lectures) where students have their own laptops and smartphones with them. At the beginning of the lecture, students are asked to (i) turn on the Wi-Fi interfaces of their devices and (ii) compile an anonymous form and insert the MAC addresses of their smartphones and laptops to serve as ground truth for our classification methods. In addition to those entries whose MAC addresses are labeled by students as belonging to either the "laptop" or "mobile" class, we also add to the database all those probe request frames from device manufactured by a laptop-only or mobile-only producer. The manufacturer is identified from the first 3 octets of the

MAC address (the so-called Organizationally Unique Identifier - OUI). In detail, probe request frames from Intel and Liteon devices are automatically marked as coming from laptops, while probe requests from Huawei, Nokia, Sony Mobile, Xiaomi and onePlus are labeled as "mobile". The data is collected using a standard laptop running Linux and equipped with a Wi-Fi card set in *monitor* mode on 802.11 channel 1. We used *tshark* (the terminal version of WireShark) to capture only probe request frames, which are stored in a local MySQL database for further analysis. Each database entry thus contains the following fields: source MAC address, OUI, timestamp of probe request frame reception, probe request sequence number, received signal strength (RSS) and the Service Set Identifier (SSID) of the probe request. Note that the latter can be either "Broadcast" or a string containing the SSID of a Wi-Fi network known to the device. In total, our database consists of more than 2×10^5 different probe request entries, spanning 10 different hours over 5 days and belonging to 279 different devices of known type (groundtruth). For simplicity, let N_s be the number of entries in the database having s as source MAC address.

3. FEATURE EXTRACTION

For each MAC address contained in the database the following features are extracted:

- *Inter-Probe Period (IPP):* Many works related to probe requests analysis have highlighted that different devices transmit probe requests with different temporal frequencies. Moreover, mobile devices vary a lot their probing pattern depending on their status. As an example, the probing frequency is generally decreased when the screen is turned off, and each time a user presses a button or unblocks the phone a new probe request is transmitted. We attempt to capture those behaviours with two specific features. In particular, all timestamps t_i of the probe request frames belonging to a single MAC address are extracted and sorted in chronological increasing order in an array $\mathbf{T} = [t_1, t_2, \ldots, t_{N_s}]$. Let $p_i = t_{i+1} - t_i$ be the i-th inter-probe period. We define the average inter-probe period as:

$$\mu_{p,s} = \frac{1}{N_s - 1} \sum_{i=1}^{N_s - 1} p_i. \tag{1}$$

Similarly, we define the standard deviation of the inter-probe period as:

$$\sigma_{p,s} = \sqrt{\frac{1}{N_s - 1} \sum_{i=1}^{N_s - 1} (p_i - \mu_{p,s})^2}. \tag{2}$$

Figure 1(a) shows the Cumulative Distribution Function of the average inter-probe period for laptops and mobile devices. We can observe that laptop devices probe more frequently than smartphones: 50% of all laptops have an inter-probe period of less than 60 seconds, and 95% of them have an IPP of less than 1000 seconds. The IPP for the same percentages of smartphones are considerably higher, 120 seconds and 2300 seconds, respectively.

- *Received Signal Strength (RSS):* The received signal strength measures the power of a probe request as seen

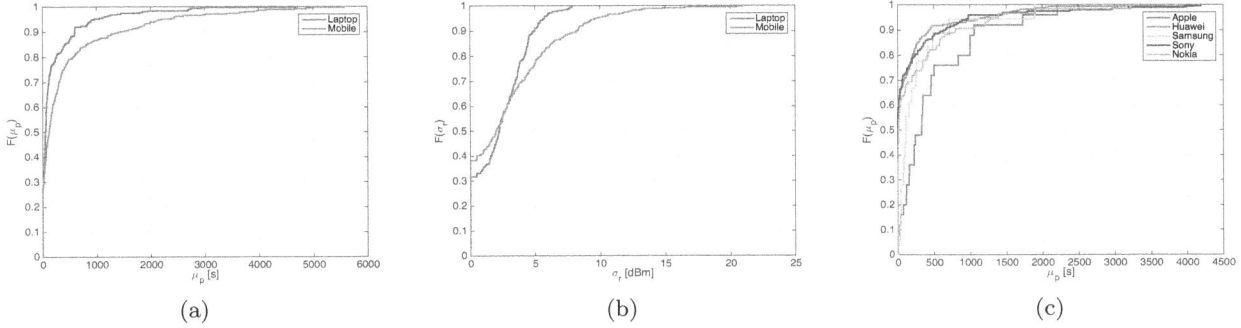

Figure 1: (a) CDF of the inter-probe period for laptops and mobile devices; (b) CDF of the standard deviation of the RSS for laptops and mobile devices; (c) CDF of the inter-probe period for mobile devices of different vendors (best viewed in color)

from the receiver (sniffer) and depends on the distance between the transmitter and the receiver as well as on other effects characterizing the radio environment (presence of obstacles, mutual antenna orientations, etc.). Similarly to the IPP, we capture the RSS using two features, namely:

$$\mu_{r,s} = \frac{1}{N_s - 1} \sum_{i=1}^{N_s - 1} r_i, \qquad (3)$$

and

$$\sigma_{r,s} = \sqrt{\frac{1}{N_s - 1} \sum_{i=1}^{N_s - 1} (r_i - \mu_{r,s})^2} \qquad (4)$$

that is, the average and standard deviation of the RSS of the captured probe request frames. The reason behind the use of such two features is the following: we posit that handheld devices exhibit a higher variance in the RSS compared to non-handheld devices. Indeed, smartphones and tablets are more frequently handled and moved than laptops, creating fluctuations in the RSS measurements captured by $\sigma_{r,s}$. Such difference is clearly illustrated in Figure 1(b): as one can see, 95% of the laptops in our dataset have standard deviation of the RSS lower than 5 dBm, while for mobile devices this value is almost double.

- *Coefficients of variation:* For both IPP and RSS features we also compute the coefficients of variation

$$c_{p,s} = \frac{\sigma_{p,s}}{\mu_{p,s}}, \qquad (5)$$

and

$$c_{r,s} = \frac{\sigma_{r,s}}{\mu_{r,s}}. \qquad (6)$$

Such coefficients are useful to provide a dimensionless feature and to compare the degree of variation of measurements from different devices regardless of their mean value.

- *Number of probe requests with broadcast/known SSID:* For each source MAC address s we store the number of probe request frames with a "Broadcast" destination SSID $N_{b,s}$ and the number of probe request frames

with a textual SSID (that is, the SSID of a Wi-Fi network to which the device associated at least once) $N_{k,s}$. Note that $N_s = N_{b,s} + N_{k,s}$. We also compute the proportion of broadcast and known probe request frames, that is $\frac{N_{b,s}}{N_s}$ and $\frac{N_{k,s}}{N_s}$. Finally, we also store the number of unique SSIDs contained in the probe request frames, that is $N_{u,s}$.

- *Device manufacturer:* Several works in the past have exploited the vendor information contained in the MAC address to infer the class of a device ([9, 10]). Given that some vendors produce only mobile or laptop devices, it is reasonable to include the vendor as a feature for classification. We observe that the set of OUIs contained in the database is limited to V different vendors. At the same time, we observe that devices from different vendors have very different probing behaviors. As an example, Figure 1(c) illustrates the CDF of the inter-probe period for 5 different vendors of mobile devices, with Huawei and Sony devices having the smallest inter-probe period while Apple devices have the largest one. To capture such differences, we create $V - 1$ dummy binary variables $d_{1,s}, d_{2,s}, \ldots, d_{V-1,s}$, such that:

$$d_{i,s} = \begin{cases} 1 & \text{if } s \text{ is from the } i\text{-th vendor} \\ 0 & \text{otherwise} \end{cases} \qquad (7)$$

Note that the V-*th* vendor is identified by having all $d_{i,s}$ equal to zero.

In summary, each device in the database is represented with the following feature feature vector:

$$\mathbf{f} = \left\{ \mu_p, \sigma_p, \mu_r, \sigma_r, c_p, c_r, N_b, N_k, \frac{N_b}{N}, \frac{N_k}{N}, d_1, \ldots, d_{V-1} \right\}, \qquad (8)$$

where we have suppressed the subscript s for simplicity. Finally, we label each entry in the dataset with its ground truth class "Laptop" or "Mobile". After the feature extraction step, our dataset consists of 279 labeled entries belonging to 150 laptops and 129 mobile devices.

4. CLASSIFICATION ALGORITHMS

We aim at solving the following problem: given a feature vector $\mathbf{f}$ belonging to a device of unknown type T (and computed through processing of sniffed probe request frames as explained in Section 3), predict wether the device is a laptop or a mobile device. We solve such a problem taking a supervised learning approach: we use different classifier algorithms that are trained with a set of labeled observations and are then evaluated on a set of completely new observations. In particular, we test the following classification algorithms:

- Naïve Bayes (NB): this simple algorithm assigns to the feature vector $\mathbf{f}$ a probability value $P(T|\mathbf{f})$, computed using the Bayes Theorem and assuming that features are independent, that is:

$$P(T|\mathbf{f}) = \frac{P(\mathbf{f}|T)P(T)}{P(\mathbf{f})} = P(T) \prod_i P(f_i|T), \quad (9)$$

where f_i denotes the i-th component of $\mathbf{f}$ and the denominator $P(\mathbf{f})$ can be ignored as it is the same for all classes. In the training phase, the Naïve Bayes classifier learns $P(f_i|T)$ by fitting probability distributions to each individual feature: for real valued features, normal (Gaussian) distributions are used, while for binary features (e.g. d_1 to d_{V-1}) binomial distributions are used to model the data. In the test phase, given a newly observed feature vector $\mathbf{f}$, the NB classifier returns the most probable class, that is the class T for which $P(T|\mathbf{f})$ is maximized.

- Support Vector Machine (SVM): SVM classifiers are very popular supervised algorithms that construct a hyperplane in the subspace of features so that observation belonging to different classes are separated by a margin as wide as possible. In addition, when the different classes are not linearly separable, SVMs allows to perform non-linear classification efficiently by first transforming the feature space with a non-linear kernel function, and then constructing a separating hyperplane in the transformed space.

- Decision tree (DT): a decision tree is a classification algorithm that returns the predicted class by iteratively making decisions on the value of the input features. Decisions are learned with a training process, starting with the most discriminative feature at the top (root) of tree and iteratively aggregating decisions in branches, finally arriving to the tree leaves (predicted classes). As a result, the learned tree can be more easily interpreted than a SVM classifier (e.g., it can be displayed graphically). As a drawback, decision trees generally do not have the same level of predictive accuracy as SVM, due to their tendency to overfit the training data.

- Random Forest (RF): this ensemble algorithm is generally used to prevent overfitting when using decision trees, and has been shown to perform very well in several machine learning tasks. A random forest classifier constructs several decision trees at training time, and outputs as a prediction the mode of the classes predicted by the individual trees (majority voting). The individual trees are obtained selecting each time a random training sample in order to decrease model variance (i.e. overfitting) and a random subset of the input features to produce weakly correlated trees.

Table 1: Classification accuracy using only dummy features

Algorithm	Accuracy
Naive Bayes	0.8029
Support Vector Machine	0.7957
Decision Tree	0.778
Random Forest	0.8129

The performance of such classifiers are obtained resorting to k-fold cross validation: first, the original set of 279 observations is divided in k complementary subsets; then, $k - 1$ subsets are used for training each classifier, while one is used for testing. The process is repeated k times, averaging the results. Here, we used $k = 5$. The performance metric used throughout the tests is the *classification accuracy*, that is the fraction of correctly classified observations over the total number of tests.

We test the performance of the different classifiers in three different scenarios:

- Quantitative features only (QF): we consider only the numerical features extracted from the database of probe requests, that is $\{\mu_p, \sigma_p, \mu_r, \sigma_r, c_p, c_r, N_b, N_k, \frac{N_b}{N}, \frac{N_k}{N}\}$, for training and testing the classifiers. This scenario reflects the case in which the OUI information of a device cannot be read. This can happen if the MAC addresses of the devices are encrypted through randomization, a solution that several vendors are gradually implementing in the operating systems of their devices (e.g., iOS8, Android 6.0).

- Dummy features only (DF): conversely, we consider only the dummy features obtained with the OUI information available from the MAC address to perform classification. This approach applies machine learning techniques to the same information available to other approaches available in the literature [9, 10].

- All features (AF): finally, in this scenario, we train and test the classifiers using both quantitative and qualitative features.

Table 1 shows the classification accuracy for the dummy features scenario. As one can see, the different classifiers have similar values of accuracy, around 80%. Note, however, that this value strongly depends on the distribution of device vendors in the dataset. As an example, if the majority of the devices in the dataset is from a vendor that produces both handheld and non handheld devices (e.g., Apple, Samsung), the accuracy of such method is expected to decrease dramatically due to the impossibility to link a vendor with a particular device class.

For the quantitative features and the all features scenarios, the tests are performed considering only those samples belonging to devices whose features are extracted starting from at least N_s probe request frames, each time increasing the value of N_s. Such value as a twofold effect on the performance of the classifiers: on one hand, increasing N_s allows to train the classifiers with more "stable" features, as those features involving mean and standard deviation operation are computed with an increasing set of samples. On the other hand, increasing N_s makes the number of samples available for training the classifiers decrease, as shown

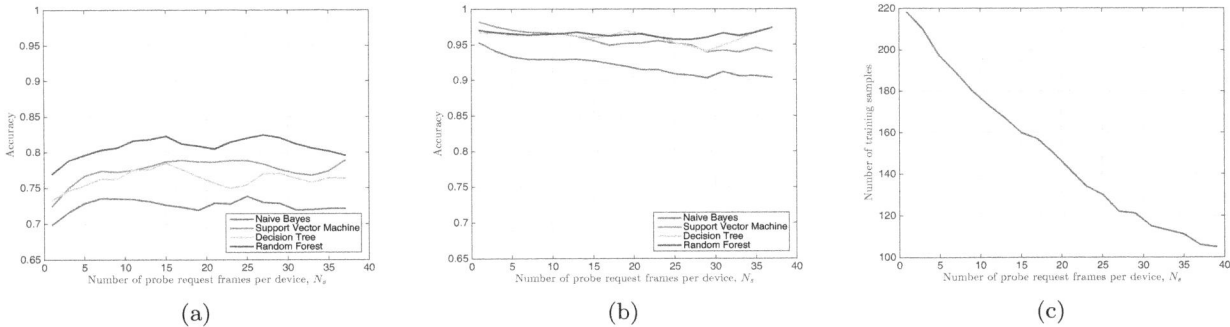

Figure 2: (a) Classification accuracy when using only quantitative features; (b) Classification accuracy when using both quantitative and dummy features. (c) Number of training samples at different values of N_s. (best viewed in color)

in Figure 2(c). Note also that N_s is related to the amount of time one should spend to capture probe request frames, which increases with N_s.

Figure 2(a) shows the classification accuracy of the different classifiers when using only quantitative features. As one can see, the accuracy of all classifier tends to increase for small values of N_s and decreases for high values of N_s. The first effect is due to the increasing stability in the computed features, while the latter effect is due to the decreasing number of training observations, as explained above. Overall, the Random Forest classifier exhibits the best performance, with a peak accuracy value of 83% for $N_s = 15$. The performance of the different classifiers in the scenario where both quantitative and qualitative features are used is illustrated in Figure 2(b). First, it is possible to appreciate the great performance increase given by using both kind of features. In this case, all methods but the Naive Bayes classifier exhibit similar performance, with the Random Forest classifier correctly classifying more than 95% of the test samples. In this case, the positive effect of increasing N_s seems shadowed by the use of dummy features. On the contrary, increasing N_s too much hurts the performance of all classifiers, due to the decrease in the number of training samples.

5. TRAFFIC ANALYSIS

This section shows the results of the analysis of network data traces extracted from the wireless network of a university campus building, performed after applying the proposed classification method to identify which traces belong to MHD or NHD. The wireless network under study is composed of 28 different wireless access points (AP) located on four different floors of the building. The access points run the AirWave Management Platform system, which allows to observe every device connected to the wireless network. For each access point, the uplink/downlink bandwidth usage and the number of connected clients are available with a sampling period of 5 minutes. Additionally, for each connected client, the following information are available: MAC address of the device, timestamp of the association with the AP, duration of the session (time elapsed from the association with the AP), average and variance of the bandwidth usage during the session [kbps] as well as average and variance of the signal quality during the session [dB]. We focus our analysis on a period of two weeks, from the 20th of May,

2016 to the 3rd of June, 2016. A single Raspberry PI 3 coupled with a Netgear WNA1100 Wi-Fi dongle in monitor mode is used to capture probe request frames. Such device is placed in an open space of the building that students use to study, work on their projects or simply pass time between two lectures. Such a place is therefore characterized with a good mix of MHD and NHD devices, whose emitted probe request frames are captured by the Raspberry PI. We analyze the frames with our classification algorithm (using the Random Forest classifier fed with both quantitative and qualitative features), labeling each observed MAC address as "Laptop" or "Mobile". Note that, differently from what proposed in Section 4, no groundtruth is available to assess the accuracy of our classification. We restrict the analysis of the data traces from the AirWave Management Platform only to those devices seen and classified by our method. Over the two weeks object of our analysis, a total of 2519 unique devices were observed, generating a total of 10287 different sessions. Figure 3 shows the distribution of different vendors in our dataset: note that Apple and Samsung, vendors who produce both laptops and smartphones, together sum up to almost 40% of the total devices seen. This confirms that approaches only based on the OUI for device classification may exclude a lot of data from the analysis. Table 2 reports the result of our classification on the available data. As one can see, over 75% percent of the observed devices and sessions are classified as non handheld devices. Considering that the university wireless network bandwidth is limited to 2 Mbps per user, the results in Table 2 can be due to a growing tendency of mobile users to use their cellular connections (e.g., LTE, 3G) instead of Wi-Fi in the university campus to experience better quality of service.

5.1 Session start time

First, we look at the distribution of starting time of sessions. We identify the minute of the day (from 1 to 1440)

Table 2: Classification results on the period of two weeks

Observed Devices	MHD	NHD
2519	658 (26.12%)	1861 (73.88%)
Observed Sessions	MHD	NHD
10287	2429 (23.61%)	7858 (76.39%)

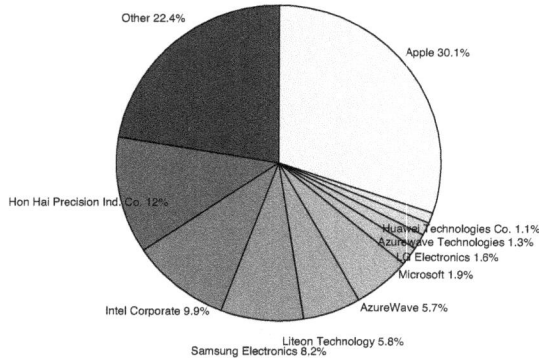

Figure 3: Distribution of the different device vendors (best viewed in color)

at which each connection starts and plot in Figure 4(a) its probability distribution for MHD and NHD device. Several observations can be made from the inspection of such distribution:

1. The global trend follows the human daily pattern, with very few sessions started during night. Two sharp peaks are visible in the morning and in the afternoon, divided by a valley corresponding to the lunch break at minute 800 (1.30 PM).

2. From minutes 1 to 180 and from 1200 to 1440, corresponding to the period 8 PM - 3 AM, the probability of a MHD starting a session is higher than that of a NHD. This can be explained taking into account that online activities at the end of a working day (chatting, email checking) are carried out more frequently with a MHD.

3. Conversely, during the day, there is no clear difference between MHD and NHD devices: in the morning (8:30 - 10:30 AM) we observe a higher probability for MHD device, while in the afternoon NHD sessions are more frequent.

5.2 Network usage

Then, we analyze how MHD and NHD devices use the network. Figure 4(b) shows the cumulative distribution function of the network usage (total volume of data exchanged with the AP divided by the duration of the session) in kbps for the two different class of devices, together with the CDF obtained considering all devices together. As one can see there is a dramatic difference between MHD and NHD usage: handheld devices have an average usage of about 50 kbps, while non-handheld devices have an average usage which is more than 4 times higher (203.9 kbps). Also, 95% of MHD have an usage below 200 kbps, while for NHD this value raises to 1 Mbps. This can be explained considering the different applications typically run on MHD (e.g., email, messaging services, quick browsing, etc...) compared to NHD (file download, heavy browsing, etc.). Indirectly, such a result confirms the goodness of our classification method in segmenting MHD and NHD devices.

5.3 Session duration

Finally, we also look at the distribution of the duration of the sessions in Figure 4(c). Differently from previous studies ([9, 10]), in which the duration of sessions of MHD was observed as notably lower than NHD, here we do not find such a great difference. The average session duration for MHD is 70.4 minutes, while for NHD is 86.5 minutes. Coupling this result with what explained previously in Sections 5.1 and 5.2, it seems that both MHD and NHD users tend to remain connected to the network for a long period of time and their behaviour differ just in the amount of data transferred over the network and partially in when they start connections with the network.

6. RELATED WORK

To the best of our knowledge, the first work analyzing differences in the traffic behavior of MHD and NHD devices is the one from Maier et al. [11], where network data from residential DSL lines spanning a period of 11 months is analyzed. To identify which DSL lines hosted MHD and hence to identify the corresponding traffic traces, the authors rely on the user-agent strings contained in HTTP headers, which are generally precise indicators of a device and its operating system. For non-HTTP traffic traces, the authors take advantage of the IP TTL field, which turns out to be different in MHD operating systems compared to the most commonly used PC OSs. As a result of such an analysis, the authors show that MHD traffic is dominated by multimedia content and downloads of mobile applications, and that MHD HTTP objects are larger on average than NHD ones.

In [8] network traffic traces from a campus wireless networks are analyzed by examining their content and flow properties (transport and application protocols used, flow length and durations, etc..). Handheld devices are filtered looking at HTTP user-agents as primary method, followed by a confirmation step using the Organizationally Unique Identifiers (OUIs) contained in the MAC addresses: 14% of the devices remain uncategorized and are excluded from the analysis. The key findings of such an analysis are that (i) the majority of handheld traffic is HTTP, (ii) the top content type for MHD is video and (iii) MHD tend to have smaller TCP flows and narrower range of flow durations, compared to NHD. A similar study with comparable results is performed by Zhu et al. in [19], where tcpdump traces from the Dalian university of technology are analyzed. Once again, device classification is performed by relying on the User-Agent field in HTTP headers.

Chen et al. in [3] analyze 3 days of WiFi network data collected by a monitor located at a gateway router fo the network. Again, MHD identification is performed by looking at keywords in the HTTP user-agent. The authors report a small increase in the percentage of HTTPS flows (4.3%), which are impossible to classify as belonging to MHD or NHD. The main findings are that MHD have longer local RTTs, and that the number of concurrent flows has negative effect on performance (and this effect is more significant on MHD than on NHD).

Papapanagiotou et al. in [15] study the web browsing behaviour of MHD and NHD devices on a 3 weeks long full-packet trace in a wireless enterprise environment. Classification is performed analyzing DHCP request header fields (Host-name, Vendor-name) and the OUIs, allowing to clas-

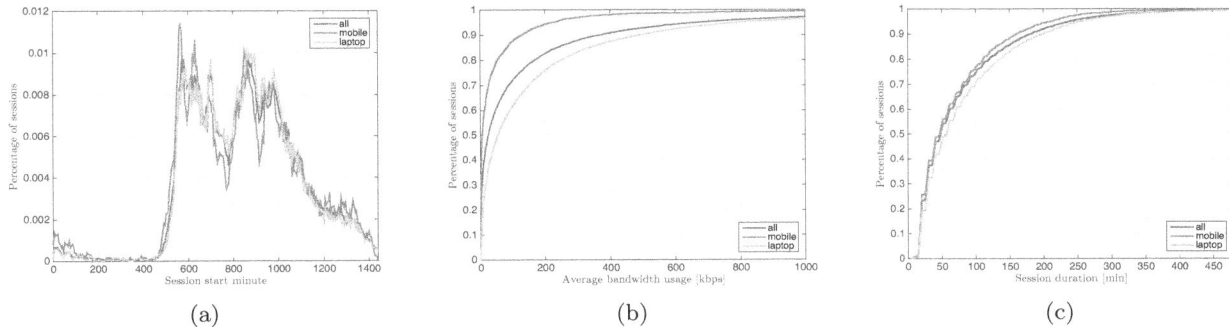

Figure 4: (a) Probability distribution of the starting minute of Wi-Fi sessions; (b) Cumulative distribution function of the average bandwidth usage for MHD and NHD devices; (c) Cumulative density function of the average session duration for MHD and NHD devices (best viewed in color)

sify 97% of the devices (although no ground truth is provided [14]). The main finding of the analysis is that (i) NHD devices have more intelligent browser caching capabilities and (ii) a 10 MB browser cache in smatphones would be enough to provide 10% - 20% bandwidth savings.

In [9] and [10] Kumar et al. analyze wireless association traces connected at hte University of Florida. Classification of MHD and NHD is done only via inspection of the OUI, since no other information is available. Since some manufacturers (e.g. Apple and Samsung) produce both MHD and NHD, the authors conduct a user survey where users of smartphones were asked to give the first 3 octets of their MAC address (i.e., the OUI). The authors performed then classification assuming that a manufacturer does not use the same MAC address range for both smart-phones and laptops. The analysis include several spatio-temporal features (average session duration, number of session per days, mobility etc.), and shows dramatic differences between MHD and NHD behaviors.

Finally, Wei et al. in [18] propose Brofiler, an approach for studying how MHD behaves along different dimensions (protocol and control plane, data plane, temporal behavior). MHD and NHD are classified with the method proposed in [14] (i.e., looking at DHCP logs). Interestingly, the authors find that 24% of MHD have 50% of their traffic encrypted. This confirms the increasing trend in the use of HTTPS, with serious implication for those classification methods that use the HTTP User-Agent field.

In the last few years, many works have focused on the analysis of Wi-Fi probe request frames sniffed with off-the-shelf hardware. Such data traces have been used for several purposes, including estimating crowd densities and pedestrian flows [17, 6], user tracking and trajectory estimation [13, 16], privacy-related issues and device-to-identity linking [12, 5, 4].

7. CONCLUSIONS

We proposed a method for classifying handheld (smartphones) and non-handheld (laptops) Wi-Fi enabled devices in a passive way, relying only on probe request frames captured with low-cost, commercially available hardware. We compared different algorithms to perform such a classification and identified a solution which correctly classifies the devices more than 95% of the times. Finally, we have used

the proposed method to classify devices and performed an analysis of the network traffic traces in a university building, identifying interesting differences in the behavior of handheld and non-handheld devices. We believe that the proposed classification method can be used as a pre-processing stage in many scenarios related to Wi-Fi network management and optimization and Wi-Fi based services. To cite an example, we plan to apply the proposed methodology to improve the performance of localization systems based on radio-map fingerprinting by constructing different radio maps for MHD or NHD devices.

8. REFERENCES

[1] Cisco visual networking index: Forecast and methodology, 2014-2019 white paper. May 2015.

[2] Google transparency report: Https at google. Jan 2016.

[3] X. Chen, R. Jin, K. Suh, B. Wang, and W. Wei. Network performance of smart mobile handhelds in a university campus wifi network. In *Proceedings of the 2012 ACM conference on Internet measurement conference*, pages 315–328. ACM, 2012.

[4] M. Cunche. I know your mac address: Targeted tracking of individual using wi-fi. *Journal of Computer Virology and Hacking Techniques*, 10(4):219–227, 2014.

[5] S. Du, J. Hua, Y. Gao, and S. Zhong. Ev-linker: Mapping eavesdropped wi-fi packets to individuals via electronic and visual signal matching. *Journal of Computer and System Sciences*, 82(1):156–172, 2016.

[6] Y. Fukuzaki, M. Mochizuki, K. Murao, and N. Nishio. Statistical analysis of actual number of pedestrians for wi-fi packet-based pedestrian flow sensing. In *Proceedings of the 2015 ACM International Joint Conference on Pervasive and Ubiquitous Computing and Proceedings of the 2015 ACM International Symposium on Wearable Computers*, pages 1519–1526. ACM, 2015.

[7] B. M. Gaff. Byod? omg! *Computer*, 48(2):10–11, 2015.

[8] A. Gember, A. Anand, and A. Akella. A comparative study of handheld and non-handheld traffic in campus wi-fi networks. In *Passive and Active Measurement*, pages 173–183. Springer, 2011.

[9] U. Kumar, J. Kim, and A. Helmy. Changing patterns of mobile network (wlan) usage: smart-phones vs.

laptops. In *Wireless Communications and Mobile Computing Conference (IWCMC), 2013 9th International*, pages 1584–1589. IEEE, 2013.

[10] U. Kumar, J. Kim, and A. Helmy. Comparing wireless network usage: laptop vs smart-phones. In *Proceedings of the 19th annual international conference on Mobile computing & networking*, pages 243–246. ACM, 2013.

[11] G. Maier, F. Schneider, and A. Feldmann. A first look at mobile hand-held device traffic. In *Passive and Active Measurement*, pages 161–170. Springer, 2010.

[12] C. Matte, J. P. Achara, and M. Cunche. Device-to-identity linking attack using targeted wi-fi geolocation spoofing. In *Proceedings of the 8th ACM Conference on Security & Privacy in Wireless and Mobile Networks*, page 20. ACM, 2015.

[13] A. Musa and J. Eriksson. Tracking unmodified smartphones using wi-fi monitors. In *Proceedings of the 10th ACM conference on embedded network sensor systems*, pages 281–294. ACM, 2012.

[14] I. Papapanagiotou, E. M. Nahum, and V. Pappas. Configuring dhcp leases in the smartphone era. In *Proceedings of the 2012 ACM conference on Internet measurement conference*, pages 365–370. ACM, 2012.

[15] I. Papapanagiotou, E. M. Nahum, and V. Pappas. Smartphones vs. laptops: comparing web browsing behavior and the implications for caching. In *ACM SIGMETRICS Performance Evaluation Review*, volume 40, pages 423–424. ACM, 2012.

[16] P. Rouveyrol, P. Raveneau, and M. Cunche. Large scale wi-fi tracking using a botnet of wireless routers. In *Workshop on Surveillance & Technology*, 2015.

[17] L. Schauer, M. Werner, and P. Marcus. Estimating crowd densities and pedestrian flows using wi-fi and bluetooth. In *Proceedings of the 11th International Conference on Mobile and Ubiquitous Systems: Computing, Networking and Services*, pages 171–177. ICST (Institute for Computer Sciences, Social-Informatics and Telecommunications Engineering), 2014.

[18] X. Wei, N. C. Valler, H. V. Madhyastha, I. Neamtiu, and M. Faloutsos. A behavior-aware profiling of handheld devices. In *Computer Communications (INFOCOM), 2015 IEEE Conference on*, pages 846–854. IEEE, 2015.

[19] M. Zhu, Z. Zeng, L. Wang, Z. Qin, A. Pan, Y. Zhang, and L. Shu. A measurement study of a campus wi-fi network with mixed handheld and non-handheld traffic. In *Electrical and Computer Engineering (CCECE), 2015 IEEE 28th Canadian Conference on*, pages 848–853. IEEE, 2015.

Do LoRa Low-Power Wide-Area Networks Scale?

Martin Bor, Utz Roedig
Lancaster University, UK
m.bor@lancaster.ac.uk
u.roedig@lancaster.ac.uk

Thiemo Voigt
Uppsala University and SICS,
Sweden
thiemo@sics.se

Juan M. Alonso
Univ. Nac. de Cuyo and Univ.
Nac. de San Luis, Argentina
jmalonso@uncu.edu.ar

ABSTRACT

New Internet of Things (IoT) technologies such as Long Range (LoRa) are emerging which enable power efficient wireless communication over very long distances. Devices typically communicate directly to a sink node which removes the need of constructing and maintaining a complex multi-hop network. Given the fact that a wide area is covered and that all devices communicate directly to a few sink nodes a large number of nodes have to share the communication medium. LoRa provides for this reason a range of communication options (centre frequency, spreading factor, bandwidth, coding rates) from which a transmitter can choose. Many combination settings are orthogonal and provide simultaneous collision free communications. Nevertheless, there is a limit regarding the number of transmitters a LoRa system can support. In this paper we investigate the capacity limits of LoRa networks. Using experiments we develop models describing LoRa communication behaviour. We use these models to parameterise a LoRa simulation to study scalability. Our experiments show that a typical smart city deployment can support 120 nodes per 3.8 ha, which is not sufficient for future IoT deployments. LoRa networks can scale quite well, however, if they use dynamic communication parameter selection and/or multiple sinks.

Keywords

LoRa, Low-Power Wide-Area Network, Scalability Analysis

1. INTRODUCTION

Large scale Internet of Things (IoT) installations are becoming a reality and networks are being deployed to realise smart city, intelligent transportation system or environmental monitoring applications. Many of these IoT installations rely on Low-Power Wide-Area Network (LPWAN) technologies. New LPWAN technologies such as Long Range (LoRa) [5], Sigfox [13], RPMA [11] and Weightless [18] are emerging which enable power efficient wireless communication over very long distances. LPWANs generally form one-hop networks where every node can reach directly one (or more) Internet connected sink nodes. Network operators see this as beneficial as constructing and maintaining a multi-hop network can be avoided. However, given the fact that LPWANs cover a wide area and that all devices communicate directly to a few sink nodes a large number of nodes have to share the communication medium. The question arises how many nodes can be operated in the same area without dissatisfying application performance requirements.

In this paper we focus on LoRa as it is the currently most widely deployed emerging LPWAN technology and is considered by a large number of industries as a base for their IoT applications. To be scalable LoRa provides for a range of communication options (carrier frequency, spreading factor, bandwidth and coding rate) from which a transmitter can choose. Many settings are orthogonal and provide simultaneous collision free communications. Nevertheless, there is a limit regarding the number of transmitters a LoRa system can support. In this paper we investigate these capacity limits combining practical experimentation and simulation. The contributions are:

- *LoRa Link Behaviour:* Using practical experiments we develop models describing (i) communication range in dependence of communication settings Spreading Factor (SF) and Bandwidth (BW) and (ii) capture effect of LoRa transmissions depending on transmission timings and power.

- *LoRa Simulator:* We use the insight from our practical experimentation to build the simulator LoRaSim. This purpose built simulation tool captures specific LoRa link behaviour and enables evaluation of large-scale LoRa networks.

- *LoRa Scalability Evaluation:* Using LoRaSim we carry out an evaluation of the scalability of LoRa networks. We show that LoRa does not scale well when using it with static settings and a single sink as typically deployed in Long Range Wide Area Network (LoRaWAN). However, we show that the usage of multiple sinks and dynamic communication parameter settings can produce very scalable solutions.

The next section gives an overview of LoRa. Section 3 describes our experiments to understand LoRa link behaviour. Section 4 describes the simulator LoRaSim and our scalability evaluation of LoRa. Section 5 describes related work and Section 6 concludes the paper.

MSWiM '16 November 13–17, 2016, Malta, Malta

© 2016 Copyright held by the owner/author(s).

ACM ISBN 978-1-4503-4502-6/16/11.

DOI: http://dx.doi.org/10.1145/2988287.2989163

2. LORA

Long Range (LoRa) is a proprietary spread spectrum modulation technique by Semtech. It is a derivative of Chirp Spread Spectrum (CSS) with integrated Forward Error Correction (FEC). Transmissions use a wide band to counter interference and to handle frequency offsets caused by low cost crystals. A LoRa receiver can decode transmissions 19.5 dB below the noise floor, thus, enabling very long communication distances. LoRa key properties are: long range, high robustness, multipath resistance, Doppler resistance and low power. LoRa transceivers available today can operate between 137 MHz to 1020 MHz, and thus can also operate in licensed bands. However, they are often deployed in ISM bands (EU: 868 MHz and 433 MHz, USA: 915 MHz and 433 MHz). The LoRa physical layer may be used with any MAC layer; however, LoRaWAN is the currently proposed MAC which operates in a simple star topology.

2.1 Transmission Options

A typical LoRa radio provides five configuration parameters: Transmission Power (TP), Carrier Frequency (CF), Spreading Factor (SF), Bandwidth (BW) and Coding Rate (CR). Energy consumption, transmission range and resilience to noise is determined by the selection of these parameters.

Transmission Power (TP). TP on a LoRa radio can be adjusted from −4 dBm to 20 dBm, in 1 dB steps, but because of hardware implementation limits, the range is often limited to 2 dBm to 20 dBm. In addition, because of hardware limitations, power levels higher than 17 dBm can only be used on a 1% duty cycle.

Carrier Frequency (CF). CF is the centre frequency that can be programmed in steps of 61 Hz between 137 MHz to 1020 MHz. Depending on the particular LoRa chip, this range may be limited to 860 MHz to 1020 MHz.

Spreading Factor (SF). SF is the ratio between the symbol rate and chip rate. A higher spreading factor increases the Signal to Noise Ratio (SNR), and thus sensitivity and range, but also increases the airtime of the packet. The number of chips per symbol is calculated as 2^{SF}. For example, with an SF of 12 (SF12) 4096 chips/symbol are used. Each increase in SF halves the transmission rate and, hence, doubles transmission duration and ultimately energy consumption. Spreading factor can be selected from 6 to 12. As we have shown in previous work, radio communications with different SF are orthogonal to each other and network separation using different SF is possible [1].

Bandwidth (BW). BW is the width of frequencies in the transmission band. Higher BW gives a higher data rate (thus shorter time on air), but a lower sensitivity (because of integration of additional noise). A lower BW gives a higher sensitivity, but a lower data rate. Lower BW also requires more accurate crystals (less ppm). Data is send out at a chip rate equal to the bandwidth. So, a bandwidth of 125 kHz corresponds to a chip rate of 125 kcps. Although the bandwidth can be selected in a range of 7.8 kHz to 500 kHz, a typical LoRa network operates at either 500 kHz, 250 kHz or 125 kHz. Also, bandwidths lower than 62.5 kHz require a temperature compensated crystal oscillator (TCXO).

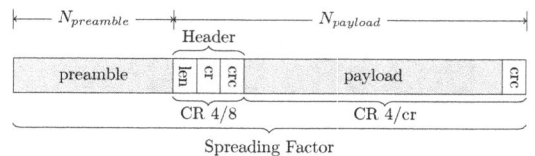

Figure 1: LoRa packet structure. Grey shaded areas are required, white shaded areas are optional.

Coding Rate (CR). CR is the FEC rate used by the LoRa modem that offers protection against bursts of interference, and can be set to either 4/5, 4/6, 4/7 or 4/8. A higher CR offers more protection, but increases time on air. Radios with different CR (and same CF, SF and BW), can still communicate with each other if they use an explicit header, as the CR of the payload is stored in the header of the packet.

2.2 Transmissions

LoRa Packet Structure. The LoRa packet structure is shown in Figure 1. A packet starts with the preamble, programmable from 6 to 65535 symbols, to which the radio adds 4.25 symbols. Thereafter follows an optional header, which describes the length and FEC rate of the payload, and indicates the presence of an optional 16-bit CRC for the payload. The header is always transmitted with a 4/8 FEC rate, and has its own CRC. After the optional header, there is the payload, which can contain 1 to 255 bytes. At the end of the payload an optional 16-bit CRC may be included.

Airtime. The airtime of a LoRa transmission depends, besides the payload size, on the combination of SF, BW, and CR. The duration of a transmission can be calculated with the Semtech LoRa modem calculator [6]. It has to be noted that depending on the selected communication settings a data packet can have significant variations in airtime. For example, a 20 byte packet can vary between 9 ms and 2.2 s. Thus, the selection of communication parameters has a tremendous impact on scalability of a LoRa deployment.

2.3 Regulatory Constraints

LoRa is classified as a Short Range Device (SRD) and usually operates in license-exempt frequency bands. There are certain restrictions on access to the physical medium, imposed by the regulatory body for the particular region. These limitations have an impact on communication performance and hence have an impact on scalability of LoRa deployments. Scalability is therefore often limited due to regulatory constraints and not due to technical limitations. Next we describe in more detail EU and US regulations; other countries such as China have their own regulations with often are modelled on EU or US standards.

Europe. The constraints in Europe regarding frequency allocation and use for SRD are defined in CEPT/ERC/REC 70–03 [3]. The license-exempt band usable for LoRa (863 MHz to 870 MHz) is referred to as 'Annex 1 h', and is subdivided in 7 (overlapping) subbands. Each subband has specific requirements regarding maximum Effective Radiated Power (ERP), spectrum access and channel spacing. For the majority of the subbands, the ERP is 25 mW (14 dBm). For spectrum access there is the option of either using a

Figure 2: NetBlocks XRange RF module.

duty cycle (often $\leq 0.1\%$) or a Listen Before Talk (LBT) transmission scheme, combined with an Adaptive Frequency Agility (AFA) depending on the specific subband and/or ERP required (see [2, chap. 9] for details).

United States. The Federal Communications Commission (FCC) regulates the use of frequencies for wireless communications in United States. Rules and regulations are stated in Title 47 of the Code of Federal Regulations (CFR). Part 15 (often referred to as 'FCC Rule 15') of this code deals with devices operating in unlicensed frequency bands. The license-exempt band usable for LoRa is 902 MHz to 928 MHz. Compared to the European regulations, the FCC allows a higher peak output power of 1 W (30 dBm), but requires a bandwidth of at least 500 kHz. For lower bandwidths, the device operates in 'hybrid mode', that combines the regulations for digital modulation techniques (like LoRa) with those for Frequency Hopping Spread Spectrum (FHSS). An important limitation for FHSS systems, is the maximum dwell time of 400 ms. This makes the lowest LoRa datarates not usable, as transmitting the preamble already takes longer than 400 ms.

3. LORA LINK BEHAVIOUR

In this section we develop a model of LoRa communication behaviour which we use subsequently in our simulation environment LoRaSim. Specifically, we develop a model describing (i) achievable communication range in dependence of communication settings SF and BW and (ii) capture effect behaviour of LoRa transmissions depending on transmission timings and power. The development process of these models is supported by practical evaluation.

3.1 Experimental Platform

For our experiments we use the XRange SX1272 LoRa module from NetBlocks[1] as shown in Figure 2. The module consists of a low-power STM32L151CC ARM Cortex-M3 microcontroller (32 MHz CPU, 32 kB RAM, 256 kB flash) and a Semtech SX1272 LoRa transceiver. Our models describing link behaviour are validated on this particular platform. However, the used communication chip is the most commonly employed LoRa chip and we believe the used models can be easily tailored to other transceiver types.

3.2 Communication Range

A transmission is successfully received if the received signal power P_{rx} lies above the sensitivity threshold S_{rx} of

[1]http://www.netblocks.eu/

the receiver. The received signal power P_{rx} depends on the transmit power P_{tx} and all gains and losses along the communication path:

$$P_{rx} = P_{tx} + G_{tx} - L_{tx} - L_{pl} - L_m + G_{rx} - L_{rx} \qquad (1)$$

P_{rx} is the received power in dB, P_{tx} is transmitted power in dB, G_{tx} is the transmitter antenna gain in dBi, L_{tx} is the transmitter loss (RF switch, non-matching circuit, connectors) in dB, L_{pl} is the path loss in dB, L_m are miscellaneous losses (fading margin, other losses) in dB, G_{rx} is the receiver antenna gain in dBi and L_{rx} are receiver losses. For the purpose of this study we simplify this general equation to:

$$P_{rx} = P_{tx} + GL - L_{pl} \qquad (2)$$

Here, GL combines all general gains and losses while L_{pl} represents the path loss, determined by the nature of the communication environment.

On the transmitter side, range can only be changed by changing the transmit power. Other parameters like SF, BW and CR do not influence the radiated power, or any other gains and losses. On the receiver side, the range is limited by the sensitivity threshold S_{rx}, which is influenced by the LoRa parameters SF and BW.

Path Loss. Many models exist to describe path loss in dependence of different environments (built-up area, free space). We use the well known log-distance path loss model [9] which is commonly used to model deployments in built-up and densely populated areas. We choose this model as it matches environments in which we expect LoRa deployments are to be found. Using this model the path loss in dependence of the communication distance d can be described as:

$$L_{pl}(d) = \overline{L_{pl}}(d_0) + 10\gamma \log\left(\frac{d}{d_0}\right) + X_\sigma \qquad (3)$$

where $L_{pl}(d)$ is the path loss in dB, $\overline{L_{pl}}(d_0)$ is the mean path loss at the reference distance d_0, γ is the path loss exponent and $X_\sigma \sim N(0, \sigma^2)$, the normal distribution with zero mean and σ^2 variance to account for shadowing.

The advertised communication range of LoRa is more than 15 km for suburban environments. Petajajarvi et al. [8] have reported a range of 15 km to 30 km in a city, where the receiver was located in a 24 m tall tower and the transmitter was on the roof of a car, and in a boat on open water. Our own experiments with the aforementioned hardware show a range of 2.6 km in rural areas. From our studies [1] in built-up environments we deduce a range of 100 m. This is significantly less than other reported ranges, probably caused by less than ideal indoor deployment, hardware and antennas, and as such represents a worst-case deployment. We also performed all the simulations using parameters reported by Petajajarvi et al. [8], and obtained similar results in terms of scalability.

Obviously, the communication range and, hence, the exact path loss model is highly dependant on the environment and a generic figure cannot be given. However, using our own empirical measurements with d_0 at 40 m, we determined that in the built up environment $\overline{L_{pl}}(d_0)$ is 127.41 dB, γ is 2.08 and σ is 3.57. We use these values in our simulation, but set $\sigma = 0$ since otherwise some transmissions might not be able to reach the sink rendering our results inconclusive.

Table 1: Measured receiver sensitivity in dBm for different bandwidths and spreading factors.

SF	Bandwidth (kHz)		
	125	250	500
7	−126.50	−124.25	−120.75
8	−127.25	−126.75	−124.00
9	−131.25	−128.25	−127.50
10	−132.75	−130.25	−128.75
11	−134.50	−132.75	−128.75
12	−133.25	−132.25	−132.25

Sensitivity. The sensitivity of a radio receiver at room temperature, as found in [12], is given by:

$$S = -174 + 10 \log_{10}(BW) + NF + SNR \qquad (4)$$

The first term describes thermal noise in 1 Hz of bandwidth and can only be influenced by changing the temperature of the receiver. BW is the receiver bandwidth. NF is the receiver noise figure, and fixed for a given hardware implementation. SNR is the signal-to-noise ratio required by the underlying modulation scheme, and is determined by the spreading factor SF. The higher the SF, the higher the SNR.

As BW is set in steps of powers of 2, we can derive from Equation 4 that increasing the bandwidth decreases the sensitivity by 3 dB and vice versa. Similar for SF, increasing the spreading factor doubles the chips per symbol, which increases the sensitivity by 3 dB.

To determine the receiver sensitivity for our experimental platform, we carry out an experiment using two nodes. Both nodes are placed in different rooms on different floors of an office building. The distance between the nodes is approximately 40 m. One node transmits a fixed number of packets, on all combinations of spreading factor (SF7 to SF12), bandwidth (125 kHz, 250 kHz, 500 kHz), coding rates (CR 4/5, CR 4/6, CR 4/7 and CR 4/8) and transmit powers (2 dBm to 17 dBm). We repeat the measurement over several days and of all the correctly received packets we record the minimal RSSI to determine the sensitivity. The results are shown in Table 1.

As expected, decreasing the bandwidth or increasing the spreading factor does improve sensitivity. The difference between each step, however, is not 3 dB, but more in the range of 0 dB to 4 dB, and 2 dB on average. Presumably this is caused by external interference, and hardware limitations other than the radio chip itself. We use these experimental determined values in our simulations.

Summary. Using Equation 2, Equation 3 and Equation 4 we can now estimate if a LoRa transmission will be received or not. The decision regarding transmission reception can be formally described as:

$$R = \begin{cases} 1, & P_{rx} > S_{rx} \\ 0, & else \end{cases} \qquad (5)$$

To determine P_{rx}, $\overline{L_{pl}}$, d_0, γ and σ must be set to parameterise the path loss model and the communication distance d must be known. In our simulations we set these parameters to the values previously described to reflect a built up environment. S_{rx} depends on the selected BW and SF. We use the measured sensitivity as shown in Table 1 in our simulations to determine sensitivity in dependence of BW and SF.

3.3 Collision Behaviour

When two LoRa transmissions overlap at the receiver, there are several conditions which determine whether the receiver can decode, one or two packets, or nothing at all. These conditions are Carrier Frequency (CF), Spreading Factor (SF), power and timing.

Reception Overlap. Packet reception starts at time a and ends at time b. We define reception interval (a_i, b_i) for packet $i \in \mathbb{N}$, that is reception i starts at a_i and ends at b_i. We define the midpoint $m_i = \frac{a_i + b_i}{2}$ and midpoint length $d_i = \frac{b_i - a_i}{2}$. Two packets, x and y, overlap when their reception intervals overlap, that is:

$$O(x, y) = |m_x - m_y| < d_x + d_y \qquad (6)$$

Carrier Frequency. When two transmissions overlap in time, but not in Carrier Frequency (CF), they do not interfere which each other and can both be decoded (assuming a receiver is listening at both carrier frequencies). The overlap in CF is defined as the absolute difference of these frequencies, and the tolerable frequency offset, which depends on the bandwidth. Therefore, we can define the condition when two transmissions collide on CF C_{freq} as:

$$C_{freq}(x, y) = \begin{cases} 1 & \text{if } |f_x - f_y| < f_{threshold} \\ 0 & \text{else} \end{cases} \qquad (7)$$

where f_x and f_y are the centre frequencies of transmission x and y, and $f_{threshold}$ is the minimum tolerable frequency offset. The minimum tolerable frequency offset for the Semtech SX1272 is 60 kHz for a bandwidth of 125 kHz, 120 kHz for a bandwidth of 250 kHz and 240 kHz for a bandwidth of 500 kHz.

Spreading Factor. The spreading factors (SF) used in LoRa are orthogonal. Transmissions with different SF (and same CF and BW) can thus be successfully decoded (assuming two available receive paths). Therefore, we define the condition on when two receptions collide on SF C_{sf} as:

$$C_{sf} = \begin{cases} 1 & \text{if } SF_x = SF_y \\ 0 & \text{else} \end{cases} \qquad (8)$$

where SF_x and SF_y are the SF of transmission x and y.

Power. As LoRa is a form of frequency modulation, it exhibits the *capture effect*. The capture effect occurs when two signals are present at the receiver and the weaker signal is suppressed by the stronger signal. The difference in received signal strength can therefore be relatively small. When the difference is too small, however, the receiver keeps switching between the two signals, effectively not able to decode either transmission. Therefore, we can define the condition on when packet x collides with packet y on received signal strength as:

$$C_{pwr}(x, y) = \begin{cases} 1 & \text{if } (P_x - P_y) > P_{threshold} \\ 0 & \text{else} \end{cases} \qquad (9)$$

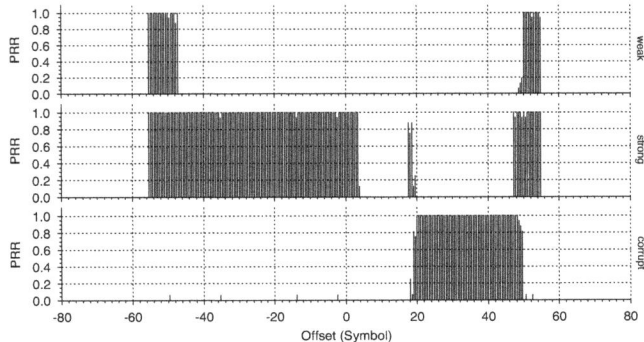

Figure 3: Capture effect. $SF = 12$, $BW = 250\,\text{kHz}$, 55.25 symbols packet length. X-axis shows the transmission offset relative to the weak node in symbols, Y-axis shows the packet reception rate.

where P_x is the received signal strength of transmission x and P_y is the received signal strength of transmission y and $P_{threshold}$ is the power threshold.

To verify the capture effect, we set up an experiment with one receiver and two transmitters (an extension of our previous experiments reported in [1]). One transmitter is set to transmit a 32-byte packet on a regular interval at a *weak* transmit power (2 dBm), while another transmitter was set to transmit a 32-byte packet at a *strong* transmit power (3 dBm). The strong transmitter sends a number of packets on a particular time offset relative to the weak transmitter, from one packet time early to one packet too late. The strong and weak transmitter are time synchronised by a packet send by the receiver that initiates the experiment. We repeat this experiment for all different combinations of SF, BW and offsets. The results of the experiment with SF12 and BW250 is shown in Figure 3. For all other combinations similar patterns are obtained.

From Figure 3 we can see that a strong transmission can be successfully decoded when it arrives one packet time early up to at most 3 symbols late, successfully suppressing the weak transmission. However, with an offset of more than +3 symbols up to the end of the packet, no transmission gets through. The receiver requires 5 symbols to detect the preamble and synchronise. The transmissions were sent with 8 preamble symbols. Therefore, after 3 symbols, the receiver has locked on to the weak transmission, but its signal is suppressed by the strong transmission and the packet is corrupted.

Timing. From the aforementioned experiments and Figure 3, we can also conclude that packets can overlap, as long there are at least 5 preamble symbols left intact (in case of a *weak* packet). In other words, the critical section of a packet reception starts at the last 5 preamble symbols, so we can redefine the interval for transmission x as $x_{cs} = (a_x + T_{sym} \cdot (N_{pp} - 5), b_x)$, where T_{sym} is the symbol time and N_{pp} is the number of programmed preamble symbols. Therefore, packet x collides with packet y when it overlaps in its critical section x_{cs}:

$$C_{cs}(x, y) = \begin{cases} 1 & \text{if } O(x_{cs}, y) \\ 0 & \text{else} \end{cases} \qquad (10)$$

Summary. When all conditions as defined in Equation 6, Equation 7, Equation 8, Equation 9 and Equation 10 are true, then packet x and y collide:

$$C(x, y) = O(x, y) \wedge C_{freq}(x, y) \wedge C_{sf}(x, y)$$
$$\wedge\, C_{pwr}(x, y) \wedge C_{cs}(x, y) \qquad (11)$$

We use this model of collision behaviour in our simulations.

4. LORA SCALABILITY

We use a simulator to examine and understand scalability of LoRa networks. It is not feasible to evaluate scalability of large-scale LoRa networks in practice as the deployment of such networks would be prohibitively expensive. Furthermore, a real deployment would not allow us to test a larger number of configurations and topologies as is needed for a general study on scalability. However, to ensure our results are of practical relevance we use the aforementioned practical experiments to calibrate our simulation.

4.1 Simulation Framework

For the purpose of this study we developed the simulation tool LoRaSim. The LoRaSim[2] is a custom-build discrete-event simulator implement with SimPy [14]. LoRaSim allows us to place N LoRa nodes in a 2-dimensional space (grid layout or random distribution). M LoRa sinks (the data collection points) can also be placed within the space.

Each LoRa node has a specific communication characteristic defined by the transmission parameters TP, CF, SF, BW and CR. For an experiment, each node's transmission behaviour is described by the average packet transmission rate λ and packet payload B. We assume a preamble length of 8 symbols, so packet airtime for a packet is given by B, SF, BW and CR. The behaviour of a node n during a simulation run is therefore described by the set $SN_n = \{TP, CF, SF, BW, CR, \lambda, B\}$.

Each LoRa sink is able to receive for a given CF multiple signals with different SF and BW combinations. This mimics the behaviour of LoRa sink chips such as the Semtech SX1301 which can receive 8 concurrent signals as long as these signals are orthogonal (i.e. as they are using different SF or BW settings). Two of such chips can be used in a sink node to ensure that concurrent signals on all orthogonal SF and BW settings can be received simultaneously.

The communication behaviour of LoRa nodes can be modelled using the equations for communication range (Equation 5) and collision behaviour (Equation 11). However, the simulator has the ability to replace both models with a simplified variant. The simple variant assumes infinite communication range and any two transmissions overlapping in time at the receiver with the same CF, SF and BW will collide and none of the two transmissions is received. The simple models allows us to establish a baseline which can be analytically described (See Experiment 1).

4.2 Evaluation Metrics

To evaluate scalability and performance of LoRa deployments we define two metrics: Data Extraction Rate (DER) and Network Energy Consumption (NEC).

DER: In an effective LoRa deployment all transmitted messages should be received by the backend system. This means that each transmitted message should be received

---

[2]Available at http://www.lancaster.ac.uk/scc/sites/lora/

Table 2: Parameter setting for Experiment Set 1.

Parameter	Set SN^1	SN^2	SN^3
TP (dBm)	14	14	14
CF (MHz)	868	868	868
SF	12	6	12
BW (kHz)	125	500	125
CR	4/8	4/5	4/5
λ (ms)	1×10^{-6}	1×10^{-6}	1×10^{-6}
B (byte)	20	20	20

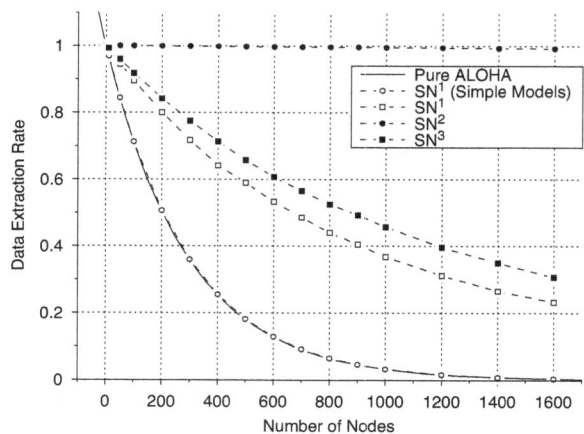

Figure 4: **Experiment Set 1 – Single Sink: Pure ALOHA and SN^1 (Simple Models) overlap. As the number of nodes increases, the DER decreases exponentially. With typical LoRaWAN settings (SN^3) and a typical $DER > 0.9$ requirement $N = 120$ nodes can be supported.**

correctly by at least one LoRa sink. We define the Data Extraction Rate DER as the ratio of received messages to transmitted messages over a period of time. The achievable DER depends on the position, number and behaviour of LoRa nodes and sinks which is defined by N, M and SN. DER is a value between 0 and 1; the closer the value is to 1 the more effective the LoRa deployment is. In a perfect deployment one would expect $DER = 1$. The metric does not capture individual node performance and is a metric looking at the network deployment as a whole.

NEC: The energy consumption of a LoRa node will depend in most scenarios mainly on the energy consumption of the transceiver. As nodes will be deployed in many scenarios on batteries it is essential to keep energy consumption for transmissions to a minimum. Transmit energy consumption for each message depends on transmit power TP and transmission duration which is influenced by SF, BW and CR. We define Network Energy Consumption NEC as the energy spent by the network to successfully extract a message. The NEC depends on the number of nodes, frequency of transmissions and transmitter communication parameters. The lower the metric, the more efficient is the deployment as lifetime of nodes is longer. The energy required to extract a message should be independent of the number of nodes deployed in the network. Again, the metric does not capture individual node behaviour and is a metric looking at the network deployment as a whole.

4.3 Experimental Evaluation

Experiment Set 1 – Single Sink. In our first set of experiments we evaluate the principle capability of LoRa using a simple setup where N nodes transmit to one sink ($M = 1$). We use in these experiments homogeneous transmitter configurations; for an experiment run all nodes use the same configuration set $SN = \{TP, CF, SF, BW, CR, \lambda, B\}$. Nodes are placed randomly around the sink such that all nodes can reach the sink with the given setting SN.

We compare the three transmitter configurations SN^1 and SN^2 and SN^3 (see Table 2). In all settings we assume a 20 byte packet is sent by each node every 16.7 min representing a realistic application. With SN^1 we choose the most robust LoRa transmitter settings leading to transmissions with the longest possible airtime of 1712.13 ms. With SN^2 we choose the transmission setting leading to the shortest airtime of 7.07 ms. With SN^3 we choose the setting use by common LoRaWAN deployments as, for example, one

trialled in Amsterdam[3]. We use SN^1 with simple channel models and our LoRa channel models to analyse the impact of these more realistic channel representations. For all subsequent experiments we use the LoRa channel representation.

Figure 4 shows the result of our first set of experiments. Each data point represents a simulation run of approximately 58 days. With an increasing number of nodes the Data Extraction Rate (DER) drops exponentially in all cases. The difference in DER is significant when comparing the configuration with longest (SN^1) and shortest airtime (SN^2). The default LoRaWAN configuration (SN^3) is very close to the configuration with the longest airtime (SN^1). We also observe a significant difference between using simple channel models (SN^1 Simple Models) and the LoRa channel representation (SN^1).

If we would assume that an application requires a $DER > 0.9$ to provide useful functionality we would be able to support $N = 120$ nodes with the default LoRaWAN configuration (SN^3). The modelled communication range here is around 100 m (as observed in our experiments in a built up environment) and we can see that many applications (such as building automation) could not be supported by a LoRa system. It is likely that in such scenarios more nodes would have to be supported within the given range of a sink.

Obviously one could use less conservative transmission settings (the extreme represented by SN^2) to accommodate more nodes. However, in this case the transmission range is reduced and little protection against burst interference is provided. For example, the average transmission range for SN^1 is 98 m compared to 37 m for SN^2.

If we assume our deployment is located in Europe the regulator would require that each node can only use the channel for 0.1% of the time (duty-cycle limitation). For our experiment using the default LoRaWAN configuration (SN^3) we would obtain a channel duty-cycle of 0.13% that is above the regulator allowance. To comply we would need

---

[3]https://thethingsnetwork.org

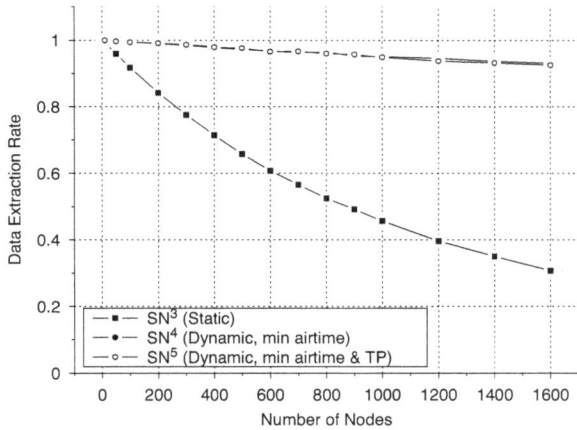

Figure 5: Experiment Set 2 – Dynamic Parameters: Lines for SN^4 and SN^5 overlap. When optimising transmission parameters for minimal airtime (or airtime and power) network capacity greatly improves. With minimised airtime (SN^4) and $DER > 0.9$, well over $N = 1600$ nodes can be supported (compared to $N = 120$ nodes with static settings).

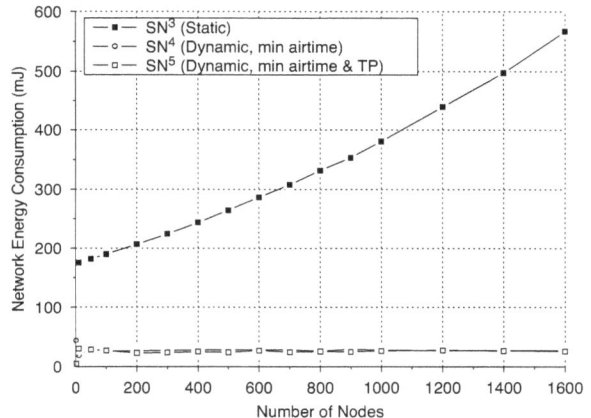

Figure 6: Experiment Set 2 – Dynamic Parameters: Lines for SN^4 and SN^5 overlap. Choosing communication parameters of nodes to minimise airtime (or airtime and power) has a significant impact on energy per extracted packet.

to reduce the data transmission rate from one 20 byte packet every 16.7 min to every 22 min.

For SN^1 Figure 4 shows results using simple channel models and LoRa models. The more realistic channel representation leads to an increase in DER as colliding transmissions may still be received due to the capture effect. For example, for $N = 200$ the DER increases from 0.51 to 0.80. This effect is significant and cannot be neglected when analysing the capacity of a LoRa network.

The setup with simple channel models corresponds to Pure ALOHA [16]. The DER for such systems is:

$$DER = e^{(-2N \cdot T_{packet} \cdot \lambda)} \qquad (12)$$

N is the number of transmitters, T_{packet} the packet airtime and λ is the transmission rate of all nodes. Figure 4 shows for SN^1 simulation results together with the analytic solution that match closely. This analytic solution can be used to describe the DER worst-case bound. More realistic channel models always result in a performance boost due to the capture effect. Equation 12 implies a lower DER for larger packets and higher transmission rates. We have verified that this is indeed the case, also in the more complex simulations such as those with multiple sinks.

Experiment Set 2 – Dynamic Parameters. In the second set of experiments we evaluate the impact of dynamic communication parameter selection on Data Extraction Rate (DER) and Network Energy Consumption (NEC). We compare three transmitter configurations SN^3, SN^4 and SN^5. SN^3 is the same as in Experiment Set 1 and is used as reference. For all settings we assume again a 20 byte packet is sent by each node every 16.7 min and CF is 868 MHz. N nodes transmit to a single sink ($M = 1$). Nodes are placed randomly around the sink within a radius that ensures that all nodes can reach the sink if they use the most robust settings. However, for each node the BW, SF, CR are set such that airtime is minimised (setting SN^4 with constant

$TP = 14$ dBm) and then such that first airtime and then Transmission Power (TP) is minimised (setting SN^5). For all experiments we use the LoRa channel representation.

As shown in Figure 5 the optimal allocated settings in terms of airtime (and airtime plus TP) has a huge impact on achievable DER. With minimised airtime (SN^4) and a $DER > 0.9$ requirement well over $N = 1600$ nodes can be supported. This is a dramatic improvement compared to $N = 120$ nodes achieved with static conservative settings as used in LoRaWAN.

However, it has to be considered that this achievement is not practical and relies on quite optimistic assumptions. First, the simulation does not consider interference and a minimum airtime setting has a low CR setting which does not provide sufficient protection. Second, the minimum setting would need to be re-evaluated from time to time due to environmental changes. A protocol would need to be used in the LoRa network to determine and adjust the settings. Although LoRaWAN specifies a *Network Manager* component to specifically deal with this issue the implementation and its protocols are not yet defined. Thus, existing LoRaWAN deployments use static and conservative transmission settings represented by SN^3.

Figure 6 shows the impact of optimal allocated settings on Network Energy Consumption (NEC). Obviously, choosing settings with shorter airtime and less TP will not only help to improve DER but helps to achieve significant energy savings. For example, for $N = 200$ energy consumption in the network is reduced by 89%. This in turn translates to a proportional longer node lifetime if they operate on battery. Again, in practice these savings may only be achieved partially due to a lack of mechanisms for transmission setting adaptation and due to other constraints such as interference.

Experiment 3 – Multiple Sinks. We have seen in the previous experiments that LoRa communication settings have a huge impact on network performance. In this set of experiments we explore the impact of the number of sinks M.

We use the previously described setting SN^1 for each experimental run (a 20 byte packet is sent by each node every

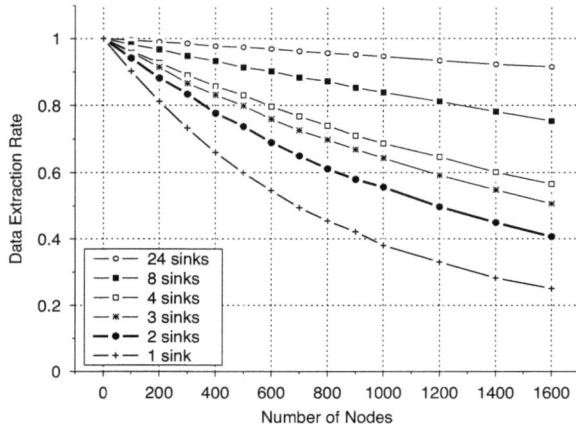

Figure 7: Experiment Set 3 – Multiple Sinks: multiple sink can significantly increase the DER.

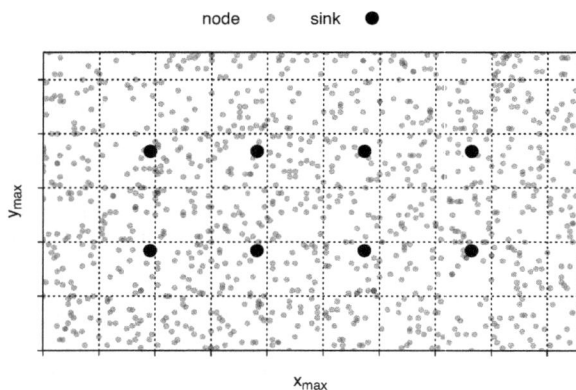

Figure 8: Example of a simulated deployment with 1000 nodes and 8 sinks.

16.7 min and CF is 868 MHz). For each run an increasing number of sinks M is used. The node placement strategy is changed as now multiple sinks are present. Nodes are placed in a rectangle with a diagonal twice the maximum transmission range d_{max}, and side lengths $x_{max} = \sqrt{3} \cdot d_{max}$ and $y_{max} = d_{max}$. This setup ensures that with communication settings SN^1 nodes within this rectangle can reach at least one sink. With four sinks or less, we space them equally over x_{max} on a straight line with $y = y_{max}/2$. Six or eight sinks are equally spaced over the two straight lines at $y = y_{max}/3$ and $y = 2 \cdot y_{max}/3$. 24 sinks are equally spaced over three straight lines at $y = y_{max}/4$ and $y = 2 \cdot y_{max}/4$ and $y = 3 \cdot y_{max}/4$. Figure 8 shows an example deployment with 1000 nodes and eight sinks. Here the bottom left point is placed at $(x_{max}/5, y_{max}/3)$ while the top right point is placed at $(x_{max} \cdot \frac{4}{5}, y_{max} \cdot \frac{2}{3})$. We intentionally chose this sink placement strategy for simplicity rather than optimality. Simulations with different node placements have led to similar results.

Our results in Figure 7 depict that increasing the number of sinks significantly increases the DER. For example, with 200 nodes, one sink is not able to support the typical $DER > 0.9$ requirement while three sinks achieve this. With eight

sinks, more than 600 nodes still obey this requirement while with one sink the DER would be as low as 0.55.

Our expectation was that with an increase in the number of sinks the network would get saturated, and the DER would actually decrease. The figure, however, shows that this is not the case. We believe that this is caused by the fact that there only needs to be one sink where the capture effect comes into play in order to ensure that a packet can eventually be received. With more sinks, the chances increase that a packet finds a sink where the capture effect plays for its advantage. With an infinite number of sinks, each node might find such a sink avoiding packet loss.

4.4 Findings

Our experiments lead to a number of findings regarding the scalability of LoRa networks:

- *Lower-Bound on Performance*: Pure ALOHA represents a good Data Extraction Rate (DER) lower-bound in single sink deployments. Equation 12. can be used to quickly estimate expected performance of a typical LoRaWAN deployment.

- *LoRaWAN Scalability*: With typical LoRaWAN settings (SF12, 125 kHz bandwidth, CR 4/5), the assumption of a 20 byte packet is sent by each node every 16.7 min and a $DER > 0.9$ requirement, $N = 120$ nodes can be supported. This is not a sufficient number for applications such as smart city deployments.

- *Dynamic LoRa Settings*: Dynamic allocation of LoRa communication settings has a tremendous impact on network scalability. However, to make use of this potential gain protocols and mechanisms for dynamic parameter selection are required. In LoRaWAN the *Network Manager* is envisioned to fulfil this role but a specification is yet to be given.

- *Capture Effect*: The capture effect has a significant impact on achievable Data Extraction Rate (DER). By far not all colliding transmissions are lost, in many situations at least one of the colliding transmissions can be received successfully. As this effect is significant it has to be taken into account when planning LoRa deployments. It also would have to be taken into account in simulation environments.

- *Multiple Sinks*: Adding additional sinks to a deployment improves Data Extraction Rate (DER). We have not observed that there is an upper bound below 1 in terms of DER when adding additional sinks.

4.5 Future Work

We have not yet investigated the full spectrum of parameters governing scalability of LoRa networks. For example, we have yet to investigate the impact of choosing different Carrier Frequency (CF) in a deployment on scalability. In a deployment area it can also be expected that we find multiple concurrent deployments that may interfere which each other; this aspect has yet to be investigated.

We have shown that dynamic transmission parameter selection and the introduction of more sinks has a dramatic impact on scalability. However, we have not investigated which of the two strategies yields a better return. Dynamic parameter selection requires implementation of complex (and potentially unstable or erroneous) protocols to facilitate this;

deployment of multiple sinks is costly and one has to find out where to deploy sinks best. For LoRa network operators it would be beneficial to determine which route to take.

5. RELATED WORK

There is limited published work discussing scalability of LoRa. Closest to this paper is the work by Petajajarvi et al. [8] and our own previous work reported in [1]. Petajajarvi et al. present an evaluation of LoRa link behaviour in open spaces. We evaluated LoRa link behaviour in built-up environments. We built upon the results reported in these papers when constructing our communication models for LoRaSim (see Section 3). This previous work, however, does not address general scalability questions of LoRa.

A vast number of generic wireless simulation tools such as ns-3 [10] or OMNet++ [17] exist. There are also simulators such as Cooja [7] or TOSSIM [4] designed for Wireless Sensor Networks (WSN) and IoT environments. These simulators can be extended by the components designed for our simulator LoRaSim to enable LoRa simulations.

The Semtech LoRa modem calculator [6] helps with analysis of LoRa transmission features (airtime of packets, receiver sensitivity) but does not enable network planning.

Siradel provides a simulation tool called *S_IOT* [15]. S_IOT relies on Volcano, a 3D-ray tracing propagation model and a portfolio of 2D and 3D geodata. The tool supports sink deployment decisions based on propagation models. This commercial tool considers the environment to a much greater detail than our simulator LoRaSim. However, it does not take into account actual traffic, collisions or details such as capture effect. Our models provided in Section 3 could be used to improve S_IOT.

6. CONCLUSION

Do Long Range (LoRa) Low-Power Wide-Area Network (LPWAN) scale? According to our study presented in the paper current installations based on LoRaWAN do not. The selected conservative transmission settings combined with the fact that in most scenarios only one sink is in range of a node scalability is limited. In a typical scenario, $N = 120$ nodes in an area of 3.8 ha can be handled which is not sufficient for future IoT deployments. However, our study also shows that LoRa networks can scale quite well if they use dynamic transmission parameter selection and/or multiple sinks. For both aspects more work is required as protocols for dynamic transmission parameter selection and strategies for useful sink deployment must be developed.

7. ACKNOWLEDGEMENTS

This research was partially funded through the Natural Environment Research Council (NERC) under grant number NE/N007808/1, VR and VINNOVA.

8. REFERENCES

[1] M. Bor, J. Vidler, and U. Roedig. LoRa for the Internet of Things. In *Proceedings of the 2016 International Conference on Embedded Wireless Systems and Networks*, EWSN '16, pages 361–366, USA, 2016. Junction Publishing.

[2] Electromagnetic compatibility and Radio spectrum Matters (ERM); Short Range Devices (SRD); Radio equipment to be used in the 25 MHz to 1000 MHz frequency range with power levels ranging up to 500 mW; Part 1: Technical characteristics and test methods, May 2012. EN 300 220-1 V2.4.1.

[3] ERC Recommendation 70-03: Relating to the use of Short Range Devices (SRD), Sept. 2015. CEPT/ERC/REC 70-03.

[4] P. Levis, N. Lee, M. Welsh, and D. Culler. Tossim: accurate and scalable simulation of entire tinyos applications. In *Proceedings of the International Conference on Embedded Networked Sensor Systems (ACM SenSys)*, Los Angeles, California, USA, 2003.

[5] LoRa. https://www.lora-alliance.org/What-Is-LoRa/Technology. Accessed: 2015-11-07.

[6] LoRa Calculator. http://www.semtech.com/apps/filedown/down.php?file=SX1272LoRaCalculatorSetup1\%271.zip. Accessed: 20-05-2016.

[7] F. Österlind, A. Dunkels, J. Eriksson, N. Finne, and T. Voigt. Cross-level sensor network simulation with cooja. In *First IEEE International Workshop on Practical Issues in Building Sensor Network Applications (SenseApp 2006)*, Tampa, Florida, USA, Nov. 2006.

[8] J. Petajajarvi, K. Mikhaylov, A. Roivainen, T. Hanninen, and M. Pettissalo. On the coverage of LPWANs: range evaluation and channel attenuation model for LoRa technology. In *ITS Telecommunications (ITST), 2015 14th International Conference on*, pages 55–59, Dec 2015.

[9] T. S. Rappaport et al. *Wireless communications: principles and practice*, volume 2. Prentice Hall PTR New Jersey, 1996.

[10] G. F. Riley and T. R. Henderson. Modeling and tools for network simulation. chapter The ns-3 Network Simulator, pages 15–34. Springer Berlin Heidelberg, Berlin, Heidelberg, 2010.

[11] Ingenu RPMA. http://www.ingenu.com/technology/rpma/. Accessed: 2016-05-09.

[12] Semtech. *AN1200.13 SX1272/3/6/7/8: LoRa Modem – Designer's Guide, Revision 1*, July 2013.

[13] Sigfox. http://www.sigfox.com. Accessed: 2015-11-07.

[14] SimPy – Event discrete simulation for Python. https://simpy.readthedocs.io. Accessed: 24-05-2016.

[15] Siradel S_IoT. http://www.siradel.com/portfolio-item/alliance-lora/. Accessed: 2016-05-29.

[16] A. S. Tanenbaum. *Computer Networks*. Upper Saddle River, NJ, USA, 3rd edition, 1996.

[17] A. Varga et al. The OMNeT++ discrete event simulation system. In *Proceedings of the European simulation multiconference (ESM'2001)*, volume 9, page 65, 2001.

[18] Weightless Open Standard. http://www.weightless.org. Accessed: 2015-11-07.

Impact of Time in Network Selection for Mobile Nodes

Tobias Rueckelt
Adam Opel AG
Bahnhofsplatz
Rüsselsheim, Germany
tobias.rueckelt@opel.com

Daniel Burgstahler
Technische Universität
Darmstadt
Rundeturmstr. 10
Darmstadt, Germany
daniel.burgstahler@kom.
tu-darmstadt.de

Florian Jomrich
Adam Opel AG
Bahnhofsplatz
Rüsselsheim, Germany
florian.jomrich@opel.com

Doreen Böhnstedt
Technische Universität
Darmstadt
Rundeturmstr. 10
Darmstadt, Germany
doreen.boehnstedt@kom.
tu-darmstadt.de

Ralf Steinmetz
Technische Universität
Darmstadt
Rundeturmstr. 10
Darmstadt, Germany
ralf.steinmetz@kom.
tu-darmstadt.de

ABSTRACT

Today, mobile nodes use multiple Internet access networks inefficiently. State-of-the-art network selection strategies distribute data traffic to available networks, but ignore an important second dimension: time. Time selection offers the opportunity to plan usage of future-available networks for delay-tolerant data traffic. We hypothesize, that concurrent selection of network and time leads to synergy effects, which reduce transmission cost and boost connectivity performance. To assess data distribution to wireless networks and time, we propose a novel rating model for joint network and time selection. The proposed model rates the satisfaction of Quality-of-Service (QoS) application requirements and trades off conflicting optimization goals. Moreover, we analyze the impact of time in network selection and present three network selection schedulers, which differ in their time selection strategy. Evaluation of the results reveals a strong impact of time selection on network performance. This gives evidence, that our initial hypothesis holds and forward-looking scheduling strategies provide a substantial benefit over state-of-the-art approaches.

Keywords

Network selection, time selection, rating model, mobile node

1. INTRODUCTION

Mobile devices are commonly equipped with multiple network interfaces, e.g. WiFi and cellular network. A method to switch and use them in parallel is provided by multi-homing capable handover schemes, which enable dynamic distribution of data flows over available networks [9][11]. This leads to the question: Which networks suit best to transmit application data?

MSWiM '16, November 13–17, 2016, Malta, Malta.

© 2016 Copyright held by the owner/author(s). Publication rights licensed to ACM.
ISBN 978-1-4503-4502-6/16/11. . . $15.00

DOI: http://dx.doi.org/mswim008

Network selection ideally aims on QoS requirement satisfaction of data flows. These QoS requirements are defined as flow-specific limits whose violation causes user-perceived service quality degradation. QoS requirement satisfaction benefits from flow distribution through qualified network selection. Networks are selected that match best to application QoS requirements. This contributes to our superordinate goal: user-perceived network quality improvement [10].

Considering a scenario of fast moving mobile nodes, network availability and transmission characteristics change frequently. Such dynamics impose challenges but also provide opportunities for substantial improvement. The question of network selection expands in time dimension: Which of the now or future-available networks suit best to transmit application data?

However, related work limits the problem to pure network selection and ignore the time selection. In contrast, the selection of proper transmission time without a view on network selection is often named resource allocation. Existing approaches usually focus on a single network connection and homogeneous data traffic. However, even these simple scenarios cover a huge optimization potential. Transmission of application data is coordinated to preload data or to use prospective available network resources. However, state-of-the-art QoS rating functions on resource allocation are not flexible enough for heterogeneous data traffic. Furthermore, no parallel networks are considered.

To the best of our knowledge, network selection and resource allocation are only considered separately in existing approaches. We hypothesize, that time selection in network selection has a strong impact on user-perceived network performance. To illustrate the impact of the time dimension, we give an example: Data transmission of a flow may be delayed to use a better-suited network, which will be available soon. Furthermore, delaying transmission or handover to another network can free up resources to finish transmission of concurrent data flows before a certain network gets out of reach. Consequently, the scenario requires tight coordination of data flows in network and time selection.

To answer our hypothesis, we need a schedule rating function that enables assessment for joint network and time selection schedulers. In this paper, we present three contributions:

1. A rating model to assess schedule quality in joint network

and time selection. It considers satisfaction of application QoS requirements and monetary cost in heterogeneous networks with heterogeneous data traffic.

2. An analysis on the impact of time in network selection. Therefore, we present three schedulers differing in time impact of their search strategy. (1) A classical Network Selection (NS) without time impact. For each data flow, it selects the best matching now-available network. (2) An Opportunistic Network Selection (ONS) with statistical time impact. It extends NS by the opportunity to delay transmission, if no well-matching network is available now. (3) A Transmission Planning (TP) with explicit time impact on search strategy. It selects the best matching network from now and future available ones and decides about transmission time in a second step. Using these three schedulers and the proposed rating model, we investigate the impact of time selection in network selection schedulers on user-perceived network performance.

3. We provide the code sources of the schedulers and our evaluation framework including the novel rating model to encourage future development of advanced schedulers.[1]

In the following section, we discuss related work and give an overview on our schedule rating approach in section 3. Subsequently, we explain the parameter space in section 4 and the rating model in section 5. These sections belong to our first contribution, the schedule rating model. The following sections focus on our second contribution, the investigation of the impact of time in network selection. To demonstrate the joint network and time selection problem complexity, we analyze it in section 6 and discuss why existing heuristics are not applicable. After that, we present three heuristic schedulers in section 7. Finally, we apply our novel rating scheme to them in section 8 to investigate the impact of time in network selection.

2. RELATED WORK

The related work in this topic is split into two domains: network selection and resource allocation. In fusion, we call it scheduling. This split preempts work from evolving synergy benefits.

2.1 Network Selection

Network selection algorithms try to select the best network to connect to and a good point in time for a soft or hard handover. Mathematical models are analyzed in [14]. We further divide the related work into network-controlled and client-controlled selection. The difference is firstly the location of the decision making and triggering and secondly the environmental knowledge that decisions are based on.

Network-controlled: In network-controlled approaches, network operators manage selection. In general, network operators aim to maximize overall throughput and their revenue. Network-controlled approaches benefit from top-level knowledge about user devices, which enables access coordination inside the controlled network [4]. Competitive and collaborative design using game theory [13] or predictive models and lead to remarkable results [7].

Client-controlled: In contrast, client-controlled approaches benefit from network operator independence. The network selection is not limited to those of the network operator. The selection uses detailed information about the user's needs. However, in the client-controlled domain, there is a lack of information about other users and the current network state. Therefore, algorithms are usually

[1] http://www.kom.tu-darmstadt.de/~trueckelt/scheduling/

based on assessment of estimated network performance [15]. Many approaches use map-attached aggregated historical data and movement estimation to derive future network availability and performance. The assessment measure in several papers is satisfaction of application QoS requirements. Popular methods are Multi-Attribute Decision Making (MADM) functions [8, 1], which apply weighted sums to assess the networks. MADM approaches provide linear models, which enable linear replacement of violations. However, linear replacement implies, that a strong violation of one requirement, is as severe as many slight or even negligible violations. Furthermore, normalization of requirements leads to fairness between data flows. However, a data flow with hard requirements should not be assessed equally to one with soft requirements, e.g. a voice-over-IP flow in comparison to a background download.

2.2 Resource Allocation

Resource allocation decides at which rate and which time data is transmitted. It focuses on collaborative link capacity use and packet preference. It is usually applied on data link layer and focuses on fairness of transmission. A well-studied subject is packet prioritization in WiFi within send buffers, to optimize transmission via a single link [5]. In contrast to this, we target collaborative use of different network interfaces. A simple L2 approach distributes packets to available networks in round robin fashion [16]. It reduces QoS requirements to interface preference and ensures fairness for scheduled flows. However, this scheduling covers only short-term delivery plans for the next few packets. The rating model is static and does not cover long-term optimization potential.

Bui and Widmer focus on bufferable video delivery [2]. They reduce device energy consumption and avoid buffer under-run. Therefore, flow control is planed for up to several minutes. Moreover, the scheduling tolerates hazy network prediction. This proactive long term scheduling provides good transmission time planning. A similar approach using opportunistic algorithms has been studied in [6]. However, authors of both papers limit their approaches to a single network and bufferable video traffic. Its QoS requirements are unchallenging and therefore mostly neglected. Thus, their schedule quality rating models lose general validity.

2.3 Discussion

In network selection, network-controlled and client-controlled schemes are often discussed as competitive approaches. In contrast, we argue that both should be applied concurrently. This way, network operators optimize performance with collaborative client information for their own network. Concurrently, users choose between optimized networks of different providers. For our scheduling, we assume this two-fold network selection model and focus on the user-controlled one.

Network selection and resource allocation both suffer from issues in rating functions. Those functions often lack validity for heterogeneous data traffic or provide only linear models. Linear models make QoS requirement violations interchangeable, regardless of their strength. A better model would avoid severe violations.

In addition, network selection and resource allocation provide only limited optimization potentials when regarded separately. Synergies evolve in a combined approach that plans both together. To assess such scheduling models and to analyze synergy effects, a combined rating model is required.

3. RATING MODEL OVERVIEW

Rating of schedules is fundamental for scheduler development. Therefore, we present a novel, well-elaborated metric that supports detailed schedule assessment for heterogeneous data traffic in joint

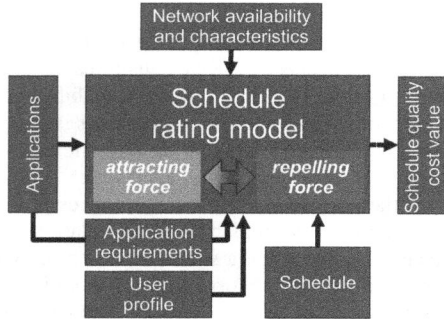

Figure 1: Schedule rating overview

network and time selection. It focuses on application QoS satisfaction with heterogeneous data traffic using heterogeneous networks.

To rate a schedule, we define a model of opposing forces. Firstly, we model an attracting force that pushes data to available networks. Secondly, we add a repelling force that pushes application data away from networks and time that violate application QoS requirements. Hence, a schedule has a certain tension of forces, for example from violation of a deadline or a minimum throughput requirement of a data flow. We express this tension in a cost function. The cost function serves as quality metric to assess schedules. A lower cost means that requirements of applications are satisfied better, and thus indicates higher schedule quality.

In a perfect schedule, data is pushed especially to QoS-matching networks. Moreover, delay tolerant data is moved to a point in time in which a matching network is available. Severe violations are avoided. As a result, the forces balance out transmissions of different applications according to user preference and to their integral QoS-defined priority.

A highlight of our schedule rating model is our novel throughput continuity model. To target the potential of time selection, it defines throughput requirements with tolerance to bursts and pauses. Bursty transfer may be more efficient in the dynamic scenario of mobile devices with fast changing network characteristics [6]. It enables data flow distribution to networks, which are available for a short time. As part of our novel schedule rating model, we therefore introduce an innovative throughput continuity model based on sliding windows.

However, the absolute cost function value provides no quantitative rating for schedule quality. For example, a scenario may have rare network capacity, which enforces violations. In this case, even the optimal schedule has a high cost function value. To make schedule quality assessable, we therefore provide a scoring system, which we call Normalized Rating Score (NRS). Instead of using absolute values, it states how much of the overall optimization potential of the scenario the scheduler exploits. This potential is defined by a relative value between two borders: the optimal score and the average score of a random scheduler as reasonable lower bound.

The schedule rating model needs information about its environment and about the data to transmit. Required information covers network availability and QoS characteristics, application QoS requirements and user preferences. A model overview is given in figure 1. Estimation or potential sources for this information are assumed to be available for offline analysis. We explicitly focus on the rating function, which assesses QoS and user preference satisfaction. This rating function enables detailed assessment of any scheduler and can be used to investigate weaknesses in model details and parameter choice for scored schedulers.

4. RATING MODEL COMPONENTS AND PARAMETER SPACE

Our schedule rating uses models for networks, data flows and user preferences. We summarize the defined parameters in table 1.

4.1 Network Model

Our network model covers throughput, latency, jitter and monetary costs. Network throughput is defined by bucket sizes in time slots. Hereby, a time slot t corresponds the time span of the current time τ divided by the time slot length $\Delta\tau$. $t = \tau/\Delta\tau$. The bucket sizes $S_{t,n}$ represent the capacity that the network $n \in N$ can provide to the mobile node in time slot $t \in T$. Furthermore, latency L_n and jitter J_n are constant abstract parameters for each network. Additionally, network use leads to monetary costs $w_{mon,n}$ for the user. We model this monetary cost as constant abstract parameter for each network.

4.2 Data Flow Model

We define data flows by data amount, latency, jitter and throughput requirements and time limits. Hereby, a requirement for property x is defined in $\widehat{x}$, e.g., $\widehat{L}_f$ is a latency requirement for flow $f \in F$. The amount of data $\widehat{s}_f$ to be scheduled is abstracted using tokens that represent equally sized data chunks. During scheduling, tokens are allocated to time-slotted network buckets.

4.2.1 Throughput

We model throughput requirements as the number of tokens, which are allocated within a time window. We define a throughput limit using firstly a window size $\Delta\widehat{t}$. Its length is measured in number of time slots. Secondly, we define the amount of data inside the window in number of tokens $\widehat{\sigma}$. Modeling throughput using time windows and token amounts $\widehat{TP}_{min,f} = \{\Delta\widehat{t}_{min,f}, \widehat{\sigma}_{min,f}\}$ enables the definition of transmission continuity requirements. For example, a bufferable stream may be transmitted using large data bursts that fill a buffer fast, followed by potentially long pauses. We model it using a large window and many data tokens. In contrast, a live-stream requires continuous data transfer that we represent by a tiny window and proportionally less data tokens.

Transmission continuity follows from the integration of the new dimension of time into scheduling. It relaxes hard throughput requirements from alternative models that arose from imprecise static throughput models.

4.2.2 Start Time and Deadline

Adding the dimension of time into the scheduling model imposes timing requirements for known data flows. To model these timing requirements, we introduce an earliest start time $\widehat{t}_{st,f}$ and a deadline $\widehat{t}_{dl,f}$ for each data flow $f \in F$. They refer to the corresponding time slots.

4.2.3 Latency and Jitter

Latency requirements $\widehat{L}_f$ and jitter requirements $\widehat{J}_f$ are constants for each flow representing abstract upper limits. For rating, they are compared to the corresponding network characteristics.

4.2.4 Weights

Data flows of applications have individual requirements that we define through the previously introduced parameters. For each requirement, we define a linear weight that determines importance of the requirement for a flow. For example, latency requirement is important for a voice call, but not for a background download. The set of flow requirement weights is given in 1. Weights scale re-

Table 1: Model parameters and variables

Description	Symbol
flow in flows to be scheduled	$f \in F$
time slot in overall planned time slots	$t \in T$
network in available networks	$n \in N$
network interface type i in interface types I	$i \in I$
number of tokens to be scheduled for flow f	$\widehat{s}_f$
capacity of network n in time slot t (network limit)	$\widehat{S}_{t,n}$
scheduled tokens of flow f in time slot t to network n	$s_{f,t,n}$
association $\in \{0, 1\}$ of flow f in time slot t to network n	$a_{f,t,n}$
unscheduled tokens of flow f	u_f
number of interfaces of type i of the mobile node	k_i
size of max. throughput window of flow f in time slots	$\Delta\widehat{t}_{max,f}$
max. amount of tokens in max. throughput window of flow f	$\widehat{\sigma}_{max,f}$
size of min. throughput window of flow f in time slots	$\Delta\widehat{t}_{min,f}$
min. amount of tokens in min. throughput window of flow f	$\widehat{\sigma}_{min,f}$
violation of min. amount of tokens in min. throughput window for flow f in time slot t	$\sigma_{min,f,t}$
deadline requirement $\in T$ of flow f	$\widehat{t}_{dl,f}$
start time requirement $\in T$ of flow f	$\widehat{t}_{st,f}$
latency requirement of flow f	$\widehat{L}_f$
latency of network n	L_n
jitter requirement of flow f	$\widehat{J}_f$
jitter of network n	J_n
weight of parameter x for flow f	$w_{x,f}$
total cost function value	c
cost for model part y	c_y

quirement violations of minimum throughput $w_{\widehat{TP}_{min,f}}$, start time $w_{\widehat{t}_{st,f}}$, deadline $w_{\widehat{t}_{dl,f}}$, latency $w_{\widehat{L}_f}$ and jitter $w_{\widehat{J}_f}$.

This model leads to prioritization of flows with tough requirements. This behavior is intended. We explicitly do not implement a normalization. Thus, application QoS requirement strengths balance flow prioritization.

$$\widehat{W}_f = \{w_{\widehat{TP}_{min,f}}, w_{\widehat{t}_{st,f}}, w_{\widehat{t}_{dl,f}}, w_{\widehat{L}_f}, w_{\widehat{J}_f}, w_{user,f}\} \quad (1)$$

4.3 User Preference Model

The user may prefer a specific application or flow. Therefore, we introduce another linear weight $w_{user,f}$ that influences prioritization of flows. This enables personalization of application priorities.

To give users a trade-off trigger between network performance and monetary transmission cost, we introduce the balancing parameter willingness-to-pay w_{wtp}. We define willingness-to-pay inversely. A low value results in a high willingness of the user to pay for more network performance. It trades off accumulated flow violations to monetary cost.

4.4 Discussion

Our network and data flow models both integrate the dimension of time. This enables accurate rating of transmission volumes and flow shapes. In particular, the novel throughput model enables flow continuity optimization, using flow rate adaption, continuous data transfer or allowing bursts. Weights provide flexible requirement definition, which enable modeling of heterogeneous data traffic with time-dependent transmission constraints.

5. BEHAVIORAL MODEL DEFINITION

In the following, we introduce the equations that define the cost function for rating and a set of schedule feasibility constraints. Within these equations, we use the identity function $\mathbb{I}(x = y)$, which is 1 if x is equal to y, else 0. Furthermore, we use signum function $sgn(x)$, which is 1 for positive x, 0 if $x = 0$ and -1 for negative x. Furthermore, all parameters and decision variables are of type integer. In addition, $a_{f,t,n}$ is limited to $[0, 1]$.

The core of our model is the cost function. We define it ac-

cording to an analogy to opposing forces. The attracting forces foster token allocation to networks. They cover a punishment for unscheduled tokens and violation of minimum throughput application requirement. In contrast, the repelling forces punish tokens that are allocated at networks or time slots, which violate application requirements. They cover firstly violation models for latency, jitter, start time and deadline and secondly monetary cost model.

5.1 Token Allocation

This model regulates how tokens of a flow can be allocated, enabling dedicated network and transmission time selection.

5.1.1 Token Scheduling

A token of flow f can either be scheduled $s_{f,t,n}$ to time slot t and network n or stay unscheduled u_f. In sum, the number of tokens of a flow is limited by $\widehat{s}_f$. We model this constraint C1 in equation 4. Scheduled tokens $s_{f,t,n}$ lead to data transmission, which implies monetary cost c_{mon} according to equation 5. This monetary cost applies a repelling force, which pushes tokens away from expensive networks. The force is scaled by willingness-to-pay w_{wtp}. In contrast, unscheduled tokens u_f lead to violation $c_{u,f}$ as shown in equation 6. They take effect in an attracting force, which pulls tokens to networks. Furthermore, the sum of scheduled flow tokens $s_{f,t,n}$ must not exceed available resources of networks, modeled by the bucket size $S_{t,n}$. Constraint C2 in equation 7 ensures this limit.

5.1.2 Available Interfaces

In our model, the mobile node has a specified number of network interfaces k_i of the type $i \in I$, e.g. WiFi or cellular network. The mobile node cannot connect to more networks of the same type i at the same time, than dedicated interfaces available. We model this constraint C3 according to equation 8.

5.1.3 Flow Migration Model

Flow migration, or handover from one network to another, leads to protocol overhead and might lead to performance degradation during the process. It contributes to the repelling forces, pushing tokens away from all networks except from the currently used. To suppress frequent and unnecessary flow migration, often referred to as ping-pong effects, each migration process contributes linearly to the cost function. Flow migration is complex to detect from our scheduling matrix, because scheduled flows can pause for a while.

5.1.4 Network Association Model

To detect flow migrations, we associate each flow at each time slot to a single network that is used for potential transmission $a_{f,t,n}$. We ensure this by equation 9. To provide coincidence between network association $a_{f,t,n}$ and scheduled tokens $s_{f,t,n}$, we introduce constraint 10. It ensures that token assignment presumes flow association to the corresponding network. In contrast, an association does not require an assignment of tokens. Therefore, a network association for each flow exists in each time slot. This enables a simple way to identify flow migration: checking of association changes in consecutive time slots. We calculate the cost from flow migration in equation 11. It counts the number of flow migrations and weights it linearly by w_{mig} to calculate flow migration cost c_{mig}.

5.2 Throughput Model

Our throughput model defines window sizes and limits for the number of tokens inside of them. The model assesses limits for each time step, sliding the window along the planned time span. This defines a crucial rating model for time slot selection and is

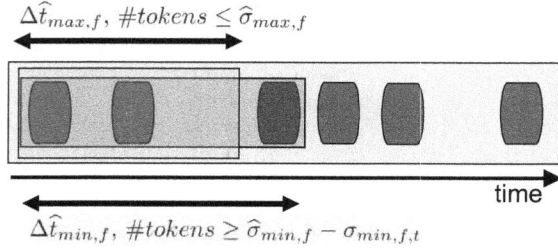

$$\Delta \widehat{t}_{max,f}, \#tokens \leq \widehat{\sigma}_{max,f}$$

$$\Delta \widehat{t}_{min,f}, \#tokens \geq \widehat{\sigma}_{min,f} - \sigma_{min,f,t}$$

Figure 2: Throughput model: window size is defined by $\Delta\widehat{t}$, number of required tokens by $\widehat{\sigma}$. #tokens stands for the number of scheduled tokens of a flow in the time window over all networks.

shown in figure 2. Many data flows require a minimum throughput. We add an attractive force to the model that pushes data tokens to networks to affirm minimum flow throughput requirement. We model this force in equation 13. It counts the number of scheduled tokens $s_{f,t,n}$ inside each window over all networks. The sum of tokens in the window should at least be equal to the required number $\widehat{\sigma}_{min,f}$. Violation is allowed by the additional term of $\sigma_{min,f,t}$, which contributes to the cost function and is therefore minimized.

Moreover, the model also requires an upper throughput model, as shown in equation 12. This constraint C4 ensures, that a scheduler does not plan a higher throughput than the source can deliver. An example is a live-stream. Data cannot be transmitted earlier with high throughput bursts because it has not been generated yet. It is a hard constraint, which cannot be violated. Therefore, it does not contribute to the cost function.

5.2.1 Throughput Violation Normalization

To derive the cost function impact for minimum throughput violation $c_{\widehat{TP}_{min,f}}$, we define a cost normalization for violation token count $\sigma_{min,f,t}$ in equation 14. To treat flows equally from their data amount, we normalize the violation cost to the number of tokens of a flow. Thus, we add the linear parameter $\widehat{\sigma}_{min,f}$ to the cost function calculation. Additionally, a token gap, which causes violation, is counted multiple times, while a window slides over it. A long window covers the gap at more sliding steps and leads to higher violation token count. To avoid violation strength dependence on window size $\Delta\widehat{t}_{min,f}$, we normalize cost to it and weight it with parameter ρ. To counteract contradiction with start time and deadline requirements, the minimum throughput requirement is only active within the time slots in between. The latter normalization underrates violation near start time and deadline, because gaps are covered fewer times by the sliding window. For example, the time slot at start time is covered once only: in the first sliding step of the window. Accordingly, the model penalizes minimum throughput violation at the start and the end lower than in the middle. Indeed, this approximates reality. It provides two advantages: Firstly, real flow control mechanisms increase throughput gradually. The model error endorses lower throughput at flow start that represents real transmission behavior. Secondly, decreasing data rate towards the deadline implies that data should be transmitted earlier. This favors conservative data buffer filling towards the deadline, which helps to finish data transmission in time.

5.3 Start Time, Deadline, Latency and Jitter

Start time, deadline, latency and jitter violations create repelling forces that push tokens away from non-matching time slots and networks. Violation contributes to the cost function with quadratic im-

pact, as shown in equations 15 - 18. Hence, a severe deadline violation causes a higher force than many slight violations. As a result, the model avoids severe violations. Note that the quadratic impact factors do not depend on the schedule, but can be pre-calculated. Therefore, the model is still linear. Corresponding weights and the number of violating tokens scale violations linearly.

5.4 Cost Function

The absolute cost c reaches its minimum at an equilibrium of forces with an optimal schedule. We define absolute cost in equation 2. It covers firstly monetary cost, secondly flow migration cost and thirdly the flow requirement violation cost from equation 3 with their user-defined weights.

Finally, the objective of the optimization is to minimize c, subject to equations 3..18.

$$c = c_{mon} + c_{mig} + \sum_{f \in F} (w_{user,f} \cdot c_f) \tag{2}$$

$$c_f = c_{u,f} + c_{\widehat{TP}_{min,f}} + c_{dl,f} + c_{st,f} + c_{L,f} + c_{J,f} \tag{3}$$

Token allocation model:

$$\texttt{C1}: \ \forall f \in F: \ \sum_{\substack{t \in T, \\ n \in N}} s_{f,t,n} + u_f = \widehat{s}_f \tag{4}$$

$$c_{mon} = w_{wtp} \cdot \sum_{n \in N} \left(w_{mon,n} \cdot \sum_{\substack{f \in F, \\ t \in T}} s_{f,t,n} \right) \tag{5}$$

$$c_{u,f} = w_{u,f} \cdot u_f \cdot w_{user,f} \tag{6}$$

$$\texttt{C2}: \ \forall t \in T, n \in N: \ \sum_{f \in F} s_{f,t,n} \leq S_{t,n} \tag{7}$$

$$\texttt{C3}: \ \forall t \in T, i \in I:$$
$$k_i \geq \sum_{n \in N} \left(\mathbb{I}(i_n = i) \cdot \sum_{f \in F} sgn(s_{f,t,n}) \right) \tag{8}$$

Network association and flow migration model:

$$\forall f \in F, t \in T: \ \sum_{n \in N} a_{f,t,n} = 1 \tag{9}$$

$$\forall f \in F, t \in T, n \in N: \ a_{f,t,n} \geq sgn(s_{f,t,n}) \tag{10}$$

$$c_{mig} = w_{mig} \cdot \sum_{\substack{f \in F, \\ n \in N}} \sum_{\substack{t \in T | \\ t \geq 2}} (1 - \mathbb{I}(a_{f,t-1,n} = a_{f,t,n})) \tag{11}$$

Throughput model:

$$\texttt{C4}: \ \forall f \in F, t_0 \in T: \widehat{\sigma}_{max,f} \geq \sum_{t=t_0}^{t_0 + \Delta\widehat{t}_{max,f}} \sum_{n \in N} s_{f,t,n} \tag{12}$$

$$\forall f \in F, t_0 \in T:$$
$$\widehat{\sigma}_{min,f} \leq \sum_{t=t_0}^{t_0 + \Delta\widehat{t}_{min,f}} \sum_{n \in N} s_{f,t,n} + \sigma_{min,f,t} \tag{13}$$

$$\forall f \in F: c_{\widehat{TP}_{min,f}} = \frac{\rho \cdot w_{\widehat{TP}_{min,f}}}{\Delta\widehat{t}_{min,f} \cdot \widehat{\sigma}_{min,f}} \cdot \sum_{t=\widehat{t}_{st,f}}^{\widehat{t}_{dl,f} - \Delta\widehat{t}_{min,f}} \sigma_{min,f,t} \tag{14}$$

Deadline, start time, latency and jitter models:

$$\forall f \in F: \quad c_{dl,f} = w_{\widehat{t}_{dl,f}} \cdot \sum_{\substack{t \in T, \\ n \in N}} sgn(s_{f,t,n}) \cdot \max(0, t - \widehat{t}_{dl,f})^2 \tag{15}$$

$$\forall f \in F: \quad c_{st,f} = w_{\widehat{t}_{st,f}} \cdot \sum_{\substack{t \in T, \\ n \in N}} sgn(s_{f,t,n}) \cdot \max(0, \widehat{t}_{st,f} - t)^2 \tag{16}$$

$$\forall f \in F: \quad c_{L,f} = w_{\widehat{L}_f} \cdot \sum_{\substack{t \in T, \\ n \in N}} sgn(s_{f,t,n}) \cdot \max(0, L_n - \widehat{L}_f)^2 \tag{17}$$

$$\forall f \in F: \quad c_{J,f} = w_{\widehat{J}_f} \cdot \sum_{\substack{t \in T, \\ n \in N}} sgn(s_{f,t,n}) \cdot \max(0, J_n - \widehat{J}_f)^2 \tag{18}$$

6. COMPLEXITY ANALYSIS

Problem definition: *Given a schedule* s, *a set of networks and a set of data flows, is* s *a feasible schedule and is* s *of minimal cost?*

The presented model defines a polynomial-time cost function in equation 2 and sub-functions and additional polynomial-time constraints C1-C4. Hence, the feasibility and the cost of a schedule s can be determined within polynomial time. However, it is not possible to verify in polynomial time if s is of minimal cost, given $P \neq NP$.

To analyze the problem complexity, we start with a separation. The effect of the cost function parameters L, J, $w_{mon,n}$ and $w_{u,f}$ follows from two factors. Firstly from the match between network and flow and secondly from the number of scheduled tokens. Time does not influence those equations. Thus, a time-independent solution subspace of the scheduling problem can be derived, when we consider only $s_{f,n}$, as shown in equation 19.

$$s_{f,n} = \sum_{t \in T} s_{f,t,n} \tag{19}$$

$$\forall f \in F, n \in N: v_{f,n} = sgn(s_{f,n}) \cdot \left(w_{\widehat{L}_f} \cdot \max(0, L_n - \widehat{L}_f)^2 \right.$$
$$\left. + w_{\widehat{J}_f} \cdot \max(0, J_n - \widehat{J}_f)^2 \right) + s_{f,n} \cdot (w_{mon,n} - w_{u,f}) \tag{20}$$

We are able to derive a time-constant value $v_{f,n}$ from the separated properties, as shown in equation 20. This separated part of the optimization is equivalent to multiple-demand bounded multiple knapsack problem. Flows with their individual network-matching $v_{f,n}$ represent multiple, different demands. Furthermore, the number of tokens of a flow is equivalent to the bounded number of equal items. Limited knapsack sizes are expressed by limited network resources, whereby multiple networks with individual capacity exist. We argue that the defined scheduling problem is NP-hard, because knapsack is a sub-problem that is NP-complete and the scheduling is not in NP.

The presented scheduling problem contains an additional dimension that makes it harder to solve: time. However, the omitted, time-dependent parts of the cost function may dominate the cost value of a knapsack solution from the split-off sub-problem. Therefore, the time-dependent parts cannot be considered separately. These parts are firstly our throughput violation model, secondly the start time and deadline violation models and finally the flow migration cost model. For scheduling, we therefore cannot apply the well-known heuristics of knapsack problem.

7. HEURISTIC SCHEDULERS

To fill the gap of heuristic schedulers, we present three approaches and a random baseline. To make the three scheduler approaches comparable, we apply the same heuristics for flow prioritization and network matching to all of them. Therefore, they only differ in time selection in their search strategy. This decision follows the goal of this work, to investigate the effect of the paradigm change of integrating time selection as explicit part into network selection. In the following, we firstly present the applied heuristics and constraint checkers and secondly explain the search strategies of the schedulers.

7.1 Heuristic Design

Substantial elements in the scheduling process are flow prioritization and network matching. We present heuristics for these two elements.

7.1.1 Flow Prioritization

For flow prioritization, we rely on the individual flow requirements. According to the well-known Most-Constrained-First theorem in search heuristics for Constrained Satisfaction Problems (CSP), we schedule flows first, which are expected to be most restricted ones. Therefore, we create a function that evaluates the restrictiveness $\widetilde{r}_f$ of a flow f. In complexity analysis in section 6, we already identified the time-invariant cost function terms. These are latency, jitter, monetary cost and number of unscheduled chunks of a flow. We use these cost function terms linearly in our restrictiveness heuristic. In addition, we linearize minimum throughput requirement by the average throughput within the corresponding time window. Our restrictiveness heuristic sums up all restrictive flow requirements, multiplied by their corresponding weights, as shown in equation 21.

$$\widetilde{r}_f = w_{user,f} \cdot \left[w_{u,f} \cdot w_{user,f} + w_{\widehat{J}_f} \cdot \widehat{J}_f^2 + w_{\widehat{L}_f} \cdot \widehat{L}_f^2 \right.$$
$$\left. + w_{\widehat{TP}_{min,f}} \cdot \widehat{TP}_{min,f,average} \right] \tag{21}$$

7.1.2 Network Matching

For network matching, we design a cost heuristic, which is based on the cost function of the proposed rating model and approximates time-dependent terms. It covers the same requirements as our restrictiveness heuristic but compares them to the characteristics of a network to estimate their match. In addition, it covers the monetary cost induced from network use. We bisect the terms into attracting and repelling forces and give the attracting forces a negative influence on the result. The derived cost heuristic is shown in equation 22 and gives an estimation of the cost $\widetilde{c}_{f,n}$ of a token assignment of a flow f to network n. Note, that this estimated cost is usually negative, since token assignment is supposed to improve the schedule.

$$\widetilde{c}_{f,n} = w_{user,f} \cdot \left[\, w_{\widehat{J}_f} \cdot \max(0, J_n - \widehat{J}_f)^2 \right.$$
$$+ w_{\widehat{L}_f} \cdot \max(0, L_n - \widehat{L}_f)^2 - w_{u,f} \cdot w_{user,f}$$
$$\left. - w_{\widehat{TP}_{min,f}} \cdot \rho \cdot \frac{TP_{n,average} - \widehat{TP}_{min,f,average}}{\Delta \widehat{t}_{min,f} \cdot \widehat{\sigma}_{min,f}} \, \right]$$
$$+ w_{mon,n} \cdot w_{wtp} \tag{22}$$

7.2 Constraint Satisfaction

All presented schedulers rely on search algorithms for constrained optimization problems. Constraints C1-C4 invalidate a large share of the solution space. To stay within the valid solution space during search, we apply a forward checking strategy for all four schedulers. The forward checking disqualifies token assignments according to the constraints of the optimization. C1, C2 and C3 limit the token amount for an assignment. For each assignment, we apply the minimum operator to remaining tokens of the flow, remaining capacity of the network in time slot and averaged maximum throughput of the flow. C4 constraints network selection based on available network interfaces of the mobile node. For each network selection, it validates if the network is already planned to be used or if for this time slot a network interface of matching type is free. In addition, we simplify start time and deadline violation model to constraints. No data is scheduled outside these limits. In applying forward checking, our search heuristics do not require a backtracking strategy for constraint satisfaction.

7.3 Schedulers

The schedulers apply the defined heuristics and differ in their strategy of time selection. We follow this approach to investigate the impact of time in search strategies on schedule quality and thereby target the main goal of this work.

7.3.1 Network Selection (NS)

The Network Selection scheduler splits the search space by time slot and treats each slot separately. Therefore, time has no impact on its search strategy. This follows the usual state-of-the-art approach of network selection schemes. It starts with sorting of flows to assess which flows should be prioritized during scheduling, using restrictiveness heuristic $\widetilde{r}_f$ according to equation 21.

For each flow, it sorts available networks according to their match determined by cost heuristic $\widetilde{c}_{f,n}$ according to equation 22 and tries to assign as many tokens of the flow as possible to the networks in the sorted list, starting with the best match. For token assignment, we apply forward checking to ensure that all constraints are satisfied and the resulting schedule is valid.

7.3.2 Opportunistic Network Selection (ONS)

Opportunistic Network Selection is based on the NS. In addition, it implements an opportunistic term for token assignment, which enables the decision to refuse scheduling to bad matching networks in the current time slot. It therefore introduces a new parameter, the cost limit c_{lim}. The algorithm only adds networks to the sorted network list, whose cost heuristic result is lower than the limit $\widetilde{c}_{f,n} < c_{lim}$. This change in strategy adds a statistical time impact because some data, which could be scheduled in current time slot, is delayed for potential later transmission. Time selection of ONS follows state-of-the-art resource allocation approaches. In addition, we combine their strategies with network selection.

7.3.3 Transmission Planning (TP)

Transmission Planning assumes to have further knowledge on future available networks. Instead of splitting the search space into independently scheduled time slots like NS and ONS, it first focuses on network matching.

TP starts with a flow prioritization. Like NS and ONS, TP applies $\widetilde{r}_f$ to sort flows according to their restrictiveness. Secondly, for each data flow, networks are sorted according to their match in network characteristics using the cost heuristic $\widetilde{c}_{f,n}$. As last step before token assignment, it selects transmission time. It therefore checks the overlap of network availability and the time window between flow start time and deadline. This novel strategy focuses on QoS satisfaction. Instead of ignoring optimization potential of time completely like NS, or covering it statistically like ONS, TP explicitly employs time selection as search strategy step.

7.3.4 Random Scheduler

The random scheduler follows the design of NS. Instead of applying heuristics for flow and network sorting, it uses a shuffle function. During token assignment, forward checking still ensures validity of the resulting schedules.

8. EVALUATION

In this evaluation, we give evidence that integrating the time domain into network selection is beneficial. As second contribution, we show how to apply our novel rating scheme to identify strengths and weaknesses of schedulers. In the following, we explain our evaluation metrics and setup and discuss the results and improvement potentials of the three heuristic schedulers.

8.1 Evaluation Metrics

Our rating model defines an appropriate quality measure in its cost function. It creates a comparable rating measure for any schedule. However, the absolute cost function values alone provide no evidence on quality of a schedule. Depending on the scenario, a schedule may have violations and therefore a high cost function value, even though it is ideal. We therefore compare scheduling cost function values to bounding values for the given scenario.

An optimization determines a schedule of minimum cost for the scenario, but has a long execution time. This is not convenient for online execution. Nevertheless, it provides the upper quality bound and is therefore a perfect candidate to analyze improvement potentials of schedulers. To assess schedule quality, we additionally require a reasonable lower quality bound. We select a random scheduler for this purpose. It provides feasible, but low quality schedules. Every reasonable scheduler should return results better than average random. The two bounds enable relative quality assessment.

We introduce the Normalized Rating Score (NRS) in equation 23. It provides a score from 0 to 1, which informs about the quality of the schedule s. 0 means, that it is as bad as average random schedules. In contrast, a score of 1 means that the scheduler reached optimal performance. From NRS, the overall optimization potential of the scheduler can be estimated. To clarify which details of the scored scheduler lead to this waste of potential, we introduce Relative Detail Score (RDS) in equation 24. It provides cost information on the rated requirement satisfaction criteria of the cost function. RDS determines the deviation of criterion v from this of the optimal schedule, normalized to the absolute cost function optimization potential of schedule s. A value of 0.2 means, that criterion v_1 (e.g. minimum throughput requirement) contributes 20% to the wasted optimization potential. In contrast, a value of -0.1 means, that the scheduler performs 10% better than the optimum in criteria v_2. This gives hint, that the scheduler should be less restrictive on criterion v_2 in order to provide space for optimization of other criteria. In these two cases, a parameter change or model refinement on criterion v should be considered. A value of 0 means, that the scheduler brings criteria v perfectly in balance to reach optimal schedules.

Additionally, computational complexity of schedulers can lead to long execution times, which could make them infeasible for real world use. Therefore, we use execution time as last evaluation metric to assess schedulers.

$$NRS(s) = \frac{c_{Rnd} - c_s}{c_{Rnd} - c_{Opt}}; \qquad (23)$$

$$RDS_v(s) = \frac{c_{v,s} - c_{v,Opt}}{c_s - c_{Opt}}; \qquad (24)$$

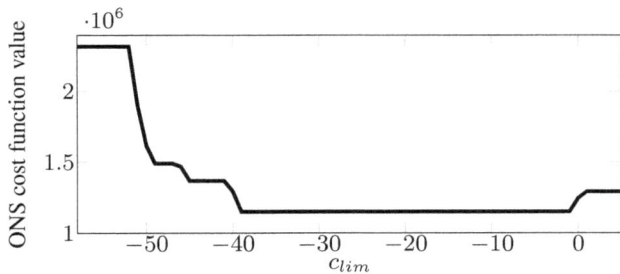

Figure 3: ONS cost function value over c_{lim}

The three evaluation metrics of NRS, RDS and execution time provide means to analyze firstly the overall scheduler performance, secondly weaknesses and optimization potential of schedulers and thirdly real-time applicability of schedulers.

8.2 Evaluation Setup

For evaluation, we generate randomized scenarios with 16 flows, eight networks and vary the scenario size by the number of time slots from 25 to 400. The simulated networks cover two cellular networks, which are always available and six WiFis, which are available only for certain time windows. In comparison to WiFi, simulated cellular networks provide higher latency, equal to lower jitter, lower to equal throughput and cause higher cost. Data flows are composed of four typical traffic classes: Live-stream, bufferable stream, interactive and background with randomized requirement values within typical ranges and traffic share [12, 3]. Mobile nodes furthermore have one cellular network interface and one WiFi interface. For each scenario size, we generate 30 randomized scenarios and measure quality and execution time. For random scheduler, we execute 100 runs for each scenario. The results show about normal distribution (Anderson-Darling test: execution time p = 0.72, cost p = 0.78). We can therefore use average values of the 100 runs for NRS. For optimization, we use IBM CPLEX Branch&Cut solver. We implemented the random and heuristic schedulers in Java. For each simulation instance, we use one core of a server machine with Intel Xeon E5-2643 v3 @ 3.4GHz and 512 GB RAM.

8.3 ONS Opportunistic Parameter Tuning

The ONS scheduler delays token assignments when expected cost $\widetilde{c}_{f,n}$ is higher than c_{lim}. Therefore, schedule quality of ONS depends on this parameter. The lower its value is, the higher is the probability to delay traffic. A too low value will always effect token assignment skipping. Figure 3 shows the cost function value depending on c_{lim}. We observe a relatively large window for optimal choice of the parameter. For evaluation, we select $c_{lim} = -10$.

8.4 Evaluation Results and Discussion

We first present absolute cost function values and execution time to give an impression on the data set and then rate the different schedulers using our novel rating scheme, consisting of the cost function and the metrics NRS and RDS. We show the Optimal Scheduler (Opt), the classical Network Selection (NS), the Opportunistic Network Selection (ONS), the Traffic Planning (TP) and the Random Scheduler (Rnd). For all plots, we vary scenario size in time slots on the x axis.

8.4.1 Absolute Cost Value and Execution Time

The absolute cost in figure 4 shows an overall increase of values towards larger scenarios for all schedulers. For cost function value, schedulers keep in a strict order in every scenario. All heuristic schedulers show approximately a linear increase of cost function

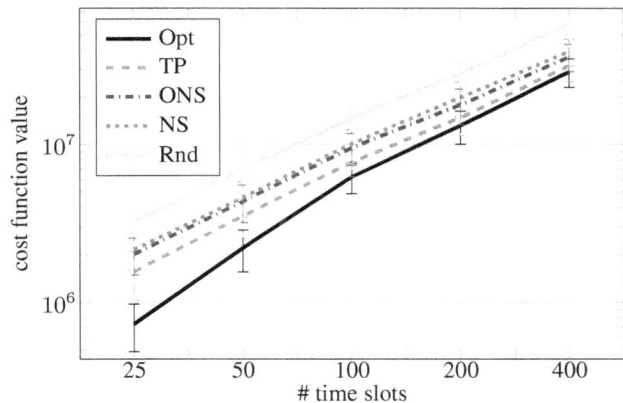

Figure 4: Cost function results of schedulers over scenario size

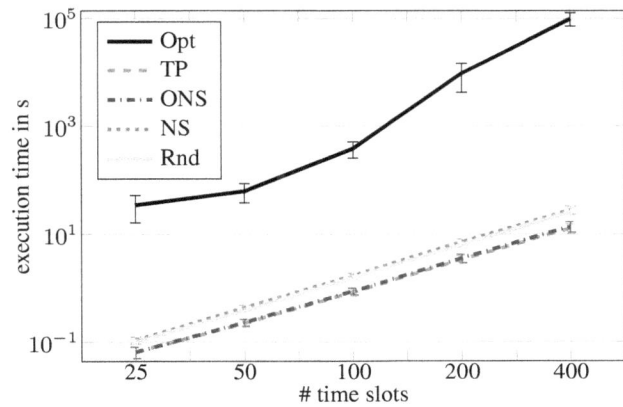

Figure 5: Execution times of schedulers over scenario size

value with scenario size while the optimization scheduler result shows a concave curve, slowly approximating to the other schedulers. This admits the claim that our heuristic results converge towards the optimum with increasing scenario size.

For execution time, we observe exponential increase for the optimization, resulting in an average execution time of 98766s (27.4h) for solving the largest simulated scenario size. In contrast, all heuristic schedulers show an average execution time of less than 29s for the same scenario size. Note, that the two online schedulers NS and ONS can distribute their workload over the real scenario duration. All three of them provide real-time compliant solutions for scheduling.

8.4.2 Rating Score Analysis

We propose to use our metric NRS in addition to absolute values and RDS for detail analysis. NRS indicates how much of the overall optimization potential the scheduler uses. RDS shows how much the model sub-function violations diverge from optimal cost distribution. This provides inference about which parameter choices or models of a scheduler contain the main weaknesses. We use these two metrics to analyze the three proposed heuristic schedulers.

Normalized Rating Score (NRS) Analysis.

In figure 6, we show the NRS of the three heuristic schedulers NS, ONS and TP. Like in absolute cost value comparison, we observe a strict order in performance of the three schedulers and a convergence towards the optimum with rising scenario size.

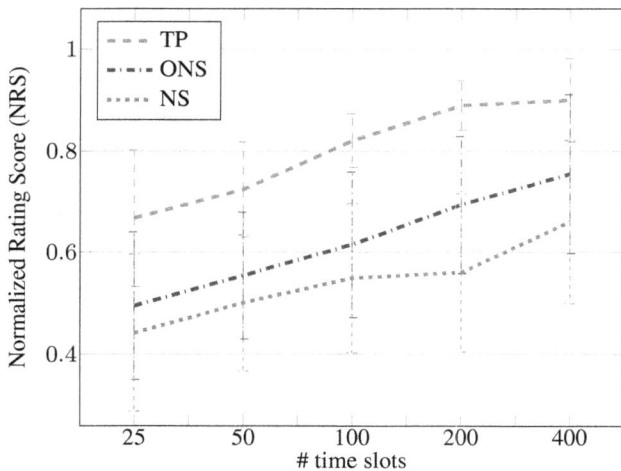

Figure 6: Normalized Rating Score (NRS) over scenario size

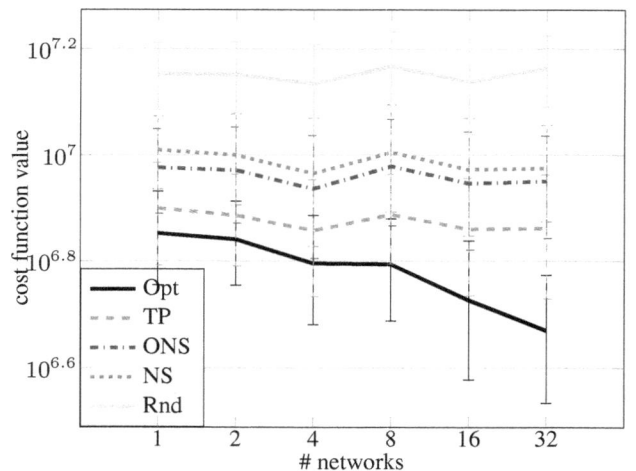

Figure 7: Absolute cost function value over number of networks, scenario size = 100 time slots

In contrast to figure 4, the used optimization potential of each scheduler gets obvious. TP uses in average 18% more of this potential than ONS and 26% more than NS. Note, that improvement of NRS gets harder with rising absolute NRS score. Since all three schedulers only differ on the impact of time in search strategy, this observation confirms our initial hypothesis: For the given scenario with non-constant network characteristics, there is a substantial impact of time in network selection.

But why do the schedulers' NRS converge towards the optimum with rising scenario sizes? The answer originates from the fixed number of networks in the scenario. With rising scenario duration, the relative number of network-changes decreases linearly. If network-changes are rare, the overall optimization potential of joint network and time selection decreases and the simplified throughput heuristics converge towards the optimum. To show this effect, we vary the number of networks and, hence, adapt the frequency of network-changes over time. This is illustrated in figure 7. The one-network case depicts the limited optimization potential of state-of-the-art resource allocation. Moreover, we see how the optimization potential, i.e. the difference between the optimal and averaged random-scheduler cost function values, increases with the number of networks. This affirms our initial hypothesis, that joint network and time selection for mobile nodes leads to synergies which provide unknown optimization potentials. However, the performance of the three heuristic schedulers stay nearly identical. This leads to a relative decrease of performance in NRS score towards scenarios with high optimization potential. The heuristic schedulers' behavior clarifies the challenge in development of new schedulers, which use the new identified optimization potential in a better way.

Relative Detail Score (RDS) Analysis.
To identify the origins of the weaknesses of the schedulers and to find out how to improve them, we analyze the RDS for the three proposed schedulers, shown in figure 8. Note that RDS is normed on individual scheduler performance and should therefore not be used for comparison of schedulers to each other. Keep in mind that the heuristics are kept simple by intention to be able to apply them equally to all three schedulers in order to investigate the impact of time in network selection. The development of more elaborated schedulers exceeds the scope of this paper.

We can observe a good balance of the heuristics for the latency and jitter model. Their performance turn out as expected since we reuse the original rating model for the heuristic.

Unsurprisingly, time limits model, namely start time and deadline violations, overperform slightly because the heuristic schedulers forbid violation of start times or deadlines. However, any overperformance can have essential impact on other categories. For example, the heuristic schedulers always hold even soft deadlines. Nevertheless, their violation provides high potentials to assign additional tokens to well-matching networks. To cope with this weakness, a trade-off heuristic for time limit violation is required.

Unscheduled tokens and throughput violation play a major role in wasted optimization potential. For the two network selection strategies NS and ONS, unscheduled token violation impact decreases with rising scenario size. This is the case because the probability for existing later time slots with free capacity in matching networks rises with higher overall scenario duration.

In addition, the heuristics select networks based on restrictiveness values of single flows only. Therefore, especially live-streams with high restrictiveness dominate the network selection and network interfaces get occupied early in process from this strategy. This behavior seems to underrate the selection of high throughput networks and causes throughput shortage. As observed, this leads to many unscheduled tokens especially from high bandwidth flows with low restrictiveness like bufferable streaming applications and background traffic. A better approach could use a collaborative throughput demand assessment to select networks based on peek demands. However, this collaborative assessment also requires new decision models for arising questions including: Which flows should share a medium in a time slot?

For ONS and TP, monetary cost contributes to the strategy of opportunistic respectively explicit time selection. We suppose that its overperformance for the two schedulers correlates with the number of unscheduled chunks. Since less chunks are scheduled from both strategies, the overall transmission cost drops as well. In NS, this effect is dominated by a much worse network selection due to the lack of time selection. The rising impact over time can be explained by the nature of the scheduler. NS assigns tokens to the best matching network available as early as possible. If suiting, cheaper networks are available at a later point in time, the optimization potential rises but stays unused by NS. Therefore, monetary cost impact rises with increasing scenario size for NS.

9. CONCLUSION

We hypothesized, that in rapidly changing network environments, time selection within network selection has a notable impact on

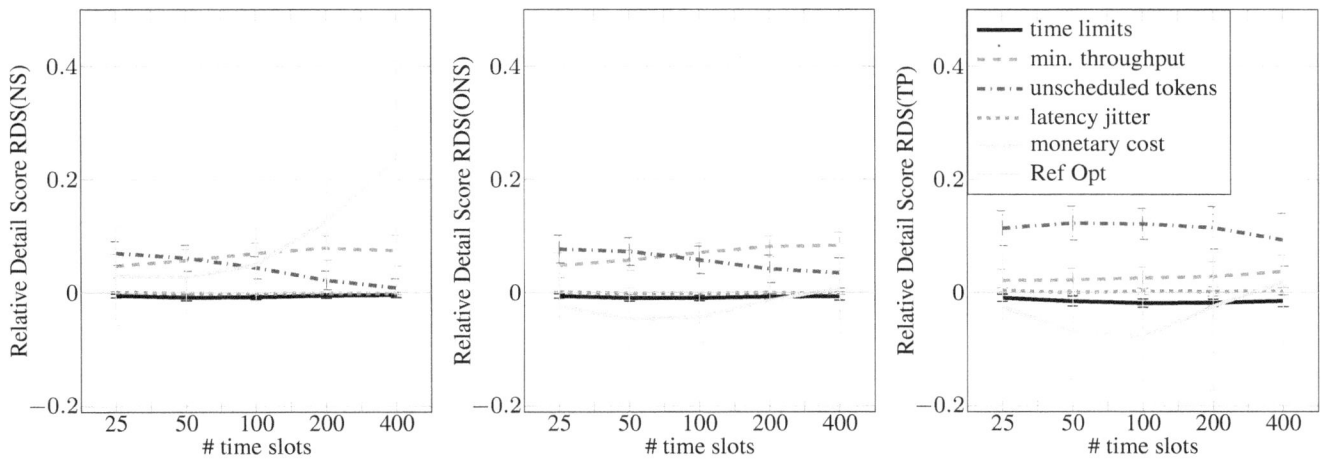

Figure 8: Relative Detail Scores (RDS) over scenario size for NS (left), ONS (center), TP (right)

user-perceived network performance. To the best of our knowledge, time selection and network selection have only been considered separately so far. To investigate our hypothesis, we define a rating scheme able to assess joint network and time selection. Our novel schedule rating scheme assesses application QoS-requirement satisfaction and provides an innovative throughput model, which integrates the impact of bursty data transfer. This novel rating scheme is flexible enough to model extensive application QoS requirements, network characteristics and user preferences. It acts as a tool to investigate our initial hypothesis and is the first contribution of this work.

To approach our second contribution, the time-impact analysis on network selection for mobile nodes, we present three heuristic schedulers, which differ in their strategy of time selection. Two of them follow state-of-the-art approaches with classical and opportunistic network selection. The third explicitly integrates time selection into network selection. We use our novel rating model to investigate the impact of time on network selection on these three schedulers. We furthermore present how to apply the new tools to analyze weaknesses of schedulers. As result, we observe a strong impact of 26% respectively 18% of improvement when using the joint selection instead of the classical respectively an opportunistic approach. This confirms our initial hypothesis. This new insight reveals a path to exploit new potentials of network usage optimization for mobile nodes: a paradigm change from classical network selection strategies towards joint network and time selection.

10. REFERENCES

[1] F. Bari and V. C. M. Leung. Automated Network Selection in a Heterogeneous Wireless Network Environment. *IEEE Network*, 21(1), 2007.

[2] N. Bui and J. Widmer. Mobile Network Resource Optimization under Imperfect Prediction. In *IEEE International Symposium on a World of Wireless, Mobile and Multimedia Networks (WoWMoM)*, 2015.

[3] Ericsson. Mobility Report. Technical report, 2016.

[4] ETSI. *TS 124 312 v13.3.0: Access Network Discovery and Selection Function (ANDSF)*. 2016.

[5] K. Johnsson and D. Cox. An adaptive cross-layer scheduler for improved QoS support of multiclass data services on wireless systems. *IEEE Journal on Selected Areas in Communications*, 23(2), 2005.

[6] Z. Lu and G. D. Veciana. Optimizing Stored Video Delivery For Mobile Networks : The Value of Knowing the Future. In *Proc. of IEEE International Conference on Computer Communications (INFOCOM)*, 2013.

[7] I. Malanchini, M. Cesana, and N. Gatti. Network Selection and Resource Allocation Games for Wireless Access Networks. *IEEE Transactions on Mobile Computing*, 12(12), 2013.

[8] K. R. Rao, Z. S. Bojkovic, and B. M. Bakmaz. Network Selection in Heterogeneous Environment : A Step toward Always Best Connected and Served. In *Proc. of International Conference on Telecommunication in Modern Satellite, Cable and Broadcasting Services (TELSIKS)*, 2013.

[9] T. Rueckelt, D. Burgstahler, D. Böhnstedt, and R. Steinmetz. MoVeNet : Mobility Management for Vehicular Networking. In *Proc. of ACM International Symposium on Mobility Management and Wireless Access (MobiWAC)*, 2016.

[10] T. Rueckelt, D. Burgstahler, F. Englert, C. Gottron, and S. Zöller. A Concept for Vehicle Internet Connectivity for Non-Safety Applications. In *Proc. of IEEE Local Computer Networks Conference (LCN)*, 2014.

[11] T. Rueckelt, F. Jomrich, D. Burgstahler, D. Böhnstedt, and R. Steinmetz. Publish-Subscribe-Based Control Mechanism for Scheduling Integration in Mobile IPv6. In *Proc. of IEEE Local Computer Networks Conference (LCN)*, 2015.

[12] Sandvine. Global Internet Phenomena Asia-Pacific & Europe. Technical report, 2015.

[13] R. Trestian, O. Ormond, and G.-M. Muntean. Game Theory-Based Network Selection: Solutions and Challenges. *IEEE Communications Surveys & Tutorials*, 14(4), 2012.

[14] L. Wang and G.-S. G. Kuo. Mathematical Modeling for Network Selection in Heterogeneous Wireless Networks - A Tutorial. *IEEE Communications Surveys & Tutorials*, 15(1), 2013.

[15] Q. Wu, S. Member, Z. Du, S. Member, and P. Yang. Traffic-Aware Online Network Selection in Heterogeneous Wireless Networks. *IEEE Transactions on Vehicular Technology*, 65(1), 2016.

[16] K.-K. Yap, T.-Y. Huang, Y. Yiakoumis, S. Chinchali, N. McKeown, and S. Katti. Scheduling Packets over Multiple Interfaces While Respecting User Preferences. In *Proc. of ACM Conference on Emerging Networking Experiments and Technologies (CoNEXT)*, 2013.

Evaluating Video Dissemination in Realistic Urban Vehicular Ad-Hoc Networks

Cristhian Iza-Paredes
Network Engineering Dept.
Universitat Politècnica de
Catalunya (UPC)
Barcelona, Spain
cristhian.iza@entel.upc.edu

Ahmad Mohamad
Mezher
Network Engineering Dept.
Universitat Politècnica de
Catalunya (UPC)
Barcelona, Spain
ahmad.mezher@entel.upc.edu

Mónica Aguilar Igartua
Network Engineering Dept.
Universitat Politècnica de
Catalunya (UPC)
Barcelona, Spain
monica.aguilar@entel.upc.edu

ABSTRACT

Video content delivery for vehicular ad hoc networks (VANETs) is envisioned to be of high benefit for road safety, traffic management as well as for providing value-added vehicle services. In this paper, we evaluate five existing dissemination mechanisms in a realistic urban scenario. We also propose RCP+ as a renovated mechanism for adaptive video streaming over VANETs. RCP+ is a cross layer dissemination mechanism for video safety messages that specifically addresses urban scenarios with zero infrastructure support. Through simulations, we compare our proposal with other distributed dissemination mechanisms. The performance evaluation shows that our proposal mechanism is more suitable for video transmission in realistic urban scenarios. The results also indicate that a modified frame coding approach provides many opportunities for multimedia services.

CCS Concepts

•Networks → Cross-layer protocols; Network simulations; Mobile ad hoc networks;

Keywords

Vehicular Ad hoc NETworks; H.265 encoded video; Video dissemination; Safety messages

1. INTRODUCTION

VANETs are a type of mobile ad-hoc networks wherein the network topology changes dynamically due to the high mobility of vehicles. The most promising application of VANET is road safety. Several operational tests have demonstrated the feasibility and effectiveness of this service. However, there are still many challenges to integrate wireless communication between vehicles.

When a car accident or incident is detected, a real–time SOS alert could be automatically generated and propagated

MSWiM '16, November 13 - 17, 2016, Malta, Malta

© 2016 Copyright held by the owner/author(s). Publication rights licensed to ACM.
ISBN 978-1-4503-4502-6/16/11. . . $15.00

DOI: http://dx.doi.org/10.1145/2988287.2989176

to inform the vehicles about the incident as well as to the appropriate emergency centers. The information can include vehicle speed, accelerator position, airbag deployment times, whether the brakes were applied, if seatbelts were worn, engine speed, steering angles, GPS location, and a few video information seconds before the crash. This type of information is spatio-temporally sensitive, which implies that the location and timing of the incident have to be taken into consideration. Supporting video transmission over VANETs is an attractive feature for many applications. In this paper, we are interested in investigating the topic of supporting video transmission over VANETs in safety applications using Vehicle to Vehicle (V2V) communications.

The main contributions of the paper are three. First, we propose a cooperative forwarding mechanism, so a set of forwarder vehicles are selected with regard to two metrics: Distance and Link Quality. Second, we use a smart algorithm able to give each metric a proper weight depending on a defined strategy. Third, we conduct simulations using real video traces to evaluate the performance of the proposed solution. The results show that the proposal can improve the perceived video quality.

The rest of the paper is organized as follows: Section 2 describes the features of our proposal. Section 3 discusses the performance evaluation and includes the results of our analysis. Finally, conclusions and future work are drawn in Section 4.

2. PROTOCOL DESCRIPTION

In this section, the design details of RCP+ will be presented. The key idea of RCP+ is to optimally select the next forwarder vehicles based on the information of the stage and an estimate of the congestion of the communication channel.

2.1 RCP+ Adaptive Video Streaming Scheme

The adaptive video stream scheme RPC+ includes three main modules: neighbor discovery, relay selection, and video quality strategy.

2.1.1 Neighbor discovery

The neighbor discovery mechanism estimates the local topology by monitoring periodic hello updates received from one hop neighbors. Each vehicle periodically announces its status to all its one-hop neighbors by broadcasting a hello packet. These packets carry the current location of the node which is acquired from the GPS. The periodic broadcasting of hello packets is a default operation provided in the IEEE 802.11p protocol for service announcements. Moreover, each vehicle maintains a neighbor table. It records the status of its one-hop neighbors by listening to hello messages within its coverage range. The recent hello time field records the time when a recent hello packet from a neighbor is received. If the elapsed time has a duration twice the length of one hello interval, that neighbor is supposed to be moving away and is removed from the neighbor table.

2.1.2 Relay selection

Relaying is an approach assigning the duty of forwarding a message to specific node or nodes that satisfy some criteria. The protocol developed by Zemouri [1] introduces the selection of the next forwarders which is performed in a decentralised manner, as each receiver of a safety message calculates a probability, which will determine its Backoff period (i.e., waiting time before retransmitting the received message) according to the following formula:

$$WT = CW \cdot (1 - p) + \delta \qquad (1)$$

where WT is the Backoff value, CW is the contention window multiplied by the time slot, p is the calculated probability, and δ is a random value in microseconds, smaller than one time slot. The vehicle with the shortest waiting time will forward the message first. If a vehicle overhears the same message before the end of its waiting time, it will consider it as an acknowledgment for the last message it received and will drop out the retransmission process. Note that the vehicle having the highest probability will be assigned the shortest Backoff period. Inspired by this proposal, we have adapted the calculation of probability as a function that combines several parameters in our framework of simulation. Unlike the work developed by Zemouri [1] and based in our previous work [2], we add an algorithm to compute the weights of the Distance factor (D) and the Link Quality factor (LQ) as a function of the variation of the values of the normalized metrics with respect to the average of those values. This gives proper weights to each metric.

We obtain the retransmission probability as a weighted sum of the Distance factor (D) and the Link Quality factor (LQ). It is calculated as follows:

$$p = LQ \cdot W_{P_1} + D \cdot W_{P_2} \qquad (2)$$

where LQ is the Link Quality factor, D is the Distance factor and W_{P_1}, W_{P_2} are the computed weights. LQ and D are factors described in Eq. 3 and Eq. 7 respectively.

The Link Quality factor (LQ): It is a function of the signal quality (sq), the channel quality (cq) and the collision probability (cp).

$$LQ = sq \cdot W_{Q_1} + cq \cdot (1 - cp) \cdot W_{Q_2} \qquad (3)$$

The **signal quality** (sq) aims at ensuring the integrity of the received message, and it is calculated as follows:

$$sq = \begin{cases} \max(0, S \cdot (1 - \frac{1}{SNR}) \cdot (1 - V)) & \text{, if } SNR > 0 \\ S & \text{, otherwise} \end{cases} \qquad (4)$$

where V is the ratio between the relative velocity and the maximum velocity allowed, SNR is the ratio between the

signal power and the noise intensity. S is the received signal strength is bounded by 1 and it is defined using the following:

$$S = \begin{cases} \min(1, \frac{RSS - RSS_{\text{th}}}{RSS_{\max} - RSS_{\text{th}}}) & \text{, if } RSS \geq RSS_{\text{th}} \\ 0 & \text{, otherwise} \end{cases} \qquad (5)$$

where RSS is the received signal strength, RSS_{th} is a threshold below which the received signal is considered too weak and $RSS_{\max}$ is the maximum value of the received signal strength.

The **collision probability** (cp) is an estimation of the likelihood of a collision occurrence if the message is forwarded by the receiver vehicle. It is calculated using the channel occupancy time (co) and a fixed windows time (tw) in which the channel is observed.

The **channel quality** (cq) estimates the state of the channel around the receiver before and at the time of the reception of the emergency message and it is calculated using the Number of Successful Transmissions (nst) and the Number of Overall Transmissions (not).

$$cp = \frac{co}{tw} \qquad cq = \begin{cases} \frac{nst}{not} & \text{, if } not > 0 \\ 0 & \text{, otherwise} \end{cases} \qquad (6)$$

The Distance factor (D): Thanks to the information from the GPS, the receiver vehicle can know the distance to the next nearest intersection Dri. The information provided by neighbor discovery allows to calculate the distance between the transmitter and receiver Dsr. If Dri is greater than the maximum range of transmission $R_{\max}$, the distance factor (D) is calculated as the ratio between them. With this, the furthest vehicle from the sender is assigned the highest distance factor without taking into account the distance to the next intersection. This case is usual in highways where the intersections are at a greater distance. On the other hand, when we consider an urban scenario, it is clear that intersections exist in the range of transmission of a vehicle, so the distance factor D is calculated as a function of the next nearest intersection Dri. With this, the closer the vehicle is to the intersection, the higher the distance factor assigned to it will be. All previous analysis is summarized in Eq. (7).

$$D = \begin{cases} \frac{Dsr}{R_{\max}} & \text{, if } Dri > R_{\max} \\ 1 - \frac{Dri}{Dri + 1} & \text{, otherwise} \end{cases} \qquad (7)$$

where Dsr is the relative distance between source s and receptor vehicle r, Dri is the relative distance between vehicle r and the next nearest intersection, and $R_{\max}$ is the maximum transmission range.

Algorithm to update the weights of the metrics. We proposed in [2] an algorithm to compute the weights of the metrics as a function of the variation of the values of the normalized metrics with respect to the average of those values. For the calculation of the weights in Eq. (2), let us denote R as the variation made in each T_{hello} seconds (each i iteration) for each metric such as:

$$R = \begin{cases} R_1 = \left| \frac{LQ_i - A_{LQ}}{LQ_i} \right| \\ R_2 = \left| \frac{D_i - A_D}{D_i} \right| \end{cases} \qquad (8)$$

where LQ_i and D_i are the current value for each metric in each T_{hello} seconds, A_{LQ} and A_D are the average value for each metric. All values entries are maintained based on their age using a timer T, which can be considered as an *age threshold*: below the threshold T, the information is considered to be up-to-date, whereas any value of the metrics set older than T are discarded. After that, we have a vector $R = [R_1; R_2]$. Suppose that the maximum value found in vector R is $[R_{1max}; R_{2max}]$. Now, we bound vector R to be between 0 and 1 and this new vector is named S. Therefore, the new normalized vector weights for the metrics is W_P.

$$S = \begin{cases} S_1 = \frac{R_1}{R_{1max}} \\ S_2 = \frac{R_2}{R_{2max}} \end{cases} \qquad W_P = \begin{cases} W_{P_1} = \frac{S_1}{S_1+S_2} \\ W_{P_2} = \frac{S_2}{S_1+S_2} \end{cases} \qquad (9)$$

The same procedure is applied for the calculation of the weights W_{Q_1} and W_{Q_2} in Eq. (3).

2.1.3 Video quality strategy

A key component to efficiently transport video with its stringent playout deadlines and bursty traffic characteristics, is using the most–efficient current encoding format. High Efficiency Video Coding (HEVC) is a new Standard for video compression developed by the ISO/IEC Moving Picture Experts Group and ITU-T Video Coding Experts Group (VCEG) [3]. According to some previous studies [4] [5], H.265 allows to transport higher quality videos with better resolution at the same bit rates of previous generation codecs, reducing overall cost of video delivery while improving on the quality of experience for consumer.

We consider a trace video encoded in All Intra mode. In this case, every frame of the video sequence is encoded as an I frame i.e. it is coded without any motion estimation/-compensation. As reported in the HEVC standard [3], AI mode is a fast coding process because no time is wasted in motion estimation. Even though this mode gets lower compression rates, B-frames introduces delays in the encoding process, and thus they are generally not used in low-delay applications such as road safety applications.

3. PERFORMANCE EVALUATION

In this section a performance assessment of dissemination protocols is carried out by means of simulations.

3.1 Simulation setup

We select VEINS [6] and INET [7] frameworks which integrate OMNeT++ [8] and SUMO [9] due to these important features: Fully-detailed models of IEEE 802.11p, IEEE 1609.4 DSRC/WAVE network layers [10], models for the Internet protocols: RTP, UDP, IP, and suppor for realistic maps. For our evaluation, we used the well-known *Highway* video stream, which is publicly available at [11]. It is the CIF (Common Intermediate Format) version which contains 2000 frames and it was encode with H.265/HEVC [3]. Constant Rate Factor (CRF=28) was selected and used to control quality level. To carry out the performance of the analysed dissemination schemes, we have provided each run with a different random scenario that fulfills the requirements of the study. For each point in all figures we have calculated the average from 10 simulation runs. This let us obtain a standard error less than 5% in a 95% confidence interval.

3.2 Scenario Description

We focus on the immediate consequences of an accident in an urban region of the city of Berlin, Germany ($1.8\ km^2$). The crashed vehicle starts to generate and transmit a real–time SOS alert in order to inform the vehicles in the network about the incident and to the appropriate emergency centers (e.g. 112 or 911). The information include a short video information of the last 80 seconds before the crash. We consider a real street environment which is imported from OpenStreetMap [12]. A set of 4 RSUs has been strategically located at 20m, 300m, 600m, 1200m and 1500m from-scene, and the distance between the RSUs and the road is 3m. RSUs are traffic sinks used to measure the quality of the received video.

3.3 Metrics

In this paper, we use two performance metrics to evaluate the quality of video transmitted over VANETs: Frame Delivery Ratio and PSNR.

Frame Delivery Ratio: It is defined as a ratio between the number of frames delivered and the total number of frames received during a time interval T

PSNR (Peak Signal-to-Noise Ratio): It is an objective metric used to assess the application-level QoS of video transmissions. PSNR measures the error between the reconstructed image and the original one, frame by frame.

3.4 Simulation Results

In this section we present some representative simulation results. Our goal is to study the capability dissemination of RCP+ under urban realistic scenarios. To do so, we have implemented the code of our RCP+ protocol. We select four state-of-the-art protocols for comparison, namely:

Road Casting Protocol (RCP) [1]: it is a cross-layer dissemination protocol for safety messages that specifically addresses urban scenarios.

Flooding [4]: We use two flooding mechanisms custom identified as *Counter* and *Distance*. The main idea of *Counter* is receiving C copies of a packet to stop rebroadcasting in a limited time *MaxTime*. In the *Distance* scheme, the time a node waits *MaxTime* before resending is inversely proportional to the minimum distance *MinDistance* between the original node and the resending node. We select the best flooding configuration based on the results presented in [4].

UV-CAST [13]: it is a protocol that specifically addresses urban scenarios with zero infrastructure support. It combines: (i) a suppression technique for dense networks that gives higher priority to vehicles near intersection points; (ii) and a gift-wrapping algorithm to select vehicles to store, carry, and forward messages.

Slotted 1-Persistence [14]: it is a mechanism of suppression of broadcast storms. The broadcast coverage is spatially divided into regions (slots), and a shorter waiting time is assigned to the nodes located in the farthest region. Each node uses the GPS information to calculate the waiting time to retransmit.

In a first set of experiments, we evaluated the performance of the frame delivery ratio. Figure. 1a shows the frame delivery rate for low vehicles density: 60 vehicles/km^2. Low density directly affects the ability of the algorithms to disseminate. In fact, only the RSU [0] located 20 meters from the accident, received the complete trace. In the RSU[1] located 300 meters from the accident, RCP+ reaches an aver-

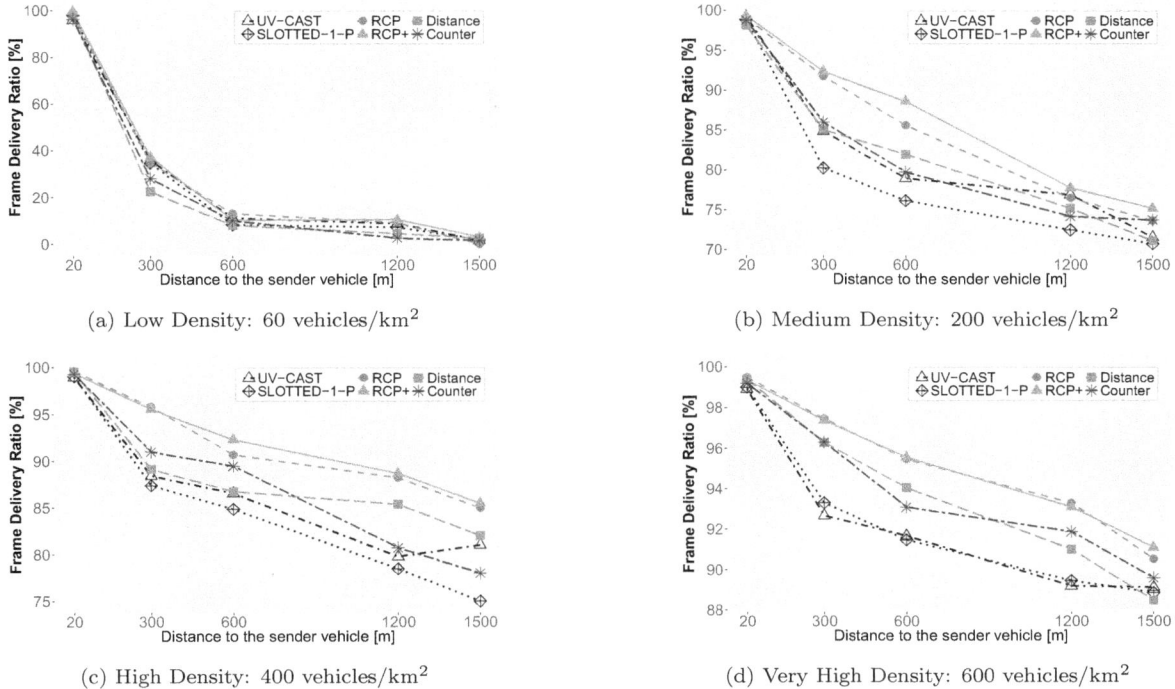

(a) Low Density: 60 vehicles/km^2

(b) Medium Density: 200 vehicles/km^2

(c) High Density: 400 vehicles/km^2

(d) Very High Density: 600 vehicles/km^2

Figure 1: Received Packets with 95% confidence intervals for different network densities in an urban scenario

age maximum rate of 35%. In the 600, 1200 and 1500 meters any protocol exceeds 15% of received frames. This result is expected, because the urban scenario shows more hostility in the packet loss due to the existence of buildings. Also, dynamic topology networks in VANET causes temporary disconnections, interrupting the dissemination and compromising the delivery of the frames. Figure. 1b shows the frame delivery rate for medium vehicles density: 200 vehicles/km^2. All the tested schemes are able to deliver more than a 70% of the frames at a distance as far as 1500 m.It is important to remember that RCP+ computes the weights of the Distance factor (D) and the Link Quality factor (LQ) as a function of the variation of the values of the normalized metrics with respect to the average of those values. This is evident in Figures 1b and 1c where the flow of vehicles allow RCP+ adapt to the changing traffic density. On the contrary, in Figure. 1d, the performance of RCP+ is similar to RCP mainly because the channel is already congested and our adaptive algorithm almost not affect the performance of the protocol. Figure 1c shows the results for the high vehicles density: 400 vehicles/km^2. In this case, we observed a minimum frame delivery rate of 85% for the RCP+ against 75%, 78%, 81%, 82% and 84% , for the Slotted-1-P, counter, UV-CAST, distance,and the RCP schemes, respectively. Low frames loss in RCP+ is thanks to a more clever use of the medium. We also notice that at a very high density level: 600 vehicles/km^2, the frame delivery ratio for the flooding schemes, does not exceed 92% of frames at a distance as far as 1500 m. In fact, at a very high density level, the number of collisions increases exponentially. This retrains the progress of the packets, and consequently the information will reach closer vehicles only.

As a next step, we evaluate PSNR. We assume that in case an individual frame was lost, the decoder would display the last successfully received frame. So if a frame is

dropped, we need to compare the source frame to the previous streamed frame. Next, we decoded each frame into its YUV[1] channels. The PSNR of the channels need to be calculated independently. We just use the Y channel, as it is the most important. From Figures. 2b, 2c and 2d, we can see that schemes: Counter, Distance, Slotted-1-P, and UV-CAST play worst, and RCP+ protocol plays best. The simulation result interprets that our proposal can better handle the video transmission. This is mainly because the RCP+ does not relay only on the maintained neighboring information but also the estimate of the congestion in the communications channel. Another interesting observation is that in the dense scenario, the average PSNR is also larger than that in sparse scenario. This is not a surprise, since the network is highly connected in the dense scenario, thus the quality of video transmitted in dense traffic scenario is better.

4. CONCLUSIONS

The recent adoption of High Efficiency Video Coding HEVC provides many opportunities for new and improved multimedia services; however there are two major difficulties. First, vehicular networks suffer greater packet loss because of its wireless nature. Second, the digital video has high requirements in terms of resources both the high volume of data handled as computing requirements needed to compress the video to be transmitted. In this paper, we proposed a renovated RCP+, and studied the performance of different schemes under different traffic scenarios. Also, we designed a proposal to update the weight values for metrics in RCP+

---

[1]YUV files contain bitmap image data stored in the YUV format, which splits color across Y, U, and V values. It stores the brightness (luminance) as the Y value, and the color (chrominance) as U and V values.

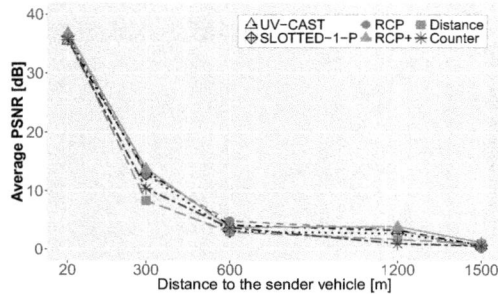

(a) Low Density: 60 vehicles/km^2

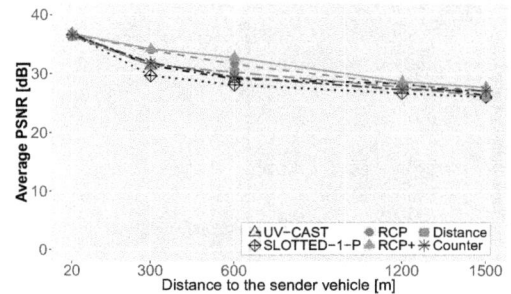

(b) Medium Density: 200 vehicles/km^2

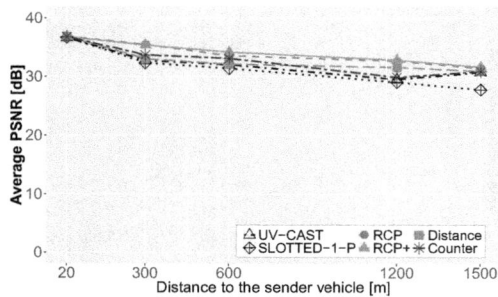

(c) High Density: 400 vehicles/km^2

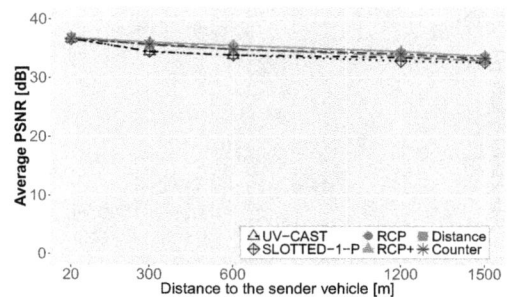

(d) Very High Density: 600 vehicles/km^2

Figure 2: PSNR with 95% confidence intervals for different network densities in an urban scenario

to provide video-streaming services. Simulation results have shown that our solution can make a good video quality in different traffic scenarios. In a future work, we will seek an efficient forwarding mechanism to guarantee enhance video QoE (Quality of Experience) according with VANETs safety applications' requirements.

5. ACKNOWLEDGMENTS

This work was partly supported by the Spanish Government through projects TEC2014-54435-C4-1-R (INcident monitoRing In Smart COmmunities. QoS and Privacy, INRISCO) and AGAUR Information Security Group (ISG) project - 2014 SGR 1504. Cristian Iza Paredes is recipient of a grant from Secretaria Nacional de Educación Superior, Ciencia y Tecnología SENESCYT. Ahmad Mohamad Mezher is a postdoctoral researcher with the Information Security Group in the Department of Network Engineering at the Universitat Politècnica de Catalunya (UPC).

6. REFERENCES

[1] Sofiane Zemouri, Soufiene Djahel, and John Murphy. A fast, reliable and lightweight distributed dissemination protocol for safety messages in urban vehicular networks. *Ad Hoc Networks*, 27:2643, Apr 2015.

[2] Ahmad Mezher, Cristhian Iza Paredes, Carolina Tripp-Barba, and Mónica Aguilar Igartua. A dynamic multimetric weights distribution in a multipath routing protocol using video-streaming services over manets. In *XII Jornadas de Ingeniería Telemática (JITEL 2015): libro de ponencias: del 14 al 16 de octubre de 2015: Palma de Mallorca*, pages 263–270, 2015.

[3] High efficiency video coding (HEVC). https://hevc.hhi.fraunhofer.de/. Accessed: 2016-05-17.

[4] A. Torres, P. Piñol, C. T. Calafate, J. C. Cano, and P. Manzoni. Evaluating H.265 real-time video flooding quality in highway V2V environments. In *Proc. IEEE Wireless Communications and Networking Conf. (WCNC)*, pages 2716–2721, April 2014.

[5] Pablo Piñol, Miguel Martínez-Rach, Otoniel López, and Manuel Pérez Malumbres. Protection of hevc video delivery in vehicular networks with raptorq codes. *The Scientific World Journal*, 2014, 2014.

[6] VEINS, Vehicular network simulations. http://veins.car2x.org. Accessed: 2015-03-22.

[7] INET framework. https://inet.omnetpp.org/. Accessed: 2015-03-22.

[8] OMNeT++, Discrete Event Simulator. http://www.omnetpp.org. Accessed: 2015-03-22.

[9] SUMO – Simulation of Urban MObility. http://goo.gl/uvvD4N. Accessed: 2015-03-22.

[10] IEEE Guide for Wireless Access in Vehicular Environments (WAVE) - Architecture, 2014.

[11] Video trace files. http://trace.eas.asu.edu/yuv/index.html. Accessed: 2016-03-22.

[12] OpenStreetMap. http://www.openstreetmap.org. Accessed: 2015-03-22.

[13] W. Viriyasitavat, O.K. Tonguz, and Fan Bai. Uv-cast: an urban vehicular broadcast protocol. 49(11):116–124, 2011.

[14] N. Wisitpongphan, O.K. Tonguz, J.S. Parikh, P. Mudalige, F. Bai, and V. Sadekar. Broadcast storm mitigation techniques in vehicular ad hoc networks. 14(6):84–94, 2007.

T-SIMn: Towards the High Fidelity Trace-Based Simulation of 802.11n Networks

Ali Abedi
University of Waterloo
ali.abedi@uwaterloo.ca

Andrew Heard
University of Waterloo
asheard@uwaterloo.ca

Tim Brecht
University of Waterloo
brecht@cs.uwaterloo.ca

ABSTRACT

In this paper, we describe the design, implementation and evaluation of a new framework for the trace-based evaluation of 802.11n networks, which we call T-SIMn. We first develop novel techniques for collecting and processing traces for 802.11n networks that incorporate Frame Aggregation (FA). We then demonstrate that the simulator portion of our framework (SIMn) accurately simulates throughput for one, two and three-antenna Physical Layer Data Rates (PL-DRs) in 802.11n with FA. Finally, we evaluate the T-SIMn framework (including trace collection) by collecting traces using an iPhone which is representative of a wide variety of one antenna devices. We show that our framework can be used to accurately simulate these scenarios and we demonstrate the fidelity of SIMn by uncovering problems with our initial evaluation methodology. We expect that the T-SIMn framework will be suitable for easily and fairly comparing algorithms that must be optimized for different and varying 802.11n channel conditions which are challenging to evaluate experimentally. These include rate adaptation, frame aggregation and channel bandwidth adaptation algorithms.

1. INTRODUCTION

With billions of WiFi devices now in use, combined with the rising popularity of high-bandwidth applications such as streaming video, demands on WiFi networks continue to rise. The 802.11n standard introduced several new physical layer features including MIMO, 40 MHz channels, denser modulations, and a shorter guard interval, to increase throughput. We refer to the combination of features as a *rate configuration*. Combinations of these features results in up to 128 different rate configurations. In order to optimize throughput in an 802.11n network, we must choose the rate configuration that results in the best trade-off between Physical Layer Data Rates (PLDRs) and error rates, which is highly dependent on environmental conditions. Because the radio spectrums are shared by WiFi devices included in computers, cell phones and tablets; as well as Bluetooth devices,

wireless keyboards/mice, cordless phones, and microwave ovens, it is challenging to experimentally evaluate and compare the performance of WiFi networks. Therefore, we need new techniques for understanding and evaluating how to best use 802.11n features.

Previously, we proposed a solution [2] that uses traces to capture environmental conditions, rather than models, to simulate 802.11g networks with high fidelity. We expected that extending this solution to 802.11n networks would be relatively simple. However, it turned out that this is actually a very interesting and challenging problem, due to *MAC layer frame aggregation (FA)* in 802.11n. The complications introduced by frame aggregation required a complete redesign of major components of our trace-based simulator. While the faster PLDRs are an important factor in the throughput gains afforded by 802.11n, it is only when they are used in combination with frame aggregation that 802.11n networks achieve significant increases in throughput when compared with 802.11g. Frame Aggregation (FA) allows multiple MAC frames to be combined into a large physical frame so that they can be transmitted and acknowledged as one aggregated packet, which results in the channel being used more efficiently.

To demonstrate the importance of FA, Figure 1 shows the maximum theoretical throughput obtained using the highest PLDRs in 802.11n for one, two and three spatial streams, respectively. Without frame aggregation throughput is limited to about 50 Mbps. However, when aggregating 32 frames, throughput increases to 350 Mbps.

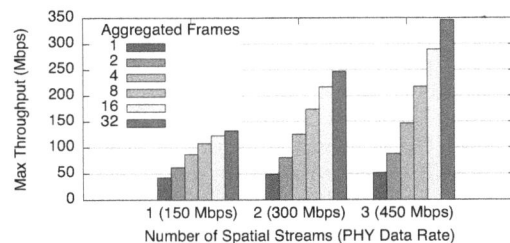

Figure 1: FA: Maximum Theoretical Throughput

Because performance is so heavily dependent on FA, accurate simulation of FA is crucial for T-SIMn to be useful in the study of a range of active research topics. This includes the evaluation of: link adaptation algorithms [15] (which studies physical layer configurations such as rate adaptation [8, 23] and channel bandwidth adaptation [7, 11]) and frame aggregation algorithms [6, 22]. We refer to link adaptation and frame aggregation algorithms collectively as *optimization algorithms*. The contributions of this paper are:

MSWiM '16, November 13-17, 2016, Malta, Malta

© 2016 ACM. ISBN 978-1-4503-4502-6/16/11. . . $15.00

DOI: http://dx.doi.org/10.1145/2988287.2989160

- We design a trace-based simulator (T-SIMn) for the realistic and repeatable performance evaluation of 802.11n networks. We evaluate a prototype implementation of T-SIMn using an iPhone and show that T-SIMn produces highly accurate results.

- Using our framework, we demonstrate that MPDUs within an A-MPDU can experience different error rates which can significantly affect throughput due to the impact losses have on the advancement of the Block-ACK window. We devise a technique for determining and accurately simulating subframe error rates.

- We demonstrate that it is possible to determine the probability of subframe losses within aggregated frames of any length using traces collected with the maximum number of aggregated frames permitted by the rate configuration. We believe this will make it possible to study and fairly compare different FAAs using our framework.

2. BACKGROUND AND RELATED WORK

2.1 Rate Configurations

In 802.11g, a transmission rate can be uniquely identified by the index of the Modulation and Coding Scheme (MCS). This index alone is no longer sufficient to uniquely identify an 802.11n rate, as the transmission rate is now also dependent on the number of Spatial Streams (SSs), the Guard Interval (GI) and the Channel Bandwidth (CB). We refer to this set of parameters as a rate configuration. In the interest of brevity, Figure 2 introduces notation used for describing a rate configuration (sometimes simply referred to as a rate).

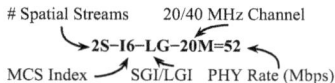

Spatial Streams   20/40 MHz Channel
2S–I6–LG–20M=52
MCS Index   SGI/LGI   PHY Rate (Mbps)

Figure 2: Rate notation

2.2 802.11n Frame Aggregation

Frame aggregation (FA) is a new MAC layer feature in 802.11n that allows multiple frames to be combined to form a larger frame. The 802.11n standard defines two types of frame aggregation: *Aggregated MAC Protocol DATA Unit (A-MPDU)* and *Aggregated MAC Service DATA Unit (A-MPDU)*. These two types of frame aggregation differ by where in the protocol stack aggregation is done. In this paper, we use A-MPDU frame aggregation as it is more widely supported by WiFi devices, including the Atheros devices used in this paper.

By sending multiple MPDUs[1] as an A-MPDU, the *sender* only performs channel sensing, backoff, Distributed Inter-Frame Space (DIFS), Short Inter-Frame Space (SIFS) and wait for an ACK once for the entire set of MPDUs. This results in a greater proportion of time being spent transmitting data, increasing the air time efficiency. The receiver sends back a *Block ACK* which acknowledges all MPDUs at once. In this work, we use MPDU and subframe interchangeably.

2.3 Related Work

Conducting experiments is a common technique for evaluating the performance of WiFi networks. The advantage of this approach is that real-world wireless channel conditions are captured. However, it is challenging to conduct repeatable experiments [3] because channel conditions can vary

---

[1]MAC header + MAC payload (IP packet)

significantly between trials due to many factors, including mobility, changes in the environment (including the movement of people who are nearby), and the presence of WiFi and non-WiFi interferers [5].

Simulation is a common technique for evaluating the performance of 802.11 networks. Since both the physical and MAC layers are simulated in this approach, comparisons are repeatable. Popular 802.11 network simulators include *ns-3* [16], OPNET Modeler [21] (renamed, Riverbed Modeler) and QualNet [18]. Unfortunately, these simulators may not reflect real-world performance due to the challenging nature of simulating wireless signals in the physical environment. WiFi signals are impacted by many factors, including the distance between devices, material types of surrounding objects and walls, wavelength, mobility and many more [20]. These simulators utilize models for signal propagation, error rates and interference and each model must trade-off computational complexity and accuracy [20]. Additionally, the complexity and time varying nature of all of the factors that can affect a frame's fate makes it incredibly challenging to obtain accurate results, especially since models of one environment (e.g., one home) may not necessarily work in another environment (e.g., an office or even a different home). In the case of environments with mobility, this model may change over time. As a result existing simulators like ns-3 suffer from practical limitations (e.g., ns-3 does not support MIMO). Rather than simulating the physical layer, we collect traces to capture the impact of the physical layer on frame fates, allowing us to handle more complex scenarios than can be accurately modeled by traditional simulators.

Emulation is another alternative for evaluating and studying 802.11 networks. The most common approach is to use real WiFi devices connected by wire to a Field-Programmable Gate Array (FPGA) which simulates signal propagation [12]. An emulation testbed by Judd and Steenkiste [13] is one of the most prominent examples of this type of system. As real devices are used, the MAC and parts of the physical layer are *not* simulated. However, signal propagation *is simulated* using the FPGA to alter the signals being transmitted between devices. The major disadvantage of this approach is that realism is again limited by the models used to simulate the physical layer.

To increase the realism of emulators, hybrid approaches using traces to simulate the physical layer and emulation for the MAC layer have also been proposed [13, 24], however these have been limited to 802.11b networks and rely on measurements of Signal-to-Noise Ratio (SNR) to simulate the physical layer. However, the SNR can not be used to accurately predict frame fates [9]. Instead, we rely on traces to directly capture the impact of the physical layer on frame fates and simulate the well-defined MAC layer. This provides an excellent combination of repeatability and fidelity.

T-RATE [2] is our trace-driven framework for evaluating Rate Adaptation Algorithms (RAAs) designed for 802.11g networks. T-RATE eschews the modeling and emulation of wireless channel conditions in favor of traces that capture channel access and channel error rate information. These traces are used to simulate RAAs using channel conditions limited only by the environment in which traces are collected. Despite the high fidelity of T-RATE, it is limited to the evaluation of RAAs in 802.11g networks. In this paper, we design and evaluate T-SIMn, a more general framework for the trace-based evaluation of 802.11n networks. The most prominent and challenging contribution in T-SIMn is the accurate handling of frame aggregation.

3. THE T-SIMN FRAMEWORK

The main goal of T-SIMn is to achieve repeatability and realism when evaluating the performance of 802.11n networks. To achieve this goal, T-SIMn records all channel conditions that affect throughput in a trace and then uses this trace to simulate different 802.11n optimization algorithms such as link adaptation and frame aggregation. As a result, T-SIM can be used to achieve repeatability by using an identical trace to evaluate different algorithms. In addition, it achieves realism since T-SIMn *relies on traces that are subject to and include information related to actual channel conditions rather than using wireless channel models*, which are known to lack realism [14, 17].

To simulate 802.11n networks with high fidelity, we need to accurately compute the transmission time of a frame and consider all factors that can affect throughput. Computing the transmission time for a frame is a relatively easy task and is done very accurately in our simulator by using timing information available in the 802.11n standard (Section 5.2 provides more details). Environmental factors may affect 802.11 channel access (i.e., CSMA/CA) and channel error rate. If a WiFi or non-WiFi device operating at the same frequency is active during channel sensing, it forces a sender device to back off and therefore limits the number of frames that can be sent. If WiFi or non-WiFi devices interfere with the receiver device, the channel error rate may increase. In T-SIMn, to accurately simulate the time required for frame transmission we need to determine: the delay (overhead) imposed by channel sensing (i.e., CSMA/CA), how long it takes to transmit a frame (including ACK reception and DCF mandatory wait times), and whether or not the transmitted frame is received correctly.

T-SIMn uses two phases to simulate 802.11n. The first phase is trace collection, where a log containing the data necessary for accurately simulating an 802.11n experiment is collected. The second phase is simulation, where the trace is used to determine frame fates, transmission delays and throughput. We now explain these two phases.

3.1 Trace Collection

The purpose of trace collection is to capture channel access and channel error rate information (i.e., a trace), for each 802.11n rate configuration. To enable the simulation of any link adaptation and frame aggregation algorithm at time t, T-SIMn must be able to simulate the transmission of an A-MPDU of any length sent with any chosen rate configuration. This requirement makes trace collection challenging, since at time t, only one particular rate configuration with a specific A-MPDU length can be transmitted. Therefore, no information is available at that time concerning the other combinations of rate configuration and frame lengths.

To address this problem we have designed a trace collection technique that samples all rate configurations in a round robin fashion. After each transmitted frame, the *sender* switches to the next rate in the set; wrapping back around after all rates have been sampled. This round-robin cycling continues for the duration of the trace collection. If we sample all rate configurations within the time a channel is considered stationary. (i.e., the channel coherence time), all configurations experience the same channel conditions.

During simulation, to obtain the error rate of a rate configuration at time t, we compute an average error rate for that configuration over a time window centered at t.

If the error rates of the MPDUs within an aggregated frame are identical, we could disable frame aggregation during trace collection and simulate aggregated frames of any size, by simply applying the error rate of (non-aggregated) collected frames to all MPDUs in an A-MPDU. However, a recent study [6] shows that the frame error rate of the MPDUs within an A-MPDU are *not identical*. More specifically, they show that the frame error rate of early MPDUs (i.e., closer to the physical header) are lower than MPDUs that appear latter in the A-MPDU. Although we confirm that individual MPDUs have different error rates, we find patterns other than the increasing error rate pattern (observed in [6]). We discuss these findings in greater detail in Section 5.4.1. Note that this problem was not an issue in our 802.11g framework since 802.11g does not support frame aggregation. One might imagine that a solution would be, during trace collection, to attempt to sample all combinations of A-MPDUs from length 1 (i.e., no frame aggregation) to the maximum number of MPDUs allowed in an A-MPDU. Since this procedure would be required for all rate configurations, it becomes impossible to sample all combinations in a sufficiently short period of time (i.e., within the channel coherence window). As a result, we design a methodology that infers the fate of MPDUs in an A-MPDU from a longer A-MPDU. Therefore, during trace collection, we only need to sample the longest possible A-MPDU for each rate configuration and infer the FERs of any shorter A-MPDU for that rate from the longer A-MPDU.

In order to record the delay imposed by channel access (CSMA/CA), we use Cycle Counter Information (CCI) reported by a modified Ath9k driver as explained in detail in Section 5.3. These counters help us infer the delay caused by WiFi and non-WiFi devices when performing channel sensing. We modify the Ath9k driver to print a log entry after each aggregated frame (A-MPDU) transmission has completed, which includes the fate of each MPDU and the CCI.

3.2 Simulation

The trace processing phase uses a trace to simulate different optimization algorithms. The simulator component of our framework (called SIMn) performs a time based simulation using a trace, where the *sender* saturates the link to the *receiver* by sending as many aggregated frames as possible.

Figures 3 illustrates the work flow of SIMn. Solid lines represent the execution flow of the simulator, with the direction being indicated by a closed (i.e., filled) arrow. Dashed lines indicate the flow of data, with the recipient of the data being indicated with an open arrow. As depicted in Figure 3, a simulation in SIMn proceeds using an event loop, starting at time $t = 0$, that performs the following steps:

1. Check the collected trace for unprocessed WiFi delays that occurred before time t. If WiFi delays exist, t is incremented by the duration of the delay. This is repeated until all WiFi delays that have occurred before t have been processed.

2. Determine any non-WiFi delays that occur at time t and increment t by the duration of the delay.

3. If there are fewer than two aggregate frames (one in transmission and one queued), create an aggregate frame and add it to the queue.

4. Compute the time to transmit the A-MPDU.

5. Determine the fate of each subframe i in the aggregate frame using the Subframe Index Error Rate (SFIER) at time t, rate r and index i. SFIERs are discussed in detail in Section 5.4.1. Failed subframes are rescheduled for retransmission if the retry limit has not been exceeded.

This process repeats until the simulation time is equal to the duration of the collected trace. To create an aggregated frame we first compute the maximum allowed size of the aggregated frame (detailed in Section 5.2.2). Then MPDUs are added to an A-MPDU in a loop until the maximum size is reached. The MPDUs are either new frames arriving from an application or failed MPDUs that are waiting for retransmission. Rescheduled frames are given priority when forming aggregate frames.

To determine the fate of a subframe with index i that needs to be sent at simulated time t with rate configuration r, T-SIMn considers all samples for the rate r and subframe index i in the averaging window (t - window_size/2) ms to (t + window_size/2) ms, from the collected trace. The averaging window should be less than the channel coherence time for the environment so that channel conditions are relatively constant with respect to the frames being used to determine the fate of packets at time t. Channel coherence time depends on many factors (e.g., the speed of movement and channel frequency). In indoor environments at walking speeds channel coherence time is reported to be approximately 200 ms for the 2.4 GHz band [19] and 100 ms for the 5 GHz band [4]. Because all experiments in this paper use the 5 GHz band, we use an averaging window of 200 ms (i.e., $t - 100$ ms to $t + 100$ ms), which corresponds to a 100 ms coherence time. Our evaluation in Section 6 shows that an averaging window of 200 ms produces accurate results in our mobile environment at walking speeds, when performing round-robin trace collection with 1 antenna. However, this parameter can be easily tailored to the environment.

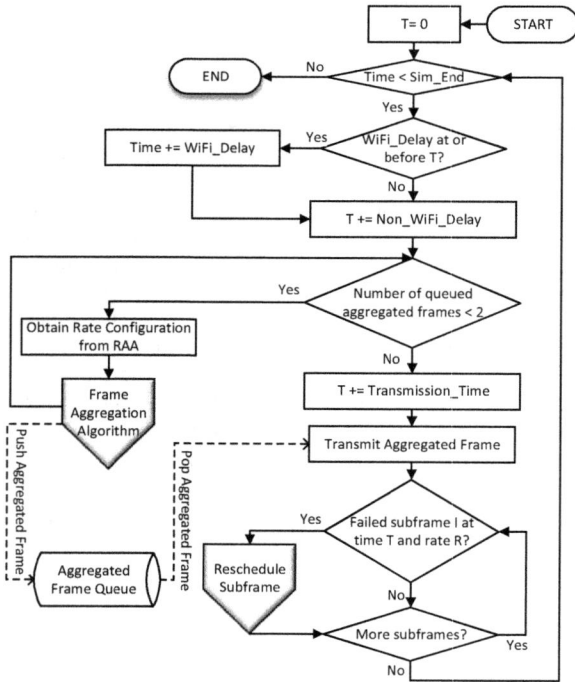

Figure 3: T-SIMn Simulation Flowchart.

3.3 Frame Aggregation Notation

To concisely describe limits on the length of an aggregated frame (i.e., the number of subframes) for a particular rate configuration, we introduce the notation:

$FA_{(SIM \mid COL)}$=*maximum number of aggregated subframes*

For example, FA_{SIM}=16 means that the *simulator* is allowed to aggregate a maximum of 16 subframes (we omit rate configuration information; it is not needed for our purposes). The number of subframes in a specific aggregated frame may be further limited by the Block-Ack window discussed in detail in Section 5.2.2. Similarly, FA_{COL}=32 means that the driver was limited to aggregating a maximum of 32 subframes *during trace collection*. We use the notation FA_{SIM}=MAX and FA_{COL}=MAX to mean that we impose no restrictions, beyond those in the 802.11n standard and the Ath9k driver (i.e., 32 MPDUs), on the aggregated frame length during simulation and trace collection, respectively. Lastly, FA_{SIM}=FA_{COL} means the limits on the aggregated frame are the same during simulation and trace collection.

4. TESTBED

Our test bed is located in cubicles in a large room, as well as some separate offices on a university campus. Our WiFi devices include two desktop computers housing identical TP-Link TL-WDN4800 PCIe cards, an Apple MacBook Pro (Retina, 15-inch, Mid 2012) and an Apple iPhone 6. The TP-Link cards use an Atheros AR9380 chipset, while the MacBook and iPhone use Broadcom BCM4331 and BCM4339, respectively. Although all five devices are dual-band (2.4 and 5 GHz), we limit our experiments to the 5 GHz band because the Apple devices used in some experiments do not support 40 MHz channel bandwidths in the 2.4 GHz spectrum. Except for the iPhone 6 which contains only one antenna, all devices contain three antennas supporting three spatial streams in a 3x3:3 MIMO configuration.

We create an 802.11n Access Point (AP) using hostapd and collect traces while that system sends packets using our modified Ath9k driver. Although the AP could be used as the *sender* or the *receiver*, we use the computer designated as the AP as the *sender* in all experiments. The major advantage of this approach is that there are fewer requirements imposed on the *receiver*, which does not need to be capable of creating an AP. In addition, the *receiver* does not need to use a modified Ath9k driver and, as a result, can be any 802.11n-capable device that runs Iperf3; this includes a wide variety of devices, even an iPhone. We create a network between the AP (*sender*) and a client, which acts as a receiver. To collect a trace the *sender* saturates the link by sending as many 1,470 byte UDP frames as possible using Iperf3. Unless otherwise noted, we aggregate the maximum number of subframes (i.e., FA_{COL}=MAX).

We use the second desktop as a *receiver* in the stationary experiments. It is located less than 1 meter from the AP with line of sight so we can collect error-free traces needed for some experiments. The MacBook and iPhone are used for mobile experiments. When it is necessary to minimize the amount of uncontrolled WiFi interference, we use channels in the 5 GHz band that are unused by other APs in the vicinity. We monitor all channels for interference using an AirMagnet Spectrum XT spectrum analyzer. For generating controlled non-WiFi interference we use an RF Explorer Handheld Signal Generator (RFE6GEN) that we control programmatically using a USB connection.

5. T-SIMN DETAILS AND EVALUATION

5.1 Experimental Methodologies

To evaluate the simulator component of the T-SIMn we use a technique that minimizes our reliance on the trace collection methodology. We conduct an experiment using a constant rate configuration which produces a constant rate configuration trace (i.e., the trace collection is also an experiment). We then use SIMn to simulate a constant rate configuration experiment (for the same rate configuration) using the collected trace. Because the simulated experiment uses the same rate configuration as the conducted experiment, simulated throughput should match throughput obtained during the conducted experiment if the simulator is accurate. There are two major advantages to this methodology: (1) It does not require experiments to be repeatable since the experiment produces a trace that is used by SIMn to simulate an experiment with exactly the same conditions and environment as the conducted experiment (i.e., the conducted experiment *is* trace collection). (2) Constant rate traces provide many samples in each averaging window, which allows us to study the accuracy of SIMn without being limited by the collected trace.

Together these properties allow us to expect, and check for, close matches between experimental and simulated throughput when evaluating SIMn. Recall that the simulation *is not simply a trace playback* as discussed in Section 3.2. Our plots include 95% confidence intervals and we consider a match to be obtained if we have overlapping confidence intervals for experimental and simulated throughput over each window of time. Note that in some plots the confidence intervals are so tight that they may not be visible. In this section, all experiments are conducted on channels free of any uncontrolled inference.

5.2 Computing Transmission Duration

Determining the time spent transmitting a frame depends on the combination of physical layer features being used (i.e., the rate configuration) and, at the MAC layer, the number of frames and method used for frame aggregation. We now describe relevant simulator details and evaluate the fidelity of the simulator with respect to these 802.11n features.

5.2.1 Physical Layer Features

The 802.11n protocol introduces many new physical layer features, namely Multiple Spatial Streams (SSs), Short Guard Intervals (SGIs), Channel Bonding and Dual-Band support. Despite being numerous, these features are relatively simple to simulate because how they influence the transmission time is either specified in or can be easily determined from the 802.11n standard. We now evaluate SIMn's ability to accurately replicate the timings, and consequently the throughput, of these 802.11n physical layer features.

Experiment Setup and Description: We create a network between the Access Point (AP) (*sender*) and the desktop client (*receiver*). We use the stationary client because it can reliably obtain error-free traces due to its close proximity and line of sight. We collect 100 second traces for the rate configurations 1S-I4-LG-20M=39, 1S-I4-SG-40M=90, 2S-I4-SG-40M=180 and 3S-I4-SG-40M=270. We choose these rate configurations because they cover both long and short Guard Intervals (GIs); 20 and 40 MHz Channel Bandwidths (CBs); as well as one, two and three spatial streams. A Modula-

tion and Coding Scheme Index (MCS index) of 4 is chosen because it is the highest index with which we could reliably obtain error-free traces. We use highest rates possible because discrepancies between experimental and simulated throughput are more likely to be seen at high rates than low rates. In this experiment, we aggregate as many MPDUs as possible during trace collection and simulation.

Experiment Results: In Figure 4, we plot pairs of throughput measurements, simulated and experimental, for each of the collected rate configurations. For all four rates, the simulated throughput tightly matches the experimental throughput. This suggests that SIMn accurately handles rate configurations using different physical layer transmission features. In other words, SIMn accurately calculates the transmission time of a frame (including ACK and DCF timing) for the combinations of the physical layer features shown. Note that we have tested other combinations (not included here) to confirm that the simulator matches the expected experimental throughput.

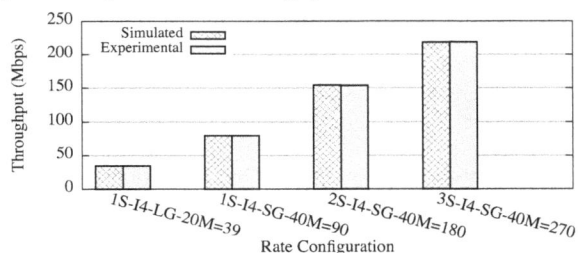

Figure 4: Fidelity of PHY layer features simulation

5.2.2 MAC Layer Features

To understand how to simulate frame aggregation, we first describe the factors that affect the length of an A-MPDU:

(a) There is an air time limit of 4 ms in the 5 GHz ISM band that prevents a single device from monopolizing the channel. This limit means that when using slower rate configurations (i.e., lower Physical Layer Data Rates (PLDRs)), aggregated frame length is limited to the number of frames that can be transmitted in 4 ms. The Ath9k driver applies the same restriction for the 2.4 GHz band.

(b) The Block-Ack Window (BAW) also plays a major role in the length of aggregated frames, as the sequence numbers of subframes can be offset by at most 64 from the starting sequence number in the BAW.

(c) There is a 64 KB limit on the size of the 802.11 PLCP. For example, if using 1,500 byte frames, a maximum of 43 frames may be aggregated.

(d) Implementation specific requirements may also limit the length of aggregated frames. For instance, although this is not dictated by the 802.11n standard, the Ath9k driver used in this paper imposes a limit of 32 subframes in an aggregate frame. This is done so that another aggregated frame can be constructed and queued while the previous frame is being transmitted. A limit of 32 MPDUs in each A-MPDU means that two aggregated frames can be created within the 64-bit BAW, one in transmission and one queued.

(e) Management frames must be transmitted as individual frames. When a time sensitive management frame, such as a beacon frame, is queued the Ath9k driver will stop aggregating subsequent frames. This allows the management frame to begin transmission sooner than if a long aggregated frame were ahead of it in the transmission queue.

Determining the time spent transmitting the frame will depend on the number of frames that have been aggregated and the time required to transmit those subframes, which can be determined from the 802.11n specification. As mentioned previously, trace collection is performed by aggregating as many subframes as possible (i.e., FA_{COL}=MAX, which is FA_{COL}=32 in Ath9k). We do not collect FA_{COL}=1, FA_{COL}=2, ..., FA_{COL}=MAX-1. However, the simulator will need to accurately simulate cases where $FA_{SIM} \leq FA_{COL}$=MAX due to the reasons listed above, in addition to permitting different frame aggregation algorithms to be implemented in the simulator (recall that a goal of this work is to enable the fair comparison of different frame aggregation algorithms). Being able to accurately simulate A-MPDUs of any length *using frames collected using only A-MPDUs of maximum length* is they key insight and critical requirement to enable trace-based simulation of 802.11n networks. Therefore, we now evaluate SIMn's accuracy when simulating the throughput of frames aggregated with fewer subframes during simulation than were obtained during trace collection.

Experiment Setup and Description: We create a network between the AP (*sender*) and desktop computer (*receiver*), which is located less than 1 meter away in order to reliably obtain error-free traces (we consider errors in Section 5.4). For all experiments, the *sender* is set to a constant rate configuration of 2S-I4-SG-40M=180. We collect a 100 second trace with FA_{COL}=MAX, as this is the aggregation limit that we will typically use for trace collection. We then conduct 100 second experiments with Frame Aggregation (FA) limited to 32, 16, 2 and 1 aggregated frames, which we use as the ground truth. We then simulate constant rate scenarios for the rate configuration 2S-I4-SG-40M=180 with FA_{SIM}=MAX, FA_{SIM}=16, FA_{SIM}=2 and FA_{SIM}=1, using the FA_{COL}=MAX trace as input to the simulator. We expect simulated throughput for FA_{SIM}=MAX, FA_{SIM}=16, FA_{SIM}=2 and FA_{SIM}=1 to match the throughput obtained directly from the experiments run with FA limited to 32, 16, 2 and 1 aggregated frames, respectively.

Experiment Results: In Figure 5, we plot pairs of simulated and experimental throughput measurements for each of the frame aggregation configurations. For all pairs of simulated and experimental throughput we see a close match, which suggests that SIMn can accurately simulate shorter aggregated frames from traces with FA_{COL}=MAX, in an error-free environment. In Section 6 we demonstrate that SIMn is also accurate in environments that are not free from errors (e.g., including uncontrolled environments). As a result, we are able to collect traces with FA_{COL}=MAX but to simulate cases where frames of shorter lengths are used.

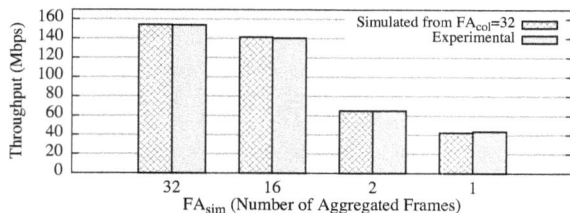

Figure 5: Simulating Shorter Aggregated Frames

5.3 Determining Channel Access

Since the 802.11 standard implements CSMA/CA, channel access is a crucial factor in determining throughput for an experiment. When a WiFi device performs channel sensing and a WiFi or non-WiFi signal is detected the transmission has to be postponed, resulting in reduced throughput. It is critical that T-SIMn measures this delay *while conducting trace collection* and accurately simulates it in order to produce realistic throughputs. Such delays can be caused by changing channel conditions and it is the ability to capture these delays that makes trace-based simulation so attractive. *Channel conditions are captured in traces, rather than simulated using computationally intensive and inaccurate models.* In T-SIMn, we compute both WiFi and non-WiFi delay using Cycle Counter Information (CCI) available on the Atheros device.

We use four counters available on the Atheros chipset which are: *tx_cycles*, which counts the number of cycles that the chip spends performing transmissions (outbound); *rx_cycles*, which counts clock cycles spent receiving (inbound); *busy_cycles*, which measures the number of cycles that the channel was busy performing transmission, receiving WiFi frames or due to non-WiFi noise; and *total_cycles*, which counts the total number of cycles for transmission, including those spent busy (i.e., waiting). We modify the driver to include cycle counts for each aggregated frame in the collected trace and compute delay as follows:

$$delay = actual\ duration - expected\ duration \quad (1)$$

The *expected duration* is determined from the 802.11n standard and includes time for transmission and the Distributed Coordination Function (we use an average backoff of 7.5 μs). The *actual duration* is the time spent transmitting the aggregated frame, as determined using the cycle counters. More details can be found in [2][10].

T-SIMn needs to determine if the source of delay was due to WiFi or non-WiFi interference in order to accurately simulate channel access because they impact delay in different ways. With non-WiFi interference each time the sender attempts to transmit a frame it may experience delay. As a result, the more frequently A-MPDUs are sent the more delay the sender may incur. Since the sender is transmitting a constant stream of packets, the frequency of A-MPDU transmission is affected by the rate configuration and the length of A-MPDUs. The situation is different for WiFi interference because all parties implement the 802.11n standard and cooperate when accessing the channel. As a result, the sender's delay before transmitting an A-MPDU does not depend on the rate configuration or the length of the A-MPDU. It only depends on the amount of time the currently transmitting device occupies the channel being used.

We have developed a simple heuristic to distinguish WiFi from non-WiFi interference. We consider delay to be due to WiFi interference if one or both of the following are true:

1. The time spent transmitting the frame is significantly longer than expected:

$$actual\ tx\ duration - expected\ tx\ duration > threshold$$

$$\frac{tx\_cycles}{clock\_speed} - data\ tx\ time > threshold$$

This handles the case where the frame is delayed due to outbound traffic on the Access Point (AP), such as transmitting a beacon frame or responding to a probe request. Our current heuristic uses a threshold of 60 μs as it is small enough to catch beacon frames, which are the shortest WiFi frames that we observed.

2. The time spent receiving the ACK for the frame is significantly longer than expected:

$$actual\ rx\ duration - expected\ rx\ duration > threshold$$

$$\frac{rx\_cycles}{clock\_speed} - ack\ rx\ time > threshold$$

This handles the case where a frame is delayed due to inbound WiFi traffic. Our heuristic uses a threshold of 10 μs because there is little variation in the *actual rx durations* in the absence of WiFi interference.

Although these values provide accurate results in the following evaluation, in future work thresholds may be tuned to improve the accuracy of the heuristic.

If the delay is due to WiFi interference, we simply increment the simulation time by the duration of delay as explained in Section 3.2. To simulate the delay caused by non-WiFi interference, we find the delay incurred when sending each frame (from the trace) and compute the average delay experienced by each frame over the 200 ms time window centered at the current simulation time (i.e., the averaging window used to compute the error rate described in Section 3.2). This average is the expected delay and is then added to the transmission time of the next frame in the simulator. Note that channel sensing does not depend on the rate configuration of the frame to be transmitted, so this computation is independent of the rate configuration.

We now evaluate the accuracy of T-SIMn in presence of WiFi interference, when the simulator must use shorter aggregated frames than those that have been collected (i.e., $FA_{SIM} < FA_{COL}$) due to the size of an A-MPDU being limited by one of the factors explained in Section 5.2.2.

Experiment Setup and Description: We create a network between the AP (*sender*) and a desktop computer client (*receiver*). We collect a trace for the rate configuration 2S-I4-SG-40M=180 with FA_{COL}=MAX. We then conduct experiments with Frame Aggregation (FA) limited to 2 and 1 aggregated frames. Using the trace collected with FA_{COL}=MAX, we simulate constant rate scenarios for the rate configuration 2S-I4-SG-40M=180 with FA_{SIM}=2 and FA_{SIM}=1. This is done to evaluate SIMn's accuracy in simulating shorter frames from traces collected with FA_{COL}=MAX, in the presence of WiFi interference. We then repeat these simulations but disable the heuristic (i.e., WiFi and non-WiFi delays are not differentiated) to demonstrate how distinguishing the two types of interference improves the accuracy of our simulator.

Experiment Results: Table 1 shows the differences between the throughput obtained with and without the heuristic for FA_{SIM}=2 and FA_{SIM}=1. In this experiment, the only WiFi interference is from beacon frames generated by the AP. We find that simulation error (i.e., the difference between simulated throughput, with and without the heuristic, and the experimental throughput), is lower when using the heuristic. With the heuristic, simulation error is less than 1% when simulating FA_{SIM}=2 from FA_{COL}=MAX, and less than 2% when simulating FA_{SIM}=1 from FA_{COL}=MAX. Without the heuristic, simulation error is roughly 6% and 10% for FA_{SIM}=2 and FA_{SIM}=1, respectively. These are significant differences, especially when considering that the only WiFi interference is beacon frames (which are relatively short in duration compared to data frames). We expect these differences to be even larger if a third-party WiFi client is added.

Table 1: Simulation Error (% Difference)

$FA_{COL} \rightarrow FA_{SIM}$	With Heuristic	Without Heuristic
32 → 2	-0.9 %	5.6 %
32 → 1	1.6 %	10.0 %

5.4 Determining Frame Error Rates

Along with the Physical Layer Data Rate (PLDR) and channel access (delay), the channel frame error rate (FER) is one of the major factors in determining the throughput for an 802.11n network. Errors can be introduced when multiple WiFi or non-WiFi devices transmit at the same time, resulting in a packet collision. Furthermore, errors may be caused by path loss when signal strength is low due to the distance between a *sender* and *receiver* or because of obstacles like walls or furniture that obscure the path between the two devices. We begin by describing the need to consider the subframe index (i.e., the location of the subframe within the A-MPDU) when computing the fate of a subframe in Section 5.4.1. Then, using path loss as an example, we demonstrate that the techniques we have devised provide accurate results (in Section 5.4.2).

5.4.1 Subframe Index Error Rates

In our initial implementation of SIMn, we treated the successes and failures of individual MPDUs (subframes) as samples in the computation of the FER over the specified time window for a particular rate configuration. For example, if we sent 5 aggregated frames, each containing 30 subframes, 15 successful and 15 failing, the FER determined to be 50% because 75 subframes were successfully transmitted and 75 failed. However, we found that simulated throughput did not always closely match experimental throughput, even though the error rates obtained in the simulator were similar to those observed in the experiments. Upon closer inspection, we found that there were significant differences between the average length of aggregated frames in the simulation and in the experiments. In our experiments the error rate of each subframe within multiple A-MPDUs varied with the index of the subframe (i.e., the error rate changed with the location of the subframe within the A-MPDU). Byeon et al. report that subframes transmitted more than 2 ms after the beginning of the transmission of an aggregated frame have a lower probability of being successfully received [6] (i.e., the pattern is that subframes with higher indices have a higher probability of failure). While some of the A-MPDUs we inspected exhibited similar behaviour, we found that the pattern of subframe error rates can differ significantly across different scenarios. As a result, we develop a technique that will work with any pattern, including environments where the pattern changes over time. SIMn now computes individual error rates for each subframe index rather than using an average FER across the entire aggregated frame. We refer to this as a Subframe Index Error Rate (SFIER). We now illustrate the importance of using the SFIERs in obtaining accurate throughput in SIMn.

Experiment Setup and Description: We take advantage of another feature of our trace-based simulator, namely the ability to generate and process synthetic traces to better understand 802.11n networks. We create two synthetic traces with *equal A-MPDU frame error rates* of 41%, but using two different SFIER patterns. The equal FERs are useful in reasoning about the expected outcome. Synthetic traces are used due to the difficulty in experimentally obtaining traces with the same overall FER with different SFIER patterns. The first trace has a linearly increasing SFIER from 0.025 at index 0 to 0.8 at index 31. The second trace uses the opposite pattern, with the SFIERs decreasing linearly from 0.8 at index 0 to 0.025 at index 31. We use SIMn to simulate the transmission of frames using these two patterns and a rate configuration of 3S-I7-SG-40M=450. We first treat all subframe indices equally, as in our initial implementation of SIMn. We then repeat the simulations using our current implementation of SIMn that considers each SFIER individually and compare the throughput obtained using these two different approaches.

Experiment Results: Figure 6 plots the throughput obtained for the two synthetic traces. The bars on the left show the results obtained using the current implementation with per-SFIERs and those on the right show results obtained using the initial implementation per-SFIERs are not considered (labelled "Original"). As expected, when using the Original implementation the throughput of the Increasing and Decreasing patterns are equal (because they have the same 41% FER. However, when using per-SFIERs, an increasing SFIER pattern results in higher throughput than a decreasing pattern, even though they have the same overall average error rate. The decreasing SFIER pattern results in lower throughput, because failures at the start of an aggregate frame prevent the Block-Ack Window (BAW) from advancing and thus reduces the average length of aggregated frames. These experiments illustrate the impact of considering individual SFIERs and their importance in obtaining accurate simulation results. This is critical because our goal is to use the simulator to evaluate link adaptation and frame aggregation algorithms, which require the correct simulation of phenomenon captured during trace collection.

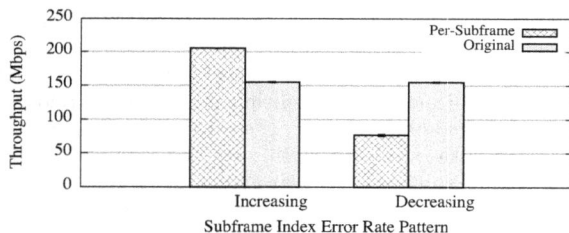

Figure 6: Impact of per-subframe error calculation

5.4.2 Path Loss

To evaluate SIMn's ability to handle channel error rate, we use a challenging mobile scenario where channel error rates vary widely due to path loss.

Experiment Setup and Description: We create a network between the Access Point (AP) (*sender*) and a Mac-Book Pro (MBP). The *sender* transmits for 100 seconds using constant rate configuration of 2S-I4-SG-40M=180 with FA_COL=MAX. We choose this rate configuration because in this mobile scenario, its error rates vary widely. In this experiment, the MBP is carried at walking speed in an office environment where cubicle walls obscure line of sight. We simulate throughput for the rate configuration 2S-I4-SG-40M=180, using the collected trace as input to the simulator. Note that during the simulation SFIERs must be computed and frames of length shorter than the maximum will be used. This tests SIMn's ability to accurately simulate throughput

with fluctuating error rates, different error rates across different subframe indices, and A-MPDUs of different length.

Experiment Results: In Figure 7, we plot pairs of throughput measurements, simulated and experimental, for this scenario. Despite the significant fluctuations during this experiment, there is a close match between simulated and experimental throughput. This suggests that the simulator can accurately determine error rates (including SFIERs) and simulate aggregated frames of different lengths.

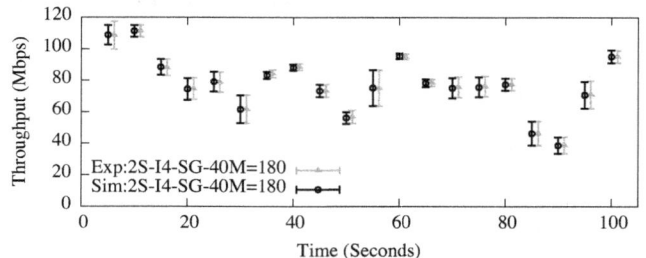

Figure 7: Mobile scenario experiencing path loss

6. EVALUATING OUR FRAMEWORK

In the previous sections, we use constant rate traces to focus our tests on the T-SIMn simulator, SIMn. Although not representative of how trace collection would be done in T-SIMn, that technique is used to ensure the accuracy of SIMn on its own. In this section, we evaluate T-SIMn as a whole, using round-robin trace collection in conditions that are representative of those in which WiFi is used.

In order to evaluate the T-SIMn framework, we use an evaluation methodology similar to that used to evaluate T-RATE [2]. That is, we conduct an experiment (which produces a trace) using a round-robin ordering of rate configurations and then in SIMn we conduct a simulation using a round-robin ordering that differs from the experiment. This experiment is designed as a means for evaluating the accuracy of the T-SIMn framework. The intuition behind this methodology is that in both the experiments and the simulation each rate will be used to send the same number of frames using each rate. Therefore, the average throughput obtained over an interval in time from the experiment should be matched by the average throughput obtained from the simulator. This will only be true if, despite not having sent a frame with rate configuration R at time t, the simulator can accurately determine the probability that the frame would be successfully sent by computing the average SFIER over the channel coherence window. Additionally, different orderings means it is extremely unlikely that the number of frames aggregated in the simulator at time t will match the number of aggregated frames collected in the trace at time t. In contrast to T-RATE, we cannot cycle through all of the available 802.11n rates (96 rates for our 3 antenna devices would take about 300 ms) because the time required to perform enough rounds to accurately compute average error rates would exceed the channel coherence time.

We instead limit our evaluation to one antenna (1-Spatial Stream (SS)) devices which includes most cell phones, tablets and other small devices. Using Long Guard Interval (LGI), Short Guard Interval (SGI), 20 and 40 MHz Channel Bandwidth (CB) results in a total of 32 rate configurations.

During trace collection, rates are grouped by a combination of the Guard Interval (GI) and the CB. Therefore, rates are sampled in the following group order LGI-20MHz, SGI-

20MHz, LGI-40MHz, SGI-40MHz. Within each group, rates are sampled in order from the lowest Modulation and Coding Scheme Index (MCS index) to the highest (i.e., MCS index $0, 1, ..., 6, 7$). We simulate round-robin in the reverse group order (i.e., SGI-40MHz, LGI-40MHz, SGI-20MHz, LGI-20MHz) and from the highest MCS index to the lowest (i.e., MCS index $7, 6, ..., 1, 0$).

Experiment Setup and Description: We create a network between the AP (*sender*) and an iPhone 6 (*receiver*). The sender is configured to sample all 32 1-SS 802.11n rate configuration, which is the entire set of rates supported by the iPhone 6. The experiment is conducted by using a mix of carrying the iPhone at walking speed and standing still in an office environment as described in Section 4.

Experiment Results: In Figure 8, we plot simulated and experimental throughput. We find that simulated throughput matches experimental throughput except for the points at times $t = 20$, $t = 60$ and $t = 100$. The largest difference is observed at $t = 60$, where average simulated throughput is roughly 11% higher than average experimental throughput. Initially, we thought that this was due to inaccuracy in SIMn. However, upon closer investigation, we realized that the simulator is in fact accurate and that the problem was with the methodology used to evaluate the accuracy of the framework. Our assumption that simulating round-robin in a different order would result in each rate configuration being used for the same proportion of time is not guaranteed in 802.11n networks, unlike a similar evaluation we conducted for 802.11g networks [2]. In the next section, we investigate and explain why the order in which rates are used in a round-robin fashion impacts throughput.

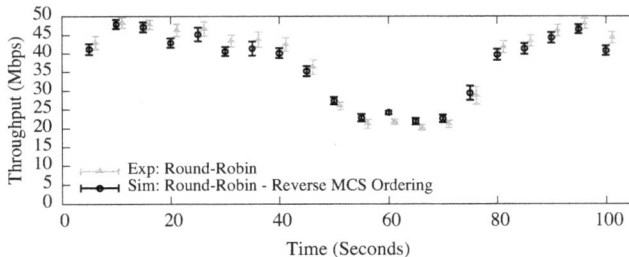

Figure 8: Simulating Reverse MCS Ordering

6.1 Effect of Rate Configuration Ordering

In 802.11n networks, the fate of one frame can impact the number of frames that can be aggregated in the next frame due to the Block-Ack Window (BAW). Failed aggregated frames or subframes limit how far forward the BAW can be advanced. Recall from Figure 1 that the number of subframes being aggregated has a significant impact on throughput, with longer aggregated frames leading to higher potential throughput. Recall that in the previous section, rates were sampled in the group order LGI-20MHz, SGI-20MHz, LGI-40MHz, SGI-40MHz. Additionally, rates are sampled in order from the lowest Modulation and Coding Scheme Index (MCS index) to the highest (i.e., MCS index $0, 1, ..., 6, 7$). This means that the most robust rates in each group are sampled first and the least robust rates are sampled last. We have examined the data shown in Figure 8 in detail and found that at times $t = 50$ to 70, the reverse ordering performed during simulation leads to longer aggregated frames on average (a mean of 15.2 subframes in each aggregated

frame during simulation compared to 14.6 in the experiment). This results in slightly higher simulated throughput during this period. Although there is a match in simulated and experimental throughput during some portions of this time interval (i.e., overlapping CIs), the simulated throughputs are visibly lower for most times t. Simulating longer frames than those that were collected may also lead to some inaccuracies because of insufficient samples in the collected trace for frames of the length being simulated.

As a result, we have had to revise our understanding and now expect different round-robin orderings to result in different throughput, unless the behavior of the Block-Ack Window (BAW) advancement and consequently Frame Aggregation (FA) is the same during trace collection and simulation. To test this hypothesis, we construct a new ordering to use in the simulation that preserves the property that the most robust rates in each group are used first and the least robust rates are used last. The simulation still uses rate groups in the reverse order from the order used when the trace is collected (i.e., simulating SGI-40MHz, LGI-40MHz, SGI-20MHz and LGI-20MHz. However, within each group, we now use rates in order from the lowest Modulation and Coding Scheme Index (MCS index) to the highest (i.e., the same order used during trace collection). We simulate a round-robin ordering with this new reverse group order and show simulated and experimental throughput in Figure 9. As the graph shows, the simulated throughput now closely matches that obtained experimentally (all pairs of confidence intervals overlap). Note that this property does not limit SIMn to simulating only certain orderings of rate configurations. It is only required for this evaluation of the accuracy of T-SIMn because we are trying to devise a methodology where the throughput of the simulator should match that of the experiment. Now that we are aware of this property, we will use the reverse group ordering in the following section, where we evaluate T-SIMn in an uncontrolled environment.

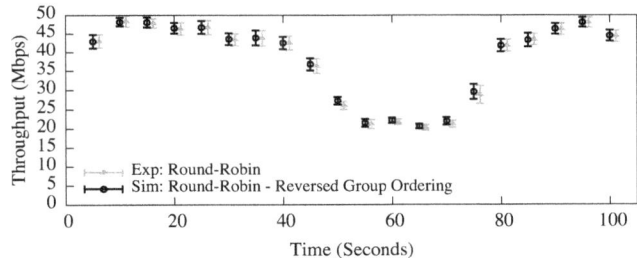

Figure 9: Simulating Reverse Group Ordering

6.2 Uncontrolled Environment

Up to this point, all experiments are performed with no neighboring Access Points (APs). We now move to a different 5 GHz channel that is in use by the university's WiFi network to evaluate T-SIMn in conditions that are typical for a shared university WiFi network. This includes interference from many third-party WiFi clients and APs.

Experiment Setup and Description: Similarly to the previous section, we create a network between the AP (*sender*) and an iPhone 6 (*receiver*). However, unlike previous experiments, we now configure the AP to use a channel occupied by one of the university's APs with the highest signal strength. As mentioned previously, we use a 5 GHz network because the iPhone does not support 40 MHz Channel

Bandwidths (CBs) in the 2.4 GHz spectrum. Note that if we had used the 2.4 GHz band, thus limiting trace collection to 20 MHz rate configurations, we would have obtained twice as many samples in each averaging window which should only improve accuracy. As in previous experiments, we sample all 1-Spatial Stream (SS) rate configurations. We collect a 100 second trace with `FA`$_{\text{COL}}$`=MAX` to test T-SIMn in an uncontrolled environment. This scenario is comprised of a mix of carrying the iPhone at walking speed and standing still in an office and hallway environment as explained in Section 4.

Experiment Results: In Figure 10, we plot pairs of throughput measurements, simulated and experimental, for the uncontrolled experiment. We find that while the *receiver* is stationary from $t = 60$ to 100 there is significantly more fluctuation in throughput when compared to Figure 8 from $t = 10$ to 40 in Figure 9. This is due to the third-party traffic on the shared channels. The close matches in throughput suggest that T-SIMn is accurately capturing and simulating third-party traffic and that it can handle conditions that are representative of those in which WiFi devices are used.

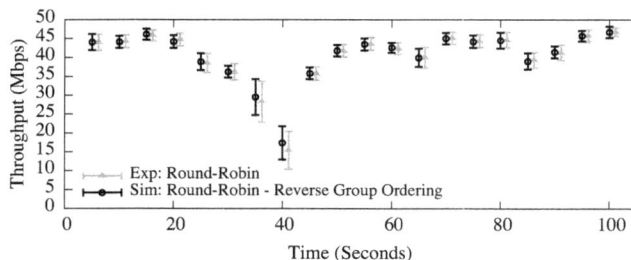

Figure 10: Uncontrolled, Mobile Scenario

7. CONCLUSIONS

In this paper, we design a trace-based simulation framework for 802.11n networks, called T-SIMn. We find that careful consideration of all factors that affect throughput such as 802.11n transmission features, channel access, and channel error rate is necessary to accurately simulate this standard. More specifically, we show that accurate handling of 802.11n frame aggregation is a key in obtaining realistic and high fidelity results. We demonstrate that SIMn accurately simulates these factors by comparing the simulator results with empirical measurements.

We demonstrate that the T-SIMn framework can be used with 1 antenna devices, including most smart phones and tablets. With so many devices being limited to 1 Spatial Stream (SS), we believe that T-SIMn is a valuable tool for studying such widely used devices and that the groundwork has been laid for simulating more SSs (i.e., support for these rates has been implemented and tested in SIMn).

We have made some traces available [1] and intend to add more traces and T-SIMn to this repository. We also plan to use T-SIMn to evaluate link adaptation and frame aggregation algorithms using a wide variety of environments.

8. ACKNOWLEDGMENTS

Funding for this project was provided in part by a Natural Sciences and Engineering Research Council (NSERC) of Canada Discovery Grant and a Discovery Accelerator Supplement in addition to an NSERC Graduate Scholarship. The authors thank Martin Karsten, Srinivasan Keshav and the anonymous reviewers for their helpful feedback on previous revisions of this work.

9. REFERENCES

[1] Sample traces. https://cs.uwaterloo.ca/~brecht/t-simn.

[2] A. Abedi and T. Brecht. T-RATE: A framework for the trace-driven evaluation of 802.11 rate adaptation algorithms. In *MASCOTS*, 2014.

[3] A. Abedi, A. Heard, and T. Brecht. Conducting repeatable experiments and fair comparisons using 802.11n MIMO networks. *ACM SIGOPS*, 49(1):41–50, 2015.

[4] J. G. Andrews, A. Ghosh, and R. Muhamed. *Fundamentals of WiMAX: understanding broadband wireless networking.* Pearson Education, 2007.

[5] R. Burchfield, E. Nourbakhsh, J. Dix, K. Sahu, S. Venkatesan, and R. Prakash. RF in the jungle: Effect of environment assumptions on wireless experiment repeatability. In *ICC*, 2009.

[6] S. Byeon, K. Yoon, O. Lee, S. Choi, W. Cho, and S. Oh. MoFA: Mobility-aware frame aggregation in Wi-Fi. In *CoNEXT*, 2014.

[7] L. Deek, E. Garcia-Villegas, E. Belding, S.-J. Lee, and K. Almeroth. Intelligent channel bonding in 802.11n WLANs. *IEEE Transactions on Mobile Computing*, 13(6):1242–1255, 2014.

[8] L. Deek, E. Garcia-Villegas, E. Belding, S.-J. Lee, and K. Almeroth. A practical framework for 802.11 MIMO rate adaptation. *Computer Networks*, 2015.

[9] D. Halperin, W. Hu, A. Sheth, and D. Wetherall. Predictable 802.11 packet delivery from wireless channel measurements. *ACM SIGCOMM Computer Communication Review*, 41(4):159–170, 2011.

[10] A. Heard. T-SIMn: Towards a Framework for the Trace-Based Simulation of 802.11n Networks. Master's thesis, University of Waterloo, 2016.

[11] P. Huang, X. Yang, and L. Xiao. Adaptive channel bonding in multicarrier wireless networks. In *MobiHoc*, 2013.

[12] G. Judd and P. Steenkiste. Repeatable and realistic wireless experimentation through physical emulation. *ACM SIGCOMM Computer Communication Review*, 2004.

[13] G. Judd and P. Steenkiste. Using emulation to understand and improve wireless networks and applications. In *NSDI*, 2005.

[14] D. Kotz, C. Newport, R. S. Gray, J. Liu, Y. Yuan, and C. Elliott. Experimental evaluation of wireless simulation assumptions. In *MSWiM*, 2004.

[15] L. Kriara and M. K. Marina. SampleLite: A hybrid approach to 802.11n link adaptation. *ACM SIGCOMM Computer Communication Review*, 45(2):4–13, 2015.

[16] M. Lacage and T. R. Henderson. Yet another network simulator. In *Proceeding from the 2006 Workshop on ns-2: The IP Network Simulator*. ACM, 2006.

[17] V. Lenders and M. Martonosi. Repeatable and realistic experimentation in mobile wireless networks. *IEEE Transactions on Mobile Computing*, 2009.

[18] Scalable Network Technologies, Inc. QualNet, 2014. http://web.scalable-networks.com/qualnet.

[19] W.-L. Shen, Y.-C. Tung, K.-C. Lee, K. C.-J. Lin, S. Gollakota, D. Katabi, and M.-S. Chen. Rate adaptation for 802.11 multiuser MIMO networks. In *Mobicom*, 2012.

[20] M. Stoffers and G. Riley. Comparing the ns-3 propagation models. In *MASCOTS*, pages 61–67. IEEE, 2012.

[21] R. Technology. SteelCentral Riverbed Modeler, 2016. http://www.riverbed.com/products/steelcentral/steelcentral-riverbed-modeler.html.

[22] P. Teymoori, A. Dadlani, K. Sohraby, and K. Kim. An optimal packet aggregation scheme in delay-constrained IEEE 802.11n WLANs. In *WiCOM*, 2012.

[23] Z. Zhao, F. Zhang, S. Guo, X.-Y. Li, and J. Han. RainbowRate: MIMO rate adaptation in 802.11n WiLD links. In *IPCCC*, 2014.

[24] J. Zhou, Z. Ji, and R. Bagrodia. TWINE: A hybrid emulation testbed for wireless networks and applications. In *INFOCOM*, 2006.

Preference and Mobility-Aware Task Assignment in Participatory Sensing

Rim Ben Messaoud
Université Paris-Est
5 Boulevard Descartes
77420 Champs-sur-Marne,
France
rim.ben_messaoud@univ-lr.fr

Yacine Ghamri-Doudane
University of La Rochelle
23 Avenue Albert Einstein
17000 La Rochelle, France
yacine.ghamri@univ-lr.fr

Dmitri Botvich
TSSG, Waterford Institute of
Technology
Waterford, Ireland
dbotvich@tssg.org

ABSTRACT

Participatory Sensing is a new paradigm of mobile sensing where users are actively involved in leveraging the power of their smart devices to collect and share information. Motivated by its potential applications, we tackle in this paper the task assignment problem for a requester encountering a crowd of participants while considering their mobility model and sensing preferences. We aim to minimize the overall processing time of sensing tasks. Hence, we introduce first the Mobility-Aware Task Assignment scheme in both oFfline (MATAF) and oNline (MATAN) models where requesters investigate the participants' arrival model in different compounds of the sensing region. Further, we enhance such schemes by jointly taking into account participants' mobility and sensing preferences. We advocate then two other task assignment models, P-MATAF (offline) and P-MATAN (online). All proposed algorithms adopt a greedy-based selection strategy and address the minimization of the average makespan of all sensing tasks. We conduct extensive performance evaluation based on real traces while varying the number of tasks and associated workloads. Results proved that our proposed schemes have achieved lower average makespan and higher number of delegated tasks.

Keywords

Participatory Sensing; task assignment; mobility-aware; preference; requester selection.

1. INTRODUCTION

In recent years, we witnessed the proliferation of smart sensors-equipped devices carried by the crowd which enhances a new paradigm of data collection and sharing defined as Crowdsensing. This emergent sensing paradigm is conducted either in an opportunistic or participatory way [1] where the users are either unaware or actively involved in the sensing process, respectively. Hence, various potential applications have been proposed in the literature in different domains such as urban traffic monitoring [2], environment management [3], activity recognition and health care [4].

Motivated by these potential applications, researchers have widely studied the problem of sensing campaigns' assignment among different users. As a matter of fact, participatory sensing can be either voluntarily or for some rewarding mechanisms, denoted as "incentives" [1], since users are dedicating their resources to perform the sensing tasks. Hence, several assignment algorithms have been proposed in the aim of minimizing the overall sensing cost in terms of energetic resources [5] and rewards provided by the crowdsensing platforms respecting a certain budget [6]. Furthermore, authors in [7] have tackled the data quality metric as an important factor required to be maximized within sensing campaigns. Along with this, we investigated in our previous works [8], [9] the fairness issue while assigning tasks in quality and energy-aware allocation schemes in order to achieve both requesters' satisfaction and users' commitment.

All the aforementioned schemes are centralized approaches, where a central unit in the cloud is responsible of assigning submitted tasks to the registered participants. The latter are supposed to collect and report samples to the platform. However, some users can be registered within different crowdsensing platforms which might lead to time-overlapping tasks assignments, thus, to a number of sensing tasks exceeding their sensing or processing capabilities. Moreover, participants may be reluctant to upload data via data networks and prefer offloading it while being in the range of Wi-Fi access points in order to optimize their data budget usage. Though, this may impact the temporal accuracy of the collected measurements. Last, potential good participants, i.e, the one who may provide high data quality, may be not reachable in the phase of assignment because of connectivity issues and can be identified later. These unpredictable issues can induce the overall sensing and processing time and consequently the sensing process.

To address these challenges, we introduce in this work a distributive crowdsensing "support" phase. We aim to better share the load among users and minimize the overall makespan of all sensing tasks. Thus, we require that the crowdsensing platform needs to identify some "supportive users" that will carry a higher number of tasks to be delegated to encountered adequate participants. That is, whenever a "requester" meets another participant, he can delegate some of his assigned tasks via direct communication

MSWiM '16, November 13-17, 2016, Malta, Malta

© 2016 ACM. ISBN 978-1-4503-4502-6/16/11. . . $15.00

DOI: http://dx.doi.org/10.1145/2988287.2989165

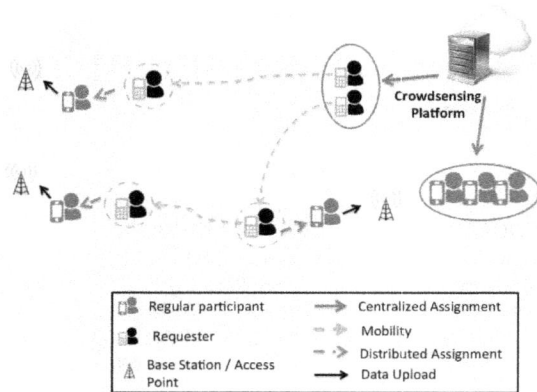

Figure 1: The hybrid assignment scenario

technologies. The latter collects and uploads data either via data or Wi-Fi networks depending on his 3G/4G budget and the data time-sensitivity as illustrated in Figure 1.

We model first the assignment of tasks as a greedy-based offline algorithm where the requester designates in advance to whom delegate the sensing tasks based on his contacts historical statistics, then assigns tasks when encountering each of the selected users. Also, we extend this model by an online strategy where each requester launches his assignment only when encountering a participant. More specifically, our major contributions are as follows:

1. We first investigate the identification of "requesters" in order to enhance the centralized existing assignment strategies by a distributed "supportive" phase based on different selection types: randomly, by-speed and by-contacts number.

2. We propose a Mobility-Aware Task Assignment scheme, **MATA**, where we study the arrival model of users within each compound of the sensing area. This variant is introduced in both offline and online models.

3. We extend our assignment policy to propose a Preference and Mobility-Aware Task Assignment scheme, **P-MATA**, where we jointly consider the users' mobility and preferences in terms of acceptance or rejection of delegated tasks. P-MATA is also introduced in both offline and online models.

4. We evaluate our assignment strategies with real-traces based simulation while varying the requesters' identification policies, the number of tasks to be assigned and their associated workloads and we show that our schemes perform well in terms of assigned tasks and overall makespan of sensing tasks.

The remainder of this paper is organized as follows. In Section 2, we list the state-of-the art work that studied the hybrid and the distributed crowdsensing scenarios. We formulate in Section 3 the users' arrival and preference models then we propose the corresponding average makespan expression to be minimized in Section 4. Sections 5 and 6 illustrate our two proposed variants of assignment: MATA and P-MATA. In Section 7, we set our simulation settings and evaluate the performance of our assignment variants. Conclusions and future work are withdrawn in Section 8.

2. RELATED WORK

By far, several assignment schemes were proposed to optimize the participatory sensing process. Yet, few works have tackled this issue in a distributed based approach.

For example, Cheung et al. [10] have introduced an asynchronous and distributed task selection (ADTS) algorithm to help users plan their task selections on their own. The basic idea is to consider users' different initial locations, movement costs, movement speeds, and reputation levels in the aim of maximizing the social surplus of the crowdsensing platform. That is, the participants designate in a non-cooperative game the paths that maximize their profit. Nevertheless, the authors did not investigate the processing time of tasks since users, even though being rewarded for their contributions, may be reluctant to perform long sensing campaigns that affect their devices' normal use.

In this context, Xiao et al. [11] have proposed to minimize the processing time of sensing tasks by letting a set of participants assign tasks on the move to other encountered participants, i.e., as an hybrid crowdsensing assignment. Authors investigated users' encountering based on their historical traces and introduced an offline and online assignment strategies. However, the proposed algorithms have considered only time-dependent crowdsensing scheme, while in fact the location of collected samples matters as much. Hence, an assignment scheme should be based on users' mobility in terms of different locations rather than estimating only their meetings. Also, authors did not consider the issue of participants' sensing preferences, i.e, the ability to accept or reject the assignment strategy. Such ability has been very recently introduced by authors in [12] in order to select the "workers" who maximize an expected sum of service quality. The proposed framework, Crowdlet, is based on dynamic programming which enhances distributed self-organized mobile crowdsensing. Though, the time cost of conducting this quality-aware sensing was not investigated.

With all this in mind, we introduce, throughout this work, two assignment variants in the aim of minimizing the overall time of sensing tasks while taking into account both users' mobility and sensing preferences. That is, each requester must consider the participants' mobility among the sensing area different compounds as well as the fact that they may reject their assignment.

3. NETWORK MODEL

We consider in this work a crowded sensing area divided into sub-regions, denoted as compounds $C = \{k, \in 1..n_C\}$. Moreover, we assume that N mobile users are moving around with various speed values between different compounds and can be at a given time with a probability q_k in a compound k. All users are registered within a crowdsensing platform and willing to collect and share information. However, some of them were designated by the crowdsensing platform to carry extra sensing tasks and start *requesting* encountered participants to share the processing load as illustrated in Figure 1. For simplicity, we denote such type of users as **requesters**, $R = \{r_1, r_2, \ldots, r_{n_r}\}$, while the rest of users are defined as **participants**, $P = \{p_1, p_2, \ldots, p_{n_p}\}$ with $n_r + n_p \leq N$. We consider users "encountering" when they move around in the same compound k and are close enough to allow direct communications such as Device-to-Device (D2D) communications. More specifically, a requester selects a participant among the ones present in its device's communication range and delegates to him a set of sensing tasks to be performed. Further, the collected data samples can be uploaded via Wi-Fi when entering an access point communication range or via data networks for only time-sensitive data. Without loss of generality, we assume here that the inter-meeting time of a requester with a user is enough for exchanging the assigned tasks. In order to better estimate this time, we investigate hereafter in details the arrival model of users.

3.1 Users' Arrival Model

The task-oriented participatory sensing depends essentially on users' mobility. Thus, we base our work on a widely-used mobility model in Mobile Social Networks (MSNs), [13], [14]. That is, we assume that the inter-meeting time between a requester r_i and a participant p_i follows an exponential distribution with a contact rate parameter λ_{p_i}. As a result, the inter-encounter time of a requester with two consecutive participants follows also an exponential distribution with parameter $\lambda = \sum_{p_i \in P} \lambda_{p_i}$, i.e, the arrival of participants to a requester follows a Poisson process. Note that λ_{p_i} can be derived from the historical encounters between a requester and each participant per time unit. Besides, we consider the fact that users can meet only while being in the same compound. Hence, we examine the probability of each user to be in a certain compound k and we model the inter-meeting time between a requester r_i and a participant p_i in this compound k by an exponential distribution with rate parameter $R_{(k,p_i)} = q_k(r_i)q_k(p_i)\lambda_{p_i}$:

$$A_i = \int_0^\infty R_{(k,p_i)} t e^{-R_{(k,p_i)}t} \, \mathrm{d}t = \frac{1}{R_{(k,p_i)}} = \frac{1}{q_k(r_i)q_k(p_i)\lambda_{p_i}}. \tag{1}$$

where $q_k(r_i)$, $q_k(p_i)$ are the probabilities of a requester r_i and a participant p_i to be in a compound k, respectively.

3.2 Acceptance/Rejection Model

The aforementioned Poisson process models the arrival of participants to a requester, however, it does not take into account the fact that a participant can accept or reject the proposed assignment. Thus, we note by p_a the probability that a participant accepts to perform the assigned sensing tasks. Consequently, the probability of rejection is defined as $p_r = 1 - p_a$. In practice, the former factor can be calculated from historical statistical data or requesters' experiences as introduced in [11]. Based on this probability, the acceptance of a task by a participant can be modeled as a Bernoulli process. That is, for each participant p_i, the set of answers are associated with the random variable X in $\{0, 1\}$, where $X = 1$ with probability p_a and $X = 0$ with probability $p_r = 1 - p_a$.

As for a requester encountering n_p participants, the number of users who have accepted to participate can be generalized to a Binomial distribution, $B(n_p, p_a)$. In the rest of this paper, we will denote by "positive" participants the ones who accept their assigned tasks. Also, we extend the arrival model of these participants as a composition of the Poisson process and the binomial distribution which leads to a Poisson distribution with parameter $(\beta_k = p_a \times R_{(k,p_i)})$ [15].

Based on this model, we proceed to compute the inter-meeting time between any requester r_i and a "positive" participant in a compound k in Lemma 1.

LEMMA 1. *The mean time, for a requester r_i, till meeting a "positive" participant, p_i, within n time slots is:*

$$\Pi_i = \Big(\sum_{l=1}^n p_r^l p_a \frac{1}{q_k(r_i)q_k(p_i)\lambda_{p_i}} \Big)'.$$

PROOF. We assume that during the assignment phase, a requester r_i is likely to meet any participant p_i more than once. However, the latter accepts the assigned tasks with p_a. Suppose that a participant will accept tasks within n meetings, thus, the mean time of meetings this "positive" participant can be expressed as: $p_a A_i + p_r p_a A_i \times 2 + \ldots + p_r^{n-1} p_a A_i \times n = p_a A_i(1 + 2p_r + 3p_r^2 + \ldots + np_r^{n-1})$. In this expression, each term of the sum can be a derivative of p_r^l with $l \in \{1, \ldots, n\}$. Hence, we can model Π_i as $p_a A_i(p_r + p_r^2 + \ldots + p_r^n)' = p_a A_i(\sum_{l=1}^n p_r^l)'$. Finally, we substitute A_i with its corresponding expression from Equation (1) to obtain the expression of Π_i. $\square$

4. PROBLEM STATEMENT

In this section, our aim is to investigate in details the two defined mobility and preference models in order to formulate the corresponding objective function.

We target to optimize the participatory sensing process by minimizing the total necessary time to perform submitted tasks. This enhances the energy consumption for all participants and lowers the burden on the ones with high number of tasks. That is, we consider the above scenario of a requester r_i carrying m sensing tasks to be assigned to encountered participants. Let $S = \{s_1, s_2, \ldots, s_m\}$ be the set of sensing tasks that a requester intends to assign. These tasks may be heterogeneous in terms of involved sensors or average workload, i.e., time of sensing and processing. Hence, we can denote their corresponding workloads as $\tau_1, \tau_2, \ldots, \tau_m$. Also, we define by makespan of a task $s_i \in S$ the time of being assigned and processed and we denote it as $M(s_i)$. Note that we exclude here the reporting phase since we assume it is instantaneous. Thus, for each assignment policy Γ, we compute the average makespan of all assigned tasks to different participants [11] by:

$$AM(\Gamma) = \frac{1}{m} \sum_{s_i \in S} M(s_i)|_\Gamma. \tag{2}$$

A task assignment strategy Γ is a set of assignments per encountered participant, i.e., $\Gamma = \{\gamma_1, \gamma_2, \ldots, \gamma_n\}$ with : $n, n \leq n_p$ is the number of encountered participants by a requester. Besides, a task is assigned only to one participant , i.e., $\gamma_i \cap \gamma_j = \emptyset \ \forall p_i, p_j \in P$. Finally, if a participant $p_i \in P$ has not received any task to be processed for a given period of assignment from encountered requesters, then his assignment set $\gamma_i = \emptyset$. In the following, we advocate how to minimize the average makespan of all tasks expressed in Equation (2) for each requester in two variants of scenarios.

First, we suppose that all encountered participants in a certain compound will accept *unconditionally* the suggested tasks. That is, we refer only to the aforementioned users' arrival model in order to formulate the objective function. We introduce this variant as the Mobility-aware Task Assignment (**MATA**) and we investigate it in two different models; offline and online assignment strategy. The former model indicates that a requester, and based on the expected arrival time for each participant, decides his assignment strategy, that we will denote in the rest of this paper as Γ_{AF}. Once the selection is done, the requester will assign the tasks to the designated participants when they meet. As for the online model, a requester starts his assignment strategy computation when he meets a participant. If the met user is among the selected ones, he receives his assignment. Otherwise, the requester keeps the set of tasks to be assigned for a next meeting. This latter strategy represents the dynamic assignment scheme whose result will be denoted as Γ_{AN}.

For the second variant, we jointly take into account the mobility of users and their sensing preferences. Then, we refer to the acceptance model of tasks where users have the ability to accept or reject an assignment. As a result, we define this variant as the Preference and Mobility-aware Task Assignment (**P-MATA**) and we develop, as for the first variant, an online and offline assignment strategies that we denote by Γ_{PN} and Γ_{PF}, respectively. Note that the offline and online assignment principles are the same for both variants. Yet, the expected arrival time of a "positive" participant is more developed.

5. MOBILITY-AWARE TASK ASSIGNMENT (MATA)

Essentially, the assignment of tasks conducted by each requester targets the minimization of the average makespan expressed in Equation (2). However, this formula varies as function of the users' arrival model. In this section, we focus on users' mobility and we ignore, for now, their ability to reject sensing campaigns. As a result, we model the corresponding objective function and we introduce a greedy-based offline and online solutions.

5.1 Offline Model (MATAF)

For the offline model, we assume that a requester can compute, based on his statistical historical meeting times with other users, the expected inter-meeting time with any participant using the expression of Equation (1). Besides, we let $\Gamma_{AF} = \{\gamma_1, \gamma_2, \ldots, \gamma_n\}$ be the assignment strategy decided by a requester r_i regarding n potential participants. We derive the average makespan of all tasks based on the approach of [11] by the following theorem:

THEOREM 1. *The average makespan of m tasks in an offline mobility-aware task assignment strategy, $AM(\Gamma_{AF})$, is expressed as follows:*

$$AM(\Gamma_{AF}) = \frac{1}{m} \sum_{i=1}^{n} \sum_{j \in \gamma_i} \left(\frac{1}{q_k(r_i)q_k(p_i)\lambda_{p_i}} + \tau_j \right).$$

PROOF. We assume that γ_i is the set of tasks to be assigned to a participant p_i and that τ_j is the workload of the task $j \in \gamma_i$. Then the makespan of all tasks assigned to the participant p_i is the sum of workloads. Plus, we consider the necessary time of meeting between a requester r_i and the participant in question which leads directly from the arrival time computed by Equation (1) as $\frac{1}{q_k(r_i)q_k(p_i)\lambda_{p_i}}$. Finally, we generalize this expression for all n met participants to consider all m tasks held by a requester, so we obtain the formula of Theorem 1. $\square$

In order to minimize the formulated average makespan, we propose a greedy-based offline solution that we denote as **MATAF** for Mobility-Aware Task Assignment oFfline. The basic idea of this assignment scheme is that a requester

---

Algorithm 1 MATAF Assignment Algorithm

Require: Set of sensing tasks $S = \{s_1, s_2, \ldots, s_m : \tau_1 \leq \tau_2 \leq \ldots \leq \tau_m\}$, Participants $P = \{p_1, p_2, \ldots, p_{n_p}\}$, EST.
Ensure: Assignment strategy $\Gamma_{AF} = \{\gamma_1, \gamma_2, \ldots, \gamma_n\}$
1: **for** $s_j \in S$ **do**
2:     **for** $k \in C$ **do**
3:         $[min_k, i_k] \leftarrow argmin(EST|_k)$
4:         **if** $min_k \leq min_e$ **then**
5:             $min_e \leftarrow min_k$
6:             $i_{min} \leftarrow i_k$
7:         **end if**
8:     **end for**
9:     Assign the task: $\gamma_{i_{min}} = \gamma_{i_{min}} + \{s_j\}$
10:     Update EST: $EST_{i_{min}}|_k = EST_{i_{min}}|_k + \tau_j; \forall k \in C$
11:     Update the set of tasks: $S = S \setminus \{s_j\}$
12: **end for**
13: Return Γ_{AF}

---

will compute the Expected Sensing Time (**EST**) for each participant in the set of registered participants P within the crowdsensing platform. This factor includes the inter-encounter time to meet a participant p_i in a certain compound k, i.e., A_i, plus the sum of the loads of the possible assigned tasks. To do so, we consider first that all tasks held by the requester in question are sorted in an ascending way. That is, $\forall s_i, s_j \in S$, if $i \leq j$ then $\tau_i \leq \tau_j$. Also, we initialize all Expected Sensing Time for all participants to their inter-meeting time with the current requester; $EST_i = A_i, \forall i \in 1 \ldots n_p$. Next, for each task $s_j \in S$, we look for the participant with the smallest EST_i, among all $EST_i|_k, \forall k \in C$, and we assign it to him then, update his $EST_i = A_i + \tau_j$ in all compounds and so on.

It is worth mentioning that the inter-meeting time varies as a function of the current compound since users have different mobility behavior in each compound. For example, a user may stay a long period in a compound representing his work/housing area but spends less time in another compound modeling a food area. Consequently, a requester may meet a participant only in certain compounds and more than once. Thus, we compute the k possible inter-meeting time between each requester and the rest of the users. As a result, we obtain the Expected Sensing Time between a certain requester and the rest of participants and we map it into a $k \times n_p$ matrix where each row presents an EST in a compound; $EST|_k = [EST_1, EST_2, \ldots, EST_{n_p}]$. As described above, EST_i is initialized to A_i and updated whenever a new task is assigned to the participant p_i. The detailed offline assignment scheme, **MATAF**, needs to be run periodically by each requester $r_i \in R$ as detailed in Algorithm 1.

5.2 Online Model (MATAN)

The second model of our Mobility-Aware Task Assignment scheme is an oNline strategy, **MATAN**. The principle here is that a requester starts his assignment process only when he encounters a participant. In other words, a requester r_i moves around in a specific compound k. Whenever he gets close to a participant p_i with a distance enabling short-distance communications, he starts requesting crowdsensing support. Hence, the requester asks first the encountered participant to update his EST_i in case he is processing tasks

Algorithm 2 MATAN Assignment Algorithm

Require: Set of sensing tasks $S = \{s_1, s_2, \ldots, s_m : \tau_1 \leq \tau_2 \leq \ldots \leq \tau_m\}$, Participants $P = \{p_1, p_2, \ldots, p_{n_p}\}$, EST.
Ensure: Assignment strategy $\Gamma_{AN} = \{\gamma_1, \gamma_2, \ldots, \gamma_n\}$
1: When the requester meets a participant p_i in a compound $k \in C$
2: Set $EST_i|_k = IST_i|_k$
3: $P = P \setminus \{p_i\}$
4: **for** $s_j \in S$ **do**
5:     **for** $k \in C$ **do**
6:        $[min_k, i_k] \leftarrow argmin(IST_i|_k + EST|_k)$
7:        **if** $min_k \leq min_e$ **then**
8:           $min_e \leftarrow min_k$
9:           $i_{min} \leftarrow i_k$
10:       **end if**
11:     **end for**
12:     **if** $(i_{min} = i)$ **then**
13:       Assign the task to this participant: $\gamma_i = \gamma_i + \{s_j\}$
14:       Update EST: $EST_i|_k = EST_i|_k + \tau_j; \forall k \in C$
15:       Update the set of tasks: $S = S \setminus \{s_j\}$
16:     **else**
17:       Temporary assignment : $\gamma_{i_{min}} = \gamma_{i_{min}} + \{s_j\}$
18:       Temporary Update of EST: $EST_{i_{min}}|_k = EST_{i_{min}}|_k + \tau_j; \forall k \in C$
19:     **end if**
20: **end for**
21: Return Γ_{AN}

---

assigned from previous met requesters. As a result, the expected sensing time is merged to an Instant Sensing Time (**IST**) which considers only the rest of workload held by the current met participant as follows:

$$IST_i = \sum_{j \in \gamma_i} \tau_j - T_{i,\gamma_i} \quad \forall i \in 1 \ldots n_p. \qquad (3)$$

where $T_{i,\gamma_i} = t_c - t_{s,\gamma_i}$ is the time passed since the participant has started performing his previous assignment γ_i, t_c is the current time and t_{s,γ_i} is the starting time of γ_i.

Further, the requester starts an assignment strategy comparable to the offline method while setting EST_i as IST_i for the encountered participant p_i to obtain a possible assignment Γ_{AN}. If the encountered participant p_i figures in the list of selected participants, then he will receive his assignment. As for the rest of selected users, this assignment can change based on the next encountered participants. Note that as in the offline model, we assume that the sensing tasks are sorted in an ascending way as a function of their loads. Moreover, the requester will adopt the same principle of assigning the current task to the participant with the smallest EST. Algorithm 2 describes the detailed steps of the online mobility-aware assignment, **MATAN**.

6. PREFERENCE & MOBILITY-AWARE TASK ASSIGNMENT (P-MATA)

In the previous section, we introduced the variant of our assignment scheme which foresees users' arrival model based on their historical mobility data and decides accordingly to whom delegate tasks. Though, this decision policy did not tackle the question of preference for each participant which may impact their commitment to the crowdsensing process.

In this section, we take this latter factor into consideration and we develop a preference and mobility aware variant which relies on participants' answers during the assignment phase and consequently guarantees their satisfaction while performing sensing campaigns.

More precisely, we resume the above detailed task assignment approach while investigating participants' sensing preferences. We propose to consider the fact that each participant can accept or reject his assignment due to many reasons such as his current sensing workload, his non availability or his constraints in terms of energetic resources or data budget. To do so, we refer to the model of acceptance probability described in Section 2 and we introduce an offline and online Preference & Mobility-Aware Task Assignment models.

6.1 Offline Model (P-MATAF)

As for the offline model, we adopt the same policy as in **MATAF** in which we introduce the probability of acceptance consideration. This new model is denoted as **P-MATAF**. However, we need to compute first the new inter-meeting time for all users based on Lemma 1. That is, each requester estimates the next time slot in which he will meet a "positive" participant based on his historical statistics of meetings and acceptance of tasks by different participants. In order to derive the corresponding average makespan, we need to jointly take into consideration the mobility and the acceptance probability of users. Hence, we consider $\Gamma_{PF} = \{\gamma_1, \gamma_2, \ldots, \gamma_n\}$ as the assignment strategy decided by a requester r_i regarding n potential "positive" participants and we propose the following theorem:

THEOREM 2. *The average makespan of m tasks in an offline preference and mobility-aware task assignment strategy, $AM(\Gamma_{PF})$, is expressed as follows:*

$$AM(\Gamma_{PF}) = \frac{1}{m} \sum_{i=1}^{n} \sum_{j \in \gamma_i} \left(\Big[\sum_{l=1}^{t} p_r^l p_a \frac{1}{q_k(r_i) q_k(p_i) \lambda_{p_i}} \Big]' + \tau_j \right).$$

PROOF. Let γ_i be the set of tasks to be assigned to a participant p_i with τ_j is the workload of the task $j \in \gamma_i$. The makespan of all tasks assigned to the participant p_i is the sum of workloads plus the passed time before the first acceptance. The latter factor can be derived from Lemma 1 as $\left[\sum_{l=1}^{t} p_r^l p_a \frac{1}{q_k(r_i) q_k(p_i) \lambda_{p_i}} \right]'$ where l is the number of time slots to get an acceptance from a participant and $[.]'$ is the derivative operator. Similarly to previous approach, we generalize this expression for all n met "positive" participants to consider all m tasks held by a requester, so we obtain the formula of Theorem 2. □

We proceed to search the set of users that minimizes the average makespan $AM(\Gamma_{PF})$ of all tasks in a crowdsensing support process for a requester r_i as follows:

- We generate the acceptance model of each participant p_i based on his sensing preferences, p_a and p_r.

- We compute the inter-encounter time Π_i, as in Lemma 1, to get the list of possible "positive" participants, i.e, the ones with the highest probabilities p_a.

- We set the Expected Sensing Time of all participants to $\Pi_i, \forall i \in 1 \ldots n$ and we look for the smallest EST_i.

- We select the corresponding participant and update his $EST_{i_{min}}$ as in Algorithm 1 until we assign all tasks carried by the requester r_i.

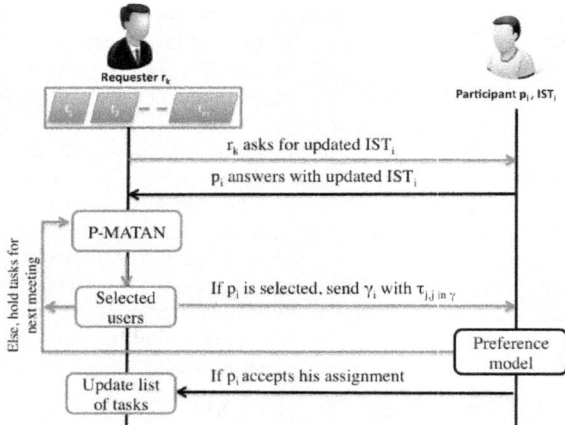

Figure 2: P-MATAN illustrative example

Note that the preference of a participant is only considered in the pre-assignment phase. Particularly, a requester estimates the behavior of each participant based on his historical data and gets the list of selected users. Further, when meeting the designated participants, the requester will only transmit to each one his assignment γ_i with no intention to wait for his confirmation or rejection which may result in a non perceived rejection and consequently some lost tasks. Also, we generalize the preference model for all compounds $k \in C$ and we compute respectively the corresponding arrival model of "positive" participants in each compound.

6.2 Online Model (P-MATAN)

To get a more realistic case, we opt for an online Preference and Mobility-aware Task Assignment, **P-MATAN**. In this model, we design the crowdsensing support process as two phases performed by both requesters and participants:

1. *The online selection phase*: a requester r_i moves around and travels between different compounds and whenever he meets a participant, he asks him to update his Instant Sensing time IST_i based on Equation (3), in order to estimate how much time he needs to perform his next assignment. After receiving the participant response, the requester conducts an online greedy-based selection as in Algorithm 2. Hence, if the current participant is identified among the list of selected users to perform the future sensing campaigns, the requester needs to send the designated tasks along with their workloads and wait for the participant's response.

2. *The after-decision phase:* the encountered participant decides to accept or reject such assignment based on his associated probability of acceptance p_a and sends back his response to the requester r_i. If the participant has accepted this assignment, then the list of tasks is updated as well as his IST_i. Otherwise, the requester r_i holds the designated tasks and continues moving until encountering another participant. This second phase highly impacts the time of assignment, since the less a requester gets rejections the faster he conducts his online assignment. To avoid such issue, we consider a list of met participants for each requester to not con-

sider a previous encountered user in the candidate list of the current online assignment.

The illustrative example given in Figure 2 details the steps of the preference and mobility-aware task assignment online model introduced in this work.

7. PERFORMANCE EVALUATION

In order to evaluate the performance of the proposed task assignment schemes **MATA** and **P-MATA** while considering the two different approaches for each, offline and online, we conducted extensive simulations. Hereafter, we detail the used traces, the simulation settings as well as the evaluation metrics and corresponding results.

7.1 Real Traces

We opt for real mobility traces to design our crowdsensing scenario. Hence, we refer to two well-known users' traces within a campus [16]. These traces include daily GPS track logs from two university campuses; North Carolina State University (NCSU) and Korea Advanced Institute of Science and Technology (KAIST).

For the first trace, the GPS readings were collected at every 10 seconds and recorded into a daily track log by 34 randomly selected students who took a course in the computer science department. Thus, we divide the corrsponding area into four major compounds where we consider the two most dense as computer science labs and the two others as food and administrative area, respectively. As for KAIST trace, the GPS readings were sampled each 10 seconds as well by students living in the dormitory of the campus between 2006 and 2007. Hence, we notice a higher density and lower speed compared to the first trace. We subdivide the KAIST area also into 4 compounds; two dormitory sections with the highest densities, one food area and one studying area in the campus.

Users have different mobility behaviors. In the beginning, we estimate their probabilities to be in different compounds q_k for each trace. Besides, we estimate the inter-meeting time between two users in a general area as $\lambda_i = N_i/T$, where N_i is the total number of times those users get close enough to exchange short-distance communication (we set it here to $10m$) and T is the total duration in the trace. These parameters will be used to estimate the inter-encounter time between different users within each compound. This is realized in both models: the one where we consider only the mobility and the one where we consider jointly users' mobility and sensing preference.

7.2 Requester Selection

We investigated the different characteristics of the above real mobility traces. Thus, we set the number of requesters to be $\simeq 5\%$ of the total number of users in a trace. As a consequence, the number of requesters in NCSU trace is equal to 7 while the one in KAIST trace is equal to 20 as illustrated in Table 1. Then, we study three different selection methods that a crowdsensing platform can use to identify, among users, the requesters for the crowdsensing support phase. First, we designate the requesters in a random way. Second, we consider the estimated number of meetings λ_i and we select the users with the highest values. Last, we select the *faster* mobile users as requesters in order to enhance the probability of them meeting other users.

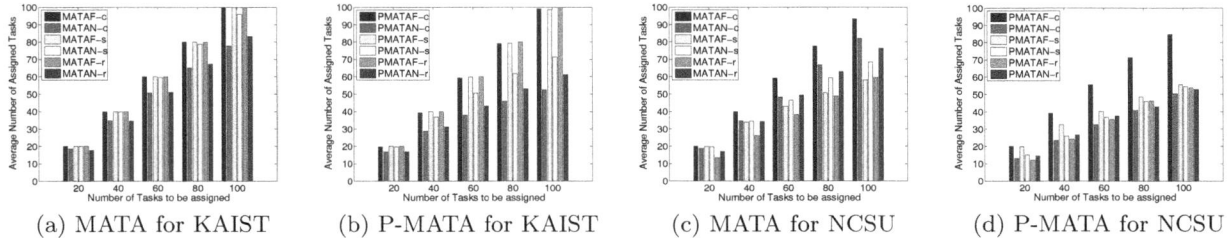

| (a) MATA for KAIST | (b) P-MATA for KAIST | (c) MATA for NCSU | (d) P-MATA for NCSU |

Figure 3: The number of assigned tasks by each scheme while varying the number of tasks

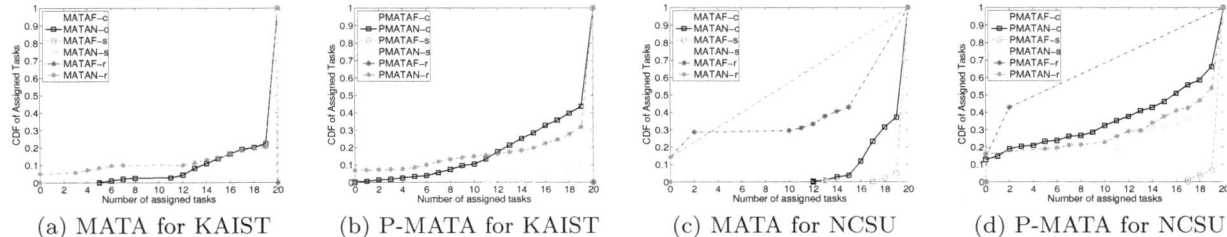

| (a) MATA for KAIST | (b) P-MATA for KAIST | (c) MATA for NCSU | (d) P-MATA for NCSU |

Figure 4: The cdf of assigned tasks while setting the number of tasks to 20 for each scheme and trace

Table 1: Real Traces characteristics

Trace	Length	Requesters	Participants	Bad_Req
NCSU	22 (h)	7	27	2
KAIST	24 (h)	20	72	0

The identification method of requesters is very important since it may highly impact the performance of our assignment scheme. For example, when selecting requesters randomly, we had *bad* ones, i.e, requesters who will not meet other users due to their mobility behavior and consequently, they can not delegate some of their sensing campaigns. This was the case of 2 requesters among the randomly selected ones in the NCSU campus trace, as illustrated in Table 1.

7.3 Simulation Settings

To simulate our crowdsensing hybrid approach, we generate a set of sensing tasks to be assigned by each of the identified requesters to the encountered participants. Besides, we vary the number of tasks and associated workloads to study their impact on our proposed assignment schemes. The number of tasks is, then, selected from $\{20, 40, 60, 80, 100\}$ and the average workload of all tasks τ is selected from $\{1, 3, 5\}$ (hours). Moreover, we vary the workload among different tasks by randomly selecting each task sensing load τ_j in the interval $[0, 2\tau]$.

Furthermore, we generate for each participant p_i his probability of acceptance p_a, and based on it his possible response an_{p_i} as a Bernoulli variable. That is, a participant accepts his assignment,i.e, $an_{p_i} = 1$, with probability p_a and rejects it with probability $p_r = 1 - p_a$ ($an_{p_i} = 0$).

We compare hereafter the performance of our different proposed variants of task assignment schemes; **MATAF**, **MATAN**, **P-MATAF** and **P-MATAN**. Also, we investigate, within each variant, the performance of the different selections of requesters: random, by-contacts and by-speed. We run two different groups of simulations; first while vary-

ing the number of tasks and setting the average workload to 1h and second while varying the average workload of tasks and fixing the number of tasks to 20. Also, we run within each group, 30 simulations for each trace (NCSU/ KAIST), each model of assignment and each method of requesters' selection. Results are illustrated by Figures $3 - 6$.

7.4 Evaluation Results

7.4.1 The Number of Assigned Tasks

First, we evaluate the performance of our proposed schemes on the two real traces KAIST and NCSU while comparing the achieved number of assigned tasks among different requesters' selection policies. Thus, we conduct simulations while varying the number of tasks and setting an average workload $\tau = 1$h.

The results illustrated in Figure 3 show that the offline model achieves the highest values of assigned number of tasks for all requesters' selection policies and for both MATA and P-MATA variants. Hence, the preference and mobility aware variant realizes slightly lower values since it considers the ability of a user to reject his assignment which reduces the total final number of assigned tasks. Nevertheless, this latter case is more realistic. Besides, for the NCSU real trace case, the number of requesters and users in general, 7 and 34, are smaller than in the KAIST trace; which limits the availability of participants for sensing and consequently impacts the final assignment results.

Similarly, we investigate the distribution of the assigned number of tasks for different requesters' selection types while setting the required tasks number to 20. The results in Figure 4 conform with our observations. That is, the offline models of mobility-aware assignment for both traces outperform the online ones by assigning all and 80% of sensing tasks for the KAIST trace and the NCSU trace, respectively. Moreover, the distribution of assigned tasks by P-MATA scheme describes the competitive achieved results when assigning, for all requesters' selection types, more than 50% of

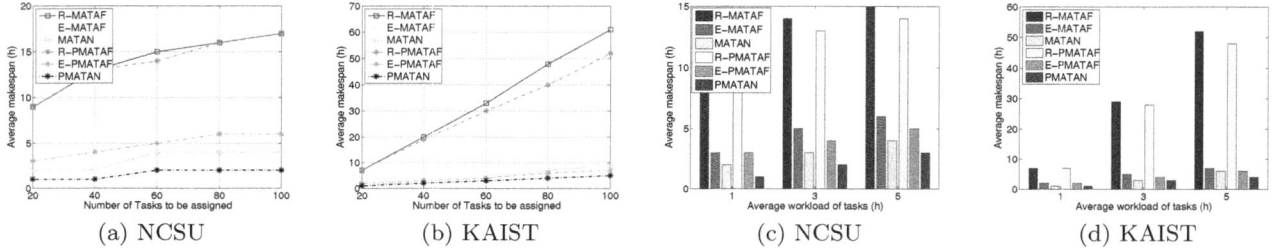

| (a) NCSU | (b) KAIST | (c) NCSU | (d) KAIST |

Figure 5: Average makespan while varying the number of tasks (a), (b) ($\tau = 1$ h) and varying the average workload (c), (d) ($m = 20$)

the required tasks in 70% of the experiments for the NCSU trace and in 80% of the cases for the KAIST trace.

Finally, we compare the achieved results among different selection policies of requesters. We observe that for the two real traces, and the different variants and models of assignment, the selected requesters by-speed are the ones with the most competitive results, especially in the online model. For instance, the identified requesters using the by-speed policies assigned by MATAF and P-MATAF methods all the tasks for the KAIST trace and more than 90% for the NCSU one. Also, this selection policy enhances the online assignment model results by realizing the most important values of assigned tasks for all traces and schemes.

As a result, we consider this policy as the main selection to identify requesters within each trace and compare the different algorithms based on this.

7.4.2 The Achieved Average Makespan

Hereafter, we evaluate the performance of our schemes by measuring the achieved value of the average makespan, the objective to be minimized in this work, while varying first the number of tasks and second the average workload. The results are shown in Figure 5 for both traces.

It is worth mentioning, that we computed the *Real* makespan for the offline models. That is, we sum the workload of all tasks for each participant at the end of each assignment phase. Then, we recompute the makespan of each requester as detailed in Theorem 1 for the MATA variant and Theorem 2 for the P-MATA variant. This is because, in the offline model the requester assigns tasks based on his only Expected Sensing Time and without considering the fact that a participant may have received other assignments from other requetsers. Hence, we denote By R-x the real makespan of a scheme, similarly for E-x to denote the estimated makespan.

Clearly, the average makespan of all algorithms increases as function of the number of tasks or the average workload. We notice also that the variance between the estimated and the real makespan is relatively important. For both real traces, the estimated makespan of the two variants MATA and P-MATA are rather close to the online achieved average makespan. This was proved to be wrong by the high values described in the real makespan measures. Consequently, the online model is proved to realize better performance when considering the updated Expected Sensing Time, EST, for all encountered participants.

Furthermore, the probability and mobility aware assignment scheme (P-MATA) has the best performance among all schemes by realizing the smallest values of the average makespan. In other words, **P-MATAN** assigns tasks in

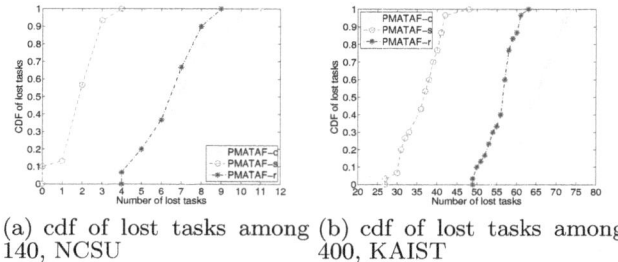

(a) cdf of lost tasks among 140, NCSU (b) cdf of lost tasks among 400, KAIST

Figure 6: cdf of lost tasks in both real traces for a simulation of all requesters' selection types with 20 tasks and 1h average workload.

a better approach. As a matter of fact, we consider in this variant and model the updated IST and the preference of the participant, which enhances the re-assignment of rejected tasks in time. Note that these results are valid for both cases, while varying the number of tasks or varying the average workload and for both traces, NCSU and KAIST.

7.4.3 The Number of Lost Tasks

Finally, we study the distribution of the number of lost tasks. As we mentioned earlier, in **P-MATAF** assignment scheme, requesters assign tasks respecting the generated Γ_{PF} strategy, however, without waiting for a response from the encountered participant which may result in a non perceived rejection and consequently some lost tasks. In Figure 6, we plot the cumulative distribution function (cdf) of the number of lost tasks for both real traces and for different types of requesters' identification.

Note that since we have 7 requesters for the NCSU trace, we measure the number of lost tasks among the total $7 \times 20 = 140$ tasks to be assigned. Similarly, for the KAIST trace we designated 20 requesters, i.e, 400 tasks. For the former trace, the number of lost tasks does not exceed 10% while for the latter one it goes up to 18%. Particularly, for both traces, we observe that the speed-based selected requesters assign better the held tasks by a percentage of only 2% of lost tasks for the NCSU trace and 11% for the KAIST trace. This conforms with the previous evaluation metrics. Besides, we emphasize the fact that the **P-MATAN** assignment scheme is proved to perform better among all variants with no lost tasks by holding back the rejected tasks and assigning them when encountering other participants.

8. CONCLUSIONS & FUTURE WORK

In this paper, we investigated the hybrid multi-task assignment in participatory sensing systems. Thus, we introduced a "support" phase where requesters identified by the central platform need to delegate sensing campaigns to adequate encountered participants. To do so, we investigated the different possible requesters' selection type to identify the most efficient ones. Moreover, we studied the participants' arrival and preference models to the requesters in order to select those who minimize the average makespan of all sensing tasks. Furthermore, we advocated two variants of assignment schemes; a mobility-aware variant and a jointly preference and mobility-aware one, and we proposed an offline as well as an online greedy-based algorithms for each variant. We showed through real traces-based simulations, that the preference and mobility-aware variant outperforms the other models, particularly, by its online model which achieves the minimum average makespan with zero lost tasks.

For future work, we will extend our solution to consider the effect of selfish participants who may repetitively reject their assignments. This can be addressed by introducing incentivizing mechanisms to enhance the cooperation between the requesters and the encountered participants.

9. REFERENCES

[1] N.D. Lane, E. Miluzzo, Hong Lu, D. Peebles, T. Choudhury, and A.T. Campbell. A survey of mobile phone sensing. *IEEE Communications Magazine*, 48(9):140–150, 2010.

[2] Prashanth Mohan, Venkata N. Padmanabhan, and Ramachandran Ramjee. Nericell: Rich monitoring of road and traffic conditions using mobile smartphones. In *Proc. ACM Sensys*, pages 323–336, 2008.

[3] Min Mun, Sasank Reddy, Katie Shilton, Nathan Yau, Jeff Burke, Deborah Estrin, Mark Hansen, Eric Howard, Ruth West, and Péter Boda. PEIR, the personal environmental impact report, as a platform for participatory sensing systems research. In *Proc. MobiSys*, pages 55–68, 2009.

[4] J. Burke, D. Estrin, M. Hansen, A. Parker, N. Ramanathan, S. Reddy, and M. B. Srivastava. Participatory sensing. In *Proc. WSW: Mobile Device Centric Sensor Networks and Applications*, pages 117–134, 2006.

[5] Xiang Sheng, Jian Tang, Xuejie Xiao, and Guoliang Xue. Leveraging GPS-less sensing scheduling for green mobile crowd sensing. *IEEE Internet of Things Journal*, 1(4):328–336, 2014.

[6] Xianling Lu, Deying Li, Biaofei Xu, Wenping Chen, and Zhiming Ding. Minimum cost collaborative sensing network with mobile phones. In *Proc. IEEE ICC*, pages 1816–1820, 2013.

[7] C. H. Liu, B. Zhang, X. Su, J. Ma, W. Wang, and K. K. Leung. Energy-aware participant selection for smartphone-enabled mobile crowd sensing. *IEEE Systems Journal*, PP(99):1–12, 2015.

[8] R. Ben Messaoud and Y. Ghamri-Doudane. Fair QoI and energy-aware task allocation in participatory sensing. In *IEEE WCNC*, 2016.

[9] R. Ben Messaoud and Y. Ghamri-Doudane. QoI and

energy-aware mobile sensing scheme: A tabu-search approach. In *IEEE 82nd VTC Fall*, pages 1–6, 2015.

[10] Man Hon Cheung, Richard Southwell, Fen Hou, and Jianwei Huang. Distributed time-sensitive task selection in mobile crowdsensing. In *Proc. ACM MobiHoc*, pages 157–166, 2015.

[11] M. Xiao, J. Wu, L. Huang, Y. Wang, and C. Liu. Multi-task assignment for crowdsensing in mobile social networks. In *Proc. IEEE INFOCOM*, pages 2227–2235, 2015.

[12] L. Pu, X. Chen, J. Xu, and X. Fu. Crowdlet: Optimal worker recruitment for self-organized mobile crowdsourcing. In *Proc. IEEE INFOCOM*, 2016.

[13] J. Wu, M. Xiao, and L. Huang. Homing spread: Community home-based multi-copy routing in mobile social networks. In *Proc. IEEE INFOCOM*, pages 2319–2327, 2013.

[14] Wei Gao, Qinghua Li, Bo Zhao, and Guohong Cao. Multicasting in delay tolerant networks: A social network perspective. In *Proc. ACM MobiHoc*, pages 299–308, 2009.

[15] K. F. Riley. *Mathematical methods for physics and engineering: a comprehensive guide*. Cambridge University Press, 2006.

[16] Injong Rhee, Minsu Shin, Seongik Hong, Kyunghan Lee, Seongjoon Kim, and Song Chong. CRAWDAD dataset ncsu/mobilitymodels (v. 2009-07-23). Downloaded from http://crawdad.org/ncsu/mobilitymodels/20090723/GPS, 2009.

Experimental Validation of a Distributed Self-Configured 6TiSCH with Traffic Isolation in Low Power Lossy Networks

Fabrice Theoleyre
CNRS, ICube lab
University of Strasbourg
Strasbourg, France
theoleyre@unistra.fr

Georgios Z. Papadopoulos
IRISA, Télécom Bretagne
Institut Mines Télécom
Rennes, France
georgios.papadopoulos@telecom-bretagne.eu

ABSTRACT

Time Slotted Channel Hopping (TSCH) is among the proposed Medium Access Control (MAC) layer protocols of the IEEE 802.15.4-2015 standard for low-power wireless communications in Internet of Things (IoT). TSCH aims to guarantee high network reliability by exploiting channel hopping and keeping the nodes time-synchronized at the MAC layer. In this paper, we focus on the traffic isolation issue, where several clients and applications may cohabit under the same wireless infrastructure without impacting each other. To this end, we present an autonomous version of 6TiSCH where each device uses only local information to select their timeslots. Moreover, we exploit 6TiSCH tracks to guarantee flow isolation, defining the concept of shared (best-effort) and dedicated (isolated) tracks. Our thorough experimental performance evaluation campaign, conducted over the open and large scale FIT IoT-LAB testbed (by employing the OpenWSN), highlight the interest of this solution to provide reliability and low delay while not relying on any centralized component.

Keywords

IoT; 6TiSCH; IEEE802.15.4-2015-TSCH; distributed reservation; self-configuration; traffic adaptive; experiments;

1. INTRODUCTION

During the last years we have experienced the emergence of a new paradigm called Internet of Things (IoT) in which smart and connected objects cooperatively construct a (wireless) network of things [1].

In an IoT deployment, energy-efficiency is one of the most important parameters, since smart objects have to save energy to meet the lifetime requirements of typical applications. Since MAC layer is responsible for controlling the main source of energy consumption [2], therefore, a strong focus has been put on the medium access: the devices should turn OFF their radio for most of the time.

Besides, many modern applications cannot accommodate the best effort approach. For instance, losing one packet for a smart meter application means the measures are incorrect for this subscriber. More importantly, several applications or even clients should cohabit under the same wireless infrastructure to reduce the cost of deployment [3]. These requirements lead researchers to design deterministic algorithms for medium access. Thus, the wireless infrastructure is able to provide *stable* and *predictable* performance.

IEEE 802.15.4-2015 standard was published in 2016 [4], to offer a certain quality of service for deterministic industrial-type applications. Among the MAC schemes defined in this standard, Time-Slotted Channel Hopping (TSCH) is for lower-power and reliable networking solutions. Indeed, by adopting a channel hopping approach, the standard makes the transmissions more reliable [5]. Besides, TSCH relies on scheduling where the contention is solved deterministically, and each radio link receives a given amount of bandwidth. Thus, TSCH is particularly efficient to save energy: a node has to stay awake only when it transmits or receives a frame.

6TiSCH IETF Working Group (WG) is currently defining a set of protocols to fill the gap between IPv6 and TSCH [6]. It aims at executing IPv6 over a reservation based MAC by reserving TSCH slots. Moreover, 6TiSCH introduces the concept of tracks, where certain timeslots are mapped to a given flow, guaranteeing thus traffic isolation. Different flows from different applications are mapped to different tracks. We consider this feature as a key enabler for reliability in IoT. Recently, Orchestra proposed an innovative way to exploit the 6TiSCH architecture, highlighting the relevance of a distributed version [7]. However, it does not guarantee traffic isolation since it does not implement any track management solution.

Our 6TiSCH version is resilient: we propose to adapt the schedule locally, based on the radio link quality and the actual amount of traffic to forward. We do not rely on a centralized component which would increase the delay to react to changes. In this paper, we present a distributed version of 6TiSCH to guarantee traffic isolation and deterministic performance.

The contributions presented in this paper are threefold:

1. We first propose a distributed implementation of 6TiSCH with traffic isolation using tracks, where each pair of nodes negotiates the required bandwidth.

2. We then describe mechanisms so that each node decides locally which timeslot to use, and for which track;

3. We perform a thorough experimental evaluation over the FIT IoT-LAB testbed, to highlight the feasibility of an high reliability and low delay solution.

2. BACKGROUND AND RELATED WORK

Hereafter, we first provide the necessary background about TSCH and 6TiSCH. We then review the existing contributions that provide high reliability with deterministic performance for Low-Power Lossy Networks (LLNs).

2.1 TSCH Overview

As previously mentioned, TSCH is among the MAC protocols defined in the IEEE 802.15.4-2015 standard [4] that provide high-level reliability and low-power operation in LLNs.

In TSCH networks, a schedule is computed and distributed among the nodes, therefore nodes must remain time synchronized throughout the network deployment. Moreover, under TSCH operation, time is divided into timeslots of equal length, large enough to transmit a frame and to receive an acknowledgement. A set of timeslots constructs a slotframe. At each timeslot, a node may transmit or receive a frame, or it may turn its radio OFF for saving energy. Finally, each timeslot is labelled with Absolute Sequence Number (ASN), a variable which counts the number of timeslots since the network was established. Thus, based on ASN and its scheduler, each node decides when to transmit or receive a frame.

Furthermore, to defeat noise and interference, and consequently to enable high reliability, TSCH proposes to implement a channel hopping scheme. To each transmission opportunity is attached a *channel offset*. In TSCH, a *cell* is a transmission opportunity described by a pair of timeslot and channel offset. Thus, at the beginning of each timeslot, the selection of the actual channel is derived from the channel offset and the ASN.

Finally, in TSCH, a cell may be either shared or dedicated, see Fig. 1. In the former mode, several interfering nodes are authorized to transmit: they must execute a slotted CSMA-CA mechanism to avoid collisions. In the latter case, a collection of non interfering transmitters are the owners of the cell: they transmit in contention-free mode.

2.2 6TiSCH Overview

6TiSCH IETF WG aims at defining protocols to bind IPv6 (i.e., 6LoWPAN) and reservation based MAC layer (i.e., TSCH). In 6TiSCH minimal [8], one shared cell is reserved at the beginning of the slotframe to exchange control packets (cf. Fig. 1). For instance, Enhanced Beacons (EBs) are transmitted during the shared timeslot so that the neighbors may associate with the existing network, while the rest of the slotframe comprises dedicated cells.

Furthermore, 6TiSCH makes a distinction between the protocol which defines how to negotiate the cells (i.e. 6P [9]) and the algorithm deciding how much cells to allocate in the schedule (the Scheduling Function such as SF0 [10]). The solution is very flexible since any scheduling algorithm may be practically implemented: a new Scheduling Function has just to be defined and interfaced with 6P. Thus, 6P may work either in a centralized manner (e.g. a node asks a Path Computation Element for new cells to use) or in a distributed manner (e.g. SF0 decides how many cells to allocate based on the local measures).

6TiSCH introduces the concept of *track* [11]. A track corresponds to dedicated radio resource, along with a multihop

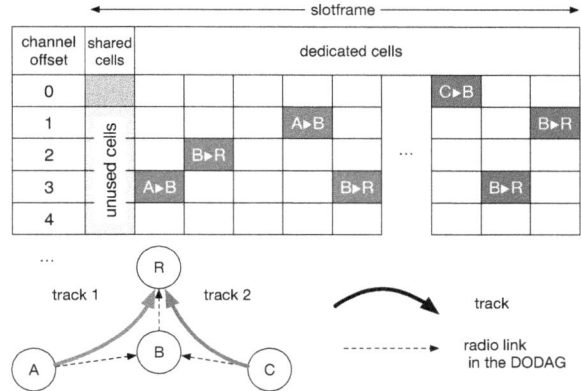

Figure 1: Schedule in a 6TiSCH network, using two different tracks for traffic isolation.

path. More precisely, a set of cells (a *bundle*) is reserved for each hop. By selecting different cells for different data flow, 6TiSCH may provide traffic isolation. A track forwarding scheme is in this case applied: when 6P receives a frame to forward, it automatically finds the outgoing bundle associated with the incoming cells.

Furthermore, 6TiSCH introduces the concept of *chunk*: each node is able to separate the scheduling matrix in non overlapping chunks[12]. Then, the churns are allocated (in a centralized or distributed manner) to different nodes, so that each of them can pick in its churn when it has to allocate new cells.

In Fig. 1, the flow from A to the border router R, via node B, will be assigned to track 1. Besides, the same node (e.g., B) may forward an additional flow, for instance from C, using a different track (i.e., 2).

2.3 Scheduling

6TiSCH may rely either on an centralized scheduler (i.e., the Path Computation Element (PCE)) or on a distributed algorithm.

2.3.1 Centralized Scheduling

Several scheduling algorithms can be used by 6P. In [13], the tradeoff between a centralized and a distributed scheduling is studied. By adopting a queue theory approach, the authors showed that a centralized one is more efficient.

Ghosh *et al.* [14] proposed to minimize the schedule length in a multichannel TDMA environment. Similarly, TASA proposed to construct a centralized scheduling for a multihop TSCH network achieving the same objective [15].

Yigit *et al.* [16] studied the impact of routing on scheduling. The nodes have to use a larger number of timeslots when the radio links are unreliable. Schedex [17] proposed to schedule additional timeslots until an end-to-end delay constraint is not anymore respected.

All these centralized approaches assume the interference can be estimated accurately. They are particularly well suited for industrial networks in controlled environments.

2.3.2 Distributed Solutions

To not rely on a centralized controller, certain distributed solutions have been proposed. DeTAS presented a decentralized version of TASA [18], assembling micro-schedules. Phung *et al.* [19] proposed to use a Reinforcement Learning based scheduling algorithm to cope with a variable traffic. However, the authors do not propose dedicated cells: the nodes have always to execute a CSMA-CA phase before transmitting their packets. In the same way, Z-MAC [20] proposes a mix between CSMA and TDMA, where timeslots are assigned distributively, solving iteratively the collisions.

Orchestra was proposed recently [7]. As exposed previously, Orchestra uses dedicated cells selected according to a pseudo-random sequence. However, it does not implement tracks (i.e., traffic isolation) and, thus, may suffer from the funneling effect [21], since each nodes reserves the same number of timeslots with its parent.

SF0 [10] proposed a Scheduling Function to compute the number of cells to allocate/remove. Palattella proposed also to use an hysteresis function to decide when new cells have to be added or removed [22]. While it presents a promising approach, they did not present experimental evaluation, and moreover, they didn't describe the integration of tracks to provide traffic isolation (the bandwidth estimation algorithm is let to a future work).

3. A FULLY DISTRIBUTED VERSION OF 6TISCH

Hereafter, we will present our distributed 6TiSCH architecture where all decisions are taken locally, and guaranteeing traffic isolation: different applications may be assigned to different tracks, and use consequently different cells.

- the shared cells are only used to transmit 6P packets (unicast) and Enhanced Beacons and DIO (broadcast);

- the other unicast packets such as DAO or data packets use dedicated cells, reserved for a given track.

In other words, data transmissions use the deterministic part of TSCH, while random access is only reserved for 6P negotiations and beacons.

3.1 Track Management

6TiSCH track consists in one track owner (64 bits) and one track ID (16 bits). We propose here a way to exploit these tracks to enable the following features:

Isolated track: a source node has to reserve one end-to-end track for its flow. To guarantee traffic isolation, the track must be only used by one data flow. Thus, the track owner is its own MAC address (64 bits) and the track ID (16 bits) corresponds to the application in execution on the node. The track ID may be assigned uniquely before the deployment, following the same approach as the well known ports. Thus, a network may support at most 65,535 different applications.

Convergent track (shared track, e.g., alarms): because data transmissions are in this case unfrequent, reserving one cell during each slotframe may waste bandwidth. However, we must guarantee small end-to-end delays for alarms, and the maximum time between two cells should be minimized. In particular, if an event is detected by several nodes, the delay of the first exemplary received by the border router is the most important one.

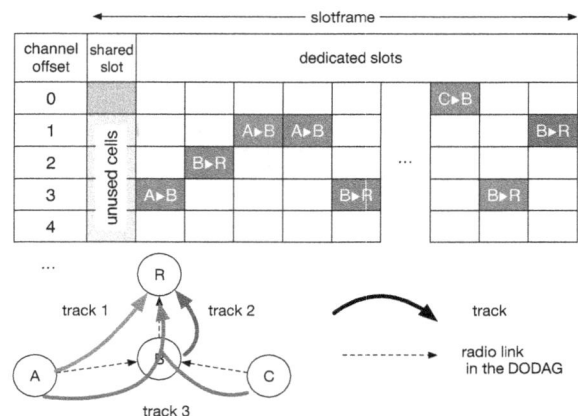

Figure 2: Mixing heterogeneous applications in the same 6TiSCH instance.

We propose for these applications to reserve a common convergecast track, shared among all the sources of the same application. Thus, the track owner is the address of the destination, and the track ID is specific to the application. All the other nodes which generate data packets to this destination will, by definition, use the same track. It is important to note that the packets from different sources do not collide: they use dedicated cells. However, the packets after the first one have to be buffered, increasing the delay, and the probability of a buffer overflow if a large amount of traffic is generated at the same time.

When packets are routed via the border router, the track owner is extracted from the RPL DAG Information Object (DIO).

Furthermore, we may mix different applications in the same network. In Fig. 2, the smart metering application uses isolated tracks (blue and green for two applications). Bandwidth reserved for the the blue track cannot be used by the *green* flow. On the contrary, the application on A and C use a convergent track (in red). Let's imagine that both A and C generate one packet during the same slotframe. B has only one outgoing cell to forward the two packets: the second one has to be forwarded in the next slotframe.

The convergent track strategy represents well the behavior of classical wireless sensor networks: each source may generate an indefinite number of packets, and the relay nodes expects to forward them in a best effort manner. However, different applications use different tracks, and therefore orthogonal radio resources. In other words, we multiplex only the transmissions from the same application (and different source nodes).

Note that we do not implement a GMPLS-like approach to manage the tracks, as advocated by [11]. We insert rather information in the 6P transaction to specify which track is associated with the cells to insert in the schedule. For this purpose, our Scheduling Function may use the `metadata` field of the 6P `Add Request` message. Later, when a node receives a data frame, it has to extract the track associated with the incoming cell, and tag the frame accordingly in the queue. We also implemented a FIFO discipline: the node picks up the first packet from the queue with the trackID corresponding to the outgoing dedicated cell.

3.2 Bandwidth Requirement Estimation with SF

We propose a simple strategy to allocate the bandwidth on-demand. The Scheduling Function SF0 [10] collects the bandwidth requirements from neighbor nodes. Note that it does not detail how per track requirements are computed. We here propose a Scheduling Function SF_{loc} which takes decisions considering only local information. Besides, SF_{loc} allocates different cells for different tracks. In this way, we are able to compute a schedule in a distributed manner while maintaining traffic isolation: two applications using different tracks will be managed independently by SF_{loc}. Besides, we do not require each application defines a priori its requirements: SF_{loc} is self-adaptive and learns from the forwarded packets.

In our explanations, we focus on the convergecast traffic pattern. A node has consequently to negotiate with its RPL preferred parent a list of cells to use for each of its tracks. A node, which has to decide how many cells to reserve, considers only its own buffer and its schedule utilization.

3.2.1 Cell insertion

We have to decide when a new cell has to be negotiated with a neighbor. We follow a similar approach to SF0, while only using the amount of forwarded traffic to compute the bandwidth requirements:

1. when a packet is inserted in the queue, SF_{loc} is triggered;

2. if the node already has an on-going 6P transaction, SF_{loc} stops: only one track may be modified at the same time;

3. for each track tr, the node computes:

   (a) the list of outgoing cells $\mathcal{C}_{out}$ toward the parent and the average number of transmissions required before receiving an acknowledgment ($\forall k \in \mathcal{C}_{out}, ETX(k)$);

   (b) the number of packets present in the queue for this track $N_{pk}(tr)$

   (c) if the following condition does not hold:

   $$\sum_{k \in \mathcal{C}_{out}} \frac{1}{ETX(k)} \geq N_{pk}(tr) \qquad (1)$$

   SF_{loc} asks 6P to reserve the following number of cells:

   $$N_{pk}(t) - \sum_{k \in \mathcal{C}_{out}} \frac{1}{ETX(k)} \qquad (2)$$

   (upper bounded by 3 since an 6P Information Element may contain at most 3 timeslots).

Our approach is robust to interference: a colliding cell will present a larger Expected Transmission Count (ETX), and will be detected quickly, using the same mechanism as [23] (tx-housekeeping feature). A bootstrapping node will reserve quickly new cells for the given track: this over-provisioning efficiently deals with lossy links. The colliding cells will be detected and removed later.

We plan in the future to implement a more sophisticated mechanism. Recently, Domingo-Prieto et al. [24] proposed to avoid oscillations by considering the dynamics of the bandwidth requirement. The solution was evaluated by simulations and seems promising.

We will detail in the next subsection how 6P selects the actual cells (timeslot and channel offset) to use.

3.2.2 Cell removal

The routing topology might changes since RPL is dynamic. In the same way, a node may be too aggressive and may have reserved too much bandwidth, when e.g., a new parent is selected and it has to empty its buffer. A node has to later remove the unused cells.

To select the cells to remove, we consider a given cell becomes useless if no ack is received during a long time. This cell is considered useless even if unicast packets are transmitted but not acknowledged. In this way, we remove both the colliding and the unused cells. Indeed, no contention is implemented for dedicated cells: the data packets will be deterministically lost if a pair of interfering radio links uses the same cell.

To this end, we propose a simple timeout based approach: when a cell is not used during at least $Timeout_{SF_{loc}-tx}$ seconds, the owner of the cell (the transmitter) asks the receiver to release this cell. More precisely, 6P sends a link-removal request, which specifies the timeslot and the channel offset to remove from the schedule.

Possibly, the radio link may not be anymore usable. Thus, the transmitter removes silently a cell if the 6P link-removal failed after all the possible retransmissions.

Inversely, a receiver removes silently a cell if it is unused during $Timeout_{SF_{loc}-rx}$. To avoid inconsistent decisions, the following condition must hold:

$$Timeout_{SF_{loc}-tx} \ll Timeout_{SF_{loc}-rx} \qquad (3)$$

In particular, it must take into account the time to transmit the link-removal request and to receive the associated ACK.

3.3 Distributed Scheduling With 6P

To make 6TiSCH entirely distributed, a pair of nodes must be able to decide which cell should be used to exchange packets, without the help of a centralized PCE.

We present here two different approaches to either reduce the number of collisions (random) or to reduce the end-to-end delay (contiguous).

3.3.1 Random Scheduling

When the nodes select autonomously the cells to use with their parent, they do not have a vision of the cells already reserved by an interfering transmitter. To reduce the probability of collision, we propose to select randomly the cells to use: we minimize the probability to have colliding cells in the global schedule. As it is shown in performance evaluation Section, this simple and greedy approach is efficient and robust.

When a node has to reserve k new cells, 6P must ask its preferred parent to reserve some additional bandwidth for a given track, using a 2-step 6P transaction:

1. the transmitter N_t selects j timeslots ($j \geq k$), selected randomly among the available timeslots in its schedule. It selects one random channel offset for each of these timeslots;

2. N_t constructs a `link-request` including these cells and transmits the packet during a shared cell;

3. the receiver N_r selects the first k cells present in the `link-request` and available in its schedule. It enqueues a `link-reply`, which will be transmitted during one shared slot. If there is not enough available cells ($< k$), N_r refuses the transaction and sends an empty negative `link-reply`. Else, the reply includes the list of the selected cells.

4. N_t receives the `link-reply` and updates its schedule with the cells allocated by its parent if the reply is positive.

Selecting randomly the cells to use minimizes the probability of collision, but tends to increase the end-to-end delay. Intuitively, the outgoing and incoming cells being chosen randomly, the end-to-end delay equals on average:

$$delay = \frac{hops * SF_{length} * T_{slot}}{2} \qquad (4)$$

With hops being the number of hops in the route, SF_{length} the slotframe length, and T_{slot} the timeslot duration (by default 15ms). Besides, a node, which forwards many flows, will have to buffer many packets since the outgoing and incoming cells may be far away. Thus, some packets may be dropped because of buffer overflows. However, as we highlighted in our experiments this effect is limited.

3.3.2 Contiguous Scheduling

In this second approach, we focus on minimizing the end-to-end delay. To this aim, we propose to minimize the buffering delay:

1. With SF_{loc}, the transmitter N_t computes the number of cells ($= k$) to reserve toward its parent for the track tr. It identifies in its schedule the last slot number $T_{rx\_last}(tr)$ which is used to receive a packet for the track tr.

   - If no incoming cell exists (i.e., N_t generated the packet), $T_{rx\_last}(tr)$ is chosen randomly;

2. N_t selects the first available cells after $T_{rx\_last}(tr)$ and chooses randomly one channel offset for each of them. It constructs a `link-request` to piggyback this list;

3. The receiver N_r selects the first k cells from the `link-request` also available in its schedule. The following cases may occur:

   (a) at least k cells are available: N_r selects the k first of them, and constructs the associated `link-reply` as usually;

   (b) not enough cells are available:

      i. N_r constructs a `link-reply` and piggybacks an Information Element which lists the *busy* cells.

      ii. N_t receives this `link-reply` and will insert in its own schedule the blacklisted cells, linked with the parent. When N_t will send another `link-request` to N_r, theses busy cells cannot be selected.

4. PERFORMANCE EVALUATION

4.1 Experimental Setup

Our experimental campaign was conducted over the FIT IoT-LAB platform in Grenoble [25]. This federated platform provides access to a large collection of motes. We employed the m3 nodes, based on a STM32 (ARM Cortex M3) microcontroller (ST2M32F103REY). It embeds an AT86RF231 radio chipset, providing thus, an IEEE 802.15.4 compliant PHY layer.

4.1.1 Topology

FIT IoT-LAB allows for several experiments to be executed concurrently. Thus, we evaluate the behavior of 6TiSCH under real-world conditions, with potential external interference. The nodes are placed in corridors, in false ceilings and floors, to mimic smart buildings scenarios. To construct multihop topologies, we select nodes sufficiently far from each other: we alternate between ceils and floors, and two consecutive nodes are separated by approximatively 1.5meters. We selected the nodes in the corridor located in the middle (cf. Fig. 3).

4.1.2 Default parameters

Furthermore, we employed the OpenWSN*, that provides an open-source implementation of the 6TiSCH stack (i.e., IEEE802.15.4-2015 TSCH, 6P, SF, 6LoWPAN and RPL). We implemented in OpenWSN our proposal to handle tracks, schedule appropriately the cells, etc. Our modifications are freely available on GitHub[†].

We use the default parameters value as depicted in Table 1. All nodes take local decisions, based on the information exchanged with their neighbors (EBs, 6P requests and replies). Each mote sends its packets to the border router according to a CBR traffic, see Table 1. To dissociate the impact of traffic and of the network size, we maintain the number of packets generated constant in the network, whatever the number of nodes. Thus, each node generates by default one data packet every $10 * nbNodes$ seconds.

4.1.3 Queue management

Because of tracks, the buffer does not follow a FIFO approach: data packets assigned to a track are buffered until the node enters in a dedicated cell for this particular track. Due to memory constraints, the data buffer is limited, and thus, it may be filled quickly. To guarantee sufficient space for the control packets in the buffer, we reserve by defaults 4 slots in a buffer of 10 frames (cf. Table 1). To avoid privileging old packets in the queues, we implemented a timeout based mechanism, where each data packet is tagged at reception and is dropped after 8 seconds ($\approx$6 slotframes) if it is still present in the queue.

---

*openwsn - open-source implementations of protocol stacks based on Internet of Things standards, https://openwsn.atlassian.net/

[†]https://github.com/ftheoleyre/openwsn-fw/ and https://github.com/ftheoleyre/openwsn-sw/

[‡]In this way, we have a constant number of packets generated in the whole network, even when increasing the number of nodes.

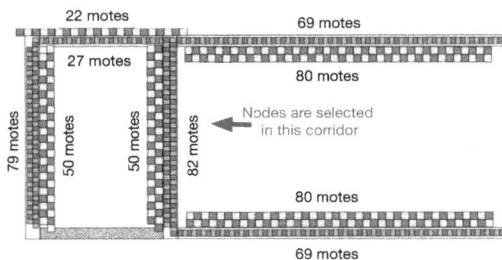

Figure 3: FIT IoT-LAB: topology in the Grenoble testbed.

Table 1: Default parameter values
(the inter-packet time depends on the number of nodes to maintain a constant load with a variable number of nodes)

Experiments	Duration	1.5 $hours$
	Topology	line (floors and ceils)
	Separation	$\approx 1.5\ meters$
TSCH	Slotframe length	101
	Nb. shared cells (N_{shared})	5
	Timeslot duration	15 ms
RPL	DAO period	50 s
	DIO period	8.5 s
CoAP	CBR	10 s * nbNodes
6TiSCH	$Timeout_{SF_{loc}-rx}$	25 s
	$Timeout_{SF_{loc}-tx}$	20 s
Queues	Timeouts	8 s
	Queue size	10 packets
	incl. data packets	at most 6 packets

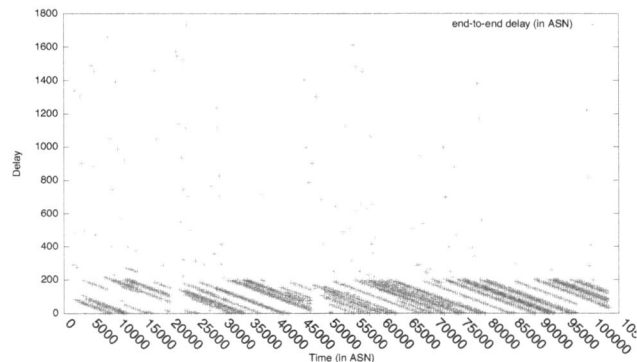

(a) End-to-end delays for each received packets

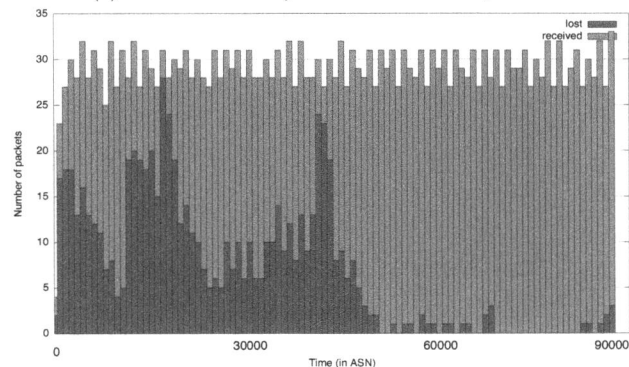

(b) Packet losses versus received

Figure 4: 6TiSCH behavior during the convergence - topology with 12 nodes and one sink (1.5 hours).

4.2 Convergence in a simple topology

We first study the network behavior during the convergence, on a simple 2 hops topology, by selecting an appropriate set of nodes in the same corridor of the Grenoble's IoT Lab topology (cf. Fig. 3). The DODAG is constructed by RPL in a distributed manner.

We first measure the delay performance (see Fig. 4a). As it can be observed, most of the packets are delivered very quickly to the border router, even for nodes several hops far from the sink. A few packets need more time to be delivered: they correspond to retransmissions, since radio links may be unreliable. Finally, only a few packets are delivered in more than 101 slots (i.e., the slotframe length, 1,010 ms).

Considering the packet losses distribution (see Fig. 4b), we can remark that most of the packets are lost at the beginning, during the convergence time. Indeed, each node has to request bandwidth to its parent, negotiating which timeslots and channel offsets should be used for the transmission. Meanwhile, the packets are buffered, and are dropped when they are stored in the buffer for a long duration (i.e., 8 seconds). However, after the convergence period, the reliability significantly increases, only a few packets are dropped, mainly due to the external interference (i.e., other experiments are executed simultaneously on the same testbed).

It is worth mentioning that medium access is deterministic after the convergence: the schedule does not change anymore, and the same cells are used for a given track (i.e., application).

4.3 Contiguous versus Uniformly Distributed Shared Cells

In 6TiSCH, a node may use a shared cell to transmit a frame under contention. Typically, these shared cells are used for EBs, broadcast packets (e.g., DIO), as well as to reserve bandwidth (`Link-Request`, and `Link-Replies`). By default, the N_{shared} first cells are shared in the slotframe (i.e., the *contiguous* scenario).

We here propose rather to distribute uniformly the shared cells. Indeed, IEEE802.15.4-2015-TSCH does not use a backoff at the beginning of a shared cell. It rather implements a CSMA-CA slotted approach *among* the shared cells: the backoff counts the number of shared cells to wait before transmitting a packet. Thus, collisions are very frequent during the shared cells.

We compare the *contiguous* and the *distributed* strategies during the convergence (Fig. 5). We measure the packet losses in a topology with 10 nodes and one sink. With contiguous cells, many collisions occur in the shared cells: `links requests` tend to be lost, retransmitted, and a node has to wait for a long time before receiving a dedicated cell to use. On the contrary, having uniformly distributed cells in the slotframe tends to reduce the collisions and to accelerate the convergence. Thus, we should either use very short slot-

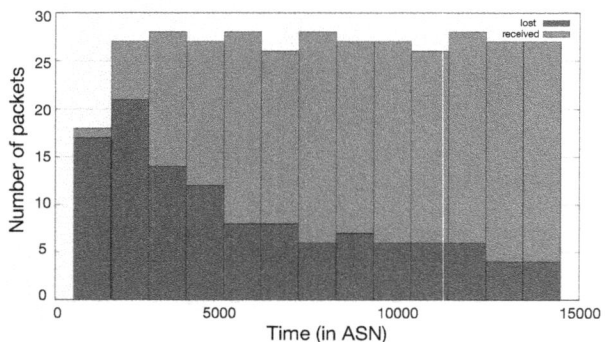

(a) Uniformly distributed cells

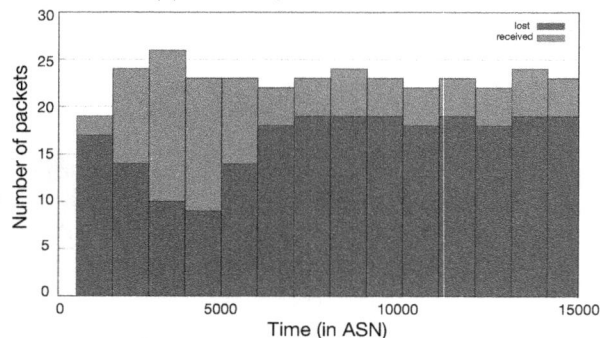

(b) Contiguous cells

Figure 5: Packet losses / received during an experiment of 30 minutes with 10 nodes and one sink.

frames with one single shared cell, or a long slotframe with uniformly distributed shared cells.

4.4 RPL metric

RPL may use any objective function to compute the DAG rank of the nodes. However, minimizing the number of hops tends to perform poorly [26]. Thus, the ETX metric is often privileged: it consists in estimating the number of transmissions before receiving an acknowledgement.

To highlight the impact of the routing metric, we evaluate the behavior of the 6TiSCH stack with the following routing metrics:

Minhops: we minimize here the number of hops: the link metric is set to `minHopRankIncrease` for all the links;

ETX: we use ETX, reported by the MAC layer: ratio of the number of acknowledged packets and the number of transmitted packets for a given neighbor;

RSSI: all links with a RSSI superior than a threshold value have the best link quality (=1). Then, the link metric is incremented for each dBm less.

To compute the DAG rank, a node sums the rank of its parent, and the link cost (i.e. the OF0 objective function in RPL).

Besides, we maintain the default blacklisting method of OpenWSN: a radio link is marked as stable when its RSSI exceeds −80 dBm for 3 consecutive different packets. Inversely, links become unstable when its RSSI is inferior than −80 dBm for 3 consecutive packets.

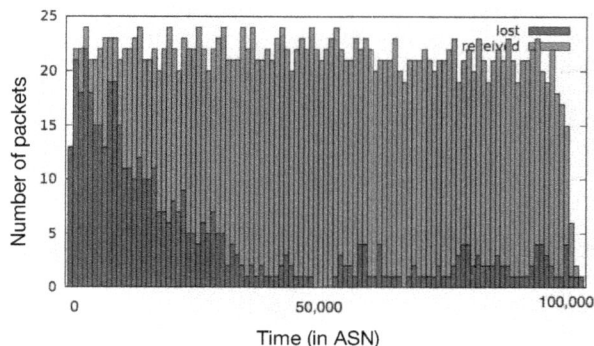

(a) ETX

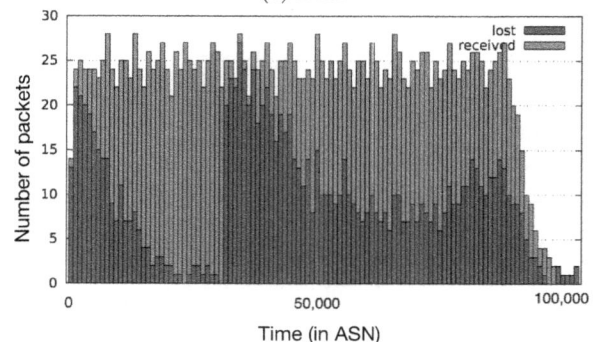

(b) MinHop

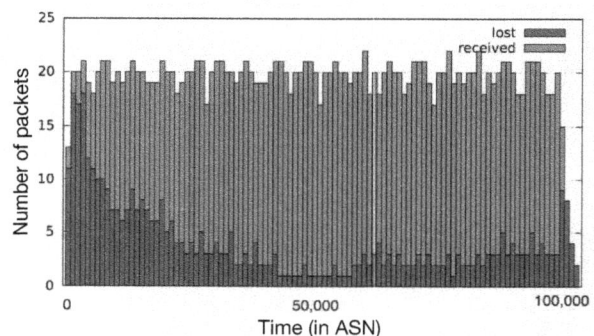

(c) RSSI

Figure 6: Packet losses / received during an experiment of 1.5 hours with 20 nodes and one sink.

Figure 6 presents the impact of the routing metric on the reliability. ETX converges slowly: a significant part of the packets is lost during the beginning (first hour). On the contrary, the packet losses decrease more quickly with `minhop`. Finally, using the RSSI metric constitutes a tradeoff between minhop and ETX.

After 20 minutes, the packet losses increase drastically with `minhop`. A link performs badly and the RPL DAG structure is reconfigured: minHop tends to select unreliable long links. Thus, a large ratio of the nodes have to change their preferred parent, and a storm of requests use the shared cells. The network re-converges very slowly to a legal state. On the contrary, RSSI and ETX perform better: the performance is more stable after 1.5 hours.

In conclusion, ETX needs more time to converge because

it represents an instantaneous metric and is subject to large variations, caused by the radio instability and the dependency on the traffic (i.e., more packets on a route impacts negatively the link quality) [27]. However, 6TiSCH achieves to exhibit stable performance after the network convergence.

4.5 Scheduling algorithm

We finally evaluated the performance of the scheduling algorithms (Fig. 7), comparing our *random* strategy and the *random contiguous* strategy.

The random contiguous strategies selects the outgoing cells to minimize the buffering delay. Mechanically, the *random contiguous* strategy achieves a smaller end to end delay than the *random* strategy.

Besides, we can remark a reconfiguration with the random strategy: after 30 minutes, the DODAG is reconfigured, leading to better performance. However, the end-to-end delay remains superior to that of the contiguous scheduling strategy.

Due to lack of space, we did not represent here the performance for larger topologies. While the random contiguous strategy keeps on reducing the buffering delay, the convergence time is longer: more `link-requests` have to be transmitted before finding an available cell. Besides, shared cells suffer from many collisions when we have more than 20 nodes. Thus, the packet delivery ratio is lower with the random contiguous strategy during the convergence time (30% versus 50% after 30 minutes). In conclusion, 6P has to be improved to enable more reliable transactions.

5. LESSONS

5.1 Guidelines

Based on our experimental results, we conclude the following guidelines should be applied in 6TiSCH:

Non contiguous shared cells: when shared cells are all placed at the beginning of the slotframe, all the requests are buffered during a whole slotframe before being transmitted in the first shared cells. The collisions are consequently very frequent.

On the contrary, we propose to distribute uniformly the shared cells in the slotframe, decreasing thus the pressure, and making 6TiSCH much more efficient.

Routing metric: a blacklisting approach is surprisingly efficient, while the minhop metric converges quickly to a legal schedule. However, it selects the *worst* radio links, which may dysfunction: these local faults impact globally the network, penalizing the convergence.

On the contrary, both the ETX and RSSI metrics perform better. However, some heuristics should be proposed to accelerate the convergence.

5.2 Open Challenges

While our distributed version of 6TiSCH works efficiently in many situations, we highlighted several challenges that still have to be addressed:

Radio link quality estimation: a node has currently to select a parent without exchanging packets (i.e., no dedicated cells has been reserved so far with this possible parent).

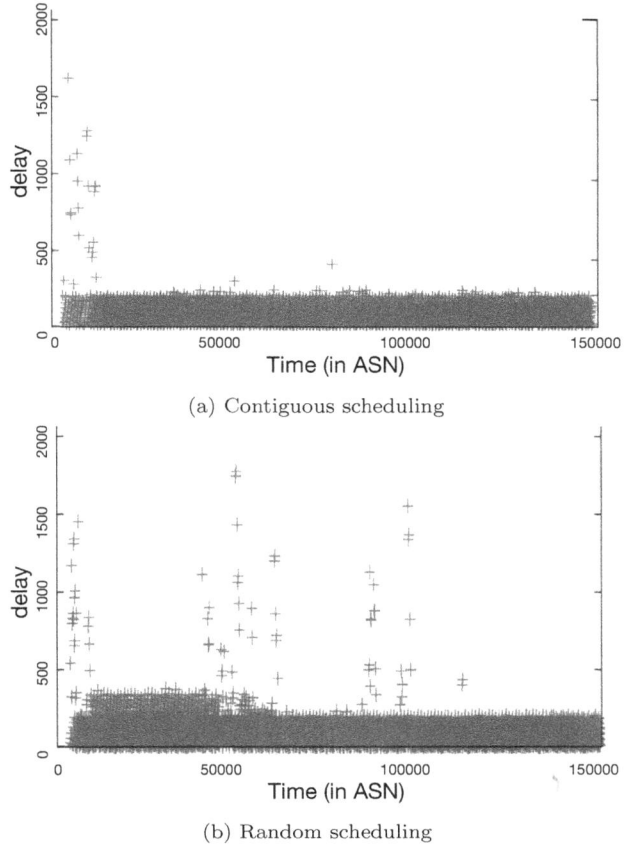

(a) Contiguous scheduling

(b) Random scheduling

Figure 7: Packet delays during an experiment of 1.5hours with 5 nodes and one sink

However, RSSI or the packet losses of EBs may be misleading to estimate the link quality [28]. Worse, the link might be asymmetrical: while EBs are received correctly, a `link-request` may never be received correctly by this parent. This process wastes bandwidth and energy.

We should propose a mechanism to estimate the link quality of a possible parent, while not being already attached to this node;

Dense topologies: the radio link quality estimation is even exacerbated with dense topologies: which neighbor should be selected as parent? While the path metric (its DAG rank) is important, the link quality is also of prime importance. We have to propose schemes, that discover an *acceptable* parent, with a tradeoff between discovery cost and optimality.

Centralized versus Distributed: we expect in the future work to compare quantitatively the performance of a centralized and a distributed scheduling solution. However, we must be able to report to the PCE the link quality of all the neighbors and to estimate the level of interference: this constitutes a challenging objective. Besides, the shared cells are subject to many collisions: how could we increase the end-to-end reliability of the communication to the PCE?

6. CONCLUSION AND PERSPECTIVES

In this paper, we presented a distributed solution of 6TiSCH: a node decides autonomously when and which cells to use with its parent. Moreover, we proposed to exploit *isolated tracks* to provide flow isolation, and to make the transmissions reliable and independent: each application has dedicated (i.e., reserved) bandwidth for its packets transmissions. Inversely, we are also able to mutualize the bandwidth reservation, using a *convergent track*: all the DAO in our experiments use the same convergent track toward the border router. This flexibility of the 6TiSCH architecture and the stability of the performance prove the relevance of a deterministic network for the low power lossy networks.

In a future work, we plan to explore the impact of very large topologies, and to study in depth the maximum distance and traffic TSCH may support efficiently. We also plan to study how we could accelerate the convergence time: we should first reduce the number of collisions among the 6P requests and replies, which increase the delay to negotiate a set of cells with its parents. Furthermore, we should explore which routing metric should be used to avoid re-changing the parent when the radio link quality is initially misestimated.

7. REFERENCES

[1] Luigi Atzori, Antonio Iera, and Giacomo Morabito. The internet of things: A survey. *Computer Networks*, 54(15):2787 – 2805, 2010.

[2] Yi Zhi Zhao et al. A Survey and Projection on Medium Access Control Protocols for Wireless Sensor Networks. *ACM Computer Surveys*, 45(1):7:1–7:37, 2012.

[3] G. Gaillard, D. Barthel, F. Theoleyre, and F. Valois. Service level agreements for wireless sensor networks: A wsn operator's point of view. In *Network Operations and Management Symposium (NOMS)*. IEEE, 2014.

[4] IEEE Standard for Low-Rate Wireless Personal Area Networks (LR-WPANs). *IEEE Std 802.15.4-2015 (Revision of IEEE Std 802.15.4-2011)*, April 2016.

[5] Thomas Watteyne, Ankur Mehta, and Kris Pister. Reliability through frequency diversity: Why channel hopping makes sense. In *PE-WASUN*. ACM, 2009.

[6] IPv6 over the TSCH mode of IEEE 802.15.4e. https://datatracker.ietf.org/wg/6tisch.

[7] Simon Duquennoy, Beshr Al Nahas, Olaf Landsiedel, and Thomas Watteyne. Orchestra: Robust mesh networks through autonomously scheduled tsch. In *SenSys*. ACM, 2015.

[8] X. Vilajosana, et al. Minimal 6TiSCH Configuration. draft-vilajosana-6tisch-minimal-16, June 2016.

[9] Q. Wang and X. Vilajosana. 6top protocol (6p). draft-ietf-6tisch-6top-protocol-02, July 2016.

[10] D. Dujovne, LA. Grieco, MR. Palattella, and N. Accettura. 6TiSCH 6top Scheduling Function Zero (SF0). draft-dujovne-6tisch-6top-sf0-00, March 2016.

[11] P. Thubert. An Architecture for IPv6 over the TSCH mode of IEEE 802.15.4. draft-ietf-6tisch-architecture-10, June 2015.

[12] D. Dujovne, T. Watteyne, X. Vilajosana, and P. Thubert. 6tisch: deterministic ip-enabled industrial internet (of things). *IEEE Communications Magazine*, 52(12):36–41, December 2014.

[13] John N. Tsitsiklis and Kuang Xu. On the power of (even a little) centralization in distributed processing. In *ACM SIGMETRICS*, pages 161–172, 2011.

[14] A. Ghosh, O.D. Incel, V.S.A. Kumar, and B. Krishnamachari. Multi-channel scheduling algorithms for fast aggregated convergecast in sensor networks. In *IEEE MASS*, pages 363–372, 2009.

[15] M.R. Palattella, et al. On Optimal Scheduling in Duty-Cycled Industrial IoT Applications Using IEEE802.15.4e TSCH. *Sensors Journal, IEEE*, 13(10):3655–3666, 2013.

[16] Melike Yigit, Ozlem Durmaz Incel, and Vehbi Cagri Gungor. On the interdependency between multi-channel scheduling and tree-based routing for WSNs in smart grid environments. *Computer Networks*, 65(0):1 – 20, 2014.

[17] Felix Dobslaw, Tingting Zhang, and Mikael Gidlund. End-to-End Reliability-aware Scheduling for Wireless Sensor Networks. *IEEE Transactions on Industrial Informatics*, pages 1–1, 2014.

[18] N. Accettura, M.R. Palattella, G. Boggia, L.A. Grieco, and M. Dohler. Decentralized traffic aware scheduling for multi-hop low power lossy networks in the internet of things. In *WoWMoM*. IEEE, 2013.

[19] Kieu-Ha Phung et al. Schedule-based multi-channel communication in wireless sensor networks: A complete design and performance evaluation. *Ad Hoc Networks*, 26(0):88 – 102, 2015.

[20] Injong Rhee, A. Warrier, M. Aia, Jeongki Min, and M.L. Sichitiu. Z-MAC: A Hybrid MAC for Wireless Sensor Networks. *IEEE/ACM Transactions on Networking*, 16(3):511–524, 2008.

[21] Chieh-Yih Wan, Shane B. Eisenman, Andrew T. Campbell, and Jon Crowcroft. Siphon: Overload traffic management using multi-radio virtual sinks in sensor networks. In *SenSys*. ACM, 2005.

[22] Maria Rita Palattella et al. On-the-Fly Bandwidth Reservation for 6TiSCH Wireless Industrial Networks. *IEEE Sensors Journal*, 16(2):550–560, November 2015.

[23] K. Muraoka, T. Watteyne, N. Accettura, X. Vilajosana, and K. S. J. Pister. Simple distributed scheduling with collision detection in tsch networks. *IEEE Sensors Journal*, 16(15):5848–5849, Aug 2016.

[24] M. Domingo-Prieto, T. Chang, X. Vilajosana, and T. Watteyne. Distributed pid-based scheduling for 6tisch networks. *IEEE Communications Letters*, 20(5):1006–1009, May 2016.

[25] Georgios Z. Papadopoulos, et al. Adding value to WSN simulation using the IoT-LAB experimental platform. In *WiMob*. IEEE, 2013.

[26] Lai Dhananjay, et al. Measurement and characterization of link quality metrics in energy constrained wireless sensor networks. In *GLOBECOM*. IEEE, 2003.

[27] O. Iova, F. Theoleyre, and T. Noel. Stability and efficiency of RPL under realistic conditions in Wireless Sensor Networks. In *PIMRC*. IEEE, 2013.

[28] Nouha Baccour et al. Radio Link Quality Estimation in Wireless Sensor Networks: A Survey. *ACM Transactions Sensor Networks*, 8(4):34:1–34:33, 2012.

A Novel Semi-Supervised Adaboost Technique for Network Anomaly Detection

Yali Yuan
Institute of Computer Science
Goldschmidtstr. 7 37077
Goettingen, Germany
Yali.Yuan@informatik.uni-goettingen.de

Georgios Kaklamanos
Gesellschaft für wissenschaftliche Datenverarbeitung mbH Goettingen (GWDG)
Am Faßberg 11, 37077
Göttingen, Germany
georgios.kaklamanos@gwdg.de

Dieter Hogrefe
Institute of Computer Science
Goldschmidtstr. 7 37077
Goettingen, Germany
hogrefe@informatik.uni-goettingen.de

ABSTRACT

With the developing of Internet, network intrusion has become more and more common. Quickly identifying and preventing network attacks is getting increasingly more important and difficult. Machine learning techniques have already proven to be robust methods in detecting malicious activities and network threats. Ensemble-based and semi-supervised learning methods are some of the areas that receive most attention in machine learning today. However relatively little attention has been given in combining these methods. To overcome such limitations, this paper proposes a novel network anomaly detection method by using a combination of a tri-training approach with Adaboost algorithms. The bootstrap samples of tri-training are replaced by three different Adaboost algorithms to create the diversity. We run 30 iteration for every simulation to obtain the average results. Simulations indicate that our proposed semi-supervised Adaboost algorithm is reproducible and consistent over a different number of runs. It outperforms other state-of-the-art learning algorithms, even with a small part of labeled data in the training phase. Specifically, it has a very short execution time and a good balance between the detection rate as well as the false-alarm rate.

Keywords

Network anomaly detection; tri-training approach; Adaboost algorithms; execution time; detection rate; false alarm rate

1. INTRODUCTION

Intrusion detection systems play an important role in defending against attacks in networks. Their basic aim is to distinguish between the normal network activities and mali-

cious network behaviors, (also known as attacks). Another aim is to classify the attacks into different categories. This functionality falls under the pattern recognition problem.

Even though a lot of effort has been invested on building effective anomaly-based detection systems, it is still an open research area. Different aspects of the problem include large scale data traffic, unbalanced data sets, ambiguous boundaries between normal and intrusive behavior, highly dynamic environments and so on. Given the variety of these problems, each researcher (and solution) is only able to address some of these issues [9].

Adaboost, as a well-known ensemble-based boosting technique, has already been used to improve the accuracy of anomaly-based detection system. In 2008, Weiming Hu et al. [3] are the first to apply the Adaboost algorithm to anomaly-based intrusion detection. In order to improve the performance, they modified the initial weights to be adaptable and also introduced some simple strategies to avoid overfitting and noise. Both the computational complexity and the error rates are low. Later, a Boosted Subspace Probabilistic Neural Network (BSPNN) was proposed by Tich Phuoc Tran et al. [8]. BSPNN combines Neural Networks and Adaboost to improve the accuracy of anomaly detection. Naive Bayes and Adaboost were used in [1], where the votes of each individual classifier, were combined to classify unknown or known examples.

As stated in [4], Jimin Li et al. proposed a semi-supervised SVM method to improve the accuracy of an anomaly detection system. This method employed three different SVMs for the classification algorithms 'of tri-training. Experiments based on KDDcup99 [5] data set showed that tri-training can improve the classification accuracy of SVMs. However, the computational complexity is very high because of the high computational cost of SVM. This renders the system impractical in many real world intrusion detection applications.

By reviewing the related work, we found that the current approaches for intrusion detection systems have the following three problems.

1) The balance of the detection rates and the false-alarm rates are not good. Some of the approaches suffer from relatively high false-alarm rates, although they can obtain high detection rates.

MSWiM '16, November 13–17, 2016, Malta, Malta
© 2016 ACM. ISBN 978-1-4503-4502-6/16/11...$15.00
DOI: http://dx.doi.org/10.1145/2988287.2989177

2) The time cost for most of the current approaches is oppressively high, which makes them impractical in real-world applications.

3) In many practical applications, labeled data are limited, while unlabeled data are in abundance. Nonetheless, most of the current approaches are unable to use unlabeled data for anomaly detection.

Based on the above, the focus of this paper is to build an anomaly-based intrusion detection system, using tri-training [10] with three different Adaboost algorithms. This combines the ensemble-based approach and semi-supervised learning methods. It minimizes the number of false positives and false negatives and improves the accuracy and efficiency of the detection system. To evaluate our proposed method, we run various simulations. The amount of the labeled and unlabeled data was varied to measure the impact of this ration to the final results. We used the KDDcup99 [5] for our experiments, since it is considered a benchmark dataset to evaluate the performance of intrusion detection systems. Compared to other classic methods, our proposed algorithm achieves high detection rate while still maintaining a low false alarm rate. Furthermore, the detection time is very short.

The structure of this paper is organized as follows: The anomaly-based detection model for the proposed method is presented in section 2. Simulation results and performance evaluation are shown in section 3. Finally, conclusions and future improvements are presented in section 4.

2. SEMI-SUPERVISED ADABOOST ALGORITHM

In this section, we describe the details of our algorithm, including the construction of the decision stumps and weak classifiers.

2.1 Implementation of Weak Classifiers

In many situations, SVMs, Neural networks, K-nearest Neighbors or Naive Bayes methods are used as weak classifiers. For our proposed algorithm, we have chosen decision stumps as the weak classifiers. A decision stump is a one node tree with only two leaves [2]. Once the single most informative feature is chosen, the decision tree will stop learning. For each feature in the input data, a decision stump is constructed. The two main reasons for choosing a decision stump are:

1) It is very simple and fast. Only one comparison operation in each decision stump for each testing sample is required.

2) Both continuous and categorical features can be implemented in a convenient way.

2.1.1 Implementation of Decision Stump Based on Categorical Features

A categorical feature f is defined with the finite discrete values. Let the set of training sample data be $\{(x_1, y_1) (x_i, y_i), ..., (x_N, y_N)\}$ where x_i is the i-th feature vector and let x_{ij} be the j-th value of the ith feature vector, $j \in \{1, 2, ..., M\}$. The label of the ith feature vector is $y_i \in \{+1, -1\}$. A value of $+1$ denotes that the sample is normal while -1 denotes the sample is an attack. The size

of the data set is n. We use a decision stump to cut the values of each feature into two non-overlapping subsets $C_p^{f_i}$ and $C_n^{f_i}$. Then the decision stump can be defined as the equation (1).

$$h_f(x_i) = \begin{cases} +1 & x_i \in C_p^{f_i} \\ -1 & x_i \in C_n^{f_i} \end{cases} \qquad (1)$$

where $C_p^{f_i}$ and $C_n^{f_i}$ are obtained by the combination method based on the values of each feature. Each feature has one decision stump and the decision stump with the smallest error rate will be chose.

2.1.2 Implementation of Decision Stump Based on Continuous Features

For the continuous feature f, given a boundary value μ, the construction of its decision stump is given by the equation (2).

$$h_f(x_i) = \begin{cases} +1 & x_i \leq \mu \\ -1 & x_i > \mu \end{cases} \qquad (2)$$

where μ is obtained by averaging the neighbor values of the feature f. The decision stump of each feature is determined by minimizing the sum of the false classification rates for normal and attack samples.

2.1.3 Implementation of Weak Classifiers

All the obtained decision stumps of each feature were integrated as one weak classifier. The weak classifier based on categorical features and continuous features is described as the equation (3).

$$h_f(x) = \frac{1}{M} \sum_{i=1}^{M} h_f(xi) \qquad (3)$$

2.2 Implementation of Semi-supervised Adaboost Algorithm

In this paper, we propose a semi-supervised Adaboost algorithm which integrates three different Adaboost algorithms to the tri-training method. The Discrete, Real and Gentle Adaboost methods were used as the three different classifiers. Although the three Adaboost algorithms are different, they are easily to integrated due to the similarity of their input and output forms.

A simple flow chart of the semi-supervised algorithm is shown in Figure 1.

3. EXPERIMENTS

For the experiments, the Knowledge Discovery and Data Mining CUP 1999 data set [5] is used to test our algorithm. This dataset includes four general types of attacks: Denial of Service Attacks (DoS), Remote to Local Attacks (R2L), User to Root Attacks (U2R) and Probing Attacks. Detailed descriptions of the four general types of attacks can be found in [6] and [7].

3.1 Simulations

To study the performance of our algorithm, we run simulations where we varied the sizes of the testing dataset and the training dataset. The training dataset included the

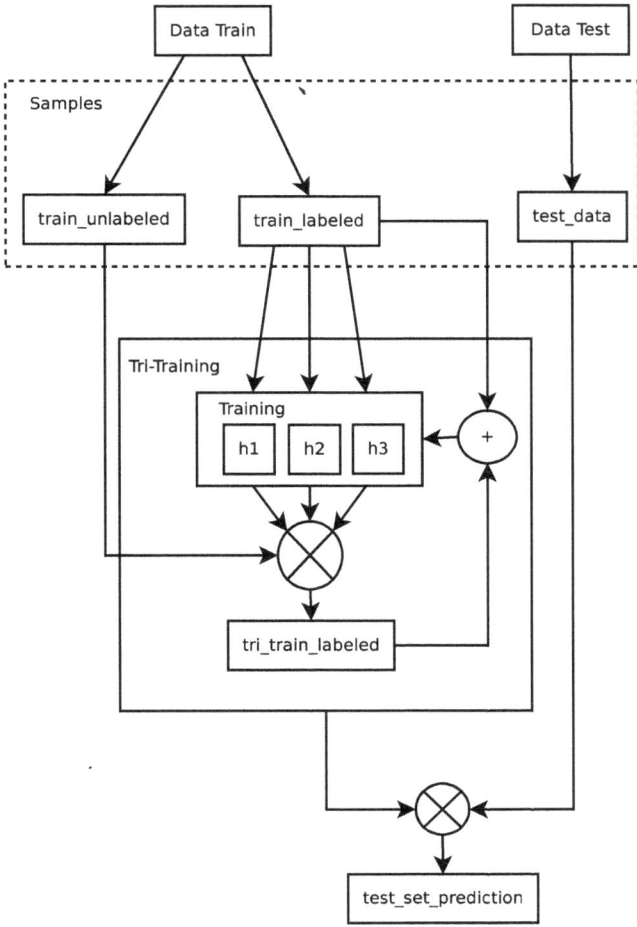

Figure 1: Semi-Supervised Adaboost algorithm

Table 1: Average results over the total number of simulations.

Metric	Average value
accuracy	96.63
precision	98.24
f-measure	97.97
g-mean	0.9452
false-alarm	0.1205
det-rate	88.58
auc	0.9341

Table 2: Results for 10% ratios of labeled and unlabeled data sets.

Testing size	5000	25000	45000
Unlabeled size	500	2500	4500
Labeled size	50	250	450
accuracy	94.47	96.71	96.88
precision	96.35	98.37	98.44
f-measure	96.59	98.09	98.13
g-mean	0.91	0.94	0.94
false-alarm	0.17	0.113	0.113
det-rate	85.1	89.1	89.09
auc	0.90	0.93	0.94

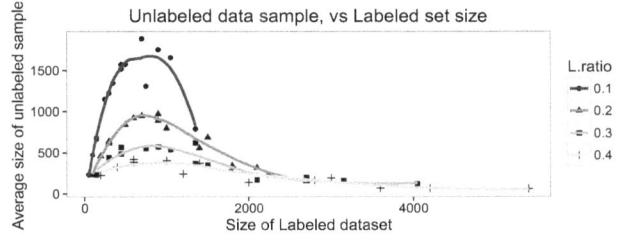

Figure 2: Sample size over a different set of Labeled/Unlabeled data ratios

labeled and the unlabeled datasets. Specifically, we used testing set sizes from 5000 to 45000 points, with a step of 10000. The size of the unlabeled data set varied to 10%, 20%, 30% or 40% of the running testing set size. Similarly, the size of the labeled data was 10%, 20%, 30% or 40% of the running labeled data set size.

The ratio of normal/attacks was 75%/25% for the labeled data set, 70%/25% for the unlabeled data set, and 83%/17% for the testing set.

For each different set of parameters, we run 30 iterations of our proposed algorithm to obtain the average results. As already mentioned above, due to the random sampling, we had different training and testing points for every iteration.

All simulation were done at a Dell Latitude E7450 laptop, with an Intel(R) Core(TM) i7-5600U CPU at 2.60GHz and 8 Gb of RAM. We used R version 3.3.0.

3.2 General Results

To evaluate our results, we use various popular metrics. The average values obtained from all the runs for all the different sizes and ratios of the labeled and unlabeled data, are shown at the table 1. Moreover, table 2 shows the results obtained, when the size of the unlabeled data set is 10% of the testing set and the size of the labeled data set is 10% of the unlabeled one. These results show that we just by

using 450 labeled examples and 4500 unlabeled ones, we can classify a testing set of size 45000, with a precision of 98.44.

3.3 Size of unlabeled data set used

The tri-training algorithm implies some restrictions on the number of samples that will be selected from the unlabeled data set based on the classifier error. A detailed analysis on that can be found at [10]. As we varied the size of labeled set and the ratios between the labeled and the unlabeled data set, we observed that even though there is an abundance of unlabeled data, tri-training deos not always utilize a big part of them. As it can be seen from figure 2, for labeled data sets with sizes greater than 2000 examples, and with a ratio of 0.4 (which implies a size of Unlabeled data set of at least 5000 examples), tri-training is using less that 250 examples. Finding the optimal ratio of of labeled/unlabeled data would be part of future work.

The precision with the different ratios of labeled data set can be seen in figure 3. Similarly, we extract the different labeled data sets with a ratio of 10%, 20%, 30% and 40%

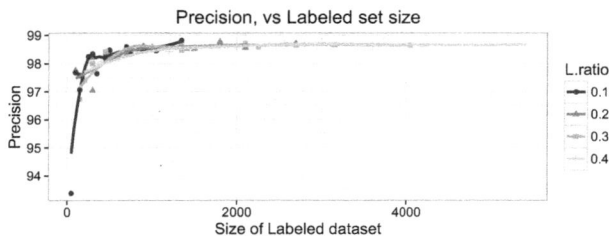

Figure 3: Precision over a different set of Labeled/Unlabeled data ratios

Table 3: Semi-Supervised Adaboost (SSA) approach and Semi-Supervised SVM (SSM) method [4]

	SSA	SSM
Detection Rate (%)	89.02	97.34
False Alarm Rate (%)	**1.38**	8.652
Precision Rate (%)	**98.63**	92.347
Detection time (s)	**8.33**	98.141

of the current labeled data set. Figure 3 shows that the proposed semi-supervised Adaboost algorithm can achieve a very good result even with only very small labeled data set.

3.4 Comparison with existing methods

Lastly, to have a comparison of our model, we compare some of our results with those obtained by [4] Jimin Li et al. This paper also uses tri-training with three different SVM algorithms, and the KDDcup99 [5] data set.

We used the same sizes/ratios for our data sets. Specifically, the labeled data set consisted of 4000 examples with 3000 normal and 1000 attacks. The unlabeled training data set had 10000 examples with 7000 normal examples and 3000 attacks. Finally the testing set consisted of 30000 examples with 25000 normal examples and 5000 attacks. Table 3 shows a basic comparison of our results.

As in the previous examples, the results shown are the average value over 30 iterations on randomly selected different initial data. We can see that our method shows a good balance between the Detection Rate and the False Alarm Rate. Moreover, it is worth noting that the detection time of our proposed algorithm is very low. This proves that our method is efficient in the aspect of time cost.

4. CONCLUSIONS

Fast detection is essential for an effective defense against anomaly attacks. Aiming to construct an anomaly detection approach based on unlabeled data with a low time cost, a high precision and a low false-alarm rate, we propose the semi-supervised Adaboost algorithm. Three different Adaboost algorithms, using decision stumps for weak classifiers (both for continuous and categorical data), are combined through the tri-training method.

Through the experiments, we show that our classifier achieves a low false alarm rate and a good detection rate, even when the size of the labeled data set is 1% of the testing data set. When using only 450 labeled examples with 4500 unlabeled ones, we can classify a testing set of size 45000, with a precision of 98.44%. This indicates that

the proposed semi-supervised Adaboost approach can obtain a very good result even with a very small labeled data set in the training phase. It is noteworthy that the detection time of our algorithm is very low which is significant in real application network detection. Moreover, we run our algorithm for 30 times to obtain the average results and the experiment result prove that our proposed algorithm is reproducible and consistent over a different number of runs. Theoretical analysis and experiments show that our proposed algorithm archives a competitive performance, as compared with the published anomaly detection algorithms, based on the benchmark sample data set.

Our future work will focus on the multi-class classification problem and attack detection.

5. ACKNOWLEDGMENTS

Yali Yuan would like to thank for the scholarship support from the China Scholarship Council (CSC).

The code used to obtain the results and the figures used on this paper are available on the github page https://github.com/gekaklam/triple_ada. The authors welcome requests for additional information regarding the material presented in this paper.

6. REFERENCES

[1] D. M. Farid, M. Z. Rahman, and C. M. Rahman. Adaptive intrusion detection based on boosting and naïve bayesian classifier. *International Journal of Computer Applications*, 24(3):12–19, 2011.

[2] R. C. Holte. Very simple classification rules perform well on most commonly used datasets. *Machine learning*, 11(1):63–90, 1993.

[3] W. Hu, W. Hu, and S. Maybank. Adaboost-based algorithm for network intrusion detection. *IEEE Transactions on Systems, Man, and Cybernetics, Part B (Cybernetics)*, 38(2):577–583, 2008.

[4] J. Li, W. Zhang, and K. Li. A novel semi-supervised svm based on tri-training for intrusition detection. *Journal of computers*, 5(4):638–645, 2010.

[5] M. Lichman. UCI machine learning repository, 2013.

[6] R. Lippmann, J. W. Haines, D. J. Fried, J. Korba, and K. Das. The 1999 darpa off-line intrusion detection evaluation. *Computer networks*, 34(4):579–595, 2000.

[7] S. Mukkamala, A. H. Sung, and A. Abraham. Intrusion detection using an ensemble of intelligent paradigms. *Journal of network and computer applications*, 28(2):167–182, 2005.

[8] T. P. Tran, L. Cao, D. Tran, and C. D. Nguyen. Novel intrusion detection using probabilistic neural network and adaptive boosting. *arXiv preprint arXiv:0911.0485*, 2009.

[9] S. X. Wu and W. Banzhaf. The use of computational intelligence in intrusion detection systems: A review. *Applied Soft Computing*, 10(1):1–35, 2010.

[10] Z.-H. Zhou and M. Li. Tri-training: Exploiting unlabeled data using three classifiers. *IEEE Transactions on knowledge and Data Engineering*, 17(11):1529–1541, 2005.

An Approach to Rule Placement in Software-Define Networks

Wenjie Li[†§]   Zheng Qin[†§]   Hui Yin[†]   Rui Li[†]   Lu Ou[†]   Heng Li[†]
[†]College of Computer Science and Electronic Engineering, Hunan University, ChangSha, China
[§]{liwenjie, zqin}@hnu.edu.cn

ABSTRACT

Software-Define Networks (SDN) is a trend of research in networks. Rule placement, a common operation for network administrators, has become more complicated due to the capacity limitation of devices in which the large number of rules are deployed. Prior works on rule placement mostly consider the influenc on rule placement incurred by the rules in a single device. However, the position relationships between neighbor devices have influence on rule placement. Our basic idea is to classify the position relationships into two categories: the serial relationship and the parallel relationship, and we present a novel strategy for rule placement based on the two different position relationships. There are two challenges of implementing our strategies: to check whether a rule is contained by a rule set or not and to check whether a rule can be merged by other rules or not. To overcome the challenges, we propose a novel data structure called $OPTree$ to represent the rules, which is convenient to check whether a rule is covered by other rules. We design the insertion algorithm and search algorithm for OPTree. Extensive experiments show that our approach can effectively reduce the number of rules while ensuring placed rules work. On the other hand, the experimental results also demonstrate that it is necessary to consider the position relationships between neighbor devices when placing rules.

Keywords

SDN; Rule Placement; Position Relationship

1. INTRODUCTION

1.1 Motivation and Problem Statement

In SDN, there are a lot of devices to control the fl w of data packets, *e.g.*, fir wall, switch, and router. In these devices, there are many rules to implement their functions. The network administrator controls the fl w of data packets by modifying the rules in the devices. If the network administrator would prohibit/permit some data packets to go through the network, he usually creates a new rule and place the rule into a suitable device. **Rule Placement** is an operation that chooses a suitable device and places a rule into it.

MSWiM '16, November 13-17, 2016, Malta, Malta
© 2016 ACM. ISBN 978-1-4503-4502-6/16/11. . . $15.00
DOI: http://dx.doi.org/10.1145/2988287.2989170

In general, network administrator simply places the rule into the firs position of the rule set in the chosen device. However, the operation is constrained by the limited capacity of devices, especially when more and more devices use the $TCAMs$ (Ternary Content Addressable Memories) to storage the rules. $TCAMs$ have good performance but their prices are expensive, so we cannot unlimitedly insert rules into the devices. As the matter of fact, we can reduce the number of rules in a device when placing rules to improve the device performance. For instance, when a rule is placed into a device, the rule may be a redundant/conflictin rule for other rules in the device and the rule can be removed to reduce the number of rules in the device. On the other hand, two rules might be merged into a new rule to reduce the number of rules in device. Therefore, reducing the number of rules as many as possible while ensuring the placed rule work for rule placement is a critical requirement.

Informally, we focus on the problem of how to place the rule into a suitable device. A suitable device should satisfy the following two conditions. First, all rules after optimizing are still able to work when placing a rule. Second, the total number of rules in the SDN is minimal. Thus, the problem of rule placement is an optimal problem in given a rule and some devices. *In this paper, we focus on the rule placement of access control list (ACL) in fi ewalls.*

However, there is a problem of rule placement that the position relationship between neighbour devices is ignored in the current researches. Obviously, the position relationship between neighbour devices has influence on rule placement. For example, if a rule has been placed into a device, then the rule will change the data packets that go through the device. Further, the rule will change the data packets that arrive at the next device according to the position relationship. Thus, when we place a rule into a device and ignore the influence of the position relationship on rule placement, the position relationship may cause some rules in next device cannot work, therefore the device is not a suitable device. In our approach, we consider the influenc of the position relationship between neighbour devices on rule placement.

1.2 Limitation of Prior Art

Recently, there are some effective works about rule placement. Casado *et al.* proposed an approach for distributing a centralized fir wall policy by placing rules for packets at their ingress switches [1], Yuan *et al.* presented a method that the edge switch config urations realize the fir wall policy [2]. However, These approaches, which do not enforce rule-table constraints on the edge switches or place rules on the internal switches, may make the load very heavy in ingress switches. DIFANE [3] and vCRIB [4] leveraged all switches in the network to enforce an endpoint policy. Specifically, DIFANE proposed a "rule split and caching" approach that increases the path length for the firs packet of a f ow. Kanizo presented the Palette distribution framework for decomposing large

SDN tables into small ones and then distributing them across the network [5]. Kang *et al.* viewed the network as "one big switch" and proposed a heuristic rule placement algorithm that distributes forwarding policies across general SDN networks while managing rule space constraints [6]. Nguyen *et al.* proposed a novel approach for rule placement using trading routing [7]. However, these works focus on the rule placement of forwarding policies deployed in router or switch. Li [8] proposed a heuristic algorithm for rule placement. However, the work focuses on the wired networks with dynamic topologies.

Similar to our solution, Zhang *et al.* proposed an Integer Linear Programming (ILP) based solution for placing rules on switches for a given fir wall policy [9]. However, the work does not consider the influenc of position relationship between the neighbor devices on rule placement.

1.3 Our Approach

In this paper, we propose a novel approach for rule placement. In our approach, we firs take the relationship of neighbor devices into consideration when placing rules. We classify the relationship of near devices into two categories: the serial relationship and the parallel relationship, and propose the rule placement strategy for each category. To implement our placement strategies, we propose a novel data structure called OPTree as well as design the insertion algorithm and query algorithm for OPTree.

1.4 Key Contributions

We make four key contributions as follows in this paper:

(1) To the best of our knowledge, we firs consider the influ ences of the position relationship between neighbour devices on rule placement. According to real condition in network, we classify the position relationship between neighbour devices into the serial relationship and the parallel relationship.

(2) We propose the rule placement strategies for different position relationships respectively.

(3) To implement our placement strategies, we propose a novel data structure called OPTree to represent the rules in devices and design the insertion algorithm and the search algorithm for OPTree.

(4) We analyze the time complexity and conduct our experiments for our approach.

2. SOLUTION APPROACH

First, we propose some operations of rules and classify the rule set in devices. In this paper, our key idea is to consider the position relationship of neighbour devices when placing rules. Second, we classify the position relationship between neighbour devices into two categories: the serial relationship and the parallel relationship. Finally, we propose the rule placement strategy for each category of position relationships respectively.

2.1 The Classificatio of Rule Set

Given a device D and a f ow of the data packet, we use D_{prev} to denote the device placed in front of D according to the fl w direction and use D_{next} to denote the device placed in behind of D according to the fl w direction. Data packets arrive at the device, and some of them are allowed to go through the device, and some of them are prohibited to go through the device. We use $P_{in}(D)$ to denote the set of data packets that arrive at the device and use $P_{out}(D)$ to denote the set of data packets that are allowed to go through the device. In this paper, we concern the ACL rule placement, so the value of action fiel is *accept* or *drop*, We use $R_a(D)$ and $R_d(D)$ to denote the rules of which the value of action fiel are accept and drop, respectively. There are some properties as follows.

1) $R(D)=R_a(D) \cup R_d(D)$.
2) $P_{in}(D)=\bigcup P_{out}(D_{prev})$.
3) Each data packet in $P_{out}(D)$ can match a rule at least in $R(D)$.

According to the principles of rule placement, we should check whether r' can work in D_i or not. If r' satisfie one of the following two conditions, then r' cannot work in D_i.

1) There does not exist data packet which can match r' in $P_{in}(D)$, we use $r' \notin P_{in}(D)$ to denote it.
2) There does exist a rule r in $R(D)$ that $r \supseteq r'$ and $A(r)=A(r')$.

2.2 The Position Relationship between Neighbour Devices

Given two devices D_i and D_j, we assume that the direction of data packets is from D_i to D_j. In other word, if $P_{out}(D_i) \cap P_{in}(D_j) \neq \emptyset$, then the position relationship between D_i and D_j is the **serial relationship**, *i.e.*, $Re(D_i, D_j)=Re_s$.

If there is not data packet that from D_i to D_j, then the position relationship between D_i and D_j is the **parallel relationship** , *i.e.*, $Re(D_i, D_j)=Re_p$.

2.3 The Rule Placement Strategy for the Parallel Relationship

Given a rule r' that would be placed and two devices D_i and D_j with the parallel relationship, *i.e.*, $Re(D_i, D_j)=Re_p$. We take the following two steps to enforce the rule placement strategy for the parallel relationship.

Step 1, we check the relationship between r' and $P_{in}(D_i)$ to determine whether r' can be placed into D_i. There are two cases as follows.

Case 1. $r' \notin P_{in}(D_i)$: In this case, we set $Pr(D_i, r')=-\infty$. We cannot place r' into D_i because any packet which arrives at D_i cannot match r', r' cannot work in D_i.

Case 2. $r' \in P_{in}(D_i)$: In this case, r' can work in D_i and we set $Pr(D_i, r')=0$. We use Step 2 to compute $Pr(D_i, r')$ further.

Step 2, we check the relationship between r' and $R(D_i)$. There are two cases as follows.

Case 1. $r' \in R(D_i)$: In this case, r' is a redundance rule for $R(D_i)$, so we set $Pr(D_i, r')=-\infty$, we cannot place r' into D_i.

Case 2. $r' \subseteq R(D_i)$ or $r' \notin R(D_i)$: In this case, r' can be placed into D_i and assume that the rule r can merged with r'. We use r_{merge} to denote the merged rule, *i.e.*, $r_{merge}=r \oplus r'$ and use r_{merge} to replace the r and r'. Note that r_{merge} maybe also merge with other rules, so this is a constant cyclic process until no rules can be merged. We let $Pr(D_i, r')$ equal to the number of merged rules.

We use the same strategy to compute $Pr(D_j, r')$ for D_j and compare $Pr(D_i, r')$ with $Pr(D_j, r')$. There are three cases as follows.

Case 1. $Pr(D_i, r')=Pr(D_j, r')=-\infty$: In this case, we skip r' because r' cannot work in the two devices.

Case 2. $Pr(D_i, r')=Pr(D_j, r') \neq -\infty$: In this case, we consider the load balancing, thus we place r' into the device D where $L(R(D))$ is minimal. If $L(R(D_i))=L(R(D_j))$, we randomly choose a device and place r' into it.

Case 3. $Pr(D_i, r') \neq Pr(D_j, r')$: In the case, we place r' into the device D where $Pr(D_i, r')$ is maximum.

2.4 The Rule Placement Strategy for the Serial Relationship

Given two devices D_i and D_j with the serial position relationship, *i.e.*, $Re(D_i, D_j)=Re_s$. According to the fl w of data packets, we assume that D_i is in front of D_j, a rule r' would be placed into one of them. The rule placement strategy for the serial relationship is similar to that of the parallel relationship.

In Case 2 of Step 2, D_i is a D_{prev} for D_j, and $P_{in}(D_j)=\bigcup P_{out}(D_i)$, if r' has been placed into D_i, $P_{out}(D_i)$ maybe change, so we should recompute $P_{in}(D_j)$, and use the same strategy to compute $Pr(D_j, r')$ for D_j, and compare $Pr(D_i, r')$ with $Pr(D_j, r')$. The process of comparing is the same as the process of comparing in the rule placement strategy for the parallel relationship.

3. OPTREE

In this paper, we propose the strategies of rule placement in section 2. There are some challenges as follows when implementing the strategies.

1) Check whether the rule is contained by a rule set or not.

2) Check whether the rule can be merged by other rules or not.

In this paper, we propose a novel data structure called OPTree to present the rules of devices.

3.1 The Properties of OPTree

OPTree is a minimal ordered predicate tree which satisfie the following properties. We use T to denote the OPTree.

1). There is one and only one vertex V that has no parent node, which is called *root* node, k vertices that have no child, which are called *terminal node*, and m vertices that have one or more children, which are called *nonterminal node*.

2). Each node except *terminal node* is labeled with a matching field The *root* is labeled with the firs matching fiel F_1, the node in the ith layer is labeled with the ith matching fiel F_i. We use $F(V)$ to denote the label of node V and use $D(F(V))$ to denote the range of values of the matching fiel F_V. The terminal nodes are labeled with a action field we use the following shorthand: a (*Accept*), d (*Drop*).

3). Each edge E is labeled with a prefix We use $I(E)$ to denote the label of edge e, i.e., $I(E) \subset D(F(V))$, where V is the starting vertex of E. We use $Edges(V)$ to denote the number of edges that start from V, and use $V(E)$ to denote the vertex that E point to .

4). The labels of the edges that share a same starting vertex are arranged in order, e.g., if the edge e_{left} is on the left side of e_{right}, then $I(e_{left}) \leq I(e_{right})$ holds.

5). We call the edge set that contains all edges in a path that starts from the *root* and ends to a *terminal node* as a *predicate path*, we use $Path$ to denote it, i.e., $Path = \{p_1 \in F_1, p_2 \in F_2, \ldots, p_n \in F_n\}$. *If a rule r whose predicate is contained by the union of some path predicates, then there must exist a predicate path that contains the predicate of r in OPTree.*

6. Given two predicate paths $p_1 = \{I(e_1^1), I(e_1^2), \cdots, I(e_1^n)\}$ and $p_2 = \{I(e_2^1), I(e_2^2), \cdots, I(e_2^n)\}$, if for each prefi $I(e_1^i)$ and $I(e_2^i)$, we have $I(e_1^i) \in I(e_2^i)$ hold, we say p_1 is redundant to p_2. There is no redundant predicate path in OPTree .

3.2 The Insertion Algorithm of OPTree

The insertion algorithm of OPTree has three steps and each step has a subalgorithm to implement it. These subalgorithms are described in detail as follows.

Step 1: Convert the rule to a direct predicate path and insert the path into the OPTree.

Step 2: When a direct predicate path has been inserted into the OPTree, the path may be merged with other paths, so the main function of step 2 is to fin which paths can be merged and merge them into a merged predicate path and insert the merged path into the OPTree by using the algorithm of **Step 1**.

Step 3: After the direct predicate path and the merged predicate path have been inserted into the OPTree, we should check the OP-Tree and remove the redundance predicate path according to the 6th property of OPTree.

3.3 The Search Algorithm of OPTree

In this paper, we usually need to check whether a rule r is contained by a rule set R in devices or not when implementing our strategy of rule placement. We use an OPTree T to represent R and use a predicate path $path$ to represent r. So we can use the search process in OPTree to represent the checking process. Obviously, the search operation of OPTree is extremely efficien according to the 5th and 6th properties of OPTree.

4. EXPERIMENTAL EVALUATION

In this section, to evaluate the performance of our approach, we perform our experiments. In our approach, we consider the influence of the position relationship between neighbour devices on rule placement. Therefore, we use two devices and change the position relationship between them to evaluate our approach.

4.1 Data Set Generation

First, we use the rule generation tool $ClassBench$ proposed in [10], which is widely used in rule generation to generate the rule sets of the two devices. The sizes of the generated rule sets range from 100 to 1000. For each size, we generate 20 rule sets.

Second, we also use $ClassBench$ to generate the rule sets that would been placed, and the sizes of the generated data sets range from 10 to 100, and for each size, we generate 10 data sets. We use S to denote the size of the rule set.

4.2 Implementation Details

In this section, we perform three kinds of experiments that use the same data set and only change the position relationship between the two devices. The firs kind of experiments is the devices with the parallel relationship, the second kind of experiment is the devices with the serial relationship, and the last kind of experiment is an comparison experiment that compares the results of the firs kind of experiments and the results of the second kind of experiments.

To evaluate the efficien y of our approach, we compute the two indicators of the experiments: the number of rules after rule placement and the number of rules that are reduced after rule placement in the three kinds of experiments. Note that the number of rules after rule placement is that the total number of rules in the device when placed into a device, so the number of rules after rule placement may more than the number of rules in device before rule placement. It indicates that our approach is effective when the number of rules after rule placement less than the number of rules in device before rule placement plus the number of rules that would been placed.

4.3 Parallel Relationship

The experimental results show that our approach can reduce the size of rules in devices with parallel relationship. For this set of experiments, we set S=10,50,100 respectively.

Figure 1(a) shows the number of rules that are reduced after rule placement, and Figure 1(b) shows the total number of rules after rule placement.

4.4 Serial Relationship

The experimental results show that our approach can reduce the size of rules in devices with serial relationship. We use the same data set in the experiments with the experiments of parallel relationship. Figure 2(a) shows the number of rules that are reduced

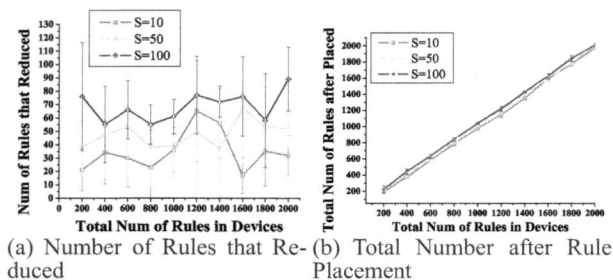

(a) Number of Rules that Reduced (b) Total Number after Rule Placement

Figure 1: Parallel Relationship

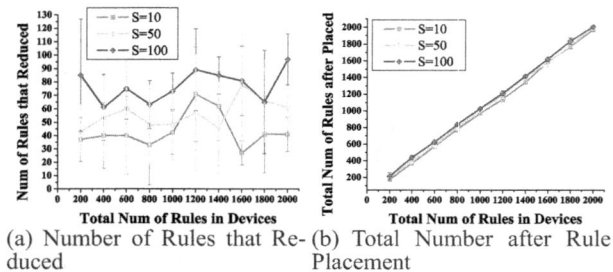

(a) Number of Rules that Reduced (b) Total Number after Rule Placement

Figure 2: Serial Relationship

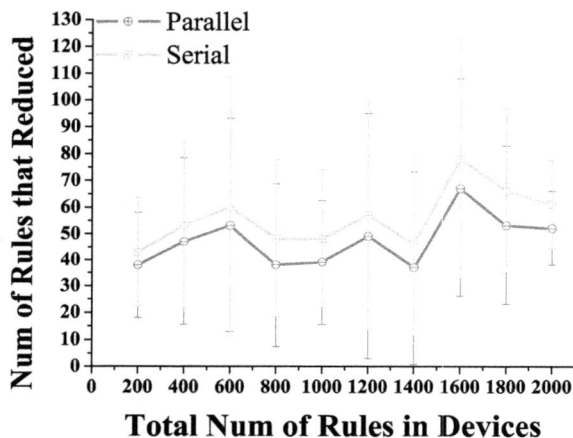

Figure 3: Parallel Relationship VS Serial Relationship

after rule placement, and Figure 2(b) shows the total number of rules after rule placement.

4.5 Serial Relationship VS. Parallel Relationship

The experimental results show that the size of rule reduction with serial relationship less than the size of rule reduction with parallel relationship, which indicates that considering the influenc of the position relationship of neighbour devices on rule placement is necessary . Figure 3 shows the result of experiment.

5. CONCLUSIONS

In this work, we consider the influenc of the position relationships of neighbour devices on rule placement, we propose the rule placement strategy for different position relationship respectively. To overcome the challenges of our strategy implementation,

we propose a new data structure called OPTree to represent rules, which is convenient to check whether a rule is covered by other rules. We design two algorithms for OPTree: insertion and search algorithms. Extensive experiments demonstrate that our approach can reduce the size of rules in device after rule placement with different position relationships. Further, the size of rule reduction with serial relationship is less than the size of rule reduction with parallel relationship, which indicates that our approach is effective and it is necessary to consider the influenc of the position relationship of neighbour devices on rule placement.

6. ACKNOWLEDGEMENTS

The research is supported by the National Natural Science Foundation of China under Grant Nos. 61472131, 61272546 and 61370226.

7. REFERENCES

[1] Martĺln Casado, Michael J. Freedman, and Justin Pettit. Rethinking enterprise network control. *IEEE/ACM TRANSACTIONS ON NETWORKING(TON)*, 17(4):1270–1283, 2009.

[2] Yossi Kanizo, David Hay, and Isaac Keslassy. Fireman: A toolkit for fir wall modeling and analysis. In *Proceedings of the of IEEE Symposium on Security and Privacy*, pages 199–213, 2006.

[3] Minlan Yu, Jennifer Rexford, Michael J.Freedman, and Jia Wang. Scalable fl w-based networking with difane. In *Proceedings of the of the SIGCOMM 2010 Conference*, pages 351–362, 2010.

[4] Masoud Moshref, Minlan Yu, Abhishek Sharma, and Ramesh Govindan. Vcrib: Virtualized rule management in the cloud. In *Proceedings of the of the 4th USENIX Conf. Hot Topics Cloud Compute*, pages 23–29, 2012.

[5] Lihua Yuan, Jianning Mai, Zhendong Su, Hao Chen, Chen-Nee Chuah, and Prasant Mohapatra. Palette: Distributing tables in software-define networks. In *Proceedings of the of IEEE Infocom Mini-conference*, pages 545–549, 2013.

[6] Nanxi Kang, Zhenming Liu, Jennifer Rexford, and David Walker. Optimizing the one big switch abstraction in software-define networks. In *Proceedings of the of the 2013 ACM International Conference on Emerging Networking Experiments and Technologies(CoNEXT)*, pages 13–24, 2013.

[7] Xuan-Nam Nguyen, Damien Saucez, Chadi Barakat, and Thierry Turletti. Optimizing rules placement in openfl w networks:trading routing for better efficien y. In *Proceedings of the of the ACM SIGCOMM 2014 Workshop on Hot Topics in Software Define Networking*, pages 127–132, 2014.

[8] He Li, Peng Li, and Song Guo. Morule: Optimized rule placement for mobile users in sdn-enabled access networks. In *Proceedings of the of the 2014 IEEE Global Communications Conference*, pages 4953–4958, 2015.

[9] Shuyuan zhang, Franjo Ivancic, and Cristian Lumezanu. An adaptable rule placement for software-define networks. In *Proceedings of the of the International Conference on Dependable Systems and Networks*, pages 88–99, 2014.

[10] David E.Taylor and Jonathan S.Turner. Classbench: A packet classificatio benchmark. In *Proceedings of the of INFOCOMM*, pages 89–99, 2005.

Association Optimization in Wi-Fi Networks: Use of an Access-based Fairness

Mohammed Amer
Univ Lyon
UCB Lyon1
Inria, ENS de Lyon
CNRS, LIP UMR 5668
mohammed.amer@ens-lyon.fr

Anthony Busson
Univ Lyon
UCB Lyon1
Inria, ENS de Lyon
CNRS, LIP UMR 5668
anthony.busson@ens-lyon.fr

Isabelle Guérin Lassous
Univ Lyon
UCB Lyon1
Inria, ENS de Lyon
CNRS, LIP UMR 5668
isabelle.guerin-lassous@ens-lyon.fr

ABSTRACT

Densification of Wi-Fi networks has led to the possibility for a station to choose between several access points (APs). On the other hand, the densification of APs generates interference, contention and decreases the global throughput as APs have to share a limited number of channels. Optimizing the association step between APs and stations can alleviate this problem and increase the overall throughput and fairness between stations. In this paper, we propose an original solution to this optimization problem based on two contributions. First, we present a mathematical model for the association optimization problem based on a realistic share of the medium between APs and stations and among APs when using the 802.11 DCF (Distributed Coordination Function) mode. Then, we introduce a local search algorithm to solve this problem through a suitable neighborhood structure. This approach has the benefit to be tuned according to the CPU and time constraints of the WLAN controller. Our evaluation, based on simulations, shows that the proposed solution improves the overall throughput and the fairness of the network.

Keywords

IEEE 802.11, wireless, association optimization

1. INTRODUCTION

Wireless LANs (WLANs) have become the first technology of access networks in terms of traffic [1]. WLANs are now extensively deployed by operators, companies, public institutions and Internet subscribers. Their success is explained by a performance increase that satisfies the users' need for bandwidth, its simplicity to access the network everywhere, and the possibility for users to be mobile. Among the existing wireless technologies, IEEE 802.11 [2] is the de facto WLAN technology. It is used mainly in infrastructure

mode where stations have to associate with access points (APs) to access the network. Most of APs use the two unlicensed bands ISM (2.4GHz) and U-NII (5.15-5.82 GHz) for which 14[1] and 8 channels are available.

Most of the Internet subscribers have a set-top box that integrates a Wi-Fi AP. On the other hand, companies / institutions deploy a large number of Wi-Fi APs to ensure an efficient coverage of the area or to allow transparent mobility. These approaches have led to a densification of WLANs, which generates congestion in terms of channel usage when several APs in detection range of each other use the same channel [3]. The number of channels being fixed, optimizations at different levels are required to efficiently manage the limited resources and ensure a sufficient throughput to Wi-Fi stations.

Among the different management operations in the IEEE 802.11 standard, the association between wireless stations and APs is a key step that has an impact on the user performance as well as on the overall wireless network performance. In a IEEE 802.11-based infrastructure network, a wireless station must be associated with one AP to be allowed to use the network. When several APs are available within its reception range, one AP must be selected. In many IEEE 802.11 products, a wireless station uses the received signal strength indicator (RSSI), from the different APs it detects, to choose the AP to associate with. This approach does not consider the number of already attached wireless stations per AP, and may consequently lead to poor performance and unfairness between stations. It does not consider either the impact of the stations' transmission rates on the user and global throughputs. Indeed, stations using a low physical transmission rate occupy the channel longer than the stations with a high physical rate [4]. High rate stations may then be significantly penalized as low and high rate stations attached to the same AP tend to have the same throughput.

Nowadays, most of the WLANs commercial solutions consist of *thin APs* combined with one or several *WLAN controllers*. In this architecture, decisions (association, security, etc.) are taken by the controller. Such an approach offers more functionalities than with autonomous APs as the controller has a centralized view of the stations parameters and their performance. These solutions are closed and not flexible, and make difficult the coexistence of heterogeneous

MSWiM '16, November 13-17, 2016, Malta, Malta
© 2016 ACM. ISBN 978-1-4503-4502-6/16/11...$15.00
DOI: http://dx.doi.org/10.1145/2988287.2989153

---

[1]It is the number of channels specified by the standard, but for some countries less channels are authorized.

network equipments. Besides these proprietary solutions, recent standards aim to provide a technological framework to allow such centralized systems. CAPWAP protocol (Control and Provisioning of Wireless Access Points) [5], standardized by IETF, allows an AC (Access Controller) to manage a collection of wireless APs. IEEE has standardized the IEEE 802.11v amendment [6] which enables the management of stations in a centralized fashion (e.g. monitoring, configuring, and updating) through a layer 2 mechanism. Also, the SDN (Software Defined Networking) paradigm [7] may offer such an approach, even if its application to WLANs is not yet defined. These different centralized approaches offer the opportunity to implement an optimized parameterization of WLANs, which is more difficult to realize in a distributed context.

In this paper, we are interested in the association step in 802.11-based wireless networks using a controller. In these architectures, the association can be solved with a centralized approach, which allows the use of an optimization model like in [8–13]. Most of the optimization models, proposed for this problem, assume a time based fairness between the AP and the stations [8–10, 13]. This assumption requires to apply an appropriate scheduling on AP that must take into account different parameters like the packet sizes and the physical transmission rates. In practice, APs use very simple scheduling policies like a FIFO scheduling and the DCF (Distributed Coordination Function) mode of IEEE 802.11 provides an access based share of the medium between APs/stations in contention. Therefore an access based fairness model for the medium share seems more appropriate. Very few solutions based on explicit optimization models use such an access based fairness scheme. This is the case in [11], but the solution goal is to minimize the maximal load on all the APs. In our work, we opt for the logarithmic utility function because of the good tradeoff that can be achieved between the overall network throughput and the fairness of user throughputs. Finally, contrary to most of the proportional fairness solutions based on optimization models (and all considering a time based fairness share), we evaluate our solution not only with an optimization solver but also with a network simulator.

The contributions of this paper are the following:

- We propose an optimization model for the association step that is based on the logarithmic utility function. In this model, we consider that an AP allocates, in average, the same number of access to the medium to each station associated with it, compared to the literature where the AP allocate the same amount of time to each station. Our approach is thus more realistic as it corresponds to the current implementation of APs and to the 802.11 DCF mode.

- A local search heuristic is proposed to solve this problem (being NP-hard). This heuristic has the benefit to be tuned according to time and CPU constraints of the WLAN controller.

- Our solution has been implemented on the network simulator ns-3. Results show that the global throughput is significantly increased compare to the default RSSI association, and leads to an improvement of fairness. A deeper analysis points out that, thanks to our optimization, stations are more homogeneously shared

among access points, and individual throughput per station is improved for almost of the stations.

This paper is organized as follows. In Section 2 we present works related to the optimization of Wi-Fi association problem. Then, in Section 3, we present our mathematical model of the optimization problem when orthogonal and non-orthogonal channels are used. In Section 3.2, the proposed approach to solve this model is described. A performance evaluation of our solution based on ns-3 simulations is carried out in Section 4. We conclude in Section 5.

2. RELATED WORK

Several papers claim that the use of the RSSI metrics is not an efficient approach for the association step and have proposed different approaches.

The association decision can be done in a central way or in a distributed way. As our work takes benefit of the presence of a controller to apply a centralized association algorithm, we only survey the centralized solutions like in [8–13]. When the solution is based on an optimization model, the solution seeks to optimize an objective function. In [8–10,13], the authors look for a proportional fair association by optimizing the logarithmic utility function which corresponds to maximizing the sum of logs of the users' throughputs. In [11], the goal is to maximize the minimal throughput among all the stations. In [12], although the proposed solution is centralized on a controller, it uses fuzzy logic and its decisions are based on metrics like, for instance, the signal quality and the packet loss rate.

Most of these works consider a specific bandwidth sharing among the users. For instance, in [8–10,13], the authors search to improve the network performance while ensuring fairness in terms of service time between stations on the same AP. It ensures that each station obtains a throughput proportional to its physical transmission rate. As explained in Introduction, this approach requires to change the AP scheduling. Other solutions, closer to the reality, consider that the share is fair in the number of channel accesses [11, 12]. As these two solutions, our model captures the access-based fairness of the IEEE 802.11 DCF mode, but, contrary to these two solutions we look for a proportional fair association.

In many solutions based on an optimization model, this latter is numerically evaluated by using a tool that solves optimization problems, like, for instance, CVX in [8] and CPLEX in [9]. In [13], approximate algorithms are designed and they are implemented in Python. In these papers, only the model/algorithm is evaluated and the performance evaluation part gives few clues on the solution performance in a more realistic networking setting, like, for instance, when the medium share is governed by the IEEE 802.11 DCF principles. On the other hand, network simulation results are provided in [10] with the OMNetpp simulator while the solution of [12] is experimentally evaluated with a homemade testbed. Contrary to most of the association solutions targeting a proportional fairness and based on an optimization model (and all considering a time based fairness medium share), we evaluate our solution with a network simulator.

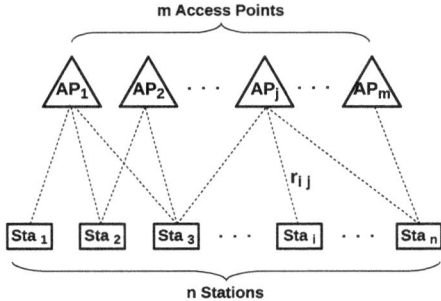

Figure 1: Access points and wireless stations in the network. Dotted lines represent the possible associations between AP and stations.

3. ASSOCIATION OPTIMIZATION

3.1 Problem Formulation

In this section, we provide the model and the notations used for the mathematical formulation of our solution. We consider a wireless network with m access points and n wireless stations as illustrated in Figure 1. We consider only downlink traffic, from the APs to the stations. The amount of uplink traffic is considered negligible, or at least not significant, with regard to the downlink traffic [14]. We also assume that the amount of data intended to the stations associated to the same AP are equal in average, or in a long term period. To this end, we assume that the mean number of frames transmitted to each station and the mean frame size are the same for each station. Obviously, it will not correspond to the reality, but it allows us to express the problem with an equal priority to each station. This assumption is motivated by different reasons: i) the optimization problem is thus addressed without privileging a station because it has more traffic than the others at a given time; ii) Internet traffic is quite sporadic and the time scale in terms of dynamics is very likely smaller than the one of the association problem, which implies that, in average, stations may receive the same amount of data; iii) the association problem output consists in associating stations with APs and the goal is not to directly set/reserve any resource for each station; consequently, stations that receive more traffic still benefit of the statistical multiplexing offered by the Wi-Fi technology. Table 1 summarizes the different notations used throughout this paper.

Table 1: Notations

Symbol	Description
m	Number of access points in the network
n	Number of wireless stations in the network
r_{ij}	Link capacity between Sta_i and AP_j
t_{ij}	Mean transmission time of one frame from AP_j to Sta_i
p_i	Mean frame size to be transmitted to Sta_i
d_{ij}	Mean throughput obtained by Sta_i when associated to AP_j
D_j	Mean overall outgoing throughput of AP_j
L_{ij}	Mean number of frames transmitted from AP_j to Sta_i
x_{ij}	1 if Sta_i is associated to AP_j, 0 otherwise
s_{ij}	1 if AP_i is in sensing range of AP_j, 0 otherwise

We model the IEEE 802.11 infrastructure based wireless network through the following steps. We consider only the IEEE 802.11 DCF mode [15].

The objective function that we optimize is based on the mean throughputs between stations and APs, denoted d_{ij} ($i \in \{1, ..., n\}$ and $j \in \{1, ..., m\}$). By convention, we set $d_{ij} = 0$ if the station i is not associated to AP_j. This throughput depends on the number of stations associated with the AP, and the corresponding link capacity. The link capacity r_{ij} is defined here as the maximum amount of data that can be exchanged between AP_j and the station i in one second. The throughput d_{ij} is the throughput when considering the other stations and, in one of the model (see Section 3.1.2), the other interfering APs. In other words, d_{ij} takes into account the fact that the medium is shared whereas r_{ij} does not.

We present our optimization problem under two variants. The first approach assumes that the channels used by the access points are orthogonal, meaning that they can not detect each other and can transmit at the same time. It is equivalent to assume that there are as many orthogonal channels as APs. Then, in the second approach, we consider that the number of orthogonal channels is limited. Consequently, APs which use the same channel and which are in the sensing range of each other share the medium. The formula that characterizes the throughput between an AP and a station is refined accordingly.

3.1.1 Orthogonal channels

We assume that all APs use different orthogonal channels, or equivalently the APs using the same channel are far enough to avoid any interference and signal detection. Therefore, each AP can be considered as an independent sub-network and the mean aggregate throughput for the whole Wi-Fi network is the sum of the mean AP throughputs. We begin by computing the mean overall throughput offered by an AP from which we derive the mean throughput between this AP and one of its stations.

The mean throughput D_j of AP_j is defined as the downlink throughput sent by this AP to the set of its associated users:

$$D_j = \sum_{i=1}^{n} d_{ij}$$

It can also be expressed as the ratio between the mean quantity of data transmitted to all wireless stations associated to it and the time required for these transmissions:

$$D_j = \frac{\sum_{i=1}^{n} L_{ij} p_i x_{ij}}{\sum_{i=1}^{n} L_{ij} t_{ij} x_{ij}} \quad (1)$$

where L_{ij} is the mean number of frames sent from AP_j to Sta_i, p_i is the mean size of these frames, x_{ij} indicates if Sta_i is associated to AP_j (it equals to 1 if it is true, and 0 otherwise) and t_{ij} is the mean time to send a frame from AP_j to Sta_i. This time is given by the ratio between the mean frame size and the link capacity:

$$t_{ij} = \frac{p_i}{r_{ij}} \quad (2)$$

By substituting (2) in (1), we get:

$$D_j = \frac{\sum_{i=1}^{n} L_{ij} p_i x_{ij}}{\sum_{i=1}^{n} L_{ij} \frac{p_i}{r_{ij}} x_{ij}} \quad (3)$$

As we assume that the mean number of frames transmitted to each station and the mean frame size are identical for each station, the mean overall throughput of an AP is then given by:

$$D_j = \frac{\sum_{i=1}^{n} x_{ij}}{\sum_{i=1}^{n} \frac{x_{ij}}{r_{ij}}} \quad (4)$$

Also, as we assume that the stations associated to the same AP receive the same amount of data in average, then the throughput of the AP is equally shared among its wireless stations. Therefore, the mean throughput d_{ij} between a station and its AP (AP_j) becomes:

$$d_{ij} = \frac{D_j}{\sum_{k=1}^{n} x_{kj}} \quad (5)$$

Substituting D_j in its formula, we get:

$$d_{ij} = \frac{1}{\sum_{k=1}^{n} \frac{x_{kj}}{r_{kj}}} \quad (6)$$

From Equation (6), we can easily see that the mean throughput d_{ij} of a Sta_i associated to AP_j is the same for all stations associated to this AP, whereas they may experience different link capacities with this AP.

Our optimization aims to maximize the throughput of the total downlink for the whole network while ensuring fairness between wireless stations. In order to introduce fairness in the objective function, we use the logarithmic utility function proposed by Kelly in [16]. The association optimization problem with orthogonal channels can then be formulated as follows:

$$\max \quad \sum_{i=1}^{n} \log \left(\sum_{j=1}^{m} d_{ij} x_{ij} \right)$$

$$\text{with} \quad d_{ij} = \frac{1}{\sum_{k=1}^{n} \frac{x_{kj}}{r_{kj}}} \qquad 1 \leq i \leq n, 1 \leq j \leq m \quad (7)$$

$$\text{subject to} \quad \sum_{j=1}^{m} x_{ij} = 1 \qquad 1 \leq i \leq n,$$
$$x_{ij} \in \{0,1\} \qquad 1 \leq i \leq n, 1 \leq j \leq m,$$
$$\text{if } r_{ij} = 0 \text{ then } x_{ij} = 0 \quad 1 \leq i \leq n, 1 \leq j \leq m.$$

The objective is thus to find the set of association variables x_{ij} that maximizes the total network throughput while ensuring a certain fairness. The two first constraints are related to the association variables x_{ij} and ensure that a station is connected to a single AP. The third constraint aims to guarantee that a wireless station cannot associate with an AP that is not within its receiving range.

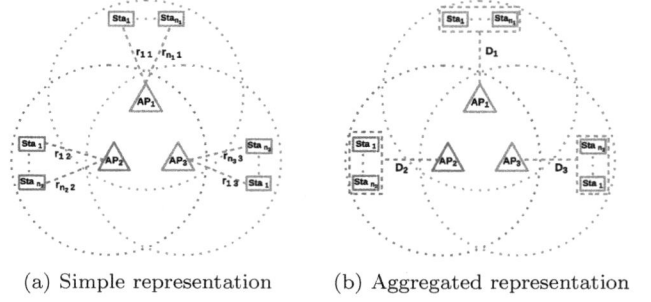

(a) Simple representation   (b) Aggregated representation

Figure 2: Wireless network with non-orthogonal channels

3.1.2 Non-orthogonal channels

We propose to refine the model by considering non-orthogonal channels. A certain number of orthogonal channels are available but their number is limited, so several APs may use the same channel.

In practice, it is difficult to know the various interferences that can undergo a radio signal in a wireless network.

A source of interference can belong to the same Wi-Fi network, e.g. a nearby AP with the same SSID, part of the same Extended Service Set (ESS), or can be external such as another wireless network, or any radio source in the same frequency band. As information on interferences and traffic are not easily available and unpredictable for external sources, we consider only interferences that exist between APs of the same ESS.

We assume that the assignment of the channels to the APs has been set. Two APs will detect transmissions of each other if they use the same channel and are in the detection range of each other. It leads to a share of the medium, as transmissions can not take place at the same time or collisions may happen if they transmit at the same time. The two APs are then in conflict.

According to the IEEE 802.11 DCF mode, APs in mutual conflict have equivalent opportunities to access the medium [17]. Therefore, we assume that the number of accesses to the medium is equal, in average, between conflicting APs. In Figure 2a, we represent three APs in mutual conflict.

To compute the mean throughput D_j^* of AP_j in presence of conflicts, we use Equation (6) and adapt it to this context. The throughput of stations associated to the same AP is seen as an aggregation, as shown in Figure 2b. d_{ij} is then replaced by D_j^*. D_j corresponds to the mean throughput of AP_j without conflict, therefore r_{kj} (which is the bandwidth obtained by one station without conflict) is replaced by D_j. Finally, in this context, the share comes from the APs in conflict: x_{kj} is replaced by s_{kj} that represents the number of APs in conflict with AP_j. Note that this adaptation of Equation (6) is possible because the opportunity to access the channel is the same for all APs in mutual conflicts (as the throughput of an AP is equally shared among its associated stations in the previous model):

$$D_j^* = \frac{1}{\sum_{k=1}^{m} \frac{s_{kj}}{D_k}} \quad (8)$$

Substituting (4) in (8), we get :

$$D_j^* = \cfrac{1}{\sum\limits_{k=1}^{m}\left(\cfrac{s_{kj}}{\sum\limits_{i=1}^{n} x_{ik}} \sum\limits_{i=1}^{n}\cfrac{x_{ik}}{r_{ik}}\right)} \qquad (9)$$

As for the case with orthogonal channels, we assume that the AP throughput is equally shared among the stations associated with it. Therefore, the mean throughput for a particular station is:

$$d_{ij}^* = \cfrac{1}{\sum\limits_{i'=1}^{n} x_{i'j}} \cdot \cfrac{1}{\sum\limits_{k=1}^{m}\left(\cfrac{s_{kj}}{\sum\limits_{i'=1}^{n} x_{i'k}} \cdot \sum\limits_{i'=1}^{n}\cfrac{x_{i'k}}{r_{i'k}}\right)} \qquad (10)$$

The formulation of the association optimization problem in a wireless network with non-orthogonal channels is given as follows:

$$\max \quad \sum_{i=1}^{n} \log\left(\sum_{j=1}^{m} d_{ij}x_{ij}\right)$$

$$\text{with} \quad d_{ij} = \cfrac{1}{\sum\limits_{i'=1}^{n} x_{i'j}} \cdot \cfrac{1}{\sum\limits_{k=1}^{m}\left(\cfrac{s_{kj}}{\sum\limits_{i'=1}^{n} x_{i'k}} \cdot \sum\limits_{i'=1}^{n}\cfrac{x_{i'k}}{r_{i'k}}\right)}$$

$$(11)$$

$$\text{subject to} \quad \sum_{j=1}^{m} x_{ij} = 1 \qquad 1 \leq i \leq n,$$
$$x_{ij} \in \{0,1\} \qquad 1 \leq i \leq n, 1 \leq j \leq m,$$
$$\text{if } r_{ij} = 0 \text{ then } x_{ij} = 0 \quad 1 \leq i \leq n, 1 \leq j \leq m.$$

The objective here is to maximize the overall network throughput while ensuring a certain fairness between the wireless stations when the APs use non-orthogonal channels. The expression of the mean throughput between an AP and an associated station has changed, compared to the orthogonal channel case, to take into account conflicts between APs. The constraints are the same as in the orthogonal channel case.

3.2 Optimization problem solving

The optimization association problem, as formulated in the previous section, is a non-linear optimization problem with discrete variables, which is known to be NP-hard [18].

We propose an heuristic, based on a local search to approach the optimal solution.

Most of the studies that deal with optimization of Wi-Fi associations, and that have been briefly present in Section 2 [8–10, 13], use approximation algorithms based on relaxation to a non-linear convex program. It allows them to apply the rounding process proposed by Shmoys and Tardos for the generalized assignment problem [19], to provide binary values of the association variable x_{ij}. This often does not allow an exact solution of the problem in a reasonable computational time.

Instead, to solve our optimization problem, we propose an iterative heuristic based on the principle of local search, also called descent or iterative improvement. Local search is an important class of heuristics used to solve combinatorial optimization problems. The key idea of a local search

algorithm is to start from an initial feasible solution and iteratively find, at each iteration, a solution called a best neighbor that improves the objective function [20]. The main benefits of local search lie in its simplicity and its iterative process which can stop the optimization process at any time to comply with a constraint like the computation time for instance. Contrary to constructive approaches, local search algorithms consider only complete feasible solutions during the search. The proposed algorithm has then the advantage to improve Wi-Fi associations at each iteration, and can be stopped at any time with a feasible solution. The time that the system spends in computing a solution can thus be bounded and tuned.

Our iterative local search method is based on two essential elements: a neighborhood structure and a procedure exploiting this neighborhood. The method can be summarized as follows:

1. It starts with an initial feasible solution.

2. At each iteration, it chooses, among all the neighbors of the current solution, one of the solutions that maximizes the objective function. This neighbor becomes the current solution on which to apply the next iteration.

A neighbor of a feasible solution $X(X = (x_{ij})_{1 \leq i \leq n, 1 \leq j \leq m})$ corresponds to a feasible solution where only a single station has changed of access point compared to the given solution X. Note that the change must respect the constraints. The condition to stop the iteration loop can be chosen according to the context. For instance, it can be stopped when it has: 1) found a local maximum (as the solution space is finite, the local search reaches a local maximum in a finite number of iterations when the current solution has no neighbor with a greater objective function), 2) reached a fixed maximum threshold for the number of iterations, or 3) exceeded a fixed maximum threshold for the runtime of the optimization program.

The two last stop conditions ensure that a feasible and better solution (compared to the initial one) may be found while respecting the time constraint of the system.

4. PERFORMANCE EVALUATION

In order to assess the effectiveness of the proposed approach, we used the $Network\ Simulator-3(ns-3.23)$ [21]. Compared to optimization tools, this tool offers a more realistic and richer environment and simulates all aspects of a network from the physical to the application layers.

Simulations are performed as follows. The first step consists in using ns-3 to create the network topologies, to compute the link capacities between the APs and the stations (r_{ij}) and to extract the initial association based on the RSSI values. A link capacity between one AP and one station corresponds to the throughput received by the station when a saturated constant bit rate (CBR) flow is generated between the two considered nodes and when all other stations and interferences from the other AP/stations are neglected. Note that these capacities are computed at the application layer of the TCP/IP stack. This has the advantage of: i) taking into account the headers generated by the sub-layers and the overhead induced by the IEEE 802.11 DCF mode (e.g. the MAC header and the Acknowledgment frame), ii) directly obtaining the useful throughput, iii) designing the proposed model independently of the standard (802.11 a/b/g/n, ...).

In a second step, we generate CBR traffic between APs and stations. This traffic is homogeneous between stations and saturates the medium. The generated payloads have a size of 1500 bytes. We then measure the throughput obtained (d_{ij}), during the ns-3 simulation, for all stations.

The last step consists in running our heuristic on the initial solution (RSSI based association). The heuristic has been integrated to ns-3. Once our heuristic has found the solution, we force the stations to associate to the APs computed by our heuristic. We then generate again the same CBR traffic between APs and stations and measure the throughput obtained (d_{ij}) for all stations.

We also compute the Jain's Index [22] to evaluate the fairness achieved in the network. It is defined as follows:

$$ Jain = \frac{\left(\sum\limits_{i=1}^{n} d_{iAP(i)} \right)^2}{n \sum\limits_{i=1}^{n} d_{iAP(i)}^2} $$

where AP(i) corresponds to the AP with which the station i is associated.

Wireless interfaces are configured to use the IEEE 802.11n standard. It allows to use the two frequency bands 2.4 GHz and 5 GHz. We use the propagation model *LogDistance-PropagationLossModel* that defines the received signal power as being the ratio between the transmitted signal power and the cube of the distance. The transmission power is 40 mW (16.00206 dBm). We use the rate adaptation algorithm *IdealHtWifiManager* of ns-3 to set the physical rate between stations and APs. We had to develop it as it was not available for 802.11n. The code may be found in [23]. This manager determines the best physical transmission rate to use between a station and its AP according to the SNR measured on packets sent from the source to the destination.

The Wi-Fi network consists of 25 (5x5) access points, deployed on a square grid such that the distance between two adjacent APs is 100 meters. This distance leads to overlapping zones. A station may then have several choices for its association. APs are then randomly moved within a circle with a diameter of 25 meters (the center being the grid points) to obtain more realistic topologies. Stations are randomly distributed in the coverage area of the access points. The distribution is Gaussian, centered in the middle of the grid. A topology sample is shown in Figure 3.

For each scenario, the number of APs is fixed (25), and we increase the number of wireless stations from 25 to 250. For each scenario, we perform 30 different configurations for a given number of stations. These configurations are obtained by randomly changing the station positions. In the different figures, each point is the mean of these 30 simulations with a confidence interval at 95%.

4.1 Orthogonal channels

Figure 4 illustrates the performance results when all APs have orthogonal channels in the 2.4 GHz band. It is very likely an unrealistic situation as they are very few orthogonal channels in this frequency band. However, it can happen in a sparse network. This scenario enables to show the solution performance when there is no radio conflict. Figure 4a represents the overall network throughput when associations are

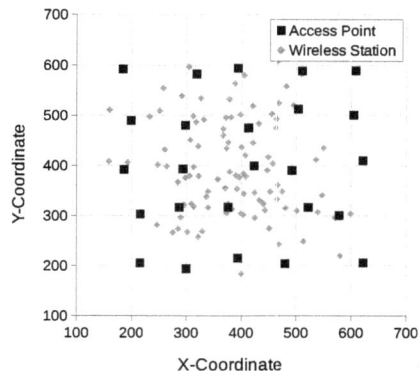

Figure 3: Placement of APs and wireless stations for one simulation.

based on RSSI values and our heuristic (based on the first model (Eq. 7)).

We observe that our algorithm improves the overall throughput by about 40% for a low number of stations, and by 20% when the number of stations reaches 250. Also, we can see that the overall throughput of the network increases until 75 stations (3 stations per access point in average) and remains stable for a greater number of stations. Figure 4b shows the evolution of the Jain's Fairness index before and after optimization. The optimization significantly improves the fairness, up to 120% for 250 stations. Moreover, we observe that, with the RSSI association, the fairness decreases with the number of stations whereas it seems to remain stable with our algorithm (at least with 75 stations and more).

Fairness is also illustrated in Figure 7, where for one simulation (250 stations), we plot the distribution of the number of stations associated to each AP, and the station throughput (d_{ij}) before and after optimization. This simulation is representative: the observed trends are similar for all simulations. In Figure 7a, we can observe that 4 APs do not have any stations associated with them with the RSSI association, whereas there is only one AP without station after optimization. With our optimization, it appears that stations are more homogeneously distributed between APs compared to the RSSI case. A more homogeneous distribution of stations among the APs leads to more balanced throughputs among stations (Figure 7b). In this figure, the x-axis represents the indexes of the 250 stations in an increasing order of the station throughput. The y-axis represents the station throughput (with a log scale). It varies from 1.15 Mb/s to 136 Mb/s for the RSSI association, and from 2.51 Mb/s to 83 Mb/s after optimization. It clearly shows a better usage of Wi-Fi resources: stations use more APs and they are more homogeneously shared between APs leading to a better fairness and a throughput increase.

4.2 Non-orthogonal channels

We simulate two cases: one with 3 orthogonal channels (in the 2.4 GHz band) and one with 8 orthogonal channels (in the 5 GHz band). We distribute channels in a way that minimizes the number of conflicts and interference. It corresponds to a scenario where the AP deployment has been planned. Figure 5a (8 orthogonal channels) shows that our optimization (based on the second model Eq. 11) improves

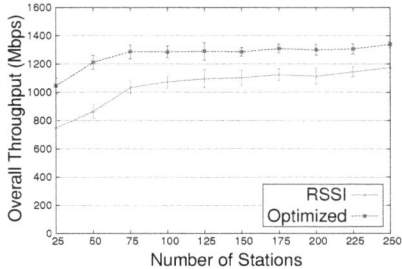

(a) Overall Network Throughput.

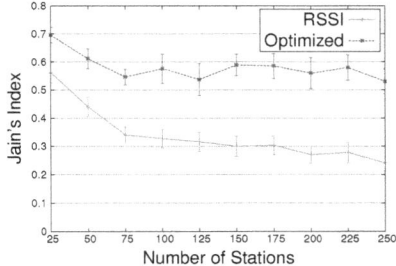

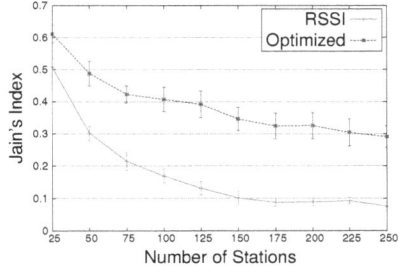

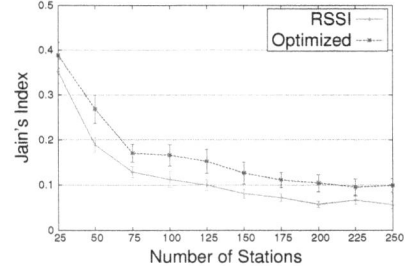

(a) Overall Network Throughput.

(a) Overall Network Throughput.

(b) Jain's Fairness Index.

(b) Jain's Fairness Index.

(b) Jain's Fairness Index.

Figure 4: All Orthogonal channels.

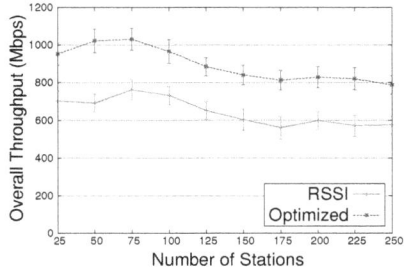

Figure 5: 8 Orthogonal channels.

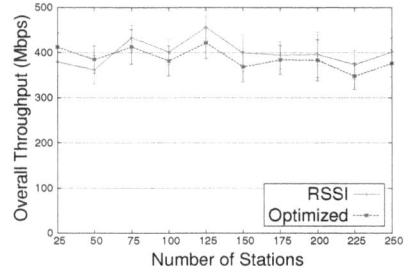

Figure 6: 3 Orthogonal channels.

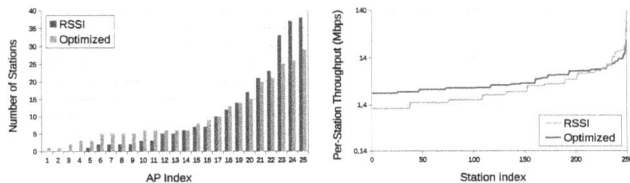

(a) Number of stations per AP.

(b) Throughput per Station.

Figure 7: Comparison of the number of stations per AP and station throughput for one simulation sample before (RSSI) and after optimization (Optimized).

the overall throughput up to 40% regardless of the number of stations. The Jain's Fairness index, shown in Figure 5b, is improved by our optimization by a factor varying from 1.2 for 25 stations to 3 for 250 stations.

Figure 6 illustrates the simulation results obtained in the 2.4 GHz band with 3 orthogonal channels. Improvements are clearly less significant than in the 8 channels case. Figure 6a shows that the optimization does not increase the overall throughput and the obtained results are almost equivalent with these two solutions, with a small advantage to the RSSI-based association. Nevertheless, we can observe an improvement of the Jain's index, with our optimization, varying from 10% to 100% (35% in average).

With our topology, the sensing range (distance at which the signal of a transmitting AP is above the clear channel assessment -or carrier sense- threshold) is approximately 221 meters. With our channel allocation, an AP detects transmissions from at most 3 APs. As we have seen during the formulation of the problem, APs/stations that share the medium tends to obtain the same throughput. Consequently, in this very constrained scenario, performance can not be significantly improved. Throughput can hardly be

increased since the high number of stations on each channel does not allow to separate stations with high and low link capacities, and fairness is already imposed by stations with low link capacities.

4.3 On-Line Optimization

Our optimization can be used, in practice, in an on-line way. More precisely, it may be run at regular interval to take into account stations that have left or joined the Wi-Fi network or that have moved. To illustrate the dynamic behavior of our approach, we simulated, on the same network topology, another scenario in which we randomly remove 50 stations among the 250 and we replace it with 50 new ones at each interval. The new stations will first associate with in function of the RSSI value, and then our optimization is applied. The results with 8 orthogonal channels are shown in Figure 8 where we evaluate the performance at the first step with and without our optimization for the 250 stations (iteration 1). Then, for each iteration (from 2 to 10), we consider 50 new stations and removed 50 existing ones. We optimize the associations and we evaluate the performance. The "Non optimized" evaluation corresponds to a configuration where the association of the 200 stations that remain come from the previous optimization and the 50 new stations are associated in function of the RSSI. Figure 8a shows the improvement of the overall network throughput after the optimization at each iteration. This improvement varies between 5% and 120%. Figure 8b shows an average improvement of 110% in fairness after each association optimization.

5. CONCLUSION

In this paper, we address the association problem in Wi-Fi networks. Our solution, based on an optimization model, aims to improve the overall network throughput while achieving a better fairness between stations, compared to the classical association based on RSSI.

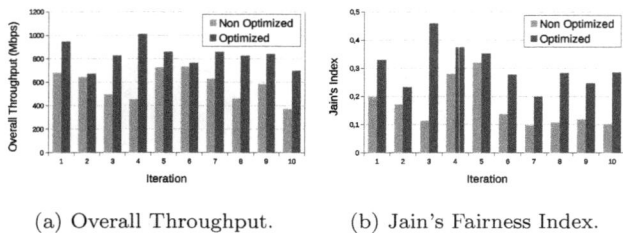

(a) Overall Throughput. (b) Jain's Fairness Index.

Figure 8: Overall throughput and Jain's index for dynamic association optimization

The main contributions of this work are the mathematical formulation of the problem and the proposed local search algorithm. The benefit of this algorithm is a convergence in a few iterations when the starting point is the default RSSI association. Moreover, the algorithm can be stopped at any time and always gives a feasible and better association. It can be easily tuned according to the CPU or time constraints of the WLAN controller. Simulation results show that the proposed optimization significantly improves the network performance. In case of orthogonal channels, our optimization increases the overall throughput up to 40% and the fairness up to 120%, and for non-orthogonal channels we observe an improvement varying from 15% to 40% for the overall throughput and from 25% to 300% for the fairness. This improvement is due to a better distribution of stations among the AP, and an improvement throughput for most of the stations.

6. REFERENCES

[1] Cisco visual networking index: Forecast and methodology, 2015-2020. *White Paper*, 2016.

[2] IEEE standard for information technology–telecommunications and information exchange between systems local and metropolitan area networks–specific requirements part 11: Wireless LAN medium access control (MAC) and physical layer (PHY) specifications. *IEEE Std 802.11-2012*, pages 1–2793, March 2012.

[3] K. Shin, I. Park, J. Hong, D. Har, and D. H. Cho. Per-node throughput enhancement in Wi-Fi densenets. *IEEE Communications Magazine*, 53(1):118–125, January 2015.

[4] M. Heusse, F. Rousseau, G. Berger-Sabbatel, and A. Duda. Performance anomaly of 802.11b. In *INFOCOM 2003*, volume 2, pages 836–843, March 2003.

[5] P. Calhoun, M. Montemurro, and D. Stanley. Control and provisioning of wireless access points (CAPWAP) protocol specification. RFC 5415, RFC Editor, March 2009.

[6] IEEE standard for information technology– local and metropolitan area networks– specific requirements– part 11: Wireless LAN medium access control (MAC) and physical layer (PHY) specifications amendment 8: IEEE 802.11 wireless network management. pages 1–433, February 2011.

[7] M. Yang, Y. Li, D. Jin, L. Zeng, X. Wu, and A. V. Vasilakos. Software-defined and virtualized future mobile and wireless networks: A survey. *Mob. Netw. Appl.*, 20(1):4–18, February 2015.

[8] O. B. Karimi, J. Liu, and J. Rexford. Optimal collaborative access point association in wireless networks. In *IEEE INFOCOM 2014. Conference on Computer Communications*, pages 1141–1149, April 2014.

[9] L. Li, M. Pal, and Y. R. Yang. Proportional fairness in multi-rate wireless LANs. In *IEEE INFOCOM 2008. Conference on Computer Communications*, April 2008.

[10] W. Li, S. Wang, Y. Cui, X. Cheng, R. Xin, M. A. Al-Rodhaan, and A. Al-Dhelaan. AP association for proportional fairness in multi-rate WLANs. *IEEE/ACM Transactions on Networking*, 2013.

[11] Y. Bejerano, S. J. Han, and L. Li. Fairness and load balancing in wireless LANs using association control. *IEEE/ACM Transactions on Networking*, 15(3):560–573, June 2007.

[12] Mario Collotta. FLBA: A fuzzy algorithm for load balancing in IEEE 802.11 networks. *Journal of Network and Computer Applications*, 53:183 – 192, 2015.

[13] H. Tang, L. Yang, J. Dong, Z. Ou, Y. Cui, and J. Wu. Throughput optimization via association control in wireless LANs. *Mobile Networks and Applications*, 21(3):453–466, 2016.

[14] A. Gupta, J. Min, and I. Rhee. WiFox: Scaling Wi-Fi performance for large audience environments. In *Proceedings of the 8th International Conference on Emerging Networking Experiments and Technologies*, CoNEXT '12, pages 217–228, 2012.

[15] G. Bianchi. Performance analysis of the IEEE 802.11 distributed coordination function. *IEEE Journal on Selected Areas in Communications*, 18(3):535–547, March 2000.

[16] F. P. Kelly. Charging and rate control for elastic traffic. *European Transactions on Telecommunications*, 1997.

[17] G. Berger-Sabbatel, A. Duda, M. Heusse, and F. Rousseau. *Short-Term Fairness of 802.11 Networks with Several Hosts*, pages 263–274. Springer US, Boston, MA, 2005.

[18] T. Bu, L. Li, and R. Ramjee. Generalized proportional fair scheduling in third generation wireless data networks. In *Proceedings IEEE INFOCOM 2006. 25TH IEEE International Conference on Computer Communications*, pages 1–12, April 2006.

[19] D. B. Shmoys and E. Tardos. An approximation algorithm for the generalized assignment problem. *Mathematical Programming*, 62(1):461–474, 1993.

[20] J. P. Walser. *Integer Optimization by Local Search: A Domain-independent Approach*. Springer-Verlag, Berlin, Heidelberg, 1999.

[21] NS-3: A discrete-event network simulator for internet systems. version3.23.https://www.nsnam.org/, 2015.

[22] R. Jain, D. M. Chiu, and W. R. Hawe. A quantitative measure of fairness and discrimination for resource allocation in shared computer system. *Digital Equipment Corporation*, 1984.

[23] NS-3 code: Ideal HT Wi-Fi manager. http://perso.ens-lyon.fr/mohammed.amer/Ideal-ht-wifi-manager.

Performance-Energy Trade-offs in Smartphones

Tiberiu S. Chis
Imperial College London
180 Queen's Gate, London, UK
tiberiu.chis07@imperial.ac.uk

Peter G. Harrison
Imperial College London
180 Queen's Gate, London, UK
p.harrison@imperial.ac.uk

ABSTRACT

In the literature, numerous works have modeled user activity on smartphones and the effects on battery life. Power-saving modes prolong battery life by saving energy, but application performance is limited as a result. We investigate performance-energy trade-offs of smartphone applications by investigating three strategies: first, we propose an M/M/1 discriminatory processor sharing queue to act as a smartphone server and measure delays of Android applications; secondly, we form a performance-energy trade-off that takes into account cellular radio transfers using an objective cost function incorporating mean delay and power consumption; and thirdly, we build an online HMM to act as a power consumption model that predicts battery life given recent data transfers. For all three strategies, we obtain logged smartphone activity of over 750 users via an open-source smartphone data-collection application. Hence, we obtain three hypotheses from our strategies: first, delay of applications is approximated well using the beta prime distribution; secondly, power consumption increases as mean delay decreases with battery life prolonged if adjustments are made to cellular radio usage; and thirdly, burstiness is captured by HMMs in both data transfers and rates of power consumption.

1. INTRODUCTION

In the last decade, smartphone technology has advanced faster than almost any other, with widespread applications in e-commerce [35], healthcare [48] and personal use [13, 14]. However, despite the development of handsets with faster multi-core CPUs, smaller physical components and high resolution displays, smartphone batteries are yet to improve at commensurate rates. As a result, multinational companies including Samsung and Apple invest millions into new battery features and capabilities [39]. Nonetheless, smartphone performance is hindered through battery misuse and poor application management, leading to elevated discharging rates [14]. Additionally, prolonged high activity via cellular radio and Wi-Fi drain battery life despite providing advantages to users [10]. Therefore, a greater aim is to understand the performance-energy trade-off: maintaining performance when running applications without severely degrading battery life.

MSWiM '16, November 13-17, 2016, Malta, Malta

© 2016 ACM. ISBN 978-1-4503-4502-6/16/11. . . $15.00

DOI: http://dx.doi.org/10.1145/2988287.2989140

One can argue that performance is driving the smartphone industry. For example, mobile users wait approximately nine seconds, on average, for a web page to load according to Google [23]. Further, smartphones are not immune to slow mobile browsers whose performance varies from device to device [25]. Whether it's using smartphones to download files, to stream web content on YouTube or to run background "apps," the same delay principle applies. From a queueing perspective, delay (i.e. the time a user waits for a job to complete) and response time (or latency, i.e. the time between a job arriving and leaving the system) are closely related, and arguably represent a vital performance metric. To meet quality of service (QoS) demands, application developers and content providers aim for fairness and quick response times to minimize performance bottlenecks. Modeling response times analytically requires a *fair* scheduling policy, such as processor sharing (PS), which gives n incoming tasks an equal share ($1/n$) of a processor that has service rate 1. PS scheduling has relevant applications in web server designs and in bandwidth-sharing protocols in packet-switched networks [19, 22]. Variants of PS queues such as discriminatory PS (DPS) queues address service differentiation and, hence, enable analytical response times to approximate queueing delays. However, simply minimizing mean response time (or how long we wait, on average, for an application to complete) is usually unacceptable nowadays because users tend to be equally frustrated with a highly variable service. Thus, users demand *predictable* response times, which makes it desirable to calculate moments and response time distributions. Surprisingly, few works address response time as a key performance metric in smartphones using queueing models.

Linked to performance, as measured principally through the delay of smartphone applications, is reducing power consumption to prolong battery life. Smartphones often run on lithium-ion (Li-ion) batteries. Users expect battery packs to tolerate many charge cycles before replacement is needed, but power-consuming applications, frequent updates and costly data transfers all degrade batteries at an accelerated rate [38]. Researchers have found that power-saving modes slow down discharge rates and prolong battery life by sacrificing levels of performance [26]. However, problems exist when low battery conflicts with high priority applications and smartphones are prohibited from entering power-saving modes. Further, users exhibit starkly different charging patterns for their device whilst transferring data over cellular radio or Wi-Fi [13]. Thus, it is important to understand the relationship between data transfers and power consumption for a wide range of mobile applications. Real data traces of smartphone battery life often provide a cheap testbed to test such performance-energy hypotheses relatively quickly. For example, one can train parsimonious models such as the hidden Markov model (HMM) [8, 29] on smartphone data usage to replicate burstiness of jobs in mobile applications and forecast power consumption. Further, an objective cost function would be useful to combine such strategies to obtain a trade-off of performance and energy metrics and experiment with optimal scenarios. In this paper, we address the aforementioned challenges to motivate three unique strategies for testing performance and energy in smartphones:

- We obtain delay distributions from smartphone applications using M/M/1-DPS queues to approximate response time moments and then apply distribution-fitting algorithms.

- We formulate a performance-energy trade-off using an objective cost function incorporating mean delay and power consumption and construct real-world experiments involving cellular radio sessions.

- We build an online power consumption model using incremental HMMs that train on traces of data transfers and can forecast battery life with some degree of accuracy.

To the best of our knowledge these strategies are novel work, combining queueing theory with real-world smartphone measurements and machine learning with battery life forecasts. From the three strategies, we discover three important findings: first, the delay of applications, which we represent by response time in queueing models, is approximated well using the beta prime distribution; secondly, the power consumption of a handset increases as the mean delay of its applications decreases and battery life can be saved by reorganizing recurrent cellular radio transfers; thirdly, HMMs capture the burstiness of data transfers and power consumption to better predict battery life compared to moving averages and regression models. The rest of the paper is organized as follows: section 2 provides background on cellular radio, existing performance-energy models and queueing theory; section 3 summarizes the data collected to test our three strategies; in sections 4 - 6, we evaluate our three main strategies; we conclude in section 7.

2. BACKGROUND

2.1 Data transfers and cellular radio

With technology companies selling more smartphones – Samsung, Apple and Huawei have each sold over 100 million handsets in 2015 [34] – wireless communication via mobile devices will only intensify. Therefore, it is important to understand the effect of asynchronous data transmission on power consumption and cost, especially from a user's point of view. Smartphones have four radios for transmitting data: cellular, Wi-Fi, bluetooth and near field communication (NFC). Techniques exist for reducing data transferred across such radios to prolong battery life. For example, "airplane mode" disables all radios and is ideal for air travel or when roaming abroad. Users might prefer to enable radios required for the relevant activity. Cellular radio is known to drain the battery when there is no access to a cellular radio tower [37] and is powered on for up to thirty seconds, irrespective of transfer size [10]. Such heavy power consumption requires further investigation of cellular radio modes. Cellular radio is controlled by a state machine that balances low latency and longer battery life: when no data is transferred via radio, it enters a low-power state, but when sending data over radio, it switches to full-power mode to initiate data transfers. The radio waits in full-power mode for data to be transferred; if no data is detected for five to ten seconds, the radio switches to an intermediate low-power state. After a minute of no data, the radio

switches to stand-by mode. Switching in between modes, or state transitions, is power-consuming and drains the battery, so must be minimized.

There exist two models for transferring data on cellular radio. The "rare-big model" downloads the largest amount of data as infrequently as possible. This model minimizes the number of mode switches for the radio states, whilst maximizing bandwidth use. The alternate "often-little model" transfers as little data as possible and performs these transfers frequently. However, this heavily fragments radio use by increasing state switching, which drains the battery since radio is on nearly constantly. Figure 1 summarizes the differences of the two techniques. Potential user interaction exists for controlling data transfers that favor the rare-big model [10, 37]. For example, users can identify cyclic data transfers and pre-fetch (i.e. load) this group of intermittent transfers. Further, updates sent to users recommending charging the device when cyclic downloads occur (i.e. application syncs and updates) are beneficial for long-term battery resource allocation. By generating graphs for battery usage, users create profiles and analyze patterns of transfers. It follows that short, cyclic periods of transfers that are identified on the graph can be batched together and transferred at a more convenient time, especially if non-time-critical.

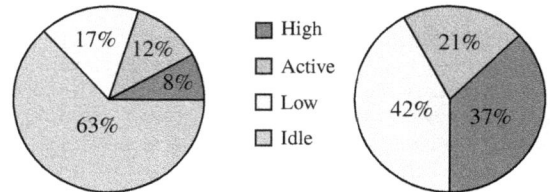

Figure 1: Defragmented network traffic showing effects of rare-big (left) and often-little (right) models on cellular radio use [10].

2.2 Existing performance-energy models

Recent studies measure application performance of smartphones [13, 14]. We extend this existing work by considering background apps as user activity, measuring delay of smartphone applications, and offering real-world strategies to reduce power consumption. More recently, smartphone benchmarking has allowed designers to select optimal processors and run tests to analyze performance and offer guidelines in energy consumption [33]. However, user preferences often ignore such guidelines, resulting in accelerated battery draw and, hence, users should be characterized by unique patterns of data usage activity and charging behavior.

Existing battery models offer power-saving modes for smartphones [3, 26], but our work focuses on lowering power consumption using performance-energy trade-offs and reducing cellular radio usage via rare-big transfer models. For example, reducing unnecessary data transfers via cellular radio on a variety of mobile handsets improves existing apps [37] as it adds cross-platform capabilities. Chen *et al* capture energy drain in the wild, but only study two smartphones [24]. Rohner *et al* simulate battery life [1], focusing on charge recovery behavior that exhibits low (4mA) and high (25mA) periodic discharge rates. However, the mode-switching of HMMs would more accurately capture the burstiness of such intermittent loads, typical of data transfer in mobile apps. Hence, this motivates our work on having an incremental HMM to act as a power consumption model that predicts expected battery life given recent data activity of the user.

2.3 Queueing theory

In computer and communication systems, simplifying core processes via queueing models is beneficial for modeling delay in a fast, efficient manner [12]. Further, one utilizes underlying continuous time Markov chain (CTMC) properties of queueing models in order to abstract dynamic processes governing such systems [27] and obtain representative performance measures (i.e. response time T). Incorporating a server with exponential service simplifies complex system processes via queueing models. The simplest model is the M/M/1-PS queue with Poisson arrivals (i.e. mean arrival rate λ), exponential service times (i.e. mean service rate μ), and one PS server. Existing research suggests that media file sizes follow exponential distributions [40]. Therefore, the assumption of exponential packet sizes is sufficient for modeling jobs from smartphone applications. By modeling multi-class jobs as part of queueing systems, one can obtain response time moments, avoid system bottlenecks and cater for efficient resource allocation in smartphones.

We justify using the processor sharing (PS) scheduling discipline to obtain response times, which approximate delays in smartphone applications. Under PS queues, a challenge is to replicate the smartphone server precisely in a numerically tractable way. Hence, to enable realistic modeling of smartphone applications, we assume PS scheduling for the following reasons: PS is popular for web server design [16] and evaluating flow-level performance of end-to-end flow control mechanisms like TCP [41]; the implicit *fairness* of PS means expected job response time is directly proportional to the job size; PS facilitates tractable asymptotic analysis of heavy-tailed distributions [28]. However, a drawback of egalitarian PS (EPS) is that it cannot cater for heterogeneous systems. Hence, there exist variants of PS such as discriminatory PS (DPS), where each job j in the system receives its own percentage of the server, therefore catering for multiple job classes. In DPS, a single processing system serving K job types is controlled by a vector of weights ($\omega_j > 0$, $j = 1, \ldots, K$). Further, assuming there are n_i class i jobs, $i = 1, \ldots, K$, in the system, each class j job is served at rate:

$$r_j(n_1, \ldots, n_K) = \frac{\omega_j}{\sum_{i=1}^{K} \omega_i n_i}, \quad j = 1, \ldots, K \tag{1}$$

Note that when $\omega_i = \omega_j, i, j = 1, \ldots, K$, DPS scheduling becomes EPS with equal job weights. DPS scheduling typically approximates fair-queueing service disciplines in communication network routers (with small number of packets flowing into the router) [42], where delays and congestion control are key measures. Important metrics for smartphone users is delay, which we define as response time obtained from steady-state DPS queues. Calculating higher moments of response time under EPS and DPS scheduling requires an advanced understanding of layered branching of incoming jobs into the system [21]. Chis and Harrison obtain unconditional response time moments [11] by considering an M/M/1-DPS queue with two job classes. For simplicity of presentation, we use equal job weights (i.e. $\omega_1 = \omega_2$), but this is not a requirement. Assuming two job classes (i.e. $K = 2$), with mean arrival rates λ_1 and λ_2, mean service rates μ_1 and μ_2, and utilization $\rho_i = \lambda_i/\mu_i$, for $i = 1, 2$, we obtain first ($\mathbb{E}[T_1]$) and second ($\mathbb{E}[T_1^2]$) response time moments as follows:

$$\mathbb{E}[T_1] = \frac{1}{\mu_1(1 - \rho_1 - \rho_2)} \tag{2}$$

$$\mathbb{E}[T_1^2] = \frac{4(\mu_1(1 + \rho_2) + \mu_2(1 - \rho_2))}{\mu_1^2(1 - \rho_1 - \rho_2)^2(\mu_1(2 - \rho_1) + \mu_2(2 - \rho_1 - 2\rho_2))} \tag{3}$$

These expressions were obtained using a multi-class automated al-

gorithm implemented in Mathematica [11]. Note, the respective moments for class 2 jobs are easily obtained by inverting the subscripts 1 and 2 in equations (2) and (3). Calculating the variance (i.e. $\sigma_i^2 = \mathbb{E}[T_i^2] - \mathbb{E}[T_i]^2$) of a class i job reveals the spread of the response time distribution from the mean. Further, calculating higher moments of response time is useful for predicting tails in delays for a variety of multi-class applications where jobs have different priorities – or shares of a DPS server. Given higher moments, it is straightforward to estimate the probability density of response time; in fact, good approximations can usually be found from the first four moments using distribution-fitting algorithms. If the DPS queue is overutilized (i.e. not in steady state), response time can typically be approximated using simulation or spectral expansion methods.

3. DATA SETS

This section provides an overview of the data sets used in this work and some pre-processing of data before building the three strategies. We use the original, unanonymized smartphone data from OpenBattery [4], which is a data collection application chronologically logging the smartphone model, the manufacturer and the timestamped battery data ranging from February 2012 to September 2014. More specifically, each row of battery data stored in the OpenBattery database consists of the following fields: a timestamp, charge level, temperature, health status, plugged status, charging status, current capacity and voltage. Additionally, we collect timestamped traces of packet data transferred for specific handsets from experiments to complement the battery data. An overview of the data statistics is shown in Table 1, where there is collectively over 1.8 million aggregate hours of battery data.

Table 1: Statistics of battery data traces analyzed.

Total smartphones	766
Total applications	4,857
Total charge cycles	> 58.2k
Total aggregate hours	> 1.8m

Table 2 presents a sample of 12 different handset models (from a total of 766) and the corresponding manufacturer, as collected by OpenBattery. Among this sample, we also record the first data log for each model. For the purpose of this work, we seasonally adjusted each time-series through decomposition by calculating the variation of seasonality (i.e. daily activity) and subtracting this variation from each smartphone trace.

Table 2: 12 handset models with manufacturer and date of first log.

Model	Manufacturer	Date
Blade	ZTE	2012-02-23
LS670	LGE	2012-03-18
LT15i	Sony Ericsson	2012-03-24
Huawei-M920	Huawei	2012-08-16
Novo10 Hero	MID	2013-04-24
Nebula 6.9	ZIGO	2013-08-07
Q800	XOLO	2013-10-19
Chaser	TeleEpoch	2013-12-28
Xperia Z C6603	Sony	2014-04-12
i867	Motorola	2014-07-04
HTC One M8	HTC	2014-07-23
GT-I8190N	Samsung	2014-09-12

Using the data sets, we investigated the charging and discharging habits of different users. More specifically, we plotted time-series of power consumption for users to find any distributions or patterns among charging behavior. For example, Figure 2 presents the distribution of session durations observed in charging and discharging patterns for different 100 users, which was a selective sample given the handset models. In the plots, the x-axis is the time of an uninterrupted action (i.e. charging for 60 minutes) and the y-axis is the frequency of this event, observed between March and July 2014. Examining the plots in Figure 2, we observe a power law distribution, where most users charge their smartphones (and allow them to discharge) in bursts of one to two hours. Let us consider the charge behavior of two specific users. Figure 3 summarizes the session durations and the corresponding increase in charge level; considering charging sessions under 100 minutes, user 329 has a positive (reasonably linear) correlation of duration vs charge, whereas user 82 offers a more uniform distribution of charge. Thus, charging (and discharging) activity are key to understanding the diurnal power consumption of smartphones.

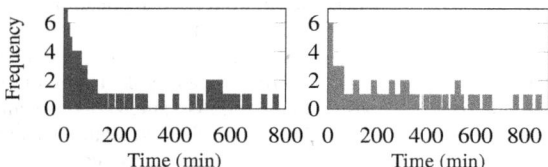

Figure 2: Charging (left) and discharging (right) sessions for 100 users.

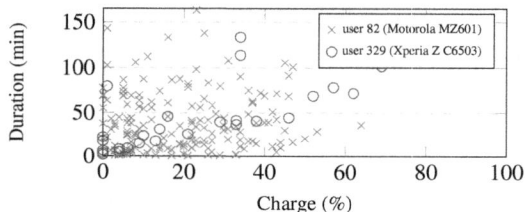

Figure 3: Charge increase with durations for two users.

Figure 4 reveals patterns in 3G data transfers for an HTC One user: on the left, the user is browsing websites using Chrome; on the right, the user is streaming YouTube videos. The bursty nature of such transfers requires parsimonious models with switching modes and capabilities to generate correlated streams, which makes the HMM suitable for data-fitting on such data.

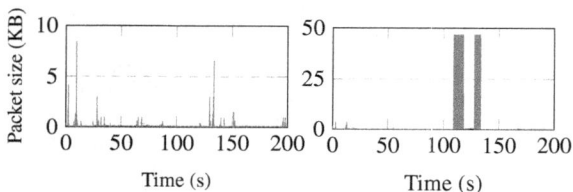

Figure 4: Data transfers for an HTC One user by browsing the Internet (left) and streaming videos online (right).

Such examples of data transfers on smartphones begs the question: what is the delay distribution of smartphone applications? Further, arguably a greater question remains: how can we reduce unnecessary data transfers and prolong battery life in the process? In subsequent sections, we investigate some of these important questions.

4. STRATEGY 1: DELAY DENSITY

Strategy 1 investigates the following question: **what is the most likely delay distribution of smartphone applications?** We aim to answer this question by approximating response time distibutions to represent delay using an M/M/1-DPS queue. Initially, we make two assumptions: first, the DPS queue is stable (i.e. utilization $\rho < 1$), where it is reasonable to assume that the total offered load at the server is less than one, which avoids saturation of resources; secondly, job service times are exponentially distributed, which is supported by existing research that media file sizes follow exponential distributions [40]. In DPS, the priority weights (ω_i) for job class i are proportional to the service requirement of that class. Given the aforementioned assumptions, the M/M/1-DPS queue abstracts the complex scheduling system of smartphone processors when serving multi-class jobs. Note that increasing the number of parallel processors physically adds a multi-core functionality, but in a DPS queueing model, all servers are considered collectively, with a single rate. This approximation is accurate at moderate to high loads where cores can be kept busy. Additionally, our DPS queue provides a means for asynchronous transmission, which is typical of smartphone data activity, and serves multiple job classes.

The DPS queue distinguishes two types of job: the aggregate class of those present under equilibrium conditions and a particular new arrival with its own specific characteristics. For example, when a job arrives at the queue, n other jobs are already present with geometric probability $(1 - \rho)\rho^n$ at equilibrium. Each of these n jobs has arrived from different smartphone applications with individual i.i.d. arrival rates λ_i, for $i = 1, \ldots, n$. Such rates are well approximated by a superposition of independent renewal processes with aggregate arrival rate $\lambda_{all} = \sum_{i=1}^{n} \lambda_i$, which is close to Poisson if no individual arrival stream dominates. On the other hand, the server treats the newly arrived job differently from the class of existing jobs in the system (with combined arrival rate λ_{all}) in that it may have any specified service demand, x. In this way, our M/M/1-DPS acts as a pseudo-multi-class queue, from which we obtain moments of response time using equations (2) and (3). With up to four moments produced, we yield response time distributions when it is too complex to numerically invert the Laplace transform. An approximation of distribution-fitting is the generalized lambda distribution (GLD) [30, 31, 17], which inputs the first four moments of response time as parameters. The goal is to find GLD parameters such that the moments of the theoretical GLD match the empirical moments from our M/M/1-DPS queue. Note, the quality-of-fit is ascertained only through a goodness-of-fit test because closed-form solutions do not exist for the GLD parameters. Further, the GLD technique produces a lower Kolmogorov-Smirnov statistic when compared to the least squares and starship methods [32].

We display the response time density for an HTC One user by conducting several 1-hour experiments. The smartphone user runs low data-intensive applications (i.e. reading messages on WhatsApp and Google searches on Chrome) and high data-intensive applications (i.e. watching segments of videos on YouTube). Figure 5 plots two arbitrary experiments and reveals that response times follow a beta time probability density. Note, the beta prime distribution has type I in the Pearson system of distribution types [44], where the F distribution (type VI) is a particular parametrization [43].

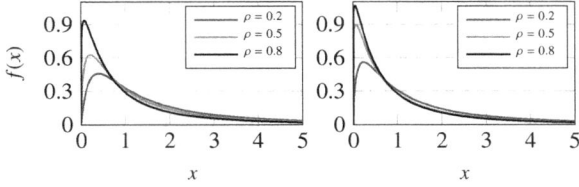

Figure 5: Response time density for HTC One user running high (left) and low (right) data-intensive applications.

Figure 5 reveals distributions with heavy tails, which increases the chance of unexpected delays whilst running applications, irrespective of utilization level. We observe that for higher system utilization the response time density is approximately exponential with parameter 1, which is useful in modeling further scenarios involving application delays. To test the applicability of our distribution-fitting approximation, we use the beta prime density functions to output the mean ($\mathbb{E}[T]$) and variance (σ^2) of delay for a number of applications on the HTC One. Further, we summarize statistics in Table 3 by comparing distributions, including Gaussian and exponential, using the mean error (%) calculated between the observed results and the approximations.

Table 3: Mean ($\mathbb{E}[T]$) and variance (σ^2) of delay (in ms) for browsing websites and YouTube videos on the HTC One.

	Browsing		YouTube		
Distribution	$\mathbb{E}[T]$	σ^2	$\mathbb{E}[T]$	σ^2	Error (%)
Observed	0.894	1.051	2.716	12.98	-
Beta prime	**0.886**	**1.044**	**2.834**	**13.11**	**1.7**
Gaussian	0.704	1.252	1.901	16.22	23.8
Exponential	0.788	0.621	2.263	5.121	32.5

The results in Table 3 reveal that only the beta prime distribution is effective in capturing the mean and the variance of delay given the two types of mobile applications. For example, the exponential distribution underestimates the observed delay and the Gaussian distribution overestimates the variance of delay for activities such as browsing Chrome and playing YouTube videos. Further, the beta prime distribution is the only distribution to exhibit heavy tails, with pronounced kurtosis. This is a realistic phenomenon occurring in data transfers as small jobs (i.e. data packets) are allowed to overtake long jobs when served by a mobile processor. Hence, we conclude that the **delays of smartphone applications are approximated well using the beta prime distribution**. Having investigated delay distributions, we plan to formulate a theoretical performance-energy trade-off of smartphone applications involving mean delay and energy terms.

5. STRATEGY 2: TRADE-OFFS

Strategy 2 investigates **the effects of cellular radio usage and mean delay of smartphone applications on power consumption rates**. To address this, we formulate an objective cost function, C, as part of a performance-energy trade-off. Recall that μ is the service rate, $\rho < 1$ is the utilization and the arrival rate $\lambda = \mu\rho$ holds at equilibrium for positive terms. Let r_{all} be the total power consumption rate for general OS processes, background applications and active power modes of cellular radio and let r_{rad} be the power consumption rate for active radio only. The rates r_{all} and r_{rad} are based on profiling hundreds of devices from the OpenBattery data set and using Li-ion manufacturers' parameters [45, 47]. Such parameters are extracted from typical Li-ion discharge curves

(i.e. voltage vs capacity) and include: voltage (~3.9V) and capacity (~1.1Ah) when the exponential zone ends; voltage (~3.6V) and capacity (~5.1Ah) when the nominal zone ends; capacity (~5.7Ah) at cut-off voltage (~2.5V); internal resistance is set to ~0.05Ohm. It is important to incorporate such realistic rates into power consumption models given varying levels of data transfers and cellular radio modes.

The performance term of the objective cost function is the mean response time under PS (for one job class): $\mu^{-1}(1-\rho)^{-1}$. The energy term is more complex: let B be the busy period, which represents the duration that the cellular radio is in active power modes continuously; let t_1 be the time needed to switch the radio to a low power mode; let I be the idle time spent with the radio in low power mode; let t_2 be the time needed to switch the radio to active power again; and define $t = t_1 + t_2$ as the total time spent switching between these states. The system operates as a sequence of $B, I, B, I, \ldots$ delay cycles and averaging over B and I yields:

$$\frac{r_{all}E[B] + r_{rad}E[I]P(I \leq t)}{E[B+I]} \quad (4)$$

where we use $P(I \leq t) = 1 - e^{-t\mu\rho}$, $\rho = E[B]/E[B+I]$ and $(1-\rho) = E[I]/E[B+I]$ to obtain:

$$r_{all}\rho + r_{rad}(1-\rho)(1 - e^{-t\mu\rho}) \quad (5)$$

Let $0 < \alpha < 1$ be a scaling parameter for performance and energy terms. Then, we define cost function C as follows:

$$C = \frac{\alpha}{\mu(1-\rho)} + (1-\alpha)(r_{all}\rho + r_{rad}(1-\rho)(1 - e^{-t\mu\rho})) \quad (6)$$

Observe that when cellular radio is in low power mode, we eliminate the term $r_{rad}(1-\rho)(1 - e^{-t\mu\rho})$ and, therefore, save energy in the process. In Figure 6, we plot μ against C for increasing values of t and fix $\rho = 0.5$, $\alpha = 0.05$, $r_{all} = 20$, $r_{rad} = 7$, where battery profiling and manufacturers' information was used as guidance. In all three cases, C has a global minimum and is essentially a minimization problem with respect to μ. Note, changing the parameter values used in the cost function would alter the slopes of the minimization curves for different values of t. Exploring both performance and energy constraints of the cost function, we need to draw conclusions from practical experiments. We set up realistic scenarios that use the theoretical cost function to measure the potential energy savings when cellular radio is reduced. We summarize our findings in two case studies as described in the next subsection.

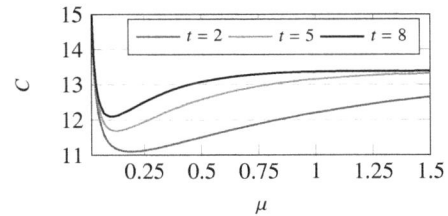

Figure 6: Cost function for varying μ.

5.1 User case studies

Each smartphone user has individual characteristics of device usage such as power consumption and data transfer activity. Since our cost function in equation (6) suggests energy consumption is influenced by cellular radio, we investigate two case studies of real smartphone users. Each user follows two cellular radio models when transferring data: the rare-big model and the often-little model. Additionally, both users charged their smartphones when the battery reached below 10% and stopped charging at 100%. We used one month's data of daily active sessions (t), where a session represents data transfers over cellular radio that lasted anywhere between ten minutes and one hour. These active sessions support the system description of busy cycles as summarized by the energy term in equation (5). We calculated the total charging hours (Hrs) and the monthly data usage (GB) of each user. Given that each user has different charging behavior and data transfers, we show that savings exist for both users when they each employ the rare-big model.

User 1 texts and calls with their ZTE Blade and has a monthly contract data limit of 1GB. Additionally, User 1 "surfs the net" rarely with less than three 4G sessions a day (with Wi-Fi off). Table 4 presents total data consumed per month (GB) for the rare-big and often-little transfer models. In cases when monthly data consumption is borderline 1GB, it is advisable to use the rare-big model to preserve monthly allowance. For example, users can organize transfers by pre-fetching bundles of data.

User 2 streams multimedia data daily on their HTC One, with up to ten significant 4G sessions per day. User 2 has a monthly contract data limit of 3GB. Table 5 presents real data consumption for User 2 for one month and supports the rare-big model for both data and battery savings. Further, the cost implications are evident with $t = 8$ daily sessions as User 2 exceeds the 3GB limit under the often-little model, but saves over 60% of data and ten hours of battery life with the rare-big model.

Table 4: Data consumed per month (GB) and charging hours (Hrs) for User 1 based on t active sessions per day using rare-big and often-little models.

	Rare-big		Often-little	
t	Hrs	Data	Hrs	Data
1	50.8	0.73	55.5	0.82
2	54.2	0.92	57.8	1.06
3	55.3	1.11	61.4	1.37

Table 5: Data consumed per month (GB) and charging hours (Hrs) for User 2 based on t active sessions per day using rare-big and often-little models.

	Rare-big		Often-little	
t	Hrs	Data	Hrs	Data
4	67.6	1.31	75.8	1.66
6	71.4	1.63	80.1	2.47
8	75.2	2.27	85.3	3.66

Evidence in Tables 4 and 5 suggests that the rare-big model has significant data savings and helps prolong battery life. As extensions to our case studies, we plan to diversify user profiles by including high number of active sessions (i.e. more than 20). From our experiments, we found that, on the whole, users charged their smartphones at night more often than during the day when data-intensive applications are run. Advice for smartphone users is to limit often-little data transfers and charge smartphones during the rare-big transfers. Given our cost function and real-world experiments, we hypothesize that **power consumption increases as mean delay decreases in mobile applications and battery life is prolonged by managing cellular radio sessions**. Further, there is a trade-off between saving energy and speeding up performance of

applications. Smartphone users typically observe small changes in delay of applications only when downloading files or waiting for a web page to load. The cost function we formulated, although theoretical, is useful when leveraging delays of non-urgent applications to reduce battery draw in bursts rather than over extended time periods. If this is coupled with careful management of cellular radio sessions, then the battery life can be extended significantly for many handset models. In the next section, we obtain another performance-energy relationship by training an online HMM to forecast power consumption given recent data activity.

6. STRATEGY 3: POWER FORECASTS

Strategy 3 focuses on **forecasting power consumption to reveal trends in data transfers and battery discharge in smartphones**. To incorporate bursty and cyclic data transfers into the power consumption model, we employ an online HMM (OnlineHMM). Notably, burstiness and mode-switching are two well-known phenomena occurring in mobile data transmission and Internet traffic [15, 20], which gives the OnlineHMM advantages over the Poisson process, for instance. Further, the incremental capabilities of the OnlineHMM provide training on live systems without re-training on data as is the case in batch learning of standard HMMs. The hidden states of the OnlineHMM represent the sizes of data transfers by various smartphone applications. For example, in a two-state OnlineHMM, if the smartphone cellular radio is frequently in active power mode (state 1), data transfers will often be larger than if the cellular radio were in low power mode (state 2). The benefit of forecasting with HMMs is knowing the most recent hidden state, which provides a likelihood of the type of forecast likely to occur given the state [7]. We summarize the OnlineHMM in subsequent sections.

6.1 Building the OnlineHMM

Online models are desirable in industry for potential analysis of live systems and resource planning, where main challenges include the dependency of model parameters on all preceding data. In mobile networks, workload arising from multiple, time-varying, correlated traffic streams may create resource bottlenecks at peak times. Therefore, it is important to model workload in a portable and efficient way and obtain representative traces for live systems, on which quantitative measurements can then be made. In terms of HMM dynamics, such online models require an approximation of the backward formula used in the forward-backward algorithm [8] to save time computing the terms for the accumulated observation set. To achieve an online power consumption model for smartphones, we first cluster traces of timestamped data transfers using the k-means algorithm and then train the OnlineHMM on the clustered traces in an incremental fashion, as described in algorithm 1. Given the user's data transfer history, the charging status of the smartphone and the current hidden state of the OnlineHMM, the model outputs the most likely change in power (approximated using real rates obtained from profiling with battery manufacturers' parameters) and updates the smartphone battery level accordingly. In this way, the OnlineHMM can predict battery life for 24 hours to allow resource planning and energy-saving strategies.

6.1.1 Backward formula

For online learning in HMMs, we seek a new backward formula in the forward-backward algorithm, which is then used as part of the Baum-Welch algorithm [9]. The reader can refer to [7] for more details of the Baum-Welch algorithm and its parameters. Through manipulation of β terms, we obtain a forward-recurrence formula such that the β probabilities for new observations O_t are easily calculated. Initially, the OnlineHMM is a standard HMM training on a fixed observation set $\{O_1, \ldots, O_T\}$, but with incoming data it updates parameters $A = \{\hat{a}_{ij}\}$, $B = \{\hat{b}_j(k)\}$, $\pi = \{\hat{\pi}_i\}$ dynamically with reduced computation. However, the difficulty lies in calculating β terms via a forward-recurrence formula. For example, by training an HMM on t observations and subsequently adding M new observations, it is straightforward to calculate:

$$\alpha_{t+1}(i) = \left[\sum_{j=1}^{N} \alpha_t(j) a_{ji} \right] b_i(O_t) \qquad (7)$$

for $i = 1, \ldots, N$. On the other hand, calculating:

$$\beta_{t+1}(i) = \sum_{j=1}^{N} a_{ij} b_j(O_{t+2}) \beta_{t+2}(j) \qquad (8)$$

for $i = 1, \ldots, N$, requires a one-step lookahead (i.e. $\beta_{t+2}(j)$). Therefore, a β approximation is needed, which we adapt from [2] – an experimental attempt on a single data trace for the $N = 2$ case. Further, we generalize this β approximation for the N-state case and collect results on real-world traces from smartphones. Once the α and β terms are updated, we define the following probability sums:

$$\xi_t(i, j) = \frac{\alpha_t(i) a_{ij} b_j(O_{t+1}) \beta_{t+1}(j)}{P} ; \; \gamma_t(i) = \sum_{j=1}^{N} \xi_t(i, j) \qquad (9)$$

where P is a normalizing constant. Then, we can iteratively calculate $\hat{a}_{ij}^{T+1}$ and $\hat{b}_j(k)^{T+1}$ as follows:

$$\hat{a}_{ij}^{T+1} = \frac{\sum_{t=1}^{T+1} \xi_t(i, j)}{\sum_{t=1}^{T+1} \gamma_t(i)} ; \; \hat{b}_j(k)^{T+1} = \frac{\sum_{t=1, O_t=k}^{T+1} \gamma_t(j)}{\sum_{t=1}^{T+1} \gamma_t(j)} \qquad (10)$$

where we only compute the $\xi_{T+1}(i, j)$ and $\gamma_{T+1}(i)$ terms for each new observation. Algorithm 1 summarizes the training process of the OnlineHMM, including the beta approximation. We present the theory behind the beta approximation in the next subsection.

6.1.2   Beta approximation

Let us assume an OnlineHMM with N hidden states. By definition of β, we re-write the system of linear equations given in equation (8) as a matrix multiplication equation. We use notation $b_i = b_i(O_{t+1})$ for a state i in order to simplify interpretation of equations. It follows that:

$$\begin{pmatrix} \beta_t(1) \\ \vdots \\ \beta_t(N) \end{pmatrix} = \begin{pmatrix} a_{11}b_1 & \cdots & a_{1N}b_N \\ \vdots & \ddots & \vdots \\ a_{N1}b_1 & \cdots & a_{NN}b_N \end{pmatrix} \begin{pmatrix} \beta_{t+1}(1) \\ \vdots \\ \beta_{t+1}(N) \end{pmatrix} \qquad (11)$$

Pre-multiplying by the inverse of the $N \times N$ matrix gives us:

$$\begin{pmatrix} a_{11}b_1 & \cdots & a_{1N}b_N \\ \vdots & \ddots & \vdots \\ a_{N1}b_1 & \cdots & a_{NN}b_N \end{pmatrix}^{-1} \begin{pmatrix} \beta_t(1) \\ \vdots \\ \beta_t(N) \end{pmatrix} = I_N \begin{pmatrix} \beta_{t+1}(1) \\ \vdots \\ \beta_{t+1}(N) \end{pmatrix} \qquad (12)$$

where I_N is the $N \times N$ identity matrix. Simplifying terms and rearranging terms in a forward-recurrence, we obtain:

$$\begin{pmatrix} \beta_{t+1}(1) \\ \vdots \\ \beta_{t+1}(N) \end{pmatrix} = \begin{pmatrix} a_{11}b_1 & \cdots & a_{1N}b_N \\ \vdots & \ddots & \vdots \\ a_{N1}b_1 & \cdots & a_{NN}b_N \end{pmatrix}^{-1} \begin{pmatrix} \beta_t(1) \\ \vdots \\ \beta_t(N) \end{pmatrix} \qquad (13)$$

Hence, terms $\beta_{t+1}(i)$, for $i = 1, \ldots, N$, are obtained from equation (13), given that the $N \times N$ matrix is invertible. In cases when the matrix is singular, we use linear approximations of $\beta_{t+1}(i)$ in terms

of $\beta_{t+1}(j)$, where $i \neq j$. In appendix 8.1, we present a linear approximation for the $N = 2$ case, which was first used by Chis in [2].

Algorithm 1 Training OnlineHMM parameters

Input: $\{O_1, \ldots, O_T\}$ = existing observation set; $\{O_{T+1}, \ldots, O_{T+M}\}$ = new observation set; N = number of hidden states; K = number of clusters in k-means; A = state transition matrix; B = emission matrix; π = initial hidden state distribution; α, β = forward-backward probabilities.
  Train HMM on $\{O_1, \ldots, O_T\}$ by calculating parameters A, B, π.
  for $t = T + 1 : T + M - 1$ **do**
    Assign a cluster value to O_t between 1 and K.
    for $i = 1 : N$ **do**
      Calculate $\alpha_{t+1}(i) = [\sum_{j=1}^{N} \alpha_t(j) a_{ji}] b_i(O_t)$.
      Calculate $\beta_{t+1}(i)$ using equation (13).
      for $j = 1 : K$ **do**
        Calculate OnlineHMM parameters iteratively until convergence:
        Update $\hat{a}_{ij}^t$ and $\hat{b}_j(k)^t$ using equation (10).
      end for
    end for
  end for
Output: $A = \{\hat{a}_{ij}\}$; $B = \{\hat{b}_j(k)\}$; $\pi = \{\hat{\pi}_i\}$

6.1.3   Convergence of the OnlineHMM

The space and time complexity for batch learning of the Baum-Welch algorithm in HMMs is $O(N^2 T)$, where T is the trace length and N is the number of hidden states. When training standard HMMs on T new data points K different times, the Baum-Welch convergence complexity is $O(N^2 T K(K + 1)/2)$. However, for OnlineHMM, the complexity is reduced to $O(N^2 T K)$. Therefore, the model parameters converge faster than in the traditional Baum-Welch algorithm. We prove this as follows: if we train a model on K sequential groups of T new observations (i.e. groups of T new data points arrive K times), the additional steps for training a standard HMM (H_1) over the OnlineHMM (H_2) is given by:

$$\begin{aligned} H_1 - H_2 &= (T + 2T + \cdots + KT) - KT \\ &= [TK(K+1)/2] - KT \\ &= TK(K-1)/2 \end{aligned} \qquad (14)$$

Hence, we justify training the OnlineHMM to forecast power consumption given the time-saving benefits in equation (14) compared to standard HMMs. Further, as we scale up by increasing T, the total training steps saved can become a quadratic product in T and K. The next section presents results of the OnlineHMM forecasting battery life compared to a moving average model and a regression model.

6.1.4   Results

Given the user's data transfer history, the charging status of the smartphone and the current hidden state, the OnlineHMM can predict battery life for 24 hours with some degree of accuracy. Using symmetric mean absolute percentage error (sMAPE) as validation (i.e. see appendix 8.2 for justification), we executed 10000 simulations with 95% confidence intervals and compared results of the two-state OnlineHMM against two models: the first is a simple regression model similar to [13], which fits a nonlinear curve of expected power consumption; the second is a moving average of recent data consumption that averages recent power consumption to forecast future consumption.

Table 6: sMAPE for three smartphone users comparing three forecast models for battery life.

	HTC One	GT-I9300	Nexus 7
OnlineHMM	**0.32 ± 2e-4**	0.28 ± 1e-4	**0.35 ± 4e-4**
Moving Avg.	0.54 ± 8e-9	**0.24 ± 4e-9**	0.44 ± 1e-8
Regression	0.40 ± 1e-8	0.33 ± 6e-9	0.44 ± 7e-9

Table 6 shows the OnlineHMM as the most consistent forecast model. The moving average model performs well on steady charging or discharging rates as observed for the GT-I9300 trace, but poorly on traces with intermittent behavior (i.e. HTC One and Nexus 7 traces). The regression model is more consistent than the moving average, but produces higher errors by over 20%, on average, than our OnlineHMM predictive model. These results highlight that HMM forecast models are useful for capturing intermittent data use and battery discharging for smartphones and, hence, can plan optimal charging times and durations. The OnlineHMM power consumption model we have investigated for three smartphone users proves that **HMMs capture burstiness and mode-switching in both smartphone data activity and battery behavior.** Further, forecasting battery life given live data transfers saves computational complexity of re-training models and is beneficial for resource planning. We conclude the paper in the next section.

7. CONCLUSION

In this work, we have pursued three strategies that analyze performance and energy in smartphone applications: first, we modeled specific smartphone applications using M/M/1-DPS queues and represented delays through response time distributions; secondly, we built a performance-energy trade-off structured as an objective cost function incorporating mean delay and energy consumption; thirdly, we created a power consumption model using an online HMM (OnlineHMM) that trained on traces of data transfers and predicted battery life of smartphones. As a result, we have formulated three hypotheses: first, that delay of smartphone applications is approximated well using the beta prime distribution; secondly, power consumption of smartphone increases as mean delay of its applications decreases with advantages to battery life brought by limiting recurrent cellular radio transfers; thirdly, HMMs capture the burstiness and hidden patterns of both data transfers and power consumption in an efficient, online manner to save resources of live systems. Important observations in data usage highlight the need to consider both performance (via response times) and energy (via power consumption) for a number of smartphone users, handsets and applications.

Extensions for this work include improvements to the three strategies. We extend strategy 1 by separating applications into classes based on their job sizes to see if there is any effect of service requirement on delay distribution tails. Further, we plan to approximate response time distributions for heavy-tailed service times (i.e. non-exponential) via an MMPP/PH/1-DPS queueing system, where PH represents a phase-type distribution. Strategy 2 can be extended by incorporating higher response time moments into the objective cost function. We extend strategy 3 by considering a wider range of mobile handsets to predict longer periods of battery life (i.e. a week) given traces of data activity and known charging times. Finally, the OnlineHMM can be adapted for training on multiple applications simultaneously by combining techniques from existing multi-input HMMs [36, 46] with new incremental approximations [5, 18].

8. REFERENCES

[1] C. Rohner, L. M. Feeney, P. Gunningberg: Evaluating Battery Models in Wireless Sensor Networks, In *Proc. LNCS WWIC*, St-Petersburg, Russia, 2013

[2] T. Chis, P. G. Harrison: Incremental HMM with an improved Baum-Welch Algorithm, In *Proc. ICCSW*, London, UK, 2012

[3] B. J. Prabhu, A. Chockalingam, V. Sharma: Performance Analysis of Battery Power Management Schemes in Wireless Mobile Devices, In *Proc. IEEE WCNC*, Florida, USA, 2002

[4] G. L. Jones: Open Battery, Department of Computing, Imperial College London, 2012

[5] T. Chis: Sliding Hidden Markov Model for Evaluating Discrete Data, In *Proc. EPEW*, Venice, Italy, 2013

[6] G. L. Jones, P. G. Harrison: Collecting battery data with Open Battery, In *Proc. ICCSW*, London, UK, 2012

[7] T. Chis: Hidden Markov Models: Applications to Flash Memory Data and Hospital Arrival Times, *MSci Thesis*, Department of Computing, Imperial College London, 2011

[8] L. E. Baum, T. Petrie: Stastical Inference for Probabilistic Functions of Finite Markov Chains, In *The Annals of Mathematical Statistics*, **37**, pp. 1554-1563, 1966

[9] L. E. Baum, T. Petrie, G. Soules, N. Weiss: A maximization technique occurring in the statistical analysis of probabilistic functions of Markov chains, In *The Annals of Mathematical Statistics*, **41**, pp. 164-171, 1970

[10] DevBytes: Efficient Data Transfers - Understanding the cellular radio, In *YouTube*, August, 2013

[11] T. Chis, P. G. Harrison: Moment-Generating Algorithm for Response Time in Processor Sharing Queueing Systems, In *Proc. EPEW*, Madrid, Spain, 2015

[12] P. G. Harrison, N. M. Patel: Performance Modelling of Communication Networks and Computer Architectures, *Addison-Wesley*, 1993

[13] A. Shye, B. Scholbrock, G. Memik, P. A. Dinda: Characterizing and Modeling User Activity on Smartphones, *Technical Report*, Northwest University, 2010

[14] J. Huang, Q. Xu, B. Tiwana, Z. M. Mao, M. Zhang, P. Bahl: Anatomizing Application Performance Differences on Smartphones, In *Proc. ACM Mobisys*, San Francisco, USA, 2010

[15] J. Domanska, A. Domanski, T. Czachorski: A HMM Network Traffic Model, In *Proc. ICNFI*, Istanbul, Turkey, 2012

[16] M. A. Kjaer, M Kihl, A. Robertsson: Response-Time Control of a Processor-Sharing System using Virtualised Server Environments, In *Proc. IFAC*, Seoul, South Korea, 2008

[17] S. W. M. Au-Yeung, N. J. Dingle, W. J. Knottenbelt: Efficient Approximation of Response time Densities and Quantiles in Stochastic Models, In *Proc. ACM WOSP*, Redwood Shores, USA, 2004

[18] T. Chis, P. G. Harrison: iSWoM: The incremental Storage Workload Model using Hidden Markov Models, In *Proc. ASMTA*, Ghent, Belgium, 2013

[19] L. Massoulie, J. W. Roberts: Bandwidth sharing and admission control for elastic traffic, In *Telecomm. Systems*, **15**, pp. 185-201, 2000

[20] B. Ciciani, A. Santoro, P. Romano: Approximate Analytical Models for Networked Servers Subject to MMPP Arrival Processes, In *Proc. IEEE NCA*, Rome, Italy, 2007

[21] S. F. Yashkov: Processor-Sharing Queues: Some Progress In Analysis, In *Queueing Systems*, **2**, pp. 1-17, 1987

[22] J. W. Roberts: A survey on statistical bandwidth sharing, In *Computer Networks*, **45**, pp. 319-332, 2004

[23] S. Lohr: For Impatient Web Users, an Eye Blink Is Just Too Long to Wait, In *New York Times*, March, 2012

[24] X. Chen, N. Ding, A. Jindal, Y. C. Hu, M. Gupta: Smartphone Energy Drain in the Wild: Analysis and Implications, In *Proc. SIGMETRICS*, Portland, USA, 2015

[25] C. Laird: 5 steps for optimizing the load time of web pages, In *Go Daddy*, May, 2015

[26] G. L. Jones, P. G. Harrison, U. Harder, T. Field: Fluid Queue Models of Battery Life, In *Proc. IEEE MASCOTS*, Singapore, 2011

[27] G. Casale, P. G. Harrison: AutoCAT: Automated Product-Form Solution of Stochastic Models, In *Matrix-Analytic Methods in Stochastic Models*, **27**, pp. 57-85, 2013

[28] R. N. Queija: Sojourn times in non-homogeneous QBD processes with processor sharing, In *Stochastic Models*, **17**, pp. 61-92, 2001

[29] P. G. Harrison, S. K. Harrison, N. M. Patel, S. Zertal: Storage Workload Modelling by Hidden Markov Models: Application to Flash Memory, In *Performance Evaluation*, **69**, pp. 17-40, 2012

[30] J. Ramberg, B. Schmeiser: An approximate method for generating asymmetrics random variables, In *Comm. ACM*, **17**, pp. 78-82, 1974

[31] J. Ramberg, E. Dudewicz, P. Tadikamalla, E. Mykytka: A probability distribution and its uses in fitting data, In *Technometrics*, **21**, pp. 201-214, 1979

[32] A. Lakhany, H. Mausser: Estimating the parameters of the General Lambda Distribution, In *Algo. Research Quarterly*, **3**, pp. 47-58, 2000

[33] Embedded Microprocessor Benchmark Consortium (EEMBC)

[34] D. Curry: Huawei surpasses local rivals Xiaomi and Lenovo in sales, In *Digital Trends*, December, 2015

[35] I. Macleod: Two-fifths of online sales to be via smartphones and tablets by 2018, In *The Drum*, June, 2014

[36] T. Chis, P. G. Harrison: Modeling Multi-user Behaviour in Social Networks, In *Proc. MASCOTS*, Paris, France, 2014

[37] J. P. Cohen: Cell Radio ShutOff, In *Google Play Store*, February, 2013

[38] R. Harlaka: How to stop your mobile app from being a serious battery drain, In *The Next Web*, August, 2013

[39] P. Sawers: Samsung drives $17M investment round in Seeo to help build better batteries for electric cars, In *VentureBeat*, December, 2014

[40] L. Guo, E. Tan, S. Chen, Z. Xiao, X. Zhang: The Stretched Exponential Distribution of Internet Media Access Patterns, In *Proc. PODC*, Toronto, Canada, 2008

[41] A. A. Kherani, A. Kumar: On Processor Sharing as a Model for TCP Controlled HTTP-like Transfers, In *Proc. IEEE ICC*, Paris, France, 2004

[42] N. Dukkipati, M. Kobayashi, R. Zhang-Shen, N. McKeown: Processor Sharing Flows in the Internet, In *Proc. IWQoS*, Passau, Germany 2005

[43] N. L. Johnson, S. Kotz, N. Balakrishnan: Continuous Univariate Distributions, Wiley, **2**, 1995

[44] K. Pearson: Mathematical Contributions to the Theory of Evolution XIX. Second Supplement to a Memoir on Skew Variation, In *Phil. Trans. Royal Society London* **216**, pp. 429-457, 1916

[45] BU-204: Lithium-based batteries, In *Battery University*, June, 2016

[46] T. Chis, P. G. Harrison: Adapting Hidden Markov Models for Online Learning, In *ENTCS*, **318**, pp. 109-127, 2015

[47] PSIM Tutorial: How To Use Lithium-Ion Battery Model, In *Powersim Tech*, March, 2016

[48] Y. Park, J. V. Chen: Acceptance and adoption of the innovative use of smartphone, In *Indust. Managmt. Data Systems*, **107**, pp. 1349-1365, 2007

8.1 Backward formula

We define the backward formula approximation inspired originially from work in [2]. Simplifying equation (11) for the $N = 2$ case, it follows that:

$$\begin{pmatrix} \beta_t(1) \\ \beta_t(2) \end{pmatrix} = \begin{pmatrix} a_{11}b_1 & a_{12}b_2 \\ a_{21}b_1 & a_{22}b_2 \end{pmatrix} \begin{pmatrix} \beta_{t+1}(1) \\ \beta_{t+1}(2) \end{pmatrix} \tag{15}$$

Pre-multiplying by the 2×2 inverse transition matrix gives us:

$$\begin{pmatrix} a_{11}b_1 & a_{12}b_2 \\ a_{21}b_1 & a_{22}b_2 \end{pmatrix}^{-1} \begin{pmatrix} \beta_t(1) \\ \beta_t(2) \end{pmatrix} = I_2 \begin{pmatrix} \beta_{t+1}(1) \\ \beta_{t+1}(2) \end{pmatrix} \tag{16}$$

For the $N = 2$ case, we display the inverse matrix explicitly in the equation, as follows:

$$\begin{pmatrix} \beta_{t+1}(1) \\ \beta_{t+1}(2) \end{pmatrix} = \begin{pmatrix} a_{22}b_2 & -a_{12}b_2 \\ -a_{21}b_1 & a_{11}b_1 \end{pmatrix} \begin{pmatrix} \beta_t(1) \\ \beta_t(2) \end{pmatrix}$$
$$\times \frac{1}{b_1 b_2 (a_{11}a_{22} - a_{21}a_{12})} \tag{17}$$

where $b_1 \neq 0$, $b_2 \neq 0$ and $a_{11}a_{22} \neq a_{21}a_{12}$.

In cases when $b_i(O_{t+1}) = 0$ for a state i, the 2×2 matrix is singular and has no inverse. Note that the third case (i.e. $a_{11}a_{22} \neq a_{21}a_{12}$) holds due to model re-parametrization, stochastic matrix properties and initialization of state transition probabilities. Adopting a simple β approximation for the $N = 2$ case, it follows that:

$$\begin{cases} \begin{pmatrix} \beta_{t+1}(1) \\ \beta_{t+1}(2) \end{pmatrix} = \begin{pmatrix} 1.0 \\ \frac{\beta_t(2)}{a_{22}b_2} \end{pmatrix}, & \text{if } b_1 = 0 \\[4mm] \begin{pmatrix} \beta_{t+1}(1) \\ \beta_{t+1}(2) \end{pmatrix} = \begin{pmatrix} \frac{\beta_t(1)}{a_{11}b_1} \\ 1.0 \end{pmatrix}, & \text{if } b_2 = 0 \end{cases} \tag{18}$$

8.2 Justification for sMAPE

A form of validating forecast models is to use the error between the model-generated time-series and the original data. A widely used metric is the mean absolute percentage error (MAPE), which measures accuracy of forecast values against actual values. The MAPE formula is expressed as a percentage for a time-series of n values:

$$\text{MAPE} = \frac{1}{n} \sum_{t=1}^{n} \left| \frac{a_t - f_t}{a_t} \right| \tag{19}$$

where a_t is the actual value and f_t is the forecast value. A variation of MAPE is the symmetric MAPE (sMAPE), which is defined as:

$$\text{sMAPE} = \frac{2}{n} \sum_{t=1}^{n} \frac{|f_t - a_t|}{|a_t| + |f_t|} \tag{20}$$

An averaged MAPE that is based on many time-series is sometimes distorted if particular time-series produce inflated values (i.e. significantly larger than one), which jeopardizes reliable comparisons. To solve such an issue, one typically uses the sMAPE formula.

A Novel Service-oriented Architecture for Information-Centric Vehicular Networks

Felipe M. Modesto
PARADISE Research Laboratory,
University of Ottawa,
Ottawa – ON – Canada,
fmode039@uottawa.ca

Azzedine Boukerche
PARADISE Research Laboratory,
University of Ottawa,
Ottawa – ON – Canada,
boukerch@site.uottawa.ca

ABSTRACT

With Vehicular mobile communication becoming an everyday requirement and an ever increasing number of services available, it is clear that vehicular networks require more efficient management. In this paper, we discuss service orientation as an architectural model for Information Centric Networking (ICN) VANETs. We discuss the limitations faced by vehicles and propose structuring communication towards as a coordinated service-centric network. Intermittent connectivity and end-to-end network delay are amongst the issues tackled by this work as we envision our network model. Additionally, we perform a set of simulations to exemplify the benefits of service coordination.

1. INTRODUCTION

Technical advances in mobile communication and the near ubiquitous presence of wireless devices have lead to significant shifts in vehicular technology. Vehicles have become service hubs where passengers experience multimedia content and drivers are assisted by a multitude of sensors and traffic information. In fact, vehicles are becoming mobile agents with increasingly vast processing power. Unlike most wireless network enabled devices, however, cars are not limited by their power supply. Hence, the major challenges faced by vehicular networks concern routing and network resource management. The limited nature of networking resources coupled with growing demand for services and further motivates the drive for more efficient communication. Furthermore, the incorporation of services provided by cloud and Internet of Things *(IoT)* will only increase the bandwidth requirements, as suggested by the recent proposal of an Internet of Vehicles *(IoV)* [2]. VANET implementations, however, are still in early stages and existing solutions consider IP-based network architectures in their majority. However, the predilection for physical addressing imposes restrictions to highly mobile agents such as vehicles [1]. Because of the high level of mobility, in order to increase performance and supply the ever increasing demand for content, VANETs require more efficient communication architectures than those provided by IP.

Information-Centric Networking (ICN) offers an alternative that tackles the many shortfalls of traditional networking models. The network structure of ICN decouples the network structure from physical addresses in favor of indexing based on information classification. Ranging from Road Safety to Information Sharing and Infotainment, it is clear that the volume of services that will become readily available will require an efficient network structure to be implemented. Implementing a system that can efficiently enable such a varied number of services is challenged by heterogeneous service requirements. Towards this goal, with this work we aim to further research in ICN VANET by analyzing the major requirements and proposing a service based architecture. The contributions of this work are summarized as follows: (1) we bring to light open issues in ICN VANETs, (2) present a general architecture to tackle existing shortcomings, (3) conduct experimentations to further denote the issues discussed.

The remainder of this works is structured as follows: Section 2 describes the system architecture proposed by this work. Section 3 discusses a set of simulations that accompany the proposed model. Finally, Section 4 discusses the work and presents the concluding remarks.

2. SYSTEM MODEL

Towards the goal of improving communication in VANETs, we consider a network designed around the principle of knowledge exchange, which we believe allows for significant improvement over existing technologies in terms of access to content as well as routing efficiency. The proposed model is designed to take advantage of the peculiarities of VANETs as well as working towards its two main uses: Road Information Sharing and Infotainment. Unlike more traditional network structures, members of the VANET network have interests that can be categorized into explicit groups. Naturally, different content groups (generally referred in this work as content categories) are defined by some of their characteristics, including a general class, popularity or network relevance and estimated bandwidth consumption. By taking advantage of classification based prefixing, the proposed model empowers its users with information, allowing them to make better networking decisions that benefit overall network performance as well as individual interests. In the

MSWiM '16, November 13–17, 2016, Malta, Malta

© 2016 ACM. ISBN 978-1-4503-4502-6/16/11...$15.00

DOI: http://dx.doi.org/10.1145/2988287.2989178

proposed model, content prefixing is structured so that content classification is rooted on content classes. In Synthesis, associated with each content class are its general characteristics, such as network priority, network popularity, average data packet size and data lifespan. These basic attributes used by routing policies and are managed by the two novel subcomponents proposed, described in Section 2.2.

It has been demonstrated that content delivery using named data can cope with a high level of mobility and maintain high request reply rates while host-to-host IP cannot maintain comparable service quality [10]. With this in mind, the work in this paper furthers the ICN research effort by proposing a service based system architecture. Following the principles proposed by the Named Data Network (NDN) model, applications are responsible for naming their data and forwarding requests to the network given they adhere to the basic naming policy scheme [3]. Prefix-based naming, in alignment with other CCN solutions, is the scheme considered as it allows for service grouping, service substitution, and fine granularity control. No further considerations are made to naming as we adhere to the consensus that applications are ultimately responsible for the namespaces of their services. This decision should empower services allowing them the flexibility to structure their content namespace to improve how service provisioning or by including additional meta-data alongside content objects [7].

2.1 Functionalities & Roles

To implement the ICN transport layer and enable the management and information sharing, the proposed model features three unique roles. Each role is performed by a separate component, namely: (*i*) Service Manager: responsible for maintaining both local and remote content and service provider lists as well as managing intermediate content caching. (*ii*) Service Orchestrator: responsible for brokering services, managing interactions with network manager and Service Manager and managing content requests. The relationship and roles of the proposed components are displayed in Figure 1. Services fulfill user demands for specific resources or needs, be them physical (*e.g.: processing, networking*) or logical (*e.g.:information*). Consider an example where a user is interested in traffic information. In this scenario, all users have partial knowledge of the system and their individual knowledge complements one another. While local information may be partial and at times conflicting, if structured properly, network load can be reduced by efficient data dissemination strategies. Requests such as the one in the example allow for geo-assisted request forwarding resulting in reduced number of messages targeting the vehicles in the requested region [6] However, the dynamic nature of VANETs and the different requirements of potential applications results in an increase in service management complexity and relevance. To cope with the existing requirements, we consider the inclusion of the aforementioned service sublayer which contains the Service Manager and Service Orchestrator and is described in the following subsection.

2.2 Service Sublayer

With data becoming independent from location and mean of transportation, content exchange can migrate to a service-like structure, in which many functionalities can

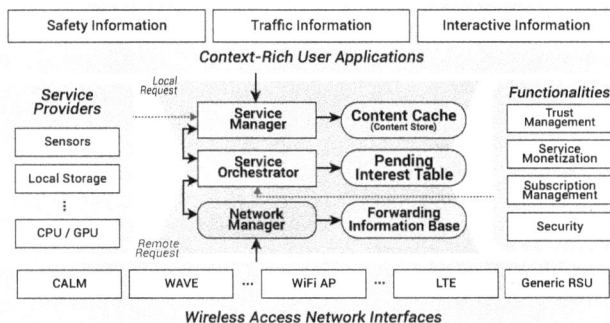

Figure 1: System Components & Interactions

be integrated. This change allows for in-network caching, content priority management and content exchange to be implemented as services. To manage local content and coordination with remote nodes, this work considers the inclusion of a service management sublayer, also known as the Service Sublayer. The Service Sublayer was designed to be responsible for service management and provisioning. As presented in the diagram available in Figure 1, the Service Sublayer is the novel component of our model and its main functions are to: Maintain local and intermediate content caches, Manage and aggregate sensor data, Broker service exchange with remote nodes whenever required, Orchestrate network coordination with remote nodes.

Two components are responsible for performing these roles, namely the Service Manager and Service Orchestrator. The main responsibility of the Service Manager is to interact with clients, either local or remote, when providing content as well as with service providers when obtaining said content. The Service Sublayer also participates in content forwarding processes regardless of local content availability as it is responsible for intermediate caching. Adhering to NDN conventions, the service sublayer maintains the three basic data structures (CS, PIT, FIB) as well as a data forwarding policy, which are managed by the Service Manager and Service Orchestrator. The main responsibility of the Service Manager is to maintain the content cache, be it by performing on-route caching or local caching. The Service Manager interacts with local service providers as part of its role as content cache manager, meaning that it mediates requests for services. Because named data allows for more efficient cache management, the Service Manager's task needs to be frequently performed.

Certain categories of content such as traffic information are not only bound by traditional cache control like freshness but also by other factors such as physical location as well as network-wide events. In the example given, a network-wide event such as a notification of an traffic incident would invalidate theoretically fresh content. Similarly, geographical location can also affect cached content. In this case, upon traveling far enough from a certain region, the reliability of the traffic data might be lowered or even considered invalid. These examples denote the importance of cache control, whose functionality is enhanced by sensor and network information. However, it is unfeasible to consider a single caching scheme capable of correctly managing a multitude of application specific content. The solution proposed by this work is for Cache Control to be implemented as a service. Basic caching is implemented by the Service Manager however, optimal caching requires explicit policies relating to local validity, explicit lifetime and local interest [5]. As caches have to operate at line-rate, coordination is significantly limited and we consider that nodes operate their cache independently from one another [11], ultimately leading to the implementation of simpler cache policies.

The Service Manager is also responsible for Local service provider coordination. As services range software to infrastructure, access to processing power, storage, and cached content are managed as resources available to a distributed system, meaning that the Service Manager operates similarly to a resource scheduler who controls and offers services to local users as well as remote entities. Access control is constantly coordinated with the network orchestrator, who exchanges access to local content for locally inaccessible resources. While the Service Manager takes on a more structural role operating similarly to a run-time infrastructure, the Service Orchestrator implements the core innovation proposed in this work. The main feature implemented by the Service Orchestrator is service brokerage, considered a practical solution for resource scarcity management. The Service Orchestrator is also tasked with communicating with a network manager, whose responsibilities can be summed as connection and interface management. We consider the inclusion of a separate component for this role, as ICN allows for interface independence allowing greater integration of multiple network interfaces which can be easily achieved as data flows can be multiplexed easily without application awareness [6].

3. EXPERIMENTAL EVALUATION

The main focus of this paper is the proposal of an ICN based network model for VANETs. To reinforce the benefits of the solution proposed a set of experimental evaluations were performed. Extensive simulation was carried out using the OMNeT++ Discrete Event Simulator coupled with the Vehicle in Network Simulation (Veins) framework and Simulation of Urban MObility (SUMO) road traffic simulator [9, 8, 4]. The purpose of this evaluation is to further illustrate the limitations in network resources and denote the benefits of managing application access to physical resources.

3.1 Simulation Setup

Simulations considered two types of data: (1) Network Traffic Information and (2) Multimedia. Network traffic information responses were set to $20kB$ each while Multimedia content responses were set to $5MB$. Upon receiving remote interest requests for Traffic information, vehicles always reply with content availability, as each vehicle is considered to have partial knowledge of local traffic. Multimedia content, is managed by local content caches. The Multimedia content cache in each vehicle is built based on a global library which contains one thousand (1000) separate individual multimedia objects. During network initialization vehicles select 10% of the items in the multimedia content library and include these items to their local cache prior. During simulation, all vehicles maintain

message request timers used to time interest broadcasts. The "popularity" value of Multimedia messages was set to $M = \{1, 2, 5, 10, 20, 40, 80\}$ while the popularity value for Network Traffic Information was set to $T = \{20\}$. Network MTU was set to 1460 $kilobytes$ and each message included a header of 32 $bytes$.

The simulation environment selected for simulation is a cross-section of Ottawa's Downtown area. This location was selected due to its grid-like nature, the presence of varied road segment types and high level of knowledge of the environment, used to ensure the simulation represented the location with the highest level of fidelity possible. To simulate realistic traffic conditions in a busy area, statistical information provided by real-world scenarios and traffic flow statistics was used as the basis for the simulation including statistical traffic flow from real world locations. Simulation configurations were produced to match daily road section averages, which range from 3.000 to 50.000 vehicles per road segment. Results were recorded for fixed periods of 600 seconds (10 minutes) after a preset warm-up time of 100 seconds.

Content considered for simulation was artificially generated based on two basic content classes: traffic information and multimedia content. For experimental evaluations we consider the following naming structure /category/service/contentidentifier. Simulation results are available for network scenarios for $\{50, 100, 150, 300, 450\}$ vehicles, however due to spacial limitations, only select results are displayed. The simulated scenarios are equivalent to vehicle densities between $2 - 20$ vehicles/km and represent low to medium traffic flows.

3.2 Evaluation

We evaluated data delivery in terms of the success rate as well as individual delivery rates for text and multimedia content. Summarized communication results are available in Figure 2 and display the cumulative results for each vehicle density scenario. The four curves in each graph represent proportionate distributions of the total of data transfers according to transfer results. Results in all five scenario configurations denote significant reduction in text data transfer success rate and growth of failures in multimedia content transfers as transfer priority shifts from smaller to larger content. Notably, the statistical prevalence of successful text transfers are replaced by failures in multimedia transfer, result of noise in network environment, transmission errors or lack of availability of content providers. In fact, the percentage of successful multimedia transmissions remains small but increases proportionate to the number of vehicles in the network. This occurs because the number of service providers for multimedia content increases and content is served closer to clients, reducing transmission failures. This trend is furthered detailed by evaluation the delivery rates. The results in these graphs make clear that unrestricted content fulfillment is not an adequate network resource management policy as it promotes network strangulation. Increases in multimedia content fulfillment significantly degrade network performance. This is because as interest in multimedia content grows, so does network load. Interestingly, text data is generally unaffected by increases in multimedia results with text delivery rates remaining stable, but fewer in numbers. Evaluation of simulation results denoted random loss of 1% to 2.5% chunks in multimedia transfers, which due to their limited size, affect text data marginally but add to the failure rate. In regards to multimedia data transfers, content delivery rates are comparatively low but increase with increases in network load. The result increases in provider availability and in-network caching, result of subsequent content requests. Interestingly, the simulations display degradation of up to 20% in delivery rate for text data as a result of increased number of vehicles in the network. This is likely the result of the increased vehicle volume in the network which increases both network noise and adds obstacles to the transmission paths. Considering that vehicle density can still be increased by up to 50% before road traffic collapse, significant degradation is expected for high-density scenarios. Ultimately, however, it is not necessary to simulate worst case scenarios to observe the need for network management in VANETs.

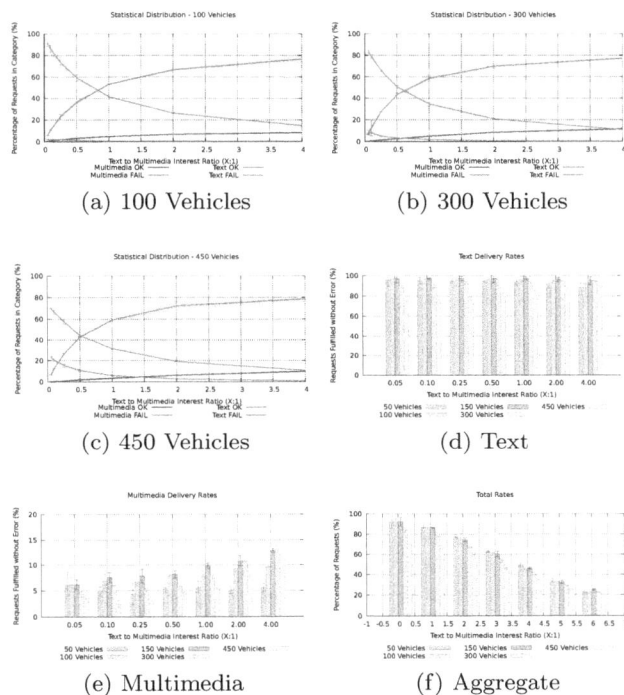

(a) 100 Vehicles   (b) 300 Vehicles

(c) 450 Vehicles   (d) Text

(e) Multimedia   (f) Aggregate

Figure 2: Simulation Results

4. CLOSING REMARKS

In this paper, we proposed a network model for ICN networks based service-centric content exchange. We argued the benefits of an information-based economy as a mean of controlling information dissemination and enabling service exchange. Based on our considerations we proposed a basic system model capable of implementing such functionalities by introducing two components of a novel service sublayer. Our model enables the delivery of content model while ensuring that service exchange promotes sharing and management of the limited network services. Our initial simulations demonstrate how easily network resources can become strangled in vehicular network and furthered evidence the need to manage content provisioning. We suggest content prioritization schemes and service based coordination which will be studied a future work.

5. ACKNOWLEDGMENTS

This work was supported by CAPES – Brazilian Federal Agency for Support and Evaluation of Graduate Education within the Ministry of Education of Brazil, NSERC, Canada Research Chairs program, NSERC DIVA Strategic Research Network and NSERC CREATE TRANSIT Network.

6. REFERENCES

[1] M. Amadeo, C. Campolo, and A. Molinaro. Content-centric networking: Is that a solution for upcoming vehicular networks? In *Proceedings of the Ninth ACM International Workshop on Vehicular Inter-networking, Systems, and Applications*, pages 99–102, June 2012.

[2] M. Gerla, E. Lee, G. Pau, and U. Lee. Internet of vehicles: From intelligent grid to autonomous cars and vehicular clouds. In *Internet of Things (WF-IoT), 2014 IEEE World Forum on*, pages 241–246, March 2014.

[3] V. Jacobson, D. K. Smetters, J. D. Thornton, M. F. Plass, N. H. Briggs, and R. L. Braynard. Networking named content. In *Proceedings of the 5th International Conference on Emerging Networking Experiments and Technologies*, pages 1–12, December 2009.

[4] D. Krajzewicz, J. Erdmann, M. Behrisch, and L. Bieker. Recent development and applications of SUMO - Simulation of Urban MObility. *International Journal On Advances in Systems and Measurements*, 5(3&4):3&4, December 2012.

[5] E. Lee, E.Lee, M. Gerla, and S. Oh. Vehicular cloud networking: Architecture and design principles. *IEEE Communications Magazine*, 52(2):148–155, February 2014.

[6] X. Liu, Z. Li, P. Yang, and Y. Dong. Information-centric mobile ad hoc networks and content routing: A survey (accepted manuscript). *Ad Hoc Networks*, April 2016.

[7] W. Quan, C. Xu, J. Guan, H. Zhang, and L. Grieco. Social cooperation for information-centric multimedia streaming in highway VANETs. In *World of Wireless, Mobile and Multimedia Networks (WoWMoM), 2014 IEEE 15th International Symposium on a*, pages 1–6, June 2014.

[8] C. Sommer, R. German, and F. Dressler. Bidirectionally Coupled Network and Road Traffic Simulation for Improved IVC Analysis. *IEEE Transactions on Mobile Computing*, 10(1):3–15, January 2011.

[9] A. Vargas. The OMNeT++ discrete event simulation system. In *Proceedings of the European simulation multiconference (ESM'2001)*, volume 9, page 65. sn, 2001.

[10] J. Wang, R. Wakikawa, and L. Zhang. Dmnd: Collecting data from mobiles using named data. In *Vehicular Networking Conference (VNC), 2010 IEEE*, pages 49–56, December 2010.

[11] G. Zhang, Y. Li, and T. Lin. Caching in information centric networking: A survey. *Computer Networks*, 57(16):3128–3141, August 2013. Information Centric Networking.

Formal Analysis and Verification of the IEEE 802.15.4 DSME Slot Allocation

Florian Kauer, Maximilian Köstler, Tobias Lübkert, Volker Turau
Institute of Telematics, Hamburg University of Technology
Am Schwarzenberg-Campus 3, 21073 Hamburg, Germany
{florian.kauer},{maximilian.koestler},{tobias.luebkert},{turau}@tuhh.de

ABSTRACT

Providing dependability is still a major issue for wireless mesh networks, which restrains their application in industrial contexts. The widespread CSMA/CA medium access can provide high throughput and low latency, but can not prevent packet loss due to collisions, especially in very large and dense networks. Time slotted medium access techniques together with a distributed slot management, as proposed by the Distributed Synchronous Multi-channel Extension (DSME) of the IEEE 802.15.4 standard, are promising to provide low packet loss, high scalability and bounded end-to-end delays. However, our implementation, openDSME, exposed some weaknesses. While the allocated slots allow for reliable data transmission, the slot management itself is conducted via CSMA/CA and is thus vulnerable to packet loss, eventually leading to an inconsistent slot allocation.

This paper uses the UPPAAL framework for formal analysis and verification of the slot management process. The analysis identifies weaknesses of the slot allocation process under communication and node failures. However, it is shown that inconsistencies are eventually resolved and improvements to the procedure are proposed that reduce the negative impact of failed slot allocation procedures significantly.

1. INTRODUCTION

The usage of wireless technology in industrial contexts promises high cost savings for installation and provides high flexibility for the deployment. In certain scenarios, the installation costs can be nearly cut by half [9]. Especially devices based on the IEEE 802.15.4 standard [3] have gained much attention in industrial automation [23] due to their low energy consumption and the availability of cost-effective hardware. This standard is one of the main pillars of the Internet of Things. As a core feature, the standard provides the possibility to build multi-hop networks for extended coverage and a high scalability. Commonly, Carrier Sense Multiple Access with Collision Avoidance (CSMA/CA) is used to access the medium. However, it is prone to collisions, es-

pecially in hidden node situations leading to low reliability in large and dense networks [21]. Thus, for industrial applications where dependability is a crucial requirement, medium access based on time slots (TDMA) and multiple channels as for example described in the WirelessHART standard [1] are advised due to a higher resilience against collisions and packet loss [25].

WirelessHART uses IEEE 802.15.4 for the lower layers, but the original IEEE 802.15.4 standard lacked the possibility to use TDMA over multiple hops. This changed with the amendment IEEE 802.15.4e [2] that was merged with the original standard in the 2015 version. It adds Time-Slotted Channel Hopping (TSCH) to the standard. TSCH has gained a lot of research attention [4][12] and is currently being merged into the 6LoWPAN stack [27]. The amendment also introduces an alternative approach for time-slotted multi-hop networks, the so-called Distributed Synchronous Multi-Channel Extension (DSME). It conforms to the already existing superframe structure and can be configured for a wide range of scenarios. This paper discusses intentional and unintentional consequences of the corresponding parameter selection. Especially the number of superframes per multi-superframe has a severe impact on the performance in terms of transmission intervals, possible network density, energy consumption and control overhead.

In [10] the similarities and differences between TSCH and DSME are presented. While TSCH relies on upper layer decisions for the management of slots, DSME provides protocols and services that allow for distributed slot management. By using a three-way handshake, pairs of nodes can allocate slots amongst each other and in doing so they inform their neighbors about occupied slots. This procedure promises highly scalable networks [19]. However, since the schedule is not managed by a central entity, inconsistencies of the slot schedule are not impossible per se. In particular, the slot allocation itself is conducted via CSMA/CA, so it possibly prone to collisions and race-conditions. Since inconsistencies in the slot schedule might thwart the original requirement of reliable communication, it is crucial to investigate the existence of inconsistencies and to reduce their influence on the performance of the overall network.

Even events that occur with a very low probability, for example every few hours, might eventually have severe impacts on the overall performance. Therefore, it is hard to find flaws in the protocol purely by testbeds and simulations, so we decided to use formal verification to allow for definitive statements for the worst case impact of lost packets during the slot allocation phase.

MSWiM '16, November 13 - 17, 2016, Malta

DOI: http://dx.doi.org/10.1145/2988287.2989148

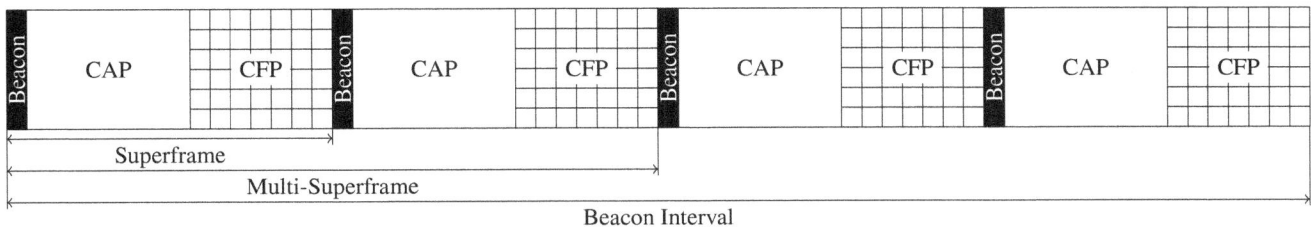

Figure 1: DSME Superframe structure for $SO = 3$, $MO = 4$ and $BO = 5$.

The contribution of this paper is a formal analysis of the IEEE 802.15.4 DSME slot allocation procedure between two nodes under consideration of communication and node failures. The analysis reveals the occurrence of inconsistencies in the slot schedule for both kinds of failures, eventually leading to broken links over a long time. The authors propose an extension of the procedure without the need of sending additional messages that reduces these durations significantly to improve the overall dependability of the network.

2. RELATED WORK

Due to asynchronicity as well as the occurrence of partial failures, distributed systems have a high potential for failures [20]. According to this article, formal verification of distributed systems is tedious and composing provably correct systems to larger systems does not necessarily result in a correct overall system. Still, multiple examples are presented where formal verification greatly helped to build stable systems, including [22] a description of how Amazon Web Services were improved by formal methods.

In order to support formal verification, multiple tools and frameworks have been developed, including generic frameworks such as TLA+ [17] and UPPAAL [18], as well as frameworks that are tailored to the needs of distributed systems such as DS2 [5] and Verdi [28].

Wireless connections are in particular challenging for distributed networks due to the unreliability and unpredictability of the wireless channel. Nonetheless, formal verification can prove conformance to industrial standards even for wireless applications [13]. In wireless mesh networks, formal verification was in particular used for routing protocol analysis such as finding loops in AODV [29] and suggesting boundary conditions for fixing these problems [8].

A more abstract verification of ad hoc networks was conducted in [11] leading to fundamental statements about the decidability of the coverability problem under node and communication failures. In [6] a formal model of the IEEE 802.11 Point Coordination Function and the Distributed Coordination Function is presented to support applications with real-time requirements. It also includes an elaborate introduction about how to model wireless networks in UPPAAL. Proving adherence to time limits in real-time systems is the motivation for many other formal models, too, such as in [26] where wired bus standards such as TTA are surveyed under the occurrence of faults.

In [14], a formal analysis of the IEEE 802.15.4 CSMA/CA procedure is conducted. Furthermore, the performance of a simple abstract slot allocation method is analyzed using formal methods, while a more sophisticated channel allocation procedure was analyzed in [7].

3. DISTRIBUTED SYNCHRONOUS MULTI-CHANNEL EXTENSION

In the following, a brief overview of DSME as specified in the IEEE 802.15.4-2015 standard is given. DSME builds upon a superframe structure as shown in Fig. 1. Every superframe starts with a beacon slot that allows dedicated coordinators in the network to send beacons for time synchronization. The precise procedure for this is not relevant for the slot allocation, so details are omitted. In the following, it is assumed that the superframes of all participating nodes are already aligned in time. The beacon slot is followed by the Contention Access Period (CAP) during which CSMA/CA is used for communication on a common channel. Within this time, the slot allocation procedure takes place.

Afterwards, the Contention Free Period (CFP) allows communication via previously allocated Guaranteed Time Slots (GTS). The slots can either be allocated on multiple channels (channel adaption mode) or the channel is regularly cycled during the CFP (channel hopping mode). Several superframes form a multi-superframe. Within one multi-superframe, every allocated GTS occurs exactly once. The structure can be optimized to the application with the parameters as given in Table 1.

Parameter	Range	Default
$macSuperframeOrder$ (SO)	$0-15$	15
$macMultisuperframeOrder$ (MO)	$0-22$	15
$aBaseSlotDuration$	60 symbols	
$aNumSuperframeSlots$	16	
$macResponseWaitTime$ (W_r)	$2-64$	32
$macDsmeGTSExpirationTime$ (M_x)	$0-255$	7

Table 1: Relevant MAC parameters.

With these parameters and the duration of a symbol in the 2.4 GHz band of 16 µs, the duration of a slot is given by

$$T_s = 16\,\mu s \cdot aBaseSlotDuration \cdot 2^{SO}.$$

In the following, SO is set to 3, resulting in $T_s = 7.68$ ms to fit one acknowledged transmission with the maximum of 127 octets within one slot. For other physical layers, the slot duration can be calculated correspondingly. The number of superframes in a multi-superframe is calculated as 2^{MO-SO} and therefore with 16 available channels and 8 CAP slots,

$$N_s = 16 \cdot (aNumSuperframeSlots - 8 - 1) \cdot 2^{MO-SO} \quad (1)$$

allocatable slots can be used in total for channel adaption mode, but of course, a device can only use one channel at a

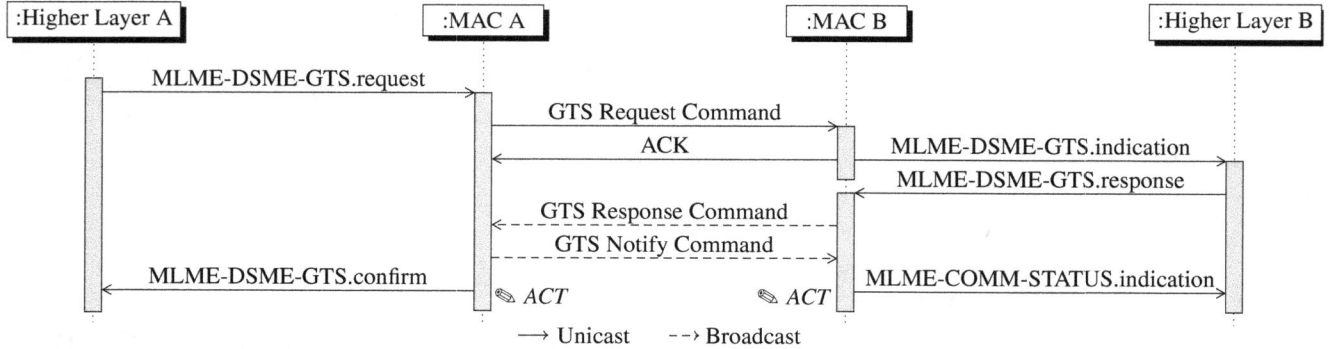

Figure 2: Sequence diagram of a successful slot allocation.

time. The duration of a multi-superframe is given by

$$T_m = T_s \cdot aNumSuperframeSlots \cdot 2^{MO-SO}.$$

Since a GTS is repeated with that interval, it is convenient to choose SO and MO so that T_m is in the order of the average transmission interval. For example, with $SO = 3$ and the default as given by the standard of $MO = 15$, a node can transmit a packet over one allocated GTS every $T_m \approx 8$ minutes.

Choosing a smaller MO leads to shorter multi-superframes and therefore, the slot occurs more often. Not sending data during a slot has two disadvantages. First, the receiving device has to turn on the transceiver unnecessarily, leading to a higher energy consumption. Secondly, if this happens too often, the receiver assumes a broken connection and deallocates the slot (cf. Sect. 8).

Furthermore, choosing a smaller MO results in fewer allocatable slots, cf. (1), so it has a negative impact on the maximum supported node density. More slots are also required to allow for the allocation of multiple slots for links with higher traffic, to support heterogeneous transmission intervals. On the other hand, MO should not be chosen too high for networks with a lot of traffic, since it increases the slot management overhead if a lot of slots have to be allocated for a single link.

4. DSME SLOT ALLOCATION

Fig. 2 shows the sequence diagram for a successful slot allocation. If a higher layer, such as the routing layer or an intermediate helper layer, decides to allocate a slot with a neighbor, it sends a request via the MAC Sublayer Management Entity (MLME) interface. A slot is always used in one direction only, but can be requested as a reception or transmission slot. The request includes a Slot Allocation Bitmap (SAB) that indicates all occupied slots in the one-hop neighborhood as well as a preferred slot. Thereupon, the MAC layer sends a GTS Request Command including the SAB as unicast to the respective destination. This takes place during the CAP and since the message is sent as unicast, it will be acknowledged.

The MAC layer of the receiver will generate an indication primitive to be sent to the higher layer. With the information from the SAB, the higher layer chooses a slot that matches both the received and the own SAB. If a matching slot is found, a response is generated that is sent via the MAC layer to the originator. This message is sent as broadcast to allow other devices in the neighborhood to update

their own SAB. The originator of the request will inform the upper layer about the response. Furthermore, it issues a notify command with the main purpose of notifying the nodes that did not receive the response because they are not in the transmission range of the responder. Moreover, the responder is now aware that the response was received by the originator. In case of a lost response or notify, the nodes will return to the idle state after a timeout of

$$T_w = macResponseWaitTime \cdot aNumSuperframeSlots \cdot T_s.$$

If all messages arrive, the GTS is considered allocated on both sides and will be written to the Allocation Counter Table (ACT), a local data structure on every node that describes which slots are allocated with other nodes. In contrast to the SAB, the ACT does not include information about allocated slots in the neighborhood, but includes further information about the own allocated slots, such as the address of the remote device. The allocated slot will be used for transmissions in the subsequent multi-superframes. One GTS is dedicated to transmission for one device and to reception for the other. So the receiver will switch to reception mode shortly before the slot begins, the transmitter will transmit its frame within the slot and wait for an acknowledgment by the receiver. Afterwards, both devices can disable the transceiver for power saving.

5. UPPAAL MODEL

The system is modeled as a network of timed automata. This is done by means of the UPPAAL tool environment [18] that allows for convenient modeling and formal verification of such a system. An overview of the involved automata is given in Fig. 4. The model includes a three layer network stack for the nodes as well as an omniscient observer and a global clock.

- The **GTS Manager** implements the core functionality of the DSME protocol, including the generation of MLME messages for the higher layers as well as MAC frames for transmission via radio.

- The **GTS Allocation Helper** implements the functionality that is dedicated to the higher layers according to the standard. That mainly covers the decision if a slot can be allocated and choosing a slot, as well as generating requests for new slots.

- A **CAP Transmission** is dedicated for the transmission of a message from one GTS Manager to another.

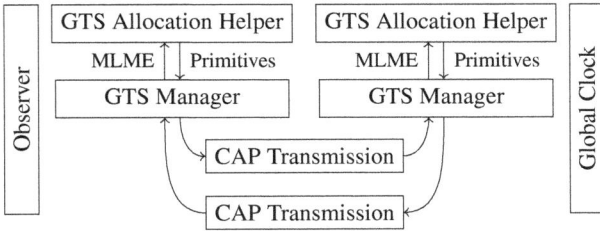

Figure 4: Overview of the system model.

It delays the message to be sent and decides the outcome of the transmission.

- The **Observer** regularly checks for inconsistencies, and measures the duration until an inconsistency is recognized by the nodes where applicable.

- The **Global Clock** generates events for every superframe. In a real implementation, the time synchronization is done via beacons, but since this is out of the scope of this model, a global clock simplifies the model and thus allows for faster verification.

UPPAAL allows for a graphical specification of the automata as shown in the appendix. Apart from the syntax, the implementations of the GTS Manager and the GTS Allocation Helper are very similar to an implementation for hardware or simulation where an equivalent state machine could be specified. However, the channel model is quite different since its purpose diverges from the one in a simulation where it is advised to closely model the probabilities for the events such as a lost packet. Instead of determining the probability that a certain event occurs, a formal analysis assumes that a certain event occurred and thereupon decides about the soundness of certain statements, for example whether the system is still in a valid state *if* a packet was lost. This is evaluated for all possible sequences of events. On the downside, this requires traversing a very large state space. On the upside, it is not required to model the probabilities, but a specification of all possible events as follows is sufficient.

Once a device has a message to transmit via the CAP phase, it senses the channel. If it was not able to sense a free channel several times in a row, the packet is not sent and an ACCESS_FAILURE is signaled. Otherwise, the packet is sent, but might not be received by the receiver due to collisions or other sources of disturbances. If it was sent as

broadcast, the transmitter does not know if the packet was received and will signal SUCCESS. If it was sent as unicast, an acknowledgment is expected. In case of such a failed transmission, NO_ACK is signaled after a timeout. This is also signaled if the transmission was properly received, but the acknowledgment is lost. Otherwise, SUCCESS is signaled if the acknowledgment is received.

The Allocation Counter Table (ACT) for storing the information about the allocated slots is denoted as

$$ACT : N \times S \to N \cup \{\circ\},$$

with N being the set of nodes, $S = \{s \in \mathbb{N}_0 \mid 0 \leq s < N_s\}$ being the set of possible slots and $\circ$ denoting that a slot is not allocated. The consistency predicate is defined as

$$\phi : \ \forall n, m \in N \land \forall s \in S :$$
$$ACT(n, s) = m \Rightarrow ACT(m, s) = n.$$

The requirement for a permanently consistent system, that is that ϕ holds for all points in time, is denoted as

$$A \square \, \phi.$$

The entry in the ACT is not absolutely synchronized, so this does not hold, but since the state of the slot allocation is only relevant during the CFP, this expression can be relaxed to

$$A \square \, (\mathrm{CFP} \Rightarrow \phi) \,, \tag{2}$$

where CFP equals true if and only if the global clock is currently in the CFP state.

6. THE LOST NOTIFY

When checking the model against (2), UPPAAL classifies it as not satisfied and gives a sequence as shown in Fig. 3 as a counterexample. If the notify is not received by B, it will never mark the slot as allocated in its ACT. Now A assumes the slot is allocated, while B assumes the slot is not allocated, leading to an inconsistent state. It is interesting to note that in the original IEEE 802.15.4e standard the slot is written to the ACT already after sending the response, but this would not change the result because in that case the inconsistent state would occur after a lost response instead of a lost notify. The reason for the modification is not mentioned in the standard, however, both versions can lead to an inconsistent state.

While this is an undesirable result, the underlying problem of attaining consensus is of general nature. Attaining common knowledge in a distributed system, such as agreeing

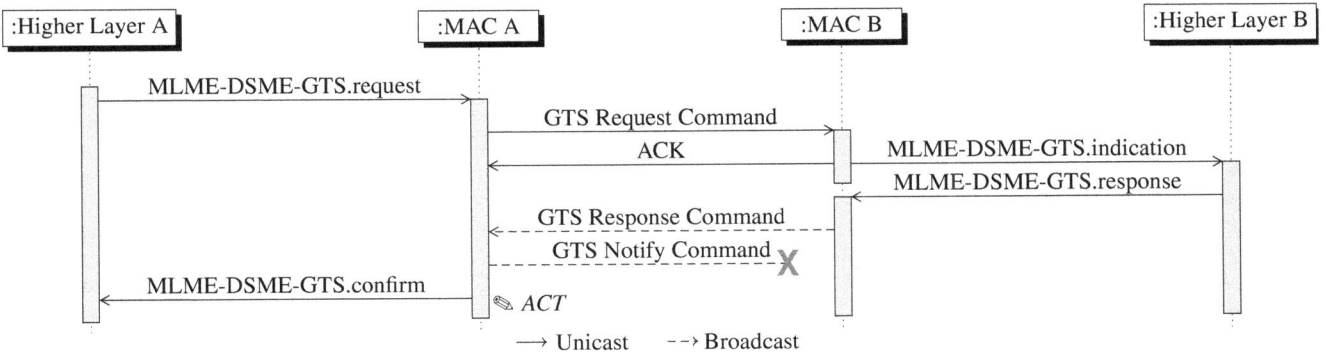

Figure 3: Sequence diagram of a failed slot allocation.

on a common GTS, is a well-studied concept and is actually proven to be impossible in the strict sense [16]. This proof also refers to the well known coordinated attack problem where two divisions of an army try to agree on a common time to attack but can only communicate via messengers that might get caught. Even with multiple messengers sent back and forth, the sender of the last messenger can not be sure that the messenger arrived and thus can not be sure that the other division will attack. Correspondingly in the DSME protocol, the sender of the notify can not know if the counterpart will eventually set the slot to allocated.

7. NODE FAILURES

A similar, but more obvious problem occurs when nodes reset during the course of the slot allocation or at a later point in time. This might be due to energy shortages in energy-harvesting applications or bugs in hard- or software. This is modeled by adding an additional transition from every state to the initial state that is fired optionally for all automata of one device at the same time. These transitions are omitted in the figures in the appendix for clarity. As soon as a node resets, the ACT is cleared, while the other node might have the slot still allocated or while it even waits for a pending message. For the latter case UPPAAL verifies that due to the timeout T_w, the other node returns to the idle state, too, and does not block. However, if the node resets after the other node has written the slot to the ACT, ϕ is no longer satisfied.

8. DSME GTS EXPIRATION

While it is not possible to establish common knowledge in a strict sense as defined by Halpern and Moses [16], they and others (e.g. [15][24]) made suggestions to weaken the requirements. For example, if a single division attacks and notices that the other division is not there as well, it might be able to escape, possibly losing some troops. Generalized, if a party will eventually recognize an inconsistency in the common knowledge and act accordingly, the system will eventually return to a consistent state. For the DSME application, this is formalized as

$$A\square\left(\neg\left(\mathrm{CFP}\Rightarrow\phi\right)\Rightarrow A\diamond\left(\mathrm{CFP}\Rightarrow\phi\right)\right)$$

with $A\diamond$ denoting that the statement will eventually hold.

In fact, the standard includes a mechanism to guarantee this property called DSME GTS expiration. If the transmitter has transmitted $macDsmeGTSExpirationTime$ (M_x) frames and has not received any acknowledgment, it will deallocate the slot with a procedure that is very similar to the slot allocation. The receiver, on the other hand, will start a deallocation if no frame was received for $macDsme$-$GTSExpirationTime$ opportunities. UPPAAL actually verifies that this mechanism eventually leads to a consistent state again, both for the case of a lost notify or of a node failure at an arbitrary point in time.

So what is the price for this, how many troops are lost? Until the slot is recognized as invalid, all communication over this slot will fail. In order to quantify this effect, the observer measures the time $\neg\phi$ holds. However, UPPAAL can only give the results *satisfied* or *not satisfied*. Therefore, it is necessary to verify the property that this clock never gets larger than a fixed value T_i. By testing multiple values, for example by using a binary search, it is possible to

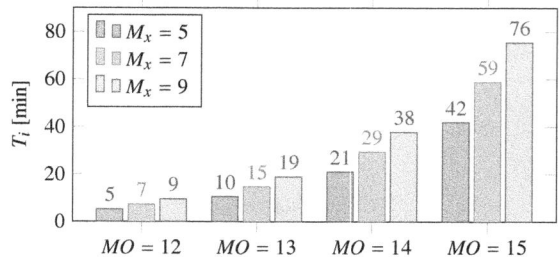

Figure 5: Duration for returning from an inconsistent to a consistent state.

determine the maximum duration $\neg\phi$ holds. The result is dependent on the parameters as shown in Fig. 5. Thereby, the parameters $M_x = 7$ and $MO = 15$ are the ones given as default by the standard, resulting in an inconsistency duration of over one hour.

9. IMPROVEMENT

While this result shows that in fact the system returns to a consistent state in finite time, the times are very long. Especially in configurations with a large MO, the timeouts are way too long for many applications. Reducing the parameters to decrease the duration is often not possible as elaborated in Sect. 3. A possible solution would be to generate additional dummy traffic in applications with low traffic demand to avoid the slot expiration for actually valid slot allocations, but of course, this leads to unnecessary channel utilization and boosts the energy consumption. Furthermore, reducing M_x would increase the probability of premature deallocation in case of short-term channel disturbance.

However, by investigating the possible outcomes of a slot allocation, we found that at least one of the participants can recognize a potential invalid state much earlier and can anticipatorily send a deallocation. In order to model this mechanism and also as a suggestion for an actual implementation, the ACT is extended with an invalid flag

$$ACT_n : N \times S \rightarrow (N \times \{\mathrm{OK}, \mathrm{INVALID}\}) \cup \{\circ\}.$$

This flag indicates that the node shall deallocate the slot again as soon as possible. The predicate is changed to

$$\psi : \forall n, m \in N \wedge \forall s \in S :$$
$$(ACT_n(n, s) = (m, OK) \Rightarrow ACT_n(m, s) = (n, OK))$$
$$\vee ACT_n(m, s) = (n, \mathrm{INVALID}).$$

Note that ψ is weaker than ϕ, because it does not imply that *both* nodes have recognized the invalid state. In the unfavorable case, the anticipatory deallocation will not reach the other node. However, this will be recognized since no acknowledgment is received and the deallocation can be repeated immediately. Furthermore, this improvement only helps in case of communication failures, but not node failures if the device sending the deallocation resets before the deallocation request was sent. Even in those cases, the expiration procedure will guarantee a consistent state as determined in Sect. 8. In any case, it is reasonable that the receiver also turns on the transceiver during invalid and unconfirmed slots, but the transmitter only transmits in slots with OK flag. Thus, packets sent during the transition period have a higher chance to get delivered even though an inconsistency exists.

In order to identify the possible events that can indicate an inconsistent state provoked by the allocation procedure, Fig. 6 shows the possible outcomes from the view of the initiator and Fig. 7 from the responding device. The possible outcomes are marked as explained in the following.

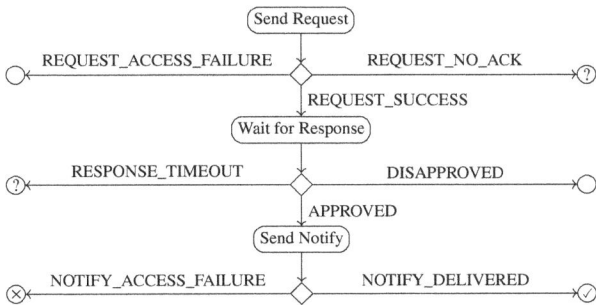

Figure 6: Possible results for the requesting device.

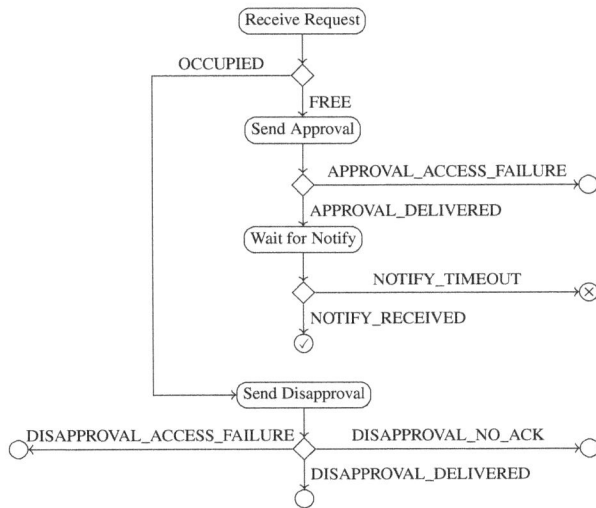

Figure 7: Possible results for the responding device.

⊘ A slot was successfully associated, at least from the perspective of the respective device.

◯ No positive response was or will be sent to the requesting device. Thus, no allocation or deallocation is necessary.

⑦ The request was sent, but no answer was received. Even if a response was sent, there is no indication for the requesting device which slot was chosen, so there is no possibility to allocate or deallocate it. In the worst case, the responder will run into a timeout when waiting for the notify. Either way, no device will allocate the slot.

⊗ The notify was not successfully delivered to the responder. The slot is actually known by both sides, but this fact is not known by the responder as explained in Sect. 6. As soon as this case is recognized, the slot should be marked as INVALID and the devices should deallocate it properly.

By marking the slot as INVALID, the inconsistency case can be easily recognized by at least one of the devices. This is the case if either a timeout occurs when waiting for the notify or the requester senses a busy channel while sending the notify. Note that even though the slot was not allocated in the NOTIFY_ACCESS_FAILURE case, the requesting device should not rely on the deallocation due to the timeout on the responding device. Otherwise, the slot would no longer be known to the requesting device and no proper deallocation will take place, therefore, the neighborhood would not be informed about the inconsistency.

The maximum duration until an inconsistent state is recognized is now mainly dependent on the $macResponseWaitTime$ (W_r), resulting in a different T_w which is the timeout for waiting for a notify. As shown in Fig. 8, the durations are lower than the ones resulting from the DSME GTS expiration by orders of magnitude. It can be minimized by choosing a low W_r, but this might lead to false negatives in case the notify is delayed, for example due to a high network load. Choosing the default $W_r = 32$ is completely sufficient.

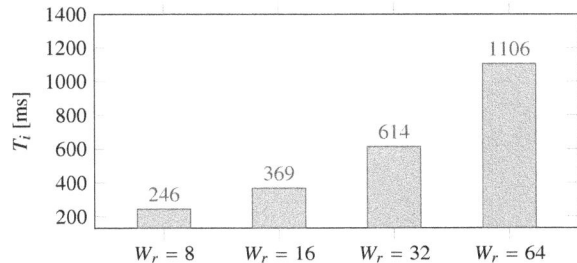

Figure 8: Duration for recognizing an inconsistent state for the improved handling.

10. CONCLUSION

This paper analyzes the distributed slot allocation procedure by means of formal verification. It was shown that in fact inconsistencies in the slot allocation can occur and are not avoidable. However, these inconsistencies are not persistent and will always be resolved. In the original standard, this is done by counting failed transmission during the contention free phase. Since this can induce delays in the order of one hour, this paper proposes to exploit the supervision of the message transmission during the slot allocation procedure to recognize the inconsistency much earlier. As a suggestion for a sound implementation, an additional flag is added to the allocation counter table to mark invalid slots. It is shown by formal verification that using the proposed optimization reduces the time until an inconsistency is recognized by several magnitudes. These results already helped to improve our DSME implementation[1] significantly, leading to much more stable and reliable networks. Future work includes the investigation of more intertwined processes that occur in large networks of demanding industrial wireless sensor and actuator scenarios.

Acknowledgments

This research was supported by the German Federal Ministry for Economic Affairs and Energy (BMWi) in the AutoR project (0325629D).

[1] http://www.openDSME.org

11. REFERENCES

[1] IEC 62591:2010 - Industrial communication networks - Wireless communication network and communication profiles - WirelessHART™, 2010.

[2] IEEE 802.15.4e™-2012 -IEEE Standard for Local and metropolitan area networks–Part 15.4: Low-Rate Wireless Personal Area Networks (LR-WPANs) Amendment 1: MAC sublayer, 2012.

[3] IEEE 802.15.4™-2015 - IEEE Standard for Local and metropolitan area networks–Part 15.4: Low-Rate Wireless Personal Area Networks (WPANs), 2016.

[4] N. Accettura, M. R. Palattella, G. Boggia, L. A. Grieco, and M. Dohler. Decentralized Traffic Aware Scheduling for Multi-hop Low Power Lossy Networks in the Internet of Things. In *International Symposium and Workshops on a World of Wireless, Mobile and Multimedia Networks (WoWMoM)*. IEEE, 2013.

[5] M. Al-Mahfoudh, G. Gopalakrishnan, and R. Stutsman. Toward Rigorous Design of Domain-Specific Distributed Systems. In *FME Workshop on Formal Methods in Software Engineering (FormaliSE)*, 2016.

[6] F. J. R. Barboza, A. M. S. Andrade, F. A. Silva, and G. Lima. Specification and Verification of the IEEE 802.11 Medium Access Control and an Analysis of its Applicability to Real-Time Systems. *Electronic Notes in Theoretical Computer Science*, 195, Jan. 2006.

[7] R. Boucebsi, F. Belala, and L. Derdouri. Modeling Channel Allocation via BRS: Case of WMNs. In *International Conference on Advanced Aspects of Software Engineering (ICAASE)*, 2014.

[8] E. Bres, R. v. Glabbeek, and P. Höfner. A Timed Process Algebra for Wireless Networks with an Application in Routing. In *Programming Languages and Systems*, number 9632 in Lecture Notes in Computer Science. Springer, Apr. 2016.

[9] J. Colpo and D. Mols. No strings attached. *Hydrocarbon Engineering*, 16, Nov. 2011.

[10] D. De Guglielmo, S. Brienza, and G. Anastasi. IEEE 802.15.4e: A Survey. *Computer Communications*, 2016. 10.1016/j.comcom.2016.05.004.

[11] G. Delzanno, A. Sangnier, and G. Zavattaro. Verification of Ad Hoc Networks with Node and Communication Failures. In *Formal Techniques for Distributed Systems*. Springer, 2012.

[12] S. Duquennoy, B. Al Nahas, O. Landsiedel, and T. Watteyne. Orchestra: Robust Mesh Networks Through Autonomously Scheduled TSCH. In *13th ACM Conference on Embedded Networked Sensor Systems (SenSys)*, 2015.

[13] S. Feo-Arenis, B. Westphal, D. Dietsch, M. Muñiz, and A. S. Andisha. The Wireless Fire Alarm System: Ensuring Conformance to Industrial Standards through Formal Verification. In *FM 2014: Formal Methods*, number 8442 in Lecture Notes in Computer Science. Springer, May 2014.

[14] M. Fruth. *Formal Methods for the Analysis of Wireless Network Protocols*. Ph. D. Thesis, University of Oxford, 2011.

[15] P. J. Gmytrasiewicz and E. H. Durfee. Decision-theoretic Recursive Modeling and the Coordinated Attack Problem. In *International Conference on Artificial Intelligence Planning Systems*, 1992.

[16] J. Y. Halpern and Y. Moses. Knowledge and Common Knowledge in a Distributed Environment. *Journal of the ACM*, 37(3), July 1990.

[17] L. Lamport. Specifying Concurrent Systems with TLA+. 2000.

[18] K. G. Larsen, P. Pettersson, and W. Yi. UPPAAL in a Nutshell. *Int. Journal on Software Tools for Technology Transfer*, 1(1–2), Oct. 1997.

[19] Y.-S. Lee and S.-H. Chung. An Efficient Distributed Scheduling Algorithm for Mobility Support in IEEE 802.15.4e DSME-Based Industrial Wireless Sensor Networks. *International Journal of Distributed Sensor Networks*, Feb. 2016.

[20] C. McCaffrey. The Verification of a Distributed System. *Communications of the ACM*, 59(2), Jan. 2016.

[21] F. Meier and V. Turau. An Analytical Model for Fast and Verifiable Assessment of Large Scale Wireless Mesh Networks. In *11th International Conference on the Design of Reliable Communication Networks (DRCN)*, Mar. 2015.

[22] C. Newcombe, T. Rath, F. Zhang, B. Munteanu, M. Brooker, and M. Deardeuff. How Amazon Web Services Uses Formal Methods. *Communications of the ACM*, 58(4), Apr. 2015.

[23] M. Paavola and K. Leivisk. Wireless Sensor Networks in Industrial Automation. In *Factory Automation*. InTech, Mar. 2010.

[24] P. Panangaden and K. Taylor. Concurrent Common Knowledge: Defining Agreement for Asynchronous Systems. *Distributed Computing*, 6(2), 1992.

[25] S. Petersen and S. Carlsen. Performance Evaluation of WirelessHART for Factory Automation. In *Conference on Emerging Technologies Factory Automation (ETFA)*. IEEE, Sept. 2009.

[26] I. Saha, S. Roy, and S. Ramesh. Formal Verification of Fault-Tolerant Startup Algorithms for Time-Triggered Architectures: A Survey. *Proceedings of the IEEE*, 104(5), May 2016.

[27] T. Watteyne, M. R. Palattella, and L. A. Grieco. Using IEEE 802.15.4e Time-Slotted Channel Hopping (TSCH) in the Internet of Things (IoT): Problem Statement. RFC 7554, May 2015.

[28] J. R. Wilcox, D. Woos, P. Panchekha, Z. Tatlock, X. Wang, M. D. Ernst, and T. Anderson. Verdi: A Framework for Implementing and Formally Verifying Distributed Systems. In *36th SIGPLAN Conference on Programming Language Design and Implementation*. ACM, 2015.

[29] B. Yousefi, F. Ghassemi, and R. Khosravi. Modeling and Efficient Verification of Wireless Ad hoc Networks. *arXiv:1604.07179 [cs]*, Apr. 2016.

APPENDIX

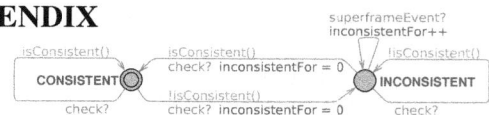

Figure 9: State diagram of the Observer.

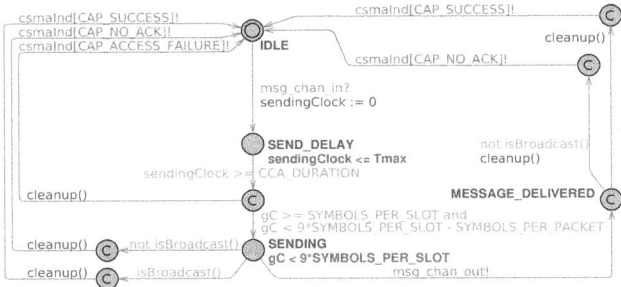

Figure 10: State diagram of the CAP Transmission.

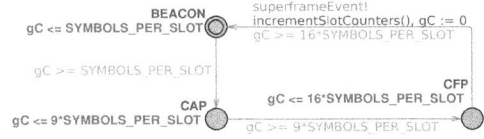

Figure 11: State diagram of the Global Clock.

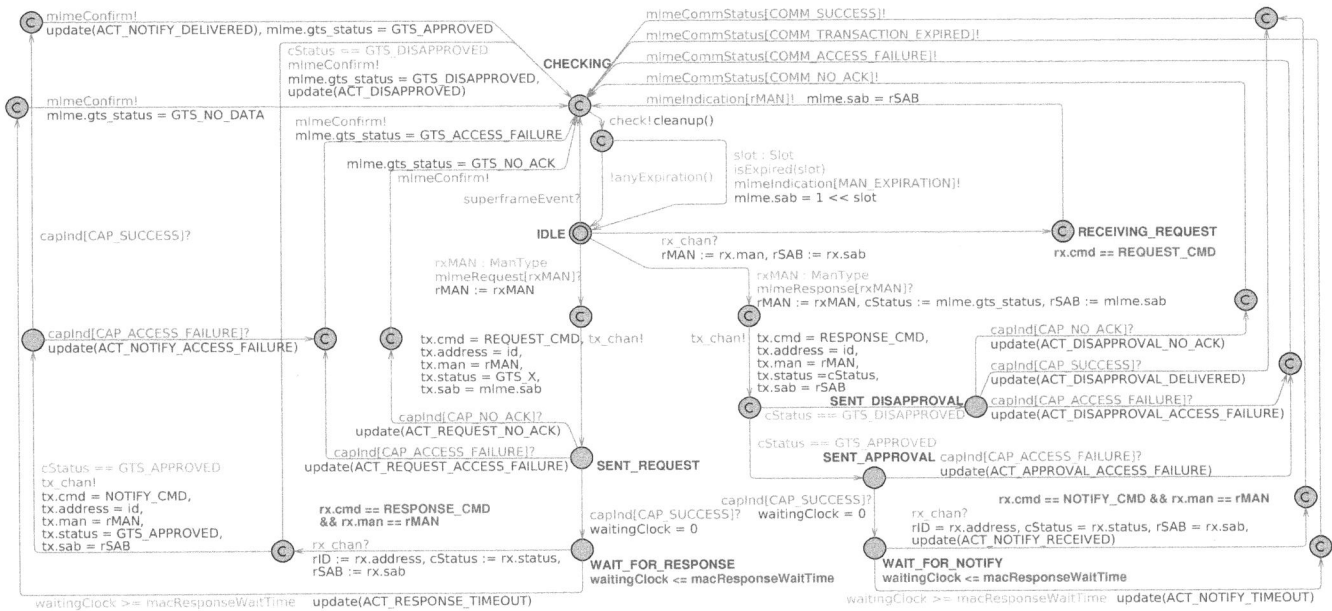

Figure 12: State diagram of the GTS Manager.

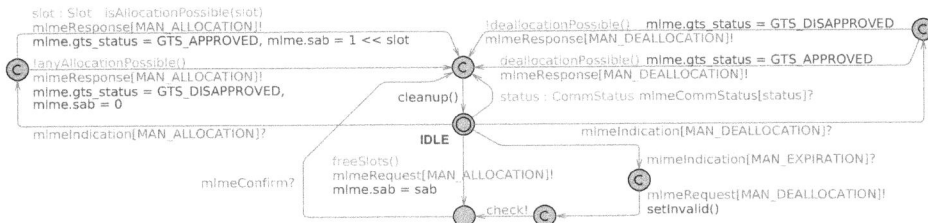

Figure 13: State diagram of the GTS Allocation Helper.

147

Analytical Models for QoS-driven VNF Placement and Provisioning in Wireless Carrier Cloud

Fatma Ben Jemaa and Guy Pujolle
Sorbonne Universités, UPMC Univ Paris 06
UMR 7606, LIP6, Paris, France
{fatma.ben-jemaa, guy.pujolle}@lip6.fr

Michel Pariente
Meteor Network
Vitry-Sur-Seine, France
mpariente@meteornetworks.com

ABSTRACT

Network Function Virtualisation (NFV) represents a promising solution for wireless network operators to improve business agility and cope with the continuing growth in data traffic. Furthermore, by virtualizing core network functions as well as radio-access network functions, NFV can effectively reduce the cost to deploy and operate large wireless networks. Face to this technology revolution, a new underlying cloud architecture is emerging. This architecture is based on the combination of edge clouds and a centralized cloud, referred to as the edge-central cloud. This notably improves user experience while ensuring scalability and load balancing. In such carrier cloud environment, efficient management mechanisms for the Virtual Network Functions (VNFs) are of crucial importance. In this paper, we introduce VNF placement and provisioning optimization strategies over an edge-central carrier cloud infrastructure taking into account QoS requirements (i.e., response time, latency constraints and real-time requirements) and using analytical and QoS models. Our main design goals are to optimize resource utilization, to prevent cloudlet overload, and to avoid violation of SLA requirements. We propose different solutions to achieve a trade-off between these conflicting objectives according to the wireless operator requirements. These solutions are evaluated through extensive simulations using different performance metrics and encouraging results are obtained.

Keywords

Analytical models; QoS; NFV; VNF placement; Edge and Cloud computing; Wireless carrier network

1. INTRODUCTION

Over the last decade, Cloud computing has gained significant popularity as a cost-effective, scalable and flexible model for hosting services in powerful data centers which provide on-demand computing, storage and networking resources. In particular, wireless network operators are considering the usage of cloud computing as a potential solution to enable more agility for the creation of new services and cope with the surging mobile data traffic [1]. Furthermore, virtualizing the core network as well as the radio access network (RAN) represents one of the key technology drivers of the next generation 5G networks. This is called Network Function Virtualisation (NFV) which promises cost efficient deployment and operation of networks by shifting network functions away from dedicated hardware appliances into software instances running on general-purpose hardware.

One of the emerging cloud architectures that will be leveraged to deploy Virtual Network Functions (VNFs) is the edge-central cloud architecture, also referred to as the two-tier cloud architecture. This architecture consists of edge clouds (i.e., a cloudlet), close to end-users, and a core cloud, located in a centralized data center. This provides low-latency and high-capacity virtualized services and resources as close as possible to end-users and ensures improved scaling and load balancing with centralized cloud resources. Moreover, it supports location- and context-aware services to improve the quality of users' experience.

In this emerging carrier-grade cloud landscape, specific requirements need to be considered for VNF management and deployment. Thereby, efficient VNF placement and provisioning strategies are needed to ensure a superior customer experience. However, deciding where to place VNFs either on the cloudlet or on the cloud is not trivial. Indeed, there are many functions (e.g., RAN functions) with strict real-time requirements and latency constraints that need to be placed on the edge cloudlet. But, the latter is constrained by capacity limits. Moreover, in order to satisfy VNF response time requirements and to improve the user-perceived QoS, several factors should be considered like the virtualization overhead, utilization level of physical hosts and network delays. To address these issues, we propose a VNF provisioning and placement strategies to determine the required resources and placement of VNFs in the two-tier carrier cloud infrastructure taking into account QoS requirements (i.e., response time, latency constraints and real-time requirements). The main goals of our proposal are i) to optimize resource utilization, ii) to prevent cloudlet overload and congestion, and iii) to avoid violation of QoS and SLA requirements. For this purpose, we use queuing and QoS models along with optimization techniques to efficiently allocate resources and place VNFs.

The rest of the paper is organized as follows. In Section 2, we present related works relevant to ours. We then describe

MSWiM '16, November 13-17, 2016, Malta, Malta

© 2016 ACM. ISBN 978-1-4503-4502-6/16/11...$15.00

DOI: http://dx.doi.org/10.1145/2988287.2989154

our performance and QoS models used in our optimization framework in Section 3. Next, we provide mathematical formulation and solutions of our problem in Section 4 and 5 respectively. Section 6 discusses the simulation results of our proposed solutions. We finally provide concluding remarks in Section 7.

2. RELATED LITERATURE REVIEW

The VNF placement problem is a kind of VM (Virtual Machine) placement problem since VNFs are virtual machines that run network functions. A plethora of research works have addressed the VM placement problem within a data center, in distributed clouds, or in hybrid clouds. The latter two architectures are the closest to our edge-central cloud architecture. Indeed, our architecture can be considered as a kind of distributed clouds. Also, it has the same aspect of an hybrid architecture where an organization operates a private *local* cloud and is able to externalize workloads to public *distant* Infrastructure Providers (InPs). However, in our case, both the local and distant clouds are managed by the same organization. We explore, in the following, relevant research works related to these two topics, namely VM placement in distributed clouds and hybrid clouds, as well as initial studies on placement of VNFs.

• VM placement across distributed clouds

Several research works have been conducted for decision on the placement of VMs in geographically distributed data centers. Son et al. [22] propose an SLA-based cloud computing framework to facilitate location- and load-aware resource allocation. According to a utility function that involves machine workload and the expected response time, the user's VM is allocated in the physical machine that is closest to the user and has a light workload to guarantee a reasonable response time. However, this work places VMs one by one and does not address the whole system performance optimization. In [25], Zhang et al. present a framework for dynamic service placement problems in multiple data centers to minimize the total resource cost while satisfying SLA requirements, taking into consideration the fluctuation of both demand and resource price. As SLA constraint, they specify a maximum delay to achieve between a data center and a user location. However, they do not deal with resource provisioning to satisfy response time requirements for each VM. In [4], authors propose a network-aware algorithm for allocation of virtual machines in distributed cloud systems. Their objective is to minimize the latency in communication between the VMs allocated for a user request when they are split over multiple data centers. Consequently, they only consider latency between VMs and do not take into account latency between user location and the different selected data centers for the placement of user's VMs.

The aforementioned works are mainly conducted under the context of a cloud computing environment where InPs tend to build large data centers in geographically distributed locations to achieve reliability while minimizing operational cost, on the one hand, and where Service Providers (SPs) leverage geo-diversity of data centers to serve customers from multiple geographical regions, on the other hand. This context differs from our study scope which focuses on carrier network architecture leveraging NFV concepts. Indeed, the first context generally involves the placement of many and small VMs in large-scale data center infrastructure while the latter involves the placement of few and resource-intensive VNFs in a two-tier cloud infrastructure with small edge cloudlets.

• VM placement in hybrid clouds

Several works have been conducted to address the VM placement in hybrid cloud scenario [5, 9, 15, 19, 24, 26]. The main objective of these works is to ensure efficient utilization of the on-premise resources and to minimize the cost of running the outsourced tasks in the cloud, while fulfilling the applications' quality of service constraints.

In our context of study, there are no costs relative to the price of VM deployment in external clouds since the whole two-tier cloud infrastructure belongs to the same organization (i.e., the wireless network carrier). However, network delay between the on-premise and the distant cloud can generate costs related to SLA violation penalties. Nonetheless, the aforementioned works can not be applied to our problematic since our objective is to minimize the maximum utilization of the edge cloud. In contrast, the cited works aim to maximize utilization of the internal data center. This approach used in hybrid clouds will be compared to our solution in the evaluation section.

• VNF placement

As NFV is becoming a hot topic across industry and academia, the problem of VNF placement has recently gained the attention of some research works. For instance, Bari et al. [6] propose a model to optimize the VNF placement problem in ISP and enterprise networks while minimizing operational costs, mainly node and link resource utilization. As SLA constraint, they only consider propagation delay and do not include processing delay at each node. In the same context, Bernadetta et al. [2] propose a VNF chaining and placement model that optimize network level (i.e. link utilization) and NFVI-level (i.e. allocated computing resources) performance metrics. For this, they consider the latency bounds at both the VNF node and the end-to-end levels. To determine the VNF forwarding latency metric, they only consider traffic load and do not take into account utilization level of the physical host (i.e. the number of VMs placed on the NFVI node) which can dramatically increase the VNF latency due to the virtualization overhead and resource sharing of the same physical host. Moreover, both of [6] and [2] do not consider the latency between VNFs and end-users and the fact that some VNFs may require to be placed in the proximity of end-users.

In [7], authors address the placement of virtual mobile core network functions (i.e; S-GW, PDN-GW, MME and HSS) excluding VNFs on the radio access network. Their optimization target is to minimize the cost of occupied link and node resources while taking as constraints VNF requirements in terms of bandwidth, processing and storage resources. However, they do not consider latency constraint on the VNF nodes and the end-to-end network. In the same context of mobile networks, Taleb et al. [23] propose algorithms to place VNFs of both PDN-GWs and S-GWs on a given topology of distributed datacenters. They deal with two conflicting objectives, namely the insurance of QoE via the placement of VNFs of PDN-GWs closer to User Equipments (UEs) and the avoidance of the relocation of S-GWs via the placement of their VNFs far enough from UEs. While their results are promising, their scope is very limited to two particular mobile core network functions (i.e., S-GW and

PDN-GW), on the one hand, and VNF resource requirements are not addressed, on the other hand.

In [21], authors investigate the VNF placement problem in the radio access network (RAN) domain which can include functions such as load-balancing, firewall, and virtual radio nodes. Their objective is to minimize the cost of mapping virtual functions to substrate network (nodes and links) while satisfying VNF requirements in terms of CPU, memory, storage, radio, and bandwidth resources. However, neither latency of VNF nodes nor end-to-end latency perceived by the user are considered.

Furthermore, none of the aforementioned works deals with the resource provisioning problem. Indeed, specific resource requirements for each VNF are determined in advance or a set of predefined VM templates are used to embed VNFs. However, these values can change as a function of workload variation and physical host performance and utilization level. So, a joint placement and provisioning problem should be considered to satisfy VNF SLA requirements with respect to the underlying infrastructure performance and status.

To the best of our knowledge, this work is the first effort to address VNF placement and provisioning problem over a two-tier carrier cloud architecture while considering SLA requirements (VNF processing delay and real-time constraints), virtualization overhead and utilization level of the physical hosts.

3. SYSTEM MODELING

We present in this section the performance and QoS models on which is based our QoS-aware VNF placement and provisioning methods for carrier edge-central cloud system.

3.1 Performance model

Performance requirements of VNFs (instantiated within VMs) are generally specified in terms of average response time. This metric depends on various factors. First, by allocating more computing resources (i.e., CPUs), virtual machines usually improve their processing power and response time. Thus, sufficient resources have to be allocated to each VNF to guarantee the requested average response time. Second, since a VNF potentially shares resources with other VMs on the same physical host, the response time also depends on the utilization level of the physical host (e.g., number of instantiated VMs, number of user requests). If the latter is under a heavy workload, the VNF response time will be degraded. Moreover, all incoming and outgoing user traffic passes through a virtualization layer (i.e., Virtual Machine Monitor (VMM) or an hypervisor), and incurs additional latency. Despite the several technologies used to reduce virtualization overhead (e.g., [10]), this still has an impact on the response time. Unless this is not explicitly modeled, response time will be inaccurate. Finally, placing VNFs in the centralized cloud is likely to result in better response times due to the high performance capacity of the cloud. However, the network delay plays very important role in the client-perceived QoS.

Taking into account these different factors, we model the performance of our system using analytical queuing models. Fig. 1 represents this model.

We define N as the number of VNFs to be initially placed in the carrier two-tier cloud network. Let n_1 and n_2 be the number of VNFs that will be placed on the edge cloudlet and the central cloud respectively. We model both the cloudlet

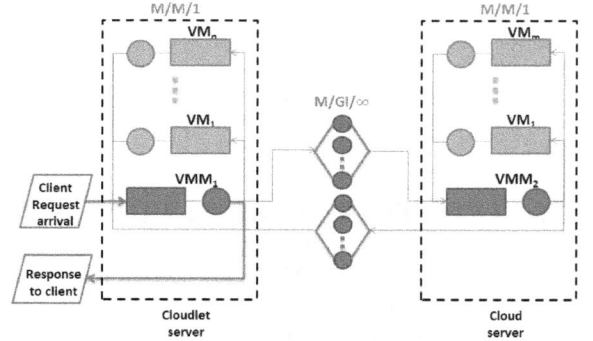

Figure 1: Two-tier cloud system model

and the cloud servers as two open Jackson networks [11]. We assume that the distribution of inter-arrival times of user requests coming from outside have a Poisson distribution. We denote the arrival rate of requests by λ. In each network, the VMM as well as VNF machines are modeled as $M/M/1$ queues.

Let p_0 (resp. q_0) be the probability that a user request, having finished being served by the cloudlet server (resp. the cloud server), goes (resp. goes back) to the cloud server (resp. cloudlet server) and p_s be the probability that a user request is accomplished. User requests arriving from the exterior first move towards VMM_1, the virtual machine manager (VMM) of the cloudlet server.

We denote by $\{p_i; 1 \leq i \leq n_1\}$ and $\{q_i; 1 \leq i \leq n_2\}$ the probability that a request having passed through VMM_1 (resp. VMM_2, the virtual machine manager of the cloud server) goes to a VNF_i machine within the cloudlet server (resp. the cloud server). Applying the *Little's Law* [11], the mean response time of VMM_1 is:

$$\mathcal{R}_{VMM_1} = \frac{1}{\mu_{VMM_1} - \frac{\lambda}{p_s}} \qquad (1)$$

and the mean response time of VMM_2 is:

$$\mathcal{R}_{VMM_2} = \frac{1}{\mu_{VMM_2} - \frac{\lambda p_0}{p_s q_0}} \qquad (2)$$

where μ_{VMM_j}, $j \in \{1, 2\}$, denotes the mean service rate of requests at VMM_i. Equation 1 and 2 actually represent the average delay induced by the virtualization layer (i.e., VMM). Besides, the mean response time of a VM_i instantiated on the cloudlet server is:

$$\mathcal{R}_{VM_{i1}} = \frac{1}{\phi_{i1}\mu_1 - \frac{\lambda p_i}{p_s}}; 1 \leq i \leq n_1 \qquad (3)$$

and the mean response time of a VM_i instantiated on the cloud server is:

$$\mathcal{R}_{VM_{i2}} = \frac{1}{\phi_{i2}\mu_2 - \frac{\lambda p_0 q_i}{p_s q_0}}; 1 \leq i \leq n_2 \qquad (4)$$

where μ_j, $j \in \{1, 2\}$, denotes the mean service rate of requests per unit of processing capacity and ϕ_{ij}, $j \in \{1, 2\}$, denotes the number of processing units allocated to VM_i on server j. Note that $\{p_i; 1 \leq i \leq n_1\}$ and $\{q_i; 1 \leq i \leq n_2\}$ respectively depend on the number of VNFs placed on the cloudlet and the cloud. For the sake of simplicity, and while taking into account the total number of VNFs placed in each server, we assume that:

$$p_i = \frac{1 - p_0 - p_s}{n_1} \text{ and } q_i = \frac{1 - q_0}{n_2}, \forall i \in [1, N] \qquad (5)$$

By defining the constants:

$$b_1 = \frac{\lambda(1 - p_0 - p_s)}{p_s} \text{ and } b_2 = \frac{\lambda p_0(1 - q_0)}{p_s q_0} \qquad (6)$$

150

we can write equation 3 and 4 as:

$$\mathcal{R}_{VM_{ij}} = \frac{1}{\phi_{ij}\mu_j - \frac{b_j}{n_j}}, \forall i \in [1, N] \text{ and } \forall j \in \{1, 2\} \quad (7)$$

Finally, based on equation 1, 2 and 7, the mean response time of VNF_i, $i \in \{1, 2 \cdots N\}$, on server j is:

$$\mathcal{R}_{VNF_{ij}} = \mathcal{R}_{VMM_j} + \mathcal{R}_{VM_{ij}} \quad (8)$$

where VM_{ij} is the virtual machine instantiated for VNF_i on server j.

Consequently, this model allows us to determine the number of processing units (i.e., CPU cores) required to achieve the requested average response time for each VNF taking into account utilization level of the physical host (i.e., arrival rate of user requests and the number of hosted VMs) and virtualization overhead.

To model the network link between the cloudlet and the cloud, we use $M/GI/\infty$ queue in which we assume that requests arrive following a Poisson process [13] with parameter $\lambda p_0 / p_s$ and the service times are General Independent (GI) with rate μ. In such queue system, when a request arrive, it is immediately served and does not wait and the average response time of this queue depends only on the mean of the service time distribution. Hence, the average network delay can be calculated as follows:

$$\mathcal{D}_{Network} = \frac{1}{\mu} \quad (9)$$

3.2 QoS model

Real-time behavior is an important aspect of network functions. Indeed, these functions have different timing requirements to maintain end-to-end QoS. For instance, management functions (e.g., OSS and off-line charging systems) have high tolerance to delays. Networks functions in the control plane (e.g., policy management, firewalling and AAA) as well as in the application plane (e.g., analytics solutions, location-based services) can tolerate small timing delays. Networking infrastructure functions (e.g., access points, routers and switches) and packet processing functions (e.g., CDN and DPI) have a very low tolerance for timing delays with a major impact on the QoS and end-user experience. Inspired by the classification of these network functions presented in [3], we define a QoS model (see Table 1) which includes three types of network functions according to their delay sensitivity: *real-time*, *near real-time*, and *non real-time* functions. Then, for each type we define *i*) a priority level, according to which network functions have to be placed in proximity to end-users, *ii*) a maximum tolerated delay, and *iii*) a penalty metric representing severity of violating this delay.

Table 1: QoS model for network functions

Type of network function	Priority level	Maximum delay	Penalty metric
Real-time	1	10 ms	5
Near real-time	2	30 ms	3
Non real-time	3	100 ms	1

4. PROBLEM DESCRIPTION AND FORMULATION

In this section, we formally define the VNF Placement problem in edge-central carrier cloud architectures as a Mixed Integer Linear Program (MILP).

The problem of placing a given VNF_i across the infrastructure involves two steps:

- First, assign VNF_i to a server j (i.e., the cloudlet or the cloud). Hence, we define the decision variable x_{ij} as:

$$x_{ij} = \begin{cases} 1 & \text{if } VNF_i \text{ is placed on server } j \\ 0 & \text{else} \end{cases} \quad (10)$$

- Second, allocate the required processing resources to each VNF_i placed on server j. To do so, we define the resource allocation variable ϕ_{ij} as the number of CPU cores allocated to the VM running VNF_i.

In addition, we define a pseudo binary variable y_i which determines if the maximum delay Max_Delay_i defined by the QoS model of VNF_i is respected ($y_i = 0$) or violated ($y_i = 1$). We assume that the delay between end-users and the cloudlet is negligible as the latter is placed in proximity to them. Thus, we only consider the network delay between the cloudlet and the cloud when VNF_i is placed on the latter. Then, y_i is defined as follows:

$$y_i = \begin{cases} 1 & \text{if } x_{i2}\mathcal{R}_{VNF_{i2}} + 2x_{i2}\mathcal{D}_{Network} \geq Max\_Delay_i \\ 0 & \text{else} \end{cases} \quad (11)$$

In our problem, a set of constraints should be respected:

- A VNF_i should be placed either in the cloudlet or the cloud:

$$\sum_{j=1}^{2} x_{ij} = 1, \forall i \in [1, N] \quad (12)$$

- If VNF_i is placed on server j, a certain amount of resources $\phi_{ij} \neq 0$ should be allocated to this VNF, else ϕ_{ij} will be equal to 0. We model this constraint as follows:

$$x_{ij} \leq \phi_{ij} \leq C_j x_{ij} \quad (13)$$
$$\forall i \in [1, N] \text{ and } \forall j \in [1, 2]$$

where Cj is the capacity of server j.

- Each server has a capacity limitation C_j. Moreover, a utilization rate U of the cloudlet server capacity C_1 should not be exceeded to prevent over provisioning and bottleneck creation at the cloudlet node. These constraints are presented as follows:

$$\sum_{i=1}^{N} \phi_{i2} \leq C_2, \text{ and } \sum_{i=1}^{N} \phi_{i1} \leq C_1 U, \forall i \in [1, N] \quad (14)$$

- The response time of each VNF_i placed on server j should not exceed a threshold value T_i defined in the SLA of this function. Based on equation 7, this constraint is presented as follows:

$$x_{ij}\mathcal{R}_{VMM_j} + \frac{x_{ij}}{\phi_{ij}\mu_j - \frac{b_j x_{ij}}{\sum_{i=1}^{N} x_{ij}}} \leq T_i, \quad (15)$$
$$\forall i \in [1, N] \text{ and } \forall j \in [1, 2]$$

and can also be written as:

$$x_{ij}\sum_{i=1}^{N} x_{ij} \leq (T_i - \mathcal{R}_{VMM_j}x_{ij})(\phi_{ij}\mu_j \sum_{i=1}^{N} x_{ij} - x_{ij}b_j)$$
$$\forall i \in [1, N] \text{ and } \forall j \in [1, 2] \quad (16)$$

This represents a non-linear quadratic constraint which can be linearized using the Big-M reformulation [17].

- Finally, we model equation (11) using the following constraints:

$$My_i \geq x_{i2}\mathcal{R}_{VNF_{ij}} + 2x_{i2}\mathcal{D}_{Network} - Max\_Delay_i \quad (17)$$
$$M(1 - y_i) \geq -(x_{i2}\mathcal{R}_{VNF_{ij}} + 2x_{i2}\mathcal{D}_{Network}$$
$$- Max\_Delay_i), \forall i \in [1, N] \quad (18)$$

where $M = \max(Max\_Delay_i, i \in [1, N])$. Based on equations 2, 7 and 8, constraints 17 and 18 can be transformed to quadratic constraints which can also be linearized using the Big-M reformulation.

Our optimization problem is based on three main objectives:

i) minimizing the maximum utilization of the edge cloudlet U to prevent over provisioning and to have spare resources for eventual new function placement and thus minimize VM migration:

$$Min\ U \qquad (19)$$

In our work, we assume that the centralized distant cloud has extensive resources. Thus, we only consider utilization level of the cloudlet as it has very limited resource capacity.

ii) minimizing allocated computing resources in the centralized cloud to only allocate sufficient resources:

$$Min \sum_{i=1}^{N} \phi_{i2} \qquad (20)$$

iii) minimizing QoS violation in terms of real time requirements of each VNF:

$$Min \sum_{i=1}^{N} y_i P_i \qquad (21)$$

where P_i is the penalty metric defined by the QoS model of VNF_i.

The third objective can be achieved by placing all the real time constrained VNFs in the cloudlet. However, in this case, it will be over-provisioned and the first objective will be violated. This results in a conflict between the two objectives and a trade-off has to be found.

5. SOLUTIONS DESCRIPTION

Our problem represents a Multiple Objective Decision Making (MODM) [12] (also known as Multiple Criteria Decision Making). We present, in the following, three solutions to resolve this MODM problem.

5.1 Trade-off between Cloudlet Utilization and QoS Violation (To-CUQV)

As the three objective functions are linear, the wireless network carrier can specify his preferences in terms of the relative importance for each objective, especially the two conflicting ones. Thus, the problem can be solved using the weighting sum method [12, 16]. To more accurately reflect the relative importance of each objective by using weights, the different objective functions should have similar orders of magnitude and ranges [16]. For this purpose, we define the aggregate objective as follows:

$$Min\ \alpha U + \beta \sum_{i=1}^{N} \frac{\phi_{i2}}{C_2} + \gamma k \sum_{i=1}^{N} \frac{y_i P_i}{P_{RT} N_{RT} + P_{NeRT} N_{NeRT}} \qquad (22)$$

where α, β and γ are the preference weights of each objective; k is a scaling factor; P_{RT} and P_{NeRT} are penalty metrics respectively defined for real-time and near real-time functions (see Table 1); and N_{RT} and N_{NeRT} are number of real-time and near real-time functions respectively. The optimization program of to-CUQV solution is formulated as follows:

```
Minimize
```
$$\alpha U + \beta \sum_{i=1}^{N} \frac{\phi_{i2}}{C_2} + \gamma k \sum_{i=1}^{N} \frac{y_i P_i}{P_{RT} N_{RT} + P_{NeRT} N_{NeRT}}$$
```
Subject to:
```
$$\sum_{j=1}^{2} x_{ij} = 1, \ \forall i \in [1, N]$$
$$x_{ij} \leq \phi_{ij} \leq C_j x_{ij}, \ \forall i \in [1, N], \ \forall j \in [1, 2]$$
$$\sum_{i=1}^{N} \phi_{i2} \leq C_2, \ \text{and} \ \sum_{i=1}^{N} \phi_{i1} \leq C_1 U, \ \forall i \in [1, N]$$
$$\mathcal{R}_{VNF_{ij}} \leq T_i, \ \forall i \in [1, N], \ \forall j \in [1, 2]$$
$$M y_i \geq x_{i2} \mathcal{R}_{VNF_{ij}} + 2 x_{i2} \mathcal{D}_{Network} - Max\_Delay_i \ \text{and}$$
$$M(1 - y_i) \geq -(x_{i2} \mathcal{R}_{VNF_{ij}} + 2 x_{i2} \mathcal{D}_{Network} - Max\_Delay_i), \ \forall i \in [1, N]$$

Problem 1: To-CUQV problem

5.2 Fixed QoS Violation Threshold (FQVT)

This solution is proposed for wireless carriers desiring to fix the QoS violation threshold in advance to guarantee a certain level of QoS. Therefore, we use the min-max approach to minimize the utilization rate of the edge cloudlet and the allocated resources while respecting the specified threshold of QoS violation. This threshold is defined as the maximum QoS penalty cost tolerated by the carrier denoted by P_{Th}. Its value is defined as a percentage of the maximum possible penalty cost. The optimization model of FQVT solution is formulated as follows:

```
Minimize
```
$\alpha U + \beta \sum_{i=1}^{N} \frac{\phi_{i2}}{C_2}$
```
Subject to:
```
$$\sum_{j=1}^{2} x_{ij} = 1, \ \forall i \in [1, N]$$
$$x_{ij} \leq \phi_{ij} \leq C_j x_{ij} \forall i \in [1, N], \ \forall j \in [1, 2]$$
$$\sum_{i=1}^{N} \phi_{i2} \leq C_2, \ \text{and} \ \sum_{i=1}^{N} \phi_{i1} \leq C_1 U, \ \forall i \in [1, N]$$
$$\mathcal{R}_{VNF_{ij}} \leq T_i, \ \forall i \in [1, N], \ \forall j \in [1, 2]$$
$$M y_i \geq x_{i2} \mathcal{R}_{VNF_{ij}} + 2 x_{i2} \mathcal{D}_{Network} - Max\_Delay_i \ \text{and}$$
$$M(1 - y_i) \geq -(x_{i2} \mathcal{R}_{VNF_{ij}} + 2 x_{i2} \mathcal{D}_{Network} - Max\_Delay_i), \ \forall i \in [1, N]$$
$$\sum_{i=1}^{N} y_i P_i \leq P_{Th}$$

Problem 2: FQVT problem

5.3 Fixed Maximum Cloudlet Utilization level (FMCU)

A common approach for resource management in enterprise computing systems is to maintain the utilization level under a pre-defined upper bound in order to guarantee optimal performance and QoS. Indeed, response time has small magnitude of change under low utilization rate, but it increases exponentially as the utilization reaches the maximum capacity [18]. From the other hand, wireless carriers may desire to limit the utilization of the cloudlet server under a sufficiently high level such that more capacity is available for hosting future functions. Thus, it is up to the wireless carrier to choose an appropriate utilization level according to his requirements. We denote by U_{max} the specified utilization level of the cloudlet. The optimization model, in this case, is formulated as follows:

```
Minimize
```
$$\beta \sum_{i=1}^{N} \frac{\phi_{i2}}{C_2} + \gamma k \sum_{i=1}^{N} \frac{y_i P_i}{P_{RT} N_{RT} + P_{NeRT} N_{NeRT}}$$
```
Subject to:
```
$$\sum_{j=1}^{2} x_{ij} = 1, \ \forall i \in [1, N]$$
$$x_{ij} \leq \phi_{ij} \leq C_j x_{ij} \forall i \in [1, N], \ \forall j \in [1, 2]$$
$$\sum_{i=1}^{N} \phi_{i2} \leq C_2, \ \text{and} \ \sum_{i=1}^{N} \phi_{i1} \leq C_1 U_{max}, \ \forall i \in [1, N]$$
$$\mathcal{R}_{VNF_{ij}} \leq T_i, \ \forall i \in [1, N], \ \forall j \in [1, 2]$$
$$M y_i \geq x_{i2} \mathcal{R}_{VNF_{ij}} + 2 x_{i2} \mathcal{D}_{Network} - Max\_Delay_i \ \text{and}$$
$$M(1 - y_i) \geq -(x_{i2} \mathcal{R}_{VNF_{ij}} + 2 x_{i2} \mathcal{D}_{Network} - Max\_Delay_i), \ \forall i \in [1, N]$$

Problem 3: FMCU problem

6. PERFORMANCE EVALUATION

In this section, we evaluate the performance of our proposals. To do so, we present the settings of the conducted simulations, the performance metrics that we have evaluated as well as the obtained results.

6.1 Simulation settings

- *Physical infrastructure*

In our experimental setup, we consider a 2.10 GHz Intel Xeon Processor E5-2620 v4 with 8 CPU cores for the edge cloudlet server and we consider a 2.50 GHz Intel Xeon Processor E7-8890 v3 with 18 CPU cores for the cloud server. We assume that the network delay between the cloudlet and the cloud servers is 15 ms.

- *VNFs*

As a practical use case, we target a carrier Wi-Fi network based on an edge-central cloud architecture [8]. Thus, the range of values that we will consider in the following particularly apply to such networks. Nevertheless, as seen in Section 3, 4 and 5, our provisioning and placement models do not make any assumption about the particular type of wireless technology and can be as well applied to any kind of carrier wireless network including mobile networks such as LTE and LTE-Advanced.

We consider a set of VNFs ($N \in [5,12]$) composed of 25% of real-time functions and 50% of near real-time functions. Response time requirements T_i are assigned to each VNF uniformly between 1 ms and 5 ms. The arrival rate of user requests (i.e., user packet flows) to the system λ is fixed to 1 request per second. We assume that a request is about 5 Mbits.

The mean service rate of requests μ_{VMM_1}, μ_{VMM_2}, μ_1 and μ_2 depend on the Processor Base Frequency (PBF) of the server (i.e., number of CPU cycles per second) and the average number of required cycles by a request. Thus, μ_{VMM_i} and μ_i are respectively fixed to $PBF_i/10^6$ and $PBF_i/4.10^6$, while assuming that the average number of CPU cycles required per request by the VMM and by a VNF's VM are respectively equal to 10^6 $cycles/request$ and 4.10^6 $cycles/request$. The average number of processing cycles required per bit is estimated to be 0.25 for the VMM and 0.8 for a VNF's VM [20].

The probability p_0 is a decreasing function of the cloudlet capacity (i.e., CPU cores) and an increasing function of the total number of VNFs. Thus we define the probability p_0 as:

$$p_0 = \exp(-\frac{C_1 + 1}{N}) \qquad (23)$$

In addition, we assume that $p_0 = q_0$ and $q_s = \frac{1}{N+1}$.

- *The simulator*

To evaluate the proposed solutions, we have developed a simulator tool based on Matlab, CPLEX and YALMIP [14]. The results are obtained over many simulation instances (100) for each scenario and are calculated with a confidence interval of 95%.

6.2 The baseline approach

Since previous proposals on VM placement and VNF placement are not directly applicable to the studied scenario (see Section 2), we developed a baseline VNF placement and provisioning algorithm similar to the approach used in hybrid clouds. Starting with VNFs having high priority level, the baseline algorithm first selects the cloudlet, if it is not-saturated, to place a VNF instance with adequate processing resources. Otherwise, the VNF instance will be placed on the cloud.

6.3 Performance metrics

The main performance metrics used to evaluate our proposals and to compare them with the baseline approach are:

- *The cloudlet utilization rate*:

One of our goals is not to overload the cloudlet. Thus, the utilization rate of processing resource capacity after VNF placement represents an important performance metric. This is calculated as follows:

$$U = \sum_{i=1}^{N} \frac{\phi_{i1}}{C_1} \qquad (24)$$

- *The number of QoS violation*:

This metric represents the number of VNFs whose maximum delay, defined in their SLAs and representing the end-user perceived latency, has been exceeded. This metric only concerns VNFs placed on the distant cloud since in our scenario the Cloudlet is placed in the end-user premises.

- *The cost function value*:

This metric represents the global cost of VNF placement in terms of resource utilization and QoS violation. It is calculated using the cumulative objective function (Equation 22).

6.4 Simulation results

In our experiments, we evaluate the different proposed solutions and we compare them to the baseline solution in terms of cloudlet utilization rate, occurrence of QoS vioaltion and cost. Moreover, we study the impact of the number of VNFs and the cloudlet computing capacity on all these performance metrics. In these experiments, we set $\alpha = \gamma = 0.45$. β is set to a low value (i.e., 0.1) since the objective of minimizing the allocated cloud resources is not conflicting with the other ones. We also set $P_{Th} = 10\%$ for FQVT solution and $U_{max} = 70\%$ for FMCU solution.

Effect of number of VNFs: Fig.2 compares the obtained results of the different solutions while varying the number of VNFs.

In Fig.2-(a), we can observe that the cloudlet becomes saturated with the baseline approach when the number of VNFs is approximately more than the number of available CPU cores (i.e., 8). In addition, as the baseline places VNFs by order of priority in the cloudlet, we can observe in Fig.2-(c) that there is no QoS violation of real-time functions but, in return, this leads to the cloudlet saturation.

On the other hand, To-CUQV always finds an optimal trade-off between the cloudlet utilization rate and the number of QoS violation while keeping the cost function as low as possible. Furthermore, compared to the baseline, To-CUQV reduces the total number of QoS violation particularly for $N > 8$ (see Fig.2-(b)). The reason is that To-CUQV may place real-time functions with heavy resource-consumption in the cloud when this enables to place additional near real-time functions in the cloudlet. Thus, To-CUQV does not only consider per-VNF QoS level but also the overall QoS level.

FMCU represents the least cloudlet utilization rate and respects the fixed maximum value (i.e., 70%). However, it generates the highest number of QoS violation (see Fig.2-(b) and (c)) and A high cost value (see Fig.2-(d)).

In Fig.2-(b) and (c), we can observe that FQVT ensures no QoS violation for $N \leq 9$. So, the cost shown in 2-(c) for this interval corresponds only to the cost of resource utilization. It is clear that FQVT has the least cost and number

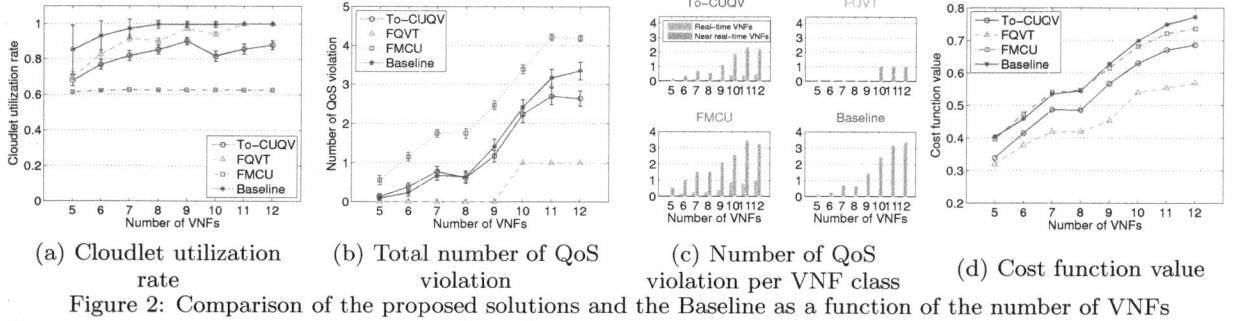

(a) Cloudlet utilization rate   (b) Total number of QoS violation   (c) Number of QoS violation per VNF class   (d) Cost function value

Figure 2: Comparison of the proposed solutions and the Baseline as a function of the number of VNFs

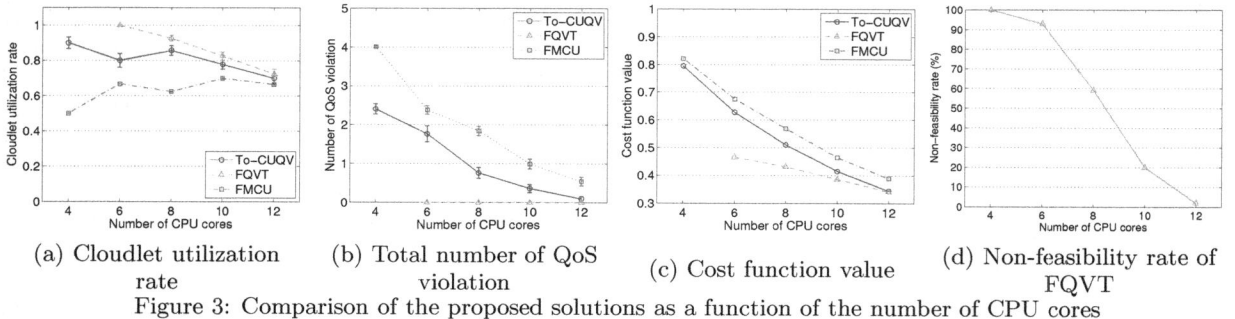

(a) Cloudlet utilization rate   (b) Total number of QoS violation   (c) Cost function value   (d) Non-feasibility rate of FQVT

Figure 3: Comparison of the proposed solutions as a function of the number of CPU cores

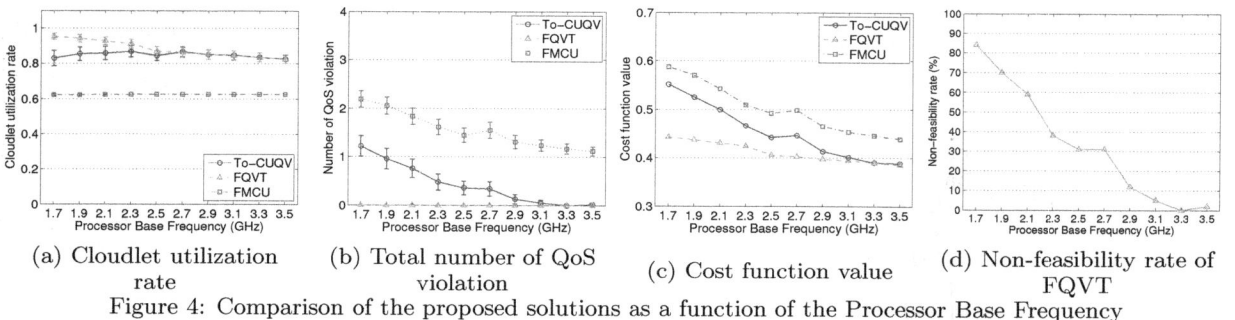

(a) Cloudlet utilization rate   (b) Total number of QoS violation   (c) Cost function value   (d) Non-feasibility rate of FQVT

Figure 4: Comparison of the proposed solutions as a function of the Processor Base Frequency

of QoS violation. However, this solution is not always feasible. Indeed, the QoS violation threshold constraint can not always be satisfied. Fig.5 shows the non-feasibility rate in our experiments for $P_{Th} = 10\%$ as well as for other values (15%, 25% and 30%). We note that this rate is higher for low value of P_{Th} and it remarkably increases when $N > 8$. Only for $P_{Th} = 25\%$ and $P_{Th} = 30\%$, the solution becomes nearly 100% feasible for $N \leq 8$.

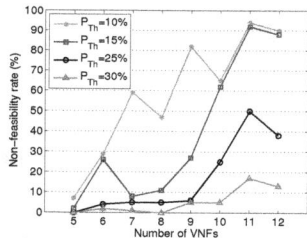

Figure 5: Non-feasibility rate

Effect of Cloudlet computing capacity: As we have noticed in the previous results, performance metrics degrade more remarkably when the number of VNFs becomes superior to the number of available CPU cores on the cloudlet. Thus, we fix the number of VNF to 8 and we vary the number of CPU cores to see more clearly the effect of this parameter on performances. As expected, Fig.3-(a), (b) and

(c) show that performance metrics are improved when the number of CPU cores increases. We notice that FQVT solution is not feasible at all with 4 CPU cores. This means that it is impossible to have a QoS violation threshold of 10% of penalty cost with only 4 CPU cores. Fig.3-(d) depicts how the non-feasibility rate decreases as the number of CPU cores increases and it becomes almost 0 for 12 CPU cores.

On the other hand, we vary the Processor Base Frequency of the cloudlet server (see Fig.4). We can observe that the PBF has much clearer impact on the QoS level than on the cloudlet utilization rate. In fact, processors with high PBF improve QoS level. Regarding FQVT solution, the effect of PBF appears on its feasibility rate. Indeed, high PBF values provide better feasibility rate.

To summarize, this part represents a deep analysis and detailed results of our system performances using different parameters and solutions. These results can help carriers to choose the appropriate solution and dimension their system according to their needs and requirements.

7. CONCLUSION

The edge-central carrier cloud architecture along with NFV technology represent a promising solution for wireless operators to address future 5G challenges. In this paper, we have presented strategies that enable QoS-driven VNF placement and provisioning in such environment using performance and QoS models. Simulation experiments and performance analysis show promising results. Indeed, our approaches are able to achieve a fair trade-off between two conflicting objectives, namely i) the optimization of resource utilization, especially in the capacity-constrained cloudlet system, and ii) the minimization of SLA violations. This trade-off depends on carrier requirements in terms of resource utilization and QoS level. In addition, an acceptable level of overall QoS is ensured. Finally, we show how our system performances depend on the number of deployed VNFs and the cloudlet computing capacities.

As future work, we will consider communication traffic requirements between VNFs and extend our approach to also support network resource provisioning during VNF placement.

8. REFERENCES

[1] Cisco visual networking index: Global mobile data traffic forecast update, 2015-2020 white paper, February 2016.

[2] B. Addis, D. Belabed, M. Bouet, and S. Secci. Virtual Network Functions Placement and Routing Optimization. In *IEEE 4th International Conference on Cloud Networking (CloudNet)*, pages 171–177, 2015.

[3] Alcatel-Lucent. White paper: Network functions virtualization - challenges and solutions, June 2013.

[4] M. Alicherry and T. Lakshman. Network aware resource allocation in distributed clouds. In *2012 Proceedings IEEE INFOCOM*, pages 963–971, 2012.

[5] J. Altmann and M. M. Kashef. Cost model based service placement in federated hybrid clouds. *Future Generation Computer Systems*, pages 79–90, 2014.

[6] F. Bari, S. R. Chowdhury, R. Ahmed, and R. Boutaba. On Orchestrating Virtual Network Functions. In *11th International Conference on Network and Service Management (CNSM)*, pages 50–56. IEEE, 2015.

[7] A. Baumgartner, V. S. Reddy, and T. Bauschert. Mobile core network virtualization: A model for combined virtual core network function placement and topology optimization. In *1st Conference on Network Softwarization (NETSOFT)*, pages 1–9. IEEE, 2015.

[8] F. Ben Jemaa, G. Pujolle, and M. Pariente. Cloudlet- and nfv-based carrier wi-fi architecture for a wider range of services. *Annals of Telecommunications*, pages 1–8, 2016.

[9] R. N. Calheiros and R. Buyya. Cost-effective provisioning and scheduling of deadline-constrained applications in hybrid clouds. *Lecture Notes in Computer Science*, pages 171–184, 2012.

[10] Y. Dong, X. Yang, J. Li, G. Liao, K. Tian, and H. Guan. High performance network virtualization with sr-iov. *Journal of Parallel and Distributed Computing*, pages 1471–1480, 2012.

[11] E. Gelenbe, G. Pujolle, and J. Nelson. *Introduction to queueing networks.* Wiley Chichester, 1998.

[12] C.-L. Hwang and A. S. M. Masud. *Multiple Objective Decision Making, Methods and Applications: a state-of-the-art survey.* Springer, 1979.

[13] J. Labetoulle, G. Pujolle, and C. Soula. Stationary distributions of flows in jackson networks. *Mathematics of operations research*, pages 173–185, 1981.

[14] J. Löfberg. Yalmip: A toolbox for modeling and optimization in matlab. In *International Symposium on Computer Aided Control Systems Design*, pages 284–289. IEEE, 2004.

[15] M. Malawski, K. Figiela, and J. Nabrzyski. Cost minimization for computational applications on hybrid cloud infrastructures. *Future Generation Computer Systems*, pages 1786–1794, 2013.

[16] R. T. Marler and J. S. Arora. The weighted sum method for multi-objective optimization: New insights. *Structural and Multidisciplinary Optimization*, pages 853–862, 2010.

[17] G. L. Nemhauser and L. A. Wolsey. Integer and combinatorial optimization. *John Wiley & Sons*, 1988.

[18] M. Pedram and I. Hwang. Power and performance modeling in a virtualized server system. *Proceedings of the International Conference on Parallel Processing Workshops*, pages 520–526, 2010.

[19] X. Qiu, W. L. Yeow, C. Wu, and F. C. M. Lau. Cost-minimizing preemptive scheduling of mapreduce workloads on hybrid clouds. In *IEEE International Workshop on Quality of Service*, pages 213–218, 2013.

[20] D. Raumer, F. Wohlfart, D. Scholz, P. Emmerich, and G. Carle. Performance exploration of software-based packet processing systems. In *Leistungs-, Zuverlässigkeits-und Verlässlichkeitsbewertung von Kommunikationsnetzen und verteilten Systemen, 8. GI/ITG-Workshop MMBnet*, 2015.

[21] R. Riggio, A. Bradai, T. Rasheed, J. Schulz-Zander, S. Kuklinski, and T. Ahmed. Virtual Network Functions Orchestration in Wireless Networks. In *11th International Conference on Network and Service Management (CNSM)*, pages 108—-116. IEEE, 2015.

[22] S. Son, G. Jung, and S. C. Jun. An SLA-based cloud computing that facilitates resource allocation in the distributed data centers of a cloud provider. *Journal of Supercomputing*, pages 606–637, 2013.

[23] T. Taleb, M. Bagaa, and A. Ksentini. User mobility-aware Virtual Network Function placement for Virtual 5G Network Infrastructure. In *IEEE International Conference on Communications (ICC)*, pages 3879–3884, 2015.

[24] R. Van Den Bossche, K. Vanmechelen, and J. Broeckhove. Cost-optimal scheduling in hybrid IaaS clouds for deadline constrained workloads. *IEEE 3rd International Conference on Cloud Computing*, pages 228–235, 2010.

[25] Q. Zhang, Q. Zhu, M. F. Zhani, R. Boutaba, and J. L. Hellerstein. Dynamic service placement in geographically distributed clouds. *IEEE Journal on Selected Areas in Communications*, pages 762–772, 2013.

[26] X. Zuo, G. Zhang, and W. Tan. Self-adaptive learning pso-based deadline constrained task scheduling for hybrid iaas cloud. *IEEE Transactions on Automation Science and Engineering*, pages 564–573, 2014.

Modeling and Analysis :
Energy Harvesting in the Internet of Things

Yu-Hsuan Chen
Department of Computer Science and
Information Engineering
National Taiwan University, Taipei, Taiwan
r03922015@ntu.edu.tw

Bryan Ng
School of Engineering and Computer Science
Victoria University of Wellington, New Zealand
bryan.ng@ecs.vuw.ac.nz

Winston K.G. Seah
School of Engineering and Computer Science
Victoria University of Wellington, New Zealand
winston.seah@ecs.vuw.ac.nz

Ai-Chun Pang
Graduate Institute of Networking and Multimedia
National Taiwan University, Taipei, Taiwan
acpang@csie.ntu.edu.tw

ABSTRACT

In the Internet of Things (IoT), the size constraint of those small and embedded devices limits the network lifetime because limited energy can be stored on these devices. In recent years, energy harvesting technology has attracted increasing attention, due to its ability to extend the network lifetime significantly. However, the performance of IoT devices powered by energy harvesting sources has not been fully analyzed and understood. In this paper, we model the energy harvesting process in IoT devices using slotted Carrier Sense Multiple Access with Collision Avoidance (CSMA /CA) mechanism of IEEE 802.15.4 standard, and analyze the performance in terms of delay and throughput. Our new model successfully integrates the energy harvesting process and binary backoff process through a unified Markov chain model. Finally, the new model is validated by simulation and the throughput errors between simulation and analytical model are no more than 6%. We demonstrate the application of the model with different energy harvesting rate corresponding to different sources such as solar and vibration energy harvesters.

Keywords

Internet of Things, Energy Harvesting, IEEE 802.15.4 standard, CSMA/CA, Markov process

1. INTRODUCTION

The uses of Internet of Things(IoT) appears in a range of different domains [23] such as structural health monitoring, animal tracking and environmental surveillance. Despite the ubiquitous deployment of IoT devices, one prevailing problem with the network is the limited energy stored on each

MSWiM '16, November 13-17, 2016, Malta, Malta

© 2016 ACM. ISBN 978-1-4503-4502-6/16/11... $15.00

DOI: http://dx.doi.org/10.1145/2988287.2989144

device. Replenishing the energy source by replacing batteries is a way to extend the network lifetime. However, in most applications it is difficult perhaps infeasible to replace the batteries because of the physical and environmental constraints. To deal with this problem, recent research efforts directed at designing energy efficient medium access control (MAC) protocols for IoT, and energy harvesting for IoT devices have emerged as a promising technique to prolong the network lifetime.

Powering IoT devices by energy harvesting technology is one half of the solution to the limited available energy while energy management is the other half. Since the energy harvesting rate is lower than the energy consumption rate [20], the sensing device stays awake for a short period of time after harvesting energy. Hence, the time spent harvesting energy must be taken into consideration when analyzing the performance of an energy harvesting IoT. Different MAC protocols for IoT with energy harvesting are analyzed through experiments, and the result shows that the energy harvesting process directly affects the performance of network throughput via the MAC protocols [5,9].

The IEEE 802.15.4 MAC protocol is widely adopted in IoT for example, 6LoWPAN and ZigBee. It specifies the semantics for low-cost and low-power sensor networks operation. One of the access mechanisms specified by IEEE 802.15.4 standard is slotted Carrier Sense Multiple Access with Collision Avoidance (CSMA/CA) mechanism, and several simulation-based studies *e.g.,* [13, 15–17], analyze this protocol through Markov chain models. The Markov models for 802.15.4 that appear in [15–17] successfully predict the performance of the protocol in terms of delay, reliability, throughput and power consumption. However, these models assume that sensing devices have unlimited power, which limits the applicability of the model and simulation result in practical settings.

Some studies *e.g.,* [4,8,11,21], have modelled the energy replenishment (recharging) process with varying degrees of success. A favoured approach for modelling the energy replenishment is the Markovian energy model which appears in [11] and [21]. The model in [11] assumes that the packet arrival and energy replenishment are both memoryless Poisson process, and the energy state transition follows the birth and death process. A further assumption is that packet transmissions are not interrupted by the energy replenishment, which is not valid in the real energy harvesting environment, but yields insights into how throughput is affected by energy harvesting process.

In [21], the energy model is modelled as a Bernoulli process and is unified with the slotted CSMA/CA mechanism of the IEEE 802.11 standard. In their model, the packet length and the backoff counter freezing time are not modelled, and the energy consumption during the channel sensing state is ignored, which does not reflect changes in residual energy correctly. In this paper, we model the slotted CSMA/CA mechanism of the IEEE 802.15.4 standard with the energy harvesting process through a unified Markov chain model. For simplicity, we assume that the network topology is a single hop network with a star topology. We derive the expressions for delay and throughput from the model, and validate the model through simulations. Through the proposed model, we characterize the effect of energy replenishment process on the performance of IEEE 802.15.4 MAC protocol, and show the effect of energy harvesting rate on the performance.

The contributions of this paper are: (i) a new model that integrates energy harvesting with slotted CSMA/CA mechanism of IEEE 802.15.4 standard within a unified Markov model, (ii) the energy harvesting process and the backoff process can take on different parameters and (iii) the energy consumption during binary backoff, clear channel assessment and packet transmission are necessarily distinct. Contributions (ii) and (iii) relaxes assumptions in existing models and reflects the real-world IoT devices behavior more closely.

The remainder of this paper is structured as follows. In Section II, we briefly describe the slotted CSMA/CA mechanism of the IEEE 802.15.4 standard, and explain how it interacts with the energy harvesting process. In Section III, we propose a Markov chain model of the slotted CSMA/CA mechanism integrated with the energy harvesting process. In Section IV, the model is validated by simulation and we compare the network performance with different energy harvesting rates. Section V concludes the paper.

2. OVERVIEW OF IEEE 802.15.4 SLOTTED CSMA/CA

In this section, we briefly explain the slotted CSMA/CA mechanism of the IEEE 802.15.4 standard [1], and highlight the interaction with an energy harvesting process. In the slotted CSMA/CA mechanism, there are three important variables [10] :

1. The *Number of Backoffs (NB)* is the number of times the algorithm has performed binary backoff before the packet transmission attempt. The value is initialized to 0 for a new transmission attempt.

2. The *Contention Window (CW)* is the number of backoff periods that the channel is required to be sensed idle before the transmission attempt. The value of CW is initialized to CW_0. If the node operation is in the Japanese 950 MHz band, CW_0 shall be set to 1; otherwise, CW_0 shall be set to 2.

3. The *Backoff Exponent (BE)* controls the number of backoff periods that the algorithm needs to backoff before sensing the channel. The number of backoff periods is a random variable between $[0, 2^{BE}-1]$.

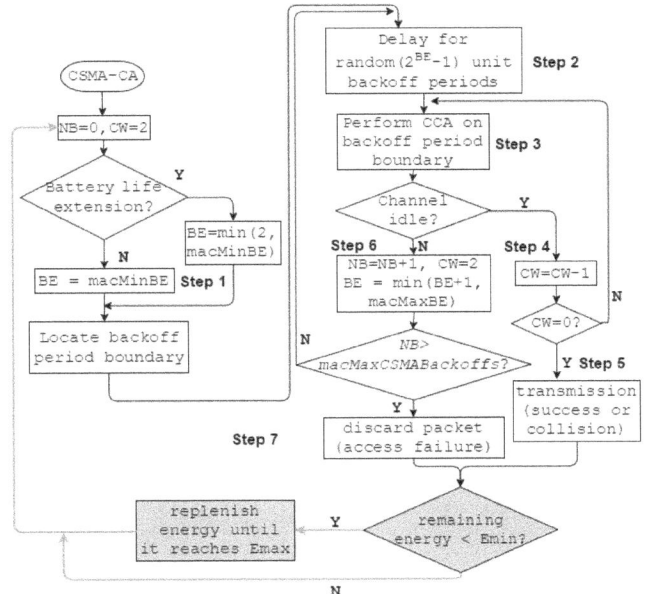

Figure 1: Slotted CSMA/CA mechanism with energy harvesting

Figure 1 is the flow chart of the slotted CSMA/CA mechanism with energy harvesting. First, the variables NB and CW are initialized to 0 and 2 respectively, while BE is initialized to min (2, $macMinBE$) or $macMinBE$ depending on the battery life extension(BLE). When BLE value is true, the MAC sublayer limits the random backoff exponent to ensure that the backoff duration, CCA and packet transmission is completed quickly (hence conserving energy). (**Step 1**). Next, the algorithm counts down a number of backoff periods which is randomly selected from $[0, 2^{BE}$-1] (**Step 2**). After counting down to 0, the algorithm performs Clear Channel Assessment (CCA) to check if the channel is idle (**Step 3**). If the channel is idle, CW is decreased by 1 (**Step 4**). If CW is equal to 0, the packet can be transmitted (**Step 5**), or the CCA is repeated. If the channel is sensed busy, NB is increased by 1, CW is reinitialized and BE is reinitialized to min($BE+1$, $macMaxBE$) (**Step 6**). If $macMaxCSMABackoffs$ is reached, the packet is discarded (**Step 7**); otherwise, the backoff process restarts.

In this paper, we assume the MAC layer checks the remaining energy of the device after the packet transmission or access failure and this is shown in the orange shaded blocks in Fig. 1. If the energy is below a threshold denoted by E_{min}, the energy harvesting process starts, and the energy is replenished before a new packet transmission attempt.

3. SYSTEM MODEL

In this section, we integrate an energy harvesting process to the IEEE 802.15.4 slotted CSMA/CA mechanism to characterize the performance of a network of IoT devices powered by energy harvesting. We focus on a single hop star network, in which every device transmits packets to the personal area network (PAN) coordinator and receives an acknowledgement (ACK). In the model, we assume that each device has a supercapacitor to store energy, and the maximum energy

Table 1: Symbols used to describe the System Model

Symbol	Description
m_0	$macMinBE$
m	$macMAXCSMABackoffs$
W_0	$2^{macMinBE}$
W_i	$2^i W_0$, for $1 \le i \le m$
$E_{\max}$	Maximum energy capacity of the supercapacitor
$E_{\min}$	Minimum energy threshold, $L_t + (m+1) + 1$
L_0	The number of idle states
L_t	Duration for packet transmission and receiving ACK
P_c	Probability that collision occurs during packet transmission
α	Probability that the channel is busy in phase CCA1
β	Probability that the channel is busy in phase CCA2
q_0	Probability that the device keeps idle

capacity of the supercapacitor is $E_{\max}$ unit.

During normal operation, defined as the MAC protocol in the following set of states: { idle, backoff, channel sensing, packet transmission }, energy is decreased. After the packet transmission process (success or collision) is finished, the device checks its remaining energy level. If the remaining energy is less than $E_{\min}$ units, the device halts operation and enters the energy harvesting process; otherwise, the device waits for a new packet arrival.

3.1 Energy harvesting process

Energy harvesting is the process by which ambient energy is captured and stored in the supercapacitor. We assume that the energy harvesting process follows the Poisson process to reflect the deployments of IoT in several sensor network scenarios such as structural health monitoring environments [6], bridge monitoring [3] and harvesting solar energy in situations whereby the solar irradiance is variable due to the passing of clouds [2]. The energy harvesting process stops when the energy level in the supercapacitor reaches $E_{\max}$ and the CSMA/CA mechanism restarts operation.

3.2 State space of the Markov model

The Markov chain model for the IEEE 802.15.4 slotted CSMA/CA mechanism with energy harvesting is shown in Fig. 2. The state space is categorized into four sets of states and each set is characterized with different indices. Let $e(t)$, $f(t)$, $h(t)$, $s(t)$ and $k(t)$ be stochastic processes representing the the backoff stage number, the state of the backoff counter, the residual energy level of a device, the energy harvested and the number of packets awaiting transmission at time t respectively. The tuple $\{\delta(t), e(t), f(t), h(t)\}$ form the set of **transmission states** whereby $\delta(t)$ is the indicator process of a successful transmission or otherwise defined in Eq.(1). This set of states are grouped and labelled as "Tx #0" and "Tx #m" in Fig.2(a).

$$\delta(t) = \begin{cases} -1 & \text{if transmission successful at time } t \\ -2 & \text{if transmission unsuccessfull at time } t \end{cases} \quad (1)$$

Transmission states $\{-1, i, j, s\}$ and $\{-2, i, j, s\}$ represent the successful and collided packet transmissions respectively with the indices bounded by $i \in [0, m]$, $j \in [0, L_t - 1]$ and

$s \in [E_{\max} - 2 - m - L_t, E_{\max} - m - 3]$.

The backoff process is characterised by stochastic processes $e(t)$, $f(t)$ and $h(t)$ and the tuple $\{e(t), f(t), h(t)\}$ denotes the set of **backoff states** and the set of **CCA states** (these sets are labelled as "Backoff" and "Idle" in Fig. 2(a). Backoff states $\{i, w, s\}$ are bounded by $i \in [0, m]$, $w \in [1, W_i - 1]$, in which i is the backoff stage, and w is the backoff counter. The first phase (CCA1) and the second phase (CCA2) of the CCA are denoted by states $\{i, 0, s\}$ and $\{i, -1, s\}$, $i \in [0, m]$ respectively.

The behaviour of an idle device waiting for a new packet arrival is modelled by $k(t)$ and $s(t)$, therefore the tuple $\{k(t), s(t)\}$ denotes the set of **idle states** with the tuple defined in the range of $\{c, s\}$, $c \in [0, L_0 - 1]$, $s \in [0, E_{\max} - 1]$. Note that the degree of traffic saturation is regulated through the parameter L_0. Finally, the energy harvesting is governed by a single process $s(t)$ with $s \in [0, E_{\max} - 1]$ and it forms a sub-chain shown in Fig.2(c).

The variable L_t denotes the number of backoff periods for packet transmission and receiving ACK and it is expressed as $L_t = L + t_{\text{ack}} + L_{\text{ack}}$, where L is the number of backoff periods for packet transmission, t_{ack} is the idle period between the packet transmission and receiving ACK, and L_{ack} is the number of backoff periods for receiving ACK. Based on the 802.15.4 standard specifications [1] we set $t_{\text{ack}} = 1$ backoff period and $L_{\text{ack}} = 2$ backoff periods. Throughout this paper, we assume that the duration for successful packet transmission and the duration for collided packet transmission are identical.

Recall that the states $s \in [0, E_{\max} - 1]$ are energy harvesting states with s representing the residual energy level of the device, and the energy harvesting is governed by a Poisson process with rate λ. The value of λ dictates the energy units harvested in a backoff period. According to the energy consumption rates in different states, we assume that there is no energy consumption in backoff states [17]. In our model, idle states collectively consume one unit of energy, thus CCA1 and CCA2 together consume one unit energy, and each of the transmission state consumes one unit of energy. The value of $E_{\min}$ is the sum of the energy consumed during packet transmission, the total number of backoff stages, and the energy consumed in idle states, thus:

$$E_{\min} = L_t + (m+1) + 1.$$

In Fig. 2(c), the constant e is equal to $E_{\min} - 1$. Table 1 lists the symbols and the meanings in the context of the Markov model.

3.3 State transitions

Our model in Fig. 2 is composed of layers, and these layers are linked to energy harvesting states. Each layer has the same structure in terms of states and transitions. When a device terminates packet transmission and the remaining energy level s is greater than $E_{\min}$, the device transits to the idle state in another layer with probability q_0, or transits to the backoff state with probability $1 - q_0$. But if s is less than $E_{\min}$ unit, the device transits to the energy harvesting state. For example, if the packet transmission is done in the state $(-1, 0, L_t - 1, E_{\max} - 2 - L_t)$ and $(E_{\max} - 2 - L_t)$ is greater than $E_{\min}$, the state of the device transits to the idle state $(0, (E_{\max} - 2 - L_t) - 1)$ with probability q_0.

The index of a layer models the remaining energy level of the device when in idle states and this index is an integer

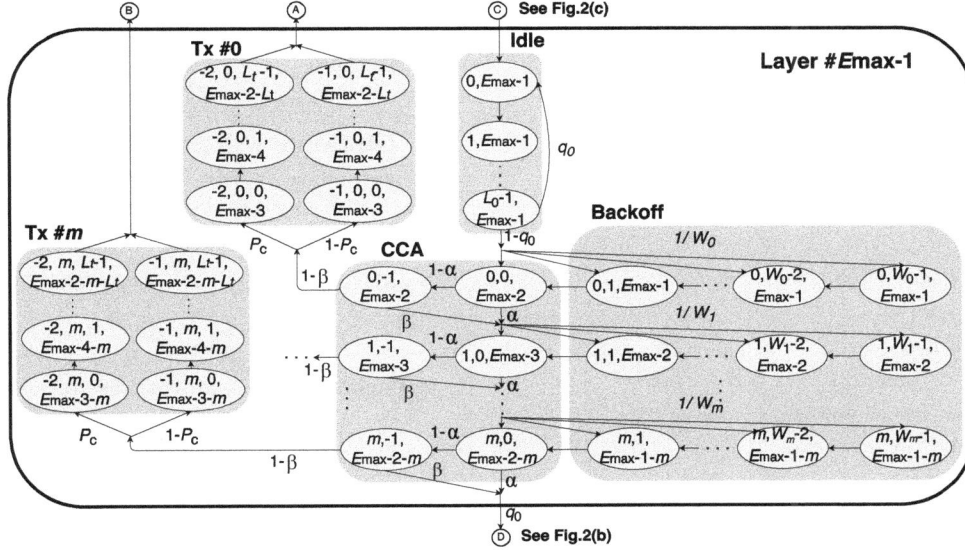

(a) Transitions and states of the Markov chain model for CSMA/CA depicted as a single layer.

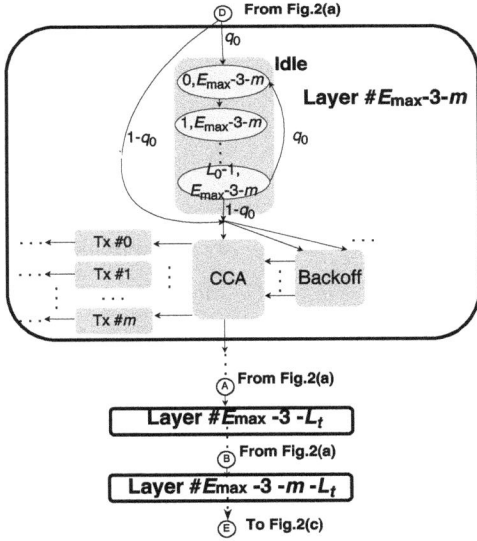

(b) Transitions between adjacent CSMA/CA backoff layers. This figure is connected to Fig. 2(a).

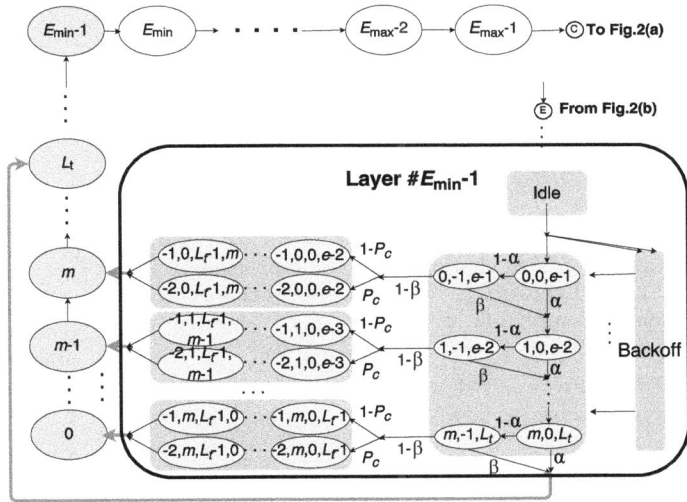

(c) Transitions and states of the energy harvesting sub-chain.

Figure 2: Markov model

defined over the range of $E_{\min} - 1$ to $E_{\max} - 1$. In energy harvesting states, the permissible state transitions are shaded (green in Fig. 2(c)) and the sojourn time of energy harvesting states follows an exponential distribution.

Using simplified notation $\Pr\{\mathcal{E}\}$ where $\mathcal{E}$ denotes a transition event of the MAC, the non-null state transition probabilities of the Markov chain are:

$\Pr\{$harvesting one unit of energy$\}$
$$= P(s+1|s) = e^{\lambda}\lambda, \quad \text{for } 0 \leq s < E_{\max} - 1, \tag{2}$$

$\Pr\{$transit to the first backoff stage from an idle state$\}$
$$= P(0, w, s|L_0, s)$$
$$= P(0, 0, s-1|L_0, s)$$
$$= \frac{1 - q_0}{W_0}, \quad \text{for } 1 \leq w < W_0, \tag{3}$$

$\Pr\{$the decrement of the backoff counter$\}$
$$= P(i, w-1, s|i, w, s)$$
$$= P(i, 0, s-1|i, 1, s)$$
$$= 1, \quad \text{for } 0 \leq i \leq m \text{ and } 1 < w < W_0, \tag{4}$$

$\Pr\{$new backoff after channel sensed busy during CCA1 or CCA2$\}$
$$= P(i, w, s|i-1, 0, s)$$
$$= P(i, 0, s-1|i-1, 0, s)$$
$$= \frac{\alpha + (1-\alpha)\beta}{W_i}, \quad \text{for } 1 \leq i \leq m \text{ and } 1 \leq w < W_i, \tag{5}$$

$\Pr\{$channel is idle during CCA1 and CCA2,
  upon a successful packet transmission$\}$
$$= P(-1, i, 0, s-1|i, 0, s)$$
$$= (1-\alpha)(1-\beta)(1-P_c), \tag{6}$$

$\Pr\{$channel is idle during CCA1 and CCA2,
  after a collision$\}$
$$= P(-2, i, 0, s-1|i, 0, s)$$
$$= (1-\alpha)(1-\beta)P_c. \tag{7}$$

The probability that the device is in the wait state (awaiting packet arrivals) or is charged after the transmission is denoted by Eq. (8) and Eq. (9) respectively. Therefore, the non-null transition probabilities are:

$\Pr\{$waiting state after a packet transmission$\}$
$$= P(0, s-1|-1, i, L_t - 1, s)$$
$$= P(0, s-1|-2, i, L_t - 1, s) = \begin{cases} q_0, & \text{if } s \geq E_{\min} \\ 0, & \text{if } s < E_{\min} \end{cases}, \tag{8}$$

$\Pr\{$energy harvesting after the packet transmission$\}$
$$= P(s|-1, i, L_t - 1, s)$$
$$= P(s|-2, i, L_t - 1, s) = \begin{cases} 0, & \text{if } s \geq E_{\min} \\ 1, & \text{if } s < E_{\min} \end{cases}. \tag{9}$$

If the remaining energy level is below $E_{\min}$, the device halts normal operation and the energy harvesting process starts. Subsequently, the probability that the device is in a wait state (awaiting packet arrival) or is charged after the access failure is given by Eq. (10) and Eq. (11). The device waits for a new packet arrival only if the remaining energy level is

above $E_{\min}$. Thus, the non-null transition probabilities are:

$\Pr\{$waiting state after an access failure$\}$
$$= P(0, s-1|m, 0, s)$$
$$= \begin{cases} q_0 \times (\alpha + (1-\alpha)\beta), & \text{if } s \geq E_{\min}, \\ 0, & \text{if } s < E_{\min} \end{cases}, \tag{10}$$

$\Pr\{$energy harvesting after the access failure$\}$
$$= P(s|m, 0, s) = \begin{cases} 0, & \text{if } s \geq E_{\min} \\ \alpha + (1-\alpha)\beta, & \text{if } s < E_{\min} \end{cases}. \tag{11}$$

3.4 Stationary distribution

The stationary distribution of the embedded Markov chain of Fig. 2 is a vector $\boldsymbol{\pi}$. For ease of presentation, we decompose the vector into four different states:

- **idle states**, the stationary probability is
$$\pi_{c,s}, c \in (0, L_0 - 1), s \in (E_{\min} - 1, E_{\max} - 1),$$

- **backoff / CCA states**, the stationary probability is
$$\pi_{i,w,s}, i \in (0, m), w \in (-1, W_i - 1),$$

- **packet transmission states**, the stationary probability is
$$\pi_{-1,i,j,s} \text{ and } \pi_{-2,i,j,s}, i \in (0, m), j \in (0, L_t - 1),$$

- **energy harvesting states**, the stationary probability is
$$\pi_s, s \in (0, E_{\max} - 1),$$

such that
$$\boldsymbol{\pi} = \left(\pi_{c,s} \cup \pi_{i,w,s} \cup \pi_{-1,i,j,s} \cup \pi_{-2,i,j,s} \cup \pi_s\right).$$

Using this notation, the transition probabilities that appear earlier in Eq. (3) and Eq. (4) are simplified to:
$$\pi_{i,w,s+1} = \frac{W_i - w}{W_i} \pi_{i,0,s}, \tag{12}$$

where w is from 1 to $W_i - 1$. Similarly, the transition probabilities in Eq. (5) are expressed as
$$\pi_{i,0,s-i} = (\alpha + (1-\alpha)\beta)^i \pi_{0,0,s}. \tag{13}$$

Summing the state probabilities for a layer indexed by s (i.e. Eq. (3) - (7), Eq. (12) and Eq. (13)), we obtain the probability the Markov chain is in layer s:

$$L_0 \times \pi_{0,s} + \frac{\pi_{0,0,s-1}}{2}\left(\frac{1 - (2x)^{m+1}}{1 - 2x}W_0 + \frac{1 - x^{m+1}}{1 - x}\right)$$
$$+ (1-\alpha)\frac{1 - x^{m+1}}{1 - x}\pi_{0,0,s-1} + L_t(1 - x^{m+1})\pi_{0,0,s-1}$$
$$= \pi_{0,s} \times L_0 + \pi_{0,0,s-1} \times$$
$$\left\{\frac{1 - (2x)^{m+1}}{2(1 - 2x)}W_0 + \frac{1 - x^{m+1}}{1 - x}\left[\frac{3}{2} - \alpha + (1-x)L_t\right]\right\}, \tag{14}$$

where $x = \alpha + (1-\alpha)\beta$.

From Eq. (14) we expand the expressions for $\pi_{0,s}$ and $\pi_{0,0,s-1}$ and this yields:

$$\pi_{0,s} = \begin{cases} \frac{\pi_{E_{\max}-1}}{1-q_0}, & \text{if } s = E_{\max} - 1 \\ \frac{q_0(Q_a(s)+Q_b(s))}{1-q_0}, & \text{otherwise} \end{cases}, \quad (15)$$

and $\pi_{0,0,s-1}$ is given by:

$$\pi_{0,0,s-1} = \begin{cases} (1-q_0)\pi_{0,s}, & \text{if } s = E_{\max} - 1 \\ (1-q_0)(Q_a(s)+Q_b(s)+\pi_{0,s}), & \text{otherwise} \end{cases}, \quad (16)$$

where $Q_a(s)$ is the state transition probability to layer s due to the packet transmission and $Q_b(s)$ is the state transition probability to s conditioned on access failure. Using Eq. (15) and Eq. (16), we establish the relationship between $\pi_{0,s}$ and $\pi_{0,0,s-1}$ which expresses the probability the Markov chain is in state s (Eq. (14)) as a function of $\pi_{0,s}$.

The derivation of $Q_a(s)$ is as follows: we introduce the auxiliary variable $r = (s+1) + L_t$, to denote the remaining energy level of the device during its successful CCA1 and CCA2. For $r+1 > E_{\max} - 1$, the corresponding $Q_a(s)$ is 0, while for $r+1 \leq E_{\max} - 1$, we obtain $Q_a(s)$ as:

$$Q_a(s) = \sum_{i=(r+1)+0}^{n} (1-\alpha)(1-\beta)\pi_{i-(r+1),0,r}$$
$$= \sum_{i=(r+1)+0}^{n} (1-\alpha)(1-\beta)x^{i-(r+1)}\pi_{0,0,i-1},$$

where $(r+1)$ and $n = \min(E_{\max}-1, (r+1)+m)$ are the respective minimum and maximum index of layers that the state transition from these layers to state $(0,s)$ after the packet transmission exists. This relationship is direct from Eq. (6) and Eq. (7). Moreover, from Eq. (10), the expression for $Q_b(s)$ is readily obtained as:

$$Q_b(s) = \begin{cases} 0, & \text{if } d > E_{\max} - 1 \\ x \times \pi_{m,0,s+1}, & \text{if } d \leq E_{\max} - 1 \end{cases}, \quad (17)$$

where $d = (s+1) + m + 1$, which is the index of the layer and the state transition from the layer to state $(0,s)$ after an access failure. When $d \leq E_{\max} - 1$, the probability the Markov chain transits to state s can be rewritten as follows:

$$Q_b(s) = x \times \pi_{m,0,s+1} = x^{m+1}\pi_{0,0,d-1}.$$

Now, we will derive the stationary distribution expressions for the energy harvesting states $\pi_s, s \in (0, E_{\max} - 1)$. Starting from the expressions in Eq. (2), Eq. (9) and Eq. (11), we have:

$$\pi_s = \begin{cases} R_a(s) + R_b(s), & \text{if } s = 0 \\ R_a(s) + R_b(s) + \pi_{s-1}, & \text{if } 0 < s \leq E_{\min} - 1 \\ \pi_{E_{\min}-1}, & \text{if } E_{\min} - 1 < s \end{cases} \quad (18)$$

where $R_a(s)$ is the probability that the device starts energy harvesting process with remaining energy level s after the packet transmission, and $R_b(s)$ is the probability that the device starts energy harvesting process with remaining energy level s after the access failure.

The derivation of $R_a(s)$ is similar to that of $Q_a(s)$. Denote the remaining energy level of the device during its successful CCA1 and CCA2 by u such that $u = s + L_t$. When $u+1 > E_{\max} - 1$, the value of $R_a(s)$ is 0. When $u+1 \leq E_{\max} - 1$,

the expression of $R_a(s)$ is

$$R_a(s) = \sum_{i=v}^{k} (1-\alpha)(1-\beta)\pi_{i-(u+1),0,u}$$
$$= \sum_{i=v}^{k} (1-\alpha)(1-\beta)x^{i-(u+1)}\pi_{0,0,i-1}, \quad (19)$$

where $v = \max(u+1, E_{\min}-1)$ and $k = \min((u+1)+m, E_{\max}-1)$ are the minimum and maximum index of those layers that can transit to state (s) after the access failure, respectively. The expression of $R_b(s)$ is

$$R_b(s) = \begin{cases} 0, & \text{if } s+m+1 < E_{\min}-1 \\ 0, & \text{if } s+m+1 > E_{\max}-1 \\ x \times \pi_{m,0,s}, & \text{if } E_{\max}-1 \geq s+m+1 \geq E_{\min}-1 \end{cases}. \quad (20)$$

When $s+m+1 \geq E_{\min}-1$, we can rewrite $R_b(s)$ as

$$x \times \pi_{m,0,s} = x^{m+1}\pi_{0,0,s+m}$$

The probability of each state in Eq. (14) - (20) can be rewritten as a function of $\pi_{0,0,s-1}$, $s \in (E_{\min}-1, E_{\max}-1)$. Given that we have derived the relations of $\pi_{0,s}$ and $\pi_{0,0,s-1}$, the sum of the stationary probability of Markov chain can further be expressed by $\pi_{0,E_{\max}-1}$.

We now derive the remaining unknowns α, β and P_c by considering the sojourn time of the states. Let $\boldsymbol{P}$ be the limiting probability of the Markov chain in Fig. 2. For CCA1 states, the limiting probability $P_{i,0,s}$ and its relationship with $\pi_{i,0,s}$ is given by:

$$P_{i,0,s} = \lim_{t \to \infty} P_{i,0,s}(t) = \frac{\pi_{i,0,s}E(T_{i,0,s})}{\sum_{k \in S} \pi_k E(T_k)},$$

where T_k is the sojourn time of state k, and S presents a set of discrete states of the Markov chain. Because the sojourn time of each state in each layer is normalized to a unit backoff period, and the sojourn time of energy harvesting states depends only on the harvesting rate λ, the limiting probability of CCA1 states is readily expressed as a function of $\pi_{0,E_{\max}-1}$.

Next, we introduce a probability τ that the device performs its CCA1 in a random backoff period, which is equal to the sum of the limiting probability of CCA1 states. Similar to [16], the value of τ is given by

$$\tau = \sum_{s=E_{\min}-2}^{E_{\max}-2} \frac{1-x^{m+1}}{1-x} P_{0,0,s}. \quad (21)$$

Now, we can derive the probabilities α, β and P_c. The conditional collision probability P_c is the probability that the collision occurs during packet transmission. In the slotted CSMA/CA mechanism, a collision occurs only if at least one of the remaining $N-1$ devices start packet transmission in a same backoff period. Hence, P_c is

$$P_c = 1 - (1-\tau)^{N-1}, \quad (22)$$

where N is the number of nodes.

The probabilities α and β are the probabilities that the channel is sensed busy during CCA1 and CCA2:

$$\alpha = \alpha_1 + \alpha_2, \quad (23)$$

where α_1 is the probability that the channel is sensed busy during CCA1 due to the packet transmission (the proof of (23) appears in [17] and [16].) Since the probability that a device starts to transmit a packet is $\tau(1-\alpha)(1-\beta)$, and $1-(1-\tau)^{N-1}$ is the probability that at least one of the $N-1$ remaining devices stay in CCA1 states, α_1 is

$$\alpha_1 = L(1-(1-\tau)^{N-1})(1-\alpha)(1-\beta)$$

and α_2 is the probability that the channel is sensed busy during CCA1 due to ACK transmission, which is expressed as:

$$\alpha_2 = L_{ack}\frac{N\tau(1-\tau)^{N-1}(1-\alpha)(1-\beta)}{(1-(1-\tau)^N)(1-\alpha)(1-\beta)}$$
$$\times (1-(1-\tau)^{N-1})(1-\alpha)(1-\beta)$$
$$= L_{ack}\frac{N\tau(1-\tau)^{N-1}}{1-(1-\tau)^N}(1-(1-\tau)^{N-1})(1-\alpha)(1-\beta),$$

where $(1-(1-\tau)^N)(1-\alpha)(1-\beta)$ is the probability that at least one device can transmit a packet, and $N\tau(1-\tau)^{N-1}(1-\alpha)(1-\beta)$ is the probability that only one device is transmitting the packet. The probability that the channel is sensed busy (denoted by β):

$$\beta = \frac{1-(1-\tau)^{N-1}+N\tau(1-\tau)^{N-1}}{2-(1-\tau)^N+N\tau(1-\tau)^{N-1}}. \quad (24)$$

Further details about deriving the probabilities α, β and P_c appear in [17]. With the complete characterization of these transition probabilities, the model is solved numerically.

4. MODEL VALIDATION

In this section, we validate the proposed model by simulation, and analyze the performance in terms of delay, throughput and reliability. The simulation is developed in Matlab.

4.1 Simulation Setup

The algorithm follows the pseudo code proposed in [17] and we extend it to accommodate acknowledgements and the unsaturated traffic conditions. Because the device only changes state at the backoff period boundaries, we normalize the simulation step to one backoff period. The total simulation time is 10^8 backoff periods. The simulation is performed 10 times with different random seeds, and it shows that the percentage differences of each result value and the average value are all less than 1%.

4.2 Expression of Throughput and Delay

The average throughput from the simulation is simply:

$$\text{Throughput(sim)} = \frac{n_s \times L}{T_{\text{simulation}}}$$

where n_s denotes the number of successfully transmitted packets, and $T_{\text{simulation}}$ refers to the total simulation time. The unit of the packet length L and the unit of simulation time are both a backoff period. Similarly to [17], we derive the average throughput from our analytical model in Section III by the following expression:

$$\text{Throughput(ana)} = LN\tau(1-\tau)^{N-1}(1-\alpha)(1-\beta)$$

Next, we derive the average delay. We define the average delay of a packet as the time from the first attempt of backoff, until the time when the ACK is received. Consistent with the analytical model, we do not consider the delay of discarded packets due to the collision or access failure. The

Table 2: energy harvesting rate with 10cm^2 or 10cm^3 harvesting material

Material	Power Density ($\mu\text{W/cm}^2$)	Energy Harvesting Rate (mW)	Energy Harvesting Rate[†]
Electromagnetic [19]	433[**]	4.33	0.144
Piezoelectric [7]	106.9[**]	1.069	0.0356
Electrostatic (Tribo-electric) [18]	0.648	0.0064	0.0002
Thermoelectric [12]	60	0.6	0.02
Solar - direct sunlight [14]	16800	168	5.6

[†] the energy units harvested in a backoff period
[**] unit is $\mu\text{W/cm}^3$

expression of the average delay is as follows:

$$\text{Delay(sim)} = \frac{T_{\text{delay}}}{n_s} \times T$$

where T_{delay} denotes the sum of packets' delay while T is the length of the backoff period. According to IEEE 802.15.4 standard [1], a backoff period is 20 symbols long (*aUnitBackoffPeriod*), and 1 symbol is 4 bits. For a typical bit rate of 250kbps, T is $\frac{80\text{bits}}{250\text{kbps}} = 0.32\text{ms}$.

The derivation of the average delay from the analytical model is similar to that in [16]. However, in our model, we assume that the packet is dropped if the collision or access failure occurs, so *macMaxFrameRetries* = 0.

4.3 Model Validation and Performance Analysis

The energy harvesting rates from different energy harvesting technologies with dimension 10cm^2 or 10cm^3 is listed in Table 2. In [19], they harvested energy through an electromagnetic transducer constructed with two permanent magnets and a 11cm^3 coil. Output power of 4.33mW is achieved with a 90Ω load resistor connected to the transducer. In [7], the energy is harvested using piezoelectric bimorph/magnet composites and an AC power line. When the power is switched on, the AC magnetic field interacts with the magnetization of the magnet inciting the piezoelectric cantilever. In [18], they implement the electrodes, diode ladder circuit and a energy harvesting circuit on skirt paddles. Due to the triboelectric effect, these paddles generate electrostatic energy when brushed rapidly against each other.

In [12], they wear the 9cm^2 thermoelectric energy harvester on the wrist. Using the temperature difference between the skin and ambient temperature, the thermoelectric energy is generated. The maximum generated power is about $60\mu\text{W/cm}^2$ indoors and about $600\mu\text{W/cm}^2$ at a temperature of 0° C. In [14], the National Institute of Water and Atmospheric Research(NIWA) conducts the SolarView calculation for a year in Kelburn, Wellington. The average Solar Energy reachers 168mW.

In this paper, we assume that the energy consumption rate for packet transmission is 30mW [16], and the actual length of a backoff period is 0.32ms. Using this relationship, the energy harvesting rate from mW is easily converted to the

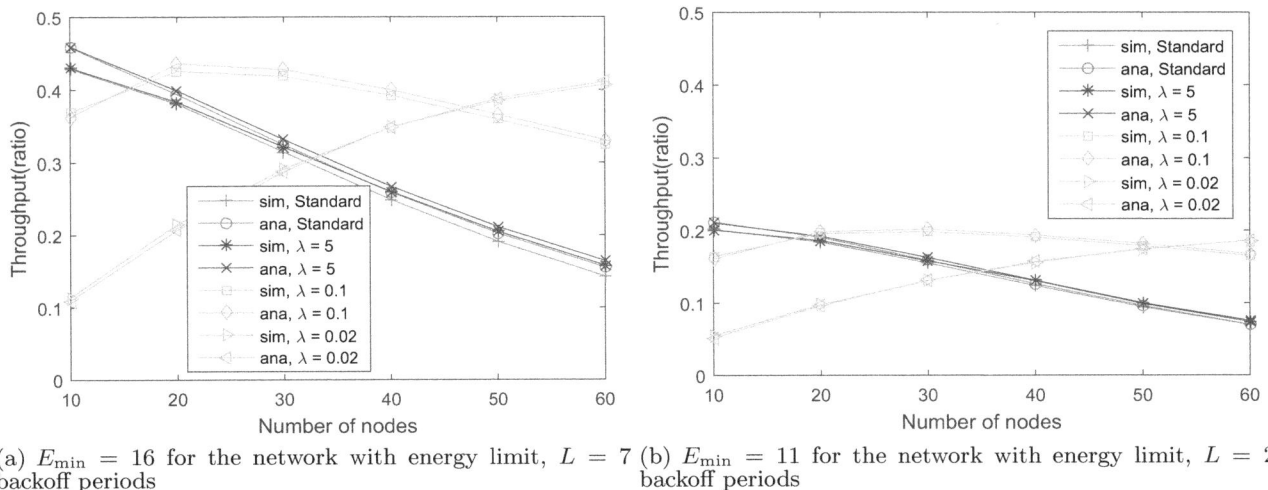

(a) $E_{\min} = 16$ for the network with energy limit, $L = 7$ backoff periods (b) $E_{\min} = 11$ for the network with energy limit, $L = 2$ backoff periods

Figure 3: The average throughput derived from the simulation (sim) and analytical model (ana) under different parameter setting. The parameter $E_{\max} = 30$ for the network with energy constraint, $q_0 = 0.3$, $m_0 = 3$ and $m = 4$

energy unit per backoff period and this is used to tabulate the harvesting rate in the fourth column of Table 2. In the paper, we choose the harvesting rate $\lambda = 5, 0.1, 0.02$ as the simulation parameter, in which the rate $= 5$ is close to the rate given by outdoor solar energy harvesters, the rate $= 0.1$ is close to the rate given by electromagnetic energy harvesters, and rate $= 0.02$ is close to the rate given by thermoelectric energy harvesters.

Fig. 3 compares the average throughput derived from the simulation and our analytical model. The analytical model matches the simulation result closely. Subsequently, we analyze the throughput of the network under different energy harvesting rate λ. The energy harvesting rate is the average unit of the energy harvested in one backoff period. In our results, the curves/points labelled "standard" refer to the basic IEEE 802.15.4 protocol in which the devices have no energy constraint (i.e. no energy harvesting state in the model). It should be noted that the evaluation is also carried out under reasonable heavy traffic (i.e. $q_0 = 0.3$).

From the performance evaluation: (i) the throughput of the network with solar energy harvesting sources is almost equal to the throughput of network without energy constraint, and (ii) a higher energy harvesting rate yields a lower throughput. In line with our expectations, there is an upper bound on the throughput. Our evaluation also agrees with results from previous studies that show that energy harvesting directly affects the throughput, but our results go one step further and show that it is range bound (as evidenced by the asymptotic levelling of throughput). The reasoning behind the better performance is that energy harvesting nodes introduce lesser contention because of their intermittent transmission attempts which essentially reduces the overall attempts on the channel. It is well known that CSMA protocols suffer throughout degradation when large number of nodes compete for access [22], and in this case, the energy harvesting states reduces the number of devices contending for channel access thus improving throughput.

Next, we analyze the throughput of the network with different packet lengths L. By comparing Fig. 3(a) and Fig.

3(b), we observe that with the same number of nodes and the same energy harvesting rate, the network with longer packet length L has better throughput. When L becomes bigger, the value of $E_{\min}$ increases, which means that the number of times a device attempts to transmit a packet before the energy harvesting process starts may decrease. But the simulation result shows that the length of a packet L has more influence than the value of $E_{\min}$ on the network throughput.

Figure 4 plots the average delay versus the number of nodes. The result of the analytical model tracks the simulation result well. We observe that the average delay of the network without the energy constraint is higher than the network with energy harvesting sources, and with the fixed number of nodes, the average delay decreases as the energy harvesting rate decreases. It is interesting that with lower energy harvesting rate, the delay increases faster as the number of nodes increases. By comparing Fig. 4(a) and Fig. 4(b), it is clear that with the same energy harvesting rate and the number of nodes, the larger packet lengths yields higher delay, and the delay is exaggerated when the number of nodes increase.

In Fig. 5, we seek to determine the network performance as a function of parameter $E_{\max}$. We compare the network throughput, delay and reliability with different energy harvesting rate and $E_{\max} = 30, 40, 50$, and 60. We find that the performance difference is insignificant with increasing $E_{\max}$. Hence, we conclude that when the energy harvesting rate λ is between 0.02 and 1 with $E_{\max}$ is between 30 to 60, $E_{\max}$ is not an important factor on the network performance.

Based on the results presented in Figs. 3–5, we demonstrated that our Markov chain model successfully predicts the behavior of the slotted CSMA/CA protocol of IEEE 802.15.4 standard with energy harvesting process. Additionally, we reaffirm previous findings [21] that the network performance is indeed different if the energy constraint of each device in considered.

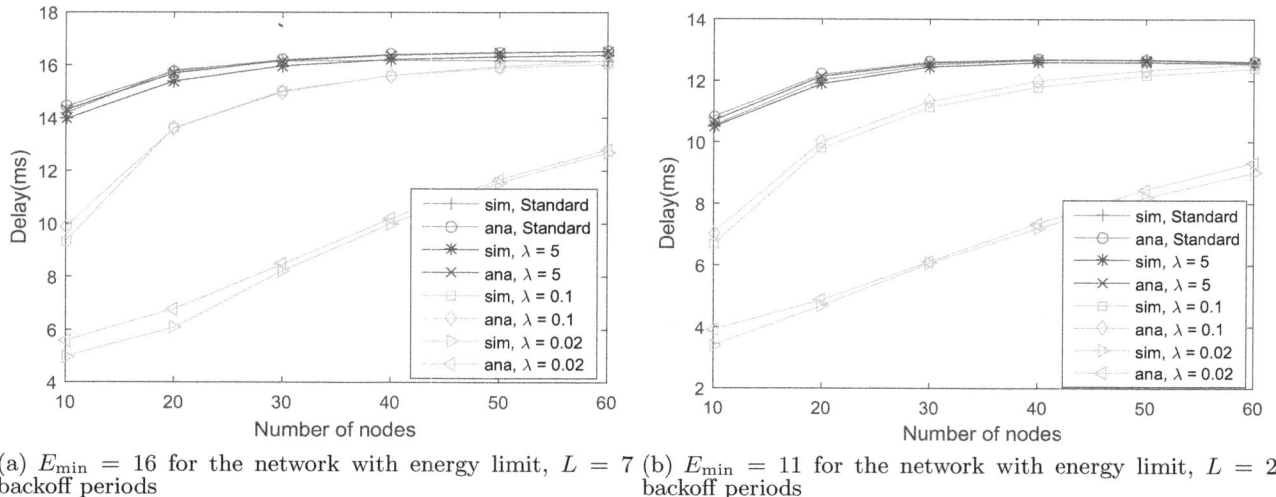

(a) $E_{\min} = 16$ for the network with energy limit, $L = 7$ backoff periods

(b) $E_{\min} = 11$ for the network with energy limit, $L = 2$ backoff periods

Figure 4: The average delay derived from the simulation(sim) and analytical model(ana) under different parameter setting. The parameter $E_{\max} = 30$ for the network with energy constraint, $q_0 = 0.3$, $m_0 = 3$ and $m = 4$

5. CONCLUSIONS

In this paper, we have analyzed the performance of the slotted CSMA/CA mechanism of the IEEE 802.15.4 standard taking into consideration the energy harvesting process in each IoT device. Insights to networked IoT performance with energy harvesting is expected to contribute to improving the prevailing energy constraints plaguing WSNs.

A Markov chain model is presented to analyze the performance of the slotted CSMA/CA mechanism with the energy harvesting process, and the performance is compared in terms of throughput, delay and reliability. The validity of the proposed model is proven by simulation. Analytical result shows that the performance of IoT devices with energy harvesting sources is different from typical CSMA/CA curves. We find that IoT devices with higher energy harvesting rate may have lower throughput if the network has large number of active nodes.

As the first attempt to incorporate energy harvesting process into the CSMA/CA mechanism for IEEE 802.15.4 standard, we make the assumption that the energy harvesting process follows the Poisson distribution and devices consume energy in discrete units. In practice, these assumptions may introduce errors into the predicted performance. Relaxing the above mentioned assumptions are immediate directions to improve the model and is left as the future work.

6. ACKNOWLEDGEMENT

This work was supported by Victoria University of Wellington's University Research Fund Grant #8-1620-207086-3468, by Excellent Research Projects of National Taiwan University under Grant 105R89082B, by Ministry of Science and Technology under Grant 105-2221-E-002-144-MY3, Information and Communications Research Laboratories of the Industrial Technology Research Institute (ICL/ITRI) and Institute for Information Industry (III).

7. REFERENCES

[1] *IEEE Std 802.15.4-2011, September, Part 15.4: Low-Rate Wireless Personal Area Networks (LR-WPANs).* IEEE, 2011.

[2] E. Arias-Castro, J. Kleissl, and M. Lave. A Poisson model for anisotropic solar ramp rate correlations . *Solar Energy*, 101:192–202, 2014.

[3] Y. Chen, C.-A. Tan, M. Q. Feng, and Y. Fukuda. A video assisted approach for structural health monitoring of highway bridges under normal traffic. *Proc. SPIE*, 6174:1–18, 2006.

[4] N. Dang, R. Valentini, E. Bozorgzadeh, M. Levorato, and N. Venkatasubramanian. A Unified Stochastic Model for Energy Management in Solar-Powered Embedded Systems. In *Proc. of the IEEE/ACM International Conference on Computer-Aided Design (ICCAD)*, pages 621 – 626, 2015.

[5] Z. Eu, H. Tan, and W. Seah. Design and performance analysis of MAC schemes for Wireless Sensor Networks Powered by Ambient Energy Harvesting. *Ad Hoc Networks*, 9(3):300–323, 2011.

[6] D. M. Frangopol. Life-cycle performance, management, and optimisation of structural systems under uncertainty: accomplishments and challenges. *Structure and Infrastructure Engineering*, 7(6):389–413, 2011.

[7] J. Han, J. Hu, Y. Yang, Z. Wang, S. X. Wang, and J. He. A nonintrusive power supply design forself-powered sensor networks in the smartgrid by scavenging energy from ac power line. *IEEE Transactions on Industrial Electronics*, 62(7):4398–4407, 2015.

[8] C. K. Ho, P. D. Khoa, and P. C. Ming. Markovian Models for Harvested Energy in Wireless Communications. In *Proc. of IEEE International Conference on Communication Systems (ICCS)*, pages 311–315, 2010.

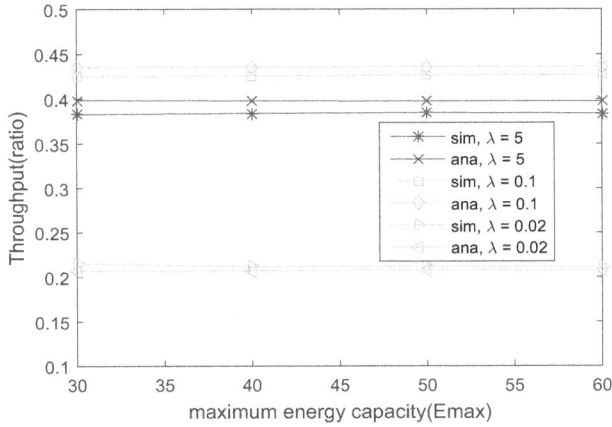

(a) Throughput

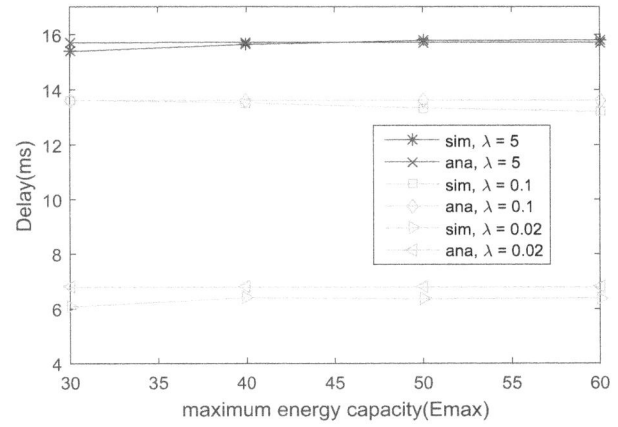

(b) Delay

Figure 5: The average throughput and delay derived from the simulation(sim) and analytical model(ana) under different parameter setting. The parameter $N = 20$, $L = 7$ backoff periods, $q_0 = 0.3$, $m_0 = 3$ and $m = 4$

[9] F. Iannello, O. Simeone, and U. Spagnolini. Medium Access Control Protocols for Wireless Sensor Networks with Energy Harvesting. *IEEE Transactions on Communications*, 60(5):1381 – 1389, 2012.

[10] A. Koubaa, M. Alves, and E. Tovar. A comprehensive simulation study of slotted CSMA/CA for IEEE 802.15.4 wireless sensor networks. In *Proc. of IEEE International Workshop on Factory Communication Systems*, pages 183–192, 28-30 June 2006.

[11] J. Lei, R. Yates, and L. Greenstein. A Generic Model for Optimizing Single-Hop Transmission Policy of Replenishable Sensors. *IEEE Transactions on Wireless Communications*, 8(2), 2009.

[12] V. Leonov. Thermoelectric energy harvesting of human bodyheat for wearable sensors. *IEEE Sensors Journal*, 13(6):2284–2291, 2013.

[13] J. Mišić, V. B. Mišić, and S. Shafi. Performance of a beacon enabled IEEE 802.15.4 cluster with downlink and uplink traffic. *IEEE Transactions on Parallel and Distributed Systems*, 17(4):361–376, 2006.

[14] NIWA. Solarview.

[15] P. Park, C. Fischione, and K. H. Johansson. Modeling and Stability Analysis of Hybrid Multiple Access in the IEEE 802.15.4 Protocol. *ACM Transactions on Sensor Networks*, 9(2), 2013.

[16] P. Park, P. D. Marco, P. Soldati, C. Fischione, and K. Johansson. A generalized Markov chain model for effective analysis of slotted IEEE 802.15.4. In *Proc. of IEEE 6th International Conference on Mobile Adhoc and Sensor Systems (MASS)*, pages 130–139, Macau, 12-15 Oct 2009.

[17] S. Pollin, M. Ergen, S. Ergen, B. Bougard, L. D. Perre, I. Moerman, A. Bahai, P. Varaiya, and F. Catthoor. Performance Analysis of Slotted Carrier Sense IEEE 802.15.4 Medium Access Layer. *IEEE Transactions on Wireless Communications*, 7(9):3359 – 3371, 2008.

[18] Post, E. Rehmi, and K. Waal. Electrostatic power harvesting for material computing. *Personal and Ubiquitous Computing*, 15(2):115–121, 2011.

[19] L. Ren, R. Chen, H. Xia, and X. Zhang. Energy harvesting performance of a broadband electromagnetic vibration energy harvester for powering industrial wireless sensor networks. *proc. SPIE*, 9799:1–11, 2016.

[20] W. K. G. Seah, Z. A. Eu, and H.-P. Tan. Wireless Sensor Networks Powered by Ambient Energy Harvesting (WSN-HEAP) - Survey and Challenges. In *Proc. of the 1st International Conference on Wireless*, pages 1–5, 2009.

[21] G. Yang, G.-Y. Lin, and H.-Y. Wei. Markov Chain Performance Model for IEEE 802.11 Devices with Energy Harvesting Source. In *Proc. of Global Communications Conference(GLOBECOM)*, pages 5212–5217, 2012.

[22] J. C. Yong, H. H. Young, S. D. Keun, and H. G. Uk. Enhanced Markov Chain Model and Throughput Analysis of the Slotted CSMACA for IEEE 802.15.4 Under Unsaturated Traffic Conditions. *IEEE Transactions on Vehicular Technology*, 58(1):473 – 478, 2009.

[23] A. Zanella, N. Bui, A. Castellani, and L. V. amd Michele Zorzi. Internet of things for smart cities. *IEEE Internet of Things Journal*, 1(1):22–32, 2014.

Holistic Small Cell Traffic Balancing across Licensed and Unlicensed Bands

Ursula Challita
ursula.challita@ed.ac.uk

Mahesh K. Marina
mahesh@ed.ac.uk

School of Informatics
The University of Edinburgh

ABSTRACT

Due to the dramatic growth in mobile data traffic on one hand and the scarcity of the licensed spectrum on the other hand, mobile operators are considering the use of unlicensed bands (especially those in 5 GHz) as complementary spectrum for providing higher system capacity and better user experience. This approach is currently being standardized by 3GPP under the name of LTE Licensed-Assisted Access (LTE-LAA). In this paper, we take a holistic approach for LTE-LAA small cell traffic balancing by jointly optimizing the use of the licensed and unlicensed bands. We pose this traffic balancing as an optimization problem that seeks proportional fair coexistence of WiFi, small cell and macro cell users by adapting the transmission probability of the LTE-LAA small cell in the licensed and unlicensed bands. The motivation for this formulation is for the LTE-LAA small cell to switch between or aggregate licensed and unlicensed bands depending on the interference/traffic level and the number of active users in each band. We derive a closed form solution for this optimization problem and additionally propose a transmission mechanism for the operation of the LTE-LAA small cell on both bands. Through numerical and simulation results, we show that our proposed traffic balancing scheme, besides enabling better LTE-WiFi coexistence and efficient utilization of the radio resources relative to the existing traffic balancing scheme, also provides a better tradeoff between maximizing the total network throughput and achieving fairness among all network flows compared to alternative approaches.

Keywords

Traffic balancing; LTE Licensed Assisted Access (LTE-LAA); small cell; WLAN; unlicensed band; proportional fairness

1. INTRODUCTION

The 3rd Generation Partnership Project (3GPP) is considering the deployment of LTE in the 5 GHz unlicensed bands, an approach known as Licensed-Assisted Access using LTE (LTE-LAA) [1], as one of the key mechanisms to cope with the dramatic growth in mobile data traffic as well as the spectrum scarcity problem, especially below 6 GHz. LTE-LAA is an attractive solution for small cells

MSWiM '16, November 13-17, 2016, Malta, Malta

© 2016 ACM. ISBN 978-1-4503-4502-6/16/11...$15.00

DOI: http://dx.doi.org/10.1145/2988287.2989143

due to the limits on maximum transmit power in unlicensed bands. It will allow the opportunistic use of the unlicensed spectrum as a complement to the licensed spectrum for offloading best-effort traffic via the LTE carrier aggregation (CA) framework, while critical control signalling, mobility, voice and control data will always be transmitted on licensed bands. Therefore, the performance experienced by mobile UEs as well as the utilization of the unlicensed spectrum will be enhanced.

LTE-LAA, however, introduces new and inter-dependent challenges of LTE-WiFi coexistence in unlicensed bands, traffic offloading from licensed to unlicensed spectrum, and inter-operator spectrum sharing in unlicensed bands [23]. LTE-WiFi coexistence depends on the extent to which LTE-LAA small cells (operating in both licensed and unlicensed bands) rely on unlicensed spectrum to meet their traffic demand, and this in turn is dependent on the nature of inter-tier interference in the licensed spectrum shared by a macro cell and small cells in its coverage area. This link between LTE small cell operation in the unlicensed band and inter-tier/inter-cell interference in the licensed spectrum is essentially the traffic balancing problem[1] and the focus of this paper. The transmission of the small cell base station (SBS) on the unlicensed band can disrupt WiFi transmissions as the latter relies on a contention-based channel access and hence starvation may occur when co-existing with LTE. On the other hand, LTE-LAA SBS transmission on the licensed band can cause inter-tier/inter-cell interference to the macro cell and other small cell users, potentially degrading their throughput. Thus addressing the traffic balancing problem is challenging as it entails a LTE-LAA small cell base station to adaptively decide on how to steer its traffic between the licensed and unlicensed bands while optimizing the overall network performance and achieving fair coexistence among the technologies operating on both bands. Though the above discussion highlights the importance of traffic balancing for optimizing the performance of co-located networks based on different technologies (LTE and WiFi) sharing same unlicensed bands, and for more effective LTE-WiFi coexistence, this problem has till date received little attention in the research literature with [14] as the only notable work. Nevertheless, the work in [14] leads to an inefficient utilization of the available resources due to the inefficient coexistence mechanism on the licensed band as well as the sequential adaptation approach for optimizing both bands, which we further discuss in Section 2.

In this paper, we take a holistic approach for LTE-LAA small cell traffic balancing across licensed and unlicensed bands. In other words, we aim to jointly address the LTE-LAA small cell operation in licensed and unlicensed bands by determining its transmission behavior on both bands in a coordinated fashion depending on the

---

[1]Traffic balancing can be seen as addressing LTE-WiFi coexistence and LTE traffic offloading challenges together.

interference/traffic levels on each of the bands. Specifically, we make the following key contributions:

- We present a formulation of the optimization problem for holistic traffic balancing that seeks proportional fair coexistence of WiFi, small cell and macro cells by deciding on the transmission probability of LTE-LAA small cell in the licensed and unlicensed bands. The intention behind this formulation is for the LTE-LAA SBS to switch between or aggregate licensed and unlicensed bands depending on the interference/traffic level and number of active UEs in each cell. We derive a closed form solution for the aforementioned optimization problem. An attractive aspect of our solution is that it can be applied online by each LTE-LAA SBS, adapting its transmission behavior in each of the bands, and without explicit communication with WiFi nodes. (Section 4)

- We also propose a transmission mechanism for the operation of SBS on the licensed and unlicensed bands. Our mechanism leverages the above mentioned traffic balancing solution and aims at avoiding the disruption to on-going WiFi transmissions while adhering to the LTE frame structure. (Section 5)

- We provide extensive numerical and simulation results using several scenarios to highlight the main capabilities of our proposed scheme. Results show that LTE-LAA SBS, aided by our scheme, would adaptively steer its traffic from one band to another or transmit on both bands simultaneously depending on the interference/traffic levels and number of active UEs on each of the bands. Simulation results additionally demonstrate the effectiveness of our proposed scheme in comparison with [14] and other approaches, representing the state-of-the-art. They reveal that approaches focusing on coexistence in one band while ignoring the other cause load imbalance and a decrease in the total network throughput and/or fairness. On the other hand, our approach, aided by its holistic nature, results in improved network performance as it achieves a better tradeoff between maximizing the total network throughput and attaining fairness among all network flows while also providing better LTE-WiFi coexistence. (Section 6)

2. RELATED WORK

LTE use of unlicensed bands has been receiving growing amount of attention within the research community in recent years. The authors in [23] provide an overview of LTE-LAA as well as the benefits and challenges it brings. Several papers have looked at the performance impact of LTE operating in unlicensed bands on WiFi. In a recent paper [13], the authors conduct an experimental evaluation for characterizing the interference impact of LTE-LAA on WiFi under various network conditions; it is shown that the impact of LTE-LAA on WiFi throughput depends on the channel bandwidth, center frequency and MIMO and can be heavily degraded for some scenarios. Concerning mechanisms for LTE-WiFi coexistence, most of the previous work uses muting (adaptive duty cycling) [2, 22, 6, 17, 10]. More crucially, much of the existing work does not consider the operation of LTE-LAA SBS in the licensed band while optimizing its use in the unlicensed bands alongside WiFi. This can however lead to a suboptimal resource allocation when seen globally. For instance, it can result in an over-utilization of the unlicensed band by LTE-LAA SBS and a decrease in WLAN performance, as it will be shown later in Section 6.

LTE-LAA small cells enable efficient and flexible use of the unlicensed spectrum, leveraging the LTE-Advanced carrier aggregation feature. Nevertheless, early work on traffic balancing across licensed and unlicensed bands (e.g., [3, 9]) focused on dual-access small cells (with both LTE and WiFi air interfaces) and thus lacking these benefits. To the best of our knowledge, [14] is the only notable traffic balancing work in the literature that applies to LTE-LAA small cells. The proposed traffic balancing technique in [14] is based on adjusting the power level in the licensed spectrum and the number of muted subframes in the unlicensed bands. We identify three aspects of the work in [14] discussed below, which together result in a lower WLAN performance and a degradation in the overall network performance compared to our proposed scheme, as shown later in Section 6.

1. *Use of power control in the licensed band.* In the context of inter-cell interference coordination (ICIC) management in HetNets, 3GPP Release 10 introduced almost blank subframes (ABS) as an efficient way to enhance the network performance. In [15], the authors evaluate the 3GPP enhanced ICIC (eICIC) techniques through realistic system-level simulations where it is shown that the ABS eICIC time method provides the best macrocell UE (MUE) protection as compared to other eICIC power methods. There is other work (e.g., [21]) which also shows that ABS muting achieves better macro-layer performance at less degradation of the SBS layer performance as compared to power adaptation. Therefore, the use of power control on the licensed band in [14] leads to a sub-optimal performance on both the licensed and the unlicensed bands given the fact that the coexistence mechanism in the licensed spectrum directly influences the optimization process in the unlicensed band.

2. *Considering a fixed level of performance for macrocell base station (MBS).* The use of a fixed and predefined interference threshold value for MBS in [14] results in prioritizing the MBS performance irrespective of the degradation level caused to the SBS layer. This uncoordinated optimization approach on the licensed band would result in an unfair share of that band which in turn could lead to an over-utilization of the unlicensed band by the SBS and thus a degradation in the WLAN performance.

3. *Sequential approach to optimizing the licensed band first then the unlicensed band.* The authors in [14] consider a sequential approach for optimizing both bands i.e., the output of the power allocation sub-problem in the licensed spectrum serves as an input to the muting sub-problem for the unlicensed bands. This results in prioritizing the licensed band and potentially over-utilizing the unlicensed band by SBS as well as degrading the total network performance.

3. SYSTEM MODEL

We consider a system model (depicted in Figure 1) similar to that in [14, 6] consisting of a macrocell base station, a small cell and multiple independently operated WiFi networks. We assume a dual band small cell that transmits on both licensed and unlicensed bands via the LTE carrier aggregation feature. The licensed band is shared between MBS and SBS where smaller portions of the spectrum, referred to as Resource Blocks (RBs), are allocated to UEs. On the other hand, SBS and WiFi networks share an unlicensed channel in the time domain and hence at a particular time, the unlicensed channel is occupied by either SBS or WiFi. This represents

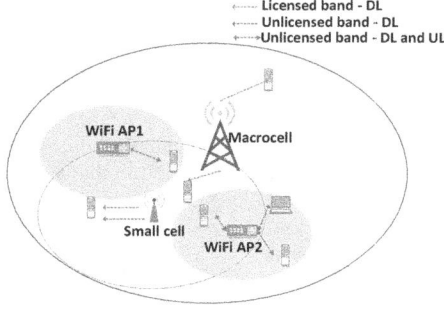

Figure 1: Illustration of the system model.

a dense WiFi deployment scenario where SBS and WiFi may need to time share the same channel.

Let N_m, N_f and N_w, respectively, denote the number of macro-cell UEs, small cell UEs (SUEs) and WiFi stations (STAs) in a given time period T. We assume the supplemental downlink (SDL) mode for the transmission of the small cell in the unlicensed band. On the other hand, traffic for WiFi STAs can be in either uplink or downlink directions. A full-buffer traffic model is assumed for the SBS, consistent with the motivation for SBS to use both licensed and unlicensed bands to meet its traffic demand.

In order to coexist with MBS on the licensed band and WLAN on the unlicensed band, we adopt in our model a holistic traffic balancing approach where SBS adjusts the proportion of time it transmits on both licensed and unlicensed bands. Therefore, at a particular time, the small cell would adaptively choose to transmit on the licensed, unlicensed or both bands depending on the interference level and traffic load of MUEs and WiFi nodes. The proposed scheme can be implemented at the MAC layer and hence the traffic assignment would be transparent to applications on the UEs. SBS would defer from transmission on the unlicensed band in order to allow WiFi transmission opportunities and on the licensed band in order to avoid inter-tier interference. Therefore, to decide on the proportion of time the small cell transmits on the licensed and unlicensed bands, the following decision variables are defined:

- $\alpha \epsilon [0, 1]$: the fraction of time SBS is *muted* on the unlicensed channel.

- $\beta \epsilon [0, 1]$: the fraction of time SBS is *transmitting* on the licensed band.

Note that upon muting on the licensed band, SBS would defer from sending data on the physical channels, however, would still send control and reference signals, an approach known as almost blank subframe [15]. On the other hand, the use of unlicensed band by the small cell is limited to data plane traffic while control and reference signals are transmitted by the SBS on a licensed carrier, which is essentially the license assisted access (LAA) aspect of LTE-LAA. Concerning the LTE-WiFi coexistence mechanism in the unlicensed band, even though the work of 3GPP LTE-LAA study group is in the direction of standardizing the listen-before-talk (LBT) mechanism, we choose muting as the coexistence mechanism in this work influenced by two observations: (i) most of the LTE-WiFi coexistence literature focuses on adaptive muting; (ii) recent work in [7] shows that conceptually both LBT and adaptive duty cycling (muting) provide the same level of fairness to WiFi transmissions when properly configured.

3.1 Throughput Modeling

In order to assess the network performance for the coexistence of LTE MBS, LTE-LAA small cell and WiFi, we define the throughput for each of the MUEs, SUEs and WiFi STAs.

Upon the transmission on the licensed band, SBS would share the frequency band with MBS. In LTE, the downlink RB allocation among UEs is via OFDMA, implying no intra-cell interference. However, frequency reuse in LTE can be one where macro and adjacent small cells may transmit on the same frequency leading to inter-cell interference. On the other hand, when SBS is transmitting on the unlicensed channel, it shares the channel with WLAN. Therefore, the downlink SINR at SUE f, served by SBS F, in our model assuming a single MBS and SBS, during the transmission of SBS on the licensed and unlicensed channels respectively, can be expressed as follows:

$$\Gamma_{F,f}^l = \frac{P_{F,f}}{\sigma^2 + I_{M,f}} \qquad \text{and} \qquad \Gamma_{F,f}^u = \frac{P_{F,f}}{\sigma^2 + I_{W,f}} \qquad (1)$$

where $P_{F,f}$ denotes the received signal power for SUE f from its serving SBS F, σ^2 is the thermal noise power, $I_{M,f}$ represents the interference power from MBS M on SUE f and $I_{W,f}$ corresponds to the aggregate interference power from neighboring WLAN APs/STAs on SUE f. Note that upon the transmission of SBS on the unlicensed channel, WLAN would defer from transmission since WiFi STAs sense the carrier, i.e. listen to the channel before transmissions, and transmit only if the channel is idle. Therefore, $I_{W,f}$ corresponds to the interference power due to WLAN hidden terminals.

Similarly, the downlink SINR at MUE m, served by MBS M, during the non-ABS and ABS periods of SBS on the licensed band respectively, can be expressed as follows:

$$\Gamma_{M,m}^{\text{noABS}} = \frac{P_{M,m}}{\sigma^2 + I_{F,m}} \qquad \text{and} \qquad \Gamma_{M,m}^{\text{ABS}} = \frac{P_{M,m}}{\sigma^2} \qquad (2)$$

where $P_{M,m}$ denotes the received signal power for MUE m from its serving MBS M, and $I_{F,m}$ represents the interference power from SBS F on MUE m.

We denote by s_k the total throughput attained by an LTE UE k (where k is m or f). An upper bound for the downlink UE throughput, based on Shannon's capacity, is computed as follows:

$$s_k(\text{bps}) = \text{BW}_k \cdot \log_2(1 + \Gamma_k) \qquad (3)$$

where BW_k is the channel bandwidth allocated to UE k and Γ_k is the SINR value of UE k.

To derive the throughput attained by a WiFi STA w when using the unlicensed band exclusively, we consider a slotted channel, as per the IEEE 802.11 modus operandi [12]. Let τ_w denote the stationary probability that station w is attempting transmission in a randomly chosen slot time. The total throughput $\hat{s}_w$ attained by a WiFi STA w when using the channel *exclusively* is:

$$\hat{s}_w(\text{bps}) = \frac{P_{w,succ} \cdot E[D_w]}{P_{w,idle} \cdot \sigma + P_{w,busy} \cdot T_b}, \qquad (4)$$

where $E[D_w]$ is the expected payload size for station w, $P_{w,succ}$ is the probability of a successful transmission and can be expressed as $P_{w,succ} = \tau_w \prod_{i=1, i \neq w}^{N_w}(1 - \tau_i)$, $P_{w,idle}$ is the probability of an idle slot and can be expressed as $P_{w,idle} = \prod_{w=1}^{N_w}(1 - \tau_w)$ and $P_{w,busy}$ is the probability of a busy slot, regardless of whether it corresponds to a collision or a successful transmission and can be expressed as $P_{w,busy} = 1 - \prod_{w=1}^{N_w}(1 - \tau_w)$ [8]. σ and T_b correspond to the average durations of an idle and a busy slot respectively and thus the denominator corresponds to the mean duration of a WiFi MAC slot.

Therefore, during an epoch T, the throughput attained by a macro, small cell and WiFi UE respectively can be expressed as follows:

$$s_m = \beta s_m^{\text{noABS}} + (1 - \beta)s_m^{\text{ABS}} \qquad (5)$$

$$s_f = \beta s_f^{\text{l}} + (1 - \alpha)s_f^{\text{u}} \qquad (6)$$

and

$$s_w = \alpha \hat{s}_w \qquad (7)$$

where s_m, s_f and s_w are the achieved throughputs of MUEs, SUEs and WiFi STAs respectively during a given period of time T. s_m^{noABS} and s_m^{ABS} correspond to the throughput achieved by MUE m during the transmission of the SBS on the licensed band and during the ABS period of SBS, respectively. s_f^{l} and s_f^{u} correspond to the throughput of SUE f during the transmission of SBS on the licensed band and an unlicensed channel, respectively.

4. HOLISTIC TRAFFIC BALANCING

In order to maximize the total network throughput while coexisting fairly with other LTE and WiFi cells, we aim in this section at proposing a traffic balancing approach that aims at providing a proportional fair coexistence of WiFi STAs, SUEs and MUEs. The rationale behind this approach is to allow SBS to either switch between or aggregate the unlicensed and licensed bands based on the interference level on each band. This will allow higher throughput for MUEs that are in the vicinity of the SBS when SBS is not transmitting on the licensed band, and similarly, more transmission opportunities for WiFi nodes when SBS is not transmitting on the unlicensed band. Therefore, the utility function can be expressed as the product of the throughputs obtained by SUEs, MUEs and WiFi STAs:

$$\mathcal{U} = \prod_{m=1}^{N_m} s_m \prod_{f=1}^{N_f} s_f \prod_{w=1}^{N_w} s_w \qquad (8)$$

$\mathcal{U}$ in turn can be expressed as the summation of the logarithmic function of the achieved rates as given below:

$$\begin{aligned} \mathcal{U}_{\log} = & \sum_{m=1}^{N_m} \log(s_m) + \sum_{f=1}^{N_f} \log(s_f) + \sum_{w=1}^{N_w} \log(s_w) \\ = & \sum_{m=1}^{N_m} \log\left[\beta s_m^{\text{noABS}} + (1 - \beta)s_m^{\text{ABS}}\right] \\ & + \sum_{f=1}^{N_f} \log\left[\beta s_f^{\text{l}} + (1 - \alpha)s_f^{\text{u}}\right] \\ & + \sum_{w=1}^{N_w} \log\left[\alpha s_w\right] \end{aligned} \qquad (9)$$

The proposed utility function $\mathcal{U}_{\log}$ corresponds to a proportional fair coexistence of MUEs, SUEs and WiFi STAs. The PF scheduling algorithm has been an attractive allocation criterion in wireless networks since it maintains a balance between maximizing the total network throughput while achieving good fairness among network flows [20]. Therefore, our optimization problem is formulated as follows:

$$\max_{\alpha,\beta} \ \mathcal{U}_{\log} \qquad (10)$$

subject to

$$\alpha \leq \overline{R}_w \qquad (11)$$

$$\alpha \leq \beta \qquad (12)$$

$$0 \leq \alpha \leq 1, 0 \leq \beta \leq 1 \qquad (13)$$

where $\overline{R}_w (\leq 1)$ corresponds to the normalized offered load across all WiFi stations; it can be obtained via long-term channel sensing where SBS would monitor the WLAN activity on the unlicensed band and estimate the average WLAN traffic load. In the above formulation, constraint (11) limits the fraction of time SBS is muted on the unlicensed band to the time it is busy due to WiFi activity. In other words, it is to make sure that the unlicensed band is not underutilized. The purpose of constraint (12) is to ensure that SBS transmits on either the licensed or the unlicensed channel at any given point in time. Constraints (13) limit the range of values variables α and β can take.

LEMMA 1. *$\log(x)$ is concave. It follows that the utility function $\mathcal{U}_{\log}$ is an affine combination of concave functions, and hence is concave. Therefore, the optimization problem defined by (10)-(13) is concave since the objective function and the feasible region defined by the constraints are concave and hence a closed form solution can be obtained using the Karush-Kuhn-Tucker (KKT) conditions at optimality [5].*

Based on the above lemma, we now aim to derive a closed form solution for the optimization problem (10)-(13) using the KKT conditions at optimality. The KKT conditions are necessary and sufficient for convex optimization problems and consist of the stationarity, primal and dual feasibility, and complementary slackness conditions [5]. Therefore, the Lagrangian of the optimization problem (10)-(13) can be written as follows:

$$\begin{aligned} \mathcal{L}(\alpha, \beta, \lambda_1, \lambda_2, \lambda_3, \lambda_4, \lambda_5, \lambda_6) = & -\mathcal{U}_{\text{total}} + \lambda_1(\alpha - \overline{R}_w) \\ & + \lambda_2(\alpha - \beta) - \lambda_3\alpha + \lambda_4(\alpha - 1) - \lambda_5\beta + \lambda_6(\beta - 1) \end{aligned} \quad (14)$$

where λ_1, λ_2, λ_3, λ_4, λ_5 and λ_6 correspond to the lagrangian multipliers of constraints (11)-(13).

In the *first step*, we compute the candidates for an optimal solution pair (α^*, β^*) from the possible combinations of feasible solutions satisfying the stationarity and complementary slackness conditions. Note that the total number of possible combinations for the Lagrangian multipliers is 64 (i.e., 2^6) where a given multiplier could be either zero (Z) or non-zero (NZ) at an optimal solution. However, for our optimization formulation, only 6 combinations are possible candidates for an optimal solution due to some infeasible and redundant combinations. For instance, the combinations that have λ_4 and λ_5 as NZ can be omitted since their corresponding solution is $(\alpha^*, \beta^*) = (1,0)$, however, this will lead to the violation of constraint (12). Similarly, if a constraint has finite values for both lower and upper bounds, one would need to consider the possible combinations when at most one of the Lagrange multipliers for that constraint is NZ. This is due to the fact that one or the other, or both, of the multipliers will always be equal to zero since only one of the bounds can be active at a time. Therefore, the combinations that have both λ_3 and λ_4 or λ_5 and λ_6 as NZ can be omitted. Moreover, we impose a non-zero muting period on the unlicensed band (i.e., restrict α to be greater than 0) in order to allow the small cell to sense WiFi activity and number of stations and thus we omit the combinations having λ_3 as NZ. Based on the above, the 6 candidate solutions for α^*, β^* and $(\lambda_1^*, \lambda_2^*, \lambda_3^*, \lambda_4^*, \lambda_5^*, \lambda_6^*)$ are as follows:
Candidate solution 1: λ=(NZ,0,0,0,0,NZ)

$$\alpha_1 = \overline{R}_w \quad \text{and} \quad \beta_1 = 1$$

$$\lambda_1 = -\sum_{f=1}^{N_f} \frac{s_f^u}{\beta_1 s_f^l + (1-\alpha_1)s_f^u} + \frac{N_w}{\alpha_1}$$

$$\lambda_6 = \sum_{m=1}^{N_m} \frac{(s_m^{\text{noABS}} - s_m^{\text{ABS}})}{\beta_1 s_m^{\text{noABS}} + (1-\beta_1)s_m^{\text{ABS}}}$$
$$+ \sum_{f=1}^{N_f} \frac{s_f^l}{\beta_1 s_f^l + (1-\alpha_1)s_f^u}$$

Candidate solution 2: λ=(0,0,0,0,0,NZ)

α_2 corresponds to the solution of the following equation:

$$\sum_{f=1}^{N_f} \frac{s_f^u}{s_f^l + (1-\alpha_2)s_f^u} - \frac{N_w}{\alpha_2} = 0$$

$$\beta_2 = 1$$

$$\lambda_6 = \sum_{m=1}^{N_m} \frac{(s_m^{\text{noABS}} - s_m^{\text{ABS}})}{\beta_2 s_m^{\text{noABS}} + (1-\beta_2)s_m^{\text{ABS}}}$$
$$+ \sum_{f=1}^{N_f} \frac{s_f^l}{\beta_2 s_f^l + (1-\alpha_2)s_f^u}$$

Candidate solution 3: λ=(NZ,NZ,0,0,0,0)

$$\alpha_3 = \overline{R}_w \quad \text{and} \quad \beta_3 = \overline{R}_w$$

$$\lambda_2 = -\sum_{m=1}^{N_m} \frac{(s_m^{\text{noABS}} - s_m^{\text{ABS}})}{\beta_3 s_m^{\text{noABS}} + (1-\beta_3)s_m^{\text{ABS}}}$$
$$- \sum_{f=1}^{N_f} \frac{s_f^l}{\beta_3 s_f^l + (1-\alpha_3)s_f^u}$$

$$\lambda_1 = -\sum_{f=1}^{N_f} \frac{s_f^u}{\beta_3 s_f^l + (1-\alpha_3)s_f^u} + \frac{N_w}{\alpha_3} - \lambda_2$$

Candidate solution 4: λ=(NZ,0,0,0,0,0)

$$\alpha_4 = \overline{R}_w$$

β_4 corresponds to the solution of the following equation:

$$-\sum_{m=1}^{N_m} \frac{(s_m^{\text{noABS}} - s_m^{\text{ABS}})}{\beta_4 s_m^{\text{noABS}} + (1-\beta_4)s_m^{\text{ABS}}} - \sum_{f=1}^{N_f} \frac{s_f^l}{\beta_4 s_f^l + (1-\alpha_4)s_f^u} = 0$$

$$\lambda_1 = -\sum_{f=1}^{N_f} \frac{s_f^u}{\beta_4 s_f^l + (1-\alpha_4)s_f^u} + \frac{N_w}{\alpha_4}$$

Candidate solution 5: λ=(0,NZ,0,0,0,0)

α_5 is equal to β_5 and their corresponding value is the solution of the following equation:

$$-\sum_{m=1}^{N_m} \frac{(s_m^{\text{noABS}} - s_m^{\text{ABS}})}{\alpha_5 s_m^{\text{noABS}} + (1-\alpha_5)s_m^{\text{ABS}}} - \sum_{f=1}^{N_f} \frac{s_f^l}{\alpha_5 s_f^l + (1-\alpha_5)s_f^u}$$
$$+ \sum_{f=1}^{N_f} \frac{s_f^u}{\alpha_5 s_f^l + (1-\alpha_5)s_f^u} - \frac{N_w}{\alpha_5} = 0$$

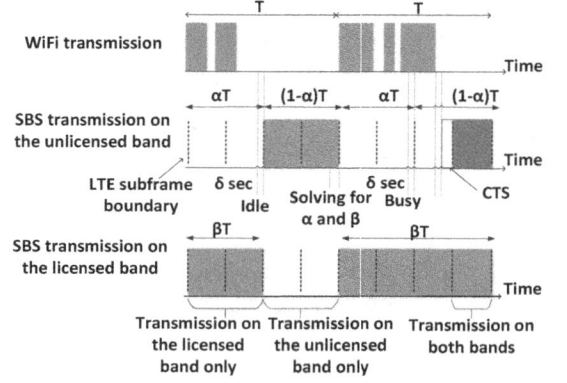

Figure 2: Illustration of the proposed SBS transmission mechanism on the licensed and unlicensed bands. The two possible states upon sensing the unlicensed channel (idle and busy) are demonstrated. SBS will remain in a sensing state when it encounters a busy channel. The three states of SBS (i.e., transmission on the licensed, unlicensed and both bands) are also shown.

$$\lambda_2 = -\sum_{f=1}^{N_f} \frac{s_f^u}{\beta_5 s_f^l + (1-\alpha_5)s_f^u} + \frac{N_w}{\alpha_5}$$

Candidate solution 6: λ=(0,0,0,0,0,0)

α_6 and β_6 correspond to the solution of the following two equations:

$$\sum_{f=1}^{N_f} \frac{s_f^u}{\beta_6 s_f^l + (1-\alpha_6)s_f^u} - \frac{N_w}{\alpha_6} = 0$$

$$-\sum_{m=1}^{N_m} \frac{(s_m^{\text{noABS}} - s_m^{\text{ABS}})}{\beta_6 s_m^{\text{noABS}} + (1-\beta_6)s_m^{\text{ABS}}} - \sum_{f=1}^{N_f} \frac{s_f^l}{\beta_6 s_f^l + (1-\alpha_6)s_f^u} = 0$$

Note that two more candidate solutions exist for λ= (NZ,NZ,0,NZ,0,NZ) and λ= (0,NZ,0,NZ,0,NZ) where α and β are both equal to 1. However, we can avoid checking these two candidate solutions as they exist only in the case when $\overline{R}_w$=1 and hence their solution matches with that of candidate solution 1.

In the *second step*, we check the primal and dual feasibility conditions for each of the 6 candidate solution pairs and the pair satisfying these conditions is the optimal solution.

Note that all the candidate solutions are independent of the WiFi throughput s_w and hence SBS needs to know only the normalized WiFi offered load as well as the number of active WiFi STAs; the SBS can learn the number of active WiFi STAs based on their corresponding MAC addresses during the sensing period [14]. The number of MUEs and their throughput can be conveyed to the SBS through the X2 interface. Using this information, SBS can determine the optimal values for α and β *locally* when needed.

5. A TRANSMISSION MECHANISM FOR LTE-LAA SBS OPERATION

LTE is designed for the exclusive use of the spectrum and hence when operating on the unlicensed band, a new channel access scheme is needed to coexist with other devices having different air interfaces. Therefore, in this section, we propose a transmission mechanism for the operation of an LTE-LAA small cell on the licensed and unlicensed bands. This mechanism builds upon the problem formulation from Section 4 and incorporates a channel access scheme on the unlicensed channel that would allow LTE-LAA SBS to transmit on the unlicensed band in a way that would not disrupt any ongoing WiFi transmissions.

For our proposed mechanism, we divide the time domain into T epochs, where in each epoch we aim at finding the optimal values of α and β using the results of Section 4. Taking into account that LTE transmits only at the beginning of a subframe, our proposed transmission mechanism is aligned with LTE frame structure where $(1-\alpha)T$ and βT are rounded to an integer multiple of an LTE subframe duration (1 msec). Moreover, we define δ as the duration of time the SBS would sense the unlicensed channel before attempting to transmit. Let δ be such that SIFS $< \delta <$ DIFS, and hence this will guarantee that the ACK of any previous WiFi transmission is received at the sender and that SBS would get access to the unlicensed channel before any other WiFi STA that would be sensing the channel at the same time. The proposed LTE-LAA transmission mechanism is illustrated in Figure 2 where the two possible states upon sensing the channel (idle and busy) are demonstrated. Moreover, the steps of the proposed mechanism are summarized as follows:

1. SBS calculates the values of α and β before the beginning of a T period based on the throughput values and number of active nodes of the previous T period and using the results of Section 4.

2. At the beginning of a T period, SBS remains silent for the period αT on the unlicensed band and transmits for the period βT on the licensed band.

3. SBS senses the unlicensed channel for δ sec before αT expires in order to detect any ongoing WiFi transmissions and guarantee alignment with LTE frame structure.

4. If the channel is idle, SBS transmits for a period of $(1-\alpha)T$.

5. If the channel is busy, SBS keeps on listening to the channel until it detects a silent period for a duration of δ sec in order to avoid the disruption to any ongoing WiFi transmission. After detecting a silent period of δ sec, SBS sends a clear-to-send (CTS) with the duration of the remaining time of the $(1-\alpha)T$ period to reserve the channel for SBS transmission on the unlicensed band. It is important to note that the maximum channel occupancy time is limited to 10 msec after which the unlicensed channel must be released and the LBT process is repeated. Therefore, for the cases where $(1-\alpha)T$ is less than 10 msec, there is a risk that the SBS will not be able to get access to the unlicensed band when the WLAN burst is larger than $(1-\alpha)T$. For such scenarios, the WLAN transmission period for the next T period is shortened accordingly to maintain the average time allocated for LTE-LAA and WLAN.

6. EVALUATION

In this section, we examine the behavior of our proposed holistic traffic balancing scheme in various scenarios using a combination of numerical and simulation results. We also conduct a comparative study of our holistic traffic balancing approach with respect to

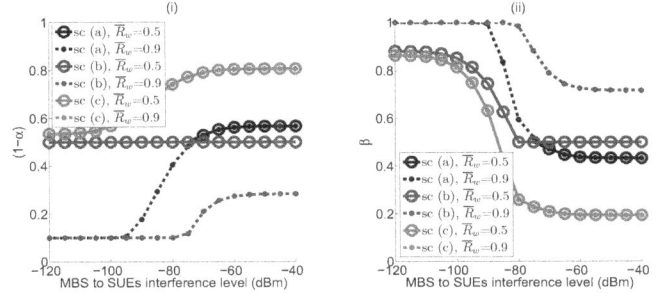

Figure 3: Numerical results for the optimal values of (i) $(1-\alpha)$ and (ii) β for varying levels of MBS to SUEs interference in three different scenarios; sc (a) considers an equal number of MUEs, SUEs and WiFi STAs, sc (b) considers the number of WiFi STAs to be three times that of each of MUEs and SUEs and sc (c) considers the number of each of MUEs and SUEs to be three times that of WiFi STAs. For the studied scenarios, we consider medium and high WiFi offered load i.e., $\overline{R}_w$=0.5 and 0.9 respectively, as well as a fixed value for SBS to MUEs interference level (-85 dBm).

[14] and other alternative approaches, representing other proposed techniques from the literature.

In simulations, for WiFi we consider the 802.11 distributed coordination function (DCF) medium access mechanism based on carrier sense multiple access with collision avoidance (CSMA/CA). We assume randomly located STAs that transmit and receive packets according to an independent Poisson process. For simplicity, we consider that all WiFi STAs use the same physical layer parameters, 64-QAM modulation with a 5/6 coding rate when using a 20 MHz channel, which provides a 65 Mbps MAC layer throughput. The simulation parameters for the 802.11 network are the same as those used in [6].

For the LTE and LTE-LAA networks, we assume the same channel conditions for all RBs on both bands and hence the same modulation and coding scheme (MCS) i.e., 64 QAM with 5/6 coding rate, is applied to all RBs of the given 20 MHz channel. Maximum MAC layer throughput for LTE with the above settings is 75 Mbps. These simulation parameters are similar to the ones used in [14]. We assume a Round Robin (RR) scheduler and equal transmit power for all OFDM symbols in a Transmission Time Interval (TTI) due to the fact that all RBs have the same MCS and thus equal number of bits are allocated to each subcarrier. The maximum transmit power for MBS and SBS is 43 dBm and 23 dBm, respectively. We consider an urban area characterized by the path loss model (for outdoor and indoor locations of the base station and UEs) as given in [16]. A constant payload size of 1500 bytes is assumed for MUEs, SUEs and WiFi STAs. Simulation results are provided for the average of 1000 runs with a 95% confidence interval.

6.1 Behavior of α and β in different scenarios

In this subsection, we study the effect of the variation of the traffic arrival rate as well as the number of active UEs on the values of α and β by conducting numerical and simulation results for different practical deployment scenarios.

For the numerical results, we consider three different scenarios with different number of MUEs, SUEs and WiFi STAs. Figure 3 shows the optimal values of $(1-\alpha)$ and β as a function of the MBS

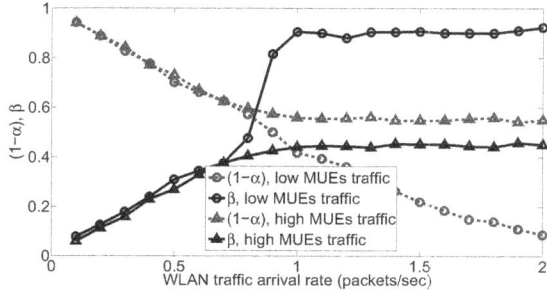

Figure 4: Simulation results for the variation of the proportion of time the SBS transmits on the licensed (β) and unlicensed bands ($1 - \alpha$) as a function of the WLAN traffic arrival rate (λ_{WLAN}) and for a low and high MUEs traffic arrival rates i.e., λ_{MUE}= 0.5 and 2 (packets/sec) respectively, for a scenario of equal number of MUEs, SUEs and WLAN STAs.

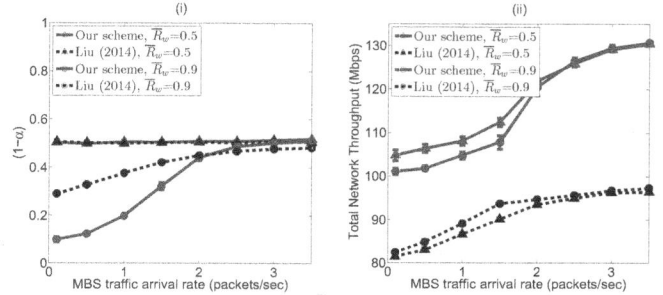

Figure 5: Simulation results for (i) the optimal value of the transmission ratio of SBS on the unlicensed band i.e., (1-α) and (ii) the total achieved network throughput as a function of the MBS traffic arrival rate (λ_{MUE}) for our proposed traffic balancing scheme (Our scheme) and the scheme in [14] (Liu (2014)). For the comparative study, we consider moderate and high WLAN offered load i.e., $\overline{R}_w$=0.5 and 0.9 respectively.

to SUE interference level on the licensed band, for a fixed value of the SBS to MUE interference level (-85 dBm) and two different WLAN traffic loads ($\overline{R}_w$=0.5 and 0.9). Note that the MBS to SUE interference and the SBS to MUE interference levels are relevant during the non-ABS period only.

For the simulation results (shown in Figure 4), we consider only scenario (a) of Figure 3 due to space limitations. Figure 4 shows the variation of the proportion of time SBS is transmitting on the licensed and unlicensed bands during the period T as a function of the WLAN traffic arrival rate (λ_{WLAN} (packets/sec)) and for a low and high MUEs traffic arrival rates, i.e., $\lambda_{\mathrm{MUE}} = 0.5$ and 2 (packets/sec) respectively. Note that λ_{WLAN} and λ_{MUE} correlate to $\overline{R}_w$ and inter-tier interference level respectively of Figure 3. Each data point in the simulation results is obtained from 1000 runs, each of length 200 msec and with T set to 20 msec.

We can make the following observations from Figures 3 and 4. First, comparing the three considered scenarios of Figure 3, we conclude that *our proposed traffic balancing scheme provides per node airtime fairness among each of the MUEs, SUEs and WiFi STAs*. For example, consider -60 dBm for the value of MBS to SUEs interference level and $\overline{R}_w$=0.5 for the WLAN load, we observe that in scenario (c), SBS transmits more on the unlicensed band (80%) and less on the licensed band (20%) as compared to scenario (b) where SBS transmits 50% on the unlicensed band and 50% on the licensed band. This is because the number of each MUEs and SUEs is larger than that of WiFi STAs in scenario (c) while in scenario (b) the number of WiFi STAs is larger than each of the number of MUEs and SUEs.

Second, *our proposed scheme copes with the interference level on both bands by adapting the values of α and β*. This can be observed for high values of inter-tier interference in Figure 3 or high values of λ_{MUE} in Figure 4. In those scenarios, WLAN shares the unlicensed band with SBS for a proportion of time larger than its idle period, i.e., larger than (1-$\overline{R}_w$), in order to decrease the effect of inter-tier interference on the UEs throughput on the licensed band. For example, in Figure 3, for scenario (a) and $\overline{R}_w$=0.9, SBS transmits for 55% of the time on the unlicensed band when the MBS to SUEs interference level is -60 dBm as compared to 10% when the MBS to SUEs interference level is -95 dBm. This can also be noted from Figure 4 where (1-α) is equal to 20% for λ_{MUE}= 0.5 (packets/sec) but increases to 55% for λ_{MUE}= 2 (packets/sec), for λ_{WLAN}=1.5.

Third, *our proposed traffic balancing scheme allows SBS to trans-*

mit on either one of the two bands or aggregate both bands through CA and thus increasing its capacity. Given that SBS is muted for the period of α and (1-β) on the unlicensed and licensed bands respectively, we can deduce that it transmits on both bands simultaneously for a period of ($\beta - \alpha$)T sec, and on one of the two bands for the remaining duration of the T period i.e., for a period of ($1-(\beta-\alpha)$)T sec, as per our proposed transmission mechanism of Section 5. For example, in Figure 3, for scenario (b), $\overline{R}_w$=0.5 and MBS to SUEs interference level of -90 dBm, α=0.5 and β=0.75 and thus SBS transmits on both bands simultaneously for 25% of the T period. This can also be shown in Figure 4 where α=0.6 and β=0.9 for λ_{WLAN}=1 and λ_{MUE}=0.5 and hence SBS transmits on both bands simultaneously for 30% of the T period.

Fourth, for all the considered scenarios of Figures 3 and 4, we notice that *the unlicensed band is always utilized by either WLAN or SBS and hence this avoids its under-utilization*. In other words, SBS is always transmitting on the unlicensed band for at least the portion of time that it is not utilized by WLAN i.e., (1-α) is always greater than or equal to (1-$\overline{R}_w$), consistent with constraint (11) in the optimization problem, irrespective of the value of inter-tier interference on the licensed band. For example, for $\overline{R}_w$=0.5 and 0.9, (1-α) is always greater than or equal to 0.5 and 0.1 respectively.

Fifth, for all the studied scenarios, *there exists an upper limit for the value of (1-α) which corresponds to the maximum proportion of time that WLAN would share its unlicensed band with LTE*. This can be observed in the cases of high inter-cell interference on the licensed band where a minimum airtime portion for WLAN, that is a function of the number of active UEs and WLAN activity, is guaranteed and thus allowing a fair LTE-WiFi coexistence. For example, in Figure 3, for an equal number of SBS and WLAN UEs (i.e. scenario (a)), the upper limit for (1-α) is approximately 0.5.

Overall, the results demonstrate that our traffic balancing scheme performs as per expectations by steering SBS traffic from one band to another or using both bands simultaneously depending on the level of inter-tier interference on the licensed band, WiFi offered load and number of UEs in each band.

6.2 Comparison with existing traffic balancing scheme [14]

In this subsection, we compare the performance of our proposed scheme with that of [14] which also studies the problem of SBS traffic balancing across licensed and unlicensed bands. Unlike our scheme that jointly optimizes the muting pattern on both bands, the work in [14] takes a sequential approach adapting the power level in the licensed band first followed by adjusting the muting pattern on the unlicensed channel. Figure 5 shows simulation results for (i) the value of $(1-\alpha)$ and (ii) the total network throughput for the two schemes as a function of the MBS traffic arrival rate for two different values of the WLAN traffic load ($\overline{R}_w$=0.5 and $\overline{R}_w$=0.9). We can make the following high-level observations from Figure 5:

Observation 1: *Overall, our proposed traffic balancing scheme achieves better LTE-WiFi coexistence.*

Observation 2: *For all the studied network scenarios, our proposed traffic balancing scheme achieves higher total network throughput.*

In what follows, we examine the reasons behind these observations. First, for scenarios of high WLAN load and when MBS is not in a full buffer state (i.e. $\lambda_{\mathrm{MUE}} < 2.5$ (packets/sec)), corresponding to candidate solutions 2 or 6, our proposed scheme provides better LTE-WiFi coexistence while also achieving higher total network throughput as compared to [14]. This gain is due to the use of subframe muting instead of power adaptation, optimizing the MBS and SBS in a coordinated fashion instead of having a fixed level of performance for MBS, and optimizing the licensed and unlicensed bands in a holistic (joint) manner instead of adopting a sequential approach (see all aspects for [14] discussed in Section 2). The gain for solving the problem holistically as compared to sequentially is characterized separately in Section 6.3 where we consider a variant of our scheme that adopts an independent muting strategy on both bands. On the other hand, the gain due to the other two differences between our scheme and that of [14] can be clearly seen from the value of α for candidate solutions 2 or 6 with N_f=1:

$$\alpha = \frac{N_w(T_f^l + s_f^u)}{s_f^u(N_w + 1)} \quad (15)$$

where T_f^l is the throughput achieved by SBS on the licensed band and corresponds to $\beta \cdot s_f^L$ for our proposed scheme and $s_f^L(P_f^*)$ (i.e., a function of the optimal allocated power) for the proposed algorithm of [14]. Therefore, from Equation (15), we can note that higher values of T_f^l result in higher values for α and thus less utilization of the unlicensed band. Given that ABS muting achieves better macro-layer performance at less degradation of the SBS layer performance as compared to power adaptation, for a specified level of performance for MUEs (e.g., minimum outage level, minimum interference level from SBSs to MUEs), ABS muting causes less degradation in the performance of the SBS layer as compared to power control, i.e., $\beta \cdot s_f^L > s_f^L(P_f^*)$. Following Equation (15), our proposed scheme results in less utilization of the unlicensed band and thus allows more WLAN transmission opportunities as compared to [14] while maximizing the total network performance.

On the other hand, in the case of a full-buffer MBS (i.e. $\lambda_{\mathrm{MUE}} \geq 2.5$ (packets/sec)) and at high WLAN load, corresponding to candidate solution 5, we can notice that the value of $(1-\alpha)$ for our proposed scheme (0.51) is slightly higher than that of [14] (0.49). This is due to the high interference level on the licensed band and thus the need to steer more traffic on the unlicensed band in order to guarantee that the SBS is transmitting on at least one of the two bands at a given time (see constraint (12) in the optimization problem). Note, however, that $(1-\alpha)$ would converge to its upper limit (i.e., ~ 0.5 for the studied scenarios) and thus allowing a fair LTE-WiFi coexistence.

Second, our proposed scheme achieves similar performance on the *unlicensed* band as that of [14] for the case of moderate WLAN

load ($\overline{R}_w = 0.5$) but it results in a higher total network throughput. For these scenarios, the value of α is limited by $\overline{R}_w$ (corresponding to candidate solutions 1, 3 or 4) and thus the increase in the total network throughput is due to the improvement in the performance on the licensed band i.e., due to the use of subframe muting instead of power adaptation and optimizing the MBS and SBS in a coordinated fashion instead of having a fixed level of performance for MBS (i.e., see aspects (1) and (2) of [14] discussed in Section 2).

In summary, our proposed scheme achieves better utilization of the available resources compared to [14] (an increase of 28.3% in the total network throughput for the studied scenarios) while increasing the transmission opportunities for WiFi on the unlicensed band.

6.3 Comparison with alternative approaches

In this subsection, we compare the performance of our proposed traffic balancing approach with a broad spectrum of alternative approaches. As performance metrics, we consider throughput and fairness obtained using each of the various different approaches. Denote by $\eta(s_i)$ the efficiency of a resource allocation scheme where $\eta(s_i)$ is defined as the sum of all the UEs throughput i.e., $\eta(s_i) = \sum_{i=1}^{N} s_i$ (where i is m, f, or w and $N = N_m + N_f + N_w$), and its fairness is given by the Jain's index defined below [19]:

$$\mathcal{J}(s_i) = \frac{\left(\sum_{i=1}^{N} s_i\right)^2}{N \cdot \sum_{i=1}^{N} s_i^2} \quad (16)$$

The value of the Jain's fairness index lies in $[\frac{1}{N}, 1]$ where the value of $(\frac{1}{N})$ corresponds to the least fair allocation in which only one UE attains a non-zero throughput and the value of (1) corresponds to the most fair allocation in which all UEs achieve equal rates. Therefore, an efficient allocation of the radio resources seeks to provide a tradeoff between $\eta(s_i)$ and $\mathcal{J}(s_i)$ [19].

We compare the throughput and fairness of our proposed scheme with the following set of approaches:

- *Case 1 - No Muting on Licensed*: SBS operates on both bands, however, considering a PF muting strategy on the unlicensed band only and hence providing a coexistence technique with WLAN only. On the licensed band, MBS and SBS transmit simultaneously, and hence inter-tier interference is not eliminated.

- *Case 2 - No Muting on Unlicensed*: SBS operates on both bands, however, considering a PF muting strategy on the licensed band only and hence providing a coexistence technique with MBS only. On the unlicensed band, SBS is transmitting all the time, and hence excluding any opportunity for WiFi transmissions.

- *Case 3 - No Transmission on Licensed*: SBS operates on the unlicensed band only and shares the spectrum with WLAN by muting adaptively. This corresponds to previously suggested approaches such as the work proposed in [2, 22, 6, 17, 10]. For this case, we specifically consider a muting pattern based on PF coexistence of SBS and WLAN on the unlicensed band which is similar to [6].

- *Case 4 - No Transmission on Unlicensed*: SBS operates on the licensed band only and shares the spectrum with MBS by muting adaptively. This corresponds to previously suggested approaches in the area of ICIC such as the work proposed in [15] based on muting (ABS). For this case, we specifically consider a muting pattern based on PF coexistence of MBS and SBS on the licensed band.

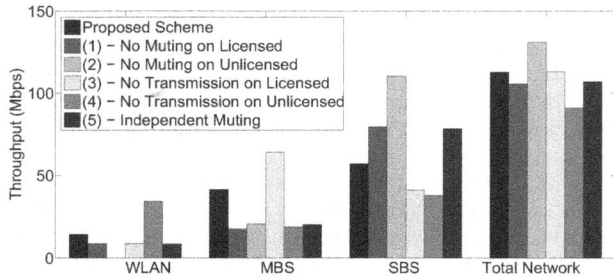

Figure 6: The aggregate throughput of the WLAN, MBS, SBS and total network for our proposed traffic balancing scheme in comparison with other approaches.

- *Case 5 - Independent Muting*: SBS operates on both bands, however, an independent mechanism is applied on each band for its coexistence with LTE and WLAN i.e., the coexistence of SBS and MBS on the licensed band and the coexistence of SBS and WLAN on the unlicensed band are solved separately. To realize this case, we consider two independent PF coexistence formulations for the muting of SBS on each of the licensed and unlicensed bands. In other words, when solving for α, we consider the WLAN and SBS throughput on the unlicensed band only, and when solving for β, we consider the MBS and SBS throughput on the licensed band only.

Note that cases 1 and 2, respectively, do not consider coexistence mechanisms on the licensed and unlicensed bands and thus are not practical solutions; however, we include them in our study for the sake of completeness.

Figure 6 shows the throughput achieved by WLAN, MBS, SBS and the total network for our proposed scheme as well as the other five studied approaches; the corresponding Jain's fairness index $\mathcal{J}(s_i)$ values are given in Table 1. We can make the following observations from these results. First, the WLAN throughput can be improved when coexisting with LTE-LAA small cells on the unlicensed band by taking into account the transmission of LTE-LAA small cells on the licensed and unlicensed bands and considering a holistic approach for the allocation of the resources on both bands i.e., optimizing both bands jointly. This can be observed from Figure 6 by comparing the total achieved throughput of WLAN for our proposed scheme with that of cases 1, 2, 3 and 5. Similarly, MBS throughput is higher with our proposed scheme compared to cases 1, 2, 4 and 5. Note that the WLAN and MBS throughputs will be, respectively, maximum when they exclusively use the unlicensed (case 4) and licensed bands (case 3), due to the absence of inter-technology interference in the former and lack of inter-tier interference in the latter. However, the total network throughput is the lowest for case 4; and case 3 results in a relatively unfair sharing of the radio resources as compared to our proposed scheme.

Second, considering an independent muting mechanism on the licensed and unlicensed bands (case 5) leads to performance degradation in terms of throughput and fairness, indicating that the effectiveness of our proposed traffic balancing scheme stems from its holistic nature. This is validated from Figure 6 and Table 1 by comparing the total network throughput and Jain's fairness index of our approach to that of case 5 i.e., $\mathcal{J}(s_i)=0.82$ and 0.57 respectively and 5.5% improvement in the total network throughput. As another observation, the independent muting approach provides very close performance for MBS to case 4 due to the fact that $\alpha=1$ and hence the optimization problem would be a function of the variable β only

Table 1: Jain's fairness index for the UEs achieved throughput of our proposed scheme and the other five cases.

Cases	Our scheme	(1)	(2)	(3)	(4)	(5)
$\mathcal{J}(s_i)$	0.82	0.55	0.45	0.73	0.92	0.57

and would correspond to the sub-problem of the coexistence on the licensed band of case 5. Similar argument applies for the WLAN throughput of case 5 which is similar to that of case 3 (where $\beta=0$).

Third, our proposed traffic balancing scheme utilizes the radio resources in the most efficient way compared to the other studied schemes as it provides a better tradeoff between efficiency (throughput) $\eta(s_i)$ and fairness $\mathcal{J}(s_i)$. In terms of efficiency, case 2 provides the maximum total network throughput since SBS will be transmitting on both bands simultaneously, however, WLAN would not be given opportunities for transmission and hence this would result in the least value of $\mathcal{J}(s_i)$ (0.45) as the radio resources are not shared fairly among the different technologies. Note also that our proposed scheme provides similar throughput as case 3; the major contribution to overall throughput in case 3 comes from MBS throughput which is maximum due to its exclusive use of the licensed band. However, comparing Jain's index fairness of our approach to that of case 3, we observe that our scheme allocates the radio resources in a more fair way unlike case 3 that causes a degradation in the WLAN and SBS throughputs. In terms of fairness, case 4 provides the most fair allocation of the licensed and the unlicensed bands as $\mathcal{J}(s_i)$ is the closest to 1 but it comes at the expense of throughput efficiency; total network throughput is the lowest with case 4. The reason for this high value of $\mathcal{J}(s_i)$ is because WLAN would have more transmission opportunities and hence its throughput would increase when using the channel exclusively as compared to sharing it with LTE-LAA SBS. On the other hand, the decrease in the value of $\eta(s_i)$ is due to the difference in the MAC layer throughputs with WiFi and LTE (65 Mbps and 75 Mbps respectively in our simulation setup) and the inter-tier interference level on the licensed band which results in the degradation of the SBS and MBS throughput.

7. DISCUSSION

In this section, we briefly discuss a couple of issues that warrant detailed exploration in future work.

7.1 Multiple Channels

Although we focus on a single unlicensed channel, our traffic balancing scheme can be extended to multiple unlicensed channels, each with a different muting variable $\{\alpha_1, ..., \alpha_c\}$, provided that the WiFi networks occupy disjoint channels (non-overlapping channels). Note that in such scenarios, the computational complexity increases due to the increase in the number of variables and thus would make it hard to obtain an online solution. An efficient extension to multiple channels is a key aspect for future work where one could potentially combine channel selection (as studied in [11, 18]) with the work in this paper in a joint framework.

7.2 Hidden Terminals

LTE use of unlicensed bands in the SDL mode gives rise to hidden terminal situations that need to be handled. In WLAN, this issue is addressed via the request-to-send/clear-to-send (RTS/CTS) messages; however, this method cannot be used for LTE-LAA since only DL transmissions are supported and hence SUEs are not able to transmit the CTS on the unlicensed spectrum. Therefore, to solve the hidden node problem, device-assisted enhancements need to be considered along with other existing mechanisms of the LTE system such as the periodic transmission of UE CSI/interference measurement over the licensed band. On the unlicensed band, a hidden terminal can be detected if SBS senses a good channel while the CSI report from the SUE shows a high interference value. This allows SBS to perform scheduling changes prior and during its operation on the unlicensed channel i.e., exclude the victim SUE for scheduling until its channel becomes idle and schedule other SUEs meanwhile. Alternatively, SBS may select another unlicensed channel to operate on [4].

8. CONCLUSION

In this paper, we have presented a formulation of the holistic LTE-LAA SBS traffic balancing across the licensed and unlicensed bands as an optimization problem that seeks to achieve a proportional fair coexistence of WiFi STAs, SUEs and MUEs. We have derived a closed form solution for the aforementioned optimization problem and proposed a transmission mechanism for the operation of the LTE-LAA SBS on both bands. Results show that LTE-LAA SBS aided by our solution would switch between or aggregate the licensed and unlicensed bands based on the interference/traffic level and number of active UEs in each band. It also provides a better performance for WLAN when coexisting with LTE and an efficient utilization of the radio resources compared to alternative approaches from the literature as it allows a better tradeoff between maximizing the total network throughput and achieving fairness among all network flows.

9. ACKNOWLEDGEMENT

We would like to thank Paul Patras for his discussions during the early stages of this research work.

10. REFERENCES

[1] 3rd Generation Partnership Project. Study on licensed-assisted access using LTE. Technical report, RP-141664, September 2014.

[2] E. Almeida, A. Cavalcante, R. Paiva, F. Chaves, F. Abinader, R. Vieira, S. Choudhury, E. Tuomaala, and K. Doppler. Enabling LTE/WiFi coexistence by LTE blank subframe allocation. *IEEE International Conference on Communications (ICC)*, June 2013.

[3] M. Bennis, M. Simsek, A. Czylwik, W. Saad, S. Valentin, and M. Debbah. When cellular meets WiFi in wireless small cell networks. *IEEE Communications Magazine*, 51(6):44–50, June 2013.

[4] A. Bhorkar, C. Ibars, and P. Zong. Performance analysis of LTE and WiFi in unlicensed band using stochastic geometry. *IEEE 25th International Symposium on Personal, Indoor and Mobile Radio Communications (PIMRC)*, September 2014.

[5] S. Boyd and L. Vandenberghe. *Convex Optimization*. Cambridge University Press, 2004.

[6] C. Cano and D. Leith. Coexistence of WiFi and LTE in unlicensed bands: a proportional fair allocation scheme. *IEEE International Conference on Communication Workshop (ICCW)*, June 2015.

[7] C. Cano and D. Leith. Unlicensed LTE/WiFi coexistence: Is LBT inherently fairer than CSAT? *IEEE International Conference on Communications (ICC)*, May 2016.

[8] K. Duffy. Mean field Markov models of wireless local area networks. *Markov Processes and Related Fields*, 16(2), April 2010.

[9] A. Elsherif, W. Chen, A. Ito, and Z. Ding. Resource allocation and inter-cell interference management for dual-access small cells. *IEEE Journal on Selected Areas in Communications*, 33(6):1082–1096, June 2015.

[10] Z. Guan and T. Melodia. CU-LTE: spectrally-efficient and fair coexistence between LTE and Wi-Fi in unlicensed bands. *IEEE Conference on Computer Communications (INFOCOM)*, April 2016.

[11] C. Ibars, A. Bhorkar, A. Papathanassiou, and P. Zong. Channel selection for licensed assisted access in LTE based on UE measurements. *IEEE 82nd Vehicular Technology Conference (VTC Fall)*, September 2015.

[12] IEEE 802.11 WG. *Wireless LAN Medium Access Control (MAC) and Physical Layer (PHY) Specifications*. IEEE Std 802.11, 2012.

[13] Y. Jian, C. Shih, B. Krishnaswamy, and R. Sivakumar. Coexistence of Wi-Fi and LAA-LTE: Experimental evaluation, analysis and insights. *IEEE International Conference on Communication Workshop (ICCW)*, June 2015.

[14] F. Liu, E. Bala, E. Erkip, M. Beluri, and R. Yang. Small cell traffic balancing over licensed and unlicensed bands. *IEEE Transactions on Vehicular Technology (TVT)*, December 2014.

[15] D. Lopez-Perez, I. Guvenc, G. de la Roche, M. Kountouris, T. Q. S. Quek, and J. Zhang. Enhanced intercell interference coordination challenges in heterogeneous networks. *IEEE Wireless Communication Magazine*, 18(3):22–30, June 2011.

[16] G. R4-092042. Simulation assumptions and parameters for FDD HeNB RF requirement. Technical report, 3GPP, 2009.

[17] S. Sagari, S. Baysting, D. Saha, I. Seskar, W. Trappe, and D. Raychaudhuri. Coordinated dynamic spectrum management of LTE-U and Wi-Fi networks. *IEEE Dynamic Spectrum Access Networks (DySPAN)*, September 2015.

[18] O. Sallent, J. Perez-Romero, R. Ferrus, and R. Agusti. Learning-based coexistence for LTE operation in unlicensed bands. *IEEE International Conference on Communication Workshop (ICCW)*, June 2015.

[19] A. Sediq, R. Gohary, R. Schoenen, and H. Yanikomeroglu. Optimal tradeoff between sum-rate efficiency and Jain's fairness index in resource allocation. *IEEE Transactions on Wireless Communications*, 12(7):3496–3509, July 2013.

[20] H. Shi, R. V. Prasad, E. Onur, and I. Niemegeers. Fairness in wireless networks: issues, measures and challenges. *IEEE Communications Surveys and Tutorials*, 16(1):5–24, First Quarter 2014.

[21] Y. Wang and K. Pedersen. Time and power domain interference management for LTE networks with macro-cells and HeNBs. In *Vehicular Technology Conference (VTC Fall)*, September 2011.

[22] M. Xing, Y. Peng, T. Xia, H. Long, and K. Zheng. Adaptive spectrum sharing of LTE co-existing with WLAN in unlicensed frequency bands. *IEEE 81st Vehicular Technology Conference (VTC Spring)*, May 2015.

[23] R. Zhang, M. Wang, L. Cai, Z. Zheng, X. Shen, and L. Xie. LTE-Unlicensed: The future of spectrum aggregation for cellular networks. 22(3):150–159, June 2015.

Learning-Based Resource Allocation Scheme for TDD-Based 5G CRAN System

Sahar Imtiaz
KTH Royal Institute of
Technology,
School of Electrical
Engineering,
Stockholm, Sweden
sahari@kth.se

Hadi Ghauch
KTH Royal Institute of
Technology,
School of Electrical
Engineering,
Stockholm, Sweden
ghauch@kth.se

M. Mahboob Ur Rahman[*]
KTH Royal Institute of
Technology,
School of Electrical
Engineering,
Stockholm, Sweden
mahboob.rahman@ee.kth.se

George Koudouridis
Radio Network Technology
Research,
Huawei Technologies,
Kista, Sweden
george.koudouridis
@huawei.com

James Gross
KTH Royal Institute of
Technology,
School of Electrical
Engineering,
Stockholm, Sweden
james.gross@ee.kth.se

ABSTRACT

Provision of high data rates with always-on connectivity to high mobility users is one of the motivations for design of fifth generation (5G) systems. High system capacity can be achieved by coordination between large number of antennas, which is done using the cloud radio access network (CRAN) design in 5G systems. In terms of baseband processing, allocation of appropriate resources to the users is necessary to achieve high system capacity, for which the state of the art uses the users' channel state information (CSI); however, they do not take into account the associated overhead, which poses a major bottleneck for the effective system performance. In contrast to this approach, this paper proposes the use of *machine learning* for allocating resources to high mobility users using only their position estimates. Specifically, the 'random forest' algorithm, a supervised machine learning technique, is used to design a learning-based resource allocation scheme by exploiting the relationships between the system parameters and the users' position estimates. In this way, the overhead for CSI acquisition is avoided by using the position estimates instead, with better spectrum utilization. While the initial numerical investigations, with minimum number of users in the system, show that the proposed learning-based scheme achieves 86% of the efficiency achieved by the perfect CSI-based scheme, if the effect of overhead is factored in, the proposed scheme performs better than the CSI-based approach. In a realistic scenario, with multiple users in the system, the significant increase in overhead for the CSI-based scheme leads to a performance gain of 100%, or more, by using the proposed scheme, and thus proving the proposed scheme to be more efficient in terms of system performance.

Keywords

5G; CRAN; TDD; resource allocation; machine learning.

1. INTRODUCTION

Increased usage of smart electronic and wireless-capable devices, such as hand-held mobile sets, tablets and laptops, in the recent years, has resulted in increased demand for higher data rates. Furthermore, the users of such devices demand full-time access to data packet connection, irrespective of their location and surrounding environment. Therefore, future communication systems are expected to have greater system efficiency and better provision of data service to the users compared to existing fourth generation (4G) technology [1]. The fifth generation (5G) systems will be designed to provide a $\times 1000$ increase in the system capacity [2], as well as almost $\times 10$ decrease in latency [3], compared to Long Term Evolution-Advanced (LTE-A) systems. Moreover, they will be able to provide high system efficiency and always-on connectivity, specially to high mobility users, in Ultra-Dense Network (UDN) deployments [4].

To achieve these goals for 5G, one possible approach is to massively increase the number of antennas (either centrally or de-centrally) [5]. Research from the last few years indicates that significant performance gain can be obtained from massive antenna deployment, if transmission from such antennas is tightly coordinated [6], [7]. This tight coordination includes phase-level synchronization, which is needed for joint transmission, as well as the synchronization needed

[*]M. Mahboob Ur Rahman was affiliated with KTH from November 2013 - April 2016. Currently, he is an Assistant Professor at Information Technology University (ITU), Lahore, Pakistan.

for coordinated precoding. Using tight synchronization between these large number of antennas leads to a coordination overhead [8]. To overcome this problem, the cloud radio access network (CRAN) architecture has been introduced, which is a centralized, cloud-computing based network architecture [9]. In CRAN, the baseband units (the main signal processing units of the network) are connected to the cloud to form a pool of centralized processors, which is then connected to the set of distributed antennas (the radio access units) in the system. Thus, separating the baseband units from the radio access units helps in achieving synchronized coordination between large sets of antennas, at a relatively reduced cost in the system. However, besides the synchronization overhead, the overhead for acquiring channel state information (CSI) of the mobile users still exists, which increases with the number of antennas, the granularity of the acquired CSI as well as the mobility of the terminal users. In real-time scenarios, consideration of this CSI acquisition overhead is necessary for evaluating the effective system performance.

The main purpose of CSI acquisition is to perform the allocation of resources such that all users can be served well. The resources include time and/or frequency resources, coding rates, modulation schemes, transmit beamforming, and many more. Much work has been done in the past few years for designing efficient resource allocation schemes, specific to certain 5G system characteristics. A non-orthogonal resource allocation scheme, called non-orthogonal multiple access (NOMA) [10], has been investigated in [11], for increased system throughput and accommodating maximum users by sharing time and frequency resources. The technique of dynamic time domain duplexing for centralized and decentralized resource allocation in 5G has been studied in [4]. In [12], a radio resource allocation scheme for multi-beam operating systems has been proposed, where the allocation of the radio resources to a user is based on its channel state and the beam serving that user. The authors in [13] propose a resource block (RB) allocation algorithm, which exploits the combination of multi-user diversity and users' CSI for allocation of RBs, with carrier aggregation, and modulation and coding scheme (MCS) for throughput maximization in 5G LTE-A network.

Exploiting CSI for high mobility users is associated with significant system overhead, which is not considered in those studies. On the other hand, the system's performance is affected if outdated CSI is used for resource allocation for high mobility users [14]. One of the network deployment architectures suited for achieving the expected targets of a 5G system is the ultra-dense small cell deployment, in which the users are expected to be in line-of-sight (LOS) with the serving base stations at almost all times. In this case, the users' position information can be used instead of their CSI [15]. More precisely, the optimal allocation of resources depends on many system parameters (including users' position, users' velocity, propagation environment, interference in the system, and so on), which are inherently correlated. One way of exploiting these hidden correlations among system parameters for efficient allocation of resources is through Machine Learning. Various machine learning algorithms have been used in the state of art for resource allocation in wireless communication systems; some examples include using support vector machines (SVMs) for power control in CDMA systems [16], prediction of the next cell of a mobile user us-

ing supervised learning techniques and CSI [17], and rate adaptation using random forests (a form of supervised machine learning technique) in vehicular networks [18]. Use of machine learning has also been investigated for orthogonal frequency division multiplex-multiple input, multiple output (OFDM-MIMO) based 5G systems [19], [20]. However, for time division duplex (TDD) MIMO systems, the resource allocation is done based on instantaneous CSI availability (without using learning, or considering the CSI acquistion overhead), where resource allocation is referred to RB assignment [13], rate allocation [21] and beamforming for joint transmission-based coordinated multipoint (CoMP) [22].

This paper proposes and evaluates a novel learning-based resource allocation scheme for TDD multi-user MIMO (MU-MIMO) CRAN systems that uses position estimates of high-mobility users for the resource allocation, instead of instantaneous CSI measurements. The output of the proposed scheme machine learning-based scheme, which is performed by means of a 'random forest' algorithm, is the assignment of resources to users including transmit beam, receive filter and packet size. The robustness of the proposed resource allocation scheme is tested by using different values in training and test datasets for random forest, such as using accurate position estimates for training the random forest and testing its performance using data having inaccurate position estimates of the users. Afterwards, the system goodput is computed for the proposed resource allocation scheme and is compared to the system goodput when instantaneous CSI of users (with a system overhead) is used for resource allocation. The results show that the proposed scheme achieves about 86% of the system performance obtained for traditional CSI-based resource allocation scheme. Furthermore, a maximum performance loss of 5% is observed when either the scatterers' density or the shadowing effect varies, thus showing the robustness of the proposed scheme to changes in the propagation environment.

For practical consideration, this paper also presents an overhead model based on the frame structure for 5G TDD proposed in [23], to evaluate the effective system throughput for both the proposed and the traditional resource allocation schemes. The results show that for minimum number of users present in the system, the proposed position-based scheme incurs a system overhead of only 2.4% compared to the traditional CSI acquisition-based resource allocation which has an overhead of 19%; and, therefore, gives better effective system throughput than the traditional CSI-based scheme. The effectiveness of using the proposed scheme improves significantly when a large number of users are present in the system, where a gain of about 100% is achieved for effective system throughput, compared to the traditional CSI-based scheme.

The structure for the rest of the paper is as follows: Section 2 presents the system model. Details of the proposed learning-based resource allocation scheme, and the 'random forest' algorithm are presented in section 3. Simulation results and relevant discussions are presented in section 4, along with the details regarding the overhead model and its effect on system throughput. Section 5 concludes the paper.

2. SYSTEM MODEL

Consider a scenario (Figure 1), based on CRAN architecture, where N users are being served by R remote radio

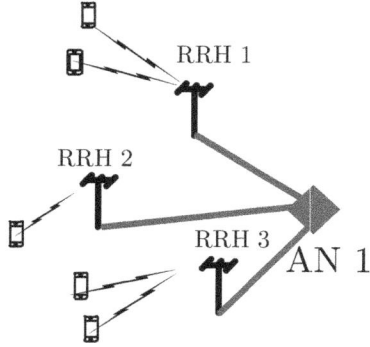

Figure 1: The CRAN architecture for 5G system

heads (RRHs), and all RRHs are connected to an aggregation node (AN). The AN is the computational hub where all baseband processing takes place, whereas RRHs mainly serve as radio frequency (RF) front ends. Further details of the CRAN based system model can be found in [24]. This work focuses on the downlink communication of the aforementioned 5G CRAN system model. A TDD based frame structure is considered for downlink communication, and the operational frequency of the CRAN system is f_c. The users are assumed to be moving at high speeds ($v_{\text{Rx}} > 50$ km/h). The RRHs are densely deployed (UDN deployment), such that the users are expected to be in LOS with the serving RRHs. Also, each user is equipped with N_{Rx} antennas, each at a height of h_{Rx} from the ground, and will be served by an RRH having R_{Tx} antennas, each at a height of h_{Tx} from the ground.

The channel between the RRH r and user n is characterized by the spatial system parameters [such as the angle of arrival (AoA) and the angle of departure (AoD)], the frequency-based system parameters (such as operational frequency of the system, and the Doppler shift), as well as the time-dependent system parameters (such as change in user's position, change in scatterers' density, propagation environment, etc.). All RRHs are expected to serve at least one user, in the same time-slot, implying that all users will experience interference from other users being served by the same RRH, as well as cross-channel interference from the neighboring RRHs. Each RRH is connected to the AN, which acts as a resource allocation unit, and consists of a set of resources, including transmit beams, receive filters, and packet sizes, to serve a given user. Full-buffer condition is assumed, which means that at each time, at least one user n needs to be allocated resources by the AN for being served by the associated RRH r. A fixed set of transmit beams B_{Tx} is available to serve the users, based on the geometry of the propagation scenario, and is also used to design a set of receive filters B_{Rx}, which will be used by the terminal users for reduced-interference reception. The position coordinates $\mathcal{P}_{n,(x,y,z)}$ of the nth user are available at the rth RRH, with some inaccuracy, and is the primary parameter used for allocation of resources by the AN connected to the RRH.

For simplifying the analysis, we consider that each RRH is serving only one user in a given time-slot, so that only cross-RRH (or inter-RRH) interference exists in the system. Based on all these parameters, the signal-to-interference-and-noise ratio (SINR) for a user n, at time t, is calculated as follows:

$$\gamma_{n,t}(\phi_n^a, \phi_n^d) = \frac{P_{n,t}(\phi_n^a, \phi_n^d)}{\sigma^2 + \sum_{\substack{m=1 \\ m \neq n}}^{N} P_{m,t}(\phi_n^a, \phi_m^d)}, \tag{1}$$

where, $P_{n,t}$ is the received signal power for a user n, at time t, and is given by:

$$\begin{aligned} P_{n,t}(\phi_n^a, \phi_n^d) = P_{\text{Tx}} h_{\text{PL}}^2 \cdot \\ \cdot \ |\boldsymbol{U}(\phi_n^a)^\dagger \boldsymbol{H}_{n,t}(\phi_n^a, \phi_n^d) \boldsymbol{V}(\phi_n^d)|^2. \end{aligned} \tag{2}$$

Here, P_{Tx} is the allocated transmit power per RRH, h_{PL}^2 denotes the pathloss, ϕ_n^a is the azimuth AoA of user n, and ϕ_n^d is its azimuth AoD. $\boldsymbol{U}(\phi_n^a)$ is the receive filter with the main beam focused in the direction closest to ϕ_n^a, and $\boldsymbol{V}(\phi_n^d)$ is the transmit beamformer with the main beam located in the direction closest to ϕ_n^d (details regarding beamforming can be found in [25]). $\boldsymbol{H}_{n,t}(\phi_n^a, \phi_n^d)$ is the channel matrix for an instance of time t for a given ϕ_n^a and ϕ_n^d, and σ^2 is the noise power. $(.)^\dagger$ denotes the Hermitian of a vector or a matrix.

The SINR computed for a given combination of $\boldsymbol{U}(\phi_n^a)$ and $\boldsymbol{V}(\phi_n^d)$, with the corresponding channel matrix $\boldsymbol{H}_{n,t}(\phi_n^a, \phi_n^d)$, is used to compute the transport capacity for user n by the following formula:

$$C_{n,t} = S \times \log_2(1 + \gamma_{n,t}(\phi_n^a, \phi_n^d)). \tag{3}$$

Here, S is the symbol length, which is the product of the transmission time interval (TTI) and bandwidth BW of the system. For determining the transmission success or failure, the error model based on Shannon's capacity (Eq. (3)) is used; if the nth user's packet size $< C_{n,t}$ then the packet is successfully transmitted, otherwise the packet transmission for user n fails.

2.1 Problem Statement

In the considered CRAN system, the task of the AN is to allocate the resources efficiently for each RRH-user link, per TTI, such that the system's sum-throughput is maximized. For this purpose, it needs to acquire the CSI of all users in the system, on per TTI basis, which incurs a large system overhead. The overhead is even larger for high mobility users who are susceptible to outdated CSI measurements.

One way of avoiding the CSI overhead is to use the position information of the high-speed users; since LOS exists, the resource allocation for users can be done based on their position information rather than using their instantaneous CSI. However, the position information alone is not sufficient for efficient resource allocation, rather, the hidden correlation among the position estimates and the other system parameters has to be exploited together for this purpose. We propose to use *machine learning* for accomplishing this task. Specifically, we use machine learning to design a resource allocation scheme for the aforementioned system, purely based on the users' position information, such that the CSI acquisition is not needed at all. We will investigate the performance of this *learning-based resource allocation scheme* in comparison to the conventional CSI-based resource allocation technique, also taking into account the system overhead. Furthermore, we want to test the robustness of our scheme when the position information for the users in the system is inaccurate. In the next section, we discuss the details regarding the design of the learning-based resource allocation

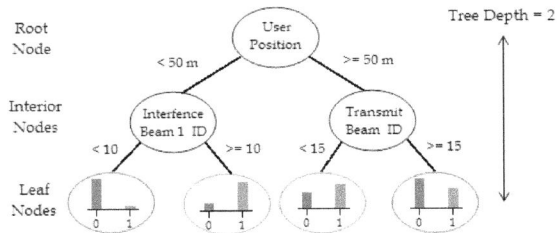

Figure 2: An example of a binary random decision tree

scheme, along with some relevant background on machine learning.

3. DESIGN OF THE LEARNING-BASED RE-SOURCE ALLOCATION SCHEME

Learning the different correlated parameters is accomplished using *machine learning*, which is defined as "the capability of a computer program or a machine to develop new knowledge or skill from the existing and non-existing data samples to optimize some performance criteria" [26]. 'Random forest algorithm' [27] is the learning technique used in this work for learning the system parameters, and predicting the probability of successful or failed transmission of data packets from a given RRH to the respective user(s). We first provide some background on the random forest algorithm, followed by the details about how can this algorithm be used for designing the learning-based resource allocation scheme.

3.1 Background on Random Forest Algorithm

The random forest algorithm is a supervised learning technique, which consists of a number of decision trees (hence the term 'forest') that are generated by using the statistical information of the supplied dataset, to develop a hypothesis for predicting the outcome of a future instance [18], [28]. Each instance x of the dataset $\boldsymbol{x}$ consists of two parts: a set of data characteristics $\boldsymbol{I}$, called *features*, and the relevant output variable y. These two parts collectively form the *input feature vector* x_i. To learn the information in the data features $\boldsymbol{I}$ (the 'training' process), the random forest algorithm constructs T_n binary random decision trees, each having a maximum depth of T_d. Each tree has one *root node* and several *interior* and *leaf nodes*. Figure 2 shows an example of a binary random decision tree, consisting of two interior and four leaf nodes. Each root node and interior node is constructed by a decision threshold based on a (randomly selected) feature subset from the set of given $\boldsymbol{I}$ input features. Thus, each tree has a different subset of features considered for decision threshold at each of its nodes. The output variable is represented by the leaf nodes of a decision tree. The instance on which the prediction has to be made, is traversed through all decision trees in the forest, to get T_n output variables, called *votes*. The output variable y is predicted by aggregating all the votes and selecting the majority class (category or value of the output variable) from among those votes.

For making each tree in the training phase, a training dataset $\boldsymbol{z}$, having the same size as the training data $\boldsymbol{x}$, is con-

structed by using training samples which are randomly chosen, with replacement, from $\boldsymbol{x}$. This random selection with replacement makes some instances from the training data to be used repeatedly, while some are not used at all. The later instances are collectively known as *out-of-the-bag* (OOB) examples and represent almost 30% of the total training data [27]. A random subset of input variables is used for every node of a decision tree from the $\boldsymbol{z}$ training examples. A decision threshold is determined for the selected input variable, based on which the left or right traversing path in the subsequent levels of the random decision tree is chosen. It is critical to select the input variable at a node, as well as the decision threshold, such that the *purity* of the subsequent levels of the random decision tree is maximized. Purity measures the extent to which the resulting child node is made up of cases having the same output variable [29]. Thus, an ideal threshold at any node would divide the data in such a way that the resulting child nodes would give distinct values of the output variable.

The generated random forest has two types of qualitative measures. First is the *prediction accuracy*, which measures how accurately the random forest predicts the output variable for a given dataset. If the prediction accuracy is evaluated on the training data, it is called the *training accuracy*, while the same when evaluated on a newly collected dataset is called the *test accuracy*. Second qualitative measure is the *importance of an input variable*, which indicates how important a particular input variable is in determining the desired output variable. It is generally proven that the random forest algorithm can cater for the missing input data variables, is robust to noisy data and is computationally efficient [27]. Also, it does not suffer from the problem of over-fitting, by using only a subset of the training data for making the random decision trees which make up the random forest. Due to all these properties, the random forest algorithm has been previously applied to system performance optimization techniques including intrusion detection for mobile devices [30], and designing a rate adaptation scheme in vehicular networks using the random forest [18].

3.2 The Learning-Based Resource Allocation Scheme

The main aim of the learning-based resource allocation scheme is to use only the position estimate of the users and learn its relationship with different system parameters and resources, such that the system resources are efficiently utilized without incurring any CSI overhead. We first explain the structure of the learning-based resource allocation scheme, and then present its working details.

3.2.1 Structure of the Learning-Based Resource Allocation Scheme

The structure of the learning-based resource allocation scheme can be divided into three parts: the pre-processing unit, the machine learning unit, and the scheduler.

The Pre-Processing Unit

The main function of the pre-processing unit is to design and produce the training dataset. The training dataset is constructed off-line, and hence the CSI as well as the position information of the users are available at the AN, along with the information for the resources to be allocated. In (off-line phase of) the pre-processing unit, the optimal transport capacity for each user is computed using its CSI (considering all the other users in the system), based on the maximization of the system's sum-transport capacity. Then, the optimal transmit beam b_{Tx} and receive filter b_{Rx} combinations for a given user position $\mathcal{P}_{n,(x,y,z)}$ are identified, for which the optimal transport capacity is obtained (i.e. the exhaustive search), and are used as the input features for the training dataset of the machine learning unit. Based on the values of the optimal transport capacity for the overall system, a set of packet sizes is designed, which consists of 5 discrete values, and the optimal transport capacity for each user is checked against those packet sizes (according to the Shannon's capacity-based error model) to generate the output variables, 0 or 1, for the training dataset. Thus, the user's ID n, its position information $\mathcal{P}_{n,(x,y,z)}$, optimal transmit beam b_{Tx}, optimal receive filter b_{Rx}, the packet size PS, and the output variable (0 or 1) form the input feature vector, and a set of those input feature vectors constitute the training dataset to be used by the machine learning unit.

The Machine Learning Unit

The training of the machine learning unit is done off-line, where the training dataset is used to learn the input features, i.e. the user's ID n, its position information $\mathcal{P}_{n,(x,y,z)}$, optimal transmit beam b_{Tx}, optimal receive filter b_{Rx}, and the packet size PS. The learning is essentially done to construct the random forest, with the parameters like number of decision trees T_n, tree depth T_d and number of random features for split at each tree node, chosen so as to optimize the training accuracy of the random forest. Here, it should be noted that the performance of the random forest is affected by the 'bias' in output variable distribution for the overall training dataset, i.e. the training accuracy is affected if, for example, a large number ($> 80\%$) of input feature vectors have class '0' as output variable than class '1', and vice versa. This bias in class distribution is being taken care of by the pre-processing unit, such that the training dataset has a balanced number of input feature vectors for both the classes '0' and '1', as the output variable. Once an optimal training accuracy is achieved, the machine learning unit is ready to be used for testing new dataset(s) generated on run-time in a realistic system.

The Scheduler

This proposed scheme includes a scheduler as the last unit, whose main task is to forward the information about the allocated resources (obtained from the machine learning unit) for each user in the system, to their corresponding RRH. This scheduler is, however, sensitive to the occurrence of false-positives in the output from the machine learning unit. Technically, a false-positive occurs when an input feature vector has '0' as its output variable realistically, but the learning algorithm wrongly predicts the output variable to be '1' for that input feature vector. In the proposed scheme, false-positive occurrence makes the algorithm more error-prone, by suggesting a higher packet size PS_{o+1} to serve a particular user, though, realistically, the highest packet size that can serve the user is PS_o. In this case, the scheduler backs-off the packet size for transmission, and transmits a packet size, chosen randomly, from the set of packet sizes one less than PS_{o+1}, i.e. the packet size for which the false-positive detection occurred. We call this a 'random back-off scheduler', which operates in combination with the output

predicted by the random forest, and thus completes the design structure of learning-based resource allocation scheme. The false-positive occurrence for an input feature vector is identified as follows: the given input feature vector is compared with the input feature vectors available in the training dataset, and the output for the closest-related input feature vector in the training data is compared with the output predicted for the given input feature vector by the machine learning unit. Based on this false-positive detection, the scheduler operates more sensitively for those input feature vectors. In this way, the resource allocation scheme ensures that erroneous predictions by the machine learning unit does not significantly impact the system's performance.

3.2.2 Working of the Learning-Based Resource Allocation Scheme

In a realistic system, the position estimate $\hat{\mathcal{P}}_{n,(x,y,z)}$ of the user n is acquired by the corresponding RRH and reported back to the AN. This position estimate is used by the pre-processing unit, where it is compared against the user position information $\mathcal{P}_{n,(x,y,z)}$ available in the training dataset, and the position information in the training data that gives the minimum value for $|\mathcal{P}_{n,(x,y,z)} - \hat{\mathcal{P}}_{n,(x,y,z)}|$ is chosen to construct the input feature vector for the test dataset. Once the closest position estimate $\mathcal{P}_{n,(x,y,z)}^o$ is obtained, it is combined with the corresponding optimal transmit beam b_{Tx}, receive filter b_{Rx}, and with the 5 discrete packet sizes PS to form a set of input feature vectors for different packet sizes corresponding to the position estimate $\hat{\mathcal{P}}_{n,(x,y,z)}$.

This set of input feature vectors is then passed to the machine learning unit, where each of the input feature vector is parsed through the random forest to obtain the *votes* for the predicted output variable by each decision tree in the forest. In essence, the votes are obtained for successful transmission (i.e for $y = 1$) of a packet size PS_p and denote the packet-size success rate (PSR) for PS_p. This PSR also denotes the tendency of the machine learning unit's predicted output variable; if the PSR $\geq T_n/2$ (T_n being the number of trees in the random forest), then the predicted output variable is '1', otherwise, it is '0'. This predicted output variable is tested for false-positive detection by the scheduler, by comparing it to the output variable for the corresponding input feature vector in the training dataset. If the prediction is correct, the scheduler retains the packet size PS_p; otherwise (in case of false-positive occurrence), it chooses a random packet size PS_r, to derive a prediction for the packet size for transmission PS_{os}. The PSR corresponding to PS_{os} is used to compute the system goodput predicted by the learning-based resource allocation scheme, as follows:

$$Goodput_{os} = PSR_{os} \times PS_{os} \tag{4}$$

Figure 3 shows the different steps of the proposed learning-based resource allocation scheme. Overall, the random forest algorithm is expected to learn the assignment of optimal packet size, transmit beam and receive filter for each user, in order to maximize the system goodput, using only the users' position information but without knowing their CSI. In reality, the position estimates of high-mobility users can be acquired with certain precision using an extended Kalman filter (EKF), along with the direction of arrival (DoA) and time of arrival (ToA) estimates of those users [31]. Since the random forest algorithm is robust to noisy

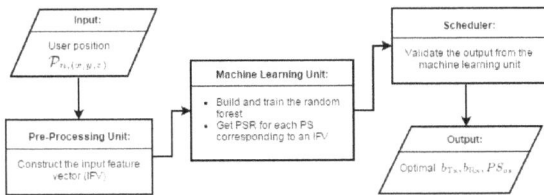

Figure 3: The proposed Learning-Based Resource Allocation Scheme

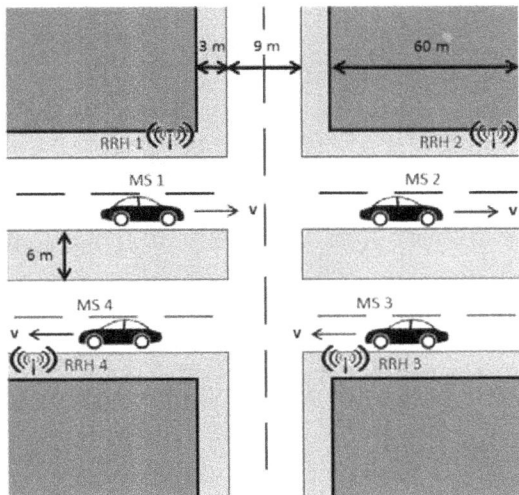

Figure 4: The simulation scenario; each RRH serves one user

Table 1: Parameter Settings for the Simulator

Parameter	Value
f_c	3.5 GHz
BW	5 MHz
R_{Tx}	8
N_{Rx}	2
h_{Tx}	10 m
h_{Rx}	1.5 m
P_{Tx}	1 mW
TTI	1 ms
v_{Rx}	30 m/s

Table 2: Training Accuracy of Random Forest for Different Parameter Settings

T_n	T_d	Training Accuracy (%)
5	3	83.3
10	**3**	**86**
10	4	86.9
20	3	86.65
20	4	87.2

data, the learning-based resource allocation scheme is expected to perform well when noisy position estimates of the users are available for either the training or test datasets (or both). The performance of the proposed resource allocation scheme is evaluated by performing system-level simulations, which are discussed in the next section.

4. RESULTS AND DISCUSSION

In this section, we first compare the performance of the proposed scheme to that of the traditional resource allocation scheme based on user's CSI. We also investigate the robustness of the proposed scheme when inaccurate position estimates are available in the test dataset, or when the propagation environment parameters vary in the training and the test datasets (specifically, change of scatterers' density and change in shadowing characteristics). Afterwards, we present the effect of overhead on the proposed and the traditional schemes on the theoretical system throughput for a 5G CRAN system.

4.1 Evaluation Methodology

The performance evaluation of the proposed scheme in section 3.2 is done by doing realistic simulations using a discrete event simulator (DES) called Horizon [32]. The propagation scenario, shown in figure 4, consists of 4 RRHs, each serving one user, and is implemented in Horizon for simulating a CRAN based multi-users, multi-RRHs communication

system (as presented in section 2). Based on the propagation scenario, a fixed set of transmit beams is designed in the following way: the transmit beams are formed using geometric beamforming, where each consecutive beam is separated by 3° angular resolution. The receive filters are, essentially, geometric beams formed by using the multiple antennas at the user end, and are designed in the same way as the transmit beams but with an angular resolution of 12°. The parametrization for system simulations is given in table 1. The channel coefficients for downlink communication are extracted from the simulator for each TTI, i.e. after every 1 ms. Ray-tracing based METIS channel model [33] for Madrid grid is implemented in Horizon for generating the channel coefficients. Details about the ray-tracer based channel model can be found in [34].

After computing the channel matrices, the training dataset is generated using the procedure explained in section 3.2.1. As mentioned earlier, the training data is used to build random forests for various parameter settings, from which the random forest with the optimal training accuracy is chosen for further processing. The random forest is constructed using the random forest implementation in WEKA software [35]. Table 2 shows the values of training accuracy obtained for different parameter settings of random forest algorithm. Based on the results, the random forest with $T_n = 10$ and $T_d = 3$ was chosen for further processing, with the number of random features used for split at each node of decision tree as $\sqrt{I}$ (I being the number of features in the input feature vector) [27]. Here, it should be noted that selecting the random forest with the highest training accuracy (from table 2, for $T_n = 20$ and $T_d = 4$) is not always the best choice; having a larger number of trees for a small set of input features I increases the correlation among the trees (thus reducing the robustness of the random forest to noisy data), as well as increases the computation time for constructing the random forest.

A total of 100 user positions (for each user) are chosen randomly from the available set of 1000 positions (for each user)

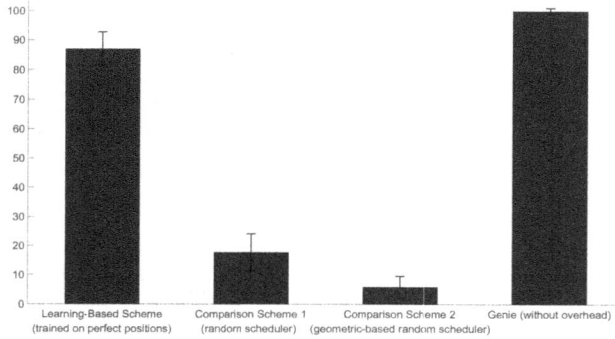

Figure 5: System goodput (in %age relative to the Genie) for perfect position information of all users

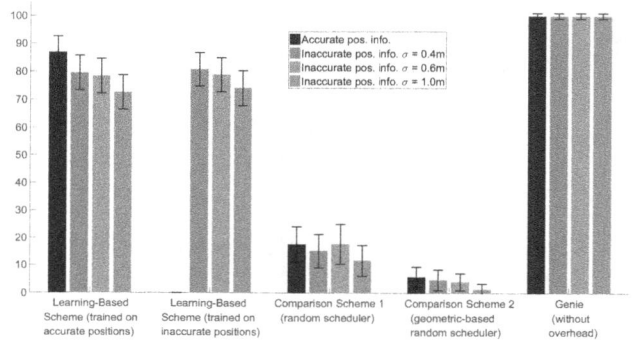

Figure 6: System goodput (in %age relative to the Genie) for different schemes and various possibilities of available position information

in the overall simulation scenario, for generating the training and test datasets, each having 0.25 million samples. The output from the random forest is combined with the scheduler, as explained in section 3.2.2, and the system goodput (in bits/TTI) is computed. The first simulation is performed by setting the scattering objects' density as $0.01/m^2$, i.e., 1 scatterer per 10×10 m^2 area. The performance of learning-based resource allocation scheme is compared against the following schemes:

- Random packet scheduler: Schedules a randomly selected packet size for each user using the optimal selection strategy for transmit beam and receive filter.

- Random packet scheduler for geometric beam and filter assignment: Schedules a randomly selected packet size for each user using the location-based assignment of transmit beam and receive filter.

- Optimal packet scheduler (the Genie): Schedules the optimal packet size for each user based on the optimal transport capacity for each user, obtained through the instantaneous CSI of the users.

4.2 Results for the Proposed Scheme

Figure 5 shows the system goodput obtained for each of the resource allocation schemes when perfect information about each user position is available. The results are shown as the system goodput relative to the one obtained by the Genie. It can be seen that the learning-based resource allocation scheme performs very well compared to the Genie, and achieves about 86% of the optimal system performance (i.e. Genie without system overhead). The training accuracy of the random forest is 86%, where the performance loss is due to the inequitable distribution of output variables in the training dataset. The random packet scheduler performs worse, which highlights the importance of learning the system parameters for optimal resource allocation. The geometric assignment-based random scheduler also shows poor performance (only 6% goodput compared to the optimal one), due to the fact that geometric-based allocation of transmit beam and receive filter is not the optimal strategy for serving a user in an interference-limited system.

In reality, the perfect position information is not always available, rather there is some inaccuracy involved in the reported coordinates for the user's position. Figure 6 shows

the relative system goodput for all resource allocation schemes when the user position is having a root mean squared error of 0.4, 0.6 and 1.0 m. It can be seen that the position inaccuracy affects the system performance for all sub-optimal resource allocation schemes due to the fact that optimal transmit beam and receive filter combination is not valid for the inaccurate position information. Despite this, the learning-based allocation scheme achieves more than 72% of the optimal system performance (for the highest position inaccuracy), which is 4 times better than any of the other comparison schemes. For having a fair performance comparison, we trained the random forests for each of the cases of inaccurate position availability, and tested their performance against the relative test data for inaccurate position information. The results show that no significant improvement in performance can be obtained if the learning is performed for inaccurate position information datasets; the random forest trained on accurate user position information can also operate effectively for any case of inaccurate user position information.

To observe the effect of randomness in the system parameters on the performance of different resource allocation schemes, the scatterers' density is varied. Figure 7 shows the relative system goodput for learning-based resource allocation scheme for different values of scattering objects' density when perfect user position is available. The random forest in the machine learning unit is trained for scatterers' density of $0.01/m^2$ (the same as used for previous simulations), and is tested for datasets generated using different values of scatterers' density. The results show that the relative system goodput is not affected severely when learning-based resource allocation scheme is used for changing scatterers' density in the propagation environment. The maximum difference with respect to the Genie is 83% (for 10 scatterers per 100 m^2 area), when the dataset generated for different densities of scattering objects is tested against the random forest generated using a fixed scatterers' density. Realistically, the goodput of the system is expected to be not affected severely by the change of scatterers' density, since LOS link exists at all times between the users and their corresponding RRHs. Keeping this into consideration, the learning-based resource allocation scheme is seen to be robust for changing scatterers' density, where the maximum performance loss compared to the Genie varies by less than

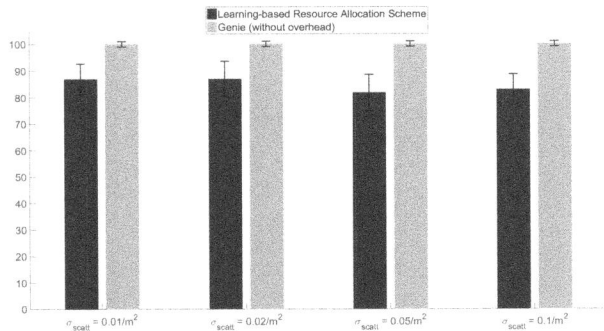

Figure 7: System goodput (in %age relative to the Genie) for different scattering densities for perfect users' position information

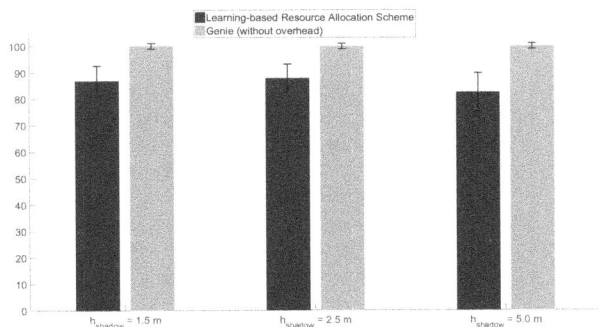

Figure 8: System goodput (in %age relative to the Genie) for different heights of the shadow object for perfect users' position information and $\sigma_{\text{scatt}} = 0.01/\text{m}^2$

5% as the number of scatterers per 100 m^2 of area is increased.

Another system parameter that can vary randomly in a realistic propagation scenario is the effect of shadowing. Figure 8 shows the performance of the proposed scheme compared to the optimal system performance when the height of shadow object is increased from 1.5 m to 5.0 m. Here, again, we observe that the performance loss does not vary significantly; maximum loss of about 5% is observed, when the shadowing effect is increased by increasing the height of the shadow object. Since LOS is existent at all times between the users and their corresponding RRHs, therefore, the channel coefficients do not vary significantly with the variation in shadowing effect, which in turn does not affect the transport capacity per user, and hence, the overall sum-goodput of the system.

4.3 Effect of Overhead on Throughput of a 5G System

After comparing the performance of the proposed learning-based scheme with the traditional CSI-based scheme for resource allocation, we now consider the effect of overhead on the overall system performance for 5G CRAN. In UDN deployment, a single RRH can either have a single user or multiple users in its vicinity. Depending on the scenario,

an RRH will have to acquire the position or CSI estimates for each user such that it can optimally serve the intended user(s). Based on this assumption, the simulation scenario in figure 4 represents the best case scenario in terms of low system overhead, where each RRH is surrounded by only one user, and thus, has to sense the position or CSI for minimal number of users. On the other hand, the worst case scenario may exist in a realistic system, where each RRH has to acquire the position or CSI estimates for a large number of users ($\sim$25), for resource allocation, thus resulting in increased system overhead.

The frame structure proposed in [23] for 5G TDD based system is considered for formulating the overhead model. The total length of the frame is 0.2 ms and it consists of 42 OFDM symbols ($T_{\text{sym,total}} = 42$), and about 833 sub-carriers ($f_{\text{sc,total}} = 833$). The position information of the users present in the system can be acquired using narrow-band pilots (also called uplink beacons), typically spanning the first symbol of the frame. The CSI for the users can be obtained using 4 full-band pilots, placed at the beginning of a frame just after the positioning beacons. The adjacent CSI-sensing pilots are scheduled based on the cyclic-prefix compensation distance, as explained in [3], to avoid inter-carrier interference. Based on these parameters, the overhead for position acquisition per user can be calculated as:

$$OH_{pos,n} = \frac{T_{\text{sym},pos,n} \times f_{\text{sc},pos,n}}{T_{\text{sym,total}} \times f_{\text{sc,total}}}. \tag{5}$$

Here, $T_{\text{sym},pos,n}$ is the number of OFDM symbols used for position estimation of user n, and $f_{\text{sc},pos,n}$ denotes the number of sub-carriers used in the positioning beacon. Similarly, for CSI acquisition per user, the overhead can be computed as:

$$OH_{CSI,n} = \frac{T_{\text{sym},CSI,n} \times f_{\text{sc},CSI,n}}{T_{\text{sym,total}} \times f_{\text{sc,total}}}, \tag{6}$$

where $T_{\text{sym},CSI,n}$ and $f_{\text{sc},CSI,n}$ denote the number of OFDM symbols and the number of sub-carriers, used for CSI acquisition of user n, respectively. The system overhead for position, or CSI, acquisition is computed by multiplying the corresponding overhead with the number of users for which the position information, or CSI, is acquired.

Figure 9 shows the theoretical system throughput for the parametrization of a TDD-based 5G system for different schemes under the aforementioned scenarios. It can be seen that the learning-based resource allocation scheme, in the best case scenario, does not suffer from the inclusion of the system overhead, where 4 RRHs serve 1 user each, after acquiring their position information. However, the theoretical system throughput for the same scenario using the traditional CSI-based resource allocation scheme is reduced by almost 19% considering the effect of the CSI acquisition overhead. In the worst case scenario, considering 24 users present in the system, the CSI overhead increases to about 57%, resulting in a significantly lower effective system throughput. The overhead for each of the cases is computed by keeping in mind the assignment of CSI acquisition pilots based on the cyclic-prefix compensation distance, as mentioned above. Overall, it can be seen that the overhead for CSI acquisition increases with the number of users, thus decreasing the effective system throughput, whereas for position acquisition, the overhead will not impact the effective system throughput since only narrow-band beacons are suf-

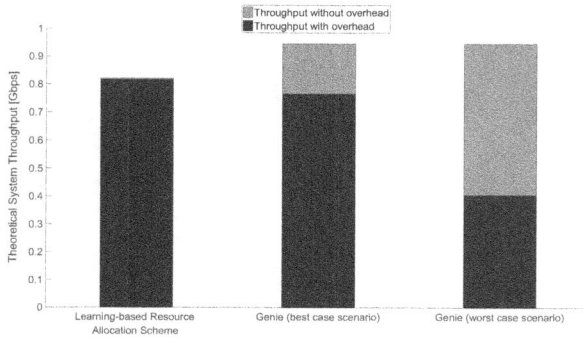

Figure 9: Effect of overhead on system throughput for the proposed learning-based scheme and the traditional CSI-based scheme

ficient for obtaining the position information for the users to be served by a given RRH. This fact suggests the position-based scheme to be a more cost-effective solution for resource allocation, compared to a conventional CSI-based approach.

5. CONCLUSION

This paper proposed a novel learning-based resource allocation scheme for 5G CRAN systems, which allocates the system resources based on only the position information of the users present in the system. An overhead model is also presented, for both the position information and CSI acquisition of the users, and its effect on system performance is evaluated. The operation of the proposed scheme based on usage of only the positioning beacons avoids the CSI acquisition overhead, while achieving close to optimal system performance. Overall, less than 15% loss in system goodput is observed when the proposed scheme is used for resource allocation, compared to the optimal CSI-based scheme. However, the proposed scheme has an overhead of only 2.4% for the presented simulation scenario, compared to an overhead of about 19% for the CSI-based scheme, and thus, has a better performance in terms of effective system throughput. The proposed scheme is robust to realistic system changes as well, where the maximum performance loss of about 30% is observed for the case when the reported user's position information has an inaccuracy of 1.0 m. The proposed resource allocation scheme is fairly robust to the changes in the propagation environment; maximum performance loss of 5% is observed when the system parameters affecting the scattering and shadowing phenomena are different for the training and test datasets used for the machine learning unit of the learning-based resource allocation scheme. The performance loss for inaccurate position information availability can be reduced by using restricted combinations of transmit beam and receive filters (for a given user position) while training the machine learning unit of the proposed scheme, which is included in the related future work. Furthermore, the performance of the proposed scheme can be evaluated when intra-RRH interference is present in addition to the inter-RRH interference, or for different transmit power settings, or when LOS link is not ensured at all times between the RRHs and the users, in the 5G CRAN system.

6. REFERENCES

[1] L. Goratti, S. Savazzi, A. Parichehreh, and U. Spagnolini. Distributed Load Balancing for Future 5G Systems On-Board High-Speed Trains. In *5G for Ubiquitous Connectivity (5GU), 2014 1st International Conference on*, pages 140–145, November 2014.

[2] Q.C. Li, Huaning Niu, A.T. Papathanassiou, and Geng Wu. 5G Network Capacity: Key Elements and Technologies. *Vehicular Technology Magazine, IEEE*, 9(1):71–78, March 2014.

[3] P. Kela, J. Turkka, and M. Costa. Borderless Mobility in 5G Outdoor Ultra-Dense Networks. *Access, IEEE*, 3:1462–1476, 2015.

[4] V. Venkatasubramanian, M. Hesse, P. Marsch, and M. Maternia. On the Performance Gain of Flexible UL/DL TDD with Centralized and Decentralized Resource Allocation in Dense 5G Deployments. In *2014 IEEE 25th Annual International Symposium on Personal, Indoor, and Mobile Radio Communication (PIMRC)*, pages 1840–1845, September 2014.

[5] G. N. Kamga, M. Xia, and S. Aïssa. Spectral-Efficiency Analysis of Massive MIMO Systems in Centralized and Distributed Schemes. *IEEE Transactions on Communications*, 64(5):1930–1941, May 2016.

[6] D. Gesbert, S. Hanly, H. Huang, S. Shamai Shitz, O. Simeone, and W. Yu. Multi-Cell MIMO Cooperative Networks: A New Look at Interference. *IEEE Journal on Selected Areas in Communications*, 28(9):1380–1408, December 2010.

[7] M. K. Karakayali, G. J. Foschini, R. A. Valenzuela, and R. D. Yates. On the Maximum Common Rate Achievable in a Coordinated Network. In *2006 IEEE International Conference on Communications*, volume 9, pages 4333–4338, June 2006.

[8] M. Sanjabi, M. Hong, M. Razaviyayn, and Z. Q. Luo. Joint Base Station Clustering and Beamformer Design for Partial Coordinated Transmission Using Statistical Channel State Information. In *2014 IEEE 15th International Workshop on Signal Processing Advances in Wireless Communications (SPAWC)*, pages 359–363, June 2014.

[9] R. Wang, H. Hu, and X. Yang. Potentials and Challenges of C-RAN Supporting Multi-RATs Toward 5G Mobile Networks. *IEEE Access*, 2:1187–1195, 2014.

[10] F. Boccardi, R. W. Heath, A. Lozano, T. L. Marzetta, and P. Popovski. Five Disruptive Technology Directions for 5G. *IEEE Communications Magazine*, 52(2):74–80, February 2014.

[11] L. Dai, B. Wang, Y. Yuan, S. Han, C. l. I, and Z. Wang. Non-Orthogonal Multiple Access for 5G: Solutions, Challenges, Opportunities, and Future Research Trends. *IEEE Communications Magazine*, 53(9):74–81, September 2015.

[12] E. S. Bae, J. S. Kim, and M. Y. Chung. Radio Resource Management for Multi-Beam Operating Mobile Communications. In *the 20th Asia-Pacific Conference on Communication (APCC2014)*, pages 184–188, October 2014.

[13] S. Rostami, K. Arshad, and P. Rapajic. A Joint Resource Allocation and Link Adaptation Algorithm with Carrier Aggregation for 5G LTE-Advanced

Network. In *Telecommunications (ICT), 2015 22nd International Conference on*, pages 102–106, April 2015.

[14] Juei-Chin Shen, Jun Zhang, Kwang-Cheng Chen, and Khaled B Letaief. High-Dimensional CSI Acquisition in Massive MIMO: Sparsity-Inspired Approaches. *arXiv preprint arXiv:1505.00426*, 2015.

[15] S. Imtiaz, G. S. Dahman, F. Rusek, and F. Tufvesson. On the Directional Reciprocity of Uplink and Downlink Channels in Frequency Division Duplex Systems. In *2014 IEEE 25th Annual International Symposium on Personal, Indoor, and Mobile Radio Communication (PIMRC)*, pages 172–176, September 2014.

[16] J.A. Rohwer, C.T. Abdallah, and C.G. Christodoulou. Machine Learning Based CDMA Power Control. In *Signals, Systems and Computers, 2004. Conference Record of the Thirty-Seventh Asilomar Conference on*, volume 1, pages 207–211 Vol.1, November 2003.

[17] Xu Chen, F. Meriaux, and S. Valentin. Predicting a User's Next Cell with Supervised Learning Based on Channel States. In *Signal Processing Advances in Wireless Communications (SPAWC), 2013 IEEE 14th Workshop on*, pages 36–40, June 2013.

[18] H. Zhou O. Punal and J. Gross. RFRA: Random Forests Rate Adaptation for Vehicular Networks,. In *Proc. of the 13th IEEE International Symposium on a World of Wireless, Mobile and Multimedia Networks 2013 (WoWMoM 2013)*, June 2013.

[19] J. P. Leite, P. H. P. de Carvalho, and R. D. Vieira. A Flexible Framework Based on Reinforcement Learning for Adaptive Modulation and Coding in OFDM Wireless Systems. In *2012 IEEE Wireless Communications and Networking Conference (WCNC)*, pages 809–814, April 2012.

[20] A. Rico-Alvariño and R. W. Heath. Learning-Based Adaptive Transmission for Limited Feedback Multiuser MIMO-OFDM. *IEEE Transactions on Wireless Communications*, 13(7):3806–3820, July 2014.

[21] A. Argyriou, D. Kosmanos, and L. Tassiulas. Joint Time-Domain Resource Partitioning, Rate Allocation, and Video Quality Adaptation in Heterogeneous Cellular Networks. *IEEE Transactions on Multimedia*, 17(5):736–745, May 2015.

[22] G. Wang and M. Lei. Enabling Downlink Coordinated Multi-Point Transmission in TDD Heterogeneous Network. In *Vehicular Technology Conference (VTC Spring), 2013 IEEE 77th*, pages 1–5, June 2013.

[23] P. Kela, X. Gelabert, J. Turkka, M. Costa, K. Heiska, K. Leppänen, and C. Qvarfordt. Supporting Mobility in 5G: A Comparison Between Massive MIMO and Continuous Ultra Dense Networks. In *2016 IEEE International Conference on Communications (ICC)*, pages 1–6, May 2016.

[24] M. M. U. Rahman, H. Ghauch, S. Imtiaz, and J. Gross. RRH Clustering and Transmit Precoding for Interference-Limited 5G CRAN Downlink. In *2015 IEEE Globecom Workshops (GC Wkshps)*, pages 1–7, December 2015.

[25] Andreas F Molisch. *Wireless Communications*, pages 157–162. John Wiley & Sons, 2007.

[26] Ethem Alpaydin. *Introduction to Machine Learning*. MIT press, 2014.

[27] L. Breiman. Random Forests. *Machine Learning*, 45(1):5–32, 2001.

[28] Zanifa Omary and Fredrick Mtenzi. Machine Learning Approach to Identifying the Dataset Threshold for the Performance Estimators in Supervised Learning. *International Journal for Infonomics (IJI)*, 3:314–325, 2010.

[29] Oracle Data Mining Concepts. 11g release 1 (11.1). *Oracle Corp*, 2007, 2005.

[30] Dimitrios Damopoulos, Sofia A Menesidou, Georgios Kambourakis, Maria Papadaki, Nathan Clarke, and Stefanos Gritzalis. Evaluation of Anomaly-Based IDS for Mobile Devices Using Machine Learning Classifiers. *Security and Communication Networks*, 5(1):3–14, 2012.

[31] J. Werner, M. Costa, A. Hakkarainen, K. Leppänen, and M. Valkama. Joint User Node Positioning and Clock Offset Estimation in 5G Ultra-Dense Networks. In *2015 IEEE Global Communications Conference (GLOBECOM)*, pages 1–7, December 2015.

[32] Georg Kunz, Olaf Landsiedel, Stefan Götz, Klaus Wehrle, James Gross, and Farshad Naghibi. Expanding the Event Horizon in Parallelized Network Simulations. In *Modeling, Analysis & Simulation of Computer and Telecommunication Systems (MASCOTS), 2010 IEEE International Symposium on*, pages 172–181. IEEE, 2010.

[33] T Jamsa et al. Deliverable D1.2 Initial Channel Models Based on Measurements. *METIS project Deliverable*, 2014.

[34] P Kela et al. Location Based Beamforming in 5G Ultra-Dense Networks. In *Proc. Vehicular Technology Conference (VTC Fall), 2016 IEEE 84th*, September 2016. accepted for publication.

[35] Mark Hall, Eibe Frank, Geoffrey Holmes, Bernhard Pfahringer, Peter Reutemann, and Ian H Witten. The WEKA Data Mining Software: An Update. *ACM SIGKDD explorations newsletter*, 11(1):10–18, 2009.

Backhaul Routing and Base Station Sleep Mode Engagement in Energy Harvesting Cellular Networks

Jorge Baranda
jorge.baranda@cttc.cat

Marco Miozzo
marco.miozzo@cttc.cat

Paolo Dini
paolo.dini@cttc.cat

José Núñez-Martínez
jose.nunez@cttc.cat

Josep Mangues-Bafalluy
josep.mangues@cttc.cat

Centre Tecnològic de Telecomunicacions de Catalunya (CTTC)
Av. Carl Friedrich Gauss 7,
Castelldefels, Barcelona, Spain

ABSTRACT

Future dense mobile networks will imply much higher costs both in access and backhaul. This paper analyzes the effect on wireless mesh backhaul routing performance when energy saving policies are present at the radio access network (RAN). We consider an heterogeneous two-tier network where small cells (SC) with energy harvesting capabilities extend the capacity of the macro base stations (MBS), and can autonomously switch on-off in order to increase the energy efficiency of the network based on a Q-learning (QL) algorithm. Instead of calculating new routes for each SCs activation pattern, we propose to agnostically adapt to the RAN traffic demands using a non-route-based backpressure routing policy for the wireless mesh backhaul to even the network resource usage amongst SCs. We used the ns-3 simulator to integrate the different mobile network segments: RAN, wireless mesh backhaul, and evolved packet core (EPC). Simulation results show an achieved reduction of the 37% of the RAN energy consumption while satisfying traffic demands with an improvement of up to a factor of 10 of delay performance in the backhaul during peak hours.

Keywords

5G, Dense Deployment, Energy Saving, Energy Harvesting, Backhauling, Routing

1. INTRODUCTION

Long Term Evolution (LTE) dense deployments formed by both Small Cells (SC) and macro base stations (MBS), known as HetNets, are expected to accommodate the rising demand of mobile data services. Being very unlikely to count with a fiber connection at each SC location, it is recognized that SCs will include wireless capabilities, allowing the deployment of wireless mesh networks between SCs for backhauling purposes.

MSWiM '16, November 13-17, 2016, Malta, Malta

© 2016 ACM. ISBN 978-1-4503-4502-6/16/11... $15.00

DOI: http://dx.doi.org/10.1145/2988287.2989175

Consequently, future large-scale/dense mesh SC topologies will substantially increase network resource redundancy. Additionally, ultra-dense SC deployments pose some concerns in terms of energy consumption. First, not all SCs may be directly connected to the power grid. Second, even if they were, this approach would not scale. Instead of connecting these SCs to the energy grid, a solution could be to equip them with energy harvesters and storage systems to reduce their energy consumption. On this matter, photovoltaic (PV) technology represents a valuable choice due to its good efficiency, competitive cost, and availabilily.

Therefore, appropriate resource management will be key for dynamic, complex, and heterogeneous future mobile networks. Their high density will imply much higher radio access network (RAN) costs, and also the need for an appropriate backhaul network. Wireless mesh networks are expected to play a key role in this respect. It is therefore fundamental to reduce RAN and backhaul resource consumption. In this paper, we evaluate the global resource consumption when combining a RAN energy management scheme and an efficient backpressure-based routing scheme in the backhaul.

State of the art routing adopted for the mobile backhaul (MPLS) uses one static single path. Such strategy can under-utilize the resources of a dense wireless mesh network. In contrast, backpressure approaches [8] offer, in theory, the possibility to exploit such resources. For instance, BP-MR [4] has shown to bring throughput and latency improvements by taking on-the-fly *per-packet* routing decisions. On the other hand, a promising method for energy-constrained radio resource management (RRM) is to dynamically reconfigure the RAN. This could be achieved by enabling sleep mode in the SC and offloading traffic to the macro cell based on the harvested energy and the traffic demand [10]. Indeed, a key question to answer is whether and how a routing strategy for the backhaul is adapting to the RAN reconfiguration triggered by the energy-constrained RRM.

In this paper, we consider a heterogeneous two-tier network where SCs with energy harvesting capabilities extend the capacity of the MBS, and that can distributedly and autonomously switch on-off in order to increase the network energy efficiency based on a distributed Q-learning (QL) algorithm presented in our previous work [10]. As for backhaul resource management, instead of calculating new routes for each SC activation pattern, we propose to independently adapt to the RAN traffic demands using a non-route-based backpressure routing policy for the wireless mesh backhaul. Overall, this combination provides resource management at two different timescales, first, by deciding SC hourly activation patterns and second, by dynamically adapting to backhaul traffic demand variations at packet-level timescale.

The analysis is performed using a flexible end-to-end cellular network test environment based on the popular ns-3 network simulator and an ad-hoc octave simulator to perform large scale energy characterization of the system.

The herein presented results demonstrate an efficient resource consumption in the RAN and backhaul when using a per-packet backpressure-based routing protocol in combination with the QL energy algorithm. Simulation results reveal remarkable gains in peak hours in throughput and latency (up to 10% and a factor of ten, respectively). Finally, we show that the distributed energy harvesting management can achieve high energy savings (up to 37%) with respect to when the SCs are connected to the electrical grid.

Up to our knowledge, this is the first attempt to study the reconfiguration capabilities of the wireless mesh backhaul to the self-organized dynamics enabled by energy-constrained RRM mechanisms. Usually, routing in meshed backhaul, energy harvesting, and BS sleep mode are not tackled together. In fact, there are several analysis made in the field of wireless mesh networks facing the routing with energy harvesting nodes, such as those in [2], [9] or [3]. However, they do not consider backhaul mesh networks for the mobile RAN. Other examples study backhaul-aware user association or load balancing with tree or star topology backhaul, as in [12] and [7].

The remainder of this paper is organized as follows. Section 2 provides an explanation of the node architecture together with background on energy-constrained RRM and flexible backpressure routing strategies, before conducting the aimed performance evaluation in Section 3. Section 4 concludes the paper with the main conclusions.

2. NODE ARCHITECTURE AND RESOURCE MANAGEMENT SCHEMES

In our vision, SCs count with a LTE radio access plus wireless backhaul capabilities to reach the EPC via a mesh topology. In addition to the standard protocol stacks, we propose to insert (i) a distributed Energy Manager module, as part of the required Operation Administration and Maintenance (OAM) activities to be conducted at the RAN level, and (ii) a backpressure-routing module taking routing decisions on a per-packet basis on IP packets. The working details of each module are covered in subsequent subsections. This decoupled, self-organized and distributed architecture allows the two modules to work independently, giving a high grade of flexibility and scalability to the system, suitable for the requirements of future 5G networks.

2.1 Energy Management

In the last years, the use of renewable energy sources (RES) in the cellular network started to generate interests in the research community [1]. The integration between renewable energies and mobile networks plays an important role in the roadmap to 5G to reduce the consumed energy used by the mobile operators. Regarding the RAN, a deployment optimization has been presented in [5], where a design for the management of k-tier HetNets powered by RES has been presented. This model optimizes the fraction of ON time of each tier. Considering on-line optimization algorithms, [13]

proposes a dynamic control of the BS power consumption as a function of the energy reserve and the expected amount of renewable energy. However, the two works above do not consider the temporal variations in traffic and in harvested energy processes, as typical in a real scenario.

In order to overcome the above mentioned problems, in [10] we proposed a distributed on-line solution based on a multi-agent Reinforcement Learning (RL) algorithm, known as *distributed Q-learning* (QL). Thanks to RL, the agents can independently learn its proper RRM policy through real-time interactions for capturing the dynamic conditions of the environment, in terms of energy inflow and traffic demand and it is able to jointly maximize the system performance in terms of throughput, drop rate and energy consumption. This paper extends this analysis interacting with a backpressure based backhaul resource management scheme.

2.2 Backpressure Routing

The origins of the backpressure concept lies on the seminal paper of Tassiulas and Ephremides [8]. The root concept consists in a centralized policy which routes traffic in a multi-hop network by minimizing the Lyapunov drift in the network, that is, minimizing the sum of the queue *backlogs* in the network amongst time slots.

Despite throughput optimality, this work presents several drawbacks: centralized control mode, high queuing complexity (per-flow queuing system), and poor delay performance. Recently, many proposals have been presented to alleviate the effect of these issues [8]. From this set of proposals, in this paper, we refer to *BP-MR* [4] because of its scalability and performance improvements in wireless mesh backhauls. Based on the Lyapunov-drift-plus penalty approach, routing decisions are taken distributively at each node on a per-packet basis combining queue backlog information (backpressure component) with geographic information.

Specifically, *BP-MR* performs dynamic per-packet routing decisions following a two-stage process: (i) data packet classification in a per-interface queue system according to its destination, and (ii) the use of geographic and congestion information to compute the best possible next-hop. The per-interface queue system presents lower complexity and a better delay performance than the original per-flow queueing system, contributing to the protocol scalability.

3. EVALUATION

This section evaluates via simulations the adaptability of the backhaul routing to the RAN reconfiguration, triggered by energy saving mechanisms. In particular, we compare *BP-MR* with *OLSR* against a distributed QL mechanism, which enables sleep mode in the SCs [10]. *OLSR* is a static single path routing protocol that, in absence of node mobility and failures, is equivalent to MPLS, a reference transport technology for mobile backhaul networks.

3.1 Scenario Description

Figure 1 shows the evaluated scenario consisting of a mesh deployment of non-overlapping SCs assisting a macrocell forming a plain grid of 2×3 elements deployed over a $1 Km^2$ according to use cases covered by 3GPP documents TR 36.872 and TR 36.842. Each SC counts with an LTE radio access plus multiple wireless interfaces simulating high directive μwave links. One of these SCs has a wired connection to the LTE Evolved Packet core (EPC), which connects to the Internet. The PV model considered is based on a Panasonic N235B solar module. Each SC is equipped with an array of 16 × 16 solar cells. The storage system is based on a battery of 2 kWh. The panel and battery sizes have been chosen so that the SC battery is replenished in a full winter day. The SolarStat tool [11] has been used for generating the hourly harvested energy profile.

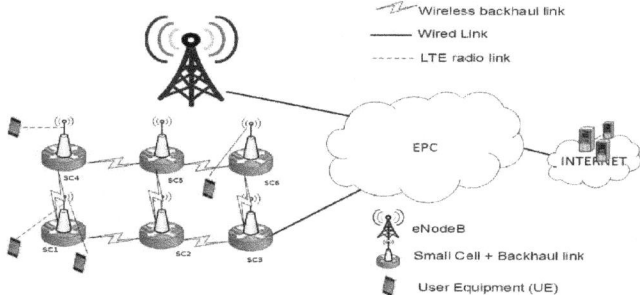

Figure 1: Mobile Network under evaluation.

The requested traffic is generated by 120 users (UEs) uniformly placed within the coverage area of each SC. We adopt the daily traffic pattern described in [6] and updated with the requirements provided by a telco operator collaborating in the EU-H2020-SANSA project [1]. According to this model, 50% of the UEs are configured as heavy users (their data volume is 2.25GB/h), while the remaining UEs are ordinary users (0.45GB/h). Furthermore, simulations consider UDP constant bit rate (CBR) downlink (DL) traffic.

Link rates in the backhaul network are dimensioned according to the mentioned traffic demands, where there is a certain percentage of active users (e.g., 16-17% during peak hour). They have been selected lower (from 12Mbps to 36Mbps) than rates offered by commercial equipment to better show the exploitation of scarce wireless resources by each of the evaluated protocols. The backhaul network is connected to the EPC through a 1Gbps wired connection.

Simulation results have been conducted with ns-3 simulator using the latest version of LENA LTE model [2] conveniently updated to include custom backhaul topologies.

3.2 Simulation Results

3.2.1 RAN Reconfiguration

In this work, the energy characterization of the system has been obtained averaging 10 runs over a simulated year to evaluate the behavior of the QL energy algorithm for different months and energy harvested inflow. We used an ad-hoc octave simulator since ns-3 does not allow simulating time frames of this range in a reasonable time.

Figure 2 presents the energy drained from the grid during each of the hours in a day and averaged during all days in a year. This figure compares the QL algorithm with when all the SCs are powered by the grid. QL guarantees an overall energy saving of 37% during the whole day. The consumption spike around hour 4 of the QL is due to the fact that many SCs are in sleep mode, generating a peak of energy consumption of the MBS. The QL algorithm decides a more intensive sleep mode in the RAN, thus saving the harvested energy in the storage system to use it later to satisfy traffic demands during peak hours.

Figure 3 depicts the energy efficiency of the system in one day and averaged during one year. QL is able to reach up

[1] http://sansa-h2020.eu/
[2] http://networks.cttc.es/mobile-networks/software-tools/lena/

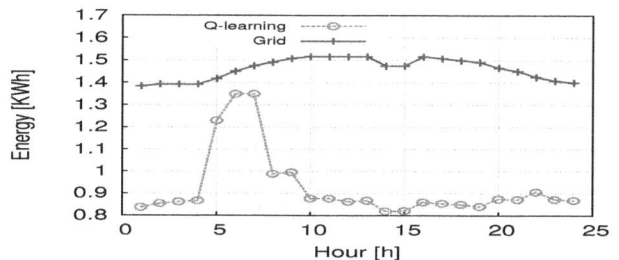

Figure 2: Average grid consumed energy evolution.

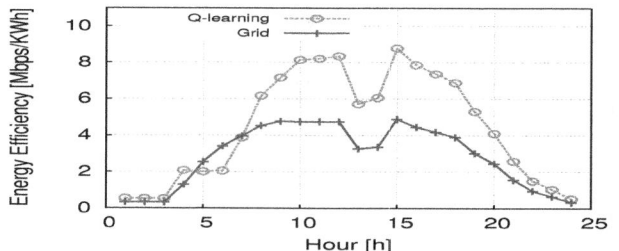

Figure 3: Average energy efficiency evolution.

to the double of the energy efficiency during peak hours, whereas it has a lower energy efficiency when the sleep behavior is more intensive (hours 5 to 7).

Figure 4 presents the daily average throughput and delay distribution variation experienced by the traffic served by the mesh network of activated SCs determined hourly by the QL algorithm. The results are obtained over 10 repetitions of a given sample day. The boxes in the statistical packet delay distribution show from the 25th to the 75th percentiles, and the whiskers from the 5th to the 95th percentiles.

BP-MR experiences significant gains both in terms of throughput and delay, especially during traffic peak hours. In particular, BP-MR increases throughput performance by up to a 10% and achieves a reduction in latency of about a factor of ten with respect to OLSR (notice the logarithmic axes on the delay graph). It distributes the traffic to follow the less congested path and is able (if needed) to deviate from the shortest path, in terms of number of hops, hence, reducing queuing delays. OLSR calculates static equivalent paths between two endpoints independently from the SC traffic requirements, hence not fully utilizing the backhaul capacity and deriving in high delays due to excessive queueing. These results indicate the compatibility of a dynamic backpressure-based protocol, such as BP-MR, with the QL energy algorithm in a mesh backhaul network providing resources redundancy.

3.2.2 Backhaul Reconfiguration

Durink peak hours, most of the SCs are active, hence requiring the full backhaul. However, when the requested capacity decreases, some of the backhaul links are partially used and they can be deactivated to save energy.

For this purpose, we setup a simulation where the link from the SC1 to the SC4 (see Figure 1) is deactivated due to reduced activity. Figure 5 shows a zoom of the temporal evolution of the average network throughput around $t = 15s$, when the link is deactivated. This event is transparent to BP-MR due to its dynamic per-packet routing approach and the enough amount of available network resources. The

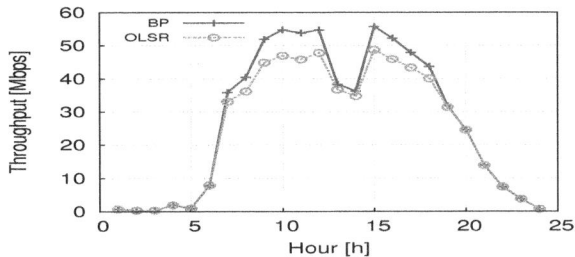

Figure 4: Throughput and delay performance evolution in the wireless mesh backhaul during a sample day.

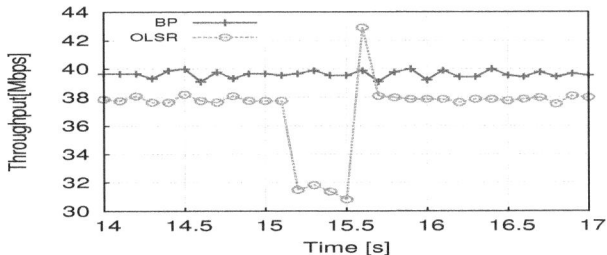

Figure 5: Evolution under backhaul reconfiguration.

behavior of OLSR is the opposite: the reconfiguration of a single wireless backhaul link yields a transitory sudden degradation in throughput performance (around $400ms$) due to the recomputation of the actual end-to-end paths, being this time directly related with the size of the network.

Concluding, *BP-MR* presents good reconfiguration capabilities, since the route is discovered on-the-fly while packets traverse the network. This trend motivates further research on energy-constrained backpressure-based routing protocols for saving energy in backhaul networks.

4. CONCLUSIONS

In this paper, we evaluate the combination of a two level resource management scheme combining 1) Q-learning-based energy management in the RAN that hourly switches ON/ OFF SCs, and 2) backhaul resource management in the form of backpressure routing in the wireless mesh network that acts on a per-packet basis. Simulation results show that the QL energy algorithm reduces network energy consumption up to 37% and that the backpressure-based protocol efficiently adapts the backhaul resource consumption to the RAN reconfigurations determined by the QL energy algorithm. More specifically, the dynamic per-packet backpressure routing policy attains delay improvements by a factor of 10 during peak hours, compared to a route-based protocol such as OLSR. The analysis performed in this paper further encourages research on schemes for energy-constrained scenarios integrated within the backpressure-based protocol to dynamically (de)activate wireless backhaul links.

5. ACKNOWLEDGMENTS

This work was partially funded by the EC under grant agreement no 645047 (H2020 SANSA project) and by the Spanish Ministry of Economy and Competitiveness under grant TEC2014-60491-R (5GNORM).

6. REFERENCES

[1] H. Al Haj Hassan, L. Nuaymi, and A. Pelov. Renewable energy in cellular networks: A survey. In *IEEE Online Conf. on Green Comms. (GreenCom)*, Oct. 2013.

[2] S. Avallone and A. Banchs. A channel assignment and routing algorithm for energy harvesting multi-radio wireless mesh networks. *IEEE JSAC*, 2016.

[3] G. H. Badawy, A. A. Sayegh, and T. D. Todd. Energy provisioning in solar-powered wireless mesh networks. *IEEE Trans. on Vehicular Tech.*, 59(8):3859–3871, Oct 2010.

[4] J. Baranda, J. Núñez-Martínez, and J. Mangues-Bafalluy. Backpressure Routing for the Heterogeneous Multi-radio Backhaul of Small Cells. In *IFIP Wireless and Mobile Networking Conf. (WMNC)*, pages 48–55, Oct. 2015.

[5] H. Dhillon, Y. Li, P. Nuggehalli, Z. Pi, and J. Andrews. Fundamentals of Heterogeneous Cellular Networks with Energy Harvesting. *IEEE Trans. on Wireless Comms.*, 13(5):2782–2797, May 2014.

[6] EU EARTH project. Deliverable D2.3. Dec. 2011.

[7] Q. Han, B. Yang, G. Miao, C. Chen, X. Wang, and X. Guan. Backhaul-aware user association and resource allocation for energy-constrained hetnets. *IEEE Trans. on Vehicular Tech.*, PP(99):1–1, 2016.

[8] Z. Jiao, B. Zhang, C. Li, and H. Mouftah. Backpressure-based routing and scheduling protocols for wireless multihop networks: A survey. *IEEE Wireless Comms.*, 23(1):102–110, Feb. 2016.

[9] S. Kwon and N. B. Shroff. Energy-efficient sinr-based routing for multihop wireless networks. *Mobile Computing, IEEE Trans. on*, 8(5):668–681, 2009.

[10] M. Miozzo, L. Giupponi, M. Rossi, and P. Dini. Distributed q-learning for energy harvesting heterogeneous networks. In *2015 IEEE Int. Conf. on Comm. Workshop (ICCW)*, June 2015.

[11] M. Miozzo, D. Zordan, P. Dini, and M. Rossi. SolarStat: Modeling Photovoltaic Sources through Stochastic Markov Processes. In *IEEE Energy Conf. (ENERGYCON)*, Dubrovnik, Croatia, May 2014.

[12] A. Prasad and A. Maeder. Backhaul-aware energy efficient heterogeneous networks with dual connectivity. *Telecommunication Systems*, 59(1):25–41, 2015.

[13] D. Valerdi, Q. Zhu, K. Exadaktylos, S. Xia, M. Arranz, R. Liu, and D. Xu. Intelligent energy managed service for green base stations. In *IEEE Global Comms. Conf. (GLOBECOM)*, Miami, US, Dec. 2010.

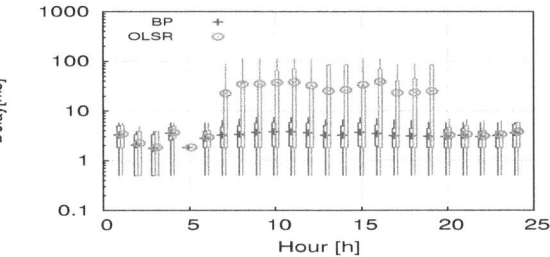

Characterizing User Activity in WiFi Networks: University Campus and Urban Area Case Studies

Larissa Oliveira
Department of Computer
Engineering
UC Santa Cruz
lmarinho@ucsc.edu

Katia Obraczka
Department of Computer
Engineering
UC Santa Cruz
katia@soe.ucsc.edu

Abel Rodríguez
Applied Mathematics and
Statistics
UC Santa Cruz
abel@soe.ucsc.edu

ABSTRACT

In this paper we investigate and characterize user activity in WiFi networks by analyzing and comparing the behavior of users that connect to two public WiFi networks, one of them deployed in a University campus and the other in a major urban area. We characterize WiFi network user activity based on two main features, namely: time users stay connected to Access Points and Access Point load. Overall, the main contributions of our work are as follows: (1) to the best of our knowledge, this is the first study comparing user activity in two different scenarios, i.e., a University campus WiFi network and an urban WiFi network; (2) our results validate previously observed characteristics of user behavior in WiFi networks, as well as unveil new behavior patterns, such as the fact that users on campus tend to stay connected to the network for longer periods of time when compared to users in an urban area; and (3) our work is the first study to formally test and validate the hypothesis that association times in WiFi networks follows a power law and to estimate the power-law's tail index.

Keywords

WiFi Networks; user Behavior; tail-distribution

1. INTRODUCTION

According to [1], mobile data traffic grew 74% worldwide in 2015 and is expected to increase almost eightfold by 2020. Additionally, by 2020, the total number of smartphones will be nearly 50% of the total number of devices and connections. This unprecedented growth demands a deeper understanding of how users move, connect, as well as generate and consume traffic. Understanding user activity in wireless access networks is essential to be able to scale and accommodate future connectivity- and traffic demand. Furthermore, better understanding mobile user behavior and activity can also greatly contribute to improve urban planning, including transit, transportation, and housing infras-

MSWiM '16, November 13-17, 2016, Malta, Malta

© 2016 ACM. ISBN 978-1-4503-4502-6/16/11...$15.00

DOI: http://dx.doi.org/10.1145/2988287.2989172

tructure, emergency response, as well as other services (e.g., food, shopping, entertainment, etc).

In this paper, our goal is to characterize user mobility- and usage patterns in WiFi networks based on data from real networks. In particular, we study traces from two different scenarios, namely a University campus and the downtown area of a major city. The former trace was obtained at the Dartmouth College campus during the 2005-06 academic year with a total of over 24,000 users and 3,300 access points. The latter trace was collected for 6 years (2004-2010) at the city of Montreal consisting of over 340 access points connecting 45,000 users. The main contributions of this study are as follows:

- To our knowledge, this is the first systematic study that compares user activity in a University campus and a major city.
- We have both validated results from previous related work and unveiled new user behavior. For example, we confirm that user connection times follow a power-law as has been observed previously; an example of a new result our study reveals is the fact that users tend to connect for longer periods of time in a university campus when compared to an urban network.
- Ours is the first study to apply statistical theory to test whether association times follow a power law and to estimate the tail index of their distribution.

2. RELATED WORK

In order to put our work in perspective, we propose a new taxonomy to classify existing studies on user mobility. We start by classifying related work into two main categories, namely studies based on descriptive- versus predictive analysis. In Table 1 we list relevant work on user activity in infrastructure-based WiFi networks and the features they investigate according to our taxonomy. Predictive studies on user mobility characterization in WiFi networks explore different features including: (1) **Association Time**: time interval during which the user stayed connected to an Access Point (AP) before moving to another AP or leaving the network; (2) **User Traffic**: amount of traffic (e.g., in number of bytes) users download and upload during the association time; (3) **Direction of Movement**: direction a user takes when moving between APs; (4) **AP Load**: access point usage, such as number of users connected to a given AP, total traffic handled by an AP, etc; (5) **Hotspots**: group users into communities according to social- and geographic features, such as popular hotspots. On the other hand, pre-

Table 1: Relevant related work divided according to proposed taxonomy

Descriptive	Association Time	Traffic	Direction of Movement	AP load	Hotspots
Google WiFi [2]	√	√		√	
Dartmouth [8]	√		√		√
SF and NY [6]	√	√			
Predictive	Fractal Waypoint	Markov	Queuing Models	Clustering	SVM
MixedQueuing [4]			√		
MHMM [5]		√			
ToGo [12]					√
SAGA [13]				√	

dictive studies of user activity in WiFi networks can be classified according to the modeling approach adopted. Notable modeling approaches used in previous work include: (1) **Markov Models**; (2) **Fractal Waypoints**; (3) **Queuing Models**;(4) **Clustering**, and (5) **Support Vector Machines (SVMs)**.

3. WIFI NETWORK TRACES

Our study explores user activity in two different WiFi network scenarios, namely a major urban center and a University campus. To this end, we study two WiFi traces which have been made publicly available from CRAWDAD. The first trace was collected over six years (2004-2010) from the WiFi network deployed in the city of Montreal, Quebec, Canada [11]. The second trace was collected at the Dartmouth College campus during the 2005-2006 academic Year [9]. In the remainder of this section, we describe the two traces in detail

3.1 Montreal Trace

Île Sans Fil (French for "Wireless Island", also known as ISF), is a non-profit organization that operates a network of WiFi hotspots in Montréal, Québec, Canada [11]. ISF provides free wireless network access to over 45,000 users and has a total of 346 unique access points (APs) deployed across Montreal's downtown area. All of the APs are located in publically accessible spaces, including cafes, restaurants, and bars, but also in libraries, funeral homes, doctors' offices, and Business Improvement Agencies (BIAs). They cover city parks and sections of popular commercial streets. While at of the end of the 6-year period, ISF had 346 APs deployed. The number of active APs per month varies, however it steadily increases during the trace collection period. At the last month of the trace, there were 185 active APs. Information available in the trace includes: users session (i.e., between login and logout) data such as account (user) id, MAC address, login- and logout times, AP id, and amount of data transferred (incoming and outgoing) for a period of six years from 2004 to 2010. The data has been sanitized in order to anonymize user-specifc information such as account id, connection id, user MAC address, and AP id.

3.2 Dartmouth Trace

The Dartmouth trace [9] was collected at the Dartmouth College campus during the 2005-2006 academic year. The campus occupies 200 acres with over 190 buildings, of which 188 had wireless coverage at the time the trace was collected. Over 3000 APs were deployed, providing WiFi coverage to the campus. Due to the compact nature of the campus, the APs installed in buildings are able to provide network coverage to most of the campus' outdoor areas. All APs share the same SSID, allowing wireless clients to roam seamlessly between APs. The 188 buildings with wireless coverage span 115 subnets, so clients roaming between buildings may be forced to obtain new IP addresses through DHCP (lease times were 6 or 12 hours at different points in the trace).

4. USER ACTIVITY PATTERNS

We analyze user activity for both the Montreal- and Dartmouth traces according to the Association Time and AP Load metrics as defined in Section 2.

4.1 AP Load

Montreal

Figure 1(left) shows the number of sessions (connections) for every user while Figure 1(right) shows the number of sessions for every unique AP for the Montreal trace. According to Figure 1(left), users have on average 14 sessions and the user that connects the most has over 13,000 sessions. The median number of sessions is 3 and the third quantile is 8. The tail index for the session distribution is 3.71, which indicates that, even though most users have very few sessions, approximately 23% of users have more than 8 sessions and 15% have more the 14 sessions. As shown in Figure 1(right), the average- and median number of sessions per AP is 692 and 218, respectively, while the maximum number of sessions per AP is over 10,000. Note that the least loaded APs have 57 sessions or less, which represents the first quantile.

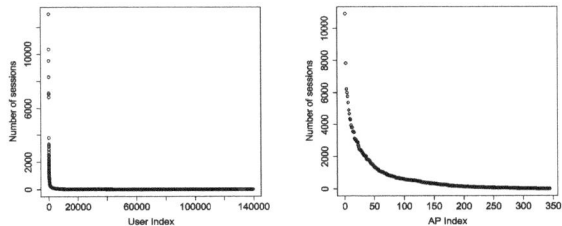

Figure 1: Montreal trace - Left: Number of sessions per user. Right: Number of sessions per AP.

Figure 2(left) shows a scatterplot of the logarithm of the total number of sessions per AP versus the logarithm of the number of users in each AP. Note that the number of users per AP represents a lower bound for the number of sessions, so all points in the graphs must lie above the 45 degree line. The graph indicates that the relationship is roughly linear (in the log-log plot), with limited- and roughly constant variability. On the other hand, in Figure 2(right), we show a scatterplot of the total number of sessions per user versus the number of APs to which a user connects. Interestingly, the relationship between these two variables is generally not linear in this case. Indeed, we see evidence of at least three clusters. One of them corresponds to what could be considered "static users", i.e., users who frequently connect to a relatively small number of APs (data points located along the vertical axis). Another cluster consists of the points located along the horizontal axis which correspond to users that connect very sporadically, but they do so to a large number of different APs. Note that the latter type of users appears to be relatively more frequent that the former. Finally, we observe the cluster represented by the points in the bottom left corner of the graph, indicating that most users connect to under 40 APs over less that 4,000 sessions.

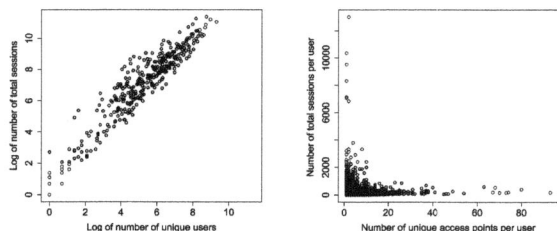

Figure 2: Montreal trace: Left: Logarithm of the total number of sessions per AP versus the logarithm of the number of users in each AP. Right: Total number of sessions per user versus number of APs a user connects to.

Dartmouth

We also analyzed AP Load for the Dartmouth trace. Again, first we study the usage patterns for users and APs separately which is plotted in Figure 3. In Figure 3(left), the number of sessions per user is shown and we can see that, on average, users have approximately 160 sessions, whereas very few users have more than 10,000 sessions. In Figure 3(right), we show the number of sessions per AP. The average load per AP for Dartmouth is 158 sessions and the highest load is 4000 sessions. When we compare Montreal and Dartmouth in terms of the number of sessions per AP, that is AP Load, we observe that access points in Montreal have on average, and overall, a higher load then Dartmouth access points. This result is to be expected since the sample population in Montreal is at least ten times higher and the number of access points in Montreal is approximately ten times lower. However, we note that users have on average a higher number of sessions in Dartmouth, a university campus, than in Montreal. The same observation also holds when comparing the number of user sessions at the Dartmouth campus to the results obtained in [2] for Google's Mountain View WiFi network.

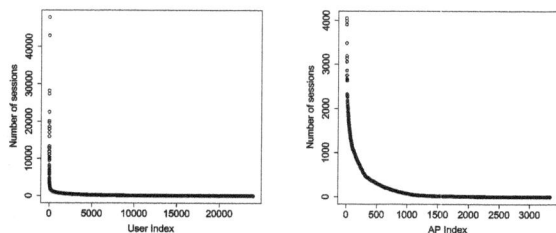

Figure 3: Dartmouth trace: Left: Number of sessions per user. Right: Number of sessions per AP.

Next, we study AP usage patterns for Dartmouth. Figure 4(left) plots the log of the total number of sessions per AP versus the log of the number of users in each AP. Similarly to the Montreal trace, we observe that the relationship is also almost linear (in the log-log plot) but exhibits much higher variability. In Figure 4(right), we plot the total number of sessions per user versus the number of APs to which users connect. Like in the Montreal case, we observe a cluster of users in the bottom left corner of the graph

who connect to less than 400 APs over less that 5,000 sessions. However, unlike Montreal, there are no other easily identifiable clusters.

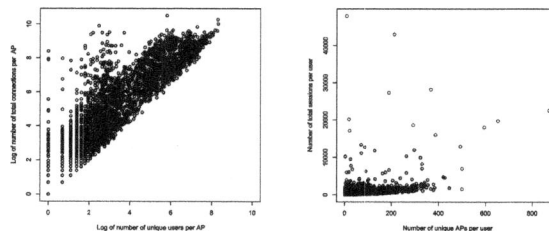

Figure 4: Dartmouth trace: Left: Logarithm of the total number of sessions per AP versus the logarithm of the number of users in each AP. Right: Total number of sessions per user versus number of APs a user connects to.

4.2 Association Time

Montreal

Figure 5 shows the histogram of the logarithm of association times for the whole Montreal trace. We observe that a little less than 30% of users spend approximately 50 min connected, while a little over 20% remain connected for approximately 20 min and another 20% remain connected for up to 2h. We also observe that a small percentage of users connect over very long or very short times. To better understand the behavior of these users, we analyze in Section 5 the tail of the association time distribution and test the hypothesis that it follows a power-law. This power-law behavior of the association times has has been observed in related work [10], [8], [4]. However, to our knowledge, our work is the first to conduct a formal analysis to test the power-law hypothesis for association times in WiFi networks, where we estimate power-law parameters such as the tail index.

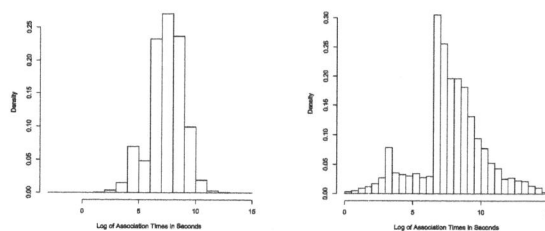

Figure 5: Left - Montreal trace: Histogram of the log of association times (in seconds). Right - Dartmouth trace: Histogram of the log of the association times (in seconds).

In our study, we also try to uncover temporal patterns in the association times. Figure 6(left) shows the distribution of the log of the median association time per day of the week for the entire trace. We divided each day of the week in 8 periods, namely: from 0am to 3am, from 3am to 6am, etc. in order to explore finer-grained temporal patterns for the time users remain connected to an AP.

Using the average median association time of 29 minutes (red horizontal line in Figure 6(left)) as baseline, we observe different behavior depending not only on the day of the week but also on time of the day. As expected, on Monday, we notice higher association times during business hours (i.e., 9am-6pm), whereas during early morning and late night, association times are lower. The median and average association times during business hours are 30- and 75 minutes, respectively. Tuesday and Wednesday show similar behavior, i.e., higher association times during business hours, however the period extends from 9am-7pm. We notice a somewhat different behavior on Thursdays and Fridays: while the median association time is still around 29min, the average association time is 60min between 9am and 3pm. Interestingly, on weekends, we observe longer average association times, which happen during the period between 6am and 3pm. We also notice that the median and average association times for the weekend in on average higher than for weekdays, namely 36 and 80 minutes, respectively. In order to explore coarser grain patterns, we also investigated the distribution of the median association times on a monthly basis throughout the year. Figure 6(center) shows a boxplot of the log of the median association time per month for the entire trace period. Here we can see that the average median association time is approximately 30min (red horizontal line in the plot). However, we observe that in the first six months after the network was deployed, i.e., from August 2004 to February 2005, the average median association time is approximately 18min. We believe this lower association time (relative to the overall average median association time of 30min) is due to the fact that the Ile San Fils network had just been deployed and was still growing.

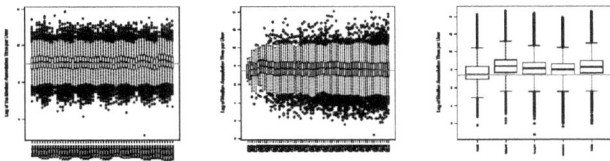

Figure 6: Montreal trace: Left: Boxplot of the log of the median association time per day of the week, and (center) per month. Dartmouth trace: Boxplot of the log of the median association time per quarter (in seconds) for the 2005-06 academic year.

Dartmouth

We also analyze the distribution of the association time for the Dartmouth trace. Dartmouth campus' WiFi network has been studied in previous work, for example [3] [13] [5] [8] [4]. To our knowledge, we are the first ones to study the most recent version of the trace available from [9]. We find that, differently from traces collected in major cities (e.g., Montreal, San Francisco and New York [6]), Dartmouth campus users tend to remain connected for longer periods of time. More specifically, on average, users spend more than 1h connected to campus APs. Figure 5 (right) shows the histogram of the log of the association time for the entire trace. Similarly to Montreal, we observe a bimodal distribution. In the first cluster, users remain connected for up to 11 min, which encompass approximately 20% of users. The second cluster encompass approximately 62% of users that remain connected for more than 20 min. Within the first cluster, we observe that 10% of users have an association time of 6 min. On the other hand, approximately 15% of users have an association time of over 2h. Similarly to Montreal, we

can identify a small percentage of users (7%) that either remain connected for very long or very short periods of time. We hypothesize that some of these longer connections times, e.g., in the order of days, might be attributed to desktop- or even laptop computers in dorms or offices which remain connected for long periods of time. To better understand the behavior of these extreme users, we analyze in Section 5 the tail of the association time distribution and test that it follows a power-law. Our results align with results from studies of the Dartmouth campus network for previous academic years [8] [2] [5].

We also investigated the distribution of the median association time during every quarter of the academic year. Here, we are interested in capturing temporal usage patterns over a shorter time scale. Figure 6 (right) shows a boxplot of the log of the median association time per quarter for the 2005-2006 academic year. Using the average median association time of 38 min (red horizontal line in Figure 6) as baseline, we can observe some variation among quarters. For the Fall quarter of 2005, we observer lower median association times, on average 28 min, whereas during Winter quarter of 2006 we observe a higher median association time 72 min. Even though the average median association time from Spring 2006 to Summer 2006 decreased (3h to 48 min), we can see they still have a very similar distribution. This is an interesting result, since we could expect that most students wouldn't remain on campus during summer vacations. Finally, we notice an increase in the median association time during the beginning of the next academic year, Fall 2006. We also observe that the average median association time for Fall 2006 and Winter 2006 have similar distributions.

5. HEAVY-TAILED ASSOCIATION TIMES

In this section, we investigate the hypothesis that the heavy-tail distribution of user association times follows a power-law as suggested by our results reported in Section 4.2 and by relevant related work [10], [8], [4]. Previous work suggests that many of the reported power-law distributions in the literature have not been rigorously validated. This is especially true when the power-law assumption is made based on log-log plots. Instead, in this paper we aim to formally test the hypothesis that association times follow a power law. We also estimate the distribution's tail index, which is key to estimate future association times.

The probability density function of the power-law distribution (also known as the Pareto distribution) is defined as:

$$f(x) = \frac{\alpha - 1}{x_{min}} \left(\frac{x_{min}}{x} \right)^{\alpha} \quad (1)$$

for $\alpha > 1$ and $x_{min} > 0$. We do not attempt to use the power-law distribution to model the full distribution of the association times. Instead, it is used to model its right tail, i.e., the distribution of large association times. The value x_{min} represents the minimum value for which the distribution follows a power-law. Note that as the value of x_{min} increases, the amount of information available about the behavior of the tail decreases. The most common approach to estimate x_{min}, also known as the threshold, is by inspecting the log-log plot of the data. However, this method is very subjective and error prone. Instead, we use a Kolmogorov-Smirnov (K-S) test, which looks at the maximum distance between the data and the cumulative density function of the power-law distribution whose parameters are estimated using maximum likelihood. This test is implemented using the R poweRlaw [7] package. The uncertainty associated with the parameters are estimated via a bootstrap procedure also available in the poweRlaw package. Figure 7(left) shows the power-law fitted to the heavy tail of the association times for Montreal while Figure 7(right) shows the same graph for Dartmouth. The tail parameters estimated for Montreal were $\alpha = 3.68$ $sd = 0.22$ and for Dartmouth $\alpha = 2.79$ $sd = 0.004$, where sd is the standard deviation. The $p - value$ associated with the K-S test was 0.06 for Montreal and 0.10 for Dartmouth.

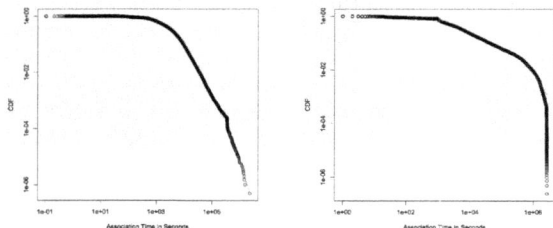

Figure 7: Montreal trace: (left) Power law fit for the tail of association times for Montreal and (right) for Dartmouth

Both K-S goodness-of-fit ($p - values$) for Montreal's and Dartmouth's association time distributions indicate that they can indeed be modeled by a power-law. We further observe that the tail of the distribution of Dartmouth's association times is heavier than Montreal's. This can be observed by inspecting Figure 7(left) and (right) as well as by their tail parameter α. Dartmouth's α is lower that Montreal's indicating a heavier tail since the lower α is, the slower the distribution decays and therefore, the heavier the distribution's tail. Consequently, large association times tend to be relatively more common for Dartmouth than Montreal. Indeed, since for the power-law distribution only moments of order $\lfloor \alpha \rfloor - 1$ exist, the tail of Dartmouth is heavy enough that the conditional variance is infinite.

6. SUMMARY AND DISCUSSION

In this section, we summarize the main findings of our study:

- **AP Load:** We find that for the Montreal trace, the relationship between number of sessions and number of users is roughly linear, whereas the relationship between number of sessions and number of APs is not. We also observed similar trends for Dartmouth. However, as expected, the AP load for Montreal is on average and overall higher than Dartmouth's. For the Montreal network, we can identify 3 different user clusters based on the number of user sessions: there are the so-called static users, i.e., users that mostly connect to a few APs (i.e., less than 5), users that are quite mobile, i.e., connect to a large number of APs (i.e., more than 50), and finally most users connect to less than 40 APs. However, for Dartmouth, we can only identify one clear cluster, which are users that connect to less than 400 APs.
- **Association Time' Heavy-Tailedness:** We test the hyphotesis that the association times for both Montreal and Dartmouth follow a power-law and confirm

that both distributions can indeed be modeled as power-laws. Dartmouth has a heavier-tail when compared to Montreal, therefore large association times tend to be more common for Dartmouth.

7. ACKNOWLEDGMENTS

Financial support was granted by the CAPES Foundation Grant ID:13428-13-6 and by NSF under project CNS 1321151.

8. REFERENCES

[1] Global mobile data traffic forecast update. http://www.cisco.com/c/en/us/solutions/collateral/service-provider/visual-networking-index-vni/mobile-white-paper-c11-520862.html.

[2] M. Afanasyev, T. Chen, G. M. Voelker, and A. C. Snoeren. Usage patterns in an urban wifi network. IEEE/ACM Trans. Netw., 18(5):1359–1372, Oct. 2010.

[3] W. Bao and B. Liang. Insensitivity of user distribution in multicell networks under general mobility and session patterns. IEEE Transactions on Wireless Communications, 12(12):6244–6254, December 2013.

[4] Y.-C. Chen, J. Kurose, and D. Towsley. A mixed queueing network model of mobility in a campus wireless network. In INFOCOM, 2012 Proceedings IEEE, pages 2656–2660, March 2012.

[5] M. Gani, H. Sarwar, and C. M. Rahman. Prediction of state of wireless network using markov and hidden markov model. Journal of Networks, 4(10):976–984, 2009.

[6] A. Ghosh, R. Jana, V. Ramaswami, J. Rowland, and N. K. Shankaranarayanan. Modeling and characterization of large-scale wi-fi traffic in public hot-spots. In INFOCOM, 2011 Proceedings IEEE, pages 2921–2929, April 2011.

[7] C. S. Gillespie. Fitting heavy tailed distributions: The poweRlaw package. Journal of Statistical Software, 64(2):1–16, 2015.

[8] M. Kim, D. Kotz, and S. Kim. Extracting a mobility model from real user traces. In INFOCOM, volume 6, pages 1–13, 2006.

[9] D. Kotz, T. Henderson, I. Abyzov, and J. Yeo. CRAWDAD dataset dartmouth(v.2009-09-09). http://crawdad.org/dartmouth/campus/20090909, Sept. 2009.

[10] K. Lee, S. Hong, S. J. Kim, I. Rhee, and S. Chong. Slaw: A new mobility model for human walks. In INFOCOM 2009, IEEE, pages 855–863, April 2009.

[11] M. Lenczner, B. Grégoire, and F. Proulx. CRAWDAD dataset ilesansfil(v.2007-08-27). http://crawdad.org/ilesansfil/wifidog/20070827, Aug. 2007.

[12] J. Manweiler, N. Santhapuri, R. Choudhury, and S. Nelakuditi. Predicting length of stay at wifi hotspots. In INFOCOM, 2013 Proceedings IEEE, pages 3102–3110, April 2013.

[13] B. Nunes, K. Obraczka, and A. Rodrigues. Saga: Socially- and geography-aware mobility modeling framework. In Proceedings of the 15th ACM International Conference on Modeling, Analysis and Simulation of Wireless and Mobile Systems, MSWiM '12, pages 367–376, New York, NY, USA, 2012. ACM.

An Experimental Study of Cross-Technology Interference in In-Vehicle Wireless Sensor Networks

Rasool Tavakoli[1], Majid Nabi[1], Twan Basten[1,2], Kees Goossens[1]
[1]Department of Electrical Engineering, Eindhoven University of Technology, the Netherlands
[2]TNO Embedded Systems Innovation, Eindhoven, the Netherlands
{r.tavakoli, m.nabi, a.a.basten, k.g.w.goossens}@tue.nl

ABSTRACT

Wireless in-vehicle networks are considered as a flexible and cost-efficient solution for the new generation of cars. One of the candidate wireless technologies for these wireless sensor networks is the IEEE 802.15.4 standard which operates in the 2.4 GHz ISM band. This is while the number of wireless devices that operate in this band is ever increasing. This broad usage of the same RF band may cause considerable performance degradation of wireless networks due to interference. There is some work on the coexistence of the IEEE 802.15.4 protocol and other standard technologies such as IEEE 802.11 (Wi-Fi) and IEEE 802.15.1 (Bluetooth), but none of it considers the highly dynamic conditions of in-vehicle networks. In this paper, we investigate the interference behavior in in-vehicle environments using real-world experiments. We consider different scenarios and measure the interference on all the 16 channels of IEEE 802.15.4 in the 2.4 GHz band. The measurement data set is available to the public. This real-world data set can be used for realistic and accurate network simulation. To study the effect of interference on in-vehicle networks, we use this data set to evaluate the performance of an IEEE 802.15.4e TSCH link. The simulation results show that the packet error rate for some interference scenarios is considerably high and dynamic over time. This shows the value of the data set and reveals the importance of using adaptive interference mitigation techniques to improve the reliability of wireless in-vehicle networks.

Keywords

Wireless sensor networks; In-vehicle networks; Interference; Wireless co-existence; IEEE 802.15.4e; TSCH

1. INTRODUCTION

Wireless communication is considered as a solution to be used in new generations of cars. This technology provides significant improvement in flexibility and reconfigurability

MSWiM '16, November 13-17, 2016, Malta, Malta
© 2016 ACM. ISBN 978-1-4503-4502-6/16/11... $15.00
DOI: http://dx.doi.org/10.1145/2988287.2989141

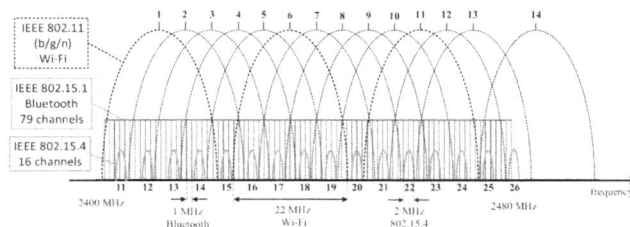

Figure 1: Usage of 2.4 GHz ISM band.

of In-Vehicle Networks (IVNs). It further reduces the manufacturing cost and enables new applications. Based on the requirements of these networks that include low data rate communications, reduced complexity of nodes and low power consumptions, the IEEE 802.15.4 standard [3] is a proper candidate to be used as the physical and Medium Access Control (MAC) layer protocols for these networks. This standard uses 16 frequency channels in the license-free 2.4 GHz ISM band. The 4e amendment [5] of this standard was developed aiming to increase the robustness of wireless communication links through guaranteed medium accesses and channel diversity. In the Time-Slotted Channel Hopping (TSCH) mode, wireless nodes hop over different channels to transmit frames of a single link. This eliminates repeated dropping of packets because of noise on a single channel. Although this standard provides guaranteed access to the medium for the network links, there is no guarantee that it can meet the stringent Quality-of-Service (QoS) requirements of the in-vehicle applications. The main reason is the common usage of the unlicensed 2.4 GHz ISM band by different standards including IEEE 802.11 WLAN [4] and IEEE 802.15.1 Bluetooth [2], which leads to cross-technology interference and packet losses. Fig. 1 shows the frequency usage of these three protocol standards in the ISM band.

Considering the low transmission power in Wireless Sensor Networks (WSNs), the IEEE 802.15.4 networks are expected to be affected considerably by the other coexisting technologies. Actually there are several experimental and analytical studies on the coexistence of IEEE 802.15.4 and other technologies, but none of them considers the in-vehicle conditions and its effect on the quality of the links in WSNs. Moreover, all of these studies focused on CSMA/CA based MAC modes of the 802.15.4 standard while our study is the first one that investigates the cross-technology interference effect on the TSCH MAC of the 4e amendment.

The cross-technology interference in in-vehicle environments can be categorized into interference of in-car and out-of-car sources. This makes in-vehicle wireless communications more challenging due to (1) high density of in-car wireless devices such as phones and music players that use both Wi-Fi and Bluetooth communications and (2) high dynamism of out-of-car interferers because of the car movements. Furthermore, each coexisting technology behaves differently w.r.t. transmission timings and power. This work is the first one to study the behavior of interference in in-vehicle environments and its effect on TSCH communications.

We investigate the interference behavior in in-vehicle environments using real-world experimental setups. We consider different scenarios and measure the interference power on all the 16 channels of IEEE 802.15.4 in the 2.4 GHz band. The measurement results are used in a simulation framework to analyze TSCH behavior under different interference scenarios. We also provide a public measurement data set for in-vehicle environments. This data set and the simulation scripts are public and available online through https://git.ics.ele.tue.nl/Public/interference-behavior-in-in-vehicle-env.

The paper is organized as follows. The next section gives an overview of related work about wireless coexistence in WSNs. Section 3 presents our measurement setup and scenarios in detail. The measurement result of in-car and out-of-car interference is discussed in Sections 4 and 5, respectively. The performance of TSCH communications under measured in-vehicle interference is studied in Section 6. Section 7 concludes.

2. RELATED WORK

The ever increasing number of the 2.4 GHz ISM band users makes wireless interference of coexisting wireless devices a challenge, especially for low power IEEE 802.15.4 WSNs. The IEEE 802.15.4 standard document [3], provides estimation of packet error rate of this standard under IEEE 802.11b, IEEE 802.15.1, and IEEE 802.15.3 networks using coexistence simulations. Some work has been done on the coexistence of IEEE 802.15.4 with other standard wireless protocols using experiments and analytic modeling. Experimental studies presented in [11, 6, 13], and [18], mainly measure and report the impact of coexistence on the network performance metrics such as Packet Reception Ratio (PRR) and latency. The authors of [16] and [19], provide analytic models of the coexistence of IEEE 802.15.4 under IEEE 802.11 interference, based on the transmission patterns of both technologies. A radio link quality estimation survey in IEEE 802.15.4 WSNs is provided in [7]. The authors present the observation that the external interference of Wi-Fi and Bluetooth has a strong impact on the quality of IEEE 802.15.4 links but the communications of Wi-Fi and Bluetooth are less affected by an 802.15.4 network.

Different WSN operating environments may lead to different coexistence and interference conditions. While some (e.g., [6, 16, 23, 17]) focus on the general coexistence, others consider specific environments such as buildings [11, 14], industrial [8], outdoor [12], and body [13] environments. There are also studies on the wireless coexistence in in-vehicle WSNs. The authors of [24] consider Wi-Fi and Bluetooth as the most likely interferers for IEEE 802.15.4-based IVNs. They provide measurements and analysis for interference of these technologies on a single channel of IEEE 802.15.4, done in an RF anechoic chamber. This makes this work similar to general coexistence studies, skipping the real-world con-

ditions. The authors of [9] do some measurements for a static in-vehicle scenario. They place some IEEE 802.15.4 sensor nodes in different parts of a car, and investigate the performance of different single channel links between them under Bluetooth communications. The results are expressed in terms of Packet Error Rate (PER) and average/peak latency. These studies only addressed the coexistence effect of devices inside a vehicle on single channel IVNs. This is while IVNs (that are operating in single or multiple channels) may also experience interference from devices out of the vehicle There is no measurement study on this.

A channel quality measurement data set for industrial wireless environments is presented in [8]. These kind of public data sets are useful for interference modeling and network performance simulation based on real-world situations. However, the authors of [8] note that these data sets are limited to the office, laboratory, and industrial environments and there is nothing like this for in-vehicle environments.

In this paper, we focus on the multi-channel in-vehicle WSNs and the effect of cross-technology interference on them. Based on real-world scenarios, we perform a set of interference measurements on all the IEEE 802.15.4 channels and provide a public data set for in-vehicle environments that can be used to estimate the performance of wireless IVNs. We also evaluate the performance of a TSCH link under real-world interference using the provided data set and simulations.

3. MEASUREMENT SETUP

To verify the performance of higher layers of a wireless protocol, we need to know about its physical layer conditions in the working environment. In this work, we aim to capture the wireless conditions of all the IEEE 802.15.4 channels in in-vehicle environments. Here we describe the requirements for such a measurement and introduce the used hardware setup for our experiments. Later we present different experiment scenarios to capture different interference behaviors.

3.1 Measurement Requirements

To perform noise measurement on the IEEE 802.15.4 channels, we need to sample each channel continuously. Each channel experiences dynamic energy levels for different periods and durations of time. This is caused by packet transmissions of different coexisting technologies. Wi-Fi and Bluetooth are considered to be two coexisting technologies that have the most impact on 802.15.4 IVNs. The data rate, packet size, and bandwidth usage of these standards vary from each other and even from version to version and application to application. Therefore, the sampling method, rate and duration can have direct impact on the extracted behavior of the wireless channels. Considering these facts, we need to sample the medium continuously and with the highest possible rate. Each sample should reflect the medium quality during the sampling duration.

We select hardware Energy Detection (ED), defined in the IEEE 802.15.4 protocol, to measure the quality of the wireless channels. Based on the IEEE 802.15.4 protocol definitions, an ED is an average of the received signal power within the bandwidth of the channel over 128 μs. Thus, lower values indicate less noisy channels while higher values indicate higher noise on the wireless channel.

3.2 Measurement Hardware Setup

To measure the interference, we used Atmel ATMEGA256-RFR2 Xplained Pro kits [1]. This kit includes an ATMEL ATMEGA256RFR2 SOC which contains an IEEE 802.15.4 compliant wireless transceiver. We assign one Atmel mote to each of the 802.15.4 channels to measure the noise level of that channel and stream the measurement results to a laptop. In the Atmel chip, each ED is done by averaging RSSI values over this period and has a value in the range of [-90, -10] dBm.

We use 16 AVR kits to measure the noise level of all the 16 IEEE 802.15.4 channels on the 2.4 GHz ISM band at the same time. All the AVR kits are placed next to each-other under the back window of a car. Since one Wi-Fi transmission can affect 3 to 5 IEEE 802.15.4 channels, we should synchronize all the samples of different channels to correctly extract the interference behavior. Clock drifts of different AVR chips make a one-time initial synchronization useless. We use wired signaling between kits to synchronize them at the beginning of each sampling interval. One of the kits works as master and triggers an output pin at the start of each sampling interval. Other nodes get this signal as input and start each sampling period when it is triggered. We set the sampling period to 500 μs which is enough to do an ED and send the results to the computer. On the computer side, we use Matlab to collect the sampling data that is sent by individual kits.

3.3 Measurement Scenarios

We categorize the interference sources for wireless IVNs into in-car and out-of-car sources. For each category we perform several measurements using different real-world scenarios. For in-car interference sources, each scenario is designed to investigate the effect of one type of interference sources and/or applications. In this case, we picked up three measurement scenarios to study the behavior of Wi-Fi and Bluetooth transmissions. The three scenarios are 1) Bluetooth connection of a mobile phone and a music player device with an audio streaming application, 2) Bluetooth connection between two smart phones with a file transfer application which requires more bandwidth and handshaking than that of scenario 1, and 3) Wi-Fi connection between two smart phones with a file transfer application.

The out-of-car interference is caused by the devices that are operating out of the car along the roads or in other cars. We defined four scenarios in this case; 1) Driving along a route near some apartments; 2) Driving along an office area in downtown; 3) Driving in a suburb area; 4) Driving along a highway with no buildings around.

4. IN-CAR INTERFERENCE MEASUREM-ENT

To study the interference behavior of in-car sources, we parked the car in an open space area with no construction within 0.5 kilometer. Using sniffers, it was confirmed that the selected environment has negligible external interference on the 2.4 GHz ISM band. We pick three measurement scenarios to study the behavior of in-car interferers (including Wi-Fi and Bluetooth devices). Each measurement is performed for 5 minutes which leads to 600k samples per channel. In the following, we discuss the result of each measurement in detail.

4.1 Bluetooth Audio Streaming

In this scenario, we use a mobile phone to stream audio to the audio system of the car using Bluetooth version 4.0. We placed the phone on the dashboard of the car, with 2.5 meters distance from the interference measuring motes. Fig. 2 depicts the captured Bluetooth interference over time on different IEEE 802.15.4 channels. Fig. 2(a) uses a contour plot to show the distribution of interference power over different channels. Each color in the plot reflects the maximum power of the captured Bluetooth signal on a channel during a period of one second. In contour plots, the width of the samples' color on the horizontal line shows the repetition of samples with that power level in that channel over time.

The first observation about Fig. 2(a) is that in this scenario there is no Bluetooth interference on the first four IEEE 802.15.4 channels in the 2.4GHz ISM band. This may be because of the blacklisting method that is used by the Bluetooth channel hopping module. It should be considered that this blacklisting method may be different in different Bluetooth devices, from version to version, and vendor to vendor. The Bluetooth channel hopping module can also be pre-programmed to not use some parts of the frequency band to prevent cross-technology interference with in-range devices. The second observation about Fig. 2(a) is that the usage of different parts of the frequency band by Bluetooth is not uniform. For instance, some of the channels, such as channel 22, experience higher power Bluetooth interference (darker parts of the plot) while some others, such as channel 19, experience lower power Bluetooth interference. To make it clearer, Fig. 2(b) shows the measured noise on channels 19 and 22 during one second. We can see that channel 22 experiences interference of more that 20 Bluetooth transmissions during this period. Channel 19 only experiences interference of 3 Bluetooth transmissions. This shows that the Bluetooth interference is not uniform over different channels, and some channels may be occupied more than others. Furthermore, the measured power of the interference signal on channel 22 is considerably higher than on channel 19. A possible reason is the cross channel interference and distance between center frequency of the Bluetooth operating channels and the measured IEEE 802.15.4 channel. Thus, different adjacent Bluetooth channels can cause interference with different signal powers on an IEEE 802.15.4 channel.

We have a more detailed look at the Bluetooth interference behavior considering the application of audio streaming that is used in this scenario. Fig. 2(c) depicts the Bluetooth interference measured on the IEEE 802.15.4 channels in a 100 ms time period in this scenario. The measured interference follows a periodic behavior with intervals of around 30 ms with each transmission lasting for 3 ms, which is the transmission time of a Bluetooth packet with the maximum size. It shows that the audio streaming application sends periodic packets that require a bandwidth of around 10% of the available Bluetooth bandwidth.

Fig. 3 shows the measured interference of one complete Bluetooth packet transmission. In this case, we can say that the first Bluetooth packet transmission fails because it is not followed by the receiver's acknowledgement. Thus, the transmitter sends the packet again within a short interval, and in this try, it is followed by an acknowledge packet. As mentioned before, the difference between measured signal powers on different IEEE 802.15.4 channels for a single (or multiple) Bluetooth transmission(s) can be because of

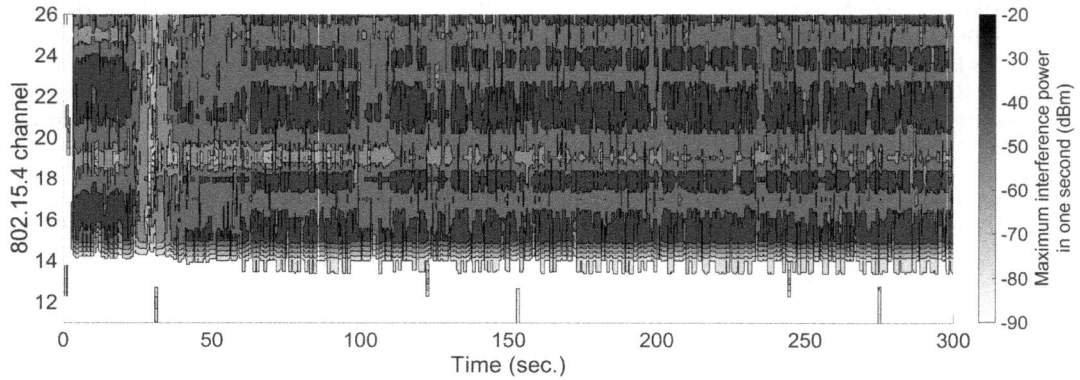

(a) Interference behavior over 300 s using contour plot.

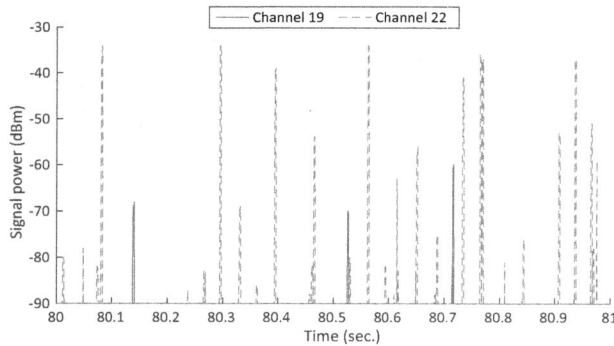

(b) Measured interference power on channels 19 and 22 over 1 s.

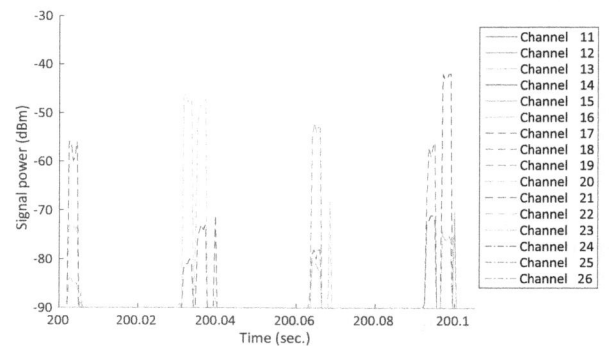

(c) Measured interference power on all channels over 100 ms

Figure 2: Effect of Bluetooth audio streaming on IEEE 802.15.4 channels

the different distance between center frequency of the Bluetooth operating channels and the measured IEEE 802.15.4 channels. For instance, the first Bluetooth packet transmission in Fig. 3 generates interference on both the IEEE 802.15.4 channels 17 and 18 with different powers.

As a conclusion, voice streaming over Bluetooth produces periodic transmissions that lead to non-uniform interference for IEEE 802.15.4 channels. Thus some IEEE 802.15.4 channels may experience less interference than other channels (as shown in Fig. 2(a)). This behavior is caused by the channel hopping of Bluetooth which follows a pseudo-random hopping sequence. The power level of this interference on each channel is often stable over substantial periods of time.

4.2 Bluetooth File Transfer

To study the Bluetooth interference on IEEE 802.15.4 channels when Bluetooth is under higher load, we use two mobile phones to transfer a large file using a Bluetooth connection. The transmitter phone was placed on the back seat of the car near the interference measuring motes. The receiver phone was placed on the dashboard with 2 meters distance from the transmitter phone. As Fig. 4(a) shows, as for the audio streaming scenario, some of the channels experience more interference than others. Furthermore, the power level of the interferer signal on a single channel varies over time (compare interference power on channel 14 at $t = 100$ and $t = 200$).

Fig. 4(b) shows the measured Bluetooth interference in channels 14 and 25 at $t = 200$ for half a second. This fig-

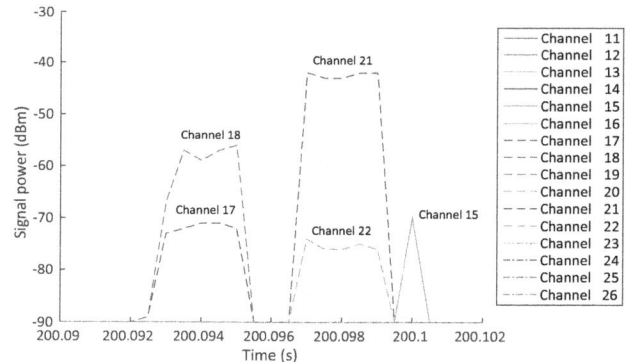

Figure 3: Interference of one Bluetooth packet transmission, one retransmission, and one acknowledgement on IEEE 802.15.4 channels

ure shows that the number of interferer signals and their power in channel 14 is considerably higher than in channel 16. This is while Bluetooth uses its full bandwidth to transfer data in this scenario (see constant transmissions in Fig. 4(c)). Considering the results of the first scenario, we can conclude that Bluetooth causes a non-uniform interference over IEEE 802.15.4 channels for different applications with different data transfer rates. The important point here is that the power of Bluetooth interference on each channel is almost stable over substantial periods of time.

198

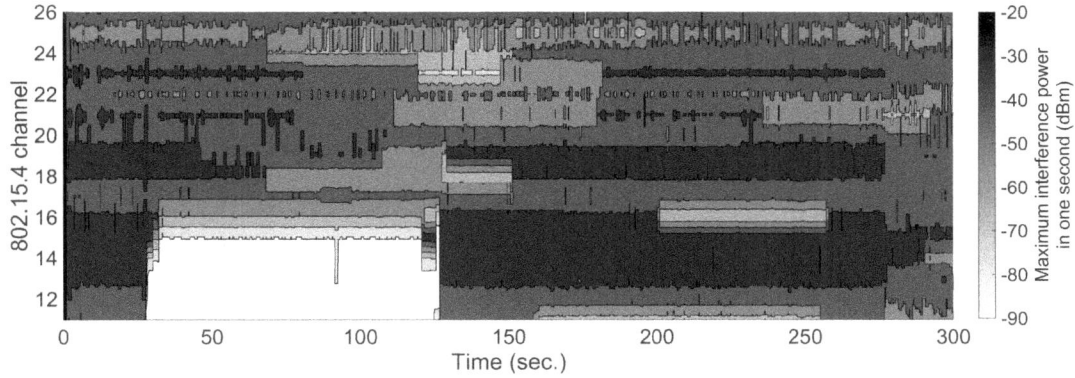

(a) Interference behavior over 300 s using contour plot.

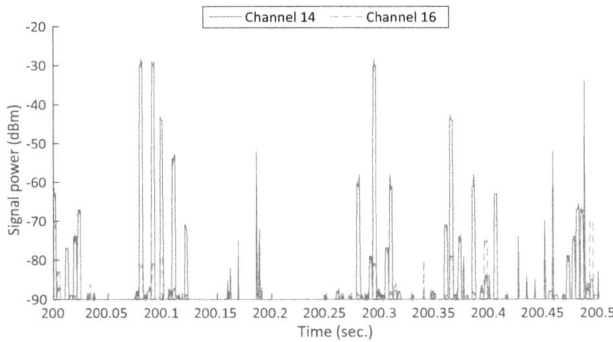

(b) Measured interference power on channels 14 and 16 over 0.5 s.

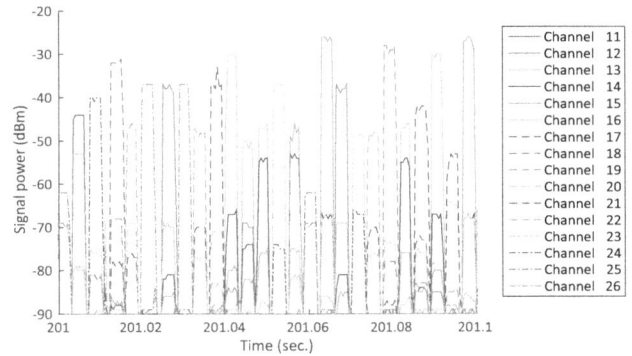

(c) Measured interference power on all channels over 100 ms.

Figure 4: Effect of Bluetooth file transfer on IEEE 802.15.4 channels

4.3 Wi-Fi Connection

In this scenario we are interested in the amount of interference from Wi-Fi communication within the vehicle on the IEEE 802.15.4 channels. To study this effect, we connect two smart phones using *Wi-Fi direct* and use this connection to transfer some large files. One of the phones is used as the transmitter and another one as the receiver of the files. During the experiment, two phones are placed in different places inside the cabin by two passengers (one passenger at the driver seat and another at one of the rear seats). We logged the generated interference of this Wi-Fi connection on the IEEE 802.15.4 channels for 300 seconds.

Fig. 5(a) shows the interference behavior over time and channels, using a contour plot. It shows that the Wi-Fi interference mostly affects a number of adjacent IEEE 802.15.4 channels and the power of this interference decreases by going far from the center frequency of the Wi-Fi operating channel. This plot also shows some transmissions at other frequencies used for the mentioned Wi-Fi connection. These are probe requests (to perform active scans) and beacons (to advertise a P2P Group) that are done on so-called social channels, namely channels 1, 6 or 11 in the 2.4 Ghz band, by *Wi-Fi direct* devices [22].

In this experiment, the center frequency of the Wi-Fi operating channel is between channels 12 and 13 of IEEE 802.15.4. As Fig. 5(a) shows, the interference strength changes over time. These changes are due to the movement of two phones which changes the distance between interferer and sensor nodes and also due to the movement of passengers

in the car that affects the path-loss of the interferer signal. Compared to Bluetooth, the observed interference on each channel is more stable over time. This is because Wi-Fi devices do not use channel hopping and a connection normally uses a fixed channel for communications.

Fig. 5(b) depicts the interference of Wi-Fi transmissions on the IEEE 802.15.4 channels over 100 ms. According to this plot, channels 11 to 14 are within the main 22 MHz bandwidth of the Wi-Fi operating channel, while channels 15 and 16 are on the sidebands of the Wi-Fi operating channel. Because the file transfer application uses the full bandwidth of the Wi-Fi connection, the captured interference on each channel is almost constant during the transmission period of a file.

4.4 In-car Interference Conclusion

In this section, we investigated the behavior of two main sources of in-car interference for wireless IVNs. The experiments show that the distribution of interference on different IEEE 802.15.4 channels is not uniform. Depending on the interferer protocol and the used application, the power of interference on each channel is almost stable over substantial periods of time. The minimum period of changes in the power of the interferer signal, that is more visible for Bluetooth, is in the order of a few seconds. We may conclude that the non-uniform interference over different channels suggests the need for a proper channel whitelisting (or blacklisting) mechanism. These mechanisms should also cope with the possible changes in the quality of each channel over time.

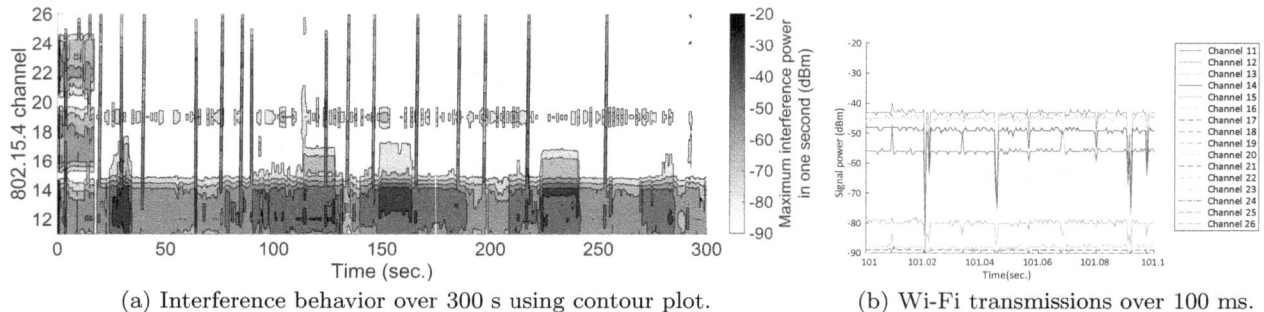

(a) Interference behavior over 300 s using contour plot.

(b) Wi-Fi transmissions over 100 ms.

Figure 5: Interference of in-car Wi-Fi communications on the IEEE 802.15.4 channels.

5. OUT-OF-CAR INTERFERENCE MEASUREMENT

To study the interference behavior of out-of-car sources, we drove the car in different environments with different density of interferer sources. During these measurements, all the in-car interferers were turned off and the car was driven with allowed speed in that district. Four scenarios are considered that include apartment area, downtown, suburb, and highway. Considering the higher transmission power of Wi-Fi compared to Bluetooth devices, we expect that the Wi-Fi devices at sides of the roads be the main source of out-of-car interference. By using a Wi-Fi analyzer application on a mobile phone, we found that the density of Wi-Fi devices in these four scenarios is decreasing from apartment areas to downtown, suburb, and highways. We take a 5 minute drive in each of the environments while the interference measuring motes measure the noise level of all 16 channels. Fig. 6 shows the captured interference in different environments using a contour plot. To make these plots more clear, for each point in the plots we show the maximum observed interference level over a window of 2000 samples (1 s) in that time.

Fig. 6(a) shows the interference behavior while driving near apartments with speed in a range of 10 to 25 kmph. As it was expected, the interference power and density in apartment areas is more than in other environments. In this figure, there are lots of overlapping ovals with a high power at their centers (some of which are marked by red ellipses). This is because when the car is in the range of one Wi-Fi device and moving toward it, the interference power will be increased and vise versa. Thus the interference of one Wi-Fi device is only visible for a few seconds. The figure shows that any time the car is in the interference range of a number of Wi-Fi devices, which they can even overlap in operating channels, each one can affect 2 to 3 IEEE 802.15.4 channels. On the other hand, some of the IEEE 802.15.4 channels are noise free over different periods of time; this can be seen as white spaces on the contour plots.

The downtown scenario (Fig. 6(b)) has two specific properties. First, the speed of the car is determined by the traffic load of the streets and the traffic lights and is in a range of 0 to 30 kmph. This affects the time that a car will be in the range of a stationary interferer and thus affects the dynamism level of the interference. For example, around time 0s to 30s in the Fig. 6(b), the car has been waiting for a traffic light and the interference is not dynamic on channels 12 and 18. This is while from time 250s to 300s, the car has been moving along the street and the observed interference

is relatively more dynamic. The second property is that the car moves next to other cars in the street in the same or opposite direction. These neighbor cars may carry some devices that are operating in the 2.4 GHz ISM band (Bluetooth, Wi-Fi, etc.). This may lead to long or short term interference. The vertical bars in Fig. 6(b) may be because of such interferences. These bars can be due to Bluetooth transmissions in the neighbor cars which affect most parts of the frequency band because of the fast channel hopping of the Bluetooth protocol. The interference of Bluetooth devices in neighbor cars is normally very short term. This is because of the low transmission power that is used in Bluetooth devices which leads to interference only when two cars are in a distance of few meters.

In the third scenario, the test car is moving in a quiet street in a suburb area with an average speed of 40 kmph. As it is clear in Fig. 6(c), the interference level in this area is less than apartment and downtown areas and there is more noise-free area left in the channel-time space. This is because of lower density of houses in suburb areas which leads to lower density of interferers. This also causes longer distances between stationary interferers and the car, which reduces the power of the observed interferer signal.

Fig. 6(d) shows the observed interference on a highway while the car is moving with a fixed speed of 115 kmph. In this scenario, the stationary interferers play the least role (only near the gas stations). The interferer devices in neighbor cars cause low level and short term interference too. The reason is the short time and high distance adjacency of cars in a highway.

Considering the mentioned observations of the out-of-car interference behavior, it can be concluded that in-vehicle wireless sensor communications may face serious problems in city environments if the operating channels and transmission power are selected blindly. In the next section, we study the effect of such interferences on the performance of the TSCH protocol by using probabilistic communication models and the collected interference database.

6. IVN SIMULATION UNDER REAL INTERFERENCE DATA SET

In this section, we propose a simulation framework that uses the measured interference data set to evaluate the performance of IEEE 802.15.4 WSNs. As a case study, we study the effect of dynamic in-vehicle interferences on the performance of multi channel wireless IVN communications.

(a) Near apartments

(b) Downtown

(c) Suburb

(d) Highway

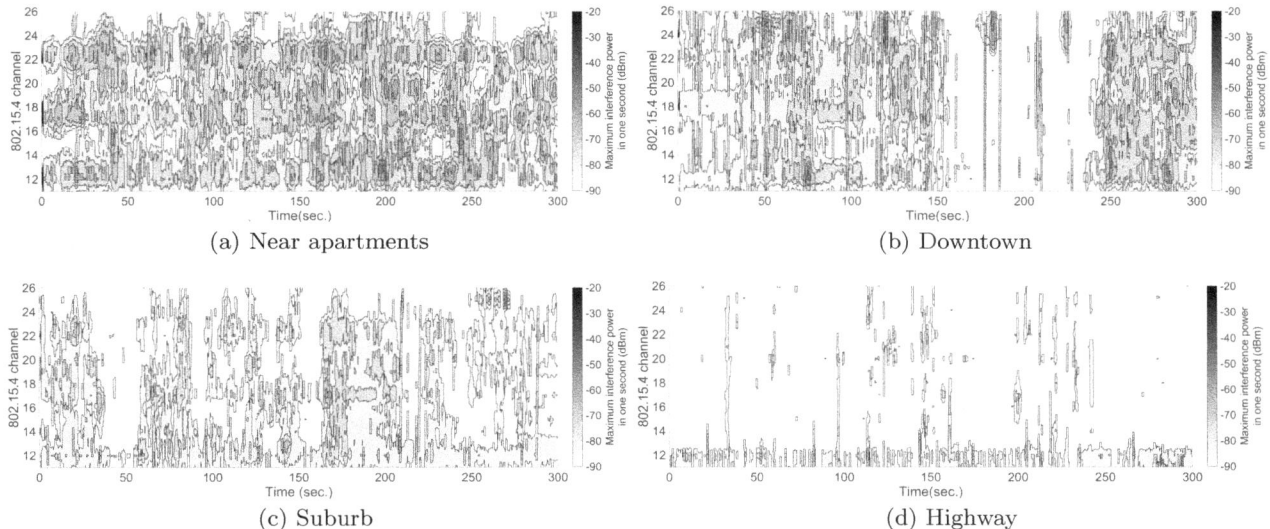

Figure 6: Behavior of out-of-car wireless interference in different city environments.

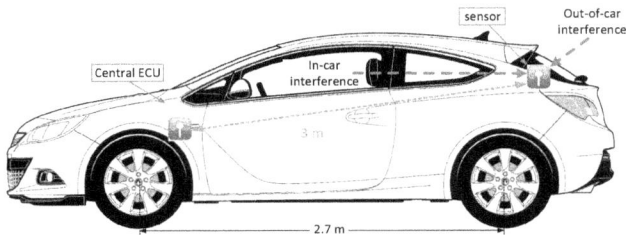

Figure 7: Interference model for packet reception probability computation.

Time Slotted Channel Hopping (TSCH) is one of the operation modes of the IEEE 802.15.4e [5] protocol standard. It uses channel hopping to eliminate blocking of wireless links caused by external interference on some frequency channels. This technique improves the reliability and connectivity of the wireless links compared to single channel communications [21]. This is the first work in the literature on the evaluation of TSCH performance under interference of in-vehicle environments. To investigate the effect of channel whitelisting, we also evaluate ETSCH [20], one of the enhancements to the TSCH protocol that uses channel whitelisting based on the interference condition of all channels. The main conclusions of [20] are confirmed, but the savings are less for the realistic scenarios, compared to the lab tests of [20].

We use a simple model to extract the communication behavior of a single wireless link in a car (shown in Fig. 7). In this model, there is an Engine Control Unit (ECU) inside the dashboard of the car which is connected, through a wireless link, to a wireless sensor node placed exactly where we placed the interference measuring motes. Considering a direct wireless link from the central ECU to the sensor node, the received signal power (P_{rx}) at the sensor node can be computed as:

$$P_{rx}[dBm] = P_{tx}[dBm] - PL(d)[dB] \qquad (1)$$

where P_{tx} is the power of the signal at the transmitter (central ECU) and $PL(d)$ is the path loss at distance d. We use the path loss model (Eqn. 2) introduced in [3] for short

range communications at 2.4 GHz band.

$$PL(d)[dB] = \gamma \left[20.1 + 10 \log(d)\right] \qquad d \le 8m \qquad (2)$$

where γ is the path-loss exponent, which has a value equal to (for free space) or greater than 2.0 (other environments).

The receiver node in our framework experiences interference from sources inside and outside the car. The probability of successful communication is related to the Signal-to-Noise Ratio (SNR) [15]. Here we focus on the effect of interference from co-existing devices and ignore other kinds of noise. Thus, the SNR is given in decibel as:

$$SNR[dB] = P_{rx}[dBm] - P_{intf}[dBm] \qquad (3)$$

where P_{intf} is the interference power at the receiver point within the same bandwidth as P_{rx}. Considering that the distance between the transmitter and receiver in our model is 3 meters, the SNR for the given link can be presented as:

$$SNR[dB] = P_{tx}[dBm] - 24.87\gamma - P_{intf}[dBm] \qquad (4)$$

For a given SNR, the expected Bit Error Rate (BER) of an IEEE 802.15.4 link can be extracted using the BER model provided in the IEEE 802.15.4 standard (Annex E part 4.2) [3]. Thus, we can compute the expected Packet Reception Probability (PRP) for a given packet length and interference level during the transmission of that packet.

We perform our simulations with $P_{tx} = 0$ dBm that is the default transmission power of the protocol and also with a higher power of $P_{tx} = 4$ dBm that is the maximum transmission power of our ATMEL wireless motes. The path-loss exponent is expected to be dynamic in an in-vehicle environment because of the dynamism in the car (e.g., number of passengers and their position). We pick 3 values of $\gamma = 2.5$, 3.0, and 3.5 for our simulations to investigate the effect of environment changes on the performance of the given wireless link. Therefore, we simulate the performance of the TSCH link for 6 different (P_{tx}, γ) combinations under all different interference scenarios.

We implemented our simulation framework in Matlab according to the communication timings of the TSCH protocol. Time is divided into $10ms$ timeslots. After an offset at the beginning of each timeslot, we compute the BER for every bit using Eqn. 4 and the measured interference sample at that time on the operating channel. We considered a packet

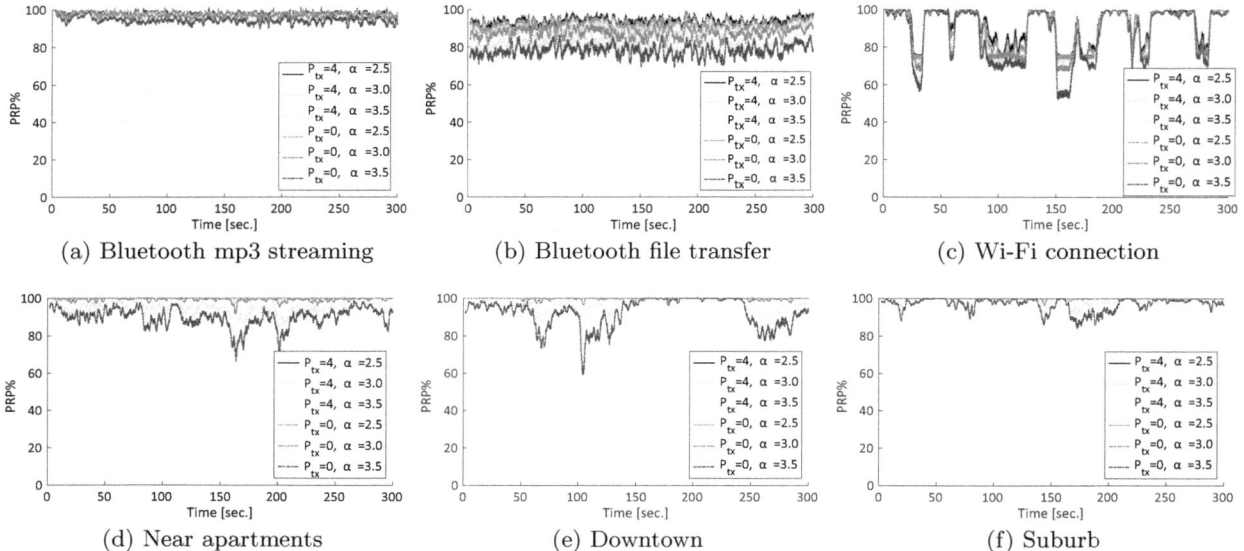

(a) Bluetooth mp3 streaming   (b) Bluetooth file transfer   (c) Wi-Fi connection

(d) Near apartments   (e) Downtown   (f) Suburb

Figure 8: Average PRP of TSCH communications over time for different interference scenarios and transmission parameters.

length of 133 bytes which is the maximum physical layer packet length in the IEEE 802.15.4 protocol. By the start of the next timeslot, we hop to the next channel according to the TSCH hopping algorithm. We use all 16 available channels for the hopping sequence.

In our interference measurements, the radio sensitivity of the used devices was -90 dBm. Considering our worst case scenario with $P_{tx} = 0$ dBm and $\gamma = 3.5$, the PRP for $P_{intf} =$ -90 dBm is more than 99.99%. Thus we can be sure that our simulations only show the effect of existing interference. Measured interference values of -90 dBm, at the radio sensitivity limit, have no effect on the results.

Fig. 8 shows the PRP for different scenarios. We skipped results of the highway scenario because for all the different sets of parameters, the PRP is close to 100%. We used a moving average function with a window of 2 s (200 transmissions) to show the average PRP over time. This is an approximation of the PRR in real-world communications.

A general observation from different scenarios in Fig. 8 is that the path-loss exponent, which is a parameter of the environment conditions, considerably affects the communications. Since this parameter is not a controllable parameter in the real-world, higher transmission powers may be a solution to increase the PRP. But WSNs are limited in power sources and thus, transmission power should be decreased as much as possible. The effect of generated interference to the neighbor networks due to this increase in transmission power should also be taken into account.

Another observation is that for almost all different (P_{tx}, γ) combinations in in-car interference scenarios (Fig. 8(a-c)), interference decreases the PRP even for a small value. In out-of-car scenarios (Fig. 8(d-f)), the impact of interference on PRP is considerably higher for $(P_{tx}, \gamma) = (4, 3.5)$ and $(0, 3.5)$ combinations, but for other combinations of (P_{tx}, γ), interference has almost no effect on the PRP. The reason is that different in-car interferers normally produce high power interference on a set of channels (due to a low distance between interferer and the wireless node in the car) and less or even no interference on other channels (Fig. 2(a),4(a), and

5(a)). Therefore even for (P_{tx}, γ) combinations with higher P_{tx} and lower path-loss exponents, the 802.15.4 link cannot overcome this high power interference on some channels and PRP will be decreased even with low values. On the other hand, in the out-of-car scenarios the interference power is usually weaker (compared to in-car interference) but distributed over most of the channels (Fig. 6). For higher P_{tx} and lower path-loss exponents, this low power interference has almost no effect on the PRP because the SNR is high enough. This is while for lower P_{tx} and higher path-loss exponents, the SNR decreases and even low power interference can affect the PRP. Because multiple channels in urban scenarios may experience interference at the same time (Fig. 6(a), (b), and (c)), packet transmission may fail in a set of channels and thus PRP decreases considerably.

Fig. 8 also shows that PRP in in-car scenarios (Fig. 8(a-c)) is almost uniform over time. This is because the user applications in in-car interferers are normally invariant and running for a long time. Thus, wireless medium usage and generated interference is almost uniform over time. For the Wi-Fi scenario in which we transmitted some files with random intervals, the uniform behavior is visible for each file transfer (the periods with reduced PRP). Due to the movement of the interferers inside the car in this scenario, each file transfer leads to different interference power and thus different levels of PRP. For the out-of-car scenarios (Fig. 8(d-f)), because of the car movements, different interferers (with different user applications) may come into range during time and even in some periods there may be no interferer in the range. Therefore, the effective interference and thus the PRP is very dynamic over time.

It should be considered that in real-world scenarios, out-of-car interference may be mixed with in-car interference, which may cause a bigger impact on the performance of a in-vehicle WSN. For example, a moving car in a downtown area may carry a mobile phone that is connected to the audio system of the car by Bluetooth to answer a phone call and at the same time a kid on rear seats may play an online video on a tablet which is connected to internet through

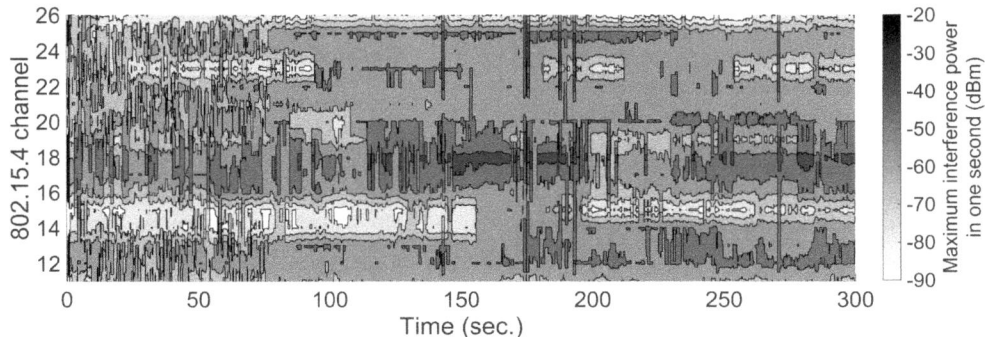

(a) Interference behavior over 300 s using contour plot.

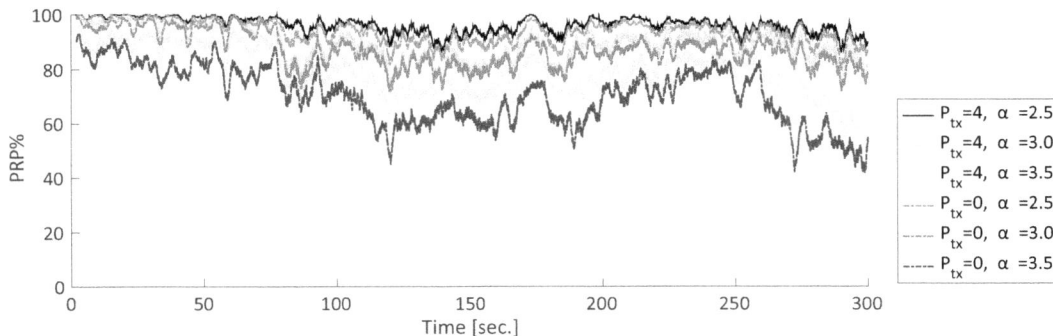

(b) Average PRP of TSCH communications over time.

Figure 9: Effect of the mixed interference scenario on the IEEE 802.15.4 channels.

a Wi-Fi hotspot link on a mobile phone. Since there can be a scenario with lots of interferers that block communications on all the channels, discussing about the possible worst case interference scenario is pointless. We consider the mentioned situation as an example real-world scenario (named mixed scenario) with multiple sources of interference for an in-vehicle WSN. Fig. 9 shows the captured interference of this scenario together with the simulation results of average PRP of TSCH communications. As it can be seen, in such a scenario the PRP of the TSCH protocol may be reduced more than 50% in some points. This makes in-vehicle WSNs an unreliable candidate for in-vehicle networks.

There are some solutions such as ATSCH [10] and ETSCH [20] to overcome packet errors (due to interference) in TSCH networks. All of these techniques dynamically pick a subset of less noisy channels for channel hopping purposes, instead of using all available channels. The ETSCH technique uses part of the offset at the beginning of each timeslot for interference measurement (one sample in our experiments) on 2 to 3 channels and assigns a quality value to each channel based on the results. In every predefined time-interval, this technique selects a subset of the best quality channels as the hopping sequence list for the network. We implemented the functionality of this technique on top of our simulation framework in Matlab to evaluate its performance under real-world interference. In our simulations, one second time-intervals are used to update the hopping sequence list of size 6. As the interference input for our simulations, we picked the scenario of Bluetooth file transfer, Wi-Fi file transfer, driving near apartments, and the mixed scenario with multiple interference sources. In the Wi-Fi scenario,

Table 1: Average PRP of TSCH and ETSCH

	P_{tx}	TSCH	ETSCH
Bluetooth file transfer	0 dBm	78.02	87.31
	4 dBm	81.86	90.01
Wi-Fi file transfer	0 dBm	74.77	99.75
	4 dBm	76.14	99.81
Driving near apartments	0 dBm	89.90	97.01
	4 dBm	94.92	98.72
Mixed interference scenario	0 dBm	70.36	84.76
	4 dBm	78.97	91.16

the connection was idle between consecutive file transfers and those periods do not reflect the effect of Wi-Fi transmission on TSCH communications. Thus in our calculations of this scenario, we only take the file transmission periods into consideration.

Table 1 shows the average PRP over 300 seconds for both TSCH and ETSCH. We only show the results for the $(P_{tx}, \gamma) = (0, 3.5)$ and $(4, 3.5)$ combinations that led to the worst PRP results in TSCH simulations. As the results show, interference of a Wi-Fi connection reduces the average PRP of TSCH protocol about 25%, but ETSCH can reduce this negative effect to less than 1%. This is because of the static channel usage by the Wi-Fi protocol. For other scenarios, which experience more dynamic interference over frequency and time, ETSCH is still able to reduce the effect of interference more than 50%. This shows the importance of using such a technique for in-vehicle WSNs to improve the reliability of the network for both dynamic out-of-car and strong in-car interferences.

To the best of our knowledge, currently there are no models for simulating interference in in-vehicle environments. In this section we showed that the logged data set can be easily used to perform realistic simulations for in-vehicle WSNs under interference of different types of sources. In these simulations, there is no need to dive into the detail of the behavior of the protocols that are used by interference sources. Moreover, the logged data set can be used in the future for developing and tuning interference models for in-vehicle environments.

7. CONCLUSION

This paper studies the cross-technology interference behavior in in-vehicle environments using real-world experiments. Different scenarios for both in-car and out-of-car interference are considered. Each measurement simultaneously captures the noise power on all the IEEE 802.15.4 channels in the 2.4 GHz band. The measurement data set is available online and can be used for research in this domain by the community. Use of this data set provides more accurate analysis than lab data and simulated data. Moreover, there is no interference model available for in-vehicle environments and data sets as the one presented in this paper can be used to develop such models.

The measurement results show that both in-car and out-of-car interference affect most of the IEEE 802.15.4 channels at the same time and the maximum power of interference on each channel typically is stable over substantial periods of time. The measurement data set is used as an input for a packet transmission model to study the behavior of the TSCH protocol under interference of different scenarios. The results show that interference of in-car sources leads to effective and almost uniform probability of packet errors over time. For out-of-car interference sources, the probability of packet errors can be highly dynamic over time. An enhanced version of the TSCH protocol [20] that uses a channel whitelisting technique is simulated using the real interference data set. The results show that this technique almost completely overcomes the less dynamic interference caused by in-vehicle Wi-Fi devices. The technique also reduces around 50% of the effect of dynamic interference caused by different sources. This result shows the importance of using such techniques for in-vehicle WSNs to improve their reliability and it illustrates the value of the collected data set.

8. ACKNOWLEDGMENTS

The research from the DEWI project (www.dewi-project.eu) leading to these results received funding from the ARTEMIS Joint Undertaking under grant agreement n° 621353.

9. REFERENCES

[1] ATmega256RFR2 Xplained Pro Evaluation Kit. http://www.atmel.com/.
[2] IEEE Standard for Information Technology - Part 15.1. *IEEE Std 802.15.1-2005*, 2005.
[3] IEEE Standard for Information technology - Part 15.4. *IEEE Std 802.15.4-2006*, 2006.
[4] IEEE Standard for Information Technology - Part 11. *IEEE Std 802.11-2007*, 2007.
[5] IEEE Standard for Local and metropolitan area networks - Part 15.4. *IEEE Std 802.15.4e-2012 (Amendment to IEEE Std 802.15.4-2011)*, 2012.
[6] L. Angrisani et al. Experimental Study of Coexistence Issues Between IEEE 802.11b and IEEE 802.15.4 Wireless Networks. *Instrumentation and Measurement, IEEE Transactions on*, 57(8):1514–1523, Aug 2008.
[7] N. Baccour et al. Radio link quality estimation in wireless sensor networks: a survey. *ACM Transactions on Sensor Networks (TOSN)*, 8(4):34, 2012.
[8] D. Block et al. Wireless channel measurement data sets for reproducible performance evaluation in industrial environments. In *Emerging Technologies Factory Automation (ETFA), IEEE 20th Conference on*, pages 1–4, Sept 2015.
[9] R. de Francisco et al. Coexistence of ZigBee wireless sensor networks and Bluetooth inside a vehicle. In *Personal, Indoor and Mobile Radio Communications, IEEE 20th International Symposium on*, pages 2700–2704, Sept 2009.
[10] P. Du et al. Spectrum-aware wireless sensor networks. In *Personal Indoor and Mobile Radio Communications (PIMRC), IEEE 24th International Symposium on*, 2013.
[11] W. Guo et al. Impacts of 2.4-GHz ISM band interference on IEEE 802.15.4 wireless sensor network reliability in buildings. *Instrumentation and Measurement, IEEE Transactions on*, 61(9):2533–2544, 2012.
[12] S. Hanna et al. Distributed sensing of spectrum occupancy and interference in outdoor 2.4 GHz Wi-Fi networks. In *Global Communications Conference (GLOBECOM)*, pages 1453–1459. IEEE, 2012.
[13] J. H. Hauer et al. Experimental study of the impact of WLAN interference on IEEE 802.15.4 body area networks. In *Wireless sensor networks*, pages 17–32. Springer, 2009.
[14] H. W. Huo et al. Coexistence of 2.4 GHz sensor networks in home environment. *The Journal of China Universities of Posts and Telecommunications*, 17(1):9–18, 2010.
[15] H. Karl et al. *Protocols and architectures for wireless sensor networks*. John Wiley & Sons, 2007.
[16] E. Ngangue Ndih et al. Analytic Modeling of the Coexistence of IEEE 802.15.4 and IEEE 802.11 in Saturation Conditions. *Communications Letters, IEEE*, 19(11):1981–1984, Nov 2015.
[17] F. Penna et al. Measurement-based analysis of spectrum sensing in adaptive WSNs under Wi-Fi and Bluetooth interference. In *Vehicular Technology Conference, VTC Spring 2009. IEEE 69th*, pages 1–5. IEEE, 2009.
[18] M. Petrova et al. Performance study of IEEE 802.15.4 using measurements and simulations. In *Wireless Communications and Networking Conference (WCNC)*, volume 1, pages 487–492. IEEE, 2006.
[19] S. Y. Shin. Throughput analysis of IEEE 802.15.4 network under IEEE 802.11 network interference. *AEU-International Journal of Electronics and Communications*, 67(8):686–689, 2013.
[20] R. Tavakoli et al. Enhanced Time-Slotted Channel Hopping in WSNs using Non-Intrusive Channel-Quality Estimation. In *Mobile Ad Hoc and Sensor Systems (MASS), 12th International Conference on*, pages 217–225. IEEE, 2015.
[21] T. Watteyne et al. Reliability Through Frequency Diversity: Why Channel Hopping Makes Sense. In *PE-WASUN*. ACM, 2009.
[22] WiFi Alliance. Wi-Fi peer-to-peer (P2P) technical specification v1.5. 2014.
[23] W. Yuan et al. Coexistence performance of IEEE 802.15.4 wireless sensor networks under IEEE 802.11 b/g interference. *Wireless Personal Communications*, 68(2):281–302, 2013.
[24] S. Zacharias et al. Coexistence measurements and analysis of IEEE 802.15.4 with Wi-Fi and bluetooth for vehicle networks. In *ITS Telecommunications (ITST), 2012 12th International Conference on*, pages 785–790, Nov 2012.

A Novel Centrality Metric for Topology Control in Underwater Sensor Networks

Rodolfo W. L. Coutinho
EECS, University of Ottawa
Ottawa, Canada
Fed. Univ. of Minas Gerais
Belo Horizonte, Brazil
rwlc@dcc.ufmg.br

Azzedine Boukerche
EECS, University of Ottawa
Ottawa, Canada
boukerch@site.uottawa.ca

Luiz F. M. Vieira
Fed. Univ. of Minas Gerais
Belo Horizonte, Brazil
lfvieira@dcc.ufmg.br

Antonio A. F. Loureiro
Fed. Univ. of Minas Gerais
Belo Horizonte, Brazil
loureiro@dcc.ufmg.br

ABSTRACT

In underwater sensor networks, the design of energy efficient and reliable data collection protocols is a daunting challenge. In this context, topology control and opportunistic routing are promising techniques for improving reliability and conserve energy. However, due to the challenges of the underwater acoustic channel, the vast knowledge acquired and the solution proposed so far in the context of terrestrial wireless ad hoc & sensor networks cannot be applied directly to underwater acoustic sensor networks. In this work, we shed light on network topology modeling from a routing viewpoint. We model the probabilistic multipath routing behavior driven by opportunistic routing protocols in underwater sensor networks. Afterward, we propose the PCen centrality metric to measure the importance of underwater sensor nodes to the data delivery task through opportunistic routing protocols. PCen is aimed to identify critical nodes that can be used to guide topology control solutions. Our simulation results consider different network densities and reveal the presence of a few number of nodes with high PCen centrality value that will have a high rate of carried traffic, being critical for the network performance.

CCS Concepts

•Networks → **Topology analysis and generation**; *Routing protocols; Network performance modeling;*

Keywords

Topology control; centrality measurement; underwater sensor networks; opportunistic routing

MSWiM '16, November 13-17, 2016, Malta

© 2016 ACM. ISBN 978-1-4503-4502-6/16/11...$15.00

DOI: http://dx.doi.org/10.1145/2988287.2989162

1. INTRODUCTION

Underwater wireless sensor network (UWSN) [1, 14] is comprised of wirelessly interconnected underwater nodes, unmanned vehicles, welding robots, underwater manipulators and several other underwater monitoring and actuator entities. UWSN will be a fundamental part of the technological apparatus for damage detection and control, for instance, of offshore industries operating in the challenging environment of deep- and ultra-deep waters and iced regions [21]. Moreover, thanks to the potential of UWSN for (almost) real-time data collection, it is envisioned a revolution on oceanographic science, offshore industrial activities and ocean's exploration, navigation and military operations, given the possibility of real-time data collection of underwater environments.

However, drawbacks arising from the use of the underwater acoustic channel have limited UWSN deployments to low-scale scenarios of restricted experimental applications. The underwater acoustic channel is considered the most difficult wireless communication technology [24]. In UWSNs, it imposes large and variable delays for packet delivery, due to the low signal propagation speed. Moreover, underwater wireless communication experiences temporary path losses, due to the shadowing zones; limited bandwidth, since path loss increases as frequency increases; high signal attenuation; noise and high bit error rate.

Underwater wireless communication is expensive in terms of energy. In fact, the energy consumption for transmitting over the underwater acoustic channel is of the order of dozen watts. The aforementioned drawbacks of underwater acoustic channel contribute to shortening the UWSN lifetime. Due to the aforementioned characteristics, the design of energy efficient and reliable data collection protocols for UWSNs is a daunting challenge. Underwater acoustic links have low reliability and even might be down during some times. Moreover, the low propagation speed of the sound underwater contributes to increasing packet collisions. These factors result in packet retransmissions and losses.

Traditionally, topology control has been extensively used in terrestrial RF-based wireless ad hoc & sensor networks for reducing energy consumption. Transmission power control, duty-cycling operation, mobility and clustering have been used for topology control in wireless sensor networks to conserve energy and prolonging their lifetime. Unfavorably, the vast knowledge acquired so far in terrestrial RF wireless sensor networks cannot be directly applied to underwater network scenarios.

In this paper, we shed light on network topology modeling in UWSNs, from a routing viewpoint. We model the probabilistic nature of multipath routing determined by opportunistic routing protocols in underwater sensor networks. Afterward, we propose the PCen centrality metric to measure the importance of each underwater sensor node for opportunistic routing. The PCen metric is aimed to identify critical nodes that would be used to guide topology control solutions. Our simulation results consider different network densities and show the presence of a few number of nodes with high PCen centrality value. These nodes will be critical for both the network performance and a high data packet forwarding rate when the network density increases. The obtained insights are helpful to the design of topology control algorithm to efficiently improve routing, medium access and energy consumption in UWSNs.

The remaining of this paper is organized as follows. Section 2 overviews some of the opportunistic routing protocols proposed for UWSNs. Section 3 describes our proposed opportunistic routing modeling and the probabilistic-based multipath centrality metric (PCen) to measure the effects of the topology on routing tasks. Section 4 shows the performance evaluation and the results achieved from the proposed model. Section 5 discusses some topology control solutions that can be employed to improve the underwater sensor network performance. Finally, Section 6 presents the final remarks and future work.

2. BACKGROUND

It was shown that opportunistic routing mitigates the drawbacks of underwater acoustic channel [27], such as high bit error, temporary losses of connectivity, shadow zones, limited bandwidth; and improves the network performance as well. In fact, several routing protocols for UWSNs were designed based on the opportunistic routing paradigm [28, 29, 18, 5, 7, 17, 6, 8]. We describe the Depth-Based Routing (DBR) [29] and Hydrocast routing protocols [16, 17] that are used in the performance evaluation section of this paper, given their characteristics in the number of generated paths that differs due to the candidate set selection heuristics employed by them.

DBR [29] and Hydrocast [16, 17] protocol are two well known pressure-based opportunistic routing protocols for underwater sensor networks. They differ in the way of how the next-hop forwarder candidates are selected. In DBR, all neighboring nodes closer to the surface and with depth difference, from the current forwarder node, of Δ meters or more, are candidates to continue forwarding the data packet. A timer-based priority is assigned to each candidate, based on the depth difference from the forwarder node. In Hydrocast, the candidate set heuristic considers the proximity of the neighbors that are likely to continue forwarding the data packet. The basic idea is to select the neighboring nodes that advance the packet towards to the surface and are closer enough such that each one can hear the transmission of the other. This is to reduce the hidden terminal problem during the prioritized data forwarding. This heuristic limits the number of neighbors in the candidate set.

To the best of our knowledge, none of the opportunistic routing (OR) protocols proposed for underwater sensor networks deal with network topological aspects that will influence the performance. For instance, none of them implements rotation priority heuristics and flow balance protocols to alleviate the traffic load at some important nodes of the network. In this sense, this work models the probabilistic nature of multipath data routing produced by OR protocols and proposes a centrality metric to measure the importance of the sensor nodes in this context. The identification of these critical nodes will be impactful for the proposals of topology control and efficient OR protocols with the goal of improving the network performance.

3. SYSTEM MODEL

In this section, we present the proposed models to investigate the network topological aspects in underwater sensor networks. We introduce (i) the underwater sensor network swarm architecture, the modeling of (ii) multihop routing using opportunistic routing protocols, (iii) probabilistic-based multipath nature of data delivery in opportunistic routing, (iv) PCen, the proposed probabilistic-based multipath routing centrality metric to identify critical nodes in opportunistic routing, and (v) the data packet generation process considered in this work.

3.1 Network architecture

We concentrate on the scenario of homogeneous sensor swarm deployment. Moreover, we concern on the static network topology, i.e., underwater sensor nodes are attached to buoys or anchors.

Accordingly, we represent the network topology as an undirected graph $G = (V \cup S, E)$, where V is the set of $v_1, \ldots, v_n$ sensor nodes, S is the set of $s_1, \ldots, s_m$ sinks, and E is the finite set of links between nodes. In our graph modeling, there exists an edge $e_{ij} \in E$ between nodes v_i and v_j if they can communicate with each other directly.

Associated to each edge e_{ij}, there is a weight p_{ij} that corresponds to the delivery probability of a packet transmitted from the node v_i to v_j. Moreover, we define $\mathcal{N}_i$ as the set of i's neighbors ($i \notin N_i$) and $\mathcal{C}_i$ as the set of neighboring nodes of i apt to continue forwarding its data packets ($\mathcal{C}_i \subseteq \mathcal{N}_i$).

3.2 Opportunistic routing modeling

In general, opportunistic routing protocols work as following. Assume that node i has a data packet to be transmitted. Firstly, it determines which ones of its neighbors are apt to continue forwarding the data packet; for instance, those neighbors leading to a positive progress towards to the destination. Secondly, from the apt neighbors, i selects the next-hop forwarder candidate nodes. A fitness function is used to rank and prioritize the candidates in order to select a few of the best ones since a large number of candidate forwarders in the set can diminish the routing performance. Finally, node i includes the unique addresses of the candidates or other indicative information into the packet header and then broadcasts it. Candidates receiving the packet forward it in a prioritized way. For this, usually, they set a packet holding time based on their priority. During the packet holding time, if a node hears the transmission of the packet from a high priority level candidate, it cancels its packet transmission. Otherwise, it broadcasts the packet after its holding time.

In modeling the aforementioned behavior, we denote $\mathcal{F}_i := \langle f_1, f_2, \ldots, f_m \rangle$ as the set of **next-hop forwarder candidate nodes**, or shortly *candidates*, of i. The set $\mathcal{F}_i$ is a subset of the i's neighbors set, i.e., $\mathcal{F}_i \subseteq \mathcal{C}_i$. Nodes in $\mathcal{F}_i$ are the i's neighbors selected to transmit coordinately, as will be described below, the data packet towards the destination. The candidates in $\mathcal{F}_i$ are ordered based on their transmission priorities as $f_1 > f_2 > \ldots > f_m$. Hence, to avoid duplicated transmissions, a next-hop forwarder candidate node having forwarder priority f_k only transmits if the high priority level nodes, $f_1 \ldots f_{k-1}$, fail in doing so.

We assume that there is a perfect coordination between candidates' transmission, i.e., a candidate can perfectly listen the transmission of a high priority level node and suppress its transmission. This assumption is commonly considered to maintain the model simple and tractable, as in [10, 15]. Under this assumption, let the candidate set $\mathcal{F}_i$ of node i having m neighbors ordered in their priority levels, candidate j forwards i's data packet with probability:

$$P_f^{ij} = \frac{p_{ij} \prod\limits_{k=1}^{j-1}(1 - p_{ik})}{1 - \prod\limits_{k=1}^{m}(1 - p_{ik})}. \tag{1}$$

In Eq. 1, the term p_{ij} (or its generalization as p_{ab}) refers to the packet delivery probability from node i to j (a to b) given by Eq. 14; the term $\prod_{k=1}^{j-1}(1 - p_{ik})$ calculates the probability of candidates with higher priority than j fail in receiving the packet.

3.3 Multipath of OR protocols modeling

Using the OR paradigm, a sender node selects a subset of its neighboring nodes to continue forwarding the data packet. Thus, at the end, the data packet transmitted from a sender node will reach the destination through one of the several possible paths determined from forwarder nodes at each hop. Let us define $\mathcal{H}(i, s)$ as the set composed of the possible routing paths from the sensor node i to the sink node s. There is a probability p_{h_i} associated to each path $h_i \in \mathcal{H}(v, s)$, which corresponds to the probability that a data packet will traverse it.

The probability p_{h_i} of each path $h_i \in \mathcal{H}(v, s)$ is determined as follows. Assume node i is the current forwarder node of a data packet to be delivered to the destination s, as depicted in Fig. 1. One of the possible paths is $h_1 = \{v_i, v_j, v_m, \ldots, v_s\}$. At each path h_i, there is a probability $P_f^{v_m v_{m+1}}$ (e.g., P_f^{ij}, P_f^{ik}, P_f^{jm}, and P_f^{jn} in Fig. 1) associated at each link between node v_m and its successor v_{m+1} in the routing path. This is the probability that node v_{m+1} forwards the data packet initially transmitted from v_i and received from the forwarder v_m, given by Eq. 1. From these associated probabilities, we can determine the probability of a data packet transmitted from v to s takes the opportunistic routing path h_i as:

$$p_{h_i} = \left(\prod_{m=1}^{|h_i|-2} P_f^{v_m v_{m+1}} \right) \times p_{v_{|h_i|-1, |h_i|}}, \tag{2}$$

where $p_{v_{|h_i|-1, |h_i|}}$ is the packet delivery probability at the last hop, i.e., between the last sensor node in the path and the sonobuoy.

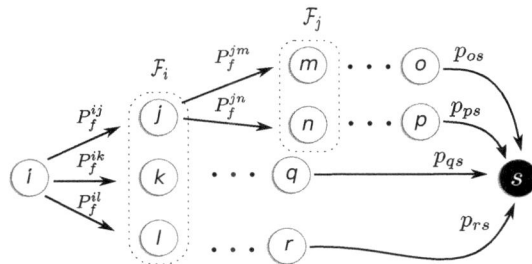

Figure 1: OR paths towards the destination.

3.4 PCen centrality metric

In multihop routing, some nodes are more demanded than others, i.e., they are more *central* for data routing task. These nodes are, therefore, critical for the network performance since, in most scenarios, they are those ones ensuring end-to-end network connectivity. This is truer for underwater sensor networks, which have low-density nodes' deployment. Consequently, it is essential to identify highly central nodes, since (i) they will suffer from high packet collisions as multiple routing paths will converge in their proximity and, more importantly, (ii) they will be the first ones to drain the battery because of the high volume of data traffic transmissions and energy consumption.

The centrality information of nodes can be used to design efficient network solutions improving wireless ad hoc & sensor network performance. The identification of central nodes could be the first step of topology control, routing, medium access control and other networking protocols aiming to conserve energy and/or balance the consumption at the nodes. Just to name a few, for instance, Vázquez-Rodas and Llopis [26] proposed a topology control protocol for wireless mesh networks, considering centrality metrics of social network analysis. Cuzzocrea et al. [9] proposed the EBC (edge betweenness centrality)-based topology control algorithm for RF wireless sensor networks. Ramos et al. [19] proposed the sink betweenness (SBet) metric, where, differently of the betweenness centrality, shortest paths used to calculate the centrality of the nodes are accounted only from sensor nodes to the sink.

To the best of our knowledge, there is no a centrality metrics presented in literature considering any path nature of the novel and promising opportunistic routing paradigm. The betweenness centrality metric [11], which has been widely used measures the importance of nodes also in the context of wireless networks, considers the shortest path of each node to all the other nodes. The SBet metric [19] considers the reverse multipath communication nature from sensor nodes to a unique sink node. However, none of them considers the probabilistic nature of wireless links, i.e., packet losses and errors occasioned by spatial and temporal factors influencing wireless link reliabilities. More critically, they have not considered multipath opportunistic routing that has been proposed to improve wireless link reliability.

Herein, we propose a probabilistic-based multipath routing centrality metric, named PCen, to measure the importance of nodes in the context of opportunistic routing. It is worth mentioning that, in this paper, we focus and restrict our analysis of PCen on the scenario of UWSNs. However, the proposed PCen metric also have a potential to be applied in several scenarios of wireless ad hoc networks, such as in RF wireless sensor networks.

The intuition behind this metric is the following. The centrality value of a node must be proportional to the number of routing paths that it is part of. However, in opportunistic routing, a packet can take one of the several paths from the sender to the destination. This is because there is a subset of nodes apt to continue forwarding the data packet at each hop, as described in Section 3.2. The priority level of forwarders and the channel conditions at each hop are the reasons that determine which path is taken by the packet. Therefore, a transmitted data packet is delivered from each one of the possible paths according to the associated probability derived in Section 3.3.

In this setting, the centrality of each node k is computed by Eq. 3. The centrality of a node k is determined from all paths initiating at each node $v \neq k$ to all sonobuoys $s \in S$. In Eq. 3, the numerator accounts the probabilities of the paths from $v \in V$ to $s \in S$ in which the node k is part of. The denominator accounts the probability of all the paths.

$$\beta(k) = \frac{\sum_{v=1}^{|V|} \sum_{s=1}^{|S|} \sum_{i=1}^{|\mathcal{H}(v,s)|} p_{h_i}(k)}{\sum_{v=1}^{|V|} \sum_{s=1}^{|S|} \sum_{i=1}^{|\mathcal{H}(v,s)|} p_{h_i}}. \tag{3}$$

3.5 Data traffic modeling

The traffic generated in a sensor network is strictly dependent of the application. We consider that each node has a set of sensors that can independently generate data traffic at different frequency sample. We denote $\mathcal{L}_i = \{l_1, \ldots, l_m\}$ the set of sensors attached at the node i. Hence, we model the packet generation of the sensor $l_j \in \mathcal{L}_i$ according to a Poisson process with average value of $\lambda_{i,j}$ pkts/min. The overall packet generation rate at node i, therefore, can be calculated as:

$$\lambda_i = \sum_{\forall j \in \mathcal{L}_i} \lambda_{i,j}. \tag{4}$$

The motivation behind the traffic model described above is twofold. First, we may have different sensor types attached at node to measure a composite event. A composite event is observed through a combination of several different properties readings (multi-modal data) that jointly determines the occurrence of the event, such as fire detection which may involve light intensity, temperature, acoustic and smoke density sensors [13]. Second, underwater nodes can be equipped with several sensors and the monitoring infrastructure can be used for data collection of applications in ocean monitoring programs, such as the Atlantic [1], Arctic [2] and Pacific [3] Canadian programs'.

In order to model the multihop nature of sensor networks, the carried traffic from a node k will be its generated data packets and those packets coming from other nodes, which the node k forwards. An example of how to calculate the

[1]http://www.dfo-mpo.gc.ca/science/oceanography-oceanographie/observations/atlantic-atlantique-eng.html
[2]http://www.dfo-mpo.gc.ca/science/oceanography-oceanographie/observations/arctic-artique-eng.html
[3]http://www.dfo-mpo.gc.ca/science/oceanography-oceanographie/observations/pacific-pacifique-eng.html

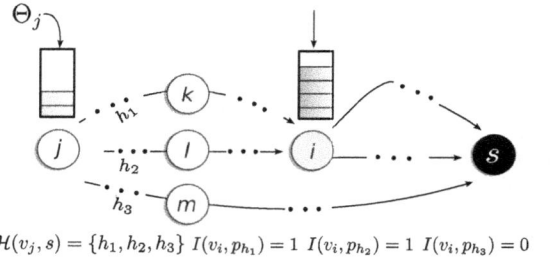

$$\mathcal{H}(v_j, s) = \{h_1, h_2, h_3\} \quad I(v_i, p_{h_1}) = 1 \quad I(v_i, p_{h_2}) = 1 \quad I(v_i, p_{h_3}) = 0$$

Figure 2: Example of the carried traffic calculation at i.

carried data traffic rate of a node i is showed in Fig. 2. Node i will forward its generated packets produced at rate of λ_i, given by Eq. 4, and a fraction of the data packets generated by nodes j, k and l that used node i as a forwarder. From node j, data packets will take one of the three possible paths h_1, h_2 or h_3 according to the respective associate probability p_{h_1}, p_{h_2} and p_{h_3} given by Eq. 2.

Therefore, the rate of the data carried traffic by each path is calculated from the nodes' traffic generation rate times the probability of the path (e.g., from the node j, $\lambda_j \times p_{h_1}$ is the data traffic rate outgoing through the path h_1). In order to devise this rate, we define $I(i, p_{h_k})$ as an indicator function, such that:

$$I(v_i, h_k) = \begin{cases} 1, & v_i \in h_k \\ 0, & \text{otherwise.} \end{cases} \tag{5}$$

Eq. 5 determines whether node i is or is not a forwarder node in the path h_k from the node k and a considered sink node.

Afterward, we need to avoid to compute redundantly the carried traffic rate. That is, in the sets $\mathcal{H}(v_j, s) \mid \forall s \in S$ of paths from the sensor node j to the sonobuoys, the prefix of the path until the node i, i.e., the set of edges from $j \rightsquigarrow i$, might be the same. Thus, only the routing paths with different set of edges from j until i should be considered, instead of considering all the paths in $\mathcal{H}(v_j, s) \mid \forall s \in S$, to compute the carried traffic in i from j. Thus, we define the set $\mathcal{K}(v_j, v_i)$ with the following characteristics:

- It is composed of the routing paths from j to the sonobuoys that have i as a vertex, i.e., $h_k \mid I(v_i, h_k) = 1$;

- It only includes the different prefix of the paths in $\mathcal{H}(v_j, s) \mid \forall s \in S$, from j until i.

Finally, we define $p_{h_k}(i)$ as the probability of the path $h_k(i)$ from its origin until it reaches node i. This probability is computed based on the Eq. 2, considering the node i as the final vertex of the paths, as follows:

$$p_{h_k}(i) = \left(\prod_{m=1}^{|h_k(i)|-1} P_f^{v_m v_{m+1}} \right). \tag{6}$$

Thus, we can recursively compute the carried traffic rate of node i as:

$$\Theta_i = \lambda_i + \sum_{\forall v_j \in V \setminus \{i\}} \sum_{\forall h_k \in \mathcal{K}(v_j, v_i)} \Theta_j \times p_{h_k}(i). \tag{7}$$

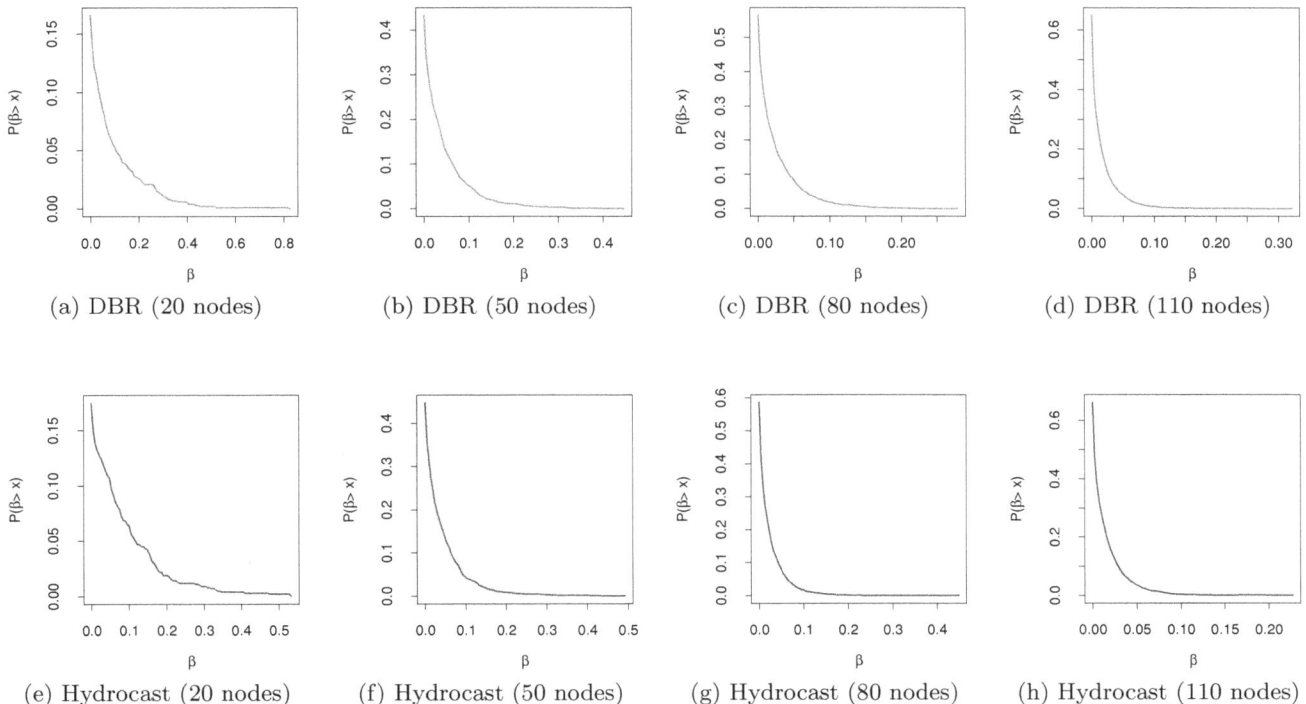

| (a) DBR (20 nodes) | (b) DBR (50 nodes) | (c) DBR (80 nodes) | (d) DBR (110 nodes) |

| (e) Hydrocast (20 nodes) | (f) Hydrocast (50 nodes) | (g) Hydrocast (80 nodes) | (h) Hydrocast (110 nodes) |

Figure 3: Complementary cumulative distribution function (CCDF) of the carried traffic load at different network densities

4. PERFORMANCE EVALUATION

In this section, we simulate different network densities from the proposed model. Our goal is to evaluate how the nodes' centrality change along different network topologies, routing protocols and traffic load. The identification of critical nodes will be helpful for further design of topology control solutions to mitigate several networking problems in underwater sensor networks, such as high and unbalanced energy consumption and high packet collisions rate.

In our experiments, we choose the Depth-based (DBR) [29] and Hydrocast [17] routing protocols to determine the opportunistic paths from each node to the surface sonobuoys. Both protocols employ the pressure-based routing methodology to route data packets. In this methodology, a current forwarder node selects its neighbors closer to the sea surface. The main difference between them, which motivates their choice in this paper, is that DBR does not restrict the number of next-hop candidate nodes whereas the Hydrocast informally do this when trying to reduce the hidden terminal problem, by selecting only neighbors distant to each other less than the communication range. These approaches will result in a different number of paths, and therefore it is worth to investigate the centrality of the nodes.

4.1 Simulations' setup

In our simulations, we consider a randomly deployment of 20, 35, 50, 65, 80, 95 and 110 underwater sensor nodes over an area of 10 km×10 km×10 km. Moreover, at the sea surface of the 10 km×10 km considered the area, we consider a pre-planned deployment of 64 sonobuoys as following. The considered surface area is divided into a grid of 2 km×2 km.

Thus, we simulate an evenly deployment of each sonobuoy, in each cell of the grid, one by one, until all of them is deployed. In these settings and with the radio's parameters described below, the average degree of the nodes is 3, 5, 8, 11, 13, 16 and 19, respectively. Our goal is to evaluate how the centrality of the nodes change along different network densities.

We consider a homogeneous data packet generation rate at the underwater sensor nodes, with the rate of 0.015 pkts/min. The packet size is set to 150 bytes. We set the radio's parameters following the specifications of the Telesonar SM-75 SMART modem of the Teledyne Benthos [25]. Accordingly, the transmission power of the nodes is set to 190 dB μ re Pa, the frequency f is set to 14 kHz and the bit rate is 18700 bps. When not otherwise specified, the results show an average value of 50 runs with 95 % confidence interval.

We use MATLAB to implement the considered scenarios, opportunistic routing and proposed modeling. In order to simulate the dynamics of underwater acoustic communication, we implement the underwater acoustic channel model described in the following. The path loss of a transmitted signal is given as $A(d, f) = d^k a(f)^d$, where d is the distance, f is the frequency, k is the spreading factor describing the propagation geometry and $a(f)$ is the absorption coefficient. The Thorp's formula given by Eq. 8 is used to determine the absorption coefficient $a(f)$ in dB/km for a signal frequency f in kHz.

$$10 \log a(f) = 0.11 \frac{f^2}{1+f^2} + 44 \frac{f^2}{4100+f^2} +$$
$$2.75 \cdot 10^{-4} f^2 + 0.003. \quad (8)$$

The average signal-to-noise ratio (SNR) over distance d can be characterized from the passive sonar equation as [30]:

$$\Gamma(d) = SL - A(d,f) - N(f) + DI, \quad (9)$$

where SL is the source level set to 190 dB μ re Pa, $N(f)$ is the noise level and DI is the directivity index.

The noise level $N(f)$ can be modeled using four sources [23]: turbulence (N_t), shipping (N_s), waves (N_w), and thermal noise (N_{th}). The overall ambient noise is $N(f) = N_t(f) + N_s(f) + N_w(f) + N_{th}(f)$. For frequency f in kHz, shipping s ranging between 0 and 1 (light to dense) and wind in m/s, the four noise components in dB re μ Pa per Hz is given by:

$$\begin{aligned}
10 \log N_t(f) &= 17 - 30 \log f \\
10 \log N_s(f) &= 40 + 20(s - 0.5) + 26 \log f \\
& \quad\quad -60 \log(f + 0.03) \\
10 \log N_w(f) &= 50 + 7.5 w^{1/2} + 20 \log f \\
& \quad\quad -40 \log(f + 0.4) \\
10 \log N_{th}(f) &= -15 + 20 \log f.
\end{aligned} \quad (10)$$

In this work, we set $s = 0.5$ and $w = 7$, respectively.

The packet delivery probability, used in Eq. 1, of a packet of m bits from a transmission between d m distant nodes is calculated as follows. Similar to the studies in [2] and [22], we use Rayleigh fading to model small scale fading where SNR has the following probability distribution:

$$p_d(X) = \int_0^\infty \frac{1}{\Gamma(d)} e^{-\frac{X}{\Gamma(d)}}. \quad (11)$$

The error probability can be evaluated as:

$$p_e(d) = \int_0^\infty p_e(X) p_d(X) dX, \quad (12)$$

where $p_e(X)$ is the error probability for an arbitrary modulation at a specific value of SNR X.

We use the binary phase shift keying (BPSK) modulation as it is widely used in the state-of-the-art acoustic modem [12]. Each symbol carries a bit in BPSK. In [20], the probability of the bit error over distance d is given as:

$$p_e(d) = \frac{1}{2} \left(1 - \sqrt{\frac{\Gamma(d)}{1 + \Gamma(d)}} \right). \quad (13)$$

Finally, for any pair of nodes i and $j \in \mathcal{V}$ distant $d_{i,j}$ meters, the delivery probability of a packet of m bits is simply given by:

$$p_{ij} = (1 - p_e(d_{i,j}))^m. \quad (14)$$

4.2 Results

Fig. 3 depicts the complementary cumulative distribution function of the PCen centrality value along the experiments for different network densities. The plots (a)-(d) concerns to the DBR and (e)-(h) to the Hydrocast routing protocol. The plots show an interesting trend of long tail behavior in the CCDFs. Despite the presence of several possible paths from a source node to the destination, the most part

of the nodes have low centrality value, but there are a few of them with a high centrality value. The highest centrality value is obtained in low-density scenarios (see Figs. 3a and b). This achievement is interesting because this behavior is well-known in single path multihop routing in wireless sensor networks, and it is also present in opportunistic routing scenarios, as observed in the results obtained from the proposed modeling and PCen metric.

The few highly central nodes, in this case of opportunistic routing, are critical, such as in the single multipath routing, for the network performance since they probably are bridge nodes interconnecting network segments and they will drain their battery first due to the transmissions to forward data packets. It is also possible to note that when the network density increases the percentage of nodes being part of a routing path, also increases. For instance, Fig. 3a shows that 85 % of the nodes do not participate (only 15 % of the nodes have centrality value higher than 0) as a forwarder, when using the DBR. There is a reduction of 52 % of these nodes when we compare with the network density scenario of 110 nodes (see Fig. 3). The same trend is observed when Hydrocast routing protocol is used. Finally, Fig. 3 shows that the centrality value of the nodes when using Hydrocast is slightly lower than in DBR. This is because it limits the number of paths by employing the heuristic to reduce the hidden terminal problem.

Fig. 4 portrays the average value of the maximum PCen centrality of each experiment for different network densities. Overall speaking, this result shows that the PCen decreases when the network density decreases. This behavior is already expected and explained by the increment of alternative paths when the network density increases. This is an important information showing that more nodes are participating in the multihop task. Interestingly, the maximum centrality value is slightly lower when the Hydrocast routing protocol was used. This is because of its behavior in restricting the number of next-hop forwarder candidates at each hop as corroborated by the results showed in Fig. 3. Moreover, we can observe an increment when we compare the scenarios of average degree of three and four nodes due to the high number of disconnected nodes when network density is very low. That is, due to the very low network density, a high fraction of the nodes do not have any routing path to any sonobuoy (destination).

Fig. 5 shows the average of the maximum carried traffic rate of each experiment for different network densities. The maximal carried traffic rate increases when the network density increases. This is due to the increment of the number of nodes using highly central nodes to deliver data packets. This is true especially for Hydrocast that limits the number of possible paths, which demands more of highly central nodes. This result particularly motivates the use of topology control solutions aiming to balance the network traffic flows along the nodes, in order to prolong the network lifetime and medium access control protocols to efficiently reduce packet collisions along central nodes.

5. DISCUSSION

The obtained results, from the proposed modeling framework and PCen centrality metric, discussed in the previous section provide interesting insights that might drive the design of topology control and opportunistic routing protocols for underwater sensor networks. In summary, our results

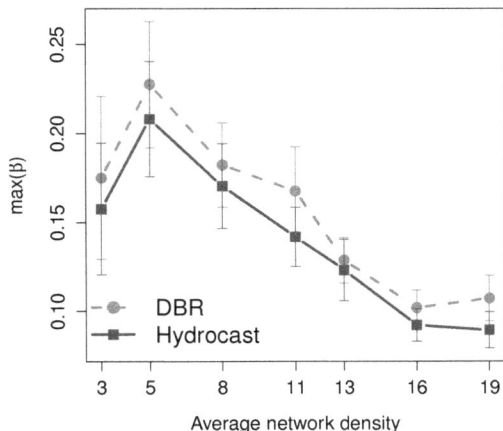

Figure 4: Average value of the maximum PCen centrality measured.

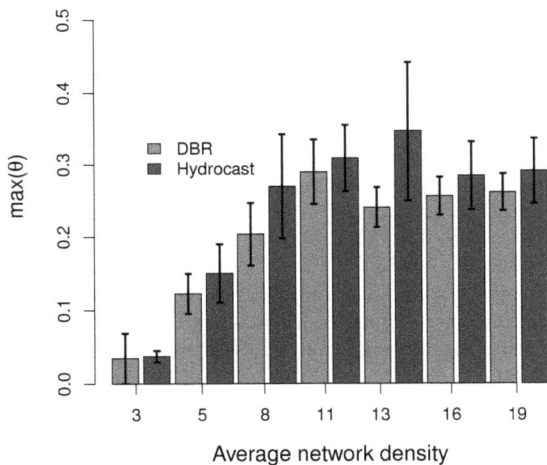

Figure 5: Traffic rate per minute for the maximal PCen node.

show the presence of a few highly central nodes from the routing viewing point that might be critical for ensuring network connectivity, especially in low-density deployments. In addition, it is worth mentioning that these central nodes will be responsible for a high volume of traffic forwarding rate.

In this situation, topology control is necessary to improve the network performance. In order to extend the network lifetime, some topology control solutions might be designed, for instance, to rotate some nodes at critical locations of the environment that lead to high PCen centrality measurement. One approach is to leverage the vertical movement capability of underwater sensor nodes and design topology control through the depth adjustment of the nodes [4, 7]. Accordingly, a node with a high centrality score could move

for a new depth towards the extremity of the network. A neighboring node with more residual energy could move to the location of the high centrality node in order to avoid disconnections.

Another approach is the deployment of heterogeneous underwater sensor networks. A few number of nodes with more capabilities (i.e., more energy budget) can be used to occupy key locations making them highly central for the routing task. In this approach, efficient deployment strategies should be investigated in order to have an adequate topology. Another strategy is the use of mobile nodes for repositioning at determined locations.

Finally, the design of opportunistic routing protocols might consider the PCen information to balance the flow between forwarder nodes. Candidate set selection procedures could use this metric to rotate the priority of the nodes. Another approach to better balance the centrality of the nodes is through the use of upward and downward routing paths instead of the classical pressure-based methodology. For instance, the authors in [3] propose a protocol that routes data through downward paths when they lead to a low delay. The motivation for this come from the fact that the acoustic signal propagation speed varies according to the temperature, salinity concentration, and the depth. A similar approach could incorporate the centrality information of the nodes to decides which data flows will go in the upward/downward direction.

6. CONCLUSION

In this paper, we investigate the importance of the network topology for opportunistic routing in various deployment scenarios of underwater sensor networks. We proposed an analytical model to capture the behavior of probabilistic-based any path transmission of opportunistic routing. Thereafter, we proposed the PCen centrality metric to measure the importance of each node relative to the opportunistic routing paths passing through it.

Our results showed that the same behavior observed in the traditional multihop routing appears in the opportunistic routing: the existence of a few number nodes highly central for the routing tasks. Moreover, when the network density increases the PCen value of the nodes decreased, due to the existence of more alternative routing paths. The general trend of the experiments showed that in several network density, there are a high number of nodes with low PCen value and a few of them with a high value. Moreover, the carried traffic rate at these highly central nodes increased as the network density increased. The identification of these nodes through this information is meaningful for the design of efficient topology control and opportunistic routing protocols aiming to improve the underwater sensor network performance and prolong the network lifetime.

As a future work, we plan to extend our model to include several other aspects of networking performance related to the topology, such as signal interference, packet collisions, mobility, delay and delivery ratio. In addition, we intend to investigate the relation between nodes' PCen centrality and energy consumption.

7. ACKNOWLEDGMENTS

This work was partially supported by the NSERC CRE-ATE TRANSIT Project and NSERC DIVA Network Research Program, ORF/MRI Program, Canada Research Chairs program, CNPq, CAPES, and FAPEMIG Brazilian research support agencies.

8. REFERENCES

[1] I. F. Akyildiz, D. Pompili, and T. Melodia. Underwater acoustic sensor networks: research challenges. *Ad Hoc Networks*, 3(3):257–279, 2005.

[2] C. Carbonelli and U. Mitra. Cooperative multihop communication for underwater acoustic networks. In *Proc. 1st ACM Int'l Workshop on Underwater Networks (WUWNet '06)*, pages 97–100, 2006.

[3] Y. D. Chen, C. Y. Lien, C. H. Wang, and K. P. Shih. Darp: A depth adaptive routing protocol for large-scale underwater acoustic sensor networks. In *Oceans - Yeosu*, pages 1–6, May 2012.

[4] R. W. L. Coutinho, A. Boukerche, L. F. M. Vieira, and A. A. Loureiro. GEDAR: geographic and opportunistic routing protocol with depth adjustment for mobile underwater sensor networks. In *Proc. IEEE Int'l Conf. on Commun. (ICC '14)*, 2014.

[5] R. W. L. Coutinho, A. Boukerche, L. F. M. Vieira, and A. A. F. Loureiro. Modeling and analysis of opportunistic routing in low duty-cycle underwater sensor networks. In *Proc. 18th ACM Int'l Conf. on Modeling, Analysis and Simulation of Wireless and Mobile Systems (MSWiM)*, pages 125–132, 2015.

[6] R. W. L. Coutinho, A. Boukerche, L. F. M. Vieira, and A. A. F. Loureiro. Design guidelines for opportunistic routing in underwater networks. *IEEE Communications Magazine*, 2016.

[7] R. W. L. Coutinho, A. Boukerche, L. F. M. Vieira, and A. A. F. Loureiro. Geographic and opportunistic routing for underwater sensor networks. *IEEE Transactions on Computers*, 65(2):548–561, Feb. 2016.

[8] R. W. L. Coutinho, A. Boukerche, L. F. M. Vieira, and A. A. F. Loureiro. Modeling the sleep interval effects in duty-cycled underwater sensor networks. In *Proc. of the IEEE Int'l Conf. on Commun. (ICC)*, pages 1997–2002, 2016.

[9] A. Cuzzocrea, A. Papadimitriou, D. Katsaros, and Y. Manolopoulos. Edge betweenness centrality: A novel algorithm for qos-based topology control over wireless sensor networks. *Journal of Network and Computer Applications*, 35(4):1210 – 1217, 2012.

[10] H. Dubois-Ferrière, M. Grossglauser, and M. Vetterli. Valuable detours: Least-cost anypath routing. *IEEE/ACM Transactions on Networking*, 19(2):333–346, April 2011.

[11] L. C. Freeman. A set of measures of centrality based on betweenness. *Sociometry*, 40(1):35–41, 1977.

[12] L. Freitag, M. Grund, S. Singh, J. Partan, P. Koski, and K. Ball. The WHOI micro-modem: An acoustic communcations and navigation system for multiple platforms. In *Proc. MTS/IEEE Oceans*, 2005.

[13] J. Gao, J. Li, Z. Cai, and H. Gao. Composite event coverage in wireless sensor networks with heterogeneous sensors. In *Proc. of the IEEE INFOCOM*, pages 217–225, Apr. 2015.

[14] J. Heidemann, M. Stojanovic, and M. Zorzi. Underwater sensor networks: applications, advances and challenges. *Philosophical Transactions of the Royal Society A: Mathematical, Physical and Engineering Sciences*, 370(1958):158–175, 2012.

[15] W. Hu, J. Xie, and Z. Zhang. Practical opportunistic routing in high-speed multi-rate wireless mesh networks. In *Proc. of the 14th ACM MobiHoc*, pages 127–136, 2013.

[16] U. Lee, P. Wang, Y. Noh, F. Vieira, M. Gerla, and J.-H. Cui. Pressure routing for underwater sensor networks. In *Proc. IEEE INFOCOM*, pages 1–9, 2010.

[17] Y. Noh, U. Lee, S. Lee, P. Wang, L. F. M. Vieira, J. H. Cui, M. Gerla, and K. Kim. Hydrocast: Pressure routing for underwater sensor networks. *IEEE Transactions on Vehicular Technology*, 65(1):333–347, Jan. 2016.

[18] Y. Noh, U. Lee, P. Wang, B. S. C. Choi, and M. Gerla. VAPR: void-aware pressure routing for underwater sensor networks. *IEEE Trans. on Mobile Comput.*, 12(5):895–908, 2013.

[19] H. S. Ramos, A. C. Frery, A. Boukerche, E. M. R. Oliveira, and A. A. F. Loureiro. Topology-related metrics and applications for the design and operation of wireless sensor networks. *ACM Trans. Sen. Netw.*, 10(3):53:1–53:35, May 2014.

[20] T. Rappaport. *Wireless Communications: Principles and Practice*. Prentice Hall, 2002.

[21] A. Shukla and H. Karki. Application of robotics in offshore oil and gas industry – a review part ii. *Robotics and Auton. Syst.*, 75, Part B:508 – 524, 2016.

[22] M. Stojanovic. Recent advances in high-speed underwater acoustic communications. *IEEE J. Oceanic Eng.*, pages 125–136, 1996.

[23] M. Stojanovic. On the relationship between capacity and distance in an underwater acoustic communication channel. In *Proc. 1st ACM Int'l Workshop on Underwater Networks (WUWNet '06)*, pages 41–47, 2006.

[24] M. Stojanovic and J. Preisig. Underwater acoustic communication channels: Propagation models and statistical characterization. *IEEE Commun. Mag.*, 47(1):84–89, 2009.

[25] Teledyne-Benthos. http://www.benthos.com, 2016.

[26] A. Vázquez-Rodas and L. J. de la C. Llopis. A centrality-based topology control protocol for wireless mesh networks. *Ad Hoc Networks*, 24, 34 – 54, 2015.

[27] L. F. M. Vieira. Performance and trade-offs of opportunistic routing in underwater networks. In *Proc. IEEE Wireless Communications and Networking Conference (WCNC)*, pages 2911–2915, 2012.

[28] P. Xie, J.-H. Cui, and L. Lao. VBF: vector-based forwarding protocol for underwater sensor networks. In *Proc. 5th Int'l IFIP-TC6 NETWORKING*, pages 1216–1221, 2006.

[29] H. Yan, Z. J. Shi, and J.-H. Cui. DBR: depth-based routing for underwater sensor networks. In *Proc. 7th Int'l IFIP-TC6 NETWORKING*, pages 72–86, 2008.

[30] H. Yang, B. Liu, F. Ren, H. Wen, and C. Lin. Optimization of energy efficient transmission in underwater sensor networks. In *Proc. IEEE Global Telecommun. Conf. (GLOBECOM)*, pages 1–6, 2009.

A Slot Sharing TDMA Scheme for Reliable and Efficient Collision Resolution in WSNs

Philip Parsch and Alejandro Masrur
Department of Computer Science
TU Chemnitz, Germany

ABSTRACT

With the advent of Internet of Things (IoT), an increasing number of devices may spontaneously communicate to exchange information. This puts emphasis on wireless sensor networks (WSNs) and, in particular, on intelligent medium access control (MAC) protocols, as there is a need to guarantee a certain quality of service (QoS) on timely data/packet delivery. Most existing approaches, however, are either of random nature, making it impossible to guarantee any bounded delay, or do not scale well for a higher number of nodes. As a result, we propose slot sharing TDMA (short s^2TDMA), a deterministic contention resolution scheme in form of generating TDMA cycles with shared slots at the event of collisions. Every TDMA slot is assigned to a range of IDs, in which the corresponding nodes can transmit. By further dividing these slots in case of collisions, we implement an *interval tree search* enabling for fast collision resolution in $\log_{\hat{s}}$-complexity, where $\hat{s}$ is the number of slots in each cycle. Since our scheme is activated upon collisions, it incurs in zero overhead during normal operation and is able to quickly react to changing traffic load such as bursty traffic. We perform a large set of detailed simulations on OMNeT++ showing that our technique offers a fast collision resolution and is able to handle a large number of nodes in the network.

CCS Concepts

•Networks → **Network protocol design;** *Network reliability; Sensor networks;*

Keywords

Medium Access Control; delay bounded communication; reliability; receiver-initiated

1. INTRODUCTION

In the era of IoT, different devices will spontaneously communicate with each other to exchange information allowing for new interesting applications. For example, wearables can

MSWiM '16, November 13-17, 2016, Malta, Malta
ⓒ 2016 ACM. ISBN 978-1-4503-4502-6/16/11... $15.00
DOI: http://dx.doi.org/10.1145/2988287.2989164

communicate with existing smart home structures to improve comfort and user experience or even call an ambulance in emergency situations.

This, however, poses a number of challenges that need to be addressed. In particular, there can be a potentially large number of nodes transmitting on a communication channel and, hence, leading to increased collisions and data loss.

While we expect IoT applications to tolerate some data loss, there is a need to guarantee a certain QoS on which they can rely. That is, devices should be able to reliably deliver data in a timely manner, which needs to be enabled from the MAC layer upwards.

In this context, CSMA-based approaches seem to be suitable, as these do not require devices to synchronize and, hence, offer good energy efficiency. In addition, they are known to be very effective in handling retransmissions in case of collisions at the communication channel. However, their effectiveness drastically reduces at high load, e.g., as the number of transmitting devices increases. That is, the retransmission delay potentially becomes unbounded and, therefore, no QoS guarantees can be given.

On the other hand, TDMA-based approaches allow for a reliable communication at high loads, but they lack the necessary flexibility, particularly, for dynamic reconfiguration — devices may join and leave the network at arbitrary points in time — apart from relying on devices to synchronize.

Hybrid MACs [2] [9] have been proposed to overcome this problem. These are based on combining CSMA and TDMA to allow for deterministic behavior, especially, at high loads and, at the same time, for reconfiguration flexibility.

Although these hybrid approaches allow guaranteeing QoS at high loads, they do not easily scale to an increasing number of devices or nodes in the network. In other words, these are effective when a few nodes produce high communication load, but rapidly degrade when multiple nodes are responsible for that communication load, as discussed later in more detail. In addition, they require control messages to be exchanged adding further delay and making them react slowly, which can be problematic for bursty traffic.

In order to allow for faster response times, other approaches have been presented [5] [7] [10]. These rely on collision resolution schemes that schedule retransmissions and therefore avoid further interference between nodes. Since they just activate on collisions, they do not result in any overhead during normal operation and allow for fast data transfers. However, they are either of random nature again making any QoS guarantees impossible, or only work for a small number of nodes.

Similar to the previously mentioned approaches, this paper proposes a hybrid MAC. However, in contrast to them, our approach better scales to an increasing number of nodes. This makes it more suitable for upcoming IoT and, in general, for WSN applications where large numbers of nodes are to be expected.

1.1 Contributions

In this paper, we propose s^2TDMA, a hybrid MAC that allows deterministic collision resolution in receiver-initiated WSNs, i.e., those where nodes only send when awakened by the receiver. Our technique consists in generating TDMA cycles — called arbitration cycles — upon collisions. The particularity of the proposed scheme is that every TDMA slot is assigned to a range of IDs, in which the corresponding nodes can transmit, i.e., slots are shared by multiple nodes.

Whenever a collision occurs, the current slot is further divided into multiple sub-slots with smaller ID ranges. This enables fast collision resolving in log_x-complexity being x the number of slots per each such cycles as illustrated later in detail.

In addition, we analyze the probability of collision and the worst-case communication delay according to the proposed scheme. Finally, extensive simulation results are presented based on OMNeT++. These compare the performance and show benefits by s^2TDMA with respect to other approaches from the literature.

1.2 Structure of the Paper

The rest of this paper is structured as follows. Related work is discussed in Section 2. Next, Section 3 explains our system model and assumptions. Section 4 introduces the proposed MAC protocol and Section 5 analyses collision probabilities and communication delays mathematically. Section 6 presents our experimental evaluation based on simulation and Section 7 concludes the paper.

2. RELATED WORK

There are many different approaches from the literature that are concerned with making WSNs more reliable and energy-efficient. In general, these can be classified into contention-based, reservation-based and hybrid schemes.

Contention-based methods are usually asynchronous protocols that can access the channel at arbitrary points in time. Whenever a collision occurs or the channel is busy during carrier sensing, they perform techniques to resolve the contention, such as random back-off schemes. Due to their low overhead, high flexibility and simplicity, they enjoy great popularity. However, since channel access is uncoordinated, contention-based approaches generally offer bad performance for high traffic loads. A widely used contention-based protocol is CSMA.

In contrast, reservation-based protocols avoid collisions by assigning nodes individual time slots to transmit. This ensures that even high numbers of nodes can transmit their data reliably and within a bounded delay. Nevertheless, reservation-based protocols generally require synchronization, which incurs in additional overhead and worsens the energy efficiency, especially during low network load. Examples of synchronous networks are TDMA and slotted Aloha [1].

Hybrid approaches try to combine the advantages of both contention and reservation-based protocols. This can, for

example, be done by switching from CSMA to TDMA in high traffic [9] or by leaving space in TDMA frames, where nodes can transmit packets with CSMA [2]. However, both methods require additional control messages for switching modes or assigning TDMA slots. Since these messages can also be lost, no real-time guarantees can be made. Further, they impose an additional delay making these schemes react only slowly to changes in traffic load.

Another contention-based approach, called Strawman, is presented in [7]. Here, nodes actively contend after collisions by sending a contention packet of random length. The receiver then selects the node with the longest contention packet and transmits an RTS-like decision message. After the actual data is transmitted, the arbitration starts anew until all collisions are resolved. In summary, Strawman allows fast adaption to changing traffic, as well as a fast collision resolution. However, its random nature makes it not suitable for real-time applications.

Similar to Strawman [7], STAIRS [5] uses active contention messages after every collision. However, instead of just picking the longest packet out of a number of contention packets, the RSSI channel is used to determine the number of contenders and, hence, create a schedule. This greatly reduces the overhead, as contention packets have to be transmitted only once in the best case. On the other hand, the use of the RSSI channel is highly error-prone and works only for a low number of contenders, as it quickly starts to saturate.

In order to manage higher number of contenders, for example, in dense sensor networks, Carlson et al. propose Flip-MAC [3]. Here, the receiver first reduces the number of contenders by a series of probe-acknowledgment cycles. In every cycle, each node randomly picks one of two possible IDs and all nodes matching the ID of the probe message send an acknowledgment while all others drop out. The receiver repeats this cycle until no more ACKs are received indicating that contenders have been reduced to a manageable level. The remaining contenders then use CSMA to transmit data.

The previously mentioned contention-based approaches were of random nature enabling fast collision resolution, but making it impossible to guarantee any bounded delay. Since some applications are delay sensitive and require deterministic behavior, different MAC protocols are needed. To this end, BIN-MAC [10] proposes a hybrid protocol that allows a delay-bounded contention resolution. More precisely, every node is assigned a unique ID and every time a collision occurs, the receiver replies with a negative acknowledgment (NAK) containing a range of IDs. Only nodes with an ID within that range can retransmit, all others have to wait. Similar to a binary tree search, this range is halved upon every collision until data is successfully transmitted. This results in a log_2-complexity allowing fast collision resolutions even for high number of contenders.

In this paper, we propose s^2TDMA, a deterministic contention resolution scheme similar to BIN-MAC [10]. However, instead of using a binary tree search, we implement an interval tree search in form of generating TDMA cycles upon collisions. This does not only speed up the collision resolution, but also allows multiple nodes to send consecutively within a cycle. We later show that our approach greatly improves the performance, such as latency, throughput, etc. of the network, which makes it, together with its high scalability, be better suited for larger networks.

3. MODELS AND ASSUMPTIONS

We consider a WSN consisting of multiple sensor nodes and one or more sink nodes that are spatially distributed. Upon activation, nodes do not transmit spontaneously, but wait for the next query/probe message from their corresponding sinks. This receiver-initiated topology, which is also used by similar approaches from the literature [3] [5] [7] [10], offers two main advantages: First, it allows the usually very resource constrained nodes to put most of the burden on the receiving node. Second, it limits the number of contending nodes as they can only participate in the communication cycle after a receiver's probe. This implicit sender synchronization prevents nodes from joining during later MAC phases, where they might interrupt the ongoing arbitration process.

In order to avoid conflicts between multiple sink nodes, we reduce contention by using multiple radio channels for operation. Similar to A-MAC [4], the initial probe messages are sent on a pre-determined channel to be receivable for all nodes. Later data transfers are then performed on other radio channels as defined in the probe message.

Transmitting a data packet takes a given amount of time, which depends on the number of bits to be transmitted and the bandwidth of the communication channel. We refer to this time to as *packet length* and denote the length of any packet of node i by l_i.

Since probe messages can wake up multiple nodes at once, data transmissions may interfere with each other leading to packet loss. As a result, to achieve reliability, the receiver node acknowledges (ACK) a packet after successful reception. We denote by l_{ack} the length of an acknowledgment packet. If the data packet is corrupt — we assume that even the slightest overlapping of two different data packets leads to data loss — the sink node replies with a negative acknowledgment (NAK). For simplicity, we set the length of NAK packets to be equal to $l_{nak} = l_{ack}$.

Every node in the system has a unique ID, which allows the sink node to distinguish between different data transmissions and to assign TDMA slots as described later. These IDs can be either be hard-programmed into the nodes memory, or be assigned dynamically by registering and de-registering in the network. However, in this paper we focus on collision resolution mechanisms and the assignment of IDs is out of scope.

4. PROPOSED SCHEME

In this section, we introduce s²TDMA, a reliable and energy-efficient collision resolution scheme for receiver-initiated WSN. As already mentioned, this consists in generating TDMA cycles upon collisions. Every TDMA slot is assigned to a range of IDs, in which the corresponding nodes can transmit. Whenever a collision occurs within a slot, it is further divided into sub-slots to resolve that collision. This allows fast collision resolution as well as multiple consecutive data transmissions in a single arbitration cycle.

4.1 Working Principle

The communication cycle starts when a sink node broadcasts a probe message. All sensor nodes — addressed in the probe — may start transmitting their data after the probe message. However, since this can potentially trigger multi-

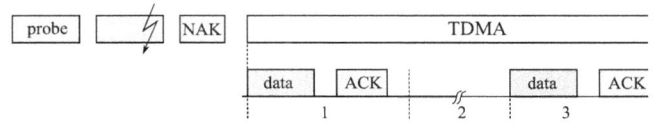

Figure 1: Different steps of the proposed contention resolution scheme: A probe message triggers 2 nodes, whose packets collide at first. After receiving a negative acknowledgment (NAK), these two nodes participate in a TDMA arbitration cycle and successfully transmit their data.

ple sensor nodes at once, there can be collisions of packets. In this case, the proposed collision scheme is activated as displayed in Fig.1.

If corrupt data is received, the sink node replies with a negative acknowledgment (NAK) to inform the sensor nodes that they have to retransmit. However, the receiver does not know the number of contending nodes a priori. If these retransmit directly and without any resolution scheme, multiple collisions can occur again. To overcome this problem, a TDMA arbitration cycle is started.

Each TDMA slot is assigned to a range of IDs in which only nodes with an ID in that range are allowed to transmit. Assuming we have a system with a set of N nodes each of which has its unique ID, the initial TDMA arbitration cycle equally splits those IDs upon $\hat{s}$ slots. For example, if we have a system of 100 nodes and therefore IDs 1 to 100, each slot would contain $|N|/\hat{s} = 100/4 = 25$ IDs, with $\hat{s} = 4$ and $|N|$ being the number of nodes in N. The first slot contains the lower IDs, in this case 1 to 25, the second contains IDs 26 to 50, the third 51 to 75 and the fourth 76 to 100. Note that whenever $|N|/\hat{s}$ produces a remainder, this is added to the last slot.

This ID splitting reduces the number of contending nodes, however, it does not yet guarantee successful transmission. To this end, a TDMA slot is further divided into equal sub-slots, whenever a collision occurred within that slot. In our previous example, a collision within slot 1 would split this slot into another $\hat{s} = 4$ sub-slots with the ID ranges of 1-6, 7-12, 13-18 and 19-25. As a consequence, the number of contending nodes is reduced from 100 to 6 after two collisions. This greatly reduces the chance of further collisions, however, it still cannot fully prevent them. In the worst case, this splitting continues until each slot contains just one ID and therefore guarantees successful communication. If, in that case, the range of IDs to be divided is smaller than $\hat{s}$, the resulting TDMA cycle will have as many slots as IDs. For example, if a slot contains 3 IDs and $\hat{s} = 4$, this slot is divided into $k = 3$ sub-slots with one ID each.

Fig 2 shows the working principle of the sub-slot creation in more detail. Here, two nodes collided first and, hence, a TDMA arbitration cycle is created. In this example, after the first empty slot has finished, they both transmit in slot 2, in which their data packets collide again. The sink then replies with a NAK indicating that a sub-cycle begins with $\hat{s} = 4$ sub-slots. Now, due to the finer ID resolution, node i can successfully transmit in slot 2 and node j in slot 3. After the last slot of the sub-cycle has finished, another new cycle is started containing the remaining IDs that have not been resolved so far. Although there are no further nodes wanting to transmit in this example, empty slots cannot be skipped and the sink will go to sleep after slot 4 of cycle 2 has finished.

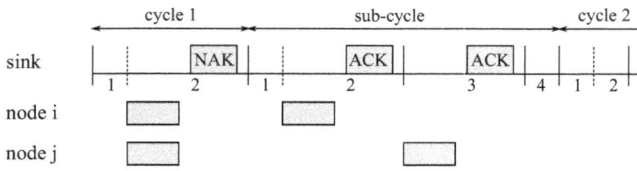

Figure 2: Illustration of the sub-cycle splitting principle: A collision within a TDMA cycle, here in slot 2, causes the immediate creation of a sub-cycle with $\hat{s} = 4$. Once these slots have been executed, the remaining IDs are processed in another full cycle (cycle 2). Note that all slots, independent of being empty or used, have the same length and have only been shortened for better illustration.

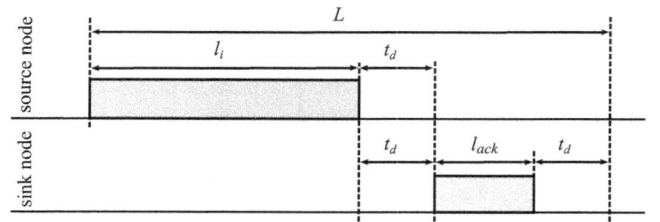

Figure 3: Timing of a successful transmission: After every data packet of length l_i, t_d is needed to process the data and to switch the operation modes of transceivers. Similarly, ACK messages (of length l_{ack}) require a processing time t_d.

Note that whenever a sub-cycle is completed, i.e., no more collisions occurred in it, a new cycle is created to resolve the remaining IDs. This is a simple and efficient solution, since other methods such as going back the interval tree, i.e., stepwise increase the slot sizes again, would require many ACK/NAK notifications. Recall that at this point of time, the sink does not know the number of nodes participating in the arbitration cycle, i.e., how many nodes have been awakened by the initial probe message, but just the already resolved IDs from previous (sub-)cycles. Therefore up to $|N| - x$ nodes can still be pending, where $|N|$ is the total number of IDs and x the number of already resolved IDs. In summary, this process can be repeated until no IDs are left to resolve, in which case the sink goes back to sleep.

All parameters needed for generating the arbitration cycle, such as the ID ranges, number of slots per cycle $\hat{s}$, etc., are specified and calculated by the sink. These are then broadcast in every ACK/NAK message to inform the contending nodes. This can be done in two possible ways: First, ACK/NAK messages only contain the current ID range of the nodes that are allowed to transmit in the next slot. This reduces complexity at the nodes side, since they only need to check whether their IDs match the given range. However, it also requires more control bytes to be send within the ACK/NAK messages as discussed later. Second, either no or only very little information is broadcast and nodes use hard coded parameters. The missing ID ranges are then calculated depending on whether ACKs or NAKs are received. This reduces the data overhead of control messages, but on the other hand, also decreases the flexible of the system regarding dynamic changes.

By assigning IDs to TDMA slots, nodes are prioritized according to these IDs. This means that lower IDs are resolved faster, whereas higher IDs can take a longer time to be resolved. This is useful in applications, where different types of nodes have different requirements regarding their maximum tolerable delay. For example, in a home automation system, critical devices such as controllers or alarm systems need to relay their data faster than lower priority devices such as wireless light switches.

4.2 Timings and Data Structures

Every action performed by the transceiver requires time and, hence, influences the total delay of the proposed scheme. Fig. 3 depicts the timings of a successful packets transmission.

After a data packet is transmitted, both the transceivers of the sink and the sensor node have to switch their oper-

ation mode: The sensor node switches to receive mode in order to be able to receive an ACK/NAK, whereas the sink node switches to transmit mode to transmit the ACK/NAK. However, the sink node has to safely detect the end of node i's data packet first. Although data packets include a length code, as discussed later, this may corrupt in case of a collision and, hence, the receiver has to sense the channel continuously to detect the end of a packet. We denote this delay by sensing and switching operation modes by t_d.

After reception/transmission of an ACK/NAK, again both nodes have to switch their transceiver modes. Although ACK/NAK messages are of constant length and, hence, sensing the end of the packet is not necessary, we still assume the same t_d for this delay. This does not only facilitate the system analysis, but also adds the possibility to dynamically change the payload of ACK/NAK messages, which might be required for future extensions.

Similar to other approaches from the literature , e.g., Bin-MAC [10], s^{2}TDMA requires additional structure fields to be sent within each packet. Besides the usual overhead, such as preamble, start frame delimiter (SFD), etc., each data packet contains a length code to define the number of payload bytes and a cyclic redundancy check (CRC) field to detect corrupt data. In case of ACK/NAK messages, we do not need the length code, since we previously assumed that both have the same length $t_{nak} = t_{ack}$, which is already known by sensor nodes. However, each NAK/ACK contains a type field defining if it is either a NAK or an ACK and an ID field for the ACK address. In addition, as discussed previously, further bytes are required for informing sensor nodes about the arbitration cycle. These can be two address fields defining the upper and lower bound on IDs or either no data or just the number of slots per cycle $\hat{s}$. In summary, this means an overhead of $2\,bytes$ for data packets and 3 to $7\,bytes$ for ACK/NAK messages, when assuming a size of $1\,byte$ for control fields and $2\,bytes$ for address fields.

5. ANALYSIS OF COMMUNICATION

The proposed s^{2}TDMA can be easily configured to meet desired requirements. In particular, at the event of a collision on the communication channel, we can adjust (i) the number of slots per arbitration cycle and (ii) the number of (sender) nodes in each slot. Clearly, this affects communication delay, i.e., the time taken from a node's activation to its packet being successfully delivered.

There are different policies one can follow to select (i) and (ii). For example, one slot can be dedicated to one node — guaranteeing that this node sends alone on that slot — and assign more nodes to other slots or one can also uniformly assign nodes to slots. The more nodes are sending on the same slot, the higher the probability of collision on that slot. On the other hand, having less nodes per slot increases the number of slots, since all nodes need to be accommodated in one arbitration cycle.

The used policy for selecting (i) and (ii) has a direct influence on communication delay and, hence, the analysis in this section depends on the used policy. As explained before, s^2TDMA uses a uniform distribution of nodes to slots. Note that other policies are also possible and can be easily derived in a similar manner, for example, where nodes may be unevenly distributed to slots.

5.1 Probability of Collision

As stated above, we consider a receiver-initiated WSN, i.e., where the receiver wakes up a given number of (sender) nodes and allows them to send. Let us denote by N the set of these nodes. Further, p_i denotes the probability that node i in N sends after waking up. We assume that this follows a random process and, hence, p_i can obtained statistically by observing the behavior of a large set of similar nodes over a large period of time.

Now, if node i is stochastically independent of all other nodes in N, the probability that it suffers no collision is given by the following expression:

$$\bar{p}_i = p_i \prod_{j \in N, j \neq i} (1 - p_j), \qquad (1)$$

where $1 - p_j$ is the probability that a node j in N does not send, i.e., (1) gives the probability that node i sends alone. As a result, node i undergoes a collision with a probability of $1 - \bar{p}_i$, i.e., at least one of the other nodes in N sends simultaneously.

In case of a collision, the receiver starts an arbitration cycle with a given number of slots $\hat{s}$. We consider the case of a uniform distribution of nodes to slots, where nodes in N are sorted in order of decreasing priority, i.e., node i has a higher priority than node j if $i < j$ holds. Node 1 to node $\left\lfloor \frac{|N|}{\hat{s}} \right\rfloor$ are allocated to the first slot, where $|N|$ is the number of nodes in N. Next, node $\left\lfloor \frac{|N|}{\hat{s}} \right\rfloor + 1$ to node $2 \cdot \left\lfloor \frac{|N|}{\hat{s}} \right\rfloor$ are allocated to the second slot and so on. Finally, node $(\hat{s} - 1) \cdot \left\lfloor \frac{|N|}{\hat{s}} \right\rfloor + 1$ to node $|N|$ are assigned to slot $\hat{s}$.

If a collision occurs in one of these slots, the receiver starts a second arbitration cycle, where the subset of nodes in the corresponding slot are now split into $\hat{s}$ slots — we consider that the same number of slots is used at every such cycle; however, s^2TDMA can also be configured for a varying number of slots. A node i may undergo a certain number of arbitration cycles until it sends without collisions. Note that, in the worst case, this may not happen until node i has exclusive use of a slot.

Now, in a given arbitration cycle ℓ, a node i's probability of sending without collisions is given by the following expression:

$$\bar{p}_{i\ell} = p_i \prod_{j \in N_{\ell s}, j \neq i} (1 - p_j), \qquad (2)$$

where $N_{\ell s}$ is the subset of nodes assigned together with node i to the same slot s being $1 \leq s \leq \hat{s}$ and $1 \leq \ell \leq \hat{\ell}$. Here, $\hat{\ell}$ is the maximum number of arbitration cycles for given N

and $\hat{s}$. Similar to before, $1 - \bar{p}_{i\ell}$ is the probability that node i suffers a collision in the arbitration cycle ℓ.

The maximum number of arbitration cycles $\hat{\ell}$ can be obtained considering that nodes are divided into $\hat{s}$ slots every time there is a collision. In the first arbitration cycle, this is $\left\lfloor \frac{|N|}{\hat{s}} \right\rfloor \leq \frac{|N|}{\hat{s}}$. In the second arbitration cycle, this is $\left\lfloor \frac{\left\lfloor \frac{|N|}{\hat{s}} \right\rfloor}{\hat{s}} \right\rfloor \leq \frac{|N|}{\hat{s}^2}$, and so on. Since no collision can happen and, hence, no further arbitration cycle will be started when there is only one node per slot, we have that $\frac{|N|}{\hat{s}^{\hat{\ell}}} = 1$ must hold. We can apply logarithm to solve for ℓ and round up to obtain an upper bound on the number of arbitration cycles as shown below:

$$\hat{\ell} = \left\lceil \frac{\ln |N|}{\ln \hat{s}} \right\rceil. \qquad (3)$$

5.2 Communication Delay

A node i's shortest communication delay is given by $l_i + l_{ack} + 2t_d$, i.e., the time needed by node i to send its packet plus the time needed by the receiver to send an acknowledgment plus the time needed by the transceiver IC to process both of them — see again Fig. 3. This happens when node i needs to send and no other node in N has anything to send, which again has a probability as per (1).

On the other hand, a node i's longest communication delay — denoted by $\hat{c}_i$ — happens when it needs to send data together with all nodes in N that (i) either have higher priority or (ii) are allocated to the same slot. This is because higher-priority nodes occupy the first slots in any arbitration cycle and lower-priority nodes send their data on node i's slot producing additional collisions. Considering again that nodes in N are sorted in order of decreasing priority, the upper bound of $\hat{c}_i$ can be computed in the following manner for $1 \leq i \leq |N|$:

$$\hat{c}_i \leq \sum_{j=1}^{i} L_{ack,j} + \sum_{j=1}^{\left\lceil \frac{i}{2} \right\rceil} \left\lceil \frac{\ln(|N| - 2j)}{\ln \hat{s}} \right\rceil \times L_{nak}, \qquad (4)$$

where $L_{ack,j} = l_j + l_{ack} + 2t_d$ and $L_{nak} = l_{max} + l_{nak} + 2t_d$.

The first term in (4) is the sum of the transmission times of packets of higher-priority nodes with their respective acknowledgments. The second term requires more explanation. As we already know, a collision is resolved when no more collisions occur in the corresponding (sub-)cycle. Since that sub-cycle can contain up to $\hat{s}$ slots, this means that up to $\hat{s}$ nodes can finish their transmission. However, the number of slots may vary in each arbitration cycle, for example, if the remaining IDs are less then $\hat{s}$, which typically happens after several ID splits. For the sake of simplification, let us pessimistically assume that every such (sub-)cycle has 2 slots. This means that only two IDs are resolved each time. This way, considering node i in N, up to $\left\lceil \frac{i}{2} \right\rceil$ sub-cycles will be generated. As previously discussed, each of these require at most $\hat{\ell}$ NAK messages — see again (3) with $\hat{s} = 2$. However, after every successful sub-cycle j, the number of remaining nodes reduces to $|N| - 2j$. Since NAK messages follow collided packets, their total duration is $(l_{max} + l_{nak} + 2t_d)$, where l_{max} is the longest among all collided packets.

Table 1: CC2420 radio and simulation parameters

Parameter	Value
Bit rate	$250\,kbps$
CCA Sampling time	$128\,\mu s$
RX/TX Switching time	$192\,\mu s$
Reception response delay t_d	$420\,\mu s$
CSMA slot length	$320\,\mu s$

In other words, whereas the first term in (4) results from the transmission times by higher-priority nodes, the second term accounts for protocol/arbitration overhead in the worst case.

6. SIMULATION RESULTS

In this section, we present the results of a simulation based on the OMNeT++ network simulation framework [12] and an extension for mobile and wireless networks named MiXiM [6]. This allows us to effectively simulate our network with different physical parameters and to record statistical values for very large numbers of transmissions.

The simulated network consists of one receiver and a selectable number of n transmitters that can either be within range of each other and, hence, interfere with each other, or simulate hidden terminals. The receiver node is a simple data sink, whereas transmitter nodes are data sources that transmit packets with a certain pattern according to the compared MACs as explained below. Note that our proposed MAC also supports multihop communication. However, for simplicity, a single hop and single sink setting is used, which also matches the requirements of Strawman [7] and Bin-MAC [10].

Our simulation is based on a receiver-initiated protocol, similar to RI-MAC [11], in which the sink periodically broadcasts probe messages to wake up transmitting nodes and trigger data communication. The number of nodes to wake up can be specified, whereas the nodes themselves are picked randomly to ensure that different possible combinations of IDs are considered. All simulation data is recorded and processed by the framework at runtime. In particular, the time stamps of the different packets sent are compared to determine whether packets overlap and, hence, get lost. Each simulation was performed with different parameters, for which at least 1,000 probe-cycles have been simulated each time.

We consider the following four MAC protocols and compare them in the simulation:

- The $s^2 TDMA$ scheme is our transmission scheme as presented in Section 4.

- The $BTCR$ scheme uses the deterministic binary tree contention resolution from BIN-MAC [10].

- The $Strawman$ scheme is a contention-based MAC of random nature as presented in [7].

- The $CSMA$ scheme is based on the non-persistent Carrier Sense Multiple Access (CSMA) method as defined in IEEE 802.15.4.

The transmission rate was fixed to $250\,kbps$ and the radio parameters were taken from the widely used transceiver

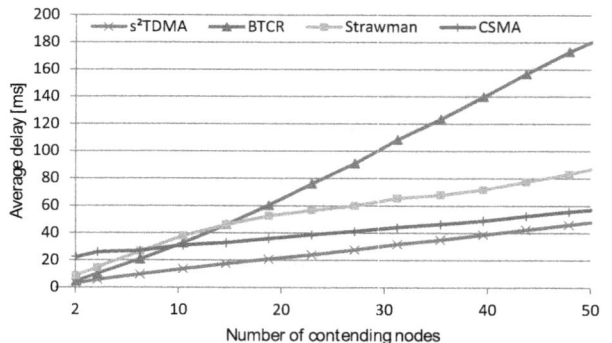

Figure 4: Average transmission delay for successful data transmission

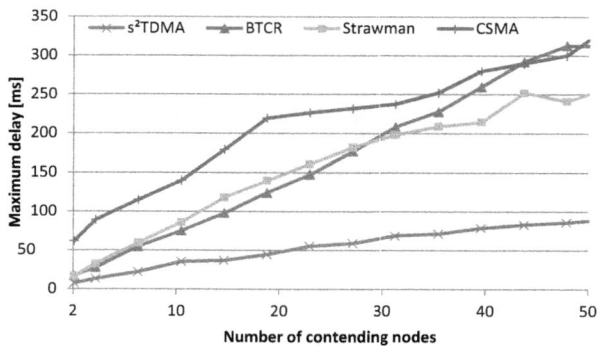

Figure 5: Maximum recorded transmission delay for successful data transmission

CC2420, as displayed in Table 1. Similar to the IEEE 802.15.4 standard, each data frame consists of $4\,bytes$ preamble, $1\,byte$ SFD (start frame delimiter), $1\,byte$ length code, $1\,byte$ CRC (cyclic redundancy check) and a number bytes for data payload, resulting in $7\,bytes$ overhead. The control messages, such as ACK, NAK, Strawman notification, etc., can omit the length field, since they are of constant size and, hence, have just $6\,bytes$ overhead.

The $Strawman$ and $CSMA$ control messages both contain a $1\,byte$ type field, defining the type of control message, and a $2\,bytes$ ACK address field. In addition, $BTCR$ and $s^2 TDMA$ require further $4\,bytes$ for address fields to specify the upper and lower ID ranges. For simplicity, we again assume that all control messages have the same length for a specific MAC, for example, $Strawman$ notification messages have the same length as $Strawman$ ACKs and NAKs.

Unless otherwise noted, the remaining parameters are set as follows: The simulated system consists of 50 nodes, of which $2 \leq N \leq 50$ nodes contend each cycle. Data packets have a fixed length of $8\,bytes$, hence, the payload is $1\,byte$. In case of $s^2 TDMA$, we set the number of TDMA slots per arbitration cycle to $\hat{s} = 4$. For $Strawman$, we use the parameters as specified in [7] and [8], resulting in a maximum contention length of $3.7\,ms$ and a maximum retransmission number of 2. For more details about $BTCR$ and $Strawman$, see Section 2.

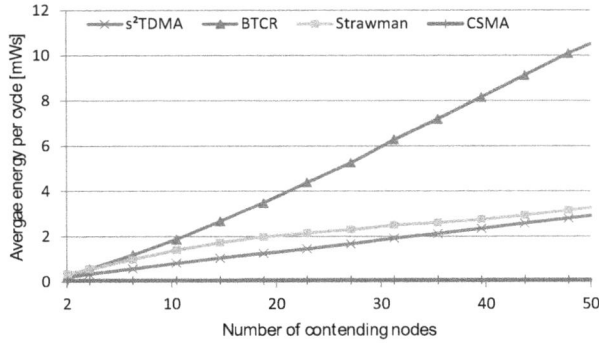

Figure 6: Average energy consumption for successful data transmission

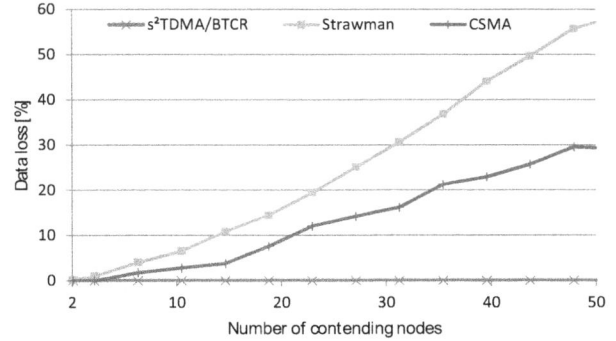

Figure 7: Amount of lost (failed) data transmissions

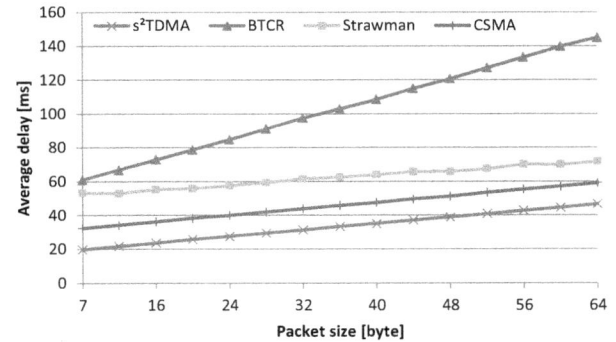

Figure 8: Average delay for a varying packet size

6.1 Delay

Let us first analyze the average transmission delay, i.e., the time from waking up the node until successful reception of its data, as depicted in Fig. 4.

Clearly, the delay rises for a greater N for all nodes, since more contenting nodes imply more collisions and, hence, a longer resolution time. In case of $s^2 TDMA$ and $BTCR$, the delays rise linearly for higher N, whereby the delay of the $BTCR$ scheme is generally higher, as its binary tree scheme needs more retransmissions for collision resolution. Similarly, $CSMA$ also rises linearly with rising N, however, it rises at a slower rate. This is because $CSMA$ starts to loose data, as we discuss later in more detail. Nodes, therefore, start to drop out of the contention resulting in (little) less load for the remaining contenders. However, for low $N < 8$, $CSMA$ has higher delays than the other schemes, as its back-off mechanism produces relatively long delays for low N.

In contrast, $Strawman$ has a relatively high delay compared to $s^2 TDMA$ and $CSMA$. This can be explained by the fact that is uses pulses instead of full packets for contention resolution, which is a much slower operation mode for most transceiver ICs (including the CC2420). For example, one CCA request with $128\,\mu s$ takes as much time as transmitting $4\,bytes$ of data. Consequently, every $Strawman$ contention pulse, which we previously set to a maximum length of $3.7\,ms$, can have a length equal to up to $115\,bytes$. This effect, however, mitigates when considering larger packet sizes, as discussed later. Similar to $CSMA$, the delay also rises at a lower rate for higher N, as $Strawman$ looses packets.

Fig. 5 shows the maximum delay that was recorded during simulation of Fig. 4. As we can see, both probabilistic approaches have a relatively high maximum delay compared to $BTCR$ and $s^2 TDMA$. This is because these are designed for simplicity and good average performance, but not for guaranteeing any QoS. During high network load these will therefore produce high loss rates and high delays. In contrast, $BTCR$ now has a relatively low maximum delay, however, $s^2 TDMA$ results again in the lowest delay of all four schemes.

6.2 Energy Efficiency

Lets us now analyze the average energy consumption of the different MAC protocols, as displayed in Fig. 6. Analogous to the delay from Fig. 4, the energy consumption curves of $BTCR$, $Strawman$ and $s^2 TDMA$ share a similar shape. This is because delay and energy consumption are directly connected to each other, since these schemes are active during the whole contention resolution and do not implement sleeping times like $CSMA$. This means that higher contention levels require the nodes to be active longer, resulting in a higher delay and energy need. On the other hand, $CSMA$ requires very little energy, since retransmission numbers are much smaller and nodes sleep during back-off times.

6.3 Reliability

Fig. 7 shows the reliability, i.e., the percentage of lost packets, for different levels of contention. As expected, both deterministic schemes result in 0 packet loss, as these are specifically designed for reliable data transfer. On the other hand, both random protocols incur in data loss, which strongly increases for higher N. Since probabilistic approaches are generally uncoordinated in channel access, a higher number of contending nodes makes collisions more likely. As a consequence, the maximum retransmission number as well as the limited back-off retries of $CSMA$ or contention packet sizes of $Strawman$, start to not be sufficient anymore and data is lost. This makes both $CSMA$ and $Strawman$ not applicable for networks, where possibly high numbers of nodes can contend simultaneously.

The reliability of $CSMA$ and $Strawman$ can be improved by increasing contention packet sizes, back-off retries or retransmission numbers. However, in return, both delay and energy consumption will increase.

6.4 Packet Size vs Performance

Next, we discuss the effects of varying the data size with respect to delay, energy consumption and data loss. To this end, we simulated a network of $N = 20$ contending nodes per probe-cycle and vary the data size from $7\,bytes$ (empty packet) to $64\,bytes$. The results regarding the average delay are depicted in Fig. 8. Since the energy consumption again shows similar behavior, we forgo to examine it separately.

Clearly, increasing the data size increases the delay and energy consumption of all four MAC protocols. For $BTCR$, this effect is the most dominant, since its contention resolution is triggered upon collisions of data packets. Increasing the packet size therefore linearly increases the delay. Similar, our s^2TDMA scheme is also based on the same principle. However, its generally faster convergence results in less collisions, hence, bigger data sizes still increase the delay, but not a strong as for $BTCR$. The delay of $Strawman$ and $CSMA$ also rises linearly for increasing data sizes, but $Strawman$ has a higher starting (offset) value due to its arbitration process.

In contrast, changing the packet sizes does not affect the loss rate of the $BTCR$ and s^2TDMA and it remains at $0\,\%$. Also for $Strawman$, no change can be observed, since its arbitration process is independent of the packet size. For $CSMA$, however, increasing the packet size slightly increases the loss rate. This is because a longer transmission time will increase the probability that nodes, which randomly want to access the channel, sense the channel as busy and perform a back-off.

7. CONCLUSION

In this paper, we proposed a MAC providing a deterministic contention resolution mechanism in form of generating spontaneous TDMA cycles upon collisions. This results in an interval tree search featuring a fast conflict resolution with $log_{\hat{s}}$-complexity, being $\hat{s}$ the number of slots in each such cycle.

The proposed scheme, called s^2TDMA, is well suited for receiver-initiated networks with high numbers of contenders, which are expected in application in the area of in Internet of Things, Cyber-Physical Systems, etc. Since s^2TDMA is only triggered on collisions and does not rely on periodic synchronization, it offers both low overhead and good energy efficiency under low contention as well as fast collision resolution under high contention.

In addition to analyzing the worst-case behavior, we performed extensive simulations using OMNeT++. The proposed technique never leads to packet losses (within the network) and shows good scalability and quick adaption to fast changing traffic load. Further, our experiments suggest that the proposed s^2TDMA is energy-efficient and significantly outperforms other approaches from the literature.

8. REFERENCES

[1] N. Abramson. The Aloha System: Another Alternative for Computer Communications. In *Proceedings of the Fall Joint Computer Conference*, 1970.

[2] J. Afonso, L. Rocha, H. Silva, and J. Correia. MAC Protocol for Low-Power Real-Time Wireless Sensing and Actuation. In *Proceedings of the IEEE International Conference on Electronics, Circuits and Systems (ICECS)*, 2006.

[3] D. Carlson and A. Terzis. Flip-MAC: A Density-Adaptive Contention-Reduction Protocol for Efficient Any-to-One Communication. In *Proceedings of the IEEE International Conference on Distributed Computing in Sensor Systems and Workshops (DCOSS)*, 2011.

[4] P. Dutta, S. Dawson-Haggerty, Y. Chen, C.-J. M. Liang, and A. Terzis. Design and Evaluation of a Versatile and Efficient Receiver-Initiated Link Layer for Low-Power Wireless. In *Proceedings of the ACM Conference on Embedded Networked Sensor Systems (SenSys)*, 2010.

[5] X. Ji, Y. He, J. Wang, W. Dong, X. Wu, and Y. Liu. Walking down the STAIRS: Efficient Collision Resolution for Wireless Sensor Networks. In *Proceedings of the IEEE Conference on Computer Communications (INFOCOM)*, 2014.

[6] A. Köpke, M. Swigulski, K. Wessel, D. Willkomm, P. T. K. Haneveld, T. E. V. Parker, O. W. Visser, H. S. Lichte, and S. Valentin. Simulating Wireless and Mobile Networks in OMNeT++: The MiXiM Vision. In *Proceedings of the International Conference on Simulation Tools and Techniques for Communications, Networks and Systems (SIMUTools)*, 2008.

[7] F. Österlind, L. Mottola, T. Voigt, N. Tsiftes, and A. Dunkels. Strawman: Resolving Collisions in Bursty Low-Power Wireless Networks. In *Proceedings of the 11th international conference on Information Processing in Sensor Networks (IPSN)*, 2012.

[8] F. Österlind, N. Wirström, N. Tsiftes, N. Finne, T. Voigt, and A. Dunkels. StrawMAN: Making Sudden Traffic Surges Graceful in Low-power Wireless Networks. In *Proceedings of the Workshop on Hot Topics in Embedded Networked Sensors (HotEmNets)*, 2010.

[9] I. Rhee, A. Warrier, M. Aia, J. Min, and M. Sichitiu. Z-MAC: A Hybrid MAC for Wireless Sensor Networks. *IEEE/ACM Transactions on Networking*, 16:511–524, 2008.

[10] V. Salmani and P. H. Chou. Bin-MAC: A Hybrid MAC for Ultra-Compact Wireless Sensor Nodes. In *Proceedings of the IEEE International Conference on Distributed Computing in Sensor Systems (DCOSS)*, 2012.

[11] Y. Sun, O. Gurewitz, and D. B. Johnson. RI-MAC: A Receiver-Initiated Asynchronous Duty Cycle MAC Protocol for Dynamic Traffic Loads in Wireless Sensor Networks. In *Proceedings of the ACM conference on Embedded Network Sensor Systems (SenSys)*, 2008.

[12] A. Varga. The OMNeT++ Discrete Event Simulation System. In *Proceedings of the European Simulation Multiconference (ESM)*, 2001.

Multisensor Data Fusion for Patient Risk Level Determination and Decision-support in Wireless Body Sensor Networks

Carol Habib
Univ. Bourgogne
Franche-Comté (UBFC)
FEMTO-ST Institute
Belfort, France
carol.habib@univ-fcomte.fr

Abdallah Makhoul
Univ. Bourgogne
Franche-Comté (UBFC)
FEMTO-ST Institute
Belfort, France
abdallah.makhoul@univ-fcomte.fr

Rony Darazi
Antonine University
TICKET Lab
Hadat-Baabda, Lebanon
rony.darazi@ua.edu.lb

Raphaël Couturier
Univ. Bourgogne
Franche-Comté (UBFC)
FEMTO-ST Institute
Belfort, France
raphael.couturier@univ-fcomte.fr

ABSTRACT

Wireless Body Sensor Networks (WBSNs) are a low-cost solution for healthcare applications allowing continuous and remote monitoring. However, many challenges are addressed in WBSNs such as limited energy resources, early detection of emergencies and fusion of large amount of heterogeneous data in order to take decisions. In this paper, we propose a multisensor data fusion approach enabling one to determine the patient risk level based on vital signs scores. Consequently, a corresponding decision is taken routinely and each time an emergency is detected. This approach is based on early warning score systems, a fuzzy inference system and a technique determining the score of a vital sign given its past and current value. We evaluate our approach on real healthcare datasets.

Keywords

WBSN; multisensor data fusion; fuzzy theory; early warning system; patient risk level; decision-making

1. INTRODUCTION

WBSNs are a subset of wireless sensor networks used for healthcare applications allowing to remotely and continuously monitor a patient's health condition, thus reducing healthcare expenditures [7]. Some monitoring scenarios include the surveillance of elderly in nursing homes and in-home monitoring of chronic or acutely ill patients. Many applications have been addressed in the literature so far such as gait analysis, monitoring vital signs, daily activities [6], fall detection systems and stress evaluation systems [4]. Such a network consists of wearable sensor nodes called biosensor nodes and a coordinator. The biosensor nodes are placed on the body of the patient or can be implanted inside the body. They sense continuously and periodically physiological signals and vital signs. The collected data are communicated to the coordinator which can be a smartphone, a pda or any other portable device. The data aggregation and fusion are performed at the coordinator level in order to take decisions routinely and when emergencies or critical events are detected such as an abnormal variation in the heart rate. The coordinator alerts the patient and sends the collected data as well as the decision to the healthcare center or any other destination [3]. Many challenges arise in WBSNs. One of the most important ones is the energy consumption at the biosensor node level due to periodic transmission and sensing. Another challenge, is the fusion of the large amount of heterogeneous data collected by several biosensor nodes in order to represent the global situation of the patient and take consequently the corresponding decision. Several approaches for the data management and processing in WBSNs have been proposed in the literature so far. To the best of our knowledge, no one has so far tackled the problem of monitoring and fusing the vital signs of a patient while taking into consideration data reduction for energy consumption requirements as well as limited computational resources. In this paper, we propose a new multisensor data fusion approach enabling the determination of the patient's risk level. The main purpose is to obtain information of greater quality by taking decisions corresponding to the patient's situation determined by the collected data. The decisions are taken routinely and when emergencies are detected, based on an early warning score system. The proposed approach, uses fuzzy sets to deal with

MSWiM '16, November 13-17, 2016, Malta, Malta

© 2016 ACM. ISBN 978-1-4503-4502-6/16/11...$15.00

DOI: http://dx.doi.org/10.1145/2988287.2989173

uncertainties and a fuzzy inference system to map the aggregate score of vital signs to the patient's risk level. We also propose a technique for keeping the information about a vital sign up-to-date while taking into consideration its past and current score. The following of the paper is organized as follows. Section 2 presents the background and related work. In section 3, the proposed data fusion model is described. In section 4, the experimental results are shown. Section 5 concludes the paper with some directions and future work.

2. BACKGROUND AND RELATED WORK

2.1 Context and WBSN Architecture

In this paper we propose a data fusion model to be implemented at the coordinator level of a WBSN. This model allows continuous monitoring of a patient's vital signs subject to acute illness. An acute disease requires immediate medical attention due to life-threatening possibilities and continuous assessment. Our proposed approach allows the early detection of emergencies, deterioration and improving condition of the patient regardless his location. The patient is equipped with biosensor nodes and a coordinator, usually being his smartphone. A biosensor node is defined as a traditional sensor node equipped with sensors that monitor vital signs. We suppose that each biosensor node senses only one vital sign and that 5 vital signs are monitored: Heart Rate (HR), Respiration Rate (RESP), Blood Temperature (BLOODT), Oxygen Saturation (SpO2) and Systolic Blood Pressure (ABP Sys). Therefore, the WBSN is composed of 5 biosensor nodes and one coordinator communicating under a star topology.

2.2 Early Warning Score System

An early warning score system (EWS) is a guide used by emergency medical services staff in hospitals to determine the severity of a patient's illness and thus, the degree of criticality of his or her situation. Once measured and recorded, the vital signs are weighed and aggregated. For each vital sign, a normal healthy range is defined ($score = 0$). Measured values outside of this range are allocated a score ranging from 1 to 3 according to the magnitude of deviation from the normal range. The weighing reflects the severity of the physiological disturbance. Since our approach aims at early detecting emergencies, such scoring systems can give the biosensor nodes the ability to locally detect criticalities and send only the important changes in vital signs to the coordinator. In our work, we have used the National EWS (NEWS) used in hospitals in the UK [1] as a scoring system.

3. MULTISENSOR DATA FUSION MODEL

The coordinator receives the measurements sent by different biosensor nodes running $Modified\ LED^*$ algorithm [5]. Its role is to perform the multisensor data fusion in order to obtain meaningful information about the patient's health condition represented by a computed patient's risk level. Depending on the computed risk, an advice or decision is given to the patient. In this paper, we propose to use a Fuzzy Inference System (FIS) which uses fuzzy set-theory in order to map inputs to outputs. Having information about how critical is the patient's health condition, a fuzzy logic system can determine the patient's risk level. Fuzzy logic is widely used as a method for representing uncertainty particularly for high-level data fusion tasks. When dealing with

medical data, these can be uncertain, ambiguous, and are interpreted in a human reasoning way.

3.1 Aggregate Score and Patient Risk Level

For health experts and doctors, it is interesting to find the aggregate score of the monitored vital signs of a given patient. This total score represents the early warning score. It allows them to determine the criticality level of the patient as well as the intervention mode that should be adopted [1]. In our work, we use the aggregate score as an input into our FIS in order to get as an output the patient's risk level. According to $Modified\ LED^*$ [5], the biosensor nodes keep the coordinator updated with changes in vital signs. At the beginning of each period p, they send the first captured measurement. Then using NEWS, each time there is a change in the score of the vital sign, the corresponding measurement is sent. Therefore, the coordinator receives several measurements for each vital sign during one round R where $R = m \times p, m \in \mathbb{N}^*$. In order to compute the aggregate score at instant t, the coordinator calculates first the up-to-date score s_t for each vital sign at instant t as follows:

$$s_t = \frac{s_{t-1} + score_t}{2} \tag{1}$$

with $s_0 = score_0$ and where $score_0$ is the score of the first measurement sent during round R, $score_t$ is the vital sign's current score at time t and s_{t-1} is the score calculated at time $t-1$. Therefore, the current score $score_t$ and the score s_{t-1}, representing the history of the vital sign, are given equal weights. Second, the aggregrate score is calculated as follows:

$$AggScore = \sum_{i=1}^{N} s_i \tag{2}$$

where s_i is the up-to-date score (equation 1) of the ith vital sign during a round R and N is the number of vital signs (biosensors). Since the analysis and the interpretation of medical data, more specifically the aggregate score of vital signs varies from one subject to another, we believe that the evaluation of the patient's health condition should be done using fuzzy theory. The aggregate score $AggScore$ is the input of the FIS. Firstly, the $AggScore$ is fuzzified, using for this purpose 3 fuzzy membership functions: Low, Medium and High as shown in Figure 1. Then, the patient's risk level determination is carried out using a set of fuzzy logic rules.

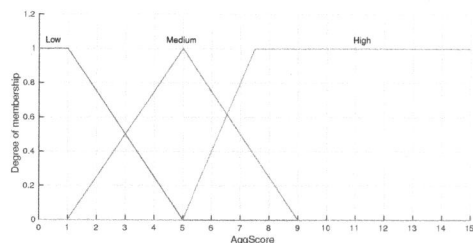

Figure 1: Aggregate Score Membership Functions

As it has already been mentioned, the objective of the proposed FIS is to determine the patient's risk level according to the received measurements of the vital signs. For this

Table 1: Fuzzy Rule Base

Rule No.	Agg Score	Patient Risk Level
1	Low	Low-Risk
2	Medium	Medium-Risk
3	High	High-Risk

Table 2: Example of an Association Table between patient risk values and decisions

Decisions	Risk value range
d1	$r < 0.25$
d2	$0.25 \leq r < 0.4$
d3	$0.4 \leq r < 0.6$
d4	$0.6 \leq r < 0.8$
d5	$r \geq 0.8$

purpose, 3 fuzzy membership functions for the evaluation of the risk are defined: Low-Risk, Medium-Risk and High-Risk as shown in Figure 2. The patient's risk level r is expressed using a quantitative variable and can range from 0 up to 1.

Table 3: Parameters settings for Modified LED^* and DFM

Modified LED^*	DFM
$p = 100$ sec $R = 2 \times p$ $\alpha = 0.05$ $r^0 = 0.9$ $SR_{max} = 50$ samples/period $SR_{min} = 10$ samples/period	$p = 100$ sec $R = 1 \times p$ $\delta_t = 1$ sec

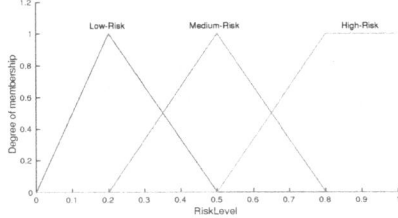

Figure 2: Patient Risk Level Membership Functions

3.2 Fuzzy Inference System

Figure 3 shows the proposed patient risk level determination block diagram. The coordinator, receiving the measurements from the m biosensors, calculates the patient's risk level in order to take a decision. This last is a predictive or corrective advice given to the patient. The input of our proposed system is the aggregate score $AggScore$ of the 5 monitored vital signs (cf. section 3.1). Using the fuzzy membership functions described in section 3.1 and the fuzzy rule base given by health experts or doctors, the FIS gives as an output the risk level of the patient. The fuzzy rule base is shown in Table 1. For example Rule 1 is: *if the aggregate score is Low then the patient risk level is Low-Risk*.

Finally, the risk level is defuzzified using the centroid method in order to obtain a crisp patient's risk level r. Depending on the value of r a decision or advice is selected.

4. EXPERIMENTAL RESULTS

Experiments are conducted on real medical datasets using a custom-based Java simulator and Matlab. In order to assess the performance of the proposed data fusion model, patient vital signs datasets are collected from Multiple Intelligent Monitoring in Intensive Care (MIMIC) II database of PhysioNet [2]. Five biosensors sense the HR, RESP, ABP Sys, BLOODT and the SpO2. The proposed data fusion model is tested based on the received measurements. Two ideas are highlighted: the score calculation for any vital sign and the patient risk level determination. *Modified LED^** is run on the biosensor nodes and the proposed data fusion model (DFM) is implemented on the coordinator. The simulation time is about 70 periods (≈ 2 hours). The parameters settings for both algorithms are shown in table 3. Figure 4 shows the scores of the received measurements from the HR biosensor nodes. In addition, it shows the up-to-date score of the HR calculated by the coordinator over 10 rounds. At the beginning of each round R, the up-to-date score of each vital sign is assigned the score of the 1st measurement sent by the corresponding biosensor nodes. Then, the up-to-date score is calculated each time a decision making process is triggered and at each refresh time δ_t. For example, at the beginning of the 1st round ($t = 0$), the coordinator receives a measurement having a score equal to 0. Thus, the up-to-date score is set to 0. Then, at $t = 36$ sec, the coordinator receives a measurement from the HR biosensor node having a score equal to 1. The up-to-date score is calculated as follows : $\frac{0+1}{2} = 0.5$, thus giving equal importance to the history represented by the last claculated score and the current score. The up-to-date score is refreshed each $\delta_t = 1$ sec, hence according to figure 4, while the current score is stable it converges to 1. For $t > 500$ sec, the HR is stable, thus the up-to-date score does not change and is stable at 0. The up-to-date score is always bounded by the scores of the two last measurements received and converges to the last one depending on δ_t and the stability of the vital sign.

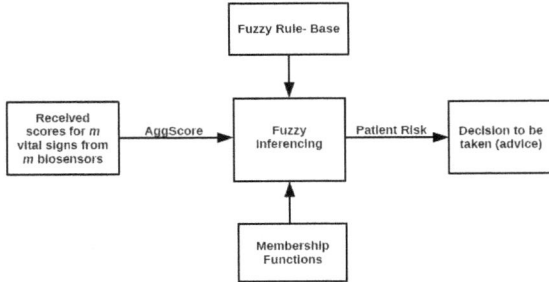

Figure 3: Patient risk level determination block diagram model

This is done using an association table between the decisions and the patient risk values as shown in Table 2. This table is set by experts or doctors. It contains simple decisions and advices such as: rest, take medicine, call the doctor etc.

Figures 5 and 6 show the aggregate score and the patient risk level respectively over 70 periods. Each time a critical score is detected by the coordinator and at the end of each round, the decision making process is launched. A decision is chosen according to the patient's risk level. This last is the output of the proposed FIS and is based on the aggre-

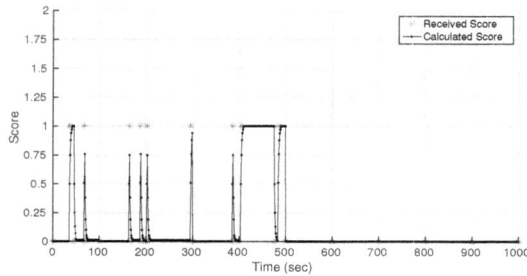

Figure 4: The scores of the received measurements from the Heart Rate biosensor node and the calculated up-to-date score by the coordinator over 10 rounds.

gate score (cf. section 3.2). Figure 5 shows the aggregate score over 70 periods. The values range between 1 and 8. The aggregate score is the sum of the up-to-date scores of the 5 vital signs. Using the rules defined in section 3.2, the patient's risk level is determined and is shown in figure 6. The higher the aggregate score, the more the patient's situation is critical. This last is characterized by the patient's risk level whose values, according to figure 6, range between 0.23 and 0.74.

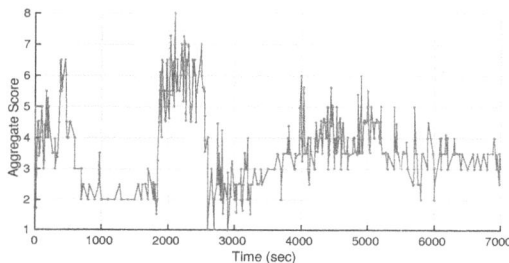

Figure 5: The aggregate score of the 5 vital signs over 70 periods.

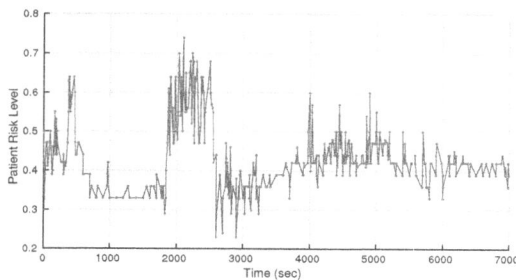

Figure 6: The patient risk level over 70 periods obtained using the proposed FIS.

Figure 7 shows the decisions that are taken each time the decision making process is triggered. Based on the patient's risk level (figure 6), a decision is selected using table 2. This table is predefined by doctors, where for each patient risk range, a decision is defined. As shown in figure 7, the deci-

sions alternate between decision 1, 2, 3 and 4 depending on the patient's risk level at a given time t.

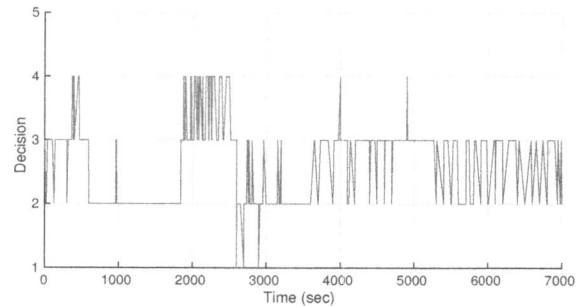

Figure 7: The decisions taken over 70 periods based on the patient's risk level.

5. CONCLUSION

In this paper, we have proposed a multisensor data fusion model allowing the coordinator of a WBSN to monitor continuously the health condition of an acutely ill patient. It takes a decision routinely and when emergencies are detected. The vital signs taken into consideration are the HR, RESP, BLOODT, SpO2 and ABP Sys. The approach takes into consideration the data reduction performed at the biosensor nodes level and uses a FIS to determine the patient's risk level. For future work, we intend to integrate other information for a better assesment of the patient's condition by adding environmental sensor nodes and motion detectors making the data fusion model context-aware.

6. REFERENCES

[1] National early warning score. http://www.rcplondon. ac.uk/resources/national-early-warning-score-news. Accessed: 9-1-2016.

[2] Physionet. https://www.physionet.org/mimic2/. Accessed: 9-1-2016.

[3] N. Bradai, L. C. Fourati, and L. Kamoun. Wban data scheduling and aggregation under wban/wlan healthcare network. *Ad Hoc Networks*, 25:251–262, 2015.

[4] G. Fortino, S. Galzarano, R. Gravina, and W. Li. A framework for collaborative computing and multi-sensor data fusion in body sensor networks. *Information Fusion*, 22:50–70, 2015.

[5] C. Habib, A. Makhoul, R. Darazi, and C. Salim. Self-adaptive data collection and fusion for health monitoring based on body sensor networks. *IEEE Transactions on Industrial Informatics*, Accepted. May 2016.

[6] I. M. Pires, N. M. Garcia, N. Pombo, and F. Flórez-Revuelta. From data acquisition to data fusion: a comprehensive review and a roadmap for the identification of activities of daily living using mobile devices. *Sensors*, 16(2):184, 2016.

[7] C. C. Poon, B. P. Lo, M. R. Yuce, A. Alomainy, and Y. Hao. Body sensor networks: In the era of big data and beyond. *Biomedical Engineering, IEEE Reviews in*, 8:4–16, 2015.

On Optimal Charger Positioning in Clustered RF-power Harvesting Wireless Sensor Networks

Dimitrios Zorbas
Univ La Rochelle
L3i Lab – France
dimitrios.zormpas@univ-lr.fr

Patrice Raveneau
Univ La Rochelle
L3i Lab – France
patrice.raveneau@univ-lr.fr

Yacine Ghamri-Doudane
Univ La Rochelle
L3i Lab – France
yacine.ghamri@univ-lr.fr

ABSTRACT

Wireless charging brings forward some new principles in designing energy efficient networks. A number of energy transmitters are placed in all over the network to recharge power constrained nodes. Since a few only nodes can remarkably benefit from the transmitter power emission, we organize the nodes in clusters and we propose an efficient localized algorithm as well as a centralized one to compute the charger position such that the cluster lifetime is maximized. Simulation results are presented to show the effectiveness of the approaches.

Keywords

RF-power harvesting; Clustering; Optimal placement

1. INTRODUCTION

A technology that has been recently developed takes advantage of the transmitted neighboring RF signals to harvest a small portion of energy. More specifically, a new type of antenna is used which can convert part of the received signal power to electricity. Depending on the transmitted power and the distance between the transmitting source and the receiver, a node can harvest from some uW to some mW of power [6]. However, this technology presents some major limitations mainly due to the low efficiency of the conversion unit [7]. First, the harvested power rapidly decreases when the receiver is moving more than few meters away from the source. Second, the conversion efficiency is substantial only for a small range of distance, and third, there is a minimum received signal power corresponding to a maximum distance, below which no conversion is possible.

In this paper, we consider networks consisting of nodes which can acquire energy from energy transmitters (chargers). We assume that a charger periodically and omnidirectionally transmits energy packets to the network. Due to the limitations of the harvesting technology, a few only nodes can substantially benefit from the energy data transmission whereas a possible use of multiple chargers in all

MSWiM '16, November 13-17, 2016, Malta, Malta
© 2016 ACM. ISBN 978-1-4503-4502-6/16/11...$15.00
DOI: http://dx.doi.org/10.1145/2988287.2989171

over the network could considerably increase the operation costs. For these reasons we organize the network in clusters so that the majority of the nodes use short communication links and the most of communication burden falls onto the shoulders of the cluster heads. By using chargers close to these nodes we can alleviate their communication cost and, thus, extend the network lifetime.

However, the question that rises up is where to place a charger so that the network lifetime is prolonged as much as possible. We explain that this placement problem is a special case of the Weber problem and we propose a local search algorithm that finds a solution close to the optimal. The algorithm can operate in both centralized or distributed manner since it uses localized information and a number of successive small steps to gradually move the charger more efficient positions. We, also, present an exhaustive search algorithm that examines a big range of possible solutions exhibiting, however, higher computation cost.

2. RELATED WORK

RF-energy harvesting networks have been extensively studied from different research aspects. For a complete literature review the reader can refer to [7] and [2]. We cite, here, the most recent research activities closer to our work.

A placement and charging problem is examined in [10]. The authors assume that a set of candidate locations for placing chargers is given and they find a charger placement and a corresponding power allocation to maximize the charging quality. The problem is proved to be NP-Complete. Moreover, a wireless charger placement problem that that takes into account the electromagnetic radiation safety is tackled in [3]. Simulations show that in terms of charging utility, the proposed algorithm presents up to 45.7% better results compared to a previous approach.

In [4], the problem of cluster head recharging by the transmissions of the cluster members is examined. The authors formulate a power resource allocation problem to maximize the energy efficiency. The reverse problem is tackled in [9]. It is assumed that the cluster heads are equipped with solar panels and they use the solar energy to recharge the cluster members. A cluster head placement problem is examined which is proved to be NP-hard.

3. SYSTEM MODEL

We consider wireless sensor nodes powered by rechargeable batteries. Each node spends its energy by taking measurements utilizing its sensing module and by communicating with other nodes. The energy spent per bit is described by $\alpha_1 + \beta d^{2b}$ for the transmissions and by α_2 for the reception. α_1 is the energy/bit consumed by the transmitter electronics, β accounts for the energy dissipated in the transmit op-amp, α_2 is the energy consumed by the receiver electronics and b is the amplitude loss exponent.

We, also, assume that all the nodes take measurements periodically and generate the same amount of data D. The data is encapsulated in a packet of size p bits and it is transmitted to the sink or to a relay node. A node can transmit k packets per time period. A relay node is capable of aggregating multiple data in one packet. We set $k' = \lceil \frac{nkD}{p} \rceil$ the number of packets transmitted per time period by a relay node, where n is the number of communicating nodes (including the relay node itself).

We define as network lifetime the time until at least one node uses up its battery. Assuming that the nodes consume energy with constant rate, the node with the highest consumption sets an upper bound on the network lifetime.

The sensor nodes are equipped with an extra RF module capable of harvesting power from transmitted signals. A charger with omni-directional antenna is used to send energy packets to the network and recharge the nodes. We used the same energy harvesting model described in [11].

We split the transmission time in rounds where each round has two phases. During the first phase, named "Sensing data phase", the nodes communicate with the sink and transmit their sensing data. In the second phase, named "Energy data phase", we allow the transmission of energy packets. The transmission time is divided in S slots and we allow only one transmission per slot within the vicinity of a single node to avoid interference. We assume that the nodes are well synchronized using a precise time synchronization protocol [8]. Each time a node is ready to transmit a packet it switches to active mode while it remains in sleep mode if it is not transmitting. In sleep mode a node consumes much less energy but it can still harvest energy from the RF-harvesting antenna.

As a consequence, the number of data transmissions during the "Sensing data phase" determines the maximum (safe) number of energy packet transmissions. Assuming a time period equal to one round and k packet transmissions per round, it holds that $\frac{p}{dr}(k(N_{max}+1) + k' + k_e) \leq \tau$, where N_{max} is the maximum number of neighbors among the nodes in the network, k_e is the energy packets, dr is the data rate, and τ is the duration of the round. The higher the node density, the higher the number of neighbors and the lower the maximum possible transmissions of energy packets.

4. THE OPTIMAL CHARGER POSITIONING PROBLEM

Finding the optimal charger position, the cluster lifetime is maximized. As it is defined in Section 3, the network lifetime is upper bounded by the node with the highest energy consumption. The most distant node to the CH, or the same the CH, set the lifetime upper bound. It practically means that in order to extend the lifetime, the charger must be placed somewhere that the CH gets enough energy to survive until one node dies, and at the same time, the most distant node (or multiple distant nodes) lasts as long as possible.

Given a group of n nodes the Optimal Charger Positioning problem (OCP) can be formulated as follows: find the best charger position $\mathcal{O}$ in the plane such that the maximum energy consumption in the cluster is minimized.

If I is the node with the highest consumption, we can distinguish two cases of the problem. First, if I is out of the harvesting range of the charger, the number of optimal charger positions is infinite. All these positions are located within a disk with center the coordinates of the CH and radius the maximum distance between the CH and charger (denoted by d_{CH}).

On the other hand, if I is in the harvesting range of the charger, then the problem is transformed to a Facility Location Problem (FLP) which in its general case is NP-hard [5]. The problem in FLP is to find facility positions that minimize the sum of transportation costs between those positions and a set of sites (nodes). A simple facility location problem is the Weber problem, in which a single facility is to be placed. In our case, as it is explained in the next section, the Weber point coincides with the center of the mass, since the maximum consumption is minimized when two or three diametrically opposed nodes have the same consumption.

5. SOLUTIONS FOR THE OCP PROBLEM

5.1 Local Search algorithm

In this section we present "Local Search" (LS), an algorithm that computes the charger's position based on local information.

The input of LS is the CH position and the initial position of the charger. The CH is chosen based on two criteria; (a) to be reachable by all the nodes of the group and (b) to be connected with the sink. Every node that satisfies these two criteria can become the CH. In LS we choose as CH a node which is closer to the centroid of the plane, in order to balance the communication cost between the nodes and the CH. Another reason is to the centroid can be computed without much cost. In the centralized case it is the average of the coordinates of the nodes while in the distributed case it can be estimated using the nodes relative position [1].

As it has been already mentioned, the CH's consumption sets an upper bound on the network lifetime if it does not have enough energy to forward multiple packets by the nodes of the group. It means that the charger must not be located far away from the CH in order to stoke it with energy. The maximum charger distance away from the CH (i.e, d_{CH}) can be calculated by taking into account the cluster size as well as the consumption and the harvesting energy of the CH. Due to the limited size of this paper, we omit the detailed equations. Note that the distance between the CH and the most distant node I is, also, involved in the equations. Hence, the optimal charger position is always found in a disk $\mathcal{A}$ with radius d_{CH} and center the coordinates of the CH. d_{CH} is, also, upper bounded by the maximum harvesting range. We have narrowed down the search space for the charger to a disk $\mathcal{A}$. However, the number of solutions in $\mathcal{A}$ remains infinite.

Based on the fact the harvesting energy is higher the closer we move to a receiver, we make two observations. First, since harvesting power depends on distance, if we move the charger towards the most distant node I the communication cost remains the same but the harvesting energy is getting higher. It means that the closer we move to distant nodes the total consumption is reduced. The second observation is that moving towards a distant node we reduce its consumption but, at the same time, we increase the consumption of other nodes located at the opposite direction from where we move to. However there is an optimal point $\mathcal{O}$ where at least two or three nodes present the same (maximum) consumption C_{max}. If w is the number of nodes with equal consumption, then all w nodes are enclosed in a minimum (weighted) circle $\mathcal{C}$ with center $\mathcal{O}$ and radius (weight) C_{max}. However, it is known that a minimum enclosing circle can be drawn by computing maximum three points (or two if the points are on the same straight line with the center of the circle). Therefore, $\mathcal{O}$ can be computed by finding three (or two) only nodes with equal weight.

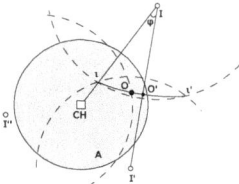

Figure 1: Example with the positions of three distant nodes, the intermediate charger positions and the optimal position on the plane.

Next, we describe how LS works in order to find a solution close to $\mathcal{O}$. Let us assume that the best solution found by LS is at point O. The algorithm works by evaluating successive charger positions with a step of ϵ, where ϵ is a small number. As it is shown in Figure 1 the charger which is initially located next to the CH, is starting moving towards I which is the most distant node and the node that presents the highest consumption. At every single point the algorithm checks if the consumption of the rest of the nodes is higher than or equal to the consumption of I. A node that satisfies this condition, let say at point ι, is the second point I' needed to define $\mathcal{C}$. If multiple nodes have higher consumption than I, the node with a consumption closer to that of I is selected. We must mention here that three subcases exist. First, if I, I' and CH are on the same straight line, no other node is needed to be found since $\mathcal{C}$ can be defined by two points (I and I'). Second, if multiple nodes exhibit the same consumption with I, it means that all these nodes belong in $\mathcal{C}$, and thus more than three points have already been found. Third, if no node I' is found, then ι is located at the intersection point of the border of $\mathcal{A}$ and the straight line defined by nodes CH and I.

At point ι the algorithm has found a solution for OCP problem, but it may not be the optimal. For example in Figure 1 if the charger moves right, the energy consumption can be improved. The algorithm's next objective is to detect a third point by moving on an arc $\overarc{\iota, \iota'}$ that connects the intersection points of the two circles with centers the coordinates of I and I', and radii $\overline{I, \iota}$ and $\overline{I', \iota}$, respectively. The energy consumption of I and I' is equal for all points on $\overarc{\iota, \iota'}$ since in fact $\iota\iota'$ is the diagonal of the (weighted) square $\iota I \iota' I'$ with a (weighted) side of $E_c^{I_\iota}$. The arc can be defined by points ι, ι' and O'. O' is the intersection point of the arc and the straight line $\overline{I, I'}$. At this point I and I' present the same consumption and $\overline{I, O} + \overline{O, I'} = \overline{I, I'}$. Similarly to the previous steps, the charger is moving on the arc $\overarc{\iota, \iota'}$ with step ϵ until a third node I'' with higher than or equal con-

sumption to that of I and I' is found. Note that the same three subcases may also exist here. Since I'' is detected, the best position has been found.

It is obvious that the lower the ϵ the closer the solution to the optimal point. We must note that there is no other $\mathcal{O}$ defined by I, I', and I'' since $\mathcal{O}$ is the center of the mass of the triangle $II'I''$ which is unique.

PROPERTY 1. *The maximum traveling distance of the charger is less than or equal to $\overline{CH, I}$.*

We omit the proof of the previous property due to the limited size of the paper.

The computation cost of the approach mainly depends on the step ϵ and the number of nodes. Apparently the lower the ϵ the more the iterations of the algorithm. If z is the number of iterations to find O, then the longest run of the algorithm is $\frac{z(n-1)}{\epsilon}$. z depends on the distance between CH and the most distant node.

In the distributed version of LS, the charger needs to communicate with the nodes before each step ϵ and to decide its movement through the nodes relative position and RSSIs. This means that the total number of exchange messages is proportional to the number of nodes and the step ϵ. Since $2(n-1)$ messages need for each step, the total number of messages is upper bounded by $\frac{2z(n-1)}{\epsilon}$.

5.2 Brute force algorithm

In this section we describe "Brute force" (BF), a simple exhaustive algorithm that examines a very wide range of possible solutions. BF divides $\mathcal{A}$ in square bits of equal size with a side of ϵ'. For every bit it assigns a point in the middle of the square. Subsequently, it checks every single point to find the minimum possible maximum consumption for all the nodes in the group.

Similar to Local Search, the lower the ϵ' the higher the precision of the best solution. BF guarantees that its best solution is $\frac{\sqrt{2}\epsilon'}{2}$ far from the optimal and, unlike LS, this solution does not depend on the nature of the harvesting module. BF's complexity depends on ϵ' and the number of nodes. Unlike Local Search, BF always checks all the possible solutions which are equal to $\frac{\pi d_{CH}^2}{\epsilon'^2}$. Hence, its complexity is $\mathcal{O}(\frac{\pi d_{CH}^2}{\epsilon'^2} n) = \Omega(\frac{\pi d_{CH}^2}{\epsilon'^2} n)$.

Due to the centralized nature of the algorithm and its high computation cost, it makes it viable only for small networks or for comparison purposes.

6. EVALUATION & DISCUSSION OF THE RESULTS

We assume a scenario with a square terrain of 25 meters side (fixed) and variable number of nodes randomly and uniformly scattered on the terrain. We measure the maximum energy consumption of the nodes (displayed as "Consumption") for one round and the execution time of the algorithms. Due to the presence of random values, we run each instance 50 times and the average results are presented. The 95% confidence intervals are, also, shown when it is feasible.

Regarding the node and station characteristics, we consider the following values (see [11] for details): $p = 127 bytes$, $D = 256 bits$, $dr = 250 Kbps$, $k = 1$ packet, $k_e = 150$ packets/sec, $\tau = 30 sec$, $P_{tx}G_T = 3W$, $R_h = 12m$ (max. harvesting range), $R_c = 40m$ (max. communication range),

$G_R = 6dBi$, $\lambda = 0.3279m$, $\sigma = 0.01$, $\rho = 1m$, $\alpha_1 = 50nJ$, $\alpha_2 = 50nJ$, $\beta = 100pJ$, and $b = 2$. We assume four transmission levels when $d < 10, 10 \leq d < 20, 20 \leq d < 30$, and $d > 30$. The steps ϵ and ϵ' are both equal to $0.05m$. Node parameters correspond to Mica2 sensor nodes using a Zigbee communication module at 915MHz. Regarding the transmitting station and the harvesting efficiency we used the values provided by Powercast corporation for P2110B model operating at the same frequency. k, k_e and node densities are chosen in that way so that no interference exists. The experiments were carried out on an Intel i7 2.5GHz CPU with 16GB RAM running Linux.

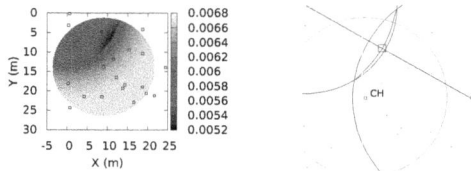

Figure 2: The range of solutions provided by BF and the best solution found by LS for a scenario with 20 nodes.

Figure 2 illustrates the range of solutions provided by BF and the best solution found by LS for a scenario with 20 nodes. The left figure pictures disk $\mathcal{A}$ centered at CH whereas the color represents the maximum consumption. The tiny squares stand for the position of the nodes. We can observe that the best solutions are gathered in an eye-shaped area while the consumption gradually increases as we move away from it. On the right figure, the solution found by LS is depicted. The tiny squares represent the nodes and the best solution is drawn with a slightly bigger square. We can see that the solution is on the arc which connects the two circles (arcs here) centered at I and I' respectively. Here, no node I'' was found, so the best solution is also located on the line which connects the I and I'.

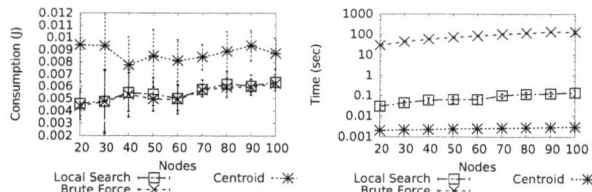

Figure 3: Maximum energy consumption (left) & execution time (right) for variable node populations.

Finally, the results of the comparison between LS, BF and "Centroid" are figured in Figure 3. "Centroid" represents the centroid of the cluster and it is the solution with the minimum computation cost. Its performance is 20-40% lower to that of BF and LS which exhibit similar results in terms of consumption. However, the computation cost of BF is 100 to 1000 times higher than that of LS.

7. CONCLUSION & FUTURE WORK

In this paper, we introduced the problem of the optimal charger placement in RF-energy harvesting networks orga-

nized in clusters. We proposed both localized and a centralized algorithms with good approximation to the optimal. Simulation results showed that the centralized algorithm exhibits a slightly better performance in terms of energy consumption but it presents high computation cost. In the future, we plan to investigate the problem of finding the optimal number of chargers so that budget and network lifetime requirements are met.

8. REFERENCES

[1] R. Aragues, C. Sagues, and Y. Mezouar. *Parallel and Distributed Map Merging and Localization: Algorithms, Tools and Strategies for Robotic Networks*. Springer, 2015.

[2] M. M. Butt, I. Krikidis, A. Mohamed, and M. Guizani. *Energy Management in Wireless Cellular and Ad-hoc Networks*, chapter RF Energy Harvesting Communications: Recent Advances and Research Issues, pages 339–363. Springer International Publishing, Cham, 2016.

[3] H. Dai, Y. Liu, A. X. Liu, L. Kong, G. Chen, and T. He. Radiation constrained wireless charger placement. In *IEEE INFOCOM 2016 - The 35th Annual IEEE International Conference on Computer Communications*, pages 1–9, April 2016.

[4] S. Guo, C. He, and Y. Yang. Resall: Energy efficiency maximization for wireless energy harvesting sensor networks. In *Sensing, Communication, and Networking (SECON), 2015 12th Annual IEEE International Conference on*, pages 64–72, June 2015.

[5] K. Jain and V. V. Vazirani. Approximation algorithms for metric facility location and k-median problems using the primal-dual schema and lagrangian relaxation. *J. ACM*, 48(2):274–296, mar 2001.

[6] A. Z. Kausar, A. W. Reza, M. U. Saleh, and H. Ramiah. Energizing wireless sensor networks by energy harvesting systems: Scopes, challenges and approaches. *Renewable and Sustainable Energy Reviews*, 38:973 – 989, 2014.

[7] X. Lu, P. Wang, D. Niyato, D. I. Kim, and Z. Han. Wireless networks with rf energy harvesting: A contemporary survey. *IEEE Communications Surveys Tutorials*, 17(2):757–789, 2nd quarter 2015.

[8] P. Sommer and R. Wattenhofer. Gradient clock synchronization in wireless sensor networks. In *Information Processing in Sensor Networks (IPSN), International Conference on*, pages 37–48, April 2009.

[9] C. Wang, J. Li, Y. Yang, and F. Ye. A hybrid framework combining solar energy harvesting and wireless charging for wireless sensor networks. In *IEEE International Conference on Computer Communications (INFOCOM '16)*, April 2016.

[10] S. Zhang, Z. Qian, F. Kong, J. Wu, and S. Lu. P3: Joint optimization of charger placement and power allocation for wireless power transfer. In *2015 IEEE Conference on Computer Communications (INFOCOM)*, pages 2344–2352, April 2015.

[11] D. Zorbas, P. Raveneau, and Y. Ghamri-Doudane. Assessing the cost of rf-power harvesting nodes in wireless sensor networks. In *2016 IEEE Global Communications Conference (GLOBECOM)*, Washington, DC, USA, Dec 2016.

Examining Relationships Between 802.11n Physical Layer Transmission Feature Combinations

Ali Abedi
University of Waterloo
ali.abedi@uwaterloo.ca

Tim Brecht
University of Waterloo
brecht@cs.uwaterloo.ca

ABSTRACT

To increase throughput the 802.11n standard introduced several physical layer transmission features including a short guard interval, wider channels, and MIMO. Since obtaining peak throughput depends on choosing the combination of physical layer features (*configuration*) best suited for the channel conditions, the large number of configurations greatly complicates the decision. A deeper understanding of relationships between configurations under a variety of channel conditions should simplify the choices and improve the performance of algorithms selecting configurations. Examples of such algorithms include: rate and channel width adaptation, frame aggregation, and MIMO setting optimization.

We propose a methodology for assessing the possibility of accurate estimation of the frame error rate (FER) of one configuration from the FER of another. Using devices that support up to 3 spatial streams (96 configurations), we conduct experiments under a variety of channel conditions to quantify relationships between configurations. We find that interesting relationships exist between many different configurations. Our results show that in 6 of the 7 scenarios studied *at most five configurations* are required to accurately estimate the error rate *of all remaining 91 configurations* and in the other scenario *at most 15 configurations are required*. Although we show that these relationships may change over time, perhaps most surprising is that relationships have been found over periods of up to *one hour*. These findings suggest optimization algorithms should not need to measure the FER of many configurations, but instead can sample a small subset of configurations to accurately estimate the FER of other configurations. To demonstrate this possibility, we make simple modifications to the Minstrel HT rate adaptation algorithm to exploit relationships and observe improvements in throughput of up to 28%.

1. INTRODUCTION

Advancements in the 802.11 standard have made gigabit per second wireless communication possible by offering

MSWiM '16, November 13-17, 2016, Malta, Malta

© 2016 ACM. ISBN 978-1-4503-4502-6/16/11... $15.00

DOI: http://dx.doi.org/10.1145/2988287.2989159

physical layer transmission features such as denser modulations, channel bonding, and MIMO, in addition to MAC layer frame aggregation. While these advancements help achieve higher data rates, efficient link adaptation in 802.11 networks is more challenging because of these options.

We use *rate configuration* (or simply *configuration*) to refer to a particular combination of physical layer transmission features such as the the modulation and coding scheme, channel width, short/long guard interval (SGI/LGI), and the number of spatial streams. The 802.11g standard offers only 8 configurations. That number has increased to as many as 128 in 802.11n networks (our work examines the 96 configurations available on devices with 3 spatial streams) and up to 640 in 802.11ac networks. Because the 802.11 standard does not specify how to choose physical layer transmission features, optimizing these choices is an active area of research. Examples of such research include: channel bonding [4], rate adaptation [9, 6], energy efficiency [17], QoS analysis [12], and STBC/SDM settings [9].

In rate adaptation studies, the combination of physical layer features used for transmission is chosen by sampling available configurations to determine their effective throughput. However, sampling can incur significant overhead [9] because probe packets are usually sent without frame aggregation. This conservative approach is used because probing often requires testing rates that may fail and the failure of a large number of frames that have been aggregated can negatively impact application performance.

In this paper, our hypothesis is that since several physical layer transmission feature combinations (rate configurations) share common features, (e.g., half use SGI and half use LGI), relationships may exist between the *average frame error rate (FER)* of different configurations. If it is possible to estimate the FER of one configuration from the measured FER of another configuration, algorithms that adapt configurations to changing channel conditions can be simpler and more effective. In this paper, we first develop a methodology for characterizing the relationship between the FER of different configurations. Then we conduct experiments in a variety of settings and report on the relationships we observe. The contributions of this paper are:

- We design a methodology for evaluating relationships among rate configurations that can be used in mobile environments with WiFi and non-WiFi interference.

- We characterize relationships under a variety of channel conditions and study changes in relationships over time. Interestingly, we find that large numbers of relationships exist, over surprisingly long periods of time, even in the presence of mobility and interference.

- Using our methodology, we find that LGI provides higher throughput than SGI in several scenarios. This is contrary to the notion that the LGI may not be required in indoor environments [5, 14, 15, 13].

- By using relationships between configurations, we demonstrate that it is feasible to improve throughput obtained using the Minstrel HT rate adaptation algorithm by up to 28%.

2. METHODOLOGY

Our relationship analysis methodology consists of the following phases: (1) collect data, (2) compute the FER for each rate configuration, and (3) compute relationships between the FER of different configurations. As demonstrated in Section 4, these steps can be used to characterize relationships between configurations.

2.1 Data Collection

To analyze the relationship between two rate configurations, the frame error rate (FER) of these rate configurations must to be measured under identical channel conditions. Hence, previous work [10] [9] has conducted experiments at night without any movement in the environment using the 5 GHz band, while also ensuring that the only interference is controlled interference (e.g., co-channel and adjacent channel interference). Additionally, theses studies use an unmodified rate adaptation algorithm. Therefore, only those rate configurations chosen by the RAA are examined and may not properly cover all configurations.

Previous work [2] has argued that repeating 802.11 experiments with identical channel conditions is difficult. More importantly, experiments from environments with only controlled interference and without mobility are unsuitable for understanding relationships between rate configurations in commonly encountered environments that include mobility and uncontrolled WiFi and non-WiFi interference.

In contrast to previous approaches, we design an experimental methodology for collecting FER information in any environment *and* that also properly covers all configurations. We have used a similar methodology previously [1] to collect representative traces for an 802.11 trace-based simulator. Our methodology does not require repeatability and can therefore be used in uncontrolled environments (including human movement and mobile devices operating in the 2.4 GHz band with WiFi and non-WiFi interference). With our technique, all configurations are sampled in a round-robin fashion. This process is continually repeated to collect information about changes in FERs over time.

Figure 1 shows a data collection example using a device with n rate configurations. Frames are sent with different configurations (denoted $R_1, R_2, ..., R_n$). The fate of each packet is denoted with 1 or 0, representing success or failure. Each sequence of n sampled configurations forms a round.

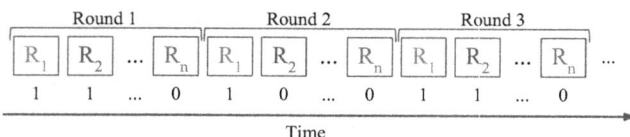

Figure 1: Round-robin data collection methodology

Since configurations in a round are subject to the same channel conditions (they are in the same channel coherence window), when interference does occur all configurations in a round experience the same conditions [2]. Changes, on average, impact each configuration equally. We implement round-robin sampling by modifying the device driver of the sending device used to collect data.

2.2 Frame Error Rate (FER) Computation

We now determine the number of packets required to compute the average FER. We use the following formula for calculating the minimum number of samples required to determine the population mean with a specified level of confidence, when the population standard deviation is known:

$$k > \left(\frac{z * \sigma}{MOE} \right)^2 \qquad (1)$$

For a 95% confidence level, $z = 1.96$. The sample size k is maximized when the standard deviation (σ) is maximized. The value of σ is maximized (i.e., $\sigma = 0.5$) when half of the frames fail and the other half succeed. Using a 10% margin of error (MOE) and confidence level of 95% the minimum sample size required is 97 frames.

Since it takes approximately 43 ms to complete a round for all 96 rate configurations and we need a minimum of 97 observations (i.e., rounds), it takes about 4.2 seconds to collect enough samples to compute an average FER. If the channel access is delayed by WiFi and non-WiFi interference, it takes more than 43 ms to complete a round and more than 4.2 seconds to conduct enough observations to compute the FER. Therefore, we calculate the average FER using a 10 second window, this means the number of samples used in all experiments is 232.

2.3 Relationships and their Computation

Many methodologies could be used to assess the relationship between two rate configurations. We first define what we mean by *relationship* and then describe the methodology used in our study. Section 8 describes several methodologies that seem appropriate but are not suitable. Note that there exist several different connotations of the term relationship and what a relationship between rate configurations might mean. It is important to understand that for the purposes of this paper, we are concerned strictly with the relationships as denoted by the following definition.

2.3.1 Relationships

> **Relationship Definition:**
> We say that there exists a relationship between rate configurations R_1 and R_2 ($R_1 \mapsto R_2$) if the FER of rate configuration R_1 can estimate the FER of rate configuration R_2 with some expected degree of accuracy. In this case, we call R_1 the *estimator* and R_2 the *estimated* configuration. Note that relationships may or may not be reflexive.

To provide the intuition behind our methodology, we first present an example of a relationship analysis between two transmission rate configurations. Using two stationary devices and the 2.4 GHz band, we collect data for all 96 rate configurations and compute the average FER over 10 second windows using the techniques described in Sections 2.1 and 2.2. Figure 3 shows the FERs for two of the 96 configurations, namely 2S-I6-LG-20M=52 (configuration R_1) and 2S-I7-LG-20M=104 (configuration R_2). The transmission rate configuration notation is described in Figure 2.

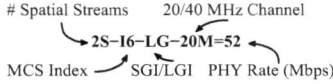

Figure 2: Transmission rate configuration notation

The changes in the FER over 30 minutes can be seen in Figure 3. One can see that the FERs of these two rate configurations seem to change together, suggesting the existence of a relationship between them.

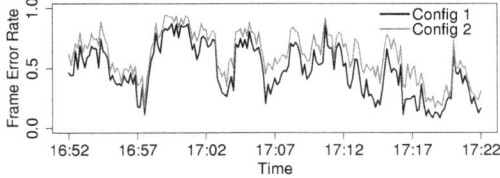

Figure 3: FER of two rate configurations changing over time

Another way to examine the relationship between the FERs of two rate configurations (irrespective of time) is to use a scatter plot with the FERs for one configuration along the x-axis and the FERs of the other configuration along the y-axis. We remove the time component because our goal is to determine relationships that persist over time *even in the presence of changing channel conditions*. If at a point in time, t, in Figure 3 the FERs of configurations R_1 and R_2 are e_1 and e_2, respectively, these two points are represented on the scatter plot (Figure 4) by one point with x and y values of e_1 and e_2, respectively.

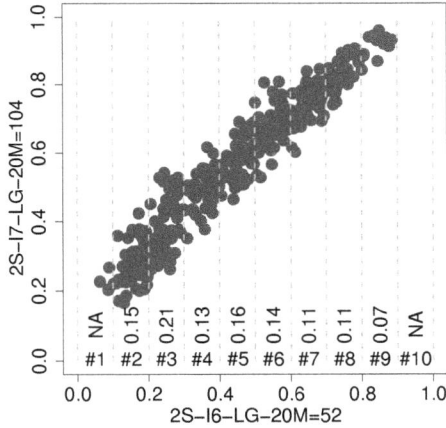

Figure 4: FERs, bins and estimation power for $R_1 \mapsto R_2$

Rate configuration R_1 can *accurately estimate* rate configuration R_2 if the FER values of R_1 are mapped to *a relatively small range* of FERs of R_2. To determine whether or not rate configuration R_1 is an estimator for rate configuration R_2, we divide the data in the scatter plot into bins, illustrated by dashed lines in Figure 4. For our analysis, we have chosen 10 bins, other values are possible and this is discussed in Section 8. Ideally, the dispersion of points (i.e., variation) in the vertical dimension is low in each bin, indicating that a reasonably accurate estimation of the FER of rate configuration R_2 from FER of rate configuration R_1 is possible. In this instance, an accurate estimate the FER of R_2 when the FER of R_1 is 0.85 is possible, because the dispersion of the points in bin #9 is relatively low. However, accurate estimation of the FER of R_2 when the FER of R_1 is 0.25, is not possible, because the corresponding FERs in bin #3 for R_2 have a fairly wide range $(0.22 - 0.57)$.

2.3.2 Estimation Power

Ideally, we would like to summarize the strength of the relationship between two rate configurations with a single quantity. We start by quantifying the variation of data points within each bin. Statistical dispersion, which determines how "stretched" or "squeezed" the distribution of data points are, is one such suitable measure. There are several measures of statistical dispersion that could be used. Range and standard deviation are two common measures. However, these measures are highly sensitive to outliers, which may be common because of potentially high variation in frame error rates over time. On the other hand, other measures such as mean absolute and quartile deviation are more robust to a small number of outliers. We have considered several robust measures of dispersion including *median* absolute deviation (MAD), *mean* absolute deviation, and interquartile range (IQR). In this paper, we have chosen to use the interdecile range which is the difference between the first and the ninth deciles (i.e., the first 10% and last 90%). This measure provides the characteristics desired for this study such as excluding some but not too many outliers. We found that other measures can provide undesirable or misleading values (discussed in more detail in Section 8).

We now provide an example of how we apply the interdecile range to the FER data to obtain a single quantity that represents the strength of the relationship between two rate configurations. As depicted in Figure 4, in each bin the vertical dispersion of the values is calculated based on the interdecile range which is written above the bin number. The interdecile range values quantify the dispersion in each bin and provide a measure of the relationship between two rate configurations based the variation of FER in each bin. Note that bins with fewer than 5 values are ignored (labeled as NA, for not applicable), as they do not contain enough data points to provide a reliable measure of dispersion. We describe the importance of bins labeled NA and how we account for them in Section 2.3.3.

To examine relationships between $96 \times 96 = 9,216$ pairs of configurations, we define *estimation power* which aggregates dispersion values from all bins for each pair of configurations.

Estimation Power: $\mathbf{EP}(R_1, R_2)$
The estimation power of a relationship between rate configurations R_1 and R_2 is a measure of the expected ability of the FER of R_1 to estimate the FER of R_2. It is calculated as the fraction of bins with an interdecile range below a specified threshold.

The total number of bins excludes those that do not have a sufficient number of data points for the interdecile range to be deemed reliable (we use 5). We use a threshold of 0.2 and discuss both choices in Section 8. In the example in Figure 4, the estimation power of rate configuration R_1 to estimate rate configuration R_2, $EP(R_1, R_2) = \frac{7}{8}$.

2.3.3 Variability Indicator

The estimation power (EP) is valuable for quantifying the relationship between two rate configurations. However, we found it beneficial to be able to differentiate types of relationships based on why they exist. We define a new metric called the *Variability Indicator* (VI) that quantifies this variation. Note that the variability indicator is not used to quantify the relationship nor to indicate the lack of a relationship but to interpret and understand the EP.

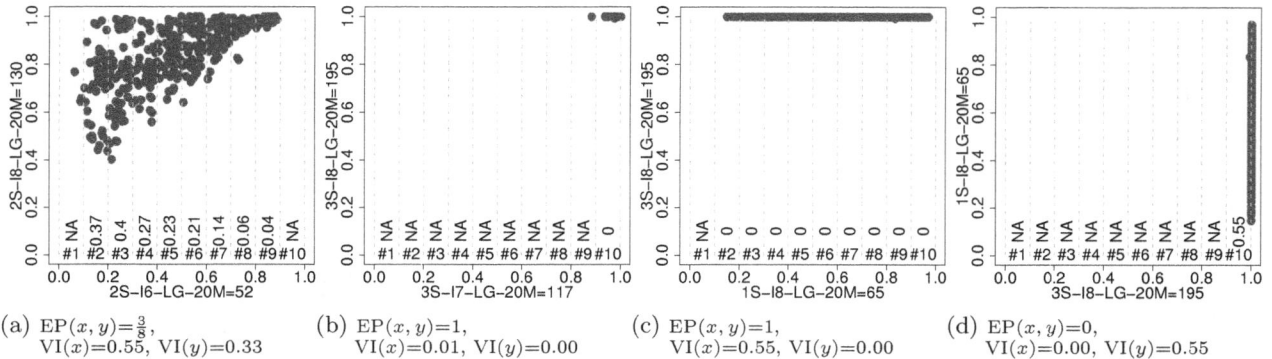

(a) EP$(x, y) = \frac{3}{8}$,
VI$(x) = 0.55$, VI$(y) = 0.33$

(b) EP$(x, y) = 1$,
VI$(x) = 0.01$, VI$(y) = 0.00$

(c) EP$(x, y) = 1$,
VI$(x) = 0.55$, VI$(y) = 0.00$

(d) EP$(x, y) = 0$,
VI$(x) = 0.00$, VI$(y) = 0.55$

Figure 5: Estimation Power (EP) and Variability Indicators (VIs)

Variability Indicator (VI):
The variability indicator is a measure of the variability of the frame error rate of a rate configuration. The metric we use is the interdecile range of the FERs of a given configuration over the course of an experiment.

As discussed in Section 2.3.2, interdecile range is a suitable metric for quantifying the variation or dispersion of frame error rates. The variability indicator helps us to better understand the underlying reasons for the existence or nonexistence of a relationship between two configurations. It is important to note that *relationships can exist regardless of the value of the variability indicator.* In Section 4.1, we use this measure to help explain the estimation power.

2.3.4 Understanding Our Metrics

To better understand the estimation power metric and the need for the variability indicator metric, we review some scatter plots for other pairs of configurations from the same experiment as used in Figure 4. The caption for each subfigure shows the values for the estimation power and variability indicator metrics. The EP metric indicates the ability of the rate configuration on the x-axis to estimate the FER of the configuration on the y-axis. The VI metric is shown for the configurations on both the x and y axes.

Figure 5a shows that within several bins the vertical dispersion of FERs is relatively high. This results in the low estimation power metric ($\frac{3}{8}$) which means that the x-axis configuration (2S-I6-LG-20M=52) is not able to estimate the y-axis configuration (2S-I8-LG-20M=130). Figure 5b and 5c show an example of one rate configuration (3S-I8-LG-20M=195, on the y-axis) with a constant FER (i.e., VI(y) = 0.00). The constant FER makes it possible to accurately estimate this configuration from all other configurations regardless of their variation in FER. For example, the estimator configuration in Figure 5b has low variation (i.e., VI(x) = 0.01), while the estimator configuration in Figure 5c has relatively high variation (i.e., VI(x) = 0.55).

Figure 5d demonstrates why an estimator configuration with a constant FER (i.e., FER is always 1) cannot estimate a configuration with highly variable FER. In this case, highly dispersed data points are all gathered in one bin (i.e., #10) making an accurate estimation impossible, as indicated by the EP value of 0. To emphasize that EP is a directional metric, Figure 5d shows the same configurations as Figure 5c, except we have switched the estimator and estimated configurations. As discussed in Section 8, symmetric measures that are oblivious to the direction of the relationship (e.g., correlation coefficient and R^2 obtained from a statistical regression), are not suitable for this study.

3. EXPERIMENTAL ENVIRONMENT

We have created a small test bed for conducting experiments. This test bed is housed within lab and office space in a building on a university campus.

Our access point and stationary clients are desktop systems, each containing a TP-Link TL-WDN4800 dual-band wireless N PCI-E adapter. These cards use the Atheros AR9380 chipset and support up to three streams (i.e., a 3x3:3 MIMO configuration). This device uses the Ath9k (Atheros) device driver. For mobile experiments, we use a laptop configured to use a TP-Link TL-WDN4200 dual-band wireless N USB adapter. This adapter contains an Ralink RT3573 chipset and also supports a 3x3:3 configuration. This device uses the rt2800usb (Ralink) device driver.

To fully utilize the network infrastructure, we use iperf [7] to generate UDP traffic from the access point to a client at as high a packet rate as possible. We have modified the Ath9k device driver to implement a rate configuration selection algorithm that transmits using each configuration in a round-robin fashion as explained in Section 2.1. To record much of the information reported in this study, we use highly detailed information obtained directly from the Ath9k driver. Since we are interested in physical layer relationships, MAC layer frame aggregation is disabled to increase the efficiency of the data collection mechanism. In future work, we plan to investigate frame aggregation.

3.1 Different Scenarios Studied

We conduct experiments under a variety of channel conditions including stationary and mobile devices both with and without interference. In some experiments, we use the 5 GHz band to examine channels that are free of interference. In this case, we use a spectrum analyzer to ensure that there is no WiFi or non-WiFi interference. For other experiments, we use the 2.4 GHz band to ensure that the channel is exposed to different types of WiFi and non-WiFi interference. We intentionally selected channel 6 which overlaps with the channel used by the campus WiFi network to test our ability to study relationships in uncontrolled environments.

In mobile experiments, a laptop (i.e., receiver) is carried at walking speed for 15 minutes. The mobile experiments are conducted in two environments (referred to as *office* and *hallway*) which we designed to exercise a variety of channel conditions. In the office environment, no line-of-sight exists between the AP and client for most of the experiment, as the signal is blocked by obstacles such as metal cabinets, cubicle partitions and walls. In these experiments, the distance between the AP and client ranges from 1 meter to about 20 meters. In the hallway experiments, a line-of-sight exists between the AP and client, and the distance between them changes from 1 meter to 60 meters.

In the stationary experiments, the AP and client are placed in different rooms in an office environment with no line of sight. All experiments are conducted during the day with people moving in and between offices (this can cause signal attenuation and influence multipath propagation).

To better understand the experimental scenarios, we present some statistical characteristics of the collected data. We classify each of the 96 rate configurations into three categories. The first two, FER < 0.1 and FER > 0.9, indicate that all frame error rate measurements for that configuration are bounded by these values. The variability indicator is low for these categories. The final category captures all configurations that do not fit into the first two categories. Table 1 shows, for each scenario, the number of configurations in each category. We observe that in the stationary 5 GHz experiment, which is our most stable environment, the FER of 71 configurations (out of 96) are either less than 0.1 (i.e., most frames are received successfully), or greater than 0.9 (i.e., most frames are lost). The same stationary experiment (with constant transmission power) using the 2.4 GHz band shows different behavior due to WiFi and non-WiFi interference; even the most robust modulation and coding schemes experience errors in presence of interference. Moreover, 11 configurations nearly almost always fail in this scenario.

	Office					Hallway	
	Stationary		Mobile			Mobile	
Scenario	1	2	3	4	5	6	7
Band (GHz)	2.4	5	5†	2.4	5	2.4	5
FER < 0.1	0	51	0	0	0	0	0
FER > 0.9	11	20	24	0	4	12	9
0.1 ≤ FER ≤ 0.9	85	25	72	96	92	84	87

Table 1: Characteristics of scenarios († = TX power cycling)

To introduce more variability in the FER for the 5 GHz stationary experiment and to increase the variability indicator in that scenario, we conduct another experiment where the transmission power is changed. Transmission starts at the default maximum setting of 30 dBm and is decreased by 1 dBm every 30 seconds until it reaches 0 dBm. It then increases transmission power by 1 dBm until it reaches 30 dBm and repeats in a round-robin fashion. The table shows that in this experiment the FER of the majority of rate configurations are now variable and even the most robust configurations experience some errors.

As mentioned previously, the mobile experiments were designed so that a variety of channel conditions are observed during the experiment. The data in Table 1 confirms that a majority of configurations experience a variable FER during the experiment. Note that in three of these four scenarios, the FER of some configurations are constantly above 0.9, even though the distance between the AP and the mobile client is about one meter during some points in the movement trajectory. A closer inspection of the raw data showed that these are the rate configurations that result in the high-

est physical data rates which never find the perfect channel conditions they need.[1]

4. CHARACTERIZATION RESULTS

In this section we utilize the proposed methodology to examine relationships among 802.11n rate configurations.

4.1 Examining Relationships

We first examine the *estimation power (EP)* and *variability indicator (VI)* of different configurations. Since 96 configurations are supported in our 802.11n cards, 9,216 (i.e., 96×96) relationships can be examined in each experiment.

Figure 6a illustrates the relationships between all 96 configurations for the 5 GHz office scenario with stationary devices (Scenario 2). The large square heat map (the EP heat map) shows the estimation power of a configuration on the x-axis for estimating the FER of the configuration on the y-axis. Each row and column in this heat map represents a rate configuration. Note that there are 96 configurations on each axis, but labels are removed as they are unnecessary for the high level view we start with. Later we present subsets of such heat maps in order to have a closer look at some particular relationships. The colors encode ranges for the estimation power (EP) as follows: high ($EP \geq 0.7$) in green, medium ($0.5 \leq EP < 0.7$) in yellow and low ($EP < 0.5$) in red. As depicted in Figure 6a the estimation power of all pairs of configurations are very high. To understand why, we study the variability of the FER of these rate configurations.

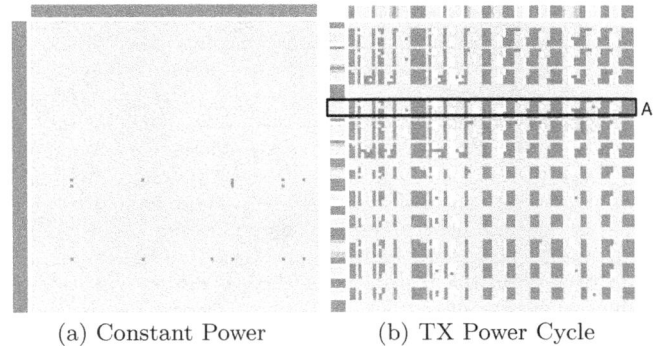

(a) Constant Power   (b) TX Power Cycle

Figure 6: Office: stationary, 5 GHz, 96x96

The thin heat maps at the top of and to the left the EP heat map represent the variability indicator for the estimator and estimated configurations and will be referred to as VI heat maps. The two VI heat maps are always identical but they are shown on both axes for readability. For the VI heat maps the colors encode ranges for the variability indicator as follows: very high ($VI > 0.75$) in green, high ($0.5 < VI \leq 0.75$) in yellow, medium ($0.25 < VI \leq 0.50$) in orange, and low ($VI \leq 0.25$) in red.

Interestingly, in Figure 6a, the variability indicator is quite low for all rate configurations. This indicates that the FERs do not change significantly. In this scenario, the main reason for so many strong relationships is because the FER of all configurations are mainly constant and are, therefore, easy to estimate. Note that in some of these cases one configuration may consistently fail (e.g., 3S-I8-SG-40M=450)

---

[1]This may be because, at short distances, the multipath field is insufficiently rich for the three antennas in the small USB WiFi adapter.

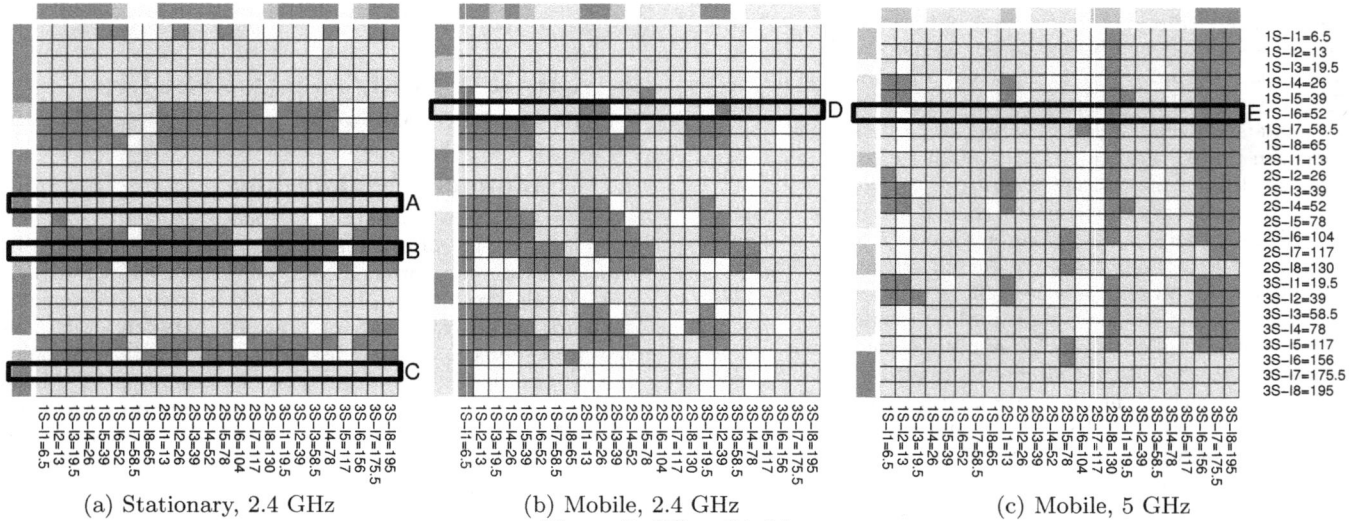

(a) Stationary, 2.4 GHz   (b) Mobile, 2.4 GHz   (c) Mobile, 5 GHz

Figure 7: Office, 24x24

while the other is consistently successful (e.g., 1S-I1-LG-20M=6.5). Nevertheless, this is a strong relationship.

In an attempt to see if any relationships exist when the FERs are variable, we program the AP to change transmission power as described in Section 3.1 (Scenario 3). The results are presented in Figure 6b. The differences between the VI heat maps in Figure 6a (which contain only red) and Figure 6b (which also contain some green, and some yellow) indicate that the changes in transmission power increase the variability of FERs. The EP heat map in Figure 6b shows that many rate configurations are still strongly related despite some FERs being highly variable. For example, although the few configurations in the rows outlined by the rectangle labelled "A" have highly variable FERs as depicted by green cells in the VI plot, we observe that there are many green cells in these rows in the EP heat map. Each green EP heat map cell indicates that the corresponding x-axis configuration can accurately estimate the y-axis configuration. As can be seen in the rectangle "A", many rate configurations can accurately estimate the y-axis configurations in those rows. Note that despite changing the transmission power, the variability of the FERs of some configurations is still low. By examining details of the collected FER data, we find that these configurations consistently fail in Scenario 2 which uses the maximum transmission power. As a result, lowering the transmission power (in Scenario 3) does not affect the FER of these configurations.

To examine some relationships in more detail, we now consider a subset of all rate configurations in the office scenarios. Figures 7a, 7b and 7c, show relationship results for the stationary (2.4 GHz) and mobile (2.4 and 5 GHz) scenarios, respectively (i.e., Scenarios 1, 4, and 5). In these scenarios, we examine only those configurations that use a long guard interval (LGI) and 20 MHz channels. This restricts the number of configurations to 24 (8 MCSes × 3 spatial streams) and the heat maps to 24 × 24 pairs of configurations.

In all graphs in Figure 7, we see patterns of colors suggesting the existence of relationships between estimation power and combinations of physical layer transmission features. The green cells (indicating a high estimation power) are not scattered randomly on the EP heat maps, but rather clustered in specific patterns based on the physical layer config-

urations indicated on the x and y axes. We now examine these plots in more detail to better understand these results.

In the stationary scenario, by comparing the relationships in the 2.4 GHz and 5 GHz bands (Scenario 1 in Figure 7a and Scenario 2 in Figure 6a), we observe more red cells in the 2.4 GHz scenario indicating a decrease in the number of related configurations. The major difference between these experiments is the lack of interference in the 5 GHz band. Figure 7a shows that some configurations, such as 2S-I4=52 (see rectangle "A"), can be estimated accurately by many configurations. The variation of the FER of this configuration is low (i.e., indicated by the red cell in the left VI heat map). Therefore, it is easy to estimate. On the other hand, configurations such as 2S-I7=117 (see rectangle "B") that have higher variation of FER (indicated by the yellow square in the left VI heat map), can be more difficult to estimate. In Figure 7a, the variability indicator is low for two groups of configurations: (a) configurations that consistently succeed (in this scenario) such as 2S-I4=52 (rectangle "A") and (b) configurations that consistently fail (in this scenario) such as 3S-I7=175.5 (rectangle "C"). Other configurations, which are not in either of these groups, experience variable FER such as 2S-I7-117 (rectangle "B").

Figures 7b and 7c show the relationships for a scenario where the client (i.e., receiver) device is moving at walking speed in an office environment using the 2.4 and 5 GHz bands (Scenarios 4 and 5). We consider these scenarios to study the effect of mobility on relationships. These are highly variable environments due to mobility. This can also be seen by the number of green cells in the VI heat maps when compared to their stationary counterparts. Figures 7b and 7c illustrate that strong relationships exist between many rate configurations. Interestingly, in both scenarios, for the estimated (y-axis) configurations with highly variable FERs (i.e., green or yellow cells in the left VI heat map), there are several (x-axis) configurations that can accurately estimate them. For example, configuration 1S-I6=52 (rectangles "D" and "E") has a highly variable FER in both scenarios as indicated by the corresponding green cells in the left VI heat maps. However, as depicted in Figures 7b, and 7c there are several green cells in the 1S-I6=52 rows ("D" and "E"), indicating the existence of several estimators for

| EP Threshold | Stat | Office: Stationary | | | | | | Office: Mobile | | | | Hallway: Mobile | | | |
| | | Scenario 1 2.4 GHz 60 minutes | | Scenario 2 5 GHz 60 minutes | | Scenario 3† 5 GHz 60 minutes | | Scenario 4 2.4 GHz 15 minutes | | Scenario 5 5 GHz 15 minutes | | Scenario 6 2.4 GHz 15 minutes | | Scenario 7 5 GHz 15 minutes | |
		$\|* \mapsto R\|$	$\|R \mapsto *\|$	$\|* \mapsto R\|$	$\|R \mapsto *\|$	$\|* \mapsto R\|$	$\|R \mapsto *\|$	$\|* \mapsto R\|$	$\|R \mapsto *\|$	$\|* \mapsto R\|$	$\|R \mapsto *\|$	$\|* \mapsto R\|$	$\|R \mapsto *\|$	$\|* \mapsto R\|$	$\|R \mapsto *\|$
0.7	Min	1	32	88	91	18	33	6	4	13	19	11	19	4	17
	Max	95	66	95	95	95	95	61	77	95	59	95	80	95	92
	Min SC	5 – 11		1		1		3		2		3		2	
1.0	Min	1	19	88	91	1	33	6	3	13	19	10	19	3	17
	Max	95	41	95	95	95	63	60	68	95	59	95	68	95	55
	Min SC	5 – 15		1		5		4		2		3		3	

Table 2: Summary of relationships. † indicates TX power cycling

this configuration. The red cells in the 1S-I6=52 rows correspond mostly to the estimators with low variability FERs (i.e., indicated by red cells in the top VI heat map), as it is difficult for their relatively constant FER to estimate a variable FER. We have highlighted a few interesting scenarios and now present an overview of the relationships.

4.2 Overview of Relationships

To provide a high level view of the number and strength of different relationships, we summarize the results from all experiments in Table 2. One measure of interest presented in this table is the count of the number of other rate configurations that can be used to estimate a particular rate configuration R, denoted $|* \mapsto R|$. Another metric we present is the count of the number of other rate configurations that a particular rate configuration R can estimate, denoted $|R \mapsto *|$. To quantify if R_1 can estimate R_2, we use a threshold for the estimation power. In the heat maps shown in this paper we have used a threshold of 0.7 to indicate a very strong relationship. As a result, we also use this threshold when computing the data presented in Table 2. The intuition is that if the estimation power of R_1 when estimating R_2 is greater than or equal to 0.7, we presume that R_1 can estimate R_2. In addition, to study the impact of that threshold on our results we also include computations using the most conservative threshold possible (1.0). Recall that this means that the dispersion metric in *all bins* must be no greater than the dispersion threshold (i.e., 0.2).

Table 2 shows a variety of information for the seven scenarios examined. For each scenario, we present the Min, Max and Min SC values for the defined measures $|* \mapsto R|$ and $|R \mapsto *|$. The Min and Max values are of interest in understanding the number of relationships that exist between different configurations (Min SC will be described later). The greater the number of relationships, the more likely we are to be able to accurately estimate the FER of one configuration from the FER of one or more other configurations.

We start by focusing on the values obtained with a threshold of 0.7. In the worst case (i.e., the lowest value) across all scenarios, there is only one estimator ($|* \mapsto R|$) for a particular rate which occurs in Scenario 1 (see the row labelled "Min" and column $|* \mapsto R|$). When examining the number of configurations that can be estimated by a single rate ($|R \mapsto *|$), the minimum value is 4, which occurs in Scenario 4 (see the row labelled "Min" and column $|R \mapsto *|$).

We now consider the minimum number of rate configurations that are required to be able to estimate (i.e., cover) all other rate configurations. This problem is equivalent to the *minimum set cover* problem which is NP-hard [8]. Interestingly, the minimum set cover in six (i.e., Scenarios 2 – 7) of the seven scenarios was small enough (the largest of these

was 3), that we were able to find them using a brute force approach that examines all sets up to size 4. These small values indicate that there are a number of strong relationships that could potentially be exploited. In Scenario 1, we have used a heuristic search to determine that the set cover size is between 5 and 11. The results for all scenarios are shown in the row labelled Min SC in Table 2.

We now focus on the values obtained in Table 2 using the most conservative threshold of 1.0. Comparing the values obtained using the two different thresholds shows that in most instances the values do not change significantly. Furthermore, the size of the minimum set cover is unchanged in three of the seven scenarios and increases only slightly in the other four. Note that the precise numbers in these tables depend on the various parameters used to determine whether relationships exist or not. The impact of these choices is discussed in Section 8.

It is interesting to note that there are large numbers of strong relationships between a variety of different configurations in the experiments conducted using the interference free, 5 GHz band. This can be seen in Figure 6 and from the data provided in Table 2. Perhaps more compelling, however, are the surprisingly large numbers of relationships in the 2.4 GHz and mobile experiments. We believe that these are intriguing results considering: (1) The complexity of the interactions of the large number of possible configurations of physical layer features. (2) The constantly changing channel conditions due to WiFi and non-WiFi interference in the uncontrolled 2.4 GHz experiments (Scenarios 1, 4 and 6). (3) The continual fluctuations in signal quality due to mobility (Scenarios 4 – 7). (4) The relatively long period of time over which these relationships hold (e.g., data for the stationary experiments covers 1 hour).

4.3 Changes in Relationships Over Time

To study if and how relationships might change over time, we start with a simple demonstration by dividing the one hour stationary 2.4 GHz experiment (i.e., Scenario 1) into four 15 minute experiments and perform the same statistical analysis over each time window. Table 3 presents the relationship data for each sub-window (EP threshold = 0.7). We observe that various measures of relationship change with time. For example, the size of the minimum set cover which was calculated to be between 5 and 11 over the full 1 hour experiments is 1, between 5 and 7, 5, and 1 for the four 15 minute sub-windows. These are significant reductions that demonstrate that a greater number of strong relationships may exist over shorter time intervals and that relationships between rate configurations vary over time. The time window over which relationships will be computed in practice will depend on the application in which they are being used.

However, because we have found evidence that relationships can be found over periods of 15 to 60 minutes in the scenarios we have examined, applications should not have to recompute relationships too frequently.

Stat	0–15 Min $\|*\mapsto R\|$	$\|R\mapsto*\|$	15–30 Min $\|*\mapsto R\|$	$\|R\mapsto*\|$	30–45 Min $\|*\mapsto R\|$	$\|R\mapsto*\|$	45–60 Min $\|*\mapsto R\|$	$\|R\mapsto*\|$	Overall $\|*\mapsto R\|$	$\|R\mapsto*\|$
Min	5	40	1	43	3	19	10	40	1	32
Max	95	75	95	77	95	72	95	95	95	66
Min SC	3		5 – 7		5		1		5 – 11	

Table 3: Changes in relationships over time, scenario 1

5. STUDYING PHY LAYER FEATURES

In this section, we use our methodology to better understand the efficacy of short and long guard intervals and then analyze the relationships that exist because of this feature.

5.1 Efficacy of LGI and SGI

Some people have argued that, for indoor environments, the 800 ns guard interval (LGI) used in 802.11 protocols prior to 802.11n was more conservative than necessary [5, 14, 15, 13]. As a result, the shorter 400 ns guard interval (SGI) was introduced in the 802.11n standard. Because we are not aware of any empirical studies that examine if there is a need for the LGI in indoor 802.11n networks, we utilize our methodology to study this issue.

Suppose we examine the FER of all rate configurations that differ only in whether they use LGI or SGI (i.e., other features are the same). If their FERs are nearly identical, it indicates that shrinking the guard interval from 800 to 400 ns for these particular rate configurations does not have an adverse effect on the FER in the scenarios examined. Therefore, SGI should be used instead of LGI, since it provides higher throughput in situations where the FERs of LGI and SGI are the same.

The FERs of a pair of rate configurations, 1S-I2-LG-20M=19.5 and 1S-I2-SG-20M=21.7, are shown in Figure 8. The only difference between these configurations is the length of their guard intervals. The data was collected using the office, mobile scenario using both the 2.4 and 5 GHz bands (i.e., Scenarios 4 and 5). When using the 5 GHz band, the FER of the SGI configuration is generally higher than the LGI configuration. We also observe this behavior for many pairs of rate configurations that differ only in their use of SGI or LGI (not shown here) in the 5 GHz band office and hallway scenarios (i.e., Scenarios 5 and 7). Interestingly, when using the 2.4 GHz spectrum (i.e., Scenarios 4 and 6), the ratio of the FERs are close to equal.

We believe different results are seen in the 2.4 and 5 GHz bands because many building materials reflect 5 GHz signals orders of magnitude better than 2.4 GHz signals [16]. Thus, the delay spread can be longer for 5 GHz signals, increasing the FER of SGI rate configurations because reflected signals arrive after the SGI and interfere with next symbol.

We now study if the observed difference in FER is significant enough to result in the inferior performance of the SGI configuration. The short guard interval provides a throughput increase of at most 11% when compared with the throughput of the corresponding LGI configuration. If the FER of the SGI configuration is too high, the extra throughput achieved from the SGI can no longer compensate for the higher FER. The blue dashed line (labeled "Threshold") shows this threshold. Points above this line indicate

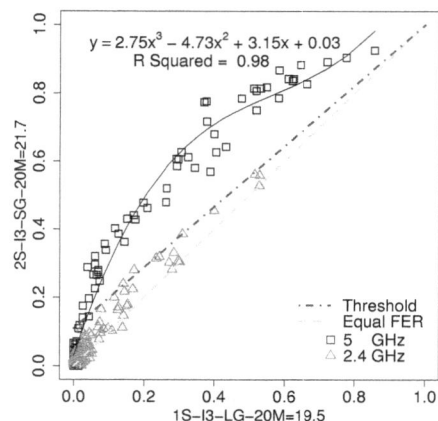

Figure 8: Office: mobile, 2.4 and 5 GHz

that the throughput of the LGI configuration is higher than the SGI configuration. As seen in Figure 8, in the 5 GHz band, many data points are above this line, indicating that the LGI configuration provides higher throughput than the SGI configuration. We observed similar results for other pairs of rate configurations and scenarios. Therefore, in the 5 GHz band, using the LGI could provide higher throughput for some configurations.

5.2 Relationship Between LGI and SGI

We now more closely examine the existence of relationships between LGI and SGI rate configurations. Figure 8 shows a non-linear relationship for the 5 GHz experiment. We found that a quadratic regression model (shown at the top of the figure) fits the data very well (i.e., $R^2 = 0.98$). To verify that LGI and SGI rate configurations are related for other combinations of physical layer transmission rate features and other scenarios, we compute the estimation power from LGI to SGI configurations and from SGI to LGI configurations for all other scenarios and rate configurations (i.e., 48 configurations). Figure 9 shows the estimation power for all configurations for Scenarios 1, 2, 4, and 5 (from top to bottom, respectively). The graphs plot the rate configuration on the x-axis and the estimation power value on the y-axis for both the LGI $\mapsto$ SGI and LGI $\mapsto$ SGI relationships. Note that we only label every 2nd rate configuration on the x-axis. The results show that the relationships are strong between all pairs of configurations that differ only by the guard interval length. Similar results were observed for the other scenarios. In the next section, we utilize the relationships between LGI and SGI configurations to demonstrate how a rate adaptation algorithm might utilize such relationships to optimize transmission rate feature configurations.

6. IMPACT ON APPLICATIONS

Many rate adaptation algorithms (RAAs), including the Minstrel HT algorithm implemented in the widely used Ath9K driver, rely on sampling to determine the best rate configuration. Unfortunately, the overhead of sampling is significant [9]. In order to reduce this overhead, the sampling frequency can be reduced by sampling a smaller subset of rate configurations and utilizing relationships between FERs to estimate the FERs of the remaining rates.

To demonstrate the impact of utilizing relationships in rate adaptation, we modify Minstrel HT to estimate the FER of LGI configurations from the SGI configurations (in-

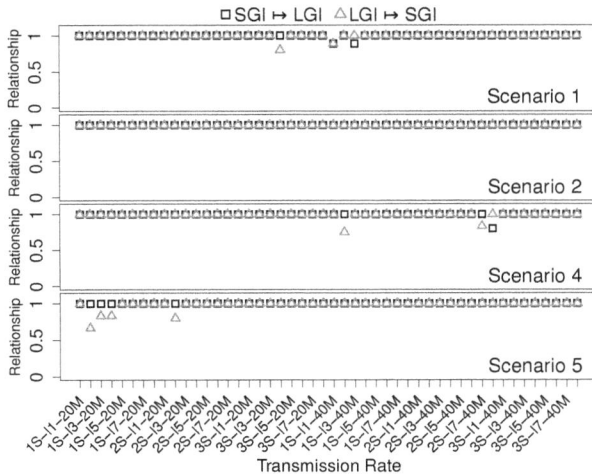

Figure 9: EP of SGI/LGI rate configurations

stead of sampling LGI configurations). In this way, we reduce the frequency at which different configurations are probed. We refer to this modified version as Minstrel HT Relationship. Our estimation function assumes that the FERs of two rate configurations are identical if the configurations only differ in the guard interval. Note that the RAA may still select LGI configurations, it just does not sample them. Although in Section 5.1 we show that in the 5 GHz bands the FER of the SGI configurations are sometimes higher, the performance results indicate that our estimation function is sufficiently accurate for this illustration. We run each experiment multiple times and present the average throughput with 95% confidence intervals in Figure 10. The two pairs of outer bars show that Minstrel HT Relationship increases throughput when compared with the vanilla version by 28% and 17%, in the stationary 2.4 GHz and mobile 5 GHz scenarios, respectively. The middle bars in each grouping show the throughput obtained using Minstrel HT when the probing frequency is reduced (Low Sample Rate) to that used by Minstrel HT Relationship. The gaps between the "Low Sample Rate" bars and the "Relationship" bars demonstrate that throughput is improved as a result of using relationships and does not come only from reducing the number of probed configurations.

These findings demonstrate the potential power of exploiting relationships among rate configurations in algorithms that optimize the selection of physical layer transmission features. Designing and comprehensively evaluating an RAA to fully utilize relationships is outside the scope of this paper and is left for future work.

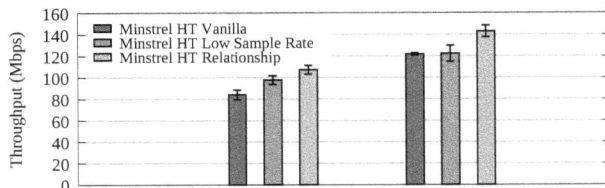

Figure 10: Impact of using relationships in RAAs

7. RELATED WORK

To better understand 802.11n networks, researchers have characterized these networks from different perspectives, such as the relationship between physical layer features and

throughput [10], jitter and energy efficiency [17]. We now review some of these 802.11n characterization studies. Although some of these studies are not directly related to our work, they help to understand different viewpoints related to the characterization of 802.11n networks.

LaCurts et al. [11] use over 1,400 access points to empirically study the correlation between sender-side SNR and throughput. The results show that SNR is not sufficient to determine the best transmission rate for a network although with sufficient training, SNR can be a good predictor of the throughput for a specific link. Halperin et al. [6] have conducted a similar study and found that due to the frequency selective fading problem,[2] the SNR is an inaccurate metric of the quality of the communication channel as it does not represent the quality of the signal received by each OFDM sub-carrier. They propose and evaluate a packet delivery prediction model that uses the effective SNR which is derived from the Channel State Information (CSI). The shortcoming of this technique is that in practice many 802.11n chipsets do not report the channel state information [3, 9] and a mechanism is required to transfer CSI data (only available at the receiver) back to the sender.

To our knowledge, the closest work to ours is the study conducted by Kriara et al. [10]. They characterize the positive and negative impacts of each physical transmission feature on throughput, FER and jitter. The authors argue that to maximize throughput all transmission features should be optimized jointly. In other words, if the transmission features are optimized one by one, a sub-optimal throughput might be achieved. This finding emphasizes the need to limit the search space when selecting the best rate configuration, as a divide and conquer approach does not work.

To limit the search space when optimizing the rate configuration, Kriara et al. [9] utilize sender side RSSI information to reduce the number rate configurations that need to be probed. In some scenarios, they are able to improve rate adaptation by reducing the overhead of probing many configurations. The data collection methodology used in [9] requires repeatability across experiments. Therefore, all experiments conducted to measure the relationship between RSSI and transmission features are done in controlled environments with no mobility and no interference other than those introduced by the experimenters. Additionally, their methodology only obtains information about rates if and when they are selected by the RAA. We postulate that this is why their algorithm does not obtain benefits in some of the uncontrolled environments they have evaluated. On the other hand, our data collection methodology examines all rates equally and can be used in controlled and uncontrolled environments without any restrictions.

In contrast with all previous work, we characterize the relationship among rate configurations in order to find how accurately the FER of one rate configuration can estimate the FER of another configuration. We show how these relationships can be used to provide new insights into the behaviour of different physical layer features (e.g., SGI and LGI). Additionally, we demonstrate how relationships might be used to reduce the search space when choosing the best combination of physical layer transmission features.

---

[2]OFDM sub-carriers suffer from different and independent fading, rendering the average SNR over all sub-carriers a very coarse and inaccurate metric for the quality of the received signal.

8. DISCUSSION

Our results are limited to the scenarios and hardware used for these experiments. However, the number of strong relationships between many configurations across the scenarios examined suggests that interesting relationships are likely to exist under a variety of channel conditions.

Our methodology utilizes several parameters such as: the number of bins (10), the minimum number of data points required for the dispersion metric to be considered reliable (5), the threshold for the interdecile range for a bin to be considered acceptable for accurate estimation (0.2) and the value used to consider the estimation power metric to be good enough to consider the relationship as strong (0.7 for the heat maps). We chose these parameters based on visual inspection of significant amounts of data and by trying to find a set of parameters and a methodology that are fairly intuitive. We believe that the chosen parameters are fairly conservative. However, the best choice of these values will depend on the purpose of the particular characterization study or the application to which it is being applied. Topics for future research include: the choice of parameters, good estimator functions and studying their accuracy.

To choose the most suitable methodology for characterizing relationships we have considered many different methodologies including but not limited to correlation, conditional entropy, and parametric and non-parametric regression. As outlined in Section 2.3 our definition of relationship is, *by necessity* a directional measure. Unfortunately, many techniques such as correlation (e.g., the Pearson product-moment correlation coefficient), and R^2 of regression provide the same value for $R_1 \mapsto R_2$ and $R_2 \mapsto R_1$ relationships which is not true of the relationships we believe are interesting for this study. In addition, correlation only detects simple linear correlations; however, we found non-linear relationships between rate configurations. For these key reasons, correlation and R^2 were not used in this study. While conditional entropy does consider the direction of the relationship, it is not defined for some special but critical cases we observe. For example, it is not defined when there is no variability in the FER of the estimator rate configuration. Therefore, it cannot be used to quantify estimation power.

We chose to focus on the 802.11n standard because it is widely used, it supports both 2.4 and 5 GHz bands and because the open source Ath9k driver made it possible to implement our data collection methodology quickly and easily. Although we believe that many of our findings will apply in 802.11ac networks because they use share many physical layer features with 802.11n networks, studying 802.11ac networks is left for future work.

9. CONCLUSIONS

In this paper, we design a methodology for evaluating the relationships between the FER of different physical layer transmission feature combinations (rate configurations). We find that in all seven scenarios examined, a surprisingly small number of rate configurations can estimate the FER of all other configurations. Interestingly, although we demonstrate that relationships can change over time, relationships are observed in uncontrolled environments over periods of up to one hour. Finally, by utilizing a small fraction of relationships, we provide a simple illustration of how the throughput of the widely used Minstrel HT algorithm can be increased

by up to 28% in the uncontrolled environments tested. This demonstrates that there are significant opportunities for utilizing relationships between rate configurations in designing algorithms that must chose the best combination of physical layer features from a large number of possibilities.

10. ACKNOWLEDGMENTS

Funding for this project was provided in part by a Natural Sciences and Engineering Research Council (NSERC) of Canada Discovery Grant and a Discovery Accelerator Supplement. The authors thank Andrew Heard for many fruitful discussions and help with some initial experiments during the early phases of this work as well as Martin Karsten, Kamal Rahimi Malekshan and the anonymous reviewers for their feedback on previous drafts of this paper.

11. REFERENCES

[1] ABEDI, A., AND BRECHT, T. T-RATE: A framework for the trace-driven evaluation of 802.11 rate adaptation algorithms. In *MASCOTS* (2014).

[2] ABEDI, A., HEARD, A., AND BRECHT, T. Conducting repeatable experiments and fair comparisons using 802.11n MIMO networks. *SIGOPS Oper. Syst. Rev. 49*, 1 (2015).

[3] BISWAS, S., BICKET, J., WONG, E., MUSALOIU-E, R., BHARTIA, A., AND AGUAYO, D. Large-scale measurements of wireless network behavior. In *SIGCOMM* (2015).

[4] DEEK, L., GARCIA-VILLEGAS, E., BELDING, E., LEE, S.-J., AND ALMEROTH, K. The impact of channel bonding on 802.11n network management. In *CoNEXT* (2011).

[5] GAST, M. S. *802.11n: A Survival Guide.* O'Reilly, 2012.

[6] HALPERIN, D., HU, W., SHETH, A., AND WETHERALL, D. Predictable 802.11 packet delivery from wireless channel measurements. In *SIGCOMM* (2010).

[7] IPERF. http://sourceforge.net/projects/iperf/.

[8] KARP, R. Reducibility among combinatorial problems. *Complexity of Computer Computations* (1972), 85–103.

[9] KRIARA, L., AND MARINA, M. Samplelite: A hybrid approach to 802.11n link adaptation. *ACM SIGCOMM Computer Communication Review* (2015).

[10] KRIARA, L., MARINA, M., AND FARSHAD, A. Characterization of 802.11n wireless LAN performance via testbed measurements and statistical analysis. In *SECON* (2013).

[11] LACURTS, K., AND BALAKRISHNAN, H. Measurement and analysis of real-world 802.11 mesh networks. In *IMC* (2010).

[12] LIU, R. P., SUTTON, G., AND COLLINGS, I. A new queueing model for QoS analysis of IEEE 802.11 DCF with finite buffer and load. *Wireless Communications, IEEE Transactions on* (2010).

[13] LORINCZ, J., AND BEGUSIC, D. Physical layer analysis of emerging IEEE 802.11n WLAN standard. In *8th International Conference Advanced Communication Technology* (2006).

[14] PRASAD, R., DIXIT, S., VAN NEE, R., AND OJANPERA, T. *Globalization of mobile and wireless communications.* Springer Netherlands, 2011.

[15] VAN NEE, R., JONES, V. K., AWATER, G., VAN ZELST, A., GARDNER, J., AND STEELE, G. The 802.11n MIMO-OFDM standard for wireless LAN and beyond. *Wireless Personal Communications* (2006).

[16] WILSON, R. Propagation losses through common building materials, 2.4 GHz vs 5 GHz. http://www.am1.us/Protected_Papers/E10589_Propagation_Losses_2_and_5GHz.pdf. Accessed: 2016-05-12.

[17] ZENG, Y., PATHAK, P., AND MOHAPATRA, P. A first look at 802.11ac in action: Energy efficiency and interference characterization. In *IFIP* (2014).

Making On-Demand Routing Efficient with Route-Request Aggregation

Maziar Mirzazad-Barijough and J.J. Garcia-Luna-Aceves
Department of Computer Engineering, University of California, Santa Cruz, CA 95064
Email: maziar@soe.ucsc.edu, jj@soe.ucsc.edu

ABSTRACT

In theory, on-demand routing is very attractive for mobile ad hoc networks (MANET), because it induces signaling only for those destinations for which there is data traffic. However, in practice, the signaling overhead of existing on-demand routing protocols becomes excessive as the rate of topology changes increases due to mobility or other causes. We introduce the first on-demand routing approach that eliminates the main limitation of on-demand routing by aggregating route requests (RREQ) for the same destinations. The approach can be applied to any existing on-demand routing protocol, and we introduce the Ad-hoc Demand-Aggregated Routing with Adaptation (ADARA) as an example of how RREQ aggregation can be used. ADARA is compared to AODV and OLSR using discrete-event simulations, and the results show that aggregating RREQs can make on-demand routing more efficient than existing proactive or on-demand routing protocols.

CCS Concepts

•Networks → Routing protocols; Mobile ad hoc networks;

Keywords

Routing; on-demand routing; MANET

1. INTRODUCTION

Many routing protocols have been proposed for mobile ad-hoc networks (MANET), and can be categorized as proactive, reactive, and hybrid routing protocols [1, 2, 12, 16, 21]. Proactive or table-driven routing protocols maintain routes to every network destination independently of the data traffic being forwarded. Reactive or on-demand routing protocols maintain routes for only this destinations for which there are data packets to be forwarded. Hybrid protocols use proactive and on-demand mechanisms.

Section 2 provides a brief summary of the basic operation of proactive and on-demand routing. The proactive

MSWiM '16, November 13-17, 2016, Malta, Malta

© 2016 ACM. ISBN 978-1-4503-4502-6/16/11...$15.00

DOI: http://dx.doi.org/10.1145/2988287.2989155

routing approach has the potential of high packet-delivery ratios and shorter end-to-end delays, because routes are established before data packets requiring those routes are offered to the network. The price paid for such responsiveness is that signaling overhead is incurred even for those destinations that are not needed, which may be too high. In theory, on-demand routing is designed to address this problem by requiring signaling overhead only for active destinations at the expense of incurring slightly longer latencies, because some data packets must wait for routes to be found. However, as prior comparative analysis of the performance of on-demand versus proactive routing schemes show [3, 5, 9, 18, 25], on-demand routing protocols end up incurring more overhead than proactive routing protocols in MANETs when topology changes that impact existing data flows increase.

Many techniques (e.g., see [1, 2, 16]) have been proposed to reduce the overhead incurred in the dissemination of each route request (RREQ), including clustering, location information, dominating sets, and virtual coordinates. However, no prior work has addressed the impact of having relay routers aggregate RREQs they need to forward when they are intended for the same destinations.

The main contribution of this paper is the introduction of a fault-tolerant approach for routers to aggregate RREQs originated by different sources and intended for the same destinations. The proposed *route-request aggregation* approach can be applied to any on-demand routing protocol (e.g., AODV or DSR [16]) and can make any routing protocol that uses on-demand routing techniques more efficient.

Section 3 introduces the Ad-hoc Demand-Aggregated Routing with Adaptation (ADARA) protocol as a specific example of the RREQ aggregation approach. Like AODV, ADARA uses destination-based sequence numbers to prevent routing-table loops and request identifiers to denote each RREQ uniquely as in AODV. ADARA introduces route-request aggregation and the use of broadcast signaling packets (RREQs, route replies and route errors) to substantially reduce signaling overhead.

Section 4 presents an example of the operation of ADARA and how it improves performance compared to AODV [16]. However, the approach used in ADARA can be applied with proper modifications to on-demand routing based on source routes (e.g., DSR [16]) or path information [8]. It can also be used in combination with prior techniques aimed at reducing signaling overhead, such as the use of geographical coordinates of destinations [11, 24], virtual coordinates, connected dominating sets [23], address aggregation [22], and clustering [2, 15].

Section 5 presents the results of simulation experiments used to compare ADARA with two routing protocols that are representative of the state of the art in proactive routing and on-demand routing for MANETs, namely OLSR [4] and AODV. The experiments were designed to study the impact of node speed, pause times, number of sources, and network size on the packet-delivery ratio, average end-to-end delay, and signaling overhead. The results show that ADARA performs better than OLSR and AODV in all cases. The key reason for this is that ADARA is able to establish routes on demand incurring far less overhead than AODV and OLSR.

2. RELATED WORK

Many MANET routing protocols have been proposed since the introduction of the routing protocol for the DARPA packet-radio network [10] and excellent surveys and comparative studies of this prior work have been presented over the years [1, 2, 9, 12, 16, 18, 21, 25].

OLSR is the best-known example of proactive routing for MANETs [4]. It uses HELLO messages to maintain neighbor connectivity, and Topology Control (TC) messages to disseminate link-state information throughout the network. To reduce signaling overhead, OLSR takes advantage of connected dominating sets. Some nodes are elected as multipoint relays (MPRs) and only MPRs forward TC messages, and only link-state information needed to connect MPRs is advertised in the network.

AODV [16] is the most popular example of the on-demand routing approach. To find a route to an intended destination, a source broadcasts a RREQ stating the source and destination nodes, the most recent sequence number known for each, a a broadcast ID, and a hop count to the source. A router that forwards a RREQ for the first time creates a record for the RREQ stating the source and broadcast-ID pair of the RREQ; and a a reverse route to the source of the RREQ stating the next hop and hop count to the source, and the sequence number of the source. It maintains any RREQ record and reverse route for a finite time. A router discards any received RREQ that states a source and broadcast-ID pair for which it has a RREQ record.

The intended destination or a router with a valid route to the destination responds to the RREQ by sending a route reply (RREP) over the reverse route from which the RREQ was received. The RREP states the destination and the source of the RREQ, the destination sequence number, and the hop count to the destination. A router receiving a RREP establishes a route record to the destination stating the destination sequence number, the next hop to it, and the neighbors using the route (precursors). A router forwards only the first copy of a RREP (based on the destination sequence number) and increments by one the hop count to the destination when it forwards a RREP.

Link failures can be recognized in AODV by the absence of HELLO messages sent periodically between neighbors. When a node detects a link failure, it sends a route error (RERR) to all neighbor nodes that are precursors of a route that is broken because of the link failure. Nodes receiving a RERR message invalidate all routes that were using the failed link and propagate the RERR message to their precursor nodes.

Hybrid routing protocols attempt to reduce the signaling overhead of proactive and on-demand schemes by combining the two. This has been done by either using clusters within which routes to destinations are maintained proactively and using on-demand routing across clusters (e.g., ZRP [16]), or by maintaining routes to certain destinations proactively and using on-demand routing for the rest of destinations [20].

Interestingly, all prior approaches proposed for on-demand and hybrid routing have assumed that a router that receives route-requests (RREQ) regarding destinations for which it does not have valid routes forwards *each* new RREQ it receives, and replicas of the same RREQ are silently dropped. This constitutes a major performance limitation for all on-demand and hybrid routing schemes proposed to date. Intuitively, as the number of destinations increase, the failure of just a few links may cause many sources to engage in the discovery of new routes to those destinations, with each source flooding RREQs. Because a router forwards each RREQ it receives as long as it does not state the same source and request ID pair, the flooding of RREQs grows linearly with the number of sources, even if the sources are seeking the same few destinations.

The following section describes our approach to address this problem crated by too many RREQs. We use a specific protocol as an example of the basic approach.

3. ADARA

The design rational for ADARA is twofold. First, for the performance of an on-demand routing protocol to be comparable to or better than the performance of a proactive routing protocol, the number of RREQs that sources initiate in the route-discovery process must be kept to a minimum when the network supports many data flows and experiences topology changes. Second, if the number of data flows intended for the same destination node is larger than the number of neighbors of that destination, the routes from the sources of the flows to the destinations *must* have some routing relays in common. Accordingly, allowing routers to aggregate RREQs intended for the same destination is bound to have a positive effect on the overall performance of the network.

ADARA (Ad-hoc Demand-Aggregated Routing with Adaptation) is the first on-demand routing protocol in which a router aggregates RREQs from different sources intended for the same destination.

ADARA adopts the use of destination-based sequence numbers as in AODV to avoid routing-table loops, as well as the use of the source address and a request identifier created by the source to identify each RREQ. Other approaches have been proposed to avoid routing-table loops when routers maintain routes on-demand [6, 8, 13, 17, 19] and can be used instead of the specific approach based on destination sequence numbers assumed in this paper.

3.1 Information Exchanged and Stored

ADARA uses four types of signaling packets, all of which are sent in broadcast mode.

A Route Request (**RREQ**) is denoted by $REQ[RID, o, on, d, dn, ho, HSN]$ and contains: A request identifier (RID), the address of the origin or source of the RREQ (o), a sequence number created by the origin (on), the address of the intended destination (d), the most recent sequence number known from d (dn), a hop count to the origin of the RREQ (ho), and a HELLO sequence number (HSN).

A Route Reply (**RREP**) is denoted by $REP[d, dn, hd, LDN, HSN]$ and contains: the address of the destination (d), the most recent sequence number known from d (dn), a hop count to the destination (hd), a list of designated neighbors (LDN) from which valid RREQs for destination d have been received, and a HELLO sequence number (HSN).

A Route Error (**RERR**) is denoted by $RE[HSN, LUA]$ and contains a HELLO sequence number (HSN) and a list of unreachable addresses (LUA).

A Hello message (**HELLO**) is denoted by $H[HSN]$ and contains the sequence number of the sending node.

Each router i maintains a routing table (RT^i) and a pending request table (PRT^i). Each entry of RT^i specifies: the address of the destination, a sequence number created by the destination, a hop count to the destination, next hop to the destination, a list of precursor neighbors for the destination, and a lifetime.

PRT^i is used to keep track of the RREQs received by router i, aggregate RREQs received for the same destination, and discard duplicates of the same RREQ. An entry in PRT^i lists a destination address, a list of precursor tuples, and a lifetime. Each precursor tuple consists of: the address of an origin node, the RID stated by that node, and the address of the precursor neighbor from which a RREQ was received.

ADARA is a soft-state protocol. Each entry in PRT^i and RT^i has a finite lifetime to allow router i to delete entries that become obsolete as a result of topology changes (e.g., the network is partitioned or a node fails).

3.2 Updating Neighbor Connectivity

Whenever a router receives a Hello message, a RREQ, a RREP, or a RERR, it calls the Hello Process function shown in Algorithm 1 to update routes to neighbor routers. This process uses the HSN included in each signaling packet. The HSN a router includes in a RREQ, RREP or RERR is simply the value of its current sequence number.

Algorithm 1 Processing Hello

---

function Process_Hello
INPUT: $sender$, r_table^i, $HelloSeqNo$;
$route = r\_table^i.lookup(sender)$;
$route.setHop(1)$;
$route.SetDes(sender)$;
$route.SetNextHop(sender)$;
$route.SetSeqNum(HelloSeqNo)$;
$route.mark(Valid)$;
$r\_table.update(route)$;

3.3 Route Discovery Process

A router originates a RREQ when it has no valid route to an intended destination as a result of topology changes or because a new destination is of interest to the router. Algorithm 2 shows the steps taken by a router to process a RREQ it receives from a neighbor.

After the neighbor information is updated according to Algorithm 1, router i updates its routing information regarding the origin of the RREQ. Router i uses Algorithm 3 to process the RREQ based on its origin, the RID created by the origin, and the entries in PRT^i.

Router i sends back a RREP to the RREQ it receives if it is the intended destination or RT^i contains a valid entry for the destination stated in the RREQ with a sequence number that is higher than or equal to the destination sequence

number stated in the RREQ. The RREP is broadcast to all neighbors and states the hop count to the destination, the destination sequence number, a HELLO sequence number for itself, and the list of designated neighbors.

If router i has no valid route to the intended destination in the RREQ and there is no entry in PRT^i for that destination, router i creates a PRT^i for the destination and broadcasts the RREQ to its neighbor routers with its own HSN and its own hop count to the origin of the RREQ. On the other hand, if there is an entry for the destination in PRT^i, there are various cases to consider.

If the RREQ is a replica of a RREQ received from the same origin (i.e., there is a pending RREQ for the destination from the same origin and with the same RID), the RREQ is silently dropped. If the RREQ is not a replica of a RREQ already received, but is a retransmission of a RREQ from one of the origins of the request, it means that the origin is retransmitting its RREQ due to a timeout expiration. Accordingly, router i updates the RID of the corresponding precursor tuple and broadcasts the RREQ to its neighbor routers. Lastly, if the RREQ is from a different source than those listed in PRT^i, router i simply adds a precursor tuple PRT^i with the address of the origin, the RID created by the origin, and the address of the neighbor that sent the RREQ. We say that the RREQ is aggregated in such a case.

Algorithm 2 Process RREQ from router s at router i

---

function Process_RREQ
INPUT: $rreq, org, r\_table^i, Destination$;
$des = rreq.getDestination()$;
$processHello(s, RREQ.HelloSeqNo)$;
$aggregated = PRT.Aggregate(RREQ)$;
$UpdateReversePath(RREQ, org)$;
$rt = r\_table^i.lookup(des)$;
if $(rt) \wedge (rt.seq \geq rreq.Seq) \wedge (rt == VALID)$ **then**
  $rrep = create\_rrep(rt)$;
  $rrep.SetHelloSeq(LocalSeq)$
  $Broadcast(rrep)$;
else
  if $!aggregated$ **then**
    $rreq.SetHelloSeq(LocalSeq)$
    $Broadcast(rreq)$;
  end if
end if

Algorithm 3 Aggregate RREQ i

---

function Aggregate_RREQ
INPUT: $rreq, PRT^i$;
$des = rreq.getDestination()$;
$org = rreq.getOrigin()$;
$id = rreq.getId()$;
if $\exists enrty \in PRT \wedge entry_{org} = org \wedge entry_{id} = id$ **then**
  $drop(rreq)$; //Duplicate RREQ
  $return\ true$;
end if
if $\exists e \in PRT \wedge e_{org} = org \wedge e_{des} = des \wedge e_{id} \neq id$ **then**
  $update(entry, rreq)$; //Retransmitted RREQ
  $return\ false$;
end if
if $\exists e \in PRT \wedge e_{org} \neq org \wedge e_{des} = des$ **then**
  $PRT.AddEntry(rreq)$; // Aggregate
  $return\ true$;
end if
$PRT.AddEntry(rreq)$;
$return\ false$;

When router i receives a RREP, it updates its neighbor information according to Algorithm 1. Router i accepts the information in the RREP and updates RT^i for the destination stated in the RREP if either the destination sequence number is higher than the destination sequence number in RT^i or the sequence numbers are the same but the hop count to the destination in the RREP is smaller than the corresponding hop count in RT^i.

For the case of a valid RREP, router i creates or updates the entry in RT^i for the destination. The entry states the destination sequence number obtained in the RREP, its hop count to the destination, and the list of precursor neighbors for the destination. The precursor neighbors are simply those neighbors listed in precursor tuples for the destination in PRT^i. If the router is a member of LDN of RREP, then the router i broadcasts the RREP to its neighbors stating its own hop count to the destination, its own HELLO sequence number, and a list of designated neighbors of router i that need to process and perhaps forward the RREP. Router i can then delete the entry for the destination in PRT^i. In case the router is not in LDN, after updating the routes, router will drop the RREP to limit the region within which the RREP is re-broadcast.

Algorithm 4 Processing RREP from router s at router i

---

function Process_RREP
INPUT: $rrep, sender, r\_table^i, Destination$;
$des = rrep.getDestination()$;
$processHello(sender, rrep.GetHelloSeqNo())$;
$rt = r\_table^i.lookup(des)$;
$intended = false$;
if $currentNode \in RREP.LDN()$ **then**
  $designated = true$;
end if
if $(rt\_des \neq empty)$ **then**
  if $(rrep.seq > rt\_des.seq) \vee (rrep.seq = rt\_des.seq \wedge rrep.hop < rt\_des.hop)$ **then**
    $rt\_des.update(rrep)$;
  end if
else
  $rt\_des = r\_table^i.AddRoute(RREP)$;
end if
if $designated \neq true \wedge PRT.lookup(Des_{RREP}).Count \leq 1$ **then**
  $return$;
end if
$RREP.ClearLDN()$;
for each $entry \in PRT.lookup(Des_{RREP})$ **do**
  $PRT.remove(des)$;
  $rt\_org = r\_table^i.lookup(entry.org)$;
  $RREP.LDN.Add(entry.PrecursorNeighbor)$;
  $rt\_des.AddPrecursor(entry.PrecursorNeighbor)$
end for
$RREP.setHelloSeq(LocalSeq)$;
$Broadcast(RREP)$;

Algorithm 5 Processing RERR from router s at router i

---

function Process_RERR
INPUT: $rerr, r\_table^i, unreachable$;
$processHello(s)$;
$rtList = $ Get All entries in r_table^i that use s toward unreachable routers;
$hasPrecursor = false$;
for each $rt \in rtList$ **do**
  if $rt.precursorCount() > 0$ **then**
    $hasPrecursor = true$;
  end if
  $invalidate(rt)$;
end for
if $hasPrecursor$ **then**
  $RERR.SetHelloSeq(LocalSeq)$;
  $Broadcast(RERR)$;
end if

3.4 Handling Errors and Topology Changes

Route error messages are created when no route is found toward a destination router or a link break is detected. A router assumes that a link with a neighbor is down when it fails to receive any signaling packet within interval defined

for the reception of signaling packets from a neighbor. An error message states all the destinations for which routes are broken as a result of the link failure.

Algorithm 5 shows the steps taken by router i to process a RERR from a neighbor. Router i invalidates all the routes to destinations listed in the RERR that require the router sending the RERR as the next hop. Router i broadcasts a RERR it receives if at least one precursor neighbor exists for the destinations listed in the RERR. Accordingly, only routers that established routes to destinations by forwarding RREQs may have to forward RERRs.

4. ADARA EXAMPLE

Figure 1 shows a small wireless network in which ADARA is used. The network consists of six relay routers (m, n, o, p, q, and r), three source routers (S, A, and B), and one destination router D. The example assumes that no router has valid routes for destination D, and shows router S generating and broadcasting a RREQ for destination D at time t_1. The propagation of this RREQ is indicated by thin arrows in the figure, and the propagation of RREPs is shown with thick blue arrows. The RREQ from router S states $REQ[RID_S, S, on_S, D, dn = 0, ho = \infty, HSN_S]$

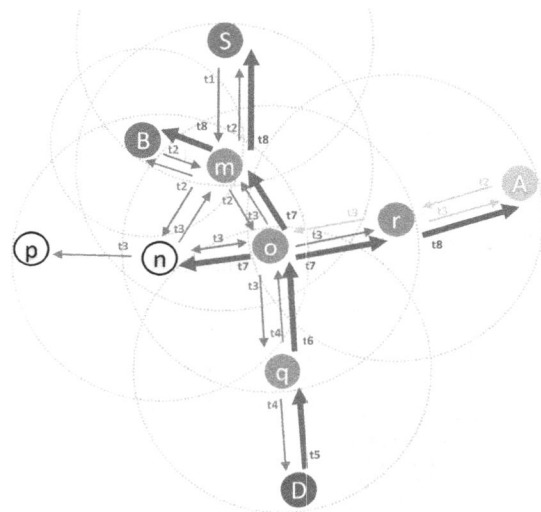

Figure 1: Dissemination of RREQs and RREPs in ADARA

When router m receives the RREQ from source S, it adds a route for destination router S as a destination in RT^m with a hop count of one and S as the next hop. Router m also creates an entry for D in PRT^m listing the precursor tuple $[S, RID_S, S]$, which states S as the origin of the RREQ with a RID equal to RID_S and source S as the neighbor from which the RREQ was received.

The example shows routers A and B originating RREQs for destination D at time $t_2 > t_1$. As the figure shows, router r forwards the RREQ at time $t_3 > t_2$. However, when router m receives the RREQ from router B for destination D shortly after time t_2, it simply aggregates the RREQ, because PRT^m contains an entry for D. Router m does this by adding the precursor tuple $[B, RID_B, B]$ to its entry for destination D in PRT^m.

Router o creates an entry for D in PRT^o after receiving the RREQ forwarded by router m, and that entry lists the precursor tuple $[S, RID_S, m]$. Accordingly, when router o receives the RREQ forwarded by router r shortly after time t_3, it can simply aggregate the RREQ. It does this by adding the precursor tuple $[A, RID_A, r]$ to the entry for destination D in PRT^o. Similarly, when router r receives the RREQ forwarded by router o (originated by source S) shortly after time t_3, it already has an entry for destination D in PRT^r and hence aggregates the RREQ received from router o by adding the precursor tuple $[S, RID_S, o]$ to its list of precursor tuples for destination D.

We note that, shortly after time t_3, routers n and o receive the RREQ originated by source S from each other. Both routers simply ignore the replicas of the RREQ originated by router S because they each have an entry for destination D in their PRTs listing a precursor tuple with the same source router and source sequence number than the ones included in the RREQ they receive from each other.

As the RREQs from sources S, A, and B are disseminated in the network, relaying routers add precursor tuples to their PRTs for destination D. These tuples allow each relay router to decide whether to broadcast a RREP for D when it receives a RREP from a neighbor. Destination D generates a RREP for itself at time t_5 when it receives the RREQ from router q. Starting with router q, the RREP is disseminated back to the sources that originated RREQs for D along the reverse paths traversed by the RREQs thanks to the precursor tuples maintained in the PRTs of routers. Each relaying router re-broadcasts the RREP for destination D if it has at least one precursor tuple for D in its PRT, which results in RREPs being disseminated along a directed acyclic graph as illustrated in Figure 1. Each router that forwards a RREP copies the precursor neighbors for D to its RT.

A RREP contains the list of designated neighbors (LDN) that may forward the RREP as needed, and is based on the precursors stated for a given destination in the PRTs of routers. In the example, the LDN of the RREP from router q lists router o, and the LDN of the RREP from router o states routers m and r. Accordingly, as shown in Figure 1, when router n receives the RREP from router o, it does not forward the RREP, given that it is not listed in the LDN of the RREP from router o. However, router n adds a routing entry for D in RT^n. Routers m and r forward the RREPs they receive from router o.

Router r forwards the RREP with an LDN listing routers o and A. Router o simply ignores the RREP from r, and source A is able to start sending data packets to D. By the same token, routers that receive RREPs from the next hops to the sources of RREQs can ignore the RREPs because they are not listed in the LDNs of those RREPs.

In contrast to the above, AODV and other on-demand routing protocols would require the dissemination of the RREQs from S, A and B throughout the entire network, and for each origin router, a RREP would be sent on the path from source to destination.

Figure 2 shows the number of signaling packets sent in the topology of Figure 1. The number of RREQs in ADARA is much smaller compared to AODV, which is a direct result of RREQ aggregation. Using ADARA, the RREQ generated by A is only sent by routers A and r, and the RREQ

from router B is sent once by router B and aggregated at router m. On the other hand, using AODV, the RREQs from routers S, B, and A are flooded in the network. The number of RREPs sent over the network in ADARA is also lower than AODV as a result of the aggregation or RREQs. In ADARA, RREPs are sent once on the path up to an aggregation point. In AODV, each RREP sent once on each path. As a result, the number of RREQs and RREPs in AODV is 2.5 times larger than in ADARA for this example. Furthermore, since all RREPs are broadcast messages, routers on the path from a source to a destination do not generate Hello messages for a time interval. For the case of AODV, Hello messages are generated independently of the RREPs being sent.

	ADARA	AODV
RREQ	11	27
RREP	5	12
SUM	16	39

Figure 2: Number of Signaling Packets Sent for ADARA and AODV

5. PERFORMANCE COMPARISON

5.1 Simulation Model and Parameters

We implemented ADARA in ns3 and used the ns3 implementations of AODV and OLSR without modifications to compare their performance. Figure 7 shows simulation-environment settings for AODV, OLSR, and ADARA.

Hello Interval	2 sec
Active Route Timeout	3 sec
Net Diameter	5
Max Queue Length	64
RREQ Rate Limit	10
RREQ Retries	2
TC Interval (OLSR)	5 sec

Figure 7: Simulation Configuration for ADARA, AODV, and OLSR.

The Distributed Coordination Function (DCF) of IEEE 802.11n 2.4 Ghz with rate of 2Mbps is used as the MAC-layer protocol for unicast data transmission. To avoid incorrect paths resulting from transmission-range differences between unicast and broadcast transmissions, we made sure that both broadcast and unicast packets are sent with the same rate (2Mbps) and range. Transmission power is adjusted to fix the transmission range to 250 meters. Both AODV and ADARA use a sending buffer of 64 packets. These buffers store packets waiting for RREP message to the desired destination for 30 seconds.

Simulations include 50 routers spread uniformly in a $300m \times 1500m$ area. For other scenarios, 25, 75, and 100 routers are uniformly spread in a $300m \times 1500m$, $300m \times 1500m$, and $300m \times 1500m$ respectively. Routers use the random-waypoint mobility model with a randomly-chosen moving speed between 0 and 20 m/s and pause time of 0 seconds. A router chooses a destination location randomly and moves

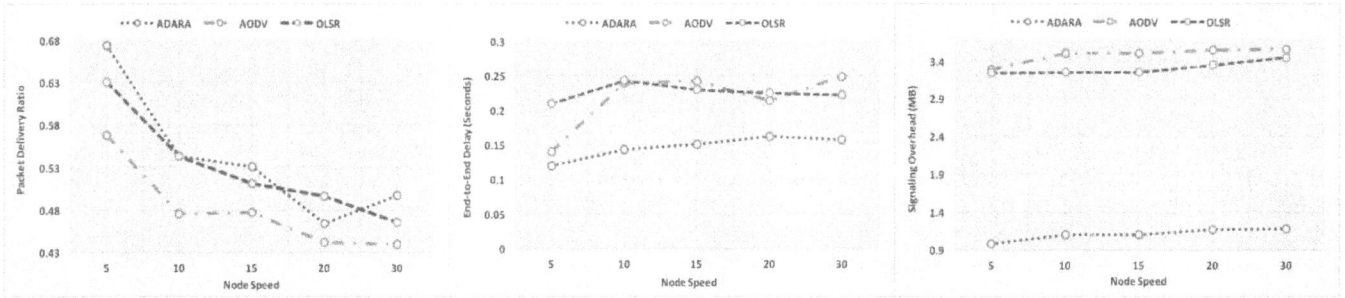

Figure 3: Performance comparison as a function of router speed.

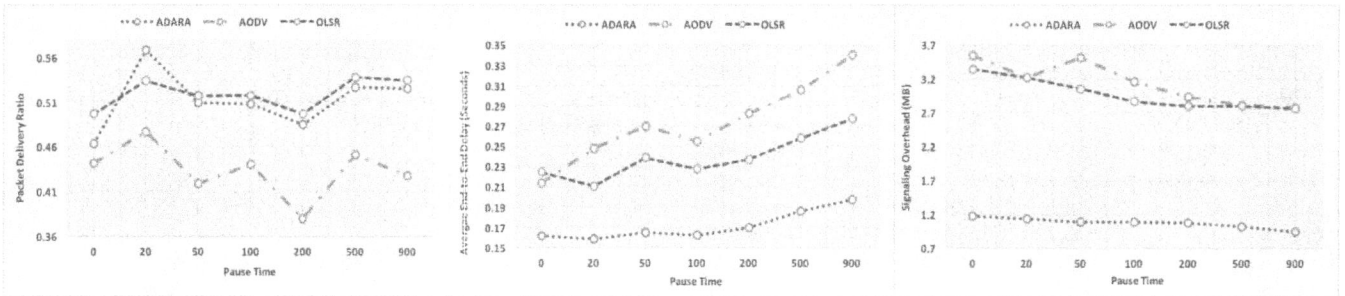

Figure 4: Performance comparison as a function of Pause Time.

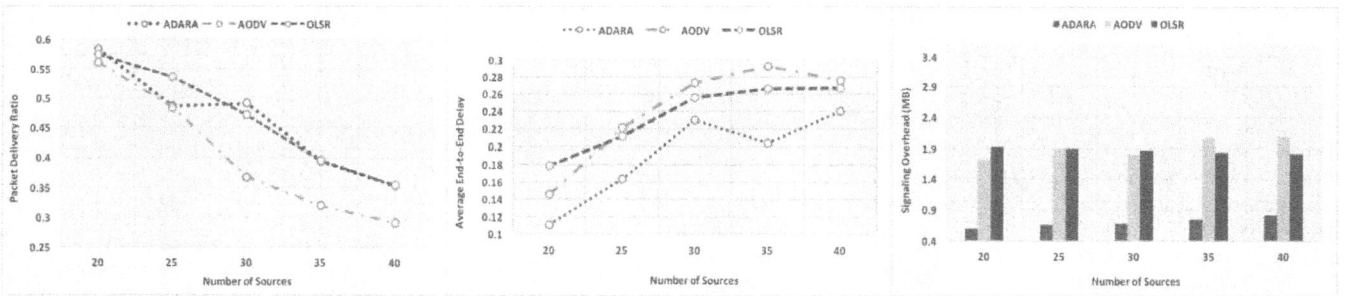

Figure 5: Performance comparison as a function Number of Sources.

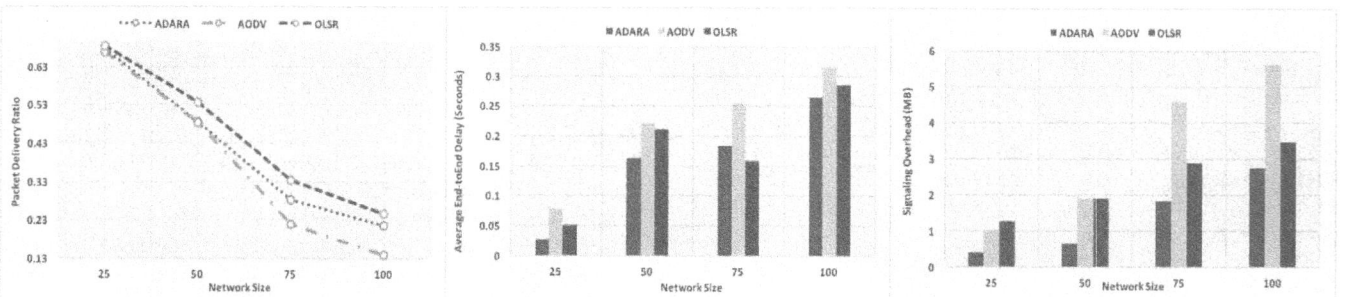

Figure 6: Performance comparison as a function Network Size.

toward that destination with a randomly chosen speed between zero and the specified maximum speed. When a destination location is reached, the router remains there for a specified pause time.

The scenarios include 25 data flows from 25 different source routers. The destination router for each flow is a specific router with probability 0.5 and is chosen randomly from all routers with probability 0.5. Traffic sources are on-off applications with on and off time of 1 second, which generate packets of size 512 bytes and rate of 15 packets per second. For network sizes of 25 and 50 routers, simulations are run for 900 seconds, and for networks sizes of 75 and 100 routers, the simulation time is 500 seconds.

The signaling overhead in AODV includes its five types of packets: RREQ, RREP, RERR, Route Reply Ack, and HELLO messages. In OLSR, the signaling overhead includes, Topology Control (TC) messages and HELLO messages. In ADARA, the signaling overhead includes all its different types of signaling packets.

We compared ADARA, AODV and OLSR based on the packet delivery ratios (PDR), the average end-to-end delay, and the number of signaling packets sent by all routers. PDR indicates the number of packets received by destination routers divided by number of packets sent by the source routers. The average end-to-end delay is the time elapsed from the time a packet is sent by a source until it is received by its destination. For the case of ADARA and AODV, this delay includes the duration packet is buffered waiting for RREPs.

The scenarios used to compare the three routing protocols were chosen to stress all three protocols, rather than to attain good performance for either on-demand or proactive routing.

5.2 Effect of Mobility

In this scenario, 50 routers are spread randomly in a $300m \times 1500m$ area, with 25 of the routers generating traffic, each with 15 packets per second. The destination for each flow is a specific router with probability of 0.5 and is chosen randomly from all routers with probability of 0.5. We tried different maximum mobility speeds of 5 m/s to 30 m/s with a zero pause.

Figure 3 shows the PDR, average end-to-end delays, and the signaling overhead incurred by the three protocols as a function of router speed.

Higher router speed results in more topology changes. The drastic drop in PDR in all protocols is due to routes breaking due to router mobility and the time needed by the routing protocols to obtain new routes. OLSR requires routers to detect link failures and additions based on the absence or reception of HELLO messages, and TC messages to inform all routers of the topology so that new routes can be established. Given that TC messages are sent periodically listing one or multiple link states, the signaling overhead in OLSR remains fairly constant as a function of router speed. However, this means that more link changes take place between periodic transmissions of TC messages as router speed increases, which results in more data packets being lost as they traverse paths that are broken.

Link failures in AODV and ADARA are detected by the absence of a number of consecutive Hello messages, and a route discovery process is done to inform sources of new routes to destinations. Because of the delays incurred in detecting link failures and in establishing new routes after that, as router speed increases more and more data packets traversing failed routes end up being dropped.

The lower delays obtained with ADARA can be attributed to the aggregation of RREQs, which reduces the number of RREQs being flooded and hence reduces network congestion, as well as the fact that each signaling packet is sent in broadcast mode containing the current sequence number of the transmitting router, which helps routers detect link failures and repair routes more quickly.

The enormous impact of RREQ aggregation in ADARA is evident in Figure 3. In OLSR, TC messages must be disseminated by MPRs throughout the network and in AODV, each RREQ is flooded throughout the network. By contrast, a RREQ in ADARA is disseminated throughout the network only when no other RREQ asking for a route for the same destination has been forwarded recently. The size of TC messages in OLSR is much larger than the size of RREQs in AODV, which accounts for the similarity in signaling overhead between the two even though routers in OLSR disseminate fewer signaling packets than in AODV.

Figure 4 shows the performance comparison of the three protocols as a function of mobility pause time. For this simulation runs, we considered 50 routers in a area of $300m \times 1500m$ with 25 flows as described previously. Pause times vary from 0 seconds (i.e., constant mobility) to to 900 seconds (i.e., almost static routers). The speed of routers is chosen randomly between zero and 20 meters per second. As it is can be seen from the figure, the packet delivery ratio for ADARA is very close to that of OLSR, while AODV is much lower for all pause times. Average delays in ADARA are much lower than those attained in OLSR and AODV over all pause times, and AODV renders the higher delays in all cases. It is also evident that ADARA incurs far less signaling overhead than OLSR and AODV for all pause times. As should be expected, less signaling overhead is incurred by all protocols as the pause time increases.

5.3 Effect of Number of Flows

Figure 5 shows the comparison of the three protocols as a function of number of sources in the network. For all cases, sources are different routers. For each flow, one specific router is selected as the destination with probability 0.5 and a random destination is selected with probability 0.5.

The PDR decreases and the average end-to-end delays increase for all three protocols as the number of sources increases. These results can be explained from the additional congestion created in the channel as a result of having more data packets when more sources are added. The results for signaling overhead as a function of the number of sources clearly show the benefits of RREQ aggregation in ADARA compared to AODV and OLSR. Although the signaling traffic in ADARA does increase as the number of sources increases, many of those sources share common destinations and this results in many RREQs being aggregated, which in turn results in much smaller overhead than with the other two protocols.

5.4 Effect of Network Size

Figure 6 shows the performance of the three protocols as a function of the number of routers. We considered different network sizes of 25, 50, 75, and 100 routers spread randomly in a area of $300m \times 1000m$, $300m \times 1500$, $300m \times 2000$, and $500m \times 2200$ with 15, 25, 40 and 50 flows respectively. Similar to the previous scenarios, a destination is a specific router with probability of 0.5 and it chosen randomly with probability of 0.5.

As we have stated, the scenarios were selected to stress all protocols, rather than to show likely operating points. For all three protocols, as the network size increases the PDR drops, end-to-end delays increase, and signaling overhead increases. This is unavoidable, given that OLSR must send more link states, and AODV and ADARA must send more route requests as the network size increases. However, it is clear that ADARA is more scalable than OLSR and AODV, and is far more efficient than AODV.

6. CONCLUSIONS

We introduced route-request aggregation as an effective mechanism to significantly reduce the signaling overhead incurred in route discovery, and presented ADARA as an example of the basic approach.

ADARA uses destination-based sequence numbers to avoid routing-table loops like AODV does, and uses RREQ aggregation and broadcast signaling packets to reduce signaling overhead. We compared the performance of ADARA, AODV, and OLSR and analyzed the effect of mobility, number of flows, and network size on the performance of the protocols. The simulation results show that, in terms of packet delivery ratio, ADARA performs much better than AODV and performs very close to OLSR in all cases. The signaling overhead incurred with ADARA is much smaller than the overhead in AODV and OLSR. Furthermore, the use of RREQ aggregation and broadcast signaling packets in ADARA leads to fewer packets contenting for the channel and results in lower end-to-end delays for ADARA compared to AODV and OLSR.

As we have stated, the basic approach of using RREQ aggregation can be applied to any on-demand routing protocol. Accordingly, our results offer a great opportunity to improve the performance of on-demand routing protocols being considered for standardization. Our results indicate that RREQ aggregation can make AODV, DSR, or other on-demand routing protocols, far more attractive compared to OLSR and other proactive routing protocols.

Our description of ADARA assumed single-path routing. However, multi-path routing [13, 19] can be easily supported as well. Furthermore, as we we have stated, RREQ aggregation can be used together with other techniques that have been proposed to improve the performance of on-demand routing in MANETs.

The next steps for our work on unicast routing include the definition and analysis of multi-path routing based on ADARA, the use of loop-avoidance techniques other than destination-based sequence numbers in the context of route-request aggregation, the use of geographical coordinates as in [11, 24], and the use of clustering techniques. In addition, it is clear that the use of route-request aggregation can be applied to improve the performance of on-demand multicast routing [2, 7].

7. ACKNOWLEDGMENTS

This work was supported in part by the Baskin Chair of Computer Engineering at UCSC.

8. REFERENCES

[1] M. Abolhasan et al., "A Review of Routing Protocols for Mobile Ad Hoc Networks," *Ad hoc networks*, 2004.

[2] A. Boukersche, *Handbook of Algorithms for Wireless and Mobile Computing*, Chapman and Hall, 2006.

[3] J. Broch et al., "A Performance Comparison of Multi-Hop Wireless Ad Hoc Network Routing Protocols." *Proc. ACM/IEEE MobiCom '98*, 1998.

[4] T. Clausen and P. Jacquet, "Optimized link state routing protocol (OLSR)" *RFC 3626*, 2003.

[5] T. Clausen, "Comparative Study of Routing Protocols for Mobile Ad-hoc networks," Research Report RR-5135, INRIA, 2004.

[6] S. Dabideen and J.J. Garcia-Luna-Aceves, "Ordering in Time: A New Routing Approach for Wireless Networks," Proc. IEEE MASS 2010, San Francisco, CA, November 8-12, 2010.

[7] J.J. Garcia-Luna-Aceves and R. Menchaca-Mendez, "PRIME: An Interest-Driven Approach to Integrated Unicast and Multicast Routing in MANETs," *IEEE/ACM Trans. on Networking*, March 2011.

[8] J.J. Garcia-Luna-Aceves and S. Roy, "On-Demand Routing in Ad Hoc Networks Using Link Vectors," *IEEE JSAC*, Vol. 23, No. 3, March 2005.

[9] H. Jiang and J.J. Garcia-Luna-Aceves, "Performance Comparison of Three Routing Protocols for Ad Hoc Networks," *Proc. IEEE IC3N '01*, Oct. 2001.

[10] J. Jubin and J. Tornow, "The DARPA Packet Radio Network Protocols," *Proc. of The IEEE*, january 1987.

[11] Y. Ko and N.Vaidya, "Location-Aided Routing (LAR) in Mobile Ad Hoc Networks," *Wireless Networks*, Vol. 6, No. 4, 2000.

[12] P. Mohapatra et al., *Ad Hoc Networks: Technologies and Protocols*, Springer, 2005.

[13] M. Mosko and J.J. Garcia-Luna-Aceves, "Multipath Routing in Wireless Mesh Networks," *Proc. IEEE WiMesh '05*, 2005.

[14] S. Murthy and J.J. Garcia-Luna-Aceves, "An Efficient Routing Protocol for Wireless Networks." *Mobile Networks and Applications*, 1996.

[15] G. Pei et al., "A Wireless Hierarchical Routing Protocol with Group Mobility," *Proc. IEEE WCNC '99*, 1999.

[16] C. Perkins et al., *Ad Hoc Networkiing*, Addison-Wesley, 2008.

[17] H. Rangarajan and J.J. Garcia-Luna-Aceves, "On-demand Loop-Free Routing in Ad hoc Networks Using Source Sequence Numbers," *Proc. IEEE MASS '05*, Nov. 2005.

[18] J. Raju and J.J. Garcia-Luna-Aceves, "A Comparison of On-Demand and Table Driven Routing for Ad-Hoc Wireless Networks," *Proc. IEEE ICC '00*, June 2000.

[19] J. Raju and J.J. Garcia-Luna-Aceves, "A New Approach to On-Demand Loop-Free Multipath Routing," *Proc. IEEE IC3N '99*, Oct. 1999.

[20] S. Roy and J.J. Garcia-Luna-Aceves, "Node-Centric Hybrid Routing for Ad Hoc Networks," *Proc. 10th IEEE/ACM MASCOTS '02*, 2002.

[21] E. Royer and C.K. Toh, "A Review of Current Routing Protocols for Ad Hoc Mobile Wireless Networks," *IEEE Personal Communications*, 1999.

[22] C. Shiflet, E. M. Belding-Royer, and C.E. Perkins. "Address Aggregation in Mobile Ad Hoc Networks," *Proc. IEEE ICC '04*, 2004.

[23] J. Wu and H. Li, "On Calculating Connected Dominating Set for Efficient Routing in Ad Hoc Wireless Networks," *Proc. ACM Int'l Workshop on Discrete Algorithms and Methods for Mobile Computing and Communications*, 1999.

[24] Y. Wang, C. Westphal, and J.J. Garcia-Luna-Aceves, "Using Geographical Coordinates To Attain Efficient Route Signaling in Ad Hoc Networks," *Proc. IEEE WoWMoM '13*, June 2013.

[25] X. Wu et al., "A Unified Analysis of Routing Protocols in MANETs," *IEEE Trans. on Communications*, March 2010.

[26] IEEE Computer Society. IEEE 802.11 and 802.11n Standards, 1999.

Neighbor Contamination to Achieve Complete Bottleneck Control

Nadav Schweitzer
Department of Information
Systems Engineering
Ben-Gurion University
Beer-Sheva, Israel
nadavsc@post.bgu.ac.il

Ariel Stulman
Dept. of Computer Science
and Engineering
Jerusalem College of
Technology
Jerusalem, Israel
stulman@jct.ac.il

Asaf Shabtai
Department of Information
Systems Engineering
Ben-Gurion University
Beer-Sheva, Israel
shabtaia@bgu.ac.il

ABSTRACT

Black-holes, gray-holes and, wormholes, are devastating to the correct operation of any network. These attacks (among others) are based on the premise that packets will travel through compromised nodes, and methods exist to coax routing into these traps. Detection of these attacks are mainly centered around finding the subversion in action. In networks, bottleneck nodes – those that sit on many potential routes between sender and receiver – are an optimal location for compromise. Finding naturally occurring path bottlenecks, however, does not entitle network subversion, and as such are more difficult to detect. The dynamic nature of mobile ad-hoc networks (MANETs) causes ubiquitous routing algorithms to be even more susceptible to this class of attacks. Finding perceived bottlenecks in an OLSR based MANET, is able to capture between 50%-75% of data. In this paper we propose a method of subtly expanding perceived bottlenecks into complete bottlenecks, raising capture rate up to 99%; albeit, at high cost. We further tune the method to reduce cost, and measure the corresponding capture rate.

Categories and Subject Descriptors

c.2.0 [**Computer-communication Networks**]: General—*Security and protection*

Keywords

wormhole; network bottlenecks; MANET; mobile; internet of things

1. INTRODUCTION

As mobile ad-hoc networks (MANETs) are becoming ubiquitous with the introduction of Internet of Things (IoT), VANETs and other self-organizing networks, attackers are turning their attention to these venues. The high volume of data expected to flow through these networks, creates and

enormous potential for profit. Conversely, compromised privacy, anonymity, loss of confidential information, etc. can be catastrophic.

One of the basic functions that successful attackers run, is the discovery of potential high-asset victims. It is not enough to develop the algorithms, exploit some fault and execute an attack. It must be done to high asset victims for maximizing attack impact (positive or negative). There may be many high-asset victims available, but invariably, when networks are under scrutiny, it is where a bottleneck exists. This creates the golden opportunity of sifting through all network traffic without having to orchestrate some sophisticated mechanism for creating a man-in-the-middle (MiTM). It simply exists by the virtue of network topology. A network bottleneck may be a single point through which all traffic must flow, or a number of nodes that as a group constitute the collection point for data. It can also be a local bottleneck through which data from specific nodes must traverse. Regardless of which it is, the ability to identify such points extends the attack surface.

In infrastructure networks such bottlenecks are easily identified, and much care is taken to harden these *single points of failure*. The lack of topology fluctuation allows for the employment of infinite time and highly complex discovery algorithms. MANETs, however, are characterized by an ever-changing topology. It is thus, much more difficult for both the attacker and defender of the network to identify and exploit or harden such points. [13] proposed a linear time algorithm that can facilitate the calculation of local or global bottleneck between a sender and receiver, on-the-fly, without additional network overhead for MANETs using the prevalent optimized link state routing (OLSR) protocol [4, 11]. This ability can be used by an attacker looking to eavesdrop or tamper a conversation between two specific nodes.

Simulated execution (using NS3 [1]), however, was only able to confirm 50%-75% packet interception success on the projected bottlenecks (see Figure 1). The missing packets (25%-50%) can be attributed to alternate optimal paths not discernable by the attacker, sender or receiver, but none-the-less existent. These hidden paths circumvent projected bottlenecks, avoiding exploitation by an attacker. They are the result of a discrepancy between the perceived topology which is composed solely of multi-point relay nodes, a subset of the entire network (see section 2.1), and the full topology.

In this paper we propose a method for an attacker to wisely contaminate a bottleneck's neighbors such that he

MSWiM '16, November 13-17, 2016, Malta, Malta

© 2016 ACM. ISBN 978-1-4503-4502-6/16/11. . . $15.00

DOI: http://dx.doi.org/10.1145/2988287.2989146

is able to turn a perceived bottleneck to a physical one. We show that by choosing a specific sub-set of nodes he is able to completely block network paths (~99.8% success); albeit, at a relatively high cost. Choosing a much smaller set, one is still able to raise the bar for bottleneck based attacks (increasing packet interception to ~89%), with a cost that is inverse to the size of the network (larger networks incur lower costs).

2. BACKGROUND AND RELATED WORK

2.1 OLSR

The optimized link state routing (OLSR) protocol [4, 11] is an optimization of the classical link state routing (LSR) protocol aimed at reducing network overhead. While the original LSR uses a flooding propagation technique in which a node, receiving any message (control or data), must re-transmit it to all its neighbors; OLSR selectively re-transmits messages based on a specified set of rules. The crux of the optimization is based upon a sub-set of 1-hop neighbors, termed multi-point relays (MPR), that are designated for the purposes of forwarding agents of control packet throughout the network.

2.1.1 MPR selection

MPRs are selected by a node as a sub-set of its 1-hop neighbors, such that the MPR set allows for coverage of all of its 2-hop neighbors. By minimizing its MPR selections, a node is able to transmit messages to all 2-hop neighbors with minimal duplication. Thus, both topology control messages and data packets are forwarded only by means of this minimal MPR set, allowing for fewer duplicate messages while maintaining network-wide coverage.

2.1.2 Topology discovery and route detection

There are two types of messages used to discover network topology in OLSR: HELLO and TC (i.e. topology control). The HELLO message, which declares a node's knowledge of its surrounding, is broadcast to all nodes within direct transmission distance. Every node that can hear the broadcast and reciprocate back to the sender is classified as a 1-hop neighbor. Consequently, each node acquires its local topology up to a two-hop range. In addition, OLSR requires that all nodes selected as MPRs periodically advertise a TC message listing all nodes that have selected the sender as its MPR. Of course, as mentioned in 2.1.1, these control messages are only propagated through MPR super-network, reducing overall network traffic. Each node in the network maintains network topology based on both the HELLO and TC messages it receives. It then calculates and stores, for each discovered node, two properties: the shortest distance (i.e. amount of hops between itself and the node) to that node and the last MPR through which the node is to be reached.

2.2 Bottleneck attacks on OLSR

There are numerous attacks on OLSR that attempt at orchestrating a bottleneck – a node or set of nodes that data traversing from source to target must pass through – within the network. The common goal of all these attacks is to coax the routing algorithm into passing data through specific malicious nodes. This does not necessarily require a network-wide bottleneck, and a perceived bottleneck by either the nodes under attack or the nodes routing the data

suffices. This gives the attacker the opportunity to examine data for useful information or to selectively drop packets creating a DOS attack. In OLSR, specifically, a bottleneck on the set of known optimal (shortest) paths between the source and the target nodes suffices for the attacks to commence. This claim is derived directly from OLSR's RFC [4] by the virtue that OLSR will transmit all data using one of the known optimal (shortest) paths found. Thus, by controlling the set of such paths, we have, in effect, created a virtual bottleneck for commencing attacks.

2.2.1 Wormhole attack

A wormhole attack is orchestrated by two colluding attackers having an out-of-band communication link between them. By broadcasting data that arrives at one side of the wormhole on its other side and vice-versa, surrounding nodes reach the conclusion that this link is more efficient than other existing links and route traffic through it. This causes all of the traffic of the MANET to be channeled through two malicious nodes, creating a virtual bottleneck in the network.

Hu, et al. [3, 10] places a packet leash on the data packets. This method allows the network to limit the travel of specific packets, rendering the wormhole useless. They point to two types of leashes: geographical leashes and temporal leashes. The geographical leash places a limit on the physical distance a packet can travel. The temporal leash assumes the existence of synchronized clocks among all network nodes and limits the time a packet can travel. Both types of leashes require assumptions that are superfluous in our work.

In [16], Capkun, et al., equipped nodes with hardware that allows them to respond to a one bit challenge in real time. The round trip time of the challenge and the response are used to accurately calculate the distance between two nodes. This method assumes that nodes have hardware capabilities for executing the challenge-response cycle, something that is not prevalent in most mobile hosts today.

Wang, et al., [17] had a source node that sends a wormhole detection packet to a specified destination. Each intermediate node on the packet's path appends to the packet a timestamp logging when it is received, when it is transmitted and it is own unique identifier for that node. The destination node then checks all the appended information in an attempt to conclude whether a wormhole exists. If one does exist, it transmits a message to stop the communication. This approach imposes overhead on the network and introduces the possibility for a malicious node to falsely advertise the existence of a wormhole; disrupting network communication.

2.2.2 Black hole attack

Black holes are well studied for AODV routing protocol [5], and are achieved by having a malicious node reply to every route request it hears. Then it selectively drops packets that are routed through it, creating a black hole in the network. This attack is easily ported into OLSR [8], and is induced by having a malicious node declare false neighbor information, thus increasing its chances of being selected as a sole MPR. A prerequisite condition for this attack to succeed is that no other paths are chosen, and that it must be based primarily on being a route bottleneck.

In [2], Al-Shurman, et al., propose two solutions for this

problem. The first requires the sender to wait until it can construct multiple paths between sender and receiver. Then, based on similarities between routes, the sender attempt to figure out which node is acting as a black hole. Assuming a bottleneck exists, the algorithm will not receive sufficient information to reach a viable conclusion. The second is based on the messages sent by AODV reactive routing protocol and it cannot be ported to OLSR.

Besides porting the attack into OLSR, Gerhards-Padilla, et al., also proposed TOGBAD as a solution to the problem [8]. By placing sensors throughout the network a topology graph is created and the number of neighbors each node has is calculated. It is then determined how many neighbors each node claims to have. This is accomplished by having every node extract the number of neighbors claimed in the HELLO message, and send it to a central TOGBAD node. The two values, the one that is recognized by TOGBAD as the true value and the one that is sent, are compared. A node will be declared malicious if the difference is greater than some predetermined value.

This solution requires sensors throughout the network, and some central all-knowing master node. Both requirements counter MANET's declared purpose: that networks can be setup ad-hoc. These networks must be pre-configured with trustworthy sensors and must have all nodes succumb to a central trusted third party.

2.2.3 Powerful broadcaster

Another method an attacker can employ to overcome OLSR, is by using a powerful receiver/transmitter for her node. Based on the routing specifications, all those who can hear her HELLO message will deduce that she is a neighbor. Thus, many distant nodes will regard the attacker as the optimal hop for the purposes of reaching any other node; after all, she is a 1-hop for a multitude of nodes. In effect, the attacker has created a virtual bottleneck.

2.3 Discovering bottlenecks

What unites the above attacks and defenses is an attempt at manipulating topologies to create bottlenecks (defenses try to detect such manipulation). We can, however, define high-value assets as those nodes that have the majority of paths between a source, s, and target, t. If all paths between s and t travel through a single node, it is a bottleneck that will hold the highest asset value. Nodes having the partial set of paths can be given an asset value, less than possible maximum, and thus can be grouped into potential fault point. Now the attack reduces to finding these nodes and contaminating them.

2.3.1 Bottleneck

Let G=(V,E) be a graph depicting the network, with a source s and a target t. It is quite intuitive, that the highest asset nodes to compromise between two nodes, s and t, are the nodes themselves. This implies that compromising either s or t would give the highest results when communication between s and t is in question. Let $x, u, v \in V$. Let $paths(u \rightarrow v, x)$ denote the number of paths that exist in the network between u and v that traverse through node x. Let $paths(u \rightarrow v, \cdot)$ denote the number of different paths between nodes u and v using any intermediate node.[1] Thus,

the maximum asset value possible for either s or t is

$$max\_asset = paths(s \rightarrow t, \cdot)$$

It is also trivial to see, that the number of paths between s and t that traverse through x, $paths(s \rightarrow t, x)$, is given by (1):

$$
\begin{aligned}
paths(s \rightarrow t, x) &= paths(s \rightarrow x, \cdot) * paths(x \rightarrow t, \cdot) \\
&\leq max\_asset \quad (1)
\end{aligned}
$$

(1) also denotes the asset value associated with every node between s and t. If a node exists such that $paths(s \rightarrow t, x) = paths(s \rightarrow t, \cdot) = max\_asset$, it is a complete bottleneck.

In the event that a max_asset node does not exist, we can still find

$$
\begin{aligned}
max(G, s, t) = \quad &\{x| \quad \forall v \in (V - \{s, t\}) \quad (2) \\
&(paths(s \rightarrow t, x) \geq paths(s \rightarrow t, v))\}
\end{aligned}
$$

These nodes have the highest potential of being on the path of the packet sent from s to t.

2.3.2 Linear bottleneck detection

[13] proposed a linear time algorithm for giving each node its asset value based on the Ford-Fulkerson method [6] for finding max-flows in a flow network.

The crux of the proposition is the understanding that in OLSR it is possible for any node to learn the network topology without actually injecting additional overhead into the network. Due to the nature of the routing protocol, all forwarding nodes (MPRs) transmit local network topology knowledge to all other nodes. As mentioned in section 2.1.2, this knowledge is used by each of the nodes to build its own "view" of the network for a given time. However, nothing stops an attacker from extracting the information needed to build the "view" of the network topology as seen by any other node from the same TC messages. The information is readily available, and it is only a matter of consuming some CPU resources. Moreover, it does not impose any additional broadcasting on the network. Thus, the algorithm proposed simply calculated in linear time asset values for nodes on the expected path from s to t choosing the highest as the location for attack.

As the method described refrains from manipulating network topology, it us much more difficult to detect.

2.3.3 Other ideas

There are a number of papers dealing with finding 'high-asset' value nodes; albeit, in different contexts and under different assumptions. In [7], a *betweenness* measure is used to calculate one's relevance in a social network. Using a min-cut max-flow on a graph representing social ties, a quadratic algorithm, based on Ford-Fulkerson's network flow algorithm [6], is devised. This algorithm searches through the entire graph to find a node with high social ties.

[9] devised a method for detecting bottleneck nodes within a random deployment of a WSN for the purpose of maximizing the energy conservation, and consequently the total life of the network. Their work aims to improve the Stoer and Wagner's [14] $\mathcal{O}\left(N^3\right)$ MINCUT algorithm by introducing DBND, a $\mathcal{O}\left(N^2\right)$ cost algorithm. The solution, however,

---

[1] As G isn't a directed acyclic graph (DAG), it is possible that $paths(u \rightarrow v, x) = \infty$. This, however, will be resolved in a real OLSR MANET as cycles are omitted.

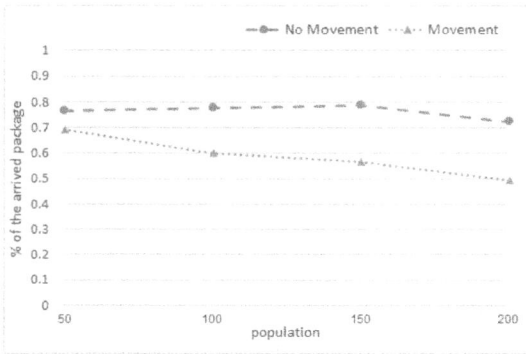

Figure 1: % of packets caught by bottleneck with [13] for different size networks with movement and without movement

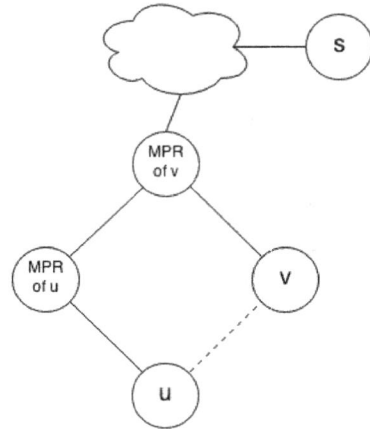

Figure 2: discrepancy between actual and perceived topologies

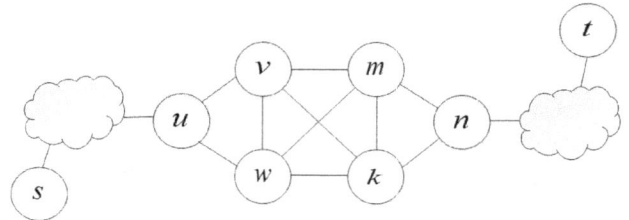

Figure 3: Alternate path around perceived bottleneck node k

is burdened with control messages (potential bottlenecks, discovery, confirmation, etc.) which consume bandwidth and resources. In addition, complete topology knowledge is achieved by dedicated control messages. Lastly, [9] does not consider bottleneck sets, i.e. two or more nodes that together comprise a bottleneck, which is a requirement for detecting colluding attackers within the network.

3. CONTAMINATION

Running[2] [13]'s on NS3 [1], a professional network simulator, produces Figure 1, showing the percentage of packets captured by attacking a projected bottleneck. It is trivial to see that with a capture rate of 50%-75%, some packets were able to circumvent the attack, reaching their destination (a number fluctuating between 20%-50% depending on the size of the network and whether movement is allowed or not).

This failure is a result of a discrepancy between what a specific node actually knows (real topology) and the topology others can deduce from TC messages. For example, in Figure 2, s will deduce that packets from v to u must flow through the two MPRs. Node v, however, knows of the edge $(v, u) \in E$ (dotted line); hence, it can utilize the direct link between them.

Characterization of this discrepancy is based on the observation that for connections to 1-hop neighbors, for which neither side was declared as MPR by the other, remote nodes will only find indirect paths between them. Thus, v's view of the network differs slightly from what can be directly deduced by simply listening to TC messages.

Similarly, in Figure 3, which represents a central portion of a path in which $u, w, k, n \in V$ are MPRs, s assumes that packet destine for t must pass through k. This is incorrect, as an alternate optimal path through v and m is equally likely.

---

[2]For the sake of completeness, we provide the parameters used for all simulations presented in this paper:
The built-in OSLR module of NS3 was used, with movement, where relevant, determined as Random Walk at a rate of 1.5-2 m/s (5.4-7.2 km/h). All value sets were run ~1000 times in an area of 750 x 1,000 m^2, with values reported as averages over these results. For each simulation round, the network topology was created randomely with a varying number of nodes, fluctuating network density from 50 to 200.

3.1 Full neighbor contamination

In order to achieve a complete, physical bottleneck, it does not suffice to takeover the perceived bottleneck node. Alternate optimal paths exist that circumvent that node. Hence, we must augment the algorithm given by [13] with a secondary step.

As a preliminary explanation, we note that routing is composed of two separate decisions: distant and local. The former is a node's decision to direct the packet to a MPR 2-hop away, who, based on current topology knowledge, is on the optimal path towards the target. The latter decides on how to route towards the chosen MPR; i.e. which of its 1-hops should be used to reach the 2-hop MPR. It is the difference between these decisions that causes circumvention of a compromised bottleneck node. For Figure 3, from a distance s believes that w will be used to transfer from u to k, while u itself might use a different node, v, to reach the same result.

Another subtle, yet important, consequence of the distant vs. local decision making, is that packets will be a distance of at most 1 from each projected MPR. Thus, as long as we contaminate all 1-hop neighbors of the perceived bottleneck node, we should be guaranteed that we capture all packets traversing from s to t. We call this group of nodes the bottleneck set, B.

Attack now reduces to the following three steps:

1. run the linear bottleneck detection algorithm given in [13],

2. overtake the perceived bottleneck node and add it to

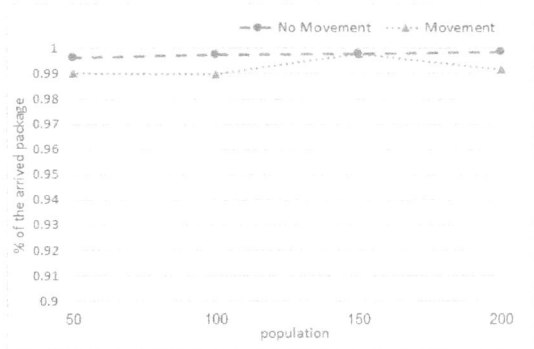

Figure 4: Data packet capture (%) with full neighbor bottleneck

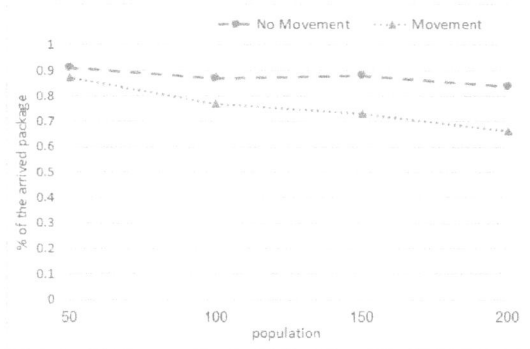

Figure 6: Data packet capture (%) with with bottleneck based on neighbor mprs only

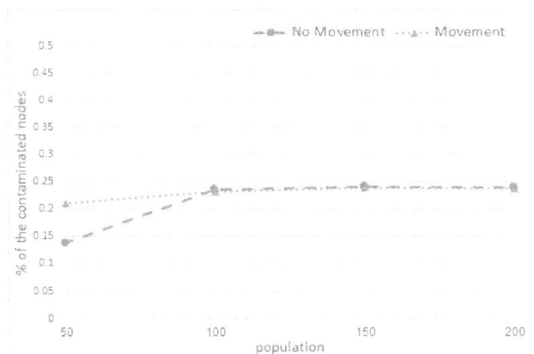

Figure 5: Estimated cost as fraction of network contaminated for full neighbor contamination

B, and

3. contaminate each of its 1-hop neighbors, and add them to B.

All nodes in B will collude on the attack, be it gray-hole, black-hole or any other MiTM attack thereof.

3.1.1 results

Running full neighbor contamination in the NS3 simulator, we measured how many packets were captured. A graph of the results can be seen in Figure 4. With over 99% success, both with movement and certainly without, such a mechanism is truly able to create a bottleneck on-the-fly, for any topology it is presented with.

Cost evaluation, however, isn't as gratifying. For each of the population sizes we measured |B|, which is the number of nodes the attacker must contaminate. Results are shown in Figure 5; fluctuating cost asymptotically centering around ~23%, irrespective of motion. This is equivalent to taking over a quarter of the network, and it's no surprise the capture rate was so high.

3.2 MPR contamination

In order to reduce the cost factor, we must minimize the number of 1-hop neighbors contaminated. As each node, at each step of the path is trying to direct traffic through MPR's 2-hops away (distant decision), contamination of the perceived bottleneck's neighbors categorized as MPR's is bound to increase success rate, reducing |B|.

Now the attack steps further reduce to the following:

1. run the linear bottleneck detection algorithm given in [13],

2. overtake a perceived bottleneck node and add it to B, and

3. contaminate and add to B each of its 1-hop neighbors that are advertised MPRs.

There is another advantage of using MPR as opposed to neighbor contamination. A distant attacker cannot see the discrepancy between what is perceived and what is real, for the same reason that this discrepancy exists; namely, only MPRs are advertised to the network. Thus, in order to execute the neighbor attack, steps 2&3 of section 3.1 must be executed sequentially. First one must take over the perceived bottleneck and only then can he know who are his clandestine 1-hop neighbors not advertised to the network.

Using MPR contamination, steps 2&3 can be executed in parallel. The perceived bottleneck node does not hold additional information regarding its 1-hop MPRs that were not advertised with TC to the network. The attacker can launch contamination of all of B's nodes at once, minimizing the time of attack setup.

3.2.1 results

Simulating MPR contamination in NS3, we expect more packets to circumvent B. Overall, as can be seen in Figure 6, there is an increase of ~10% to 20% (without and with movement, respectively) in captured packets when compared to what is achieved by [13] alone.

Evaluation of the cost of this technique, however, shows more gratifying results. Again, for each of the population sizes we measured |B|, and observed a decrease in cost as network size increased (see Figure 7). As OLSR was specifically developed for larger networks [4], a inversely decreasing cost factor is constant with the protocol goals.

4. DISCUSSION AND FUTURE RESEARCH

Turning a perceived bottleneck into a physical one, is a powerful tool in an attacker's arsenal. The ability for an external attacker to calculate a precision attack point on a conversation between targeted parties and expanding it to a complete path blockade, increases attack surface tremendously.

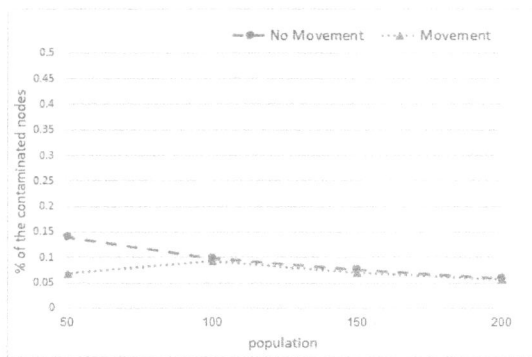

Figure 7: Estimated cost as fraction of network contaminated for mpr only contamination

With the basic capability calculated in linear time, we are not required to have an "all powerful" attacker. Mobile agents of all types (smartphone, smart sensors, etc.) can participate in the attack not sustaining penalties associated with high computations. Remote participants, not directly on the communication path, have the capability to diminish the inherent security that can be gained by a fluctuating topology. By exploiting 0-day's and the like, precision insertion of eavesdropping points is preferable to complete network overtake, as it dismisses the probability of detection.

In addition, in [12, 15] a spraying technique for secure key exchange is proposed. By spreading packets over multiple paths, the authors attempt at diffusing the single path MiTM risk. Our method, however, will allow an attacker to create complete bottlenecks (if one exists in the network), rendering such spraying as futile. We leave this exploration for future research.

Conversely, the ability for a source node to self-decide on the security potential of a future connection is a much required trait. As compared to other methods mentioned in section 2.3.3, our method is able to accomplish that without adding to the control overhead of the network. As it turns out, OLSR control traffic suffices for this purpose as well. A sender node can imitate an attacker, and discover, in linear time, the bottleneck characteristics of the path it wants to use.

This ability can be manipulated and built upon in a number of ways. First, a node can decide to abort a conversation if the topology changes over time. Nodes that were not considered a threat at specific times can evolve into a threat through a hostile takeover. They can, however, be discovered on-the-fly by the potential victim and circumvented.

The results of this research can be the basis for further research in a number of ways: First, smarter avoidance techniques can be developed and deployed based on route high-asset bottleneck detection. Second, bottleneck detection algorithms can be generated and potential high-traffic, high-asset nodes strengthened and monitored. Last, finding the balance between $|B|$ and capture ratio is left for future research.

5. REFERENCES

[1] The ns-3 simulator. http://www.nsnam.org.

[2] Mohammad Al-Shurman, Seong-Moo Yoo, and Seungjin Park. Black hole attack in mobile ad hoc networks. In *Proceedings of the 42Nd Annual Southeast Regional Conference*, ACM-SE 42, pages 96–97, New York, NY, USA, 2004. ACM.

[3] Yih chun Hu, Adrian Perrig, and David B. Johnson. Wormhole attacks in wireless networks. *IEEE Journal on Selected Areas in Communications*, 24:370–380, 2006.

[4] T. Clausen and P. Jacquet. Optimized Link State Routing Protocol (OLSR). RFC 3626 (Experimental), October 2003. [Online]. Available: http://www.ietf.org/rfc/rfc3626.txt. (Access Date: 6 September 2012).

[5] Hongmei Deng, W. Li, and D.P. Agrawal. Routing security in wireless ad hoc networks. *Communications Magazine, IEEE*, 40(10):70–75, Oct 2002.

[6] Lester R Ford and Delbert R Fulkerson. Maximal flow through a network. *Canadian Journal of Mathematics*, 8(3):399–404, 1956.

[7] Linton C Freeman, Stephen P Borgatti, and Douglas R White. Centrality in valued graphs: A measure of betweenness based on network flow. *Social networks*, 13(2):141–154, 1991.

[8] Elmar Gerhards-Padilla, Nils Aschenbruck, Peter Martini, Marko Jahnke, and Jens Tölle. Detecting black hole attacks in tactical manets using topology graphs. In *LCN*, pages 1043–1052. IEEE Computer Society, 2007.

[9] Haosong Gou and Younghwan Yoo. Distributed bottleneck node detection in wireless sensor network. In *Computer and Information Technology (CIT), 2010 IEEE 10th International Conference on*, pages 218–224, June 2010.

[10] Yih-Chun Hu, A. Perrig, and D.B. Johnson. Packet leashes: a defense against wormhole attacks in wireless networks. In *INFOCOM 2003. Twenty-Second Annual Joint Conference of the IEEE Computer and Communications. IEEE Societies*, volume 3, pages 1976–1986 vol.3, March 2003.

[11] P. Jacquet, P. Muhlethaler, T. Clausen, A. Laouiti, A. Qayyum, and L. Viennot. Optimized link state routing protocol for ad hoc networks. In *Multi Topic Conference, 2001. IEEE INMIC 2001. Technology for the 21st Century. Proceedings. IEEE International*, pages 62–68, 2001.

[12] Wenjing Lou. Spread: Enhancing data confidentiality in mobile ad hoc networks. In *Proceedings IEEE INFOCOM*, pages 2404–2413, 2004.

[13] N. Schweitzer, A. Stulman, T. Hirst, R.D. Margalit, M. Armon, and A. Shabtai. Detecting bottlenecks on-the-fly in olsr based manets. In *Electrical Electronics Engineers in Israel (IEEEI), 2014 IEEE 28th Convention of*, pages 1–5, Dec 2014.

[14] Mechthild Stoer and Frank Wagner. A simple min-cut algorithm. *J. ACM*, 44(4):585–591, July 1997.

[15] Ariel Stulman, Jonathan Lahav, and Avraham Shmueli. Spraying diffie-hellman for secure key exchange in manets. In Bruce Christianson, James A. Malcolm, Frank Stajano, Jonathan Anderson, and Joseph Bonneau, editors, *Security Protocols Workshop*, volume 8263 of *Lecture Notes in Computer Science*, pages 202–212. Springer, 2013.

[16] Srdjan Čapkun, Levente Buttyán, and Jean-Pierre

Hubaux. Sector: Secure tracking of node encounters in multi-hop wireless networks. In *Proceedings of the 1st ACM Workshop on Security of Ad Hoc and Sensor Networks*, SASN '03, pages 21–32, New York, NY, USA, 2003. ACM.

[17] Weichao Wang, Bharat Bhargava, Yi Lu, and Xiaoxin Wu. Defending against wormhole attacks in mobile ad hoc networks: Research articles. *Wirel. Commun. Mob. Comput.*, 6(4):483–503, June 2006.

Distributionally Robust Relay Beamforming in Wireless Communications

Shimin Gong
Shenzhen Institutes of
Advanced Technology
Chinese Academy of
Sciences, China
sm.gong@siat.ac.cn

Sissi Xiaoxiao Wu
Dept. of Systems Engineering
and Engineering Management
The Chinese University of
Hong Kong, Hong Kong
xxwu@ee.cuhk.edu.hk

Anthony Man-Cho So
Dept. of Systems Engineering
and Engineering Management
The Chinese University of
Hong Kong, Hong Kong
manchoso@se.cuhk.edu.hk

Xiaoxia Huang
Shenzhen Institutes of
Advanced Technology
Chinese Academy of
Sciences, China
xx.huang@siat.ac.cn

ABSTRACT

We consider a wireless network with densely deployed user devices (e.g., a device-to-device or wireless sensor network) underlaying a cellular system, in which some user devices act as relays to facilitate data transmissions between a distant transceiver pair under imperfect channel information. Motivated by the observation that most of the channel distributions are unimodal, we formulate a novel distributionally robust beamforming problem, in which the random channel coefficient follows a class of unimodal distribution with known first- and second-order moments. Our design objective is to maximize the worst-case signal-to-noise ratio (SNR) at the dedicated user device while satisfying a probabilistic interference constraint at the cellular user equipment (CUE). Though such a unimodal distributionally robust (UDR) beamforming problem is non-convex, we show that an approximate solution can be computed efficiently using semidefinite programming. Our simulation results show that under mild conditions, the UDR model yields significant beamforming performance improvement over conventional robust models that merely rely on first- and second-order moments of the channel distribution.

CCS Concepts

•**Networks** → *Network performance analysis; Mobile ad hoc networks;*

Keywords

Relay beamforming; distributional uncertainty; robust optimization

MSWiM '16, November 13-17, 2016, Malta, Malta

© 2016 ACM. ISBN 978-1-4503-4502-6/16/11...$15.00

DOI: http://dx.doi.org/10.1145/2988287.2989137

1. INTRODUCTION

As wireless devices (e.g., smart phones, wearable devices, sensors, etc.) become ubiquitous, device-to-device (D2D) communication is a promising way to increase data rates, extend network coverage, and reduce energy consumptions in cellular networks. It is proposed primarily to offload data traffic between the cellular base station (CBS) and the cellular user equipment (CUE) within or beyond the cellular coverage [12, 17]. With the upsurge of social applications (e.g., interactive gaming, file sharing, video streaming, etc.), D2D communication has become especially advantageous for a local social network, as the access to local contents is more frequent than that to the core network via the CBS. In this paper, instead of emphasizing on the performance improvement of cellular systems, we focus on the D2D communications and aim to improve the quality-of-service (QoS) of a local D2D network within the cellular coverage.

The dense deployment of D2D user equipment (DUE) allows us to achieve spatial diversity by employing multiple DUE as collaborative relays. It has been shown in [4] that the use of relays can significantly improve network performance while causing insignificant increase in end-to-end delay. However, the dense DUE makes the spectrum usage more crowded. An economical and spectrally efficient solution is to let the DUE share the same spectrum with the cellular system [7, 9]. This requires an efficient power control strategy at the DUE relays to manage the interference among the DUE and CUE. By analyzing the interference to the CUE, a strategy for selecting different D2D operating modes is proposed in [23]. In [18], the power of each DUE relay is controlled separately while the interference to the CUE is controlled by selecting the number of relays. The authors in [8] considered an ad hoc D2D network, in which the interference to the cellular system is kept below a certain interference temperature. In general, to achieve optimal relay performance, one needs to design a distributed beamformer according to different relays' channel conditions [15,24]. However, most of the aforementioned works rely on the unrealistic assumption that the channel information is precisely known. In practice, the channel information is usually unreliable due to quantization errors, processing delay, or lack of coordination between the CUE and numerous DUE. Thus, there has been a growing effort in modeling the channel uncertainty, so that proactive strategies can be developed to avoid sharp performance deterioration. Broadly speaking, there are three different types of channel uncertainty models. A *stochastic* (STO) model assumes that the channel estimate follows an explicit distribution, such as Rician or Rayleigh [11]. Under this model, we can formulate the QoS metric in a probabilistic manner and obtain a chance-constrained robust beamforming problem [16, 22]. The *worst-case robust* (WCR) model assumes that the channel error lies in a bounded convex set and gives rise to a max-min beamforming problem [5, 6]. A less conservative approach is to build the channel models based on partial distributional information that is easy to estimate with high accuracy, such as low-order moments of the channel error. The *distributionally robust* (DRO) model was recently employed to study robust beamforming by leveraging the first- and second-order moments of the channel distribution [10]. However, such an approach can still be too conservative, as the worst-case channel distribution is shown to be discrete and hardly observed in practice [21].

The above discussion motivates us to impose additional requirements on the shape or structure of the channel distribution. Empirically, we find that the channel distribution is typically smooth, symmetric, unimodal, or even similar to some known patterns [2]. Such structural information can be extracted and exploited to further mitigate the conservatism of the DRO model. In this work, we focus on the unimodal structure and propose the *unimodal distributionally robust* (UDR) model to improve the relays' beamformer design. Our goal is to maximize the DUE receiver's SNR subject to the CUE's probabilistic interference constraints. The main contributions of this paper are summarized as follows:

- *Unimodal distributionally robust model*: Motivated by the observation that most channel distributions are unimodal, we introduce a novel UDR model, which assumes that the random channel follows a class of unimodal distributions with known first- and second-order moments. By leveraging the generalized notion of unimodality [20], we parameterize a class of unimodal distributions by a positive scalar α, which allows us to derive an upper bound on the worst-case interference violation probability. To the best of our knowledge, our work is the first to adopt the UDR model in the relays' robust beamforming problem.

- *Heuristic beamforming algorithm*: As we shall see, different values of α correspond to different levels of conservatism in channel modeling, and the UDR model degenerates into the DRO model as α approaches infinity. This observation motivates us to design an iterative algorithm to tackle the relays' beamforming problem by alternately solving the well-known DRO-based beamforming problem and updating the beamformer based on a feasibility check on the UDR-based beamforming problem. Our simulation results show that the UDR model significantly improves the DUE's throughput performance.

The rest of this paper is organized as follows. We describe the system model and the channel uncertainty in Section 2.

In Section 3, we propose the relays' robust beamforming problem and design the beamforming algorithm based on the proposed UDR model. Simulations and conclusions are given in Sections 4 and 5, respectively.

2. SYSTEM MODEL

We consider a D2D network with densely deployed user devices underlaying a downlink cellular system, in which each DUE transmitter (DTx), DUE relay, and DUE receiver (DRx) are equipped with a single antenna. We assume that a direct link between the DTx and DRx is not available due to the long transmission distance and limited power at the DTx, and the DUE's data transmission is assisted by a group of DUE relays, denoted by the set $\mathcal{N} = \{1, 2, \ldots, N\}$. The relays' transmissions also introduce interference to the CUE. Without loss of generality, we consider one CUE in the system for simplicity. The system model is illustrated in Figure 1. The CUE will not be interrupted if the interference from the DUE relays is less than a prescribed threshold. The downlink transmissions from the CBS to the CUE may also introduce interference to the D2D communications. Herein, we assume that such interference is constant and treat it as background noise.

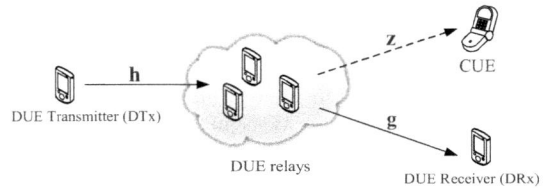

Figure 1: System model

Let $\mathbf{h} \triangleq [h_1, h_2, \ldots, h_N]^T$ and $\mathbf{g} \triangleq [g_1, g_2, \ldots, g_N]^T$ denote the channel coefficients from the DTx to the relays and from the relays to the DRx, respectively, and $\mathbf{z} \triangleq [z_1, z_2, \ldots, z_N]^T$ denote the channel coefficients from the relays to the CUE. We assume that all channels are frequency-flat and block fading [1]; i.e., the channel coefficients remain constant during one data frame and may change independently during different data frames. We assume that there is a coordinator in the system that schedules one DTx to transmit at a time to avoid conflicts between different DUE [19]. Thus, we can focus on one DUE transceiver pair each time.

2.1 Nominal Beamforming Problem

In the system, the relays' information delivery follows a two-hop amplify-and-forward (AF) protocol. In the first hop, the DTx broadcasts a symbol s to the nearby relays. The received signal at relay n is $m_n = h_n s + \sigma_n$, where $\sigma_n \sim \mathbb{N}(0, 1)$ is the Gaussian noise with zero mean and unit variance. In the second hop, relay n forwards the signal m_n amplified by a weight w_n and thus $\mathbf{w} = [w_1, w_2, \ldots, w_N]^T$ constitutes the relays' beamformer. The received signal at the DRx is

$$y = \sum_{n=1}^{N} g_n w_n h_n s + \sum_{n=1}^{N} g_n w_n \sigma_n + v_d,$$

where $v_d \sim \mathbb{N}(0, 1)$ is the noise at the DRx. Note that the first term of the received signal y contains the useful information while the second term is the noise signal forwarded by the relays. Assuming unit transmit power at the DTx (i.e., $\mathbb{E}[|s|^2] = 1$), the SNR at the DRx is given by

$$\gamma(\mathbf{w}) = \left| \sum_{n=1}^{N} w_n g_n h_n \right|^2 \bigg/ \left(1 + \sum_{n=1}^{N} |w_n|^2 |g_n|^2 \right). \quad (1)$$

We observe that it may not be optimal for all the relays to transmit at their peak power, as the relays also amplify and forward the noise signals. Let $\mathbf{a} = \mathbf{g} \circ \mathbf{h}$ be the component-wise product of the channels $\mathbf{g}$ and $\mathbf{h}$. Then, we can rewrite the DUE's SNR $\gamma(\mathbf{w})$ more compactly as $\gamma(\mathbf{w}) = \frac{\mathbf{w}^T \mathbf{A} \mathbf{w}}{1 + \mathbf{w}^T \mathbf{B} \mathbf{w}}$, where $\mathbf{A} = \mathbf{a}\mathbf{a}^T$ and $\mathbf{B} = \mathrm{D}(\mathbf{g} \circ \mathbf{g})$ are positive semidefinite matrices. Here, $\mathrm{D}(\mathbf{g})$ is a diagonal matrix with the diagonal elements specified by $\mathbf{g}$.

To ensure harmonic coexistence with the cellular system, the DUE relays' transmit beamforming has to restrict the aggregate interference to the CUE. As the transmit power at relay n is $|w_n|^2(1+|h_n|^2)$, the aggregate interference received by the CUE can be expressed as $\phi(\mathbf{w}) = \sum_{n=1}^{N} |z_n|^2 |w_n|^2 (1+|h_n|^2)$. Let $\Lambda_{\mathbf{w}} = \mathrm{D}(\mathbf{k} \circ \mathbf{k})\mathrm{D}(\mathbf{w} \circ \mathbf{w})$, where $\mathbf{k} = [(1+h_n^2)^{1/2}]_{n \in \mathcal{N}}$ is the known information at the relays. Then, we have $\phi(\mathbf{w}) = \mathbf{z}^T \Lambda_{\mathbf{w}} \mathbf{z}$. Our target is to maximize the DUE's SNR by optimizing the relays' beamformer $\mathbf{w}$, subject to the CUE's interference constraint; i.e.,

$$\max_{\mathbf{w}} \left\{ \frac{\mathbf{w}^T \mathbf{A} \mathbf{w}}{1 + \mathbf{w}^T \mathbf{B} \mathbf{w}} : \mathbf{z}^T \Lambda_{\mathbf{w}} \mathbf{z} \leq \bar{\phi} \right\}, \quad (2)$$

where $\bar{\phi}$ is a prescribed threshold that represents the CUE's sensitivity to interference. We can also add individual or sum power budget constraints at the relays, but this would not affect our subsequent analysis. Thus, we only consider the CUE's interference constraint for simplicity. Our formulation can be easily extended to the setting where there are multiple CUE. Each CUE would then have its own interference constraint, thus ensuring protection for the most vulnerable CUE.

2.2 Channel Uncertainty Model

The solution to problem (2) requires exact knowledge of the channel coefficients. In this paper, we assume that $\mathbf{h}$ in the first hop is perfectly known by the relays' channel estimation; e.g., the DTx can broadcast a known pilot signal to facilitate the relays' channel estimation. However, due to limited or untimely responses from the DRx and CUE, the relays are unable to estimate $\mathbf{g}$ and $\mathbf{z}$ accurately. To model the uncertainties in $\mathbf{g}$ and $\mathbf{z}$, we assume that $\mathbf{g}$ and $\mathbf{z}$ are random variables following distributions $\mathbb{P}_{\mathbf{g}}$ and $\mathbb{P}_{\mathbf{z}}$, respectively. Since it is relatively easy to estimate the mean $\mathbf{u}_{\mathbf{g}}$ and covariance $\mathbf{S}_{\mathbf{g}}$ of the channel coefficient $\mathbf{g}$, we can define the distributional uncertainty set of $\mathbf{g}$ as

$$\mathbb{P}_{\mathbf{g}} \in \mathcal{P}(\mathbf{u}_{\mathbf{g}}, \mathbf{S}_{\mathbf{g}}) \subset \mathcal{P}_{\infty}, \quad (3)$$

where $\mathcal{P}(\mathbf{u}_{\mathbf{g}}, \mathbf{S}_{\mathbf{g}})$ is a set of distributions having the same moment statistics $(\mathbf{u}_{\mathbf{g}}, \mathbf{S}_{\mathbf{g}})$ and $\mathcal{P}_{\infty}$ is the set of all probability distributions. In the same vein, we can define the distributional uncertainty set of $\mathbf{z}$ as $\mathbb{P}_{\mathbf{z}} \in \mathcal{P}(\mathbf{u}_{\mathbf{z}}, \mathbf{S}_{\mathbf{z}})$, where $(\mathbf{u}_{\mathbf{z}}, \mathbf{S}_{\mathbf{z}})$ is the first- and second-order moments of the channel coefficient $\mathbf{z}$, which are known to the DUE relays. The distributional uncertainty set defined in (3) gives rise to a typical DRO model [10].

In this work, we aim to mitigate the conservatism of the DRO model by incorporating additional structural information that can be extracted from channel measurements.

Specifically, we require $\mathbb{P}_{\mathbf{g}}$ or $\mathbb{P}_{\mathbf{z}}$ to be unimodal, which is a commonly observed property in the area of wireless communications and signal processing [13]. Intuitively, unimodality implies a single local maxima (referred to as the mode) in the density function. For *univariate* unimodal distributions, the density function is non-decreasing to the left of the mode and non-increasing to the right of the mode. In particular, Gaussian, Rayleigh, and Rician distributions are examples of univariate unimodal distribution. By incorporating unimodality in the DRO model, we can remove those hardly observed multi-modal distributions from the uncertainty set (3), thereby leading to more practical distributional uncertainty sets for $\mathbf{g}$ and $\mathbf{z}$. To fulfill this purpose, we first need an analytical characterization of unimodality for *multivariate* distributions. This can be achieved using the notion of α-unimodality [20]:

DEFINITION 1. *Suppose that $\mathbb{P} \in \mathcal{P}_{\infty}$ has a continuous probability density function f on $\mathbb{R}^N$. We say that $\mathbb{P}$ is α-unimodal with mode $\mathbf{0}$ for some $\alpha > 0$ if $t^{N-\alpha} f(t\mathbf{x})$ is non-increasing in $t > 0$ for all $\mathbf{x} \neq \mathbf{0}$. The set of all α-unimodal distributions with mode $\mathbf{0}$ is denoted as $\mathcal{P}_{\alpha}$.*

When $\alpha = N$, α-unimodality implies that the density function is non-increasing along the rays emanating from its mode, which coincides with our intuition for univariate unimodal distributions. When $\alpha > N$, the density function f may increase along the rays emanating from its mode, but $t^{N-\alpha} f(t\mathbf{x})$ is still non-increasing in $t > 0$. The rate of increase of f is controlled by the parameter α. Hence, α-unimodality is a more general characterization of unimodal distributions. Now, we can define the unimodal distributionally robust (UDR) model for $\mathbf{g}$ and $\mathbf{z}$ as follows:

$$\mathbb{P}_{\mathbf{g}} \in \mathcal{P}_{\mathbf{g}}^{\alpha} \triangleq \mathcal{P}_{\mathbf{g}}(\mathbf{u}_{\mathbf{g}}, \mathbf{S}_{\mathbf{g}}) \bigcap \mathcal{P}_{\alpha}, \quad (4a)$$

$$\mathbb{P}_{\mathbf{z}} \in \mathcal{P}_{\mathbf{z}}^{\alpha} \triangleq \mathcal{P}_{\mathbf{z}}(\mathbf{u}_{\mathbf{z}}, \mathbf{S}_{\mathbf{z}}) \bigcap \mathcal{P}_{\alpha}. \quad (4b)$$

The parameterized sets $\mathcal{P}_{\mathbf{g}}^{\alpha}$ and $\mathcal{P}_{\mathbf{z}}^{\alpha}$ allow flexibility in modeling the uncertainties in $\mathbf{g}$ and $\mathbf{z}$ under different channel conditions. When α is equal to the number of DUE relays, most of the practically observed distributions will fall in the set $\mathcal{P}_{\alpha}$ [20]. When α approaches infinity, every distribution belongs to the set $\mathcal{P}_{\infty}$. In this case, the UDR model (4) degenerates into the DRO model (3).

3. ROBUST BEAMFORMING PROBLEM

Both the SNR performance $\gamma(\mathbf{w})$ and the aggregate interference $\phi(\mathbf{w})$ are functions of the channel conditions. Thus, they become stochastic when the channels $\mathbf{g}$ and $\mathbf{z}$ are drawn from $\mathbb{P}_{\mathbf{g}}$ and $\mathbb{P}_{\mathbf{z}}$, respectively. Considering the UDR model (4), we formulate the robust counterpart of (2) as follows:

$$\max_{\mathbf{w}} \quad \min_{\mathbb{P}_{\mathbf{g}} \in \mathcal{P}_{\mathbf{g}}^{\alpha}} \frac{\mathbb{E}_{\mathbb{P}_{\mathbf{g}}}[\mathbf{w}^T \mathbf{A} \mathbf{w}]}{1 + \mathbb{E}_{\mathbb{P}_{\mathbf{g}}}[\mathbf{w}^T \mathbf{B} \mathbf{w}]} \quad (5a)$$

$$s.t. \quad \max_{\mathbb{P}_{\mathbf{z}} \in \mathcal{P}_{\mathbf{z}}^{\alpha}} \mathbb{P}_{\mathbf{z}}\left(\mathbf{z}^T \Lambda_{\mathbf{w}} \mathbf{z} \geq \bar{\phi} \right) \leq \eta. \quad (5b)$$

Here, we optimize the relays' beamformer $\mathbf{w}$ to maximize the DUE's worst-case SNR while limiting the CUE's worst-case (with respect to all distributions with the given structural and moment information) interference violation probability below a prescribed probability threshold η.

Due to the non-convex probabilistic constraint (5b), the UDR beamforming problem (5) is generally difficult to solve optimally. To simplify it, we introduce the SNR target $\rho \geq 0$ and observe that (5a) is equivalent to maximizing ρ subject to the following QoS constraint:

$$\rho + \max_{\mathbb{P}_{\mathbf{g}} \in \mathcal{P}_{\mathbf{g}}^{\alpha}} \mathbb{E}_{\mathbb{P}_{\mathbf{g}}} \left[\mathbf{g}^T \left(\rho \mathrm{D}(\mathbf{w} \circ \mathbf{w}) - \mathbf{q}\mathbf{q}^T \right) \mathbf{g} \right] \leq 0, \quad (6)$$

where we denote $\mathbf{q} = \mathrm{D}(\mathbf{h})\mathbf{w}$ for simplicity. Note that the SNR constraint (6) only involves the second-order moment $\mathbf{S}_g$ and not the particular structure of the distribution $\mathbb{P}_{\mathbf{g}}$. Hence, we can simplify (6) as

$$\rho + \rho\mathbf{Tr}(\mathrm{D}(\mathbf{w} \circ \mathbf{w})\mathbf{S}_{\mathbf{g}}) - \mathbf{q}^T\mathbf{S}_{\mathbf{g}}\mathbf{q} \leq 0. \quad (7)$$

To simplify the probabilistic constraint (5b), let $e(\mathbf{z}) = \mathbf{1}(\mathbf{z}^T\mathbf{\Lambda}_{\mathbf{w}}\mathbf{z} \geq \bar{\phi})$, where $\mathbf{1}(\cdot)$ is the indicator function. Define

$$B_{\alpha}(\mathbf{u}_{\mathbf{z}}, \mathbf{S}_{\mathbf{z}}) = \max_{\mathbb{P}_{\mathbf{z}} \in \mathcal{P}_{\mathbf{z}}^{\alpha}} \mathbb{E}_{\mathbb{P}_{\mathbf{z}}} \left[e(\mathbf{z}) \right] \quad (8)$$

to be the worst-case interference violation probability on the LHS of (5b). Since the maximization in (8) is semi-infinite and the constraint $B_{\alpha}(\mathbf{u}_{\mathbf{z}}, \mathbf{S}_{\mathbf{z}}) \leq \eta$ has no known closed-form convex equivalence, we shall focus on deriving an upper bound on $B_{\alpha}(\mathbf{u}_{\mathbf{z}}, \mathbf{S}_{\mathbf{z}})$ in the sequel. To proceed, we first study the approximation of $B_{\alpha}(\mathbf{u}_{\mathbf{z}}, \mathbf{S}_{\mathbf{z}})$ in a special case of the UDR model; namely, the DRO model (which corresponds to α approaching infinity). After getting some insights from this special case, we then consider the UDR model in its full generality.

3.1 A Special Case of the UDR Model

When α approaches infinity, the UDR model degenerates into the DRO model. In this case, we have the following equivalence [25]:

$$B_{\infty}(\mathbf{u}_{\mathbf{z}}, \mathbf{S}_{\mathbf{z}}) = \min_{\mathbf{M}, \nu} \mathbf{Tr}(\mathbf{\Sigma}_{\mathbf{z}}\mathbf{M}) \quad (9a)$$

$$s.t. \quad \mathbf{M} \succeq \begin{bmatrix} \nu\mathbf{\Lambda}_{\mathbf{w}} & \mathbf{0} \\ \mathbf{0} & 1 - \nu\bar{\phi} \end{bmatrix}, \quad (9b)$$

$$\mathbf{M} \succeq \mathbf{0}, \quad \nu \geq 0, \quad (9c)$$

where $\mathbf{M}, \nu$ are dual variables and $\mathbf{\Sigma}_{\mathbf{z}} = \begin{bmatrix} \mathbf{S}_{\mathbf{z}} & \mathbf{u}_{\mathbf{z}} \\ \mathbf{u}_{\mathbf{z}}^T & 1 \end{bmatrix}$ denotes the second-order moment matrix of the channel $\mathbf{z}$. For any fixed $\mathbf{w}$, (9b) is a linear matrix inequality. Hence, problem (9) is a semidefinite program (SDP) and provides a tractable reformulation of $B_{\infty}(\mathbf{u}_{\mathbf{z}}, \mathbf{S}_{\mathbf{z}})$. Upon replacing (5b) by (9), the optimal beamformer $\mathbf{w}^{\star}$ can be obtained as follows:

$$\max_{\rho \geq 0, \mathbf{w}} \rho \quad (10a)$$

$$s.t. \quad \rho + \rho\mathbf{Tr}(\mathrm{D}(\mathbf{w} \circ \mathbf{w})\mathbf{S}_{\mathbf{g}}) - \mathbf{q}^T\mathbf{S}_{\mathbf{g}}\mathbf{q} \leq 0, \quad (10b)$$

$$\mathbf{Tr}(\mathbf{\Sigma}_{\mathbf{z}}\mathbf{M}) \leq \nu\eta, \quad (10c)$$

$$\mathbf{M} \succeq \begin{bmatrix} \mathrm{D}(\mathbf{k} \circ \mathbf{k})\mathrm{D}(\mathbf{w} \circ \mathbf{w}) & \mathbf{0} \\ \mathbf{0} & \nu - \bar{\phi} \end{bmatrix}, \quad (10d)$$

$$\mathbf{M} \succeq \mathbf{0}, \quad \nu \geq 0. \quad (10e)$$

Unfortunately, problem (10) is still non-convex, as the constraints (10b) and (10d) are quadratic in $\mathbf{w}$. To circumvent this difficulty, we apply the semidefinite relaxation (SDR) technique [14]. Specifically, by first introducing the rank-one matrix $\mathbf{W} = \mathbf{w}\mathbf{w}^T$ and then dropping the non-convex rank-one constraint on $\mathbf{W}$, we obtain the following SDR of

problem (10):

$$\text{(SUB)} : \max_{\rho \geq 0, \mathbf{W} \succeq \mathbf{0}} \rho \quad (11a)$$

$$s.t. \quad \rho + \rho\mathbf{Tr}(\mathbf{\Delta}(\mathbf{W})\mathbf{S}_{\mathbf{g}}) - \mathbf{q}^T\mathbf{S}_{\mathbf{g}}\mathbf{q} \leq 0, \quad (11b)$$

$$\mathbf{Tr}(\mathbf{\Sigma}_{\mathbf{z}}\mathbf{M}) \leq \nu\eta, \quad (11c)$$

$$\mathbf{M} \succeq \begin{bmatrix} \mathrm{D}(\mathbf{k} \circ \mathbf{k})\mathbf{\Delta}(\mathbf{W}) & \mathbf{0} \\ \mathbf{0} & \nu - \bar{\phi} \end{bmatrix}, \quad (11d)$$

$$\mathbf{M} \succeq \mathbf{0}, \quad \nu \geq 0, \quad (11e)$$

where $\mathbf{\Delta}(\mathbf{W}) = \mathrm{D}(\mathbf{w} \circ \mathbf{w})$ is the diagonal matrix by setting all off-diagonal elements of $\mathbf{W}$ to zero.

Problem (SUB) can be solved optimally by a bisection method. Indeed, for a given target SNR ρ, it is clear that (11b) and (11c) are linear inequalities and (11d) is a linear matrix inequality. This implies that checking the feasibility of the constraints (11b)–(11e) is an SDP, which can be solved efficiently by the interior-point algorithms embedded in some well-known optimization toolbox, such as SeDuMi and CVX [3]. In particular, we can increase or decrease ρ depending on whether the constraints (11b)–(11e) are satisfied or not, until convergence is achieved. Now, suppose that the bisection method converges to the optimal beamforming matrix $\mathbf{W}^{\star}$. If $\mathbf{W}^{\star}$ happens to be a rank-one matrix, then the optimal beamformer $\mathbf{w}^{\star}$ to problem (10) can be extracted by eigen-decomposition. Otherwise, an approximate rank-one solution can be extracted from $\mathbf{W}^{\star}$ by, e.g., a Gaussian randomization method [14].

3.2 The General Case of the UDR Model

Now, let us focus on the general UDR model and derive an upper bound on $B_{\alpha}(\mathbf{u}_{\mathbf{z}}, \mathbf{S}_{\mathbf{z}})$ for finite values of α. By definition of α-unimodality, a finite α imposes non-trivial structure on the distribution $\mathbb{P}_{\mathbf{z}}$, and a smaller α implies more stringent structural requirement; i.e., $\mathcal{P}_{\alpha_1} \supset \mathcal{P}_{\alpha_2}$ for $\alpha_1 \geq \alpha_2 > 0$. Therefore, by tuning the value of α, we can construct a flexible robust model that captures the information uncertainty in different channel conditions. However, the lack of a concrete representation of $\mathcal{P}_{\mathbf{z}}^{\alpha}$ makes it very difficult to solve problem (8) in closed-form. A simplification of $\mathcal{P}_{\mathbf{z}}^{\alpha}$ relies on the construction of a special class of the α-unimodal distributions.

DEFINITION 2. *For any $\alpha > 0$ and $\mathbf{x} \in \mathbb{R}^n$, the radial α-unimodal distribution supported on the line segment $[\mathbf{0}, \mathbf{x}] \subset \mathbb{R}^n$, denoted by $\delta_{[\mathbf{0},\mathbf{x}]}^{\alpha}(\cdot)$, is a distribution with the property that $\delta_{[\mathbf{0},\mathbf{x}]}^{\alpha}([\mathbf{0}, t\mathbf{x}]) = t^{\alpha}$ for $t \in [0,1]$.*

LEMMA 1 ([20]). *For any $\mathbb{P} \in \mathcal{P}_{\alpha}$, there exists a unique distribution $\mathbf{m} \in \mathcal{P}_{\infty}$ such that $\mathbb{P}(\cdot) = \int_{\mathbb{R}^n} \delta_{[\mathbf{0},\mathbf{x}]}^{\alpha}(\cdot)\mathbf{m}(d\mathbf{x})$.*

Lemma 1 maps any α-unimodal distribution $\mathbb{P}_{\mathbf{z}} \in \mathcal{P}_{\mathbf{z}}^{\alpha}$ to a general distribution $\mathbf{m} \in \mathcal{P}_{\infty}$ without the unimodality constraint. This mapping allows us to reformulate (8) as a conventional moment constrained problem:

$$B_{\alpha}(\mathbf{u}_{\mathbf{z}}, \mathbf{S}_{\mathbf{z}}) = \max_{\mathbf{m} \in \mathcal{P}_{\infty}} \mathbb{E}_{\mathbf{m}} \left[p_{\alpha}(\mathbf{x}) \right] \quad (12a)$$

$$s.t. \quad \mathbb{E}_{\mathbf{m}} \begin{bmatrix} \mathbf{x}\mathbf{x}^T & \mathbf{x} \\ \mathbf{x}^T & 1 \end{bmatrix} = \begin{bmatrix} \bar{\mathbf{S}}_{\mathbf{z}} & \bar{\mathbf{u}}_{\mathbf{z}} \\ \bar{\mathbf{u}}_{\mathbf{z}}^T & 1 \end{bmatrix}, \quad (12b)$$

where $p_{\alpha}(\mathbf{x}) = \int_{\mathbb{R}^n} e(\mathbf{z})\delta_{[\mathbf{0},\mathbf{x}]}^{\alpha}(d\mathbf{z})$ and the moment statistics $\bar{\mathbf{S}}_{\mathbf{z}}$ and $\bar{\mathbf{u}}_{\mathbf{z}}$ are given by $\frac{2+\alpha}{\alpha}\mathbf{S}_{\mathbf{z}}$ and $\frac{1+\alpha}{\alpha}\mathbf{u}_{\mathbf{z}}$, respectively. The equivalence between problems (8) and (12) is straightforward by applying Lemma 1 to (8). Such equivalence implies that once we find an $\mathbf{m}$ that is feasible for (12), we can construct an α-unimodal distribution $\mathbb{P}_\mathbf{z}$ that is feasible for (8). Thus, in the sequel, we shall focus on problem (12).

Although problem (12) has a similar structure to that in the DRO model, the Lagrangian method does not give a tractable dual form of (12). Instead, we resort to the following approximation:

PROPOSITION 1. *An upper bound on $B_\alpha(\mathbf{u}_\mathbf{z}, \mathbf{S}_\mathbf{z})$ is given by*

$$\max_{\mathbf{Y}\succeq\mathbf{0}, \mathbf{y}\geq\mathbf{0}, \lambda, \tau\geq 0} \quad \lambda - \tau \tag{13a}$$

$$s.t. \quad \begin{bmatrix} \bar{\mathbf{S}}_\mathbf{z} & \bar{\mathbf{u}}_\mathbf{z} \\ \bar{\mathbf{u}}_\mathbf{z}^T & 1 \end{bmatrix} - \begin{bmatrix} \mathbf{Y} & \mathbf{y} \\ \mathbf{y}^T & \lambda \end{bmatrix} \succeq \mathbf{0}, \tag{13b}$$

$$\begin{bmatrix} \mathbf{Y} & \mathbf{y} \\ \mathbf{y}^T & \lambda \end{bmatrix} \succeq \mathbf{0}, \tag{13c}$$

$$\tau^2 \big(\mathbf{Tr}(\mathbf{\Lambda}_\mathbf{w}\mathbf{Y})\big)^\alpha \geq \lambda^{\alpha+2}\bar{\phi}^\alpha. \tag{13d}$$

PROOF. We need to show that for any feasible solution $\mathbf{m}$ to problem (12), we can construct a feasible solution $(\mathbf{Y}, \mathbf{y}, \lambda, \tau)$ to problem (13) such that it achieves at least the same probability bound as $\mathbf{m}$. Towards that end, let $\mathbb{P}_\mathbf{z}$ be a feasible α-unimodal distribution for (8) and $\mathbf{m}$ denote the corresponding mixture distribution in (12). Let $\Xi \triangleq \{\mathbf{x} \mid \mathbf{x}^T\mathbf{\Lambda}_\mathbf{w}\mathbf{x} < \bar{\phi}\}$ and $\bar{\Xi} = \mathbb{R}^n \setminus \Xi$. Then, we can construct a feasible solution to problem (13) by the following rules:

$$\begin{bmatrix} \mathbf{Y} & \mathbf{y} \\ \mathbf{y}^T & \lambda \end{bmatrix} = \int_{\bar{\Xi}} \begin{bmatrix} \mathbf{x}\mathbf{x}^T & \mathbf{x} \\ \mathbf{x}^T & 1 \end{bmatrix} \mathbf{m}(d\mathbf{x}) \succeq \mathbf{0}, \tag{14a}$$

$$\tau = \int_{\bar{\Xi}} \big(1 - p_\alpha(\mathbf{x})\big)\mathbf{m}(d\mathbf{x}) \geq 0. \tag{14b}$$

Obviously, we have $\lambda \leq 1$ and

$$\begin{bmatrix} \bar{\mathbf{S}}_\mathbf{z} & \bar{\mathbf{u}}_\mathbf{z} \\ \bar{\mathbf{u}}_\mathbf{z}^T & 1 \end{bmatrix} = \int_{\mathbf{x}\in\Xi\cup\bar{\Xi}} \begin{bmatrix} \mathbf{x}\mathbf{x}^T & \mathbf{x} \\ \mathbf{x}^T & 1 \end{bmatrix} \mathbf{m}(d\mathbf{x}) \succeq \begin{bmatrix} \mathbf{Y} & \mathbf{y} \\ \mathbf{y}^T & \lambda \end{bmatrix}.$$

Note that $p_\alpha(\mathbf{x}) = \int_{\mathbb{R}^n} \mathbf{1}(\mathbf{z}^T\mathbf{\Lambda}_\mathbf{w}\mathbf{z} \geq \bar{\phi})\delta^\alpha_{[\mathbf{0},\mathbf{x}]}(d\mathbf{z})$. Moreover, by the construction of Ξ, we have

$$1 - p_\alpha(\mathbf{x}) = \begin{cases} \left(\dfrac{\bar{\phi}}{\mathbf{x}^T\mathbf{\Lambda}_\mathbf{w}\mathbf{x}}\right)^{\frac{\alpha}{2}} & \text{for } \mathbf{x} \in \bar{\Xi}, \\ 1 & \text{for } \mathbf{x} \in \Xi, \end{cases} \tag{15}$$

which implies $\tau \geq \left(\frac{\bar{\phi}}{\int_{\bar{\Xi}} \mathbf{x}^T\mathbf{\Lambda}_\mathbf{w}\mathbf{x}\,\mathbf{m}(d\mathbf{x})}\right)^{\frac{\alpha}{2}} \geq \lambda\left(\frac{\lambda\bar{\phi}}{\mathbf{Tr}(\mathbf{Y}\mathbf{\Lambda}_\mathbf{w})}\right)^{\frac{\alpha}{2}}$. The first inequality comes from the Jensen inequality and the second inequality is due to the fact that $\int_{\bar{\Xi}} \mathbf{x}\mathbf{x}^T\mathbf{m}(d\mathbf{x}) = \mathbf{Y}$ and $\lambda \leq 1$. The final step is to verify that the same objective can be achieved by the construction in (14): $\mathbb{E}_\mathbf{m}[p_\alpha(\mathbf{x})] = \int_{\bar{\Xi}}\mathbf{m}(d\mathbf{x}) - \int_{\bar{\Xi}}\big(1 - p_\alpha(\mathbf{x})\big)\mathbf{m}(d\mathbf{x}) = \lambda - \tau$. This completes the proof. □

Proposition 1 implies that we can find a safe approximation of (5b) by solving the upper bound problem (13). However, the nonlinear constraint in (13d) is non-convex and depends on the value of α. To further simplify it, we can introduce an auxiliary variable $s \geq 0$ such that

$$\big(\mathbf{Tr}(\mathbf{\Lambda}_\mathbf{w}\mathbf{Y})\big)^\alpha s^\alpha \geq \lambda^{2\alpha}\bar{\phi}^\alpha, \tag{16a}$$

$$\tau^2\lambda^{\alpha-2}s^{2^l-\alpha} \geq s^{2^l}, \tag{16b}$$

where $l = \lceil\log_2(\alpha)\rceil$ is the smallest integer such that $2^l - \alpha \geq 0$. By imposing mild conditions on α, we can derive an equivalent convex formulation of (16a)–(16b) as follows:

PROPOSITION 2. *Let $\alpha \geq 2$ be an integer. By introducing auxiliary variables $t_{2^k+m} \geq 0$, where $k = 0, 1, \ldots, l-1$, the constraints (16a)–(16b) are equivalent to*

$$\begin{bmatrix} \mathbf{Tr}(\mathbf{\Lambda}_\mathbf{w}\mathbf{Y}) & \lambda\bar{\phi}^{\frac{1}{2}} \\ \lambda\bar{\phi}^{\frac{1}{2}} & s \end{bmatrix} \succeq \mathbf{0}, \tag{17a}$$

$$\begin{bmatrix} t_{2^{k+1}+2m} & t_{2^k+m} \\ t_{2^k+m} & t_{2^{k+1}+2m+1} \end{bmatrix} \succeq \mathbf{0}, \tag{17b}$$

$$t_1 \geq s \tag{17c}$$

for $m = 0, 1, \ldots, 2^k - 1$ and $k = 0, 1, \ldots, l-1$, where

$$t_{2^l+m} = \begin{cases} \tau & \text{for } m = 0, 1, \\ \lambda & \text{for } m = 2, \ldots, \alpha-1, \\ s & \text{for } m = \alpha, \ldots, 2^l - 1. \end{cases} \tag{18}$$

PROOF. It is easy to see that (17a) is equivalent to (16a). Thus, we only need to show the equivalence between (16b) and (17b)–(17c). By the construction (18) and the inequalities in (17b)–(17c), all power exponents in (16b) are non-negative. Thus, we have

$$\tau^2\lambda^{\alpha-2}s^{2^l-\alpha} = \prod_{m=0}^{2^l-1} t_{2^l+m} \geq \left(\prod_{m=0}^{2^{l-1}-1} t_{2^{l-1}+m}\right)^2$$

$$\geq \cdots \geq t_1^{2^l} \geq s^{2^l}.$$

The converse is also true. For any (τ, λ, s) that is feasible for (16b), we can simply construct a set of values $\{t_{2^{l-1}+m}\}_{0\leq m\leq 2^{l-1}-1}$ such that $t_{2^l+2m}t_{2^l+2m+1} = t^2_{2^{l-1}+m}$ and

$$\tau^2\lambda^{\alpha-2}s^{2^l-\alpha} = \prod_{m=0}^{2^{l-1}-1} t^2_{2^{l-1}+m} \geq s^{2^l}.$$

The same construction applies to the second inequality and yields $(\tau^2\lambda^{\alpha-2}s^{2^l-\alpha})^{2^{-l}} = \cdots = t_1 \geq s$. □

Given a fixed beamformer $\mathbf{w}$, both constraints (17a) and (17b) are linear matrix inequalities. Hence, we can solve problem (13) efficiently by leveraging on the SDP reformulation (17).

3.3 UDR-based Beamforming Algorithm

In view of the approximation of $B_\alpha(\mathbf{u}_\mathbf{z}, \mathbf{S}_\mathbf{z})$, we can reformulate the general UDR-based beamforming problem as the following bi-level optimization problem:

$$(\text{GUB}) : \max_{\rho \geq 0, \mathbf{w}} \quad \rho \tag{19a}$$

$$s.t. \quad \rho + \rho\mathbf{Tr}(\mathbf{D}(\mathbf{w}\circ\mathbf{w})\mathbf{S}_\mathbf{g}) - \mathbf{q}^T\mathbf{S}_\mathbf{g}\mathbf{q} \leq 0, \tag{19b}$$

$$\eta \geq \max\{\lambda - \tau : (13b), (13c), (17a)\text{–}(17c)\}. \tag{19c}$$

On the upper-level of problem (GUB), we optimize the rank-one beamformer $\mathbf{w}$ to maximize the target SNR ρ. The constraint (19b) ensures the target SNR at the designated DUE and the constraint (19c) bounds the CUE's worst-case interference violation probability, which is the optimum of the lower-level optimization problem as in (13). In particular, similar to problem (SUB), we can again pinpoint the maximum target SNR $\rho^\star$ by checking the feasibility of (19b)–(19c) for a given ρ and applying a bisection method. However, the feasibility check now requires solving the lower-level optimization problem, which is non-convex due to the coupling between $\mathbf{w}$ and $\mathbf{Y}$ in the matrix inequality (17a). Nevertheless, note that problems (GUB) and (SUB) differ only in the interference constraint. By exploiting the connection between problems (GUB) and (SUB), we aim to design a simpler algorithm that can bypass checking the feasibility of (19b)–(19c) directly.

PROPOSITION 3. *The upper bound on $B_\alpha(\mathbf{u_z}, \mathbf{S_z})$ derived in problem (13) is an increasing function of α.*

PROOF. For any $\alpha \geq 2$ and $\mathbf{\Gamma} = (\mathbf{Y}, \mathbf{y}, \lambda, \tau)$ that is feasible for problem (13), let $u_b(\alpha, \mathbf{\Gamma}) = \lambda - \tau$ denote the objective value of $\mathbf{\Gamma}$. Now, consider a fixed $\alpha \geq 2$ and let $\mathbf{\Gamma}^\star = (\mathbf{Y}^\star, \mathbf{y}^\star, \lambda^\star, \tau^\star)$ be an optimal solution to problem (13). Note that the inequality constraint (13d) is satisfied as an equality at $\mathbf{\Gamma}^\star$; i.e., $\tau^\star = \lambda^\star \left(\frac{\lambda^\star \bar{\phi}}{\mathbf{Tr}(\mathbf{\Lambda_w Y}^\star)} \right)^{\frac{\alpha}{2}}$. Hence, we have $\frac{\mathbf{Tr}(\mathbf{\Lambda_w Y}^\star)}{\lambda^\star \bar{\phi}} = \left(\frac{\lambda^\star}{\tau^\star} \right)^{\frac{2}{\alpha}} \geq 1$, which implies that

$$\frac{\partial u_b(\alpha, \mathbf{\Gamma}^\star)}{\partial \alpha} = \frac{\lambda^\star}{2} \left(\frac{\lambda^\star \bar{\phi}}{\mathbf{Tr}(\mathbf{\Lambda_w Y}^\star)} \right)^{\frac{\alpha}{2}} \log \left(\frac{\mathbf{Tr}(\mathbf{\Lambda_w Y}^\star)}{\lambda^\star \bar{\phi}} \right) \geq 0.$$

In particular, for any $0 < \alpha_1 \leq \alpha_2$, we have $u_b(\alpha_1, \mathbf{\Gamma}_1^\star) \leq u_b(\alpha_2, \mathbf{\Gamma}_1^\star) \leq u_b(\alpha_2, \mathbf{\Gamma}_2^\star)$, where the first inequality is due to the monotonicity of $u_b(\alpha, \mathbf{\Gamma}_1^\star)$ with respect to α and the second inequality is due to the fact that $\mathbf{\Gamma}_2^\star$ is an optimal solution corresponding to α_2. This completes the proof. □

Proposition 3 implies that (SUB) produces the largest evaluation of $B_\alpha(\mathbf{u_z}, \mathbf{S_z})$ and thus it is a restricted version of (GUB); i.e., any beamformer $\mathbf{w}$ that is feasible for (SUB) is also feasible for (GUB). Moreover, since the added structural information in (GUB) mitigates the conservatism in channel estimation, (GUB) will achieve a better SNR target than that of (SUB) for the same beamformer $\mathbf{w}$. This observation motivates us to approximate (GUB) by iteratively checking the feasibility of (SUB). The basic idea is to start from a beamformer $\mathbf{w}$ that is feasible for (SUB). Then, we fix $\mathbf{w}$ and solve the lower-level problem (13). Once we obtain an upper bound on $B_\alpha(\mathbf{u_z}, \mathbf{S_z})$, we check the feasibility of (19c), which then facilitates the update of $\mathbf{w}$. The entire procedure is summarized in Algorithm 1.

Algorithm 1 UDR-Based Beamforming Algorithm

1: initialize $\tilde{\eta}_{\min} = \eta$, $\tilde{\eta}_{\max} = 1$, and $\tilde{\eta} = \eta$
2: **while** $|\tilde{\eta}_{\max} - \tilde{\eta}_{\min}| \geq \varepsilon$
3:     find $(\rho, \mathbf{W})$ by solving (SUB) with $\tilde{\eta}$
4:     extract rank-one beamformer $\mathbf{w}$ from $\mathbf{W}$
5:     evaluate $B_\alpha(\mathbf{u_z}, \mathbf{S_z})$ by solving SDP (13)
6:     **if** $B_\alpha(\mathbf{u_z}, \mathbf{S_z}) \leq \eta$
7:         $\tilde{\eta}_{\min} \leftarrow \tilde{\eta}$
8:     **else**
9:         $\tilde{\eta}_{\max} \leftarrow \tilde{\eta}$
10:     **end if**
11:     $\tilde{\eta} \leftarrow (\tilde{\eta}_{\max} + \tilde{\eta}_{\min})/2$
12: **end while**
13: return convergent $(\rho, \mathbf{w})$

Given the CUE's probability threshold η (e.g., $\eta = 0.1$), we initialize $(\rho, \mathbf{W})$ in line 3 by solving (SUB) with the ini-

tial threshold $\tilde{\eta} = \eta$. The rank-one solution $\mathbf{w}$ can be extracted from $\mathbf{W}$ by the Gaussian randomization method [14]. Simulation results reveal that problem (SUB) always gives rank-one solutions and a similar observation has been reported in [10]. Next, fixing the beamformer $\mathbf{w}$, we check the feasibility of (19c) in problem (GUB) and update the probability threshold $\tilde{\eta}$ by the bisection method shown in lines 6–11. Then, we solve (SUB) again to update $(\rho, \mathbf{W})$. Note that Algorithm 1 always returns a feasible rank-one solution to (GRB), which provides a lower bound on the optimal value of problem (5) for any integer $\alpha \geq 2$.

4. NUMERICAL RESULTS

In this section, we demonstrate the efficacy of the proposed UDR beamforming design and compare it with some existing robust models. For simplicity, we consider 3 DUE relays collaboratively amplifying and forwarding the received signal to the DUE receiver. The noise at each relay and at the DUE has zero mean and unit variance. The channel coefficients $\mathbf{g}$ and $\mathbf{z}$ are random variables with known mean and covariance, but their exact distribution functions are unknown. We require the channel distributions to be α-unimodal. Since our safe approximation of (5b) is valid only when $\alpha \geq 2$ is an integer, we shall consider integer values of α in the simulations. By setting α to be the number of relays, the UDR model contains those commonly observed unimodal distributions in practice.

4.1 Comparing with the DRO Model [10]

In the general UDR model, an upper bound on $B_\alpha(\mathbf{u_z}, \mathbf{S_z})$ is obtained by solving problem (13) with a fixed beamformer $\mathbf{w}$. This leads to a safe approximation of the probabilistic constraint (5b). When α approaches infinity, the UDR model degenerates into the DRO model [10], which admits the equivalent SDP formulation (9) and gives an exact evaluation of $B_\alpha(\mathbf{u_z}, \mathbf{S_z})$. To compare the UDR and DRO models, we fix the same beamformer $\mathbf{w}$ in both problems (9) and (13) and then numerically evaluate the interference violation probability and the DUE's data rate. The comparison results are presented in Figure 2, where the DRO model is denoted by "$\alpha \to \infty$". We observe that a larger α implies less stringent structural requirement and a larger (thus more conservative) evaluation of $B_\alpha(\mathbf{u_z}, \mathbf{S_z})$, thus resulting in over-protection for the CUE and performance loss at the DUE. As a result, the DRO model significantly overestimates the interference violation probability; see Figure 2(a). Next, we set the probability threshold at $\eta = 0.2$ and show the data rate of the D2D communications in Figure 2(b). We see that although the general UDR model can only be solved by a heuristic method (i.e., Algorithm 1), it still provides the DUE a significantly higher data rate than the exactly solvable DRO model.

4.2 Comparing with the BER model [22]

The BER model assumes that the channel coefficients follow a Gaussian distribution. Under this model, a safe approximation of the constraint $B_\alpha(\mathbf{u_z}, \mathbf{S_z}) \leq \eta$ can be developed using the Bernstein-type inequality [22]. Since the Gaussian distribution is α-unimodal for any α greater than the dimension of the channel vector [20], the BER model demands more stringent structural information than that of the UDR model. To compare these two models, we first optimize the beamformer $\mathbf{w}$ in different models and then

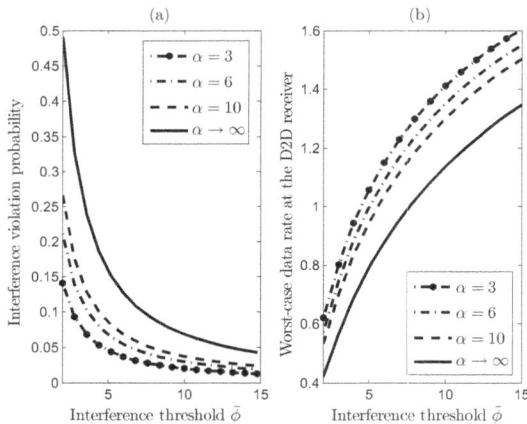

Figure 2: The UDR model outperforms the DRO model

check their throughput performance with randomized channel realizations of $\mathbf{g}$ and $\mathbf{z}$. We set the CUE's probability threshold at $\eta = 0.2$ and generate 10^6 realizations of the uncertain channel coefficients $\mathbf{g}$ and $\mathbf{z}$ according to their moment information in each simulation run. For each interference threshold $\bar{\phi}$, we record the CUE's interference violation probabilities in Table 1 and show the DUE's data rate in Figure 3. We observe that the interference violation probabilities corresponding to different models do not vary too much with the increase of $\bar{\phi}$. We also notice that the interference violation probability in the DRO model is much smaller than that of the BER and UDR models due to the lack of structural information. This explains the DRO model's conservative DUE throughput performance in Figure 3.

Table 1: Simulation results with different $\bar{\phi}$

ϕ	5	6	7	8	9	10
DRO	0.71%	0.65%	0.67%	0.65%	0.60%	0.66%
BER	2.01%	1.98%	2.09%	2.05%	2.00%	2.08%
UDR	6.43%	6.32%	6.46%	6.34%	6.31%	6.29%

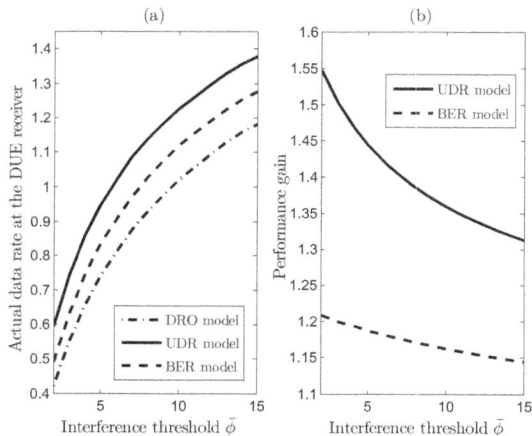

Figure 3: Throughput performance in three robust models

A counter-intuitive observation in Table 1 is that the UDR

model has the highest interference violation probability and consequently a better throughput performance than that of the BER model; see Figure 3. Though the BER model demands more structural information than that of the UDR model, the looser approximation in the Bernstein-type inequality results in an over-estimation of the interference violation probability. Therefore, the robust beamformer design in the BER model is more conservative than that of the UDR model. In Figure 3(b), the performance gain of the UDR (or BER) model is defined as the expected ratio $\mathbb{E}[\rho_U/\rho_D]$ (or $\mathbb{E}[\rho_B/\rho_D]$), where ρ_D and ρ_U (or ρ_B) denote the optimal SNR targets of the DRO and UDR (or BER) models, respectively. We find that the UDR model improves the DUE's performance significantly by exploiting the additional structural information in channel estimation, especially when the CUE has a small interference threshold.

By tuning the value of α, the UDR model has the flexibility to model the channel uncertainty. To show this, we vary the value of α and record the actual performance of these robust models in Table 2. In the simulation, we set $\bar{\phi} = 6$ and $\eta = 0.2$. Note that the DRO and BER models do not take the unimodal structure into account. Thus, we record nearly constant interference violation probabilities in the first two rows of Table 2. By the same reason, the performance gain $\mathbb{E}[\rho_B/\rho_D]$ is also a constant for different α. However, when we reduce α and thus impose more stringent structural requirement on the distribution $\mathbb{P}_\mathbf{z}$, the UDR model achieves higher SNR for the DUE by pushing the actual interference violation probability closer to its target level η. Hence, we observe an increasing value of $\mathbb{E}[\rho_U/\rho_D]$ as α decreases. When α approaches infinity, the UDR model degenerates into the DRO model and the performance gain $\mathbb{E}[\rho_U/\rho_D]$ tends to unity. A practical choice of the parameter α is to relate it to the dimension of the channel coefficients. Specifically, by setting $\alpha = N$, the set $\mathcal{P}_\mathbf{z}^\alpha$ contains most of the commonly observed distributions in wireless systems, and the UDR model achieves a significant performance improvement (around 50%) over the DRO model; see Table 2.

Table 2: Simulation results with different α values

α	3	4	5	6	10
DRO	0.96%	0.94%	0.97%	1.06%	1.13%
BER	1.90%	1.92%	1.91%	1.99%	2.02%
UDR	7.56%	6.49%	5.98%	5.37%	3.96%
$\mathbb{E}[\rho_B/\rho_D]$	1.151	1.151	1.152	1.153	1.152
$\mathbb{E}[\rho_U/\rho_D]$	1.556	1.487	1.452	1.415	1.305

5. CONCLUSIONS

In this work, we studied DUE relays' beamforming in a cellular network under imperfect channel information, where our goal is to maximize the DUE's worst-case SNR subject to the CUE's probabilistic interference constraint. Based on the notion of α-unimodality, we proposed the UDR model that can significantly mitigate the conservatism of the conventional DRO and BER models in robust beamforming design. As a future work, we may incorporate more structural information into the channel uncertainty model and study the more involved setting where the channel information in both hops of a D2D relay network is uncertain.

6. ACKNOWLEDGMENTS

This work was supported jointly by the National Natural Science Foundation of China under Grant No. 61503368, 61601449, U1501255, and U1301256; the Guangdong Science and Technology Project under Grant No. 2015A010103009; the Shenzhen Science and Technology Project under grant No. CXZZ20150401152251212, JCYJ20150401150223648, and JCYJ20150401145529016.

7. REFERENCES

[1] F. Gao, R. Zhang, and Y.-C. Liang. Channel estimation for OFDM modulated two-way relay networks. *IEEE Trans. Signal Process.*, 57(11):4443–4455, November 2009.

[2] S. Gong, P. Wang, and L. Duan. Distributed power control with robust protection for PUs in cognitive radio networks. *IEEE Trans. Wireless Commun.*, 14(6):3247–3258, June 2015.

[3] M. Grant and S. Boyd. CVX: Matlab software for disciplined convex programming, version 2.1. http://cvxr.com/cvx, March 2014.

[4] M. Hasan and E. Hossain. Distributed resource allocation for relay-aided device-to-device communication: A message passing approach. *IEEE Trans. Wireless Commun.*, 13(11):6326–6341, November 2014.

[5] M. Hasan and E. Hossain. Distributed resource allocation for relay-aided device-to-device communication under channel uncertainties: A stable matching approach. *IEEE Trans. Wireless Commun.*, 63(10):3882–3897, October 2015.

[6] M. Hasan, E. Hossain, and D. I. Kim. Resource allocation under channel uncertainties for relay-aided device-to-device communication underlaying LTE-A cellular networks. *IEEE Trans. Wireless Commun.*, 13(4):2322–2338, April 2014.

[7] K. Jayasinghe, P. Jayasinghe, N. Rajatheva, and M. Latva-Aho. Linear precoder-decoder design of MIMO device-to-device communication underlaying cellular communication. *IEEE Trans. Wireless Commun.*, 62(12):4304–4319, December 2014.

[8] B. Kaufman, J. Lilleberg, and B. Aazhang. Spectrum sharing scheme between cellular users and ad-hoc device-to-device users. *IEEE Trans. Wireless Commun.*, 12(3):1038–1049, March 2013.

[9] P. Li, S. Guo, T. Miyazaki, and W. Zhuang. Fine-grained resource allocation for cooperative device-to-device communication in cellular networks. *IEEE Wireless Commun.*, 21(5):35–40, October 2014.

[10] Q. Li, A. M.-C. So, and W.-K. Ma. Distributionally robust chance-constrained transmit beamforming for multiuser MISO downlink. In *Proc. of IEEE ICASSP*, pages 3479–3483, May 2014.

[11] M. Lin, J. Ouyang, and W. P. Zhu. Joint beamforming and power control for device-to-device communications underlaying cellular networks. *IEEE J. Sel. Areas Commun.*, 34(1):138–150, January 2016.

[12] J. Liu, Y. Kawamoto, H. Nishiyama, N. Kato, and N. Kadowaki. Device-to-device communications achieve efficient load balancing in LTE-advanced networks. *IEEE Wireless Commun.*, 21(2):57–65, April 2014.

[13] S. Loyka, V. Kostina, and F. Gagnon. On convexity of error rates in digital communications. *IEEE Trans Inf. Theory*, 59(10):6501–6516, October 2013.

[14] Z.-Q. Luo, W.-K. Ma, A. M.-C. So, Y. Ye, and S. Zhang. Semidefinite relaxation of quadratic optimization problems. *IEEE Signal Process. Mag.*, 27(3):20–34, May 2010.

[15] D. H. N. Nguyen, H. H. Nguyen, and T. T. Pham. Distributed beamforming in multiuser multi-relay networks with guaranteed QoS. In *Proc. of IEEE GLOBECOM*, November 2009.

[16] Y. Qin, M. Ding, M. Zhang, H. Yu, and H. Luo. Relaying robust beamforming for device-to-device communication with channel uncertainty. *IEEE Commun. Lett.*, 18(10):1859–1862, October 2014.

[17] Y. A. Sambo, M. Z. Shakir, K. A. Qaraqe, E. Serpedin, and M. A. Imran. Expanding cellular coverage via cell-edge deployment in heterogeneous networks: Spectral efficiency and backhaul power consumption perspectives. *IEEE Commun. Mag.*, 52(6):140–149, June 2014.

[18] S. H. Seyedmehdi and G. Boudreau. An efficient clustering algorithm for device-to-device assisted virtual MIMO. *IEEE Trans. Wireless Commun.*, 13(3):1334–1343, March 2014.

[19] M. N. Tehrani, M. Uysal, and H. Yanikomeroglu. Device-to-device communication in 5G cellular networks: Challenges, solutions, and future directions. *IEEE Commun. Mag.*, 52(5):86–92, May 2014.

[20] B. P. G. Van Parys, P. J. Goulart, and D. Kuhn. Generalized Gauss inequalities via semidefinite programming. *Mathematical Programming*, 156(1):271–302, 2016.

[21] L. Vandenberghe, S. Boyd, and K. Comanor. Generalized Chebyshev bounds via semidefinite programming. *SIAM Review*, 49(1):52–64, 2007.

[22] K.-Y. Wang, A. M.-C. So, T.-H. Chang, W.-K. Ma, and C.-Y. Chi. Outage constrained robust transmit optimization for multiuser MISO downlinks: Tractable approximations by conic optimization. *IEEE Trans. Signal Process.*, 62(21):5690–5705, November 2014.

[23] L. Wang, T. Peng, Y. Yang, and W. Wang. Interference constrained D2D communication with relay underlaying cellular networks. In *Proc. of IEEE VTC Fall*, September 2013.

[24] Y. Wang, B. Ji, Y. Huang, T. Ban, and L. Yang. Robust collaborative relay beamforming design for two-way relay systems with reciprocal CSI. *Wireless Networks*, 21(7):2209–2221, October 2015.

[25] S. Zymler, D. Kuhn, and B. Rustem. Distributionally robust joint chance constraints with second-order moment information. *Mathematical Programming*, 137(1-2):167–198, 2013.

Control-theoretic Scalable Device-to-Device Offloading System for Video Streaming Services

Gi Seok Park
Division of IT Convergence Engineering, Pohang University of Science and Technology (POSTECH), Pohang, Republic of Korea
kiseok@postech.ac.kr

Wan Kim
Cloud Technology Lab., Software R&D Center, Samsung Electronics, Suwon, Republic of Korea
wan318.kim@samsung.com

Hwangjun Song
Department of Computer Science and Engineering, Pohang University of Science and Technology (POSTECH), Pohang, Republic of Korea
hwangjun@postech.ac.kr

ABSTRACT

This work presents a control-theoretic scalable device-to-device offloading system that provides seamless video streaming services to clients by effectively offloading parts of the video traffic to D2D networks in order to alleviate the cellular network traffic load. In the proposed system, the main functionalities of the content centric networking (CCN) technology are employed to simultaneously download the video content from multiple wireless networks. A two-stage PID-based LTE traffic controller is proposed to determine the amount of traffic to be offloaded to the D2D network among the cellular operator, the D2D servers, and the D2D clients. The proposed system is fully implemented using a CCNx open source and C/C++. Experimental results are provided to demonstrate the performance improvement of the proposed system.

Keywords
Content Centric Networking; Scalable Device-to-Device Offloading; Two-Stage PID-based LTE Traffic Controller

1. INTRODUCTION

There has been a tremendous increase in mobile data traffic at a rapid pace owing to the widespread use of smart mobile devices and the explosive growth of mobile multimedia services such as mobile video streaming, mobile gaming, and social networking. Recently, Cisco visual network index has estimated that the overall mobile data traffic will grow at a compound annual growth rate (CAGR) of 57% from 2014–2019, reaching 24.3 exabytes per month by 2019, nearly a tenfold increase over 2014 [1]. Ericsson also estimates that the mobile data traffic will increase by around six times over the period 2014–2019 [2], and that the mobile broadband subscriptions will reach 7.7 billion globally by 2020, growing at a CAGR of 20% per year for the period 2014–2020 [3]. Unfortunately, this explosive growth in mobile data traffic has caused severe traffic overload problems in cellular networks. To accommodate a significant amount of mobile data traffic, few effective cellular networking technologies such as the long term

evolution (LTE), the LTE-Advanced (LTE-A), and the worldwide interoperability for microwave access (WiMAX) have been developed, and 5G technology is still under development for improving the channel/network capacity. However, accommodating the extensive increase in the mobile data traffic fueled by the increasing popularity of smart mobile devices and the growing demand for advanced multimedia mobile applications such as YouTube and Dailymotion remains challenging.

To handle this problem, a mobile traffic offloading technology has been proposed as a promising solution to support the massive growth in mobile data traffic. The mobile traffic offloading technology uses other available access networks such as the WiFi, femtocells, and picocells to deliver a part of the mobile data traffic over the cellular network. Recently, 3GPP has been focusing on the device-to-device (D2D) communication technology as a new data offloading solution [4]. D2D communication is a direct communication between devices in close physical proximity without going through the infrastructure. D2D communication can significantly reduce the traffic volume in a cellular network by taking advantage of the physical proximity of the communicating devices [4, 5]. Hence, mobile D2D traffic offloading technology can play an important role in reducing the traffic load of cellular networks, especially when there is a correlation between the proximity on the social graph and the geographical proximity [6].

In recent years, considerable research has been devoted for effectively offloading mobile traffic onto D2D communications. In [7], Belouanas et al. introduced a content centric networking (CCN)-based system for D2D communication under infrastructure assistance. They proposed a framework of high-level architecture to support CCN-based D2D offloading. However, they did not verify the proposed high-level architecture. In [8], Wang et al. proposed a game-theoretic approach for source selection and for a power control scheme that enhances the multimedia transmission quality with latency constraints. The most beneficial source devices are selected by analyzing the interactions between the base station's reward strategy and the devices' contributing behaviors using the Stackelberg game model. In [9], Liu et al. proposed a D2D communication-based load balancing algorithm in a LTE-A network that utilizes D2D communications as bridges to offload traffic among the different tier cells. The congested eNB offloads the data traffic to the adjacent uncongested picocells or macrocells via D2D relays. However, they have difficulties in offloading traffic because of the algorithm complexity and the incentive stimulation for the relay devices.

So far, most of the existing offloading schemes have not considered scalable data offloading in which only parts of the mobile user data are offloaded onto the complementary networks, while the remaining data is transferred across the cellular network. In general, scalable data offloading outperforms the full data offloading in terms of the end-to-end throughput because the mobile user data can be offloaded onto complementary networks on a flexible scale by considering the network states [10].

In this work, we propose a scalable D2D offloading system for video streaming services. In the proposed scalable D2D offloading system, content centric networking (CCN) [11] technology is deployed to accomplish a scalable data offloading. The CCN includes main functionalities such as the segmentation of the content into uniquely identified chunks, receiver-driven content retrieval protocol, in-network caching, and name-based routing. These characteristics are considerably useful for partially offloading the mobile user data onto complementary networks. The major contributions of this work can be summarized in the below:

- The proposed system is designed to support multipath routing. To implement this function, the FIB of the CCN forwarding engine is appropriately updated to forward the interest packet via multiple wireless networks.
- The amount of traffic to be offloaded is determined through negotiations among the cellular operator, the D2D server, and the D2D client. A two-stage PID-based LTE traffic controller is adopted to satisfy the desired LTE traffic load constraint.
- The proposed system is fully implemented using a CCNx open source [12] and C/C++, and the proposed system is examined in a real CCN environment.

The rest of the work is organized as follows. The concept of the CCN technology is introduced in Section 2. The details of the proposed scalable D2D offloading system are presented in Section 3 and the experimental results are given in Section 4. Finally, the concluding remarks are provided in Section 5.

2. BRIEF REVIEW OF THE CCN

The CCN is a class of information centric network (ICN) that employs a receiver driven communication model. A CCN addresses the contents using unique hierarchical names. The contents are split into chunks and each chunk is addressed by names that contain the content name and the chunk identifier. There are two types of CCN packets, the interest packet, and the data packet. To download content, a client pulls the content chunks by issuing an interest packet. Any node, on hearing the interest packet, transmits the content chunk requested by the interest packet through the data packet. The CCN forwarding engine consists of three main modules: the forwarding interest base (FIB), the pending interest table (PIT), and the content store (CS). The FIB is used to forward interest packets towards the potential node having the content. The PIT keeps track of the forwarded interest packets to avoid repeated delivery of the same interest and to send back the corresponding data packet. The CS is

used as a content cache to hold the content. The content retrieval procedure in the CCN is as follows: (1) a client sends out an interest packet with the content name. (2) the node receiving an interest packet checks whether the requested content is present in its CS. If there is a hit, the node forwards the interest and sends out the matched content chunk along the reverse path. Otherwise, the interest packet is forwarded to the interfaces determined by the FIB, where the FIB is updated according to the forwarding strategy. The PIT records the forwarded interest packet for sending back the received content chunk later. (3) When the data packets are received, the CS determines if the content is to be replicated according to the caching strategy.

3. PROPOSED CONTROL-THEORETIC SCALABLE DEVICE-TO-DEVICE OFFLOADING SYSTEM

The goal of the proposed scalable D2D offloading system is to control the LTE traffic load by scalable offloading to the D2D network while providing seamless video streaming services. In the proposed system, CCN technology is employed to simultaneously download the video content from multiple wireless networks by changing the interface list in the FIB [13]. The overall architecture of the proposed system is presented in Fig. 1. As shown in the figure, the base station (BS) and the D2D nodes include two main components, i.e., the CCN forwarding engine module and the D2D controller module. The CCN forwarding engine module performs the basic operations of the CCN such as packet routing and content caching. The D2D controller module executes the negotiation process among the cellular operator, the D2D servers, and the D2D clients. Based on the negotiation result, the D2D controller in the D2D client separately assigns the interest packets to the LTE network and the D2D network. To implement this function, the FIB of the CCN forwarding engine is appropriately updated to forward the interest packet via multiple wireless networks.

In the proposed scalable D2D offloading system, the ultimate goal of the cellular operator is to control the LTE traffic load by partially offloading the video traffic of all the D2D clients through the D2D network on a flexible scale. To achieve the objective of the operator, the active participation of the D2D server that contains the content requested by the D2D client is essential. Generally, D2D servers are unwilling to commit their own resources such as the device power without a sufficient reward. In the proposed system, a reward-based incentive mechanism is adopted to encourage the participation of the D2D servers [14]. In a reward-based incentive mechanism, it is guaranteed that the D2D clients will make a payment to the D2D servers according to the quantity of data packets they contribute. Fig. 2 represents an example of the proposed scalable D2D offloading system.

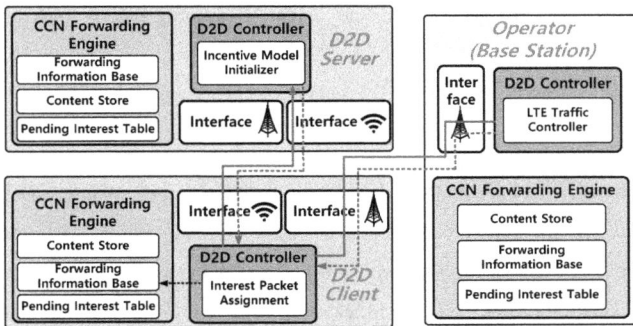

Figure 1. Proposed scalable D2D offloading system architecture.

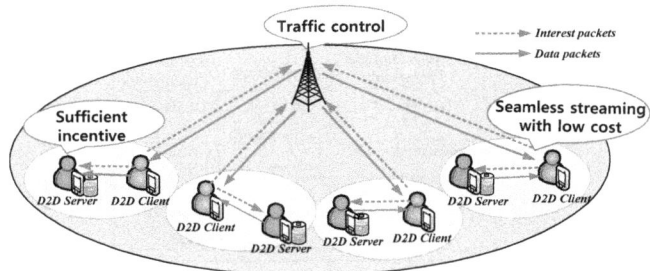

Figure 2. Proposed scalable D2D offloading system with a BS and multiple D2D pairs.

3.1 Problem Description

In this section, we describe the negotiation problems among the operator, the D2D servers, and the D2D clients, in detail. Before presenting a detailed description of the proposed system, we define the revenue model for the operator as follows:

$$p_{BS} \cdot n_i^{BS} + p_{BS} \cdot \left(n_i^{BS} - n_{BS}^{thr}\right)^{\omega_{BS}} \cdot H_{step}\left(n_i^{BS} - n_{BS}^{thr}\right), \quad (1)$$

where p_{BS} is the unit price per data packet, n_{BS}^{thr} is the packet threshold that specifies the boundary between the linear and the exponential range in the revenue model, ω_{BS} is the exponential factor that is set to be greater than 1, n_i^{BS} is the number of data packets transmitted to the i_{th} D2D client, and $H_{step}(\cdot)$ is the unit step function. Revenue parameters such as p_{BS}, n_{BS}^{thr}, and ω_{BS} are equally applied to all the D2D clients in order to ensure the fairness of the LTE network subscription. The revenue in the linear range, ($n_i^{BS} \le n_{BS}^{thr}$), linearly increases as n_i^{BS} becomes larger but the revenue in the exponential range, ($n_i^{BS} > n_{BS}^{thr}$), exponentially increases. This revenue model is similar to the real revenue models adopted by cellular operators [15]. Then, the incentive model for the D2D server is defined by

$$p_{D2D_i} \cdot n_i^{D2D} + p_{D2D_i} \cdot \left(n_i^{D2D} - n_{D2D_i}^{thr}\right)^{\omega_{D2D_i}} \cdot H_{step}\left(n_i^{D2D} - n_{D2D_i}^{thr}\right), \quad (2)$$

where p_{D2D_i} is the unit price per data packet, $n_{D2D_i}^{thr}$ is the packet threshold that specifies the boundary between the linear and the exponential range in the incentive model, ω_{D2D_i} is the exponential factor that is set to be greater than 1, and n_i^{D2D} is the number of data packets transmitted to the i_{th} D2D client. In the proposed system, p_{D2D_i}, $n_{D2D_i}^{thr}$, and ω_{D2D_i} are differently set by each D2D server. For example, they can be determined based on the remaining battery life of the i_{th} D2D server.

Fig. 3 shows the diagram of the proposed negotiation process. The operator tries negotiating with the D2D nodes when a traffic load is expected to occur over the LTE network. The blue box in Fig. 5 illustrates the internal logic flow and the information exchanges among the operator, the D2D server, and the D2D client. During the first stage, the operator and the D2D server simultaneously submit their own pricing model parameter values to the D2D client, then, the D2D client sends back the number of interest packets determined by the following interest packet

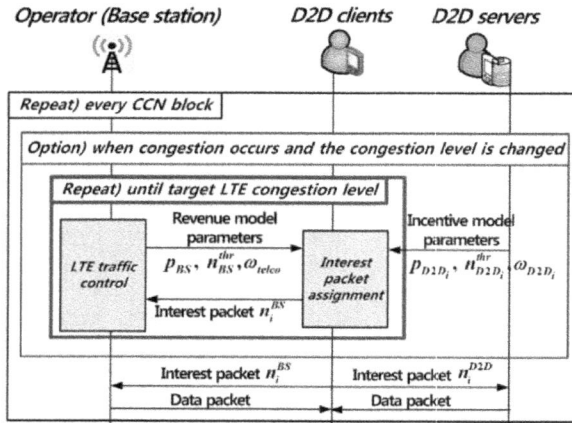

Figure 3. Diagram of the interaction process between the operator, the D2D servers, and the D2D clients.

assignment algorithm (the details are studied in section 3.2). When the amount of requested interest packets cannot be accommodated, the operator updates its revenue parameters under the assumption that the pricing model parameter values of the D2D servers are fixed, and submits new revenue parameter values. The negotiation process is repeated until the revenue parameters and the corresponding number of interest packets is not changed further at the equilibrium point.

3.2 Interest Packet Assignment Algorithm for the D2D Client

In this section, we formulate the interest packet assignment of the D2D client to minimize its networking cost, while receiving a seamless video streaming service. The networking cost of the D2D client is only the sum of the payment paid to the operator and the corresponding D2D server.

Problem Formulation for the Interest Packet Assignment: Determine n_i^{BS} and n_i^{D2D} to minimize the following the overall networking cost.

$$p_{BS} \cdot n_i^{BS} + p_{BS} \cdot \left(n_i^{BS} - n_{BS}^{thr}\right)^{\omega_{BS}} \cdot H_{step}\left(n_i^{BS} - n_{BS}^{thr}\right) +$$
$$p_{D2D_i} \cdot n_i^{D2D} + p_{D2D_i} \cdot \left(n_i^{D2D} - n_{D2D_i}^{thr}\right)^{\omega_{D2D_i}} \cdot H_{step}\left(n_i^{D2D} - n_{D2D_i}^{thr}\right), \quad (3)$$

subject to

$$n_i^{BS} + n_i^{D2D} = N_{chunk}^{block}, \quad (4)$$

and

$$\max\left\{\frac{S_{chunk} \cdot n_i^{BS}}{b_{LTE}} + RTT_{LTE}, \frac{S_{chunk} \cdot n_i^{D2D}}{b_{D2D}} + RTT_{D2D}\right\}$$
$$\le \frac{T_{video} \cdot N_{chunk}^{block}}{N_{chunk}^{total}}, \quad (5)$$

where n_i^{BS} and n_i^{D2D} are the number of interest packets sent to the operator and to the D2D server through the LTE network and the D2D network respectively, b_{LTE} and b_{D2D} are the estimated bandwidth values over the LTE and the D2D network respectively, RTT_{LTE} and RTT_{D2D} are the RTT (round trip time) of the LTE and the D2D path, S_{chunk} is the data packet size, N_{chunk}^{total} is the total number of video chunks, T_{video} is the total video duration, and N_{chunk}^{block} is the number of chunks in a block that is simultaneously sent to both the operator and the D2D server. Eq. (5) is the block download time required for a seamless video streaming. To calculate the block download time, the available bandwidth should be estimated over the LTE and the D2D networks. In this work, the ARMA (autoregressive moving average) model is employed [16]. That is,

$$\tilde{b}_{LTE}[k+1] = \left(1 - \theta_{LTE}\right) \cdot \tilde{b}_{LTE}[k] + \theta_{LTE} \cdot b_{LTE}^{obs}[k], \quad (6)$$
$$\tilde{b}_{D2D}[k+1] = \left(1 - \theta_{D2D}\right) \cdot \tilde{b}_{D2D}[k] + \theta_{D2D} \cdot b_{D2D}^{obs}[k], \quad (7)$$

where k indicates the CCN block index, $\tilde{b}_{LTE}[k]$ and $\tilde{b}_{D2D}[k]$ are the estimated bandwidths at the k_{th} block, and $b_{LTE}^{obs}[k]$ and $b_{D2D}^{obs}[k]$ are the observed LTE and D2D network bandwidths, respectively, at the k_{th} block that can be measured by the download time. θ_{LTE} and θ_{D2D} are the averaging parameters. The details of the interest packet assigning algorithm are presented below. Basically, the gradient descent method [17] is adopted to find the optimal solution because the networking cost in Eq. (3) is convex, whose required computational complexity for the interest packet assignment is $O\left(N_{chunk}^{block}\right)$.

Step 1) Initialize the step size λ and determine the search range of n_i^{BS} as follows.

$$n_{min}^{BS} \leq n_i^{BS} \leq n_{max}^{BS}, \quad (8)$$

$$n_{min}^{BS} = \max\left\{\left\lceil\left(N_{chunk}^{block} - \left(\frac{T_{video} \cdot N_{chunk}^{block}}{N_{chunk}^{total}} - RTT_{D2D}\right) \cdot \frac{b_{D2D}}{S_{chunk}}\right\rceil, 0\right\},$$

and $n_{max}^{BS} = \min\left\{\left\lfloor\left(\frac{T_{video} \cdot N_{chunk}^{block}}{N_{chunk}^{total}} - RTT_{LTE}\right) \cdot \frac{b_{LTE}}{S_{chunk}}\right\rfloor, N_{chunk}^{block}\right\}.$

The initial search point, x, is set to n_{min}^{BS} and the networking cost function is defined by

$$c\left(n_i^{BS}\right) = p_{BS} \cdot n_i^{BS} + p_{BS} \cdot \left(n_i^{BS} - n_{BS}^{thr}\right)^{\omega_{BS}} \cdot H_{step}\left(n_i^{BS} - n_{telco}^{thr}\right) +$$
$$p_{D2D_i} \cdot \left(N_{chunk}^{block} - n_i^{BS}\right) + \quad (9)$$
$$p_{D2D_i} \cdot \left(\left(N_{chunk}^{block} - n_i^{BS}\right) - n_{D2D_i}^{thr}\right)^{\omega_{D2D_i}} \cdot H_{step}\left(\left(N_{chunk}^{block} - n_i^{BS}\right) - n_{D2D_i}^{thr}\right).$$

Step 2) Set $\tilde{x}$, n_i^{BS}, and n_i^{D2D} to $x - \lambda \cdot c'(x)$, $\tilde{x}$, and $N_{chunk}^{block} - \tilde{x}$, respectively. If the search range given in Eq. (8) is satisfied by the updated n_i^{BS}, replace x with $\tilde{x}$. Otherwise, set n_i^{BS} and n_i^{D2D} to $\lfloor x \rfloor$ and $N_{chunk}^{block} - \lfloor x \rfloor$, respectively and then terminate the process.

Step 3) If the stopping criterion, $c'(x) \approx 0$, is satisfied, set n_i^{BS} and n_i^{D2D} to $\lfloor x \rfloor$ and $N_{chunk}^{block} - \lfloor x \rfloor$, respectively and then terminate the process. Otherwise, go back Step 2.

3.3 LTE Traffic Control for the Operator

In this section, we describe how to control the revenue parameters of the operator to regulate the traffic load over the LTE network. The proposed two-stage PID-based LTE traffic controller is illustrated in Fig. 4. As shown in the figure, the overall controller consists of three subsystems: the operator system, the D2D server system, and the D2D client system. The proposed two-stage PID-based LTE traffic controller is used for rapidly converging to the target LTE traffic load, i.e., p_{BS} and

n_{BS}^{thr} of the LTE revenue model are adjusted based on the feedback information given by the clients because it is empirically observed that ω_{BS} has a smaller influence on the LTE traffic than p_{BS} and n_{BS}^{thr}. The details of the proposed controller are presented below.

Step 1) Initialize the parameter values of the revenue model and the coefficients of the two-stage PID-based LTE traffic controller. Then, set the maximum number of interest packets, N_{BS}^{desire}, that the operator can support.

Step 2) Submit the parameter values of the revenue model to all the D2D clients.

Step 3) Calculate the error, $err[n]$, with the responses of the D2D clients as follows.

$$err[n] = N_{BS}^{desire} - \sum_{i=1}^{N_{clients}^{total}} n_i^{BS}[n], \quad (10)$$

where $N_{clients}^{total}$ is the number of D2D clients and $[n]$ denotes the iteration stage.

Step 4) Update the unit price as follows.

$$p_{BS}[n] = \alpha_{BS} \cdot p_{BS}[n-1] - C_P^{price} \cdot err[n] -$$
$$C_I^{price} \cdot \sum_{n=1}^{n} err[n] - C_D^{price} \cdot \left(err[n] - err[n-1]\right), \quad (11)$$

where C_P^{price}, C_I^{price}, C_D^{price}, and α_{BS}. are the PID coefficients and the forgetting factor to update the unit price.

Step 5) If $err[n]$ is saturated, update the packet threshold value as follows.

$$n_{BS}^{thr}[n] = \beta_{BS} \cdot n_{BS}^{thr}[n-1] + C_P^{thr} \cdot err[n] +$$
$$C_I^{thr} \cdot \sum_{n=1}^{n} err[n] + C_D^{thr} \cdot \left(err[n] - err[n-1]\right), \quad (12)$$

where C_P^{thr}, C_I^{thr}, C_D^{thr} are the PID coefficients and β_{BS} are the forgetting factor to update the packet threshold.

Step 6) Increase the iteration stage and go back Step 2 until $err[n] \approx 0$.

4. EXPERIMENTAL RESULTS

During the experiment, a real D2D offloading testbed is constructed using a CCNx (version 0.8.0) open source platform as

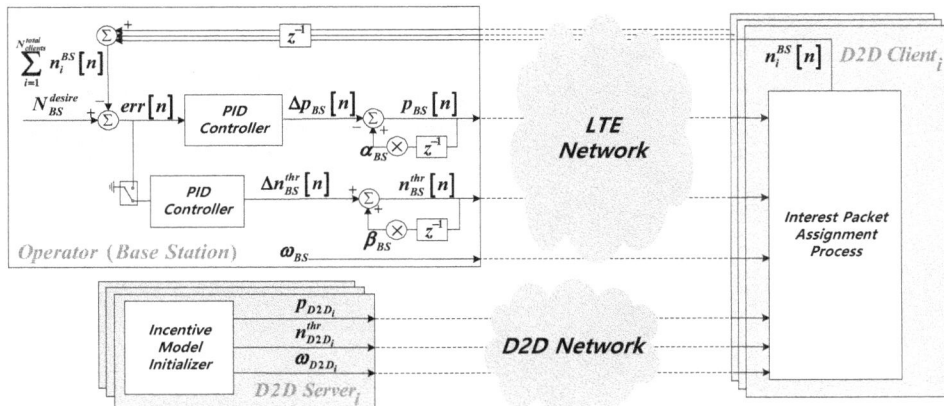

Figure 4. Block diagram of the two-stage PID-based LTE traffic controller.

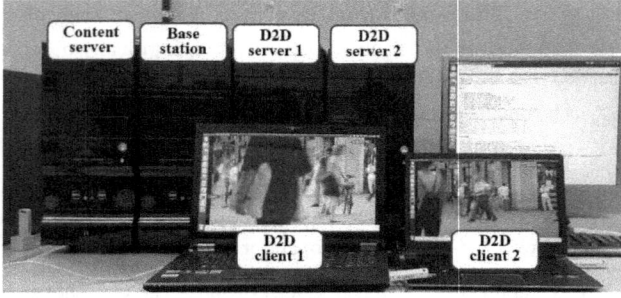

Figure 5. D2D offloading system test bed.

shown in Fig. 5. The BS and D2D servers are configured by setting up a WiFi access point on a desktop running on Ubuntu 12.04, and the wireless network states are emulated using NetEM [18]. The D2D modules is fully implemented in C/C++. Fig. 6 shows the test environment of the implemented system. The video content consists of three test video sequences: pedestrian area, rush hour, and sunflower videos [19], which is encoded by MPEG-2 Transport Stream (TS) [20] with an average 5.96 Mbps bit rate and 25 frames per second and distributed to the D2D servers and the BS. The encoding structure is IPPPPPPPPPPP (i.e., 1 GOP includes 12 frames). During the experiments, the number of chunks in a CCN block is set to 100 and the CCN chunk size is set to 8 KB that is widely used in CCN environments [21].

4.1 Performance Verification of the Two-Stage PID-based LTE Traffic Controller

We investigate the effect of the control parameters, p_{BS} and n_{BS}^{thr}, on the LTE traffic load with one hundred D2D pairs. The parameter values of the incentive model are randomly set in the range (i.e., $0.001 < p_{D2D_i} < 0.1$, $0 < n_{D2D_i}^{thr} < 100$, and $1 < \omega_{D2D_i} < 1.5$). First, it is observed in Fig. 7 that the number of interest packets requested by the D2D clients monotonically decrease over the entire range of the LTE traffic load as p_{BS} becomes larger or n_{BS}^{thr} becomes smaller.

Now, we verify the performance of the proposed two-stage PID-based LTE traffic controller. During the experiment, the parameter values of the incentive model and the PID coefficients of the two-stage PID-based LTE traffic controller are set as shown in Table 1 and Table 2, respectively (the PID coefficients are determined on the basis of the well-known Ziegler-Nichols method [22]). The target LTE traffic load, N_{BS}^{desire}, of the cellular operator is set to 85. The values of p_{BS} and n_{BS}^{thr} for every iteration are presented in Figs. 8 (a) and (b), respectively, and the

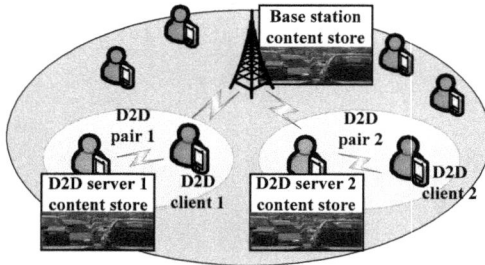

Figure 6. Test environment of the implemented system.

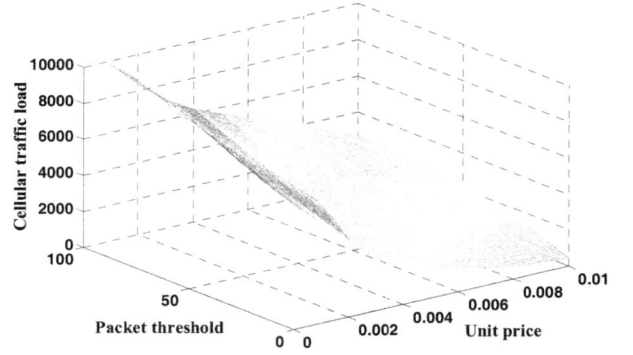

Figure 7. LTE traffic load according to p_{BS} and n_{BS}^{thr}

resulting number of interest packets are provided in Fig. 8 (c). It is observed that the number of interest packets requested to the operator decreases and the number of interest packets requested to the D2D server increases as p_{BS} becomes larger. As the iteration stage becomes longer, the fluctuation in p_{BS} gradually decreases. However, the LTE traffic load may not change, although p_{BS} is updated in every iteration. A similar phenomenon is observed at the 7th iteration stage, i.e., the total number of interest packets does not change from the 7–10th iteration stage, although p_{BS} is adjusted. In this case, n_{BS}^{thr} as well as p_{BS}, are adjusted to regulate the LTE traffic load, i.e., n_{BS}^{thr} is adjusted at the 11th iteration stage. Finally, the equilibrium point is attained at the 42th iteration stage, where the parameter values of the revenue model and the number of interest packets are never changed after the 42th stage. At this point, the number of interest packets requested from the

Table 1. Parameter values of the revenue and incentive model

Model Parameters		Value
Incentive model parameters for D2D server 1	p_{D2D_1}	0.005 [$]
	$n_{D2D_1}^{thr}$	45
	ω_{D2D_1}	1.3
Incentive model parameters for D2D server 2	p_{D2D_2}	0.006 [$]
	$n_{D2D_2}^{thr}$	40
	ω_{D2D_2}	1.2
Revenue model parameter for the operator	ω_{BS}	1.2

Table 2. Parameter values of the two-stage PID-based LTE traffic controller

Controller Parameters		Value
PID coefficients for unit price control	C_P^{price}	$0.1 \cdot 10^{-4}$
	C_I^{price}	$0.2 \cdot 10^{-4}$
	C_D^{price}	$0.125 \cdot 10^{-5}$
PID coefficients for packet threshold	C_P^{thr}	0.08
	C_I^{thr}	0.16
	C_D^{thr}	0.01
Forgetting factors	α_{BS}	0.99999
	β_{BS}	0.99

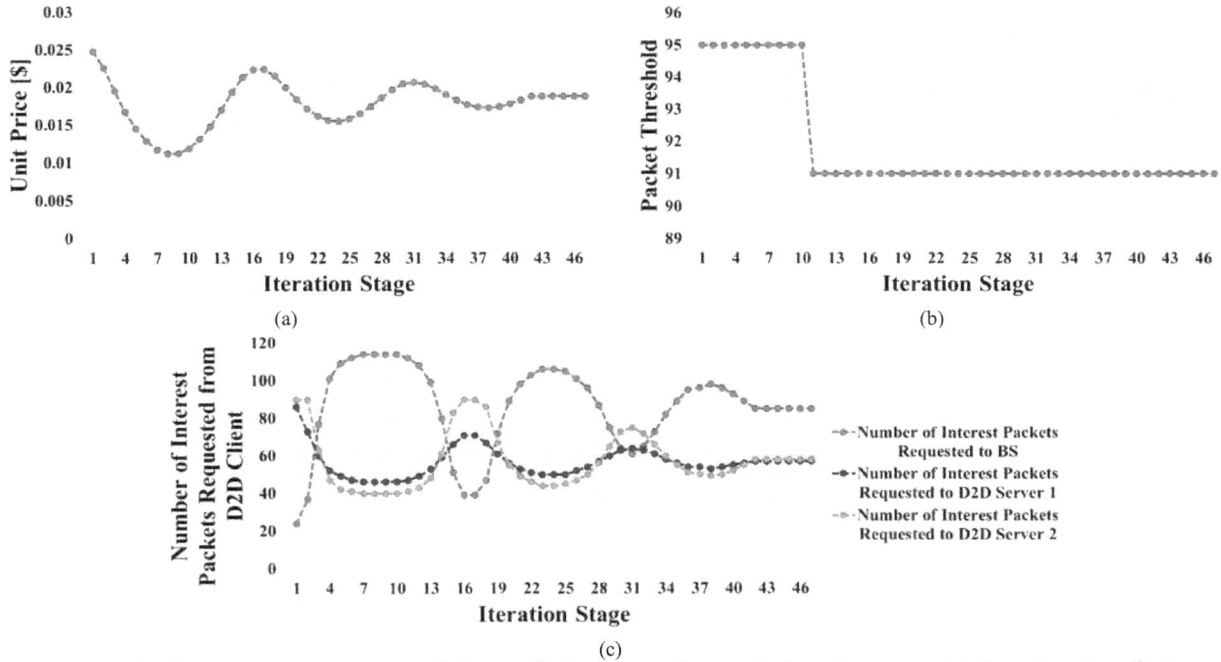

Figure 8. Change in the revenue parameters and the traffic load according to the iteration stage: (a) the unit price, (b) the packet threshold, and (c) the number of interest packets.

operator is equal to N_{BS}^{desire}. Consequently, by adjusting p_{BS} and n_{BS}^{thr}, the LTE traffic rapidly converges to N_{BS}^{desire}.

4.2 Performance Comparison with the Existing Systems

The performance of the proposed scalable D2D offloading system is compared with those of the three existing systems, namely the no offloading, only D2D offloading, and the fixed-rate D2D offloading. In the no offloading system, the client sends out interest packets only through the LTE network interface. In the only D2D offloading system, the client transmits interest packets only through the D2D network interface. In the fixed-rate D2D offloading, the client assigns the same number of interest packets to the LTE network and the D2D network. At the receiver side, the initial buffering size before the video playout is fixed to 1600 KB. When a video buffer underflow occurs during the video playback, the video is frozen until the buffered video data reaches 1600 KB. During the experiment, the capacity of the LTE network is set to 70 Mbps, the throughput between D2D pair 1 is set to 6 Mbps, and the throughput between D2D pair 2 is set to 5 Mbps. To emulate a time-varying LTE traffic load, background traffic is inserted into the LTE network. The network condition scenario is shown in Table 3.

Now, we investigate the cumulative curves of the received video data and the consumed video data at D2D client 1 and D2D client 2 to measure the temporal quality of the video streaming services. The cumulative curves at client 1 and client 2 are presented in Figs. 9 and 10, respectively. It is observed that receiver buffer underflows frequently occur in the no offloading and the only D2D offloading systems because no offloading suffers from congestion over the LTE network and the only D2D offloading experiences relatively unstable D2D network conditions. In the fixed-rate D2D offloading system, receiver buffer underflows and the buffering duration are decreased because the video data is transmitted through both the LTE and the D2D networks, simultaneously. However, a frozen video is

detected especially when the network state is dynamically changing. On the other hand, as shown in Fig. 9 (d) and Fig. 10 (d), the proposed system significantly reduces the receiver buffer underflows and the buffering duration because the interest packets are adaptively assigned to each network according to the time-varying network states. The experimental results are summarized in Table 4. LTE network utilization is defined as the ratio of the total number of interest packets requested from the D2D clients to the target LTE traffic load, i.e., $\sum_{i=1}^{N_{clients}^{total}} n_i^{BS} \Big/ N_{BS}^{desire}$. Existing offloading systems cannot make effective use of the LTE network because the traffic is not offloaded on a flexible scale considering the time-varying LTE traffic load. On the other hand, the LTE network in the proposed system is almost fully utilized because the total amount of LTE traffic is dynamically adjusted to the target LTE traffic load that the operator can support. Thus, the proposed system significantly reduces the buffer underflow and the buffering duration while improving the LTE network utilization.

TABLE 3. Network Condition Scenarios

Network	Time (sec.)	Back-ground traffic (Mbps)	Wireless Channel Status	
			Signal Strength	Packet Loss Rate (%)
LTE Network	0~50	60	Good	0~0.1
	50~100	58		
	100~	62		
D2D Network A (Pair 1)	0~40	–	Normal	0.1~0.5
	40~80		Good	0.1
	80~		Normal	0.1~0.5
D2D Network B (Pair 2)	0~30	–	Bad	0.5~2
	30~60		Normal	0.1~0.5
	60~		Good	0~0.1

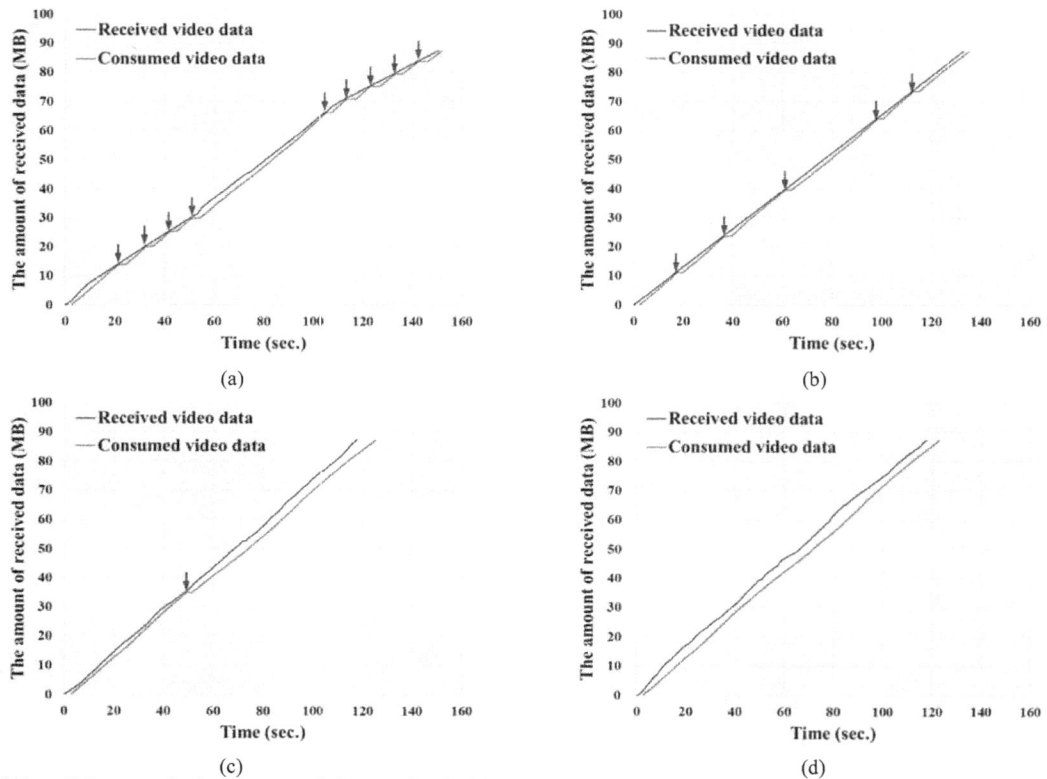

Figure 9. Client #1's cumulative curves of the received video data and the consumed video data according to the offloading system: (a) No offloading, (b) Only D2D offloading, (c) Fixed-rate D2D offloading, and (d) Proposed scalable D2D offloading (The blue arrows indicate a buffer underflow.).

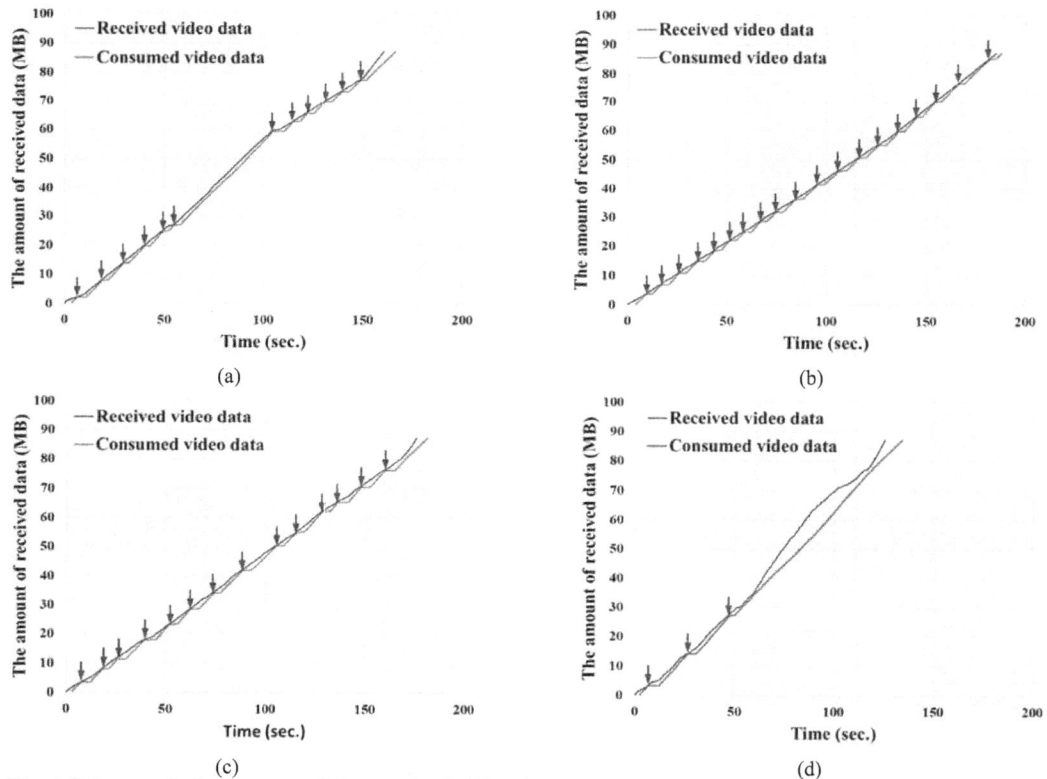

Figure 10. Client #2's cumulative curves of the received video data and the consumed video data according to the offloading system: (a) No offloading, (b) Only D2D offloading, (c) Fixed-rate D2D offloading, and (d) Proposed scalable D2D offloading (The blue arrows indicate a buffer underflow.).

TABLE 4. Goodput, buffer underflow, buffering duration, and average LTE network utilization according to the offloading system

Measurement	Offloading System	No offloading	Only D2D offloading	Fixed-rate D2D offloading	Proposed Scalable D2D offloading
Goodput (Mbps)	#1	4.642	5.263	5.937	5.934
	#2	4.362	3.769	3.967	5.562
No. of Buffer Under-flows	#1	9	5	1	0
	#2	12	19	14	3
Buffering Duration (sec.)	#1	28.86	12.45	2.15	0
	#2	42.55	63.43	58.36	11.82
Average LTE Network Utilization		1.655	0	0.707	0.974

5. CONCLUSION

In this work, we have proposed a control-theoretic scalable D2D offloading system for video streaming services to control the LTE traffic load while supporting a smooth video streaming service. The proposed system is designed considering the scalable traffic offloading and the incentive model for the D2D server's participation that are the challenging issues in traffic offloading via D2D communications. A two-stage PID-based LTE traffic controller is designed to improve the convergence speed while achieving the target LTE traffic load. The experimental results demonstrate that the two-stage PID-based LTE traffic controller is able to attain the target LTE traffic load while providing seamless video streaming services.

6. ACKNOWLEDGMENTS

This work was partly supported by the ICT R&D program of MSIP/IITP (B0101-16-0033, Research and Development of 5G Mobile Communications Technologies using CCN-based Multi-dimensional Scalability) and the National Research Foundation of Korea (NRF) grant funded by the Korea government (MSIP) (No. 2016R1A2B4007812).

7. REFERENCES

[1] Cisco White Paper, "Cisco Visual Networking Index – Global mobile data traffic forecast, update, 2014–2019," 2015.

[2] Ericsson Annual Report, "Welcome to the networked society," 2014.

[3] Ericsson, "Ericsson mobility report," 2015.

[4] M. Yang, S. Lim, H. Park, and N. Park, "Solving the data overload: Device-to-device bearer control architecture for cellular data offloading," IEEE Vehicular Technology Magazine, Vol. 8, Issue 1, pp. 31–39, Feb. 2013.

[5] A. Asadi, Q. Wang, and V. Mancuso, "A survey on device-to-device communication in cellular networks," IEEE Communications Surveys & Tutorials, Vol. 16, Issue 4, pp. 1801–1891, Apr. 2014.

[6] F. Malandrino, M. Kurant, A. Markopoulou, C. Westphal, and U. Kozat, "Proactive seeding for information cascades in cellular networks," Proceedings of IEEE INFOCOM, pp. 1719–1727, Mar. 2012.

[7] S. Belouanas, K. Thai, P. Spathis, M. Amorim, F. Rousseau, and A. Duda, "Content centricity in constrained cellular-assisted D2D communications," Lecture Notes of the Institute for Computer Sciences, Social Informatics and Telecommunications Engineering, Vol. 140, pp. 134–145, Nov. 2014.

[8] Q. Wang, W. Wang, S. Jin, H. Zhu, and N. Zhang, "Quality-optimized joint source selection and power control for wireless multimedia D2D communication using Stackelberg game," IEEE Transactions on Vehicular Technology, Vol. 64, Issue 8, pp. 3755–3769, Sep. 2014.

[9] J. Liu, Y. Kawamoto, H. Nishiyama, N. Kato, and N. Kadowaki, "Device-to-Device communications achieve efficient load balancing in LTE-advanced networks," IEEE Wireless Communications, Vol. 21, Issue 2, Apr. 2014.

[10] X. Duan, A. Akhtar, and X. Wang, "Software-defined networking-based resource management: data offloading with load balancing in 5G HetNet," EURASIP Journal on Wireless Communications and Networking, Dec. 2015.

[11] V. Jacobson, D.K. Smetters, J.D. Thornton, M.F. Plasee, N. Briggs, R. Braynard, "Networking named content", Proceedings of ACM CoNEXT, pp. 1–12, 2009.

[12] CCNx. [Online]. Available: http://blogs.parc.com/ccnx/.

[13] A. Detti, B. Ricci, and N. Blefari-Melazzi, "Mobile peer-to-peer video streaming over information-centric networks," Computer Networks, Vol. 81, pp. 272–288, Apr. 2015.

[14] W. Lin, H. Zhao, and K. Liu, "Incentive cooperation strategies for peer-to-peer live multimedia streaming social networks," IEEE Transactions on Multimedia, Vol. 11, Issue 3, pp. 396–412, Apr. 2009.

[15] LTE pricing model, http://koreajoongangdaily.joins.com/news/article/Article.aspx?aid=3003941.

[16] G. Lee and H. Song, "Cross-layer optimized video streaming based on IEEE 802.11 multi-rate over multi-hop mobile ad hoc networks," ACM/Springer Mobile Networks and Applications, Vol. 15, Issue 5, pp. 652–663, Oct. 2010.

[17] S. Boyd and L. Vandenberghe, "Convex optimization," Cambridge University Press, 2004.

[18] NetEM, http://www.linuxfoundation.org/collaborate/workgroups/networking/netem.

[19] Video test sequence, http://cs-nsl-wiki.cs.surrey.sfu.ca/wiki/Video_Library_and_Tools.

[20] ISO/IEC 13818 (MPEG-2), "Generic coding of moving pictures and associated audio information," Nov. 1994.

[21] C. Ghali, A. Narayanan, D. Oran, G. Tsudik, and C. A. Wood, "Secure fragmentation for content-centric networks," proceedings of IEEE international symposium on network computing and applications, 2015.

[22] J. Ziegler and N. Nichols, "Optimum settings for automatic controllers," Journal of Dynamic Systems, Measurement, and Control, Vol. 115, pp. 220–222, Jun. 1993.

Performance of D2D Underlay and Overlay for Elastic Traffic

Prajwal Osti
Aalto University, Finland
prajwal.osti@aalto.fi

Pasi Lassila
Aalto University, Finland
pasi.lassila@aalto.fi

Samuli Aalto
Aalto University, Finland
samuli.aalto@aalto.fi

ABSTRACT

We explore the performance of different resource allocation schemes for transferring elastic traffic in a cellular network that is either overlaid or underlaid with D2D traffic. To this end, we model a single cell during uplink transmissions and jointly consider the presence of a randomly varying number of D2D and cellular users in the system. We use different processor sharing queueing models to characterize the performance of the overlaying and underlaying schemes and measure the performance as the mean flow level delay. In the overlaying approach, depending on the load a certain fraction of the radio resources is reserved for the D2D traffic and the cellular traffic, and hence there is no interference between the D2D and cellular users. In the underlaying approach, the D2D users are allowed to opportunistically transmit unless being interfered by a cellular user nearby. Our numerical studies reveal that the underlaying D2D traffic scheme provides a good performance compared to other methods, especially if the interference range of a cellular user is small compared with the cell dimensions. Moreover, the so-called dynamic overlay method we propose appears to perform better than the static overlay scheme.

Keywords

Device-to-device; D2D; Markov process; Processor sharing; Queueing theory

1. INTRODUCTION

As the demand for data traffic is expected to grow exponentially over the next few years, new areas are being explored to accommodate this demand in the forthcoming fifth generation (5G) wireless networks. One such method is called Device-to-device (D2D) communication, whose adoption can provide not only tremendous advantage in handling the data traffic but also aid in improving energy efficiency of the network.

In all traditional methods, data communication occurs only between the user equipment (UE) and the base station (BS) or the access point (AP), which is then responsible for taking the data to the desired destination. However, in D2D communications, the devices themselves are able to directly communicate with each other, without involving the network as an intermediary. This is more effective when the users are physically close to each other. This way the precious radio resources of the network are freed up, which can then be utilized in other areas.

Since the communication occurs between physically proximal devices, comparatively less power is consumed to support a high data rate, especially at the cell edge. Obviously the latency is improved when there is a direct communication link between the communicators. More importantly, the method scales up very well even in disaster scenarios, when the network infrastructure is not working or under enormous strain. The role of the network in all such D2D scenarios is to provide the proper authentication and authorization, including the radio resources, for D2D communication to run smoothly.

D2D communications can be implemented in a number of ways. Outband D2D communication uses a band outside the cellular spectrum. While this appears to be a good strategy, since it eliminates interference in the cellular band, very limited spectrum may be available for the actual D2D communication. This is because other bands may already be occupied or there may be a huge competition for their use for some other purposes. This shrinks the scope of the application of the method.

On the other hand, in inband transmissions the spectrum allocated for the usage by the cellular network is utilized by the D2D users as well. This can obviously lead to interference between the cellular and the D2D users, and various interference management methods have to be employed for efficiently utilizing the spectrum. One way to use the inband method is to overlay D2D over the cellular users (called the *D2D overlay* hereafter), where the available cellular spectrum is partitioned in such a way that the D2D users and the ordinary cellular users use non-overlapping portions of the spectrum. This eliminates the possibility of interference between cellular and D2D users. This, however, may lead to inefficiency in utilization of spectrum.

In a second method of inband D2D, called *D2D underlay* hereafter, the D2D users are underlaid with respect to the cellular users. In this scheme, the D2D users opportunistically use the spectrum for communication when they sense that the possible interferers, which are located in close proximity to these devices, are not utilizing the spectrum. Therefore, more robust interference management schemes

MSWiM '16, November 13 - 17, 2016, Malta, Malta

© 2016 Copyright held by the owner/author(s). Publication rights licensed to ACM.
ISBN 978-1-4503-4502-6/16/11...$15.00

DOI: http://dx.doi.org/10.1145/2988287.2989157

need to be employed for this mode to work properly. Moreover, since very little power is used for D2D communications, they tend not to interfere with the ordinary cellular devices.

Although the application of D2D communications has received a lot of attention in the context of small data transfer and multi-hop relays of small packets of data, etc., very little work has been done in this area related to the transfer of elastic traffic. When a large volume of data needs to be transferred between a D2D pair then flow-level analysis of such transfer, taking into account the constraints of D2D communications, is a useful technique. The key idea in the flow-level approach is to model the impact of the randomly varying number of users in the system on the system performance. This approach has been used extensively for analyzing traditional cellular systems.

In this paper, we model a single cell during uplink transmissions and jointly consider the presence of a randomly varying number of D2D and cellular users in the system. We develop processor sharing (PS) queueing models to characterize the performance of the overlaying and underlaying schemes and measure the performance as the mean flow level delay (or the mean file transfer delay). In our model, each D2D user represents a pair of D2D devices in very close proximity so that they are able to transmit data at a very high practically constant rate. On the other hand, the cellular users are communicating with a receiver somewhere in the Internet (not in the same cell).

In the overlaying approach, depending on the load a certain fraction of the radio resources is reserved for the D2D traffic and the cellular traffic, and hence there is no interference between the D2D and cellular users. Here we consider two variants. In the static overlay approach, the fraction depends only on the average load. Additionally, we propose a new scheme, the so-called *dynamic overlay*, where the fraction of resources varies dynamically with the number of cellular users. This guarantees that D2D always gets some service but the fraction decreases the more there are cellular users. In the underlaying approach, the D2D users are allowed to opportunistically transmit unless being interfered by a cellular user nearby. Our numerical studies reveal that the underlaying D2D traffic scheme provides a good performance compared to other methods, especially if the interference range of a cellular user is small compared with the cell dimensions. Moreover, the so-called dynamic overlay method we propose appears to perform better than the static overlay scheme.

This paper is organized as follows: We present the related work in Section 2. Then we describe the system model in Section 3, following which we analyze the D2D overlay and underlay approaches in Sections 4 and 5 respectively. Then, we present the numerical results in Section 6 and finally conclusions are presented in Section 7.

2. RELATED WORK

A comprehensive survey of literature related to D2D communications can be found in [2]. According to [2], the concept of D2D communication was first introduced in [12] in the context of Multihop Cellular Networks. The various uses of D2D communication, e.g., video transfer [6], machine-type communication [13], relaying [14], cellular offloading [1], etc., have been proposed in literature. Moreover, standardizing bodies such as 3GPP have studied D2D communications as Proximity Services (ProSe) [10] and QualComm's

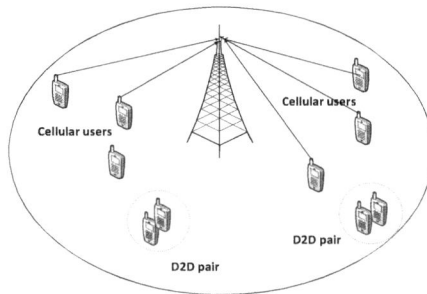

Figure 1: D2D and cellular users in a cell.

FlashLinQ [15] implements D2D communications underlaying the cellular network.

Moreover, [17] provides studies of the spectral as well as energy efficiency aspects of D2D communications. The concepts of inband/outband and underlay/overlay are discussed in [11]. Specific interference management techniques have been discussed in [16]. However, these and many others similar studies typically focus on the performance at the physical layer or the MAC layer for a fixed number of users.

Flow-level analysis for elastic traffic in cellular systems has received considerable attention, and different PS models have been used to study the flow-level performance of these systems, see, e.g., [4, 5]. As mentioned, flow-level models consider the system at the time scale where the number of users varies randomly, i.e., at the network (session) level. These flow-level models have recently been applied to D2D overlay and underlay networks in [8, 9]. We also apply similar flow-level models, but our interference model is different from that given in [8, 9]. As a result, we are able to derive more explicit results. In addition, we introduce and study a novel dynamic overlay scheme by these flow-level models.

3. SYSTEM MODEL

We consider the uplink transmission in a single cell of radius $r_{\max}$ (Figure 1) in a time-slotted system, where the time slots are indexed by $t = 1, 2, \ldots$. The users are classified either as cellular users or as D2D users denoted by $k \in \{c, d\}$. The cellular users transmit to the base station while the D2D users always exist in pairs and transmit data only to their respective partners. The members of D2D pairs are assumed to be located so close to each other that they effectively share the same physical location. In addition, we assume that the transmission power of a D2D user is so low that it is not disturbing any other transmission in the cell area.

We assume that the cellular users and the D2D user pairs arrive randomly at any location in the cell according to independent Poisson processes of rates λ_c and λ_d, respectively. The users transmit elastic traffic, which can, e.g., be files that are transferred utilizing the system's radio resources using protocols such as TCP. These transmissions are referred to as jobs or flows. After their jobs complete, the users leave the system. Let $\mathcal{N}_c(t)$ and $\mathcal{N}_d(t)$ denote the set of cellular users and D2D pairs, respectively, present in the cell at the beginning of time slot t. The cellular users are indexed by $i \in \mathcal{N}_c(t)$ and the D2D pairs by $j \in \mathcal{N}_d(t)$.

We study both the D2D overlay and the D2D underlay schemes. In the overlay scheme, the resources are allocated in such a manner that no interference is possible between the two classes of users. For the underlay scheme, we adopt a Boolean interference model in which the D2D pair either does not transmit at all (when the interference from cellular users is too high), or transmit at a constant rate, as a result of their close physical proximity (when the interference from the nearby cellular users is low). We also assume that the interference is dependent only on the distance of the cellular users from the D2D users and that the transmission power of cellular users is much higher than that of the D2D users. Due to this *power asymmetry*, the D2D pair does not cause any interference to the cellular users' operations. On the other hand, the presence of even a single cellular user in the vicinity destroys a D2D pair's transmission. Thus, the communication between a D2D pair $j \in \mathcal{N}_d(t)$ in time slot t is possible only if there is no cellular user transmitting within a radius δ of the pair in that time slot. Mathematically, the condition reads

$$\min_{i \in \mathcal{N}_c(t)} d(j, i) \geq \delta, \tag{1}$$

where $d(j, i)$ denotes the distance between D2D pair j and cellular user i. Here δ is the *interference range*, and the region around the D2D pair where a cellular user's transmission can interfere with the D2D pair is called the *interference region* of that D2D pair.

The base station allocates resources that enable communications for the two classes. When all the radio resources are allocated to the D2D class, we assume that each D2D pair is able to have a transmission between them simultaneously. The transmission rate r_d is assumed to be constant due to the close proximity of the members of the D2D pairs. On the other hand, when all the resources are allocated to the cellular class, these resources are shared among the cellular users in a fair way, e.g., scheduling the resources to the cellular users in the round-robin manner. In addition, we assume that each cellular user transmits with a constant rate r_c when scheduled. In practice, this transmission rate depends on the location of the cellular user in the cell. However, in our model, it is assumed to be constant for the sake of simplicity of analysis.

Let Y_k denote the size of a class-k job. Its service time S_k is defined by $S_k = Y_k / r_k$, and the mean service time $E[S_k] = E[Y_k]/r_k$ is denoted by $1/\mu_k$. In addition, let $\rho_k = \lambda_k / \mu_k$ denote traffic load of class k.

In Sections 4 and 5, we discuss the two ways (i.e., overlay and underlay) by which the available resources in the system can be utilized by the cellular and the D2D users so that the two can simultaneously coexist in the system. Our aim is to determine the mean delay $\mathbb{E}[T_k] = \bar{T}_k$ for both classes $k \in \{c, d\}$ under different resource allocation schemes. From these class-wise mean delays, we get the overall mean delay $E[T]$ as follows:

$$\mathbb{E}[T] = \frac{1}{\lambda_c + \lambda_d}(\lambda_c \bar{T}_c + \lambda_d \bar{T}_d). \tag{2}$$

In our study, we assume that the time slots of the system are very small compared to the time it takes for the jobs to complete (i.e., their service times). Because of this *time-scale separation* and the fair sharing of the available resources, the dynamics of the cellular user population can be modeled by processor-sharing (PS) queues of type M/G/1 [4,5]. Similarly, the time-scale separation and the lack of interference between the D2D pairs allows us to model the dynamics of

the D2D user population by so-called infinite-server queues of type M/G/∞.

4. D2D OVERLAY ANALYSIS

In the overlay scheme, the resources are allocated in such a manner that no interference is possible between the cellular users and the D2D pairs. Thus, we do not have to take into account the locations of the cellular users when the transmission of a D2D pair is considered, which considerably simplifies the analysis.

4.1 Static overlay

In the static overlay, a constant fraction p of the resources is always allocated to the cellular users while the rest, fraction $1 - p$, is allocated to the D2D pairs. Since there is no possibility of interference between cellular and D2D users, they are served at transmission rates pr_c and $(1 - p)r_d$, respectively.

The cellular users share the same resources in a fair way so that their population dynamics can be modeled by an M/G/1-PS queue with service rate $p\mu_c$, which results in the mean cellular delay equal to

$$\bar{T}_c = \frac{1}{p\mu_c - \lambda_c}.$$

On the other hand, the D2D pairs do not interfere with each other so that all the resources allocated for the D2D users can be utilized simultaneously by each pair. Thus, their population dynamics can be modeled by an M/G/∞ system with service rate $(1 - p)\mu_d$, which implies that

$$\bar{T}_d = \frac{1}{(1 - p)\mu_d}.$$

By (2), the overall mean delay of this system is given by

$$\mathbb{E}[T] = \frac{1}{\lambda_c + \lambda_d}\left(\frac{\rho_c}{p - \rho_c} + \frac{\rho_d}{1 - p}\right).$$

Clearly, $\mathbb{E}[T]$ can be minimized by choosing a proper value of splitting fraction p. By an elementary optimization analysis, we obtain the optimal value as

$$p^* = \frac{\sqrt{\rho_c} + \rho_c\sqrt{\rho_d}}{\sqrt{\rho_c} + \sqrt{\rho_d}}.$$

It follows that the minimum mean delay is given by

$$\mathbb{E}[T]_{p=p^*} = \frac{1}{\lambda_c + \lambda_d}\frac{(\sqrt{\rho_c} + \sqrt{\rho_d})^2}{1 - \rho_c}.$$

4.2 Dynamic overlay

In the dynamic overlay, the resources allocated to the cellular and D2D users still do not overlap, and they are partitioned taking into account the instantaneous number of cellular and D2D users in the system at any time.

We consider a specific dynamic overlay scheme where a fraction $1/(X_c(t)+1)$ of the resources is allocated to the D2D users while the rest, fraction $X_c(t)/(X_c(t) + 1)$, is allocated to the cellular users, where $X_c(t)$ denotes the number of cellular users in the system at time t. In the analysis of this dynamic overlay scheme, we assume that the class-k service times, S_k, are exponentially distributed for both classes k.

In this case, the cellular user population in the system can be modeled by a modified M/M/1-PS queue with one permanent user. On the other hand, since all D2D pairs can utilize all the allocated resources simultaneously, their population can be modeled by a modified M/M/∞ queue where the service rate for each D2D pair depends on the number of cellular users present in the system. It follows that the pair $(X_c(t), X_d(t))$, where $X_d(t)$ denotes the number of D2D users in the system at time t, is a two-dimensional Markov process with state space $\mathbb{N}^2$. Let $\boldsymbol{x} = (x_c, x_d) \in \mathbb{N}^2$ denote an arbitrary state of this process. The state transition rates $q(\boldsymbol{x}, \boldsymbol{y})$ from state $\boldsymbol{x}$ to state $\boldsymbol{y}$ are as follows:

$$q(\boldsymbol{x}, \boldsymbol{x} + \boldsymbol{e}_c) = \lambda_c, \quad q(\boldsymbol{x}, \boldsymbol{x} - \boldsymbol{e}_c) = \frac{x_c}{x_c + 1}\mu_c,$$

$$q(\boldsymbol{x}, \boldsymbol{x} + \boldsymbol{e}_d) = \lambda_d, \quad q(\boldsymbol{x}, \boldsymbol{x} - \boldsymbol{e}_d) = \frac{x_d}{x_c + 1}\mu_d,$$

where $\boldsymbol{e}_c = (1, 0)$ and $\boldsymbol{e}_d = (0, 1)$.

The mean delay under this dynamic overlay scheme can be calculated as

$$\mathbb{E}[T] = \frac{1}{\lambda_c + \lambda_d}\left(\sum_{x_c=0}^{\infty}\sum_{x_d=0}^{\infty} \pi(x_c, x_d)(x_c + x_d)\right),$$

where $\pi(x_c, x_d)$ is the steady state probability that the system is in state $\boldsymbol{x} = (x_c, x_d)$. However, the calculation of the mean delay can be simplified by utilizing the fact that the cellular user population can be modeled by an M/M/1-PS queue with one permanent user. The steady state probability π_i that there are i cellular users in the system is obtained by solving the following detailed balance equations:

$$\frac{i}{i + 1}\mu_c \pi_i = \lambda_c \pi_{i-1}, \quad i = 1, \ldots,$$

From these equations and the normalizing condition we obtain

$$\pi_i = (i + 1)(1 - \rho_c)^2 \rho_c^i.$$

The average number of cellular users in the system is thus

$$\mathbb{E}[X_c] = (1 - \rho_c)^2 \sum_{i=1}^{\infty} i(i + 1)\rho_c^i = \frac{2\rho_c}{1 - \rho_c},$$

which implies, by Little's result, that

$$\bar{T}_c = \frac{\mathbb{E}[X_c]}{\lambda_c} = \frac{2}{\mu_c - \lambda_c}.$$

As said, the service rate of the D2D users changes with the changing number of cellular users. Let $t_d(n)$ denote the conditional mean delay experienced by a D2D pair whose service starts when there are n cellular user. Now, due to the well-known PASTA property of Poisson arrivals, the mean delay for the D2D pairs is equal to

$$\bar{T}_d = \sum_{n=0}^{\infty} \pi_n t_d(n). \tag{3}$$

The conditional mean delays $t_d(n)$ can be determined by exploiting the Markov property of the system as follows: The D2D pair stays in the system for a minimum of

$$\frac{1}{\lambda_c + n\mu_c/(n + 1) + \mu_d/(n + 1)}$$

time units on average. After this, it can either leave the system or stay there. If it stays, the system moves either to

state $n + 1$ or state $n - 1$. These latter events occur with probabilities

$$\frac{\lambda_c}{\lambda_c + n\mu_c/(n + 1) + \mu_d/(n + 1)} \quad \text{and}$$

$$\frac{n\mu_c/(n + 1)}{\lambda_c + n\mu/(n + 1) + \mu_d/(n + 1)},$$

respectively. If the system moves to state $n + 1$ [$n - 1$], then, by the Markov property, the remaining delay for the D2D pair is equal to $t_d(n + 1)$ [$t_d(n - 1)$]. Taking into account all these possibilities, we get

$$
\begin{aligned}
t_d(n) =\ & \frac{n + 1}{(n + 1)\lambda_c + n\mu_c + \mu_d} \\
& + \frac{(n + 1)\lambda_c}{(n + 1)\lambda_c + n\mu_c + \mu_d} t_d(n + 1) \\
& + \frac{n\mu_c}{(n + 1)\lambda_c + n\mu_c + \mu_d} t_d(n - 1),
\end{aligned}
\tag{4}
$$

which is an infinite set of independent linear equations with $n \in \{0, 1, \ldots\}$. In practice, the conditional mean delays $t_d(n)$ can be determined (as precisely as needed) by appropriately truncating the process and then solving the resulting finite set of linear equations. Finally, by (2), the overall mean delay of this dynamic overlay scheme is given by

$$\mathbb{E}[T] = \frac{1}{\lambda_c + \lambda_d}\left(\frac{2\rho_c}{1 - \rho_c} + \lambda_d \bar{T}_d\right), \tag{5}$$

where $\bar{T}_d$ is given in (3).

5. D2D UNDERLAY ANALYSIS

In the underlay scheme, the same resources are shared among the cellular users and D2D pairs so that interference is possible between cellular and D2D users. Since the transmission from cellular users interferes with the D2D pairs that are sufficiently near, such a D2D pair can communicate only opportunistically when there is no cellular user at a distance of δ from the pair. On the other hand, the D2D pairs do not disturb the cellular users, which effectively gives an absolute priority to the cellular users. Therefore, the cellular users form an M/G/1-PS queue with service rate μ_c, which results in the mean cellular delay equal to

$$\bar{T}_c = \frac{1}{\mu_c - \lambda_c}. \tag{6}$$

The D2D delay is highly sensitive to the location of the D2D pair in the cell and the interference distance δ. In what follows, we analyze how different values of δ affect the mean delay of the D2D pairs.

5.1 Small δ analysis

Consider a D2D pair whose distance from the base station is denoted by r. Let $\bar{T}_d(r)$ denote the mean delay experienced by this D2D pair. Since the users appear randomly anywhere in the cell, the probability that an arbitrary cellular user is interfering with the D2D pair is given by

$$p(r, \delta) = \frac{A(r, \delta)}{A}, \tag{7}$$

where $A(r, \delta)$ denotes the area of the intersection between the circle of radius δ around the D2D pair and the circle of radius $r_{\max}$ around the base station (i.e., the whole cell area) and $A = \pi r_{\max}^2$ is the total area of the cell. When

273

$r \leq r_{\max} - \delta$, the D2D pair is located so near the center of cell that the interference region is completely inside the cell. Thus, in this case, the area of the interference region is independent of r and we may define

$$p_\delta = p(r, \delta)|_{0 \leq r \leq r_{\max} - \delta} = \left(\frac{\delta}{r_{\max}} \right)^2. \qquad (8)$$

Assume now, for a while, that $r \leq r_{\max} - \delta$. For the D2D pair, the cellular users evolve as a PS queue with two classes of users—one inside the interference region and the other outside of it. Let $X_{c,\delta}(t)$ and $X_{c,\bar{\delta}}(t)$ denote the number of cellular users inside and outside, respectively, of the interference region of this D2D pair at time t. Assuming that the service times S_c are exponentially distributed with mean $1/\mu_c$, the pair $(X_{c,\delta}(t), X_{c,\bar{\delta}}(t))$ constitutes a two-dimensional Markov process with state space $\mathbb{N}^2$. Let $\boldsymbol{x} = (x_{c,\delta}, x_{c,\bar{\delta}}) \in \mathbb{N}^2$ denote an arbitrary state of the system with $x_{c,\delta}$ cellular users in the interference region and $x_{c,\bar{\delta}}$ outside of it. The state transition rates $q(\boldsymbol{x}, \boldsymbol{y})$ from state $\boldsymbol{x}$ to state $\boldsymbol{y}$ are as follows:

$$q(\boldsymbol{x}, \boldsymbol{x} + \boldsymbol{e}_\delta) = p_\delta \lambda_c, \ q(\boldsymbol{x}, \boldsymbol{x} - \boldsymbol{e}_\delta) = \frac{x_{c,\delta}}{x_{c,\delta} + x_{c,\bar{\delta}}} \mu_c,$$

$$q(\boldsymbol{x}, \boldsymbol{x} + \boldsymbol{e}_{\bar{\delta}}) = (1 - p_\delta) \lambda_c, \ q(\boldsymbol{x}, \boldsymbol{x} - \boldsymbol{e}_{\bar{\delta}}) = \frac{x_{c,\bar{\delta}}}{x_{c,\delta} + x_{c,\bar{\delta}}} \mu_c,$$

where $\boldsymbol{e}_\delta = (1, 0)$ and $\boldsymbol{e}_{\bar{\delta}} = (0, 1)$. Since this is a two-class M/M/1-PS queue with loads $\rho_\delta = p_\delta \rho_c$ and $\rho_{\bar{\delta}} = (1 - p_\delta) \rho_c$, the steady state probabilities are given by [3]

$$\pi(\boldsymbol{x}) = \binom{x_{c,\delta} + x_{c,\bar{\delta}}}{x_{c,\delta}} (1 - \rho_c) \rho_\delta^{x_{c,\delta}} \rho_{\bar{\delta}}^{x_{c,\bar{\delta}}}. \qquad (9)$$

Let $t_d^\delta(i, j)$ denote the conditional mean delay experienced by the D2D pair (with $r \leq r_{\max} - \delta$) whose service starts when the Markov process $(X_{c,\delta}(t), X_{c,\bar{\delta}}(t))$ is in state (i, j). Now, due to the PASTA property, the mean delay for the D2D pair at distance r is equal to

$$\bar{T}_d(r) = \bar{T}_d^\delta = \sum_{i=0}^\infty \sum_{j=0}^\infty \pi(i, j) t_d^\delta(i, j). \qquad (10)$$

As before, the conditional mean delays $t_d^\delta(i, j)$ can be determined by exploiting the Markov property of the system. Note, however, that in this case the D2D pair's service may complete only when there are no cellular users in the vicinity, i.e., $x_{c,\delta} = 0$.

If the D2D pair enters the system in state $(0,0)$, then it stays there for a minimum of $1/(\mu_d + \lambda_c)$ time units on average. After this, it can either leave the system or stay there. If it stays, the system moves either to state $(1, 0)$ or $(0, 1)$ and remains there (on average) for a further $t_d^\delta(1, 0)$ or $t_d^\delta(0, 1)$ time units, respectively. These events occur with probabilities $p_\delta \lambda_c / (\mu_d + \lambda_c)$ and $(1 - p_\delta) \lambda_c / (\mu_d + \lambda_c)$, respectively. Thus,

$$t_d^\delta(0, 0) = \frac{1}{\mu_d + \lambda_c} + \frac{p_\delta \lambda_c}{\mu_d + \lambda_c} t_d^\delta(1, 0) + \frac{(1 - p_\delta) \lambda_c}{\mu_d + \lambda_c} t_d^\delta(0, 1). \qquad (11)$$

In state $(0, j)$, where $j > 0$, the departure of a cellular user can also occur in addition to the same events as in state

$(0, 0)$. Thus, by a similar reasoning as in state $(0, 0)$, we get

$$t_d^\delta(0, j) = \frac{1}{\mu_d + \lambda_c + \mu_c} + \frac{p_\delta \lambda_c}{\mu_d + \lambda_c + \mu_c} t_d^\delta(1, j) + \frac{(1 - p_\delta) \lambda_c}{\mu_d + \lambda_c + \mu_c} t_d^\delta(0, j + 1) + \frac{\mu_c}{\mu_d + \lambda_c + \mu_c} t_d^\delta(0, j - 1). \qquad (12)$$

If there are cellular users inside the interference region, i.e., in state (i, j), where $i > 0$, the D2D pair cannot leave the system. There can, however, be arrivals and departures in the cellular queue, both inside the interference region and outside of it. Thus $t_d^\delta(i, j)$ for state $(i, j), i > 0$ satisfies

$$t_d^\delta(i, j) = \frac{1}{\lambda_c + \mu_c} + \frac{p_\delta \lambda_c}{\lambda_c + \mu_c} t_d^\delta(i + 1, j) + \frac{(1 - p_\delta) \lambda_c}{\lambda_c + \mu_c} t_d^\delta(i, j + 1) + \frac{i \mu_c}{i + j} \frac{1}{\lambda_c + \mu_c} t_d^\delta(i - 1, j) + \frac{j \mu_c}{i + j} \frac{1}{\lambda_c + \mu_c} t_d^\delta(i, j - 1). \qquad (13)$$

Clearly (11), (12) and (13) constitute an infinite set of linear equations when the whole state space $\mathbb{N}^2$ is considered. However, by appropriately truncating the state space, we can approximate the conditional mean values $t_d^\delta(i, j)$ as precisely as needed.

Consider now the case $\delta \ll r_{\max}$. In this case, $p(r, \delta) = p_\delta$ almost everywhere inside the cell so that the (unconditional) mean delay $\bar{T}_d$ for the D2D pairs is essentially the same as $\bar{T}_d^\delta$. Thus, by (2), we conclude that the overall mean delay of the underlay scheme for $\delta \ll r_{\max}$ is equal to

$$\mathbb{E}[T] = \frac{1}{\lambda_c + \lambda_d} \left(\frac{\lambda_c}{\mu_c - \lambda_c} + \lambda_d \bar{T}_d^\delta \right), \qquad (14)$$

where $\bar{T}_d^\delta$ given in (10).

5.2 Medium δ analysis

Now we discuss the general case where the interference region cannot be approximated by the interior of the whole circle if $r > r_{\max} - \delta$. In this case, the analysis in Section 5.1 must take into account the border effect. This can be done by conditioning on the event that the D2D pair arrives at a given distance r from the base station and modifying the interference probability accordingly. The area of the interference region $A(r, \delta)$ when $r_{\max} - \delta < r < r_{\max}$ is given by

$$A(r, \delta) = 2 \left[\int_{r - \delta}^{x'} \sqrt{\delta^2 - (x - r)^2} \, dx + \int_{x'}^{r_{\max}} \sqrt{r_{\max}^2 - x^2} \, dx \right],$$

where

$$x' = \frac{r_{\max}^2 + r^2 - \delta^2}{2r}.$$

By (7), we now observe that $p(r, \delta)$ explicitly depends on r. Therefore, for each distance $r_{\max} - \delta < r < r_{\max}$, a Markov process has to be constructed using $p(r, \delta)$ instead of p_δ and the whole analysis has to be carried to get the mean distance-based D2D delay, $\bar{T}_d(r)$, analogously as in

Section 5.1. After that, the mean delay for D2D pairs is calculated as

$$\bar{T}_d = \frac{1}{r_{\max}^2} \left((r_{\max} - \delta)^2 \bar{T}_d^\delta + 2 \int_{r_{\max}-\delta}^{r_{\max}} r \, \bar{T}_d(r) \, dr \right), \quad (15)$$

where $\bar{T}_d^\delta$ is given in (10). Finally, by (2), the overall mean delay in this case is equal to

$$\mathbb{E}[T] = \frac{1}{\lambda_c + \lambda_d} \left(\frac{\lambda_c}{\mu_c - \lambda_c} + \lambda_d \bar{T}_d \right),$$

where $\bar{T}_d$ is given in (15).

5.3 Large δ analysis

For the special case where the interference distance of the cellular user spans the whole cell, i.e., $\delta \geq 2r_{\max}$, we have an exact expression for the mean D2D delay. We can again analyze the delay of the D2D users by considering a single D2D user and how it is affected by the presence of the cellular users in the cell.

In the following analysis, the service times S_k do not need to obey exponential distributions, i.e., the analysis holds for generally distributed service times. When $\delta \geq 2r_{\max}$, a D2D user can transmit only during the idle periods of the M/G/1-PS queue representing the cellular users. Thus, the average D2D delay can be determined by using the law of total expectation as follows

$$\bar{T}_d = \mathbb{E}[T_d \,|\, X_c = 0] \mathbb{P}\{X_c = 0\} + \mathbb{E}[T_d \,|\, X_c > 0] \mathbb{P}\{X_c > 0\}$$
$$= \mathbb{E}[T_d \,|\, X_c = 0] (1 - \rho_c) + \mathbb{E}[T_d \,|\, X_c > 0] \rho_c. \quad (16)$$

To derive the conditional mean delays $\mathbb{E}[T_d \,|\, X_c > 0]$ and $\mathbb{E}[T_d \,|\, X_c = 0]$, we can utilize the busy period analysis of the standard M/G/1 queue. Let B_c denote the length of a busy period in the M/G/1 queue with service times S_c. The first and second moments of B_c are given by [7]

$$\mathbb{E}[B_c] = \frac{\mathbb{E}[S_c]}{1 - \rho_c}, \quad \mathbb{E}[B_c^2] = \frac{\mathbb{E}[S_c^2]}{(1 - \rho_c)^3}. \quad (17)$$

If the arriving D2D user enters the system during the busy period of the cellular users, i.e., $X_c > 0$, the D2D user needs to wait until the end of the residual busy period, which has the mean length of $\mathbb{E}[B_c^2]/(2\mathbb{E}[B_c])$, before starting the transmission to its pair. Due to Poisson arrivals, the conditional mean delay $\mathbb{E}[T_d \,|\, X_c > 0]$ then becomes

$$\mathbb{E}[T_d \,|\, X_c > 0] = \frac{\mathbb{E}[B_c^2]}{2\mathbb{E}[B_c]} + \mathbb{E}[T_d \,|\, X_c = 0]$$
$$= \frac{\mathbb{E}[S_c^2]}{2\mathbb{E}[S_c](1 - \rho_c)^2} + \mathbb{E}[T_d \,|\, X_c = 0].$$

On the other hand, if the arriving D2D pair enters during the idle period of the cellular users, i.e., $X_c = 0$, then it can start transmitting immediately to its pair, which requires S_d time units to complete. However, the transmission can be interrupted at any time by the arrival of a cellular user. Let N_{S_d} denote the random number of interruptions (or cellular user arrivals) during S_d. Due to the Poisson arrival process of cellular users, by conditioning on the S_d, it is easy to see that

$$\mathbb{E}[N_{S_d}] = \mathbb{E}[\mathbb{E}[N_{S_d} \,|\, S_d]] = \lambda_c \mathbb{E}[S_d].$$

Each interruption initiates its own sub-busy period in the M/G/1 queue representing the cellular users with service

times S_c. Let $B_{c,n}$ denote the length of the sub-busy period initiated by the n:th interruption during S_d. The conditional mean delay $\mathbb{E}[T_d \,|\, X_c = 0]$ can be expressed as

$$\mathbb{E}[T_d \,|\, X_c = 0] = \mathbb{E}[S_d] + \mathbb{E}\left[\sum_{n=0}^{N_{S_d}} B_{c,n}\right].$$

Each $B_{c,n}$ is i.i.d. with mean as given by (17). Also, the random variable N_{S_d} is independent of sub-busy periods $B_{c,n}$. Thus, by Wald's lemma, we obtain

$$\mathbb{E}[T_d \,|\, X_c = 0] = \mathbb{E}[S_d] + \mathbb{E}[N_{S_d}] \mathbb{E}[B_c]$$
$$= \frac{\mathbb{E}[S_d]}{1 - \rho_c}.$$

By combining the results together, we obtain that the mean D2D delay is given by

$$\bar{T}_d = \mathbb{E}[T_d \,|\, X_c = 0] + \rho_c \frac{\mathbb{E}[S_c^2]}{2\mathbb{E}[S_c](1 - \rho_c)^2},$$
$$= \frac{\mathbb{E}[S_d]}{1 - \rho_c} + \frac{\lambda_c \mathbb{E}[S_c^2]}{2(1 - \rho_c)^2}.$$

Again, by (2), we see that the overall mean delay in this case is equal to

$$\mathbb{E}[T] = \frac{1}{\lambda_c + \lambda_d} \left(\frac{\rho_c + \rho_d}{1 - \rho_c} + \frac{\lambda_d \lambda_c \mathbb{E}[S_c^2]}{2(1 - \rho_c)^2} \right),$$

In the special case where the S_c obey the exponential distribution with mean $1/\mu_c$, we get

$$\mathbb{E}[T] = \frac{1}{\lambda_c + \lambda_d} \left(\frac{\rho_c + \rho_d}{1 - \rho_c} + \frac{\lambda_d \rho_c}{\mu_c(1 - \rho_c)^2} \right).$$

6. NUMERICAL RESULTS

In this section, we study the performance of the different resource-sharing schemes between cellular and D2D users using the models we have described in Section 4 and 5 through simulations and numerical calculations. For this purpose, we define a baseline scenario with parameter values $\lambda_c = 8.0$, $\lambda_d = 5.0$, $\mu_c = 10.0$, $\mu_d = 10.0$, $\delta = 0.1$ and $r = 1.0$. Clearly, μ_k and λ_k have the same units and δ and $r_{\max}$ have the same units. In the following figures, the different schemes have the following labels: static overlay (sOL), dynamic overlay (dOL) and underlay (UL).

In *Scenario 1*, we vary only λ_c and observe the performance of the different schemes. From Figure 2, we see that the average delay increases as the load of the cellular traffic increases and the performance of both overlay schemes are almost identical when the overall delay is considered (Figure 2, right panel).

Moreover, dynamic overlay provides some gain for the D2D users compared to the static overlay in the D2D delay (Figure 2, middle panel), while the two perform almost the same for the cellular delay (Figure 2, left panel), as well as in the total mean delay (Figure 2, right panel). However, the underlay scheme is clearly performing the best. At low cellular loads, the delay of D2D users is almost constant for underlay scheme (Figure 2, middle panel). As the traffic of the cellular users grows, the probability that there is at least one interferer in the interference region of a D2D pair also increases. Consequently, at the high values of cellular loads,

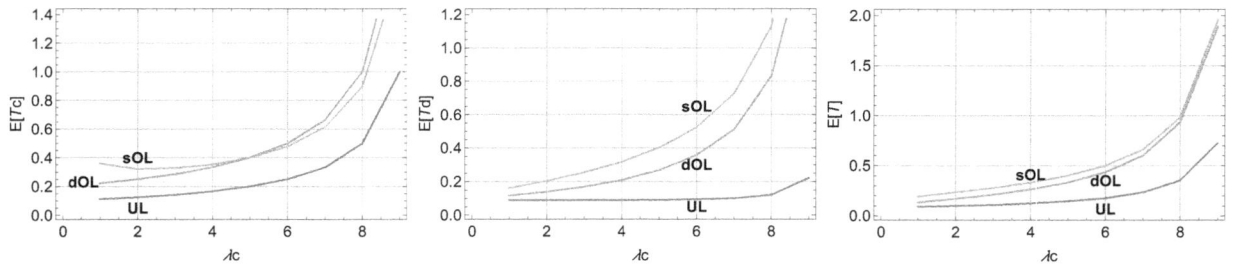

Figure 2: Performance of various schemes in Scenario 1. The left panel shows the average delay of the cellular users, the middle panel shows the average delay of the D2D users and the right panel shows the overall delay. Here, the labels "sOL", "dOL" and "UL" represent the static overlay, the dynamic overlay and the underlay schemes, respectively.

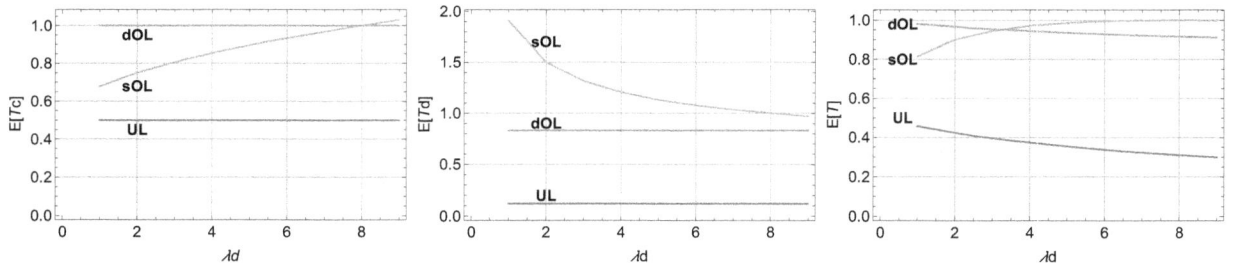

Figure 3: Performance of various schemes in Scenario 2. The left panel shows the average delay of the cellular users, the middle panel shows the average delay of the D2D users and the right panel shows the overall delay. Here, the labels "sOL", "dOL" and "UL" represent the static overlay, the dynamic overlay and the underlay schemes, respectively.

the performance of the D2D users starts to deteriorate for the underlay scheme.

In *Scenario 2* (Figure 3), we vary only λ_d and observe the performance of the different schemes. We notice that delay of the D2D and cellular users are constant for underlay and dynamic overlay schemes (Figure 3, left and middle panel). In these schemes, the cellular users either receive an absolute priority over the D2D users, or the share of resources allocated to the users depends only on the population of the cellular users. Since the cellular traffic is constant, the resources allocated for their service is also constant, and therefore, the respective delays for the cellular users is constant as well (Figure 3, left panel).

Moreover, in these schemes, the D2D pairs are served by an M/G/∞ queue with a constant service rate. Thus, their average delay is constant, irrespective of the arrival rate of the D2D pairs (Figure 3, middle panel). However, when the volume of the D2D traffic increases, it contributes more to the overall delay. In the scenarios selected, the flow level delay of the D2D users is smaller than the that of the cellular users (Figure 3, left and middle panels). Thus, the overall average delay decreases with increasing the D2D load (Figure 3, right panel).

In static overlay, a larger fraction of load is allocated to the D2D pairs with increasing D2D load. As a result, the average delay of the D2D users decreases with increasing D2D load (Figure 3, middle panel). On the other hand, the delay of the cellular users increases with increasing D2D load (Figure 3, left panel). The overall delay thus increases with increasing D2D load but quickly levels off to a constant value, as the changes in the delay of the two kind of users

appear to compensate each other (Figure 3, right panel).

In *Scenario 3*, we vary only δ and observe the performance of the different schemes. The delay of the cellular users is constant for all schemes, because cellular users get an absolute priority over the system's resource usage (Figure 4, left panel). For the D2D traffic, the delays in the overlay schemes stay constant since the interference between cellular users and D2D users has been eliminated (Figure 3, middle panel). However, in the underlay mode the D2D traffic delay is significantly affected by the interference range: as it grows the interference probability increases and hence the D2D delay also increases quickly. Thus also in the overall delay, for the overlay schemes the delay remains constant but increases for the underlay scheme (Figure 4, right panel). For comparison in the figures we have also given the asymptotic value of the delay, as obtained from the analysis in Section 5.3, labelled as 'aUL'. As can be seen, already at $\delta = 0.9$ the result is quite close to the asymptotic case.

7. CONCLUSIONS

In this paper we have proposed various queueing models to study the performance of different resource sharing schemes when D2D traffic is either underlaid or overlaid with ordinary cellular traffic and elastic data is being transmitted. We have observed that the performance of the different schemes is sensitive to the load levels in the cell as well as interference range of cellular users. Our numerical studies indicate that in almost all cases, the underlay scheme appears to provide the best performance.

As a continuation of this work in future, we can explore

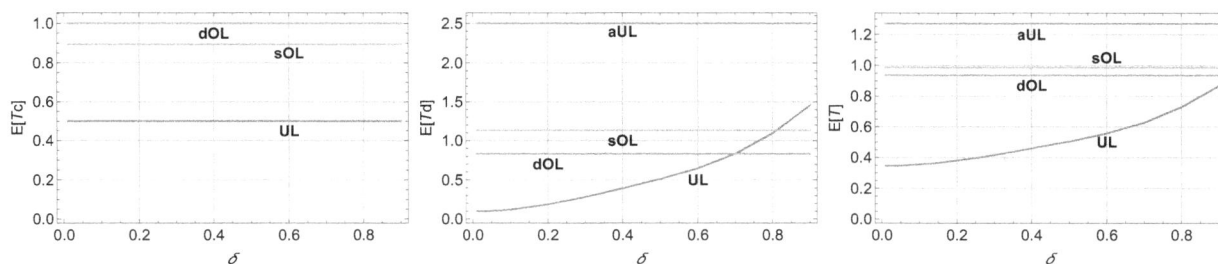

Figure 4: Performance of various schemes in Scenario 3. The left panel shows the average delay of the cellular users, the middle panel shows the average delay of the D2D users and the right panel shows the overall delay. Here, the labels "sOL", "dOL" and "UL" represent the static overlay, the dynamic overlay and the underlay schemes, respectively. The label "aUL" represents the asymptotic performance of the UL scheme when the interference range δ spans the whole cell.

other resource sharing schemes using similar queueing models in similar context. More complicated interference models could be considered in future work. Moreover, we can also explore the ways to estimate the average service rate parameter used here from the operation parameters of the system.

Acknowledgments

This research has been partially supported by EIT Digital under the HII FNS project and by the Academy of Finland under the ITTECH5G project (Grant No. 284735).

8. REFERENCES

[1] S. Andreev, A. Pyattaev, K. Johnsson, O. Galinina, and Y. Koucheryavy. Cellular traffic offloading onto network-assisted device-to-device connections. *IEEE Communications Magazine*, 52(4):20–31, 2014.

[2] A. Asadi, Q. Wang, and V. Mancuso. A survey on device-to-device communication in cellular networks. *IEEE Communications Surveys & Tutorials*, 16(4):1801–1819, 2014.

[3] T. Bonald and M. Feuillet. *Network Performance Analysis*. Wiley, 2011.

[4] T. Bonald and A. Proutière. Wireless downlink data channels: user performance and cell dimensioning. In *Proceedings of the 9th annual international conference on Mobile computing and networking*, pages 339–352. ACM, 2003.

[5] S. Borst. User-level performance of channel-aware scheduling algorithms in wireless data networks. *IEEE/ACM Transactions on Networking (TON)*, 13(3):636–647, 2005.

[6] K. Doppler, M. Rinne, C. Wijting, C. B. Ribeiro, and K. Hugl. Device-to-device communication as an underlay to LTE-advanced networks. *IEEE Communications Magazine*, 47(12):42–49, 2009.

[7] L. Kleinrock. *Queueing Systems, Volume 1: Theory*. Wiley, 1975.

[8] L. Lei, H. Wang, X. S. Shen, N. Cheng, and Z. Zhong. Flow-level performance of device-to-device underlaid OFDM cellular networks. In *2015 IEEE/CIC International Conference on Communications in China (ICCC)*, pages 1–6. IEEE, 2015.

[9] L. Lei, H. Wang, X. S. Shen, Z. Zhong, and K. Zheng. Flow-level performance of device-to-device overlaid OFDM cellular networks. In *Wireless Algorithms, Systems, and Applications*, pages 305–314. Springer, 2015.

[10] X. Lin, J. Andrews, A. Ghosh, and R. Ratasuk. An overview of 3GPP device-to-device proximity services. *IEEE Communications Magazine*, 52(4):40–48, 2014.

[11] X. Lin and J. G. Andrews. Optimal spectrum partition and mode selection in device-to-device overlaid cellular networks. In *IEEE Global Communications Conference (GLOBECOM), 2013*, pages 1837–1842. IEEE, 2013.

[12] Y.-D. Lin and Y.-C. Hsu. Multihop cellular: A new architecture for wireless communications. In *INFOCOM 2000. Nineteenth Annual Joint Conference of the IEEE Computer and Communications Societies. Proceedings. IEEE*, volume 3, pages 1273–1282. IEEE, 2000.

[13] N. K. Pratas and P. Popovski. Underlay of low-rate machine-type D2D links on downlink cellular links. In *IEEE International Conference on Communications (ICC) Workshops, 2014*, pages 423–428. IEEE, 2014.

[14] K. Vanganuru, S. Ferrante, and G. Sternberg. System capacity and coverage of a cellular network with D2D mobile relays. In *2012 Military Communications Conference, 2012-MILCOM*, pages 1–6. IEEE, 2012.

[15] X. Wu, S. Tavildar, S. Shakkottai, T. Richardson, J. Li, R. Laroia, and A. Jovicic. FlashLinQ: A synchronous distributed scheduler for peer-to-peer ad hoc networks. *IEEE/ACM Transactions on Networking (TON)*, 21(4):1215–1228, 2013.

[16] C.-H. Yu and O. Tirkkonen. Device-to-device underlay cellular network based on rate splitting. In *IEEE Wireless Communications and Networking Conference (WCNC), 2012*, pages 262–266. IEEE, 2012.

[17] Z. Zhou, M. Dong, K. Ota, J. Wu, and T. Sato. Energy efficiency and spectral efficiency tradeoff in device-to-device (D2D) communications. *IEEE Wireless Communications Letters*, 3(5):485–488, 2014.

A Virtual Local-hub Solution with Function Module Sharing for Wearable Devices

Hsin-Peng Lin
Telecommunication
Laboratories, Chunghwa
Telecom Co., Ltd.
Department of Computer
Science and Information
Engineering, National Taiwan
University
Taipei, Taiwan
hplin@cht.com.tw

Yuan-Yao Shih
Research Center for
Information Technology
Innovation, Academia Sinica
Taipei, Taiwan
ckm@citi.sinica.edu.tw

Ai-Chun Pang
Department of Computer
Science and Information
Engineering
Graduate Institute of
Networking and Multimedia,
National Taiwan University
Research Center for
Information Technology
Innovation, Academia Sinica
Taipei, Taiwan
acpang@csie.ntu.edu.tw

Yuan-Yao Lou
Graduate Institute of
Networking and Multimedia,
National Taiwan University
Taipei, Taiwan
r04944027@csie.ntu.edu.tw

ABSTRACT

Wearable devices, which are small electronic devices worn on a human body, are equipped with low level of processing and storage capacities and offer some types of integrated functionalities. Recently, wearable device is becoming increasingly popular, various kinds of wearable device are launched in the market; however, wearable devices require a powerful local-hub, most are smartphone, to replenish processing and storage capacities for advanced functionalities. Sometime it may be inconvenient to carry the local-hub (smartphone); thus, many wearable devices are equipped with Wi-Fi interface, enabling them to exchange data with local-hub though the Internet when the local-hub is not nearby. However, this results in long response time and restricted functionalities. In this paper, we present a virtual local-hub solution, which utilizes network equipment nearby (e.g., Wi-Fi APs) as the local-hub. Since migrating all applications serving the wearable devices respectively takes too much networking and storage resources, the proposed solution deploys function modules to multiple network nodes and enables remote function module sharing among different users and applications. To reduce the impact of the solution on the network bandwidth, we propose a heuristic algorithm for function module allocation with the objective of minimizing total bandwidth consumption. We conduct series of experiments, and the results show that the proposed solution can reduce the bandwidth consumption by up to half and still serve all requests given a large number of service requests.

Keywords

Wearable device; local-hub; virtualization; edge computing; fog computing

1. INTRODUCTION

There is no doubt that wearable devices, which are clothing or accessories worn on a human body incorporating computer and advanced electronic technologies, are becoming increasingly popular [1,2]. These devices are often equipped with sensors and can monitor vital signs of a human body and surrounding environment; also, the devices may have touch screens, microphones, or speakers to interact with their users. Along with the popularity of wearable devices, various innovative applications, such as health monitoring, real-time notification/navigation, and speech/gesture recognition, emerge. Those applications need powerful processing and communication capability on a tiny wearable device; however, wearable devices have limited computing and power capacities since they need to be light-weight and with low energy consumption for superb user experience. To tackle these limitations, a coordinator, or called *local-hub*, is required [3,4].

As shown in Fig. 1(a), generally, a local-hub is a smartphone, installed with applications related to the wearable devices, and the devices are connected with a local-hub via low-power wireless technologies, such as Bluetooth Low Energy (BLE). There are two kinds of applications for wearable devices: cloud-related applications and local applications. For cloud-related applications, the local-hub can pre-process the raw data (e.g., the recorded voice) and send the processed data, whose size is smaller than that of the raw data, to the cloud, reducing the bandwidth consumption between the

MSWiM '16, November 13–17, 2016, Malta, Malta.
© 2016 ACM. ISBN 978-1-4503-4502-6/16/11...$15.00
DOI: http://dx.doi.org/10.1145/2988287.2989150

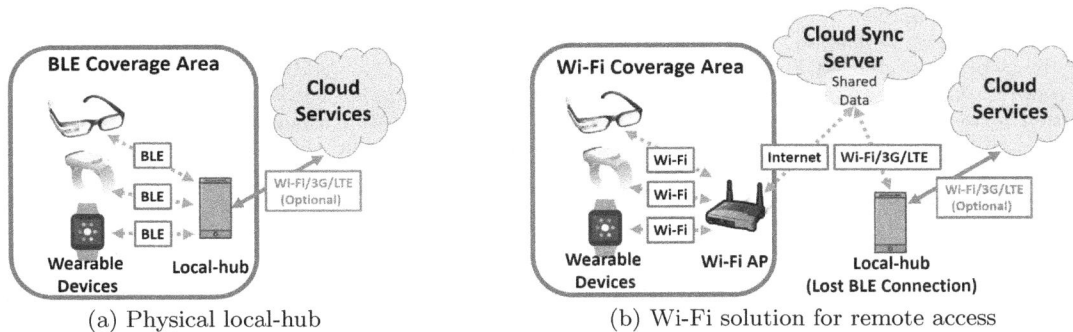

(a) Physical local-hub   (b) Wi-Fi solution for remote access

Figure 1: Current local-hub solutions for wearable devices

local-hub and the cloud. On the other hand, the local-hub can provide full computing and storage resources to local applications to process personal information (e.g., health and fitness tracking data) without connecting to the cloud. To activate cloud-related and local applications, wearable devices must be within the wireless coverage area of the local-hub. For example, an ASUS ZenWatch smartwatch requires its user to install "Android Wear", "ZenWatch Manager", "ZenWatch Wellness", "ZenWatch Face", and other related Android applications on a smartphone (as the local-hub) for the ZenWatch. Without the local-hub, the smartwatch is just an ordinary digital time-telling device. However, in many situations, it is inconvenient for users to carry their local-hubs. For instance, when people work out in the gym or swim in the pool, they would like to check the real-time body-sensing or training information on their wearable devices, but their smartphones may not be nearby.

To overcome the limitation, many manufacturers make their products of wearable devices be equipped with Wi-Fi interface so that they can directly connect to the Wi-Fi networks [5,6]. As shown in Fig. 1(b), the wearable devices not covered by their local hubs connect to the cloud sync server via Wi-Fi connections. Those solutions either migrate all tasks handled by the local-hub to the cloud or connect the wearable devices to the local-hub through the cloud; thus raw data needs to travel among the wearable device, the cloud, and the local-hub over the Internet. As a result, users suffer from long response time, and the longer response time for applications on the wearable devices not only affects the quality of user experience but also reduces the battery life of devices due to longer screen-on time.

Recently, an evolved architecture, labeled as fog computing, emerges to shift computing from the cloud to the edge of the network [7–9]. The idea of fog computing enables another possible solution: via the virtualization and migration to move tasks on the local-hub to the edge of the network, wearable devices can utilize network edge nodes (e.g., Wi-Fi APs) nearby to serve as their local-hub instead of smartphones. Then for cloud-related applications, the size of data sent to the cloud is reduced since pre-processing of the raw data can be done at the edge of the network, and applications originally processed by the local-hub alone (local applications) can be handled at network nodes near the wearable devices without being sent to the distant cloud. The application response time can thus be shortened thanks to the reduction on the transmission time between the devices and the cloud over the Internet.

Intuitively, we can virtualize all the applications for wear-

able devices in a smartphone as a virtual machine (VM) and migrate the whole VM to the network node nearby the user. However, this approach can only serve a limited number of user service requests since the size of a VM is quite large (about hundreds of MBs), and it will consume too much already-scarce network bandwidth and node storage space. Inspired by an observation that the applications can be decomposed by several *function modules* and some of the modules (e.g., speech recognition, map, localization service) are common for different applications, we propose to consider the function module as the basic unit for migration instead of a whole VM and to enable multiple applications using common function modules can share the same function module instances on different network nodes. This approach can reduce the migration cost and the consumption of the node storage; however, since an application is decomposed into multiple function modules whose instances may be hosted by different network nodes, it may consume additional network bandwidth (inter-function module communication) while serving a service request of the application. Thus, it is important to decide which nodes should host which function module instances and which service requests to serve for each function module instance with as low total network bandwidth consumption, comprising the migration cost and the inter-function module communication, as possible.

The contribution of this paper are as follows. First, we propose a virtual local-hub solution, which utilizes the storage and computing resource of the network equipment at the edge of the network to execute applications for wearable devices originally hosted by the local-hub. Second, we advocate enabling remote function module sharing, which can reduce the migration cost and the consumption of the node storage, and thus, more service requests can be fulfilled with limited network, computing, and storage resources of the network nodes. Third, given the fact that remote function module sharing may incur additional network bandwidth consumption due to the inter-function module communication, we define a function module allocation problem for deploying function module instances and assigning service requests with the objective of minimizing total network bandwidth consumption and propose a heuristic algorithm to solve it. Finally, we conduct extensive simulations to evaluate the performance of the proposed algorithm. The simulation results demonstrate that when there are so many service requests that over 80% of the requests cannot be fulfilled without remote function module sharing, the proposed algorithm can still serve all the requests. Also, the proposed algorithm can reduce the bandwidth consumption by up to 40%, compared with random allocation.

The rest of the paper is organized as follows. Section 2 reviews some related works. Section 3 presents the system model and formal formulation of the target problem. We present the design of an efficient heuristic algorithm based on several insights in Section 4. Section 5 reports some experimental results, and Section 6 concludes this paper.

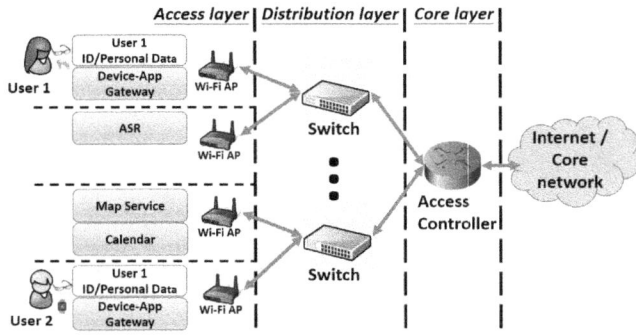

Figure 2: The architecture of an VLH network

2. RELATED WORKS

In this section, we provide a comprehensive review of related works for computation offloading and function module allocation.

One of the ideas to do computation offloading is mobile cloud computing (MCC) [10] [11]. MCC, combining cloud computing, mobile devices and wireless networks, leverages dynamic resources of varied clouds and network technologies for offering powerful computing and storage capabilities to a multitude of mobile devices anywhere, anytime through network connection. The difference between MCC and traditional client-server approach is that in MCC, mobile devices always migrate their computing tasks to remote servers, but not use the existing services in those servers. Chun et al. proposed the CloneCloud [12], a system that enables unmodified applications running in a container to offload part of their computing tasks from physical devices onto device clones (VMs) operating in the cloud. However, transferring the whole VM to the cloud results in unnecessary network bandwidth consumption and server storage since, typically, an application can be subdivided into multiple function modules, some of which need to be run on a physical device and some can be offloaded to a remote server. Cuervo et al. proposed the MAUI [13], a system that enables fine-grained offload of mobile application code to the cloud. MAUI allows a mobile device migrating partial code of a process to remote servers for energy saving. In addition, Ghorpade et al. designed a framework for migrating Android activities from a mobile device to Android emulator on server side [14]. These works migrate applications for each user to remote servers on the distant cloud without the ability to share modules among multiple applications and users; as a result, some service requests may not be fulfilled if there are too many requests. Instead, our solution utilizes the edge of the network to reduce network bandwidth consumption and thus the application response time; also, we propose to enable function module sharing among multiple network nodes, which can leverage the resources of the network edge efficiently with much lower service rejection rate (i.e., the percentage of unfulfilled service requests).

The function module allocation problem studied in this paper is similar with that of virtual network embedding (VNE) [15] [16], which is to map multiple virtual networks (VNs) to specific nodes and links in the substrate network. A number of algorithms have been developed for VNE. In general, three heuristic approaches are commonly used to solve the VNE problem: backtracking [17], simulated annealing [18] and approximation algorithms [19]. However, these approaches do not consider the migration cost and function module sharing (VNs are isolated from other VNs); thus, they are not applicable for our problem.

3. SYSTEM MODEL AND PROBLEM FORMULATION

In this section, we introduce our system model, network architecture, and assumptions underlying the system model. Then, we formally define the design objective and the problem under investigation.

3.1 System Model

A typical personal network of wearable devices is comprised of some wearable devices, equipped with both low-power (e.g., BLE) and Wi-Fi radios, and a local-hub (smartphone). These wearable devices are connected with the local-hub when the hub is within the devices' communication range. When the local-hub is not nearby, the wearable devices will try to connect to the Wi-Fi networks providing virtual local-hub (VLH) service, labeled as *VLH networks*.

As shown in Fig. 2, a VLH network, deployed by the operators with the technology of virtualization and fog computing, is with a hierarchical network architecture of three layers: access, distribution, and core layer. The access layer is formed by a group of powerful Wi-Fi APs, which are capable of executing applications migrated from the local-hub (i.e., smartphone). The distribution layer consists of switches, and the core layer is the gateway to the Internet or core network.

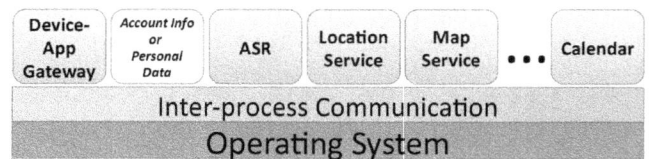

Figure 3: Modular architecture of a mobile system

The modern mobile platform provides a modular programming environment where developers can include existing function modules to build the applications for wearable devices. As shown in Fig. 3, the system fulfills a service request from a user for a specific application by calling a series of function modules. We treat a service request as a call graph [20], which is a directed graph that represents calling relationships between function modules in a service request. The same type of service requests from different users will have the same call graph, and different type of service requests may share some function modules. Without loss of generality, we assume that operators pre-install all function modules in some APs; thus, migrations from the cloud or from the local-hub to the VLH network are not considered.

3.2 Problem Formulation

The function module sharing results in additional bandwidth consumption to the VLH network due to inter-function module communication; thus, for the function module allocation, we are interested in minimizing the total bandwidth consumption with respect to the sufficient quantity of function module instances. The problem under consideration can be formulated as follows.

The VLH network. We denote the VLH network by a directed graph $\mathbb{G}^v = (\mathbb{N}^v, \mathbb{L}^v, \mathbb{A}_\mathbb{N}{}^v, \mathbb{A}_\mathbb{L}{}^v)$, where $\mathbb{N}^v$ and $\mathbb{L}^v$ is the set of nodes, including Wi-Fi APs and switches, and links on the VLH network, respectively. Those nodes and links are associated with their attributes, denoted by $\mathbb{A}_\mathbb{N}{}^v$ and $\mathbb{A}_\mathbb{L}{}^v$, respectively. In this paper, we consider computing capacity and the list of function module instances already running on the node for node attributes and bandwidth capacity for link attribute.

Function modules. We denote $\mathbb{F}$ as the set of function modules. Each function module has three properties, including package size, computing requirement and sharing limitation, denoted by $\mathbb{P}^s$, $\mathbb{P}^c$ and $\mathbb{P}^l$ respectively. The maximum quantity of service requests that a instance of a function module can serve is restricted by the sharing limitation. Given this limitation, an instance requires fixed computing resource on a node regardless of the number of serving requests. Once the number of service requests requiring the same function module is lager than the module's sharing limitation, the system has to allocate a new instance for the module on the VLH network. Moreover, we consider a migration time limitation z. If the system tries to initiate a new instance for a specific function module on a node without its package, the system has to migrate the package of the function module within the time limit z.

Call graphs and service requests. We model each call graph type as a directed graph $\mathbb{G}^c = (\mathbb{N}^c, \mathbb{L}^c, \mathbb{A}_\mathbb{N}{}^c, \mathbb{A}_\mathbb{L}{}^c)$. Every graph has a special node called traffic aggregation point (TGP), a special function module that needs to be allocated on the Wi-Fi AP that the user connect with. Every node has an attribute, denoted by $\mathbb{A}_\mathbb{N}{}^c$, indicating that the node is representing a normal function module or a TGP. In addition, every link is with an attribute, denoted by $\mathbb{A}_\mathbb{L}{}^c$, representing the bandwidth requirement of each link. Finally, we denote $\mathbb{C}$ and $\mathbb{R}$ as the set of all call graph types and the list of total service requests, of which each is a call graph belong to a graph type, on the VLH network, respectively.

The allocation and migration decisions. The function module allocation problem is defined as two group of decisions, including which function module instances should run on which nodes (allocation decisions) and how should those modules be migrated internally (migration decisions). We denote $\mathcal{A}$ and $\mathcal{M}$ as a collection of all allocation and migration decisions, respectively. Each allocation decision $(\mathbb{R} \mapsto \mathbb{N}', \mathbb{N}' \subset \mathbb{N}^v)$ indicates mapping all call graph nodes of service requests to some nodes of the VLH network. Besides, between each call graph node of service requests, inter-function module communication exists, and we denote $C^\mathcal{A}$ as the bandwidth consumption of the communication. On the other hand, each migration decision is represented as $m_d(f_s, n_j^v, n_k^v)$ for migrating a function module $f_s \in \mathbb{F}$ from $n_j^v \in \mathbb{N}^v$ to $n_k^v \in \mathbb{N}^v$. Also, each migration decision has a bandwidth consumption, denoted by $C^\mathcal{M}$.

Constraints. The allocation and migration decisions are feasible if the following constraints are met.

(1) Sharing limitation of a function module: We denote p_s^i as the number of instances for function module $f_s \in \mathbb{F}$

Table 1: Summary of Notations

$\mathbb{G}^v$	The VLH network
$\mathbb{N}^v$	Nodes of the VLH network
$\mathbb{L}^v$	Links of the VLH network
$\mathbb{A}_\mathbb{N}{}^v$	Node attribute of the VLH network
$\mathbb{A}_\mathbb{L}{}^v$	Link attribute of the VLH network
$\mathbb{F}$	The set of function modules
$\mathbb{P}^s$	Package size of function modules
$\mathbb{P}^c$	Computing requirement of function modules
$\mathbb{P}^l$	Sharing limitation of function modules
z	Migration time limitation
$\mathbb{C}$	The set of all call graph types
$\mathbb{G}^c$	A call graph type
$\mathbb{N}^c$	Nodes of a call graph type
$\mathbb{L}^c$	Links of a call graph type
$\mathbb{A}_\mathbb{N}{}^c$	Node attribute of a call graph type
$\mathbb{A}_\mathbb{L}{}^c$	Link attribute of a call graph type
$\mathbb{R}$	The list of total service requests
$\mathcal{A}$	The set of allocation decisions
$\mathcal{M}$	The set of migration decisions
$C^\mathcal{A}$	The b.w. consum. of inter-func. module comm.
$C^\mathcal{M}$	The b.w. consum. of func. module migration
p_s^i	# of instances for func. module f_s at node n_i^v
u_s^i	# of service requests req. f_s at node n_i^v

running on the node $n_i^v \in \mathbb{N}^v$. We also denote u_s^i as the total number of service requests that require $f_s \in \mathbb{F}$ on the node $n_i^v \in \mathbb{N}^v$. The quantity of instances of each function module running on each node should be sufficient to serve all requests.

$$p_s^i \cdot \mathbb{P}_{f_s}^l \geq u_s^i, \forall f_s \in \mathbb{F} \tag{1}$$

(2) Computing capacity of a node on the VLH network: The computing requirement of all instances running on the node $n_i^v \in \mathbb{N}^v$ cannot exceed its available computing capacity.

$$\sum_s (p_s^i \cdot \mathbb{P}_{f_s}^c) \leq \mathbb{A}_{n_i^v}^v, \forall f_s \in \mathbb{F} \tag{2}$$

(3) Bandwidth capacity of a link on the VLH network: The total traffic on each link $(n_i^v, n_j^v) \in \mathbb{L}^v$ cannot exceed its available bandwidth capacity.

$$\sum_{(n_i, n_j)} (C^\mathcal{A} + C^\mathcal{M}) \leq \mathbb{A}_{(n_i, n_j)}^v, \forall (n_i, n_j) \in \mathbb{L} \tag{3}$$

Minimum Network Bandwidth Function Module Allocation Problem

Input: The VLH network $\mathbb{G}$, a set of function modules $\mathbb{F}$, a set of call graph types $\mathbb{C}$, the list of total service requests on VLH network $\mathbb{R}$.

Output: $\mathcal{A}$ and $\mathcal{M}$ (collections of all allocation and migration decisions respectively).

Objective: Minimize the total network bandwidth consumption. The objective function is expressed as follows.

$$\text{Min} \quad \sum_\mathcal{A} C^\mathcal{A} + \sum_\mathcal{M} C^\mathcal{M}$$

subject to constraints (1)-(3).

Table 1 summarizes the notations used in the problem formulation.

4. FUNCTION MODULE ALLOCATION ALGORITHM

In this section, we propose an efficient heuristic algorithm for allocating instances of required function modules. First we depict the design rationale of the proposed algorithm; then we show and explain the pseudo-code of the proposed algorithm.

4.1 Algorithm Design

The concept of our algorithm fellows a greedy approach. First, to allocate an instance of a function module, we estimate the total bandwidth consumption of the instance for each candidate node (Wi-Fi AP) of the network. Then, we allocate the instance on the node with the lowest bandwidth consumption subject to the constraints of available computing and bandwidth resources. The bandwidth consumption of a function module instance is consisted of the in/output data traffic (inter-function module communication) and the migration cost of the module. With the objective of minimizing "total" bandwidth consumption, the proposed algorithm considers these two factors jointly when deciding a function module instance should be migrated to a network node with service requests that need the module (no inter-function module communication but with migration cost), or just let those service requests access the module remotely (with inter-function module communication but no migration cost).

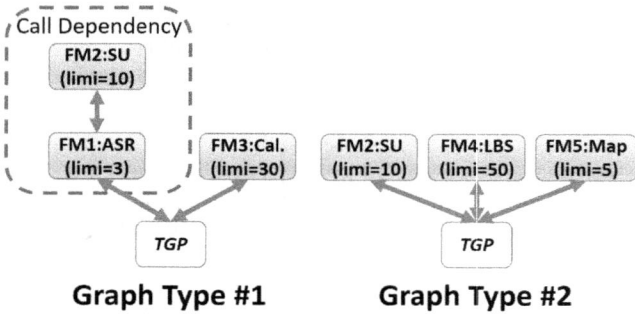

Figure 4: Call graph types with or without call dependency

Then, some service requests may need a series of function modules (i.e., *call dependency*). For example, as shown in Fig. 4, FM1 is an automatic speech recognition (ASR) function module with sharing limitation 3 for transferring voice data to text string, and FM2 is a semantic understanding (SU) function module with sharing limitation 10 for transferring text string to meaningful command. Graph type #1 and #2 represent call graphs of retrieving calendar by speech and getting local map by text respectively, and both graphs require FM2. As a result, the bandwidth consumption of the FM2 will depend on not only where the TGPs are but also the locations of the FM1. The proposed algorithm handles this challenge by de-constructing the call graphs with call dependency such that all modules are pretended to be directly connected with the TGP. For instance, the proposed algorithm considers FM2 in graph type #1 to be connected with the TGP instead of FM1.

Finally, the proposed algorithm's allocation procedure, which decides the location and nearest serving requests of a function module instance one after another, works properly

only if the capacities of the VLH network can fulfill all requirements of allocated function modules. Otherwise, some service requests will be rejected due to insufficient function modules (i.e., these requests get only partial function modules they need.). Therefore, we design a capacity testing subroutine to ensure the input service requests can all be fulfilled in the allocation procedure of our main algorithm given the capacities of the VLH network.

4.2 Algorithm Description

Algorithm 1

Input: $\mathbb{G}^v$, $\mathbb{F}$, z, $\mathbb{C}$, and $\mathbb{R}$
Output: $\mathcal{A}$ and $\mathcal{M}$

1: $\bar{\mathbb{R}} = \mathbb{R}$
2: De-construct $\mathbb{C}$ to $\mathbb{C}'$.
3: **while** Available computing capacity of $\mathbb{G}^v \geq 0$ and Available bandwidth capacity of $\mathbb{G}^v \geq 0$ and $\bar{\mathbb{R}} \neq \emptyset$ **do**
4:     Get subset $\bar{\mathbb{R}}'$ from $\bar{\mathbb{R}}$ based on Algorithm 2
5:     Calculate the quantity Q as the number of function modules that need to be allocated for $\bar{\mathbb{R}}'$, and store these function modules as a set $\mathbb{FM\_INS}$.
6:     Sort set $\mathbb{FM\_INS}$ by round-robin for allocation order.
7:     **for** $i = 1$ to Q **do**
8:         Take fm_ins_i from $\mathbb{FM\_INS}$.
9:         **for all** $n_j^v \in \mathbb{N}^v$ **do**
10:           Find the nearest node n_k^v with fm_ins_i and make migration decision $m_j(fm\_ins_i, n_k^v, n_j^v)$
11:           $k \leftarrow \mathbb{P}_{fm\_ins_i}^l$
12:           $\mathbb{SRV\_REQS}_j \leftarrow$ NEAREST-NODES(fm_ins_i, k)
13:           Calculate $C_{n_j^v}^{\mathcal{A}} \leftarrow \mathbb{SRV\_REQS}_j$
14:           $Cost_j \leftarrow (C_{m_j}^{\mathcal{M}} + C_{n_j^v}^{\mathcal{A}})$
15:         Sort $n_j^v \in \mathbb{N}^v$ by increasing priority with lower $Cost_j$
16:         **for all** $n_j^v \in \mathbb{N}^v$ by lower $Cost_j$ first order **do**
17:           **if** $(\mathbb{A}_{n_j^v}^v -= \mathbb{P}_{fm\_ins_i}^c) < 0$ **then**
18:               continue
19:           **for all** $TGP_t \in \mathbb{SRV\_REQS}_j$ **do**
20:              **if** $(\mathbb{A}_{path(n_j^v, TGP_t)}^v -= C_{n_j^v}^{\mathcal{A}}) < 0$ **then**
21:                continue
22:            Add m_j to $\mathcal{M}$
23:            Add $\mathbb{SRV\_REQS}_j$ and n_j^v to $\mathcal{A}$
24:            break
25:     $\bar{\mathbb{R}} = \bar{\mathbb{R}} - \bar{\mathbb{R}}'$
26: Calculate the total bandwidth consumption by $\mathbb{C}$, $\mathcal{M}$, and $\mathcal{A}$.
27: **return** $\mathcal{A}$ and $\mathcal{M}$

In this section, we present the pseudo-codes of the main proposed algorithm (Algorithm 1) and the capacity testing subroutine (Algorithm 2).

In Algorithm 1, we first store all service request to the set $\bar{\mathbb{R}}$ as the unserved service request set. Since we assume that the best location of function module should be as near to the location of service request as possible, we transform the call graph set $\mathbb{C}$ to $\mathbb{C}'$ for de-constructing the call dependency between function modules in line 2. Our proposed algorithm allocates all function modules for the subset of service requests that pass the capacity testing subroutine from line 3 to line 25 repeatedly, unless we use out of capacities, or no more unserved service requests left. In the allocation procedure, first we get a subset of service requests

Algorithm 2

Input: $\mathbb{G}^v$, $\mathbb{F}$, z, $\mathbb{C}'$, $\bar{\mathbb{R}}$, $\check{p}$ and $\check{m}$

Output: $\bar{\mathbb{R}}'$

1: $\mathbb{U}_{comp}$ = (Available computing capacity of $\mathbb{G}^v$) $\times \check{p}$
2: $\mathbb{U}_{band}$ = (Available bandwidth capacity of $\mathbb{G}^v$)
3: **for all** $\bar{r}_i \in \bar{\mathbb{R}}$ **do**
4:    Store all function modules that $\bar{r}_i$ needs as a set $\mathbb{K}$
5:    **for all** $k_j \in \mathbb{K}$ **do**
6:       $\mathbb{U}_{comp}\;{-}{=}\;\mathbb{P}_{k_j}^c \div \mathbb{P}_{k_j}^l$
7:       $\mathbb{U}_{band}\;{-}{=}\;((\mathbb{P}_{k_j}^s \div z) \times \check{m}) \div \mathbb{P}_{k_j}^l + C_{path(k_j,TGP_i)}^{\mathcal{A}}$
8:    **if** $\mathbb{U}_{comp} \geq 0$ and $\mathbb{U}_{band} \geq 0$ **then**
9:       Add $\bar{r}_j$ to $\bar{\mathbb{R}}'$
10: **return** $\bar{\mathbb{R}}'$

Table 2: Simulation Parameter Setting

Parameter	Value
Number of Wi-Fi APs	100
Available bandwidth capacity	1 Gbps
Available computing capacity	1000
Number of function module (f.m.) types	20
Bandwidth requirement of f.m. types	1-150 Kbps
Computing requirement of f.m. types	5-100
Package size of f.m. types	1-15 MB
Number of call graph types	20
Number of service requests	500

from the capacity testing subroutine (Algorithm 2) . After that, we calculate the number of function module instances needed to serve all service requests according to the sharing limitation of each module, and then store these function module instances to the allocation list $\mathbb{FM\_INS}$. We define a procedure NEAREST-NODES(f_s, k) to find the k-nearest nodes with remaining service requests that need $f_s \in \mathbb{F}$ and return these service requests. $\mathbb{SRV\_REQS}$ is the best serving list that f_s can serve on this node. In $\mathbb{C}'$, inbound and outbound links of a function module are connected to the TGP, so the procedure NEAREST-NODES will find nodes where TGPs of service requests belong to. We sort the allocation list $\mathbb{FM\_INS}$ such that the instances of each function module follows the round-robin ordering. In line 7 to line 24, we allocate each function module instance fm_ins_i one by one as every node is the candidate node. For each function module instance, we estimate the corresponding migration cost and find the serving list by the procedure NEAREST-NODES and its communication cost on each node. In particular, the communication cost is calculated by $\mathbb{C}'$. Note that it is the expedient cost for heuristic strategy, not the real cost, which will be calculated in line 26 based on the real call graph $\mathbb{C}$ and final decisions. After we get the decision and cost for each node, we re-arrange the order of each node by its cost and choose the node with the lowest cost as the final decision of this instance if the constraints of computing and bandwidth capacities are met. Finally, after we allocate all function module instances, we return the migration decision $\mathbb{M}$ and the allocation decision $\mathbb{A}$.

For Algorithm 2, it filters out service requests that capacities of VLH network can handle from the unserved service request set $\bar{\mathbb{R}}$ and then return a subset of service requests $\bar{\mathbb{R}}'$. $\check{p}$ adjusts the upper bound of computing resource usage, and $\check{m}$ estimates the migration cost. The values of $\check{p}$ and $\check{m}$ depend on the characteristics of the VLH network

(In our experiments, we set $\check{p}$ as 0.97 and $\check{m}$ as 0.1.). First, we calculate the upper bounds of computing and bandwidth resources. Then we test each unserved request from line 3 to line 9, and add unserved request to $\bar{\mathbb{R}}'$ if it passed the computing capacity test and bandwidth capacity test. For the computing capacity test, we split computing usage of a function module to service requests based on its computing requirement and sharing limitation; for the bandwidth capacity test, we assume that all service requests connect to the needed function modules remotely and share the migration cost based on $\check{m}$.

5. PERFORMANCE EVALUATION

In this section, we report the results of extensive experiments conducted to validate the performance of the proposed scheme and suggest some useful insights for practice.

5.1 Simulation Setups

For the simulation environment, we consider the VLH network of 100 Wi-Fi APs and five switches, and with the hierarchical topology, each switch has 20 APs [21]. The capacity of each network link is 1Gbps. Based on previous researches [22, 23], we can estimate the relative gap between the computing capacity of low-end Intel Atom processor and the computing requirement of applications for wearable devices; thus, the computing capacity of each AP is set as 1000, as well as the computing requirements and package sizes of different function module types range from 5 to 100 and from 1M to 15MB respectively. The bandwidth requirements of inter-function module communication for different function module types range from 1Kbps to 150Kbps based on the real measurements by [3, 4, 24, 25]. Finally, the default number of service requests is 500. The simulation parameters are listed in Table 2.

To validate our advocating on the remote sharing of function modules, we compared the proposed algorithm *Nearest Serving Nodes (NSN)* to other approaches of mobile computation off-loading without or with limited function module sharing. The performance metric used for the sharing strategies comparison is the rejection rate, which is the percentage of un-satisfied service requests in the VLH network due to the capability limits of the network. Then, to study the efficacy of the proposed algorithm, we compared *NSN* with two algorithms of different allocation strategies under the situation of zero rejection rate. Here we adopt the total bandwidth consumption, i.e., the objective of the studied problem, as the metric for the comparison. More detailed settings will be specified in the following subsections. The derived simulation result is the average of the output values of 100 independent runs.

5.2 Comparison of Different Sharing Strategies

To assess the impact of different function module sharing strategies on the rejection rate, we compared our approach *NSN* with *Non-shareable* (all function modules are packed into a VM for single user and are not shareable among different users), *Local-shareable* (service requests in the same Wi-Fi AP can share function module instances on that AP), and *Remote-shareable* (service requests can share function module instances on remote Wi-Fi APs only when the local Wi-Fi AP does not have enough capacity to host the needed function module instances).

Figure 5 shows the impacts of different function mod-

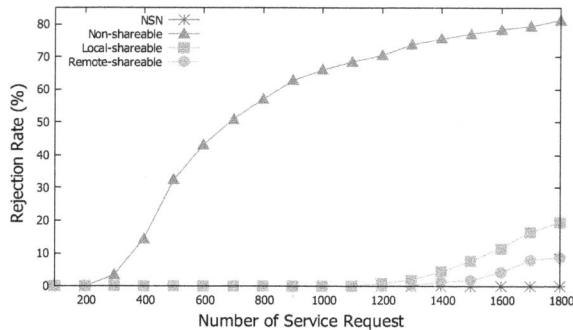

Figure 5: Rejection rate of different function module sharing strategies

ule sharing strategies on the rejection rate against different numbers of service requests. *Non-shareable* suffers from high rejection rate, up to 80% service requests cannot be accommodated in the VLH network. This is because without any form of function module sharing, the system cannot fulfill a service request when the local AP (i.e., the AP the user of the service request connects to) does not have enough resource even if other APs have plenty of resources. *Local-shareable* performs better than *Non-shareable*. The reason is that *Local-shareable* allows service requests on the same AP to share function module instances on the local AP; thus, an AP can serve more service requests. Moreover, *Remote-shareable* has lower rejection rate than *Local-shareable* since *Remote-shareable* enables service requests to use function module instances on remote Wi-Fi APs. Note that *NSN* achieves zero rejection rate regardless the number of service requests since, unlike the *Remote-shareable*, *NSN* allows remote function module sharing even if local Wi-Fi AP does have enough resource to host the needed function module instance. The result verifies that remote function module sharing can reduce rejection rate significantly.

5.3 Comparison of Different Allocation Strategies

To investigate the performance of the proposed algorithm, we compared the proposed approach *NSN* with two algorithms of different allocation strategies under the situation of zero rejection rate. The first algorithm, denoted as *First In First Out (FIFO)*, is designed to allocate resources for each service request one by one in a "first come, first serve" manner. The algorithm will not allocate a new function module instance for a new-coming service request unless the serving number of the existing function module instance reaches its sharing limitation. Once the algorithm decides to allocate a function module instance, it will take migration cost and inter-function module communication into consideration and find the best location in the VLH network for the instance. The second algorithm, denoted as *Random*, is designed as an intuitive baseline. The algorithm randomly chooses an AP in the VLH network to allocate the function module instance. When allocating a function module instance, the algorithm will assign the nearest service requests to it. We investigate the impacts of the loading (indicated by the number of service requests) and the percentage of hotspots with unbalanced loads on the network bandwidth consumption. Specifically, we considered two different cases of scenarios: In Case I, we assume that the storage size of Wi-Fi

APs is restricted, so Wi-Fi APs will remove function module packages once their service duty is completed. Note that, under this assumption, the migration cost is very high and dominates the bandwidth consumption. For Case II, we consider a situation that every Wi-Fi AP in the VLH network has sufficient storage space to keep all the packages of different kinds of function modules. There is no need to migrate packages of function module from remote nodes; thus, there is no migration cost in this case.

5.3.1 Impact of the number of service requests

Figure 6(a) shows the impacts of number of service requests on the total bandwidth consumption under Case I. In this figure, *Random* has much more bandwidth consumption than *NSN* and *FIFO*. This is because *Random* randomly selects the location of each function module instance without considering the migration cost. Besides, both *NSN* and *FIFO* have low bandwidth consumption since they will allocate function module instances on the same Wi-Fi AP as many as possible due to the high migration cost. Moreover, *NSN* delivers lower total bandwidth consumption compared to *FIFO* since *FIFO* forces the late-coming service requests to use previous-allocated function module instances without considering the bandwidth consumption of the inter-function module communication. The results show that the proposed algorithm is effective under the case of migration cost.

Figure 6(b) shows the bandwidth consumption of inter-function module communication under Case I. *Random* has lower bandwidth consumption of inter-function module communication than *NSN* and *FIFO*. This is because *Random* selects the locations of the function module instances randomly while both *NSN* and *FIFO* consider the migration cost when selecting the locations. Moreover, *NSN* introduces lower bandwidth consumption than *FIFO*. The reason is similar to that for the total bandwidth consumption (shown in Fig. 6(a)). Although *Random* has lower bandwidth consumption of inter-function module communication than *NSN*; however, as shown in Fig 6(a), *NSN* has the lowest total bandwidth consumption. This is because a trade-off exists between migration cost and inter-function module communication, and *NSN* considers both the migration cost and inter-function module communication when deciding the locations of function module instances and assigning service requests to those instances.

Figure 6(c) shows the impacts of different numbers of service requests on total bandwidth consumption under the assumption of Case II. Compared with Case I (Fig. 6(a)), *Random* performs better than *FIFO*. This is because although *Random* decides the locations of the function modules randomly, it will assign the nearest service requests to each instance of function modules while *FIFO* forces the late-coming service requests to use previous-allocated function module instances without considering the bandwidth consumption of the inter-function module communication. Nevertheless, the performance of the proposed algorithm, compared with *FIFO* and *Random*, is more efficient in reducing total bandwidth consumption regardless the numbers of service requests. This is because *NSN* tries to optimize both the locations of the function modules and which requests they serve.

5.3.2 Impact of unbalanced loads

The Wi-Fi AP is considered as a hotspot if it has a higher quantity of service requests. To simulate hotspots, here we

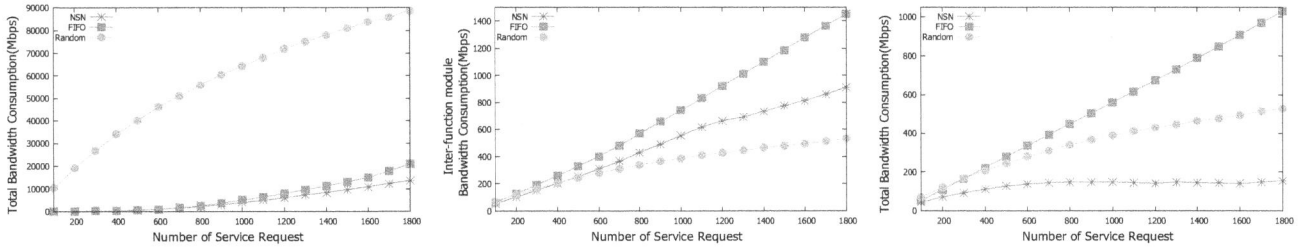

(a) Total bandwidth consumption (with migration cost)

(b) The bandwidth consumption of inter-function module communication (with migration cost)

(c) Total bandwidth consumption (no migration cost)

Figure 6: The impact of the number of service requests

assign one service request to each non-hotsopt APs, and the hotspot APs share the remaining requests. We define the percentage of hotspot as the ratio of the number of hotspot APs to the number of all APs. Higher the percentage of hotspot, more balanced the service requests across the network. For example, 10% for the percentage of hotspot means 10% of APs are the hotspots while the remaining 90% APs are not the hotspots.

Figure 7(a) and 7(b) shows the results of the impact of unbalanced loads on the bandwidth consumption under the assumption of Case I. Without considering the migration cost, as shown in fig 7(a), the total bandwidth consumption of *Random* is extremely high. Figure 7(b) further shows the impact of unbalanced loads for *NSN* and *FIFO*. When loads are concentrated on fewer hotspot APs, total bandwidth consumption of *FIFO* is relatively high. This is because early-coming service requests use all the resources on the hotspots and late-coming service requests are forced to allocate new function module instances, which come with a price of migration cost. In addition, total bandwidth consumption of *NSN* is relatively stable even under extremely load unbalancing situations since *NSN* decides the allocation of function module instances with both the considerations of migration cost and the locations of serving requests.

Figure 7(c) shows the result of the impact of unbalancing load on the bandwidth consumption for Case II. The performance of *Random* is getting better as the percentage of hotspot increases and even surpasses *FIFO* when the percentage of hotspot is higher than 70%. This is because as *Random* selects the locations of function modules randomly, more evenly the service requests distribute, better *Random* performs when there is no migration cost. In addition, the performance of *FIFO* is slightly better when percentage of hotspot is less than 20%. This is because all service requests are concentrated on few hopspot APs such that there are few inter-function module communications. The proposed algorithm achieves a notable bandwidth saving (about 40%) compared with two other algorithms, and the lowest bandwidth consumption of *NSN* happens when the percentage of hotspot is 30%. The reason is that when service requests are concentrated on few hotspot APs, those hotspot APs may not have enough resource to host all needed function module instances, and thus, some instances need to be hosted in remote APs, resulting in higher bandwidth consumption due to more inter-function module communication. On the other hand, when the service requests are scattered on the whole network, it also incurs more inter-function module communication. In conclusion, the distribution of the service requests can have a positive or negative impact on the

performance of our scheme in the case of no migration cost. Nevertheless, *NSN* incurs the lowest bandwidth consumption regardless of the percentage of hotspot. The results of Fig. 7 show that the proposed algorithm is still effective even when the loads are unbalanced.

6. CONCLUSION

We propose a virtual local-hub solution to overcome the usage limits of the local-hub for wearable devices. The solution adopts the idea of fog computing, migrating the applications serving wearable devices on the local-hub to the edge of the network. As many applications for wearable devices share the same function modules, we advocate to enable remote function module sharing for increasing the serving capacity of the network. We design heuristic algorithms to reduce the additional network bandwidth consumption due to the remote function module sharing. We conduct extensive simulations based on practical parameter settings to evaluate the efficacy of the proposed approach. The simulation results indicate that when over 80% of the requests cannot be fulfilled without remote function module sharing, the proposed algorithm can still serve all the requests. Also, the proposed algorithms can reduce the bandwidth consumption by up to 40%. Future research will extend to consider the data cache and storage capacity of the network nodes. Also, we plan to develop a testbed for more realistic performance evaluation under real-world scenarios.

7. ACKNOWLEDGMENTS

This work was supported in part by Excellent Research Projects of National Taiwan University under Grant 105R89-082B, by Ministry of Science and Technology under Grant 105-2221-E-002-144-MY3, Information and Communications Research Laboratories of the Industrial Technology Research Institute (ICL/ITRI) and Institute for Information Industry (III).

8. REFERENCES

[1] IDC. Idc forecasts worldwide shipments of wearables to surpass 200 million in 2019, driven by strong smartwatch growth and the emergence of smarter watches. https://www.idc.com/getdoc.jsp? containerId=prUS41100116, 2016. [Online; accessed 20-April-2016].

[2] Research and Markets. Wearable device market forecasts - 2016 edition. http://www.researchandmarkets.com/research/

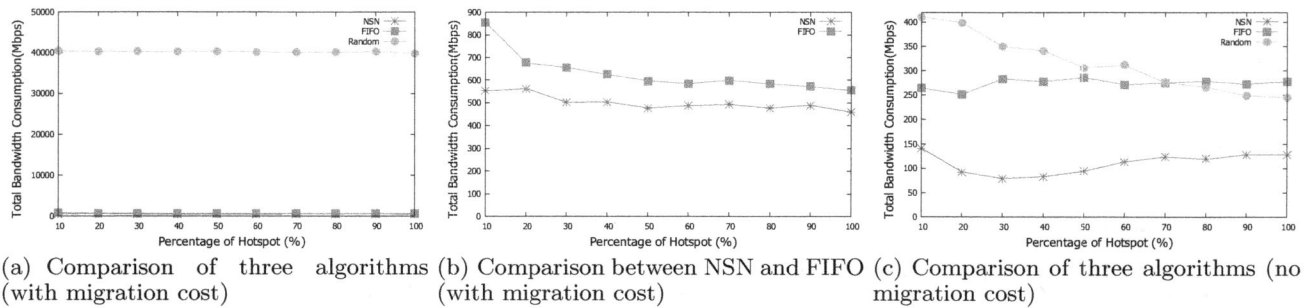

(a) Comparison of three algorithms (with migration cost)   (b) Comparison between NSN and FIFO (with migration cost)   (c) Comparison of three algorithms (no migration cost)

Figure 7: The impact of unbalanced loads on the total bandwidth consumption

lwpd7k/_wearable_device, 2016. [Online; accessed 20-April-2016].

[3] S. Movassaghi, M. Abolhasan, J. Lipman, D. Smith, and A. Jamalipour. Wireless Body Area Networks: A Survey. *IEEE Communications Surveys & Tutorials*, 16(3):1658–1686, 2014.

[4] A. M. Nia, M. Mozaffari-Kermani, S. Sur-Kolay, A. Raghunathan, and N. K. Jha. Energy-Efficient Long-term Continuous Personal Health Monitoring. *IEEE Transactions on Multi-Scale Computing Systems*, 1(2):85–98, 2015.

[5] Apple. Use apple watch without its paired iphone. https://support.apple.com/en-us/HT205547, 2016. [Online; accessed 20-April-2016].

[6] Google. Android wear help: Connect your watch to wi-fi. https://support.google.com/androidwear/answer/6207505?hl=en$\&$ref_topic=6056389, 2016. [Online; accessed 20-April-2016].

[7] CISCO. White paper: Fog computing and the internet of things: Extend the cloud to where the things are. http://www.cisco.com/c/dam/en_us/solutions/trends/iot/docs/computing-overview.pdf, 2015. [Online; accessed 20-April-2016].

[8] M. Zhanikeev. A Cloud Visitation Platform to Facilitate Cloud Federation and Fog Computing. *Computer*, 48(5):80–83, 2015.

[9] A. Al-Fuqaha, M. Guizani, M. Mohammadi, M. Aledhari, and M. Ayyash. Internet of Things: A Survey on Enabling Technologies, Protocols, and Applications. *IEEE Communications Surveys & Tutorials*, 17(4):2347–2376, 2015.

[10] Z. Sanaei, S. Abolfazli, A. Gani, and R. Buyya. Heterogeneity in Mobile Cloud Computing: Taxonomy and Open Challenges. *IEEE Communications Surveys & Tutorials*, 16(1):369–392, 2014.

[11] A. u. R. Khan, M. Othman, S. A. Madani, and S. U. Khan. Survey of Mobile Cloud Computing Application Models. *IEEE Communications Surveys & Tutorials*, 16(1):393–413, 2014.

[12] B. Chun , S. Ihm, P. Maniatis, M. Naik, and A. Patti. CloneCloud: elastic execution between mobile device and cloud. In *Proc. of EuroSys*, pages 301–314, 2011.

[13] E. Cuervo, D. Cho, A. Wolman, S. Saroiu, R. Chandra, and P. Bahl. MAUI: Making Smartphones Last Longer with Code Offload. In *Proc. of ACM MobiSys*, pages 49–62, 2010.

[14] S. Ghorpade, N. Chavan, A. Gokhale, and D. Sapkal. A Framework For Executing Android Applications On

The Cloud. In *Proc. of IEEE ICACCI*, pages 230–235, 2013.

[15] A. Fischer, J. F. Botero, M. T. Beck, H. de Meer, and X. Hesselbach. Virtual Network Embedding: A Survey. *IEEE Communications Surveys & Tutorials*, 15(4):1888–1906, 2013.

[16] M. Yu, Y. Yi, J. Rexford, and M. Chiang. Rethinking Virtual Network Embedding: Substrate Support for Path Splitting and Migration. *ACM SIGCOMM Computer Communication Review*, 38(2):17–29, 2008.

[17] J. Lischka, and H. Karl. A virtual network mapping algorithm based on subgraph isomorphism detection. In *Proc. of ACM VISA*, pages 81–88, 2009.

[18] R. Ricci, C. Alfeld, and J. Lepreau. A solver for the network testbed mapping problem. *ACM SIGCOMM Computer Communications Review*, 33(2):65–81, 2003.

[19] N. Chowdhury, M. Rahman, and R. Boutaba. Virtual network embedding with coordinated node and link mapping. In *Proc. of IEEE INFOCOM*, pages 81–88, 2009.

[20] B. G. Ryder. Constructing the Call Graph of a Program. *IEEE Transactions on Software Engineering*, SE-5(3):216–226, 1979.

[21] CISCO. Ap group. http://www.cisco.com/c/en/us/support/docs/wireless-mobility/wireless-vlan/71477-ap-group-vlans-wlc.html, 2016. [Online; accessed 20-April-2016].

[22] C. Seeger, K. Van Laerhoven, and A. Buchmann. MyHealthAssistant: An Event-driven Middleware for Multiple Medical Applications on a Smartphone-Mediated Body Sensor Network. *IEEE Journal of Biomedical and Health Informatics*, 64(10):752–760, 2015.

[23] S. H. Hung, C. S. Shih, J. P. Shieh, C. P. Lee, and Y. H. Huang. An Online Migration Environment for Executing Mobile Applications on the Cloud. In *Proc. of IMIS*, pages 20–27, 2011.

[24] R. Cavallari, F. Martelli, R. Rosini, C. Buratti, and R. Verdone. A Survey on Wireless Body Area Networks: Technologies and Design Challenges. *IEEE Communications Surveys & Tutorials*, 16(3):1635–1657, 2014.

[25] E. Rebeiz, G. Caire, and A. F. Molisch. Energy-Delay Tradeoff and Dynamic Sleep Switching for Bluetooth-Like Body-Area Sensor Networks. *IEEE Transactions on Communications*, 60(9):2733–2746, 2012.

Dynamic Adaptive Access Barring Scheme For HeavilyCongested M2M Networks

Meriam Bouzouita
University of Rennes 1, France
Mediatron, SUP'COM, Tunisia
mariem.bouzouita@supcom.tn

Yassine Hadjadj-Aoul
University of Rennes 1, France
yhadjadj@irisa.fr

Nawel Zangar
Mediatron, SUP'COM, Tunisia
nawel.zangar@insat.rnu.tn

Gerardo Rubino
INRIA Rennes, France
Gerardo.Rubino@inria.fr

Sami Tabbane
Mediatron, SUP'COM, Tunisia
Sami.Tabbane@insat.rnu.tn

ABSTRACT

The massive deployment of Machine-to-machine (M2M) communications may overwhelm the cellular network by imposing strong constraints on the Radio Access Network (RAN). As the base station cannot accurately get the exact number of M2M arrivals, it cannot really predict the overload status. Consequently, a better estimation of this number would efficiently help to overcome the risk of congestion. In this paper, we proposed a novel fluid model for M2M communications, which allows gaining an enhanced understanding of the dynamics of such systems. The provided analysis of the model was used to devise a new method to estimate accurately the number of M2M devices. We proposed, then, a novel implementation of the ACB process, which dynamically computes the ACB factor according to the network's overload conditions while includes a corrective action adapting the controller action based on the mismatch existing between the computed and the targeted mean load. The simulation results show that the proposed algorithms allow improving considerably the estimation of the number of M2M devices' arrivals, while outperforming existing techniques.

Keywords: M2M, Random access, fluid model, Congestion avoidance.

1. INTRODUCTION

The next mobile generation, is planned to create a networked and smart society in which the Internet of Things (IoT) will certainly play an important role [1]. Furthermore, the success of the forthcoming 5G standard is closely related to the efficient support of such devices, and particularly machine-to-machine (M2M) communications, which represent a key component of the IoT paradigm[2][3].

Owing to the massive deployment of M2M communications, in the near future, M2M devices may overwhelm the cellular network by causing congestion at both the Radio Access Network (RAN) and the Core Network (CN). Nonetheless, the RAN constitutes the most claiming part because of the radio resources' scarcity. In this way, new network access approaches are required to anticipate the congestion and the system overload by managing more efficiently the simultaneous Random Access (RA) of M2M devices, and hence tackling their explosive growth. This constitutes our main focus in this paper.

The congestion control problem due to competing M2M devices was considered very early as one of the priorities of the 3GPP. Indeed, the 3GPP standardizing body proposed many solutions to tackle such problem, including the Access Class Barring (ACB) concept [4], which is considered as one of the most efficient ways to tackle these types of congestion [5]. These works have been precursors of many other highly effective solutions, which succeeded in avoiding the congestion of the access network [6], [7]. However, these proposals present many limits when dealing with baseline congestion. Indeed, in such a condition, these techniques fail to avoid a synchronized access of M2M devices, which may results in some cases to a congestion collapse. Substantively, the base station cannot accurately estimate the number of M2M devices willing to connect and, hence, cannot predict the overload status. Consequently, a better estimation of this number would efficiently help to treat the congestion trouble.

The main issue addressed in this article is related to improving channel access for M2M communications in LTE-A networks and beyond. To face the identified challenges, we proposed a mechanism to better exploit channel utilization, a novel access protocol that adapts dynamically the access attempts of M2M devices according to the network congestion's level. Hence, we propose a new approach to estimate the RA attempts under the developed dynamic access algorithm, based on M2M new arrivals and backlogged equipment's estimation. A corrective action to the Proportional Integral Derivative (PID)[8][9] controller was added to better mismatch the estimated and the targeted payload.

The remainder of this paper is organized as follows. Section 2 is dedicated to describe a fluid model for M2M networks and to study the steady-state performance of such dynamic system. Section 3 portrays our new adaptive access protocol in addition to the proposed estimation algorithm. Section 4 is dedicated to the simulation setup and the analysis of our proposition. Finally, conclusions are presented in Section 5 with a summary recapping the main advantages and achievements of the proposed access protocol.

MSWiM '16, November 13-17, 2016, Malta, Malta
© 2016 ACM. ISBN 978-1-4503-4502-6/16/11... $15.00
DOI: http://dx.doi.org/10.1145/2988287.2989174

2. A MODEL FOR M2M NETWORKS

2.1 A simple fluid model

Having described briefly how M2M devices access the mobile networks, we now direct our focus on representing the whole system using a simple fluid model, described below.

Note that, for the sake of simplification, the model represented in Fig. 1 does not consider the case where the M2M devices reach the maximal number of attempts. This phenomenon should be avoided in a properly dimensioned or controlled system. Indeed, an efficient controller should minimize the number of re-attempts, whatever the number of terminals, to maximize the resources utilization. In the performance evaluation section[1], it can be clearly observed that the proposed approach presents only a few abandons.

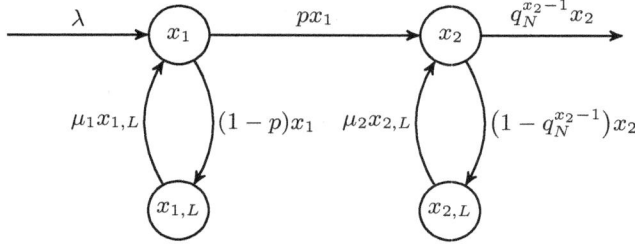

Figure 1: System model

The following quantities are used to capture the M2M devices behavior:

$x_1(t)$ number of backlogged devices at time t;

$x_{1,L}(t)$ number of blocked devices at time t, after having failed an ACB check and waiting for re-attempting;

$x_2(t)$ number of devices at time t having passed the ACB check and waiting to attempt the RA;

$x_{2,L}(t)$ the number of blocked devices at time t after a failed RA attempt and waiting to try again;

λ the arrival rate of devices;

θ the abandon rate after reaching maximum number of RA attempts.

μ_1 the rate of ACB re-attempts;

μ_2 the rate of RA re-attempts;

p the ACB factor.

When attempting the random access, the M2M devices contend for the N available preambles. In each RACH opportunity, these preambles are split into successful (i.e. chosen by only one device), collided (i.e. chosen by two or more devices) and idle (i.e. selected by none of the devices). In the following, we recall the average values of these quantities that we determined in [6]. These quantities will be used in the proposed model and algorithms.

Let's define $q_N = 1 - 1/N$. The average number of successful preambles, N_S, during the RACH opportunities is given by $N_S = q_N^{x_2-1} x_2$. The average number of idle preambles is $N_I = N q_N^{x_2}$. From these expressions, we obtain the

expected number of failed preambles N_F just by writing $N_F = N - (N_S + N_I)$.

Since the number of units considered in these systems is relatively high, we will use a fluid model (continuous state variables), that has the benefit of simplicity. In the sequel we will describe the dynamics that define the evolution of the four state variables x_1, $x_{1,L}$, x_2 and $x_{2,L}$ (all functions of time) based on the model described in Fig. 1.

The system's dynamics is described by the following system of differential equations:

$$\frac{dx_1}{dt} = \lambda - x_1 + \mu_1 x_{1,L},$$

$$\frac{dx_2}{dt} = px_1 + \mu_2 x_{2,L} - x_2,$$

$$\frac{dx_{1,L}}{dt} = (1-p)x_1 - \mu_1 x_{1,L},$$

$$\frac{dx_{2,L}}{dt} = \left(1 - q_N^{x_2-1}\right)x_2 - \mu_2 x_{2,L}.$$

The considered parameters are the following: N with $4 \leq N \leq 64$, $\lambda > 0$, p with $0 < p < 1$, $\mu_1 > 0$, $\mu_2 > 0$ along with the obvious constraint that $x_1(t)$, $x_{1,L}(t)$, $x_2(t)$ and $x_{2,L}(t)$ should be non-negative.

2.2 Steady-state performance analysis

To study the steady-state performance of our system, we replace the derivatives by 0. We obtain the equations for finding the stationary points of the dynamical system:

$$0 = \lambda - \bar{x}_1 + \mu_1 \bar{x}_{1,L}, \tag{1}$$

$$0 = p\bar{x}_1 + \mu_2 \bar{x}_{2,L} - \bar{x}_2, \tag{2}$$

$$0 = (1-p)\bar{x}_1 - \mu_1 \bar{x}_{1,L}, \tag{3}$$

$$0 = \left(1 - q_N^{\bar{x}_2-1}\right)\bar{x}_2 - \mu_2 \bar{x}_{2,L}. \tag{4}$$

From (1) and (3), we obtain

$$\bar{x}_1 = \frac{\lambda}{p}.$$

Replacing the value of $\bar{x}_1$ in (1), we have

$$\bar{x}_{1,L} = \frac{1-p}{p}\frac{\lambda}{\mu_1}.$$

From (2), $\mu_2 \bar{x}_{2,L} = \bar{x}_2 - p\bar{x}_1$, and from (4), $\mu_2 \bar{x}_{2,L} = \left(1 - q_N^{\bar{x}_2-1}\right)\bar{x}_2$. Eliminating $\mu_2 \bar{x}_{2,L}$ and using the obtained expression of $\bar{x}_1$, we have

$$\bar{x}_2 - p\frac{\lambda}{p} = \left(1 - q_N^{\bar{x}_2-1}\right)\bar{x}_2,$$

leading to the equation

$$\bar{x}_2 q_N^{\bar{x}_2-1} = \lambda. \tag{5}$$

The analysis of this nonlinear equation is a bit out of the focus of the paper, but it is straightforward. We provide a short summary here following a direct approach, avoiding the classical use of the Lambert W function defined on any complex number z by $W(z) = w \iff z = we^w$ [11].

Define the function f by means of $f(x) = xq^{x-1}$ for $x \geq 0$, where $0 < q < 1$. We have $f(0) = f(\infty) = 0$ and $f'(x) = q^{x-1}(1 + x\ln q)$, giving a maximum at $x = x^* = -1/\ln q$, whose value is $M = -1/(eq \ln q)$. This already gives us the stability condition of the "right side" of the model (the "left side", variables x_1 and $x_{1,L}$, is always stable): $\lambda \leq M$, if we use a generic q in the model, or $\lambda \leq -1/(eq_N \ln q_N)$ for our

[1]This will be a part of a future work to consider the dynamics related to M2M devices abandoning the system.t

288

specific value $q_N = 1 - 1/N$. If $\lambda < M$ then we have two solutions r_a and r_b to the equation, say $0 < r_a < x^* < r_b$, where r_a leads to stability and r_b to instability. Knowing that $0 < r_a < x^*$ allows to easily find r_a numerically, for instance using a Newton scheme.

3. DYNAMIC ACB FOR HEAVILY OVER-LOADED NETWORKS

In this section, we proposed a comprehensive solution, which consists in the two following phases. The first phase allows estimating accurately the states' space variables (i.e. x_1 and x_2) based on the mathematical model developed in the previous section. These variables are used, then, in the second phase to calculate dynamically the ACB factor using an adapted PID controller for an optimized resources management.

Algorithm 1 States' estimation

1: **global:** $\hat{x}_1, \hat{x}_2, \bar{x}_2, x_2^*, N_S, N_S^*, N_F, N_I, N_I^*, P_{\text{acb}}$
2:
3: **function** X2ESTIMATE(n)
4:     **require:** $\delta, \eta, \alpha_1 \in [0,1], \alpha_2 > 1$
5:     $x_{2,min}[n] \leftarrow N_S[n] + 2N_F[n]$
6:     **if** $N_I[n] \neq 0$ **then**
7:         $x_{2,\text{idle}}[n] \leftarrow \frac{\ln(\frac{N_I[n]}{N})}{\ln q_N}$
8:         $\tilde{x}_2[n] \leftarrow \max(x_{2,min}[n], x_{2,\text{idle}}[n])$
9:     **else**
10:         **if** $N_S[n] > 20$ **then**
11:             $N_S[n] = 19$
12:         $x_{2,\text{success}}[n] \leftarrow \frac{W(q_N \ln q_N N_S[n])}{\ln q_N}$
13:         $\tilde{x}_2[n] \leftarrow \max(x_{2,min}[n], x_{2,\text{success}}[n])$
14:     $e[n] \leftarrow e[n-1] + \delta(x_2^* - \tilde{x}_2[n])$
15:     $\bar{x}_2 \leftarrow (1-\eta)\bar{x}_2 + \eta\tilde{x}_2[n]$
16:     **if** $N_S > N_S^*$ **then**
17:         $N_S = N_S^*$
18:     $correction \leftarrow -N\frac{N_S - N_S^*}{N_S^*}$
19:     $N_{I,min} \leftarrow \alpha_1 N_I^*$
20:     $N_{I,max} \leftarrow \alpha_2 N_I^*$
21:     **if** $N_I \leq N_{I,min}$ **then**
22:         **return** $\hat{x}_2[n] \leftarrow \bar{x}_2 + e[n] + correction$
23:     **else**
24:         **if** $N_I \geq N_{I,max}$ **then**
25:             **return** $\hat{x}_2[n] \leftarrow \bar{x}_2 + e[n] - correction$
26:         **else**
27:             **return** $\hat{x}_2[n] \leftarrow \bar{x}_2 + e[n]$
28:
29: **function** X1ESTIMATE(n)
30:     **require:** $\epsilon = 10^{-6}$
31:     **if** $P_{\text{acb}[n-1]} < \epsilon$ **then**
32:         **return** $\hat{x}_1[n] = \hat{x}_1[n-1]$
33:     $\hat{x}_1[n] \leftarrow \frac{\hat{x}_2[n] - (\hat{x}_2[n-1] - N_S[n])}{P_{\text{acb}}[n-1]}$
34:     **return** $\hat{x}_1[n] > 0?\hat{x}_1[n] : \hat{x}_1[n-1]$

In contrast with existing approaches, the enhancements we suggest, in this paper, allow a more accurate estimation of the number of M2M devices attempting the random access through an iterative convergence of the estimates to the real values for an improved resources' management.

3.1 An accurate estimation of the states' space variables

In realistic use cases, the eNodeB is unaware of the devices present in the states x_1 and x_2, as no connection is established with them yet. To remedy this situation, we propose, in the following, a methodology allowing to estimate the number of devices in these two states (see Alg. 1 for more details).

For the sake of simplicity we are referring here by N_S, N_I and N_F to the average values calculated during 1 second (i.e. 100 RACH opportunities). The values N_S^*, N_I^*, and N_F^* represent the values obtained for the optimal x_2 (i.e. x_2^*).

During each RACH opportunity n, the eNodeB calculates the number of successful preambles $N_S[n]$, the idle ones $N_I[n]$ and the collided ones $N_F[n]$. Given that the number of successful preambles is also equal to the expected number of devices accomplishing the RA process, and given that a failed preamble is chosen by at least two M2M devices, one can deduce the minimal x_2 value (i.e. $x_{2,min}$), as expressed in line 5. In presence of at least one idle preamble (i.e. $N_I \neq 0$), the x_2 estimate, denoted by $x_{2,\text{idle}}$, is obtained using the solution to equation $N_I = Nq_N^{x_2}$, seen in previous subsection. Otherwise, it is estimated (i.e. $x_{2,\text{success}}$) using expression $N_S = q_N^{x_2-1}$ with the constraint that $N_S[n] <= 19$, in order to guarantee a real solution of the obtained Lambert W function [11], which is analyzed in previous Subsection 2.2. This will allow calculating the value of $\tilde{x}_2$ and its moving average $\bar{x}_2$. Therefore, the mismatch existing between $\tilde{x}_2$ and the optimal value x_2^* can be computed to correct the value of $\hat{x}_2$.

Note that a corrective action is added when the average number of idle preambles N_I during the last second is bigger or smaller than predefined threshold.

Once x_2 estimation is accomplished, the eNodeB can use $\hat{x}_2$ and N_S to estimate x_1 according to the code in line 33.

3.2 Adaptive ACB calculation

In this subsection, we will describe in details the proposed adaptive ACB algorithm, named DACB, which is performed at each RACH opportunity and illustrated in Alg. 2.

In the first phase of the DACB algorithm, the eNodeB adjusts dynamically the set point x_2^{ref} according to the overload situation. The main idea here is to compute the moving average value of the estimate $\hat{x}_2$ and to check if the value is bigger than the optimal value x_2^* (i.e. too much M2M devices in the state x_2) or smaller than it (i.e. too few M2M devices in the state x_2). To provide more stability, an action is taken only when the average is bigger or small than predefined thresholds. Thus, when the average value is considered as too big with a risk of congestion, the controller action reinforced by reducing the targeted objective x_2^{ref}, which enables blocking more devices from attempting the random access in the subsequent step. Besides, when the average value is considered as too small with a risk of resources' under-utilization, the controller action is relaxed by increasing the targeted objective, which enables accepting more devices. Note that we consider only values within the interval $[0; x_2^*]$.

Once the dynamic targeted load determined, the eNodeB executes the second phase to generate the ACB factor at step n. If the average of x_2 is less than x_2^* at step n, P_{acb} in the next step, is computed using equation in line 21, based on the estimation of $\hat{x}_1$. Otherwise, the eNodeB applies a PID controller to make the total number of M2M devices x_2, contending for RA, converges to the optimal value x_2^{ref}

Algorithm 2 Dynamic ACB calculation (DACB)

1: **global:** $\hat{x}_1, \hat{x}_2, \bar{x}_2, x_2^{\text{ref}}, x_2^*$
2:
3: **function** REFUPDATE(n)
4:     **require:** $\theta, \beta \in [0,1], \alpha > 1$
5:         $\bar{x}_2 \leftarrow (1-\theta)\bar{x}_2 + \theta\hat{x}_2[n]$
6:     **if** $\bar{x}_2 > \alpha x_2^*$ **then**
7:         $x_2^{\text{ref}}[n] \leftarrow x_2^{\text{ref}}[n-1] - 1$
8:     **else**
9:         **if** $\bar{x}_2 < \beta x_2^*$ **then**
10:             $x_2^{\text{ref}}[n] \leftarrow x_2^{\text{ref}}[n-1] + 1$
11:     $x_2^{\text{ref}}[n] \leftarrow \min\left(\max\left(x_2^{\text{ref}}[n], 0\right), x_2^*\right)$
12:
13: **procedure** DACB
14:     $n \leftarrow 1$
15:     $x_2^* \leftarrow N$
16: *loop:*
17:     $\hat{x}_2[n] \leftarrow \text{X2ESTIMATE}(n)$
18:     $\hat{x}_1[n] \leftarrow \text{X1ESTIMATE}(n)$
19:     REFUPDATE(n)
20:     **if** $(\bar{x}_2[n] \leq x_2^*)$ **and** $(\hat{x}_1[n] \neq \text{NaN})$ **then**
21:         $P_{\text{acb}}[n] \leftarrow \frac{x_2^{\text{ref}}[n]}{\hat{x}_1[n]}$
22:     **else**
23:         $e[n] \leftarrow x_2^{\text{ref}}[n] - \hat{x}_2[n]$
24:         $P_{\text{acb}}[n] \leftarrow k_{\text{p}}e[n] + k_{\text{i}} \sum_{k=0}^{n} e[k] + k_{\text{d}}(e[n] - e[n-1])$
25:     $P_{\text{acb}}[n] \leftarrow \min\left(\max\left(P_{\text{acb}}[n], 0\right), 1\right)$
26:     $n \leftarrow n + 1$
27:     **goto** *loop*

determined at step n. As P_{acb} is a probability, we apply: $\min\left(\max\left(P_{acb}, 0\right), 1\right)$ in (line 25).

Both the dynamic adjustment of the set point and the ACB factor generation are repeated in the following step (i.e. next RACH opportunity).

4. PERFORMANCE EVALUATIONS

4.1 Simulations' parameters

In this section, we evaluate the proposed solutions and highlight their technical benefits. In order to evaluate the accuracy of the estimations' and the efficiency of the dynamic ACB calculation's algorithm, we built a discrete events' simulator in C, which was validated in a previous study [6]. The developed simulator models the whole system described in section 2. Besides, we added the possibility for an M2M device to abandon the connection after reaching a maximal number of attempts $R_{max} = 10$.

We assume that there is one eNodeB and that M2M devices are activated according to a Poisson traffic model where inter-arrivals are exponentially distributed. We also adopt an RACH configuration where one RACH opportunity occurs every $10ms$ with $N = x_2^* = 54$ preambles at each opportunity. The simulation duration, the backoff parameter, the ac-BarringTime are respectively equal to 30s, 20ms and 4s [10].

4.2 Controller efficiency for various loads

To show the behaviour of our proposed DACB algorithm, we compare, in this sub-section, its performance with the PID controller for various network's loads [8]. Let's recall that the average load is represented here for a period of $10ms$. We consider the following performance's metrics: the average number of abandons, the average number of successful RA attempts and the average access delay. Here, we define the random access delay as the duration from the first RA attempt until a successful access. The obtained average values and the confidence intervals were computed for 50 experiments for each load value.

Fig. 2 depicts the average number of abandons for different network loads. In relaxed network conditions, the results obtained with the PID controller are comparable to our approach (i.e. *DACB*) and remain acceptable. Indeed, in such conditions there is no impact of the proposed adaptation mechanism, and the two approaches have the same behavior. When considering *DACB*, we note that this number remains very close to 0 even if the network's load increases, which proves the effectiveness and the stability of DACB. It can also be seen that the number of abandons increases rapidly when applying the PID controller.

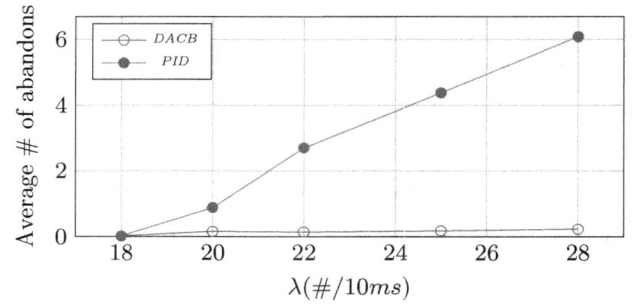

Figure 2: Evolution of the number of abandons versus λ

Another way to test the performance improvements achieved by *DACB* can be reached by comparing the numbers of successful RA attempts in function of network loads. The obtained results are depicted in Fig. 3. We first observe a very small variation, with *DACB*, of these numbers even if the number of M2M devices increases (≥ 16). Whereas, in case of the PID controller, the number of successful RA attempts decreases gradually and becomes intolerable (around 5 devices per RACH opportunity), when the network is undergoing a heavy congestion. Nevertheless, this number remains acceptable when the network is in relaxed conditions.

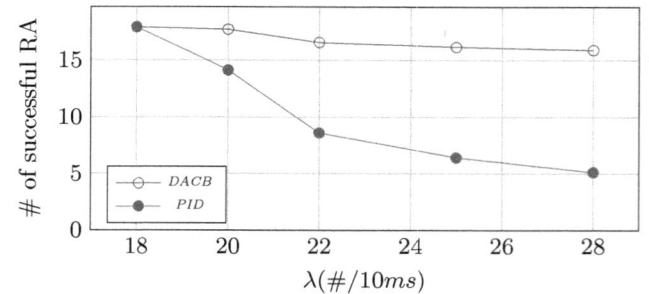

Figure 3: Evolution of the average number of successful RA attempts versus λ

Another important performance parameter is the average

random access delay illustrated in Fig. 4. If DACB method is applied, we observe that the average delays for different loads are not much different and don't exceed $45ms$. Whereas, with the PID controller, we can easily observe that the delays reach $80ms$ when the network is in heavily congested situations. This is a direct consequence of the important number of connections' reattempts, which is also reflected by the number of abandons as it can be seen in Fig. 2.

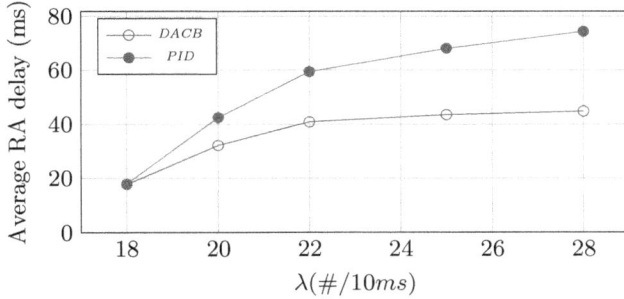

Figure 4: Evolution of RA delay versus λ

4.3 Estimation accuracy for various loads

We compare, in this sub-section, the accuracy of the proposed scheme with the *MCSA-OE* algorithm [12] for various network's loads.

Fig. 5 depicts the evolution of the estimation error for various loads. It can be clearly seen that when the network's load increases, the average estimation error decreases and then we obtain a more accurate estimation. In fact, when the network is more congested, x_2 tends to reach stable values and then the estimation's error is reduced. Nevertheless, the obtained average deviation remains very small near to 0 when a *DACB* algorithm is considered. However, this fluctuation varies between 20% and 50% in case of *MCSA-OE* scheme.

Note that the error bars are obtained for 95% confidence intervals, which show the accuracy of the obtained values.

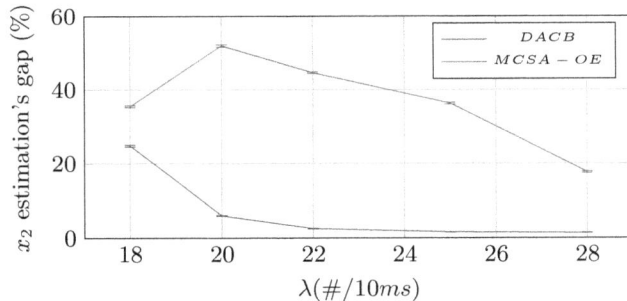

Figure 5: Evolution of the average estimation error of x_2 versus λ

5. CONCLUSIONS

In this paper, we have addressed the issue of heavily congested M2M networks, where a risk of congestion collapse appears. To treat more efficiently this trouble and improve the network's performances, we have proposed a new access control strategy for M2M random accesses.

We first presented a simple fluid model for M2M devices' accesses. Then, based on this mathematical model, we designed a novel implementation of the ACB scheme, which combines three steps performed every RA opportunity: (i) an accurate estimation of the network status, (ii) a dynamic adjustment of the model's parameters depending on the RA congestion level (e.g. the number of RA attempts that maximize the success access probability) and (iii) finally a dynamic ACB probability's calculation according to the expected network's overload situations.

The simulation results showed a reduced random access delay and also a reduced number of RA preambles' retransmissions which is one of the most important factors impacting the M2M energy consumption. Furthermore, results proved the efficiency of the proposed estimation method, as we obtained estimated values near to the actual ones.

6. REFERENCES

[1] M. R. Palattella et al., "Internet of Things in the 5G Era: Enablers, Architecture, and Business Models," in IEEE JSAC, vol. 34, no. 3, pp. 510-527, March 2016.

[2] A. Biral, M. Centenaro, A. Zanella, L. Vangelista, M. Zorzi, *The challenges of M2M massive access in wireless cellular networks*, Digital Com. and Networks, Vol. 1, Issue 1, Pages 1-19, 2015.

[3] R. Ratasuk, A. Prasad, L. Zexian, A. Ghosh, M. Uusitalo, *Recent advancements in M2M communications in 4G networks and evolution towards 5G*, ICIN 2015 , vol., no., pp.52,57, 2015.

[4] 3GPP TS 36.331 : *Evolved Universal Terrestrial Radio Access (E-UTRA); Radio Resource Control (RRC); Protocol specification* V.12.5.0 Release 10, April 2015.

[5] A. Ksentini, Y. Hadjadj-Aoul, T. Taleb, *Cellular-based machine-to-machine: overload control,*" IEEE Network, vol.26, no.6, pp.54,60, November 2012.

[6] Bouzouita M, Hadjadj-Aoul Y, Zangar N, Rubino G and Tabbane S, *Multiple Access Class Barring factors Algorithm for M2M communications in LTE-Advanced Networks*, ACM/MSWIM, 2015.

[7] Arouk O., Ksentini A. and Taleb T., *Group Paging-based Energy Saving for Massive MTC Accesses in LTE and Beyond Networks*, IEEE JSAC, 2016.

[8] Bouzouita M, Hadjadj-Aoul Y, Zangar N, Tabbane S and Viho C, *A random access model for M2M communications in LTE-advanced mobile networks*, Modeling and Simulation of Computer Networks and Systems, Elsevier, 2015.

[9] Astrom K.J., Hagglund T., *Advanced PID Control*, ISA-The Instrumentation, Systems, and Automation Society, ISBN 1556179421, 2006.

[10] 3GPP TS 36.321, *LTE; Evolved Universal Terrestrial Radio Access (E-UTRA); Medium Access Control (MAC) protocol specification*, V.11.3.0 Release 11, July 2013.

[11] Corless, R., Gonnet, G., Hare, D., Jeffrey, D. and Knuth, D., *On the Lambert W function*, Advances in Computational Mathematics (Berlin, New York: Springer-Verlag) 5: 329–359, 1996.

[12] Arouk O. and Ksentini A., *Multi-Channel Slotted Aloha Optimization for Machine-Type-Communication*, ACM/MSWiM, 2014.

A Real-time Indoor Tracking System in Smartphones

Jose Luis Carrera
University of Bern
Institute of Computer Science
carrera@inf.unibe.ch

Zan Li
University of Bern
Institute of Computer Science
li@inf.unibe.ch

Zhongliang Zhao
University of Bern
Institute of Computer Science
zhao@inf.unibe.ch

Torsten Braun
University of Bern
Institute of Computer Science
braun@inf.unibe.ch

Augusto Neto
Federal University of Rio
Grande do Norte
augusto@dimap.ufrn.br

ABSTRACT

The rapid growth area of ubiquitous applications and location-based services has made indoor localization an interesting topic for research. Some indoor localization solutions for smartphones exploit radio information and Inertial Measurement Units (IMUs), which are embedded in most of the modern smartphones. In this work, we propose to fuse WiFi Receiving Signal Strength Indicator (RSSI) readings, IMUs, and floor plan information in an enhanced particle filter to achieve high accuracy and stable performance in the tracking process. We provide an efficient double resampling method to mitigate errors caused by off-the-shelf IMUs and WiFi sensors embedded in commodity smartphones. The algorithms are designed in a terminal-based system, which consists of commercial smartphones and WiFi access points. We evaluate our system in two complex environments along moving paths. Experiment results show that our tracking method can achieve the average tracking error of 1.01 meters and 90% accuracy of 1.7 meters.

Keywords

Inertial Measurement Units (IMU); Particle Filter; WiFi; Received Signal Strength Indicator (RSSI)

1. INTRODUCTION

Nowadays, a growing number of ubiquitous mobile applications has increased the attention in indoor location-based services. In indoor environments, location-based services can be applied in many fields such as entertainment, logistic management, e-health, etc. In outdoor environments, Global Positioning System (GPS) is the most attractive and effective technology to perform object positioning. However, in indoor scenarios, the performance of GPS is degraded because of the unavailability of the GPS signals to penetrate through building materials. In contrast to GPS for outdoor

positioning, currently there is not a simple and accurate solution for indoor positioning. Therefore, indoor positioning is still considered an open challenging problem.

Radio-based positioning is one of the most widely used approaches for indoor localization. Radio-based positioning relies on the measured radio parameters, such as signal power, to estimate the absolute positions of targets. WiFi signals are often used because they are ubiquitously available indoor. RSSI is the most widely used radio parameter for indoor localization. However, RSSI is easily affected by the temporal and spatial variance due to the multipath effect [14], which is severe in indoor environments due to the presence of diverse kinds of elements and obstacles e.g., ceiling, walls, floor and furniture.

Most of the modern smartphones have various types of embedded inertial sensors, such as accelerometer, gyroscope and magnetic field sensors. These sensors can be used to estimate the relative movement of the target by detecting steps, estimating stride length and heading orientation. Pedestrian Dead Reckoning (PDR) systems exploit IMU readings to track the target by integrating the estimated relative movement at sequential time intervals. However, PDR-based tracking is prone to accumulated errors. Even small errors in each time interval can be magnified because of the integration in PDR [5].

Some approaches have been proposed to improve the positioning accuracy by combining radio-based positioning and PDR. For example, PDR can be used as a complementary method for localization. These two positioning methods (PDR and radio-based methods) are complementary because PDR can provide information about the relative movement between sequential intervals, e.g., velocity, heading orientation, which are missing in range-based methods. Additionally, the absolute location information provided by range-based methods can be used to mitigate integrating errors in PDR. Moreover, the floor plan of the area of interest can be integrated to further improve the tracking accuracy.

The vision of real-time indoor tracking on commodity smartphone devices, however, entails big challenges. For example, the noise in low-cost IMUs on commodity smartphones will introduce some errors in the process of numeric integration during tracking [5]. The sampling frequency of inertial sensors can achieve 100Hz. However, the sampling rate of the WiFi sensor is much lower, which is approximately 4Hz [5]. The limited computational resources (processor, memory, battery capacity, etc.) in commodity

MSWiM '16, November 13-17, 2016, Malta, Malta

© 2016 ACM. ISBN 978-1-4503-4502-6/16/11...$15.00

DOI: http://dx.doi.org/10.1145/2988287.2989142

smartphones bring additional challenges to run complex algorithms.

In this work, we propose an indoor tracking approach to support continuous positioning and tracking. Our approach is able to provide high accuracy by fusing IMU, radio, and floor plan information in an enhanced particle filter. Additionally, we introduce a double resampling method that is able to mitigate the errors caused by the low WiFi sampling rate on commodity smartphones.

We prototype our approach on commodity smartphones. Our approach can indicate the real-time location of a target without deploying an extra server, since all the tracking algorithms run on the smartphone itself. To validate our tracking system, we conduct extensive experiments in two indoor environments along complex moving paths. Evaluation results show that our infrastructure can achieve an average tracking error of $1.01m$ with standard deviation of $0.62m$.

The main contributions of this work are summarized as follows.

- We propose an enhanced particle filter to fuse range information estimated from RSSI, IMUs as well as floor plan information for indoor tracking.

- We incorporate a double resampling method in the particle filter. This double resampling is a continuous and asynchronous process, which is able to mitigate the tracking errors caused by unstable RSSI readings and low sampling frequency experimented in WiFi sensors of commodity smartphones.

- We implement and evaluate a real-time terminal-based positioning system, which runs our proposed tracking algorithms on commodity smartphones. Our solution does not require any interaction with an additional external server.

- We conduct a set of extensive experiments to evaluate the system in complex indoor environments with long tracking paths. In addition, several configuration parameters, such as the number of particles, commodity smartphone models and number of WiFi access points are tested in our experiments.

The rest of the paper is organized as follows. In Section II we present some related work. Some preliminaries for particle filters are reviewed in section III. The proposed enhanced particle filter is presented in section IV. Section V presents ranging and PDR methods. Implementation of the terminal-based system is presented in Section VI. Section VII presents the evaluation results of our approach. Section VII concludes the paper.

2. RELATED WORK

Indoor positioning has been investigated for decades and many solutions have been proposed. Among these solutions, radio-based positioning and inertial sensor-based tracking (i.e., PDR) have been widely investigated.

2.1 Pedestrian Dead Reckoning

Due to the fast development of modern smartphones, PDR relying on IMUs has attracted research interests. Basically,

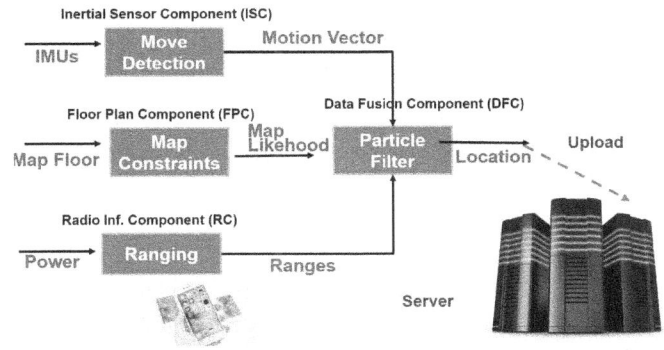

Figure 1: Indoor Localization System Architecture.

PDR systems derive the new location based on the previously determined location by using sensor readings. Inertial sensors can be adopted to implement pedestrian movement detection such as step recognition, stride length estimation, and heading orientation estimation. The authors of [4, 3] determined the heading orientation based on gyroscope measurements, whereas the displacement is estimated from accelerometer readings. In [3], authors defined a method named Heuristic Drift Elimination (HDE), which is intended to deal with the accumulated errors. However, HDE requires specialized sensors deployed on the foot of the pedestrian. The authors of [6] adopted magnetic field sensor and accelerometer readings to estimate the heading orientation. In this work authors defined a walking and running model based on accelerometer measurements. In [10], authors used readings of the gyrospcope to identify physical turns of the pedestrian user, whereas the walking distance is determined by readings of the accelerometer. PDR systems measure position changes rather than the absolute position, which results in an accumulation of sensor errors over time. Therefore, these systems must consider additional information like WiFi signals or floor plan information to deal with this kind of errors.

2.2 Radio-based Indoor Localization

Because of its ubiquitous availability, radio signals are often used in indoor positioning. Different parameters of radio signals can be used to locate the targets, such as RSSI [15] and time information [9]. Radio-based indoor localization can be classified as range-based and range-free methods. Range is defined as the propagation distance from the target to Anchor Nodes (AN). Fingerprinting [2] is very often used because of its robustness to multipath propagation. However, it is very time consuming to build up a radio map, which is required to locate the targets in fingerprinting. Range-based localization methods [7] need to first calculate the propagation distances, which is called ranging. It requires much less labor efforts than fingerprinting. Then, different positioning algorithms can be used to estimate the absolute locations of the targets, such as trilateration and multilateration [7].

2.3 PDR and WLAN Integration for Indoor Tracking

Besides the methods solely relying on PDR and radio-based positioning, some work has been proposed to combine these two methods to track indoor targets. In [12], authors proposed a fingerprinting-based solution by combining digital compass and WiFi information. The authors of [5] proposed a tracking system by exploiting particle filter features. This work adopted a particle filter to combine PDR, and floor plans together. A WiFi component records RSSI values periodically from all available access points on a floor. WiFi information is used to perform room recognition and turn verifying. The PDR component outputs a human motion vector model, which is used as input for the particle filter component.

3. PARTICLE FILTER

Particle filters are often used for indoor tracking and positioning. Indoor tracking can be modeled as estimating system state by processing a sequence of noisy measurements.

To derive the system state from all the observations so far, we have to define a system equation to model the system state changing over time and an observation model to abstract the observations on the system state. Thus, at time t we define the system state vector X_t, and the observation vector $Z_{1:t}$. We define, $X_t = [x_t, y_t]$, where x_t and y_t are the 2-dimensional location coordinates and $Z_{1:t}$, is the discrete sequence of all measurements obtained from $time = 1$ until $time = t$.

The system model is defined by the movement pattern of the target object as a non-linear function. In this case, the target object is the pedestrian who is holding a smartphone.

$$X_t = F(X_{t-1}) + v_t \tag{1}$$

v_t is the noise introduced by the system at time t.

Measurements observed at time t are modeled according to a non-linear function as follows:

$$Z_t = H(X_t) + u_t \tag{2}$$

where u_t is the noise included in the measurements at time t.

The goal of the tracking problem is to obtain the belief of the system state conditioned on the observations, i.e., posterior probability. This posterior probability can be represented as a set of particles. Therefore, the current state of the system can be determined by the probabilities of the particles. Particle filters can deal with non-Gaussian posterior probability via Monte Carlo simulations. The required posterior probability is represented by a set of random samples with associated weights with the following function:

$$p(X_t \mid Z_{1:t}) \approx \sum_{i=0}^{N_s} w_t^i \delta(X_t - X_t^i), \tag{3}$$

where N_s is the number of particles. X_t^i is the ith particle and w_t^i is its associated weight at time t.
The associated weights can be calculated as follows:

$$w_t^i \propto w_{t-1}^i * p(Z_t \mid X_t^i), \tag{4}$$

where $p(Z_t \mid X_t^i)$ is the *likelihood* function calculated from the observation measurements vector at time t.

4. ENHANCED PARTICLE FILTER WITH DOUBLE RESAMPLING

Noise in IMUs on commodity smartphones introduces errors in the localization process. RSSI in smartphones tends

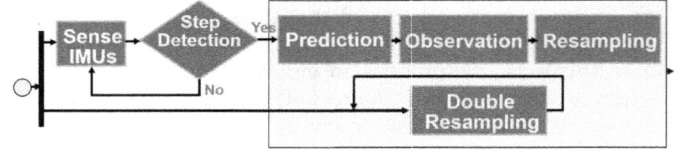

Figure 2: Particle Filter Structure

to be unstable due to multipath effects, which are severe in indoor environments [14]. Moreover, observations show that RSSI values often fluctuates over time even if the device is stationary. Unstable and vulnerable RSSI values introduce undesirable localization errors. Another issue is the achievable sampling rate of RSSI readings in WiFi sensors. The sampling rate of inertial sensors can achieve 100Hz. However, the sampling frequency of WiFi sensors is approximately 4Hz on commercial smartphones [5]. Therefore, inaccuracy of inertial sensors, instability, and low sampling frequency in WiFi sensors introduce errors in the location estimation process. Figure 1 summarizes the structure of our proposed approach and Figure 2 depicts our enhanced particle filter structure.

To mitigate these intrinsic errors, we propose an enhanced particle filter approach by fusing PDR, WiFi, and floor plan information. In our approach, an additional resampling method is incorporated in order to further mitigate the errors caused by off-the-shelf WiFi sensors embedded on commodity smartphones. The state vector at time t is defined as follows:

$$X_t = [x_t, y_t, \theta_t, \ell_t], \tag{5}$$

where (x_t, y_t) are the Cartesian coordinates of the target object, θ_t is the heading orientation and ℓ_t is the stride length. We define the motion vector as $Mv_t = [\theta_t, \ell_t]$.

The set of N weighted particles can be defined as

$$P_t = [X_t^i, W_t^i], i = 1, ..., N, \tag{6}$$

where X_t^i is the state vector with weight W_t^i of the ith particle at time t. Thus, the prediction function can be written as

$$X_t = F \cdot X_{t-1} + \eta, \tag{7}$$

where

$$F = \begin{pmatrix} 1 & 0 & 0 & 0 \\ 0 & 1 & 0 & 0 \\ 0 & 0 & 0 & 0 \\ 0 & 0 & 0 & 0 \end{pmatrix}, \eta = \begin{pmatrix} \ell * cos(\theta) & 0 \\ 0 & \ell * sin(\theta) \\ \theta & 0 \\ 0 & \ell \end{pmatrix}$$

$$\theta = \theta' + \varepsilon'$$
$$\ell = \ell' + \varepsilon''$$

Both θ and ℓ values are given by IMUs. Heading orientation and stride length are assumed to interfere by zero-mean Gaussian random noises. Therefore, ε' and ε'' are the errors introduced in the calculation process of θ and ℓ respectively. State X_t^i vector of each particle is updated based on Equation (7) from the particles at the previous time interval X_{t-1}^i. Thus, the new set P_t is calculated from P_{t-1}, and the current system state belief is calculated through four phases as follows:

4.1 Prediction Phase

Each particle is updated based on Equation (7). Floor plan restrictions are applied in this phase. Any particle is allowed to move through movement-restricted areas, e.g., movement through walls is not allowed. Prediction function (7) depends on the motion vector M_{v_t}.

The heading orientation θ can be statistically described as follows:

$$\theta_t = \hat{\theta}_t + \theta_{bs,t} + \theta_{be,t} + \epsilon_{\theta,t}, \tag{8}$$

where $\hat{\theta}_t$ is the actual heading orientation value, $\theta_{bs,t}$ is an angular bias introduced by uncalibrated sensors, $\theta_{be,t}$ is an angular bias due to local magnetic field perturbations, and $\epsilon_{\theta,t}$ is a measured random error [11].

The stride length ℓ can be statistically described as follows,

$$\ell_t = \hat{\ell}_t + \ell_{bs,t} + \epsilon_{\ell,t}, \tag{9}$$

where $\hat{\ell}_t$ is the actual stride length value, $\ell_{bs,t}$ is the bias introduced by the use of uncalibrated sensors, and $\epsilon_{\ell,t}$ is a measured random error [11].

To compensate the bias and error values introduced by the environment and uncalibrated sensors, in this work we assume the heading direction θ and stride length ℓ as random normal variables whose values can be obtained from $\mathcal{N}(\theta_t, \sigma_\theta^2)$ and $\mathcal{N}(\ell_t, \sigma_\ell^2)$, respectively.

4.2 Observation Phase

The associated weight w_t^i of the propagated particles must be corrected after updating their positions. The associated weight should be updated based on the likelihood of the observations conditioned on each particle $p(Z_t \mid X_t^i)$ at time t. The observation vector is defined by the estimated ranges to different ANs. Thus, the observation vector at time t is defined as $Z_t = [d_t^j], j = 1...N$, where N is the number of ANs. Then, the probability $p(Z_t \mid X_t^i)$ can be determined as follows:

$$p(Z_t \mid X_t^i) = p(d_t^j \mid X_t^i) \tag{10}$$

In this phase, the associated weight w_t^i of each particle is given by the ranging information. The particle at position (x_t, y_t) with low probability to observe d_t^j in their position will be assigned a small weight. In this way particles with large associated weights will have a stronger contribution in the determination of the state belief of the system. In order to avoid confusion between different likelihoods used in this work, hereafter we refer to $p(d_t \mid X_t^i)$ as the ranging likelihood and $p(Z_t \mid X_t^i)$ as the overall likelihood.

We can assume that the ranges to different ANs are independent from each other. Therefore, the ranging likelihood can be defined as follows:

$$p(Z_t \mid X_t^i) = \prod_{j=1}^{N} (\hat{d}_{j,t} \mid X_t^i), \tag{11}$$

where $\hat{d}_{j,t}$ is the measured distance to the AN j at time t. Hereafter, $p(\hat{d}_{j,t} \mid X_t^i)$ will be referred as the individual likelihood.

Each individual likelihood can be written as:

$$p(\hat{d}_{j,t} \mid X_t^i) = \frac{1}{\sigma_j \sqrt{2\pi}} \exp^{\frac{[\hat{d}_{j,t} - \sqrt{(x^i - x_j)^2 + (y^i - y_j)^2}]^2}{2\sigma_j^2}}, \tag{12}$$

where (x_j, y_j) are the coordinates of the jth AN.

In complex indoor environments WiFi signals suffer from some random variations during transmission. This random behaviour is produced by the presence of multiple obstacles such as walls, furniture, ceiling, etc. Obstacles introduce a mixed transmission between Line of Sight (LOS) and Non-LOS (NLOS) conditions. NLOS propagation induces significant bias in power-based ranging [13]. To mitigate the influence of ranging errors on the definition of the ranging likelihood $p(d_k \mid X_t^i)$, we propose to adopt the same weighting technique used in our previous work [8]. The weighting technique magnifies the contribution of the individual likelihood with smaller errors and suppress the contribution of larger ranging errors. Therefore, the weighted technique is defined on each individual likelihood as follows:

$$p(Z_t \mid X_t^i) = \prod_{j=1}^{N} p(\hat{d}_j \mid X_t^i)^{m_j}, \tag{13}$$

where m_j is the exponential weight for the individual likelihood of the jth AN. In general, estimation of larger distances introduce more errors than small distances. Thus, the exponential weight m_j can be defined as inversely proportional to the estimated range outputs [8]:

$$m_j = \frac{\frac{1}{d_j}}{\sum_{n=1}^{N_{ap}} \frac{1}{d_n}}, \tag{14}$$

where N_{ap} is the number of ANs.

4.3 Resampling Phase

The resampling step is a crucial but computationally expensive component of a particle filter approach. This phase is adopted to eliminate particles with small associated weights by repeating particles with large associated weights. Therefore, after updating each particle in the prediction phase, we perform a resampling process in a systematic manner. The resampling process in this phase relies only in the individual likelihood $p(d_t \mid X_t^i)$. It means that the associated weight of each particle is calculated by using observations related to range estimations. Afterwards, the weighted center given by all the particles is calculated as the estimated position of the current step.

4.4 Double Resampling (Correction Phase)

Range estimation is often shifted from the ground truth range [8]. Moreover, we mentioned in previous sections that unlike inertial sensors, WiFi sensors can achieve a sampling frequency of approximately 4Hz. Additionally, we observe that RSSI values registered at the smartphone side can fluctuate over time even when the smartphone is held in a static position. Thus, determination of the associated weight of each particle is not accurate since the Resampling Phase as described in Section 4.3 relays on ranging information. Therefore, individual likelihoods $p(\hat{d}_{j,t} \mid X_t^i)$ are often biased from the real individual likelihood $p(d_{j,t} \mid X_t^i)$.

This phase is intended to mitigate the errors introduced by WiFi instability and the low sampling rate experimented in smartphones. To correct the associated weight of each particle, we include a second resampling method called Correction Phase. The Correction phase implements a continuous asynchronous resampling method with three main processes as follows:

- The ranging process is executed when a new RSSI reading is available.

- The weight of each particle is continuously recalculated. In this phase the associated weight is determined based on the individual likelihood ($p(\hat{d}_{j,t} \mid X_t^i)$) and the floor plan information. It is worth to mention that $p(\hat{d}_{j,t} \mid X_t^i)$ is determined by using ranging information.

- Particles are continuously resampled in a systematic method.

To summarize, the double resampling phase is aimed to make a continuous correction of the level of influence that each particle contributes to the determination of the state of the system. Algorithm 1 describes this phase.

Algorithm 1: Asynchronous Continuous Resampling

Input : Floor Plan Constraints, $R\hat{S}SI$
Output: Particle's corrected weights
1 Scan WiFi network.
2 **if** *new $R\hat{S}SI$ reading is available* **then**
3   Determine $R\hat{S}SI$ mean ($mRSSI$) of the latest 4 $R\hat{S}SI$ readings:
4     $mRSSI = \frac{\sum_{k=0}^{3} RSS_{t-k}}{4}$
5   **foreach** AN_j **do**
6   calculate $d_j = \alpha_j \cdot e^{\beta_j \cdot mRSSI_j}$
7   **end**
8   Calculate the individual likelihood: $p(d_j \mid X_t^i)$
9   *Check position of each particle:*
10   **foreach** *Paricle P_t* **do**
11   **if** *Paticle position is in restricted area* **then**
12             $W_t = 0$
13   **end**
14   **end**
15   *Normalize weights of each particle:*
16   **foreach** *Paricle P_t* **do**
17         $W_t = \hat{W}_t / \sum_{n=1}^{N} \hat{W}_n^i$
18   **end**
19   Resample particles P_t based on systematic resampling method.
20 **end**
21 Go to 1

---

5. RANGING AND PDR METHODS

This section introduces how to estimate the observation parameter (ranges) and the motion vector (M_{v_t}) in our proposed particle filter.

5.1 Ranging Estimation Process

In order to achieve high ranging accuracy, we adopt the Non-Linear Regression (NLR) model presented in [7]. The NLR model is defined as follows:

$$d_{j,t} = \alpha_j * e^{RSS_{j,t} * \beta_j}, \qquad (15)$$

where $d_{j,t}$ is the distance between the target object and the jth AN at instant t. Both α_j and β_j are environmental variables defined for the jth AN. $RSSI_{j,t}$ is the signal power measured from the jth AN at time t.

Accurate estimation of ranges is a prerequisite to achieve high accuracy on the estimation of the individual likelihood $p(\hat{d}_{j,t} \mid X_t^i)$. Therefore, the raw values of RSSI received from the WiFi sensor are smoothed by approximating the real $RSSI$ value with the mean of the latest four raw RSSI readings.

The first step in ranging estimation is to take the initial measurements, which are aimed to train the environmental parameters α and β required for the NLR model defined in [7]. In our experiments we defined several stationary points spread over the whole floor plan as shown in Figure 3. Please find details about the ranging method in our previous work [7].

5.2 Motion Vector Estimation Process

The mobile target needs to determine the movement of the pedestrian. Therefore, in order to estimate the pedestrian displacement, we use two sensors, the accelerometer and the geomagnetic field sensor. The displacement of the pedestrian at time t is defined by the motion vector $M_{v_t} = [\theta_t, \ell_t]$. The motion vector M_{v_t} is passed from the PDR component to the Particle Filter component at instant t when a step of the pedestrian is recognized in the target mobile object. Thereby, step recognition and heading orientation methods are implemented in the PDR component. To develop the step recognition method, we use linear acceleration readings. Figure 4 shows linear acceleration behaviour in axis X,Y,Z of the smartphone when a step is executed. Therefore, based on these observations, we develop a step recognition method shown in Algorithm 2.

To estimate the heading orientation, we rely on a digital compass developed from the geomagnetic field and accelerometer sensors embedded in Android smartphones. For further details about heading orientation implementation in Android smartphones, please refer to [1].

Digital compass measures the clockwise angle between the magnetic north and the Y axis of the smartphone at time t. This value is called Azimuth (α_t). Therefore, the heading orientation (θ_t) in the local coordinate system can be determined as follows:

$$\theta_t = OffsetX - \alpha_t, \qquad (16)$$

where $OffsetX$ is the clockwise angle between the X axis of our local coordinate system and the magnetic north.

Although the stride length value can vary along the trajectory, in this work we assume that ℓ is a constant value in order to focus on the tracking algorithm. Nevertheless, the determination of a possible relation between the characteristics of human walking and stride length bias could be the subject of future work.

The frequency sampling rate in both accelerometer and magnetic field sensors are set to 14Hz.

6. IMPLEMENTATION

We have implemented a terminal-based system for accurate indoor tracking. The system comprises two main components: Mobile Target and Anchor Nodes (ANs). The pro-

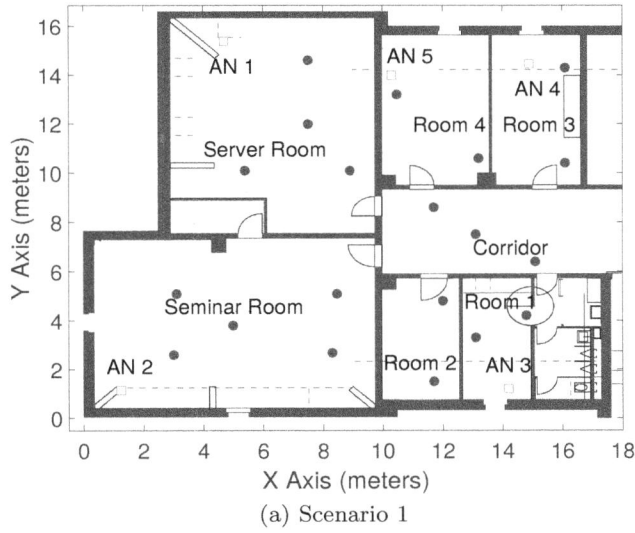

(a) Scenario 1

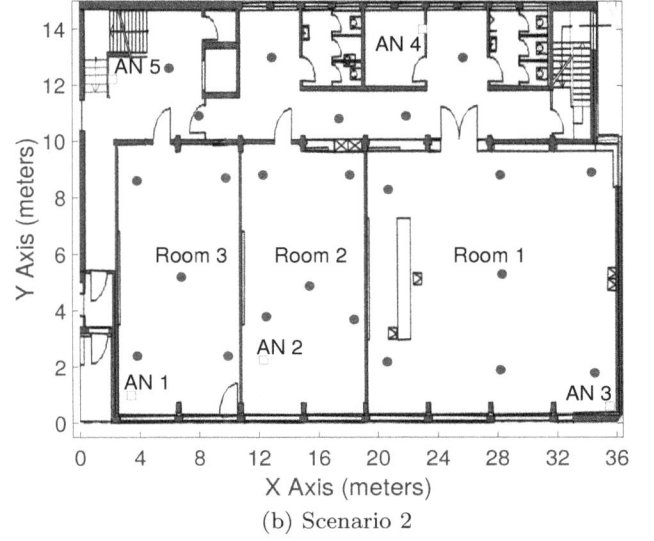

(b) Scenario 2

Figure 3: Anchor Nodes distribution and ranging training points (Square Points: Anchor Nodes; Circle Points: Ranging Training Positions)

Algorithm 2: Step Recognition Method

Input : Inertial sensor readings
Output: Step announcement

1 Sense IMUs;
2 **if** *IMUs come from Linear Acceleration sensor* **then**
3   Read $\hat{a}[x, y, z]_t$ vector;
4   **if** $\hat{a}[z]_t > threshold$ *and* $\hat{a}[z]_{t-1} < \hat{a}[z]_t$ *and* $\hat{a}[x]_t < \hat{a}[z]_t$ *and* $\hat{a}[y]_t < \hat{a}[z]_t$ **then**
5   Report a Step;
6   **end**
7 **end**
8 Go to step 1;

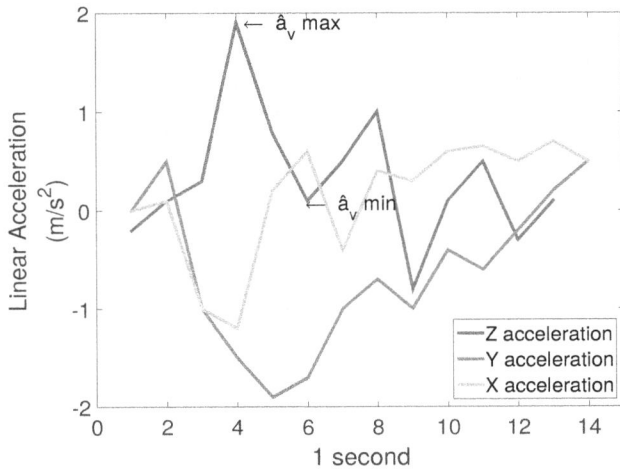

Figure 4: Step Recognition, Linear Acceleration Readings

---

posed tracking algorithms are running on the mobile target. Figure 5 presents the overview of the system.

ANs are some commercial WiFi access points deployed at known locations along the area of interest. Positions of ANs are chosen to provide the maximum coverage inside the area of interest. Thus, the location of AN are defined on the boundary corners and the boundary itself.

We have adopted D-Link D-635 and D-Link DAP-2553 as ANs in this work. The beacon period is configured to $100ms$ in ANs.

Mobile targets are some commercial Android smartphones, which support WiFi, inertial, and magnetic field sensors. We have deployed the tracking algorithms in two different models of smartphones, Motorola Nexus 6 and LG Nexus 4. Hereafter, we refer to Motorola Nexus 6 as Mobile Target 1 (MT1) and LG Nexus 4 as Mobile Target 2 (MT2).

In order to save resources in the smartphone, we set the sampling rate of inertial sensors to 14Hz. However, the WiFi sampling frequency is much lower, 3Hz and 4Hz in MT2 and MT1 respectively. Table 1 shows the main characteristics of the mobile targets used in this work.

Additionally, it is necessary to know the floor plan of the area of interest. The system requires information related with restricted areas such as walls. Particles are not allowed to be spread through restricted areas. The system reports the location of the target in real time.

7. PERFORMANCE EVALUATION

To evaluate the performance of our proposed system, we have conducted a set of experiments in office-like indoor environments.

The set of experiments was designed to determine the parameter configuration that leads to the best performance of our indoor tracking system. To do so, we varied the system configuration parameters as follows:

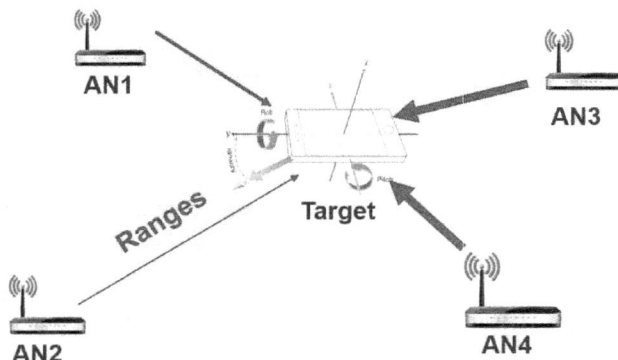

Figure 5: Indoor Localization System Overview.

Table 1: Mobile Targets

Table 1: Mobile Targets

Model	Platform
MT 1	**Model:** Motorola Nexus 6; **OS:** Android 5.1.1 **CPU:** Quad-core 2.7 GHz; **RAM:** 3GB **WLAN:**WiFi a/b/g/n **Accelerometer:** Resolution:0.039 Range:19.613 **Magnetometer:** Resolution: 0.150 Range:9830
MT 2	**Model:**LG Nexus 4; **OS:** Android 5.1.1 **CPU:** Quad-core 1.5 GHz; **RAM:** 2GB **WLAN:**WiFi a/b/g/n **Accelerometer:** Resolution:0.001 Range: 39.227 **Magnetometer:** Resolution:0.150 Range:4912

- Target object: as we mentioned in previous sections, we deployed our localization algorithm in two different models of smartphone. Therefore, different processing capabilities are taken into account in the experiments. Table 1 shows the main characteristics of the smartphones utilized in our experiments.

- Number of particles: we conducted a set of experiments to achieve the best performance related to the number of particles. The goal of this experiment is to define the number of particles that yields the highest accuracy in the tracking in the process.

- Double resampling: we validated the tracking accuracy of our system by including the double continuous asynchronous resampling proposed in this work.

- Number of ANs: we designed a set of experiments by varying the number of ANs from 5 to 4.

- Area of interest: experiments were conducted in two different indoor environments along complex and larger trajectories.

7.1 Experiment Setup

Experiments were conducted in two buildings of the Institute of Computer Science (INF) at the University of Bern. The first scenario used an area of $288m^2$ and the second scenario $540m^2$. In each scenario, the target object was held by a person moving along the trajectories as depicted in Figure 6. In order to determine the localization errors, some checking points were defined along the trajectories.

Experiments were repeated five times. Therefore, 90 and 55 checking points were analysed in scenario 1 and 2 respectively. The pedestrian was asked to walk through the trajectories and check his current position on the tracking system when he walked through a checking point. The difference between positions reported by the tracking system and ground truth positions are considered as localization error. Figure 6 shows the AN distribution, trajectories and checking points defined in both scenarios. Blue points define the path of the trajectories, whereas red points define the checking points over the moving path. We evaluated also the PDR along these moving paths.

7.2 Experiment Results

Experiments were first conducted in scenario 1. Once the configuration that yields to the best performance was defined, we tested our tracking approach in scenario 2. Validation of our proposed double resampling method was made by using the best configuration parameters defined in the experiments conducted in scenario 1.

7.2.1 Performance vs Number of Particles

This set of experiments was conducted in scenario 1, with 5 ANs. Details about the environment configuration can be seen in Figure 6. The different choices regarding the number of particles are 100, 200, 300, 400, 500, 1000, 1500, 2000, 2500. Figure 7 shows the confidence intervals resulting from the experiments conducted in both MTs. Location accuracy can be theoretically boosted by using more particles, that is, the more particles, the better is the accuracy [5]. However, we can see in our experiments that after a certain number of particles the tracking errors remain almost constant. Thus, the accuracy in both MTs is slightly improved after a certain number of particles. In the case of MT1, we can see that the minimum mean error $1.01m$ is achieved with 1500 particles which spend approximately $51.9\mu s$ of processing time. In MT2, the minimum mean error $1.18m$ is accomplished with 1000 particles, which take $49.81\mu s$ of processing time. It is worth noting that these mentioned configurations also yield the lowest standard deviation; $0.62m$ and $0.65m$ in MT1 and MT2 respectively.

7.2.2 Performance vs Number of ANs

In this experiment we selected the number of particles that yields the best performance of our localization approach. Hence, the chosen number of particles in this experiment is 1500 for MT1 and 1000 for MT2. Figure 8 shows CDF (Cumulative Distribution Function) of positioning errors of our proposed indoor tracking approach in scenario 1. Figure 9 shows CDF of tracking errors of our approach and the PDR system. Since PDR performance is independent of the number of ANs and number of particles, the CDF of PDR summarizes all the experiments in both scenarios that are utilized in this work. Table 2 summarizes the mean tracking error, standard deviation and 90% accuracy.

It is well known that PDR is prone to accumulated errors because it estimates the current location of the target by in-

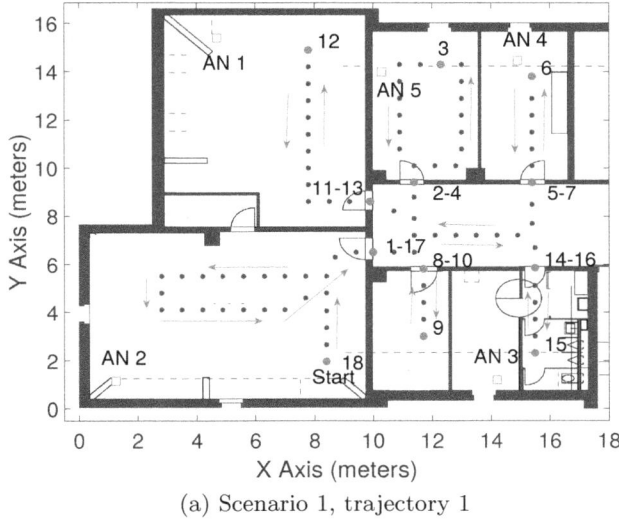

(a) Scenario 1, trajectory 1

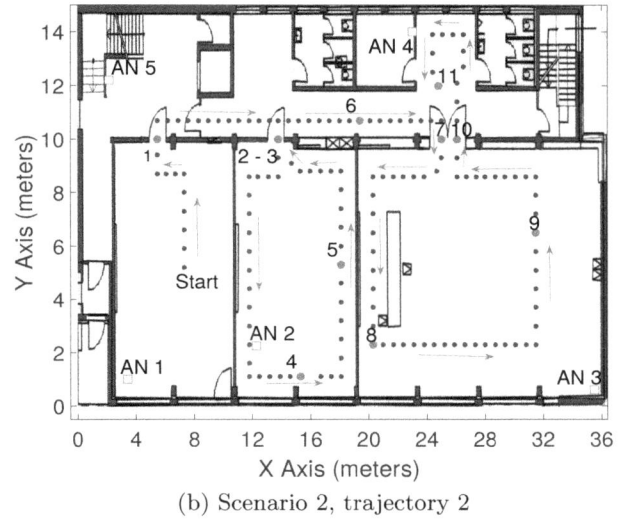

(b) Scenario 2, trajectory 2

Figure 6: Trajectories and Check point distribution (Square Points: Anchor Nodes; Red Points: Check points; Blue Points: Trajectory path)

Table 2: Performance vs Number of ANs

Configuration	Mean error	S.D	90% Acc.
MT1 1500 Ptc. (5ANs)	1.01m	0.62m	1.7m
MT2 1000 Ptc. (5ANs)	1.18m	0.65m	2.1m
MT1 1500 Ptc. (4ANs)	1.16m	0.7m	2.3m
MT2 1000 Ptc. (4ANs)	1.43m	0.86m	2.7m
PDR	8.6m	5.49m	17.2m

tegrating the relative movement from the previous locations [5]. Therefore, the larger the trajectory is, the bigger are the average of localization errors in a PDR system. Experiment results show that our proposed indoor tracking approach achieves more stable and higher accuracy than a PDR system. In order to further evaluate our tracking approach, we have designed large and complex trajectories. Our experiment results show $17.2m$ for 90% accuracy using PDR because of accumulative errors. However, our tracking approach deals efficiently with the accumulative errors even when the number of ANs is decreased to 4. Our tracking approach achieves around $1.7m$ for 90% accuracy, which outperforms PDR system by around 90.1% along trajectory 1. The mean error of our tracking approach is $1.01m$, which is 88.2% better than PDR. Standard deviation is 0.62 which is 88.7% smaller than PDR. Thus, our proposed approach outperforms PDR for accuracy and stability.

7.2.3 Performance vs Resampling Methods

Figure 10 shows the CDF of positioning errors for the tracking algorithms. Our tracking approach along double resampling method achieves higher accuracy and more stable performance compared to the single resampling approach. Table 3 summarizes the average of tracking errors, standard deviation and 90% accuracy. Our tracking approach along double resampling method achieves around $1.7m$ for 90% accuracy, whereas the single resampling method achieves around $3m$. The mean error of the double resampling method

Table 3: Double resampling and single resampling methods, scenario 1

Tracking Approach	Mean error	S.D	90% Acc.
Double Resampling	1.01m	0.62m	1.7m
Single Resampling	1.61m	1.02m	3m

is $1.01m$, whereas the mean error of single resampling is $1.61m$. Standard deviation is $0.62m$ and $1.02m$ in double and single resampling method respectively.

Based on these results, we can find the following observations. First, our tracking approach outperforms the single resampling approach by around 43.3% considering 90% accuracy. Second, the mean error of our tracking approach is 37.3% better than single resampling method. Third, standard deviation is 39.2% smaller than the single resampling method. Therefore, experiment results show that because of the continuous resampling method, our tracking approach is able to faster correct the mobile target position along the moving paths compared to single resampling. The double resampling approach outperforms the single resampling approach for accuracy and stability.

7.2.4 Performance vs Area of Interest

This experiment validates the environment independence of our approach. Thus, we chose a second scenario to deploy of tracking system. As mentioned in previous sections, scenario 2 is placed on different buildings at the University of Bern. The area of interest is 46.7% bigger than the area in scenario 1. However, we set up our approach with the configuration that achieved the best performance on experiments executed in scenario 1. That is, the tracking algorithms are deployed on MT1 with 1500 particles and 5 ANs distributed along the area of interest. Figure 6b depicts scenario 2 and trajectory 2.

Table 4 summarizes the mean tracking error, standard deviation and 90% accuracy. Figure 11 depicts the CDF of

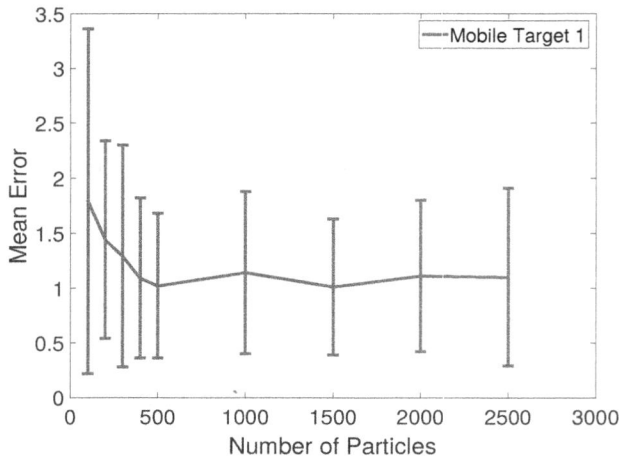

(a) Confidence Interval MT1

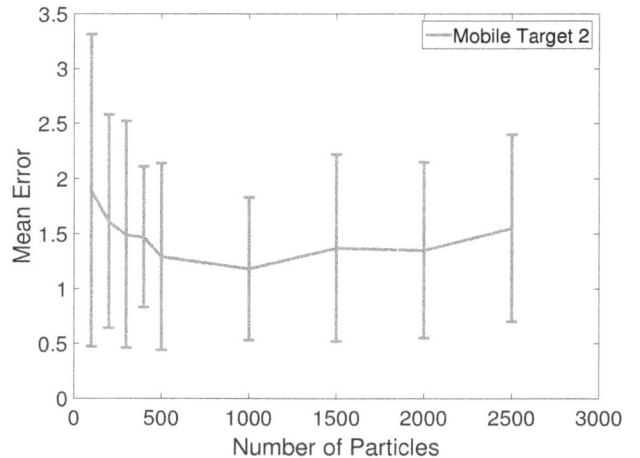

(b) Confidence Interval MT2

Figure 7: Confidence Interval

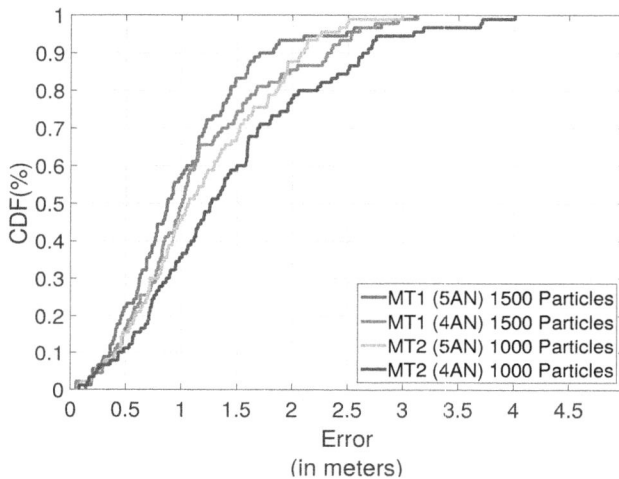

Figure 8: Configuration Parameters

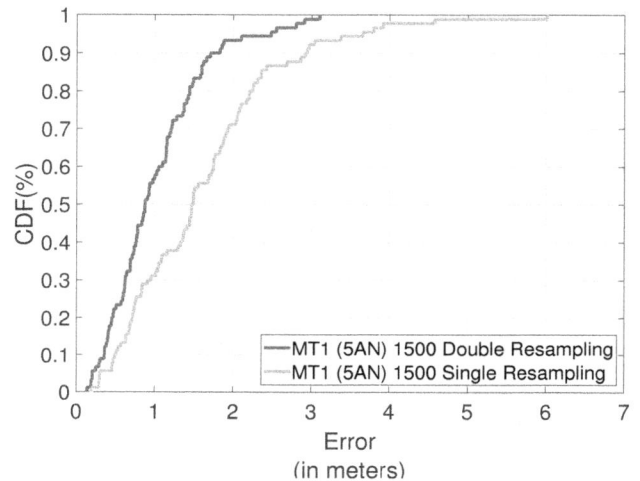

Figure 10: Tracking error CDF on double resampling vs single resampling method

positioning errors for our tracking approach tested in scenario 2. Our tracking approach using the double resampling method achieves around $3m$ for 90% accuracy, which outperforms PDR by around 86.36% along trajectory 2. The mean error is $1.6m$, which is 88.28% better than PDR. Standard deviation is $0.9m$, which is 84.62% smaller than the PDR system.

Based on these observations, we can highlight that despite the bigger area of interest, our proposed tracking approach achieves high accuracy and stable performance.

However, the mean error and standard deviation were slightly increased compared to experiments in scenario 1. This reflects that the density, positions and coverage of ANs along the area of interest influence the tracking precision.

8. CONCLUSIONS AND FUTURE WORKS

This work exploits an enhanced particle filter approach to fuse radio signals, inertial sensors and physical informa-

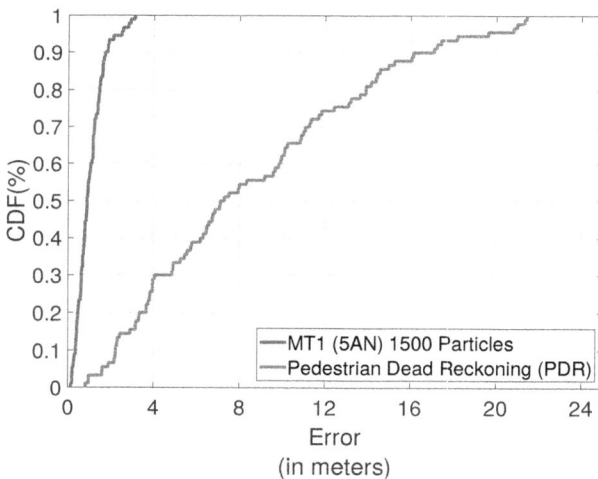

Figure 9: Particle Filter vs PDR, scenario 1

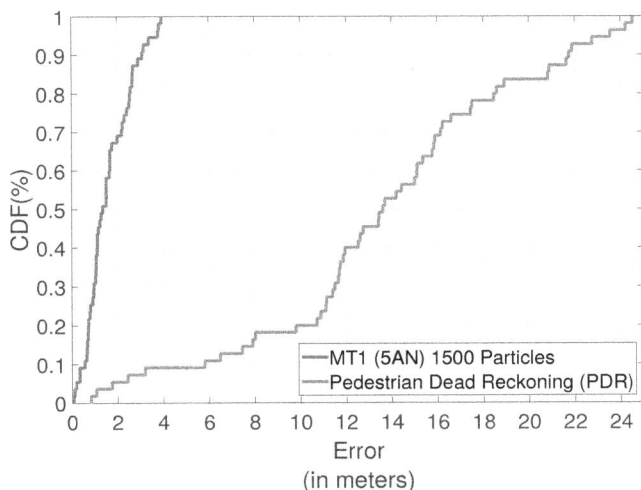

Figure 11: Tracking error CDF on scenario 2.

Table 4: Double resampling and PDR methods, scenario 2

Tracking Approach	Mean error	S.D	90% Acc.
Double Resampling	1.6m	0.9m	3m
PDR	13.66m	5.85m	22.3m

tion of the environment, to achieve high localization and tracking accuracy in complex indoor scenarios using commodity smartphones. Additionally, our work presents an asynchronous continuous resampling method that is able to tackle with the low sampling rate problem of WiFi sensors on the smartphone side. We evaluated our localization system in two complex large trajectories in different indoor scenarios. Experiments show that our approach can achieve an average tracking error of $1.01m$ and 90% accuracy is $1.7m$. Thus, our tracking approach is more accurate and stable than pedestrian dead reckoning and the commonly used particle filter with single resampling. Furthermore, our proposed approach enables real-time tracking in the smartphone side without assistance of any additional external server.

In the future, we will analyse the relation between anchor nodes' position with system performance, and also the impact of the stride length.

Acknowledgment

This work was partly supported by the Swiss National Science Foundation via the SwissSenseSynergy project under grant number 154458 and the COST AAPELE Action IC1303

9. REFERENCES

[1] Android Documentation. 2016. Android Position Sensors. Retrieved Jun 7, 2016 from developer.android.com/guide/topics/sensors/.

[2] P. Bahl and V. Padmanabhan. Radar: an in-building rf-based user location and tracking system. *INFOCOM 2000. Joint Conference of the IEEE Computer and Communications Societies. Proceedings. IEEE*, (19), 2000.

[3] J. Borestein and L. Ojeda. Heuristic drift elimination for personnel tracking systems. *The Journal of Navigation*, 63(4):591–606, 2010.

[4] F. Hong, H. Chu, L. Wang, Y. Feng, and Z. Guo. Pocket mattering: Indoor pedestrian tracking with commercial smartphone. *International Conference on Indoor Positioning and Indoor Navigation*, November 2012.

[5] F. Hong, Y. Zhang, M. Wei, Y. Feng, and Z. Guo. Wap: Indoor localization and tracking using wifi-assited particle filter. *Annual IEEE Conference on Local Computer Networks LCN*, (39):210–217, June 2014.

[6] N. Kakiuchi and S. Kamijo. Pedestrian dead reckoning for mobile phones trhough walking and running mode recognition. *Proceedings of the 16th International IEEE Annual Conference on Intelligent Transportation Systems (ITSC 2013)*, pages 261–267, October 2013.

[7] Z. Li, T. Braun, and D. Dimitrova. A passive wifi source localization system based on fine-grained power-based trilateration. *IEEE International Symposium on a World of Wireless, Mobile and Multimedia Networks (WoWMoM)*, 2015.

[8] Z. Li, D. Burbano, Z. Zhao, J. Carrera, and T. Braun. Fine-grained indoor tracking by fusing inertial sensor and physical layer information in wlans. *IEEE International Conference on Communications (ICC)*, 2016.

[9] Z. Li, D. Dimitrova, and T. Braun. A time-based passive source localization system for narrow-band signal. *The IEEE International Conference on Communications (ICC)*, (39):4599–4605, June 2015.

[10] A. Mariakakis, S. Sen, J. Lee, and K. Kim. Sail: Single access point-bases indoor localization. *Proceedings of the 12th annual conference on Mobile systems, applications, and services MobiSys 14 '*, (14):315–328, June 2014.

[11] A. Masiero, A. Guarnieri, F. Pirotti, and A. Vettore. A particle filter for smartphone-based indoor pedestrian navigation. www.mdpi.com/journal/micromachines, 2014. ISSN 2072-666X.

[12] P. Nagpal and R. Rashidzadeh. Indoor positioning using magnetic compass and accelerometer of smartphones. *'International Conference on Selected Topics in Mobile and Wireless Networking MoWNet*, pages 140–145, 2013.

[13] C. Wu, Z. Yang, Z. Zhou, K. Qian, Y. Yunhao, and M. Liu. Phaseu: Real-time los identification with wifi. *IEEE Conference on Computer Communications (INFOCOM)*, 2015.

[14] K. Wu, J. Xiao, Y. Yi, M. Gao, and L. Ni. Fila: Fine-grained indoor localization. *INFOCOM Proceedings IEEE*, pages 2210–2218, 2012.

[15] M. Youssef and A. Agrawala. The horus wlan location determination system. *Proceedings of the International Conference on Mobile Systems, Applications, and Services (MobiSys05)*, (3):205–218, 2005.

Matrix: Multihop Address Allocation and Dynamic Any-to-Any Routing for 6LoWPAN

Bruna S. Peres
bperes@dcc.ufmg.br

Otavio A. de O. Souza
oaugusto@dcc.ufmg.br

Bruno P. Santos
bruno.ps@dcc.ufmg.br

Edson R. A. Junior
edsonroteia@dcc.ufmg.br

Olga Goussevskaia
olga@dcc.ufmg.br

Marcos A. M. Vieira
mmvieira@dcc.ufmg.br

Luiz F. M. Vieira
lfvieira@dcc.ufmg.br

Antonio A.F. Loureiro
loureiro@dcc.ufmg.br

Computer Science Department, Universidade Federal de Minas Gerais, Brazil

ABSTRACT

Standard routing protocols for IPv6 over Low power Wireless Personal Area Networks (6LoWPAN) are mainly designed for data collection applications and work by establishing a tree-based network topology, which enables packets to be sent upwards, from the leaves to the root, adapting to dynamics of low-power communication links. The routing tables in such unidirectional networks are very simple and small since each node just needs to maintain the address of its parent in the tree, providing the best-quality route at every moment. In this work, we propose Matrix, a platform-independent routing protocol that utilizes the existing tree structure of the network to enable reliable and efficient any-to-any data traffic. Matrix uses hierarchical IPv6 address assignment in order to optimize routing table size, while preserving bidirectional routing. Moreover, it uses a local broadcast mechanism to forward messages to the right subtree when persistent node or link failures occur. We implemented Matrix on TinyOS and evaluated its performance both analytically and through simulations on TOSSIM. Our results show that the proposed protocol is superior to available protocols for 6LoWPAN, when it comes to any-to-any data communication, in terms of reliability, message efficiency, and memory footprint.

CCS Concepts

•Networks → Network protocol design; Network layer protocols;

Keywords

6LoWPAN; IPv6; CTP; RPL; any-to-any routing; fault tolerance

MSWiM '16, November 13-17, 2016, Malta, Malta

© 2016 ACM. ISBN 978-1-4503-4502-6/16/11...$15.00

DOI: http://dx.doi.org/10.1145/2988287.2989139

1. INTRODUCTION

IPv6 over Low-power Wireless Personal Area Networks (6LoWPAN) is a working group inspired by the idea that even the smallest low-power devices should be able to run the Internet Protocol to become part of the Internet of Things. Standard routing protocols for 6LowPAN, such as CTP (Collection Tree Protocol [6]) and RPL (IPv6 Routing Protocol for Low-Power and Lossy Networks [19]), have two distinctive characteristics: communication devices use unstructured IPv6 addresses that do not reflect the topology of the network (typically derived from their MAC addresses), and routing lacks support for any-to-any communication since it is based on distributed collection tree structures focused on bottom-up data flows (from the leaves to the root). The problem with such one-directional routing is that it makes it inefficient to build important network functions, such as configuration routines and reliable mechanisms to ensure the delivery of end-to-end data.

Even though CTP does not support any-to-any traffic, the specification of RPL defines two modes of operation for top-down data flows: the non-storing mode, which uses source routing, and the storing mode, in which each node maintains a routing table for all possible destinations. This requires $O(n)$ space (where n is the total number of nodes), which is unfeasible for memory-constrained devices.

Some works have addressed this problem from different perspectives. In [15], the authors proposed a hierarchical IPv6 address allocation scheme, referred to as MHCL, to enable any-to-any routing by incorporating network topology information into the IPv6 address, assigned to each node in a multihop fashion. MHCL was implemented as a subroutine of RPL and showed to enable any-to-any routing using compact routing tables. MHCL stores the IPv6 address range of the entire subtree rooted at a child node in a single routing table entry, which results in $O(k)$ memory space, where k is the number of one-hop descendants of a node in the collection tree. The downside of MHCL is that it was not designed to deal with network faults and dynamic network topologies since a message can be dropped whenever a node or link failure occurs in the address hierarchy.

In this work, we build upon the idea of using hierarchical IPv6 address allocation and propose Matrix, a routing scheme for dynamic network topologies and fault-tolerant any-to-any data flows in 6LoWPAN. Matrix assumes there is an underlying collection tree topology (provided by CTP or RPL, for instance), in which nodes have static locations, i.e., are not mobile, and links are dynamics, i.e., nodes might choose different parents according to link quality dynamics. Matrix uses only one-hop information in the routing tables and implements a local broadcast mechanism to forward messages to the right subtree when node or link failures occur.

After the network has been initialized and all nodes have received an IPv6 address range, three simultaneous distributed trees are maintained by all nodes: the collection tree (Ctree), the IPv6 address tree (IPtree), and the reverse collection tree (RCtree). Initially, any-to-any packet forwarding is performed using Ctree for bottom-up and IPtree for top-down data flows. Whenever a node or link fails or Ctree changes, the new link is added in the reverse direction into RCtree and is maintained as long as this topology change persists. Top-down data packets are then forwarded from IPtree to RCtree via a local broadcast. The node that receives a local-broadcast checks whether it knows the subtree of the destination IPv6 address: if yes then it forwards the packet to the right subtree via RCtree and the packet continues its path in the IPtree until the final destination.

Why is this approach robust to network dynamics? Routing is performed using the address hierarchy represented by the IPtree, so whenever a link or node fails, messages addressed to destinations in the corresponding subtree may be lost. Matrix uses the (dynamic) reverse collection tree and the local broadcast mechanism to forward messages to the right subtree, as long as an alternative route exists. Note that this local rerouting mechanism does not guarantee that all messages will be delivered. We argue that the probability that the message will be forwarded to the appropriate subtree is high, as long as there is a valid path, due to the geometric properties of wireless networks. Our simulations showed that this intuition is, in fact, correct.

Why does this approach scale? Each node stores only one-hop neighborhood information, namely: the id of its parent in Ctree, the IPv6 address ranges of its children in the IPtree, and the IPv6 address ranges of its (temporary) children in the RCtree. Therefore, the memory footprint at each node is $O(k)$, where k is the number of children at any given moment in time. The impact of such low memory footprint on the end-to-end routing success is impressive: whereas RPL delivers less than 20% of packets in some scenarios, Matrix delivers 99% of packets successfully, without end-to-end mechanisms.

We evaluated the proposed protocol both analytically and by simulation. Even though Matrix is platform-independent, we implemented it as a subroutine of CTP on TinyOS and conducted simulations on TOSSIM. The results showed that, when it comes to any-to-any communication, Matrix presents significant gains in terms of reliability (higher any-to-any message delivery) and scalability (presenting a constant, as opposed to linear, memory complexity at each node) at a moderate cost of additional control messages, when compared to other state-of-the-art protocols, such as RPL.

To sum up, Matrix achieves the following essential goals that motivated our work:

- **Any-to-any routing**: Matrix enables end-to-end connectivity between hosts located within or outside the 6LoWPAN.

- **Memory efficiency**: Matrix uses compact routing tables and, therefore, is scalable to very large networks.

- **Reliability**: Matrix achieves 99% delivery without end-to-end mechanisms, and delivers $\geq$ 95% of end-to-end packets when a route exists under challenging network conditions.

- **Communication efficiency**: Matrix uses adaptive beaconing based on Trickle algorithm [11] to minimize the number of control messages in dynamic network topologies (except with node mobility).

- **Hardware independence**: Matrix does not rely on specific radio chip features, and only assumes an underlying collection tree structure.

- **IoT integration**: Matrix allocates global (and structured) IPv6 addresses to all nodes, which allow nodes to act as destinations integrated into the Internet, contributing to the realization of the Internet of Things.

The rest of this paper is organized as follows. In Section 2 we describe the Matrix protocol design. In Section 3, we analyze the message complexity of the protocol. In Section 4 we present our analytical and simulation results. In Section 5 we discuss some related work. Finally, in Section 6 we present the concluding remarks.

2. DESIGN OVERVIEW

The objective of Matrix is to enable any-to-any routing in an underlying data collection protocol for 6LoWPAN, such as CTP and RPL, while preserving memory and message efficiency, as well as adaptability to networks topology dynamics[1]. Matrix is a network layer protocol that works together with a routing protocol. Figure 1 illustrates the protocol's architecture, which is divided into: *routing engine* and *forwarding engine*. The routing engine is responsible for the address space partitioning and distribution, as well as routing table maintenance. The forwarding engine is responsible for application packet forwarding.

Matrix is comprised of the following execution phases:

1. Collection tree initialization: the collection tree (Ctree) is built by the underlying collection protocol; each node achieves a stable knowledge about who its parent is; adaptive beaconing based on Trickle algorithm [11] is used to define stability;

2. Descendants convergecast, IPv6 tree broadcast: once the collection tree is stable, the address hierarchy tree (IPtree) is built using MHCL [16]; this phase also uses adaptive beaconing to handle network dynamics; by the end of this phase, each node has received an IPv6 address range from its parent and each non-leaf node has partitioned its own address space among its children; the resulting address hierarchy is stored in the distributed IPtree, which initially has the same topology as Ctree, but in reverse, top-down, direction.

3. Standard routing: bottom-up routing is done using the collection tree, Ctree, and top-down routing is done using the address hierarchy represented by the IPtree; any-to-any

---

[1]Note that Matrix is not designed to address scenarios with node mobility, but only to work with network topology dynamics caused by changes in link quality, as well as node and link failures.

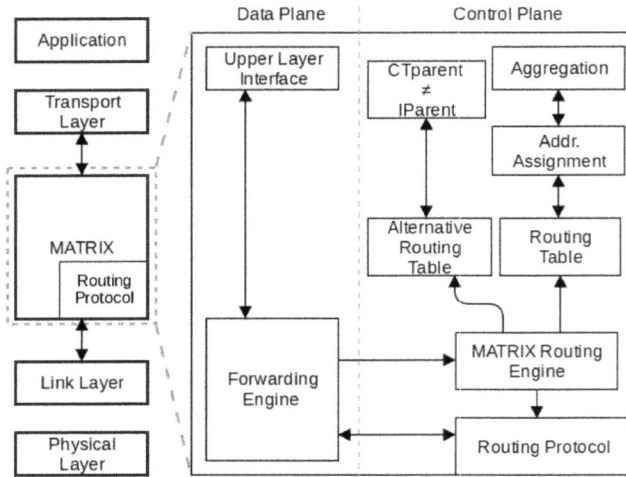

Figure 1: Matrix protocol's architecture.

routing is performed by combining bottom-up forwarding, until the least common ancestor of sender and receiver, and then top-down forwarding until the destination.

4. Alternative top-down routing table upkeep: whenever a node changes its parent in the initial collection tree, it starts sending beacons to its new parent in Ctree, requesting to upkeep an entry in its routing table with its own IPv6 range; such new links in Ctree, in reverse direction, comprise the RCtree routing tables for alternative (top-down) routing;

5. Alternative top-down routing via local broadcast: whenever a node fails to forward a data packet to the next hop/subtree in the IPtree, it broadcasts the packet to its one-hop neighborhood; upon receiving a local broadcast, all neighbors check if the destination IPv6 belongs to an address range in their RCtree table; if positive, the packet is forwarded to the correct subtree of IPtree, otherwise, the packet is dropped; we give a geometric argument and show through simulations that such events are rare.

Next we describe the architecture of Matrix in more detail.

2.1 IPv6 multihop host configuration

Matrix is built upon the idea of IPv6 hierarchical address allocation, proposed in [16, 15]. Once the collection tree is stable, the address space available to the border router of the 6LoWPAN, for instance the 64 least-significant bits of the IPv6 address (or a compressed 16-bit representation of the latter), is hierarchically partitioned among nodes in the collection tree. The (top-down) address distribution is preceded by a (bottom-up) convergecast phase, in which each node counts the total number of its descendants, i.e., the size of the subtree rooted at itself, and propagates it to its (preferred) parent. Each node saves the number of descendants of each child.

Once the root has received the (aggregate) number of descendants of its k children, it partitions the available address space into k ranges of size proportional to the size of the subtree rooted at each child, leaving a portion of the space as reserve for possible late coming connections (see Figure 2). Each node repeats the address space partitioning procedure upon receiving its own address range from the parent and sends the proportional address ranges to the respective chil-

dren, until all nodes have received an address. If a new node connects to the tree after the aggregation phase, it receives an address range from the reserved space of the respective parent node (the details of the communication routines used in this phase are described in detail in [15]).

Since the address allocation is performed in a hierarchical way, each entry in the routing table aggregates the addresses of all destination nodes in the subtree rooted at the corresponding child node.

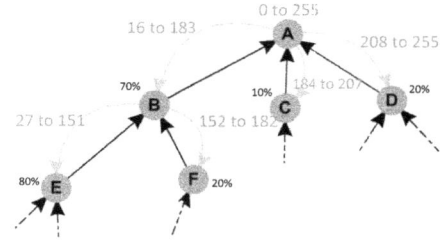

Figure 2: Example of hierarchical address assignment: (simplified) scenario with 8-bit available address space at the root and 6.25% of address reserve for delayed connections at each node.

After the address configuration phase, the network initialization is done. Each node has built the IPtree routing table with the address range of each child. All table entries are disjoint and sorted in increasing order of addresses. In this way, message forwarding can be performed in linear time using one comparison operation per table entry.

2.2 Control plane: distributed tree structures

After the network is initialized and all nodes have received an IPv6 address range, three simultaneous distributed trees are maintained on all nodes in the 6LoWPAN: **Ctree:** the collection tree, maintained by the underlying collection protocol (CTP/RPL). **IPtree:** the IPv6 address tree, built during the network initialization phase and kept static afterwards, except when new nodes join the network, in which case they receive an IPv6 range from the reserve space of the respective parent node in the collection tree. **RCtree:** the reverse collection tree, reflecting the dynamics of the collection tree in the reverse direction.

Initially, IPtree has the same topology as the reverse-collection tree $Ctree^R$, and RCtree has no links (see Figure 3(a) and 3(b)).

$$IPtree = Ctree^R \text{ and } RCtree = \emptyset$$

Whenever a change occurs in one of the links in Ctree, the new link is added in the reverse direction into RCtree and maintained as long as this topology change persists (see Figures 3(c) and 3(d)).

$$RCtree = Ctree^R \setminus IPtree$$

Therefore, RCtree is not really a tree since it contains only the reversed links present in Ctree but not in IPtree. Nevertheless, its union with the "working" links in IPtree is, in fact, a tree, which is used in the alternative top-down routing:

$$RCtree \cup (IPtree \cap Ctree^R) : \text{alternative routing tree.}$$

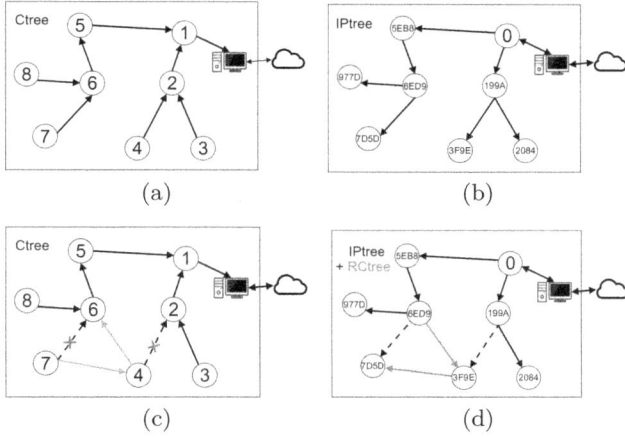

(a)

(b)

(c)

(d)

Figure 3: RCtree example: before and after two links change in the collection tree.

Each node n_i maintains the following information:

- $CTparent_i$: the ID of the current parent in the dynamic collection tree;

- $IParent_i$: the ID of the node that assigned n_i its IPv6 range initially $CTarent_i = IParent_i$);

- $IPchildren_i$: the *standard* (top-down) routing table, with address ranges of each one-hop descendent of n_i in the IPtree;

- $RChildren_i$: the *alternative* (top-down) routing table, with address ranges of one-hop descendants in the RC-tree.

Note that, each node stores only one-hop neighborhood information, so the memory footprint is $O(k)$, where k is the number of a node's children at any given moment in time, which is optimal, considering that any (optimal) top-down routing mechanism would need at least one routing entry for every (current) child in the tree topology to reach all destinations.

The routing engine (see Figure 1) is responsible for creating and maintaining the IPtree and RCtree routing tables. IPtree is created during the network initialization phase, while RCtree is updated dynamically to reflect changes in the network's link qualities. Whenever a node n_i has its $CTparent_i$ updated, and the current parent is different from its $IParent_i$ ($IParent_i \neq CTparent_i$), n_i starts sending periodic beacons to its new parent, with regular intervals (in our experiments, we set the beacon interval to $\delta/8$, where δ is the maximum interval of the Trickle timer used in CTP). Upon receiving a beacon (from a new child in the collection tree), a node ($n_j = CTparent_i$) creates and keeps an entry in its alternative routing table $RChildren_j$ with the IPv6 address range of the subtree of n_i. As soon as n_i stops using n_j as the preferred parent, it stops sending beacons to n_j. If no beacon is received from n_i after $2 \times \delta$ ms, its (alternative) routing entry is deleted. Therefore, links in RCtree

are temporary and are deleted when not present in neither the collection nor the IP trees.

2.3 Data plane: any-to-any routing

The forwarding engine (see Figure 1) is responsible for application packet forwarding. Any-to-any routing is performed by combining bottom-up forwarding, until the least common ancestor of sender and receiver, and then top-down forwarding until the destination. Upon receiving an application layer packet, each node n_i verifies whether the destination IPv6 address falls within some range $j \in IPchildren_i$: if yes then the packet is forwarded (downwards) to node n_j, otherwise, the packet is forwarded (upwards) to $CTparent_i$. Note that, since each node has an IPv6 address, in contrast to collection protocols, such as CTP and RPL, in Matrix, every node can act as a destination of messages originated inside and outside of the 6LoWPAN.

Each forwarded packet requests an acknowledgment from the next hop and can be retransmitted up to 30 times (similarly to what is done in CTP [6]). If thereafter no acknowledgment is received, then the node performs a *local broadcast*, looking for an alternative next hop in the RCtree table of a (one-hop) neighbor. The *alternative routing* process is described in detail below.

2.4 Fault tolerance and network dynamics

So why is Matrix robust to network dynamics? Note that, since routing is based on the hierarchical address allocation, if a node with the routing entries necessary to locate the next subtree becomes unreachable for longer than approximately one second (failures that last less than 1s are effectively dealt with by retransmission mechanisms available in standard link layer protocols), messages with destinations in that subtree are dropped.

When a node or link fails or changes in Ctree, RCtree reflects this change, and packets are forwarded from IPtree to RCtree via a local broadcast. The node that receives a local-broadcast checks in its RCtree whether it knows the subtree of the destination IPv6 address: if yes then is forwards the packet to the right subtree and the packet continues its path in the IPtree until the final destination.

Consider the following scenario: node X receives a packet with destination IPv6 address D (see Figure 4(a)). After consulting its standard routing table $IP - children_X$, X forwards the packet to C. However, the link X $\Rightarrow$ C fails, for some reason, and C does not reply with an acknowledgment. Then, X makes a constant number (e.g., 30 times in CTP) of retransmission attempts. Meanwhile, since node C also lost its connection to X, it decides to change its parent in the collection tree to node A (see Figure 4(b)). Having changed its parent, C starts sending beacons to A, which creates an entry in its alternative routing table $RC - children_A$ for the subtree rooted at C, and keeps it as long as it receives periodic beacons from C (which will be done as long as $CTparent_C = $ A).

Having received no ack from C, X activates the *local broadcast* mode: it sets the message's type to "LB" and broadcasts it to all its one-hop neighbors (see Figure 4(c)). Upon receiving the local broadcast, node A consults its alternative routing table and finds out that the destination address D falls within the IPv6 address range C. It then forwards the packet to C, from where the packets follows along its standard route in the subtree of C (see Figure 4(d)).

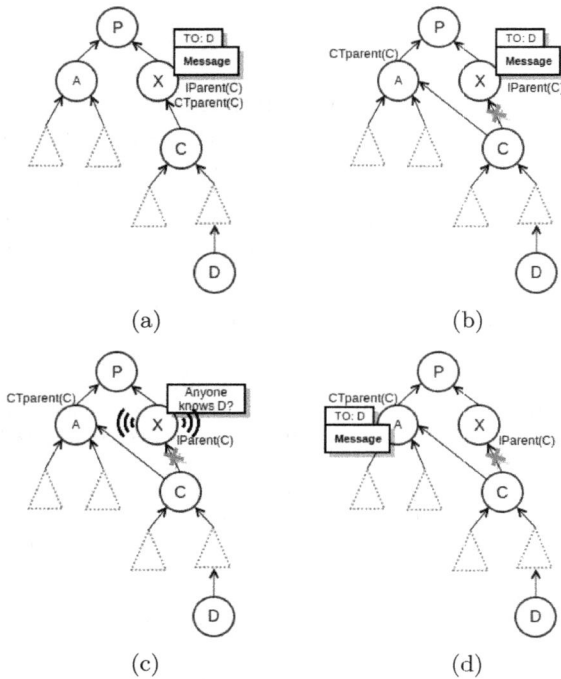

Figure 4: Alternative top-down routing.

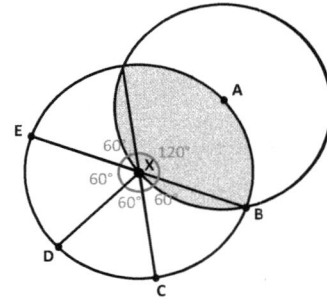

Figure 5: UDG model: the number of independent neighbors of X is at most 5.

that starts at B, and so on. This procedure can be repeated no more than 5 times, before the 360 degrees around X are covered.

Given that the maximum number of neighbors that do not know each other is very small, for any possible node distribution and density around X, the probability that two neighbors of X are independent is low. In Figure 4(c), since both X and A are neighbors of C, the probability that they are themselves neighbors is high. Similar arguments can be used to back the effectiveness of the local broadcast mechanism when dealing with different non-adjacent link and node failures.

Note that this reasoning is only valid in an open space without obstacles and, even then, does not guarantee that the message will be delivered. Nevertheless, our experiments show that this intuition is in fact correct, and Matrix has a 95%–99% message delivery success in scenarios with node failures of increasing frequency and duration.

2.5 Alternative routing: geometric rationale

The success of the local broadcast mechanism lies in the ability to forward messages top down along the IPtree, in spite of one or more link or node failures on the way. Matrix is designed to handle (non-adjacent) link or node failures and relies on a single local broadcast and temporary reverse collection links (RCtree).

Consider once again the scenario illustrated in Figure 4. When a node X is unable to forward a packet to the next hop, it activates the local broadcast mechanism, and it becomes essential that one of X's one-hop neighbors (in this case A) has replaced X as a parent of C in the collection tree. Therefore, given that the new parent of C is A, it becomes essential that X and A are neighbors. We argue that it is unlikely that this is not the case.

Our argument is of geometric nature. Since the considered 6LoWPAN is wireless, we show our argument in a unit disk graph (UDG) model [2]. We use the fact that the number of independent neighbors of any node in a UDG is bounded by a small constant, namely 5. The proof of this fact is sketched in Figure 5: consider a node X and its neighbor A. Any node located inside the gray region is a neighbor of both X and A, so any neighbor of X that is independent of (not adjacent to) A has to be outside the gray area and inside the circle around X. Let's call this neighbor B. The next independent neighbor of X has to be located outside the 60 degree sector

3. COMPLEXITY ANALYSIS

In this section, we assume a synchronous communication model with point-to-point message passing. In this model, all nodes start executing the algorithm simultaneously and time is divided into synchronous rounds, i.e., when a message is sent from node v to its neighbor u at time-slot t, it must arrive at u before time-slot $t + 1$.

We first analyze the message and time complexity of the IPv6 address allocation phase of Matrix. Then, we look into the message complexity of the control plane of Matrix after the network initialization phase.

Note that Matrix requires that an underlying acyclic topology (Ctree) has been constructed by the network before the address allocation starts, i.e., every node knows who is its parent in the Ctree is. Moreover, one of the building blocks of Matrix is the IPv6 multihop host configuration, performed by MHCL [15].

THEOREM 1. *[15] For any network of size n with a spanning collection tree Ctree rooted at node root, the message and time complexity of Matrix protocol in the address allocation phase is $Msg(Matrix^{IP}(Ctree, root)) = O(n)$ and $Time(Matrix^{IP}(T, root)) = O(depth(Ctree))$, respectively. This message and time complexity is asymptotically optimal.*

PROOF. The address allocation phase is comprised of a tree broadcast and a tree convergecast. In the broadcast operation, a message (with address allocation information) must be sent to every node by the respective parent, which needs $\Omega(n)$ messages. Moreover the message sent by the root must reach every node at distance $depth(Ctree)$ hops away, which needs $\Omega(depth(Ctree))$ time-slots. Similarly, in the convergecast operation, every node must send a message to its parent after having received a message from its children, which needs $\Omega(n)$ messages. Also, a message sent by every leaf node must reach the root, at distance $\leq depth(Ctree)$, which needs $\Omega(depth(Ctree))$ time-slots. $\square$

Next, we examine the communication cost of the routines involved in the alternative routing, performed in the presence of persistent node and link failures.

THEOREM 2. *Consider a network with n nodes and a failure event that causes $\mathcal{L}_{CT}$ links to change in the collection tree Ctree for at most Δ ms. Moreover, consider a beacon interval of δ ms. The control message complexity of Matrix to perform alternative routing is $Msg(Matrix^{RC}) = O(n)$.*

PROOF. Consider the $\mathcal{L}_{CT}$ link changes in the collection tree Ctree. Note that $\mathcal{L}_{CT} = O(n)$ since Ctree is acyclic and, therefore, has at most $n-1$ links. Every link that was changed must be inserted in the RCtree table of the respective (new) parent and kept during the interval Δ using regularly sent beacons from the child to the parent. Given a beacon interval of δ, the total number of control messages is bounded by $\Delta/\delta \times \mathcal{L}_{CT} = O(n)$. $\square$

Note that, in reality, the assumptions of synchrony and point-to-point message delivery do not hold in a 6LoWPAN. The moment in which each node joins the tree varies from node to node, such that nodes closer to the root tend to start executing the address allocation protocol earlier than nodes farther away from the root. Moreover, collisions, node and link failures can cause delays and prevent messages from being delivered. We analyze the performance of Matrix in an asynchronous model with collisions and transient node and link failures of variable duration through simulations in Section 4.

4. EVALUATION

In this section, we evaluate the performance of Matrix through simulations.

4.1 Simulation setup

Matrix was implemented as a subroutine of CTP in TinyOS [10] and the experiments were run using the TOSSIM simulator [9]. We compare Matrix with and without the local broadcast mechanism, to which we refer as MHCL (note that the implementation is different from that in [15], where it was implemented as a subroutine of RPL). RPL was implemented in Contiki [4] and was simulated on Cooja [5]. Table 1 lists the default simulation parameters used for each protocol, in a non-faulty scenario. We use the *LinkLayerModel* tool from TinyOS to generate the topology and connectivity model. We simulated a range of faulty scenarios, based on experimental data collected from TelosB sensor motes, deployed in an outdoor environment [1]. In each scenario, after every 60 seconds of simulation, each node shutdowns its radio with probability σ and keeps the radio off for a time interval uniformly distributed in $[\varepsilon - 5, \varepsilon + 5]$ seconds (see Table 2). The first scenario ($Scn1$) represents a network

without node failures. The remaining scenarios represent a combination of values of σ and ε. Note that these are all node-failure scenarios, which are significantly harsher than models that simulate link or per-packet failures only.

On top of the network layer, we ran an application, in which each node sends 10 messages to the root, and the root relies with an ack. Nodes start sending application messages 90 seconds after the simulation has started. The entire simulation takes 20 minutes. Each simulation was run 10 times. In each plot, the curve or bars represent the average, and the error bars the confidence interval of 95%.

Table 1: Simulation parameters

Parameter	Value
Base Station	1 center
Number of Nodes	100
Radio Range (m)	100
Density $(nodes/m^2)$	10
Number of experiments	10
Path Loss Exponent	4.7
Power decay (dB)	55.4
Shadowing Std Dev (dB)	3.2
Simulation duration	20 min
Application messages (node to root + ack)	10 per node
Max. Routing table size	20 entries

4.2 Results

Firstly, we turn our attention to memory efficiency of each protocol. To evaluate the usage of routing tables, we compare the number of entries used by each protocol. Each node was allocated a routing table of equal maximum size: 20 entries. In Figure 6, we show the CDFs (cumulative distribution functions) of the percentage of routing table usage among nodes[2]), and compare Matrix, RPL, and MHCL. In this plot, Matrix was simulated in the faulty scenario #10 (Table 2). Note that $> 35\%$ of nodes are leaves, i.e., do not have any descendants in the collection tree topology, and therefore use zero routing table entries. As we can see, RPL is the only protocol that uses 100% of table entries for some nodes ($\geq 30\%$ of nodes have their tables full). This is due to the fact that RPL, in the storing mode, pro-actively maintains an entry in the routing table of every node on the path from the root to each destination, which quickly fills the available memory and forces packets to be dropped. The difference between MHCL and Matrix is small: MHCL stores only the IPtree structure, whereas Matrix stores IPtree and RCtree data; the latter is kept only temporarily during parent changes in the collection tree, so its average memory usage is low.

---

[2]We measured the routing table usage of each node in one-minute intervals, then took the average over 20 minutes.

Table 2: Faulty network scenarios

$\sigma \backslash \varepsilon$	10 sec.	20 sec.	40 sec.
1%	Scenario 2	Scenario 3	Scenario 4
5%	Scenario 5	Scenario 6	Scenario 7
10%	Scenario 8	Scenario 9	Scenario 10

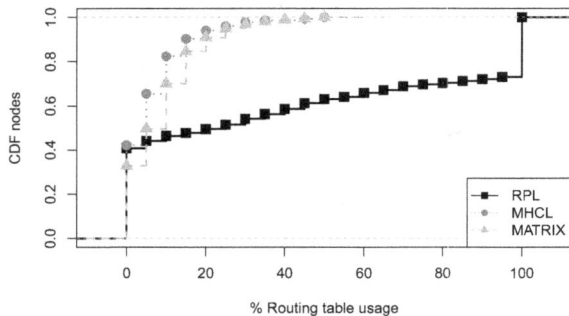

Figure 6: Routing table usage CDF. (Maximum table size = 20)

Figure 7 illustrates the amount of control traffic in our experiments (the total number of beacons sent during the entire simulation). Matrix sends fewer control packet than RPL, because it only sends additional beacons during network initialization and in case of collection tree topology updates, whereas RPL has a communication intensive maintenance of downward routes during the entire execution time.

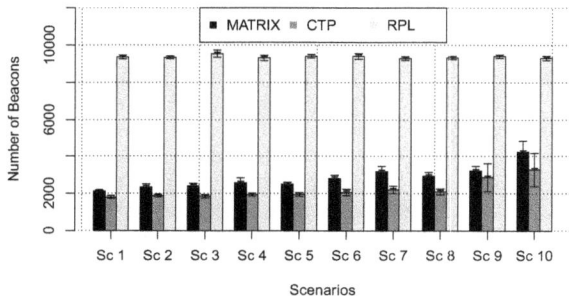

Figure 7: Number of control packets.

Figure 8 compares RAM and ROM footprints in the protocol stack of CTP, RPL and Matrix. We can see that Matrix adds only a little more than 7KB of code to CTP, allowing this protocol to perform any-to-any communication with high scalability. When compared with RPL, the execution code of Matrix requires less RAM.

Our main result is illustrated in Figure 9, which compares top-down routing success rate. We measured the total number of application (ack) messages sent downwards and successfully received by the destination.[3] In the plot, "inevitable losses" refers to the number of messages that were lost due to a failure of the destination node, in which case, there were no valid path to the destination and the packet loss was inevitable. The remaining messages were lost due to wireless collisions and node failures on the packet's path.

---

[3]We do not plot the success rate of bottom-up traffic, since it is done by the underlying collection protocol, without any intervention from Matrix .

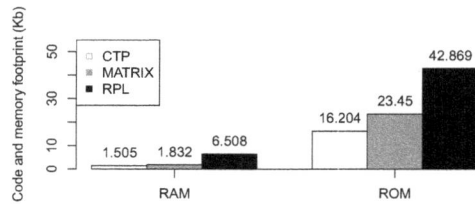

Figure 8: Code and memory footprint in bytes.

We can see that, when a valid path exists to the destination, the top-down success rate of Matrix varies between 95% and 99%. In the harshest faulty scenario 10, without the local broadcast mechanism, MHCL delivers 85% of top-down messages. With the local broadcast activated, the success rate increases to 95%, i.e., roughly 2/3 of otherwise lost messages succeed in reaching the final destination. RPL, on the other hand, delivered less than 20% of messages in all simulated scenarios, which occurs due to lack of memory to store all the top-down routes.

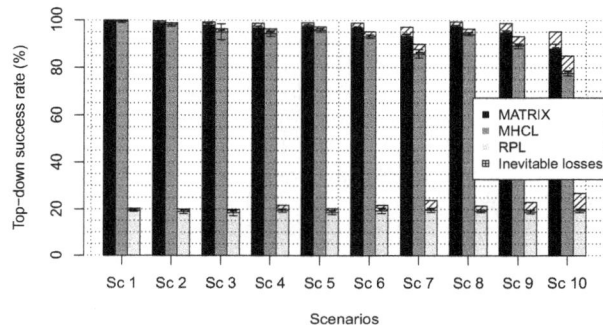

Figure 9: Top-down routing success rate.

5. RELATED WORK

AODV[17] and DSR[7] are traditional wireless protocols that allow any-to-any communication, but they were designed for 802.11 and require too many states or apply several overheads on the packet header. In the context of low-power and lossy networks, CTP[6] and CodeDrip[8] were designed for bottom-up and top-down data flows, respectively. They support communication in only one direction.

State-of-the-art routing protocols for 6lowPAN that enable any-to-any communication are RPL[19], XCTP[18], and Hydro[3]. RPL allows two modes of operation (storing and non-storing) for downwards data flows. The non-storing mode is based on source routing, and the storing mode proactively maintains an entry in the routing table of every node on the path from the root to each destination, which is not scalable to even moderate-size networks. XCTP is an extension of CTP and is based on a reactive reverse collection route creating between the root and every source node. An entry in the reverse-route table is kept for every data flow at each node on the path between the source and the destination, which is also not scalable in terms of memory footprint. Hydro protocol, like RPL, is based on a DAG (directed acyclic graph) for bottom-up communication. Source nodes need to periodically send reports to the border router, which builds a global view (typically incomplete) of the network topology.

Some more recent protocols [14, 13, 12] modified RPL to include new features. In [14], a load-balance technique is applied over nodes to decrease power consumption. In [13, 12], they provide multi-path routing protocols to improve throughput and fault tolerance.

Matrix differs from previous work by providing a reliable and scalable solution for any-to-any routing in 6LoWLAN, both in terms of routing table size and control message overhead. Moreover, it allocates global and structured IPv6 addresses to all nodes, which allow nodes to act as destinations integrated into the Internet, contributing to the realization of the Internet of Things.

Acknowledgments

This work was supported in part by CAPES, CNPq and FAPEMIG.

6. CONCLUSIONS

In this paper, we propose Matrix: a novel routing protocol that is built upon a data collection structure and is comprised of two phases: (1) network initialization, in which hierarchical IPv6 addresses, which reflect the topology of the underlying wireless network, are assigned to nodes in a multihop way; and (2) reliable any-to-any communication, which enables message and memory-efficient implementation of a wide range of new applications for 6LoWPAN.

7. REFERENCES

[1] N. Baccour, A. Koubâa, L. Mottola, M. A. Zúñiga, H. Youssef, C. A. Boano, and M. Alves. Radio link quality estimation in wireless sensor networks: A survey. *ACM Trans. Sen. Netw.*, 8(4):34:1–34:33, Sept. 2012.

[2] B. N. Clark, C. J. Colbourn, and D. S. Johnson. Unit disk graphs. *Discrete Math.*, 86(1-3):165–177, Jan. 1991.

[3] S. Dawson-Haggerty, A. Tavakoli, and D. Culler. Hydro: A hybrid routing protocol for low-power and lossy networks. In *Smart Grid Communications (SmartGridComm)*. IEEE, 2010.

[4] A. Dunkels, B. Gronvall, and T. Voigt. Contiki - a lightweight and flexible operating system for tiny networked sensors. In *IEEE LCN*, pages 455–462, Washington, DC, USA, 2004. IEEE Computer Society.

[5] J. Eriksson, F. Österlind, N. Finne, N. Tsiftes, A. Dunkels, T. Voigt, R. Sauter, and P. J. Marrón. Cooja/mspsim: Interoperability testing for wireless sensor networks. In *Proceedings of the 2Nd International Conference on Simulation Tools and Techniques*, Simutools'09, pages 27:1–27:7, 2009.

[6] O. Gnawali, R. Fonseca, K. Jamieson, D. Moss, and P. Levis. Collection tree protocol. In *Proceedings of the 7th ACM Conference on Embedded Networked Sensor Systems*, SenSys '09, pages 1–14, 2009.

[7] D. Johnson, Y. Hu, and D. Maltz. The dynamic source routing protocol (DSR) for mobile ad hoc networks for IPV4. *RFC: 4728*, 2007.

[8] N. d. S. R. Júnior, M. A. Vieira, L. F. Vieira, and O. Gnawali. Codedrip: Data dissemination protocol with network coding for wireless sensor networks. In *Wireless Sensor Networks*, pages 34–49. Springer, 2014.

[9] P. Levis, N. Lee, M. Welsh, and D. Culler. Tossim: Accurate and scalable simulation of entire tinyos applications. In *Proceedings of the 1st International Conference on Embedded Networked Sensor Systems*, SenSys '03, pages 126–137, New York, NY, USA, 2003. ACM.

[10] P. Levis, S. Madden, J. Polastre, R. Szewczyk, K. Whitehouse, A. Woo, D. Gay, J. Hill, M. Welsh, E. Brewer, et al. Tinyos: An operating system for sensor networks. In *Ambient intelligence*. Springer, 2005.

[11] P. Levis, N. Patel, D. Culler, and S. Shenker. Trickle: A self-regulating algorithm for code propagation and maintenance in wireless sensor networks. In *Proceedings of the 1st Conference on Symposium on Networked Systems Design and Implementation - Volume 1*, NSDI'04, pages 2–2, 2004.

[12] M. A. Lodhi, A. Rehman, M. M. Khan, and F. B. Hussain. Multiple path rpl for low power lossy networks. In *Wireless and Mobile (APWiMob), 2015 IEEE Asia Pacific Conference on*, pages 279–284, Aug 2015.

[13] M. N. Moghadam, H. Taheri, and M. Karrari. Multi-class multipath routing protocol for low power wireless networks with heuristic optimal load distribution. *Wirel. Pers. Commun.*, 82(2):861–881, May 2015.

[14] U. Palani, V. Alamelumangai, and A. Nachiappan. Hybrid routing and load balancing protocol for wireless sensor network. *Wireless Networks*, pages 1–8, 2015.

[15] B. Peres and O. Goussevskaia. MHCL: IPv6 Multihop Host Configuration for Low-Power Wireless Networks . http://arxiv.org/abs/1606.02674, 2016.

[16] B. S. Peres and O. Goussevskaia. Alocacao de Enderecos IPv6 em Redes Multi-hop de Radios de Baixa Potencia. In *Computer Networks and Distributed Systems (SBRC), 2015 Brazilian Symposium on*, May 2015.

[17] C. Perkins, E. Belding-Royer, and S. Das. Ad hoc on demand distance vector (AODV) routing (RFC 3561). *IETF MANET Working Group*, 2003.

[18] B. P. Santos, M. A. Vieira, and L. F. Vieira. extend collection tree protocol. In *Wireless Communications and Networking Conference (WCNC), 2015 IEEE*, pages 1512–1517, March 2015.

[19] T. Winter, P. Thubert, A. Brandt, J. Hui, R. Kelsey, P. Levis, K. Pister, R. Struik, J. Vasseur, and R. Alexander. RPL: IPv6 Routing Protocol for Low-Power and Lossy Networks. RFC 6550 (Proposed Standard), 2012.

Updating Wireless Signal Map with Bayesian Compressive Sensing

Bo Yang   Suining He   S.-H. Gary Chan
Department of Computer Science and Engineering,
The Hong Kong University of Science and Technology, Hong Kong, China
boyang@ust.hk, {sheaa, gchan}@cse.ust.hk

ABSTRACT

In a wireless system, a signal map shows the signal strength at different locations termed reference points (RPs). As access points (APs) and their transmission power may change over time, keeping an updated signal map is important for applications such as Wi-Fi optimization and indoor localization. Traditionally, the signal map is obtained by a full site survey, which is time-consuming and costly. We address in this paper how to efficiently update a signal map given sparse samples randomly crowdsourced in the space (e.g., by signal monitors, explicit human input, or implicit user participation).

We propose Compressive Signal Reconstruction (CSR), a novel learning system employing Bayesian compressive sensing (BCS) for online signal map update. CSR does not rely on any path loss model or line of sight, and is generic enough to serve as a plug-in of any wireless system. Besides signal map update, CSR also computes the estimation error of signals in terms of confidence interval. CSR models the signal correlation with a kernel function. Using it, CSR constructs a sensing matrix based on the newly sampled signals. The sensing matrix is then used to compute the signal change at all the RPs with any BCS algorithm. We have conducted extensive experiments on CSR in our university campus. Our results show that CSR outperforms other state-of-the-art algorithms by a wide margin (reducing signal error by about 30% and sampling points by 20%).

Categories and Subject Descriptors

C.2.1 [**Network Architecture and Design**]: Wireless Communication

Keywords

Signal map learning; signal change; Bayesian compressive sensing; crowdsourcing; database reconstruction.

MSWiM '16, November 13-17, 2016, Malta, Malta
© 2016 ACM. ISBN 978-1-4503-4502-6/16/11...$15.00
DOI: http://dx.doi.org/10.1145/2988287.2989132

1. INTRODUCTION

Received signal strength indicator (RSSI) exhibits spatial variation, which forms the so-called *signal map* (or *signal heat map*). Knowing the signal map in a timely manner is important for many applications. For example, in a Wi-Fi network, the signal of an access point (AP) may change over time due to AP introduction, removal, migration, power adjustment, etc. The system administrator would be interested in the current signal map so as to understand the Wi-Fi coverage, or to adjust/tune Wi-Fi settings. In fingerprint-based indoor localization, keeping its signal database updated would lead to improved localization accuracy.

Signal map is often obtained through site survey, where a professional surveyor walks through the site to measure signal values at many predefined locations termed "reference points" (RPs). As signal may evolve over time, this survey has to be conducted frequently; this is laborious, time-consuming and costly.

We consider in this paper the following problem: given a previously obtained signal map and some sparse signals newly sampled at random points in the site, how can we online update, or *reconstruct*, the signal map (in terms of signal values at RPs)? Addressing this problem can substantially cut the survey cost to keep the signal map up-to-date. As each AP signal may be considered independently, in the following we will focus on a single arbitrary AP in the site.

Signals may be *crowdsourced* in space in several ways. For example, one may install sensors [7] or monitors at different locations which report signals over time. One may also conduct explicit user input [24], where a dedicated surveyor or a volunteer samples the space at random points. Alternatively, implicit user participation may be used, where naive users may unknowingly report signals measured at their locations (as in some indoor localization system [16, 24]).

Reconstructing signal map given random sparse samples is challenging. Existing learning approaches often assume a certain RSSI signal propagation model (e.g., a log-distance path loss model), line of sight or open space [1, 15] which does not work well in complex indoor environments. Furthermore, as the measured signal is noisy, it is desirable that the reconstructed signal map has confidence interval indicating the likely RSSI range at a point.

We propose Compressive Signal Reconstruction (CSR), a novel online signal learning scheme based on *Bayesian compressive sensing* (BCS). CSR is a generic standalone module which may be integrated with any existing wireless system to keep signal map updated. CSR uses a kernel function to model the signal correlation between any pair of RPs in

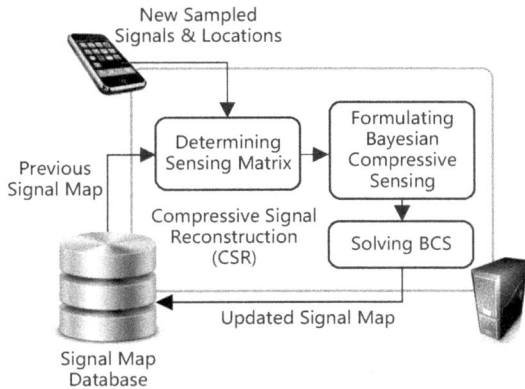

Figure 1: System framework of CSR, an online learning module for signal map reconstruction.

Table 1: Major symbols used in CSR.

Notations	Definitions
M	Number of sample neighbors (the nearest RPs)
N	Number of reference points (RPs) in the site
$(\boldsymbol{y}_t)_{M\times 1}$	$M \times 1$ vector of crowdsourced RSSI samples at time t
$(\boldsymbol{\Delta y}_t)_{M\times 1}$	Vector of crowdsourced signal map change of M RPs at time t
$(\boldsymbol{x}_{t-1})_{N\times 1}$	Vector of RSSIs at N RPs at time $t-1$
$(\boldsymbol{\Delta x}_t)_{N\times 1}$	Vector of full signal map change at N RPs at t
$\boldsymbol{e}_{M\times 1}$	Vector of additive noise in compressive sensing
$\boldsymbol{\Phi}_{M\times N}$	$M \times N$ sensing matrix in compressive sensing
$\boldsymbol{\psi}_m$	Correlation coefficients of the m-th sample neighbor and the N RPs in the signal map
$\boldsymbol{\mu}$	Vector of the mean predicted signal change
$\boldsymbol{\Sigma}$	Variance matrix of predicted signal change
$\boldsymbol{\alpha}$	Vector of reciprocals for variance of predicted $(\boldsymbol{\Delta x}_t)_{N\times 1}$
β	Reciprocal of additive noise e_m variance

the signal map (where the correlation value is high if their locations and RSSIs are similar). A new crowdsourced sample is first mapped to its closest RP location. Such RP is termed the *sample neighbor*. Using the correlations between the sample neighbor and all the other RPs, a *sensing matrix* is then formed for all the samples. Given the sensing matrix, CSR computes the signal change for all the RPs using compressive sensing.

To the best of our knowledge, this is the first work applying BCS to address online signal map learning. Note that CSR is general enough to apply upon any wireless signal, though most of the discussions and experiments in the paper are in the context of Wi-Fi. Unlike other signal reconstruction schemes, the BCS in CSR does not assume any radio propagation model or line-of-sight condition. Furthermore, BCS provides estimation uncertainty, in terms of a confidence bar, for each reconstructed RSSI at an RP.

We show the system framework of CSR in Figure 1. CSR may be executed periodically (say, in every hour) or in fixed batches (after collecting say a certain number of samples). The flow is as follows:

1) *Signal Map Initialization*: The signal map is initialized by an offline site survey. Pairs of <location, RSSI>'s are stored in the database and form the initial signal map which may evolve over time with CSR.

2) *Determining Sensing Matrix for Newly Sampled Signals*: In the online phase, given the location of a newly crowdsourced RSSI, CSR first finds its sample neighbor. Given this RP, CSR computes its correlation with all the other RPs using a kernel function. With multiple samples, a sensing matrix for compressive sensing is then formed based on these correlation values.

3) *Formulating Bayesian Compressive Sensing*: With the sample neighbor, CSR first calculates the RSSI change between the original signal and the newly sampled RSSI. Given all such RSSI changes and the sensing matrix, CSR then formulates the signal map reconstruction into a Bayesian compressive sensing problem.

4) *Solving BCS*: CSR solves the above BCS (via some existing algorithm), and finds all the signal changes at the RPs in the map. The updated <location, RSSI>'s are then returned to the database.

We have conducted extensive experiments on CSR in our university campus. Our results validate and confirm that CSR adapts to signal changes for different indoor environments. CSR outperforms other state-of-the-art algorithms such as the Basis Pursuit [8] and the Log-distance Path Loss

model [1, 25] with substantially lower RSSI error (by more than 30%) and fewer sampling points (often by more than 20%). By integrating CSR with a Wi-Fi fingerprint-based localization system [2], we also reduce the localization error significantly (by more than 40%).

This paper is organized as follows. We first discuss the background and preliminary of CSR in Section 2. After that, the signal map reconstruction problem and determining sensing matrix are presented in Section 3. Then the algorithm of CSR in solving BCS is discussed in Section 4. We finally illustrate our experimental results in Section 5, followed by conclusion in Section 6.

2. BACKGROUND & PRELIMINARY

We review previous work in this section, first on survey reduction and signal map construction with crowdsourcing (Section 2.1), followed by the algorithms in signal reconstruction (Section 2.2). Finally we review the basic principles of Bayesian compressive sensing (Section 2.3). We show the important symbols used in this paper in Table 1.

2.1 Survey Reduction with Crowdsourcing

In order to save time and labor in the signal map construction, a number of crowdsourcing approaches have been proposed [11,14]. Recent crowdsourcing studies focus on explicit user participation and implicit update through extra-infrastructure.

Users may explicitly input her/his current locations and RSSIs to update the signal map [5]. In practice, such explicit participation may be inconvenient for users.

To address this, implicit approaches have been studied, which make use of a wide range of extra devices or sensing techniques such as RFID [13], inertial navigation systems [28], and Wi-Fi sniffers [20]. These infrastructures estimate user locations and their RSSIs. Then the system generates the updated signal map.

Our signal map reconstruction with CSR is orthogonal to above works. CSR focuses on reconstructing the outdated signal map regardless of how the signals are crowdsourced. Explicit user input or implicit sensor-assisted crowdsourcing in above studies can be easily integrated with CSR to achieve survey reduction. For example, crowdsourced <RSSI, location>'s may be easily accumulated through above approaches and form the initial signal map (initial input) for our CSR. Furthermore, CSR does not assume, and hence is not restricted to any sensor measurement model or crowdsourcing user mobility like [7]. Therefore, it is more general and can be applied in more complex indoor environments.

2.2 Signal Map Reconstruction Algorithms

Signal reconstruction has been widely studied in recent years [18]. Gaussian process (GP) [1,12] has been proposed for signal map construction. Early works like [12] utilize GP to reconstruct signal map. Later works utilize GP to model spatial distribution in the site [1]. In contrast to GP, our work on Bayesian compressive sensing does not assume any signal propagation model. Therefore, it is more general and can be applied in more complex indoor environments.

More recent works study signal reconstruction using matrix completion [17,23].Some have studied using matrix completion to construct missing RSSI values in signal map [17]. The work in [23] also utilizes matrix completion in order to reduce site survey. Given limited site survey where not all AP signals are covered, these works consider the signal map in the site as an incomplete matrix and recover the unknown matrix elements, i.e., the unknown AP signals through the matrix completion. However, the matrix completion constructs the signal map in a deterministic manner. Our BCS considers the uncertainty in signals and is more robust towards the noisy measurements. Furthermore, CSR provides the confidence interval of estimation, which can be used in many probabilistic applications such as the Horus localization system [29]. Note that, in contrast to the work in [7], CSR does not assume any knowledge on environmental factors (building structure change, AP power alteration, etc.) which cause the signal map change; it updates the signal map simply based on the signal difference. Therefore, it is general enough to apply in complex signal environments.

2.3 Compressive Sensing

Compressive Sensing (CS) is a novel signal reconstruction approach which takes in far fewer samples than required in traditional Nyquist paradigm [8]. It has been applied in a wide range of areas including signal processing and image reconstruction.

The objective of CS framework is to find a sparse solution $x \in \mathbb{R}^N$ of linear equation $y = \Phi x$, where the measurement vector $y \in \mathbb{R}^M$ and the $M \times N$ sensing matrix Φ are known. Note that $M \le N$, i.e., the linear system is underdetermined. Given the vector x, let ℓ_0-norm be the number of nonzero entries of x. One simple way to pose a CS framework is to solve the following optimization problem [10],

$$\hat{x} = \arg\min_{x \in \mathbb{R}^n} \|x\|_0, \quad \text{subject to} \quad y = \Phi x. \quad (1)$$

As above ℓ_0-minimization problem is NP-hard, an alternative solution is to use ℓ_1-norm of x (i.e., $\|x\|_1 = \Sigma_{n=1}^N |x_n|$) under a sufficient constraint Restricted Isometry Property (RIP) [6] based on the convex optimization. Many other optimization-based greedy algorithms are developed to reconstruct sparse signal x, such as OMP [27] and CoSaMP [22].

In practice, the CS measurements y are usually corrupted by the environmental noises, denoted as $e \in \mathbb{R}^M$. This noise can be approximated as a zero-mean Gaussian distribution

with unknown variance σ^2. Then the CS model can be expressed as $y = \Phi x + e$. We can consider the Gaussian likelihood function of signal y given x and e, i.e.,

$$p\left(y|x, \sigma^2\right) = \frac{1}{(2\pi\sigma^2)^{m/2}} \exp\left(-\frac{\|y - \Phi x\|^2}{2\sigma^2}\right). \quad (2)$$

Given Φ and measurements y, and considering prior knowledge about sparse vector x and noise variance σ^2, the above CS reconstruction becomes a Bayesian learning problem, or the so-called *Bayesian compressive sensing* (BCS). Particularly, BCS aims to seek the full posterior values of x and σ^2, given the corresponding prior knowledge and the new measurements. BCS outperforms the traditional deterministic CS by the following two aspects:

Traditional CS requires RIP in order to be solvable, which may not be satisfied in many application scenarios [21]. Unlike traditional CS, BCS only relies on the priori statistical sparse properties of signals, which can be easily satisfied for signal map reconstruction.

Traditional CS outputs only the reconstructed signal map. BCS further provides confidence levels in terms of error bars for reconstructed signals [21], which can be further utilized in other application scenarios such as probabilistic localization algorithms [29].

3. PROBLEM OF SIGNAL MAP LEARNING

We first present the signal map reconstruction problem based on compressive sensing (CS) in Section 3.1. Given this problem and CS formulation, we then present in Section 3.2 how to determine coefficients of the sensing matrix.

3.1 Signal Map Reconstruction Problem

Suppose there are N RPs in the site map for an AP, which are labeled by $n \in \{1, 2, \ldots, N\}$. We show in Figure 2 a survey site with RPs (locations may not be regular). The signal of the n-th RP at time $t-1$ is given by $\boldsymbol{f}_{t-1}^n = ([L_x^n, L_y^n], x_{t-1}^n)$, where x_{t-1}^n represents RSSI of that RP. The RSSIs of the entire signal map can then be represented as an N-dimensional vector $\boldsymbol{x}_{t-1} \in \mathbb{R}^N$, or $\boldsymbol{x}_{t-1} = [x_{t-1}^1, \ldots, x_{t-1}^N]^T$.

Over a period of time, RSSIs $\boldsymbol{x}_{t-1}$ of the signal map evolves to $\boldsymbol{x}_t$. The N-dimensional vector of *full signal changes* on all N RPs from $t-1$ to t are given by $\boldsymbol{\Delta x}_t = \boldsymbol{x}_t - \boldsymbol{x}_{t-1}$, where $\boldsymbol{\Delta x}_t = [\Delta x_t^1, \ldots, \Delta x_t^N]^T$. The objective of the signal map reconstruction problem is to estimate $\boldsymbol{\Delta x}_t$.

In the online reconstruction phase, a batch of new samples are crowdsourced and aggregated from time $t-1$ to t. Each new sample is first mapped to its physically nearest RP (with the smallest Euclidean distance on the 2-D map), which is the red point shown in Figure 3. If there are multiple new crowdsourced samples mapped to the same RP, their RSSIs are averaged and stored for that RP. After that, the batch of new samples are mapped to M different RPs, forming the M crowdsourced sample neighbors (M RPs which are nearest to the crowdsourced samples). Each sample neighbor contains the new signal sample y_t^m. These are the sparse sampling points on the whole signal map.

Specifically, similar to $\boldsymbol{f}_{t-1}^n$, we define the m-th crowdsourced sample neighbor at time t as $\widehat{\boldsymbol{f}}_t^m = ([\widetilde{L}_x^m, \widetilde{L}_y^m], y_t^m)$, where its coordinates $[\widetilde{L}_x^m, \widetilde{L}_y^m]$ represent the location of the nearest RP in the map.The crowdsourced RSSIs of M sample neighbors are aligned as $\boldsymbol{y}_t \in \mathbb{R}^M$, or $\boldsymbol{y}_t = [y_t^1, \ldots, y_t^M]^T$.

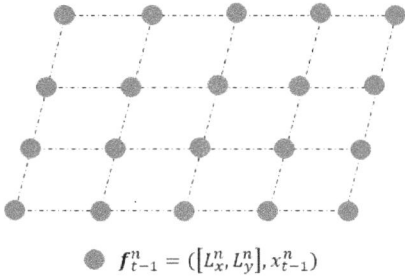

Signal map at time $t-1$

$\bullet$ $\boldsymbol{f}_{t-1}^n = ([L_x^n, L_y^n], x_{t-1}^n)$

Figure 2: The signal map at time $t-1$. Each RP contains $\boldsymbol{f}_{t-1}^n = ([L_x^n, L_y^n], x_{t-1}^n)$.

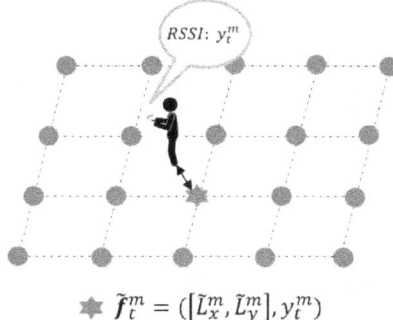

RSSI: y_t^m

$\bigstar$ $\widetilde{\boldsymbol{f}}_t^m = ([\widetilde{L}_x^m, \widetilde{L}_y^m], y_t^m)$

Figure 3: Finding the nearest RP as one crowdsourced sample neighbor.

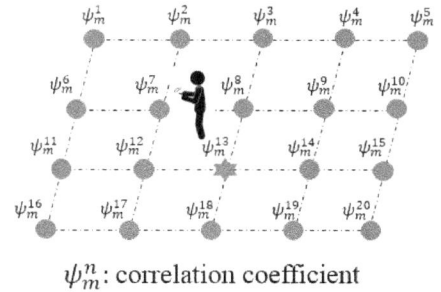

ψ_m^n: correlation coefficient

Figure 4: The correlation coefficients between the sample neighbor and all RPs.

The RSSI change on the m-th sample neighbor can be calculated as the RSSI difference between new sample y_t^m crowdsourced at time t, and the previous RSSI $\widetilde{x}_{t-1} \in \boldsymbol{x}_{t-1}$ of the nearest RP on the previous signal map, i.e., $\Delta y_t^m = y_t^m - \widetilde{x}_{t-1}$. Then the vector $\Delta \boldsymbol{y}_t \in \mathbb{R}^M$ represents the total *crowdsourced signal changes* of the M sample neighbors, i.e., $\Delta \boldsymbol{y}_t = [\Delta y_t^1, \ldots, \Delta y_t^M]^T$. We consider that each RSSI change in $\Delta \boldsymbol{y}_t$ has additive measurement noise $e_m \sim \mathcal{N}(0, \sigma^2)$.

Given a previous signal map $\boldsymbol{x}_{t-1}$ and sparse crowdsourced samples $\boldsymbol{y}_t$, we first determine the crowdsourced signal changes $\Delta \boldsymbol{y}_t$ at the sample neighbors (the nearest RPs). Then the signal map reconstruction learns the full signal changes $\Delta \boldsymbol{x}_t$ based on these sparse $\Delta \boldsymbol{y}_t$. The key problem of signal map reconstruction is how to determine $\Delta \boldsymbol{x}_t$ given only $\Delta \boldsymbol{y}_t$. Similar to compressive sensing, we consider that an individual crowdsourced signal change Δy_t^m can be formulated as a subsample from the full signal changes $\Delta \boldsymbol{x}_t$. Then we can leverage the compressive sensing to recover the entire signal map from these sparse samples.

Specifically, for each sample neighbor $\widetilde{f}_t^m$, we find its correlation with all other RPs in the site, as illustrated in Figure 4. Let ψ_m^n be the sampling or sensing coefficient between crowdsourced signal change Δy_t^m and the n-th full signal change Δx_t^n. For each individual crowdsourced signal change Δy_t^m, we consider the linear sampling relationship between it and the full signal changes $\Delta \boldsymbol{x}_t$ in the entire signal map as

$$\Delta y_t^m = \boldsymbol{\psi}_m \Delta \boldsymbol{x}_t + e_m, \tag{3}$$

where $\boldsymbol{\psi}_m = [\psi_m^1, \quad \psi_m^2, \quad \ldots, \quad \psi_m^n, \quad \ldots, \quad \psi_m^N]$, and $\sum_{n=1}^N \psi_m^n = 1$, $0 \le \psi_m^n \le 1$. In other word, the crowdsourced signal change is considered as the weighted sum of full signal changes at all RPs. We consider that the higher ψ_m^n is, the more likely that the crowdsourced signal change is near the n-th RP and their signals are correlated. Such a formulation is valid as significant signal map change happens in a close region (due to, for example, crowds of people and new wall partition).

Let $\boldsymbol{e}_{M \times 1} = [e_1, \ldots, e_m, \ldots, e_M]^T$. To summarize, for M crowdsourced signal changes $\Delta \boldsymbol{y}_t$, the whole subset sampling relationship with full signal changes $\Delta \boldsymbol{x}_t$ is given by

$$(\Delta \boldsymbol{y}_t)_{M \times 1} = \boldsymbol{\Phi}_{M \times N} (\Delta \boldsymbol{x}_t)_{N \times 1} + \boldsymbol{e}_{M \times 1}, \tag{4}$$

where the sensing matrix Φ is

$$\boldsymbol{\Phi} = [\boldsymbol{\psi}_1, \quad \boldsymbol{\psi}_2, \quad \ldots, \quad \boldsymbol{\psi}_m, \quad \ldots, \quad \boldsymbol{\psi}_M]^\mathsf{T} \tag{5}$$

Our signal map reconstruction problem finally becomes *how to find $\Delta \boldsymbol{x}_t$ in Equation (4) given $\Delta \boldsymbol{y}_t$ and $\boldsymbol{\Phi}$.* Then given full signal changes, we construct the full signal map $\boldsymbol{x}_t$ as

$$\boldsymbol{x}_t = \boldsymbol{x}_{t-1} + \Delta \boldsymbol{x}_t. \tag{6}$$

3.2 Forming the Sensing Matrix

In this section, we discuss how to determine the sensing matrix $\boldsymbol{\Phi}$ in above BCS formulation. Recall that for each new sample, we find in the signal map the nearest RP to form the sample neighbor $\widetilde{\boldsymbol{f}}_t^m$. Then we need to find other RPs in the signal map whose signals are correlated with this crowdsourced sample neighbor (the nearest RP). We consider that two RPs are highly correlated based on the following two criteria:

Criterion I. Small physical distance from the sample neighbor $\widetilde{\boldsymbol{f}}_t^m$: The physical distance $\mathcal{D}_m^n$ (unit: m) between $\widetilde{\boldsymbol{f}}_{t-1}^m$ and $\boldsymbol{f}_{t-1}^n$ is calculated by $\mathcal{D}_m^n = \sqrt{(\widetilde{L}_x^m - L_x^n)^2 + (\widetilde{L}_y^m - L_y^n)^2}$. The smaller distance $\mathcal{D}_m^n$ is, the signals at these two locations may be more correlated as they have similar distances from APs and their surrounding environments are similar [1]. After calculating the distance for each RP, we normalize each $\mathcal{D}_m^n$ by $\mathcal{D}_m^n = \mathcal{D}_m^n / \left(\sum_{n=1}^N \mathcal{D}_m^n \right)$.

Criterion II. Small difference between RSSIs at two reference points (RPs): Absolute RSSI difference $\mathcal{R}_m^n$ (unit: dB) between $\widetilde{\boldsymbol{f}}_{t-1}^m$ and $\boldsymbol{f}_{t-1}^n$ is calculated by $\mathcal{R}_m^n = |\widetilde{x}_{t-1} - x_{t-1}^n|$. The smaller RSSI difference $\mathcal{R}_m^n$, the more likely that these two locations share similar signal change in the signal space of the new signal map [23]. Similar to $\mathcal{D}_m^n$, we normalize each $\mathcal{R}_m^n$ by $\mathcal{R}_m^n = \mathcal{R}_m^n / \left(\sum_{n=1}^N \mathcal{R}_m^n \right)$.

Combining above criteria, we implement an RBF kernel function [9] to evaluate correlation between the sample neighbor and other RPs. Formally, the correlation between $\widetilde{\boldsymbol{f}}_{t-1}^m$ and $\boldsymbol{f}_{t-1}^n$ is given by $s_m^n \triangleq \exp\left\{ -\eta \left[(\theta \mathcal{D}_m^n)^2 + ((1-\theta)\mathcal{R}_m^n)^2 \right] \right\}$, where parameter η represents the sensitivity and θ ($0 \le \theta \le 1$) represents the weight between physical distance $\mathcal{D}_m^n$ and RSSI difference $\mathcal{R}_m^n$ (both η and θ are determined empirically and will be described in our experiment). For an individual crowdsourced signal change Δy_t^m, each of the correlation coefficients s_m^n is normalized as $\psi_m^n = \frac{s_m^n}{\sum_{n=1}^N s_m^n}$. To summarize, given a signal map $\boldsymbol{x}_{t-1}$ and RP locations, we map the new samples $\boldsymbol{y}_t$ to their corresponding nearest RPs. Then we find the crowdsourced signal changes $\Delta \boldsymbol{y}_t$ at those sample neighbors. Then based on Δy_t and sensing matrix Φ, through some compressive sensing algorithm we find the full signal changes Δx_t.

4. BCS FOR SIGNAL RECONSTRUCTION

Based on the problem in Equation (4), in this section we present how to formulate BCS for signal reconstruction. In Section 4.1, we present how to formulate BCS to learn signal changes. Then in Section 4.2, we discuss how to solve the compressive sensing, followed by complexity analysis in Section 4.3.

4.1 Formulating BCS

In the following, we first discuss the probabilistic preliminaries in our BCS formulation. Firstly, RSSI value of each RP at time $t-1$ is modeled as a Gaussian distribution, i.e.,

$$x_{t-1}^n \sim \mathcal{N}\left(\bar{x}_{t-1}^n, (\sigma_{t-1}^n)^2\right), \quad (7)$$

where $\bar{x}_{t-1}^n$ represents mean value and $(\sigma_{t-1}^n)^2$ is RSSI variance. Then RSSI change $\Delta x_t^n = x_t^n - x_{t-1}^n$ from time $t-1$ to t is also a Gaussian distribution, i.e., $\Delta x_t^n \sim \mathcal{N}\left(\Delta \bar{x}_t^n, (\sigma_{t-1}^n)^2 + (\sigma_t^n)^2\right)$, where $\Delta \bar{x}_t^n$ represents mean value of Δx_t^n. Δx_{t-1} can be considered as prior distribution of Δx_t. Based on Equation (2), we consider

$$p\left(\Delta y_t | \Delta x_t, \sigma^2\right) = \frac{1}{(2\pi\sigma^2)^{\frac{M}{2}}} \exp\left(-\frac{\|\Delta y_t - \Phi \Delta x_t\|^2}{2\sigma^2}\right). \quad (8)$$

From Bayesian point of view, the objective is to find full posterior density function of Δx_t, given prior distribution of full signal changes $p(\Delta x_t)$ and the crowdsourced signal changes Δy_t. The signal map reconstruction in CSR becomes a problem of finding Δx_t in order to

$$\begin{aligned} \arg\max_{\Delta x_t} \quad & p\left(\Delta x_t | \Delta y_t, \sigma^2\right), \\ \text{subject to} \quad & \Delta x_t \sim p(\Delta x_t). \end{aligned} \quad (9)$$

Based on Equations (7) and (8), posterior distribution of Δx_t is also Gaussian distribution, i.e.,

$$p(\Delta x_t | \Delta y_t, \sigma^2) \sim \mathcal{N}(\mu, \Sigma), \quad (10)$$

where μ and Σ are the mean of posterior full signal changes Δx_t and corresponding covariance, respectively. Once μ and Σ are determined, full signal values are updated by Equation (6). The variance Σ, representing the confidence level, is also stored for later use.

4.2 Solving BCS

In this section, we present how to learn posterior $p(\Delta x_t)$ based on sparse crowdsourced signal changes Δy_t and prior distribution of Δx_t and σ^2. Let α_n be the reciprocal of $(\sigma_{t-1}^n)^2 + (\sigma_t^n)^2$, and $\alpha = [\alpha_1, \ldots, \alpha_n]$. Given $\Delta x_t^n \sim \mathcal{N}(\Delta \bar{x}_t^n, \alpha_n^{-1})$, we have $p(\Delta x_t | \alpha) = \prod_{n=1}^N \mathcal{N}\left(\Delta \bar{x}_t, \alpha_n^{-1}\right)$. Let β be the precision of noise e (i.e., $\beta = \sigma^{-2}$). Initial Δx_0 and β can be either extracted from the initial version of signal map at time 0, or be simply defined as general prior probability distribution such as hierarchical prior [4].

Posterior distribution of full signal changes Δx_t and parameters α, and β is denoted as $p(\Delta x_t, \alpha, \beta | \Delta y_t)$, given crowdsourced signal changes Δy_t. Then

$$p(\Delta x_t, \alpha, \beta | \Delta y_t) = p(\Delta x_t | \alpha, \beta, \Delta y_t) p(\alpha, \beta | \Delta y_t). \quad (11)$$

In above Equation (11), $p(\Delta x_t | \alpha, \beta, \Delta y_t)$, the posterior distribution, can be computed analytically [26] as

$$p(\Delta x_t | \alpha, \beta, \Delta y_t) = \frac{p(\Delta y_t | \Delta x_t, \beta) p(\Delta x_t | \alpha)}{p(\Delta y_t | \alpha, \beta)}$$

$$= (2\pi)^{-\frac{N}{2}} |\Sigma|^{-\frac{1}{2}} \exp\left(-\frac{1}{2}(\Delta x_t - \mu)^\mathsf{T} \Sigma^{-1} (\Delta x_t - \mu)\right),$$

where posterior mean μ and covariance Σ are

$$\mu = \beta \Sigma \Phi^\mathsf{T} \Delta y_t, \quad \Sigma = (\beta \Phi^\mathsf{T} \Phi + A)^{-1}, \quad (12)$$

and $A = \mathrm{diag}(\alpha_1, \alpha_2 \ldots \alpha_n \ldots, \alpha_N)$.

As μ and Σ rely on parameters α and β, we now need to find α and β to maximize posterior distribution $p(\alpha, \beta | \Delta y_t)$, i.e., the second term on right side of Equation (11).

We apply the type II maximum likelihood [26] to estimate the above parameters. Let Σ_{nn} be the n-th diagonal value of Σ, i.e., the n-th signal RSSI change variance as shown in Equation (12). We can obtain the updated α_n^{new} as

$$\alpha_n^{\mathrm{new}} = \frac{1 - \alpha_n \Sigma_{nn}}{\mu_n^2}, \quad n \in \{1, 2 \ldots N\}, \quad (13)$$

where μ_n is the n-th entry of vector μ. Similar to α_n^{new}, we have

$$\beta^{\mathrm{new}} = \frac{M - Tr(I - A\Sigma)}{\|\Delta y_t - \Phi \mu\|_2^2}, \quad (14)$$

where $Tr(A)$ is defined as the trace (the sum of diagonal elements) of matrix A. Given the initial values of α and β, μ and Σ can be calculated through Equation (12), and then α and β can be further iteratively updated by Equation (13) and (14) until convergence.

To summarize, to reconstruct the signal map x_t at time t, BCS learns the full signal changes Δx_t based on the sample neighbors y_t and the previous signal map x_{t-1} at time $t-1$. After finding Δx_t, CSR returns the updated x_t to signal map database for other applications such as Wi-Fi monitoring or indoor localization.

4.3 Complexity Analysis

We briefly analyze the reconstruction complexity as follows. At time $t-1$, we have a signal map for each AP and we consider $\mathcal{O}(N)$ RPs to be reconstructed at time t. Suppose there are M' pairs of <RSSI, location>'s fed to CSR and they are mapped to M crowdsourced sample neighbors ($M' \geq M$) in $\mathcal{O}(M'N)$ time. During each reconstruction (i.e., at time t), M crowdsourced RSSI samples are accumulated. Determining sensing matrix Φ for M crowdsourced samples takes $\mathcal{O}(MN)$ (Section 3.2). It takes $\mathcal{O}(M)$ to find the crowdsourced signal changes Δy_t (Section 3.1). In our experiment, when determining Δx_t for signal map reconstruction, we leverage variational Bayesian algorithm [3,19], which takes $\mathcal{O}(M^3)$ (Section 4.2).

To summarize, reconstructing the signal map of one AP over N RPs in CSR takes

$$\mathcal{O}(M'N + M^3). \quad (15)$$

5. EXPERIMENTAL EVALUATION

In this section, we present the experimental evaluation over CSR in our HKUST campus. In Section 5.1, we show the experimental settings and performance metrics of CSR. Then in Section 5.2, we evaluate the performance of CSR compared with state-of-the-art algorithms.

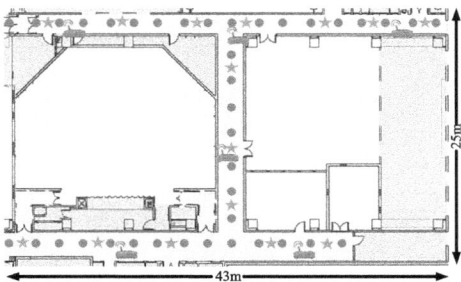

Figure 5: Floor map of the corridor area for experiment (red points are RPs, green stars illustrate crowdsource points). The deployed APs are also marked on the map.

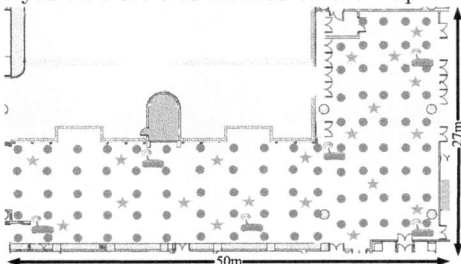

Figure 6: Floor map of the hallway area for experiment (red points are RPs, green stars illustrate crowdsource points). The deployed APs are also marked on the map.

5.1 Settings and Performance Metrics

We conduct all experiments on two indoor scenarios on our university campus. One is a typical corridor environment ($43 \times 25\ m^2$) with many wall partitions, whose floor plan is shown in Figure 5. Another one is a spacious hallway ($50 \times 27\ m^2$), whose floor plan is shown in Figure 6.

Besides environmental disturbance such as metal objects, crowds of people, etc., we also consider the AP power alteration in our experiment to enrich the signal map change studies. In Figures 5 and 6, we show the locations of deployed APs. 6 TP-Link TL-MR3020 APs are installed in each site. We manually adjust the transmission power of 3 APs and move physical locations of other 3 APs over time ($3 \sim 5$ meters apart from previous locations). In this way, we simulate the AP transmission power adjustment (due to firmware update or hardware degradation, etc.) and AP physical location changes (due to introduction/removal of wall partition or decoration, etc.). We take into account these possible factors on signal map change, and do not differentiate them in our signal map reconstruction for generality. Meanwhile, the official APs deployed by our university may also experience unknown signal fluctuation or alteration. In our experiment,we evaluate the RSSI reconstruction error with both our own APs and the official ones deployed by the university.

To construct an initial signal map, we conduct RSSI collection on 38 RPs in corridor and 86 RPs in hallway. The density of RPs (the distance between two neighboring RPs) is 3 m in both sites. At each RP, at each of the 4 directions (north, south, west and east) we form 1 RSSI vector. Then we have respectively 152 and 344 RSSI vectors in these two sites. We utilize Xiaomi Red Mi 2 for data collection. Red dots in Figure 5 and 6 represent locations of RPs.

Besides the initial signal map, we randomly collect RSSI samples every 0.5 h to simulate the crowdsourcing process. In Figures 5 and 6, the ground-truth locations of crowd-

sourced RSSIs are illustrated as green stars. The RSSI crowdsourcing is conducted in the corridor between April 7th and April 25th, 2016, while in the hallway it is conducted between February 24th and February 29th, 2016. Meanwhile, a manual site survey is conducted every day and the collected fingerprints are used as ground truth to evaluate the reconstruction accuracy.

We present the performance metrics as follows. For each AP, we denote the RSSI at the n-th RP in the previous signal map at time $t-1$ as x_{t-1}^n. At time t, let the ground-truth RSSI at the n-th RP as $\dot{x}_t^n$. Meanwhile, we denote the reconstructed RSSI through a certain scheme as x_t^n at that RP. Then for each RP n, the *reconstruction error* (dB) is defined as the absolute difference between the ground-truth RSSI and the reconstructed one at time t, i.e., $e_{\mathrm{rec}}^n = |\dot{x}_t^n - x_t^n|$. If e_{rec}^n is close to 0, the reconstructed RSSI closely match the ground-truth. We also find the cumulative density function (CDF) and the mean of the reconstruction errors e_{rec}^n's on all RPs of all APs in each survey site. To illustrate the signal change, we also evaluate the RSSI difference between the current and previous signals when no signal map reconstruction is conducted, i.e., $e_{\mathrm{true}}^n = |\dot{x}_t^n - x_{t-1}^n|$. We also compare CSR with the following state-of-art reconstruction algorithms:

Basis Pursuit (BP) Reconstruction: BP algorithm is one of deterministic reconstruction methods for compressive sensing framework [8]. Similar to matrix completion method, BP uses convex optimization to predict the signals.

Log-distance Path Loss (LDPL) Reconstruction: In LDPL reconstruction, propagation model is widely used to predict signals [1,25]. In our experiment, we implement least squares to estimate the parameters in the propagation model and then predict RSSI in the site.

An initial signal map is used as the "*Without Reconstruction*" case to illustrate the actual change of signal map RSSIs. To evaluate the performance in dynamic environment, we also vary the number of crowdsourced samples and location input error among crowdsourced signals.

To evaluate the benefits over WLAN application, we incorporate CSR into a Wi-Fi fingerprint-based indoor localization system [2]. Experiments are also conducted at the same corridor shown in Figure 5. The initial fingerprint database or the outdated signal map was constructed in September 2015. To update fingerprints, in the first week of April 2016 we randomly collect new samples at sparse locations covering 25% of the site. We append RSSI readings of newly detected APs and remove those APs which are no longer detected. Given the fingerprints updated by CSR, a weighted k-nearest neighbors algorithm (WKNN) is applied to estimate the user locations. The *localization error* is calculated by the Euclidean distance between the ground-truth location and the estimated one.

5.2 Illustrative Experimental Results

Figure 7 illustrates the signal map reconstruction results of an AP using CSR in the corridor environment. We also show the prediction error bars in the figure. We leverage 30% crowdsourced samples in the whole site. In this figure, black crosses represent the original and outdated RSSIs, while the blue diamonds are the ground-truth signals. Their difference in signal level indicates that the signal map has changed. The signal map is then updated by CSR, and the red circles are the adapted RSSI values. We can observe that

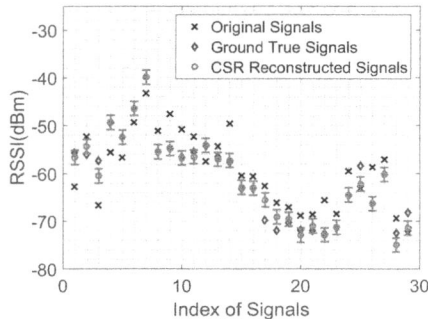

Figure 7: RSSI reconstruction results using CSR for one AP at different RPs.

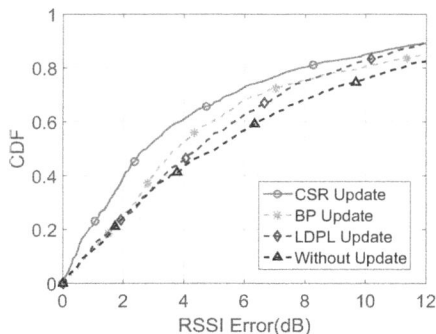

Figure 8: CDF of RSSI reconstruction error (dB) in corridor.

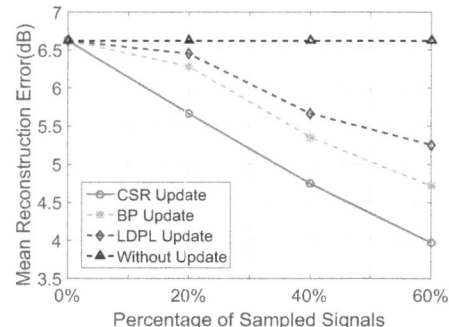

Figure 9: Mean reconstruction error versus percentage of samples in corridor.

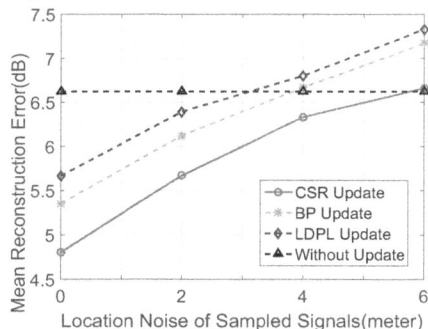

Figure 10: Mean reconstruction error versus location input error in corridor.

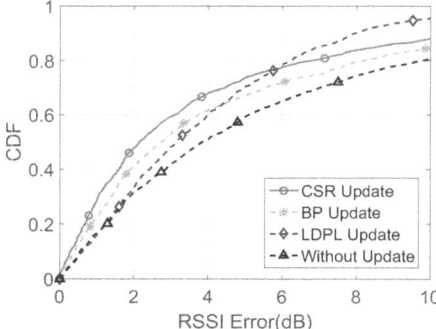

Figure 11: CDF of RSSI reconstruction error (dB) in the hallway.

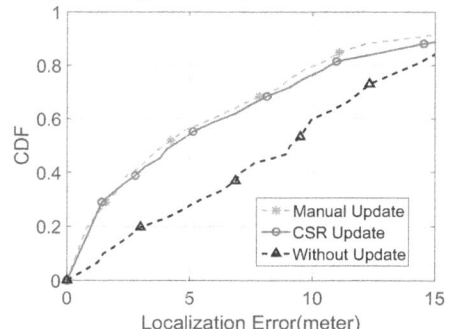

Figure 12: Cumulative errors of the Wi-Fi fingerprint-based localization system integrated with CSR.

the predicted RSSIs (red circles) closely match ground truth (blue diamonds). It shows that CSR successfully adapts the signal map towards the ground truth, significantly reduces the difference with the altered signal map.

Figure 8 shows the CDF of signal map reconstruction error (e_{rec}^n in dB) using LDPL, BP and CSR in the corridor environment. We also show the actual RSSI change (e_{true}^n) in the signal map, denoted as "Without Update". CSR improves the mean reconstruction error by around 29% (from 6.6 dB to 4.7 dB) in the corridor. Given the same number of crowdsourced samples (only 40% samples in the whole site), we can observe that CSR outperforms LDPL and BP schemes. It is because unlike LDPL reconstruction the BCS in CSR does not rely on any radio propagation model or line-of-sight condition. Furthermore, the probabilistic formulation in CSR tolerates the signal noise and is more robust than the deterministic BP scheme.

Figure 9 shows the mean signal map reconstruction error (dB) versus different number of crowdsourced signals in the corridor environment. When no crowdsourced data are fed initially, the RSSI reconstruction error is high for all schemes. As more crowdsourced samples are given, the RSSI reconstruction accuracy increases. We can observe that CSR already achieves high RSSI reconstruction accuracy even given 40% of all crowdsourced samples. We can see that CSR achieves similar reconstruction accuracy to LDPL and BP given at least 20% fewer crowdsourced signals. It is because CSR sufficiently leverages the crowdsourced signals to reconstruct RPs with high correlation and the entire signal map gets updated. In our deployment setting, we set 40% by default to achieve balance between the RSSI error and the crowdsourcing efficiency.

Figure 10 shows the mean signal map reconstruction error (dB) versus the location input error in the corridor environment. We simulate the scenario when the location of the RSSI vector is fed to CSR. We consider a Gaussian location error upon the ground-truth coordinate. Clearly, the RSSI reconstruction error increases as larger location input error is added. We can observe that even under large location input error (say, up to 6 m), CSR can still achieve better reconstruction accuracy than the other schemes.

Figure 11 shows the CDF of signal map reconstruction error in the hallway environment (see Figure 6). Similar to Figure 8, CSR achieves much lower RSSI reconstruction error compared with LDPL and BP. As the signal reconstruction results are qualitatively similar to those in the corridor, for brevity we do not repeat them here.

In the following, we present the improvement in Wi-Fi fingerprint-based localization accuracy using CSR. Figure 12 shows the CDF of localization errors using the Wi-Fi fingerprints updated by different signal map reconstruction schemes. We can observe that CSR improves the localization error by at least 40%, and the updated localization accuracy with CSR is close to that with manual site survey (the ground-truth signal map). It shows that CSR effectively updates the Wi-Fi fingerprint database and improves the adaptivity of indoor localization systems towards the environmental change.

6. CONCLUSION

In this paper, we propose Compressive Signal Reconstruction (CSR), a novel signal map online learning scheme using Bayesian compressive sensing (BCS) and crowdsourcing. Via the BCS formulation, CSR not only finds the signal changes for radio map update, but also provides error bars for confidence inference. Besides, CSR does not rely on any radio propagation model, and can be easily integrated with any wireless applications such as Wi-Fi monitoring or indoor localization systems. We have deployed CSR in our university campus. Extensive experiments show that CSR achieves more than 30% improvement in RSSI reconstruction accuracy compared with other state-of-the-art schemes. We have shown that CSR is also robust to location input errors (as much as 6 meters) in the crowdsourced signals.Furthermore, we have also integrated CSR with existing Wi-Fi fingerprint-based indoor localization systems. Given the changed signal map, CSR effectively reconstructs the fingerprint database and improves the localization accuracy by at least 40%.

7. REFERENCES

[1] M.M. Atia, A. Noureldin, and M.J. Korenberg. Dynamic online-calibrated radio maps for indoor positioning in wireless local area networks. *IEEE Trans. Mobile Computing*, 12(9):1774–1787, Sept 2013.

[2] P. Bahl and V.N. Padmanabhan. RADAR: An in-building RF-based user location and tracking system. In *Proc. IEEE INFOCOM*, volume 2, pages 775–784, 2000.

[3] M. J. Beal. Variational algorithms for approximate Bayesian inference. *PhD Thesis*, pages 1–281, 2003.

[4] C. M. Bishop and M. E Tipping. Variational relevance vector machines. In *Proc. UAI*, pages 46–53. Morgan Kaufmann Publishers, 2000.

[5] P. Bolliger. Redpin - adaptive, zero-configuration indoor localization through user collaboration. In *Proc. MELT*, pages 55–60. ACM New York, NY, USA, 2008.

[6] E. J. Candes and T. Tao. Decoding by linear programming. *IEEE Trans. Information Theory*, 51(12):4203–4215, 2005.

[7] Yi-Chao Chen, Ji-Rung Chiang, Hao-hua Chu, P. Huang, and A. W. Tsui. Sensor-assisted Wi-Fi indoor location system for adapting to environmental dynamics. In *Proc. ACM MSWiM*, pages 118–125, 2005.

[8] D. L. Donoho. Compressed sensing. *IEEE Trans. Information Theory*, 52(4):1289–1306, 2006.

[9] Ke-Lin Du and M. N. S. Swamy. Radial basis function networks. In *Neural Networks and Statistical Learning*, pages 299–335. Springer London, 2014.

[10] M. F. Duarte and Y. C. Eldar. Structured compressed sensing: From theory to applications. *IEEE Trans. Signal Processing*, 59, 2011.

[11] M. Elhamshary, M. Youssef, A. Uchiyama, H. Yamaguchi, and T. Higashino. TransitLabel: A crowd-sensing system for automatic labeling of transit stations semantics. In *Proc. ACM MobiSys*, 2016.

[12] B. Ferris, D. Fox, and N. Lawrence. WiFi-SLAM using gaussian process latent variable models. In *Proc. IJCAI*, pages 2480–2485. Morgan Kaufmann Publishers Inc. San Francisco, CA, USA, 2007.

[13] M. Gunawan, B. Li, T. Gallagher, and G. Retscher. A new method to generate and maintain a WiFi fingerprinting database automatically by using RFID. In *Proc. IPIN*, pages 1–6. IEEE, 2012.

[14] B. Guo, C. Chen, D. Zhang, Z. Yu, and A. Chin. Mobile crowd sensing and computing: when participatory sensing meets participatory social media. *IEEE Communications Magazine*, 54(2):131–137, February 2016.

[15] Suining He and S. H. G. Chan. Wi-Fi fingerprint-based indoor positioning: Recent advances and comparisons. *IEEE Communications Surveys Tutorials*, 18(1):466–490, Firstquarter 2016.

[16] Suining He, Bo Ji, and S.-H. Gary Chan. Chameleon: Survey-free updating of fingerprint database for indoor localization. *IEEE Pervasive Magazine*, to appear.

[17] Y. Hu, W. Zhou, Z. Wen, Y. Sun, and B. Yin. Efficient radio map construction based on low-rank approximation for indoor positioning. *Mathematical Problems in Engineering*, 2013, 2013.

[18] Qideng Jiang, Yongtao Ma, Kaihua Liu, and Zhi Dou. A Probabilistic Radio Map Construction Scheme for Crowdsourcing-Based Fingerprinting Localization. *IEEE Sensors Journal*, 16(10):3764–3774, 2016.

[19] Shaoyang Li, Xiaoming Tao, and Jianhua Lu. A variational Bayesian em approach to structured sparse signal reconstruction. In *Proc. IEEE VTC Fall*, pages 1 – 5. IEEE, 2014.

[20] C. Luo, L. Cheng, M. C. Chan, Y. Gu, J. Li, and M. Zhong. Pallas: Self-bootstrapping fine-grained passive indoor localization using WiFi monitors. *IEEE Trans. Mobile Computing*, 2016.

[21] Andrea Massa, Paolo Rocca, and Giacomo Oliveri. Compressive sensing in electromagnetics - a review. *IEEE Antennas and Propagation Magazine*, 57(1):224–238, 2015.

[22] D Needell and J A Tropp. CoSaMP: Iterative signal recovery from incomplete and inaccurate samples. *Applied and Computational Harmonic Analysis*, 26(3):301–321, 2009.

[23] S. Nikitaki, G. Tsagkatakis, and P. Tsakalides. Efficient multi-channel signal strength based localization via matrix completion and Bayesian sparse learning. *IEEE Trans. Mobile Computing*, 14(11):2244–2256, Nov 2015.

[24] Jun-geun Park, Ben Charrow, Dorothy Curtis, Jonathan Battat, Einat Minkov, Jamey Hicks, Seth Teller, and Jonathan Ledlie. Growing an organic indoor location system. In *Proc. ACM MobiSys*, pages 271–284. ACM New York, NY, USA, 2010.

[25] Hyojeong Shin, Yohan Chon, Yungeun Kim, and Hojung Cha. MRI: Model-based radio interpolation for indoor war-walking. *IEEE Trans. Mobile Computing*, 14(6):1231–1244, 2015.

[26] Michael E Tipping. Sparse Bayesian learning and the relevance vector machine. *The Journal of Machine Learning Research*, pages 211–244, 2001.

[27] Joel a. Tropp and Anna C. Gilbert. Signal recovery from random measurements via orthogonal matching pursuit. *IEEE Trans. Information Theory*, 53(12):4655–4666, 2007.

[28] C. Wu, Z. Yang, and Y. Liu. Smartphones based crowdsourcing for indoor localization. *IEEE Trans. Mobile Computing*, 14(2):444–457, Feb 2015.

[29] Moustafa Youssef and Ashok Agrawala. The Horus WLAN location determination system. In *Proc. ACM MobiSys*, pages 205–218, 2005.

An Energy-Detection-based
Cooperative Spectrum Sensing Scheme
for Minimizing the Effects of NPEE and RSPF

Oladiran Olaleye, Muhammad A Iqbal, Ahmed Aly, Dmitri Perkins, Magdy Bayoumi
The Center for Advanced Computer Studies
University of Louisiana at Lafayette, LA 70504, USA
{ogo8842, mxi1678, axa5234, perkins, mab}@cacs.louisiana.edu

ABSTRACT

For improved spectrum utilization, the key technique for acquiring spectrum situational awareness (SSA) — spectrum sensing — is greatly improved by cooperation among the active spectrum users, as network size increases. However, the many cooperative spectrum sensing (CSS) schemes that have been proposed are based on the assumptions of accurate noise power estimates, characterizable variation in noise level and absence of false or malicious users. As part of a series of SSA research projects, in this research work, we propose a novel scheme for minimizing the effects of noise power estimation error (NPEE) and received signal power falsification (RSPF) by energy-based reliability evaluation. The scheme adopts the Voting rule for fusing multiple spectrum sensing data. Based on simulation results, the proposed scheme yields significant improvement, 68.2—88.8%, over the conventional CSS schemes, when compared on the basis of the schemes' stability to uncertainties in noise and signal power.

CCS Concepts

●Networks → **Network performance analysis**;

Keywords

Cognitive Radio Networks, Cooperative Spectrum Sensing, Energy Detection, Received Signal Power, Spectrum Sensing Data Falsification Attacks, Noise Uncertainty, Noise Power Estimation, Reliability Evaluation.

1. INTRODUCTION

The current trend in demand and usage has exposed the vast underutilization of the available spectrum resources. As reported in a Federal communications commission (FCC) submission [1], for example, at least 80 percent of the spectrum below 3 GHz is unexploited the United States. As a result, methods and techniques have been proposed in literature, under the umbrella of cognitive radio networking, for improving spectrum utilization. To achieve that objective, assumptions about the state of the system are required, especially due to the heterogeneous and dynamic nature of future communication systems. One such assumption is the accuracy of noise power estimate, a highly variable parameter and one of the key metrics for achieving spectrum situational awareness (SSA) through spectrum sensing by energy detection. Although collaboration among multiple users helps to improve the performance of energy detection, the current cooperative spectrum sensing (CSS) schemes were formulated based on systematic and predictable noise component sources. Hence, in order to minimize the overall effects of noise for improved energy detection performance, a sensing scheme that considers the randomness and volatility of noise is required.

A number of techniques for minimizing the effects of noise power estimation error (NPEE) and received signal power falsification (RSPF) have been proposed. Some are based on individual secondary user (SU) properties such as signal-to-noise ratio (SNR), some are based on the interaction among SU's such as cluster index and consensus), while some are based on the detection threshold [2] [3]. Incorporating NPEE into threshold settings is one step to correctly adapt the process of energy detection to the random distribution of noise power. However, presetting the detection threshold to vary over a predetermined range, in order to conform to noise variation, would mean constraining the variation of noise between bounds, which are indeterminable to precision and irreproducible in variation. On the other hand, energy detection threshold can be modeled to adapt to the dynamics of noise power but the approach would also require making certain assumptions: identical distribution of noise samples, known noise average power fluctuation factor [2], and uniform SNR [3].

Hence, the novelty of this research work lies in the consideration of unsystematic and unpredictable inaccuracies in signal and noise power during spectrum sensing by energy detection. The rest of the paper is organized as follows: section II describes the system models, including the radio propagation, energy detection, noise and signal attack models; section III explains the proposed CSS scheme — energy-based reliability evaluation; the simulation experiments and results are discussed in section IV; while the conclusion and future works are stated in section V.

MSWiM '16, November 13-17, 2016, Malta, Malta
© 2016 ACM. ISBN 978-1-4503-4502-6/16/11...$15.00
DOI: http://dx.doi.org/10.1145/2988287.2989169

2. SPECTRUM SENSING

2.1 System Model

Considering a n-secondary-user cognitive radio network (CRN), deployed in a region covered by a 50 dBm (100 Watt) EIRP primary user (PU) transmitter with a coverage radius R km. The secondary users (SU's) are assumed to be independent and stationary. A SU is r km away from the PU transmitter with received SNR γ. To detect the presence of a PU transmission, a SU: measures the power of the received signal P_S^{meas}; computes the estimated noise power P_N^{est}; then transmits the P_S^{meas} and P_N^{est} to the data fusion center (DFC) where the two energy parameters are corrected for error to obtain P_S^{corr} and P_N^{corr} respectively. At the DFC, the detection threshold λ is computed based on a pre-fixed probability of false alarm P_{FA} and P_N^{corr}, followed by a comparison with P_S^{corr}. If $P_S^{\text{corr}} > \lambda$ the DFC concludes for the SU, with a detection probability P_D, that there is a PU transmission in progress, else that the channel is free. The DFC then combines the probabilities by the Voting rule to obtain the fused probability of detection Q_D and false alarm Q_{FA}.

2.2 Radio Propagation Model

The simulation environment is developed using the irregular terrain model (ITM) [4], a radio propagation model developed by the Institute for Telecommunication Sciences, National Telecommunications and Information Administration, U.S. Department of Commerce. The PU transmits at 600 MHz from a height of 305 m with location and time reliability of 50% each while the receiver antenna height is 9 m, with 2 dBi antenna gain and horizontal polarization. The average terrain height is 90 m, the surface refractivity is 301 N-units and the ground dielectric constant and conductivity are 15 and 0.005 S/m respectively.

2.3 Energy Detection Model

Compared to other methods of detecting signals, such as the matched filter method and the cyclic feature detection method, the energy detection method requires no knowledge of the signal characteristics nor it's periodicity; it is simple and requires less computation but highly susceptible to variation in noise power. To characterize the impact of noise variation on energy detection, the detection process is modeled as a binary hypothesis testing problem:

$$\begin{cases} H_0 : x(k) &= n(k) \\ H_1 : x(k) &= h(k)s(k) + n(k), k = 1, 2, ..., M \end{cases} \quad (1)$$

Where $x(k)$ represents the received signal; $s(k)$, the transmitted signal; $h(k)$, the channel gain; $n(k)$, zero-mean additive white Gaussian noise with variance σ^2; M, the number of samples; and H_0 and H_1, the hypothesis of the absence and presence of PU signal respectively.

Assuming: $x(k)$ and $s(k)$ are independent; $h(k)$ is constant during the detection process; SU channels are independent; and the PU and SU's share the same spectrum allocation, the test statistics for the energy detection process, which is equivalent to an estimate of the received signal power, measured by applying a band-pass filter to the received signal in a particular frequency region in time domain [5], is given by:

$$x_E = \frac{1}{M} \sum_{i=1}^{M} |x_i|^2, \quad M = 2tB \quad (2)$$

Where, x_i is the $i - th$ received signal sample i, t is the sensing time and B is the bandwidth.

Based on the Central Limit Theorem, when $M >> 1$, the test statistics can be approximated as a Gaussian random variable [5], giving:

$$P_{\text{FA}} = Q\left(\sqrt{M}(\lambda - 1)\right) \quad (3)$$

$$P_D = Q\left(\frac{\sqrt{M}(\lambda - (\gamma + 1))}{\sqrt{2}(\gamma + 1)}\right) \quad (4)$$

Where, λ is the energy detection threshold; $\gamma = P_S^{\text{meas}}/P_N^{\text{est}}$ and $Q(x)$ is the Marcum-Q function.

2.4 Noise and Attack Model

2.4.1 Noise

The estimation of noise power is based on ambient temperature, which is unstable in time domain. Hence, noise power estimates suffer from random error with severe impact on energy detection for CRN's. In this research work, the range of noise power estimates is modeled as an open set, with positive and negative deviations from an assumed average P_N^{avg} thus,

$$P_{N,i}^{\text{est}} - P_N^{\text{avg}} = \{\Delta_{N,1}^-, ..., 0, ..., \Delta_{N, N_{\text{SU}}-1}^+, \Delta_{N, N_{\text{SU}}}^+\} \quad (5)$$

$$P_N^{\text{avg}} = P_{\text{TN}} + SG + NF \quad (6)$$

$$P_{\text{TN}} = 10 log_{10}(1000kTB) \quad (7)$$

Where $P_{N,i}^{\text{est}}$ is the estimated noise power at the i-th SU; $\Delta_{N,i}^+$ and $\Delta_{N,i}^-$ are the positive and negative deviation, respectively, from the average noise power; $|\Delta_{N,i}^+|$ and $|\Delta_{N,i}^-|$ are not necessarily equal; N_{SU} is the total number of SU's present in the network; P_{TN} is the thermal noise in dBm; SG is the System Gain in dBm; NF is the noise figure in dBm; k is the Boltzmann constant (1.3807×10^{-23} joules/K); T is the Ambient Temperature in Kelvin; and B is the Bandwidth in Hz.

For a comprehensive analysis of the effects of NPEE and the proposed minimization approach, a spectrum of different combinations of NPEE's are considered: when all the SU's experience the same negative NPEE; when all the SU's experience the same positive NPEE; and random combinations of positive and negative NPEE.

2.4.2 Attack

As in the IEEE 802.22 standard [5], the DFC is aware of each SU's location and orientation and by the radio propagation model [4] and dynamic signal strength mapping, can predict the received signal power P_S^{pred}. While honest SU's report the actual P_S^{meas} and P_N^{est}, malicious SU's may report any combination of false P_S^{meas} and P_N^{est}. However, the main factors that determine the impact of spectrum sensing data falsification (SSDF) on the performance of energy detection include the number of honest SU's $N_{\text{SU}}^{\text{honest}}$, the number of malicious SU's $N_{\text{SU}}^{\text{malicious}}$, the magnitude of NPEE and

RSPF, and the distribution and cooperation among the malicious SU's in the network. The simple and self-correcting approach to minimizing the effects of malicious SU's would be by having a large ratio of honest SU's to malicious SU's. However, that approach is not always realizable since the number of malicious SU's in a network, at any time, is beyond the control of the DFC. Hence, for a complete investigation of the effects of malicious SU's and analysis of the minimization approach, the extremes of attack (from a large $N_{\text{SU}}^{\text{honest}}/N_{\text{SU}}^{\text{malicious}}$ ratio to the emulation of honest SU's) are considered. The range of possibilities includes: $N_{\text{SU}}^{\text{honest}} > N_{\text{SU}}^{\text{malicious}}$; $N_{\text{SU}}^{\text{honest}} < N_{\text{SU}}^{\text{malicious}}$; SU emulation; and positive, negative and random RSPF.

3. PROPOSED COOPERATIVE SPECTRUM SENSING SCHEME

The conventional method for fusing sensing data combines the raw computations from SU's without testing for authenticity. That approach is prone to error and susceptible to infiltration by faults from noise and signal data. Hence, to boost the dependability of the final decision made at the DFC, the SU sensing data must be corrected for faults. In our proposed scheme, we consider the range of possible governing factors that could affect a SU sensing data reliability (R_i): the SNR at the SU γ_i, the distance of the SU from the PU or incumbent device transmitter r_i, the intention of the SU (honest or malicious) I_i, measurement error $M_{\text{err},i}$, device error $D_{\text{err},i}$, computational error $C_{\text{err},i}$ and environmental error $E_{\text{err},i}$.

$$R_i = f(\gamma_i, r_i, I_i, M_{\text{err},i}, D_{\text{err},i}, C_{\text{err},i}, E_{\text{err},i}) \quad (8)$$

Where the impact of γ_i and r_i are dependent and those of I_i, $M_{\text{err},i}$, $D_{\text{err},i}$, $C_{\text{err},i}$ and $E_{\text{err},i}$ are cumulative.

Hence, in order to minimize the effects of NPEE and achieve a dependable probability of incumbent transmission detection, the proposed scheme, shown in Fig. 1, adopts an energy-based reliability evaluation approach.

3.1 Energy-based Reliability Evaluation

For the purpose of this work: the value of a parameter obtained by direct physical measurement (e.g. sampling and analysis) is referred to as a measured quantity; the value

obtained indirectly by measuring a related parameter is referred to as an estimated quantity; while the value obtained from an existing mathematical model is referred to as a predicted quantity. In order to determine the true value of a parameter, its estimated and measured equivalents are weighted and adapted based on its predicted value and the observed absolute deviation; the observed quantity is corrected and adapted based on a more reliable equivalent.

Let P_{corr} be the corrected value of a parameter P; P_{meas}, the measured value of P; P_{pred}, the predicted value of P; P_{est}, the estimated value of P; r_{meas}, the weighted reliability of P_{meas}; r_{pred}, the weighted reliability of P_{pred}; and r_{est}, the weighted reliability of P_{est}. Hence,

$$P_{\text{corr}} = r_{\text{meas}} P_{\text{meas}} + r_{\text{pred}} P_{\text{pred}} + r_{\text{est}} P_{\text{est}} \quad (9)$$

Where r_{meas}, r_{pred} and r_{est} are adapted to the variation of P_{meas}, P_{pred} and P_{est} respectively.

3.1.1 Detection and minimization of noise power estimation error

Based on the assumption that all the SU's in the network are honest ($N_{\text{SU}}^{\text{malicious}} = 0$), the corrected noise power is calculated from (9) thus,

$$P_{\text{N}}^{\text{corr}} = r_{\text{N}}^{\text{est}} P_{\text{N}}^{\text{est}} + r_{\text{NS}}^{\text{meas}} P_{\text{N+S}}^{\text{meas}} - r_{\text{S}}^{\text{pred}} P_{\text{S}}^{\text{pred}} \quad (10)$$

Where $r_{\text{N}}^{\text{est}}$ is the weighted reliability of noise power based on the measured ambient temperature; and $P_{\text{N}}^{\text{est}}$ is the estimated noise power based on ambient temperature; $r_{\text{NS}}^{\text{meas}}$ is the weighted reliability of the measured signal plus noise power; $P_{\text{N+S}}^{\text{meas}}$ is the measured signal plus noise power; $r_{\text{S}}^{\text{pred}}$ is the weighted reliability of the predicted signal power based on the pathloss model; and $P_{\text{S}}^{\text{pred}}$ is the predicted signal power based on the pathloss model.

If the estimated noise power is equal to the expected value, that is, the NPEE $\Delta_{\text{N}} = 0$, then

$$\begin{cases} P_{\text{N}}^{\text{est}} &= P_{\text{N+S}}^{\text{meas}} + P_{\text{S}}^{\text{pred}} \\ r_{\text{N}}^{\text{est}} &= r_{\text{NS}}^{\text{meas}} = r_{\text{S}}^{\text{pred}} = 0.5 \end{cases} \quad (11)$$

Otherwise,

$$\begin{cases} r_{\text{N}}^{\text{est}} &= 0.5 - 0.5 * \frac{|P_{\text{N}}^{\text{est}} - P_{\text{N+S}}^{\text{meas}} + P_{\text{S}}^{\text{pred}}|}{P_{\text{N+S}}^{\text{meas}} - P_{\text{S}}^{\text{pred}}} \\ r_{\text{NS}}^{\text{meas}} &= r_{\text{S}}^{\text{pred}} = 1.0 - r_{\text{N}}^{\text{est}} \end{cases} \quad (12)$$

Where,

$$r_{\text{N}}^{\text{est}} = \begin{cases} 0.0 < r_{\text{N}}^{\text{est}} \leq 0.5 \\ 0.0 \quad otherwise \end{cases}$$

3.1.2 Detection and minimization of received signal power falsification

Based on the assumption of accurate noise estimate ($\Delta_{\text{N}} = 0$), the corrected signal power is calculated from (9) thus,

$$P_{\text{S}}^{\text{corr}} = r_{\text{NS}}^{\text{meas}} P_{\text{N+S}}^{\text{meas}} - r_{\text{N}}^{\text{est}} P_{\text{N}}^{\text{est}} + r_{\text{S}}^{\text{pred}} P_{\text{S}}^{\text{pred}} \quad (13)$$

If the reported measured signal power is equal to the predicted signal power, that is, the RSPF $\Delta_{\text{S}} = 0$, then

$$\begin{cases} P_{\text{N+S}}^{\text{meas}} - P_{\text{N}}^{\text{est}} = P_{\text{S}}^{\text{pred}} \\ r_{\text{NS}}^{\text{meas}} = r_{\text{N}}^{\text{est}} = r_{\text{S}}^{\text{pred}} = 0.5 \end{cases} \quad (14)$$

Otherwise,

$$\begin{cases} r_{\text{NS}}^{\text{meas}} &= r_{\text{N}}^{\text{est}} = 0.5 - 0.5 * \frac{|P_{\text{N+S}}^{\text{meas}} - P_{\text{N}}^{\text{est}} - P_{\text{S}}^{\text{pred}}|}{P_{\text{S}}^{\text{pred}}} \\ r_{\text{S}}^{\text{pred}} &= 1.0 - r_{\text{NS}}^{\text{meas}} \end{cases} \quad (15)$$

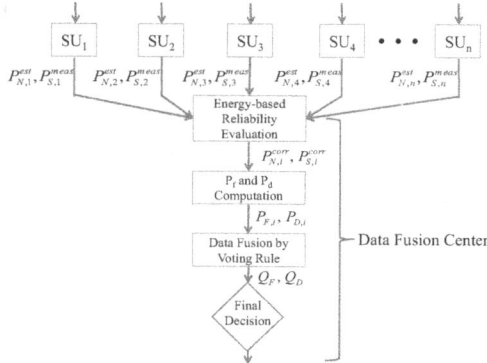

Figure 1: The proposed cooperative spectrum sensing scheme. It is based on the use of estimation, prediction and measurement for minimizing the impacts of NPEE and RSPF on signal detection.

Where,

$$r_{\mathrm{NS}}^{\mathrm{meas}} = r_{\mathrm{N}}^{\mathrm{est}} = \begin{cases} & 0.0 < r_{\mathrm{NS}}^{\mathrm{meas}} \leq 0.5 \\ 0.0 & otherwise \end{cases}$$

3.2 Data fusion by voting rule

Having corrected the energy parameters, the probabilities of false alarm and detection is computed from (3) and (4), and then combined based on Voting rule — a preferable weighted-data fusion method [5]. Thus,

$$Q_{\mathrm{D}} = \sum_{k \geq (\tau * N)}^{N} \left(\frac{N!}{k!(N-k)!} (P_{\mathrm{D},i})^k (1 - P_{\mathrm{D},i})^{N-k} \right) \quad (16)$$

Where N is the number of SU's being considered; τ is the voting threshold for k successes and was set at 0.5 for the simulation experiment; while $P_{\mathrm{D},i}$ is the detection probability for the i-th SU. The global decision is made based on Q_{D} and Q_{FA}, which is also calculated from (16) by replacing $P_{\mathrm{D},i}$ with $P_{\mathrm{FA},i}$.

4. SIMULATION RESULTS AND ANALYSIS

Different combinations of NPEE and RSPF were simulated in MATLAB in order to characterize the effects of uncertainties on the performance of energy detection for spectrum sensing and also demonstrate the efficiency of the proposed approach. For the simulation, $P_{\mathrm{N}}^{\mathrm{avg}}$ is set at -65 dBm while the channel bandwidth B is 6 MHz (for minimal multipath fading [5]).

As shown in Fig. 2(a), negative NPEE increases the probability of detection for a fixed probability of false alarm and vice versa. The figure also reveals the sensitivity of the detection probability to a unit magnitude decibel error as seen in the rapid spread of the receiver operating characteristics curves (ROC) curves from the average noise power. At $Q_{\mathrm{F}} = 0.1037$, the actual probability of detection is 0.5052 but when the magnitude of NPEE is varied between $-3 \leq \Delta_{\mathrm{N}}(dBm) \leq 3$, the detection probability fluctuates between $0.7922 \leq Q_{\mathrm{D}} \leq 0.3473$ respectively. With the proposed scheme, however, the fluctuation is reduced to $0.5512 \leq Q_{\mathrm{D}} \leq 0.5044$ (Fig. 2(b)), an equivalent of 88.8% improvement based on stability to NPEE. To demonstrate the efficacy of the scheme in a more practical scenario, NPEE's at the different SU's is made to vary randomly between $-5 \leq \Delta_{\mathrm{N}}(dBm) \leq 5$ (Fig. 2(c)). The results obtained are similar to those of equal NPEE.

Fig. 3(a) and 3(b) show the performance of the proposed scheme over the conventional method when all the SU's in the network had equal magnitude of RSPF while in Fig. 4, the simulation is carried out with different combinations of the honest and malicious users: 100 percent honest users; 50 and 100 percent malicious users all with -2 dBm RSPF; and 50 and 100 percent malicious users with the malicious users emulating the absence of PU transmission. The figures reveal the upshot of error in P_{S} by replicating the effect of the RSPF from a single SU as a cumulative effect from all the SU's in the network. As expected, positive RSPF results in increased probability of detection, and vice versa, while an increase in the number of malicious users (from 0 to 5 to 10 in the 10-user network) results in a pronounced corresponding effect in the detection probability. Based on the simulation parameters, with an even number of honest and malicious users in the network and $\Delta_{\mathrm{S}} = -2dBm$ (Fig.

4(a)), at $Q_{\mathrm{F}} = 0.1037$, the actual probability of detection is 0.5052 (as in the previous cases) but when the number of malicious users increases to 5 and 10, the detection probability are 0.5052 and 0.3871 correspondingly, while the proposed scheme (Fig. 4(b)) reduces the instability to 0.5052 and 0.4676 respectively — approximately 68.2% improvement based on stability to RSPF. On the other hand, when all the SU's in the network have equal RSPF (Fig. 3(a) and 3(b)), the improvement is similar to that in Fig. 2(a) and 2(b). For the cases where individual malicious users have random RSPF, Fig. 3(c) illustrates the efficiency of the proposed scheme in minimizing the impact of RSPF. From the plots (Fig. 3(c)), the scheme also proves to be better than the conventional method in stabilizing the detection probability with the potential to completely detect and eliminate all RSPF, provided $P_{\mathrm{S}}^{\mathrm{pred}}$ is accurate.

5. CONCLUSIONS

In this paper, we have presented a novel cooperative spectrum sensing scheme, based on radio propagation models, measured signal power and estimated noise power, for minimizing the effects of NPEE and RSPF. NPEE and RSPF were detected and corrected based on reliability metrics obtained by comparing the measured signal power and the estimated noise power to the predicted received signal power. Simulation results revealed the behavior of the ROC curve in different cases and combinations of NPEE and RSPF. The performance of the proposed scheme over the conventional method varies between 68.2 and 88.8% when compared using the resulting ROC curves. While the scheme relies on the accuracy of the predicted received signal power, we have designed and initiated our next research plan with the main focus of improving the prediction accuracy using machine learning techniques.

6. ACKNOWLEDGMENTS

This work was supported in part by the National Science Foundation (NSF) under NSF Career Grant No. 1454835.

7. REFERENCES

[1] M. Calabrese, "The End of Spectrum Scarcity: Building on the TV Bands Database to Access Unused Public Airwaves," New America Foundation's Wireless Future Program, Working Paper #25, June 2009.

[2] G. Yu, C. Long, M. Xiang and W. Xi, "A Novel Energy Detection Scheme Based on Dynamic Threshold in Cognitive Radio Systems," Journal of Computational Information Systems, Vol. 8, pp. 2245-2252, Mar. 2012.

[3] A. Gorcin, K. A.Qaraqe, H. Celebi, and H. Arslan, "An adaptive threshold method for spectrum sensing in multichannel cognitive radio networks," Telecommunications (ICT), 2010 IEEE 17th International Conference on, vol., no., pp. 425, 429, 4-7 April 2010.

[4] G. Hufford, "The ITS Irregular Terrain Model Algorithm, Version 1.2.2, The Algorithm," http://www.its.bldrdoc.gov/resources/radio-propagation-software/itm/itm.aspx, 2016.

[5] "IEEE standard for information technology-telecommunications and information

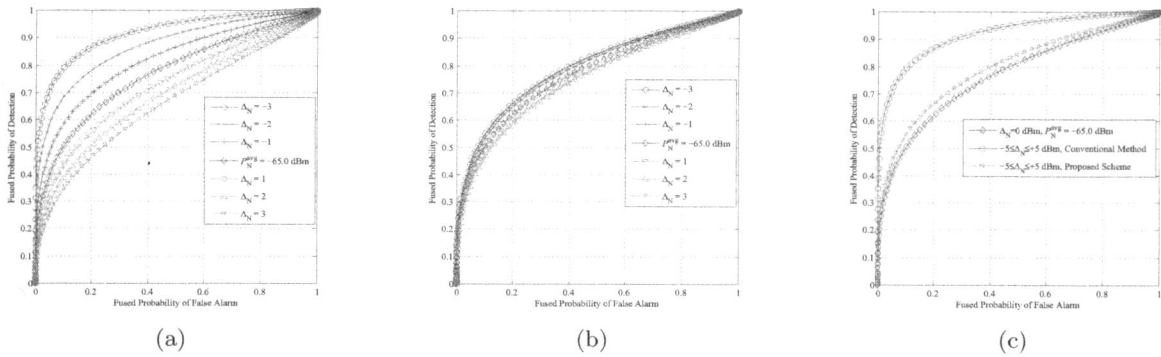

(a)   (b)   (c)

Figure 2: ROC curves comparing the proposed scheme to the conventional method based on the performance in minimizing the effects of positive and negative uncertainties in noise power estimates for a 10-SU cognitive radio network. (a) and (b) simulates the scenario with equal NPEE at each SU while (c) simulates constrained but random NPEE.

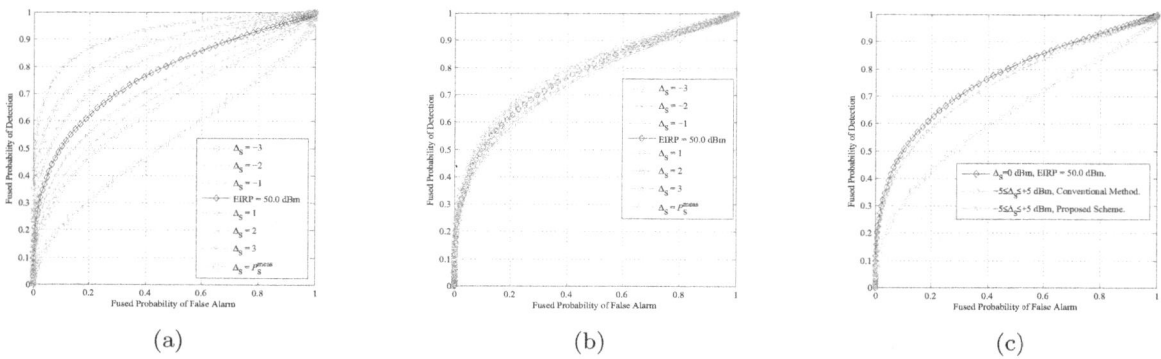

(a)   (b)   (c)

Figure 3: ROC curves comparing the proposed scheme to the conventional method based on the performance in minimizing the effects of positive and negative deviations from the actual received signal power for a 10-SU cognitive radio network. (a) and (b) assumed each SU's received signal power had equal magnitude of deviation while (c) assumed random deviations. The emulation of SU for the absence of PU transmission was simulated with $\Delta_S = P_S^{meas}$.

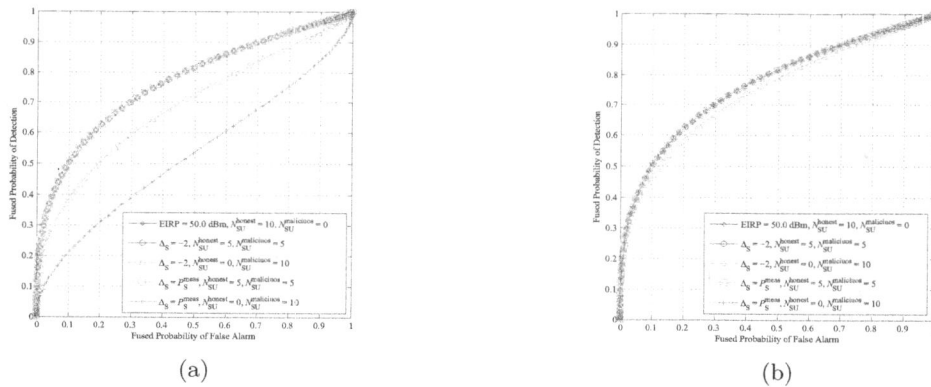

(a)   (b)

Figure 4: ROC curves comparing the proposed scheme, in (b), to the conventional method, in (a), based on the performance in minimizing the effects of a slight and total deviation from the actual received signal power, for a 10-SU cognitive radio network with different combinations of honest and malicious users: 100% honest SU's, 50% honest SU's; and 100% malicious SU's respectively.

exchange between systems wireless regional area networks (wran)-specific requirements part 22: Cognitive wireless ran medium access control (mac) and physical layer (phy) specifications: Policies and procedures for operation in the TV bands," IEEE Std 802.22-2011, pp. 1-680, 1 2011.

Dynamic Sensitivity Control to improve Spatial Reuse in Dense Wireless LANs

Parag Kulkarni
Telecommunications Research Laboratory
Toshiba Research Europe Ltd.
32 Queen Square, Bristol BS1 4ND.
parag.kulkarni@toshiba-trel.com

Fengming Cao
Telecommunications Research Laboratory
Toshiba Research Europe Ltd.
32 Queen Square, Bristol BS1 4ND.
fengming.cao@toshiba-trel.com

ABSTRACT

With the proliferation of wireless LANs, we are in an era of densification. Whilst densification could lead to increased coverage (neighbouring APs belonging to the same administrative domain), which is good news, it could also lead to increased interference (neighbouring APs not belonging to the same administrative domain). In particular, in the latter case, nodes (both APs and STAs) in neighbouring networks could carrier sense each other and resist from transmitting when in fact a parallel transmission could have been harmless. Thus, improving spatial reuse in such scenarios is crucial to improving performance in dense deployments otherwise the efficiency is likely to take a hit. This paper elaborates on dynamic sensitivity control (DSC), a way of adapting the carrier sensing threshold dynamically to address the aforementioned issue and presents results from a simulation based study aimed at evaluating the proposed method. Findings indicate that the gains achievable from deploying DSC vary significantly depending on the operating conditions and therefore, choosing a fixed conservative threshold at design time, as has been the case traditionally, may not be an appropriate decision. We also show that enabling DSC at the AP may bring benefits with the performance approaching that of the traditional method (of not adapting sensitivity) in the conservative case.

CCS Concepts

•Networks → **Wireless local area networks**;

Keywords

dynamic sensitivity control (DSC); CCA adaptation; IEEE 802.11ax; dense wireless LANs

1. BACKGROUND

The ever growing popularity of Wireless LANs is leading to significant densification of these networks. Since these networks operate in the unlicensed band where resources are scarce, this can lead to substantial interference amongst neighbouring networks. The IEEE 802.11ax group has tasked itself with devising solutions to challenges arising from densification. One of the items on the agenda is to improve spatial reuse through dynamic sensitivity adaptation. In principle, the idea is to vary the carrier sensing range of the STA to overcome the effect of simultaneous ongoing transmissions in neighbouring networks (called Overlapped Basic Service Set or OBSS). Such OBSS transmissions could lead to link suppression (a node which carrier senses an OBSS transmission will keep quiet by default). In dense deployments this could mean keeping quite most of the time for no good reason. The key question in such a situation is how to choose an appropriate carrier sensing threshold so as to avoid such unnecessary periods of silence and how often to adapt the same. The topology and link conditions being variable, a common threshold may not be appropriate for all STAs. Therefore, each STA should adapt its threshold dynamically.

A good survey of adaptive carrier sensing approaches by Thorpe et al. can be found in [12]. As highlighted in this paper, the ultimate objective of prior efforts has been the identification of the best CCA threshold, one that will work irrespective of the underlying network conditions. To accomplish this objective, most work has focused on analysing the problem theoretically making several assumptions about the topology, node distributions, interference models, use of fixed modulation and coding schemes etc. As shown in [12], not all of these assumptions are realistic and therefore, have a bearing on both the performance that is achievable in practice and the practical ability to deploy these in the first place. Whilst it seems intuitive that one needs to identify the best CCA threshold, a single such threshold is unlikely to be fit for purpose forever. Thus, a 'fix-and-forget' approach may not be practical. There is a need to keep adapting this threshold value as the underlying topology, link characteristics and traffic conditions may change thereby rendering the previously identified fixed CCA threshold not so effective.

Dynamic sensitivity control has been acknowledged by the IEEE 802.11ax task group to be an important issue to consider when addressing the problems arising from densification in WLANs. Discussions are ongoing with consensus yet to be reached on the best way forward. One of the early proposals from Smith et al. [8] (referred to as 'Baseline' in the remainder of this paper) advocates that each STA measure the RSSI of the signals from the AP, add a fixed margin to this value and set this as its CCA threshold. Whilst this proposal not only appeals to intuition, it is also simple from

MSWiM '16, November 13-17, 2016, Malta, Malta
© 2016 ACM. ISBN 978-1-4503-4502-6/16/11...$15.00
DOI: http://dx.doi.org/10.1145/2988287.2989138

an implementaton perspective. However, the issue of choosing a suitable margin does not have a trivial solution and is an open problem. A smaller value of margin will lead to an STA setting an aggressive CCA threshold whereas using a larger value of margin will lead to a more conservative CCA threshold. The former might result in increased collisions in the cell whereas the latter might negate the benefits of using adaptive carrier sensing in the first place leading to performance similar to using the default CCA threshold. There have been several follow up studies such as [9] [10] [2] [7] [3] [1] [11] [5] exploring performance of the proposal in [8] and other proposals with different fixed CCA thresholds using different margin values in different topologies yielding mixed results. Whilst a conclusive finding that has emerged from these studies is that different thresholds perform differently in different settings, a method to accomplish the adaptation remains elusive. The work in this paper as an attempt to plug this gap.

In the remainder of this paper, we elaborate on the details of a method to dynamically adapt the CCA threshold. We then point to merits of employing DSC not only at the STA side but also on the AP side and throw light on a minor admendment to the CCA threshold adaptation method to make it applicable on the AP side. Subsequently, performance of the proposed techniques are compared against that of the aforementioned Baseline method and the legacy way of choosing a fixed CCA threshold through a simulation study conducted using the network simulator ns3. Findings from this study highlight the promise and pitfalls of employing the proposed technique and assess these in light of the status-quo.

2. DYNAMIC SENSITIVITY CONTROL ALGORITHM

In our earlier work [6], we had outlined an algorithm for dynamically changing the CCA threshold in response to changes in the loss rate. This algorithm mandated that an STA increases its sensitivity when loss rate goes up and decreases its sensitivity when the loss rate goes down. Such a probing based approach was found to be too sensitive (react immediately by increasing/decreasing the CCA threshold) which had an effect on its performance. Following on from this work, we have explored two additional pathways - 1) A simple amendment to provide more stability to the algorithm wherein the STA does not change its sensitivity if the loss rate does not change significantly and 2) Investigating the effect of enabling DSC on the AP side. The focus of this paper is on these two aspects. In particular, we show the benefits that these seemingly simple optimisations can bring.

Figure 1 highlights the method to adapt the CCA threshold at a node. The intuitive principle underpinning this algorithm is that if the loss rate goes up, this could be a sign of poor carrier sensing which implies the need for a more conservative CCA threshold and therefore sensitivity is increased. Similarly, if the loss rate goes down, this could be a sign that interference has reduced which implies that the node could experiment with a more aggressive CCA threshold and therefore sensitivity is decreased. The 'maintain status quo' pathway can assist in dealing with transient fluctuations by ensuring that the algorithm does not react to minor changes in the loss rate. The value of X governs

how quickly the algorithm will react to changes in loss rate. Clearly, there is an assumption that losses are due to collisions. Whilst it would be beneficial to know the cause of losses, such support is not assumed in this work. One may argue that this will make the algorithm more conservative in that it may sometimes react unnecessarily. For instance, if the loss rate goes up, the algorithm will decide to increase sensitivity foreseeing the need for improving carrier sensing. However, the use of an adaptive approach provides the algorithm with the ability to recover from the impact of such unnecessary reaction, e.g., if these losses were due to a temporary deterioration in the channel and the channel subsequently improves, so will the loss rate statistics which will lead the algorithm to reduce sensitivity to try and pick a more aggressive CCA threshold.

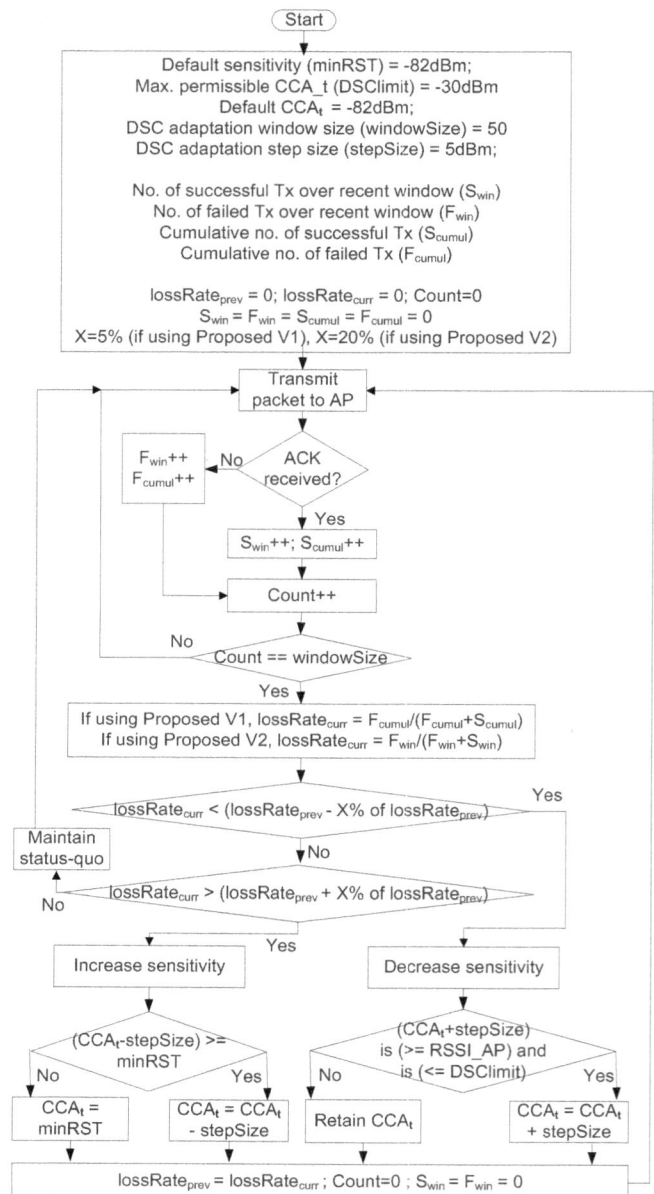

Figure 1: An algorithm to realise DSC at the STA

As a starting point, each STA picks the highest sensitivity supported by the wireless network interface card, gradually builds neighbourhood information (using loss rate as a proxy) and adjusts its CCA threshold to respond to changing operating conditions. After each transmission attempt, if an ACK is received, the number of successful transmission count is increased. In the absence of an ACK, failure statistics are updated such as the number of failed transmissions. Depending on whether short term or long term statistics are employed, there are two variants of the proposed algorithm.

Proposed V1: This variant employs long term statistics wherein cumulative counters are used in the calculation of loss rate. The use of long term statistics leads to a smoothed value of loss rate. At the end of each adaptation window (of size $windowSize$ as shown in Figure 1), the loss rate computed using cumulative counters (cumulative failures / cumulative(success + failures)) is compared against the loss rate computed at the end of the previous window. This then guides the sensitivity adaptation. When comparing the change in loss rate, it is important to bear in mind that a lower value of X should be used in this variant as long term statistics being smoothed, are less likely to vary dramatically over adjacent windows. The value of X chosen in this case was 5% which implies that no change in sensitivity is brought into force until the loss rate changes by at least 5%

Proposed V2: This variant employs short term statistics wherein counters over a window are used in the calculation of loss rate. The use of short term statistics implies the algorithm will react to short term variations in loss rate which may be desirable from a responsiveness perspective but may affect stability. At the end of each adaptation window, the loss rate is computed as the number of failures over the window divided by the sum total of transmissions over the window. This value is then compared against a similar value computed during the previous window. Any changes over subsequent windows using short term statistics then guides the sensitivity adaptation. As opposed to Variant V1, a higher value of X should be used in this case as the short term statistics may change dramatically. The value of X chosen in this case was 20% which implies that no change in sensitivity is brought into force until the loss rate changes by at least 20%

When increasing/decreasing the CCA threshold, it is necessary to ensure that 1) An increase in CCA threshold still ensures that the STA can hear its serving AP. Therefore, the condition $CCAthreshold + stepSize < RSSIofAP$ should always hold. 2) A decrease in the CCA threshold should ensure that the STA does not cross the limit of the wireless interface. Therefore, before decreasing the CCA threshold, the condition $CCAthreshold - stepSize >= -82dBm$ should also hold.

In addition to employing DSC on the STA side, we also explored the feasibility of enabling DSC on the AP side (see Figure 2). Traditionally, APs would use a default CCA threshold of -82dBm which would lead to roughly a fixed carrier sensing range. However, in dense environments where APs may be overcrowded in an area, it might be beneficial to shrink the range of the AP so that it can avoid carrier sensing OBSS nodes. This is accomplished in a simple way by the AP measuring the RSSI of all its associated STAs, choosing the RSSI of the farthest STA and adding a small margin to this value and setting this as its CCA threshold. As will be shown later in this paper, such a seemingly simple opti-

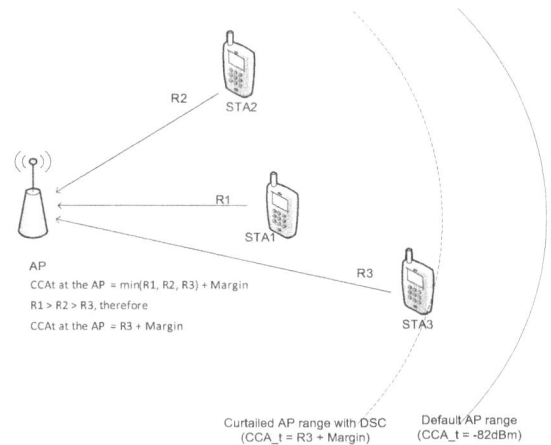

Figure 2: An example depicting use of DSC at the AP

misation can provide significant performance improvements at the same time ensuring full backwards compatibility as there is no change required to the legacy APs and STAs and the devices with the proposed modifications can gracefully coexist with legacy nodes.

3. PERFORMANCE EVALUATION

The proposed techniques along with the baseline approach were implemented in the network simulator ns-3 and their performance was evaluated through a simulation study considering a variety of scenarios. The legacy approach of using a fixed CCA threshold was also evaluated in these simulations. Simulations using different fixed CCA thresholds such as -82dBm, -72dBm, -62dBm were studied. When running a simulation for a fixed CCA threshold, the chosen CCA threshold was retained throughout the simulation whereas for simulations involving baseline and the proposed techniques, the CCA threshold varied during each simulation depending on the changes in the underlying network conditions.

The infrastructure mode of 802.11 was employed and the log distance propagation loss model (using default values) was used to simulate propagation conditions during the simulations. Ten repetitions were carried out for different seed values for each setup and the results shown are an average over these unless stated otherwise. To evaluate the performance under different network density levels, simulations with different number of STAs per cell for a given intercell distance (distance between neighbouring APs) were conducted. The AP was located at the centre of each cell with the STAs being randomly distributed around it. The node locations remained the same throughout a simulation instance. Each STA was configured to transmit 1000 packets/second with each packet payload being 1000 bytes long. Each simulation was run for 60 seconds and the performance metrics used to benchmark the different approaches are the system throughput and Jain's fairness index [4].

The evaluation was carried out under the most conservative scenario wherein all cells use the same frequency. Clearly, if some form of channel selection were to be employed, this will reduce the conflict for the scarce resource and should certainly yield better performance than what we observed in the case of a single channel scenario.

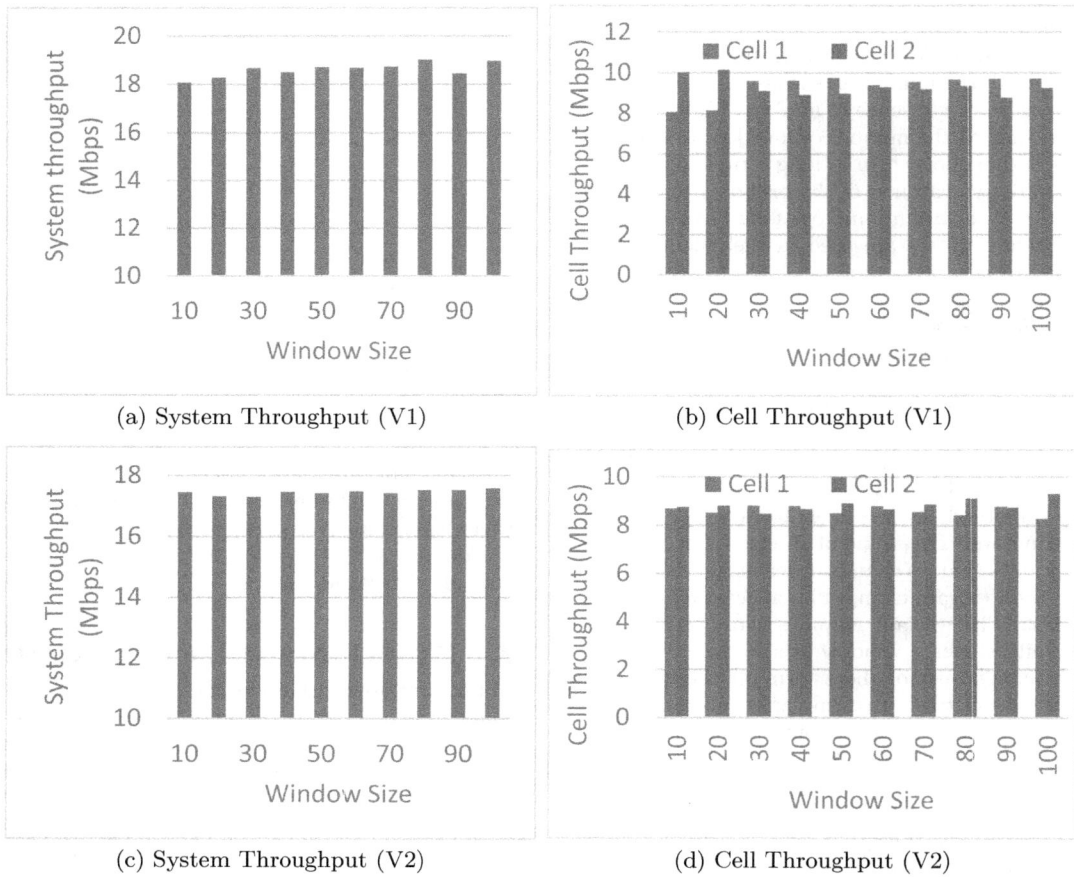

(a) System Throughput (V1)

(b) Cell Throughput (V1)

(c) System Throughput (V2)

(d) Cell Throughput (V2)

Figure 3: Effect of different window sizes on performance

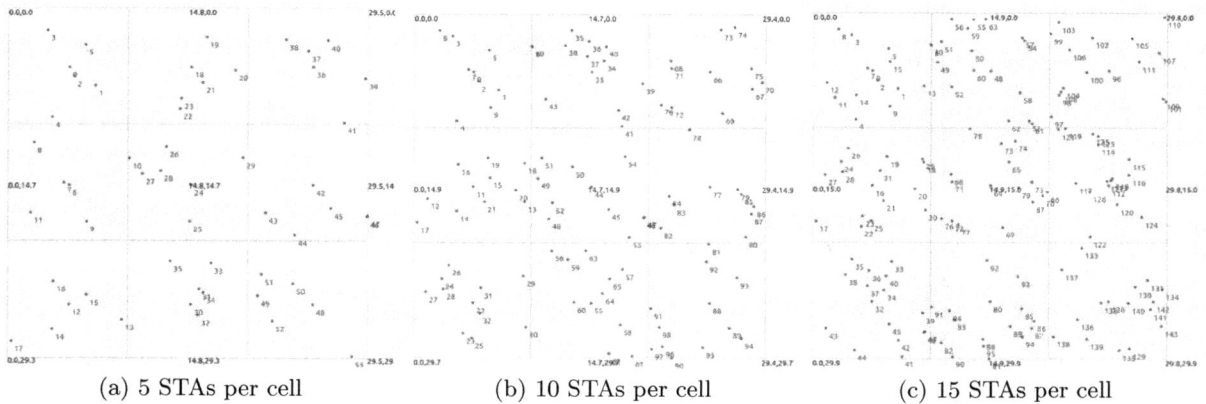

(a) 5 STAs per cell

(b) 10 STAs per cell

(c) 15 STAs per cell

Figure 4: 9 cell topology with a fixed inter-cell distance

3.1 Effect of different adaptation window sizes on the performance

To study the effect of different window sizes on the performance of the proposed algorithms, we ran simple experiments involving 2 APs with three nodes in the cell of each AP. Each experiment was repeated five times and the results shown in Figure 3 are an average. Figure 3 shows the system throughput and cell throughput for the two proposed variants V1 and V2 for different window sizes. We observe from the figures that whilst the performance varies for different window sizes, the difference does not appear to be significant. Even though the throughput for larger window sizes seems to be higher, the improvement appears to be marginal at best. This seems to suggest that any of these window size could be chosen. The choice is essentially a tradeoff between overhead and responsiveness. The smaller the window the more fine grained the adaptation at an increased computation overhead. On the other hand, the larger the window size the lower the computational overhead at the cost of relatively less frequent adaptation. A window size of 50 was chosen in this work to strike a balance between the two conflicting requirements of overhead vs responsiveness.

3.2 Benchmarking performance of the proposed techniques

Figure 4 shows the topology used in the simulation study. The node density increases as we move from Figure 4(a) to Figure 4(c). Two different inter-cell distances (30 and 40 metres) were considered in the simulation study. Figure 5 shows the performance of the legacy fixed threshold approach, the baseline approach and the proposed approaches. As evident from this figure, both variants of the enhanced algorithm outperform the legacy approaches (using fixed CCA thresholds of -82, -72 and -62 dBm respectively) and the baseline approach (RSSI of AP + Fixed Margin). The improvement over the fixed -82dBm approach varies from 2% to 12%. In all but one scenario corresponding to 5 nodes per cell and an inter cell distance of 40m, the legacy approach with a fixed threshold of -82dBm does slightly better than the proposed variants by 2-4%. This is attributed to the sparsity of the scenario (5 STAs/cell and inter cell distance of 40 metres). With few nodes in the cell and cells spaced far apart, there may not be a need for employing DSC given the less likelihood of inter-cell interference. DSC will primarily bring benefit in dense scenarios. In fact if DSC is employed in sparse scenarios, there may be a likelihood that nodes may not hear other nodes within the same cell as they are pushed out of their listening range resulting in increased intra-cell collisions thereby impinging on the throughput.

Turning the attention to the performance of the proposed variants against the baseline technique, a significant improvement is observed. In particular, improvements from 15-45% are observed which are quite significant. A key point worth bearing in mind is that the scenario considered in these simulations is the most conservative setting wherein each cell uses the same channel. Thus, if performance gains can be achieved in such a conservative setting, it is not hard to imagine that using channel selection/allocation is likely to further improve performance.

Figure 6 shows the fairness index observed in the 9 cell topology for the scenarios with different inter cell distance. Fairness index is a term defined in [4] which takes on a value between 0 and 1 with the fairness being the best if the value

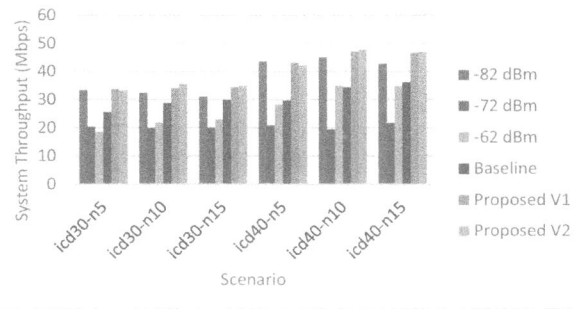

Figure 5: System throughput for a 9 cell scenario for different network densities and different inter-cell distances.

is 1 and worst if the value is 0. As observed from this figure, none of the techniques achieve fairness closer to 1. However, the proposed method achieves better fairness performance compared to other methods considered in the study and similar to that achieved by the legacy approach of using a fixed CCA threshold of -82dBm.

3.3 Benchmarking performance with DSC enabled at the AP

We now elaborate on findings in scenarios wherein DSC was enabled at the AP side. A number of different scenarios were considered encompassing STAs using fixed CCA thresholds, STAs using the baseline method and STAs using the proposed method. Figure 7 and 8 shows the performance in all the aforementioned scenarios. As evident from these figures, DSC employed at the AP in conjunction with either variant of the proposed algorithm outperforms the legacy and baseline approaches. The improvement over the legacy approach varies from 2-15%. Similar to the observations earlier, in all but one scenario corresponding to 5 nodes per cell and an inter cell distance of 40m (Figure 8), the legacy approach does better than the proposed variants with DSC enabled at the AP side by 2-4%. This could potentially be attributed to the sparsity of the scenario as explained earlier. In comparison to both baseline method enabled on the STA side only and that on both STA and AP side, significant gains are observed with the magnitude of improvement varying. Again, the scenario simulated was the one where all cells use the same channel. In scenarios with channel selection enabled, one is likely to witness better performance in comparison to the results reported here.

Figure 9 shows the fairness index observed for the scenario with DSC enabled on the AP side in the 9 cell topology considering different inter cell distance. We observe from these figures that none of the approaches including legacy are able to achieve fairness closer to 1. The proposed method with DSC enabled at the AP outperforms both the baseline technique as well as the aggressive fixed threshold approaches (-72dBm and -62 dBm) in most cases while achieving similar fairness performance as the legacy approach. Despite this, it still manages to improve the system throughput over the baseline and legacy approaches.

Overall, the results indicate that there are gains to be had from deploying DSC. The magnitude of these gains however vary and largely depend on the topology/network conditions. In sparse scenarios, there may not be much benefit

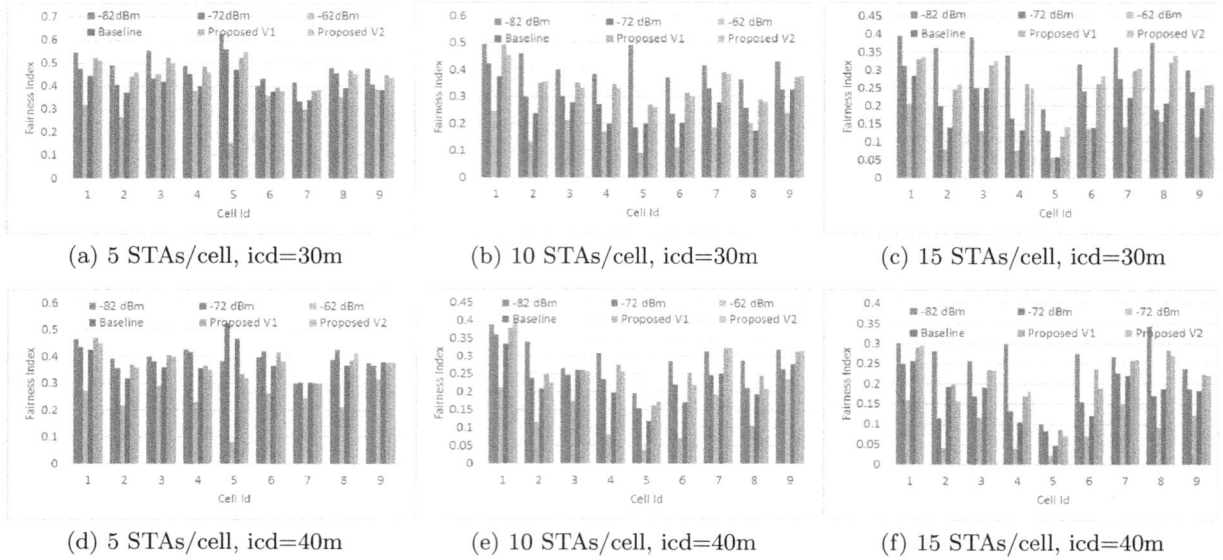

(a) 5 STAs/cell, icd=30m   (b) 10 STAs/cell, icd=30m   (c) 15 STAs/cell, icd=30m

(d) 5 STAs/cell, icd=40m   (e) 10 STAs/cell, icd=40m   (f) 15 STAs/cell, icd=40m

Figure 6: Fairness index observed in the 9 cell topology (no DSC at the AP)

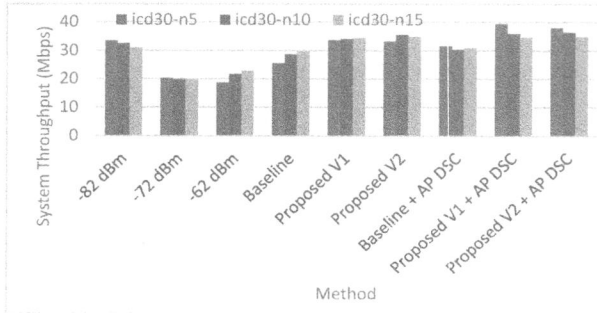

Figure 7: System throughput for a 9 cell scenario with DSC enabled at each AP (icd=30m)

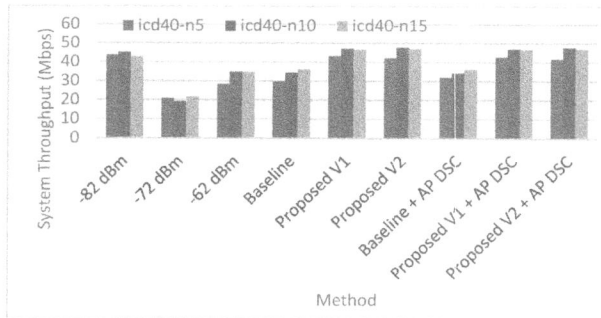

Figure 8: System throughput for a 9 cell scenario with DSC enabled at each AP (icd=40m)

from deploying DSC. However, as the network density increases, DSC may bring benefits. It is worth emphasising that choosing a static threshold at design time may not be the right approach for practical deployments and that a dynamic method for managing the CCA threshold is highly desirable. Further, depending on the node distribution, the AP could itself use DSC as a lever to improve performance. The work in the 802.11ax standards working group so far seems to be coming out with conflicting opinion of DSC. Whilst there may not be consensus on a common technique for managing the CCA threshold, the flexibility to amend the CCA threshold will be provisioned in the standard.

4. CONCLUSIONS

In a dense deployment where nodes are more likely to carrier sense neighbours not belonging to the same network, there is merit in employing dynamic sensitivity control to curtail the carrier sensing range of such nodes. This paper explored the merits and pitfalls of dynamic sensitivity control, in particular, the implications when DSC is enabled on the AP side to curtail the carrier sensing range of the AP itself in addition to that of the STAs connected to the AP. Findings indicate that whilst the gains of such a strategy vary depending on the node distributions, in the worst case it comes close to the performance of the legacy approach. Given the topology and link conditions are dynamic in a wireless network, the principle of employing a static carrier sensing range does not appeal intuitively as there are gains to be had from enabling spatial reuse wherein nodes belonging to adjacent networks could engage in parallel transmissions without interfering with each other. The work ongoing in the IEEE 802.11ax group acknowledges the pros and cons of DSC and continues its pursuit to come up with a commonly acceptable solution to enable spatial reuse ensuring that legacy nodes are not disadvantaged in the process.

With respect to future work, there are several directions worth exploring. It is clear from the work so far that using a default CCA threshold leads to lost spatial reuse oppor-

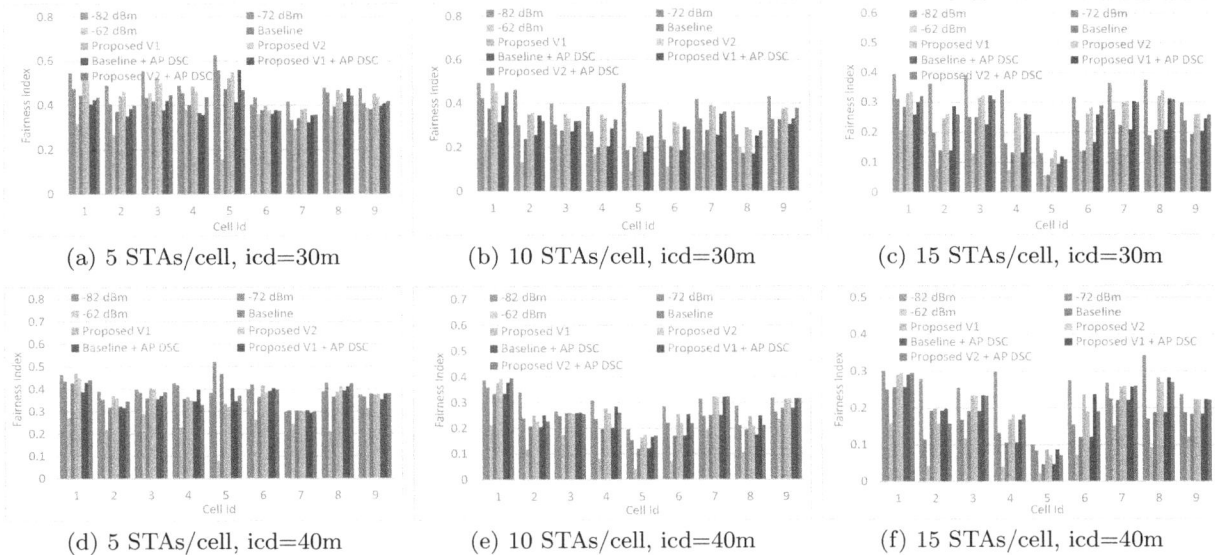

(a) 5 STAs/cell, icd=30m   (b) 10 STAs/cell, icd=30m   (c) 15 STAs/cell, icd=30m

(d) 5 STAs/cell, icd=40m   (e) 10 STAs/cell, icd=40m   (f) 15 STAs/cell, icd=40m

Figure 9: Fairness index observed in the 9 cell topology (DSC used at the AP)

tunities. Whilst the use of DSC has shown promise, how to ensure that this does not lead to unfair advantage to the nodes that use DSC is an avenue worth investigating. In particular, there may be other nodes in the cell who may or may not use DSC. Therefore, nodes with a slightly more aggressive carrier sensing threshold risk pushing other nodes within their own cell out of their carrier sensing range thereby trying to grab opportunities more often which could potentially lead to increased collisions thereby impinging on the overall system performance. Devising solutions to mitigate such problems would be immensely useful. Secondly, the use of sensitivity adaptation is one of the levers to facilitate spatial reuse. There may be other avenues such as using transmit power control with and without sensitivity adaptation, which are also being discussed within the IEEE 802.11ax standard. Devising practical solutions encompassing such techniques would also be valuable contributions to the discussions ongoing in the standardisation process.

5. REFERENCES

[1] M. S. Afaqui, E. Garcia-Villegas, E. Lopez-Aguilera, G. Smith, and D. Camps. Evaluation of dynamic sensitivity control algorithm for ieee802.11ax. In *IEEE WCNC, New Orleans, USA*, March 2015.

[2] W. Carney, Y. Morioka, K. Sakoda, M. Mori, T. Itagaki, B. Hart, T. Adachi, S. Coffey, and G. Hiertz. Dsc and legacy coexistence. IEEE doc. 802.11-14/0854r0, July 2014.

[3] S. Choudhury, A. Cavalcante, F. Chaves, E. Almeida, F. Abinader, E. Tuomaala, K. Doppler, and J. Kneckt. Impact of cca adaptation on spatial reuse in dense residential scenario. IEEE doc. 802.11-14/0861r0, July 2014.

[4] R. Jain, D. Chiu, and W. Hawe. A quantitative measure of fairness and discrimination for resource allocation in shared computer systems. DEC Research Report TR-301, Sept 1984.

[5] I. Jamil, L. Cariou, and J. Helard. Efficient mac

protocols optimisation for future high density wlans. In *IEEE WCNC, New Orleans, USA*, Mar 2015.

[6] P. Kulkarni and F. Cao. Taming the densification challenge in next generation wireless lans: An investigation into the use of dynamic sensitivity control. In *IEEE WiMob, Abu Dhabi, UAE*, Oct 2015.

[7] F. Sita, P. Xia, J. Levy, and R. Murias. Residential scenario sensitivity and transmit power control simulation results. IEEE doc. 802.11-14/0833r0, July 2014.

[8] G. Smith. Dynamic sensitivity control for hew sg. IEEE doc. 802.11-13/1290r0, Nov 2013.

[9] G. Smith. Dynamic sensitivity control channel selection and legacy sharing. IEEE doc. 802.11-14/0294r1, March 2014.

[10] J. Soder, F. Mestanov, L. Wilhelmsson, H. Persson, K. Agardh, W. Carney, K. Sakoda, and S. Coffey. Ul & dl dsc and tpc mac simulations. IEEE doc. 802.11-14/0868r0, July 2014.

[11] S. Tayamon, G. Wikstrom, K. Perez-Moreno, J. Soder, Y. Wang, and F. Mestanov. Analysis of the potential for increased spatial reuse in wireless lan. In *IEEE PIMRC, Hong Kong, China*, Aug 2015.

[12] C. Thorpe and L. Murphy. A survey of adaptive carrier sensing mechanisms for ieee 802.11 wireless networks. *IEEE Communications Surveys Tutorials*, 16(3):1266–1293, Third 2014.

Normalization of Application Performance in IEEE 802.11 Networks

Joseph Beshay and Ravi Prakash
The University of Texas at Dallas
Richardson, Texas
{joseph.beshay,ravip}@utdallas.edu

Andrea Francini
Nokia Bell Labs
Chapel Hill, North Carolina
andrea.francini@nokia-bell-labs.com

ABSTRACT

The IEEE 802.11 standards define a distributed scheme for Wi-Fi access points and stations to fairly share the wireless medium. Even if fully standard-compliant, Wi-Fi devices from different vendors have implementation differences that lead to disparities in their ability to access the medium. Erratic upper-layer behaviors become manifest when devices that exhibit such disparities inter-operate within one network. In this paper we show examples of those behaviors based on common use cases. We find that a primary cause of performance inconsistency for most network applications is the uneven ability of different IEEE 802.11 devices to access the shared medium for transmission of TCP acknowledgments, further aggravated by the excessive size of the buffers where those packets are queued before transmission. We devise and validate in a real network an effective solution for Linux hosts that is based on the link-layer priorities of IEEE 802.11e. This solution allows researchers conducting Wi-Fi experiments to collect device-independent results, and application providers to guarantee a consistent experience to their users across different devices.

1. INTRODUCTION

Wi-Fi (IEEE 802.11) is the technology most commonly used for network access by today's vast array of communication and computing devices. High capacity, ease of deployment, and untethered connectivity have made it the link layer of choice for phones, tablets, computers, TV sets, gaming consoles, and lately also for the mounting wave of Internet-of-Things (IoT) devices [8]. Wi-Fi hotspots are considered fixtures in public spaces. Wi-Fi access points (APs) and client devices (stations) come from various manufacturers. While it would be reasonable to expect equivalent or at least comparable performance from all network cards that comply with IEEE 802.11, in reality it is not unusual to observe striking disparities when comparing Wi-Fi devices from different vendors.

MSWiM '16, November 13 - 17, 2016, Malta

© 2016 Copyright held by the owner/author(s). Publication rights licensed to ACM.
ISBN 978-1-4503-4502-6/16/11. . . $15.00

DOI: http://dx.doi.org/10.1145/2988287.2989147

Transport layer protocols, such as the Transmission Control Protocol (TCP), view the link layer as an abstract best-effort packet delivery service, regardless of the link being wired or wireless. This assumption is necessary for transport protocols to achieve consistency in the provision of their services, such as reliable packet delivery and fair bandwidth sharing, to the application layer. However, differences between IEEE 802.11 and wired links do exist and are substantial. A Wi-Fi device operates in a radio frequency band that is shared not only with other devices in the same network, but also with devices in other 802.11 networks and other types of networks, such as Bluetooth and ZigBee. In order to coordinate the use of the medium, IEEE 802.11 devices employ a medium access control (MAC) scheme called carrier sense multiple access with collision avoidance (CSMA/CA) where each device must ensure that the medium remains unused for some time before it can try to occupy it for a data transmission. Accordingly, the AP and the station communicate over a half-duplex channel where both sides contend for the shared wireless medium. The ability of the upper layers of the protocol stack to meet their service expectations depends on the assumption that all active devices have equal opportunities to access the shared medium.

In a variety of practical experiments we have observed that small differences in the implementation of devices that communicate over a Wi-Fi link may cause severe imbalance in their utilization of the shared medium. Such imbalance can have significant impact on the performance of the transport layer and thus on the application. Recognizing these differences and handling them appropriately is beneficial to both research and commercial network players. For ordinary users, the degree of consistency in the performance of different devices directly affects the quality of experience that they receive from the application. Lacking the ability to troubleshoot individual user environments, application providers are best protected from user disaffection when their product performance is the same irrespective of the particular set of devices that share the IEEE 802.11 medium. Researchers need experiments that are repeatable to generate results with narrow confidence intervals. This is hard to achieve if the results depend heavily on the vendor makeup of the experiments.

In this paper we highlight inconsistencies that we have observed in simple experiments, identify their root causes, and propose solutions. Awareness of our findings can help application developers improve the robustness of their designs. Our recommendations for host configuration afford

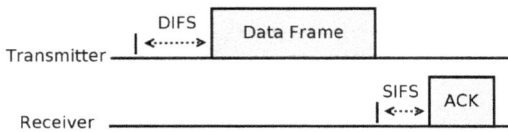

Figure 1: Transmission of a data packet using DCF.

researchers a way to enhance the consistency of their experimental results without purchasing new hardware.

The paper is organized as follows. Section 2 presents essential background about IEEE 802.11. Section 3 shows examples of performance inconsistencies between heterogeneous IEEE 802.11 devices. We investigate the cause of the observed behavior in Section 4 and propose and evaluate solutions in Section 5. In Section 6 we relate our findings to the notion of bufferbloat. In Section 7 we compare our work with two examples of previous research on TCP performance in Wi-Fi networks. We draw our conclusions in Section 8.

2. BACKGROUND

The large majority of IEEE 802.11 networks deployed in homes and businesses operate in infrastructure mode; an AP provides a number of stations with access to the wired portion of an IP network. All wireless data transfers occur between the stations and the AP without direct communication between stations. The AP transmits periodic beacons to advertise its presence and specify the parameters required for stations to join the network. In between beacon transmissions, the AP and the stations share the wireless medium using a contention-based CSMA/CA method called distributed coordination function (DCF). A device wishing to transmit a frame has to monitor the activity on the wireless medium for a time called the DCF Inter-Frame Space (DIFS). If it detects activity on the medium during the DIFS, the device calculates a random back-off interval after which it attempts to access the medium once again. If it senses no activity, the device transmits its data frame and waits for an acknowledgement (ACK) from the receiver. The receiver verifies the integrity of the frame and responds with an ACK after a time called the Short Inter-Frame Space (SIFS). SIFS is shorter than DIFS to ensure that the receiver can send the link-layer ACK before other stations send new data frames. Figure 1 shows the timing diagram of the transmission of one packet using the DCF. The scope of these data and ACK frames is fully confined within the link layer. A link-layer ACK is required for every data frame regardless of the type of upper-layer payload carried by the frame. Accordingly, the link layer treats a TCP ACK as a data frame whose reception must always be confirmed by a link-layer ACK.

The IEEE 802.11e extension of the standard [11] introduces support for Quality of Service (QoS) in the Wi-Fi medium by means of four Arbitration Inter-Frame Space (AIFS) values. AIFS1 and AIFS2 are longer than SIFS but shorter than DIFS, AIFS3 is the same as DIFS, and AIFS4 is longer than DIFS. The shorter the inter-frame space that a device associates with a frame, the higher the priority that the frame receives for accessing the medium: AIFS1 and AIFS2 are used instead of DIFS for higher-priority frames, while AIFS4 is used for low-priority background traffic. Two devices that transmit frames with the same AIFS should

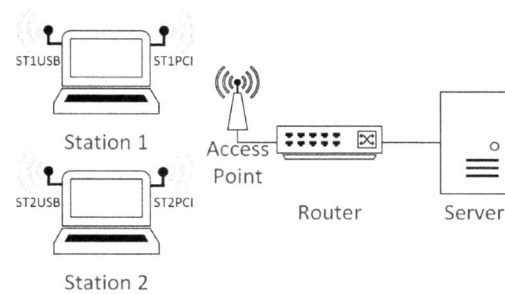

Figure 2: Network topology for the experiments.

have equal chances of accessing the medium; if both keep transmitting the same types of frames over a long time, they should end up with similar shares of the available capacity.

The IEEE 802.11 standards define the DIFS, SIFS, and AIFS values. These values have decreased gradually with the introduction of new extensions for higher link capacity (first 802.11b, then 802.11g, 802.11n, and 802.11ac). Devices that claim compliance with a particular extension should conform to the corresponding values and therefore achieve similar performance when working side-by-side.

3. WI-FI INCONSISTENCIES

We use TCP to study Wi-Fi link anomalies because it is by far the most used protocol for end-to-end transport and because its performance is highly sensitive to conditions that develop at a single link along the end-to-end data path, called the bottleneck link. We focus on the case where the TCP bottleneck is the Wi-Fi link between AP and station.

TCP does not make assumptions about the properties of the links of the end-to-end network path. The performance of the TCP connection is generally better when the contribution of packet queueing to the round-trip time (RTT) is small, the bottleneck bandwidth is stable at timescales ranging from the RTT upward, and packet losses are caused exclusively by link congestion, not by link impairments [15]. TCP finds a Wi-Fi bottleneck link comparable to a wired one when any asymmetry in connection throughput between the two directions is determined by temporary traffic conditions or by the configuration of link parameters, not when it originates from hidden differences in the implementation of the IEEE 802.11 standards at the link endpoints.

In this section we describe simple experiments where we observed erratic TCP performance due to inconsistencies in the behavior of different IEEE 802.11 interfaces. The scenarios are common ones for both researchers and ordinary users. The network topology is shown in Fig. 2. The server and the hosts of both stations are Intel x86 machines running Linux 4.4.6. The server connects to a router using 1 Gb/s Ethernet. The AP is an ASUS RT-AC55U running in IEEE 802.11g mode with WPA2 encryption. Station 1 is equipped with a mini-PCI IEEE 802.11 interface with an Atheros AR9285 chipset and a USB 802.11 interface with a Realtek RT8187B chipset. Station 2 is equipped with a mini-PCI IEEE 802.11 interface with a Ralink RT3090 chipset and USB 802.11 interface with an Atheros AR9271 chipset. Throughout the paper we use the labels in Table 1 to refer to the different station configurations.

Label	Station	Chipset	Bus	Driver
ST1PCI	1	AR9285	mini-PCI	ath9k
ST1USB	1	RT8187B	USB 2.0	rtl8187
ST2PCI	2	RT3090	mini-PCI	rt2800pci
ST2USB	2	AR9271	USB 2.0	ath9k_htc

Table 1: Labels for station configurations.

The following subsections describe the experiments and their results. We defer the analysis of the results and the identification of their root causes to the next section.

3.1 Throughput Discrepancy

In the first scenario we measure the throughput of a TCP connection between the server and a client host for each of the station configurations in Table 1. No other traffic is present. Every run of the experiment begins with the station associating with the AP. Then the server starts an iPerf TCP session to the client host that lasts 60 seconds. The station detaches from the AP after the iPerf session is finished. During each run we keep track of the congestion window size (CWND) at the TCP source using the tcp_probe module of Linux. Figure 3 shows the average, minimum, and maximum throughput achieved over five runs with each station. Figure 4 shows the evolution of CWND in one of the runs for each station. For each configuration the base RTT between server and client, measured with ICMP ping when no other traffic is present, is never larger than 3 ms.

The average TCP throughput varies between the different configurations. Switching from ST1PCI to ST1USB the average throughput to the first client host increases by 10%, from 25.44 Mb/s to 27.84 Mb/s. The second client achieves almost equal throughput with both the mini-PCI and the USB interfaces, but lower than both configurations of the first client. All connections keep CWND much higher than their bandwidth-delay product (BDP),but experience packet losses differently. ST1PC1 and ST2USB suffer not a single packet loss: CWND saturates to the maximum value advertised by the receiver while the sender is still in the slow-start phase. For ST1USB and ST2PCI, the sender exhibits the typical congestion avoidance behavior of CUBIC TCP, with losses occurring regularly when CWND is about 500 packets, well below the levels that the same sender holds persistently while serving the other configurations.

3.2 Bandwidth Sharing Unfairness

Long-term fairness in the sharing of bandwidth at the bottleneck link is a primary goal for any TCP source design. If two connections with identical source type and RTT share the bottleneck link, they are expected to settle around similar throughput levels over the course of a few RTTs. Our second scenario, as described below, shows that identical client hosts with different Wi-Fi stations can fail to achieve the long-term fairness goal by a wide margin.

In this experiment the client hosts of station 1 and station 2 concurrently receive TCP traffic from the server. Just like in the previous experiment, the shared bottleneck is the Wi-Fi medium. After both stations associate with the AP using one of their interfaces, the server concurrently starts two iPerf TCP sessions for 60 seconds, one to each client host. This scenario is common to home and business IEEE 802.11 deployments where two or more users concurrently run bandwidth intensive applications. We record the aver-

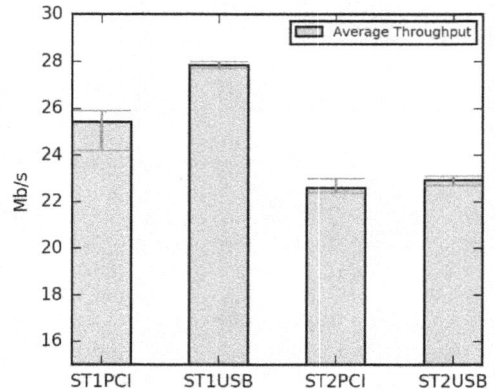

Figure 3: Average/minimum/maximum throughput achieved by each station over five iPerf TCP runs.

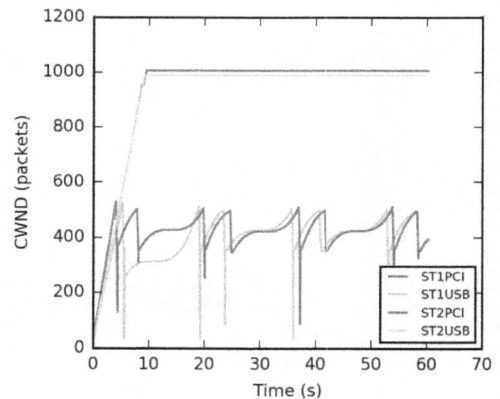

Figure 4: CWND traces in representative runs for each station configuration.

age throughput achieved with each station. We run this experiment with the four possible combinations of the configurations available for station 1 and station 2, five times per combination. The average results are shown in Fig. 5. The standard deviation of all the results is less than 0.5 Mb/s.

Two combinations show major bias in the distribution of bandwidth to the competing TCP connections over their wireless links: ST2USB is practically starved when competing with ST1USB; ST1PCI is in a similar situation against ST2PCI. The other two combinations produce more balanced outcomes: ST1USB and ST2PCI achieve ideal fairness, while ST2USB is only marginally inferior to ST1PCI. The aggregate average throughput of the four experiments is not the same, ranging from 23.73 Mb/s (ST1PCI vs. ST2PCI) to 28.97 Mb/s (ST1USB vs. ST2USB).

4. ROOT CAUSE ANALYSIS

In all scenarios of the previous section most of the traffic is flowing downstream from the server to the client hosts, and therefore from the AP to the stations. The only packets flowing in the opposite direction are the TCP ACKs. Since the downstream traffic is all transmitted by one interface, the throughput discrepancy observed in the experiments of

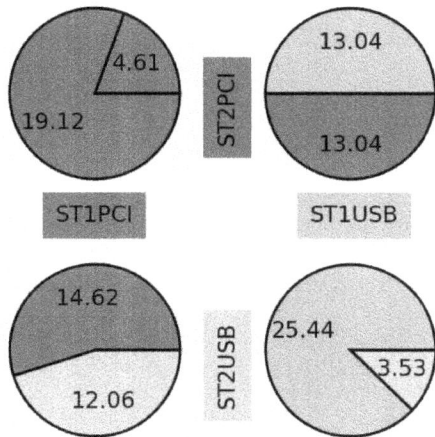

Figure 5: Throughput shares for concurrent TCP transmissions [Mb/s].

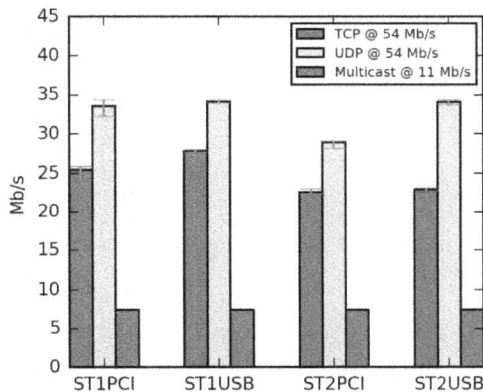

Figure 6: Average throughput achieved per station with TCP over unicast Wi-Fi, UDP over unicast, and UDP over multicast.

Section 3.1 is likely rooted in the transmission of ACKs (either TCP or link-layer) by the Wi-Fi station. To verify this conjecture we repeat scenario 1 twice, but replace the iPerf TCP session with a UDP session and use one time the unicast link layer and the other time the multicast link layer for transmissions over the Wi-Fi medium. In both cases we set the rate of the UDP traffic source well above the capacity of the Wi-Fi link to keep the medium always busy. Compared to TCP over unicast Wi-Fi, UDP over unicast removes the transport-layer ACKs but keeps the procedure for link-layer transmission the same as shown in Fig. 1, where the link-layer transmitter can dispatch a new frame only after the receiver has acknowledged the previous one. UDP over multicast additionally removes the link-layer acknowledgments. To maximize the likelihood of all clients receiving a multicast packet, the AP transmits the packet at the lowest bit rate available for the network. In our setup the AP transmits multicast packets at 11 Mb/s and unicast packets at 54 Mb/s.

Figure 6 shows the average throughput achieved with UDP over unicast and UDP over multicast for the same configurations that produced the results of Fig. 3 with TCP over unicast (plotted here again for easier comparison). The throughput of UDP over multicast is the same for all stations, at about 7.5 Mb/s (the maximum payload rate achievable by Wi-Fi over the 11 Mb/s physical layer). However some discrepancies remain with UDP over unicast. ST1PCI, ST1USB, and ST2USB achieve almost full link capacity at about 34 Mb/s while ST2PCI trails at 28.9 Mb/s. The difference between multicast and unicast suggests that the performance discrepancies originate from the link-layer behavior of the stations (the multicast scenario is the only one where no link-layer transmissions occur in the stations).

To take a closer look at the link-layer behavior of the different stations, we repeat scenario 1 with iPerf TCP sessions, but this time we also track the number of packets in the link buffer of each station. We observe that ST1PCI and ST2USB have an average standing queue of 232 and 322 link-layer frames respectively, while ST1USB and ST2PCI do not have a standing queue. The frames queued in the uplink are only for TCP ACKs.

Having ACKs queued and dropped differently at each station explains the profile diversity for the CWND traces of Fig. 4. A shorter ACK queue reflects a faster drain rate, which in turn indicates a better ability for the station to compete with the AP for access to the shared Wi-Fi medium. ST1USB and ST2PCI are more effective than ST1PCI and ST2USB at transmitting the frames carrying TCP ACKs. A shorter ACK queue also implies a shorter RTT, and therefore a smaller CWND needed for saturation of the downstream packet queue at the AP. This explains the presence of packet losses in the ST1USB and ST2PCI traces despite their lower CWND levels in the set. With ST1PCI and ST2USB, instead, the TCP ACKs are delayed long enough to cause CWND to saturate to its maximum allowed value before even overflowing the downstream AP queue. With these stations the transmission rate of data packets by the TCP source is controlled entirely by the rate of arrival of the TCP ACKs. When no packets are lost in the link layer this translates into high downlink throughput (but only in the single-station scenarios).

The following observations summarize the evidence from our experiments:

1. Different IEEE 802.11 interfaces have unequal ability to access the Wi-Fi medium. The throughput results with UDP over unicast indicate that this is true for both data and ACK link-layer frames. Less aggressive interfaces form longer packet queues.

2. With a TCP connection, a large buffer in the Wi-Fi interface may create a large queue of TCP ACKs. The large queue increases the RTT of the connection and may cause CWND to saturate at its maximum allowed value before ever incurring a packet loss. Without packet losses the TCP source may never enter the congestion avoidance phase, opening the way to unpredictable and inconsistent behavior. Contention for the shared wireless medium by multiple interfaces is a form of network congestion that the TCP sources should detect as soon as possible; large queues of TCP ACKs produce the opposite effect. This is in essence an uplink version of the bufferbloat problem [7].

5. PROPOSED SOLUTIONS

In this section we describe solutions that can help normalize the performance of applications across IEEE 802.11 interfaces from different vendors. We first present fixes for the two root causes that we have identified in the previous section, then show how the fixes contribute to better performance consistency in our reference experiments.

5.1 Solving: Medium Access Disparity

While most wireless drivers in Linux implement the MAC layer inside the kernel, control of the physical access to the medium is implemented in firmware to meet its tight timing requirements. Medium access performance is definitely sensitive to hardware quality (such as clock accuracy) and firmware details. However, modifying the hardware or firmware to re-balance the interaction of interfaces from multiple vendors is out of the scope of this paper. Instead, we focus exclusively on solutions that are fully confined within the software domain because they are much easier for end users to apply to their Wi-Fi interfaces.

As discussed in Section 2, the IEEE 802.11 medium access priority is controlled by the length of the time interval during which the station has to sense that the medium is continuously idle before it can transmit a data frame. The 802.11e extension defines four priority levels, or access categories (ACs), which correspond to different intervals (AIFS values). A packet is mapped onto one of the 802.11e ACs based on the value of the Differentiated Services Code Point (DSCP) field [9] in its IP header as specified in Table 2. We resort to 802.11e for resolution of the medium access disparity. In experiments where we play with modulating the 802.11e priority of packets based on their type we observe that the symptoms of medium access disparity are most evident when all interfaces use the same AIFS value for all packets. We find that a single modification in the mapping for AIFS assignment yields large improvements towards normalizing the performance of most applications across Wi-Fi station vendors and models.

Access Category	DSCP Value	AIFS
Voice	38, 56	AIFS1
Video	32, 40	AIFS2
Best effort	0, 24	AIFS3/DIFS
Background	8, 16	AIFS4

Table 2: DSCP to 802.11e AC mapping.

In most IEEE 802.11 deployments, downlink traffic constitutes the large majority of the data volume that moves across the shared medium. The uplink is primarily used for TCP ACKs. The AP is the source of the downlink traffic to all stations. In the downlink, contention between packets destined for different stations is resolved within the AP without MAC contention. In the uplink, instead, contention between packets arriving from different stations invokes the distributed MAC method that involves multiple stations and the AP itself. When the stations and the AP do not share the medium fairly, the performance of TCP-based applications that depend primarily on downlink data transfers is impaired by uplink shortcomings even though the uplink is only carrying TCP ACKs. *To enable fairness among receivers and to even out the performance of applications across different IEEE 802.11 interface models, we elevate the priority of all uplink TCP ACKs that carry no data payload.* We apply this change to the stations that are less aggressive in accessing the medium, that is, the stations that consistently incur the accumulation of a standing queue in the uplink. With higher link-layer priority, TCP ACKs clear their queues before the AP can transmit new downlink packets, erasing the contribution of the uplink packet queue to the RTT of all TCP connections. This improves the reactivity of the TCP sender to changes in the congestion state of the end-to-end data path, and therefore enables a closer approximation of the long-term fairness goal when TCP connections to different client hosts share the Wi-Fi medium.

We assign the higher priority to ACK packets using the Linux user-space program called iptables. On the client hosts we run the command shown in Listing 1, where *wlan1* is the name of the Wi-Fi interface. The first step of the command makes iptables intercept all packets bound to the *wlan1* interface that have the TCP ACK flag set and length not larger than 64 bytes (large enough to include the Ethernet, IP, and TCP headers, and small enough to exclude any significant data payload). In the second step, right before sending the intercepted packet to the *wlan1* interface, iptables modifies its DSCP field, promoting the packet to the AC that uses AIFS2 instead of the default AIFS3. This version of the command assumes that the DSCP marking is 0 for all TCP traffic. If deemed necessary, the command could easily be extended to elevate the ACK priority by one level when the original DSCP marking maps onto an AC between AIFS2 and AIFS4. Also in this version of the command, iptables intercepts only ACKs where no other TCP flag is set. Whether ACKs where other TCP flags (*e.g.*, the ECE flag) are also set should also be promoted is the object of further investigation, not covered here.

Listing 1: Iptables command for increasing the link-layer priority of TCP ACK packets.
```
iptables -t mangle -A OUTPUT -o wlan1 -p tcp \\
    --tcp-flags ALL ACK -m length \\
    --length 0:64 -j DSCP --set-dscp 32
```

We propose to execute the iptables command of Listing 1 only on Linux hosts where the Wi-Fi interface consistently experiences extensive queueing in the uplink (the presence of such queueing can be easily detected by measuring the RTT in the single-flow experiment of Section 3.1). When the AP runs a Linux distribution that is accessible to the end user, also the AP should be configured to elevate the Wi-Fi priority of payload-free TCP ACKs traveling downstream. Indeed, increasing the link-layer priority of downlink TCP ACKs has previously been shown to help correct a variety of other TCP performance issues over Wi-Fi [14, 10, 3].

The method that we propose for increasing the priority of TCP ACKs over the Wi-Fi medium modifies the IP header of the ACK and therefore has scope beyond the Wi-Fi access link. Unless the DSCP field is re-encoded at the AP or another intermediate network node, the ACK may be treated with higher priority than forward TCP packets or ACKs from other TCP receivers up to the remote TCP sender. More work will be needed to get experimental proof of the practical effects of broadening the scope of the priority elevation. However, the following considerations suggest that any effect, when at all tangible, would be beneficial more likely than harmful:

- The bandwidth consumed by the type of TCP ACKs with modified DSCP is a small fraction (at most 4%) of the bandwidth consumed by the corresponding packets in the opposite direction. Even in links that are heavily asymmetric in capacity or traffic load, it is very unlikely that the presence of high-priority ACKs can penalize the performance of other flows.

- In many cases the Wi-Fi access link is the network bottleneck for the TCP connection with the high-priority ACKs. This means that the rate of generation of the ACKs is paced by the congestion conditions at the Wi-Fi link. Everywhere else in the data path the high-priority ACKs are very unlikely to find other packets waiting in standing queues.

- The most likely case where the Wi-Fi link is not the network bottleneck is when the Wi-Fi network is connected to the Internet via a low-rate digital subscriber line (DSL) or cable modem link. Cable modem products that support prioritization of uplink TCP ACKs have been available for many years [16]. While the prioritization of TCP ACKs over the cable modem uplink does not extend to the broader Internet, it is the expression of a clear functional necessity in bottleneck links of all kinds.

Given that the benefits of TCP ACK prioritization have been exposed in multiple applications and that proven arguments against it are not readily accessible, it appears that a broad discussion on TCP prioritization and narrow guidelines for its operation should soon resume within the scientific community and standardization bodies like the IETF, extending preliminary work [2] that clearly identified the need but did not generate a standard solution.

5.2 Solving: Unnecessary Buffering

As shown in Fig. 7, by default in Linux an outgoing packet passes through two buffers: the queueing discipline (qdisc) buffer and the device driver buffer. The qdisc facility generally offers the ability to run sophisticated queue management and traffic shaping schemes inside the kernel on packets that have not yet reached the network interface (more detailed information can be found in [5] and [13]). The drivers of Wi-Fi interfaces with QoS support (802.11e) associate one FIFO queue with each AC. The size of the device driver queues is not always accessible for read and write operations. We have managed to retrieve the hard-coded queue size for three drivers in the Linux kernel (carl9170, ath9k, and ath9k_htc drivers), finding always large values (48, 123, and 246 packets per AC queue).

Unless traffic shaping rules are explicitly configured for the Wi-Fi interface, Linux creates for each AC queue in the device driver a corresponding first-in-first-out (FIFO) qdisc instance (pfifo_fast) that holds up to 1000 packets. The configuration of each qdisc and the status of the corresponding buffer can be queried using the Linux traffic control (tc) tool as shown in Listing 2.

Listing 2: Status query for qdisc buffer.
```
tc -s show qdisc dev wlan1
```

Coupled with the disparity in the ability to access the shared medium, the large qdisc buffers result in less aggressive stations incurring severe bufferbloat conditions in the

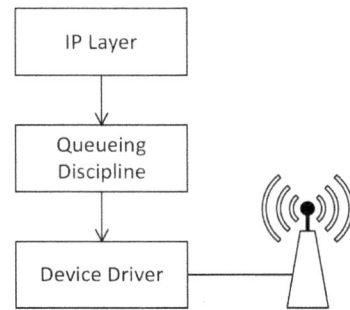

Figure 7: Outward queueing path in Linux.

uplink. While well aware of the unavoidable limitations imposed by the hard-coded size of the queues in the device driver, we can at least mitigate the detrimental effects of the oversized qdisc buffer by replacing the default configuration of the *wlan1* qdisc with a flow-queueing qdisc that enables fair distribution of bandwidth within each AC at times of congestion. Looking exclusively for flow isolation, in order to protect TCP ACKs with increased priority from unresponsive traffic that uses the same AC we choose to apply the stochastic fairness queueing (sfq) [12] qdisc to the kernel buffers that feed the four AC instances in the Wi-Fi interface (since sfq generally provides better fairness than pfifo, it makes sense to apply it to all ACs, not just the AC of the ACKs with increased priority). The tc commands to replace the default qdisc configuration are shown in Listing 3. The commands apply the default configuration of the sfq qdisc with the exception of the maximum length allowed for any flow queue, set at 20 packets, well below the 1000 packets of the default pfifo. This configuration should be applied to all stations in the Wi-Fi network. Further optimization of the sfq qdisc configuration, or comparison of sfq with other flow-queueing qdiscs like fq_codel, is beyond the scope of this paper and has no impact on the results of the experiments that we present.

Listing 3: Replacement of default qdiscs.
```
tc -s qdisc replace dev wlan1 parent :1 \\
sfq depth 20
tc -s qdisc replace dev wlan1 parent :2 \\
sfq depth 20
tc -s qdisc replace dev wlan1 parent :3 \\
sfq depth 20
tc -s qdisc replace dev wlan1 parent :4 \\
sfq depth 20
```

5.3 Performance Improvement

After replacing the default qdisc with sfq for all our test stations and increasing the priority of payload-free TCP ACK packets only for ST1PCI and ST2USB (the two stations that experienced standing uplink queues), we rerun both scenarios from section 3. The results are shown in Figs. 8 and 9.

Figure 8 shows that our solutions improve the iPerf TCP throughput for the two stations with elevated ACK priority. Increasing the priority of uplink TCP ACKs for access to the shared medium and making the queues shorter means that the TCP ACKs either return to the sender with minimal delay or get dropped (dropping otherwise late ACKs can be

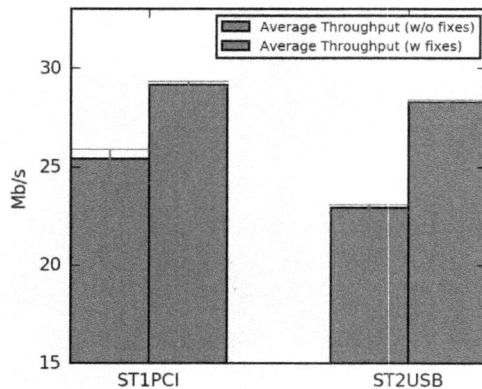

Figure 8: Average iPerf TCP throughput before and after applying our solutions (ST1PCI and ST2USB).

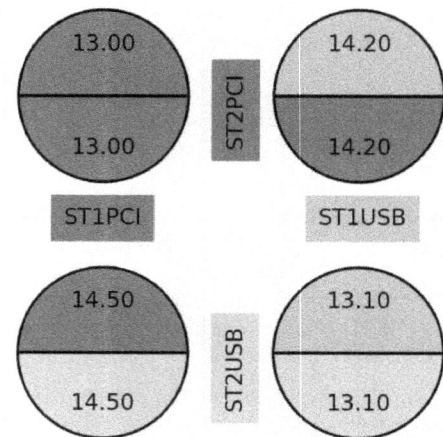

Figure 9: Throughput shares for concurrent TCP transmissions after applying our fixes [Mb/s].

viewed as a form of TCP ACK suppression, also supported in cable modem uplinks [16]). The wireless medium is no longer occupied by unneeded ACKs and allows the AP to send more packets in the downlink.

Figure 9 shows ideal bandwidth fairness for all combinations of Wi-Fi stations. Providing the TCP sender with timely ACKs ensures that the TCP source reaches and maintains operation in the congestion avoidance state, which is best equipped to fulfill the long-term fairness goal. The AP is now the only arbiter for bandwidth distribution to the two competing flows: by alternating the transmission of their packets it enforces ideal fairness for all pairs of stations.

In an attempt to assess the ability of our solutions to overcome more serious issues in device behavior, we also try to apply them to an Atheros AR9170 interface (carl9710 driver), which is known to have significant limitations [1]. Unfortunately this interface consistently under-performs all others in both individual throughput and bandwidth fairness. A close look at the kernel logs reveals that the hardware locks up repeatedly during the experiments, forcing the driver to reinitialize it. We fail to achieve ideal throughput in both single- and dual-station scenarios even when we assign all the uplink packets from the interface to AC1 and keep the priority of all packets from other stations at AC3 (the station throughput only increases by 25-30%). The shortcoming is caused by fundamental hardware issues that cannot be fully resolved with upper-layer fixes of the kind that we propose.

6. UPLINK ACK BUFFERBLOAT

Bufferbloat denotes the accumulation of excessive queuing delay in network buffers that are oversized for the traffic that they handle [7]. The effect has been studied extensively over the last five years, but most efforts have focused exclusively on the forward path of application packets (which typically includes the Wi-Fi downlink). This paper shows that the flow of those packets is also obstructed by the excessive queueing delay that the TCP ACKs can incur in the Wi-Fi uplink (*uplink ACK bufferbloat* is how we call this effect). The observation that long queues of TCP ACKs are detrimental to application performance is far from new [2] and fixes for asymmetric access links have been broadly deployed in consumer devices for quite a while [16]. We show

evidence that recognition of the problem is still not common in the Wi-Fi interface market.

The iptables and tc commands that we propose offer Linux end users, and especially networking researchers, an option that they can try for normalization of application performance before a standardized solution becomes available in Wi-Fi equipment. However, they exert no control over the size of the queues in the device driver. We have observed that Linux 802.11 drivers allocate buffers with different sizes, set without a clear common criterion. As noted earlier, we found that the ath9k driver has a 123-frame queue for each AC level, ath9k_htc has 246-frame queues, and carl9170 has 48-frame queues as observed in the source code of Linux 4.4.6. The differences between devices contribute to the inconsistency in application performance, while the large capacity of all buffer sizes contributes to performance degradation by means of bufferbloat. We plan to review the common wireless drivers in the Linux kernel and submit a kernel patch that unifies the queue sizes across the drivers. Another step forward would be ensuring that all Linux 802.11 drivers support the byte queue limits (BQL) feature [13], which is today broadly available in drivers for wired Ethernet.

Our study highlights an interesting difference in the operation of the TCP sender and receiver. The TCP sender never overflows the qdisc buffer associated with the network interface. Saturation of the qdisc buffer space simply blocks the network function calls, throttling the rate at which the application layer passes packets [4] to the stack. Throttling does not apply instead to the TCP receiver that generates ACKs in response to incoming TCP packets: the receiver passes every ACK to the stack, which then drops every ACK that finds the qdisc buffer full. The unmanaged ACK suppression associated with the onset of uplink ACK bufferbloat may confuse the remote TCP sender and further impair the performance of the application.

7. RELATED WORK

The effects of IEEE 802.11 link-layer behavior on the performance of TCP have been studied for many years. We discuss here two examples of past research that help us highlight the peculiarity of our work.

A broad survey of early approaches to enhancing the performance of TCP in single-hop and multi-hop Wi-Fi networks can be found in [6]. The approaches covered in the survey date back to the time when the IEEE 802.11 standard was in its early stage of adoption, so their focus is on performance issues inherent to the nature of the wireless medium and MAC layer protocol and not on the differences between device implementations that we address in this paper.

The issue of medium access contention between packets of the same TCP connection was studied thoroughly in [3], in the context of single- and multi-hop Wi-Fi networks. Inter-flow self-contention occurs between data packets and ACKs of the same TCP connection that try to access the Wi-Fi link in opposite directions. The paper proposes a DCF extension called *quick exchange* where the receiver of a link-layer data frame uses the link-layer ACK to carry the first packet it has available for the transmitter of the acknowledged data frame. This way a single link-layer exchange delivers two packets instead of one across the Wi-Fi medium. MAC-layer solutions like quick exchange require extensions of the 802.11 standard and new hardware to support them. Our solutions can instead be applied immediately on existing hardware and are likely to remain beneficial as the link-layer specification keeps improving.

8. CONCLUSION AND FUTURE WORK

We showed that tangible application performance inconsistencies may emerge when different IEEE 802.11 devices share the same Wi-Fi medium. We believe that the observed disparity in the ability to gain control of the shared wireless medium derives from differences in the implementation of the IEEE 802.11 standards. We proposed solutions that use 802.11e and well-known Linux tools to increase the link-layer priority of payload-free TCP ACKs and to revise the default configuration of the packet buffer that feeds the Wi-Fi interface. They work to minimize the queueing delay of the uplink TCP ACKs and thus restore the leading role of TCP congestion control in defining application performance. Our solutions can benefit end users in general and can be mostly appreciated by researchers that need consistent performance for reproduction of their experimental results irrespective of the Wi-Fi hardware available in the lab.

We realize that our fixes do not always guarantee deterministic outcomes because of factors that are beyond their control. First, implementation peculiarities of the devices, just like those that create disparities in access to the medium, can also work against the fixes. We have shown the example of a device that does not respond as expected because of a well-known anomaly in its general operation. Second, the size of the queues in the device driver is not controlled by the rest of the Linux kernel. If the buffer is too large, only a revision of the driver can change it.

We also recognize that our fixes can create networking conditions that, although not openly disruptive, could have surprising effects. First, the priority modification that we apply to the TCP ACKs can survive in the end-to-end data path beyond the Wi-Fi network if not reversed immediately by the AP. More work is needed to fully understand the implications of this extension of the scope for ACK priority promotion. Second, in a TCP connection where ACKs are both with and without payload, the priority promotion may cause the latter to overtake the former. We need to assess if altering the ACK order may have unintended consequences. As a way to eliminate all uncertainties, we plan to explore an approach for minimization of the ACK queueing delay that is fully contained within TCP and does not differentiate the link-layer transmission priority for packets of the same connection.

9. REFERENCES

[1] ArchLinux. *carl9170 problems.* Online: https://bbs.archlinux.org/viewtopic.php?id=163724.

[2] H. Balakrishnan, V. N. Padmanabhan, G. Fairhurst, and M. Sooriyabandara. TCP Performance Implications of Network Path Asymmetry. RFC 3449, December 2002.

[3] D. Berger, Z. Ye, P. Sinha, S. Krishnamurthy, M. Faloutsos, and S. K. Tripathi. TCP-friendly medium access control for ad-hoc wireless networks: Alleviating self-contention. In *Proceedings of IEEE MASS 2004*, pages 214–223. IEEE, October 2004.

[4] J. D. Beshay, A. Francini, and R. Prakash. On the fidelity of single-machine network emulation in Linux. In *Proceedings of IEEE MASCOTS 2015*, pages 19–22. IEEE, October 2015.

[5] M. A. Brown. Traffic control HOWTO. *The Linux Documentation Project*, 2006.

[6] X. Chen, H. Zhai, J. Wang, and Y. Fang. A survey on improving TCP performance over wireless networks. In *Resource Management in Wireless Networking*, pages 657–695. Springer, 2005.

[7] J. Gettys and K. Nichols. Bufferbloat: Dark buffers in the Internet. *Queue*, 9(11):40, 2011.

[8] J. Gubbi, R. Buyya, S. Marusic, and M. Palaniswami. Internet of things (IoT): A vision, architectural elements, and future directions. *Future Generation Computer Systems*, 29(7):1645–1660, 2013.

[9] K. Nichols *et al.* Definition of the Differentiated Services Field (DS Field) in the IPv4 and IPv6 Headers. RFC 2474, December 1998.

[10] D. J. Leith, P. Clifford, D. Malone, and A. Ng. TCP fairness in 802.11e WLANs. *IEEE Communications Letters*, 9(11):964–966, 2005.

[11] S. Mangold, S. Choi, P. May, O. Klein, G. Hiertz, and L. Stibor. IEEE 802.11e wireless LAN for quality of service. In *Proceedings of European Wireless*, volume 2, pages 32–39, February 2002.

[12] P. McKenney. Stochastic fairness queueing. In *Proceedings of IEEE Infocom 1990*, volume 2, pages 733–740. IEEE, June 1990.

[13] D. Siemon. Queueing in the Linux network stack. *Linux Journal*, 2013.

[14] A. Thangaraj, Q.-A. Zeng, and X. Li. Performance analysis of the IEEE 802.11e wireless networks with TCP ACK prioritization. *Telecommunication Systems*, 45(4):303–312, 2010.

[15] Y. Tian, K. Xu, and N. Ansari. TCP in wireless environments: Problems and solutions. *IEEE Comm. Mag.*, 43(3):S27–S32, March 2005.

[16] G. White. Latency in DOCSIS networks. May 2013. Online: http://www.internetsociety.org/sites/default/files/ISOC_latency_docsis.pdf.

An Efficient Content Delivery Infrastructure Leveraging the Public Transportation Network

Qiankun Su
IRIT-INPT/ENSEEIHT
University of Toulouse
Toulouse, France
qiankun.su@enseeiht.fr

Katia Jaffrès-Runser
IRIT-INPT/ENSEEIHT
University of Toulouse
Toulouse, France
kjr@enseeiht.fr

Gentian Jakllari
IRIT-INPT/ENSEEIHT
University of Toulouse
Toulouse, France
jakllari@enseeiht.fr

Charly Poulliat
IRIT-INPT/ENSEEIHT
University of Toulouse
Toulouse, France
charly.poulliat@enseeiht.fr

ABSTRACT

With the world population becoming increasingly urban and the multiplication of mega cities, urban leaders have responded with plans calling for so called smart cities relying on instantaneous access to information using mobile devices for an intelligent management of resources. Coupled with the advent of the smartphone as the main platform for accessing the Internet, this has created the conditions for the looming wireless bandwidth crunch.

This paper presents a content delivery infrastructure relying on off-the-shelf technology and the public transportation network (PTN) aimed at relieving the wireless bandwidth crunch in urban centers. Our solution proposes installing WiFi access points on selected public bus stations and buses and using the latter as data mules, creating a delay tolerant network capable of carrying content users can access while using the public transportation. Building such an infrastructure poses several challenges, including congestion points in major hubs and the cost of additional hardware necessary for secure communications. To address these challenges we propose a 3-Tier architecture that guarantees end-to-end delivery and minimizes hardware cost. Trace-based simulations from three major European cities of Paris, Helsinki and Toulouse demonstrate the viability of our design choices. In particular, the 3-Tier architecture is shown to guarantee end-to-end connectivity and reduce the deployment cost by several times while delivering at least as many packets as a baseline architecture.

Keywords

public transportation networks; XOR network coding; content delivery; urban data offloading, smart cities.

ACM acknowledges that this contribution was authored or co-authored by an employee, contractor or affiliate of a national government. As such, the Government retains a nonexclusive, royalty-free right to publish or reproduce this article, or to allow others to do so, for Government purposes only.

MSWiM '16, November 13-17, 2016, Malta, Malta

© 2016 ACM. ISBN 978-1-4503-4502-6/16/11...$15.00

DOI: http://dx.doi.org/10.1145/2988287.2989152

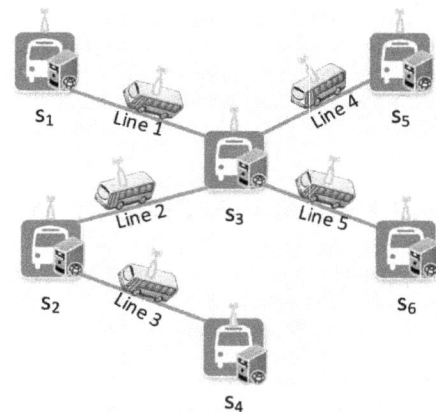

Figure 1: Content delivery using PTNs.

1. INTRODUCTION

The world has experienced tremendous urban growth in recent decades with 70% of the world's population expected to live in urban areas by 2050 [1]. Cities are responding to the environmental, transportation and infrastructure challenges this poses by becoming more intelligent, interconnected and efficient, making information and communications technologies (ICTs) crucial to their success [3]. At the same time the emergence of the smartphone as the main platform for Internet access has placed a big strain on the ICT infrastructure in urban areas. Globally, mobile data traffic has grown 4,000-fold over the past 10 years and will increase nearly 8-fold at a annual growth rate of 53% between 2015 and 2020, reaching 30.6 exabytes per month by 2020 [8]. 5G is envisioned to address the looming bandwidth crunch. However, significant 5G deployments are not expected until 2020 or beyond due to still unresolved regulatory, spectrum availability and new infrastructure deployment challenges [7].

In this paper, we propose a novel content delivery infrastructure that relies on off-the-shelf technology and the public transportation network (PTN) to help relieve the bandwidth crunch in urban areas. Our proposal is based on the observation that a significant part of the mobile content is consumed in urban areas while people are commuting using public transportation. The solution, depicted in Figure 1, proposes to install WiFi access points on buses and bus stations. The buses act as data mules creating a data mule delay tolerant network capable of carrying content that PTN customers can access while on the bus or waiting at selected stations. Data is updated onboard buses when they connect to wireless access points deployed at selected bus stops in the network. Similarly, data stored on buses can be pushed to the bus stop access points to be routed or disseminated further in the network. Mobile users connect to the platform on the bus to download different kinds of content, including videos, books, news, etc., and in turn publish new content.

The main advantage of the proposed content delivery infrastructure is that it relies on inexpensive WiFi technology and an extensive public transportation network already in place. However, public transportation networks are built around the concept of hubs with many bus lines converging on few major stops around city centers. As a result, the network can suffer from congestion points, such as the one shown in Figure 1. Four buses are shown to converge on stop S_3 and in the short time of a normal stop they all need to upload traffic to the bus station access point who in turn needs to push traffic to all four buses. Medium access control protocols, including IEEE 802.11 MAC, are designed to share the channel fairly among stations, leading to a situation where S_3 needs to communicate to all four buses but gets only a fifth of the channel capacity.

To address the challenge of congestion points, we propose to use network coding, which has been shown to significantly improve the system throughput in such scenarios [11]. Relay nodes, such as the station S_3, linearly combine sets of messages into a new network coded message (i.e. encode). Typically, a coded message m_c is obtained as the weighted sum of a set of K messages $m_{i,i\in[1..K]}$ following $m_c = \sum_{i=1}^{K} \alpha_i m_i$, where the coefficient $\alpha_i, i = 1 \cdots K$, are randomly chosen scalar elements from a finite field $\mathbb{F}_q$. In this paper, we consider basic XOR-network coding where messages are simply xor-ed together: $m_c^{xor} = \oplus_{i=1}^{K} m_i$. The destination nodes, the four buses in our example, extract the desired messages (i.e. decode) by solving the linear system created by these coded messages and their coefficients. However, network coding is suffering from a new security thread, naming pollution attacks. It spreads the pollution by combining legitimate messages with polluted ones and therefore limiting the recovery probability of legitimate messages [10]. It is possible to mitigate pollution attacks with advanced message authentication strategies but at the cost of complex cryptographic operations [4] requiring sophisticated and more expensive hardware.

To address the challenge arising from constructing a secure and cost-effective platform, we introduce an architecture that classifies bus stops in PTNs into 3 tiers. The first tier groups the biggest number of bus stops and on which we will not install any wireless access points. The second biggest group consists of bus stops on which we install basic wireless access points that are capable of relaying data traffic but cannot implement secure network coding. Finally, to minimize cost, a very limited number of bus stations belonging to the third tier will be equipped with powerful access points implementing secure network coding. Implementing such architecture, however, introduces several challenges, chief among them, how to assign the bus stops into

every tier such that end-to-end connectivity in guaranteed, packet delivery is maximized and the infrastructure cost is minimized. In short, we address these challenges by using a constructive method. First, we identify bus stops that do not need to relay any data, making them good candidates for the first tier. Second, we populate the second tier by identifying the minimum number of bus stops for guaranteeing end-to-end connectivity. Finally, among the bus stops from the second tier, we select a very small subset, judged to be the most important, to be included in the third tier.

Throughout this paper we make the following contributions: *i*) in Section 3, we introduce the content delivery infrastructure leveraging PTNs ; *ii*) in Section 4, we introduce our solution for using network coding and provide bounds on its throughput gains ; *iii*) in Section 5, we introduce a 3-Tier architecture for a secure and cost effective content delivery using PTNs and *iv*) in Section 6, we use real traces and bus schedules from three major European cities to evaluate the performance of our content delivery infrastructure.

2. RELATED WORK

Leveraging public transportation to carry delay tolerant data has been proposed in the past. Main motivations were to offer connectivity to remote locations in underdeveloped countries or to provide a disaster-relief communication infrastructure. Real deployments have been tested. DakNet [15] provides a low-cost Internet access to remote villages in India and Cambodia. The UMass DieselNet [6] has equipped up to 40 buses with access points in Amherst where data is delivered by bus-to-bus communications, leveraging their intermittent connectivity. This work has led to the design of the well known MaxProp routing protocol. The motivation of our work is different as we envision the PTN to become a content provider for its customers. And instead of leveraging vehicle to vehicle communications, we focus on the design of a fixed infrastructure to push and receive content to bus customers. In other words, no direct inter-vehicle communications are performed here and buses only communicate with the PTN access network while waiting at selected bus stops.

Routing data in delay tolerant networks (DTN) usually leverages intermittent contacts between mobile entities using the so-called "store-carry-forward" paradigm. Transfer of data is done on a per-encounter basis: two nodes carry content and exchange it upon contact such as to rapidly diffuse a copy of it to the destination. This baseline protocol is the epidemic protocol [22], which is known to be way too resource consuming due to its elevated replication rate. Main DTN routing protocols have been designed for entities that exhibit a non-predictable mobility pattern [18]. In our case, the mobility of buses is predictable and thus, leading to more efficient routing solutions [6] where vehicle to vehicle communications are exploited to create a village communication network. The difficulty with vehicle to vehicle communications, even in our predictable setting, is the harsh communication environment induced by buses moving and communicating at the same time. To favor stable and predictable transmissions, we opt for a design where buses carry data between two access points. Routing paths can be calculated a priori knowing the bus line topology, final transfer being adjusted to actual arrival and departures dates of buses on the fly.

As pinpointed earlier, our content delivery infrastructure

City	Nodes	NLN	Edges	Buses
Toulouse	44	16	46	297
Paris	213	99	236	3056
Helsinki	217	90	266	1512

Table 1: Investigated PTN topologies

Term	Description
NC	network coding
NLN	non leaf nodes, $deg(v) \neq 1$
BW	betweenness centrality
CDS	connected dominating set
$G(V', E')$	a graph induced by CDS
Δ	message creation period, $\Delta > 0$
$bw(v)$	the betweenness centrality of the node v

Table 2: Notations and definitions

usually holds several points of congestion that can be relieved by network coding [2]. Network coding solutions for DTNs were mostly discussed in the context of people-centric networks [9, 13, 17, 19, 23], where mobility of nodes is non-predictable. In these solutions, intra- or inter-flow network coding techniques have been proposed to route end-to-end flows. Messages are encoded by source or relay nodes and generally only decoded by the destination node. Complex decisions have to be made to select the messages to encode together such as to maximise the probability of decoding at the destination. Recent solutions have leveraged social routing information to improve the coding procedure at relays [19], but at the cost of memorizing the full social graph information captured by the protocol in the nodes.

On our side, we have opted for a solution where hop-by-hop encoding and decoding is performed using simple XOR operations. This approach has been successfully implemented in practice for wireless mesh networks in COPE [11]. This scheme is less effective for DTNs than for wireless mesh networks because it is rarely possible to overhear neighbors' transmissions [17]. However, it is still possible to apply the XOR scheme of COPE to pairwise communications crossing at a node of the network [13]. Exploiting this feature, we have demonstrated theoretically in previous works [20] that the maximum delivery probability could be increased of up to 50% in a village-to-village communication network.

To provide a cost-efficient design of our content delivery infrastructure, a reduced number of wireless access points have to be rolled out. Maintaining full connectivity with a reduced number of routing enabled nodes is possible by selecting the ones forming a connected dominating set of the graph (CDS). In this case, all non-CDS nodes push their traffic to the closest CDS node. CDS is then in charge of routing data [21] to the destination. In our paper, we leverage CDS to select the stations where access points are rolled out. Selecting the minimum subset of nodes forming a connected dominating set cannot be solved in polynomial time. As such, we build our solution on a previously proposed heuristic [16] whose main idea is to form a connected dominating set by traversing all nodes (either with a breadth first search or depth first search), beginning with the node with the highest degree, and continuously removing the node v if $G(V - \{v\})$ is still connected. This heuristic is modified by accounting for different centrality measures of the graph such as betweenness [5] and page rank [14]. Next, we present in details our contributions, starting with the global architecture description of our content delivery infrastructure.

3. PTNs FOR CONTENT DELIVERY

3.1 Overall architecture

The content delivery infrastructure envisioned in this paper leverages public transportation networks where public vehicles such as buses act as data mules. Data mules carry

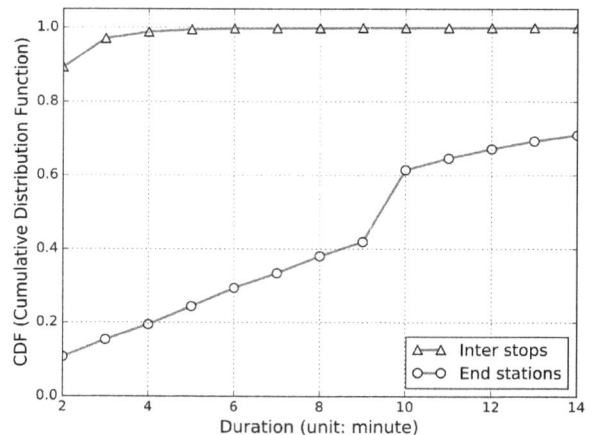

Figure 3: The CDF of the duration of inter stops and waiting time at end stations in Paris.

content that PTN customers can access over wireless (e.g. WiFi) on the bus or waiting at selected stations. Therefore, each bus is equipped with a wireless access point (AP) and local data storage capabilities. Data is updated onboard buses when they connect to wireless access points deployed at relevant bus stops of the network. Similarly, data stored on vehicles can be pushed to the bus stop AP to be routed or disseminated further in the network. Of course, AP enabled bus stops are equipped as well with storage capabilities.

Our data mules travel on a fixed schedule back and forth between two end stations, stopping along the way at different intermediary locations for a very short period of time. We count the duration of inter stops for the public bus network of the city of Paris using publicly available traces to estimate the contact time between buses and intermediate stops since the contact time is not recorded in the trace. The statistics are plotted in Figure 3, showing the duration of almost all inter stops is within 4 minutes, not to mention the contact time between the bus and intermediate stops. In contrast, Figure 3 shows that around 40% of the buses wait at the end stations for more than 10 minutes. End stations are thus particularly interesting elements of the PTN. At end stations, conductors usually rest for an extended period of time before engaging into the next journey. Moreover, multiple bus lines usually cross at such stations. This results into an extended contact duration between bus lines at end stations. We have shown in [20] that it is beneficiary to leverage such extended contact duration for exchanging data between the buses. Thus, in our architecture, we only deploy access points at the final stops of bus lines, and do not consider intermediary stops for such purpose.

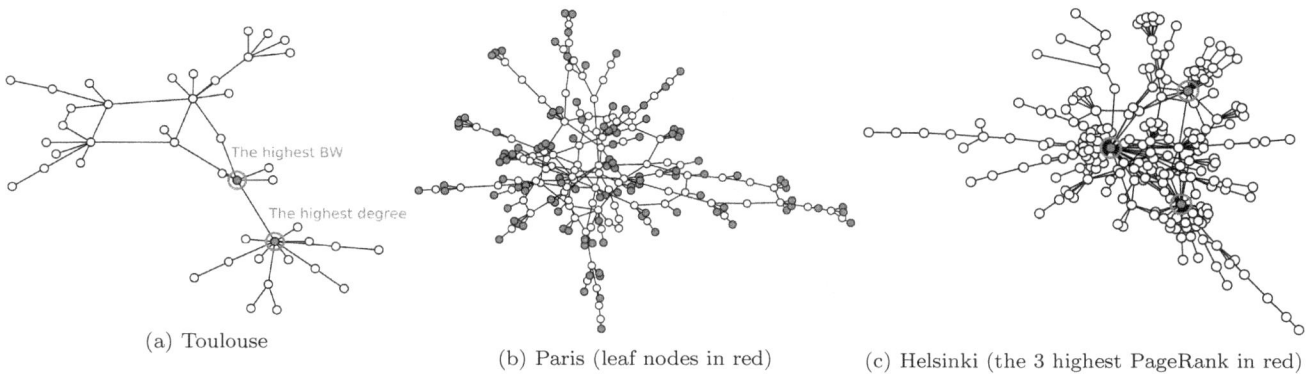

(a) Toulouse   (b) Paris (leaf nodes in red)   (c) Helsinki (the 3 highest PageRank in red)

Figure 2: The biggest connected component of public transportation networks.

3.2 Models and assumptions

PTN model and topologies.

The content delivery infrastructure can be modeled as an undirected graph $G(V, E)$ where edges represent bus lines and vertices represent corresponding end stations. Formally, there is an edge $e = (s_i, s_j)$ in E if there exists a bus service between two end stations s_i and s_j. A bus b_k of the PTN is associated with an edge (s_i, s_j).

In this paper, our derivations hold for a connected graph. If G is not connected, all computations can be applied to the individual connected components of the PTN of interest. Examples of such graphs are given in Figure 2, showing the largest connected components of three different PTNs serving as case studies in this work: a small-scale PTN from the city of Toulouse, and two large-scale ones for Paris and Helsinki, respectively. Table 1 lists the main characteristics of these networks which have been extracted from the open dataset of PTN providers[1] in GTFS[2]. Thanks to the popularity of GTFS, our scheme is easy to adapt to other cities.

Traffic model.

Users of this content delivery service connect to a platform on the bus that offers different pieces of content (videos, books, news, etc.). It is possible to update the content available on the bus using the delay tolerant network described earlier. Users may (*i*) publish new content to the on-board platform which can be spread to other nodes of the network, or (*ii*) subscribe to new content to be fetched from another node. Content not available in the PTN may be obtained from a node connected to the Internet. To save deployment costs, only one or two end stations have an Internet access.

This paper leaves for further investigation how content is actually updated, requested and fetched. The aim of this paper is to show the pure networking benefit of using PTNs for carrying delay tolerant content in a cost-efficient manner.

As such, we simplify the network traffic model by assum-

[1]Toulouse: https://data.toulouse-metropole.fr/explore/dataset/tisseo-gtfs/
Paris: http://dataratp.opendatasoft.com/explore/dataset/offre-transport-de-la-ratp-format-gtfs/
Helsinki: http://developer.reittiopas.fi/pages/en/other-apis.php
[2]GTFS (General Transit Feed Specification) is a format for public transportation schedules and associated information

ing that each node of the network pushes a constant flow of messages to be routed into the PTN. Messages are generated periodically at every node with a creation period of Δ time units. Every time a new message is created by end station s_i, its destination end station s_j $(j \neq i)$ is selected at random among possible ones. With such a traffic model, we are able to capture the maximum throughput the PTN offers to all possible flows of the network.

It is interesting to note that this type of content delivery infrastructure can be leveraged as well to offload delay-tolerant data from regular access networks (e.g., cellular, ADSL) to remote and poorly connected locations using long range bus transportation networks.

3.3 Underlying protocols

DTN routing.

From the connected graph G, we are able to pre-calculate routing tables for each station by using Dijkstra's shortest path algorithm. The routing metric to minimize is the basic hop count metric. Thus, a route between s_i and s_j is given by the sequence of stations $(s_i, s_{i+1}, ..., s_j)$ that minimizes the number of buses used. Corresponding routing tables are stored at the end stations composing G.

When a bus arrives at a station, it uploads as many messages as possible to the station's AP until it leaves, possibly sharing the bandwidth with other buses. After receiving a message m from a bus, the station extracts m's destination s_j and looks up its next hop s_k in the routing table. Then, m is placed into a virtual queue Q_k that stores only packets going to next hop s_k.

In parallel, the station tries to empty the messages stored in its queues to the set of buses currently connected to its access point. From the list of buses, it extracts the set of next hop nodes that can be reached through them, and corresponding virtual queues. In a round-robin manner, a message is dequeued from one of these queues and sent to the corresponding bus.

Medium access control.

To be fair, we assume a medium access control at the base station that divides the bandwidth equally between the contending nodes. Thus, any fair medium access control mechanism such as CSMA or TDMA can be implemented in practice.

As such, if N buses are connected to a station, $N + 1$

emitters are concurrently contending for the communication bandwidth. In other words, a station only gets a $1/(N+1)$ share of the bandwidth at the MAC layer. However, to drain N messages coming from the N connected buses on the uplink, the station's AP has to send N messages on the downlink as well. But it only has a $1/(N+1)$ bandwidth share, while it has N times more data to send than a bus. Such an imbalance results in a significant drop in throughput under heavy traffic conditions.

4. NETWORK CODING FOR PTNs

4.1 Motivation

It is possible to mitigate the unbalanced bandwidth demand by leveraging inter-session XOR network coding at stations as underlined in [20]. Main concept is represented in Figure 4.

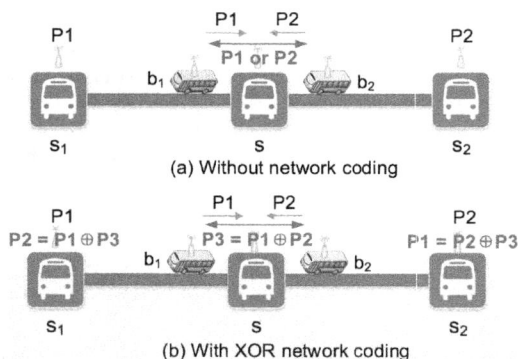

Figure 4: Exchange two packets via a station.

Figure 4-(a) illustrates the standard solution to exchange packets at relay nodes. It takes 4 transmissions to exchange two packets $P1, P2$ between two buses b_1, b_2 via the station s without network coding. In this case, s needs twice as many transmissions as b_1 or b_2. As shown in Figure 4-(b), if the station s broadcasts a coded packet $P3 = P1 \oplus P2$ in a single transmission, both buses can extract a new packet by xor-ing $P3$ with the packet they have previously sent. For instance, s_1 obtains $P2$ by calculating $P3 \oplus P1 = P2$. With XOR network coding, the base station needs a single transmission instead of two, providing the most efficient use of the underlying fair communication MAC protocol.

4.2 XOR network coding implementation

This section presents our implementation of XOR network coding for our content delivery infrastructure. Encoding and decoding operations are only performed at the stations. Buses are carrying coded messages that are decoded at the next hop station. Thus, they don't store any previously carried messages. This feature is important as a bus may not possess the message necessary to decode XOR-ed ones by simply keeping the history of previously carried message. This is typically the case if previous messages were carried by a different bus of the same bus line.

If network coding is performed at a station, the virtual message queue Q_j defined for the messages routed to next hop s_j is further divided into several network coding queues. These network coding queues are indexed by a 2-tuple key (s_i, s_j) where s_i and s_j denote the previous hop and the

next hop identifier of a message. A network coding queue is referred to using notation Q_{ij}.

For instance on Figure 4, $P1$ is stored in queue Q_{12} and $P2$ in queue Q_{21}. Encoding and decoding algorithms are introduced next. All network coding operations are limited to the 1-hop neighborhood of the station s where buses enter in contact. Encoding is done at the station s and decoding is done at next-hop stations.

Encoding.

The pseudo-code is listed in Algorithm 1. We assume that at the time of encoding, a station s has a list of buses currently waiting at the station. It can easily obtain a list of the next hop stations S that are reachable with all buses currently waiting.

The station goes through S to find two non-empty message queues: Q_{ij} and Q_{ji} $(i \neq j)$[3]. With this selection, two local cross communications are identified that can directly benefit from network coding. Next, the two head-of-line messages m_i and m_j are picked from Q_{ij} and Q_{ji} respectively. A new message m_c is created by xor-ing m_i and m_j together (i.e. $m_c = m_i \oplus m_j$). Station s broadcasts m_c in a single transmission. With this selection, we ensure that m_c can be decoded at both next-hop stations s_i and s_j.

If no cross communication is found, basic unidirectional forwarding operations are performed to reduce delays.

Algorithm 1 Coding procedure

$B = \{$Buses waiting at the station $\}$
$S = \{$Next hop nodes to be reached by B $\}$
for all $s_i \in S$ **do**
  for all $s_j \in S, j \neq i$ **do**
    if $Q_{ij} \neq \varnothing$ and $Q_{ji} \neq \varnothing$ **then**
      m_i is picked at the head of Q_{ij}
      m_j is picked at the head of Q_{ji}
      return $m_c = m_i \oplus m_j$
    end if
  end for
end for

Decoding.

Each station keeps the messages that it has given to buses. The messages are stored in a hash table keyed on message identifier. When a station receives a XOR-ed message $m_c = m_i \oplus m_j$, it looks through the hash table to get the previously sent message, say m_i. A new message m_j is retrieved from m_c by XOR-ing it with m_i, i.e. $m_j = m_c \oplus m_i$. Once the message m_j is decoded, it is stored into the virtual network coding queue. The previous station and the next station of m_j are extracted to store it in the appropriate virtual network coding queue.

Bound on throughput gains.

In [20], a theoretical analysis has been conducted to derive an upper bound on the throughput gain such a XOR network coding strategy can offer for a realistic PTN. Main results are drafted to introduce the gains we can expect for the PTNs of Toulouse, Paris and Helsinki if they are leveraged for content delivery. These gains will be ascertained in this paper using fine-grained simulations in Section 6.

---

[3]Complexity of getting these two non-empty queues is of $|S|^2/4$ steps on average.

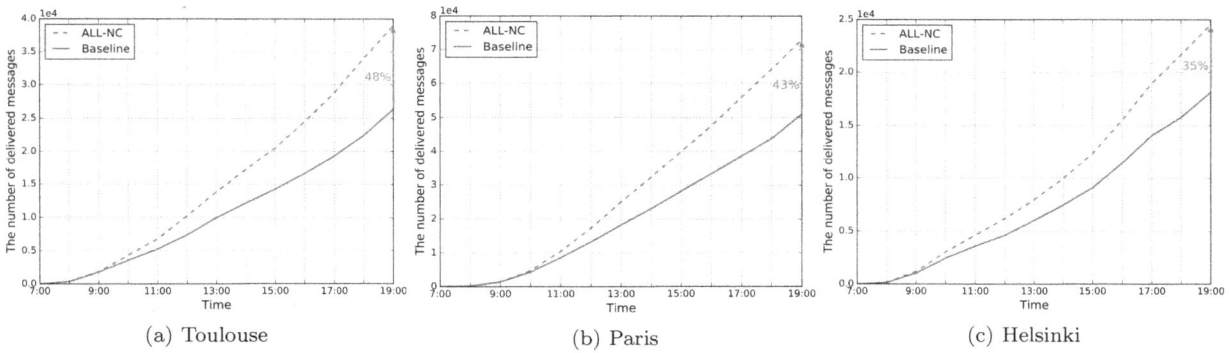

Figure 5: Network coding benefit: number of delivered messages.

In our model, we calculate, for all pairs of bus lines in the PTN and at each station they cross, the total duration buses spend waiting alone (t_1 for line 1, t_2 for line 2) and the time they spend waiting together t_{12}. From this information, we can derive the amount of data that a pair of bus lines can exchange with and without network coding using Eq. (1) and Eq. (2) respectively.

$$D_{nc} = [min(t_1, t_2) + \frac{2}{3} \cdot t_{12}] \cdot R \qquad (1)$$

$$D = [min(t_1, t_2) + \frac{1}{3} \cdot t_{12}] \cdot R \qquad (2)$$

where R denotes the data rate. From these values, an upper bound on the throughput gain that can be expected with our pairwise inter-session XOR network coding solution can be established. Table 3 shows the overall network throughput for the Toulouse, Paris and Helsinki topologies using $R = 100Mb/s$. The expected maximum throughput gains G_t is defined as $(D_{nc} - D)/D$ and the overlapping ratio r is defined as $r_{12}/(r_1 + r_{12} + r_2)$.

The potential gain is really important and thus, XOR-network coding is a promising solution for improving the performance of our content delivery infrastructure.

This upper bound is calculated assuming all pairwise bus encounters arise without other buses being present at the same time at the station. In reality, this is not the case. Additional buses will bring more congestion to the station AP and reduce the benefit of pairwise network coding. Next, we calculate the exact XOR network-coding benefit using fine grained simulations.

4.3 Network coding benefit

In this section, we aim at evaluating the benefit that can be brought if all PTN stations perform the XOR network coding strategy of Algorithm 1. Extensive simulations are carried out using the simulation setup described in Section 6.1. Two figures of merit are evaluated: (i) the number of delivered messages and (ii) the overhead ratio. The overhead ratio is defined as the ratio of the number of times

any message was transferred at any station to the number of messages delivered.

The XOR network coding strategy is compared to the *baseline* strategy where all nodes are equipped with a wireless AP and simply forward packets. The strategy where all nodes perform network coding is named ALL-NC.

Figure 5 shows the number of delivered messages for baseline and ALL-NC strategies from 7 : 00 to 19 : 00. Clearly, ALL-NC outperforms the baseline strategy as expected. Improvements reach 48%, 43% and 35.5% in Toulouse, Paris and Helsinki, respectively. These gains are significant but not as large as the upper bound presented in Table 3 (that are respectively of 82.5%, 80.5% and 75%). As already explained, this upper bound is optimistic since the pair-wise network coding can't totally compensate the traffic imbalance if more than two buses are in contact at the station.

This gain could be improved if the station could XOR more than two packets together as done in the wheel topology of [11]. But this is unfortunately not possible as the 1-hop decoding stations can't overhear the remote message emissions of the buses as done in a pure wireless setting.

Anyway, the benefit of ALL-NC is really significant: messages get delivered much faster with network coding since stations are capable of draining twice as many packets as without network coding. The number of delivered messages obtained with network coding reach the same level as the one obtained for non network coding about 2.5 hours earlier.

The overhead ratio is also reduced with network coding, as shown in Figure 6. In this plot, the message creation period Δ is increased to reduce traffic. The overhead is nicely reduced since two stations can extract desired messages with

City	$r(\%)$	D(TB)	D_{nc}(TB)	$G_t(\%)$
Toulouse	71.5	21	39	82.5
Paris	71.5	102	185	80.5
Helsinki	58.0	393	688	75

Table 3: The potential improvements: upper bound

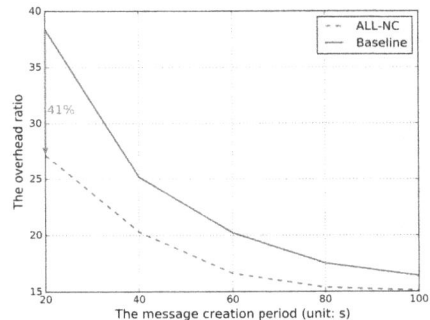

Figure 6: The overhead ratio in Paris.

XOR network coding in a single transmission instead of two with baseline. In the Paris topology, the decrease reaches 29% which is captured at $\Delta = 20$. With Δ increasing, the gap between baseline and ALL-NC is narrowed since traffic is reduced and thus, coding opportunities become less frequent.

5. A COST-EFFICIENT AND SECURE DESIGN

Section 4.3 demonstrated the benefit of using XOR network coding in PTNs. However, before adapting it as part of our content delivery infrastructure, two main challenges have to be addressed:

1. Installing network coding enabled APs at all PTN end stations is expensive – it requires specialized hardware plus extended storage capabilities.

2. Network coding is threatened by the specific pollution attack. A malicious user could inject in the network a junk message to be XOR-ed with others. Subsequent XOR operations that include this message will pollute the rest of the network.

It is possible to mitigate pollution attacks with advanced message authentication strategies [4] but at the cost of complex cryptographic operations. Thus, installing a *secure* network coding AP is even more expensive than solely installing a network coding AP. In this section, we will concentrate on reducing the overall deployment cost such as to thwart pollution attacks. Three subsequent improvements are discussed: leaf stations removal, the 2-Tier architecture and finally the 3-Tier architecture.

5.1 Leaf stations removal

In Section 3, we proposed to leverage public transportation networks for content delivery by deploying wireless APs at all end stations. However, note that leaf stations ($deg(v) = 1$) do not need to relay any message. Thus, it is not necessary to install wireless APs at the leaf stations, leading to a drastic reduction in hardware cost. Leaf nodes are highlighted in red in Figure 2-(b) for the Paris topology. Looking at Table 1, it can save 63.5%, 53% and 52% of wireless APs in Toulouse, Paris and Helsinki, respectively. More importantly, after the leaf stations removal, the number of delivered packets in the network is unchanged – only the hardware cost is reduced.

5.2 2-Tier Architecture

The number of wireless interfaces is further reduced by calculating a connected dominating sets V' for the graph G. V' induces a connected subgraph $G'(V', E')$ of $G(V, E)$, representing a virtual backbone of the network. Only the stations belonging to V' are required to be equipped with wireless transceivers. Connected dominating sets make sure that the communication network is still connected.

Figure 7 is used to demonstrate how messages are delivered in such a network. A message m is carried by a bus b_i to the station s_i ($s_i \in V'$) that dominates the leaf station s. m is relayed to s_j following the shortest path of G' and finally carried by another bus b_j to the destination t.

The main idea of MCDS-NON-DISTRIBUTED [16] is to form a connected dominating set by transversing all nodes (either breadth first search or depth first search), beginning with the node with the highest degree, and continuously removing the node v if $G(V - \{v\})$ is still connected. However,

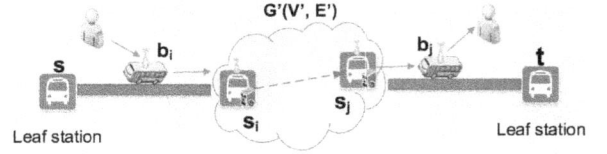

Figure 7: Relay messages in 2-tier architecture.

degree centrality sometimes can be deceiving for a purely local measure. Thus, we design another heuristic algorithm to construct a CDS with betweenness centrality. A connected dominating set is formed by iterating over nodes on ascending order based on betweenness centrality and continuously removing the node v if $G(V - \{v\})$ is still connected. The algorithm includes two steps: i), compute the shortest-path betweenness centrality for nodes V and sort them by betweenness centrality on ascending order; ii), transverse all nodes and continuously remove the node v if $G(V - \{v\})$ is still connected. The pseudo code is given in algorithm 2.

Algorithm 2 CDS with betweenness centrality

Require: A connected graph $G(V, E)$
  $d \leftarrow \{v : bw(v)\}, v \in V$, sort by BW on ascending order
  $V' \leftarrow \varnothing$, connected dominating sets
  for all $v : bw(v), v \notin V'$ **do**
    if $bw(v) = 0$ OR $G(V - \{v\})$ is connected **then**
      $V' \leftarrow V' \cup MAX - BW(N(v))$
    else
      $V' \leftarrow V' \cup \{v\}$
    end if
    $V \leftarrow V - \{v\}$
  end for

We first compute the shortest-path betweenness centrality for nodes V, and then sort the key-value pairs by value (i.e. betweenness centrality) on ascending order. Iterate over this sorted collection of node-betweenness pairs. A node whose betweenness centrality is equivalent to 0 (i.e. $bw(v) = 0$, v is a leaf node) can be directly removed from G. Because of this, unlike MCDS-NON-DISTRIBUTED, the leaf nodes are deleted from G without checking if the rest graph is connected, leading to improvement, especially for sparse graph. If $G(V - \{v\})$ is not connected, obviously, v must be included in the connected dominating sets V'. Otherwise, v is removed from G and the node with the highest betweenness centrality of v's neighbours is added to V'.

5.3 3-Tier Architecture

In this section, we explore how to further reduce the number of nodes performing network coding so as to improve the network security at little cost to network performance.

Motivated by the well known 80-20 rule, we examine how many nodes performing network coding are needed to achieve the performance similar to that of 2-tier architecture described in Section 5.2. Three metrics, degree, betweenness centrality and PageRank, are explored to select a subset of nodes. PageRank computes a ranking of the nodes in the graph G based on the structure of the incoming links. Since PageRank is applied to directed graphs, our undirected graph $G(V, E)$ is turned into a directed graph by assigning two directions to each edge.

Key	Value
simulation duration	12 hours
update interval	1s
time-to-live	12 hours
buffer size	infinite
message interval	20s

Table 4: Simulation parameters.

We compute the degree, betweenness centrality and PageRank for nodes in G, and then select the top n nodes that belong to CDS. The empirical results on three real traces are given in Section 6.3.

6. PERFORMANCE EVALUATION

In this section, we evaluate the performance of the proposed architectures in terms of packet delivery and cost effectiveness. In short, we make the following observations:

i) In Section 6.2, we show that 2-Tier is able to reduce the number of wireless access points required to cover 3 major cities by approximately a factor of 3. This significant cutback in infrastructure is achieved while the packet delivery never drops below that of Baseline.

ii) In Section 6.3, we show that 3-Tier reduces the number of wireless access points capable of performing network coding required to cover 3 major cities by over an order of magnitude. 3-Tier accomplishes this cutback while delivering essentially the same performance in terms of messages delivered.

iii) In Section 6.4, we show that 3-Tier improves the cost-effectiveness by over 100% on average when compared to 2-Tier, its closest competitor.

6.1 Experimental setup

The performance evaluation are carried out on the ONE (Opportunistic Network Environment) simulator [12]. We added the broadcast mechanism to the ONE to support network coding leveraging the broadcast nature of wireless transmissions. The simulation parameters are summarized in Table 4.

City	Baseline	ALL-NC	2-Tier
Toulouse	44	44	13
Paris	213	213	85
Helsinki	217	217	60

Table 5: Number of wireless access points required to cover 3 different cities. The 2-Tier architecture reduces the required number of interfaces by approximately a factor of 3.

Real traces: Real traces of the public transportation networks of Toulouse, Paris, and Helsinki are used for this evaluation, selected so as to represent cities of different scales. All traces are in GTFS (General Transit Feed Specification), developed by Google, a common format for public transportation schedules and associated geographic information. To get the mobility model, a bus ID is assigned to each trip using the schedules available in the traces. For instance, if there is a record in the dataset of a bus trip from the station s_i to s_j for the bus route r, a new bus id is assigned to

City	2-Tier	3-Tier
Toulouse	13	2
Paris	85	10
Helsinki	60	3

Table 6: Number of wireless access points capable of performing network coding required to cover 3 different cities. The 3-Tier architecture reduces the number of such interfaces by over an order of magnitude.

this trip if there is no bus available at the station s_i for r. Otherwise, the bus waiting at s_i is assigned to this trip. In general, public bus services run according to schedules that are different between working days, Saturdays, Sundays and holidays. In this paper, we use working day schedules. A subset of schedules is chosen from the trace, time period ranging from 7:00 to 19:00.

Data flows: A message is created at every station at a given time period, Δ (set to 20 s for the data presented here), while the simulation is running. The message destination is selected uniformly at random among all the stations.

Routing: For all three topologies, route tables are generated for each router before the simulation starts so that messages are relayed based on the shortest paths.

Basis for comparison: We compare the 2-Tier and 3-Tier architectures with **Baseline**, where all nodes are equipped with a wireless access point and forward packets without performing network coding and **ALL-NC**, wherein all nodes are equipped with a wireless access point and all implement network coding.

6.2 Evaluation of the 2-Tier architecture

In this section, we evaluate the 2-Tier architecture in terms of the cost of its deployment and packet delivery.

Results: Table 5 shows the number of wireless access points necessary to cover 3 major cities using the Baseline, ALL-NC and 2-Tier architectures. The results show that 2-Tier is able to reduce the number of interfaces by approximately a factor of 3. This results in the more impressive when looking into the packets delivered, shown in Figure 8. As expected, ALL-NC, equipped with over 3 times as many wireless access point and using network coding, delivers the most packets. However, the 2-Tier architecture, with a fraction of interfaces is still capable of outperforming Baseline in all 3 cities and being very competitive when compared to ALL-NC in 2 out of 3 cities.

For a better understanding as to the differences in performance observed in the three cities, Figure 9 shows the average hop count of the routes utilized by all packets delivered during the simulation. Baseline and ALL-NC have the same number of access points so the routes selected are the same and shown in Figure 9 under the label "ALL". The data shows that for Toulouse, on average, the packets were delivered over routes of similar hop count for all architectures, explaining the similar performance of ALL-NC and 2-Tier in terms of packets delivered. For Paris and Helsinki, however, the 2-Tier's dramatic reduction in deployed access points does lead to packets taking longer paths, explaining why the number of packets delivered drops when compared to ALL-NC. Nevertheless, 2-Tier, thanks to network coding always outperforms Baseline despite the longer paths.

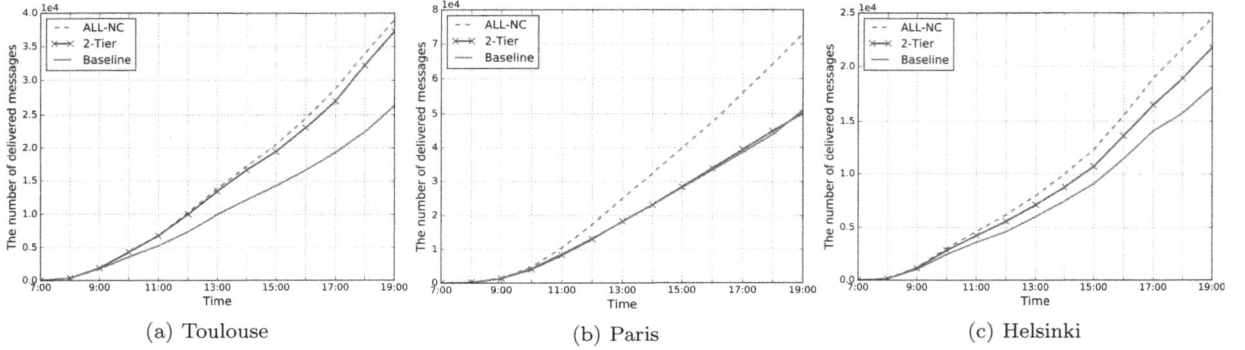

(a) Toulouse   (b) Paris   (c) Helsinki

Figure 8: Number of messages delivered for Baseline, ALL-NC and 2-Tier.

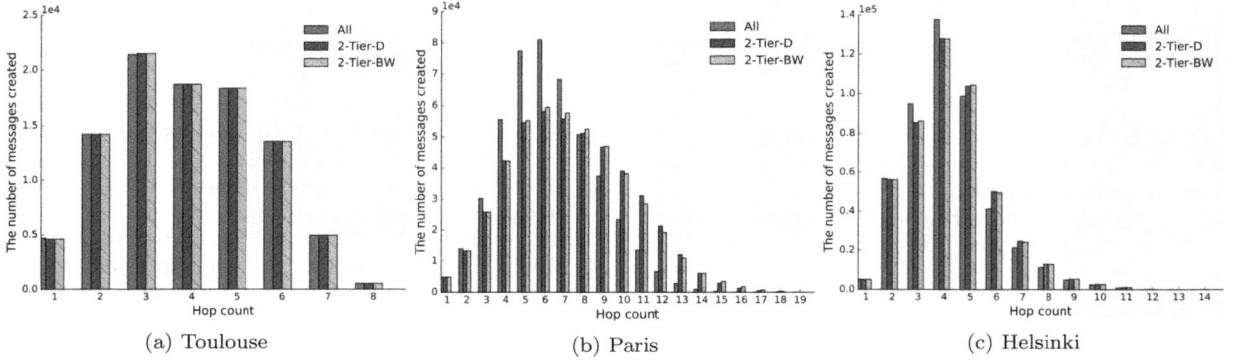

(a) Toulouse   (b) Paris   (c) Helsinki

Figure 9: The hop count(s) of the routes taken by the messages created during the simulation.

6.3 Evaluation of the 3-Tier architecture

In this section, we evaluate the performance of the 3-Tier architecture in terms of packets delivered and the number of access points deployed.

Results: Table 6 shows the number of wireless access points capable of performing network coding that 2-Tier and 3-Tier need to deploy to cover the 3 cities. The data shows that the 3-Tier architecture reduces the need for such access points by over an order of magnitude, which as we show in Section 6.4 has the potential to dramatically reduce the cost of deployment. Fortunately, this significant cutback in infrastructure does not affect performance. Figure 10 shows that 3-Tier delivers the same number of packets as 2-Tier.

6.4 Cost-effectiveness analysis

In this section, we evaluate the potential cost of different architectures for PTNs.

Method: We define the cost effectiveness of an architecture as the ratio between delivered messages and the deployment cost. To quantify the deployment cost without resorting to using specific dollar amounts, we use a simple cost function which assigns the cost of 1 to a simple wireless access point and 3 to a wireless access points capable of performing network coding.

Results: Figure 11 shows the cost effectiveness for all architectures. 3-Tier improves the cost effectiveness by 99.4%, 114.5%, and 115.28% for Toulouse, Paris and Helsinki, respectively over 2-Tier, its closest competitor. This validates our choice of using a 3-Tier architecture for a cost effective content delivery network leveraging the PTNs.

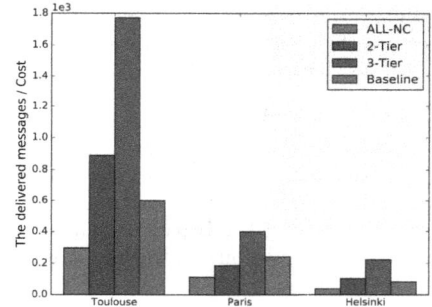

Figure 11: The cost effectiveness for all architectures.

7. CONCLUSION

We presented a secure and cost effective content delivery infrastructure leveraging existing public transportation networks aimed at relieving the looming congestion crunch in urban areas. The key novelty of our design is that it relies on inexpensive and off-the-shelf technology and infrastructure already in place. To address the challenges involved in implementing such a network, we introduced a 3-Tier architecture that is guaranteed to provide end-to-end connectivity, high packet delivery and minimizes hardware cost. We evaluated our design choices and the proposed architecture using real traces. The results showed that the 3-Tier architecture achieved a factor of 3 reduction in the number of access points required while delivering more messages than a baseline architecture.

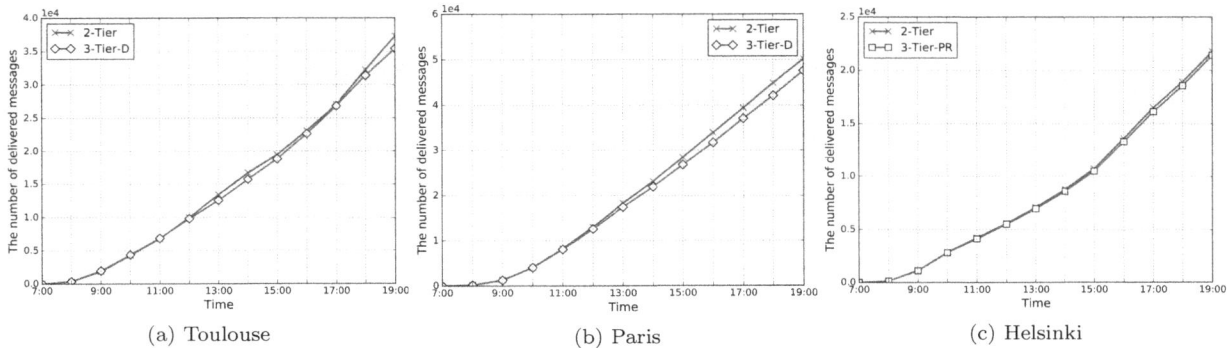

(a) Toulouse   (b) Paris   (c) Helsinki

Figure 10: Packets delivered for 2-Tier and 3-Tier.

Acknowledgements

This work is supported in part by CHIST-ERA MACACO project, ANR-13-CHR2-0002-06 and in part by China Scholarship Council (CSC).

8. REFERENCES

[1] United Nations, World Urbanization Prospects: The 2014 Revision, https://esa.un.org/unpd/wup.

[2] R. Ahlswede, N. Cai, S.-Y. R. Li, and R. W. Yeung. Network information flow. *Information Theory, IEEE Transactions on*, 46(4):1204–1216, 2000.

[3] V. Albino, U. Berardi, and R. M. Dangelico. Smart cities: Definitions, dimensions, performance, and initiatives. *Journal of Urban Technology*, 22(1), 2015.

[4] A. Apavatjrut, W. Znaidi, A. Fraboulet, C. Goursaud, K. Jaffrès-Runser, C. Lauradoux, and M. Minier. Energy efficient authentication strategies for network coding. *Concurrency and Computation: Practice and Experience*, 24(10):1086–1107, 2012.

[5] U. Brandes. On variants of shortest-path betweenness centrality and their generic computation. *Social Networks*, 30(2):136–145, 2008.

[6] J. Burgess, B. Gallagher, D. Jensen, and B. N. Levine. Maxprop: Routing for vehicle-based disruption-tolerant networks. In *INFOCOM*, volume 6, pages 1–11, 2006.

[7] S. Chen and J. Zhao. The requirements, challenges, and technologies for 5G of terrestrial mobile telecommunication. *Communications Magazine, IEEE*, 52(5):36–43, 2014.

[8] V. N. I. Cisco. Global mobile data traffic forecast update, 2015–2020. *white paper*, Feb 2016.

[9] M. Heindlmaier, D. Lun, D. Traskov, and M. Medard. Wireless inter-session network coding - an approach using virtual multicasts. In *Proceedings of IEEE ICC*, pages 1–5, 2011.

[10] K. Jaffres-Runser and C. Lauradoux. Authentication planning for XOR network coding. In *Proceedings of NetCod'11*, pages 1–6. IEEE, 2011.

[11] S. Katti, H. Rahul, W. Hu, D. Katabi, M. Médard, and J. Crowcroft. XORs in the air: practical wireless network coding. *IEEE/ACM Transactions on Networking (ToN)*, 16(3):497–510, 2008.

[12] A. Keränen, J. Ott, and T. Kärkkäinen. The ONE simulator for DTN protocol evaluation. In *Proceedings of SIMUTools'09*, page 55, 2009.

[13] A. Khreishah, W. Chih-Chun, and N. B. Shroff. Rate control with pairwise intersession network coding. *IEEE/ACM Transactions on Networking*, 18(3):816–829, June 2010.

[14] L. Page, S. Brin, R. Motwani, and T. Winograd. The pagerank citation ranking: bringing order to the web. *Technical report. Stanford InfoLab*, 1999.

[15] A. S. Pentland, R. Fletcher, and A. Hasson. Daknet: Rethinking connectivity in developing nations. *Computer*, 37(1):78–83, 2004.

[16] M. Rai, N. Garg, S. Verma, and S. Tapaswi. A new heuristic approach for minimum connected dominating set in adhoc wireless networks. In *Proceedings of IACC 2009*, pages 284–289. IEEE, 2009.

[17] S. Ahmed and S. S. Kanhere. Hubcode: hub-based forwarding using network coding in delay tolerant networks. *Wireless Communication and Mobile Computation*, 13(9), May 2011.

[18] M. R. Schurgot, C. Comaniciu, and K. Jaffres-Runser. Beyond traditional DTN routing: social networks for opportunistic communication. *IEEE Communications Magazine*, 50(7):155–162, 2013.

[19] N. Shrestha and L. Sassatelli. Inter-session network coding in delay tolerant mobile social networks: An empirical study. In *Proceedings of IEEE WoWMoM, 2015*, pages 1–6. IEEE, 2015.

[20] Q. Su, K. Jaffrès-Runser, G. Jakllari, and C. Poulliat. XOR network coding for data mule delay tolerant networks. In *Proceedings of ICCC'15*, Nov 2015.

[21] M. T. Thai, F. Wang, D. Liu, S. Zhu, and D.-Z. Du. Connected dominating sets in wireless networks with different transmission ranges. *Mobile Computing, IEEE Transactions on*, 6(7):721–730, 2007.

[22] A. Vahdat, D. Becker, et al. Epidemic routing for partially connected ad hoc networks. Technical report, Technical Report CS-200006, Duke University, 2000.

[23] X. Zhang, G. Neglia, J. Kurose, D. Towsley, and H. Wang. Benefits of network coding for unicast application in disruption-tolerant networks. *Networking, IEEE/ACM Transactions on*, 21(5):1407–1420, 2013.

Coverage Properties of One-Dimensional Infrastructure-Based Wireless Networks

K.P. Naveen
Dept. of Electrical Engineering,
Indian Institute of Technology Madras,
Chennai 600 036, India.
naveenkp@ee.iitm.ac.in

Anurag Kumar
Dept. of Electrical Communication Engineering,
Indian Institute of Science,
Bangalore 560 012, India.
anurag@ece.iisc.ernet.in

ABSTRACT

We consider an infrastructure-based wireless network comprising two types of nodes, namely, *relays* and *sinks*. The relay nodes are used to extend the network coverage by providing multi-hop paths to the sink nodes that are connected to a wireline infrastructure. Restricting to the one-dimensional case, our objective is to characterize the fraction of covered region for given densities of sink and relay nodes. We first compare and contrast our infrastructure-based model with the traditional setting, where a point is said to be covered if it simply lies within the range of some node. Then, drawing an analogy between the connected components of the network and the busy periods of an $M/D/\infty$ queue, and using renewal theoretic arguments we obtain an explicit expression for the average vacancy (which is the complement of coverage). We also compute an upper bound for vacancy by introducing the notion of *left-coverage* (i.e., coverage by a node from the left). We prove a lower bound by coupling our model with an *independent-disk model*, where the sinks' coverage regions are independent and identically distributed. Through numerical work, we study the problem of minimizing network deployment cost subject to a constraint on the average vacancy. We also conduct simulations to understand the properties of a general notion of coverage, obtained by introducing hop-counts into the definition.

Keywords

Infrastructure-based networks, coverage processes, Poisson processes, $M/D/\infty$ queues, renewal reward theory (RRT).

1. INTRODUCTION

Seamless wireless access, referred to as *coverage*, is a critical performance metric for any wireless network. In cellular networks, coverage is ensured by carefully planning base-stations' (BS) placement so that a large fraction of the deployment region has good signal strength to at least one BS. Wireless connectivity among the BSs is not required in this case as all BSs are connected to a wireline infrastructure.

MSWiM '16, November 13-17, 2016, Malta, Malta

© 2016 ACM. ISBN 978-1-4503-4502-6/16/11. . . $15.00

DOI: http://dx.doi.org/10.1145/2988287.2989135

On the other hand, there are ad hoc networks (e.g., wireless sensor networks, wireless mesh networks, etc.) where, in addition to providing good coverage, connectivity among the network nodes is required to enable multi-hop communication to a sink node (or a control center) which is solely connected to an infrastructure. In this work, we generalize the latter setting by providing more infrastructure support (i.e., introducing more sink nodes) to an ad hoc network. Our work is also applicable to a femto-cellular setting, where a large number of (infrastructure-less) femto-cell BSs are deployed to extend the coverage of the existing cellular BSs.

Formally, we consider a one-dimensional wireless network comprising two types of nodes: *sinks* and *relays*. We assume that the nodes of both types are distributed along the positive real line according to two independent Poisson processes. The sink nodes are connected to an infrastructure, while the relay nodes are used to extend the network coverage by providing multi-hop connectivity to the sink nodes. Thus, a location (i.e., a point on the positive real line) is said to be covered if it lies within the communication range of some node that is eventually connected (possibly via multiple hops) to a sink node. A generalization of the above definition is obtained by imposing a constraint on the number of hops within which a sink node can be reached. For such an infrastructure-based wireless network, we are interested in characterizing the fraction of covered region as a function of sink and relay node densities. Such a characterization will be useful for planning network deployment, where the objective is to minimize the average (per unit-length) node-cost of the network subject to a constraint on the average coverage.

A remark on one-dimensional (1D) network follows. Although for mathematical-tractability reasons we have restricted our study to 1D networks, however these are already useful for modeling some real-world applications. For instance, sensor nodes deployed along the border line for intrusion detection constitutes a 1D network. If some of these sensor nodes are equipped with satellite radios (in addition to their small range transceivers), the network can be further classified as a 1D infrastructure-based wireless network. A vehicular network along a highway is another example of a 1D infrastructure-based wireless network. Here, vehicles constitute relay nodes, and the base-stations installed along

This work was supported by an INSPIRE Faculty Award, granted to the first author by the Department of Science and Technology, Government of India. The work of the second author was supported by a J.C. Bose Fellowship of the Department of Science and Technology, Government of India.

the highway are the sink nodes. In the remainder of this section we briefly survey some related literature, following which we will discuss our main technical contributions.

Related Work: Traditional coverage processes, where all nodes are of same type (or, in our terminology, comprising only sink nodes), have been extensively studied. A classical reference on this topic is the book by Hall [1]. Application of coverage processes to wireless communication have been discussed in [2, 3, 4]. For instance, Andrews et al. in [2] consider an SINR (Signal to Interference plus Noise Ratio) based model where the region covered by a node depends on its signal power as well as the interference power received from all other nodes. Formally, a location is covered by a node if the SINR received at the location is greater than a threshold value. The above setting is extended in [3] to a scenario where the nodes are heterogeneous in terms of their transmit power and their SINR threshold. These *SINR based models* are a generalization of the *Boolean model* studied in [1] where the nodes' coverage regions are independent and identically distributed (i.i.d.); the coverage regions are further independent of node locations.

A quantity that is closely related to coverage is connectivity. A key result concerning connectivity in wireless networks is that by Gupta and Kumar [5]. Specifically, for a network deployed uniformly on an unit disk, to guarantee asymptotic connectivity they obtain the scale at which the (deterministic) transmission radius should reduce with the number of nodes. Connectivity results of similar asymptotic flavour are studied in [6, 7], while the problem of connectivity in the presence of channel randomness (so that the transmission radii are random) is addressed in [8, 9].

All the above work, however, assume that either all nodes are sinks so that coverage by any one node suffices, or seek multi-hop connectivity between every pair of nodes in the network. This is in contrast to our work where we introduce relay nodes and say that a point is covered if and only if it has a multi-hop connectivity to at least one sink node; thus, relay nodes connected to different sinks may not have a multi-hop path between them. Although we assume a Boolean model like in [1], our work can be considered as an extension of the model in [1] to the infrastructure-based network setting, but restricted to the one-dimensional case.

There are already extensive work in the literature studying the problem of coverage and connectivity in one-dimensional networks. In the following we survey some of these work. For a network with a finite number of nodes deployed on a line of finite length, Desai and Manjunath in [10] obtain the exact formula for the probability that the entire network is connected. Miorandi and Altman in [11] consider a queueing theoretic approach to compute the coverage probability for one-dimensional networks. For a general inter-node distance distribution (not limiting to exponential distribution), the authors in [11] show the equivalence between the coverage probability and the probability that an equivalent $GI/D/1$ queue is busy. We will exploit a similar equivalence for the infrastructure-based network.

One of the early work considering an infrastructure-based architecture is that of Dousse et al. [12]. In [12], although the relay nodes are Poisson distributed, the sink nodes are placed equi-distance from each other (which is in contrast to our work where the sink nodes are also Poisson distributed). A point located between two sink nodes is connected if it has a multi-hop path to at least one of them. Thus, the model essentially reduces to the one with two sink nodes placed at the end points of a finite length line segment. The authors in [12] obtain a lower bound on the probability that a location within the line segment is connected. For a similar model, motivated by vehicular networks, Suo in [13] obtains the probability that all vehicles (equivalently, relay nodes) within a road segment of finite length are connected to both *road side units* (equivalently, sink nodes) located at either ends of the road segment.

More recently, the authors in [14] consider a model where more than two sink nodes are deployed at arbitrary locations within a segment of finite length; the relay nodes are Poisson distributed as in the earlier models. The probability that the entire network is connected is obtained. Further, the authors show that uniform sink placement maximizes the connectivity probability. Assuming different ranges for sink and relay nodes, zhang et al., in [15], obtain the uplink (relay to sink) and downlink (sink to relay) connection probabilities. However, the setting is again restricted to the scenario where two sink nodes are place at the either ends of a finite length line segment.

In contrast to all these work, we consider a model where both sink and relay nodes are Poisson distributed along the positive real line. We are interested in obtaining explicit expression for the fraction of region that is covered (i.e., coverage probability) as a function of sink and relay node densities. To the best of our knowledge, the particular model we consider and the coverage characterization we obtain are not available in the literature.

Outline and Our Contributions: In Section 2 we describe our infrastructure-based network model in detail. In Section 3 we discuss the traditional case where every node is a sink. The general case, comprising both sink and relay nodes, is studied in Section 4. In Section 5, we define an hop-count constrained notion of coverage. Numerical and simulation results are presented in Section 6.

Our main technical contributions are the following:

1) Using renewal theoretic arguments we obtain an explicit expression for the average vacancy created in an infrastructure-based wireless network. The key challenge here is to identify appropriate renewal instants. Specifically, drawing an analogy between the covered/ vacant regions and the busy/idle periods of an equivalent $M/D/\infty$ queue, we define renewal instants such that a renewal cycle comprises a random (geometric) number of successive busy/idle periods.

2) Defining *left-coverage*, where a location is said to be covered if it is covered by a sink-connected node from its left, we obtain a simple upper bound for the average vacancy. More interestingly, we show that the average vacancy created in an alternate Boolean model, where the coverage regions of successive sink nodes are i.i.d., serves as a lower bound for the average vacancy in the original model (where the coverage regions are dependent). The proof is based on a coupling argument.

3) Through numerical work we study the characteristics of average vacancy as a function of sink and relay node densities. We also numerically investigate the problem of minimizing the network deployment cost subject to a constraint on the average vacancy. Finally, we conduct simulations to study the average vacancy created in the hop-count constrained model.

We summarize our work in Section 7. For the ease of presentation, we have moved some details to the Appendix.

2. SYSTEM MODEL

We consider a scenario where the sink and the relay nodes are located along a line. The point process of these locations is modeled as a Poisson process of rate λ. It is assumed that any point of this Poisson process is independently a sink with probability $\beta \in (0, 1]$. Thus, the point processes of sink locations and relay locations are independent Poisson processes of rates $\beta\lambda$ and $(1-\beta)\lambda$, respectively. The wireless *range* of each node is $r > 0$. Thus, we assume that the ranges of both sink and relay nodes are identical. This assumption can be justified by considering scenarios where both sink and relay nodes are equipped with identical digital radios, while the sink nodes have additional backhaul connectivity (e.g., ethernet or satellite radios).

Connectivity: Given two nodes whose locations are x and y ($x \neq y$), we say that the *nodes are connected* if there are nodes at locations $x_1 = x, x_2, \cdots, x_{h+1} = y$, $h \geq 1$, such that $|x_i - x_{i+1}| \leq r$ for $i = 1, \cdots, h$; otherwise the nodes are said to be *disconnected*. Further, when the above condition is satisfied, the nodes at x and y are said to be *at most h-hops away* (this definition of hop counts will be useful in Section 5 while defining hop-constrained coverage).

We define a *connected component*, $\mathcal{C}$, to be the maximal set of nodes such that any pair of nodes in the set are connected. Formally, $\mathcal{C}$ is a connected component if (i) for all $u, v \in \mathcal{C}$, u and v are connected, and (ii) for all $u \in \mathcal{C}$ and $w \notin \mathcal{C}$, u and w are disconnected.

Since we are working with an infrastructure-based network, a node is operationally useful only if it is eventually connected to a sink node. Thus, we introduce the following definition: A node is said to be *sink-connected* if it is connected to at least one sink node; otherwise we say that the node is *sink-disconnected*. For instance, node u in Figure 1 is sink-connected, while node v is sink-disconnected. For completeness, we define a sink node to be sink-connected.

Coverage and Vacancy: We finally introduce the definition of coverage for an infrastructure-based wireless network.

DEFINITION 1. *A location $\ell \in \Re_+$ is said to be **covered** if it is within the range of a sink-connected node; otherwise ℓ is said to be **vacant**.*

Let $\mathcal{I}_V : \Re_+ \to \{0, 1\}$ denote the indicator function that represents whether a location $\ell \in \Re_+$ is vacant or not. Formally, $\mathcal{I}_V(\ell) = 1$ if ℓ is vacant; $\mathcal{I}_V(\ell) = 0$ otherwise (i.e., if ℓ is covered); see Figure 1 for an illustration. Then, the *average vacancy* (i.e., fraction of vacant region) created in the infrastructure-based wireless network (of node intensity λ and sink probability β) is given by,

$$v_{\lambda,\beta} = \lim_{L \to \infty} \frac{1}{L} \int_0^L \mathcal{I}_V(\ell) d\ell. \tag{1}$$

By identifying renewal points in the network, it is possible to establish that the above limit exists a.s. (almost surely). For instance, locations of the sink nodes constitute one set of renewal points. Formally, if $\{Y_k : k \geq 1\}$ are the locations of the successive sink nodes (define $Y_0 = 0$) then the inter-sink distances, $\{X_k = Y_k - Y_{k-1} : k \geq 1\}$, is a *renewal sequence*. Define the *reward* in the k-th renewal cycle ($k \geq 1$) as,

$$R_k = \int_{Y_{k-1}}^{Y_k} \mathcal{I}_V(\ell) d\ell. \tag{2}$$

Note that, $\{R_k : k \geq 1\}$ is an i.i.d. sequence since R_k is a function solely of the Poisson points located within the k-th

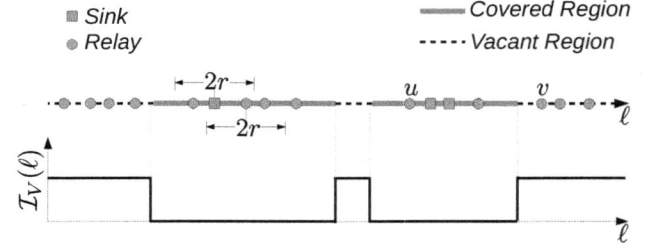

Figure 1: Covered and vacant regions in an infrastructure-based wireless network.

renewal cycle. Thus, using renewal reward theory (RRT) [16] we have,

$$v_{\lambda,\beta} = \frac{\mathbb{E}[R_k]}{\mathbb{E}[X_k]} \text{ a.s.} \tag{3}$$

Although the above procedure provides an expression for $v_{\lambda,\beta}$, it is not a workable definition as it is not easy to obtain an explicit formula for $\mathbb{E}[R_k]$ when $\beta \in (0, 1)$ ($\beta = 1$ case can be easily solved; see Section 3). Thus, our objective is to identify alternate renewal points that can enable us to characterize $v_{\lambda,\beta}$ as an explicit function of (λ, β); see Section 4.

Cost Optimization: Finally, we are interested in deploying a cost efficient network. Suppose c_S and c_R denote the costs of a sink and a relay node, respectively. Then, the average (per unit-length) cost of the network is, $c_{\lambda,\beta} := \lambda\beta c_S + \lambda(1-\beta)c_R$. The objective is to minimize the average network cost subject to an average vacancy constraint:

$$\begin{aligned}
&\text{Minimize}_{(\lambda,\beta)} \quad c_{\lambda,\beta} \\
&\text{Subject to} \quad v_{\lambda,\beta} \leq \overline{v}.
\end{aligned} \tag{4}$$

Optimal network cost is denoted as c_{λ^*,β^*} where (λ^*, β^*) is an optimal point. We will numerically study the above problem in Section 6.

3. AVERAGE VACANCY: $\beta = 1$ CASE

This section is essentially a review of some existing results. The case $\beta = 1$ corresponds to a scenario where every node is a sink. Thus, a location $\ell \in \Re_+$ is covered if it is simply within the range, r, of some node. Standard results from coverage processes [1] can now be evoked to obtain the average vacancy as $v_{\lambda,1} = e^{-\lambda 2r}$, where $2r$ is the length of the disk around each node, as shown in Figure 1 (i.e., the range on either side of a node is r).

The above result can also be obtained using (3) as follows. First, note that a location ℓ in the k-th renewal cycle is vacant only if it is not within the range r of both sinks at either ends of this cycle (i.e., nodes at Y_{k-1} and Y_k). Hence, the reward expression in (2) can be expressed as $R_k = (X_k - 2r)^+$, where $(x)^+ = \max\{0, x\}$. Next, since $\{X_k\}$ are exponential random variables of rate λ, the average reward and average renewal cycle length are given by,

$$\mathbb{E}[R_k] = \frac{e^{-\lambda 2r}}{\lambda} \text{ and } \mathbb{E}[X_k] = \frac{1}{\lambda}.$$

Thus, from (3) we have $v_{\lambda,1} = e^{-\lambda 2r}$.

As mentioned earlier, the above technique is not useful when $\beta < 1$ since it is then not easy to obtain an explicit expression for $\mathbb{E}[R_k]$. This motivates us to look for alternate renewal sequences. One idea is to view the successive covered and vacant regions in the network as being analogous to the successive busy and idle periods in an $M/D/\infty$ queuing system [16]. Then, identifying that the starting instants of the busy periods constitute renewal points, the average vacancy expression can be alternatively obtained using results from $M/D/\infty$ queues [11]. Details of this approach are discussed below.

Borrowing terminology from queuing theory, we identify the *busy* and *idle* periods of an infrastructure-based network as follows. Let $\mathcal{C}_k$ be the k-th connected component with the positions of the leftmost and the rightmost nodes in $\mathcal{C}_k$ being denoted as x_k and y_k, respectively (see Figure 2 for an illustration). Then, the *busy period* corresponding to $\mathcal{C}_k$ is the region $[x_k, y_k + r]$, i.e., it is the region starting from the leftmost node in $\mathcal{C}_k$ to the rightmost node in $\mathcal{C}_k$, and then extending up to the region of length r towards the right of the rightmost node. The *idle period* of $\mathcal{C}_k$ is the region $(y_k + r, x_{k+1})$, where x_{k+1} is the location of the leftmost node in the next connected component $\mathcal{C}_{k+1}$. Let B_k and I_k, $k \geq 1$, denote the lengths of the busy and idle periods corresponding to the k-th connected component, respectively.

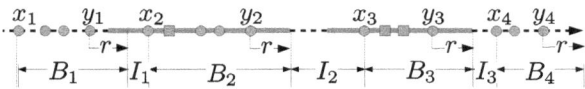

Figure 2: Illustration of the successive busy-idle periods in an infrastructure-based wireless network.

We refer to the k-th busy-idle period as the k-th renewal cycle. Thus, $B_k + I_k$ is the length of the k-th renewal cycle. The reward in the k-th renewal cycle, denoted R'_k, is the fraction of region vacant in the k-th cycle. R'_k can be evaluated as follows. First, note that when $\beta = 1$ the busy periods are always completely covered since every node is a sink. Next, when the length of an idle period is less than r then the idle period is completely covered by the first node in the next busy period. Thus R'_k is simply the portion of the idle period that is not covered, which is given by $R'_k = (I_k - r)^+$.

The renewal cycle lengths, $\{B_k + I_k : k \geq 1\}$, is an i.i.d. sequence. The reward sequence, $\{R'_k : k \geq 1\}$, is also i.i.d. Hence, using renewal reward theory we can write

$$v_{\lambda,1} = \frac{\mathbb{E}[(I_k - r)^+]}{\mathbb{E}[B_k] + \mathbb{E}[I_k]} \quad \text{a.s.} \tag{5}$$

Since I_k is an exponentially distributed random variable of rate λ, we have $\mathbb{E}[I_k] = \frac{1}{\lambda}$ and $\mathbb{E}[(I_k - r)^+] = \frac{e^{-\lambda r}}{\lambda}$. $\mathbb{E}[B_k]$ is the average busy period of an $M/D/\infty$ queuing system with constant service times r, which is given by [11]

$$\mathbb{E}[B_k] = r + \frac{\int_0^r t f_X(t) dt}{1 - F_X(r)}$$

where f_X and F_X are the p.d.f. and c.d.f., respectively, of the inter-arrival times. The inter-arrival times in our case are the inter-node distances, which are exponentially distributed random variables of rate λ, i.e., $f_X(t) = \lambda e^{-\lambda t}$ and $F_X(r) = (1 - e^{-\lambda r})$. Hence, we have

$$\mathbb{E}[B_k] = \frac{(1 - e^{-\lambda r})}{\lambda e^{-\lambda r}}. \tag{6}$$

Using the above quantities in (5), we obtain $\boxed{v_{\lambda,1} = e^{-\lambda 2r}}$.

4. AVERAGE VACANCY: $\beta < 1$ CASE

The case $\beta < 1$ yields an infrastructure-based network, comprising both sink and relay nodes. Here, a location within the range of a relay node is covered only if the relay is connected to a sink node.

Continuing the discussion from the previous section, when $\beta < 1$, it is possible for a connected component to not contain a sink node (for instance, $\mathcal{C}_1$ in Figure 2 does not contain a sink). Hence, the corresponding busy period must be treated as being vacant. Let $\mathcal{S}_k$ denote the event that there exists a sink in the k-th connected component. Let $\mathcal{S}_k^c$ be the complement of $\mathcal{S}_k$. Note that the events $\mathcal{S}_k, k \geq 1$, are independent and have the same probability.

Unlike in the $\beta = 1$ case, here it is not useful to regard the successive busy-idle periods as renewal cycles. This is because the reward R'_k, which is the fraction of region uncovered within the k-th busy-idle period, is given by ($\mathbb{I}_A$ denotes the indicator function of event A)

$$R'_k = B_k \mathbb{I}_{\mathcal{S}_k^c} + (I_k - r)^+ \mathbb{I}_{\mathcal{S}_{k+1}} + I_k \mathbb{I}_{\mathcal{S}_{k+1}^c}. \tag{7}$$

Thus, the reward in the k-th busy-idle period depends on whether the $(k+1)$-th busy-idle period contains a sink node or not. Hence, the sequence $\{R'_k : k \geq 1\}$ is not i.i.d., which is essential for applying RRT.

A simple upper bound for vacancy can however be obtained by neglecting, in the reward expression R'_k, the region covered by the $(k+1)$-th busy period (in case a sink is present in the corresponding connected component). We derive this upper bound first (in Section 4.1) before proceeding to obtain the exact expression for vacancy (in Section 4.2). In Section 4.3 we prove a lower bound for vacancy by coupling our model with a traditional Boolean model where i.i.d. coverage disks are placed around the sink nodes.

4.1 An Upper Bound for Vacancy

We begin with the following definition.

DEFINITION 2. *A location $\ell \in \Re_+$ is said to be covered from the left or **left-covered** if ℓ is within the range of a sink-connected node towards the left of ℓ, i.e., ℓ is left-covered if there is a sink-connected node at some location x such that $x \leq \ell$ and $|x - \ell| \leq r$. If there is no such sink-connected node we say that ℓ is vacant from the left or **left-vacant**.*

Let $\mathcal{I}_U : \Re_+ \to \{0, 1\}$ denote the function indicating whether a location $\ell \in \Re_+$ is left-vacant or not; see Figure 3 for an illustration. Then, the fraction of region that is left-vacant is given by,

$$u_{\lambda,\beta} = \lim_{L \to \infty} \frac{1}{L} \int_0^L \mathcal{I}_U(\ell) d\ell. \tag{8}$$

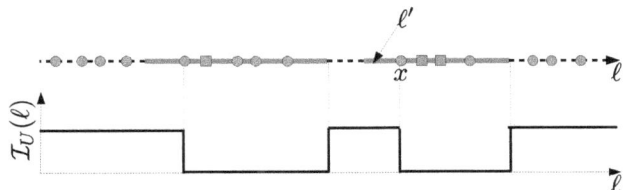

Figure 3: Illustration of the left-vacant process, $\mathcal{I}_U(\ell)$. Location ℓ', although covered, is left-vacant since the relay at x is towards its right.

We immediately obtain the following result.

THEOREM 1. *Fraction of left-vacant region is an upper bound for the fraction of vacant region, i.e., $v_{\lambda,\beta} \leq u_{\lambda,\beta}$ for all (λ, β).*

PROOF. Note that, for any $\ell \in \Re_+$ we have

$$\mathcal{I}_V(\ell) \leq \mathcal{I}_U(\ell).$$

The above relation can be easily deduced by noting that ℓ being vacant ($\mathcal{I}_V(\ell) = 1$) always implies that ℓ is left-vacant ($\mathcal{I}_U(\ell) = 1$). However, it is possible that ℓ is covered by a node towards its right ($\mathcal{I}_V(\ell) = 0$), but is not left-covered ($\mathcal{I}_U(\ell) = 1$). Thus, $v_{\lambda,\beta}$ is upper bounded by $u_{\lambda,\beta}$. □

We now proceed to obtain an explicit expression for $u_{\lambda,\beta}$. We identify the k-th renewal cycle with the busy-idle periods corresponding to the k-th connected component. Let the reward in the k-th busy-idle period, denoted R_k'', be the region that is left-vacant. Then,

$$R_k'' = B_k \mathbb{I}_{\mathcal{S}_k^c} + I_k. \tag{9}$$

The sequence $\{R_k'' : k \geq 1\}$ is i.i.d. unlike the $\{R_k' : k \geq 1\}$ sequence in (7). Hence, we can now apply RRT to obtain

$$u_{\lambda,\beta} = \frac{\mathbb{E}[B_k \mathbb{I}_{\mathcal{S}_k^c}] + \mathbb{E}[I_k]}{\mathbb{E}[B_k] + \mathbb{E}[I_k]}. \tag{10}$$

For notational simplicity, define $p := \mathbb{P}(\mathcal{S}_k^c)$ and $Q := \mathbb{E}[B_k | \mathcal{S}_k^c]$. Thus, p is the probability that a connected component does not contain a sink, and Q is the average busy period length conditioned on the event that it does not contain a sink. Hence, we have

$$\mathbb{E}[B_k \mathbb{I}_{\mathcal{S}_k^c}] = \mathbb{P}(\mathcal{S}_k^c) \mathbb{E}[B_k \mathbb{I}_{\mathcal{S}_k^c} | \mathcal{S}_k^c]$$
$$= pQ$$

Substituting the above expression in (10) along with the identities $\mathbb{E}[I_k] = \frac{1}{\lambda}$ and $\mathbb{E}[B_k] = \frac{1-e^{-\lambda r}}{\lambda e^{-\lambda r}}$, we obtain

$$\boxed{u_{\lambda,\beta} = \left(\lambda p Q + 1\right) e^{-\lambda r}.} \tag{11}$$

For simplicity, we have presented the computation of p and Q in Appendix A.

4.2 Exact Vacancy Analysis

To obtain $v_{\lambda,\beta}$ exactly we modify the definition of a renewal cycle to be the region between two successive connected components that do not contain a sink node (see Figure 4 for an illustration). Thus, a renewal cycle now comprises a random number of successive busy-idle periods, where the first busy period does not contain a sink while the following ones contain a sink.

Let M_n denote the number of busy-idle periods within the n-th such renewal cycle. By definition, $M_n = m$ ($m \geq 1$) if, after the first busy period (which does not contain a sink), there are $m-1$ successive sink-containing busy periods followed by a non-sink-containing busy period (the latter busy period is not part of the current renewal cycle). Thus, M_n is a geometric random variable with success probability $p = \mathbb{P}(\mathcal{S}_k^c)$, i.e., for $m \geq 1$

$$\mathbb{P}(M_n = m) = (1-p)^{m-1}p. \tag{12}$$

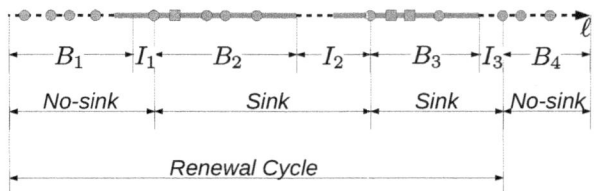

Figure 4: Illustration of a renewal cycle when $\beta < 1$.

Let $B_i^{(n)}$ and $I_i^{(n)}$, $1 \leq i \leq M_n$ represent the lengths of the i-th busy and idle periods within the n-th renewal cycle. Then, the length of the n-th renewal cycle is given by,

$$\hat{X}_n = \sum_{i=1}^{M_n} (B_i^{(n)} + I_i^{(n)}). \tag{13}$$

The reward $\hat{R}_n$ is simply the length of the vacant region within the n-th renewal cycle, which can be expressed as

$$\hat{R}_n = \begin{cases} B_1^{(n)} + I_1^{(n)}, \text{ if } M_n = 1 \\ (B_1^{(n)} + I_1^{(n)} - r) + \sum_{i=2}^{M_n-1}(I_i^{(n)} - r)^+ \\ \qquad + I_{M_n}^{(n)}, \text{ if } M_n > 1. \end{cases} \tag{14}$$

We now proceed to compute the expectation of the above quantities. For simplicity, define $\overline{Q} := \mathbb{E}[B_k | \mathcal{S}_k]$, which is the average busy period length conditioned on the event that it contains a sink node. The expectation of $\hat{X}_n$ can now be simplified as follows:

$$\mathbb{E}[\hat{X}_n] = \mathbb{E}\left[\sum_{i=1}^{M_n}(B_i^{(n)} + I_i^{(n)})\right]$$
$$= \sum_{m=1}^{\infty} \mathbb{P}(M_n = m) \, \mathbb{E}\left[\sum_{i=1}^{M_n}(B_i^{(n)} + I_i^{(n)}) \middle| M_n = m\right]$$
$$\overset{(a)}{=} \sum_{m=1}^{\infty} \mathbb{P}(M_n = m)\left(Q + (m-1)\overline{Q} + \frac{m}{\lambda}\right)$$
$$= \sum_{m=1}^{\infty} (1-p)^{m-1}p\left(Q + (m-1)\overline{Q} + \frac{m}{\lambda}\right)$$
$$\boxed{\mathbb{E}[\hat{X}_n] \overset{(b)}{=} \frac{\lambda p Q + \lambda(1-p)\overline{Q} + 1}{\lambda p}.} \tag{15}$$

To obtain (a) note that, conditioned on $(M_n = n)$, the first busy period does not contain a sink (and hence its average length is Q), while each of the remaining $(m-1)$ busy periods contain a sink (the average length of each is $\overline{Q}$), and the mean length of each of the m idle periods is $\frac{1}{\lambda}$. Equality (b) is obtained by using the identities (corresponding to a geometric distribution)

$$\sum_{m=1}^{\infty}(1-p)^{m-1}p = 1, \quad \sum_{m=1}^{\infty}m(1-p)^{m-1}p = \frac{1}{p}$$

and then simplifying.

Similarly, conditioning on $(M_n = m)$ and simplifying, we obtain the following expression for $\mathbb{E}[\hat{R}_n]$:

$$\mathbb{E}[\hat{R}_n] = \mathbb{P}(M_n = 1)\left(Q + \frac{1}{\lambda}\right) + \sum_{m=2}^{\infty} \mathbb{P}(M_n = m) \times$$
$$\left(Q + \frac{1}{\lambda} - r + (m-2)\frac{e^{-\lambda r}}{\lambda} + \frac{1}{\lambda}\right)$$

$$\mathbb{E}[\hat{R}_n] = \frac{\lambda p Q - p(1-p)\lambda r + p(2-p)(1-e^{-\lambda r}) + e^{-\lambda r}}{\lambda p}.$$

RRT can now be evoked to express average vacancy as $v_{\lambda,\beta} = \frac{\mathbb{E}[\hat{R}_n]}{\mathbb{E}[\hat{X}_n]}$. However, explicit formulas for p, Q and $\overline{Q}$ are required to obtain $v_{\lambda,\beta}$ as a function of (λ, β). Computation of these quantities is presented in Appendix A.

4.3 A Lower Bound for Vacancy

In this section we will show that the average vacancy in an *independent-disk model*, which is obtained by placing i.i.d. coverage regions (or disks) around the sink nodes, will serves as a lower bound for the average vacancy in the original model (henceforth referred to as the *dependent-disk model*) where the coverage disks are not independent. We begin by introducing some notation.

Let $Y_k \in \Re_+$ ($k \geq 1$) denote the location of the k-th sink node. For simplicity, with a slight abuse of notation we will use Y_k to also refer to the k-th sink node. Defining $X_k = Y_k - Y_{k-1}$ (with $Y_0 = 0$), note that $\{X_k : k \geq 1\}$ constitutes a Poisson (renewal) process of rate $\beta\lambda$. The location of the relay nodes are instead represented using Λ, where Λ is a Poisson (counting) process of rate $(1-\beta)\lambda$ (i.e., for any interval I, $\Lambda(I)$ denotes the number of points within I). To avoid boundary effects occurring at the origin, let us assume that the relays are distributed along the entire real line. Thus, Λ is a Poisson process on $\Re$.

The *coverage disk* of Y_k is obtained as follows. Retaining Y_k and the relay nodes, remove all other sink nodes from the network. The *coverage disk* of Y_k is defined as the set of all locations that are either (1) directly within the range of Y_k, or (2) within the range of some relay node that is connected to Y_k. Let U_k (respectively, V_k) denote the length of the coverage disk towards the right (respectively, left) of Y_k. Thus, the coverage disk of Y_k is the region $\mathcal{W}_k := [Y_k - V_k, Y_k + U_k]$.

Given that the relay nodes are distributed according to Λ, U_k is simply the length of the busy period duration of an $M/D/\infty$ queue with arrival rate $(1-\beta)\lambda$ and constant service times r. Recalling (6), the average length of U_k can be written as

$$\overline{C} := \mathbb{E}[U_k] = \frac{(1 - e^{-(1-\beta)\lambda r})}{(1-\beta)\lambda e^{-(1-\beta)\lambda r}}. \tag{16}$$

Since the process Λ is independent and identically distributed on either side of Y_k, it follows that V_k is independent and identically distributed as U_k. Thus, the average length of the coverage disk around Y_k is $2\overline{C}$. However, as mentioned earlier, the coverage disks around Y_k and Y_{k+1}, although identically distributed, are not independent. This is because these disks are constructed using the same Poisson process, Λ, of relay nodes. Hence, we refer to our original model as the *dependent-disk model*.

Now, suppose we consider an alternate *independent-disk model* where, in fact, i.i.d. coverage disks of mean length $2\overline{C}$ are placed around the sink nodes. Then, we are in the regime of the traditional coverage processes with grain density $\beta\lambda$ and disk length $2\overline{C}$. Let $w_{\lambda,\beta}$ denote the fraction of vacancy created in this coverage process. Then, from [1] we have

$$w_{\lambda,\beta} = e^{-\beta\lambda 2\overline{C}}. \tag{17}$$

Our key result here is to show that $w_{\lambda,\beta}$ is a lower bound for $v_{\lambda,\beta}$.

THEOREM 2. *Fraction of vacancy created in the independent-disk model is a lower bound for that created in the dependent-disk model, i.e., $w_{\lambda,\beta} \leq v_{\lambda,\beta}$ for all (λ, β).*

PROOF. The proof is based on a coupling argument. Given the dependent-disk model, we will iteratively construct an independent-disk model such that the region covered by the latter is larger. In fact, we will show that a larger coverage is obtained by placing i.i.d. coverage disks around a carefully chosen subset, $\{Y_{k_n} : n \geq 1\}$, of sink nodes. The details of the proof are available in Appendix B. □

5. HOP-CONSTRAINED COVERAGE

Recall from Definition 1 that a location is said to be covered if it simply lies within the range of a sink-connected node, irrespective of the number of hops between the node and the sink. This definition of coverage may be restrictive for delay sensitive applications where a strict constraint is imposed on the number of hops (which is proportional to the delay incurred) within which a packet is expected to reach a sink node for processing. Hence, in this section we will introduce a general notion of coverage by incorporating hop constraint into the definition.

DEFINITION 3. *A location $\ell \in \Re_+$ is said to be h-**covered**, $h \geq 0$, if ℓ is within the range of a sink-connected node that is at most h-hops away from a sink node; otherwise ℓ is said to be h-**vacant**.*

Let $\mathcal{I}_{V_h} : \Re_+ \to \{0, 1\}$ denote the indicator function that represents whether a location $\ell \in \Re_+$ is left-vacant or not. An illustration of these functions for $h = 0$ and $h = 1$ is shown in Figure 5. The fraction of h-vacant region is defined as,

$$v_{\lambda,\beta,h} = \lim_{L \to \infty} \frac{1}{L} \int_0^L \mathcal{I}_{V_h}(\ell) \mathrm{d}\ell. \tag{18}$$

For $h = 0$, a location ℓ is 0-covered if it is simply within the range of a sink node. In this case, the relay nodes do not contribute in extending the coverage. Thus, we are in the framework of a standard coverage process, comprising sink nodes (whose density is $\beta\lambda$) with disks of length $2r$ placed around them. Hence, we readily have $v_{\lambda,\beta,0} = e^{-\beta\lambda 2r}$.

However, for $h \geq 1$ the analysis of $v_{\lambda,\beta,h}$ is not straight forward, although some properties can be easily deduced.

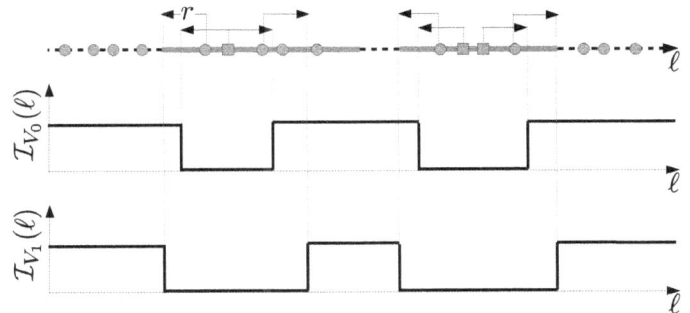

Figure 5: Hop-constrained vacancy process, $\mathcal{I}_{V_h}(\ell)$, plotted for $h = 0$ and $h = 1$.

For instance, it is easy to see that $v_{\lambda,\beta,h}$ is decreasing with h. In fact, we can also obtain a corollary to Theorem 2, yielding a lower bound on $v_{\lambda,\beta,h}$. We make a formal note of the above results.

LEMMA 1. *The fraction of h-vacant region is decreasing with h, i.e., for $h > h'$ we have $v_{\lambda,\beta,h} \leq v_{\lambda,\beta,h'}$ for all (λ, β). Further, $v_{\lambda,\beta,h} \to v_{\lambda,\beta}$ as $h \to \infty$.*

PROOF. A location $\ell \in \Re_+$ being h'-covered ($\mathcal{I}_{V_{h'}}(\ell) = 0$) implies that ℓ is h-covered ($\mathcal{I}_{V_h}(\ell) = 0$). However, it is possible for ℓ to be h'-vacant ($\mathcal{I}_{V_{h'}}(\ell) = 1$) while being h-covered ($\mathcal{I}_{V_h}(\ell) = 0$). Thus, we have $\mathcal{I}_{V_h}(\ell) \leq \mathcal{I}_{V_{h'}}(\ell)$, yielding $v_{\lambda,\beta,h} \leq v_{\lambda,\beta,h'}$. Further, since $\mathcal{I}_{V_h}(\ell) \to \mathcal{I}_V(\ell)$ as $h \to \infty$, we have $\lim_{h\to\infty} v_{\lambda,\beta,h} = v_{\lambda,\beta}$. □

COROLLARY 1. *Fraction of h-vacant region is lower bounded as follows: $w_{\lambda,\beta,h} \leq v_{\lambda,\beta,h}$, for all (λ, β, h), where*

$$w_{\lambda,\beta,h} = e^{-\beta\lambda 2\overline{C}_h}$$

with $2\overline{C}_h$ (analogous to $2\overline{C}$) being the expected length of the h-covered disk around a sink node, when all other sink nodes are removed.

PROOF. The proof is exactly along the lines of the proof of Theorem 2. □

We leave the exact analysis of $v_{\lambda,\beta,h}$ as future work. However, we resort to simulations in Section 6 to gain some insights into the properties of $v_{\lambda,\beta,h}$.

6. NUMERICAL & SIMULATION WORK

Without loss of generality we assume a normalized range of $r = 1$ unit. Thus, the node density λ is in the units of number-of-nodes/range.

Average Vacancy, Upper and Lower Bounds: In Figure 6 we plot the average vacancy $v_{\lambda,\beta}$ as a function of λ for different values of β. As expected, $v_{\lambda,\beta}$ is a decreasing function of λ for any given β. Similarly, for a given λ, $v_{\lambda,\beta}$ decreases with β. Also shown in Figure 6 are the upper-bound ($u_{\lambda,\beta}$ vs. λ) and lower-bound curves ($w_{\lambda,\beta}$ vs. λ), for different values of β.

We observe that the upper-bound curves are a good approximation for the exact vacancy curves for small values of β, while the quality of the approximation deteriorates as β increases. This is because, as β increases more connected components contain sink nodes so that the region of length r preceding the connected components are actually covered while they remain left-vacant in the upper bound process, thus increasing the contribution of the term that was left out in order to obtain the bound.

The lower bound curves should be understood as follows (although these appear to be a good approximation for the exact curves for larger values of β). For a given node density λ, observe that the difference between $v_{\lambda,\beta}$ and $w_{\lambda,\beta}$ increases as β increases. For instance, fixing $\lambda = 3$ we see that the difference, $v_{\lambda,\beta} - w_{\lambda,\beta}$, increases as β increases from $\beta = 0.001$ to $\beta = 0.1$ (curves corresponding to $\beta = 0.5$ have already saturated to 0). Hence, the lower bound is actually a good approximation for the average vacancy for smaller values of β. This is because, smaller β implies a larger distance of separation between successive sink nodes, so that the probability of adjacent coverage disks overlapping is small. Thus, essentially it appears as if i.i.d. coverage disks are placed around each sink node. Hence, the

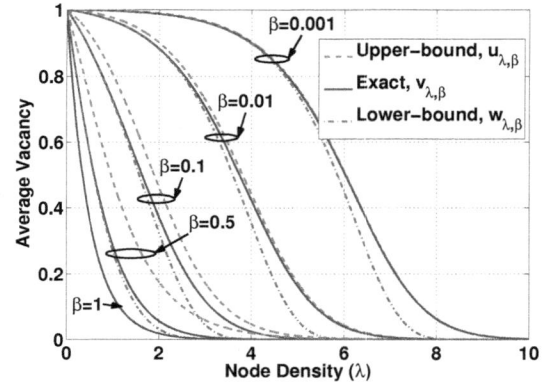

Figure 6: Average vacancy as a function of λ for different values of β. The respective upper and lower bound curves are also shown.

original dependent-disk model approaches the independent-disk model as β decreases, so that the respective average vacancies are comparable. However, the above effect gets nullified as λ increases with β remaining fixed. This observation can be made from Figure 6 where we see that, for a fixed β, the lower-bound's approximation deteriorates as λ increases. This is essentially due to the increase in the length of the coverage disk as λ increases. As a result, the probability that the adjacent disks overlap increases, thus increasing the dependency in the model.

Cost Optimization: In Figure 7(a) we depict the optimal network cost, c_{λ^*,β^*}, as a function of the vacancy constraint, $\overline{v}$. The curves are shown for different values of sink to relay cost ratios (c_S/c_R), where without loss of generality we have normalized the relay cost to 1 unit. For a given vacancy constraint (e.g., 0.1 in Figure 7(a)), note that the network cost reduces as the cost of a sink node is reduced. However, a small reduction in the sink-node's cost does not significantly reduce the network cost unless the sink-node's cost is already less. For instance, fixing $\overline{v} = 0.1$, we see that the network cost reduces only by 6% (from 5.4 to 5.1) when c_S reduces from $10c_R$ to $8c_R$, while it is more than 40% (4 to 2.3) for $c_S = 4c_R$ to $2c_R$ reduction. Thus, when the backhaul is inexpensive (so that the cost of installing a sink node is less), further gains can be achieved by optimizing the backhaul design; Otherwise (i.e., when the backhaul is expensive), incremental optimization of the backhaul is not necessary as it does not result in significant gains.

Further insights into the structure of the optimal network can be gained through Figure 7(b) and 7(c), where (for $c_S = 4c_R$ and $c_S = 10c_R$, respectively) we have shown how λ^* and β^* (optimal node density and sink probability) varies with the vacancy constraint $\overline{v}$. From these figures we observe that there is a cut-off value of $\overline{v}$ beyond which $\beta^* = 1$. Thus, if a vacancy of more than the cut-off is tolerable then the optimal network design comprises only sink nodes. The respective cut-offs in Figure 7(b) and 7(c) are (approximately) $\overline{v} = 0.3$ and $\overline{v} = 6.5$. Hence, there is a shift in the cut-off towards the right as the cost of the sink nodes increases. This is expected because as the sink-node's cost increases it is important to be cautious about using more sink nodes in the network.

On the other hand, if the vacancy constraint is less than the cut-off, the optimal network comprises both sink and relay nodes. In fact, the fraction of sink nodes required re-

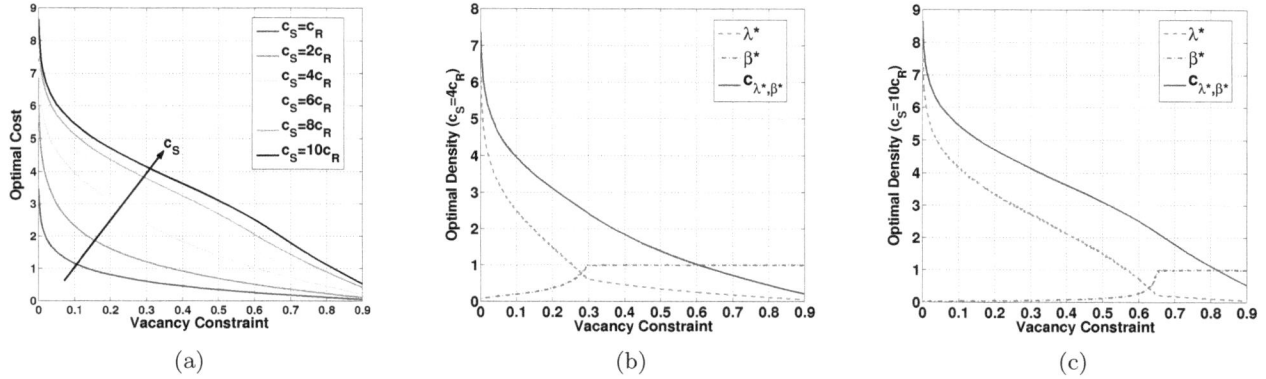

Figure 7: Deployment cost optimization: (a) Optimal cost as a function of the vacancy constraint for different values of sink and relay costs; (b) and (c): Optimal node density as a function of the vacancy constraint for $c_s = 4c_R$ and $c_s = 10c_R$, respectively.

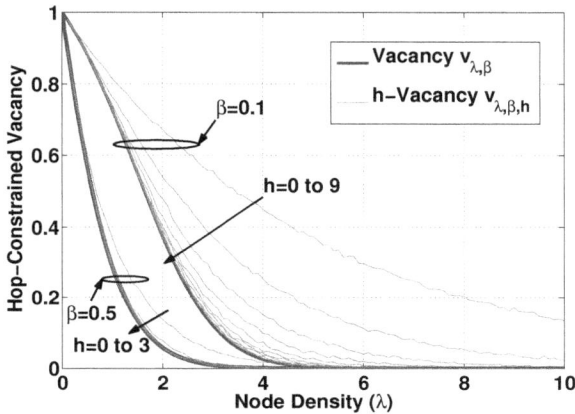

Figure 8: Hop-constrained vacancy as a function of node density.

duces as the vacancy constraint is lowered. For instance, from Figure 7(b) we see that $\beta^* = 0.37$ when $\bar{v} = 0.2$ as compared to $\beta^* = 0.19$ for $\bar{v} = 0.1$. However, the respective λ^* are 1.5 and 2.5 so that the network cost is much lower when $\bar{v} = 0.2$ although the corresponding β^* is more. Similar observations can be made from Figure 7(c).

In summary, an infrastructure-based design is necessary to achieve cost optimization whenever stringent (lower than cut-off) constraints are imposed on the average vacancy.

Hop-Constraint Vacancy: Finally, through simulations we compute the hop-constrained vacancies, $v_{\lambda,\beta,h}$. These results are reported in Figure 8 where, for $\beta = 0.1$ and $\beta = 0.5$, $v_{\lambda,\beta,h}$ are shown as functions of λ for different values of h (the direction along which h increases are shown in Figure 8 using arrowed lines). Also shown in the figure are corresponding vacancy curves, $v_{\lambda,\beta}$. As expected we observe that as h increases the hop-constrained curves, $v_{\lambda,\beta,h}$, converge to the respective vacancy curves, $v_{\lambda,\beta}$. However, the value of h for which good approximation to $v_{\lambda,\beta}$ is achieved is larger for $\beta = 0.1$ than for $\beta = 0.5$ ($h = 9$ and $h = 3$, respectively). This is because, when $\beta = 0.1$ the successive sink nodes are farther apart so that a larger value of h is required to completely cover the sink-containing busy periods (which are always completely covered when h is unconstrained).

7. CONCLUSION

We formulated the problem of characterizing average vacancy (complement of coverage) in an infrastructure-based wireless network comprising sink and relay nodes. Using renewal theoretic arguments, exact expression for average vacancy was derived. A simple upper bound was obtained by assuming left-vacancy, where a node is restricted to be covered by a sink-connected node towards its left. Through an interesting coupling argument we showed that the average region covered by an independent-disk model, where i.i.d. coverage regions are placed around the sink nodes, serves as a lower bound for the average vacancy in our original dependent-disk model. A novel notion of hop-constrained coverage was introduced. We finally conducted numerical experiments to characterize average vacancy as a function of sink and relay node densities. The problem of minimizing average deployment cost subject to a constraint on the average vacancy was also numerically explored.

APPENDIX

A. EXPRESSIONS FOR p, Q AND $\overline{Q}$

Recall that $p = \mathbb{P}(\mathcal{S}_k^c)$, $Q = \mathbb{E}[B_k|\mathcal{S}_k^c]$, and $\overline{Q} = \mathbb{E}[B_k|\mathcal{S}_k]$, where $\mathcal{S}_k$ is the event that the k-th connected component contains a sink node, and $\mathcal{S}_k^c$ is the complement of $\mathcal{S}_k$. Thus, p is the probability that the k-th connected component does not contain a sink, while Q (respectively, $\overline{Q}$) is the expected length of the k-th busy period conditioned on $\mathcal{S}_k^c$ (respectively, $\mathcal{S}_k$).

Let N_k denote the number of nodes in the k-th busy period. Note that N_k is a geometric random variable with success probability $e^{-\lambda r}$ (which is the probability that the region of length r towards the right of the N_k-th node is empty, thus terminating the busy period). Conditioning on $(N_k = n)$ we can write

$$p = \sum_{n=1}^{\infty} \mathbb{P}(N_k = n)\, \mathbb{P}(\mathcal{S}_k^c|N_k = n)$$

$$= \sum_{n=1}^{\infty} (1 - e^{-\lambda r})^{n-1}\, e^{-\lambda r}\, (1 - \beta)^n$$

$$= (1 - \beta)e^{-\lambda r} \sum_{n=1}^{\infty} [(1 - e^{-\lambda r})(1 - \beta)]^{n-1}$$

355

$$p = \frac{(1-\beta)e^{-\lambda r}}{\beta + e^{-\lambda r} - \beta e^{-\lambda r}}. \tag{19}$$

Computation of Q is along similar lines, although it is more involved. Denoting $Q_n := \mathbb{E}[B_k | \mathcal{S}_k^c, N = n]$, we have

$$
\begin{aligned}
Q &= \sum_{n=1}^{\infty} \mathbb{P}(N_k = n | \mathcal{S}_k^c) Q_n \\
&= \frac{1}{p} \sum_{n=1}^{\infty} \mathbb{P}(N_k = n) \mathbb{P}(\mathcal{S}_k^c | N_k = n) Q_n \tag{20}
\end{aligned}
$$

Now, let $D_i, i = 1, \cdots N_k - 1$, denote the distance between the i-th and $(i+1)$-th node in the k-th connected component. Note that, $\{D_i\}$ are i.i.d. exponentially distributed random variables of rate λ. Hence, we can write

$$
\begin{aligned}
Q_n &= \mathbb{E}\left[\sum_{i=1}^{N_k-1} D_i + r \,\middle|\, \mathcal{S}_k^c, N_k = n \right] \\
&= (n-1)\overline{D} + r \tag{21}
\end{aligned}
$$

where

$$
\begin{aligned}
\overline{D} &= \mathbb{E}\left[D_1 \,\middle|\, D_1 \leq r \right] \\
&= \frac{(1 - e^{-\lambda r} - \lambda r e^{-\lambda r})}{\lambda(1 - e^{-\lambda r})}. \tag{22}
\end{aligned}
$$

Substituting (21) in (20) and simplifying we obtain

$$
\begin{aligned}
Q &= \frac{p(1 - e^{-\lambda r})}{e^{-\lambda r}} \overline{D} + r \\
&= \frac{p(1 - e^{-\lambda r})}{\lambda e^{-\lambda r}} + (1-p)r.
\end{aligned}
$$

Recalling the expression for $\mathbb{E}[B_k]$ from (6), we have

$$Q = p\mathbb{E}[B_k] + (1-p)r. \tag{23}$$

Finally, $\overline{Q}$ can be easily obtained using the total expectation identity:

$$
\begin{aligned}
\mathbb{E}[B_k] &= \mathbb{P}(\mathcal{S}_k)\mathbb{E}[B_k | \mathcal{S}_k] + \mathbb{P}(\mathcal{S}_k^c)\mathbb{E}[B_k | \mathcal{S}_k^c] \\
&= (1-p)\overline{Q} + pQ.
\end{aligned}
$$

Thus,

$$\overline{Q} = \frac{\mathbb{E}[B_k] - pQ}{(1-p)}. \tag{24}$$

Discussion: Since $\mathbb{E}[B_k] \geq r$, from (23) we see that $Q \leq \mathbb{E}[B_k]$, which implies that $\overline{Q} \geq \mathbb{E}[B_k]$. Thus, the busy periods not containing sink nodes are shorter in length than the busy periods containing sink nodes. Indeed, as $\beta \to 1$, from (19) we see that $p \to 0$, yielding $Q \to r$ and $\overline{Q} \to \mathbb{E}[B_k]$. Thus, as β approaches 1, the busy periods not containing sink nodes are essentially the ones consisting of an isolated relay node (thus, $Q \approx r$), while the regular busy periods always contain sink nodes (so that, $\overline{Q} \approx \mathbb{E}[B_k]$).

B. PROOF OF THEOREM 2

PROOF. Let $\{Y_k : k \geq 1\}$ be the locations of the sink nodes in the independent-disk model. Thus, the sink node locations are coupled in both models. We will use $\widehat{U}_k$ and $\widehat{V}_k$, respectively, to denote the lengths of the coverage disk towards the right and left of Y_k in the independent-disk model.

Thus, $\widehat{\mathcal{W}}_k := [Y_k - \widehat{V}_k, Y_k + \widehat{U}_k]$ is the coverage disk around Y_k in the independent-disk model. These quantities are iteratively obtained as follows.

Define $k_1 = 1$. Let $\widehat{U}_{k_1} = U_{k_1}$ and $\widehat{V}_{k_1} = V_{k_1}$. Thus, we have $\widehat{\mathcal{W}}_{k_1} = \mathcal{W}_{k_1}$. Define $T_1 := Y_{k_1} + \widehat{U}_{k_1}$. Note that, given the sequence $\{Y_k\}$, T_1 is a *stopping time* for Λ, i.e., $\{T_1 \leq t\}$ depends only on the process $\{\Lambda([0, \tau]) : \tau \leq t\}$. Thus, the process, $\Lambda' := \{\Lambda([T_1, T_1 + t]) : t \geq 0\}$ is a one-sided Poisson process of rate $(1 - \beta)\lambda$, independent of $(\widehat{V}_{k_1}, \widehat{U}_{k_1})$.

Let Ω_1 denote a Poisson process on $\Re$ of rate $(1-\beta)\lambda$, that is independent of Λ. Construct a new point process, Λ_1, by concatenating the points of Ω_1 and Λ as follows:

$$
\Lambda_1([a,b]) = \begin{cases} \Omega_1([a,b]) & \text{if } b \leq T_1 \\ \Lambda([a,b]) & \text{if } a \geq T_1 \\ \Omega_1([a, T_1]) + \Lambda((T_1, b)) & \text{otherwise.} \end{cases} \tag{25}
$$

It follows that Λ_1 is also a Poisson process of rate $(1 - \beta)\lambda$ [17, Section 3.3]. Further, Λ_1 is independent of $(\widehat{V}_{k_1}, \widehat{U}_{k_1})$ (since Λ' and Ω_1 are independent of $(\widehat{V}_{k_1}, \widehat{U}_{k_1})$).

Now, define $k_2 = \min\{k > k_1 : Y_k > T_1 - r\}$. Using the points of Λ_1 as the location of the relay nodes, obtain the coverage disk, $\widehat{\mathcal{W}}_{k_2} := [Y_{k_2} - \widehat{V}_{k_2}, Y_2 + \widehat{U}_{k_2}]$, where $\widehat{V}_{k_2}$ and $\widehat{U}_{k_2}$ denote the disk's length towards the left and right of Y_{k_2}, respectively. $(\widehat{V}_{k_2}, \widehat{U}_{k_2})$ is independent and identically distributed as $(\widehat{V}_{k_1}, \widehat{U}_{k_1})$, since the process Λ_1 is independent of the latter. In the following we will show that

$$\bigcup_{k=1}^{k_2} \mathcal{W}_k \subseteq \widehat{\mathcal{W}}_{k_1} \cup \widehat{\mathcal{W}}_{k_2}. \tag{26}$$

First, recalling the definition of k_2, note that we have $Y_{k_1} \leq Y_k \leq T_1 - r$, for all $k_1 < k < k_2$. Thus, Y_k is surrounded by the same set of relay nodes that determine U_{k_1}. Hence, U_k satisfies, $Y_k + U_k = Y_{k_1} + U_{k_1}$. On the other hand, there are two cases possible for V_k: (i) $Y_k - V_k > Y_{k_1} - V_{k_1}$, if the connectivity between the relay nodes on either side of Y_{k_1} is affected after removing Y_{k_1}; otherwise (ii) $Y_k - V_k = Y_{k_1} - V_{k_1}$. In general, V_k satisfies, $Y_k - V_k \geq Y_{k_1} - V_{k_1}$. Thus, we have

$$\mathcal{W}_k \subseteq \mathcal{W}_{k_1} = \widehat{\mathcal{W}}_{k_1}, \text{ for all } k_1 < k < k_2. \tag{27}$$

Next, we proceed to characterize the coverage disk around Y_{k_2}. We need to consider two cases: (i) $Y_{k_2} \in (T_1 - r, T_1)$ and (ii) $Y_{k_2} \geq T_1$.

Case-(i): If $U_{k_2} = r$ (implying $\Lambda([Y_{k_2}, Y_{k_2} + r]) = 0$) then $\widehat{U}_{k_2} \geq U_{k_2}$. This is because, if $\Omega_1([Y_{k_2}, T_1]) > 0$ then it is possible that a point of Ω_1 in $[Y_{k_2}, T_1]$ is connected to a point of Λ in $[Y_{k_2} + r, \infty)$, thus extending the right coverage disk of Y_{k_2} in the independent-disk model. On the other hand, if $U_{k_2} > r$ then $\widehat{U}_{k_2} = U_{k_2}$, since in both models these quantities are determined by the points of Λ in $[T_1, \infty)$. Thus, in general, we have

$$[Y_{k_2}, Y_{k_2} + U_{k_2}] \subseteq [Y_{k_2}, Y_{k_2} + \widehat{U}_{k_2}] \subseteq \widehat{\mathcal{W}}_{k_2}. \tag{28}$$

Recalling the argument used for V_k ($k_1 < k < k_2$), we have, $Y_{k_2} - V_{k_2} \geq Y_{k_1} - V_{k_1}$, so that

$$[Y_{k_2} - V_{k_2}, Y_{k_2}] \subseteq \mathcal{W}_{k_1} = \widehat{\mathcal{W}}_{k_1}. \tag{29}$$

Combining (28) and (29) we see that, $\mathcal{W}_{k_2} \subseteq \widehat{\mathcal{W}}_{k_1} \cup \widehat{\mathcal{W}}_{k_2}$. Using the above along with (27), we obtain (26).

Case-(ii): Recall that this case corresponds to $Y_{k_2} \geq T_1$. Since $\Lambda_1 = \Lambda$ in $[T_1, \infty)$, U_{k_2} and $\widehat{U}_{k_2}$ are obtained using the same Poisson points of relay nodes. Hence, we readily have $\widehat{U}_{k_2} = U_{k_2}$. To obtain $\widehat{V}_{k_2}$, note that V_{k_2} satisfies $Y_{k_2} - V_{k_2} > T_1 - r$ (since $\Lambda([T_1 - r, T_1]) = 0$). If $Y_{k_2} - V_{k_2} > T_1$ then $\widehat{V}_{k_2} = V_{k_2}$ since $\Lambda_1 = \Lambda$ on $(T_1, Y_{k_2}]$. In contrast, if $Y_{k_2} - V_{k_2} \in (T_1 - r, T_1]$ then $\widehat{V}_{k_2} \geq V_{k_2}$ since it is possible that a point of Ω_1 in $(T_1 - r, T_1]$ is connected to a point of Λ in (T_1, ∞) so that the left coverage disk of Y_{k_2} gets extended in the independent-disk model. Thus, we have

$$\mathcal{W}_{k_2} \subseteq \widehat{\mathcal{W}}_{k_2}. \tag{30}$$

Combining (27) and (30) we see that (26) is satisfied for case-(ii) as well.

We complete the proof through an induction argument. Suppose for some $n \geq 2$ we have inductively obtained i.i.d. coverage disks, $\widehat{\mathcal{W}}_{k_m} = [Y_{k_m} - \widehat{V}_{k_m}, Y_{k_m} + \widehat{U}_{k_m}]$, for $m = 1, 2, \cdots, n$, satisfying,

$$\bigcup_{k=1}^{k_n} \mathcal{W}_k \subseteq \bigcup_{m=1}^{n} \widehat{\mathcal{W}}_{k_m}. \tag{31}$$

Define $T_k = Y_{k_n} + \widehat{U}_{k_n}$ and $k_{n+1} = \min\{k > k_n : Y_k > T_k - r\}$. Let Ω_k be a Poisson process of rate $(1 - \beta)\lambda$, independent of Λ and $\Omega_m, m = 1, 2, \cdots, k - 1$. Analogous to the construction of Λ_1 in (25), obtain the Poisson process Λ_k by concatenating the processes Ω_k and Λ at T_k. Since T_k is a stopping time for Λ, it follows that Λ_k is independent of $\widehat{\mathcal{W}}_{k_m}, m = 1, 2 \cdots, n$. Using the points of Λ_k as the location of the relay nodes, we can obtain i.i.d. coverage disk, $\widehat{\mathcal{W}}_{k_{n+1}} = [Y_{k_{n+1}} - \widehat{V}_{k_{n+1}}, Y_{k_{n+1}} + \widehat{U}_{k_{n+1}}]$, around $Y_{k_{n+1}}$.

Now, for all k such that $k_n < k < k_{n+1}$ we have $Y_{k_n} \leq Y_k \leq T_k - r$. Hence, as in $n = 2$ case, U_k and V_k, respectively, satisfies $Y_k + U_k = Y_{k_n} + U_{k_n}$ and $Y_k - V_k \geq Y_{k_n} - V_{k_n}$, thus yielding,

$$\mathcal{W}_k \subseteq \mathcal{W}_{k_n}, \text{ for all } k_n < k < k_{n+1}. \tag{32}$$

Again, using the arguments analogous to the $n = 2$ case, we can show that $\mathcal{W}_{k_{n+1}}$ satisfies,

$$\mathcal{W}_{k_{n+1}} \subseteq \begin{cases} \bigcup_{m=1}^{n+1} \widehat{\mathcal{W}}_{k_m} & \text{if } Y_{k_{n+1}} \in (T_k - r, T_k) \\ \widehat{\mathcal{W}}_{k_{n+1}} & \text{if } Y_{k_{n+1}} \geq T_k. \end{cases} \tag{33}$$

Using (31), (32) and (33) we finally obtain,

$$\bigcup_{k=1}^{k_{n+1}} \mathcal{W}_k \subseteq \bigcup_{m=1}^{n+1} \widehat{\mathcal{W}}_{k_m}.$$

thus completing the induction argument. $\square$

C. REFERENCES

[1] P. Hall, *Introduction to the Theory of Coverage Processes*, ser. Wiley Series in Probability and Mathematical Statistics. New York: Wiley, 1988.

[2] J. G. Andrews, F. Baccelli, and R. K. Ganti, "A Tractable Approach to Coverage and Rate in Cellular Networks," *IEEE Transactions on Communications*, vol. 59, no. 11, pp. 3122–3134, November 2011.

[3] H. S. Dhillon, R. K. Ganti, and J. G. Andrews, "A Tractable Framework for Coverage and Outage in Heterogeneous Cellular Networks," in *ITA 11', Information Theory and Applications Workshop*, Feb 2011.

[4] F. Baccelli and B. Bartlomiej, "On a Coverage Process Ranging from the Boolean Model to the Poisson-Voronoi Tessellation with Applications to Wireless Communications," *Advances in Applied Probability*, vol. 33, no. 2, pp. 293–323, 2001.

[5] P. Gupta and P. R. Kumar, *Stochastic Analysis, Control, Optimization and Applications: A Volume in Honor of W.H. Fleming.* Boston, MA: Birkhäuser Boston, 1999, ch. Critical Power for Asymptotic Connectivity in Wireless Networks, pp. 547–566.

[6] R. S. Ojha, G. Kannan, S. N. Merchant, and U. B. Desai, "On Optimal Transmission Range for Multihop Cellular Networks," in *GLOBECOM 08', IEEE Global Telecommunications Conference*, Nov 2008.

[7] P. Santi, "The Critical Transmitting Range for Connectivity in Mobile Ad Hoc Networks," *IEEE Transactions on Mobile Computing*, vol. 4, no. 3, pp. 310–317, May 2005.

[8] D. Miorandi, E. Altman, and G. Alfano, "The Impact of Channel Randomness on Coverage and Connectivity of Ad Hoc and Sensor Networks," *IEEE Transactions on Wireless Communications*, vol. 7, no. 3, pp. 1062–1072, March 2008.

[9] C. Bettstetter and C. Hartmann, "Connectivity of Wireless Multihop Networks in a Shadow Fading Environment," *Wireless Networks*, vol. 11, no. 5, pp. 571–579, September 2005.

[10] M. Desai and D. Manjunath, "On the Connectivity in Finite Ad Hoc Networks," *IEEE Communications Letters*, vol. 6, no. 10, pp. 437–439, Oct 2002.

[11] D. Miorandi and E. Altman, "Connectivity in One-Dimensional Ad Hoc Networks: A Queueing Theoretical Approach," *Wireless Networks*, vol. 12, no. 5, pp. 573–587, 2006.

[12] O. Dousse, P. Thiran, and M. Hasler, "Connectivity in Ad-Hoc and Hybrid Networks," in *INFOCOM 02', Twenty-First Annual Joint Conference of the IEEE Computer and Communications Societies*, 2002.

[13] S. I. Sou, "A Power-Saving Model for Roadside Unit Deployment in Vehicular Networks," *IEEE Communications Letters*, vol. 14, no. 7, pp. 623–625, July 2010.

[14] S. C. Ng, G. Mao, and B. D. O. Anderson, "On the Properties of One-Dimensional Infrastructure-Based Wireless Multi-Hop Networks," *IEEE Transactions on Wireless Communications*, vol. 11, no. 7, pp. 2606–2615, July 2012.

[15] W. Zhang, Y. Chen, Y. Yang, X. Wang, Y. Zhang, X. Hong, and G. Mao, "Multi-Hop Connectivity Probability in Infrastructure-Based Vehicular Networks," *IEEE Journal on Selected Areas in Communications*, vol. 30, no. 4, pp. 740–747, May 2012.

[16] R. W. Wolff, *Stochastic Modeling and the Theory of Queues*, ser. Prentice-Hall International Series in Industrial and Systems Engineering. Englewood Cliffs, N.J. Prentice Hall, 1989.

[17] G. Lindgren, *Stationary Stochastic Processes: Theory and Applications*, ser. Texts in Statistical Science. Chapman and Hall, 2012.

Author Index

www.ingramcontent.com/pod-product-compliance
Lightning Source LLC
Chambersburg PA
CBHW080716220326
41598CB00033B/5433